BLACK PANTHER

THE COMPLETE COLLECTION
BY REGINALD HUDLIN

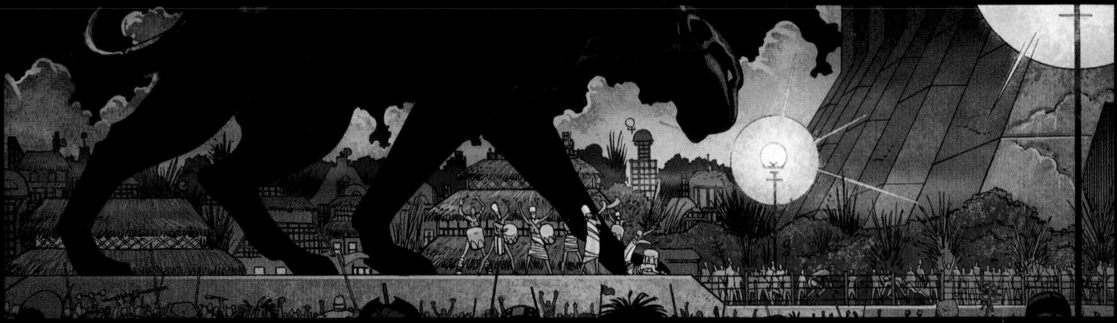

BLACK PANTHER

WRITTEN BY

REGINALD HUDLIN (BLACK PANTHER #1-18)
& **PETER MILLIGAN** (X-MEN #175-176)

BLACK PANTHER #1-6

"WHO IS THE BLACK PANTHER?"

PENCILS BY

JOHN ROMITA JR.

INKS BY

KLAUS JANSON

BLACK PANTHER #7

"SOUL POWER IN THE HOUSE OF M"

PENCILS BY

TREVOR HAIRSINE

INKS BY

JOHN DELL

X-MEN #175-176 & BLACK PANTHER #8-9

"WILD KINGDOM"

PENCILS BY

SALVADOR LARROCA (X-MEN) &
DAVID YARDIN (BLACK PANTHER)

INKS BY

DANNY MIKI WITH **ALLEN MARTINEZ** (X-MEN) AND
JAY LEISTEN (BLACK PANTHER)

BLACK PANTHER #10-13

"TWO THE HARD WAY"

BLACK PANTHER #14-18

"BRIDE OF THE PANTHER"

PENCILS BY

SCOT EATON WITH **KAARE ANDREWS** (#18 PP 21-24)

INKS BY

KLAUS JANSON WITH **KAARE ANDREWS** (#18 PP 21-24)

COLORS BY

DEAN WHITE & **LIQUID!** (X-MEN #175-176) WITH **MATT MILLA**
RICHARD ISANOVE & **KAARE ANDREWS**

LETTERS BY

CHRIS ELIOPOULOS (#1-2), **VC's RANDY GENTILE** &
VC's CORY PETIT (X-MEN #175-176)

COVERS BY

JOHN ROMITA JR., KLAUS JANSON & **DEAN WHITE** (#1); **ESAD RIBIĆ** (#2);
FRANK CHO & **DEAN WHITE**; **JOHN CASSADAY** (#4);
TERRY DODSON, RACHEL DODSON & **DEAN WHITE**; **KAARE ANDREWS**;
ANDY BRASE & **DEAN WHITE**; **GARY FRANK, JONATHAN SIBAL** & **DEAN WHITE** (#10); **MIKE DEODATO JR.** & **DEAN WHITE**;
MIKE DEODATO JR. & **RAIN BEREDO** (#12); **JAE LEE** & **JUNE CHUNG** (#13);
SCOT EATON & **DEAN WHITE** (#14); **LEINIL FRANCIS YU**;
OLIVIER COIPEL, TIM TOWNSEND & **DEAN WHITE**;
JOSEPH MICHAEL LINSNER; **SALVADOR LARROCA** & **LIQUID!** (X-MEN #175-176)

ASSISTANT EDITORS

CORY SEDLMEIER, SEAN RYAN & **DANIEL KETCHUM**

ASSOCIATE EDITORS

NICK LOWE & **CORY SEDLMEIER**

EDITORS

AXEL ALONSO & **MIKE MARTS**

SPECIAL THANKS TO

PROCTER & **GAMBLE, CBS DAYTIME, ALAN LOCHER, ELLEN WHEELER, MARIA AGUERO, ALYSON HUI** & **SHAWN DUDLEY** FOR THE DESIGN OF STORM'S WEDDING GOWN

BLACK PANTHER CREATED BY **STAN LEE** & **JACK KIRBY**

COLLECTION EDITOR **MARK D. BEAZLEY**
ASSISTANT EDITOR **CAITLIN O'CONNELL**
ASSOCIATE MANAGING EDITOR **KATERI WOODY**
ASSOCIATE MANAGER, DIGITAL ASSETS **JOE HOCHSTEIN**
SENIOR EDITOR, SPECIAL PROJECTS **JENNIFER GRÜNWALD**

VP PRODUCTION & SPECIAL PROJECTS **JEFF YOUNGQUIST**
RESEARCH **DARON JENSEN**
LAYOUT **JEPH YORK**
BOOK DESIGNER **ADAM DEL RE**
SVP PRINT, SALES & MARKETING **DAVID GABRIEL**

EDITOR IN CHIEF **AXEL ALONSO**
CHIEF CREATIVE OFFICER **JOE QUESADA**
PRESIDENT **DAN BUCKLEY**
EXECUTIVE PRODUCER **ALAN FINE**

BLACK PANTHER BY REGINALD HUDLIN: THE COMPLETE COLLECTION VOL. 1. Contains material originally published in magazine form as BLACK PANTHER #1-18 and X-MEN #175-176. First printing 2017. ISBN# 978-1-302-90771-6. Published by MARVEL WORLDWIDE, INC., a subsidiary of MARVEL ENTERTAINMENT, LLC. OFFICE OF PUBLICATION: 135 West 50th Street, New York, NY 10020.

Printed in the U.S.A. DAN BUCKLEY, President, Marvel Entertainment; JOE QUESADA, Chief Creative Officer; TOM BREVOORT, SVP of Publishing; DAVID BOGART, SVP of Business Affairs & Operations, Publishing & Partnership; C.B. CEBULSKI, VP of Brand Management & Development, Asia; DAVID GABRIEL, SVP of Sales & Marketing, Publishing; JEFF YOUNGQUIST, VP of Production & Special Projects; DAN CARR, Executive Director of Publishing Technology; ALEX MORALES, Director of Publishing Operations; SUSAN CRESPI, Production Manager; STAN LEE, Chairman Emeritus. For information regarding advertising in Marvel Comics or on Marvel.com, please contact Vit DeBellis, Integrated Sales Manager, at vdebellis@marvel.com. For Marvel subscription inquiries, please call [illegible]. **Manufactured between 9/8/2017 and 10/10/2017 by LSC COMMUNICATIONS INC., KENDALLVILLE, IN, USA.**

10 9 8 7 6 5 4 3 2 1

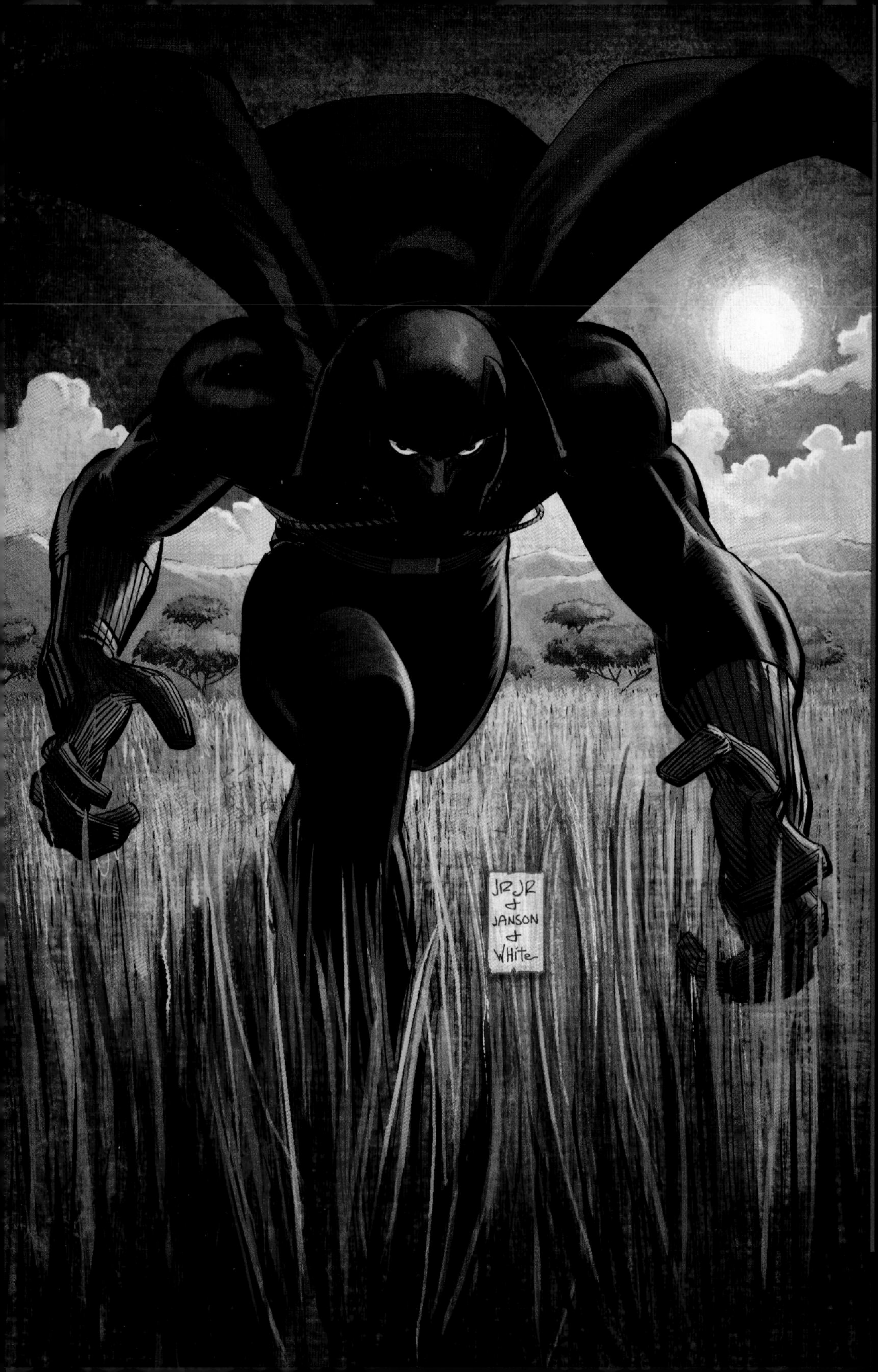
JRJR & JANSON & WHITE

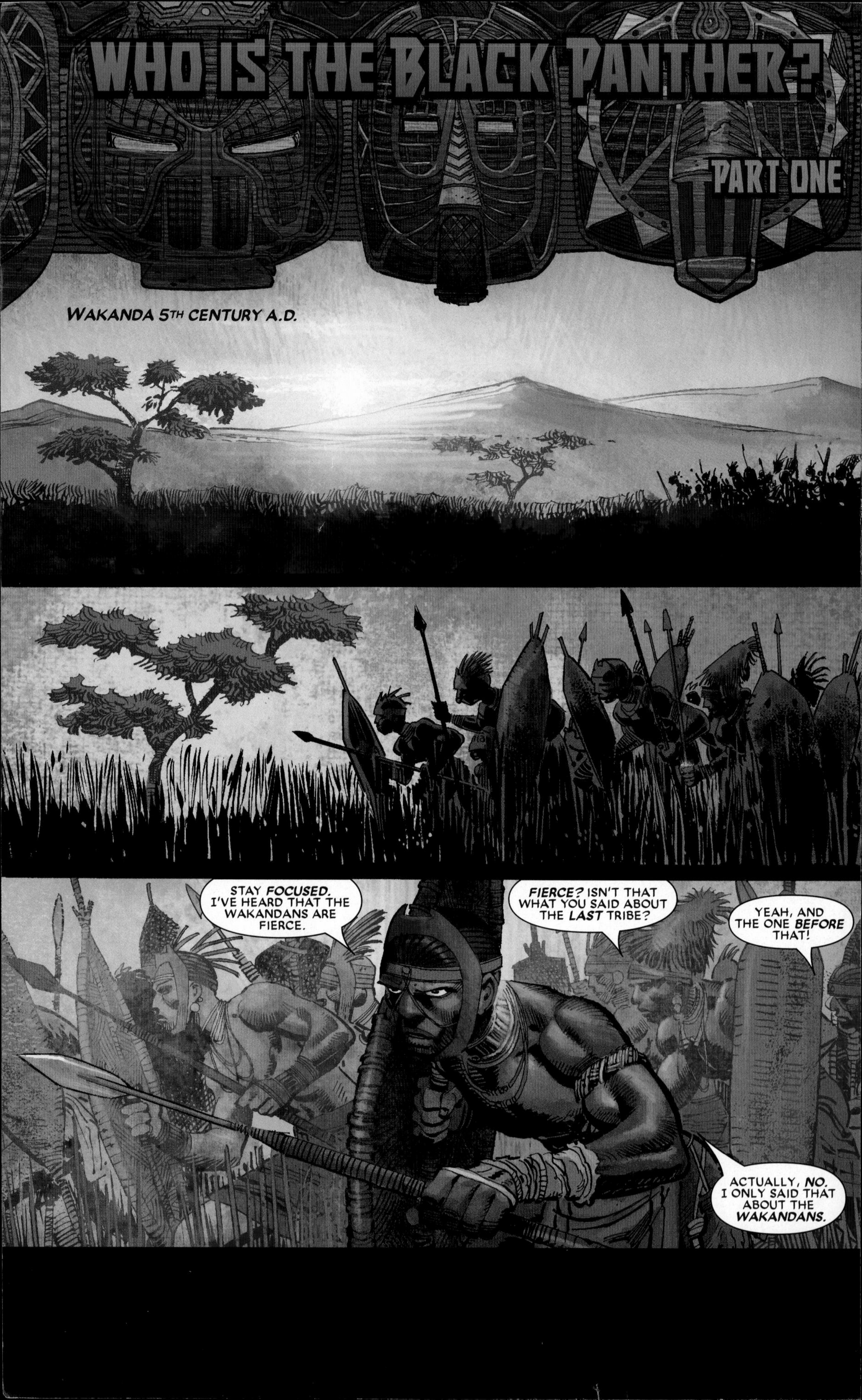
WHO IS THE BLACK PANTHER?
PART ONE
WAKANDA 5TH CENTURY A.D.
STAY FOCUSED. I'VE HEARD THAT THE WAKANDANS ARE FIERCE.
FIERCE? ISN'T THAT WHAT YOU SAID ABOUT THE LAST TRIBE?
YEAH, AND THE ONE BEFORE THAT!
ACTUALLY, NO. I ONLY SAID THAT ABOUT THE WAKANDANS.

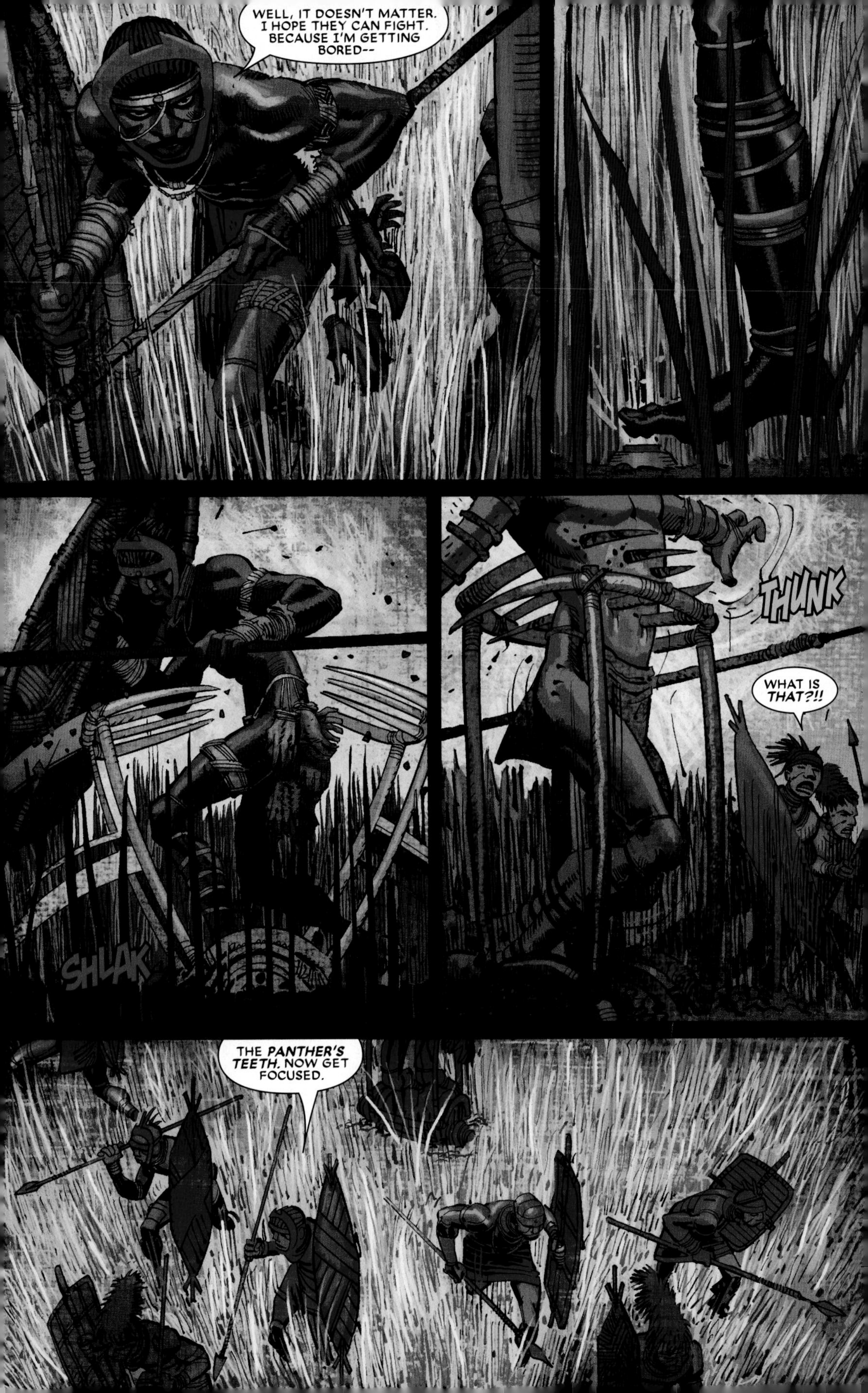

WELL, IT DOESN'T MATTER. I HOPE THEY CAN FIGHT. BECAUSE I'M GETTING BORED--
SHLAK
THUNK
WHAT IS THAT?!!
THE PANTHER'S TEETH. NOW GET FOCUSED.

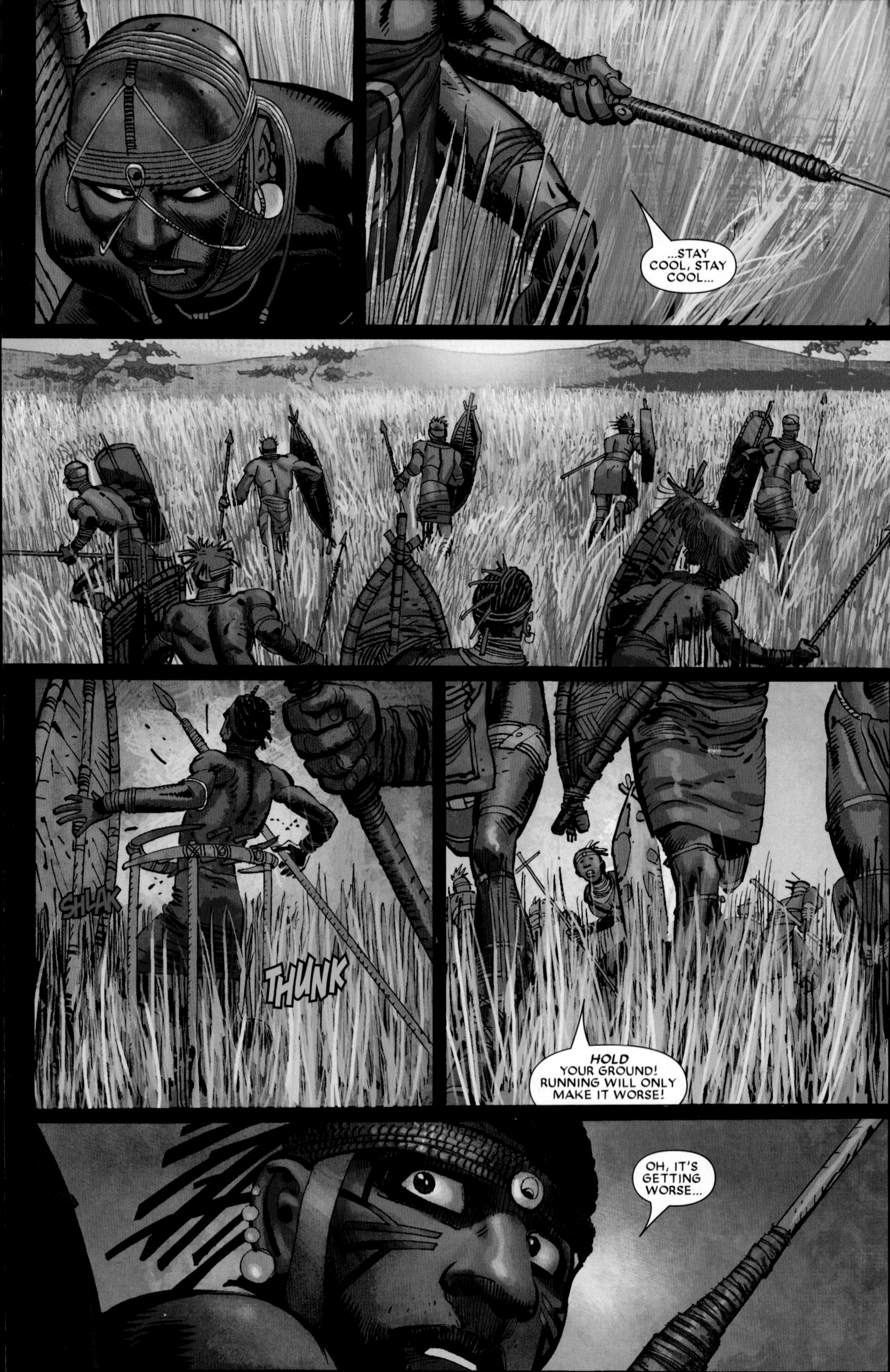
...STAY COOL, STAY COOL...
SHLAK
THUNK
HOLD YOUR GROUND! RUNNING WILL ONLY MAKE IT WORSE!
OH, IT'S GETTING WORSE...

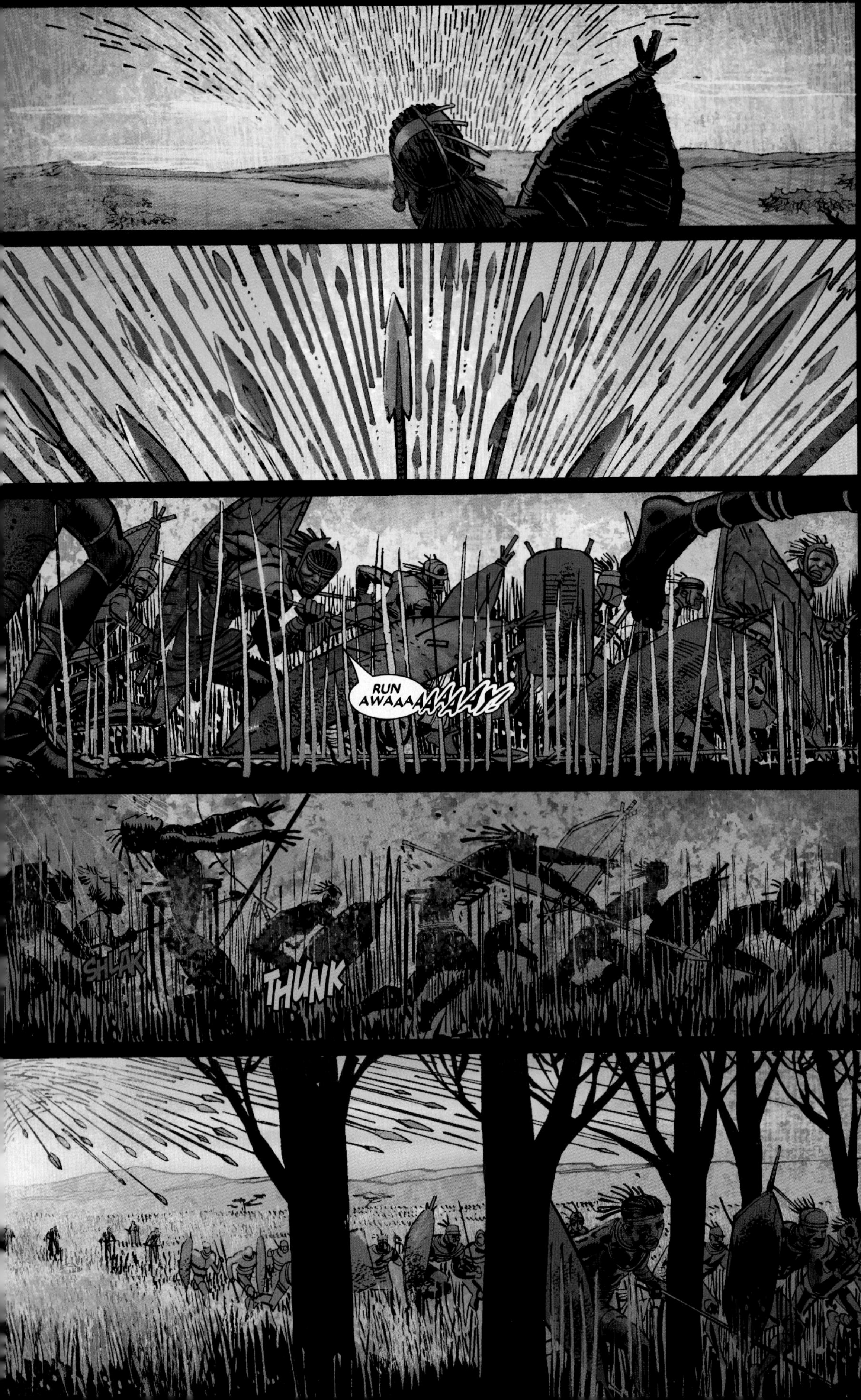
RUN AWAAAAAAAAY!
SHLAK
THUNK

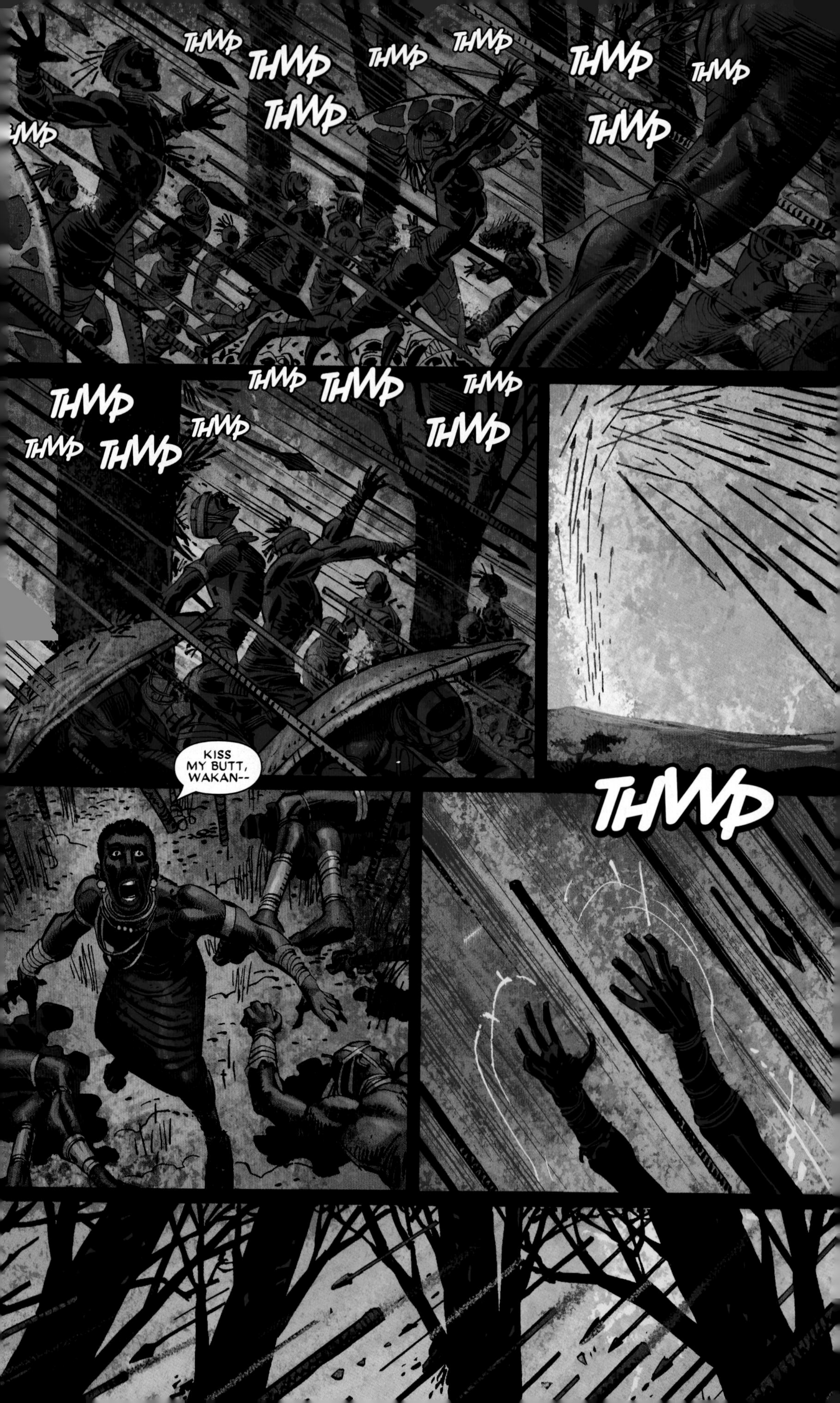
THWP
THWP
THWP
THWP
THWP
THWP
THWP
THWP
THWP
THWP
THWP
THWP
THWP
THWP
THWP
THWP
THWP
THWP
KISS MY BUTT, WAKAN--
THWP

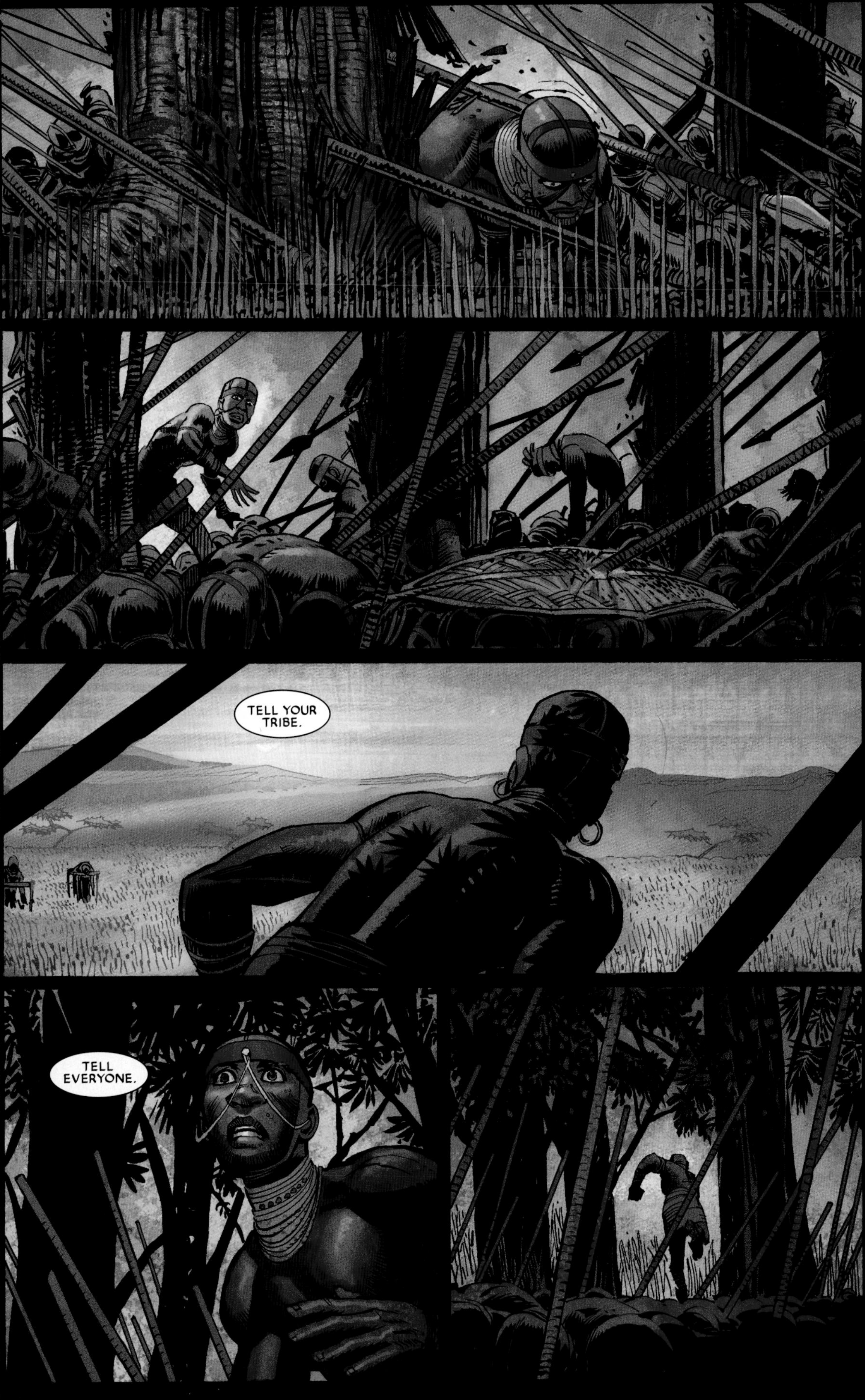
TELL YOUR TRIBE.
TELL EVERYONE.

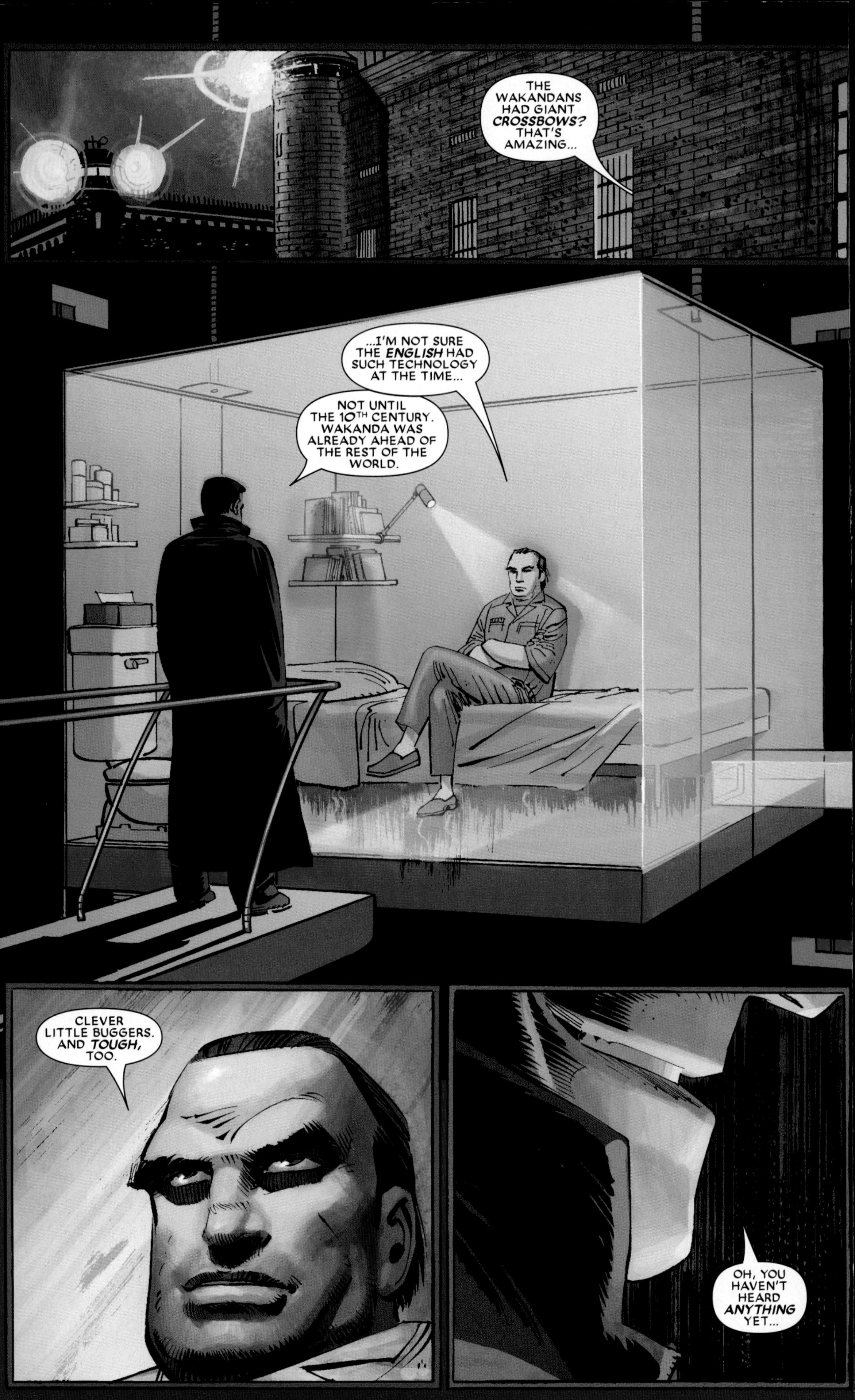
THE WAKANDANS HAD GIANT CROSSBOWS? THAT'S AMAZING...
...I'M NOT SURE THE ENGLISH HAD SUCH TECHNOLOGY AT THE TIME...
NOT UNTIL THE 10TH CENTURY. WAKANDA WAS ALREADY AHEAD OF THE REST OF THE WORLD.
CLEVER LITTLE BUGGERS. AND TOUGH, TOO.
OH, YOU HAVEN'T HEARD ANYTHING YET...

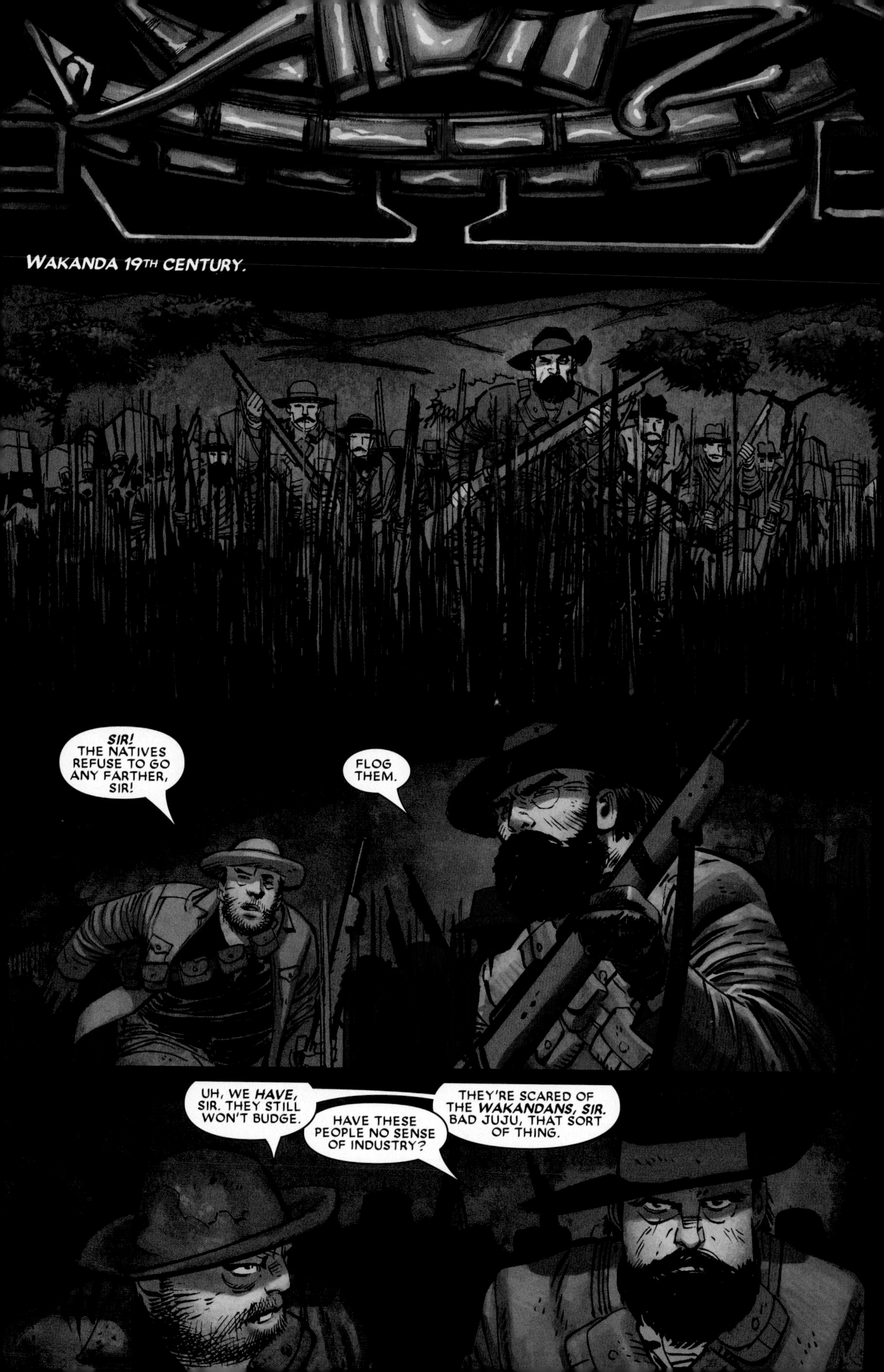
WAKANDA 19TH CENTURY.
SIR! THE NATIVES REFUSE TO GO ANY FARTHER, SIR!
FLOG THEM.
UH, WE HAVE, SIR. THEY STILL WON'T BUDGE.
HAVE THESE PEOPLE NO SENSE OF INDUSTRY?
THEY'RE SCARED OF THE WAKANDANS, SIR. BAD JUJU, THAT SORT OF THING.

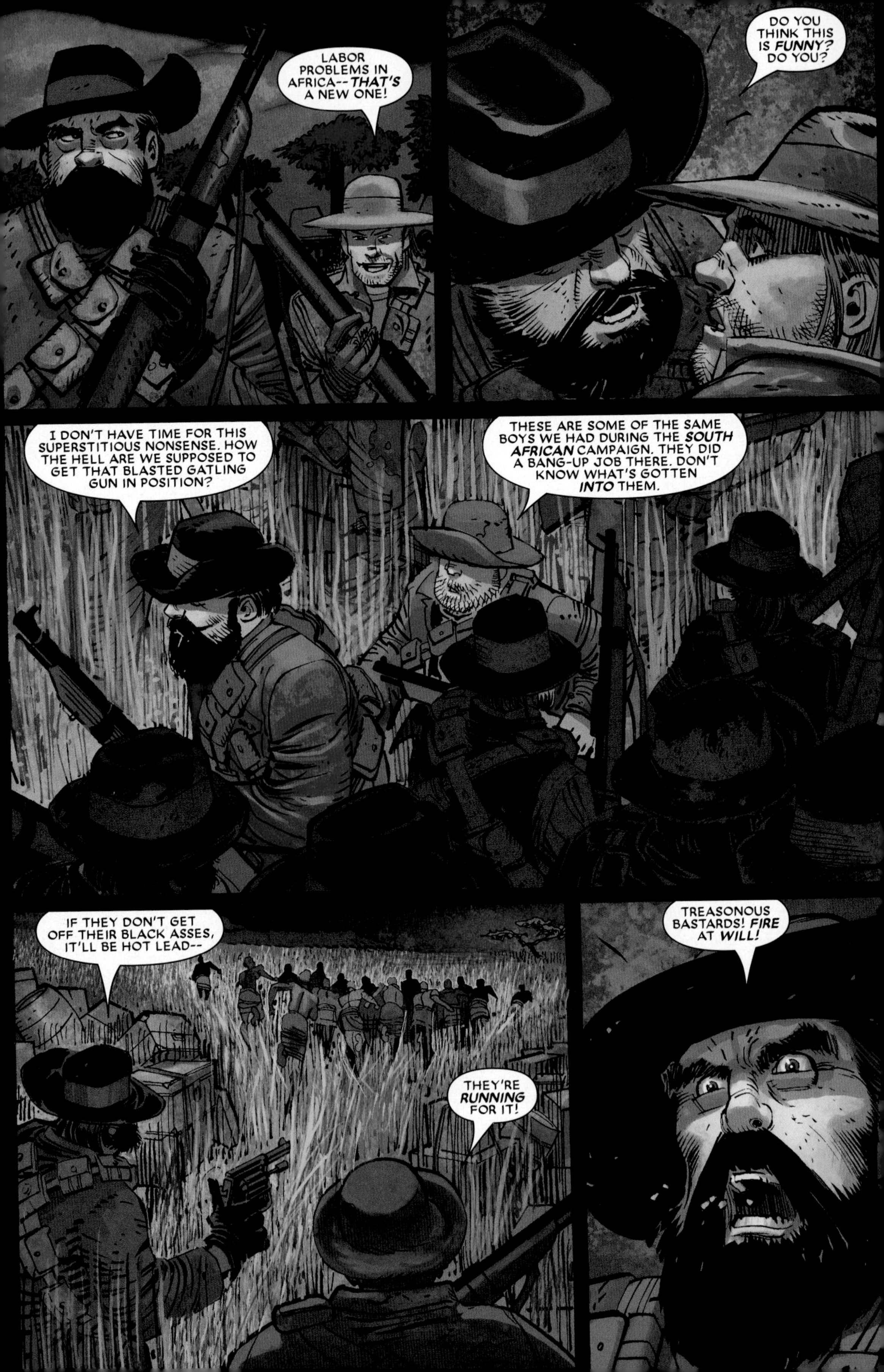
LABOR PROBLEMS IN AFRICA--THAT'S A NEW ONE!
DO YOU THINK THIS IS FUNNY? DO YOU?
I DON'T HAVE TIME FOR THIS SUPERSTITIOUS NONSENSE. HOW THE HELL ARE WE SUPPOSED TO GET THAT BLASTED GATLING GUN IN POSITION?
THESE ARE SOME OF THE SAME BOYS WE HAD DURING THE SOUTH AFRICAN CAMPAIGN. THEY DID A BANG-UP JOB THERE. DON'T KNOW WHAT'S GOTTEN INTO THEM.
IF THEY DON'T GET OFF THEIR BLACK ASSES, IT'LL BE HOT LEAD--
THEY'RE RUNNING FOR IT!
TREASONOUS BASTARDS! FIRE AT WILL!

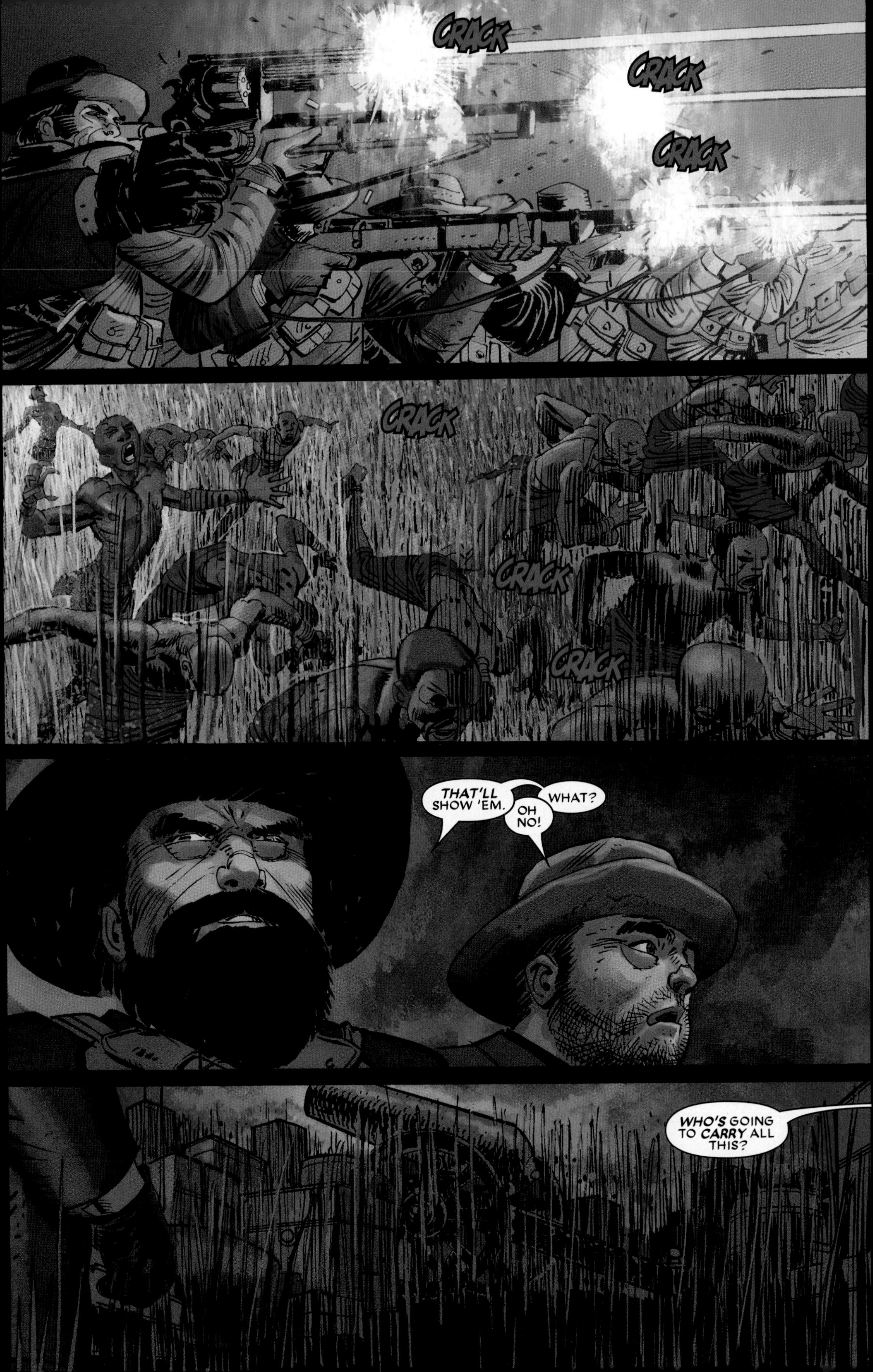
CRACK
CRACK
CRACK
CRACK
CRACK
CRACK
THAT'LL SHOW 'EM.
WHAT?
OH NO!
WHO'S GOING TO CARRY ALL THIS?

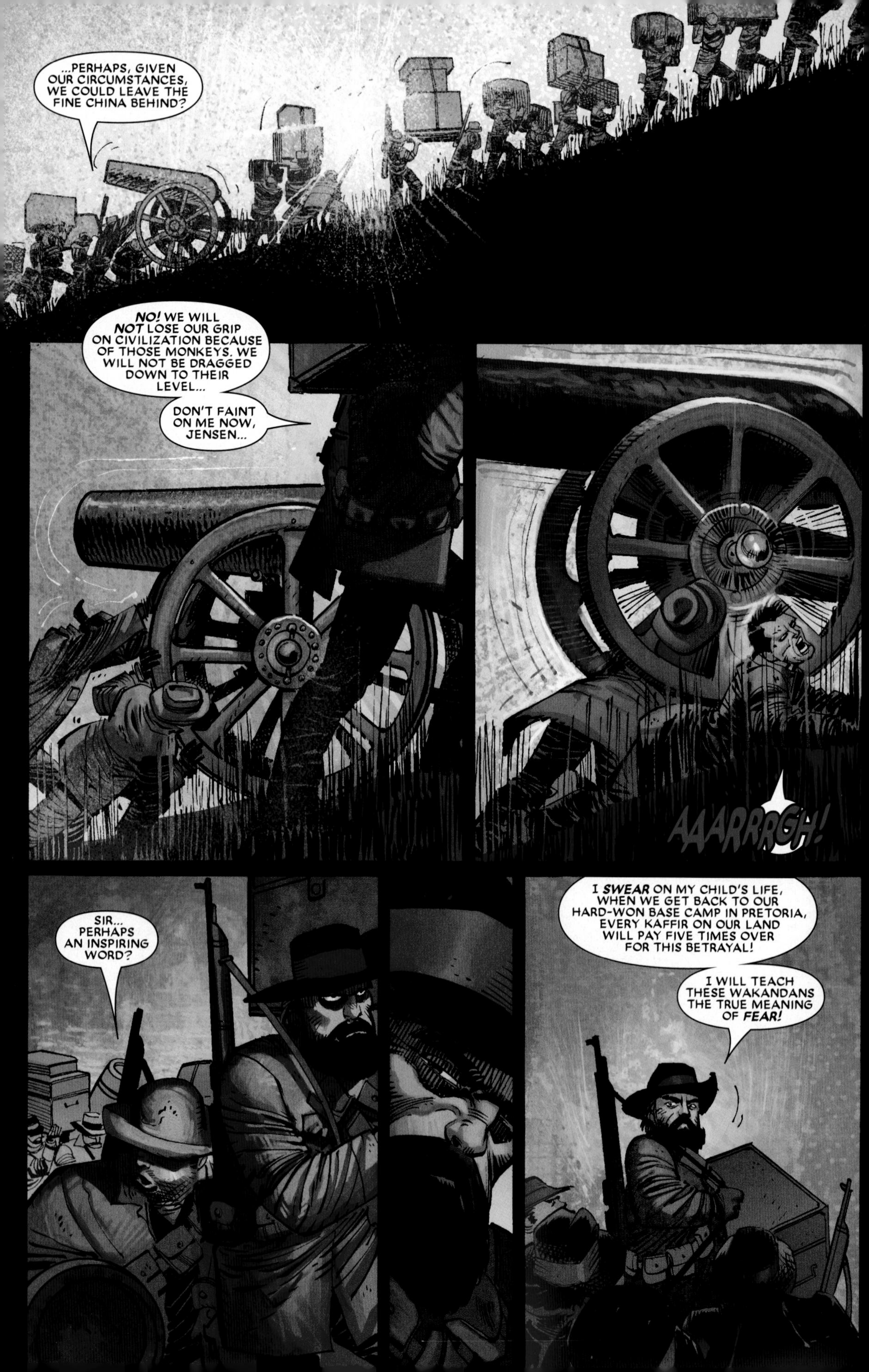
...PERHAPS, GIVEN OUR CIRCUMSTANCES, WE COULD LEAVE THE FINE CHINA BEHIND?
NO! WE WILL NOT LOSE OUR GRIP ON CIVILIZATION BECAUSE OF THOSE MONKEYS. WE WILL NOT BE DRAGGED DOWN TO THEIR LEVEL...
DON'T FAINT ON ME NOW, JENSEN...
AAARRRGH!
SIR... PERHAPS AN INSPIRING WORD?
I SWEAR ON MY CHILD'S LIFE, WHEN WE GET BACK TO OUR HARD-WON BASE CAMP IN PRETORIA, EVERY KAFFIR ON OUR LAND WILL PAY FIVE TIMES OVER FOR THIS BETRAYAL!
I WILL TEACH THESE WAKANDANS THE TRUE MEANING OF FEAR!

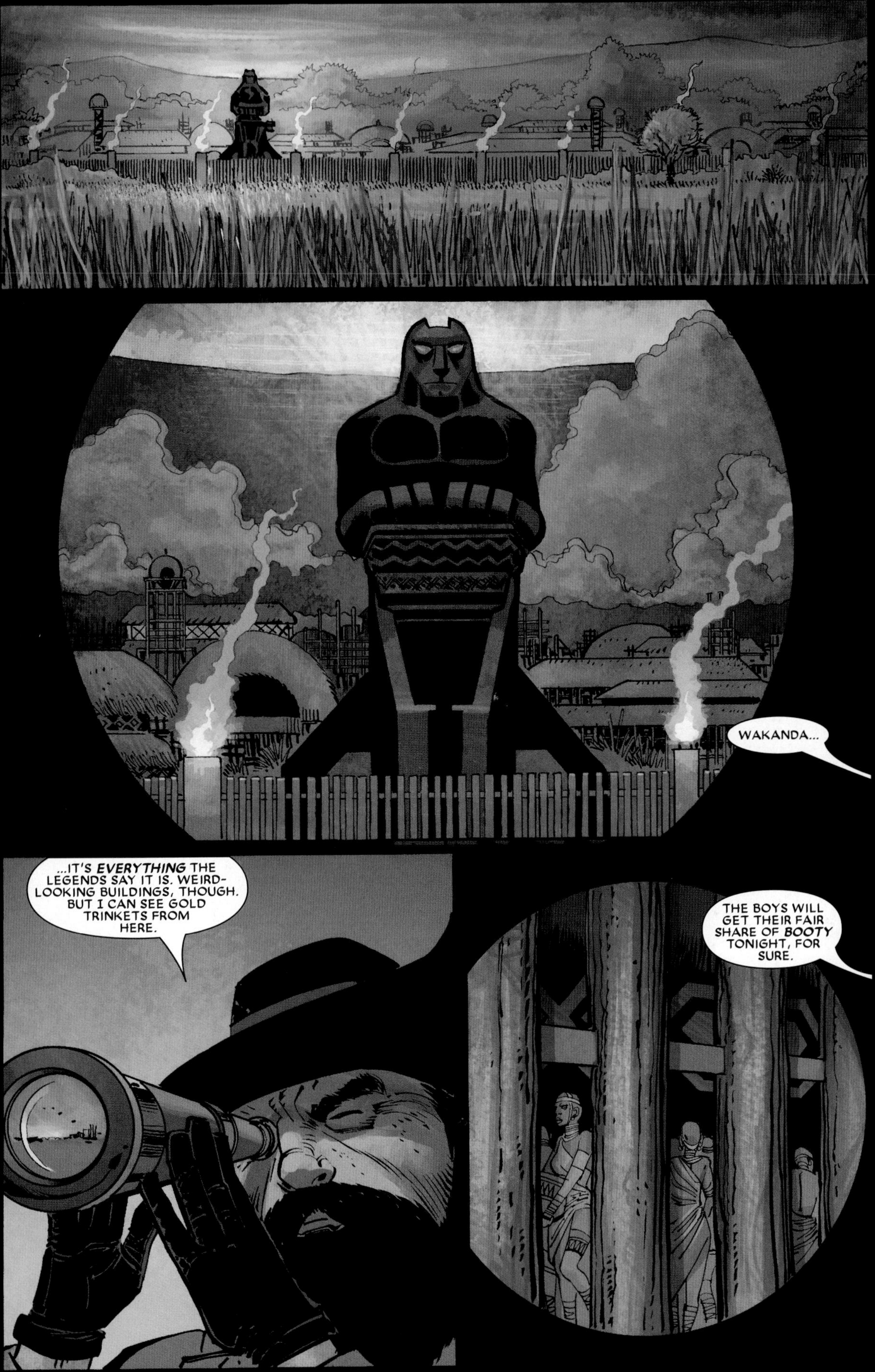
WAKANDA...
...IT'S EVERYTHING THE LEGENDS SAY IT IS. WEIRD-LOOKING BUILDINGS, THOUGH. BUT I CAN SEE GOLD TRINKETS FROM HERE.
THE BOYS WILL GET THEIR FAIR SHARE OF BOOTY TONIGHT, FOR SURE.

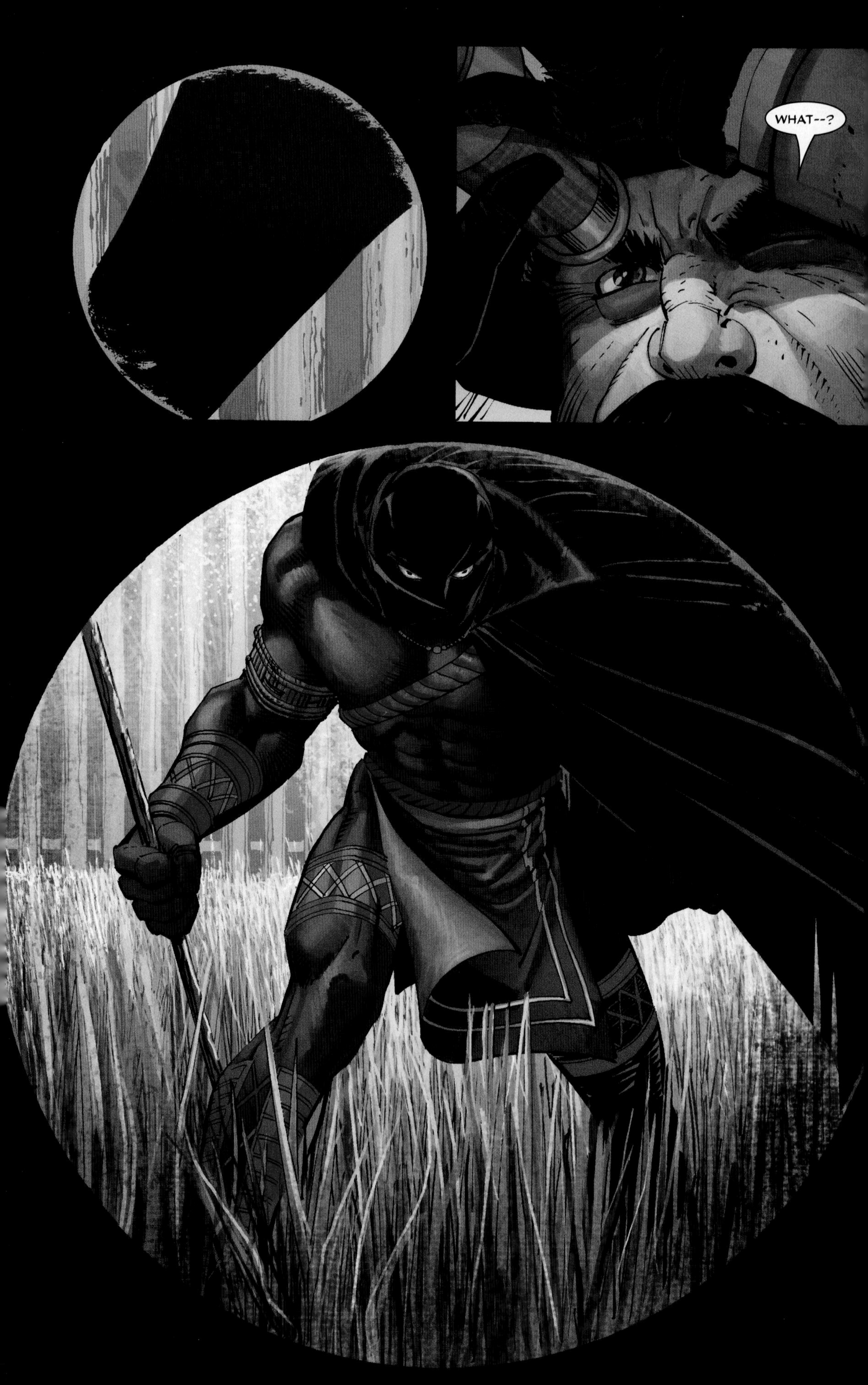
WHAT--?

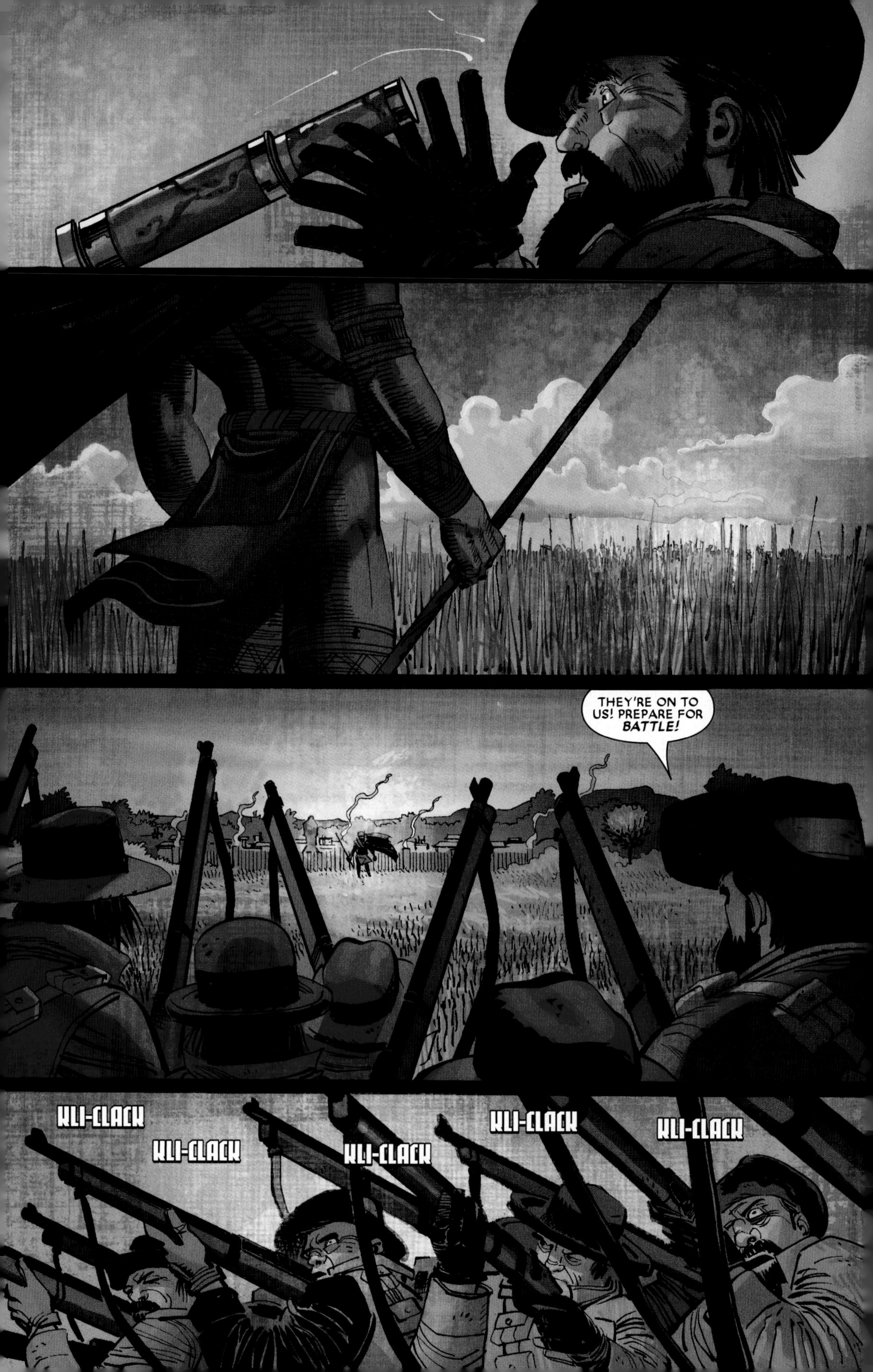
THEY'RE ON TO US! PREPARE FOR BATTLE!
KLI-CLACK
KLI-CLACK
KLI-CLACK
KLI-CLACK
KLI-CLACK

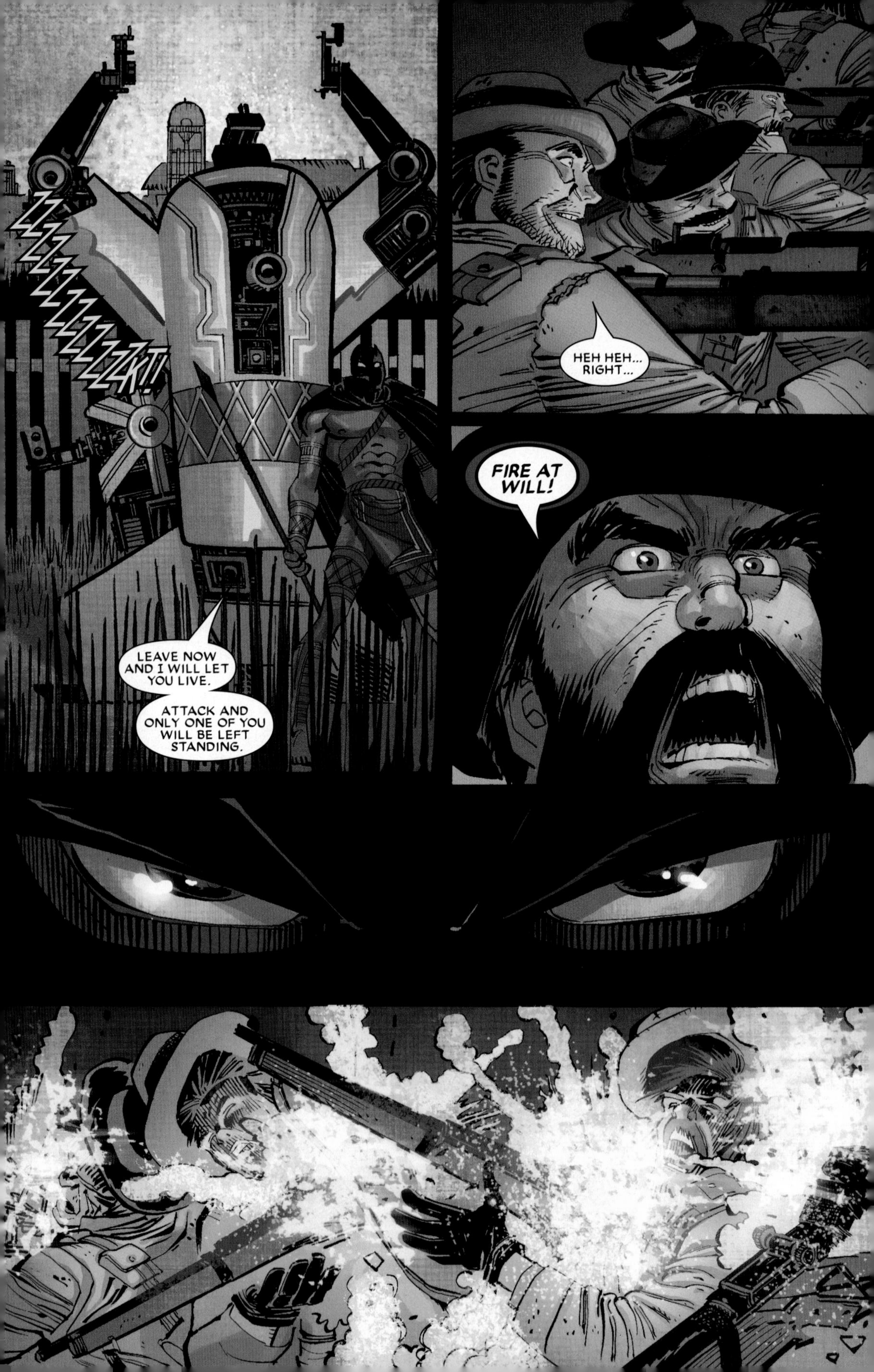
ZZZZZZZZZZZZZZKT!
LEAVE NOW AND I WILL LET YOU LIVE.
ATTACK AND ONLY ONE OF YOU WILL BE LEFT STANDING.
HEH HEH... RIGHT...
FIRE AT WILL!

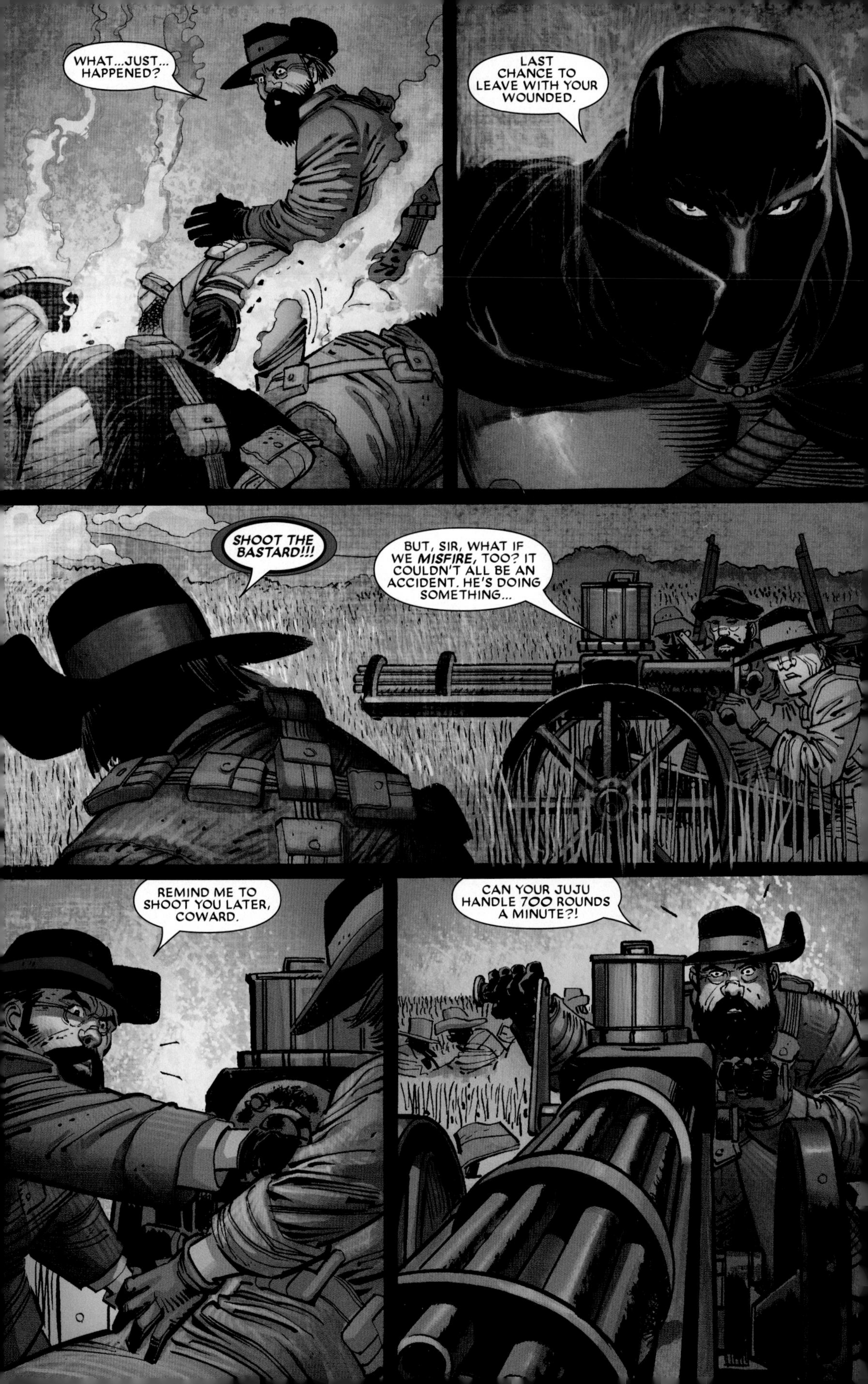
WHAT...JUST... HAPPENED?
LAST CHANCE TO LEAVE WITH YOUR WOUNDED.
SHOOT THE BASTARD!!!
BUT, SIR, WHAT IF WE MISFIRE, TOO? IT COULDN'T ALL BE AN ACCIDENT. HE'S DOING SOMETHING...
REMIND ME TO SHOOT YOU LATER, COWARD.
CAN YOUR JUJU HANDLE 700 ROUNDS A MINUTE?!

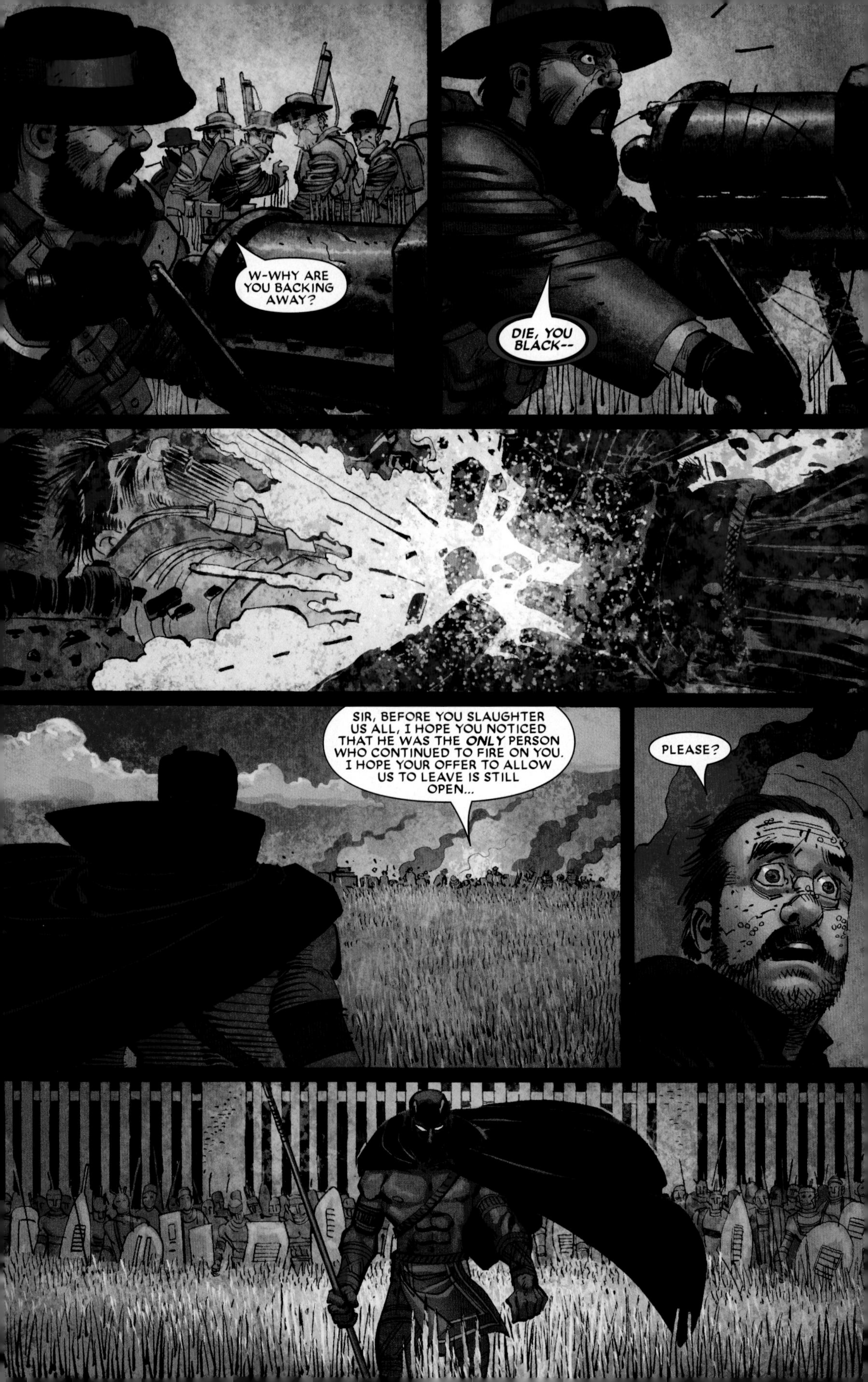
W-WHY ARE YOU BACKING AWAY?
DIE, YOU BLACK--
SIR, BEFORE YOU SLAUGHTER US ALL, I HOPE YOU NOTICED THAT HE WAS THE ONLY PERSON WHO CONTINUED TO FIRE ON YOU. I HOPE YOUR OFFER TO ALLOW US TO LEAVE IS STILL OPEN...
PLEASE?

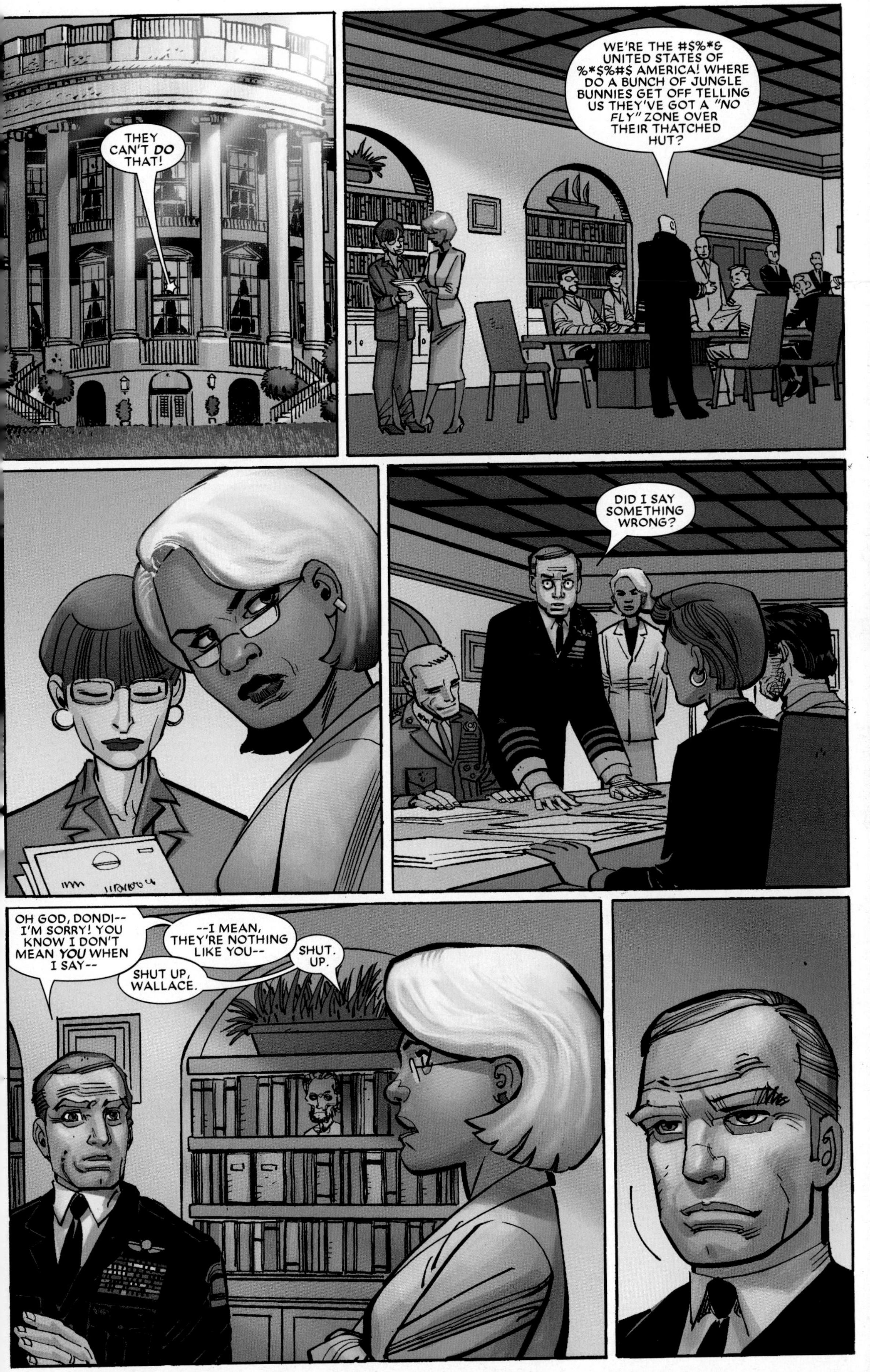
THEY CAN'T DO THAT!
WE'RE THE #$%*& UNITED STATES OF %*$%#$ AMERICA! WHERE DO A BUNCH OF JUNGLE BUNNIES GET OFF TELLING US THEY'VE GOT A "NO FLY" ZONE OVER THEIR THATCHED HUT?
DID I SAY SOMETHING WRONG?
OH GOD, DONDI-- I'M SORRY! YOU KNOW I DON'T MEAN YOU WHEN I SAY--
SHUT UP, WALLACE.
--I MEAN, THEY'RE NOTHING LIKE YOU--
SHUT. UP.

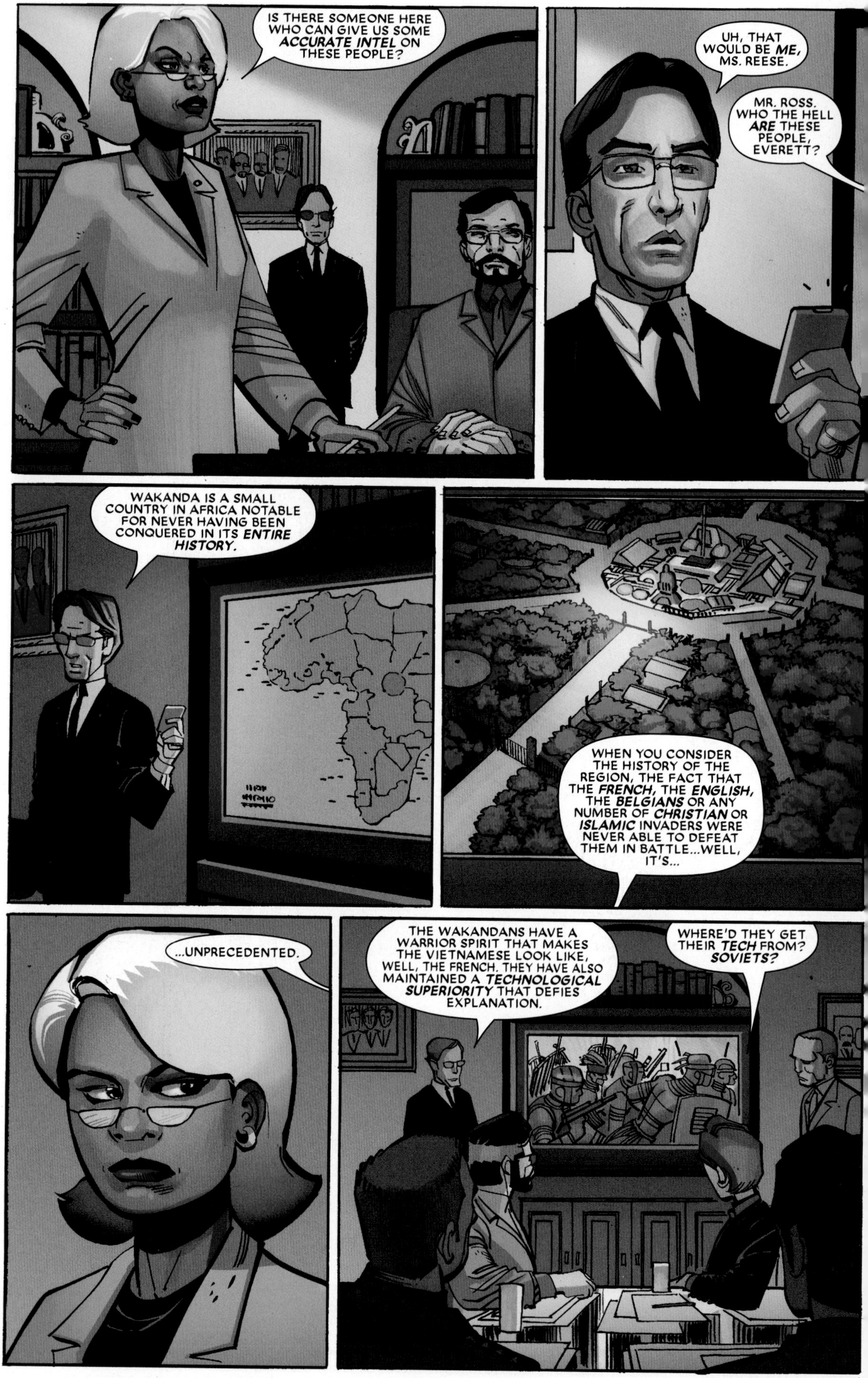
IS THERE SOMEONE HERE WHO CAN GIVE US SOME ACCURATE INTEL ON THESE PEOPLE?
UH, THAT WOULD BE ME, MS. REESE.
MR. ROSS. WHO THE HELL ARE THESE PEOPLE, EVERETT?
WAKANDA IS A SMALL COUNTRY IN AFRICA NOTABLE FOR NEVER HAVING BEEN CONQUERED IN ITS ENTIRE HISTORY.
WHEN YOU CONSIDER THE HISTORY OF THE REGION, THE FACT THAT THE FRENCH, THE ENGLISH, THE BELGIANS OR ANY NUMBER OF CHRISTIAN OR ISLAMIC INVADERS WERE NEVER ABLE TO DEFEAT THEM IN BATTLE...WELL, IT'S...
...UNPRECEDENTED.
THE WAKANDANS HAVE A WARRIOR SPIRIT THAT MAKES THE VIETNAMESE LOOK LIKE, WELL, THE FRENCH. THEY HAVE ALSO MAINTAINED A TECHNOLOGICAL SUPERIORITY THAT DEFIES EXPLANATION.
WHERE'D THEY GET THEIR TECH FROM? SOVIETS?

NO COLD WAR ALLIANCES WITH EITHER SIDE, AND NO CONTEMPORARY ALLIANCES WITH THE ARAB WORLD--INCLUDING O.P.E.C. DESPITE GEOLOGISTS' ESTIMATES THAT THEY HAVE LARGE OIL DEPOSITS--

THAT'S WHAT OUR BOYS AT HALLIBURTON SAID--

--THEY DON'T EVEN PUMP IT.

THAT'S CRAZY.

APPARENTLY THEY DON'T NEED IT AS AN ENERGY SOURCE OR A FINANCIAL BASE. THEY HAVE A VARIETY OF ECO-FRIENDLY ALTERNATIVE POWER SOURCES LIKE SOLAR AND HYDROGEN--

...BAD EXAMPLE...

...MONEY JUST LYING THERE...

...PUBLIC OPINION...

...BIGGER THAN NIGERIA...

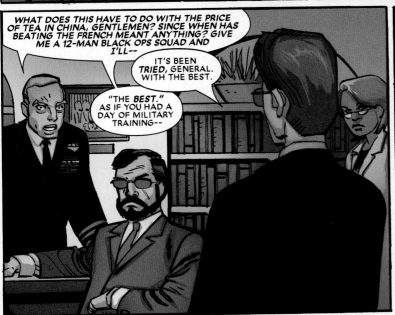

WHAT DOES THIS HAVE TO DO WITH THE PRICE OF TEA IN CHINA, GENTLEMEN? SINCE WHEN HAS BEATING THE FRENCH MEANT ANYTHING? GIVE ME A 12-MAN BLACK OPS SQUAD AND I'LL--

IT'S BEEN TRIED, GENERAL. WITH THE BEST.

"THE BEST." AS IF YOU HAD A DAY OF MILITARY TRAINING--

THE BEST.

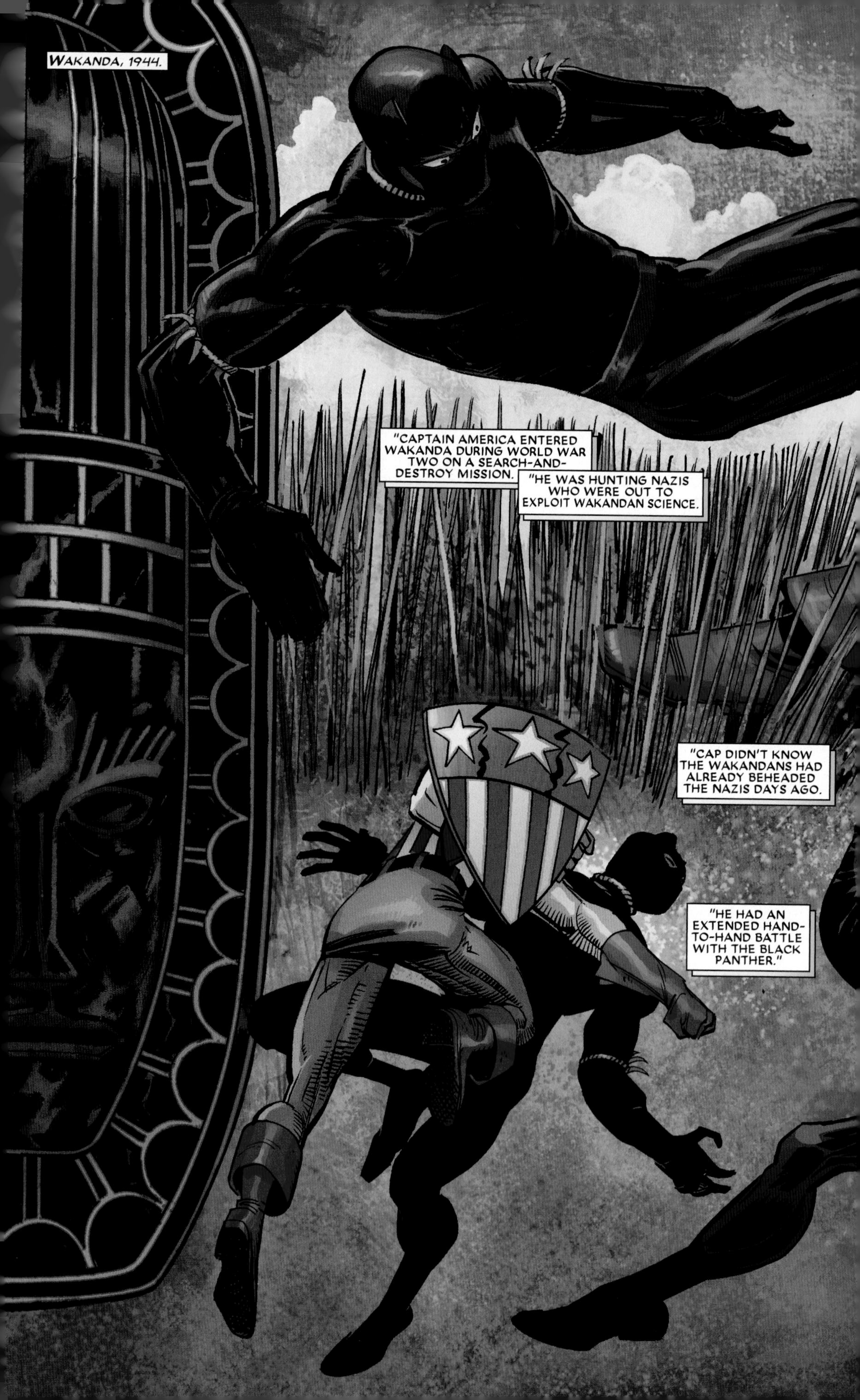
WAKANDA, 1944.
"CAPTAIN AMERICA ENTERED WAKANDA DURING WORLD WAR TWO ON A SEARCH-AND-DESTROY MISSION.
"HE WAS HUNTING NAZIS WHO WERE OUT TO EXPLOIT WAKANDAN SCIENCE.
"CAP DIDN'T KNOW THE WAKANDANS HAD ALREADY BEHEADED THE NAZIS DAYS AGO.
"HE HAD AN EXTENDED HAND-TO-HAND BATTLE WITH THE BLACK PANTHER."

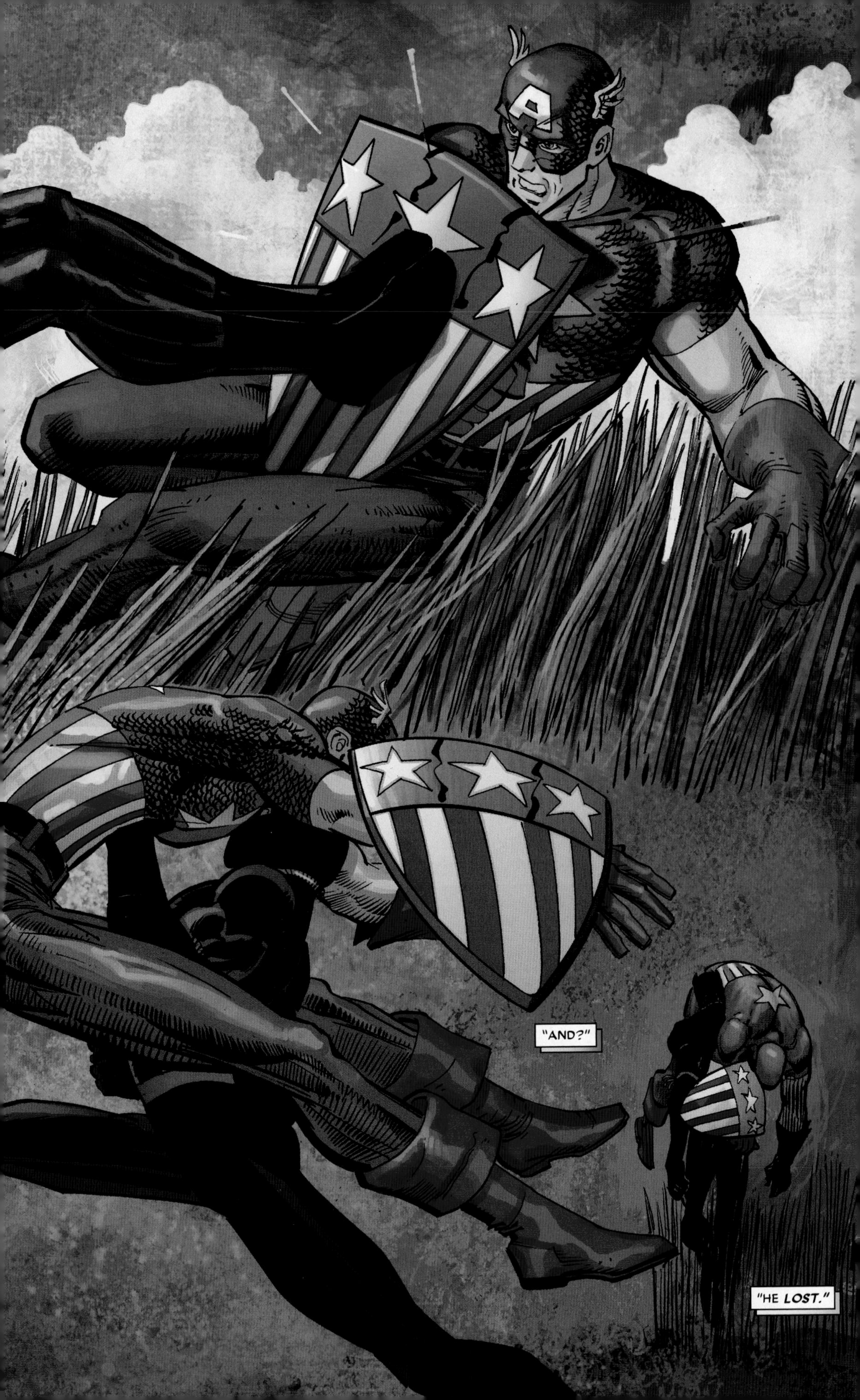
"AND?"
"HE LOST."

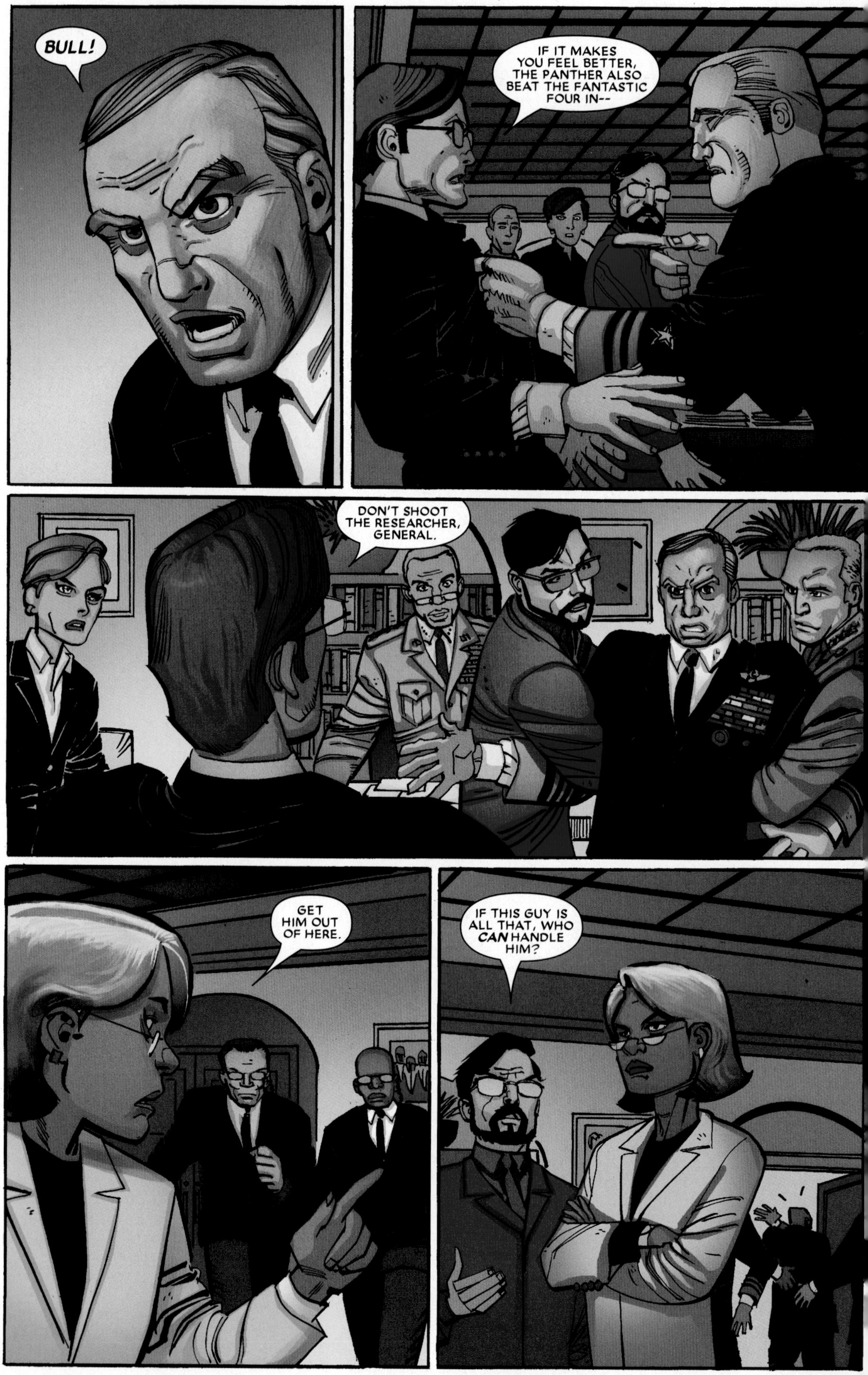
BULL!
IF IT MAKES YOU FEEL BETTER, THE PANTHER ALSO BEAT THE FANTASTIC FOUR IN--
DON'T SHOOT THE RESEARCHER, GENERAL.
GET HIM OUT OF HERE.
IF THIS GUY IS ALL THAT, WHO CAN HANDLE HIM?

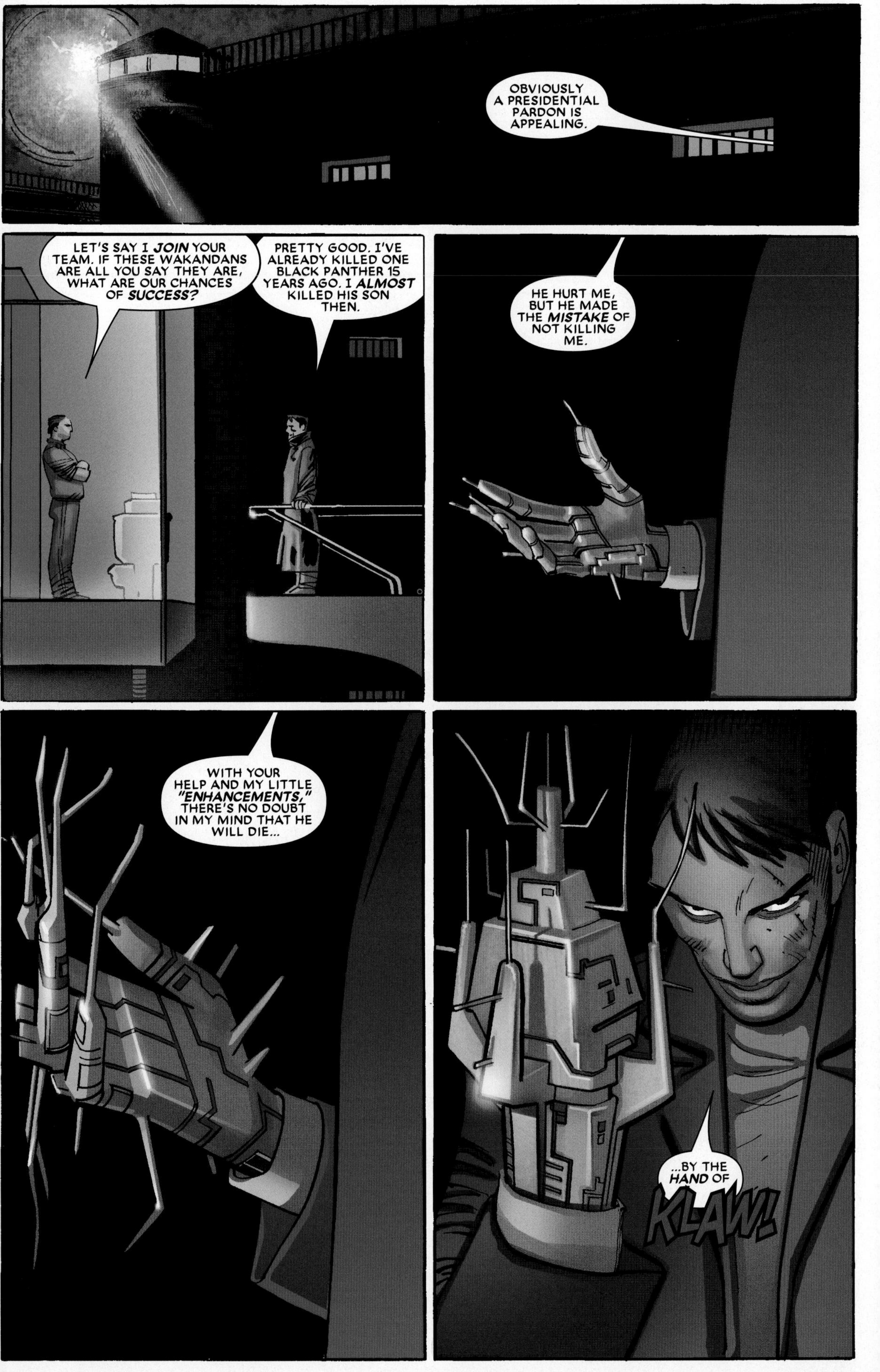
OBVIOUSLY A PRESIDENTIAL PARDON IS APPEALING.
LET'S SAY I *JOIN* YOUR TEAM. IF THESE WAKANDANS ARE ALL YOU SAY THEY ARE, WHAT ARE OUR CHANCES OF *SUCCESS?*
PRETTY GOOD. I'VE ALREADY KILLED ONE BLACK PANTHER 15 YEARS AGO. I *ALMOST* KILLED HIS SON THEN.
HE HURT ME, BUT HE MADE THE *MISTAKE* OF NOT KILLING ME.
WITH YOUR HELP AND MY LITTLE *"ENHANCEMENTS,"* THERE'S NO DOUBT IN MY MIND THAT HE WILL DIE...
...BY THE *HAND* OF
KLAW!

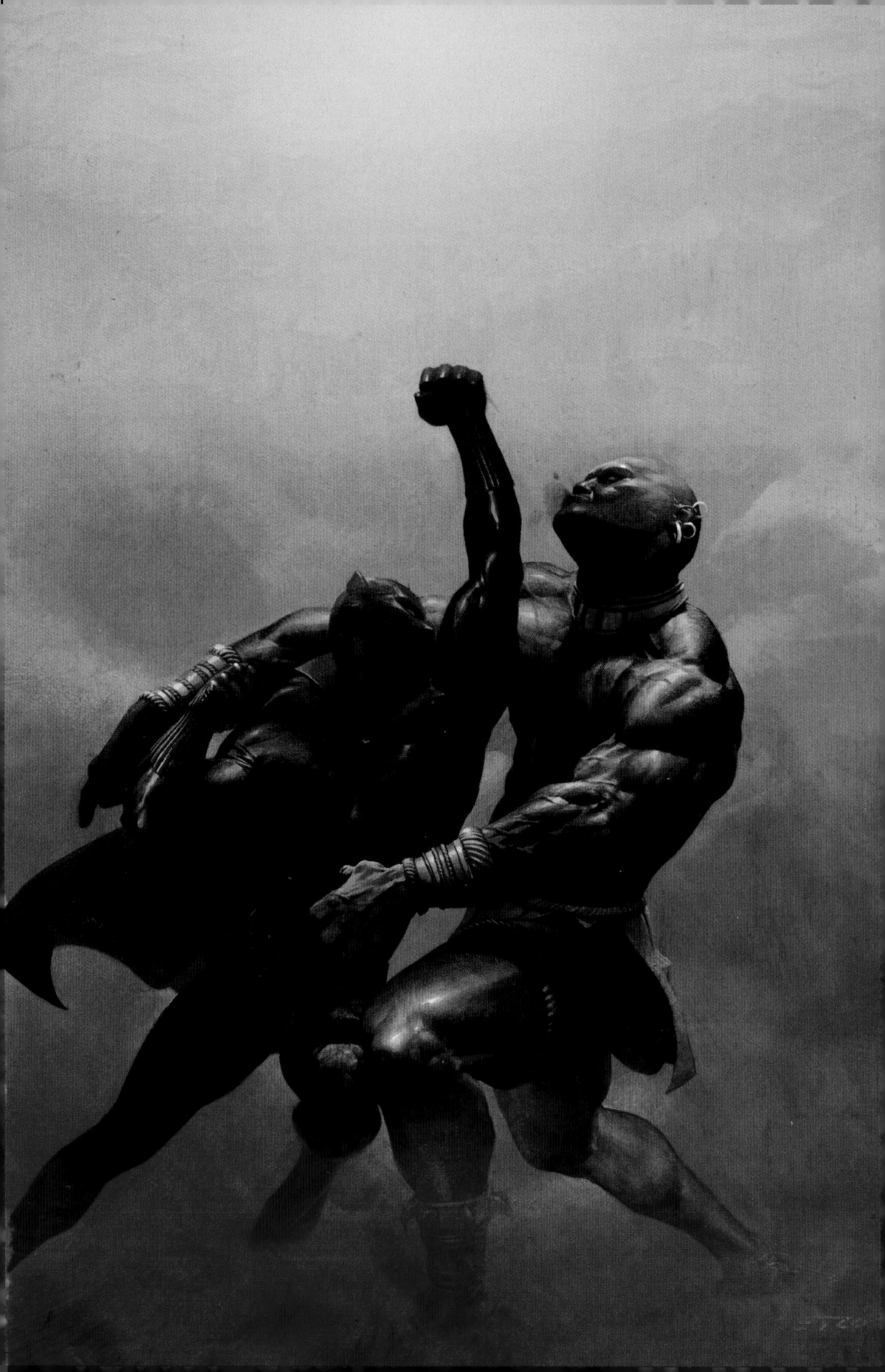

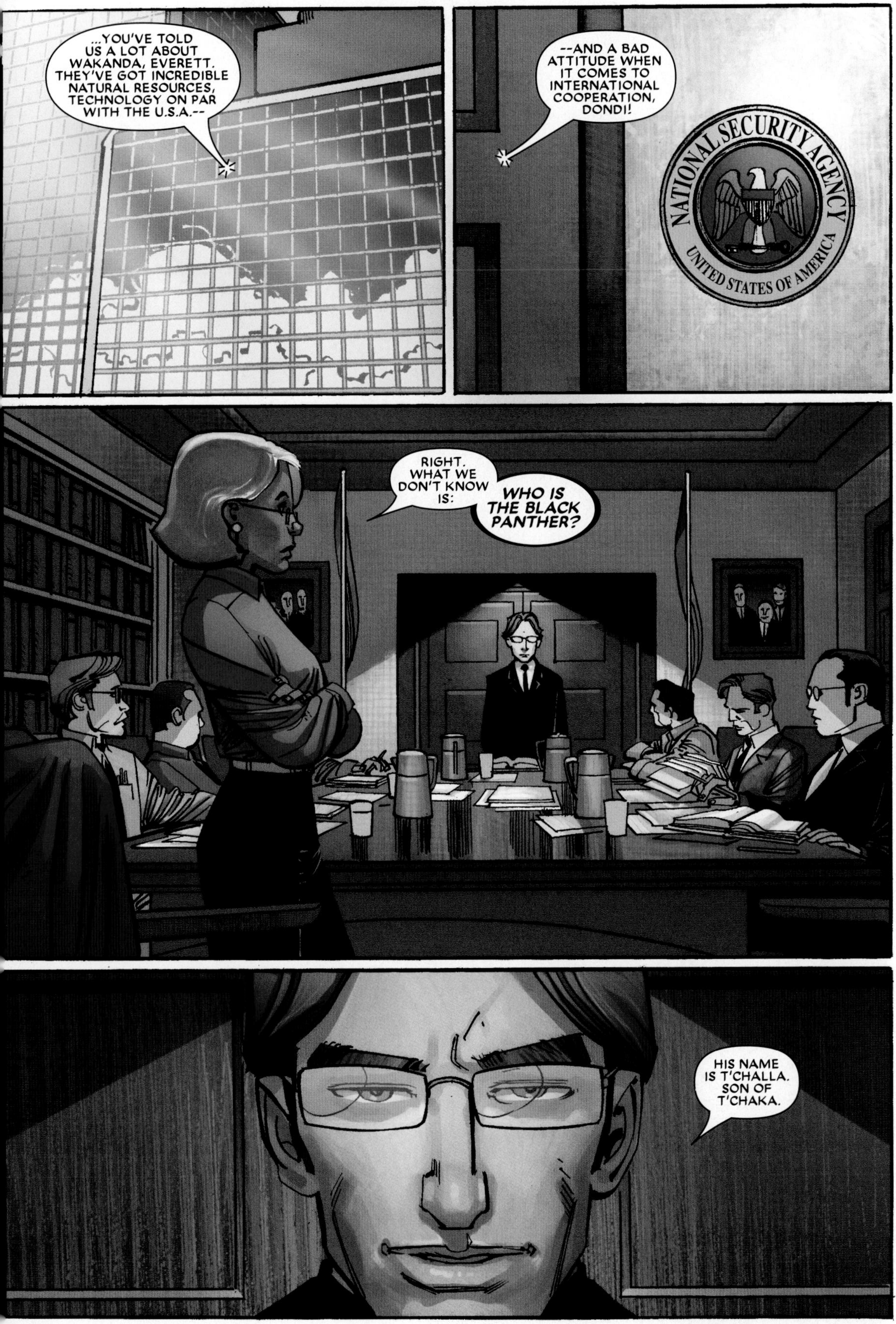
...YOU'VE TOLD US A LOT ABOUT WAKANDA, EVERETT. THEY'VE GOT INCREDIBLE NATURAL RESOURCES, TECHNOLOGY ON PAR WITH THE U.S.A.--
--AND A BAD ATTITUDE WHEN IT COMES TO INTERNATIONAL COOPERATION, DONDI!
NATIONAL SECURITY AGENCY
UNITED STATES OF AMERICA
RIGHT. WHAT WE DON'T KNOW IS:
WHO IS THE BLACK PANTHER?
HIS NAME IS T'CHALLA. SON OF T'CHAKA.

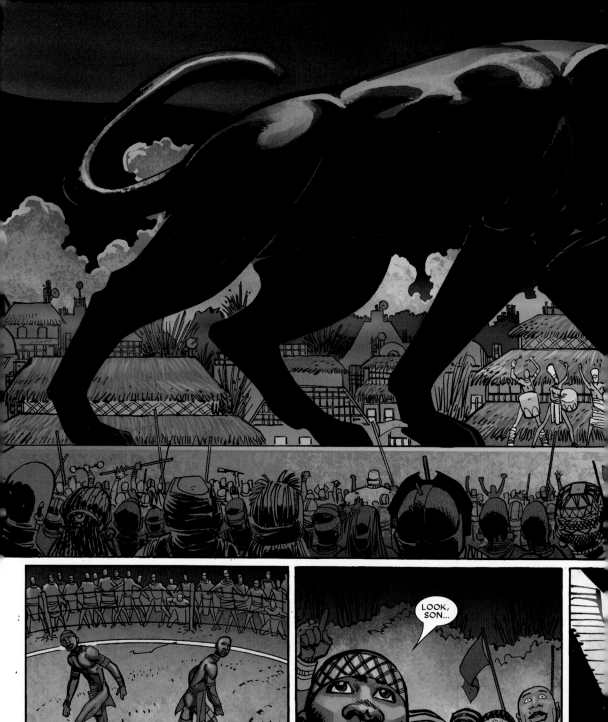

LOOK, SON...

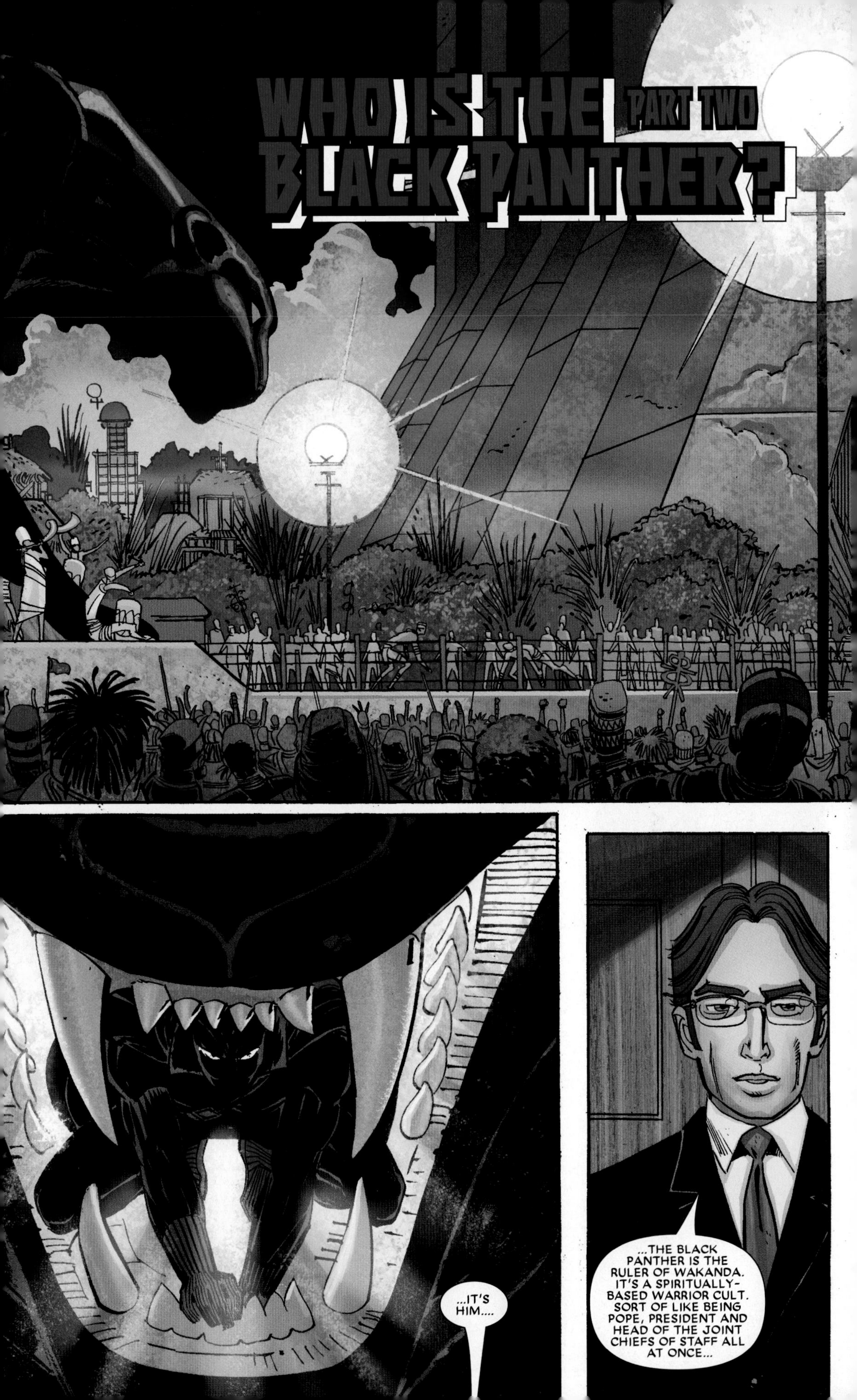
WHO IS THE BLACK PANTHER?
PART TWO
...IT'S HIM....
...THE BLACK PANTHER IS THE RULER OF WAKANDA. IT'S A SPIRITUALLY-BASED WARRIOR CULT. SORT OF LIKE BEING POPE, PRESIDENT AND HEAD OF THE JOINT CHIEFS OF STAFF ALL AT ONCE...

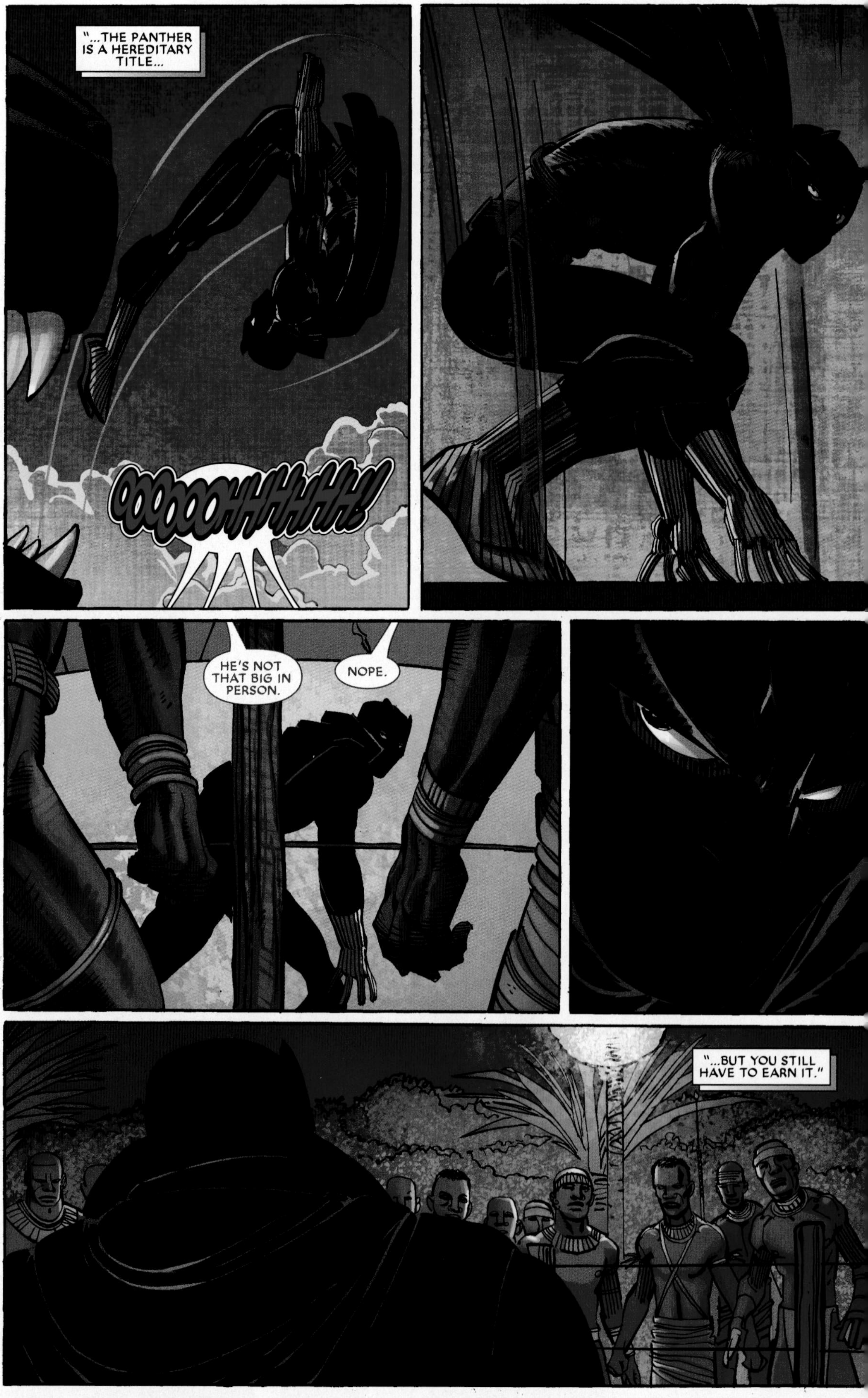
"...THE PANTHER IS A HEREDITARY TITLE...
OOOOOOOHHHHHHH!!
HE'S NOT THAT BIG IN PERSON.
NOPE.
"...BUT YOU STILL HAVE TO EARN IT."

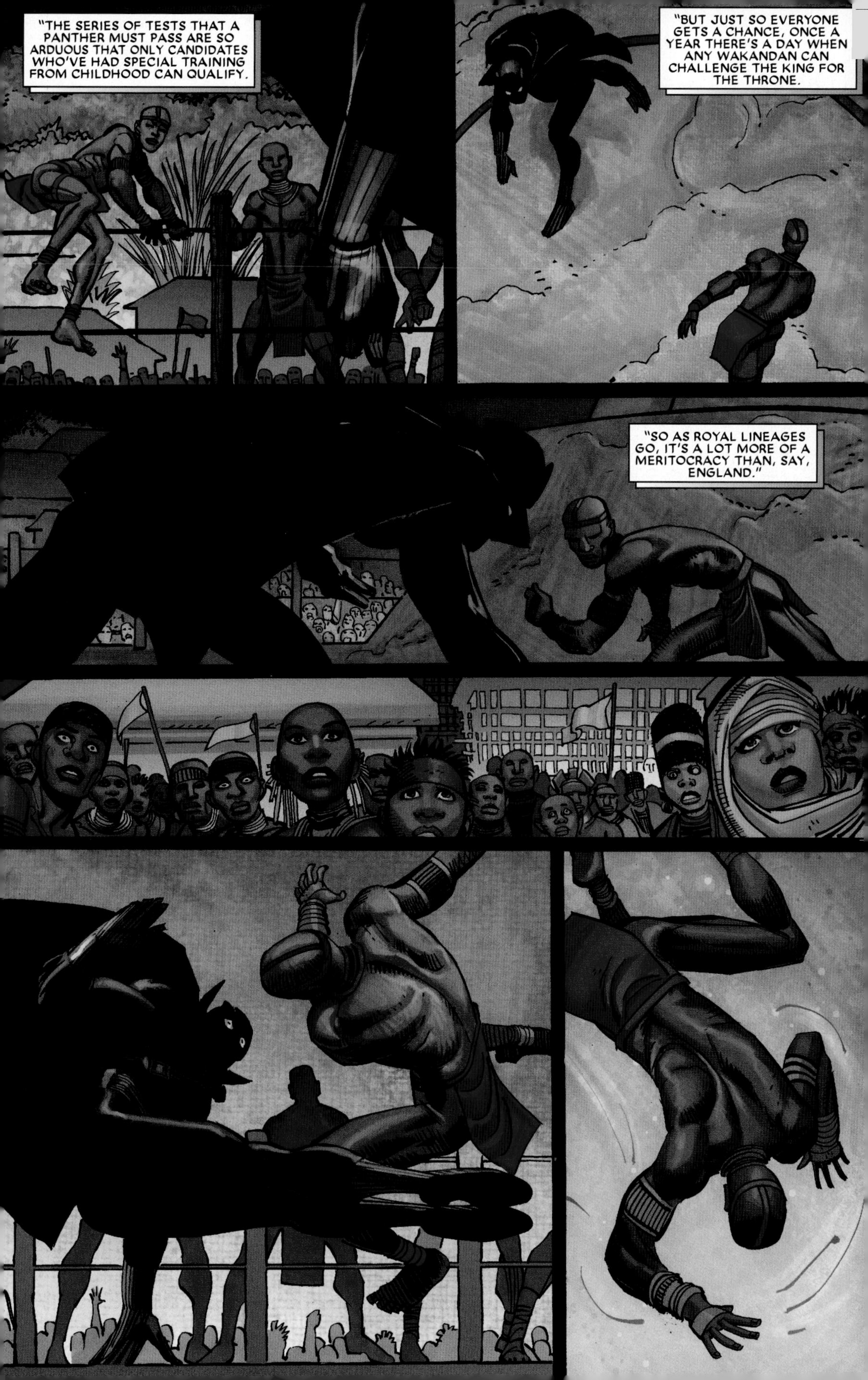
"THE SERIES OF TESTS THAT A PANTHER MUST PASS ARE SO ARDUOUS THAT ONLY CANDIDATES WHO'VE HAD SPECIAL TRAINING FROM CHILDHOOD CAN QUALIFY.
"BUT JUST SO EVERYONE GETS A CHANCE, ONCE A YEAR THERE'S A DAY WHEN ANY WAKANDAN CAN CHALLENGE THE KING FOR THE THRONE.
"SO AS ROYAL LINEAGES GO, IT'S A LOT MORE OF A MERITOCRACY THAN, SAY, ENGLAND."

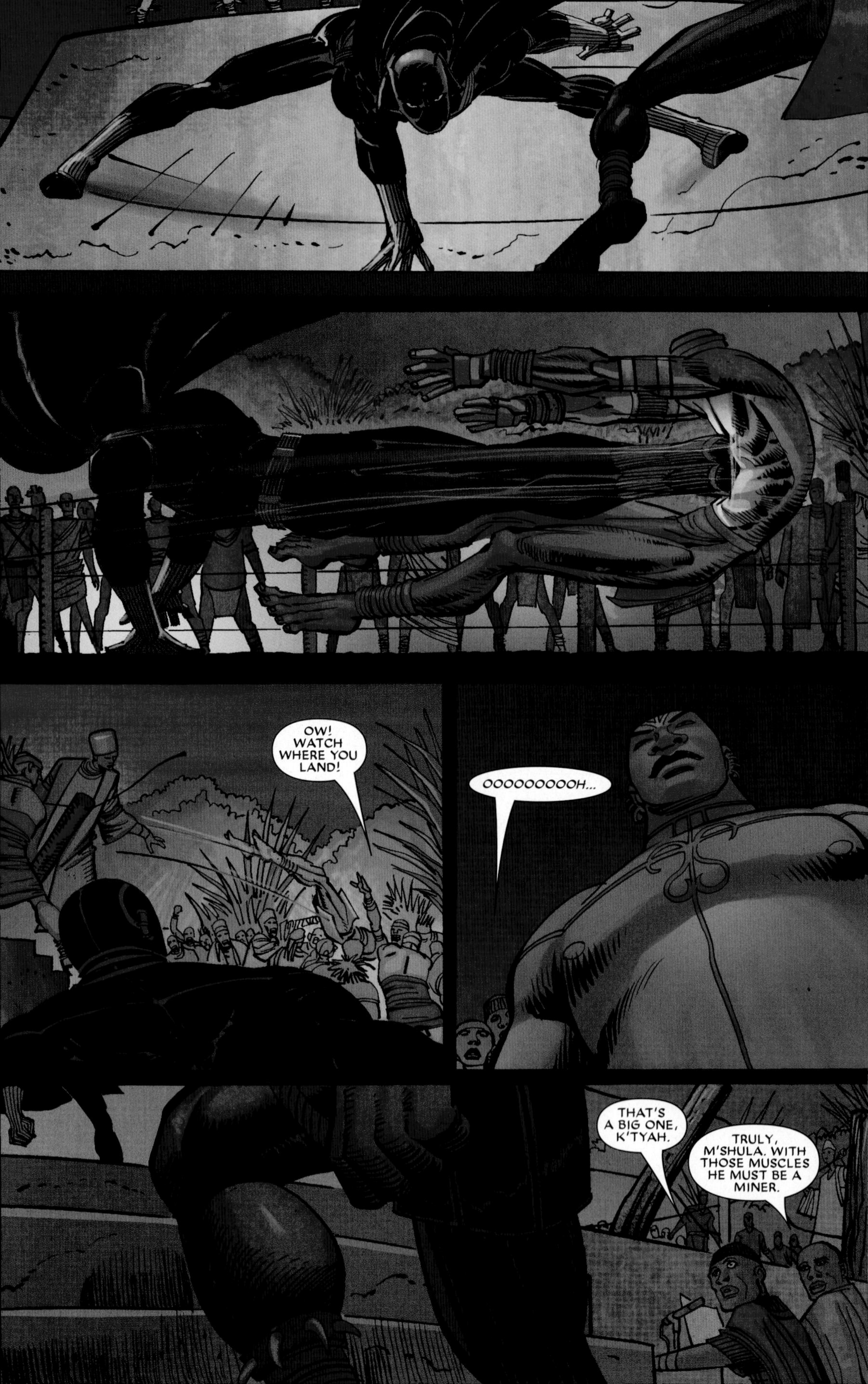
OW! WATCH WHERE YOU LAND!
OOOOOOOOOH...
THAT'S A BIG ONE, K'TYAH.
TRULY, M'SHULA. WITH THOSE MUSCLES HE MUST BE A MINER.

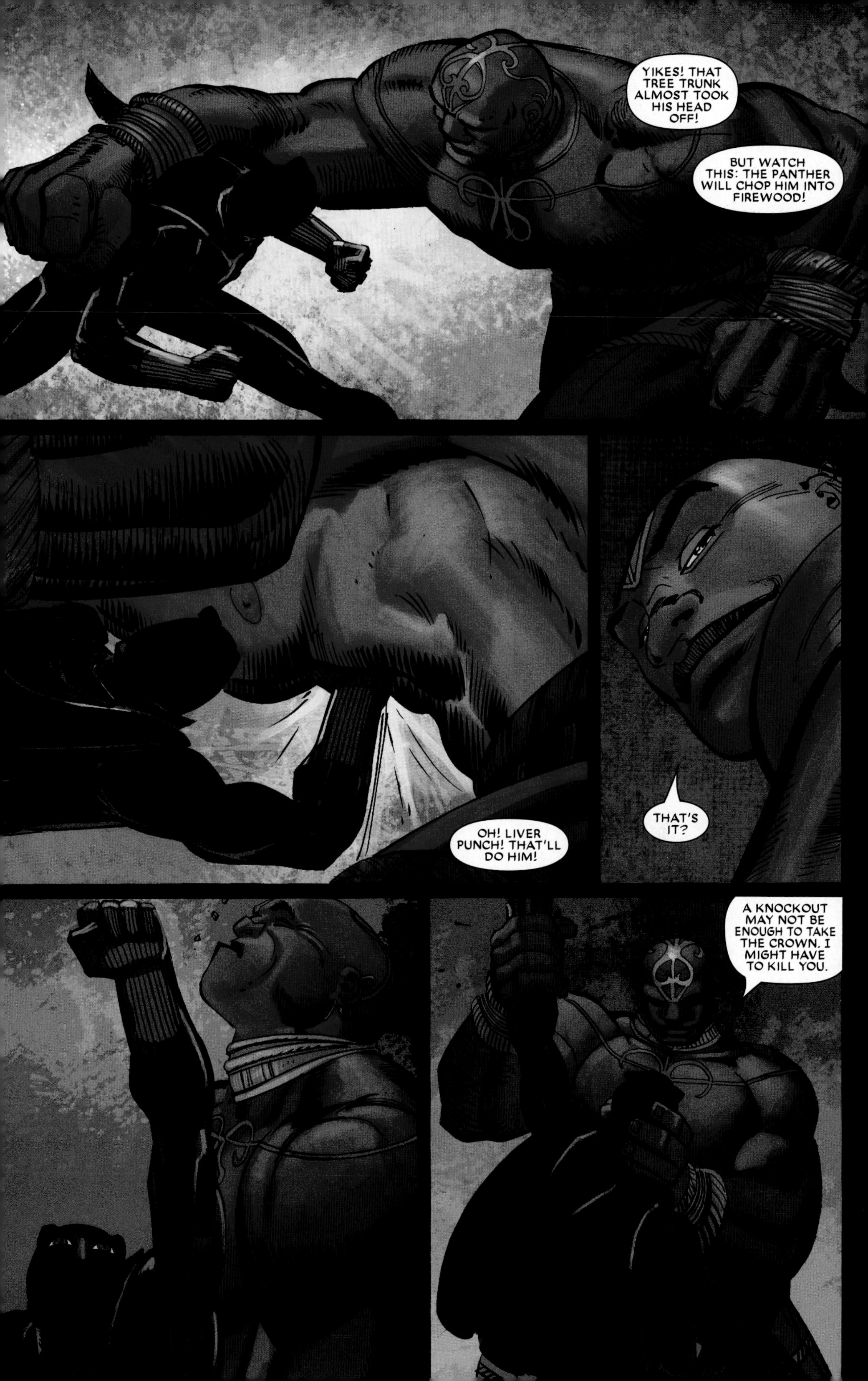
YIKES! THAT TREE TRUNK ALMOST TOOK HIS HEAD OFF!
BUT WATCH THIS: THE PANTHER WILL CHOP HIM INTO FIREWOOD!
OH! LIVER PUNCH! THAT'LL DO HIM!
THAT'S IT?
A KNOCKOUT MAY NOT BE ENOUGH TO TAKE THE CROWN. I MIGHT HAVE TO KILL YOU.

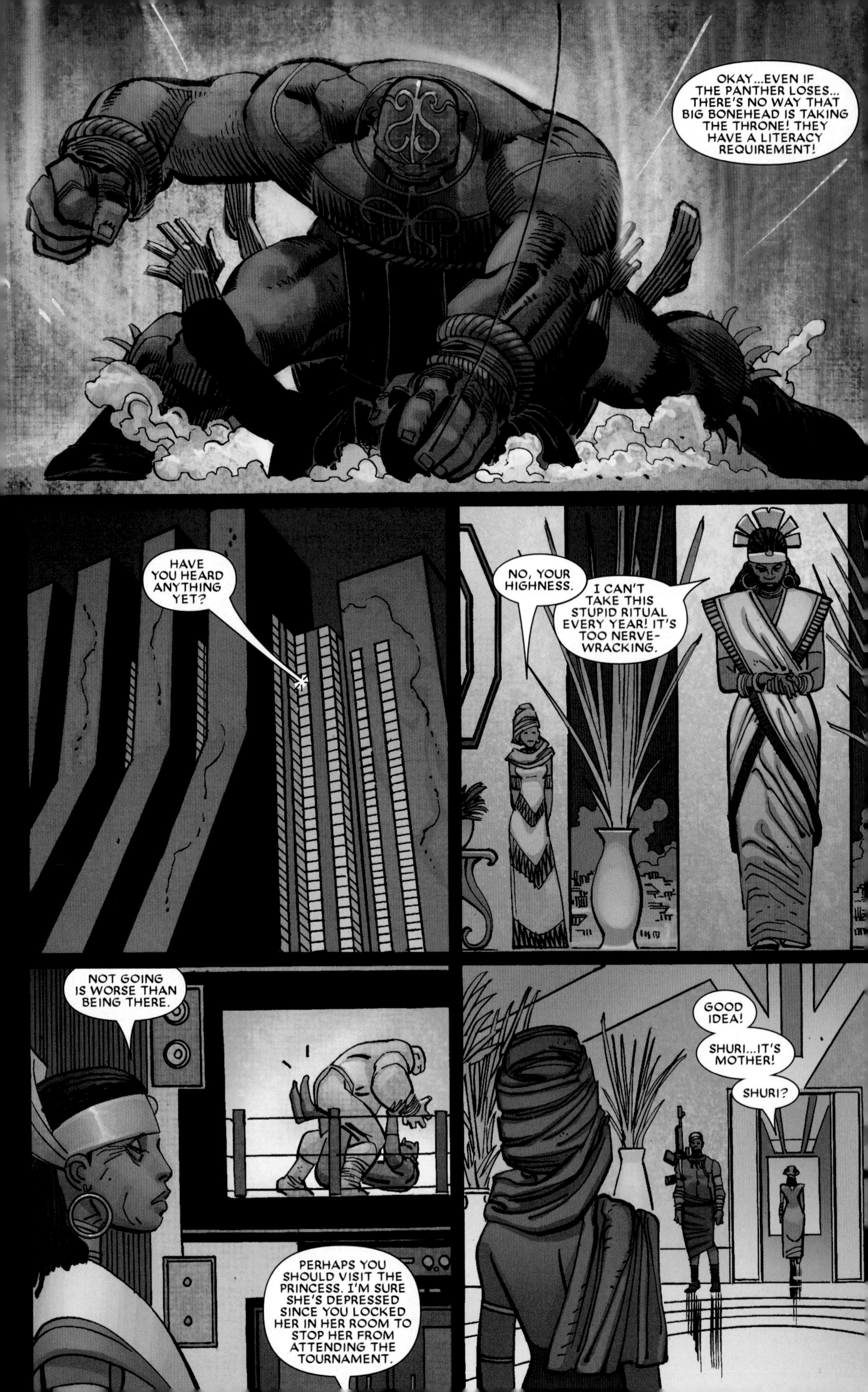
OKAY...EVEN IF THE PANTHER LOSES... THERE'S NO WAY THAT BIG BONEHEAD IS TAKING THE THRONE! THEY HAVE A LITERACY REQUIREMENT!
HAVE YOU HEARD ANYTHING YET?
NO, YOUR HIGHNESS.
I CAN'T TAKE THIS STUPID RITUAL EVERY YEAR! IT'S TOO NERVE-WRACKING.
NOT GOING IS WORSE THAN BEING THERE.
PERHAPS YOU SHOULD VISIT THE PRINCESS. I'M SURE SHE'S DEPRESSED SINCE YOU LOCKED HER IN HER ROOM TO STOP HER FROM ATTENDING THE TOURNAMENT.
GOOD IDEA!
SHURI...IT'S MOTHER!
SHURI?

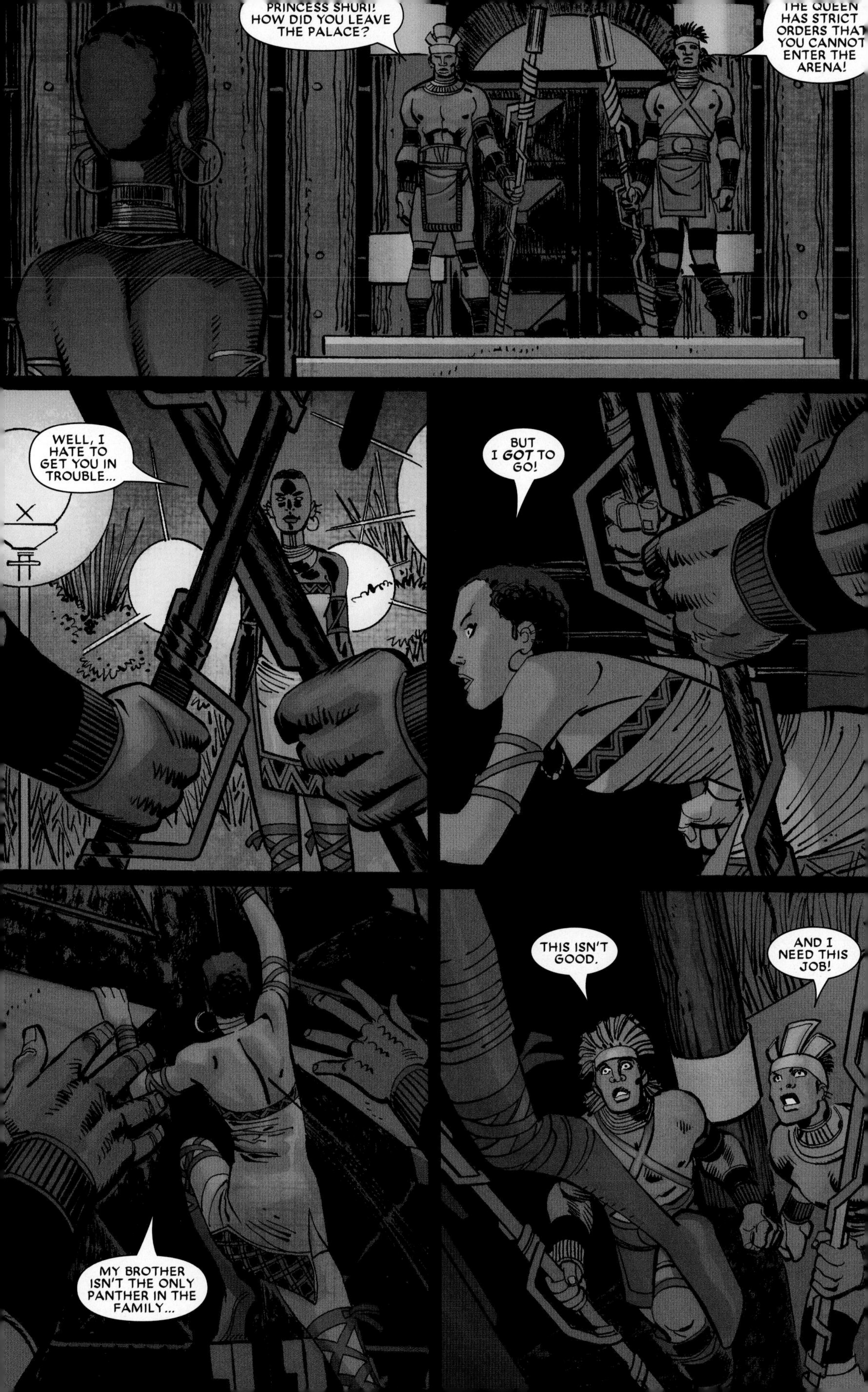
PRINCESS SHURI! HOW DID YOU LEAVE THE PALACE?
THE QUEEN HAS STRICT ORDERS THAT YOU CANNOT ENTER THE ARENA!
WELL, I HATE TO GET YOU IN TROUBLE...
BUT I *GOT* TO GO!
MY BROTHER ISN'T THE ONLY PANTHER IN THE FAMILY...
THIS ISN'T GOOD.
AND I NEED THIS JOB!

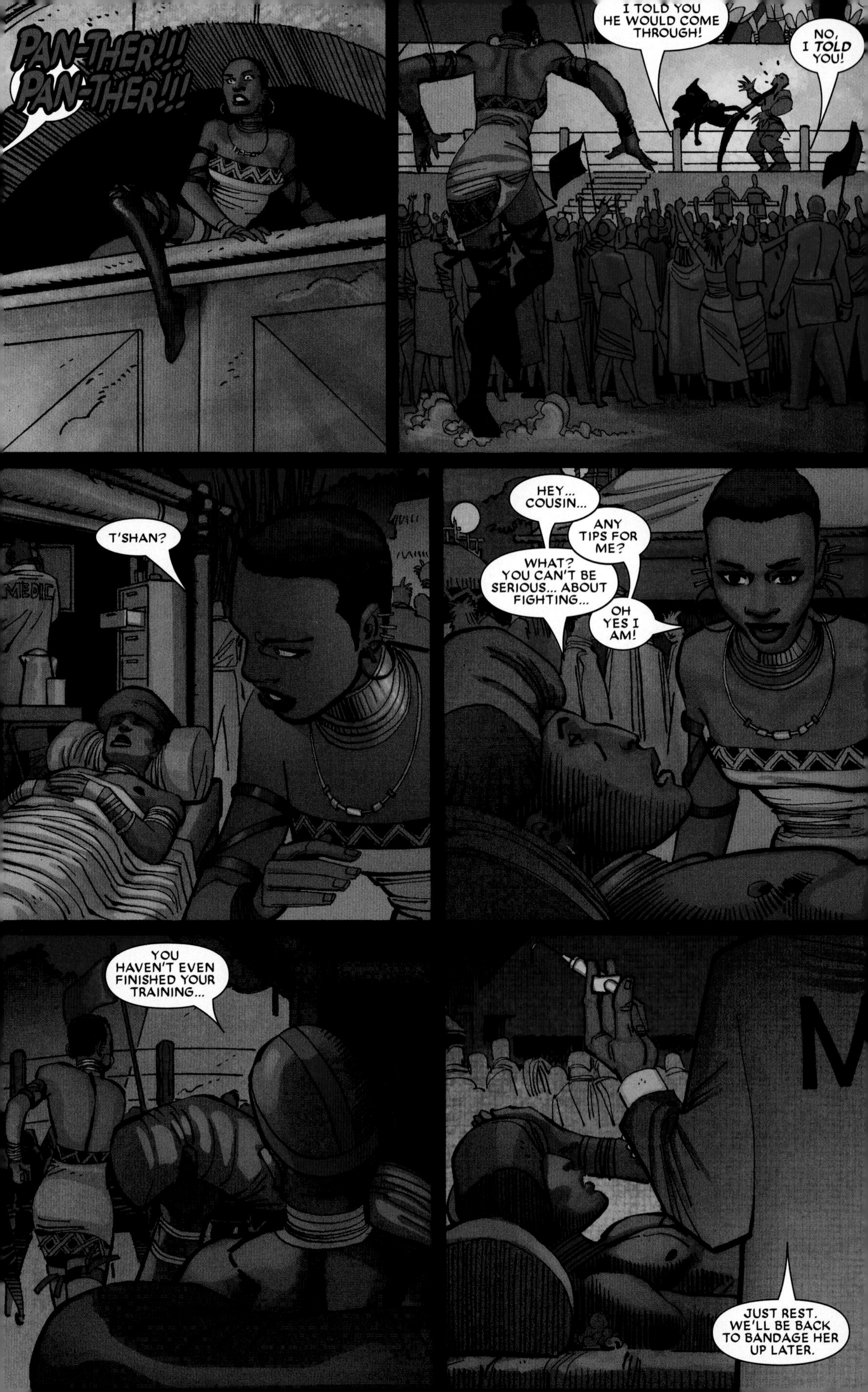
PAN-THER!!! PAN-THER!!!
I TOLD YOU HE WOULD COME THROUGH!
NO, I TOLD YOU!
T'SHAN?
MEDIC
HEY... COUSIN...
ANY TIPS FOR ME?
WHAT? YOU CAN'T BE SERIOUS... ABOUT FIGHTING...
OH YES I AM!
YOU HAVEN'T EVEN FINISHED YOUR TRAINING...
JUST REST. WE'LL BE BACK TO BANDAGE HER UP LATER.

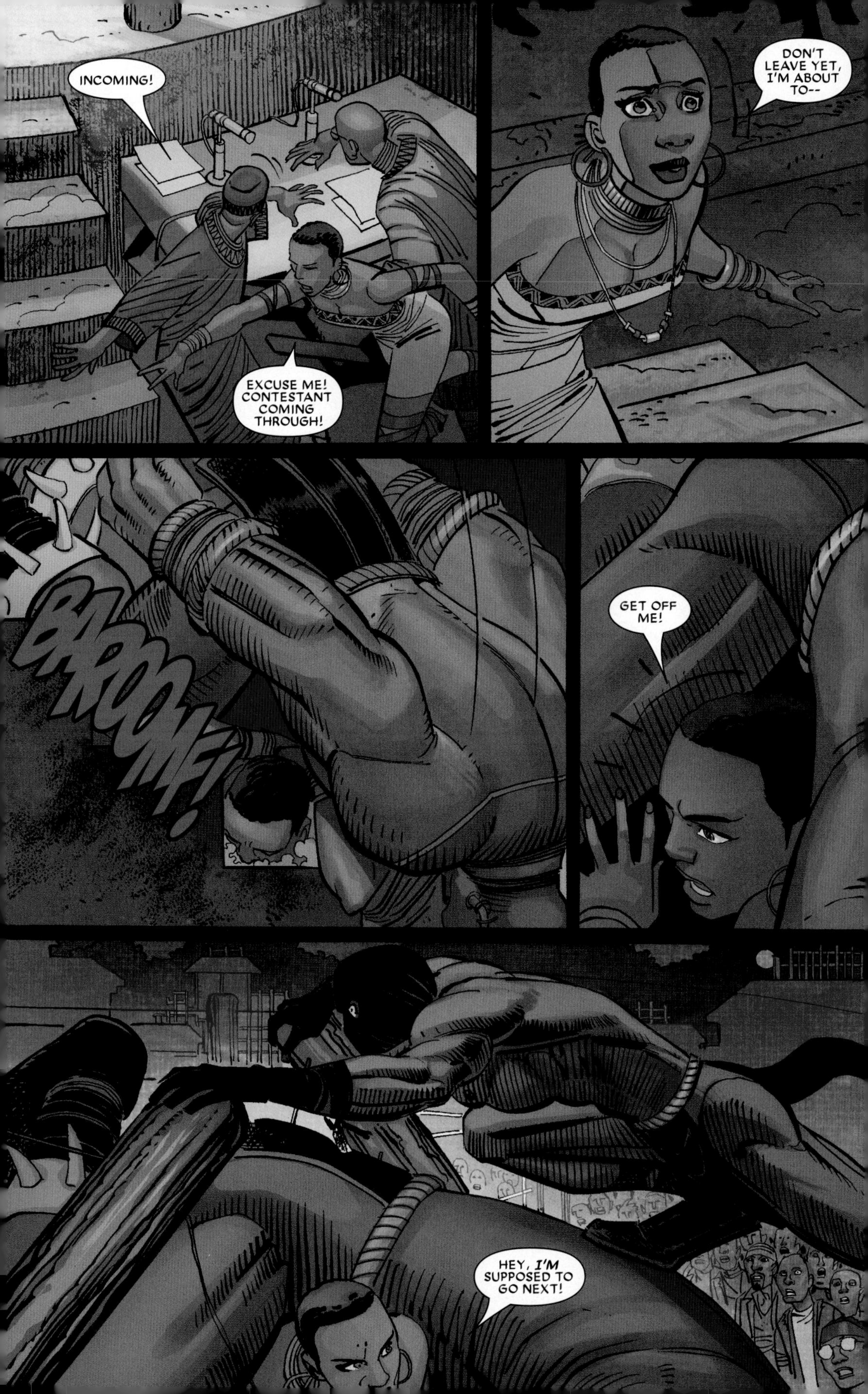
INCOMING!
EXCUSE ME! CONTESTANT COMING THROUGH!
DON'T LEAVE YET, I'M ABOUT TO--
BAROOM!
GET OFF ME!
HEY, I'M SUPPOSED TO GO NEXT!

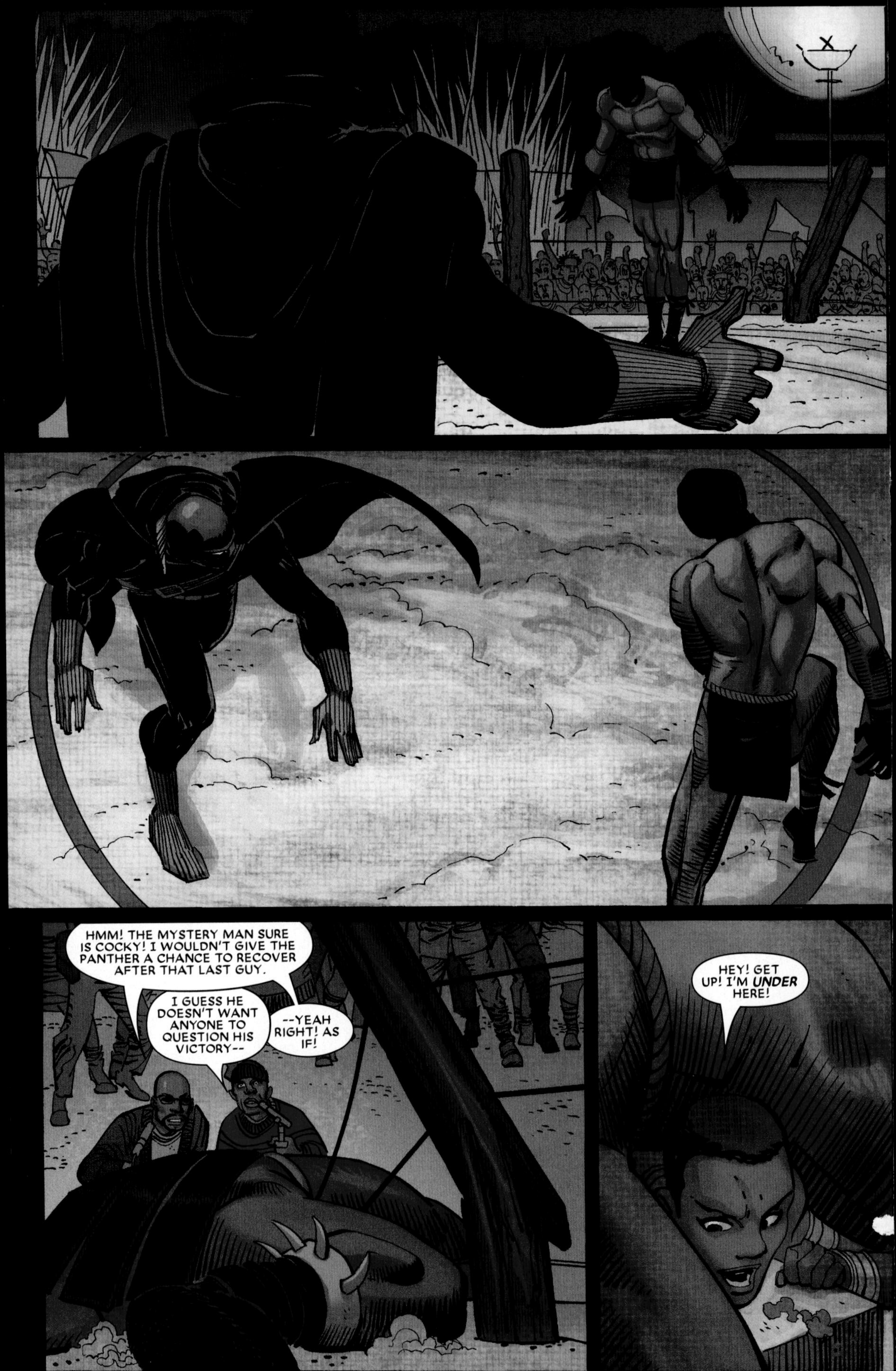
HMM! THE MYSTERY MAN SURE IS COCKY! I WOULDN'T GIVE THE PANTHER A CHANCE TO RECOVER AFTER THAT LAST GUY.
I GUESS HE DOESN'T WANT ANYONE TO QUESTION HIS VICTORY--
--YEAH RIGHT! AS IF!
HEY! GET UP! I'M UNDER HERE!

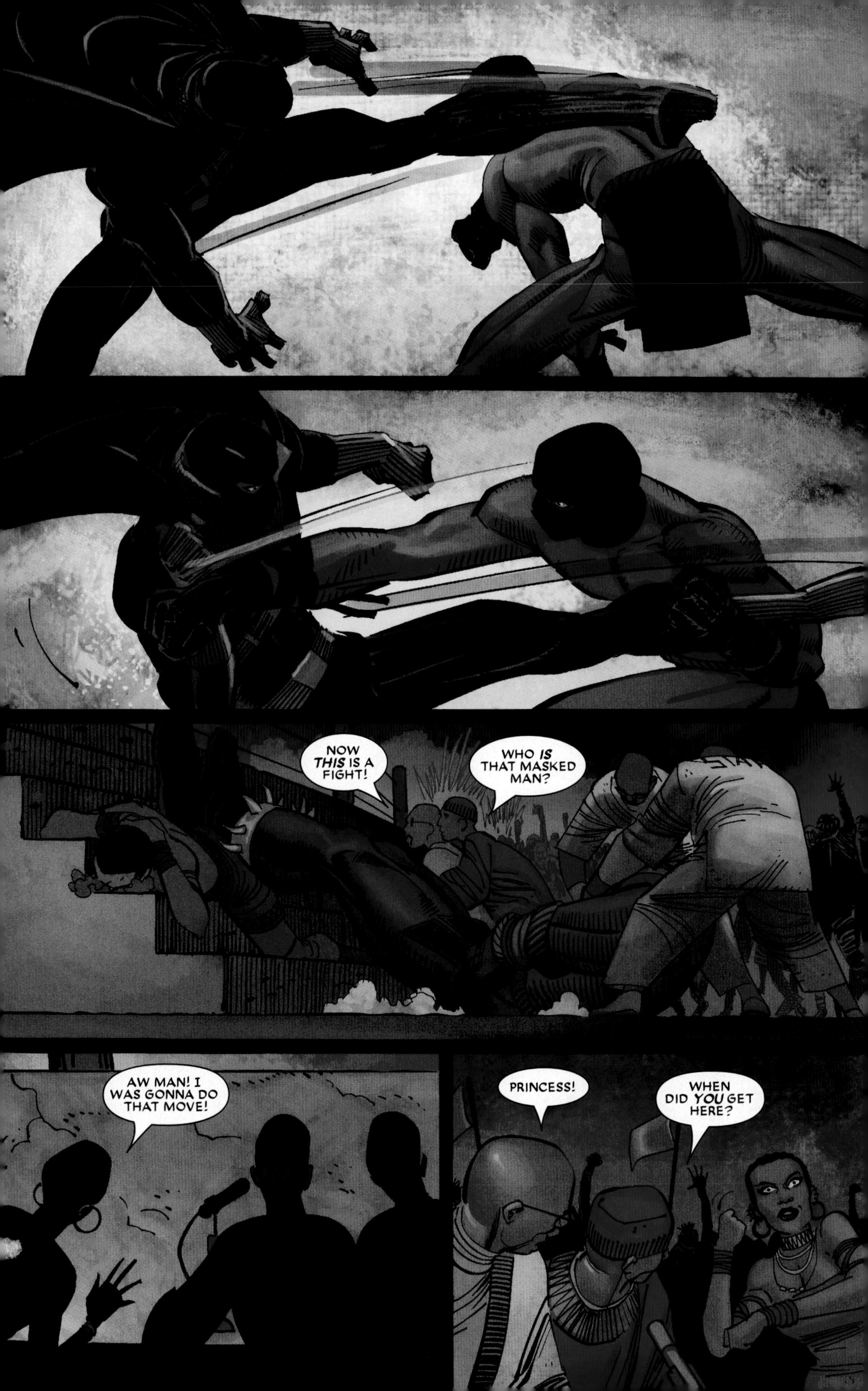
NOW THIS IS A FIGHT!
WHO IS THAT MASKED MAN?
AW MAN! I WAS GONNA DO THAT MOVE!
PRINCESS!
WHEN DID YOU GET HERE?

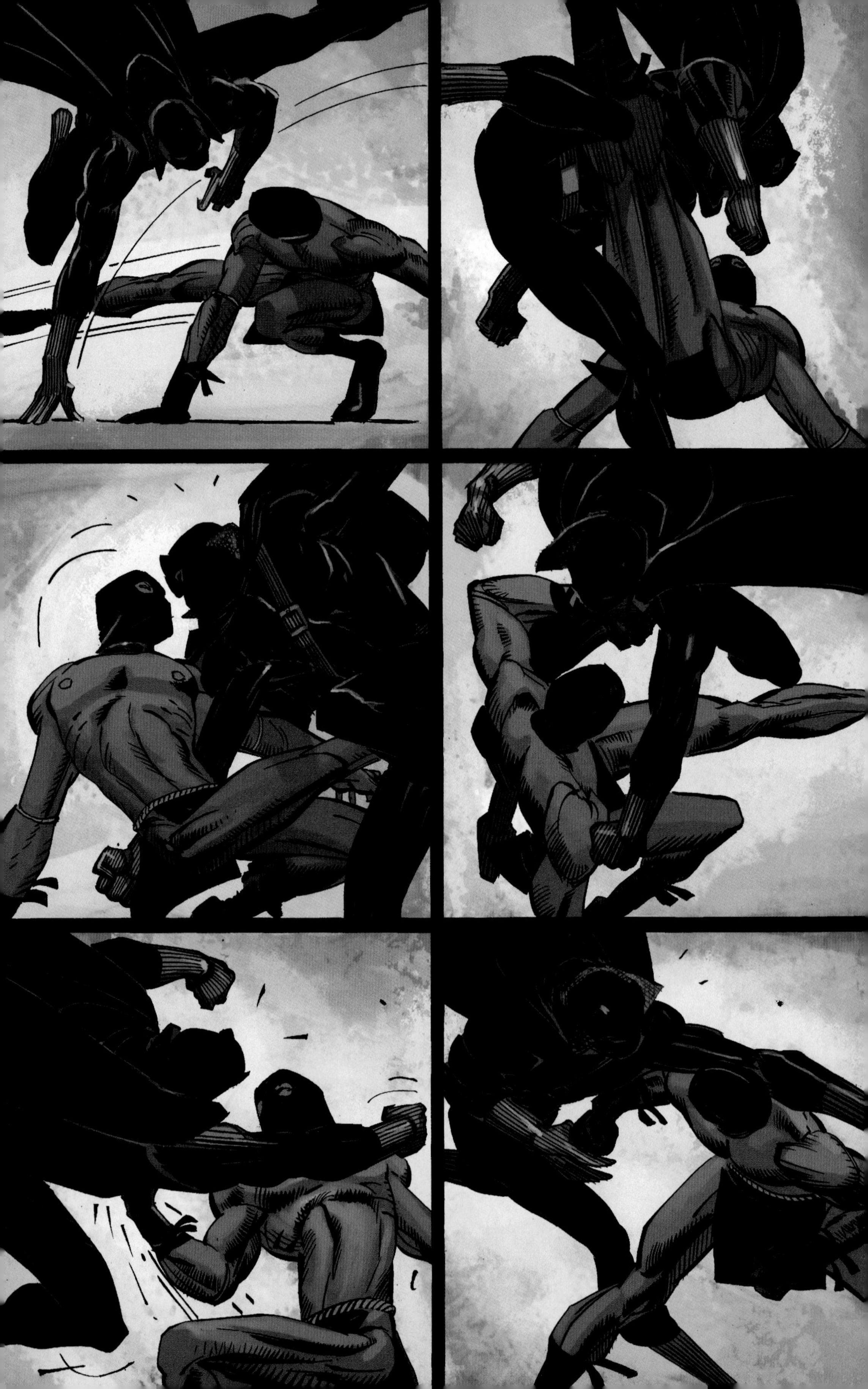

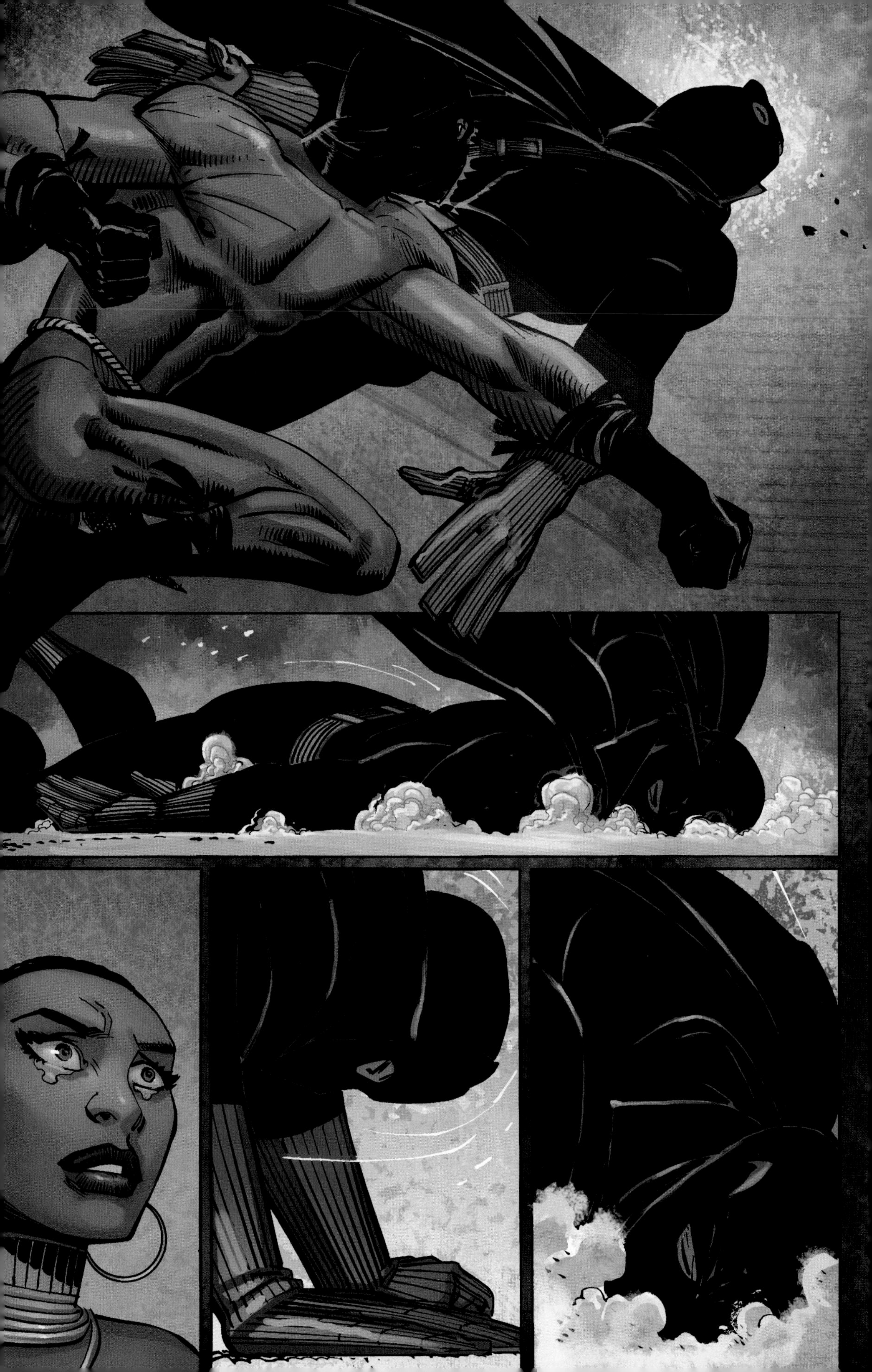

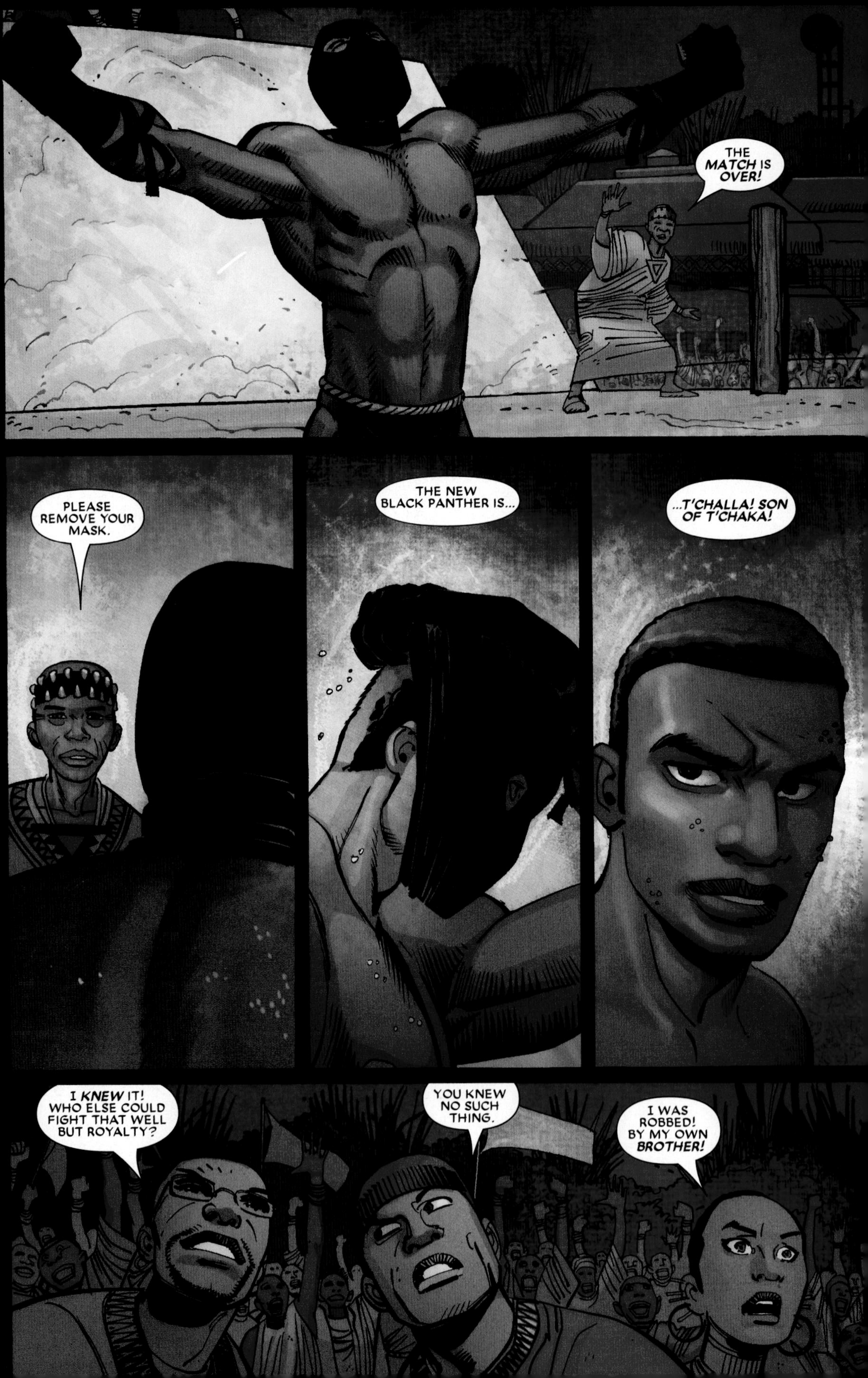
THE MATCH IS OVER!
PLEASE REMOVE YOUR MASK.
THE NEW BLACK PANTHER IS...
...T'CHALLA! SON OF T'CHAKA!
I KNEW IT! WHO ELSE COULD FIGHT THAT WELL BUT ROYALTY?
YOU KNEW NO SUCH THING.
I WAS ROBBED! BY MY OWN BROTHER!

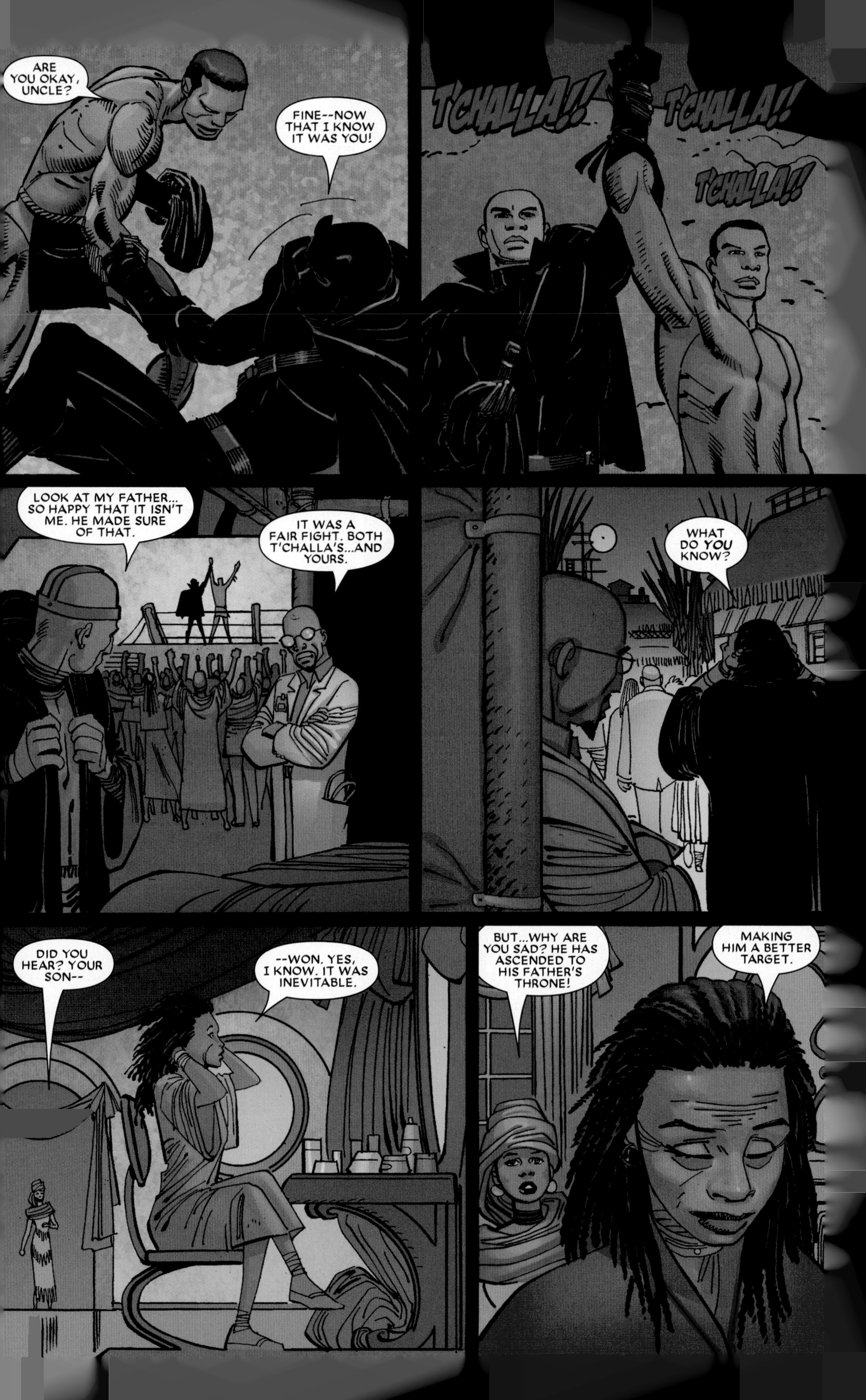
ARE YOU OKAY, UNCLE?
FINE--NOW THAT I KNOW IT WAS YOU!
T'CHALLA!!
T'CHALLA!
T'CHALLA!!
LOOK AT MY FATHER... SO HAPPY THAT IT ISN'T ME. HE MADE SURE OF THAT.
IT WAS A FAIR FIGHT. BOTH T'CHALLA'S...AND YOURS.
WHAT DO YOU KNOW?
DID YOU HEAR? YOUR SON--
--WON. YES, I KNOW. IT WAS INEVITABLE.
BUT...WHY ARE YOU SAD? HE HAS ASCENDED TO HIS FATHER'S THRONE!
MAKING HIM A BETTER TARGET.

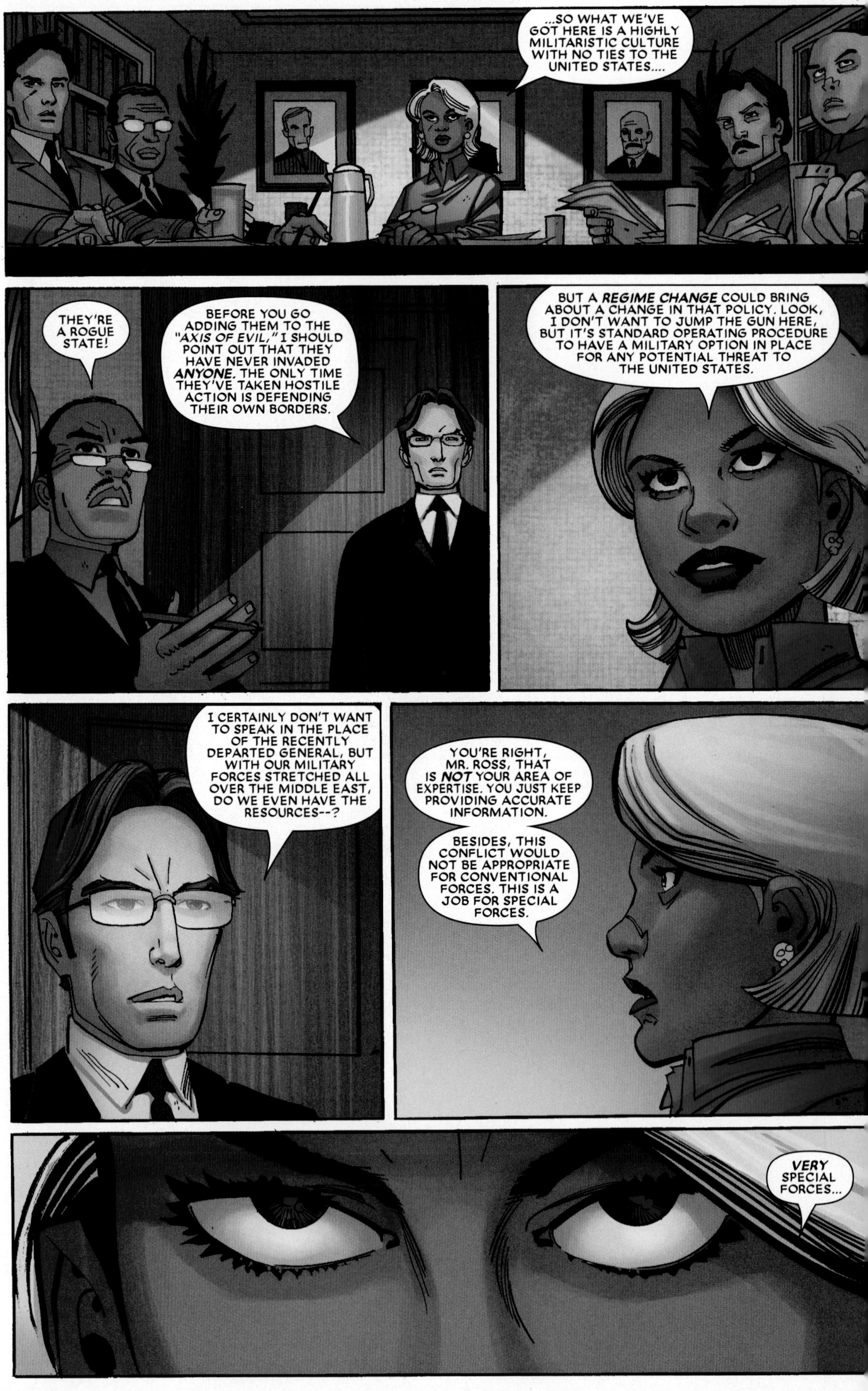
...SO WHAT WE'VE GOT HERE IS A HIGHLY MILITARISTIC CULTURE WITH NO TIES TO THE UNITED STATES....
THEY'RE A ROGUE STATE!
BEFORE YOU GO ADDING THEM TO THE "AXIS OF EVIL," I SHOULD POINT OUT THAT THEY HAVE NEVER INVADED ANYONE. THE ONLY TIME THEY'VE TAKEN HOSTILE ACTION IS DEFENDING THEIR OWN BORDERS.
BUT A REGIME CHANGE COULD BRING ABOUT A CHANGE IN THAT POLICY. LOOK, I DON'T WANT TO JUMP THE GUN HERE, BUT IT'S STANDARD OPERATING PROCEDURE TO HAVE A MILITARY OPTION IN PLACE FOR ANY POTENTIAL THREAT TO THE UNITED STATES.
I CERTAINLY DON'T WANT TO SPEAK IN THE PLACE OF THE RECENTLY DEPARTED GENERAL, BUT WITH OUR MILITARY FORCES STRETCHED ALL OVER THE MIDDLE EAST, DO WE EVEN HAVE THE RESOURCES--?
YOU'RE RIGHT, MR. ROSS, THAT IS NOT YOUR AREA OF EXPERTISE. YOU JUST KEEP PROVIDING ACCURATE INFORMATION.
BESIDES, THIS CONFLICT WOULD NOT BE APPROPRIATE FOR CONVENTIONAL FORCES. THIS IS A JOB FOR SPECIAL FORCES.
VERY SPECIAL FORCES...

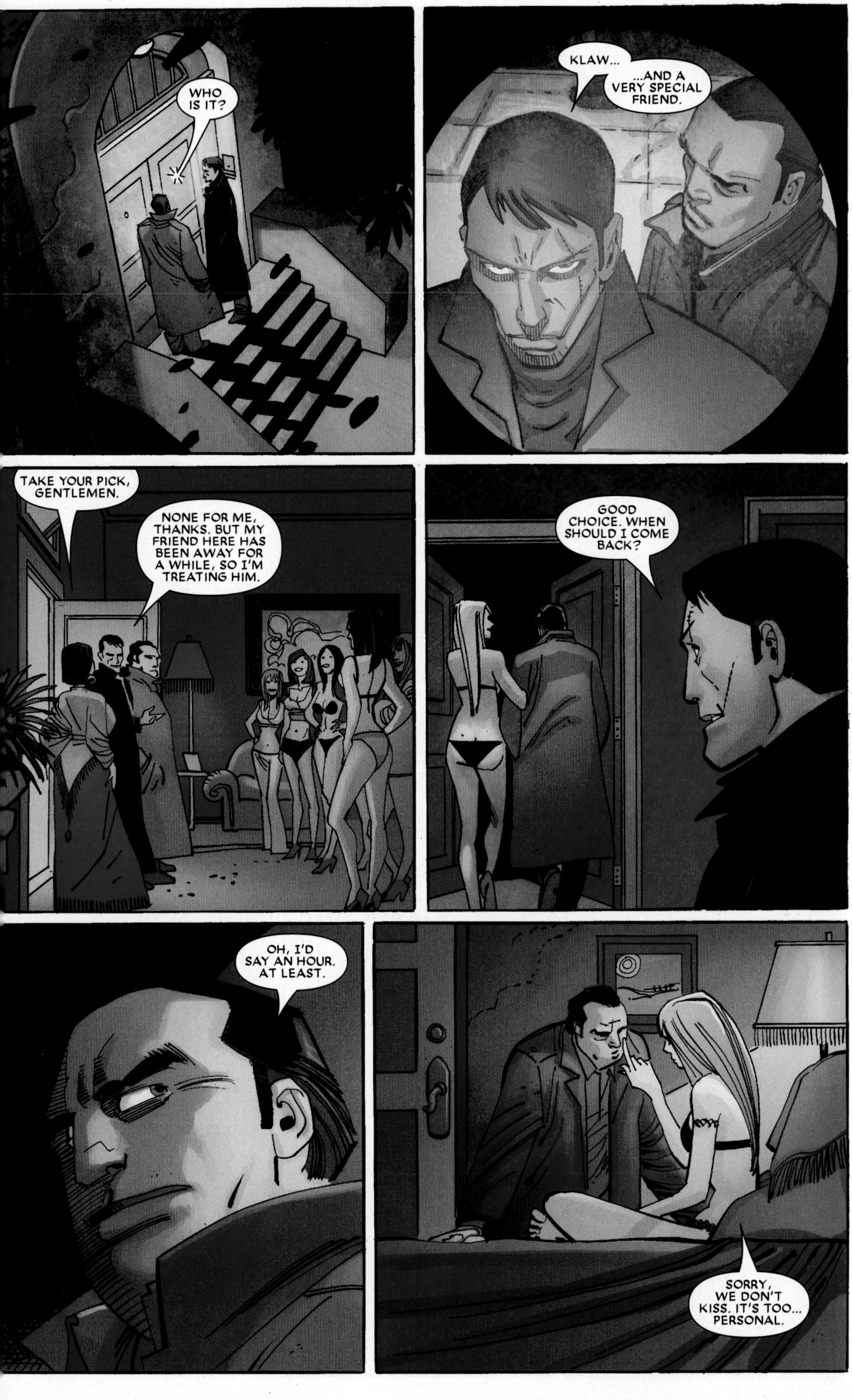
WHO IS IT?
KLAW...
...AND A VERY SPECIAL FRIEND.
TAKE YOUR PICK, GENTLEMEN.
NONE FOR ME, THANKS. BUT MY FRIEND HERE HAS BEEN AWAY FOR A WHILE, SO I'M TREATING HIM.
GOOD CHOICE. WHEN SHOULD I COME BACK?
OH, I'D SAY AN HOUR. AT LEAST.
SORRY, WE DON'T KISS. IT'S TOO... PERSONAL.

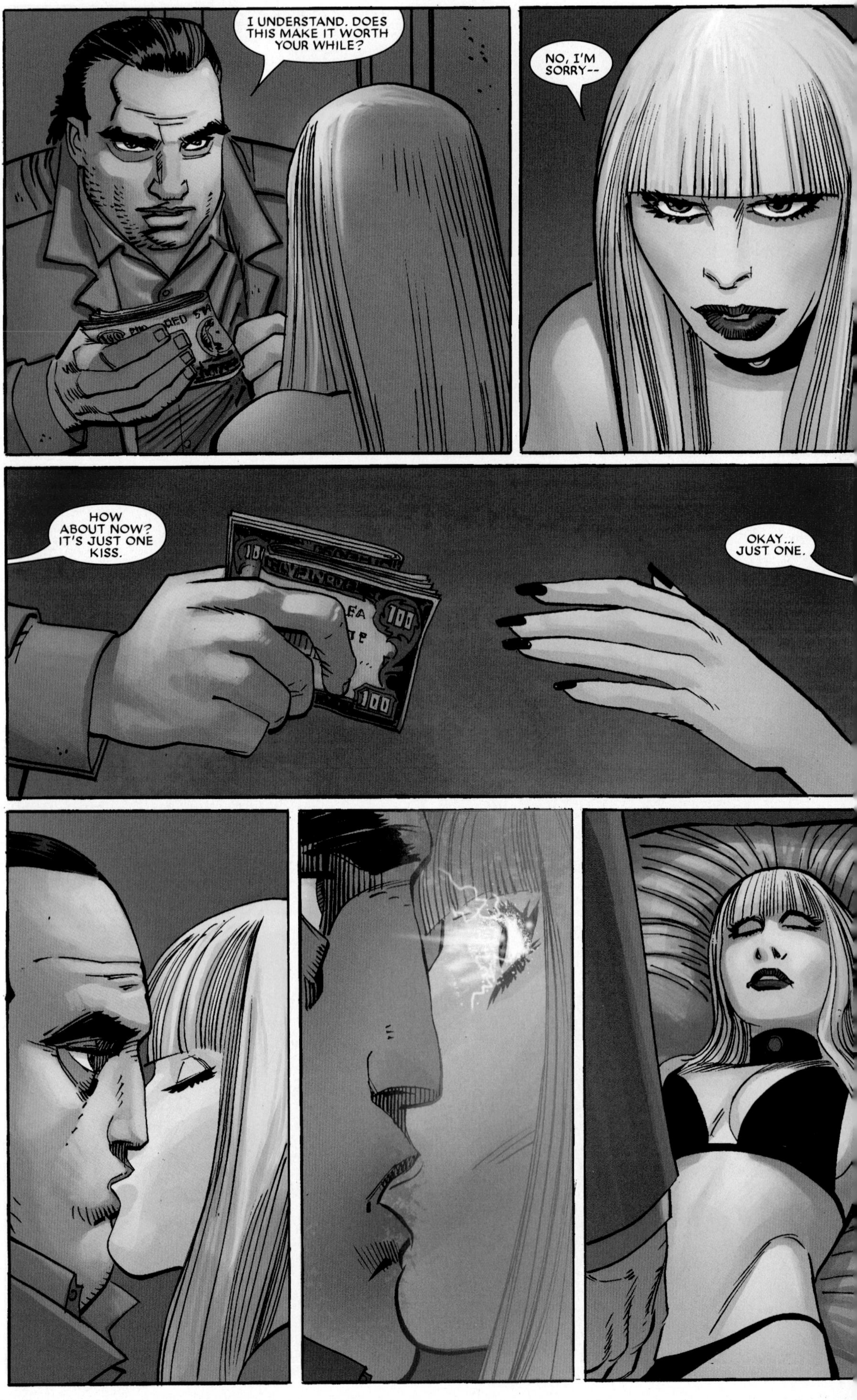
I UNDERSTAND. DOES THIS MAKE IT WORTH YOUR WHILE?
NO, I'M SORRY--
HOW ABOUT NOW? IT'S JUST ONE KISS.
OKAY... JUST ONE.

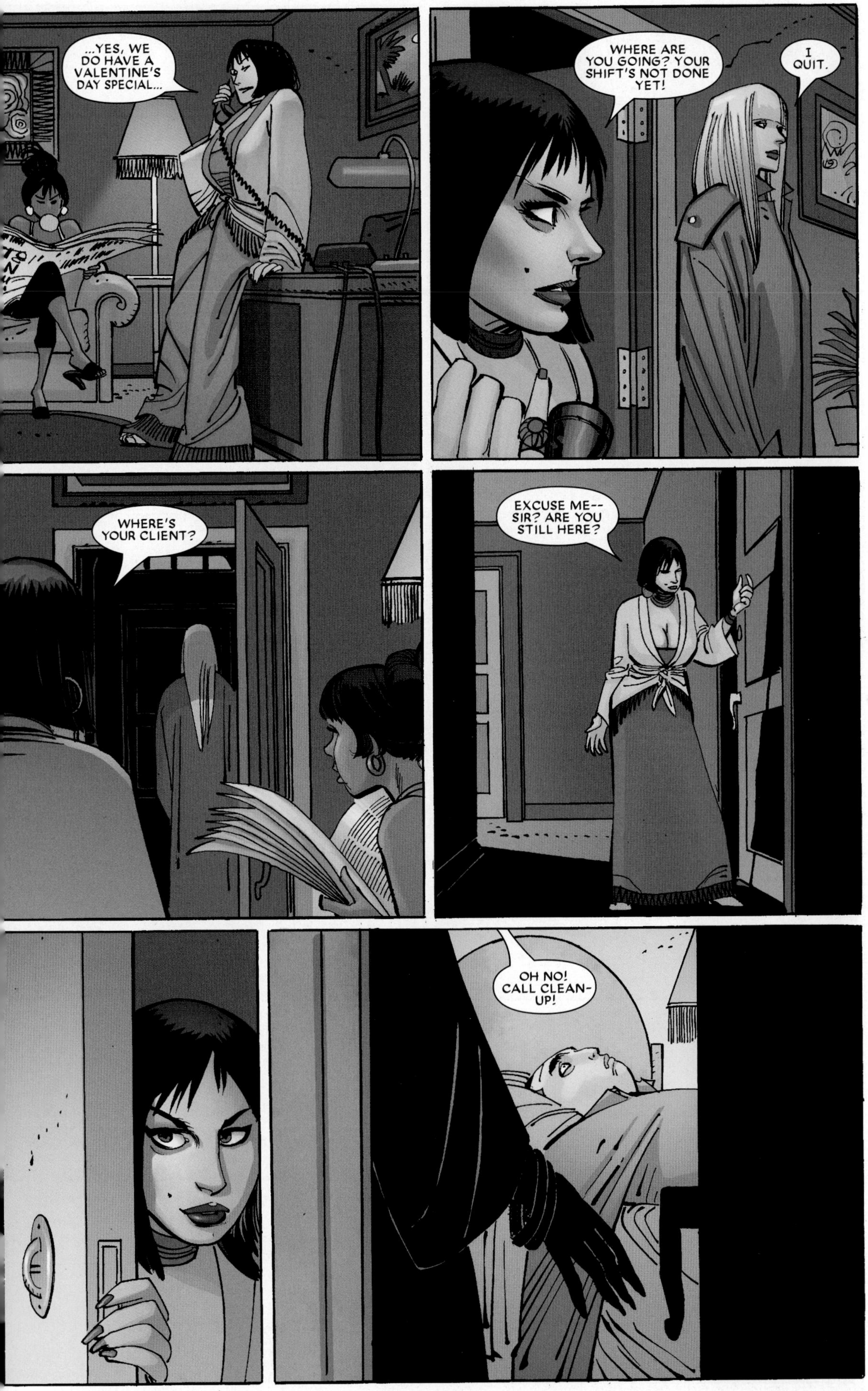
...YES, WE DO HAVE A VALENTINE'S DAY SPECIAL...
WHERE ARE YOU GOING? YOUR SHIFT'S NOT DONE YET!
I QUIT.
WHERE'S YOUR CLIENT?
EXCUSE ME-- SIR? ARE YOU STILL HERE?
OH NO! CALL CLEAN-UP!

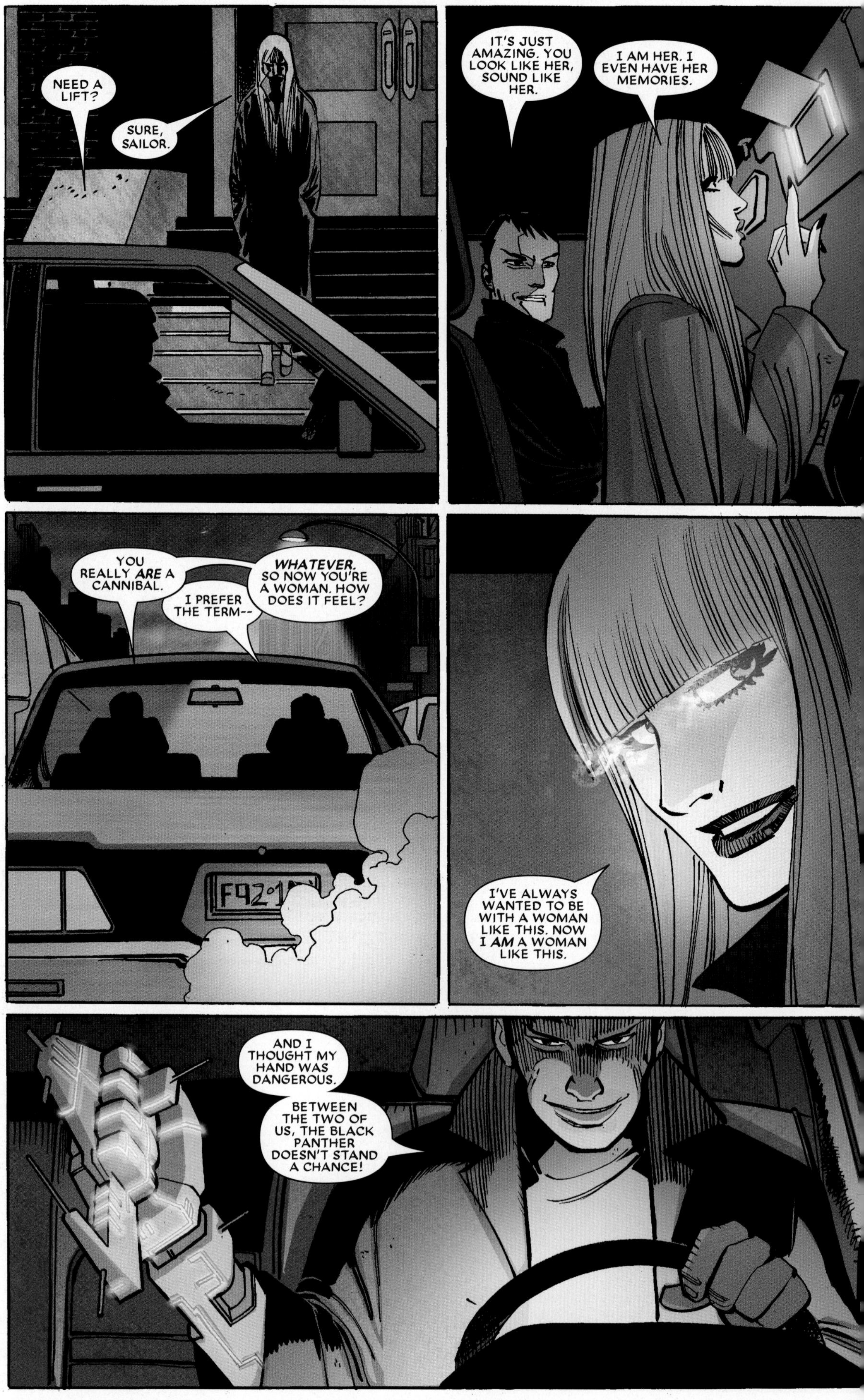
NEED A LIFT?
SURE, SAILOR.
IT'S JUST AMAZING. YOU LOOK LIKE HER, SOUND LIKE HER.
I AM HER. I EVEN HAVE HER MEMORIES.
YOU REALLY ARE A CANNIBAL.
I PREFER THE TERM--
WHATEVER. SO NOW YOU'RE A WOMAN. HOW DOES IT FEEL?
I'VE ALWAYS WANTED TO BE WITH A WOMAN LIKE THIS. NOW I AM A WOMAN LIKE THIS.
AND I THOUGHT MY HAND WAS DANGEROUS.
BETWEEN THE TWO OF US, THE BLACK PANTHER DOESN'T STAND A CHANCE!

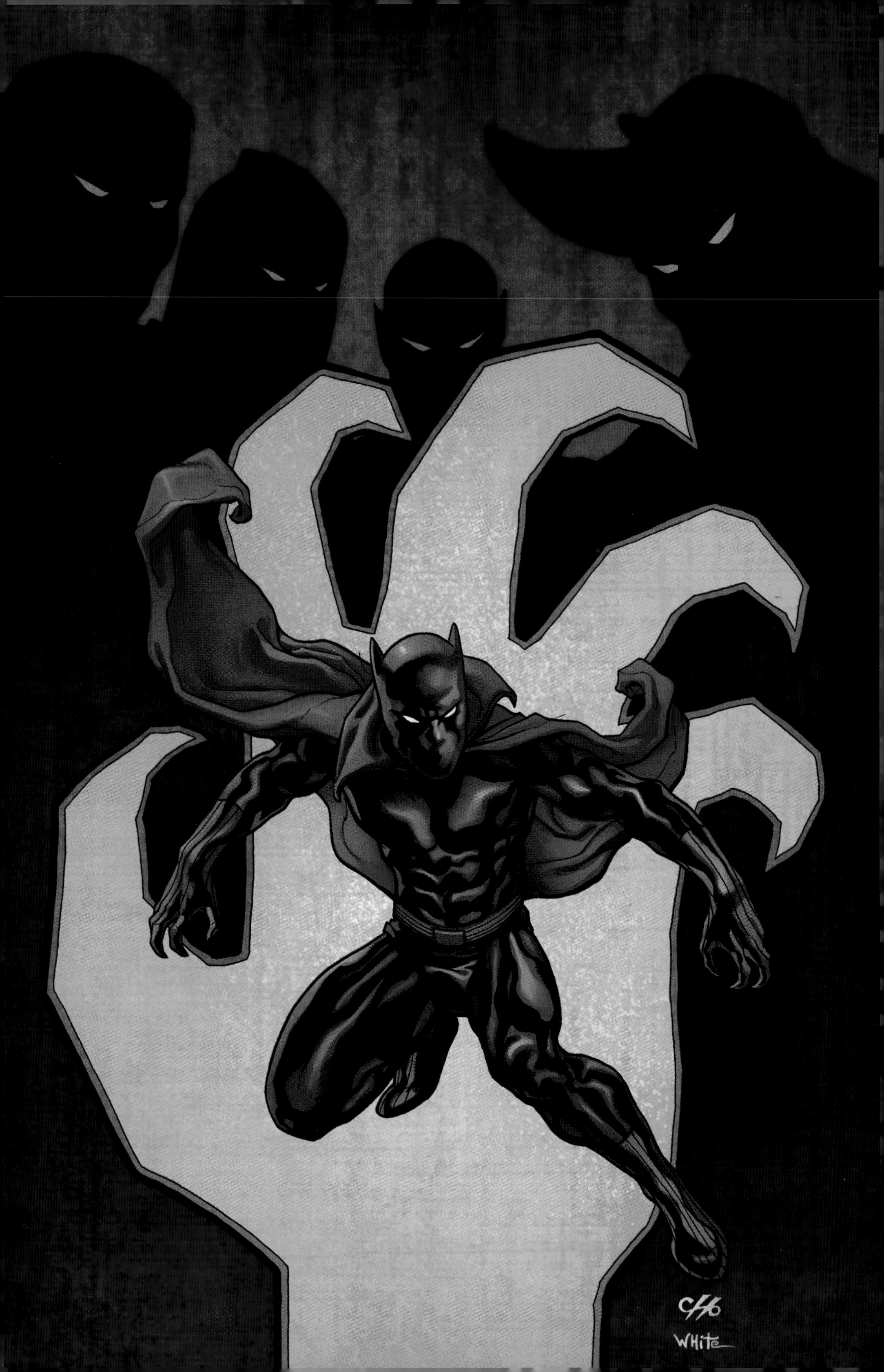
WHITE

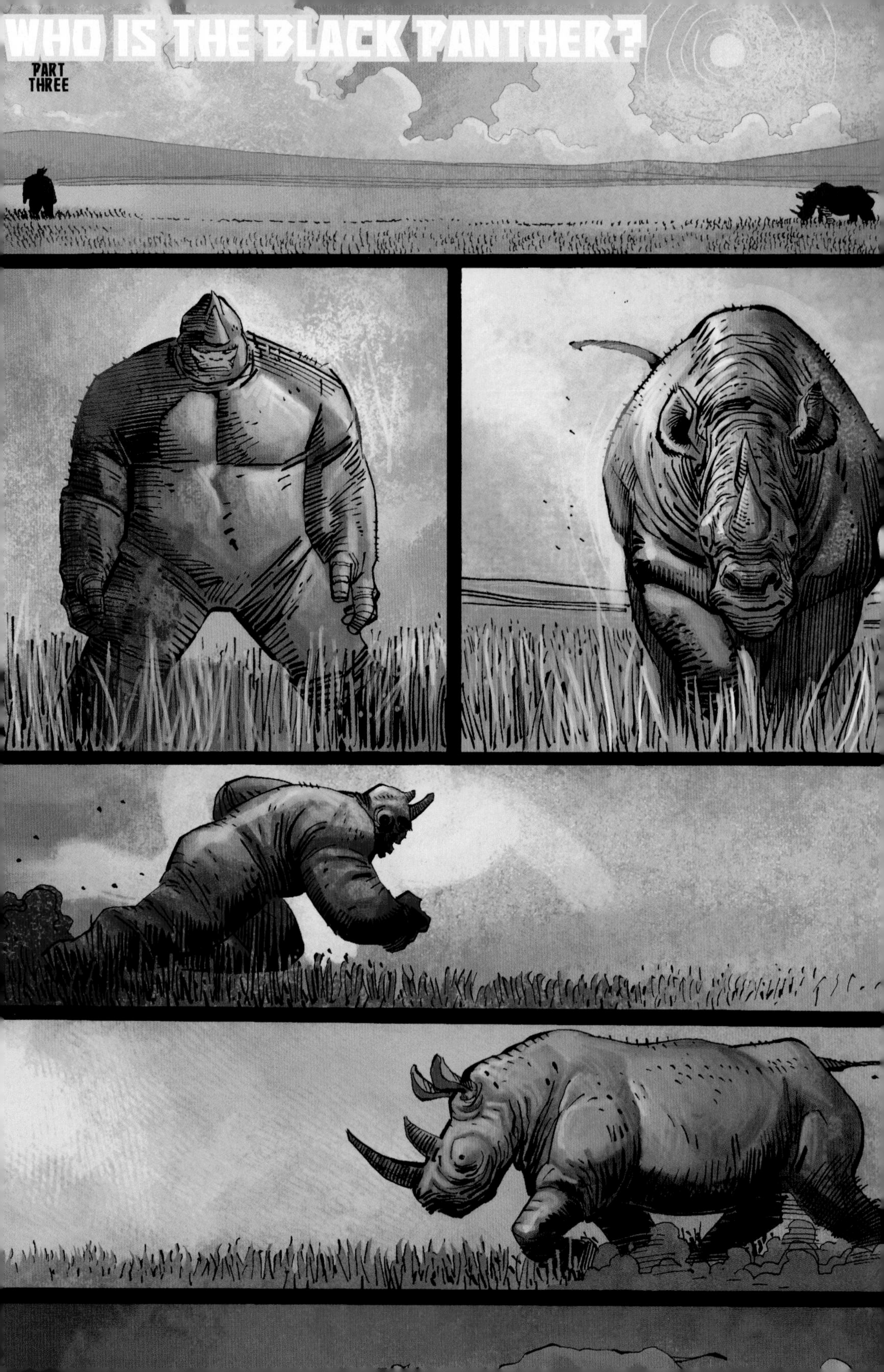
WHO IS THE BLACK PANTHER?
PART THREE

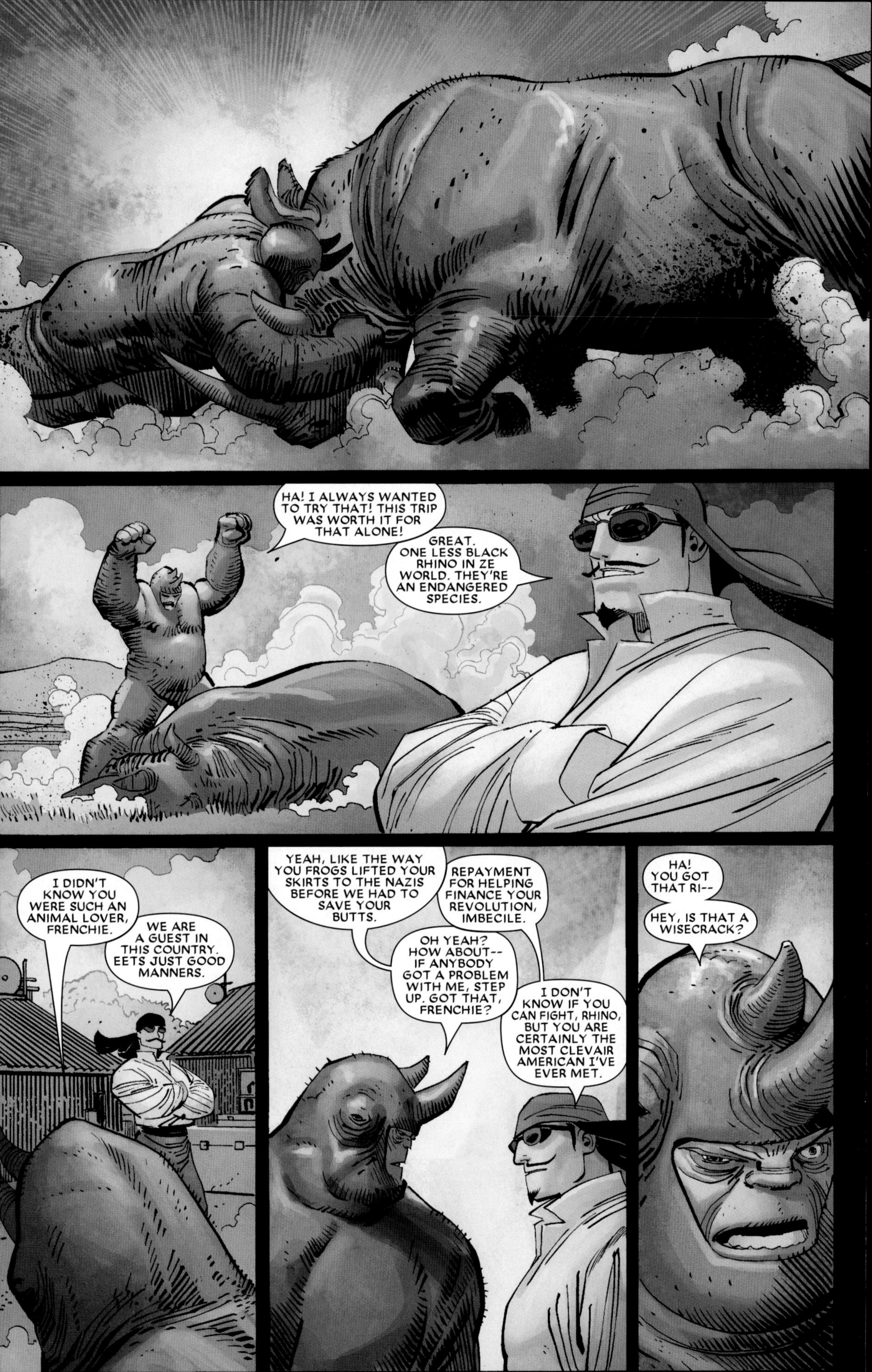
HA! I ALWAYS WANTED TO TRY THAT! THIS TRIP WAS WORTH IT FOR THAT ALONE!
GREAT. ONE LESS BLACK RHINO IN ZE WORLD. THEY'RE AN ENDANGERED SPECIES.
I DIDN'T KNOW YOU WERE SUCH AN ANIMAL LOVER, FRENCHIE.
WE ARE A GUEST IN THIS COUNTRY. EETS JUST GOOD MANNERS.
YEAH, LIKE THE WAY YOU FROGS LIFTED YOUR SKIRTS TO THE NAZIS BEFORE WE HAD TO SAVE YOUR BUTTS.
REPAYMENT FOR HELPING FINANCE YOUR REVOLUTION, IMBECILE.
OH YEAH? HOW ABOUT-- IF ANYBODY GOT A PROBLEM WITH ME, STEP UP. GOT THAT, FRENCHIE?
I DON'T KNOW IF YOU CAN FIGHT, RHINO, BUT YOU ARE CERTAINLY THE MOST CLEVAIR AMERICAN I'VE EVER MET.
HA! YOU GOT THAT RI--
HEY, IS THAT A WISECRACK?

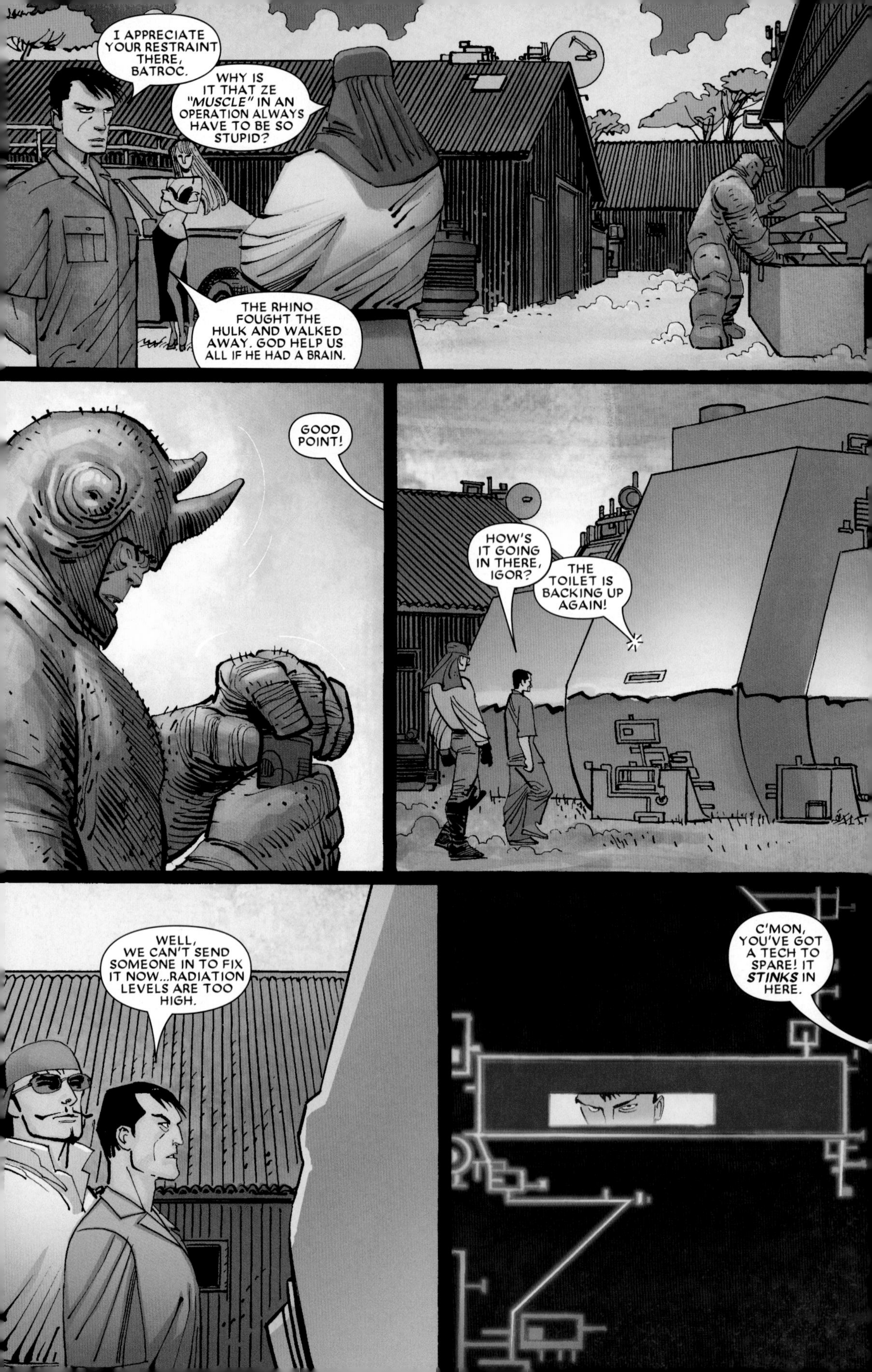
I APPRECIATE YOUR RESTRAINT THERE, BATROC.
WHY IS IT THAT ZE "*MUSCLE*" IN AN OPERATION ALWAYS HAVE TO BE SO STUPID?
THE RHINO FOUGHT THE HULK AND WALKED AWAY. GOD HELP US ALL IF HE HAD A BRAIN.
GOOD POINT!
HOW'S IT GOING IN THERE, IGOR?
THE TOILET IS BACKING UP AGAIN!
WELL, WE CAN'T SEND SOMEONE IN TO FIX IT NOW...RADIATION LEVELS ARE TOO HIGH.
C'MON, YOU'VE GOT A TECH TO SPARE! IT *STINKS* IN HERE.

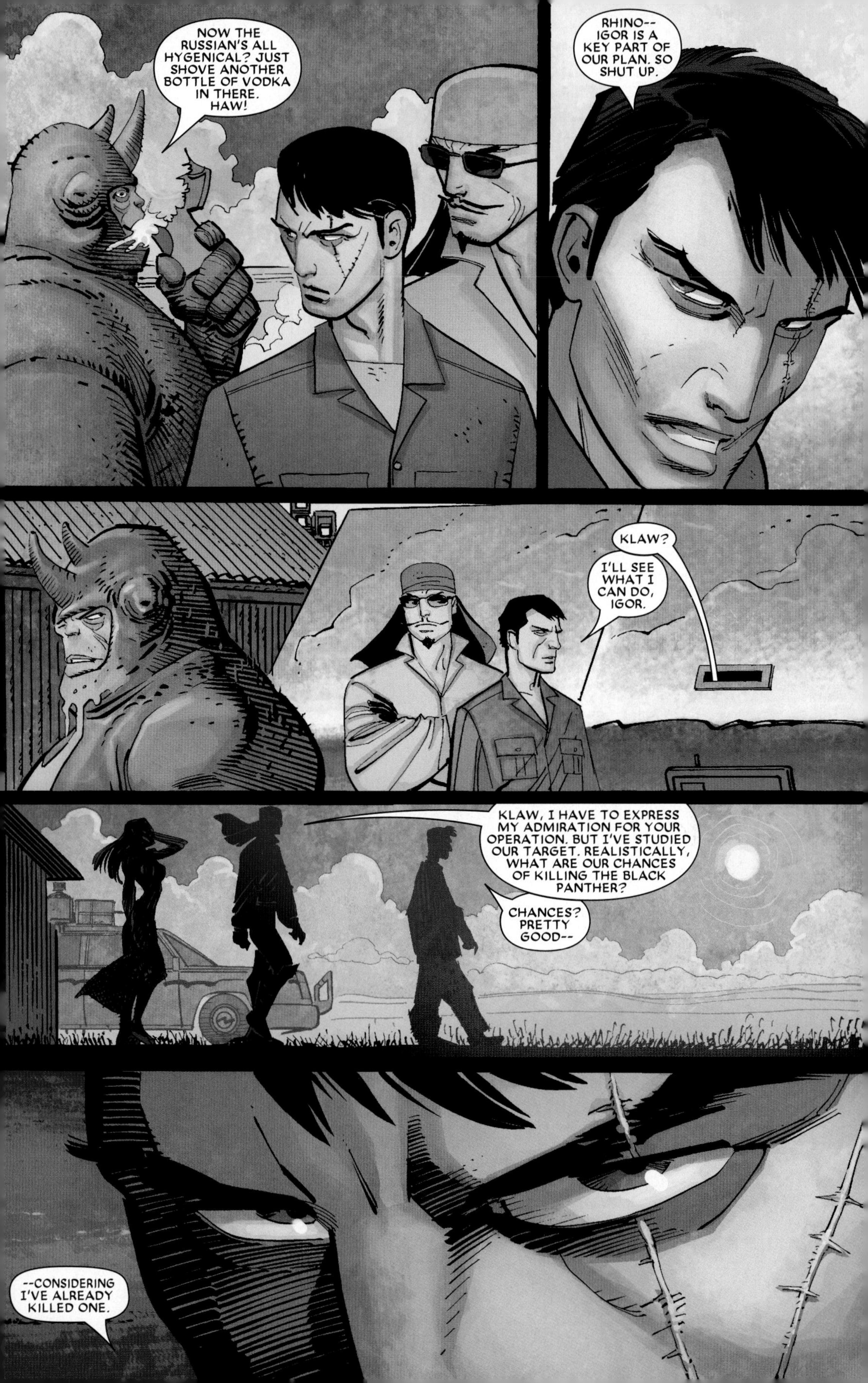
NOW THE RUSSIAN'S ALL HYGENICAL? JUST SHOVE ANOTHER BOTTLE OF VODKA IN THERE. HAW!
RHINO-- IGOR IS A KEY PART OF OUR PLAN. SO SHUT UP.
KLAW?
I'LL SEE WHAT I CAN DO, IGOR.
KLAW, I HAVE TO EXPRESS MY ADMIRATION FOR YOUR OPERATION. BUT I'VE STUDIED OUR TARGET. REALISTICALLY, WHAT ARE OUR CHANCES OF KILLING THE BLACK PANTHER?
CHANCES? PRETTY GOOD--
--CONSIDERING I'VE ALREADY KILLED ONE.

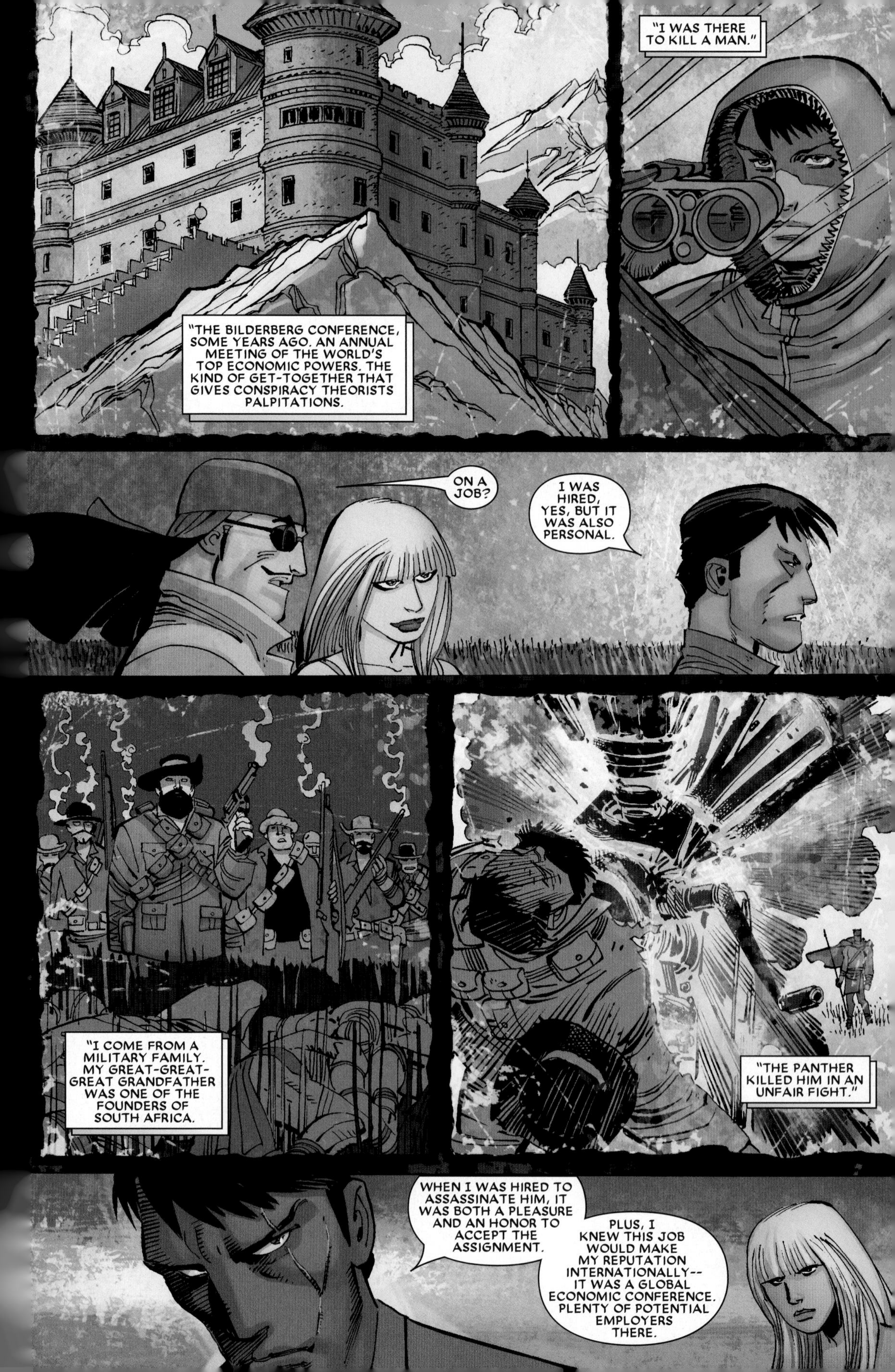
"THE BILDERBERG CONFERENCE, SOME YEARS AGO. AN ANNUAL MEETING OF THE WORLD'S TOP ECONOMIC POWERS. THE KIND OF GET-TOGETHER THAT GIVES CONSPIRACY THEORISTS PALPITATIONS.
"I WAS THERE TO KILL A MAN."
ON A JOB?
I WAS HIRED, YES, BUT IT WAS ALSO PERSONAL.
"I COME FROM A MILITARY FAMILY. MY GREAT-GREAT-GREAT GRANDFATHER WAS ONE OF THE FOUNDERS OF SOUTH AFRICA.
"THE PANTHER KILLED HIM IN AN UNFAIR FIGHT."
WHEN I WAS HIRED TO ASSASSINATE HIM, IT WAS BOTH A PLEASURE AND AN HONOR TO ACCEPT THE ASSIGNMENT.
PLUS, I KNEW THIS JOB WOULD MAKE MY REPUTATION INTERNATIONALLY-- IT WAS A GLOBAL ECONOMIC CONFERENCE. PLENTY OF POTENTIAL EMPLOYERS THERE.

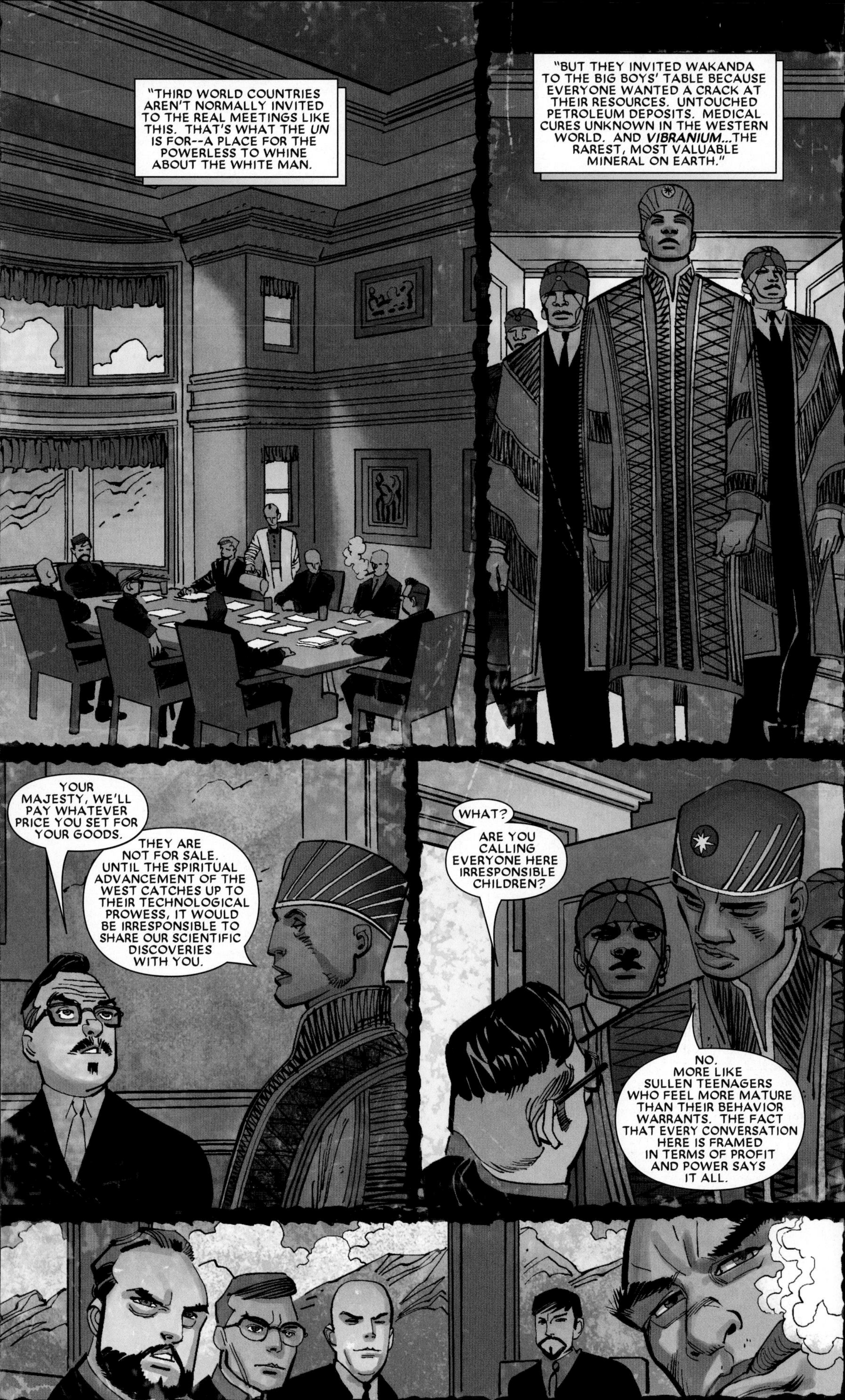
"THIRD WORLD COUNTRIES AREN'T NORMALLY INVITED TO THE REAL MEETINGS LIKE THIS. THAT'S WHAT THE *UN* IS FOR--A PLACE FOR THE POWERLESS TO WHINE ABOUT THE WHITE MAN.
"BUT THEY INVITED WAKANDA TO THE BIG BOYS' TABLE BECAUSE EVERYONE WANTED A CRACK AT THEIR RESOURCES. UNTOUCHED PETROLEUM DEPOSITS. MEDICAL CURES UNKNOWN IN THE WESTERN WORLD. AND ***VIBRANIUM...*** THE RAREST, MOST VALUABLE MINERAL ON EARTH."
YOUR MAJESTY, WE'LL PAY WHATEVER PRICE YOU SET FOR YOUR GOODS.
THEY ARE NOT FOR SALE. UNTIL THE SPIRITUAL ADVANCEMENT OF THE WEST CATCHES UP TO THEIR TECHNOLOGICAL PROWESS, IT WOULD BE IRRESPONSIBLE TO SHARE OUR SCIENTIFIC DISCOVERIES WITH YOU.
WHAT?
ARE YOU CALLING EVERYONE HERE IRRESPONSIBLE CHILDREN?
NO. MORE LIKE SULLEN TEENAGERS WHO FEEL MORE MATURE THAN THEIR BEHAVIOR WARRANTS. THE FACT THAT EVERY CONVERSATION HERE IS FRAMED IN TERMS OF PROFIT AND POWER SAYS IT ALL.

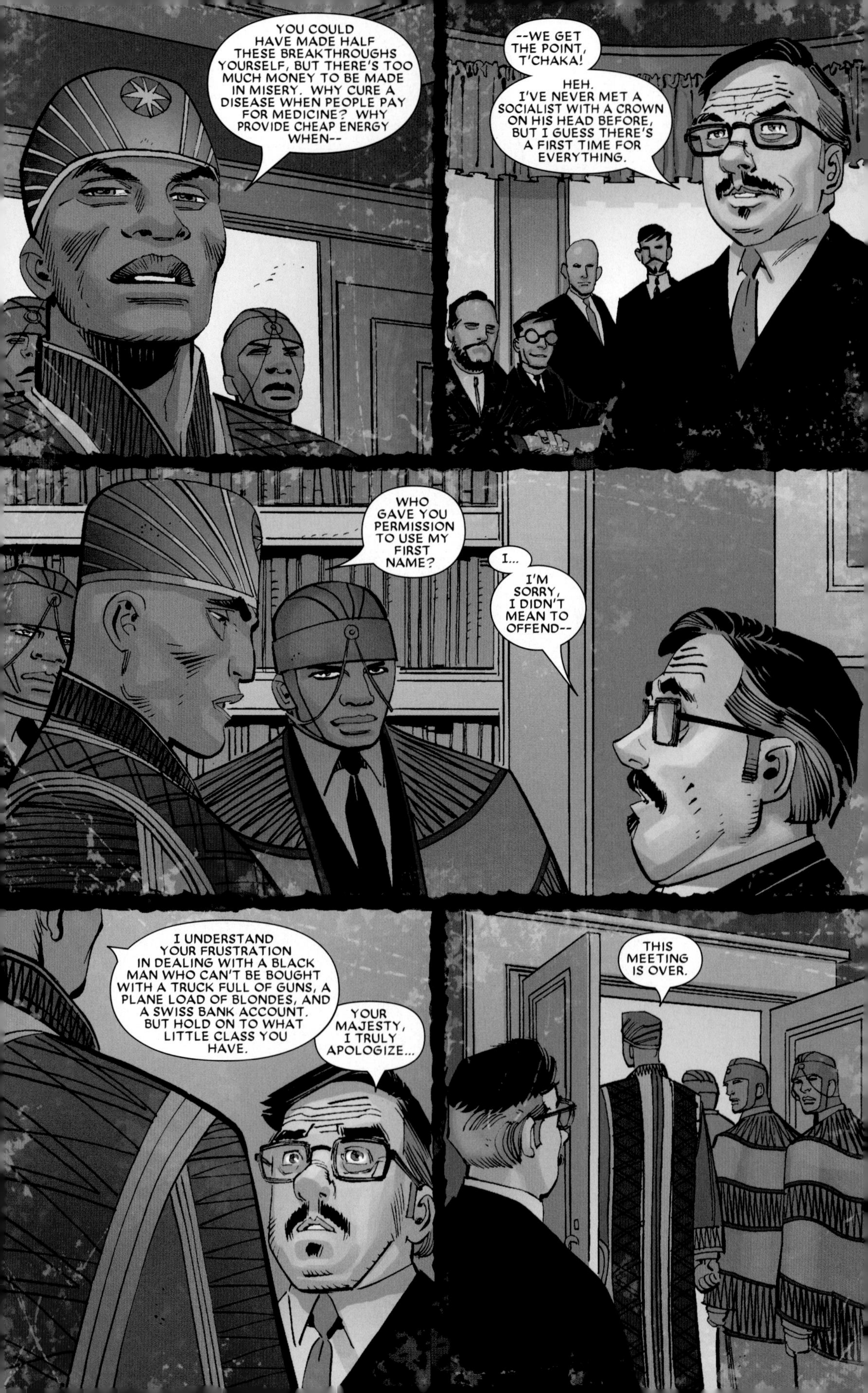
YOU COULD HAVE MADE HALF THESE BREAKTHROUGHS YOURSELF, BUT THERE'S TOO MUCH MONEY TO BE MADE IN MISERY. WHY CURE A DISEASE WHEN PEOPLE PAY FOR MEDICINE? WHY PROVIDE CHEAP ENERGY WHEN--
--WE GET THE POINT, T'CHAKA!
HEH. I'VE NEVER MET A SOCIALIST WITH A CROWN ON HIS HEAD BEFORE, BUT I GUESS THERE'S A FIRST TIME FOR EVERYTHING.
WHO GAVE YOU PERMISSION TO USE MY FIRST NAME?
I...
I'M SORRY, I DIDN'T MEAN TO OFFEND--
I UNDERSTAND YOUR FRUSTRATION IN DEALING WITH A BLACK MAN WHO CAN'T BE BOUGHT WITH A TRUCK FULL OF GUNS, A PLANE LOAD OF BLONDES, AND A SWISS BANK ACCOUNT. BUT HOLD ON TO WHAT LITTLE CLASS YOU HAVE.
YOUR MAJESTY, I TRULY APOLOGIZE...
THIS MEETING IS OVER.

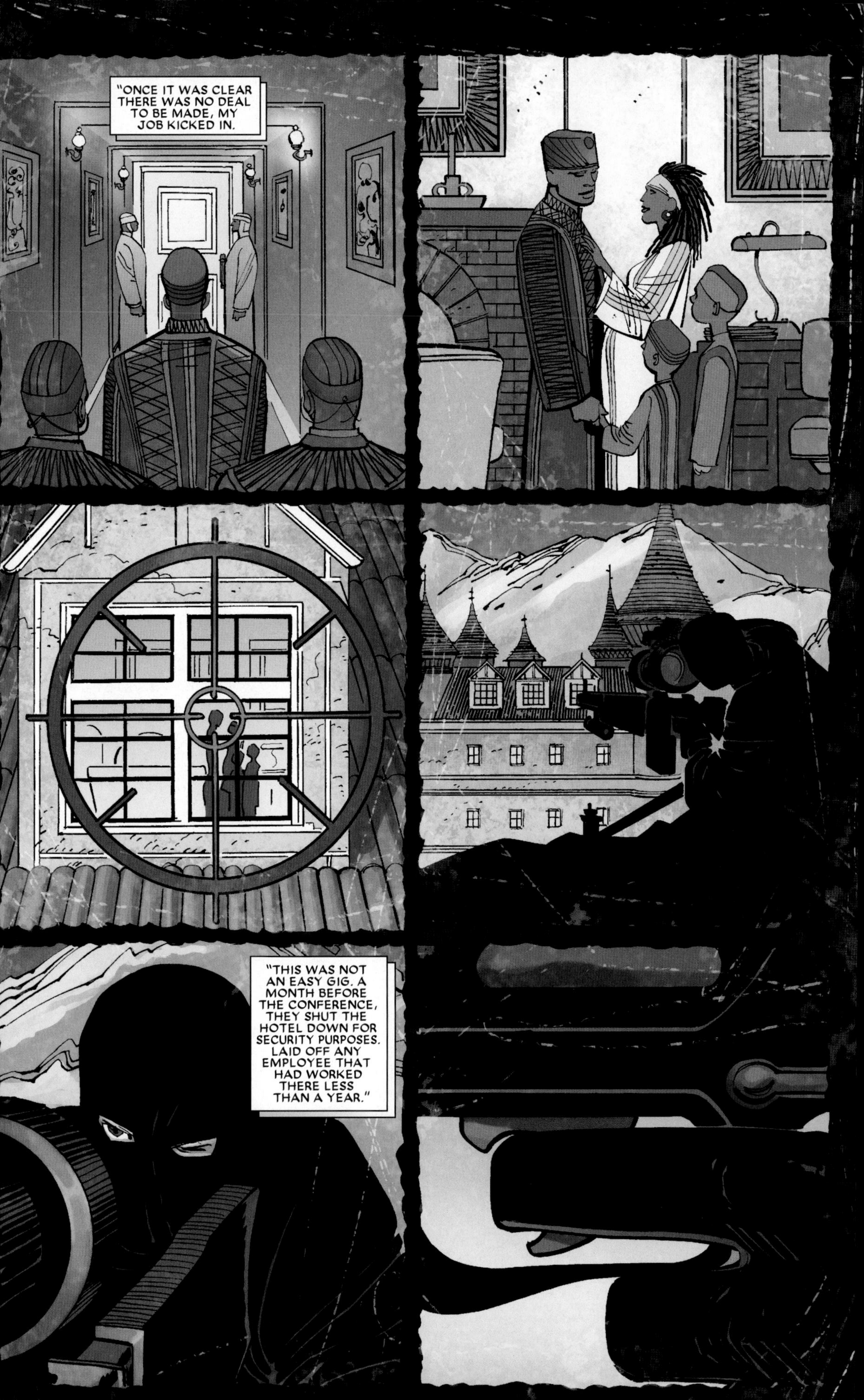
"ONCE IT WAS CLEAR THERE WAS NO DEAL TO BE MADE, MY JOB KICKED IN.
"THIS WAS NOT AN EASY GIG. A MONTH BEFORE THE CONFERENCE, THEY SHUT THE HOTEL DOWN FOR SECURITY PURPOSES. LAID OFF ANY EMPLOYEE THAT HAD WORKED THERE LESS THAN A YEAR."

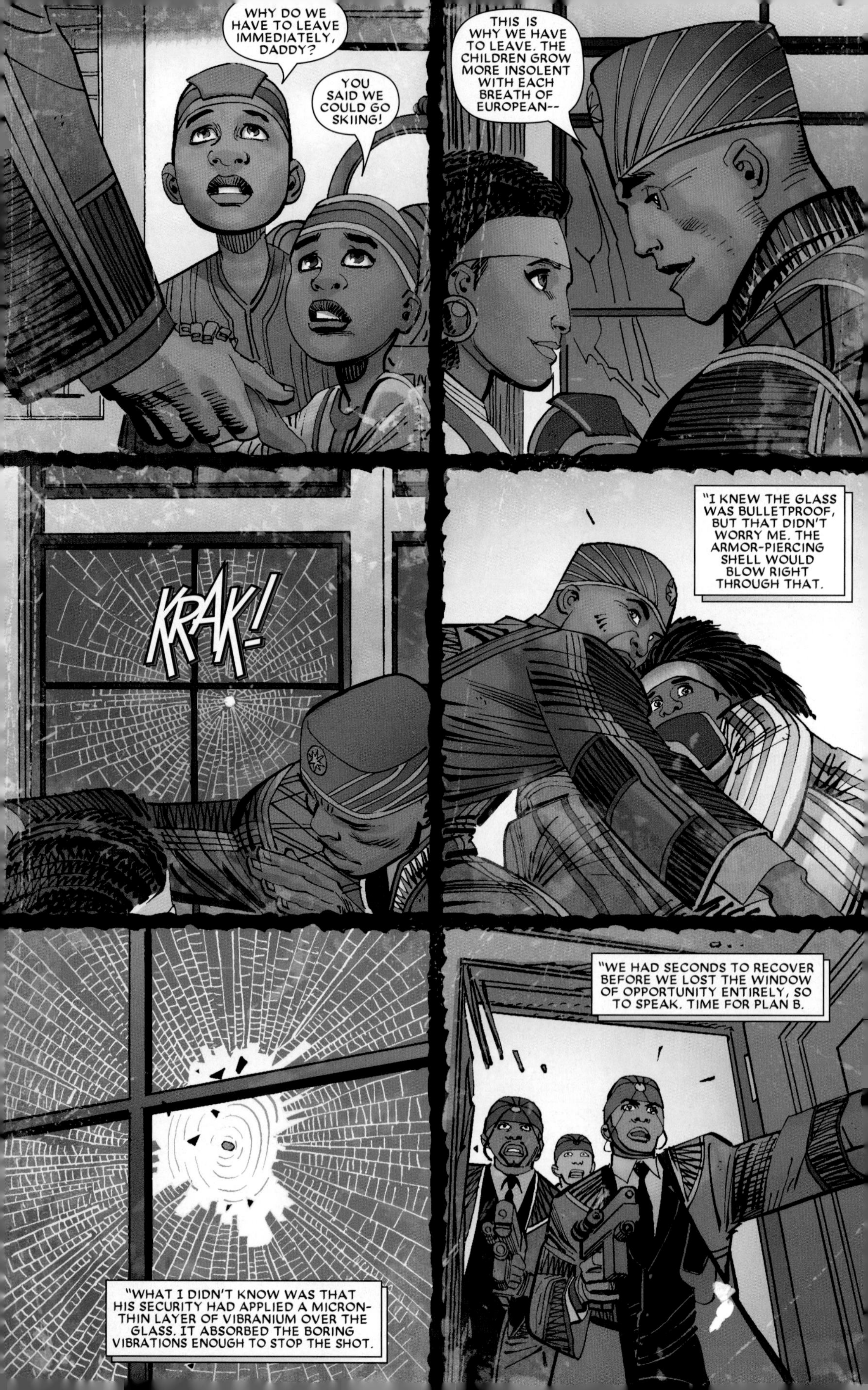
WHY DO WE HAVE TO LEAVE IMMEDIATELY, DADDY?
YOU SAID WE COULD GO SKIING!
THIS IS WHY WE HAVE TO LEAVE. THE CHILDREN GROW MORE INSOLENT WITH EACH BREATH OF EUROPEAN--
KRAK!
"I KNEW THE GLASS WAS BULLETPROOF, BUT THAT DIDN'T WORRY ME. THE ARMOR-PIERCING SHELL WOULD BLOW RIGHT THROUGH THAT.
"WHAT I DIDN'T KNOW WAS THAT HIS SECURITY HAD APPLIED A MICRON-THIN LAYER OF VIBRANIUM OVER THE GLASS. IT ABSORBED THE BORING VIBRATIONS ENOUGH TO STOP THE SHOT.
"WE HAD SECONDS TO RECOVER BEFORE WE LOST THE WINDOW OF OPPORTUNITY ENTIRELY, SO TO SPEAK. TIME FOR PLAN B.

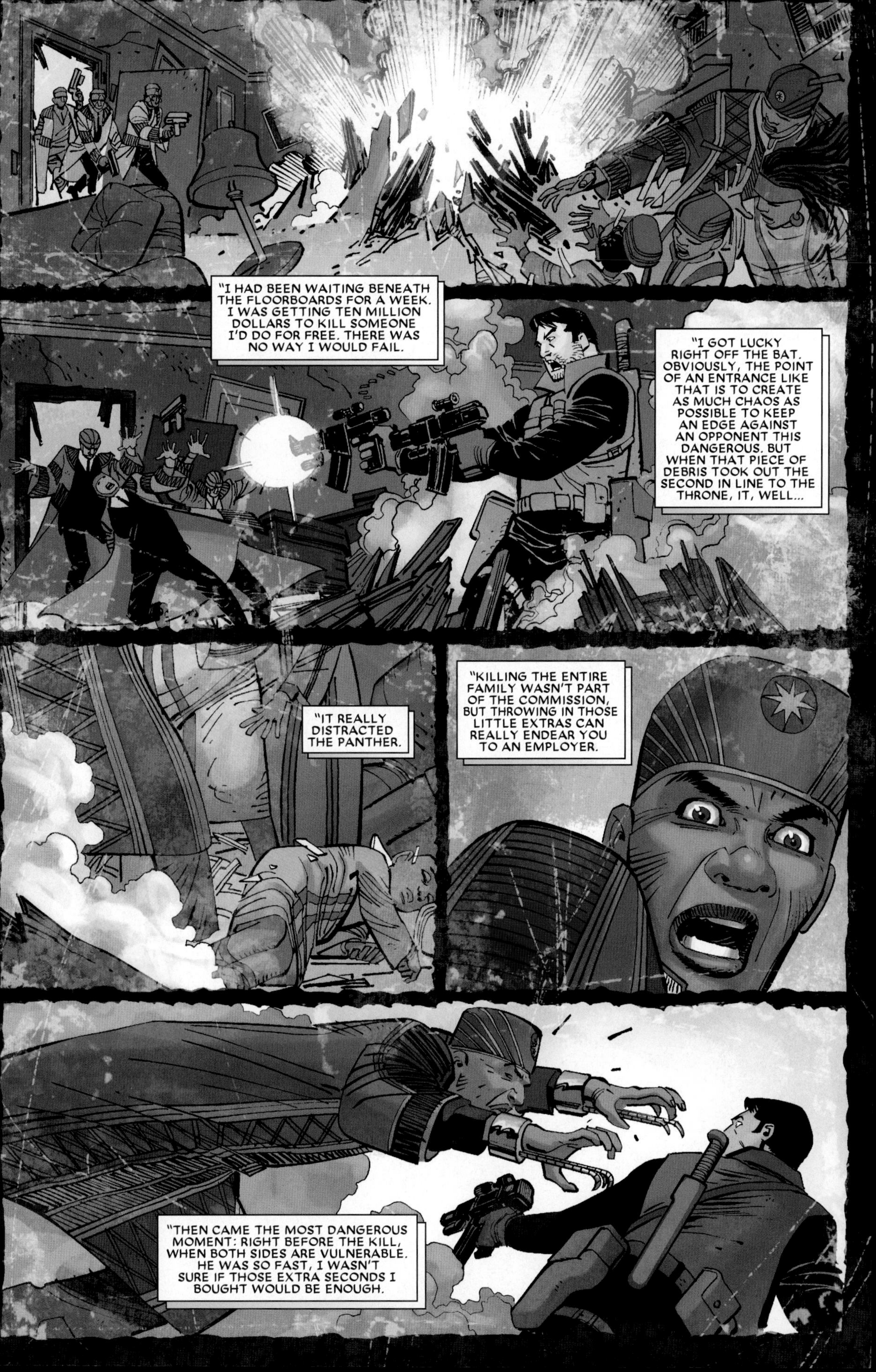
"I HAD BEEN WAITING BENEATH THE FLOORBOARDS FOR A WEEK. I WAS GETTING TEN MILLION DOLLARS TO KILL SOMEONE I'D DO FOR FREE. THERE WAS NO WAY I WOULD FAIL.
"I GOT LUCKY RIGHT OFF THE BAT. OBVIOUSLY, THE POINT OF AN ENTRANCE LIKE THAT IS TO CREATE AS MUCH CHAOS AS POSSIBLE TO KEEP AN EDGE AGAINST AN OPPONENT THIS DANGEROUS. BUT WHEN THAT PIECE OF DEBRIS TOOK OUT THE SECOND IN LINE TO THE THRONE, IT, WELL...
"IT REALLY DISTRACTED THE PANTHER.
"KILLING THE ENTIRE FAMILY WASN'T PART OF THE COMMISSION, BUT THROWING IN THOSE LITTLE EXTRAS CAN REALLY ENDEAR YOU TO AN EMPLOYER.
"THEN CAME THE MOST DANGEROUS MOMENT: RIGHT BEFORE THE KILL, WHEN BOTH SIDES ARE VULNERABLE. HE WAS SO FAST, I WASN'T SURE IF THOSE EXTRA SECONDS I BOUGHT WOULD BE ENOUGH.

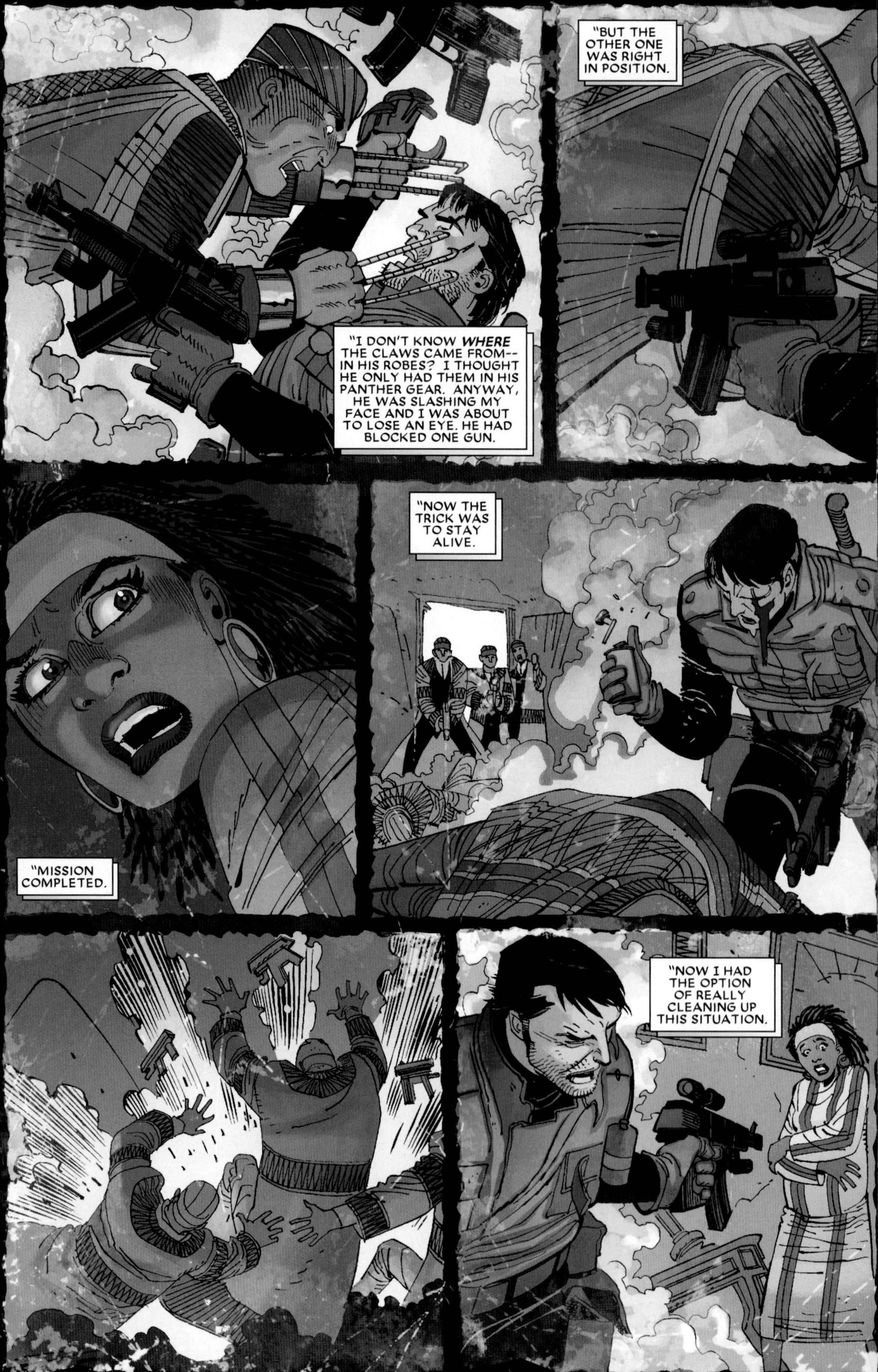

"I DON'T KNOW *WHERE* THE CLAWS CAME FROM-- IN HIS ROBES? I THOUGHT HE ONLY HAD THEM IN HIS PANTHER GEAR. ANYWAY, HE WAS SLASHING MY FACE AND I WAS ABOUT TO LOSE AN EYE. HE HAD BLOCKED ONE GUN.
"BUT THE OTHER ONE WAS RIGHT IN POSITION.
"MISSION COMPLETED.
"NOW THE TRICK WAS TO STAY ALIVE.
"NOW I HAD THE OPTION OF REALLY CLEANING UP THIS SITUATION.

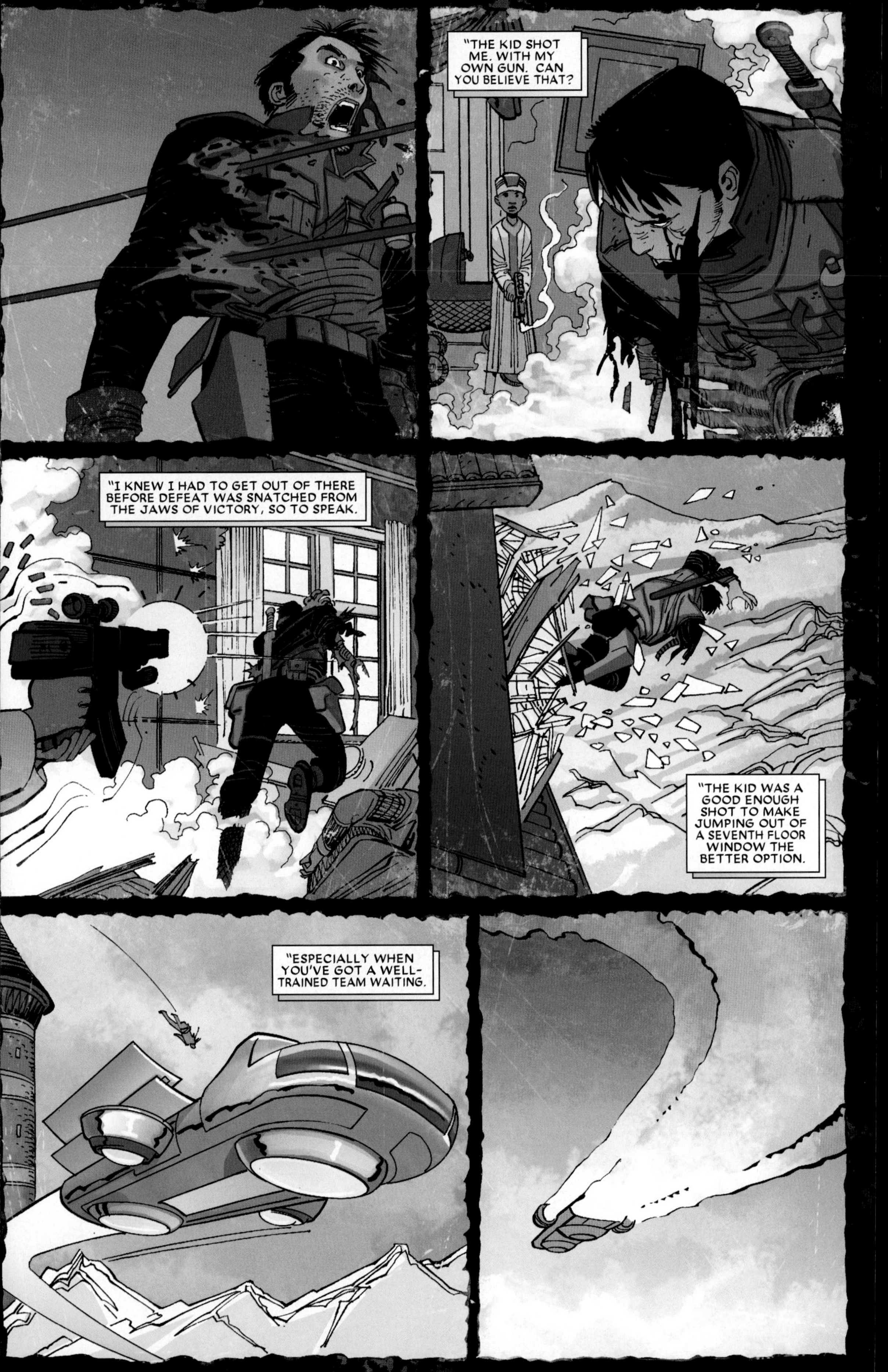
"THE KID SHOT ME. WITH MY OWN GUN. CAN YOU BELIEVE THAT?
"I KNEW I HAD TO GET OUT OF THERE BEFORE DEFEAT WAS SNATCHED FROM THE JAWS OF VICTORY, SO TO SPEAK.
"THE KID WAS A GOOD ENOUGH SHOT TO MAKE JUMPING OUT OF A SEVENTH FLOOR WINDOW THE BETTER OPTION.
"ESPECIALLY WHEN YOU'VE GOT A WELL-TRAINED TEAM WAITING.

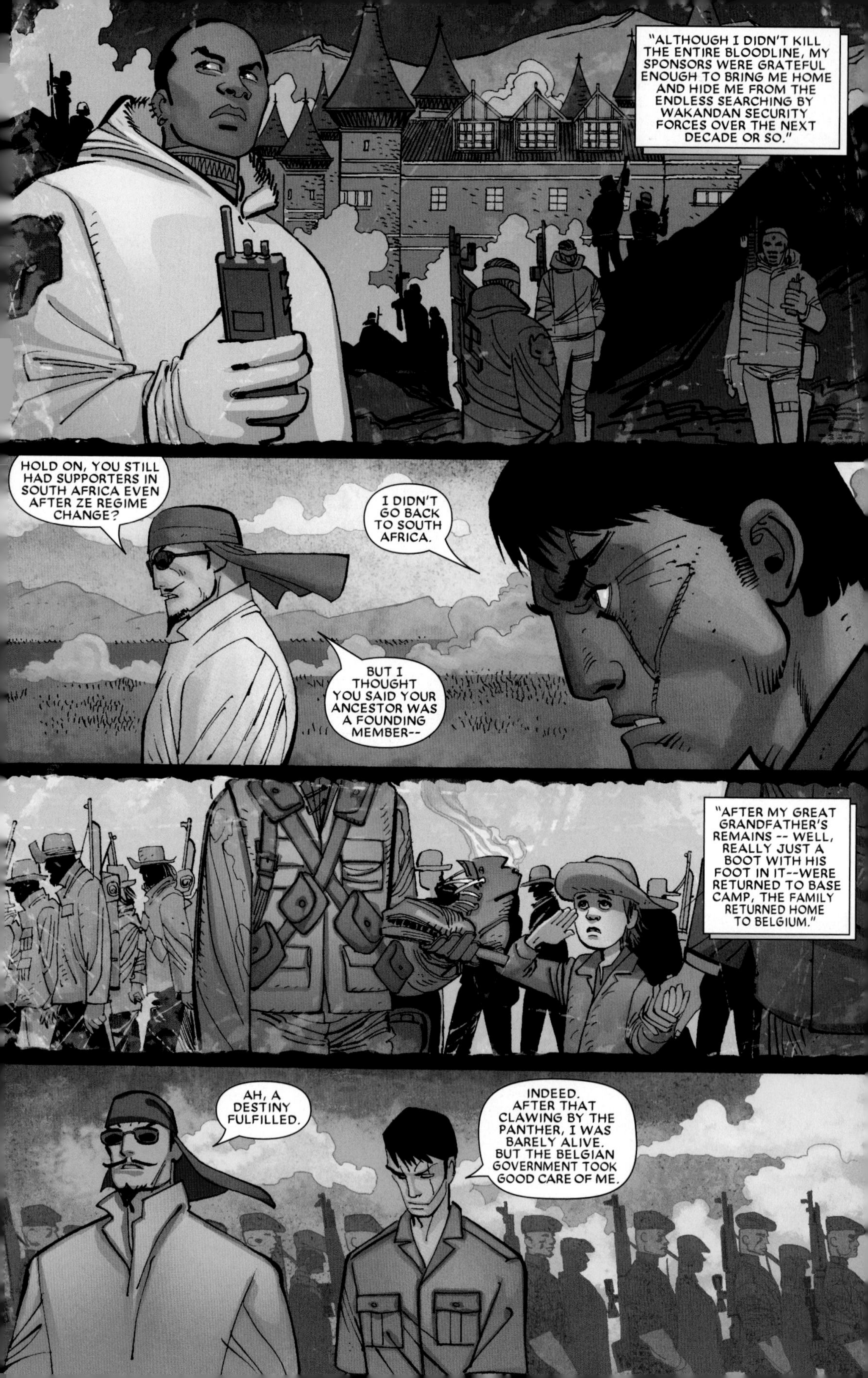
"ALTHOUGH I DIDN'T KILL THE ENTIRE BLOODLINE, MY SPONSORS WERE GRATEFUL ENOUGH TO BRING ME HOME AND HIDE ME FROM THE ENDLESS SEARCHING BY WAKANDAN SECURITY FORCES OVER THE NEXT DECADE OR SO."
HOLD ON, YOU STILL HAD SUPPORTERS IN SOUTH AFRICA EVEN AFTER ZE REGIME CHANGE?
I DIDN'T GO BACK TO SOUTH AFRICA.
BUT I THOUGHT YOU SAID YOUR ANCESTOR WAS A FOUNDING MEMBER--
"AFTER MY GREAT GRANDFATHER'S REMAINS -- WELL, REALLY JUST A BOOT WITH HIS FOOT IN IT--WERE RETURNED TO BASE CAMP, THE FAMILY RETURNED HOME TO BELGIUM."
AH, A DESTINY FULFILLED.
INDEED. AFTER THAT CLAWING BY THE PANTHER, I WAS BARELY ALIVE. BUT THE BELGIAN GOVERNMENT TOOK GOOD CARE OF ME.

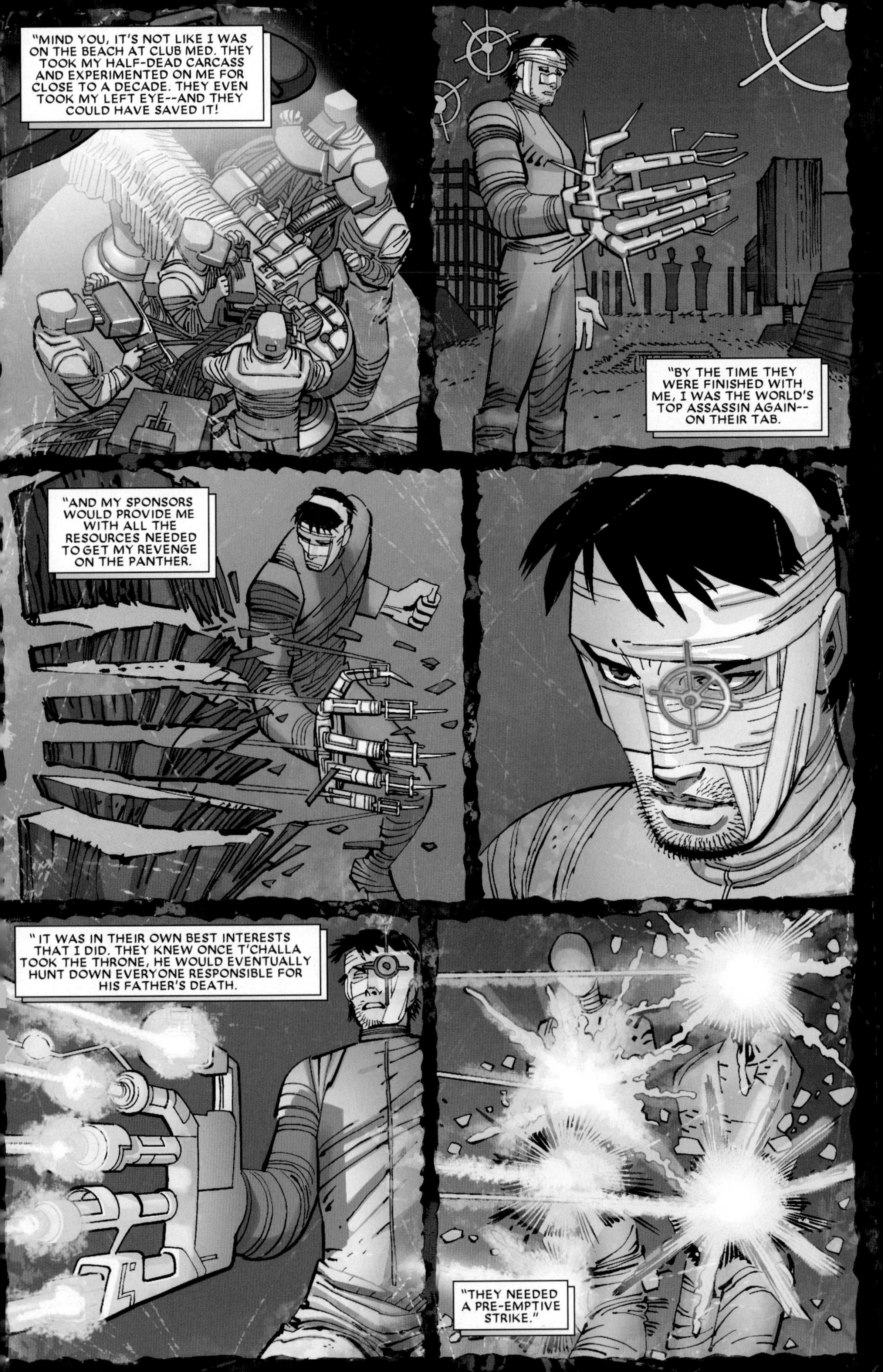
"MIND YOU, IT'S NOT LIKE I WAS ON THE BEACH AT CLUB MED. THEY TOOK MY HALF-DEAD CARCASS AND EXPERIMENTED ON ME FOR CLOSE TO A DECADE. THEY EVEN TOOK MY LEFT EYE--AND THEY COULD HAVE SAVED IT!
"BY THE TIME THEY WERE FINISHED WITH ME, I WAS THE WORLD'S TOP ASSASSIN AGAIN-- ON THEIR TAB.
"AND MY SPONSORS WOULD PROVIDE ME WITH ALL THE RESOURCES NEEDED TO GET MY REVENGE ON THE PANTHER.
"IT WAS IN THEIR OWN BEST INTERESTS THAT I DID. THEY KNEW ONCE T'CHALLA TOOK THE THRONE, HE WOULD EVENTUALLY HUNT DOWN EVERYONE RESPONSIBLE FOR HIS FATHER'S DEATH.
"THEY NEEDED A PRE-EMPTIVE STRIKE."

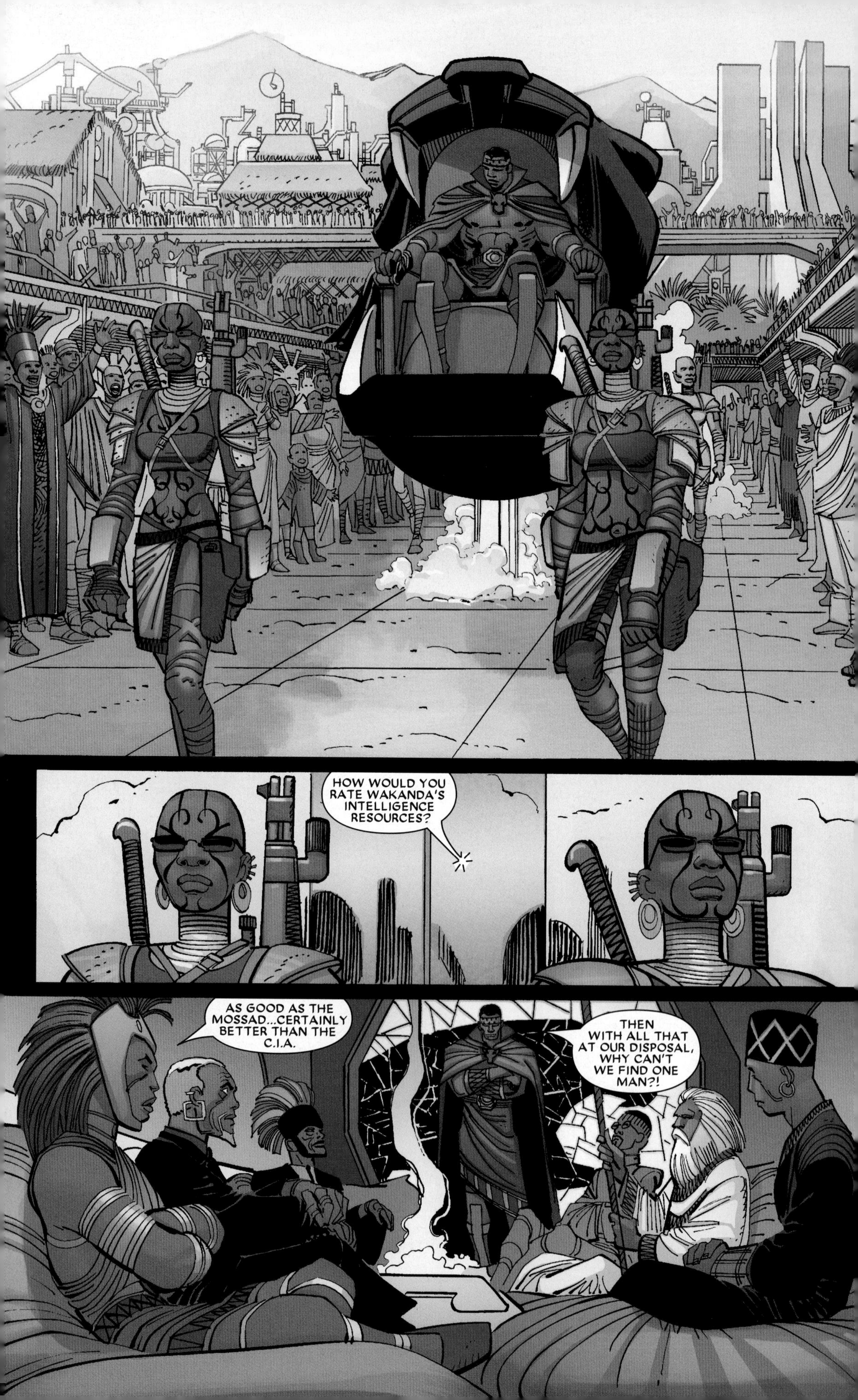
HOW WOULD YOU RATE WAKANDA'S INTELLIGENCE RESOURCES?
AS GOOD AS THE MOSSAD...CERTAINLY BETTER THAN THE C.I.A.
THEN WITH ALL THAT AT OUR DISPOSAL, WHY CAN'T WE FIND ONE MAN?!

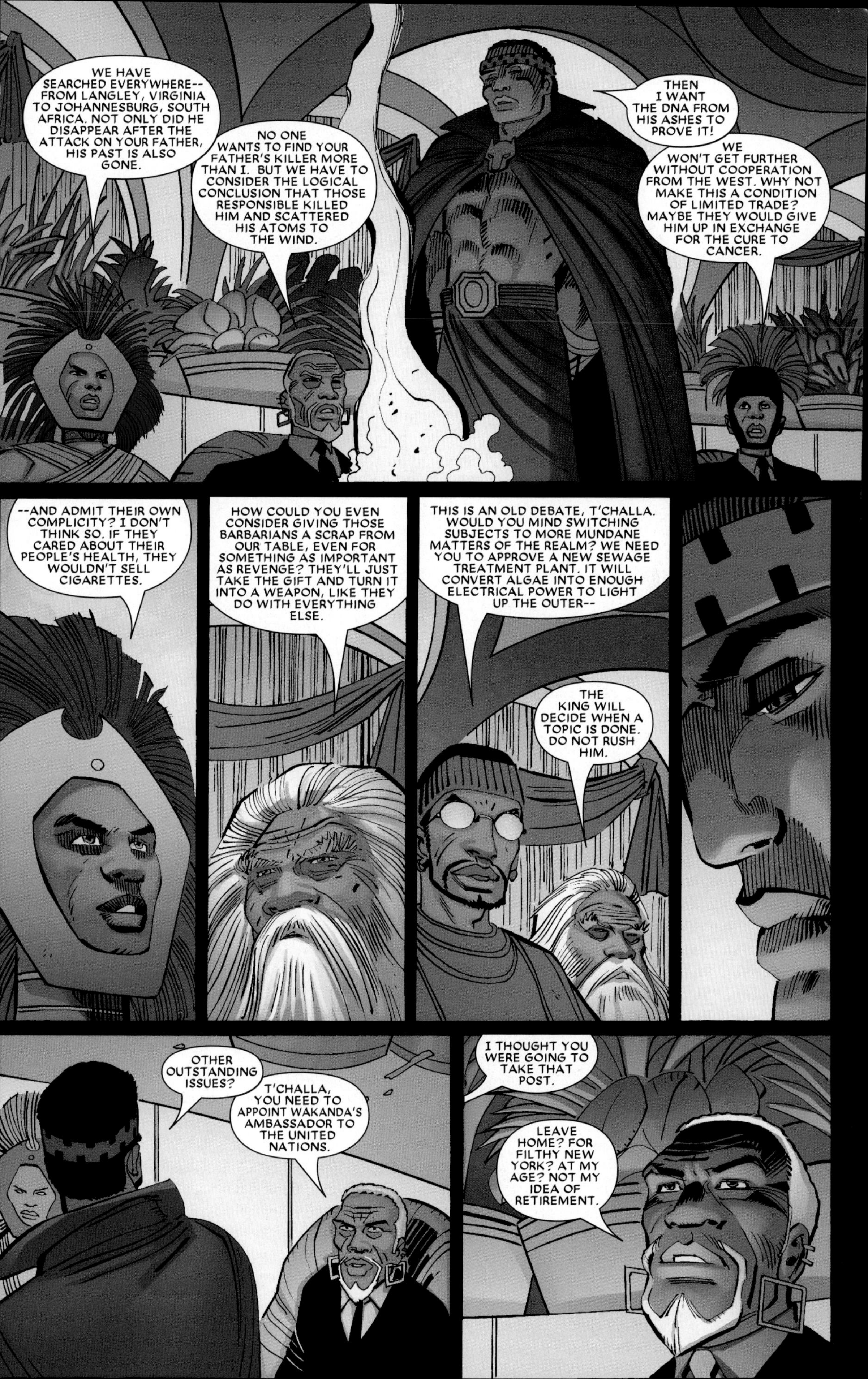
WE HAVE SEARCHED EVERYWHERE-- FROM LANGLEY, VIRGINIA TO JOHANNESBURG, SOUTH AFRICA. NOT ONLY DID HE DISAPPEAR AFTER THE ATTACK ON YOUR FATHER, HIS PAST IS ALSO GONE.
NO ONE WANTS TO FIND YOUR FATHER'S KILLER MORE THAN I. BUT WE HAVE TO CONSIDER THE LOGICAL CONCLUSION THAT THOSE RESPONSIBLE KILLED HIM AND SCATTERED HIS ATOMS TO THE WIND.
THEN I WANT THE DNA FROM HIS ASHES TO PROVE IT!
WE WON'T GET FURTHER WITHOUT COOPERATION FROM THE WEST. WHY NOT MAKE THIS A CONDITION OF LIMITED TRADE? MAYBE THEY WOULD GIVE HIM UP IN EXCHANGE FOR THE CURE TO CANCER.
--AND ADMIT THEIR OWN COMPLICITY? I DON'T THINK SO. IF THEY CARED ABOUT THEIR PEOPLE'S HEALTH, THEY WOULDN'T SELL CIGARETTES.
HOW COULD YOU EVEN CONSIDER GIVING THOSE BARBARIANS A SCRAP FROM OUR TABLE, EVEN FOR SOMETHING AS IMPORTANT AS REVENGE? THEY'LL JUST TAKE THE GIFT AND TURN IT INTO A WEAPON, LIKE THEY DO WITH EVERYTHING ELSE.
THIS IS AN OLD DEBATE, T'CHALLA. WOULD YOU MIND SWITCHING SUBJECTS TO MORE MUNDANE MATTERS OF THE REALM? WE NEED YOU TO APPROVE A NEW SEWAGE TREATMENT PLANT. IT WILL CONVERT ALGAE INTO ENOUGH ELECTRICAL POWER TO LIGHT UP THE OUTER--
THE KING WILL DECIDE WHEN A TOPIC IS DONE. DO NOT RUSH HIM.
OTHER OUTSTANDING ISSUES?
T'CHALLA, YOU NEED TO APPOINT WAKANDA'S AMBASSADOR TO THE UNITED NATIONS.
I THOUGHT YOU WERE GOING TO TAKE THAT POST.
LEAVE HOME? FOR FILTHY NEW YORK? AT MY AGE? NOT MY IDEA OF RETIREMENT.

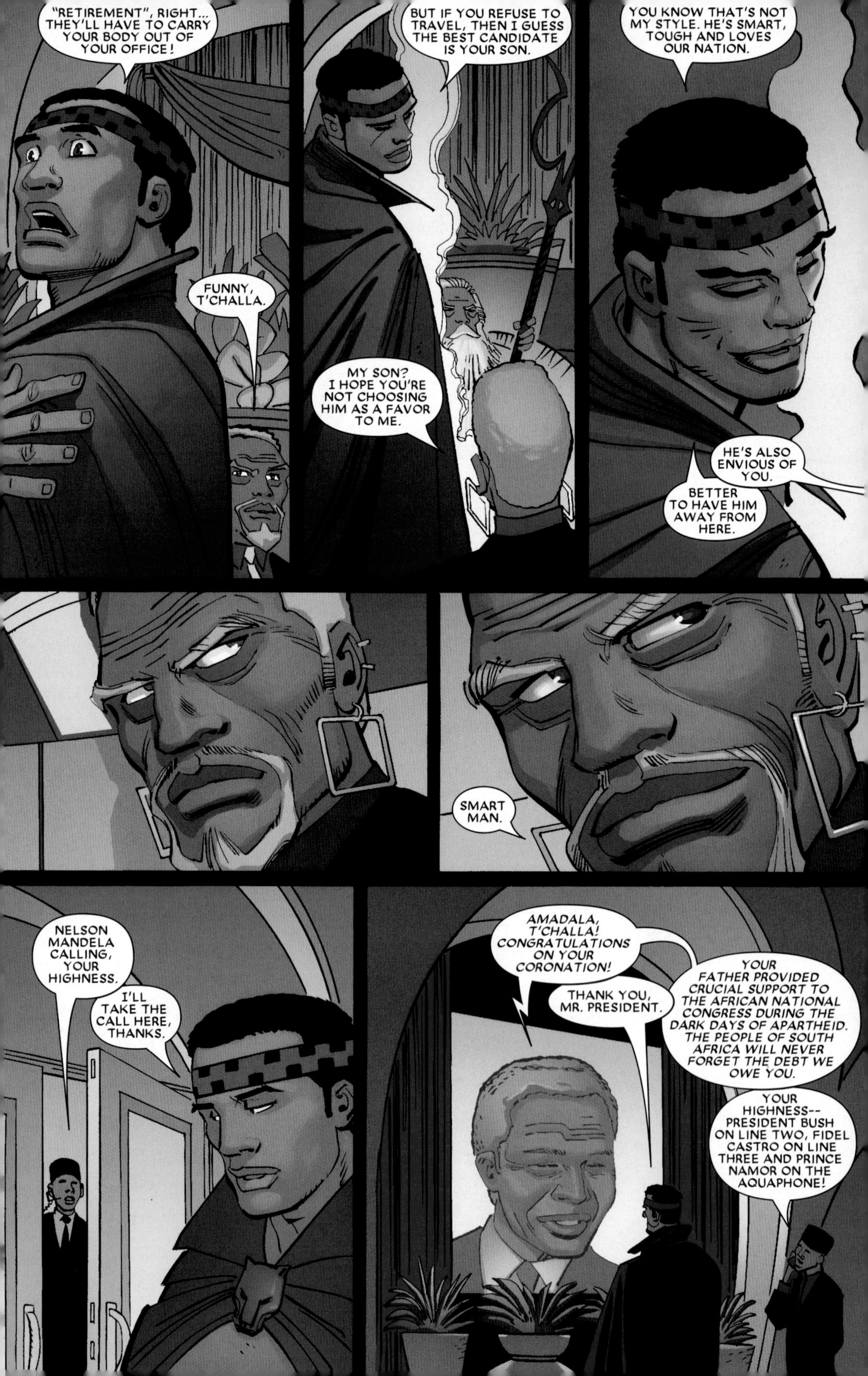
"RETIREMENT", RIGHT... THEY'LL HAVE TO CARRY YOUR BODY OUT OF YOUR OFFICE!
FUNNY, T'CHALLA.
BUT IF YOU REFUSE TO TRAVEL, THEN I GUESS THE BEST CANDIDATE IS YOUR SON.
MY SON? I HOPE YOU'RE NOT CHOOSING HIM AS A FAVOR TO ME.
YOU KNOW THAT'S NOT MY STYLE. HE'S SMART, TOUGH AND LOVES OUR NATION.
HE'S ALSO ENVIOUS OF YOU.
BETTER TO HAVE HIM AWAY FROM HERE.
SMART MAN.
NELSON MANDELA CALLING, YOUR HIGHNESS.
I'LL TAKE THE CALL HERE, THANKS.
AMADALA, T'CHALLA! CONGRATULATIONS ON YOUR CORONATION!
THANK YOU, MR. PRESIDENT.
YOUR FATHER PROVIDED CRUCIAL SUPPORT TO THE AFRICAN NATIONAL CONGRESS DURING THE DARK DAYS OF APARTHEID. THE PEOPLE OF SOUTH AFRICA WILL NEVER FORGET THE DEBT WE OWE YOU.
YOUR HIGHNESS-- PRESIDENT BUSH ON LINE TWO, FIDEL CASTRO ON LINE THREE AND PRINCE NAMOR ON THE AQUAPHONE!

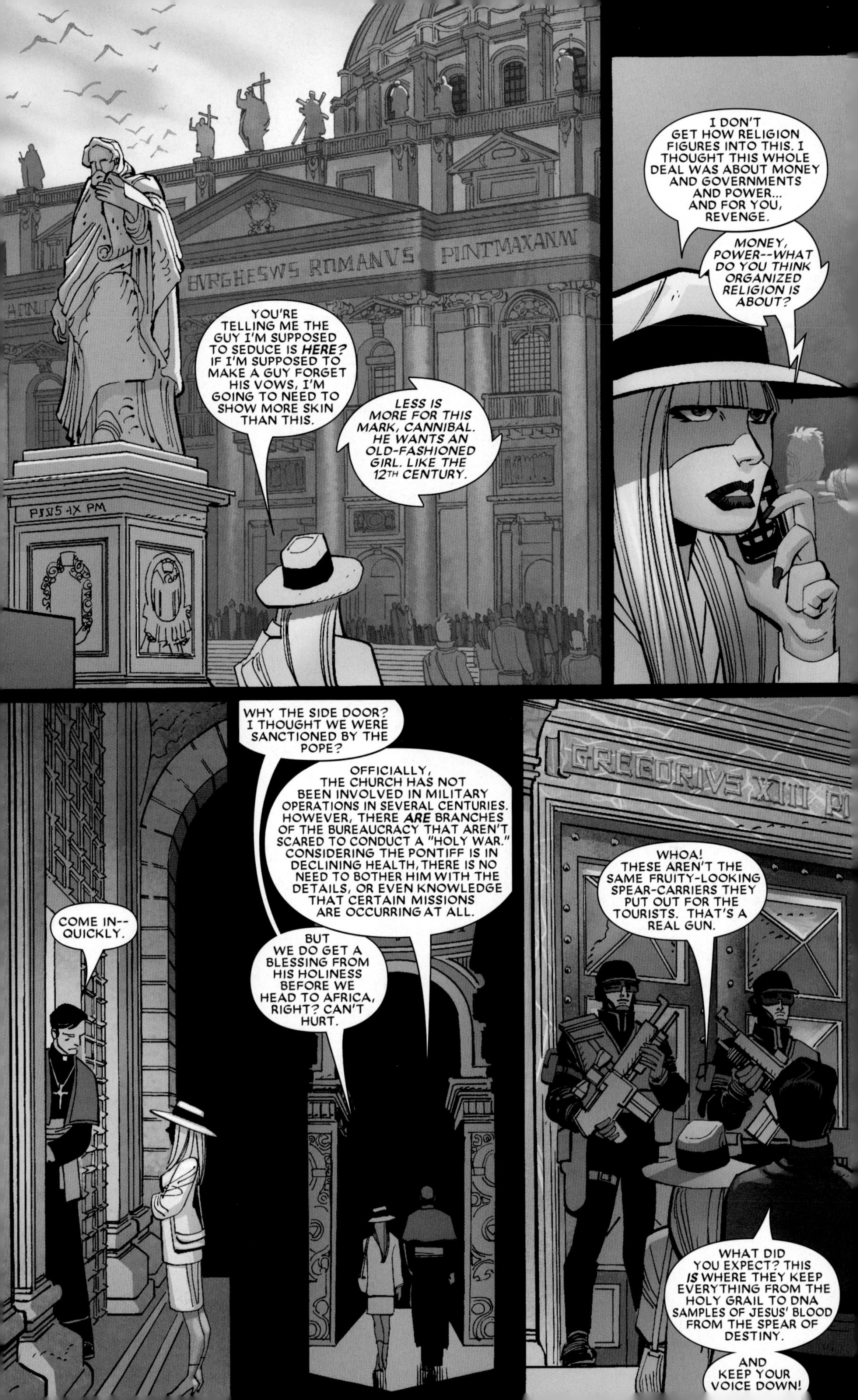
BVRGHESWS ROMANVS PINTMAXANM
PIVS IX PM
YOU'RE TELLING ME THE GUY I'M SUPPOSED TO SEDUCE IS HERE? IF I'M SUPPOSED TO MAKE A GUY FORGET HIS VOWS, I'M GOING TO NEED TO SHOW MORE SKIN THAN THIS.
LESS IS MORE FOR THIS MARK, CANNIBAL. HE WANTS AN OLD-FASHIONED GIRL. LIKE THE 12TH CENTURY.
I DON'T GET HOW RELIGION FIGURES INTO THIS. I THOUGHT THIS WHOLE DEAL WAS ABOUT MONEY AND GOVERNMENTS AND POWER... AND FOR YOU, REVENGE.
MONEY, POWER--WHAT DO YOU THINK ORGANIZED RELIGION IS ABOUT?
COME IN--QUICKLY.
WHY THE SIDE DOOR? I THOUGHT WE WERE SANCTIONED BY THE POPE?
OFFICIALLY, THE CHURCH HAS NOT BEEN INVOLVED IN MILITARY OPERATIONS IN SEVERAL CENTURIES. HOWEVER, THERE ARE BRANCHES OF THE BUREAUCRACY THAT AREN'T SCARED TO CONDUCT A "HOLY WAR." CONSIDERING THE PONTIFF IS IN DECLINING HEALTH, THERE IS NO NEED TO BOTHER HIM WITH THE DETAILS, OR EVEN KNOWLEDGE THAT CERTAIN MISSIONS ARE OCCURRING AT ALL.
BUT WE DO GET A BLESSING FROM HIS HOLINESS BEFORE WE HEAD TO AFRICA, RIGHT? CAN'T HURT.
GREGORIVS XIII P
WHOA! THESE AREN'T THE SAME FRUITY-LOOKING SPEAR-CARRIERS THEY PUT OUT FOR THE TOURISTS. THAT'S A REAL GUN.
WHAT DID YOU EXPECT? THIS IS WHERE THEY KEEP EVERYTHING FROM THE HOLY GRAIL TO DNA SAMPLES OF JESUS' BLOOD FROM THE SPEAR OF DESTINY.
AND KEEP YOUR VOICE DOWN!

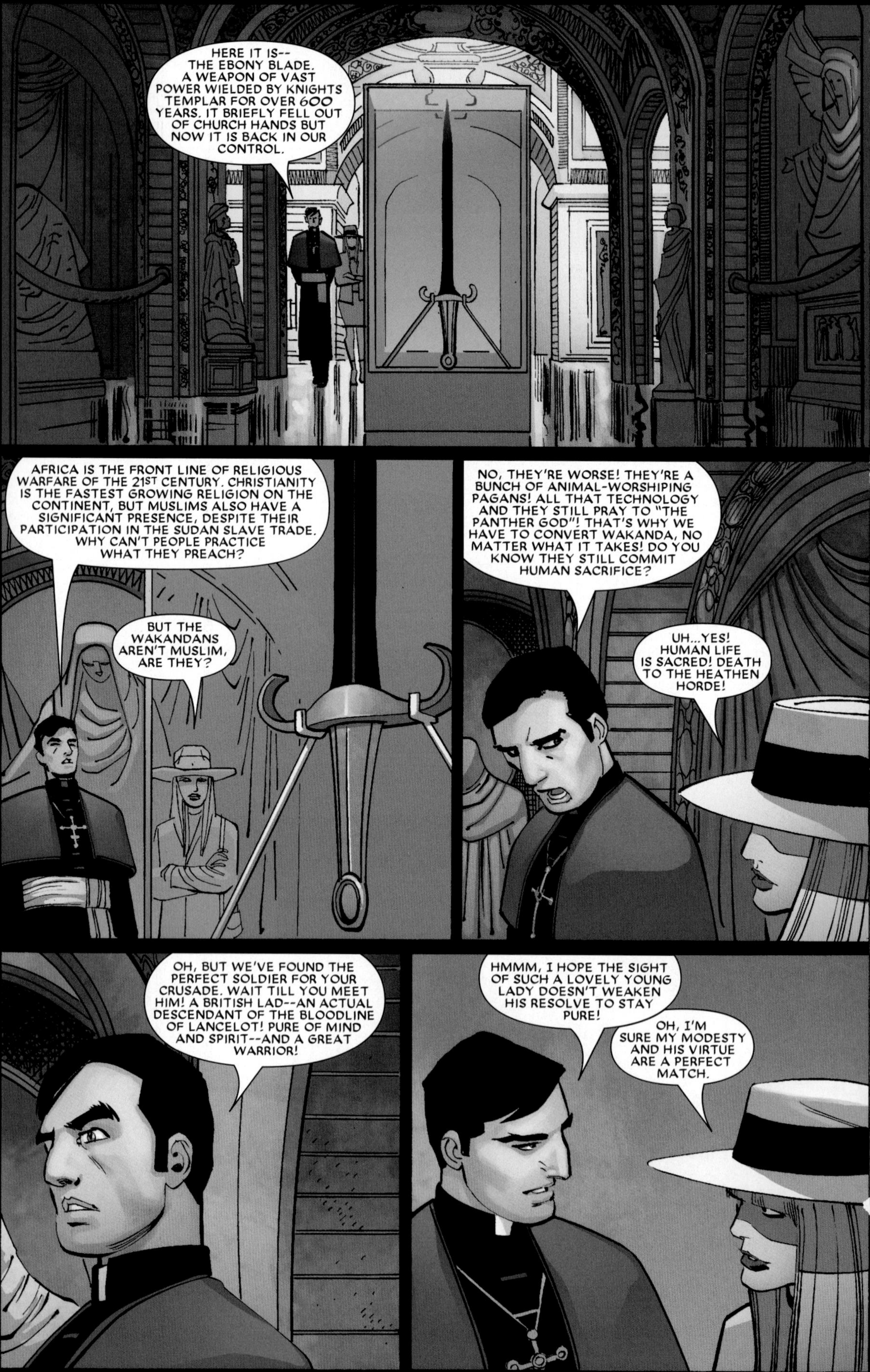
HERE IT IS-- THE EBONY BLADE. A WEAPON OF VAST POWER WIELDED BY KNIGHTS TEMPLAR FOR OVER 600 YEARS. IT BRIEFLY FELL OUT OF CHURCH HANDS BUT NOW IT IS BACK IN OUR CONTROL.
AFRICA IS THE FRONT LINE OF RELIGIOUS WARFARE OF THE 21ST CENTURY. CHRISTIANITY IS THE FASTEST GROWING RELIGION ON THE CONTINENT, BUT MUSLIMS ALSO HAVE A SIGNIFICANT PRESENCE, DESPITE THEIR PARTICIPATION IN THE SUDAN SLAVE TRADE. WHY CAN'T PEOPLE PRACTICE WHAT THEY PREACH?
BUT THE WAKANDANS AREN'T MUSLIM, ARE THEY?
NO, THEY'RE WORSE! THEY'RE A BUNCH OF ANIMAL-WORSHIPING PAGANS! ALL THAT TECHNOLOGY AND THEY STILL PRAY TO "THE PANTHER GOD"! THAT'S WHY WE HAVE TO CONVERT WAKANDA, NO MATTER WHAT IT TAKES! DO YOU KNOW THEY STILL COMMIT HUMAN SACRIFICE?
UH...YES! HUMAN LIFE IS SACRED! DEATH TO THE HEATHEN HORDE!
OH, BUT WE'VE FOUND THE PERFECT SOLDIER FOR YOUR CRUSADE. WAIT TILL YOU MEET HIM! A BRITISH LAD--AN ACTUAL DESCENDANT OF THE BLOODLINE OF LANCELOT! PURE OF MIND AND SPIRIT--AND A GREAT WARRIOR!
HMMM, I HOPE THE SIGHT OF SUCH A LOVELY YOUNG LADY DOESN'T WEAKEN HIS RESOLVE TO STAY PURE!
OH, I'M SURE MY MODESTY AND HIS VIRTUE ARE A PERFECT MATCH.

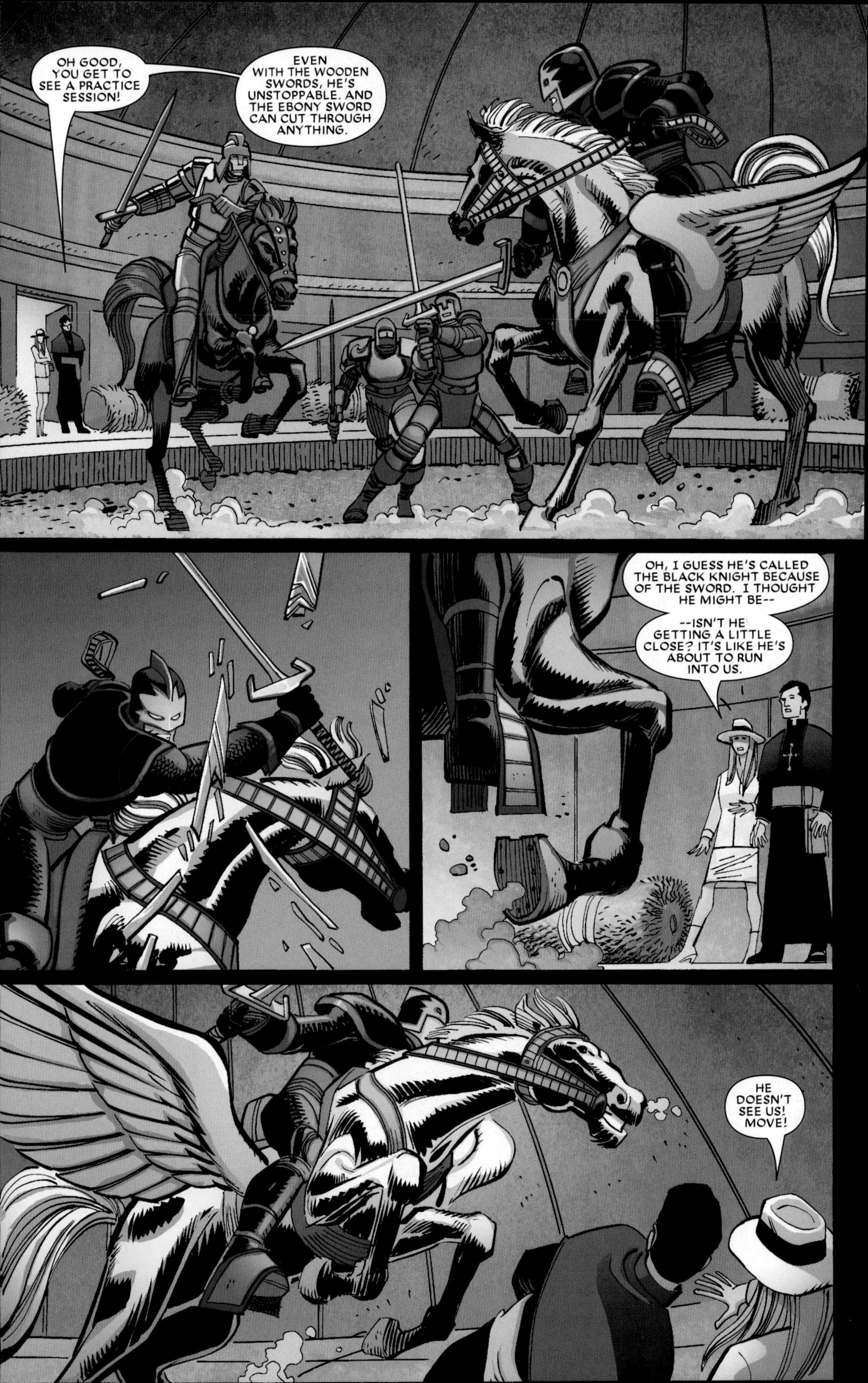
OH GOOD, YOU GET TO SEE A PRACTICE SESSION!
EVEN WITH THE WOODEN SWORDS, HE'S UNSTOPPABLE. AND THE EBONY SWORD CAN CUT THROUGH ANYTHING.
OH, I GUESS HE'S CALLED THE BLACK KNIGHT BECAUSE OF THE SWORD. I THOUGHT HE MIGHT BE--
--ISN'T HE GETTING A LITTLE CLOSE? IT'S LIKE HE'S ABOUT TO RUN INTO US.
HE DOESN'T SEE US! MOVE!

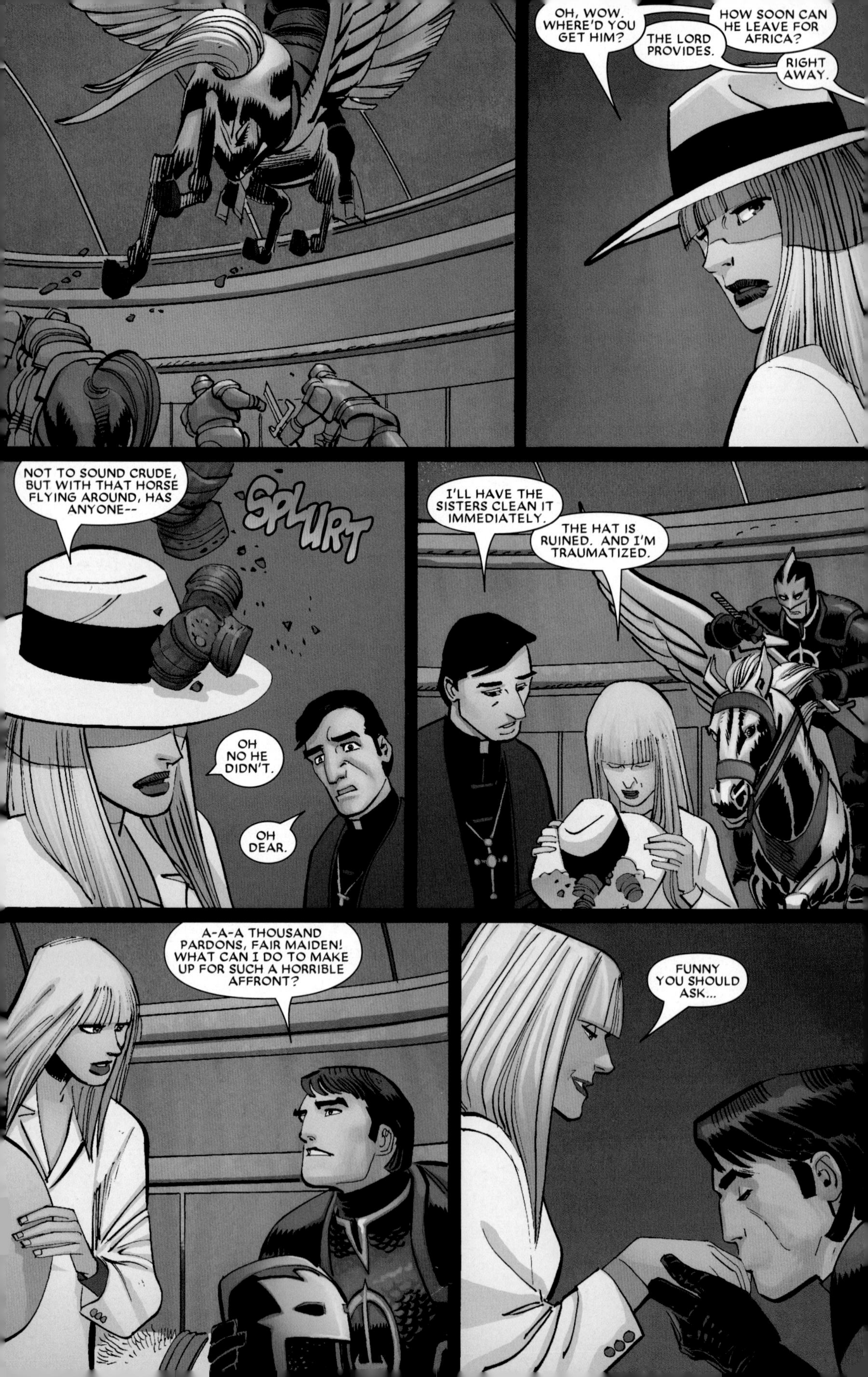
OH, WOW. WHERE'D YOU GET HIM?
THE LORD PROVIDES.
HOW SOON CAN HE LEAVE FOR AFRICA?
RIGHT AWAY.
NOT TO SOUND CRUDE, BUT WITH THAT HORSE FLYING AROUND, HAS ANYONE--
SPLURT
OH NO HE DIDN'T.
OH DEAR.
I'LL HAVE THE SISTERS CLEAN IT IMMEDIATELY.
THE HAT IS RUINED. AND I'M TRAUMATIZED.
A-A-A THOUSAND PARDONS, FAIR MAIDEN! WHAT CAN I DO TO MAKE UP FOR SUCH A HORRIBLE AFFRONT?
FUNNY YOU SHOULD ASK...

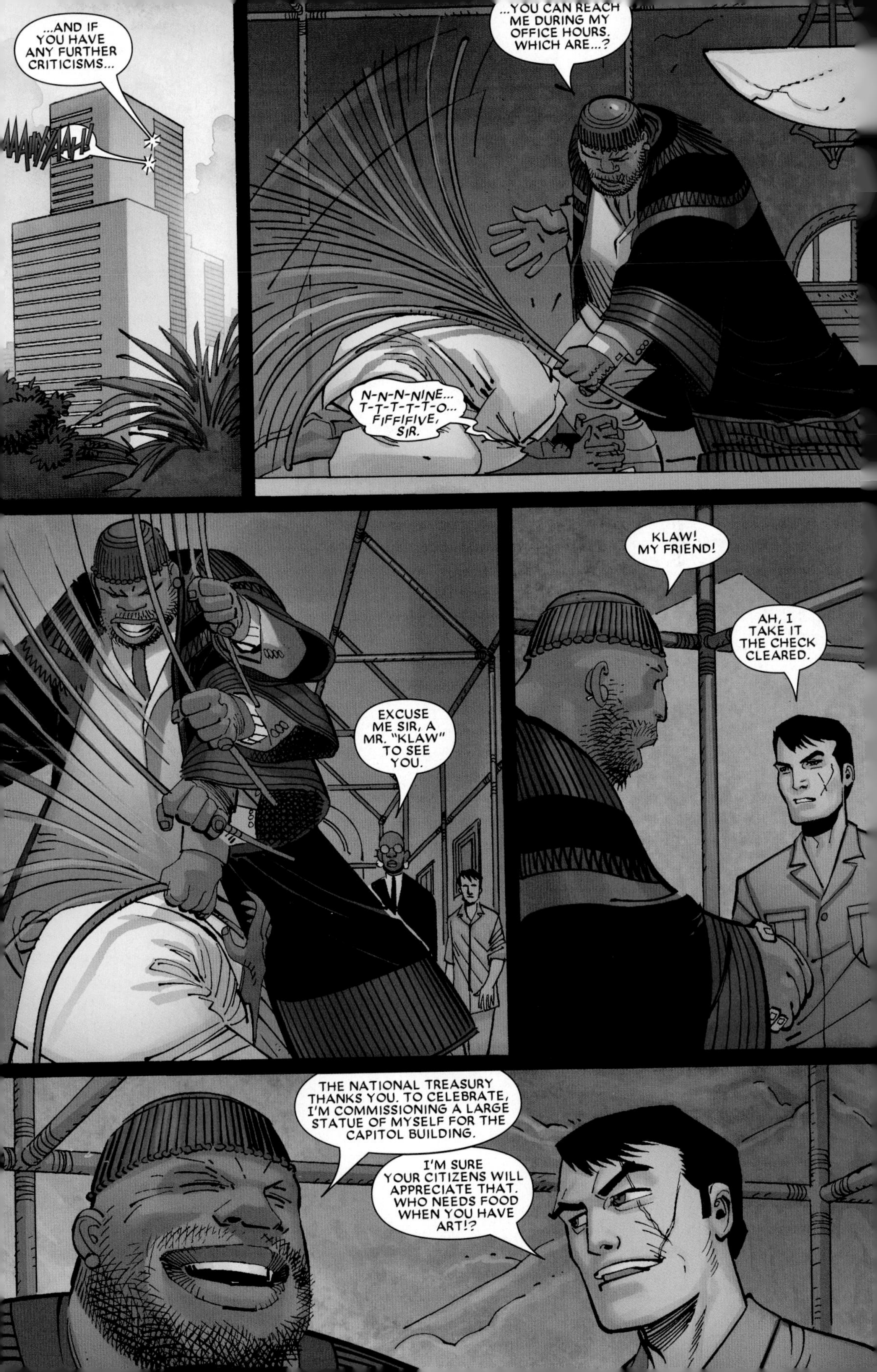
...AND IF YOU HAVE ANY FURTHER CRITICISMS...
AAAIIIYYAAH!!
...YOU CAN REACH ME DURING MY OFFICE HOURS. WHICH ARE...?
N-N-N-NINE... T-T-T-T-T-O... FIFFIFIVE, SIR.
EXCUSE ME SIR, A MR. "KLAW" TO SEE YOU.
KLAW! MY FRIEND!
AH, I TAKE IT THE CHECK CLEARED.
THE NATIONAL TREASURY THANKS YOU. TO CELEBRATE, I'M COMMISSIONING A LARGE STATUE OF MYSELF FOR THE CAPITOL BUILDING.
I'M SURE YOUR CITIZENS WILL APPRECIATE THAT. WHO NEEDS FOOD WHEN YOU HAVE ART!?

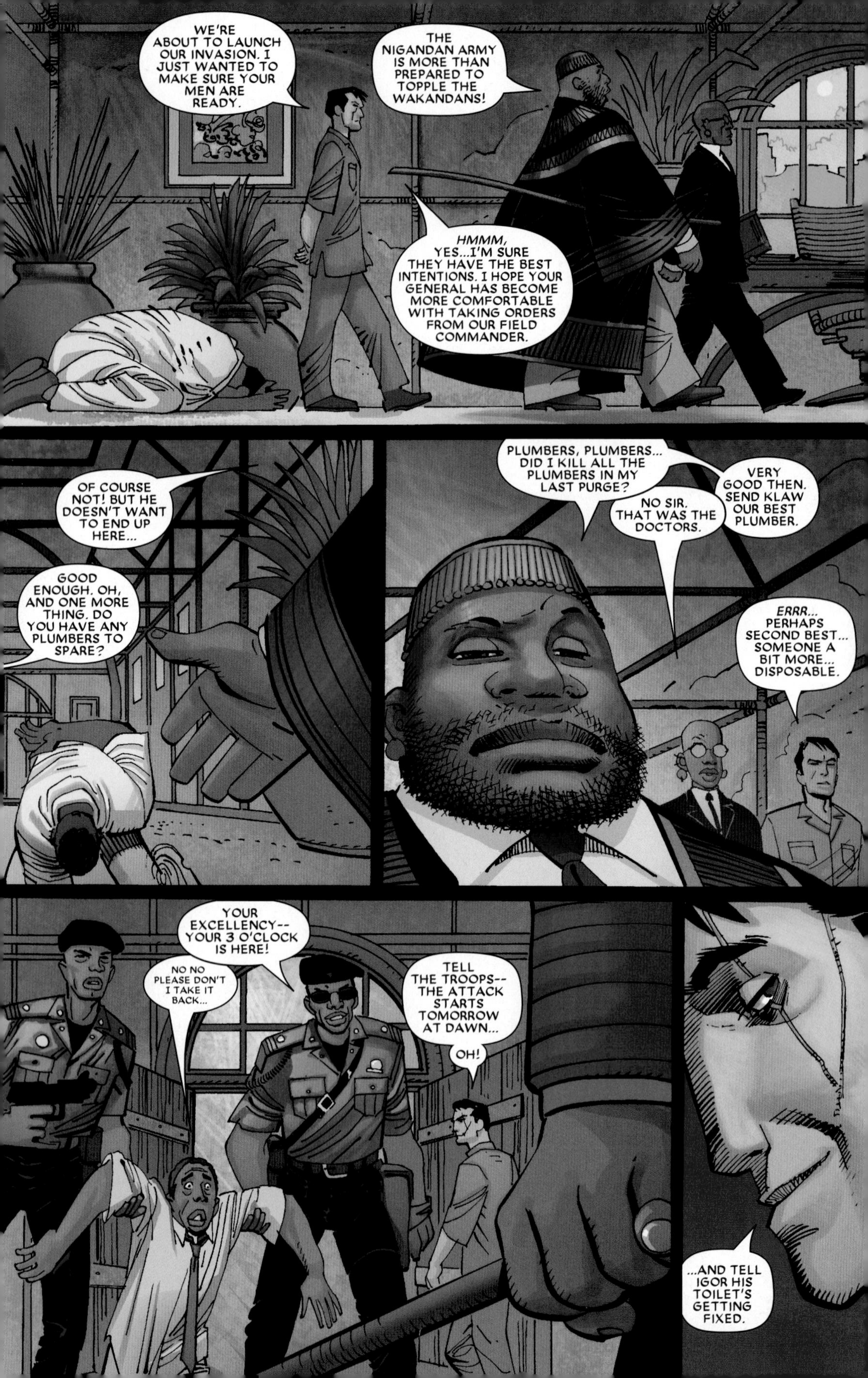
WE'RE ABOUT TO LAUNCH OUR INVASION. I JUST WANTED TO MAKE SURE YOUR MEN ARE READY.
THE NIGANDAN ARMY IS MORE THAN PREPARED TO TOPPLE THE WAKANDANS!
HMMM, YES...I'M SURE THEY HAVE THE BEST INTENTIONS. I HOPE YOUR GENERAL HAS BECOME MORE COMFORTABLE WITH TAKING ORDERS FROM OUR FIELD COMMANDER.
OF COURSE NOT! BUT HE DOESN'T WANT TO END UP HERE...
GOOD ENOUGH. OH, AND ONE MORE THING. DO YOU HAVE ANY PLUMBERS TO SPARE?
PLUMBERS, PLUMBERS... DID I KILL ALL THE PLUMBERS IN MY LAST PURGE?
NO SIR. THAT WAS THE DOCTORS.
VERY GOOD THEN. SEND KLAW OUR BEST PLUMBER.
ERRR... PERHAPS SECOND BEST... SOMEONE A BIT MORE... DISPOSABLE.
YOUR EXCELLENCY-- YOUR 3 O'CLOCK IS HERE!
NO NO PLEASE DON'T I TAKE IT BACK...
TELL THE TROOPS-- THE ATTACK STARTS TOMORROW AT DAWN...
OH!
...AND TELL IGOR HIS TOILET'S GETTING FIXED.

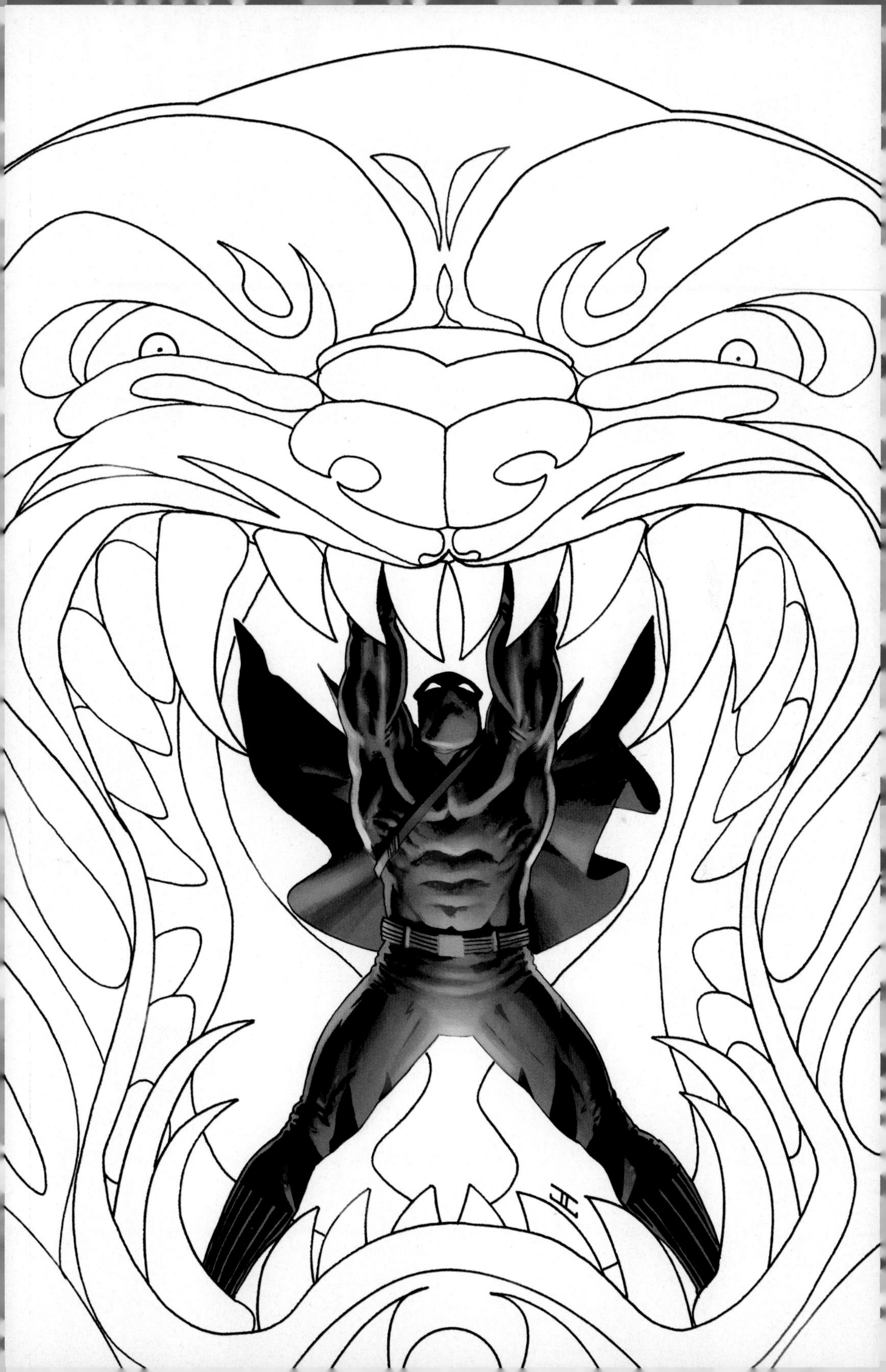

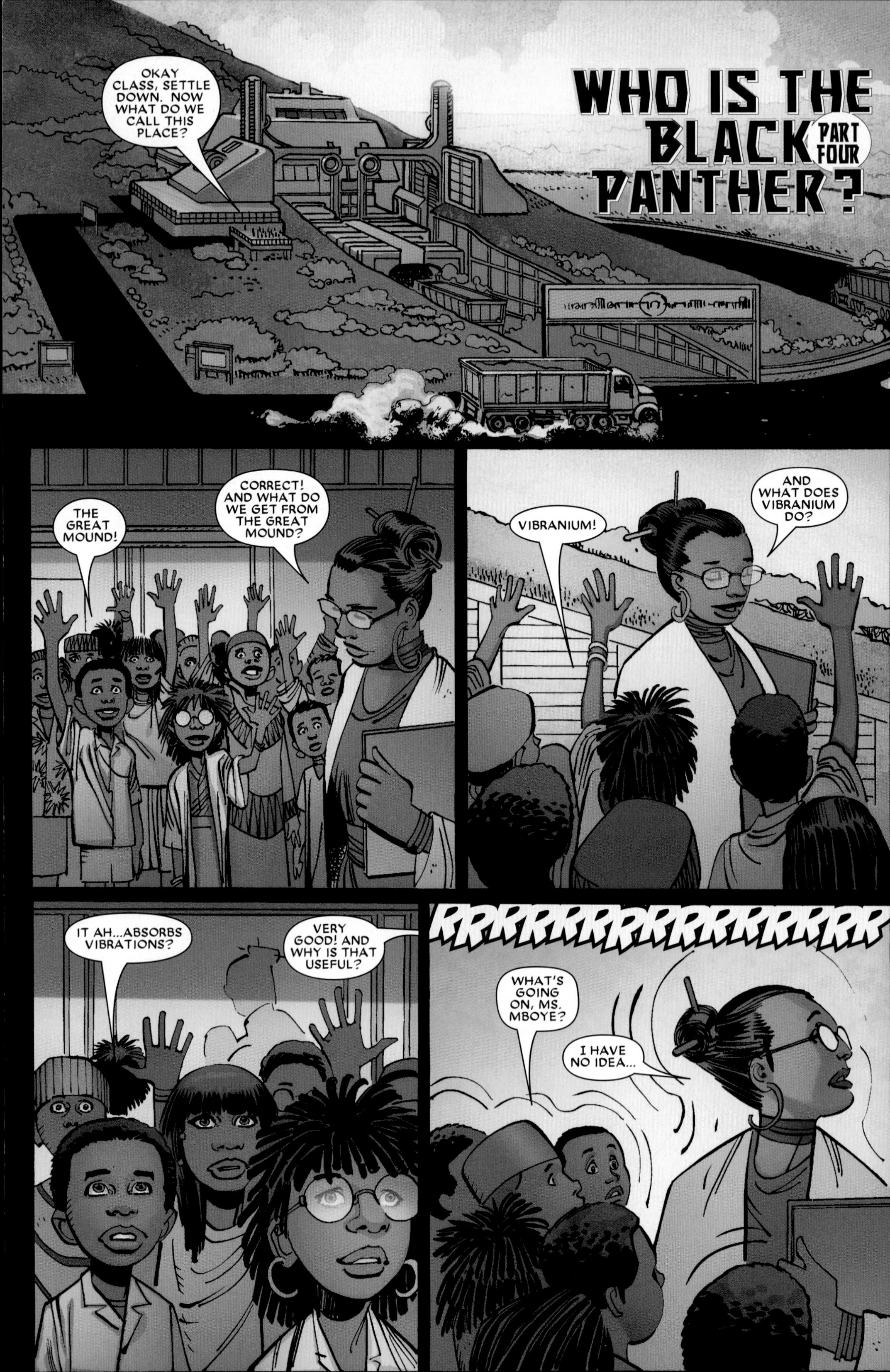
WHO IS THE BLACK PANTHER?
PART FOUR
OKAY CLASS, SETTLE DOWN. NOW WHAT DO WE CALL THIS PLACE?
THE GREAT MOUND!
CORRECT! AND WHAT DO WE GET FROM THE GREAT MOUND?
VIBRANIUM!
AND WHAT DOES VIBRANIUM DO?
IT AH...ABSORBS VIBRATIONS?
VERY GOOD! AND WHY IS THAT USEFUL?
RRRRRRRRRRRRRRRRR
WHAT'S GOING ON, MS. MBOYE?
I HAVE NO IDEA...

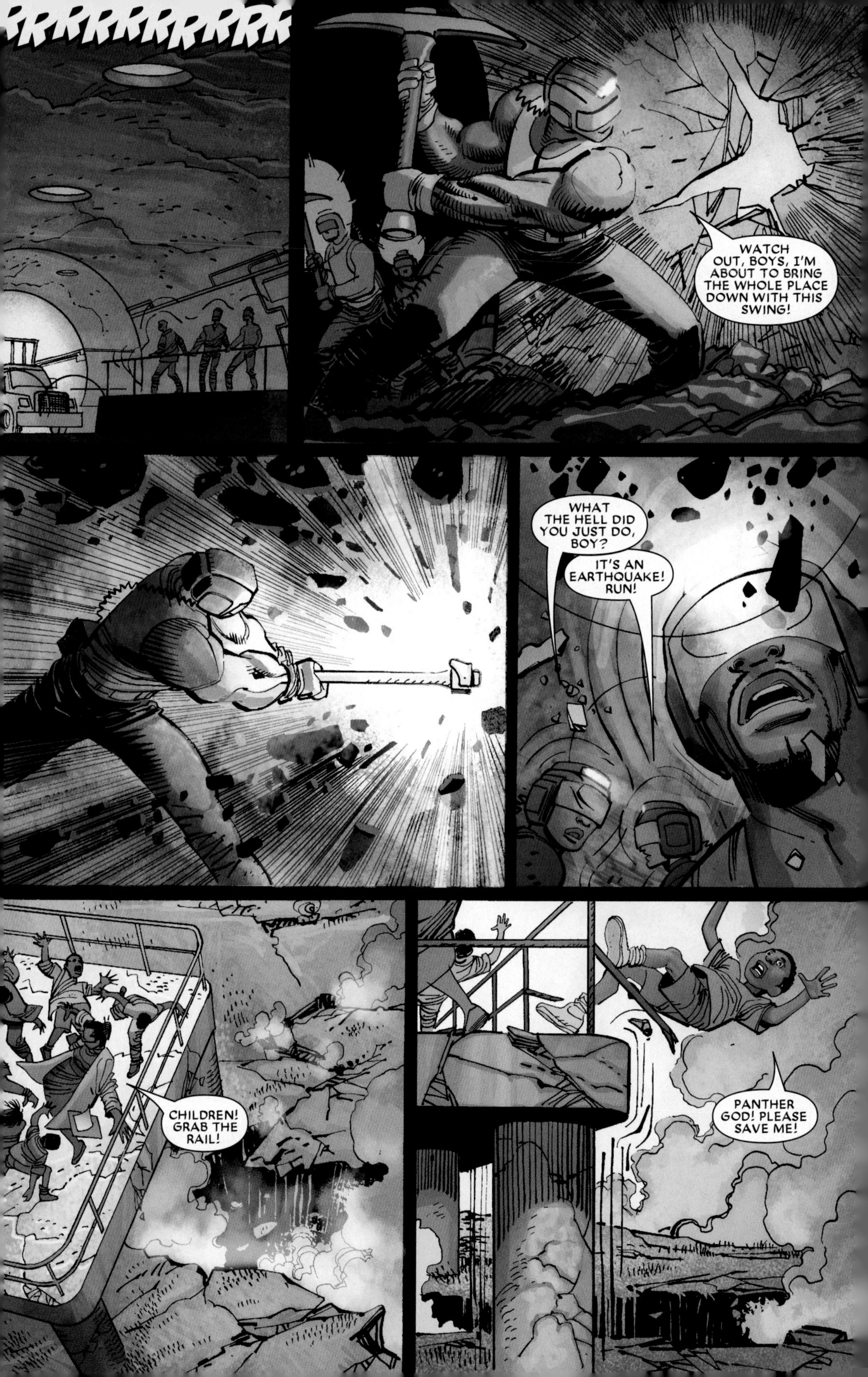

RRRRRRRRRRRR
WATCH OUT, BOYS, I'M ABOUT TO BRING THE WHOLE PLACE DOWN WITH THIS SWING!
WHAT THE HELL DID YOU JUST DO, BOY?
IT'S AN EARTHQUAKE! RUN!
CHILDREN! GRAB THE RAIL!
PANTHER GOD! PLEASE SAVE ME!

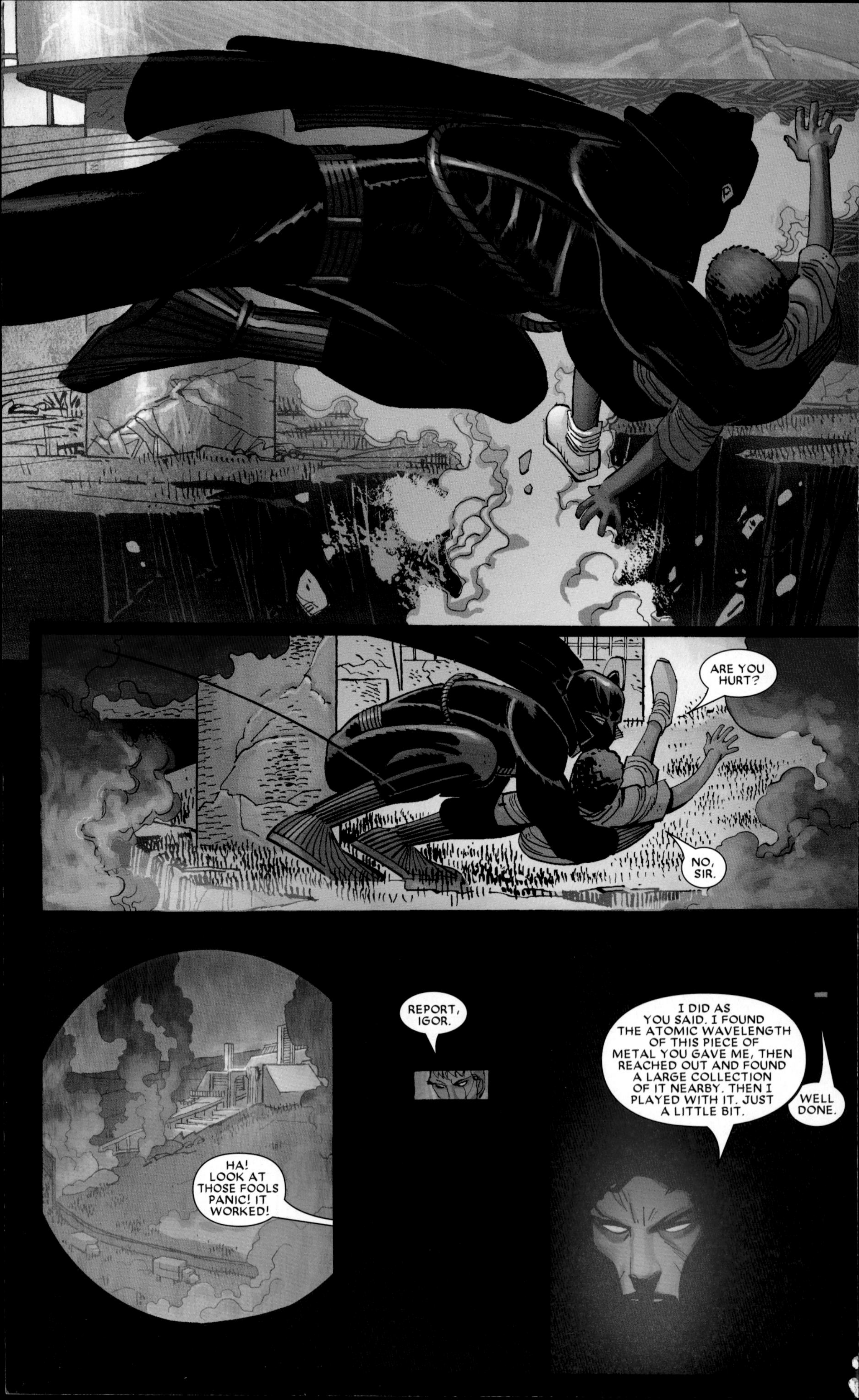
ARE YOU HURT?
NO, SIR.
HA! LOOK AT THOSE FOOLS PANIC! IT WORKED!
REPORT, IGOR.
I DID AS YOU SAID. I FOUND THE ATOMIC WAVELENGTH OF THIS PIECE OF METAL YOU GAVE ME, THEN REACHED OUT AND FOUND A LARGE COLLECTION OF IT NEARBY. THEN I PLAYED WITH IT. JUST A LITTLE BIT.
WELL DONE.

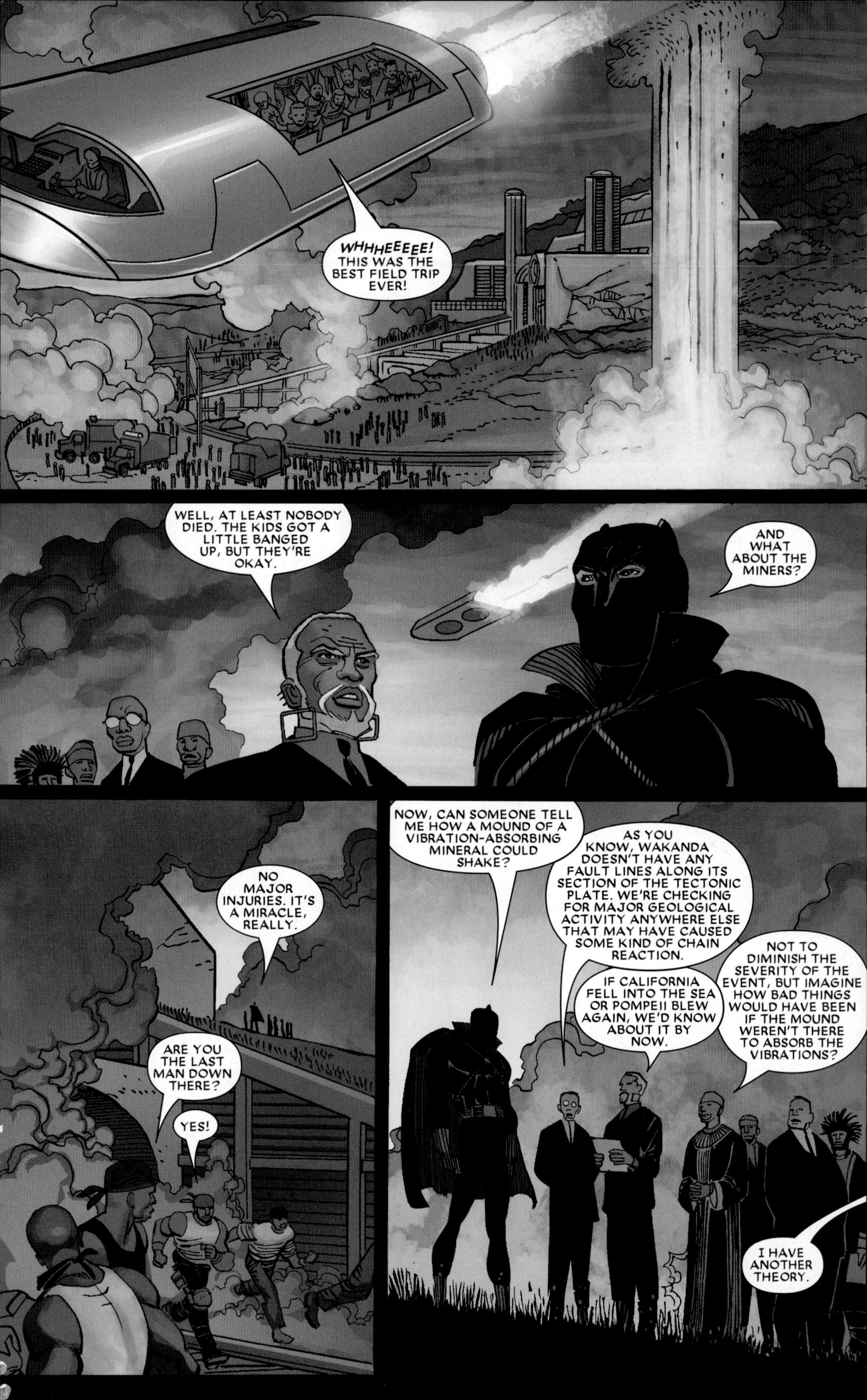

WHHHEEEEE! THIS WAS THE BEST FIELD TRIP EVER!
WELL, AT LEAST NOBODY DIED. THE KIDS GOT A LITTLE BANGED UP, BUT THEY'RE OKAY.
AND WHAT ABOUT THE MINERS?
NO MAJOR INJURIES. IT'S A MIRACLE, REALLY.
ARE YOU THE LAST MAN DOWN THERE?
YES!
NOW, CAN SOMEONE TELL ME HOW A MOUND OF A VIBRATION-ABSORBING MINERAL COULD SHAKE?
AS YOU KNOW, WAKANDA DOESN'T HAVE ANY FAULT LINES ALONG ITS SECTION OF THE TECTONIC PLATE. WE'RE CHECKING FOR MAJOR GEOLOGICAL ACTIVITY ANYWHERE ELSE THAT MAY HAVE CAUSED SOME KIND OF CHAIN REACTION.
IF CALIFORNIA FELL INTO THE SEA OR POMPEII BLEW AGAIN, WE'D KNOW ABOUT IT BY NOW.
NOT TO DIMINISH THE SEVERITY OF THE EVENT, BUT IMAGINE HOW BAD THINGS WOULD HAVE BEEN IF THE MOUND WEREN'T THERE TO ABSORB THE VIBRATIONS?
I HAVE ANOTHER THEORY.

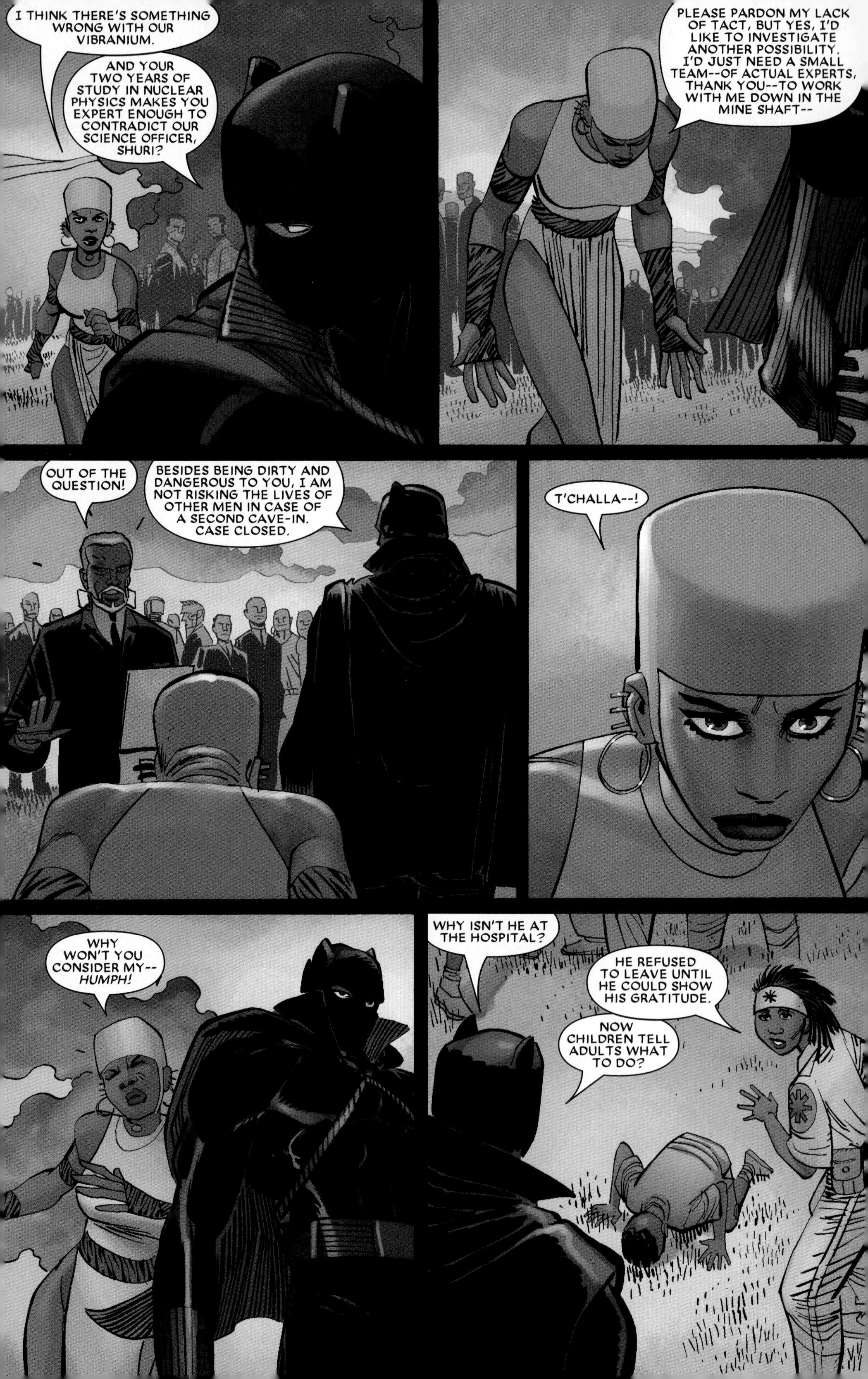
I THINK THERE'S SOMETHING WRONG WITH OUR VIBRANIUM.
AND YOUR TWO YEARS OF STUDY IN NUCLEAR PHYSICS MAKES YOU EXPERT ENOUGH TO CONTRADICT OUR SCIENCE OFFICER, SHURI?
PLEASE PARDON MY LACK OF TACT, BUT YES, I'D LIKE TO INVESTIGATE ANOTHER POSSIBILITY. I'D JUST NEED A SMALL TEAM--OF ACTUAL EXPERTS, THANK YOU--TO WORK WITH ME DOWN IN THE MINE SHAFT--
OUT OF THE QUESTION!
BESIDES BEING DIRTY AND DANGEROUS TO YOU, I AM NOT RISKING THE LIVES OF OTHER MEN IN CASE OF A SECOND CAVE-IN. CASE CLOSED.
T'CHALLA--!
WHY WON'T YOU CONSIDER MY-- *HUMPH!*
WHY ISN'T HE AT THE HOSPITAL?
HE REFUSED TO LEAVE UNTIL HE COULD SHOW HIS GRATITUDE.
NOW CHILDREN TELL ADULTS WHAT TO DO?

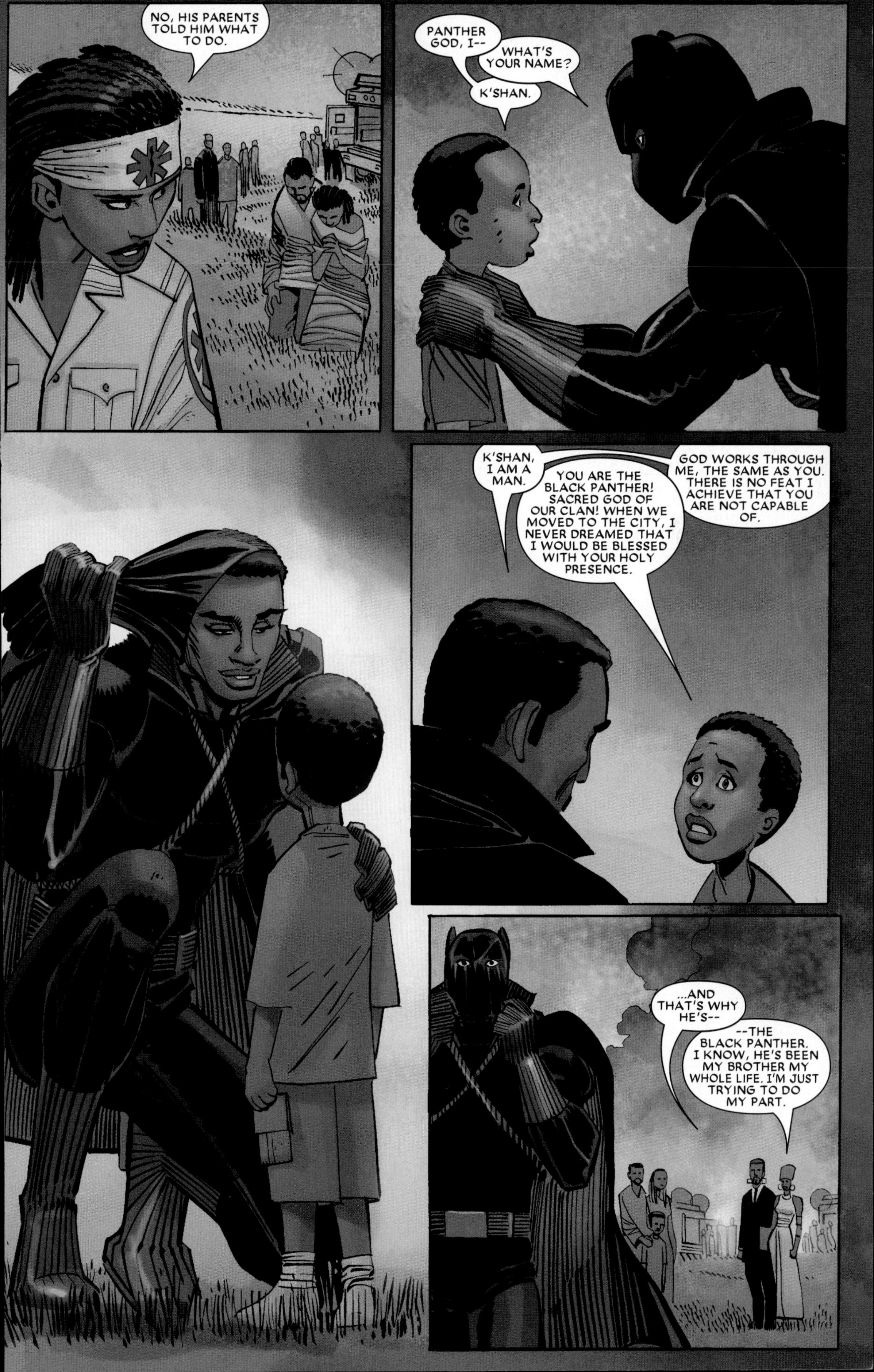
NO, HIS PARENTS TOLD HIM WHAT TO DO.
PANTHER GOD, I--
WHAT'S YOUR NAME?
K'SHAN.
K'SHAN, I AM A MAN.
YOU ARE THE BLACK PANTHER! SACRED GOD OF OUR CLAN! WHEN WE MOVED TO THE CITY, I NEVER DREAMED THAT I WOULD BE BLESSED WITH YOUR HOLY PRESENCE.
GOD WORKS THROUGH ME, THE SAME AS YOU. THERE IS NO FEAT I ACHIEVE THAT YOU ARE NOT CAPABLE OF.
...AND THAT'S WHY HE'S--
--THE BLACK PANTHER. I KNOW, HE'S BEEN MY BROTHER MY WHOLE LIFE. I'M JUST TRYING TO DO MY PART.

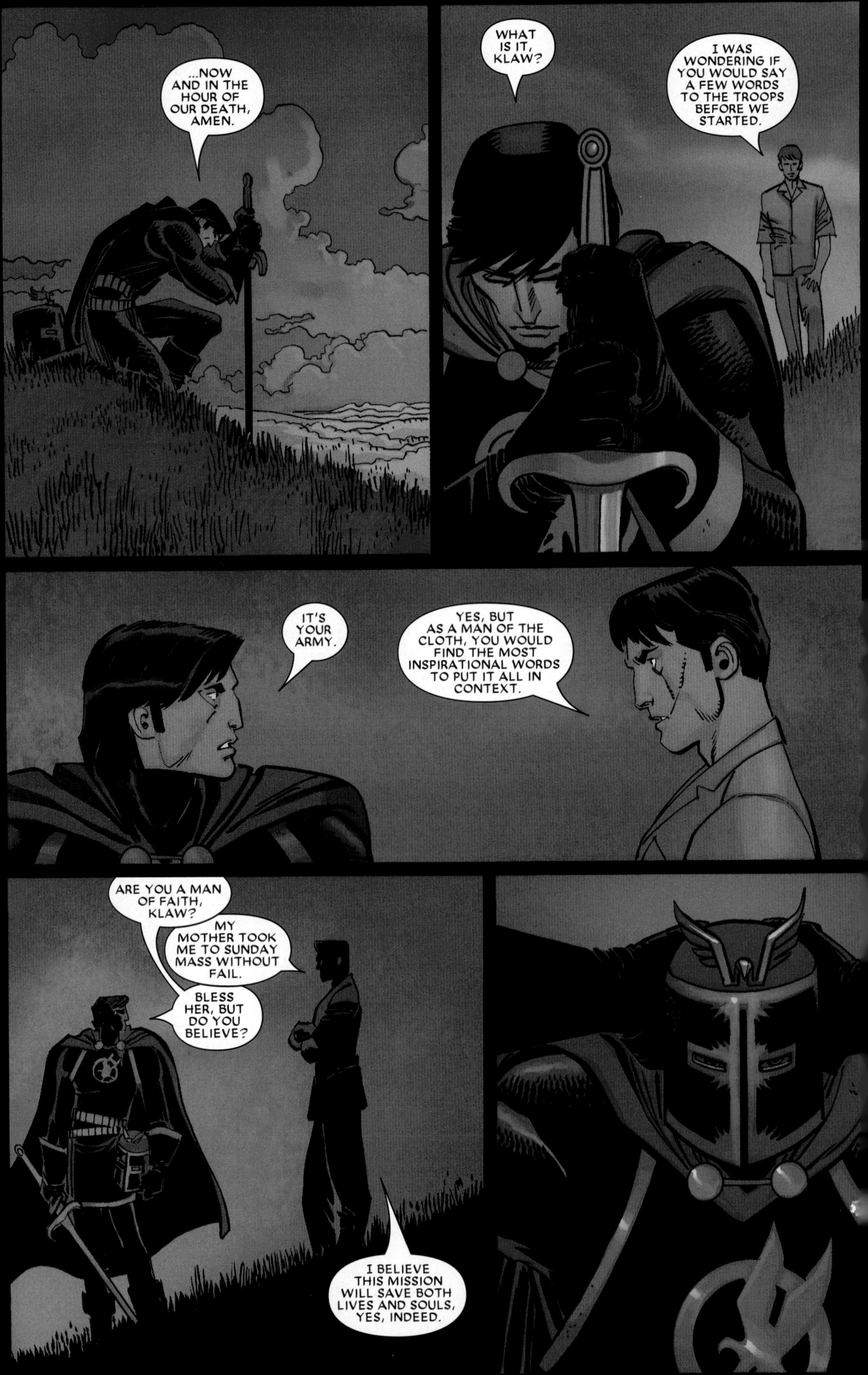
...NOW AND IN THE HOUR OF OUR DEATH, AMEN.
WHAT IS IT, KLAW?
I WAS WONDERING IF YOU WOULD SAY A FEW WORDS TO THE TROOPS BEFORE WE STARTED.
IT'S YOUR ARMY.
YES, BUT AS A MAN OF THE CLOTH, YOU WOULD FIND THE MOST INSPIRATIONAL WORDS TO PUT IT ALL IN CONTEXT.
ARE YOU A MAN OF FAITH, KLAW?
MY MOTHER TOOK ME TO SUNDAY MASS WITHOUT FAIL.
BLESS HER, BUT DO YOU BELIEVE?
I BELIEVE THIS MISSION WILL SAVE BOTH LIVES AND SOULS, YES, INDEED.

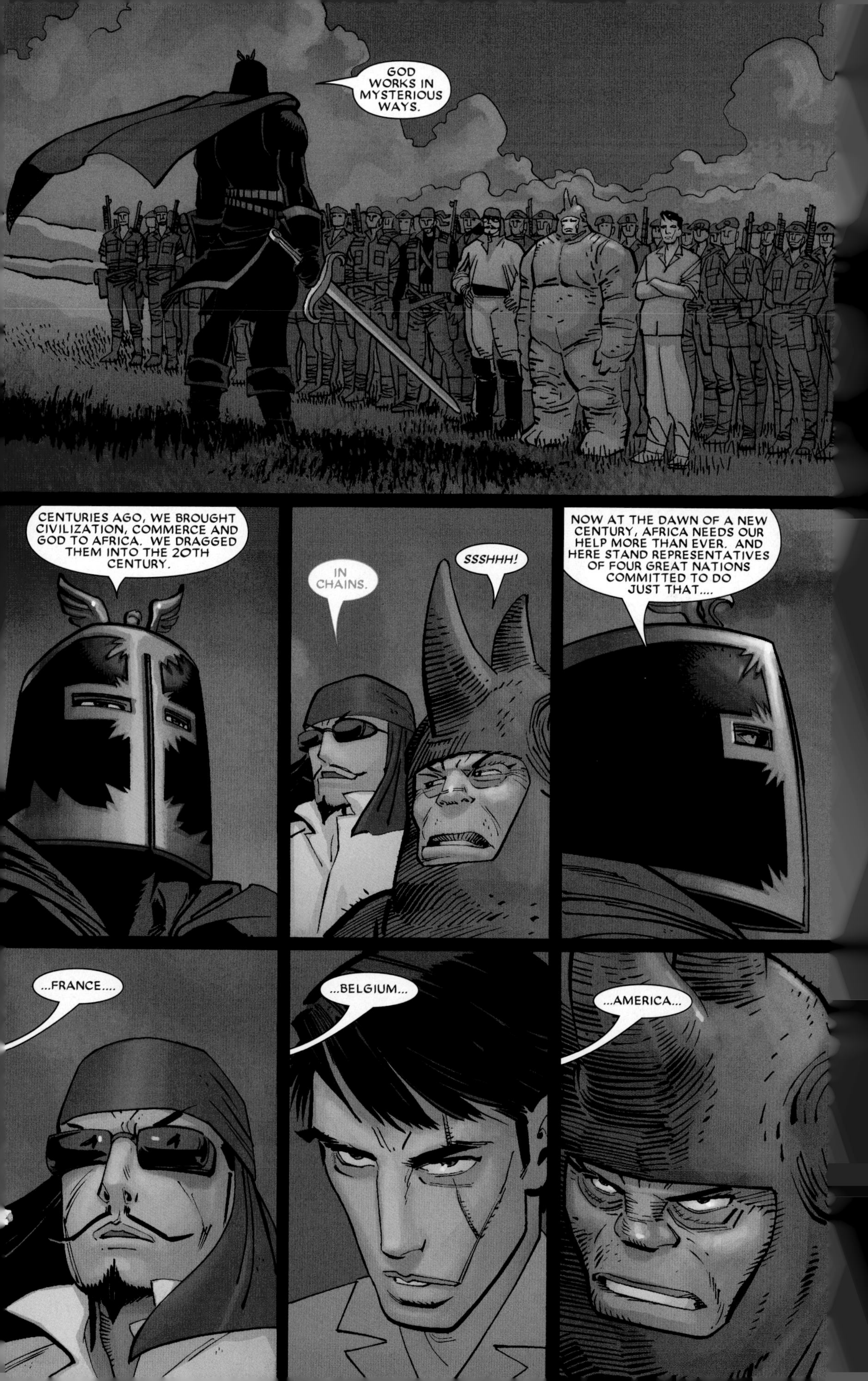
GOD WORKS IN MYSTERIOUS WAYS.
CENTURIES AGO, WE BROUGHT CIVILIZATION, COMMERCE AND GOD TO AFRICA. WE DRAGGED THEM INTO THE 20TH CENTURY.
IN CHAINS.
SSSHHH!
NOW AT THE DAWN OF A NEW CENTURY, AFRICA NEEDS OUR HELP MORE THAN EVER. AND HERE STAND REPRESENTATIVES OF FOUR GREAT NATIONS COMMITTED TO DO JUST THAT....
...FRANCE....
...BELGIUM...
...AMERICA...

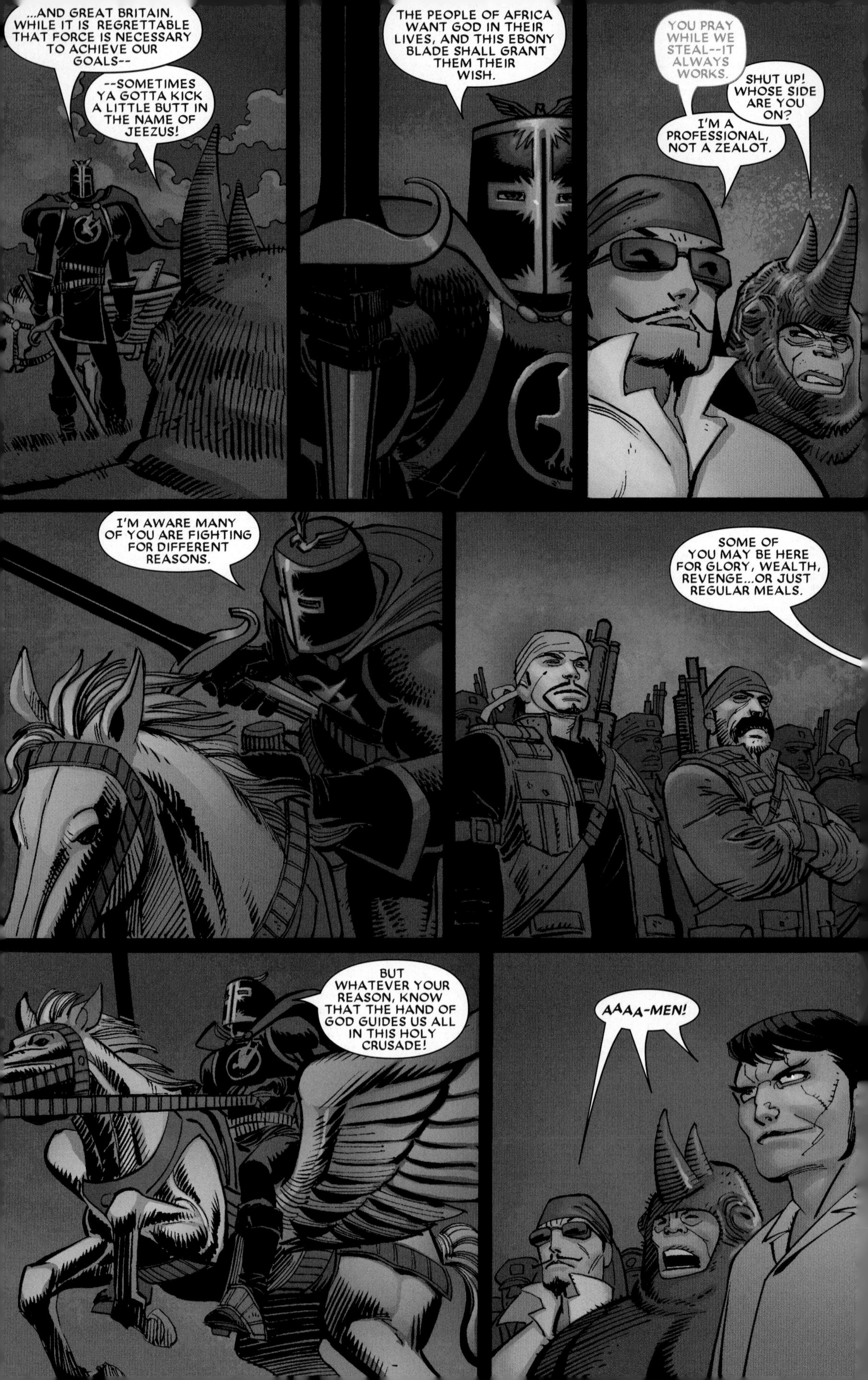
...AND GREAT BRITAIN. WHILE IT IS REGRETTABLE THAT FORCE IS NECESSARY TO ACHIEVE OUR GOALS--
--SOMETIMES YA GOTTA KICK A LITTLE BUTT IN THE NAME OF JEEZUS!
THE PEOPLE OF AFRICA WANT GOD IN THEIR LIVES, AND THIS EBONY BLADE SHALL GRANT THEM THEIR WISH.
YOU PRAY WHILE WE STEAL--IT ALWAYS WORKS.
I'M A PROFESSIONAL, NOT A ZEALOT.
SHUT UP! WHOSE SIDE ARE YOU ON?
I'M AWARE MANY OF YOU ARE FIGHTING FOR DIFFERENT REASONS.
SOME OF YOU MAY BE HERE FOR GLORY, WEALTH, REVENGE...OR JUST REGULAR MEALS.
BUT WHATEVER YOUR REASON, KNOW THAT THE HAND OF GOD GUIDES US ALL IN THIS HOLY CRUSADE!
AAAA-MEN!

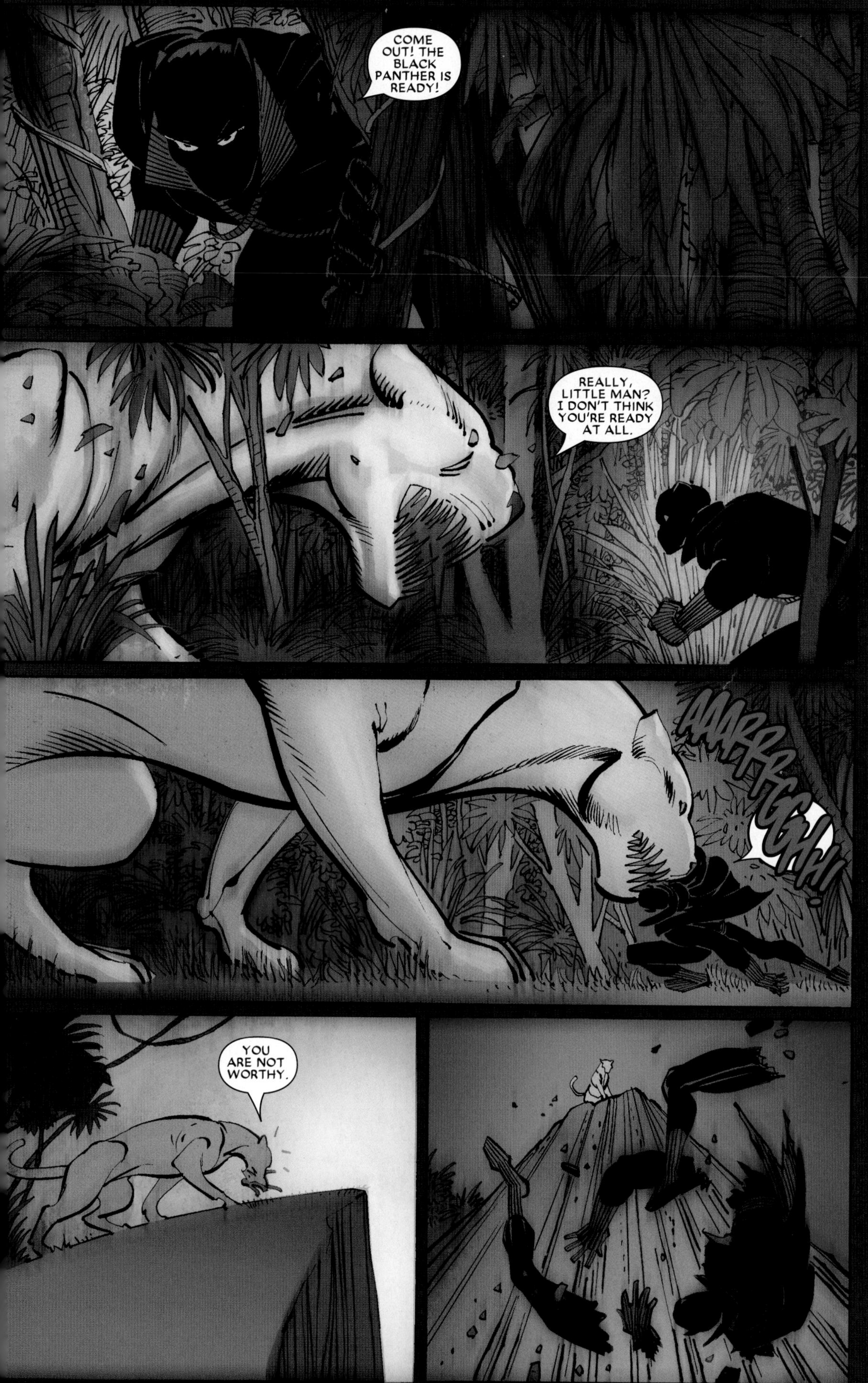
COME OUT! THE BLACK PANTHER IS READY!
REALLY, LITTLE MAN? I DON'T THINK YOU'RE READY AT ALL.
AAARRRGGHH!
YOU ARE NOT WORTHY.

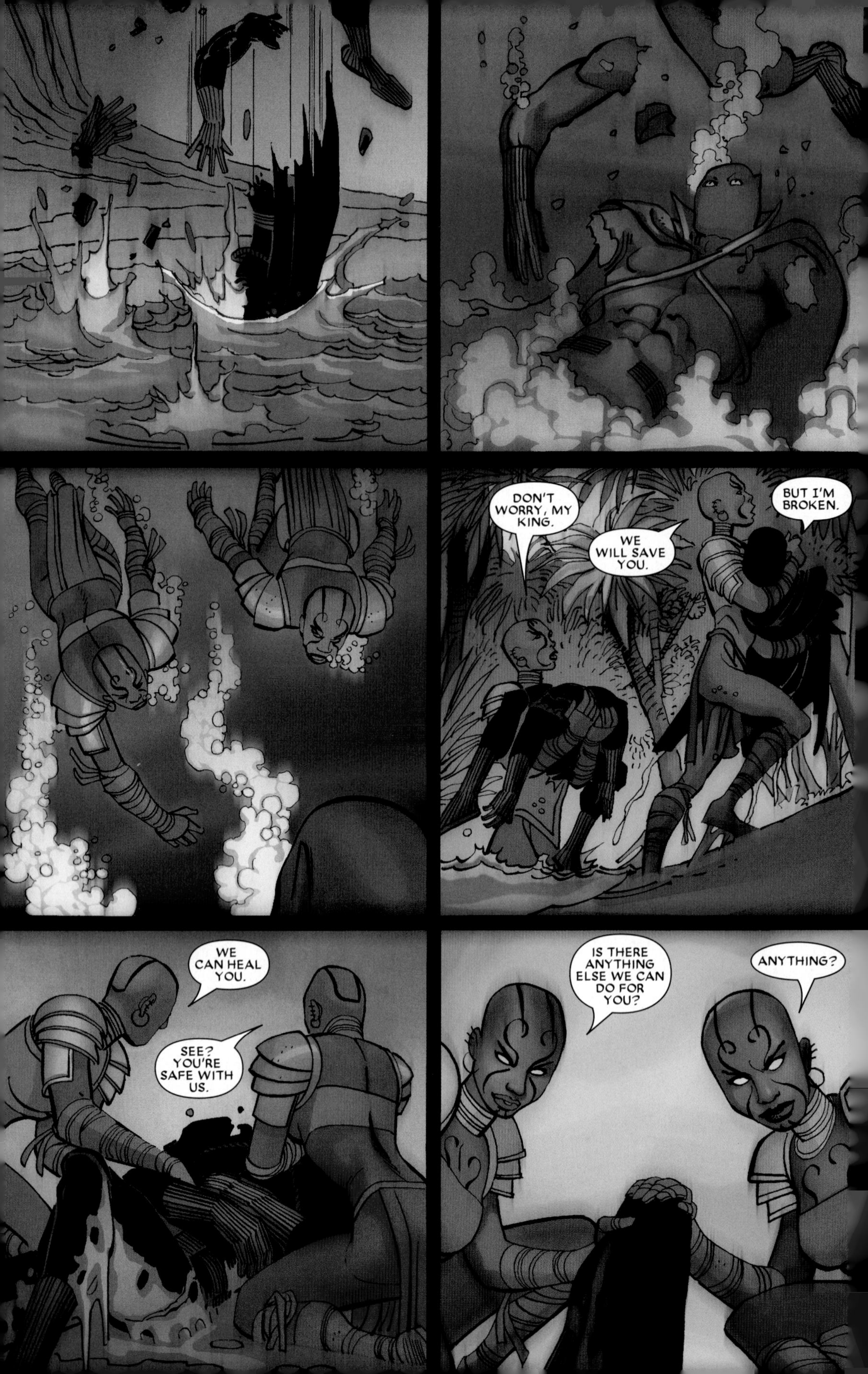
DON'T WORRY, MY KING.
WE WILL SAVE YOU.
BUT I'M BROKEN.
WE CAN HEAL YOU.
SEE? YOU'RE SAFE WITH US.
IS THERE ANYTHING ELSE WE CAN DO FOR YOU?
ANYTHING?

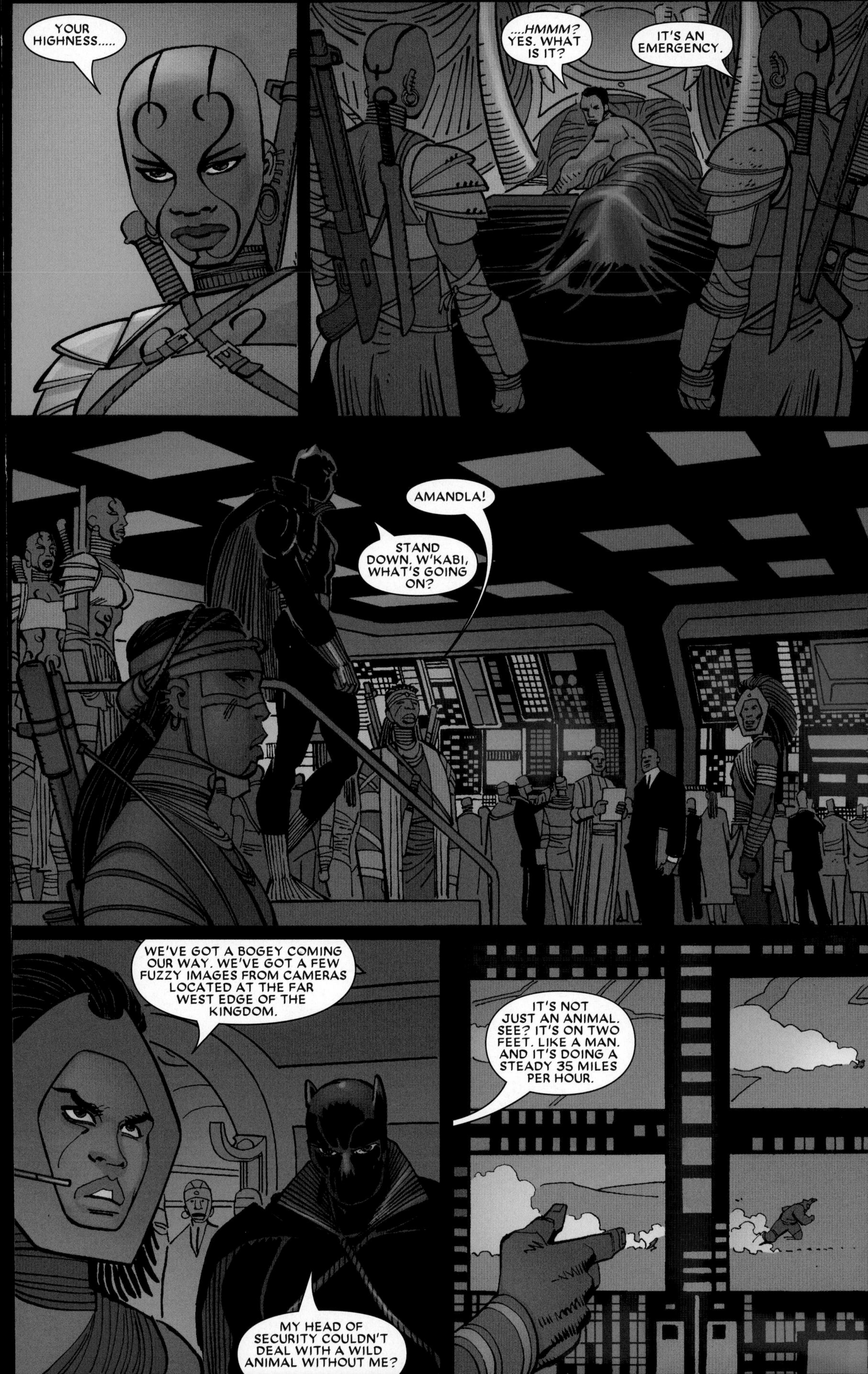
YOUR HIGHNESS.....
...HMMM? YES. WHAT IS IT?
IT'S AN EMERGENCY.
AMANDLA!
STAND DOWN. W'KABI, WHAT'S GOING ON?
WE'VE GOT A BOGEY COMING OUR WAY. WE'VE GOT A FEW FUZZY IMAGES FROM CAMERAS LOCATED AT THE FAR WEST EDGE OF THE KINGDOM.
IT'S NOT JUST AN ANIMAL. SEE? IT'S ON TWO FEET. LIKE A MAN. AND IT'S DOING A STEADY 35 MILES PER HOUR.
MY HEAD OF SECURITY COULDN'T DEAL WITH A WILD ANIMAL WITHOUT ME?

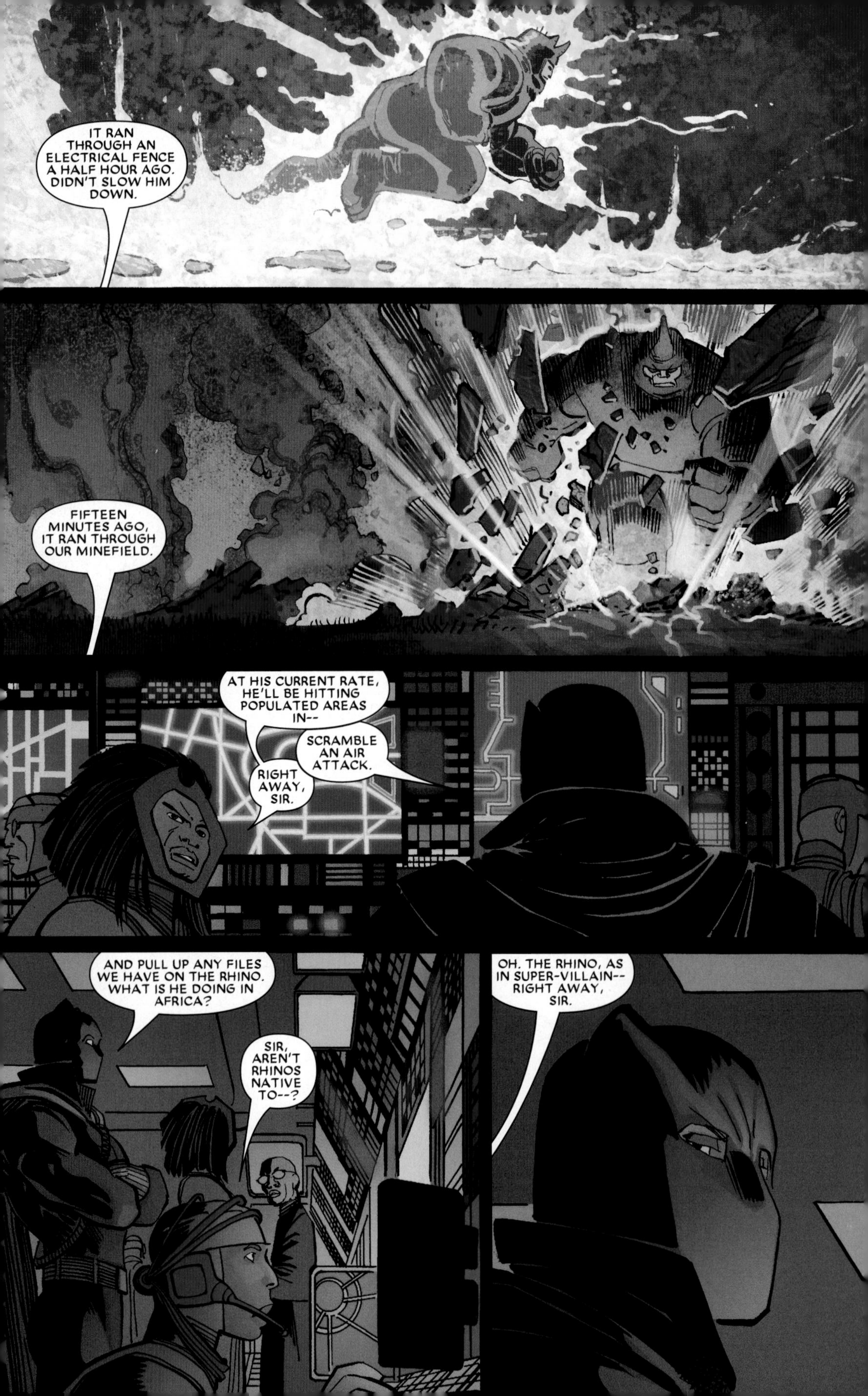
IT RAN THROUGH AN ELECTRICAL FENCE A HALF HOUR AGO. DIDN'T SLOW HIM DOWN.
FIFTEEN MINUTES AGO, IT RAN THROUGH OUR MINEFIELD.
AT HIS CURRENT RATE, HE'LL BE HITTING POPULATED AREAS IN--
SCRAMBLE AN AIR ATTACK.
RIGHT AWAY, SIR.
AND PULL UP ANY FILES WE HAVE ON THE RHINO. WHAT IS HE DOING IN AFRICA?
SIR, AREN'T RHINOS NATIVE TO--?
OH. THE RHINO, AS IN SUPER-VILLAIN-- RIGHT AWAY, SIR.

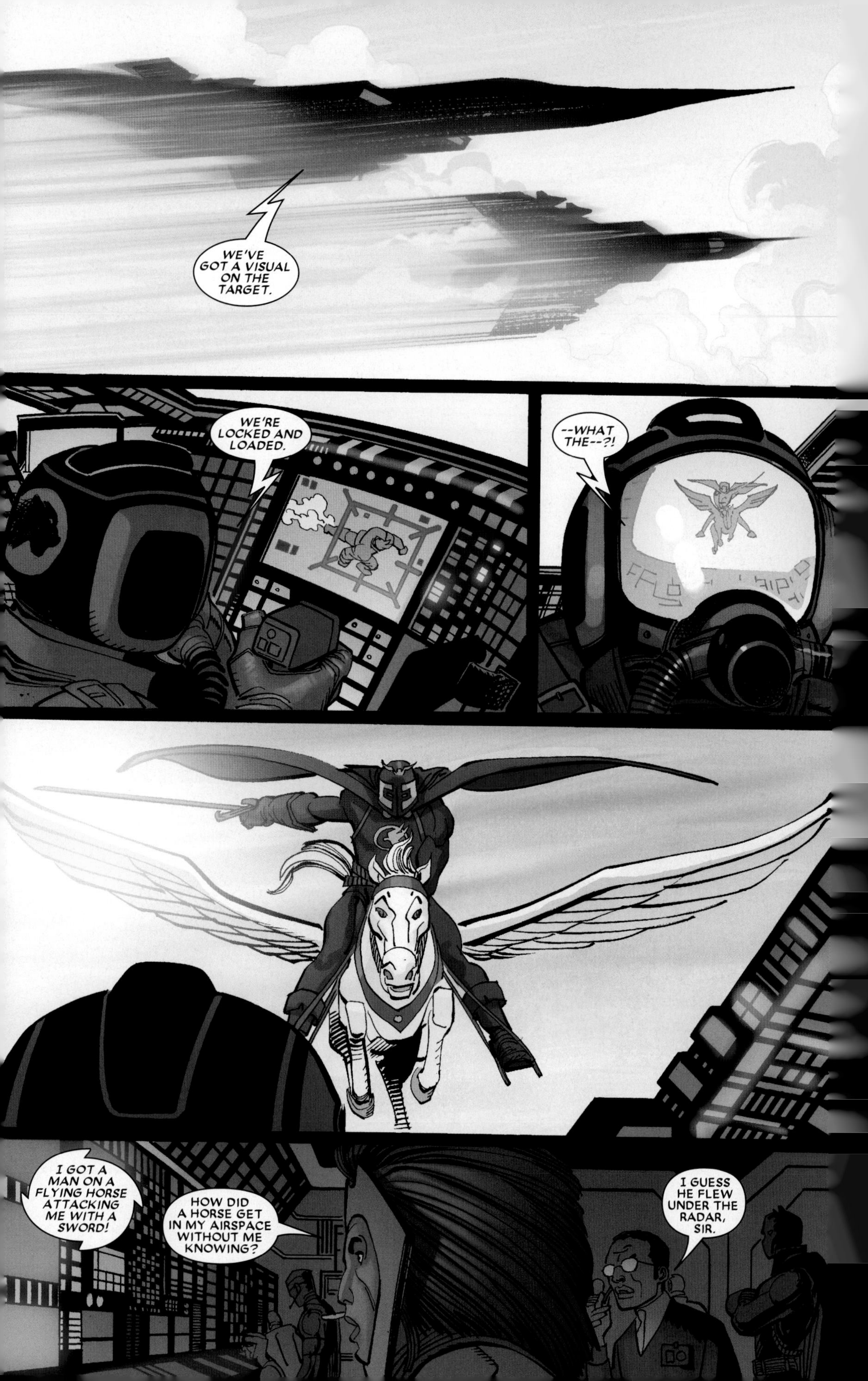
WE'VE GOT A VISUAL ON THE TARGET.
WE'RE LOCKED AND LOADED.
--WHAT THE--?!
I GOT A MAN ON A FLYING HORSE ATTACKING ME WITH A SWORD!
HOW DID A HORSE GET IN MY AIRSPACE WITHOUT ME KNOWING?
I GUESS HE FLEW UNDER THE RADAR, SIR.

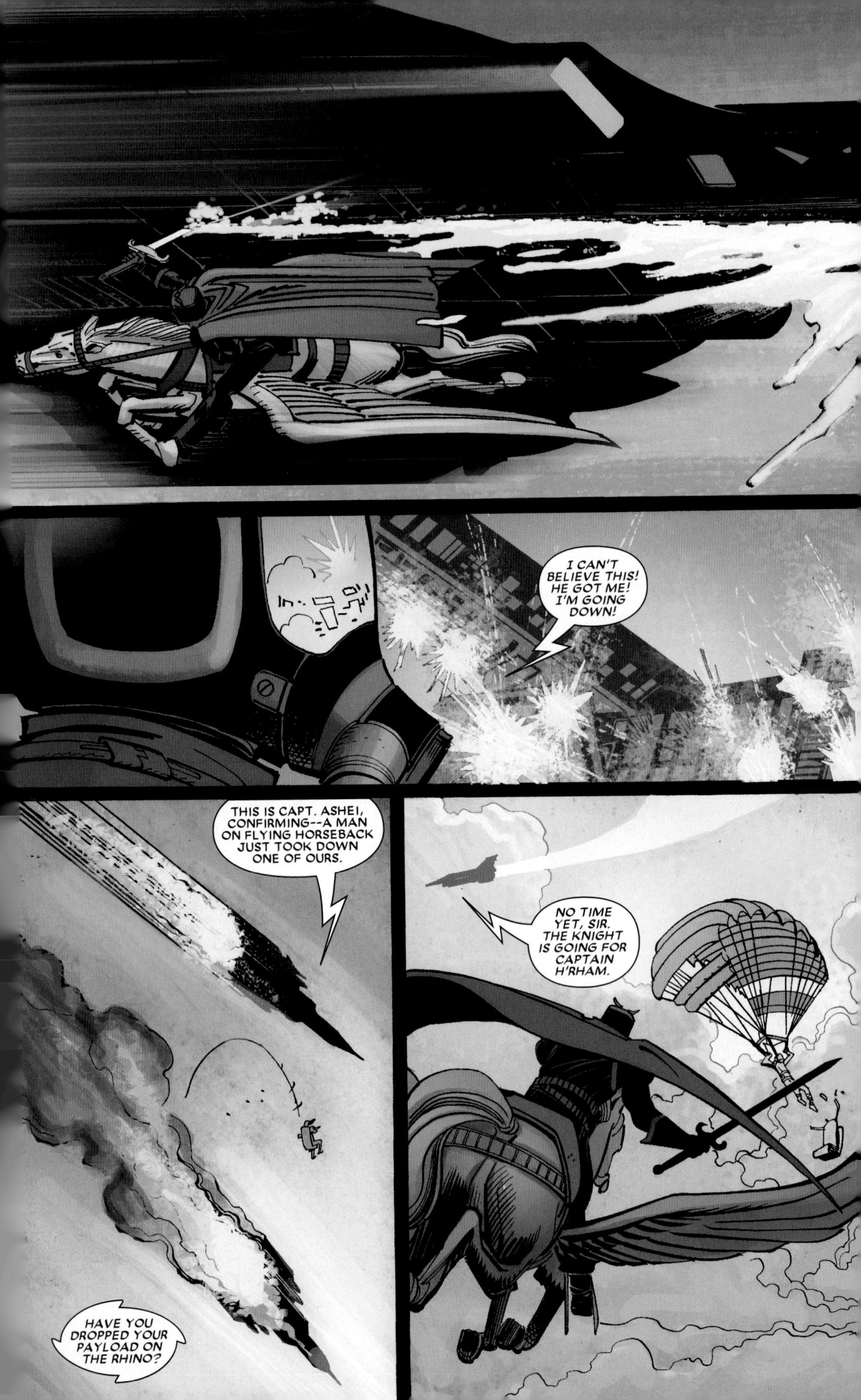
I CAN'T BELIEVE THIS! HE GOT ME! I'M GOING DOWN!
THIS IS CAPT. ASHEI, CONFIRMING--A MAN ON FLYING HORSEBACK JUST TOOK DOWN ONE OF OURS.
HAVE YOU DROPPED YOUR PAYLOAD ON THE RHINO?
NO TIME YET, SIR. THE KNIGHT IS GOING FOR CAPTAIN H'RHAM.

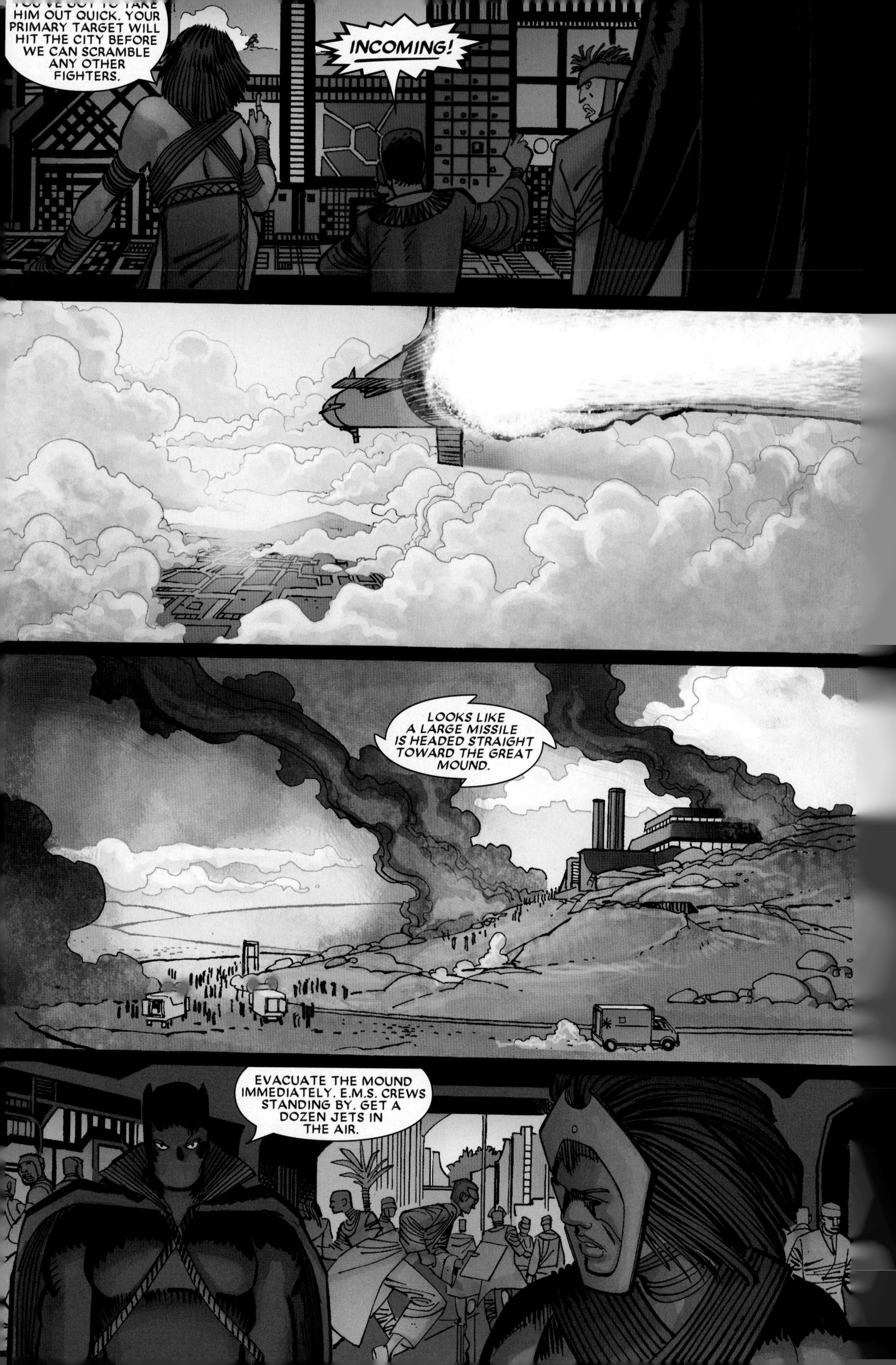
HIM OUT QUICK. YOUR PRIMARY TARGET WILL HIT THE CITY BEFORE WE CAN SCRAMBLE ANY OTHER FIGHTERS.
INCOMING!
LOOKS LIKE A LARGE MISSILE IS HEADED STRAIGHT TOWARD THE GREAT MOUND.
EVACUATE THE MOUND IMMEDIATELY. E.M.S. CREWS STANDING BY. GET A DOZEN JETS IN THE AIR.

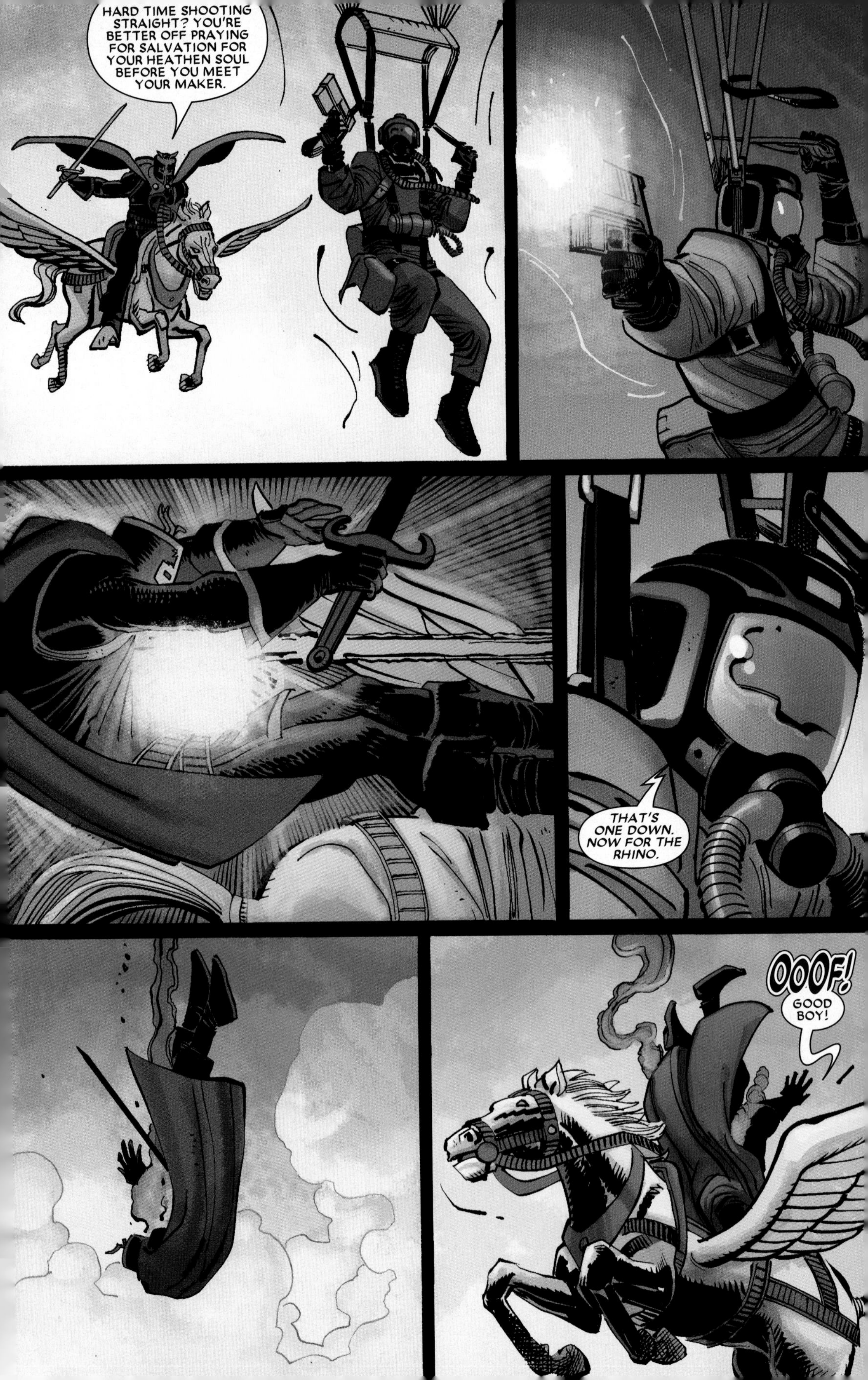
HARD TIME SHOOTING STRAIGHT? YOU'RE BETTER OFF PRAYING FOR SALVATION FOR YOUR HEATHEN SOUL BEFORE YOU MEET YOUR MAKER.
THAT'S ONE DOWN. NOW FOR THE RHINO.
OOOF!
GOOD BOY!

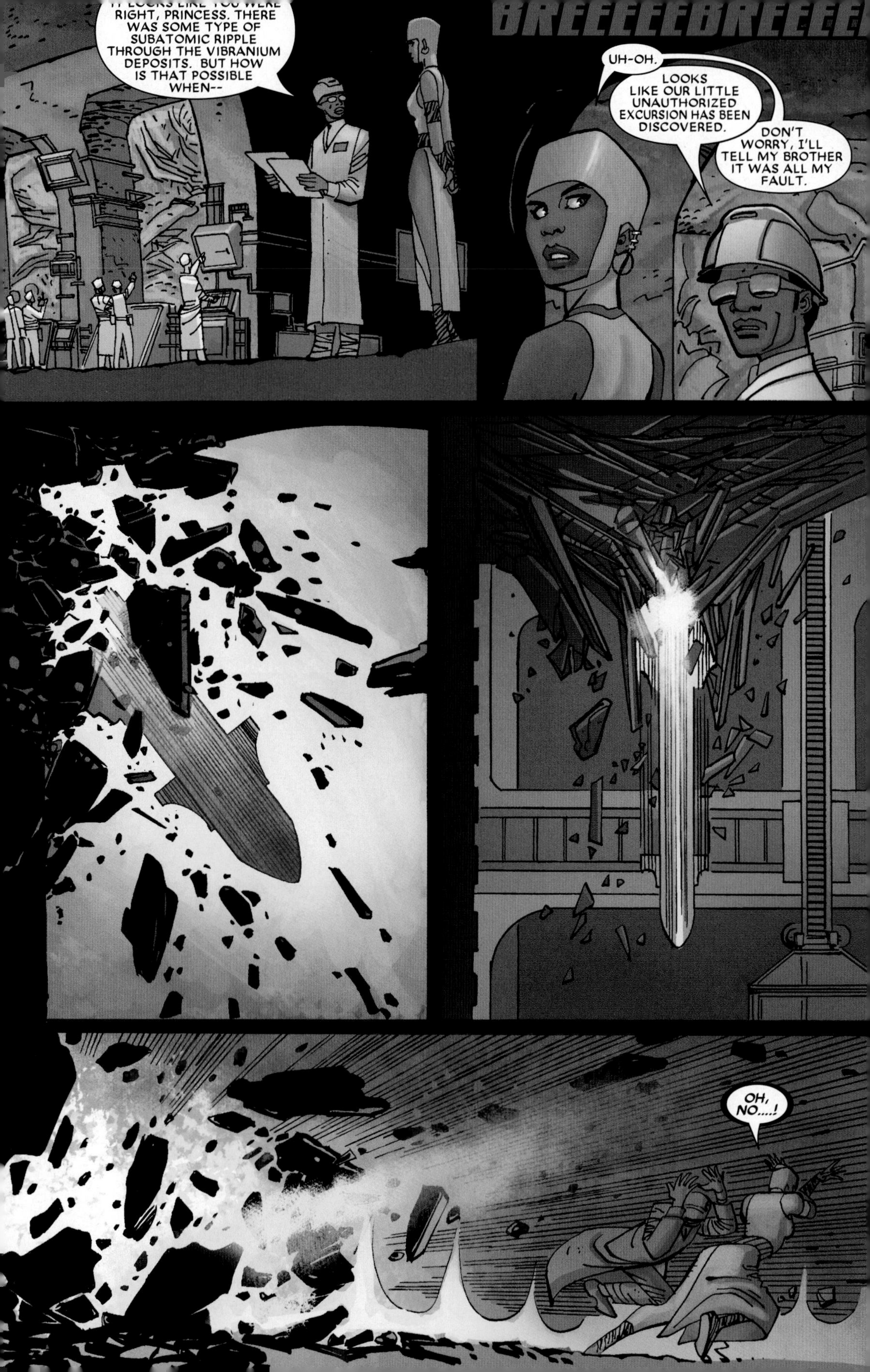
RIGHT, PRINCESS. THERE WAS SOME TYPE OF SUBATOMIC RIPPLE THROUGH THE VIBRANIUM DEPOSITS. BUT HOW IS THAT POSSIBLE WHEN--
UH-OH.
LOOKS LIKE OUR LITTLE UNAUTHORIZED EXCURSION HAS BEEN DISCOVERED.
DON'T WORRY, I'LL TELL MY BROTHER IT WAS ALL MY FAULT.
OH, NO....!

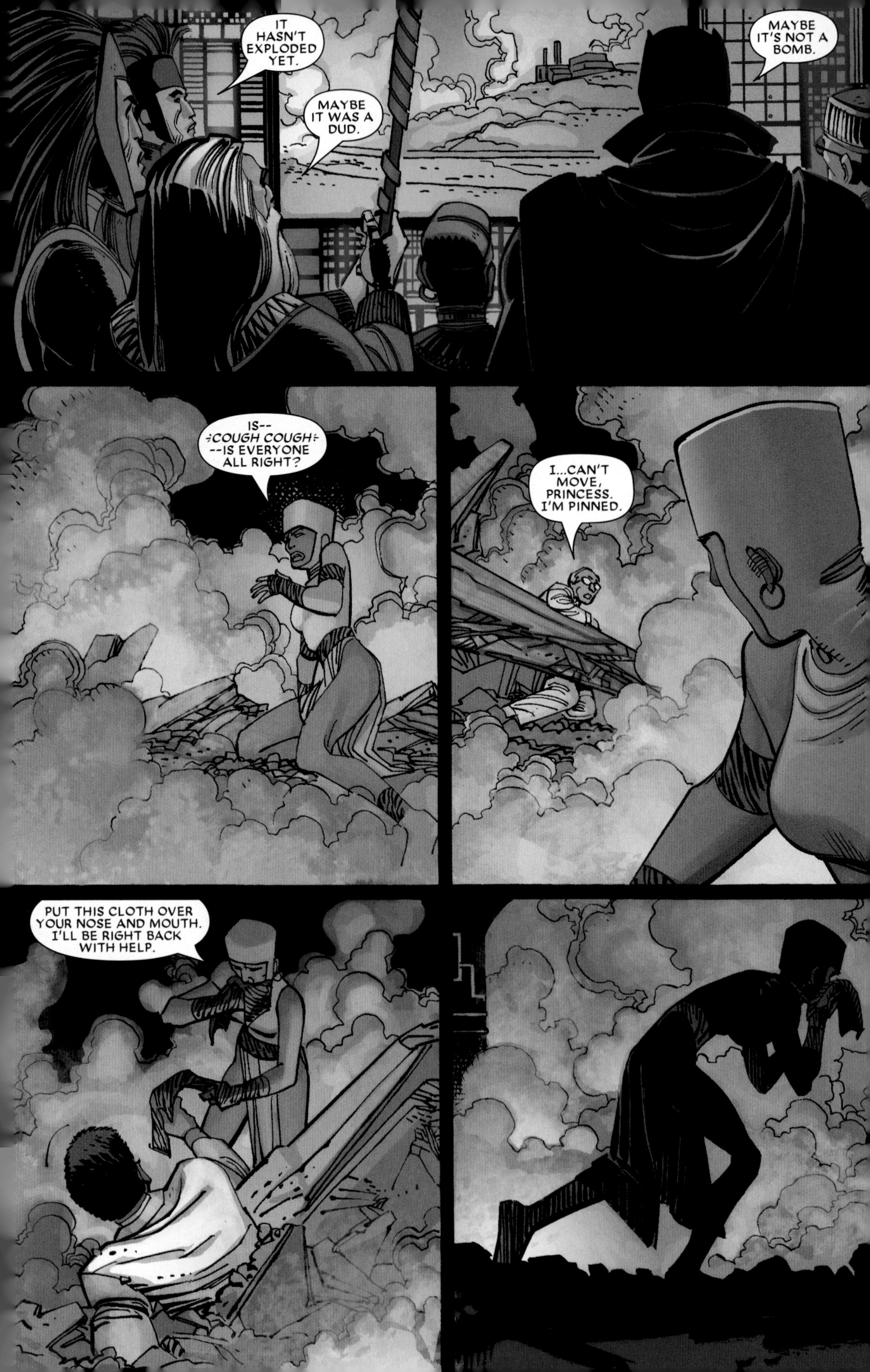
IT HASN'T EXPLODED YET.
MAYBE IT WAS A DUD.
MAYBE IT'S NOT A BOMB.
IS-- *COUGH COUGH* --IS EVERYONE ALL RIGHT?
I...CAN'T MOVE, PRINCESS. I'M PINNED.
PUT THIS CLOTH OVER YOUR NOSE AND MOUTH. I'LL BE RIGHT BACK WITH HELP.

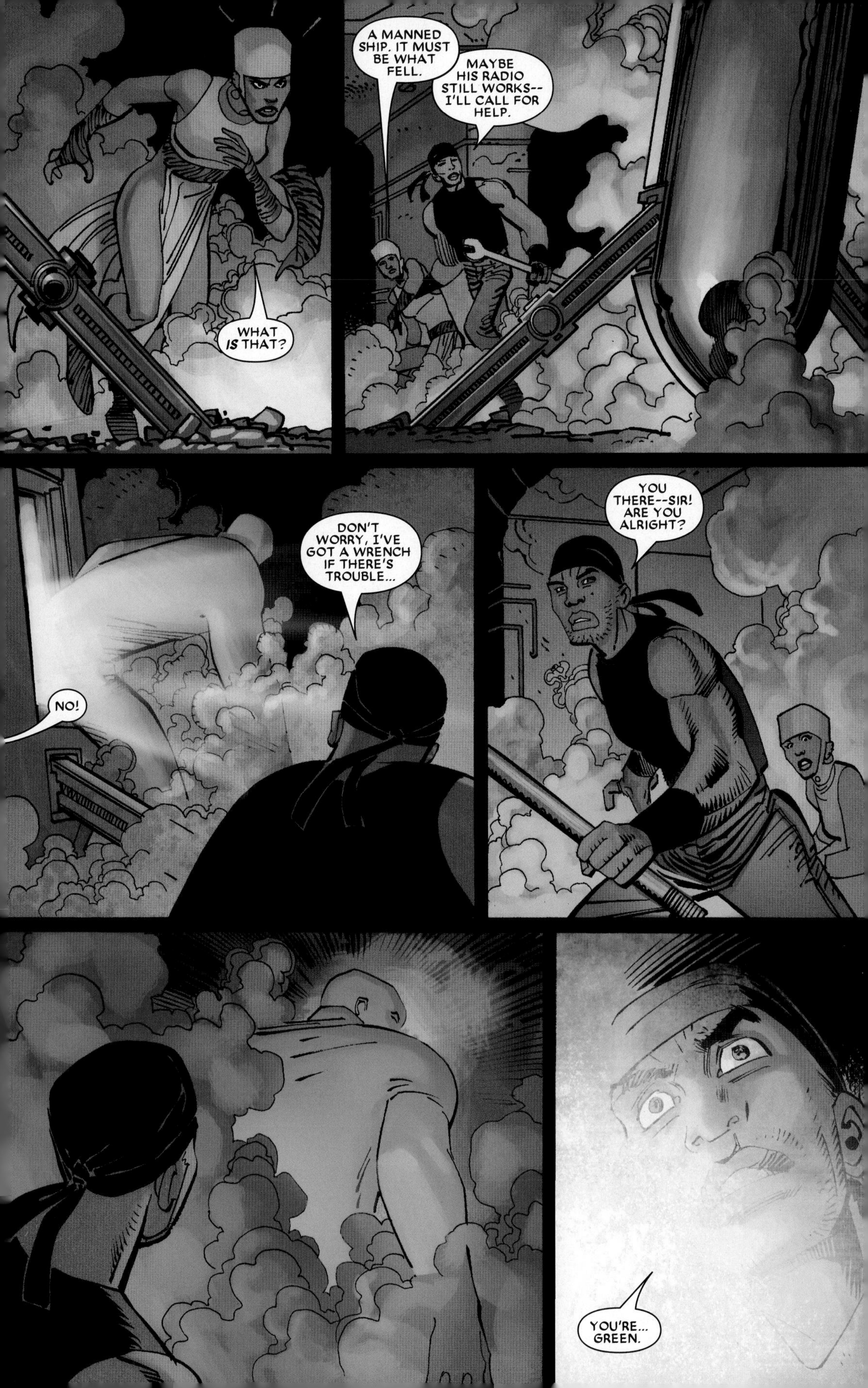
WHAT IS THAT?
A MANNED SHIP. IT MUST BE WHAT FELL.
MAYBE HIS RADIO STILL WORKS-- I'LL CALL FOR HELP.
DON'T WORRY, I'VE GOT A WRENCH IF THERE'S TROUBLE...
NO!
YOU THERE--SIR! ARE YOU ALRIGHT?
YOU'RE... GREEN.

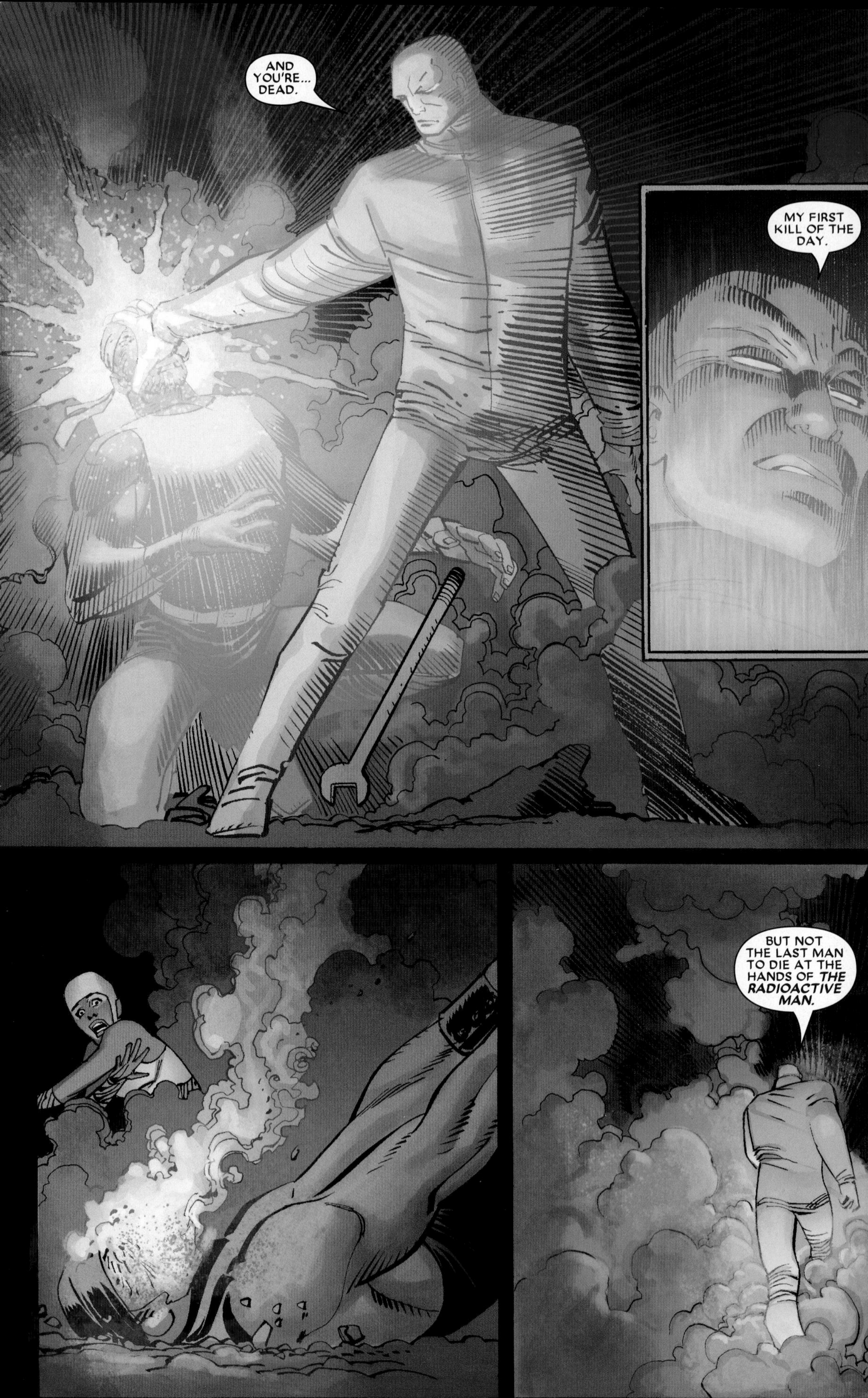
AND YOU'RE... DEAD.
MY FIRST KILL OF THE DAY.
BUT NOT THE LAST MAN TO DIE AT THE HANDS OF *THE RADIOACTIVE MAN.*

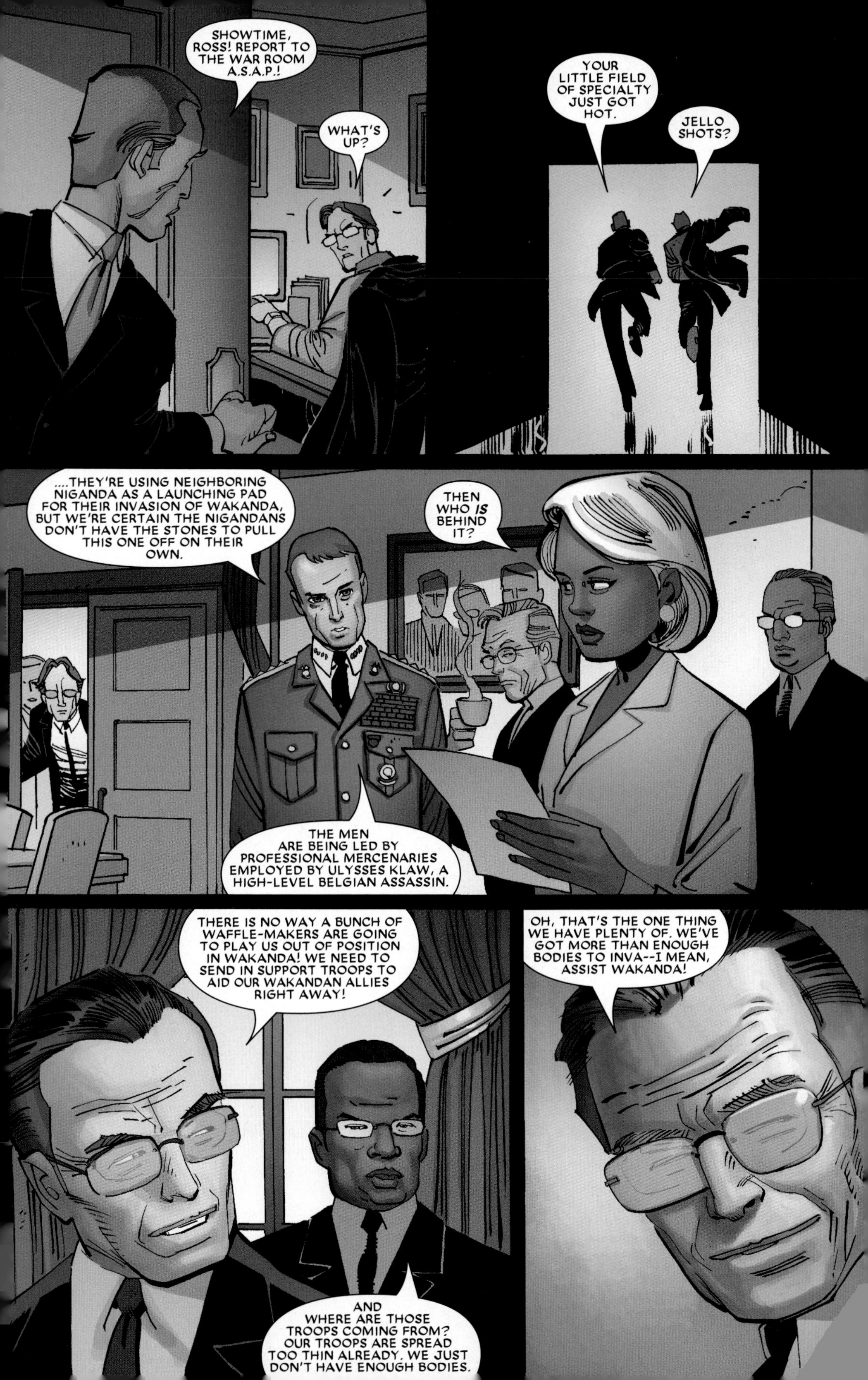
SHOWTIME, ROSS! REPORT TO THE WAR ROOM A.S.A.P.!
WHAT'S UP?
YOUR LITTLE FIELD OF SPECIALTY JUST GOT HOT.
JELLO SHOTS?
....THEY'RE USING NEIGHBORING NIGANDA AS A LAUNCHING PAD FOR THEIR INVASION OF WAKANDA, BUT WE'RE CERTAIN THE NIGANDANS DON'T HAVE THE STONES TO PULL THIS ONE OFF ON THEIR OWN.
THEN WHO *IS* BEHIND IT?
THE MEN ARE BEING LED BY PROFESSIONAL MERCENARIES EMPLOYED BY ULYSSES KLAW, A HIGH-LEVEL BELGIAN ASSASSIN.
THERE IS NO WAY A BUNCH OF WAFFLE-MAKERS ARE GOING TO PLAY US OUT OF POSITION IN WAKANDA! WE NEED TO SEND IN SUPPORT TROOPS TO AID OUR WAKANDAN ALLIES RIGHT AWAY!
AND WHERE ARE THOSE TROOPS COMING FROM? OUR TROOPS ARE SPREAD TOO THIN ALREADY. WE JUST DON'T HAVE ENOUGH BODIES.
OH, THAT'S THE ONE THING WE HAVE PLENTY OF. WE'VE GOT MORE THAN ENOUGH BODIES TO INVA--I MEAN, ASSIST WAKANDA!

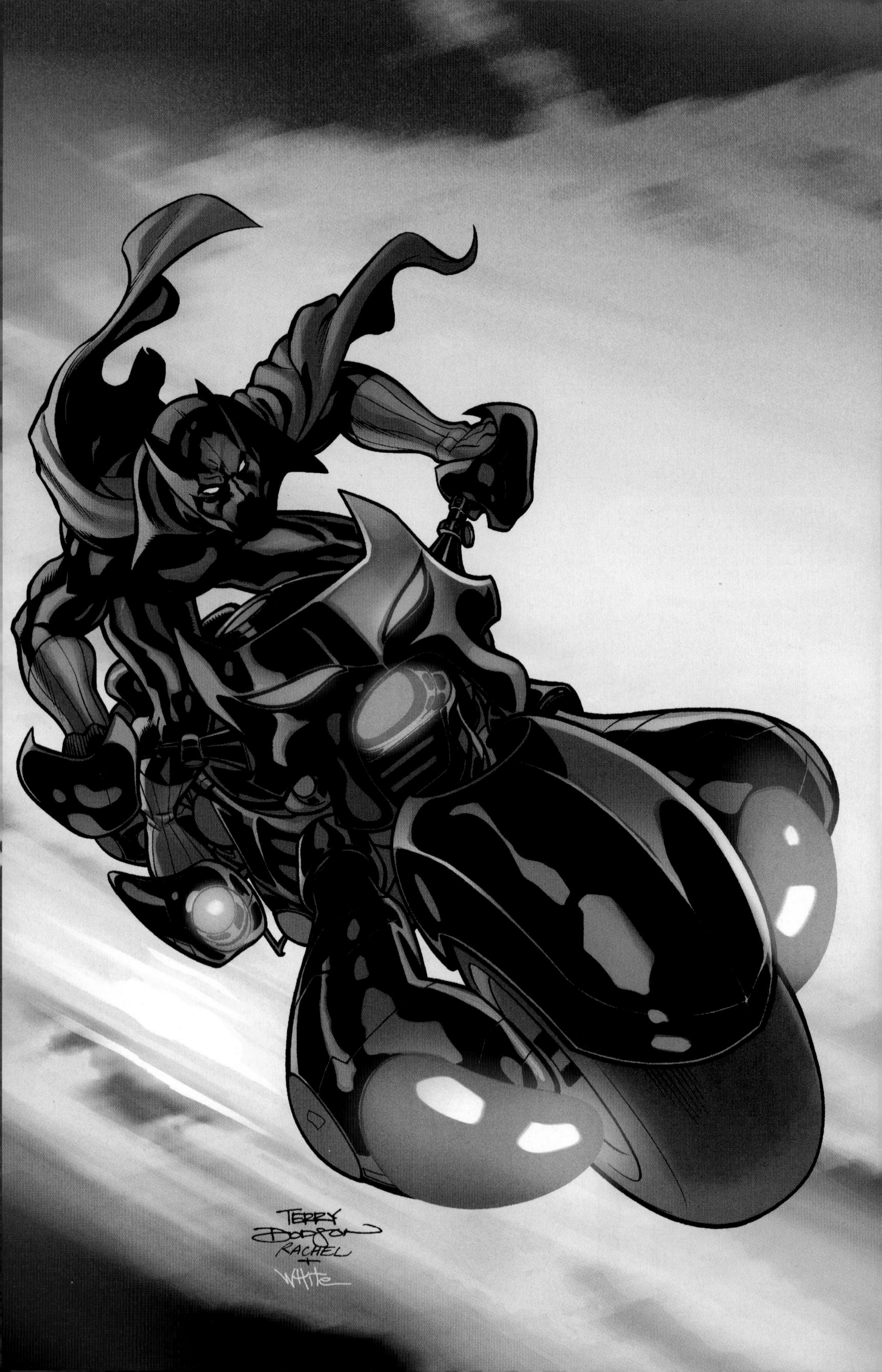
TERRY
DODSON
RACHEL
+
White

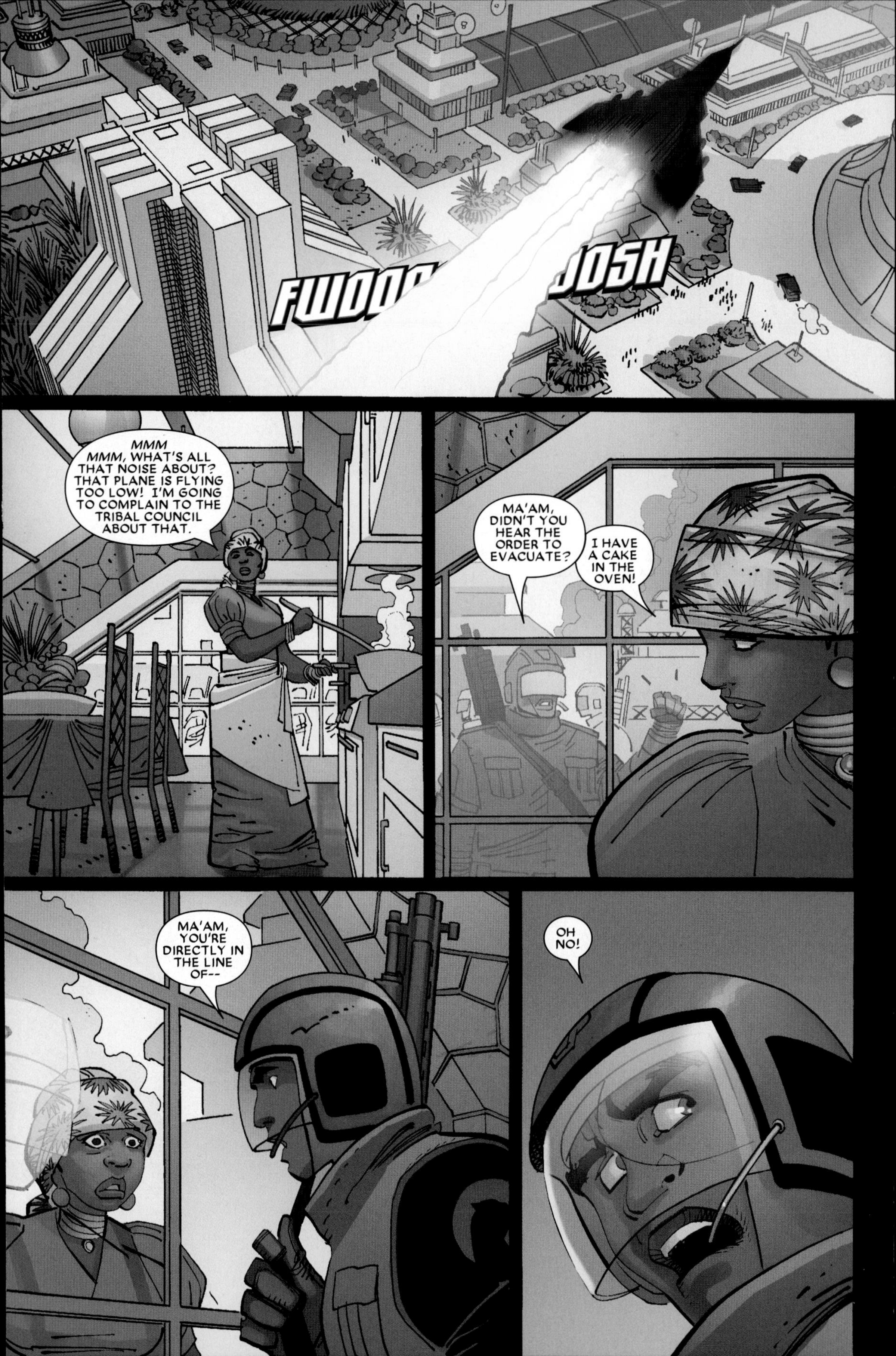
FWOOO
JOSH
MMM MMM, WHAT'S ALL THAT NOISE ABOUT? THAT PLANE IS FLYING TOO LOW! I'M GOING TO COMPLAIN TO THE TRIBAL COUNCIL ABOUT THAT.
MA'AM, DIDN'T YOU HEAR THE ORDER TO EVACUATE?
I HAVE A CAKE IN THE OVEN!
MA'AM, YOU'RE DIRECTLY IN THE LINE OF--
OH NO!

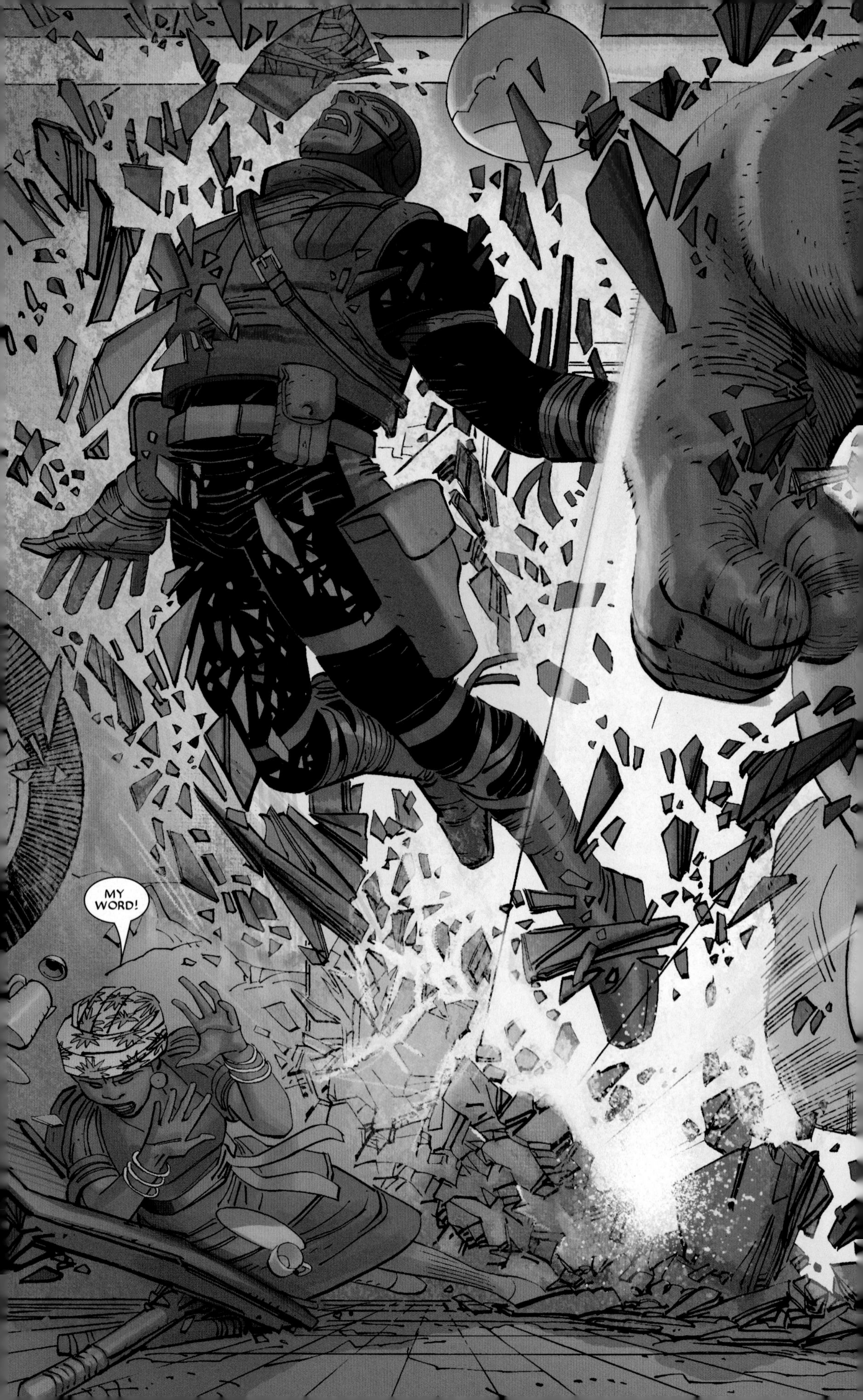
MY WORD!

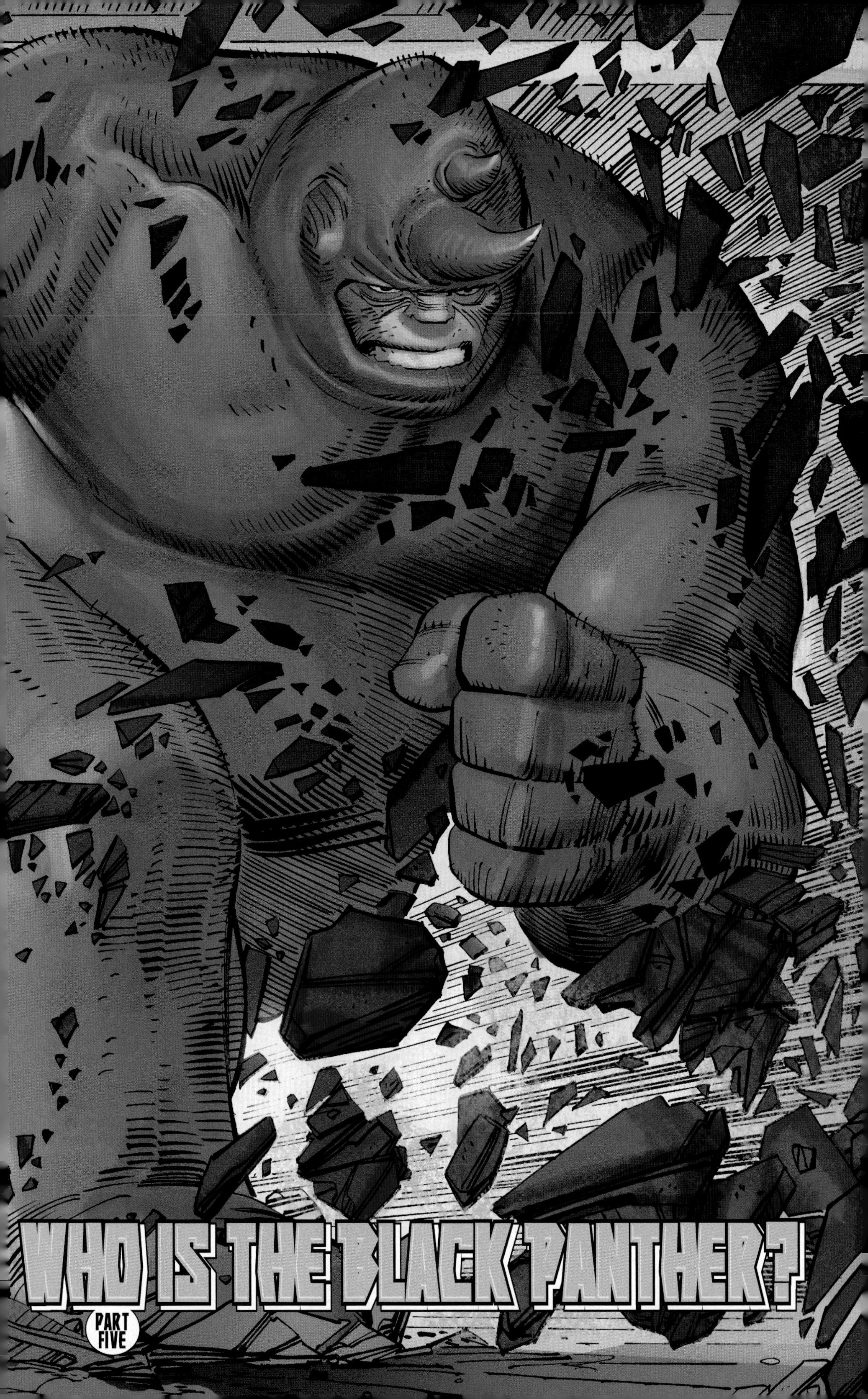
WHO IS THE BLACK PANTHER?
PART FIVE

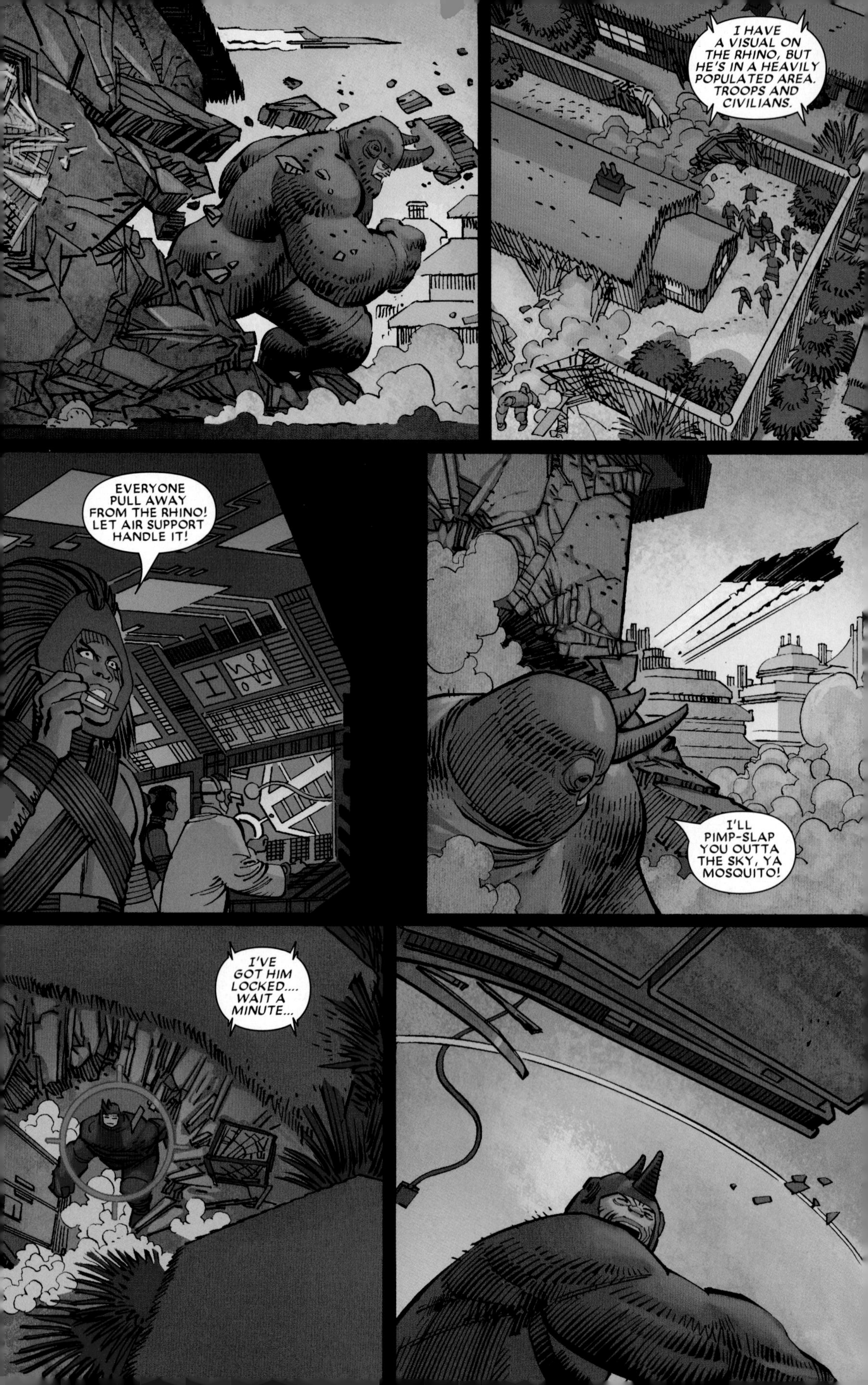
I HAVE A VISUAL ON THE RHINO, BUT HE'S IN A HEAVILY POPULATED AREA. TROOPS AND CIVILIANS.
EVERYONE PULL AWAY FROM THE RHINO! LET AIR SUPPORT HANDLE IT!
I'LL PIMP-SLAP YOU OUTTA THE SKY, YA MOSQUITO!
I'VE GOT HIM LOCKED.... WAIT A MINUTE...

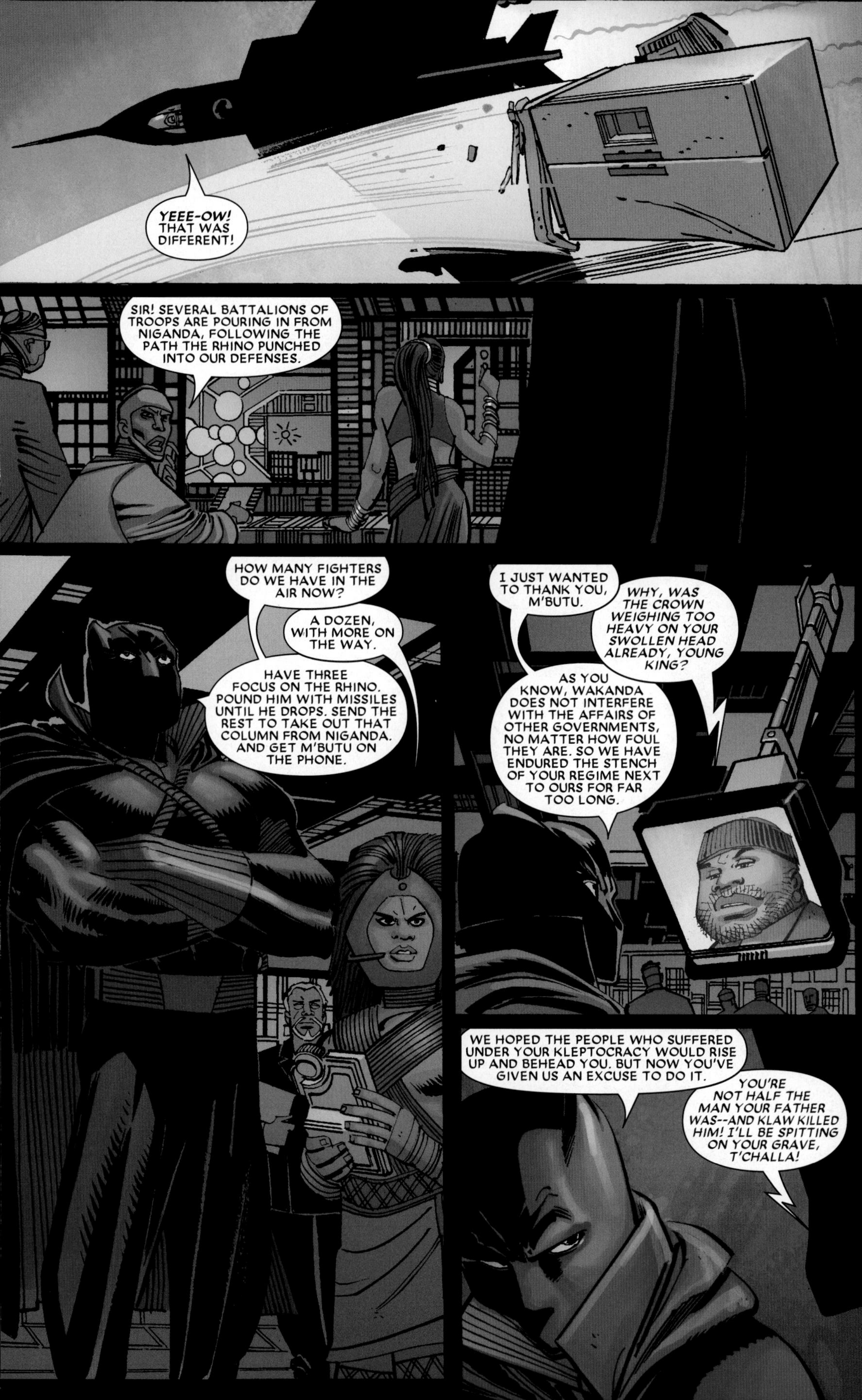
YEEE-OW! THAT WAS DIFFERENT!
SIR! SEVERAL BATTALIONS OF TROOPS ARE POURING IN FROM NIGANDA, FOLLOWING THE PATH THE RHINO PUNCHED INTO OUR DEFENSES.
HOW MANY FIGHTERS DO WE HAVE IN THE AIR NOW?
A DOZEN, WITH MORE ON THE WAY.
HAVE THREE FOCUS ON THE RHINO. POUND HIM WITH MISSILES UNTIL HE DROPS. SEND THE REST TO TAKE OUT THAT COLUMN FROM NIGANDA. AND GET M'BUTU ON THE PHONE.
I JUST WANTED TO THANK YOU, M'BUTU.
WHY, WAS THE CROWN WEIGHING TOO HEAVY ON YOUR SWOLLEN HEAD ALREADY, YOUNG KING?
AS YOU KNOW, WAKANDA DOES NOT INTERFERE WITH THE AFFAIRS OF OTHER GOVERNMENTS, NO MATTER HOW FOUL THEY ARE. SO WE HAVE ENDURED THE STENCH OF YOUR REGIME NEXT TO OURS FOR FAR TOO LONG.
WE HOPED THE PEOPLE WHO SUFFERED UNDER YOUR KLEPTOCRACY WOULD RISE UP AND BEHEAD YOU. BUT NOW YOU'VE GIVEN US AN EXCUSE TO DO IT.
YOU'RE NOT HALF THE MAN YOUR FATHER WAS--AND KLAW KILLED HIM! I'LL BE SPITTING ON YOUR GRAVE, T'CHALLA!

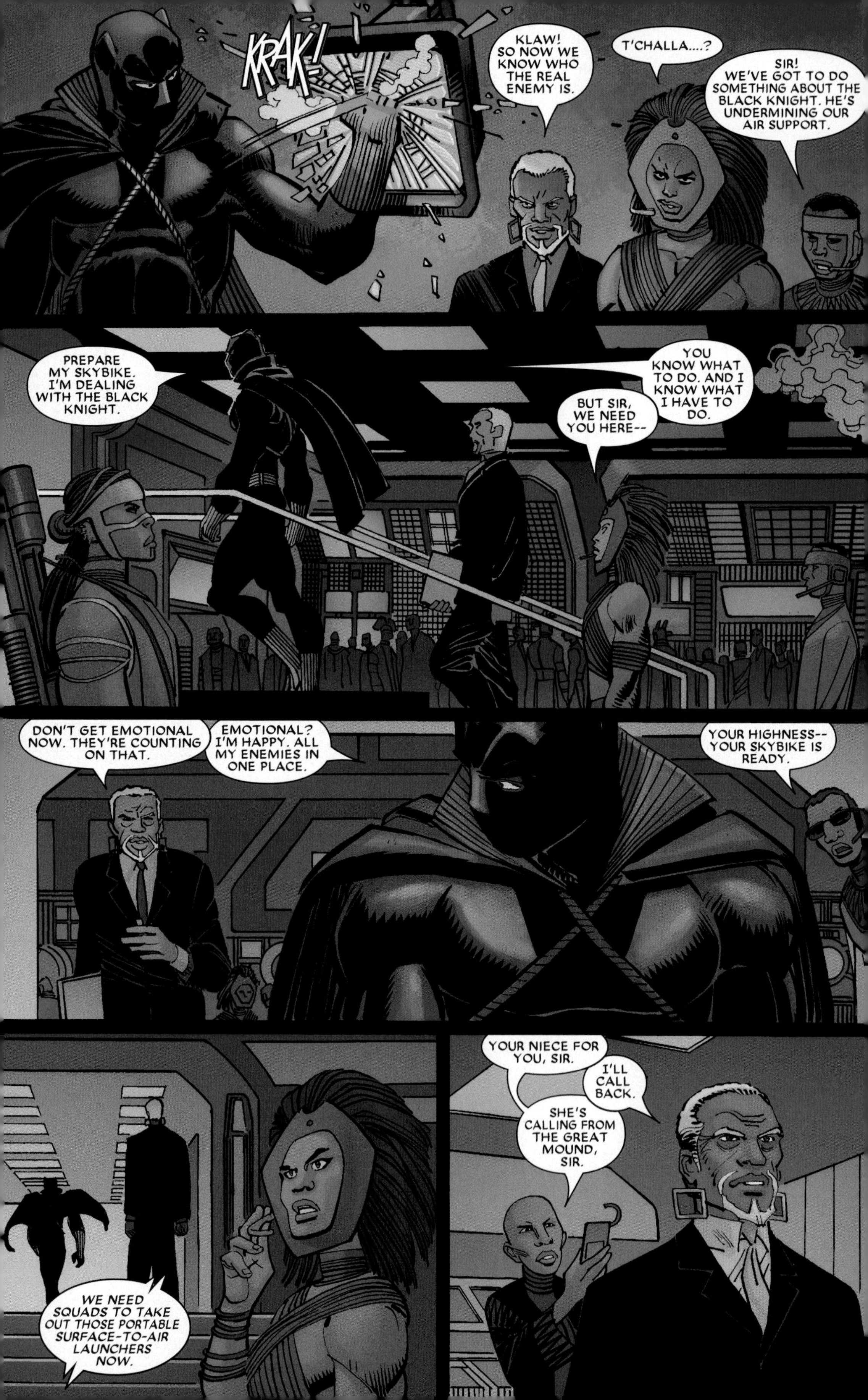
KRAK!
KLAW! SO NOW WE KNOW WHO THE REAL ENEMY IS.
T'CHALLA....?
SIR! WE'VE GOT TO DO SOMETHING ABOUT THE BLACK KNIGHT. HE'S UNDERMINING OUR AIR SUPPORT.
PREPARE MY SKYBIKE. I'M DEALING WITH THE BLACK KNIGHT.
BUT SIR, WE NEED YOU HERE--
YOU KNOW WHAT TO DO. AND I KNOW WHAT I HAVE TO DO.
DON'T GET EMOTIONAL NOW. THEY'RE COUNTING ON THAT.
EMOTIONAL? I'M HAPPY. ALL MY ENEMIES IN ONE PLACE.
YOUR HIGHNESS-- YOUR SKYBIKE IS READY.
WE NEED SQUADS TO TAKE OUT THOSE PORTABLE SURFACE-TO-AIR LAUNCHERS NOW.
YOUR NIECE FOR YOU, SIR.
I'LL CALL BACK.
SHE'S CALLING FROM THE GREAT MOUND, SIR.

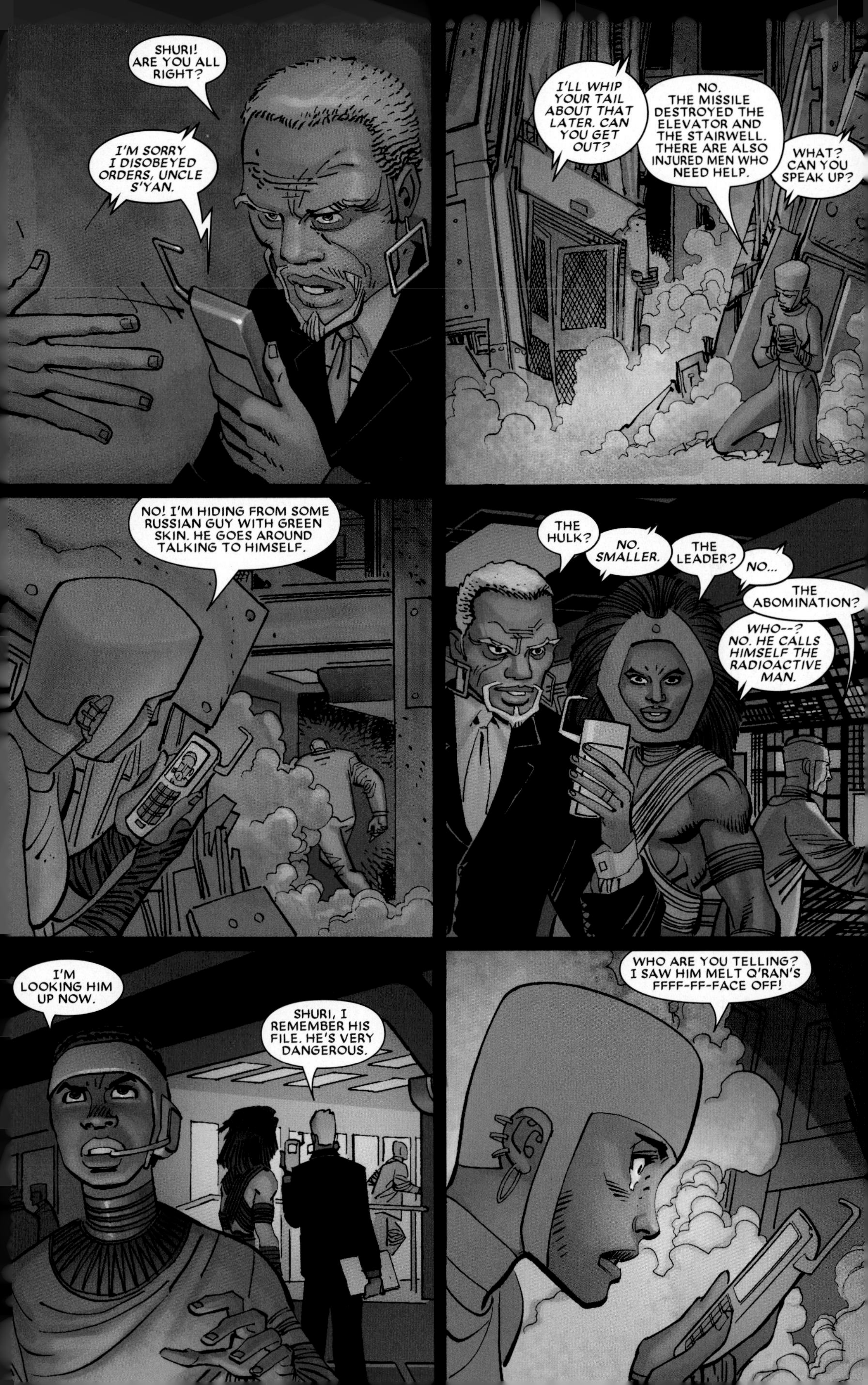
SHURI! ARE YOU ALL RIGHT?
I'M SORRY I DISOBEYED ORDERS, UNCLE S'YAN.
I'LL WHIP YOUR TAIL ABOUT THAT LATER. CAN YOU GET OUT?
NO. THE MISSILE DESTROYED THE ELEVATOR AND THE STAIRWELL. THERE ARE ALSO INJURED MEN WHO NEED HELP.
WHAT? CAN YOU SPEAK UP?
NO! I'M HIDING FROM SOME RUSSIAN GUY WITH GREEN SKIN. HE GOES AROUND TALKING TO HIMSELF.
THE HULK?
NO. SMALLER.
THE LEADER?
NO...
THE ABOMINATION?
WHO--? NO. HE CALLS HIMSELF THE RADIOACTIVE MAN.
I'M LOOKING HIM UP NOW.
SHURI, I REMEMBER HIS FILE. HE'S VERY DANGEROUS.
WHO ARE YOU TELLING? I SAW HIM MELT Q'RAN'S FFFF-FF-FACE OFF!

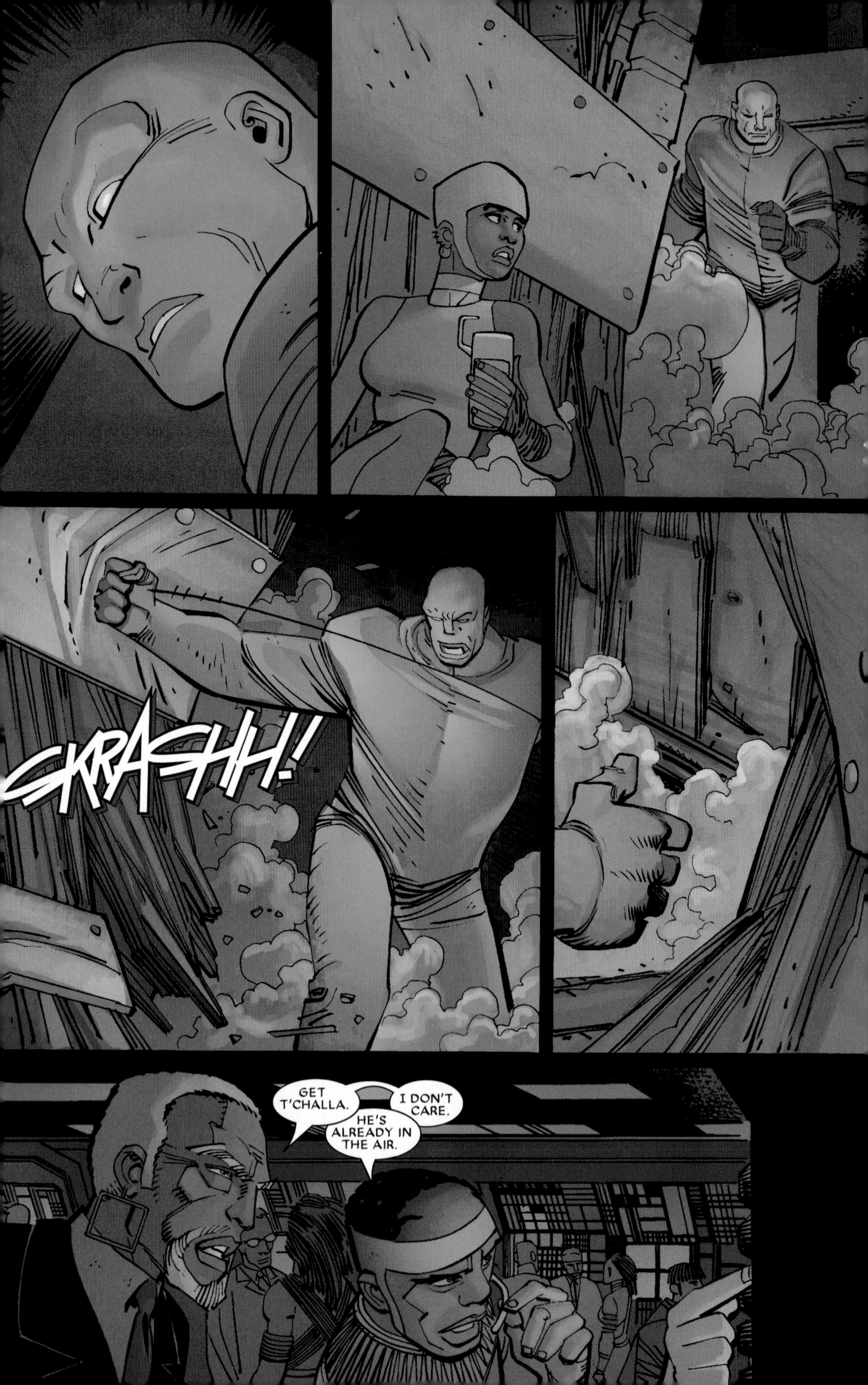
SKRASHH!
GET T'CHALLA.
I DON'T CARE.
HE'S ALREADY IN THE AIR.

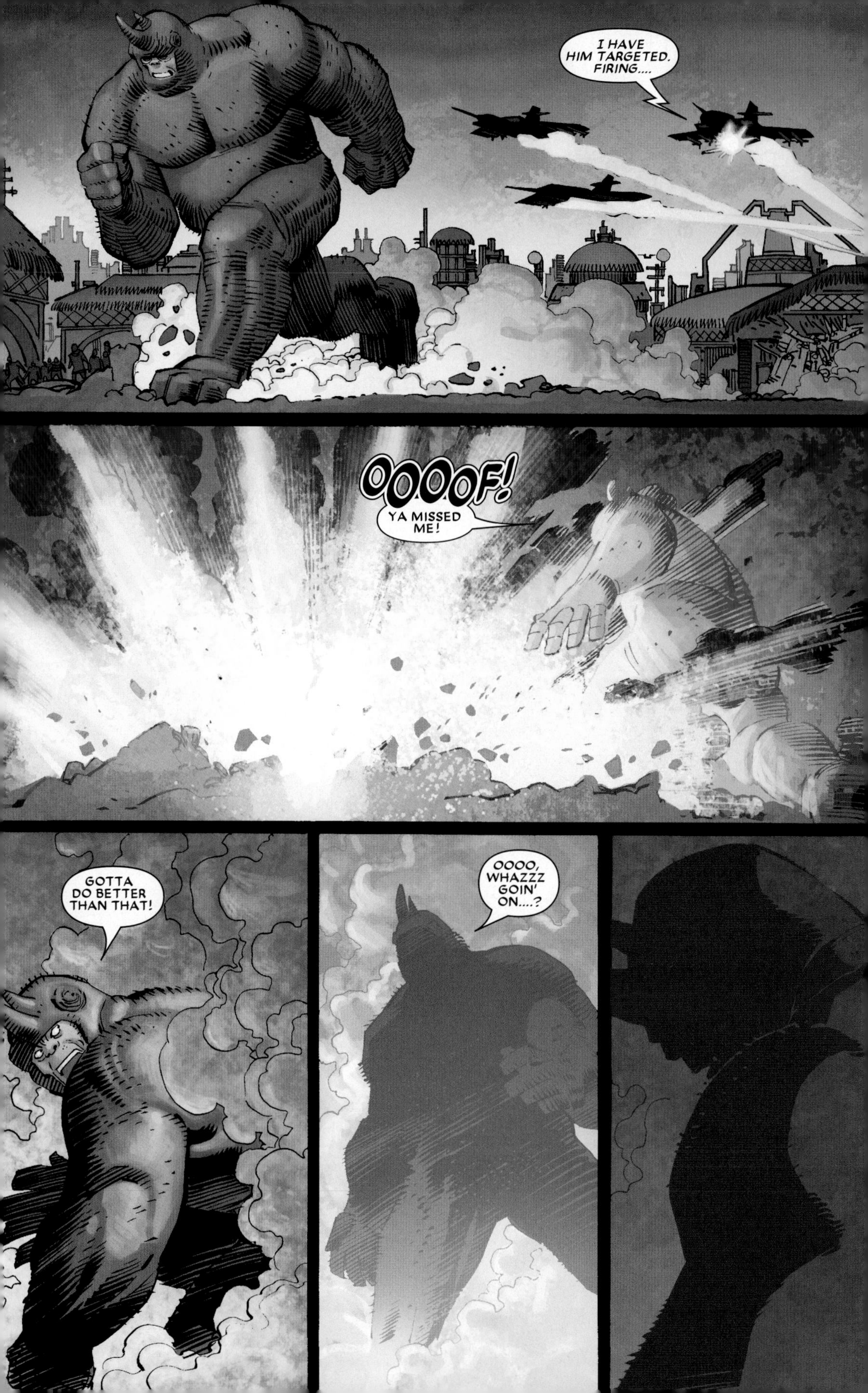
I HAVE HIM TARGETED. FIRING....
OOOOF!
YA MISSED ME!
GOTTA DO BETTER THAN THAT!
OOOO, WHAZZZ GOIN' ON....?

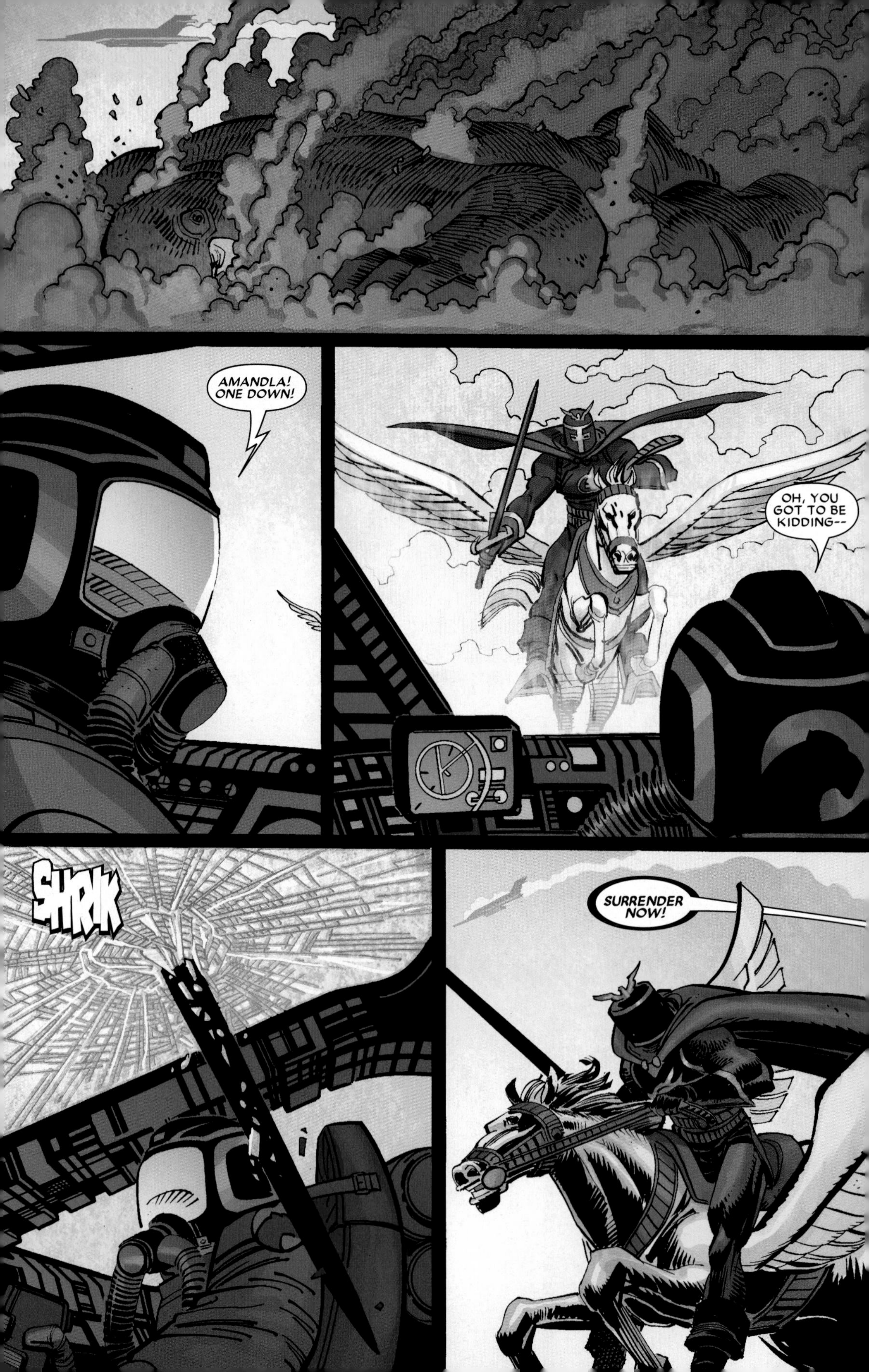
AMANDLA! ONE DOWN!
OH, YOU GOT TO BE KIDDING--
SHRIK
SURRENDER NOW!

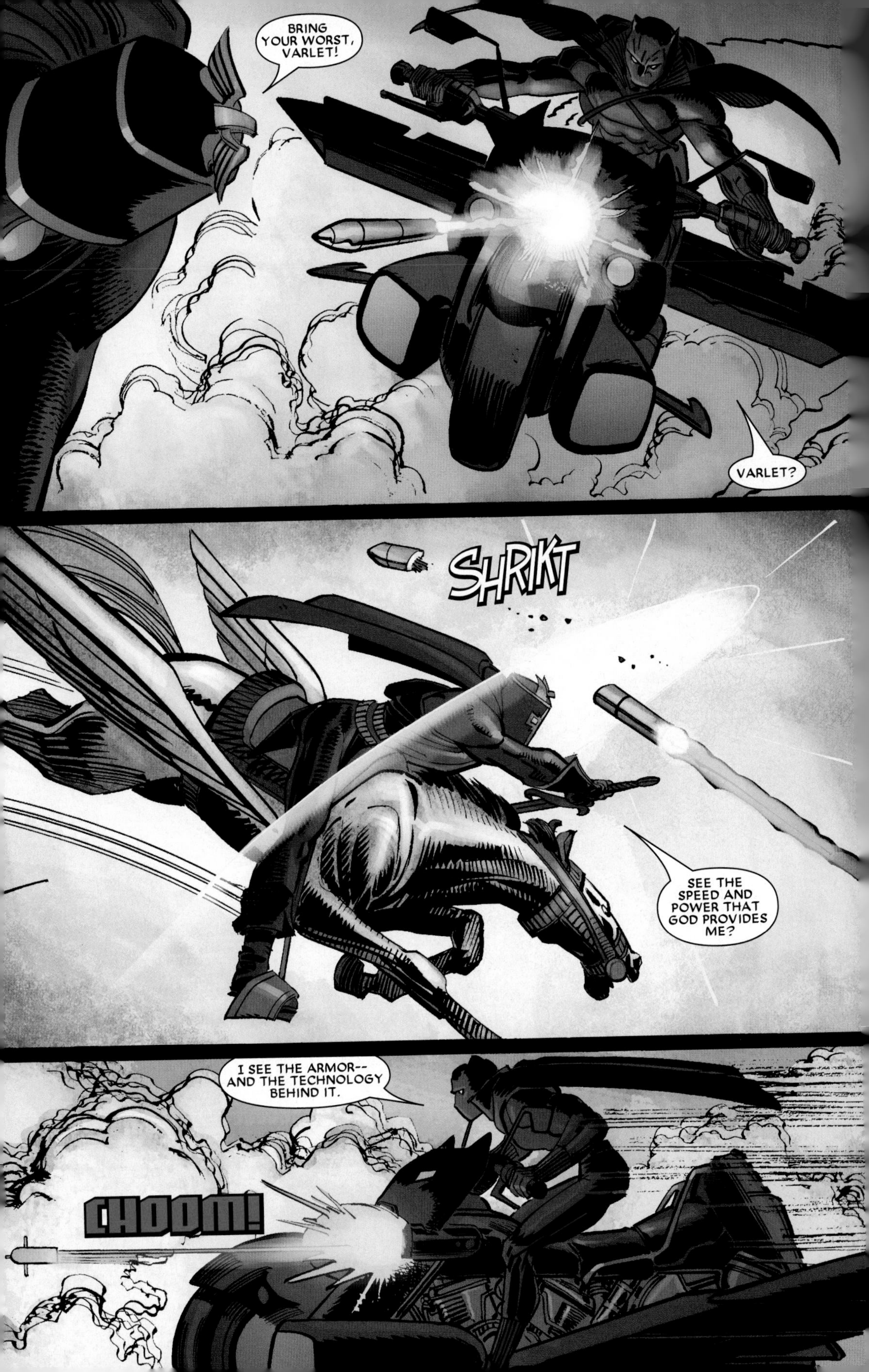
BRING YOUR WORST, VARLET!
VARLET?
SHRIKT
SEE THE SPEED AND POWER THAT GOD PROVIDES ME?
I SEE THE ARMOR-- AND THE TECHNOLOGY BEHIND IT.
CHOOM!

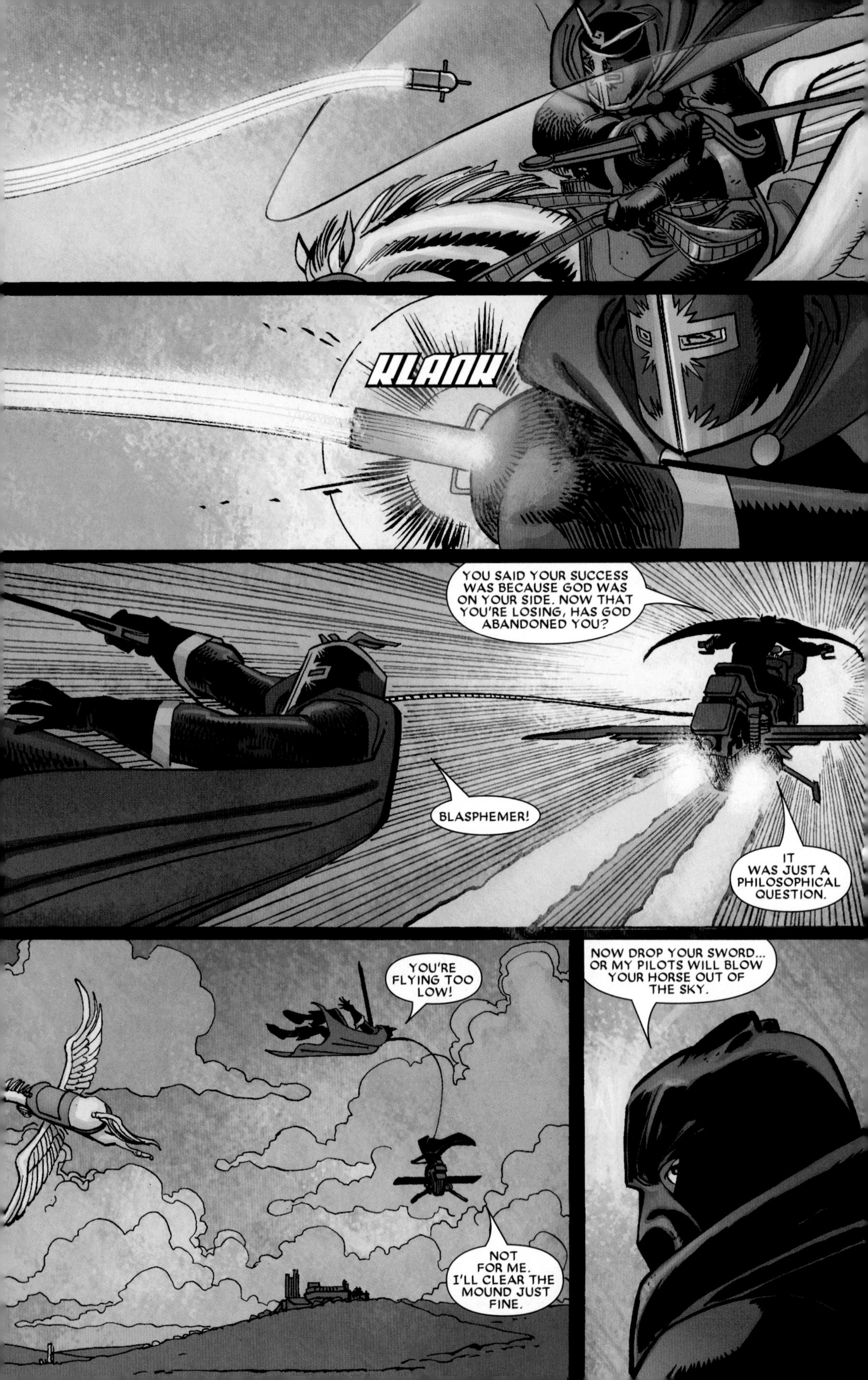
KLANK
YOU SAID YOUR SUCCESS WAS BECAUSE GOD WAS ON YOUR SIDE. NOW THAT YOU'RE LOSING, HAS GOD ABANDONED YOU?
BLASPHEMER!
IT WAS JUST A PHILOSOPHICAL QUESTION.
YOU'RE FLYING TOO LOW!
NOT FOR ME. I'LL CLEAR THE MOUND JUST FINE.
NOW DROP YOUR SWORD... OR MY PILOTS WILL BLOW YOUR HORSE OUT OF THE SKY.

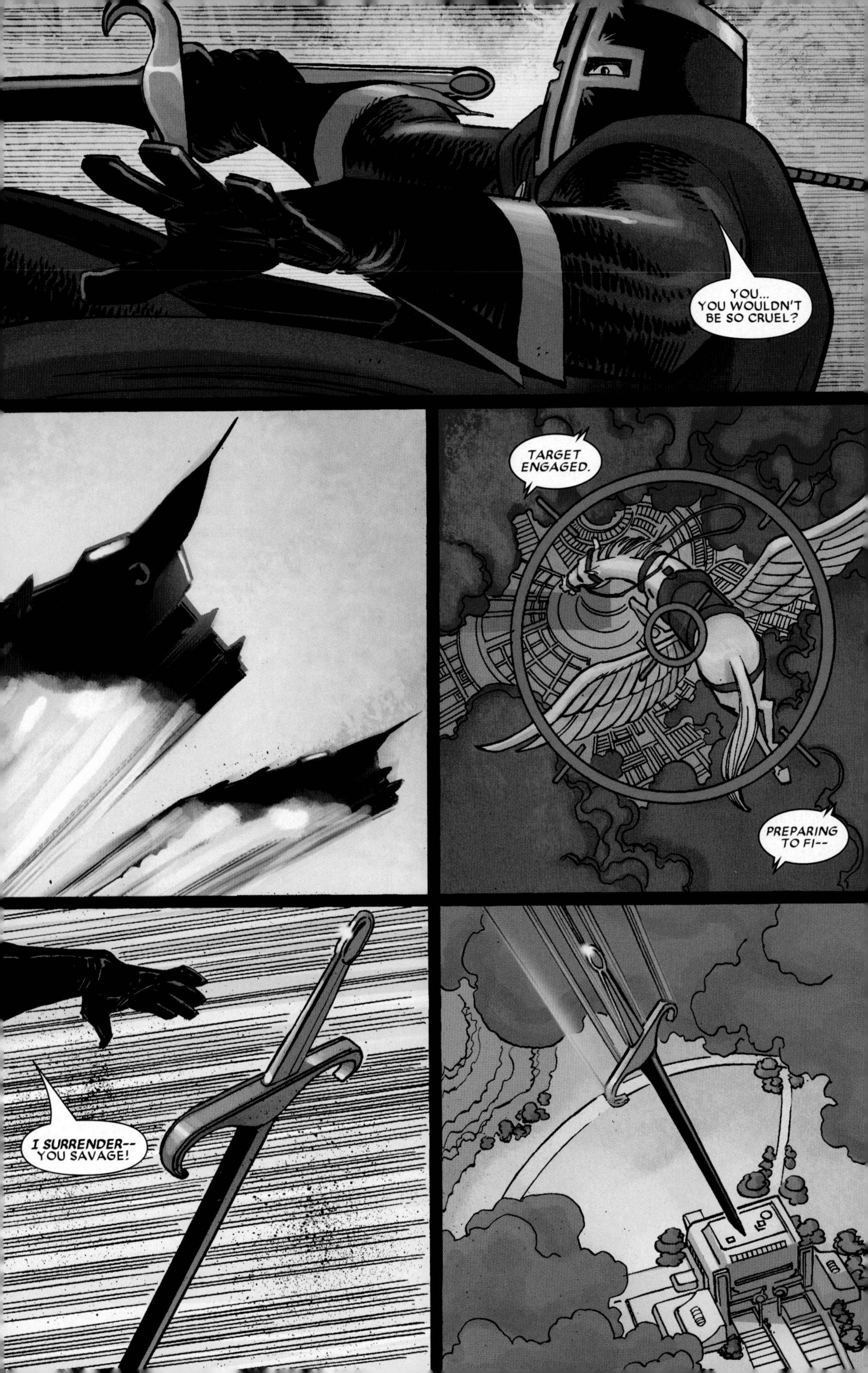
YOU... YOU WOULDN'T BE SO CRUEL?
TARGET ENGAGED.
PREPARING TO FI--
I SURRENDER-- YOU SAVAGE!

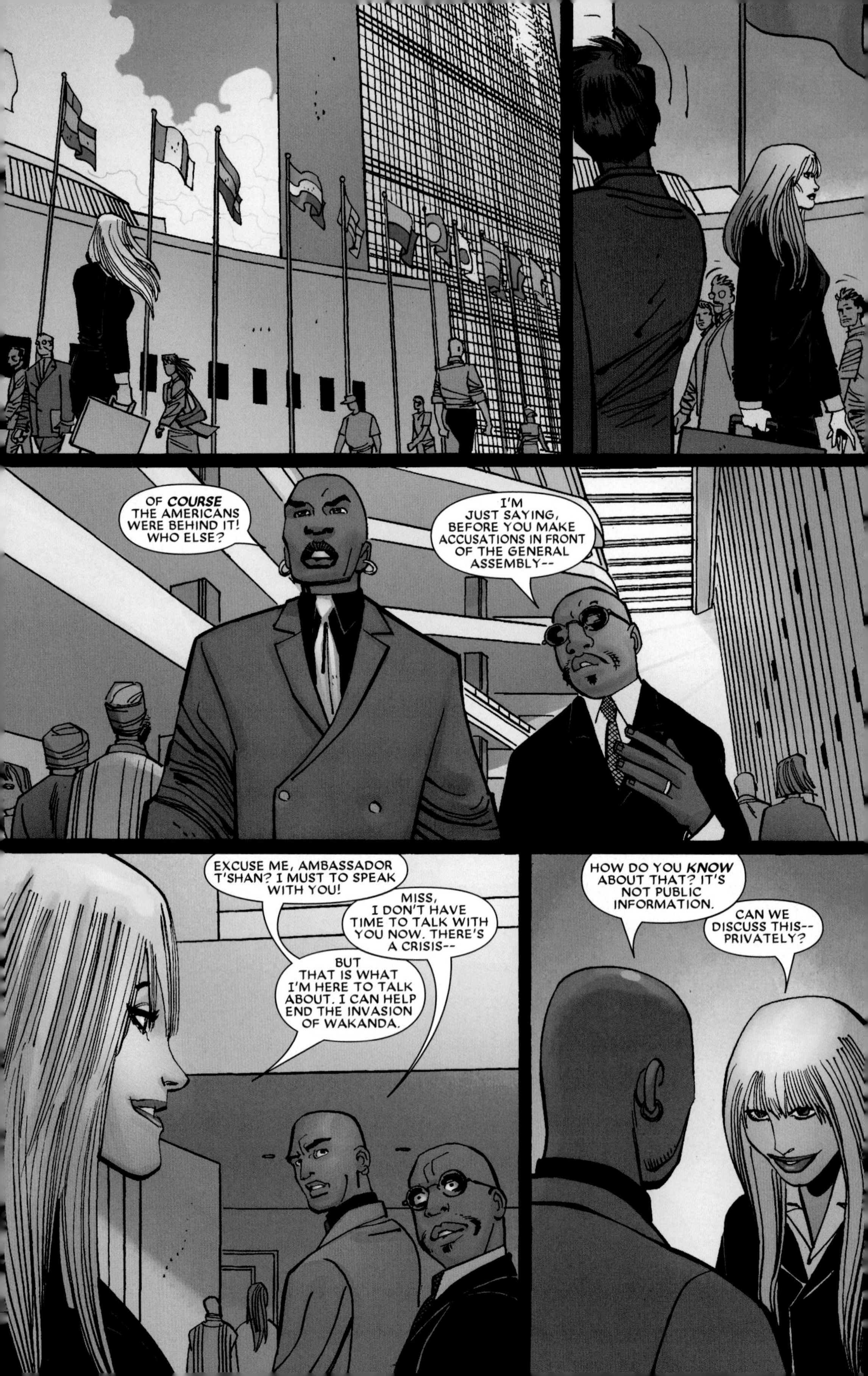

OF COURSE THE AMERICANS WERE BEHIND IT! WHO ELSE?
I'M JUST SAYING, BEFORE YOU MAKE ACCUSATIONS IN FRONT OF THE GENERAL ASSEMBLY--
EXCUSE ME, AMBASSADOR T'SHAN? I MUST TO SPEAK WITH YOU!
MISS, I DON'T HAVE TIME TO TALK WITH YOU NOW. THERE'S A CRISIS--
BUT THAT IS WHAT I'M HERE TO TALK ABOUT. I CAN HELP END THE INVASION OF WAKANDA.
HOW DO YOU KNOW ABOUT THAT? IT'S NOT PUBLIC INFORMATION.
CAN WE DISCUSS THIS-- PRIVATELY?

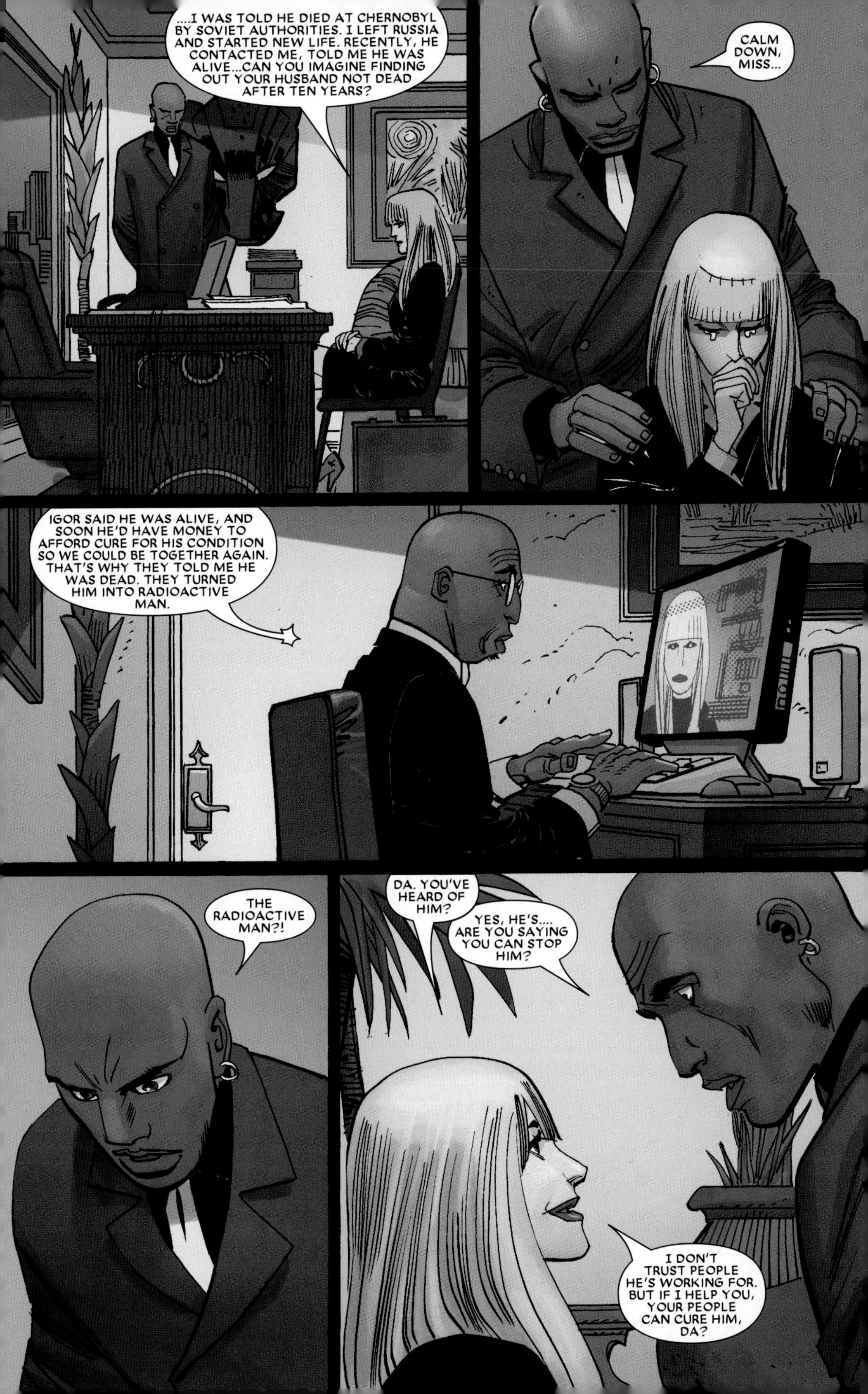
....I WAS TOLD HE DIED AT CHERNOBYL BY SOVIET AUTHORITIES. I LEFT RUSSIA AND STARTED NEW LIFE. RECENTLY, HE CONTACTED ME, TOLD ME HE WAS ALIVE...CAN YOU IMAGINE FINDING OUT YOUR HUSBAND NOT DEAD AFTER TEN YEARS?
CALM DOWN, MISS...
IGOR SAID HE WAS ALIVE, AND SOON HE'D HAVE MONEY TO AFFORD CURE FOR HIS CONDITION SO WE COULD BE TOGETHER AGAIN. THAT'S WHY THEY TOLD ME HE WAS DEAD. THEY TURNED HIM INTO RADIOACTIVE MAN.
THE RADIOACTIVE MAN?!
DA. YOU'VE HEARD OF HIM?
YES, HE'S.... ARE YOU SAYING YOU CAN STOP HIM?
I DON'T TRUST PEOPLE HE'S WORKING FOR. BUT IF I HELP YOU, YOUR PEOPLE CAN CURE HIM, DA?

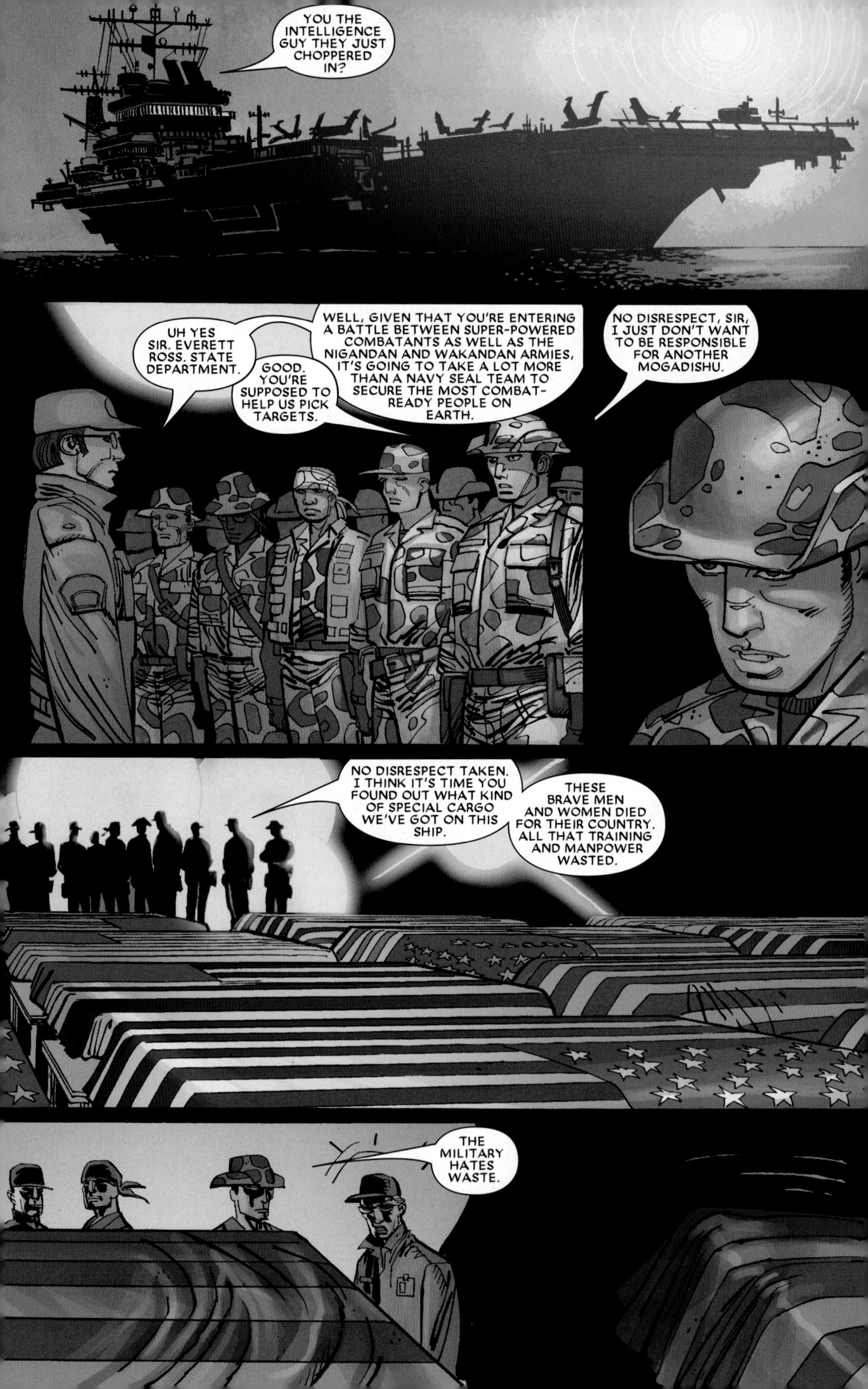
YOU THE INTELLIGENCE GUY THEY JUST CHOPPERED IN?
UH YES SIR. EVERETT ROSS. STATE DEPARTMENT.
GOOD. YOU'RE SUPPOSED TO HELP US PICK TARGETS.
WELL, GIVEN THAT YOU'RE ENTERING A BATTLE BETWEEN SUPER-POWERED COMBATANTS AS WELL AS THE NIGANDAN AND WAKANDAN ARMIES, IT'S GOING TO TAKE A LOT MORE THAN A NAVY SEAL TEAM TO SECURE THE MOST COMBAT-READY PEOPLE ON EARTH.
NO DISRESPECT, SIR, I JUST DON'T WANT TO BE RESPONSIBLE FOR ANOTHER MOGADISHU.
NO DISRESPECT TAKEN. I THINK IT'S TIME YOU FOUND OUT WHAT KIND OF SPECIAL CARGO WE'VE GOT ON THIS SHIP.
THESE BRAVE MEN AND WOMEN DIED FOR THEIR COUNTRY. ALL THAT TRAINING AND MANPOWER WASTED.
THE MILITARY HATES WASTE.

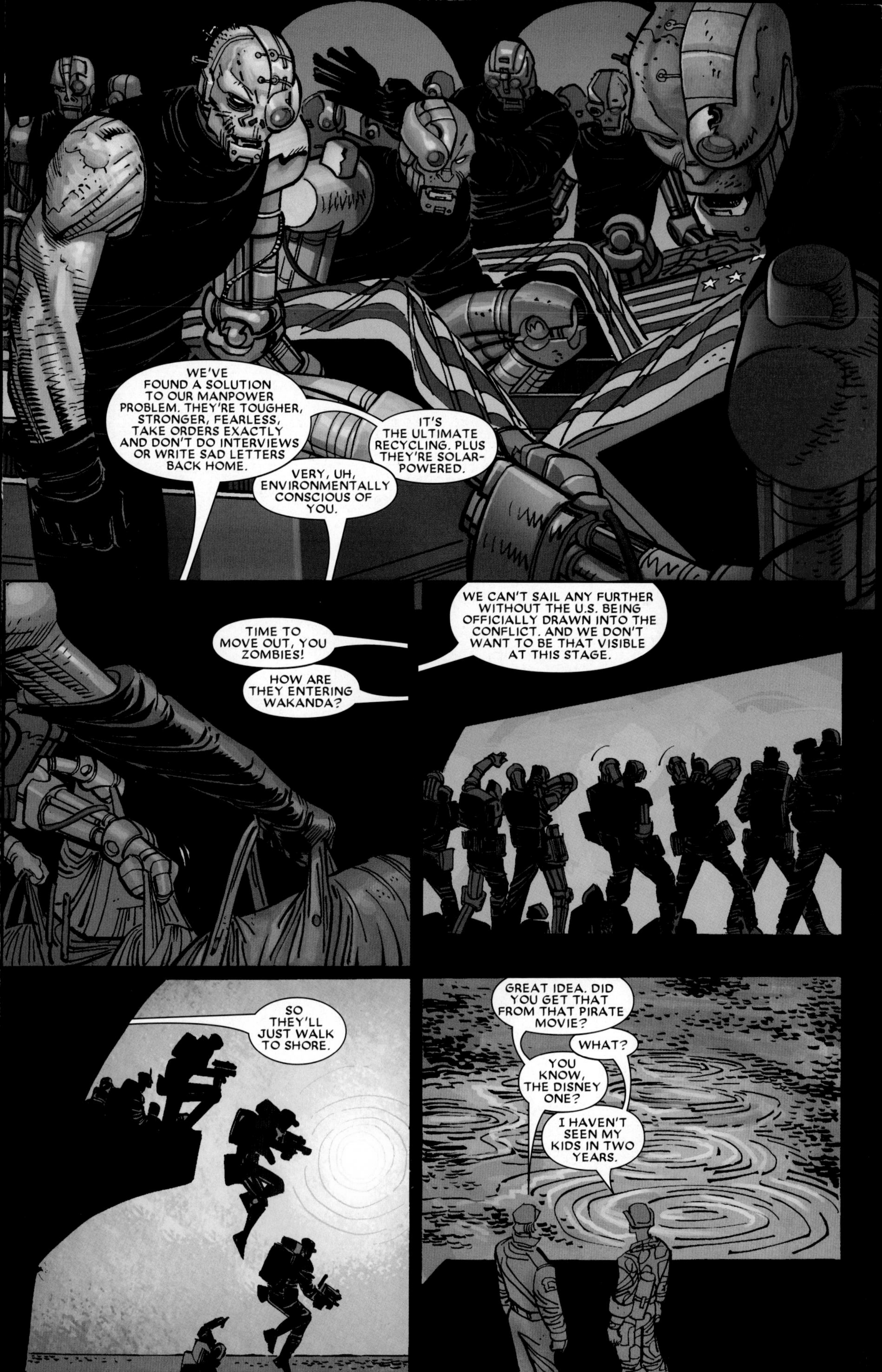
WE'VE FOUND A SOLUTION TO OUR MANPOWER PROBLEM. THEY'RE TOUGHER, STRONGER, FEARLESS, TAKE ORDERS EXACTLY AND DON'T DO INTERVIEWS OR WRITE SAD LETTERS BACK HOME.
IT'S THE ULTIMATE RECYCLING. PLUS THEY'RE SOLAR-POWERED.
VERY, UH, ENVIRONMENTALLY CONSCIOUS OF YOU.
TIME TO MOVE OUT, YOU ZOMBIES!
HOW ARE THEY ENTERING WAKANDA?
WE CAN'T SAIL ANY FURTHER WITHOUT THE U.S. BEING OFFICIALLY DRAWN INTO THE CONFLICT. AND WE DON'T WANT TO BE THAT VISIBLE AT THIS STAGE.
SO THEY'LL JUST WALK TO SHORE.
GREAT IDEA. DID YOU GET THAT FROM THAT PIRATE MOVIE?
WHAT?
YOU KNOW, THE DISNEY ONE?
I HAVEN'T SEEN MY KIDS IN TWO YEARS.

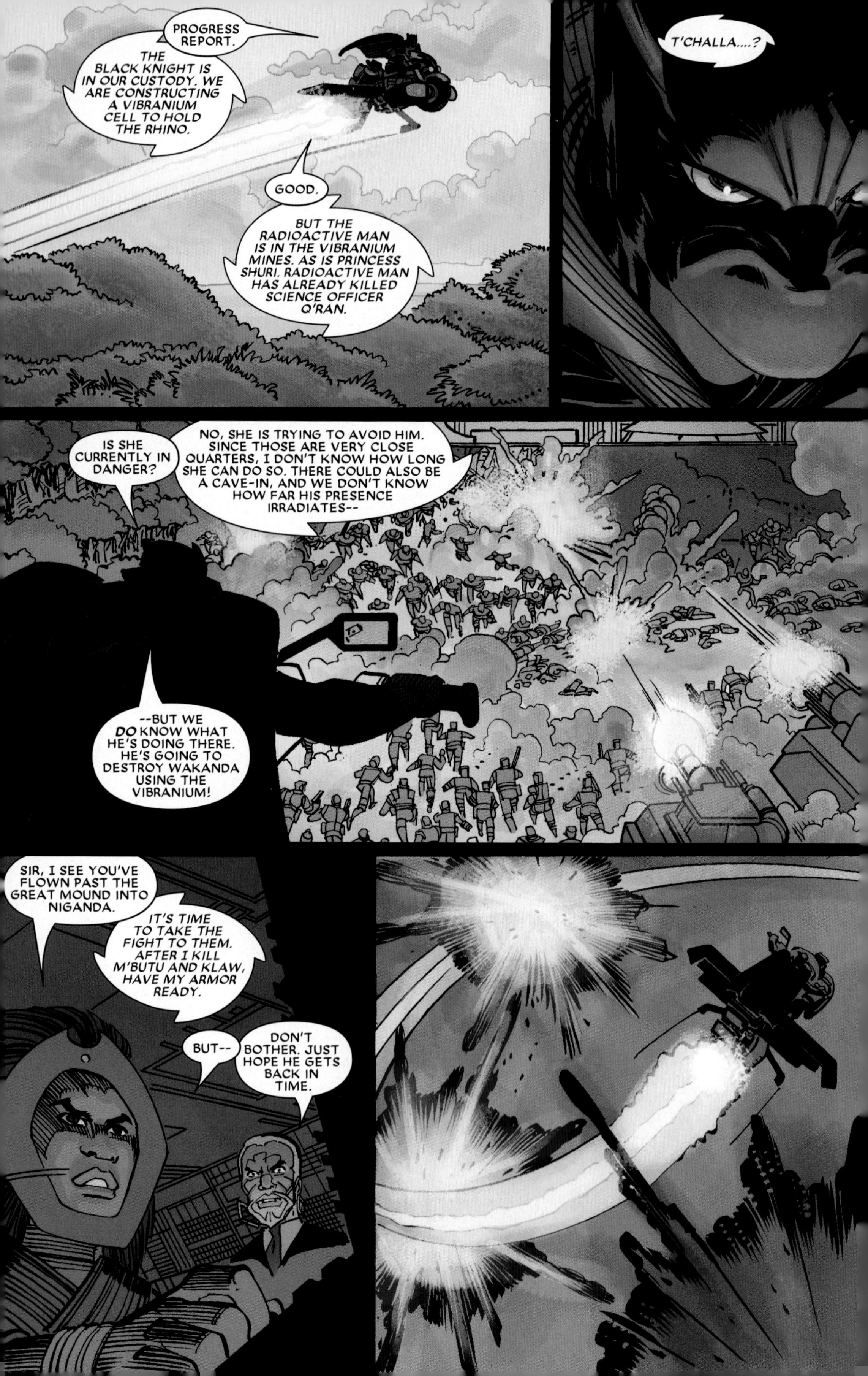

PROGRESS REPORT.
THE BLACK KNIGHT IS IN OUR CUSTODY. WE ARE CONSTRUCTING A VIBRANIUM CELL TO HOLD THE RHINO.
GOOD.
BUT THE RADIOACTIVE MAN IS IN THE VIBRANIUM MINES. AS IS PRINCESS SHURI. RADIOACTIVE MAN HAS ALREADY KILLED SCIENCE OFFICER Q'RAN.
T'CHALLA....?
IS SHE CURRENTLY IN DANGER?
NO, SHE IS TRYING TO AVOID HIM. SINCE THOSE ARE VERY CLOSE QUARTERS, I DON'T KNOW HOW LONG SHE CAN DO SO. THERE COULD ALSO BE A CAVE-IN, AND WE DON'T KNOW HOW FAR HIS PRESENCE IRRADIATES--
--BUT WE *DO* KNOW WHAT HE'S DOING THERE. HE'S GOING TO DESTROY WAKANDA USING THE VIBRANIUM!
SIR, I SEE YOU'VE FLOWN PAST THE GREAT MOUND INTO NIGANDA.
IT'S TIME TO TAKE THE FIGHT TO THEM. AFTER I KILL M'BUTU AND KLAW, HAVE MY ARMOR READY.
BUT--
DON'T BOTHER. JUST HOPE HE GETS BACK IN TIME.

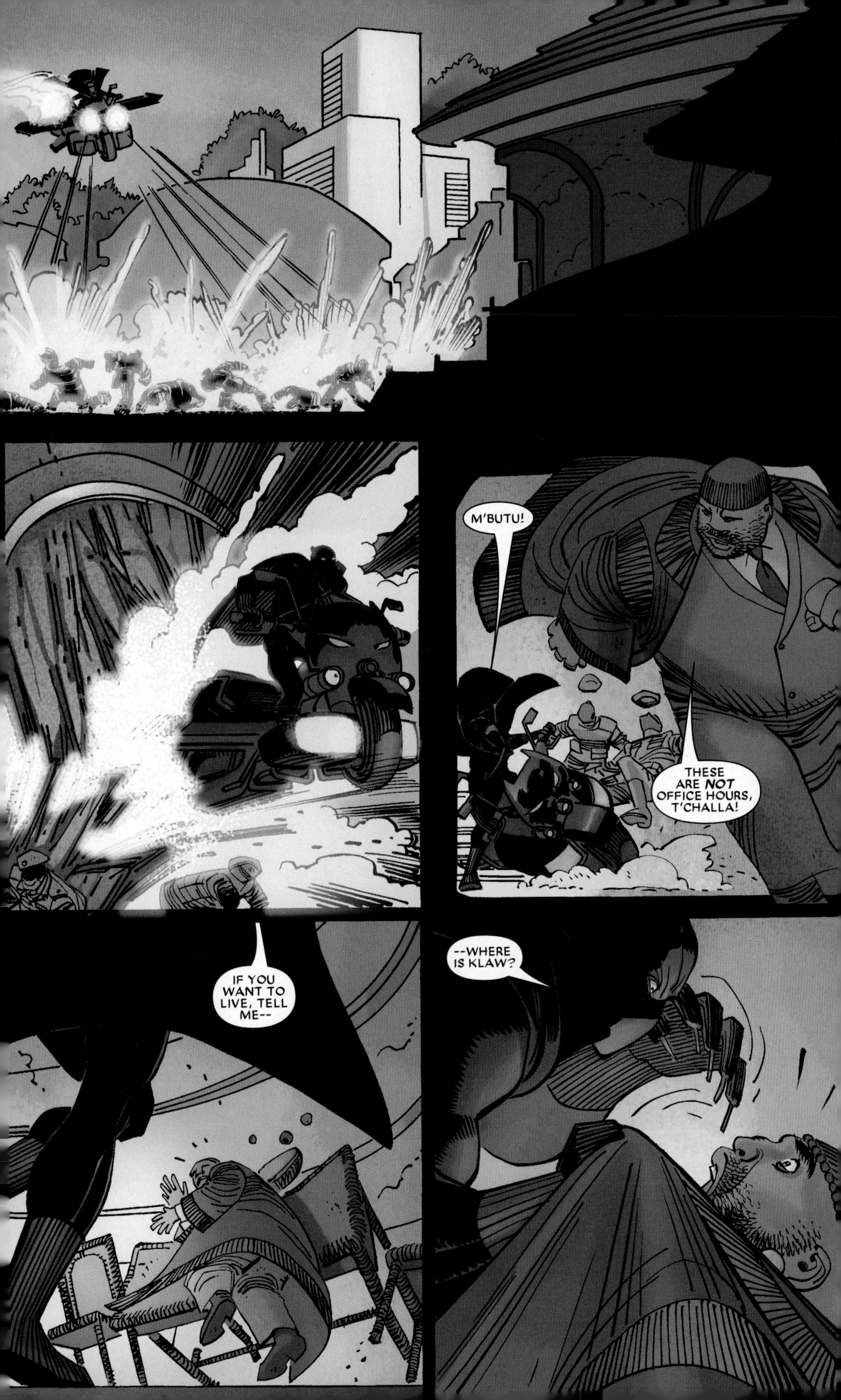
M'BUTU!
THESE ARE NOT OFFICE HOURS, T'CHALLA!
IF YOU WANT TO LIVE, TELL ME--
--WHERE IS KLAW?

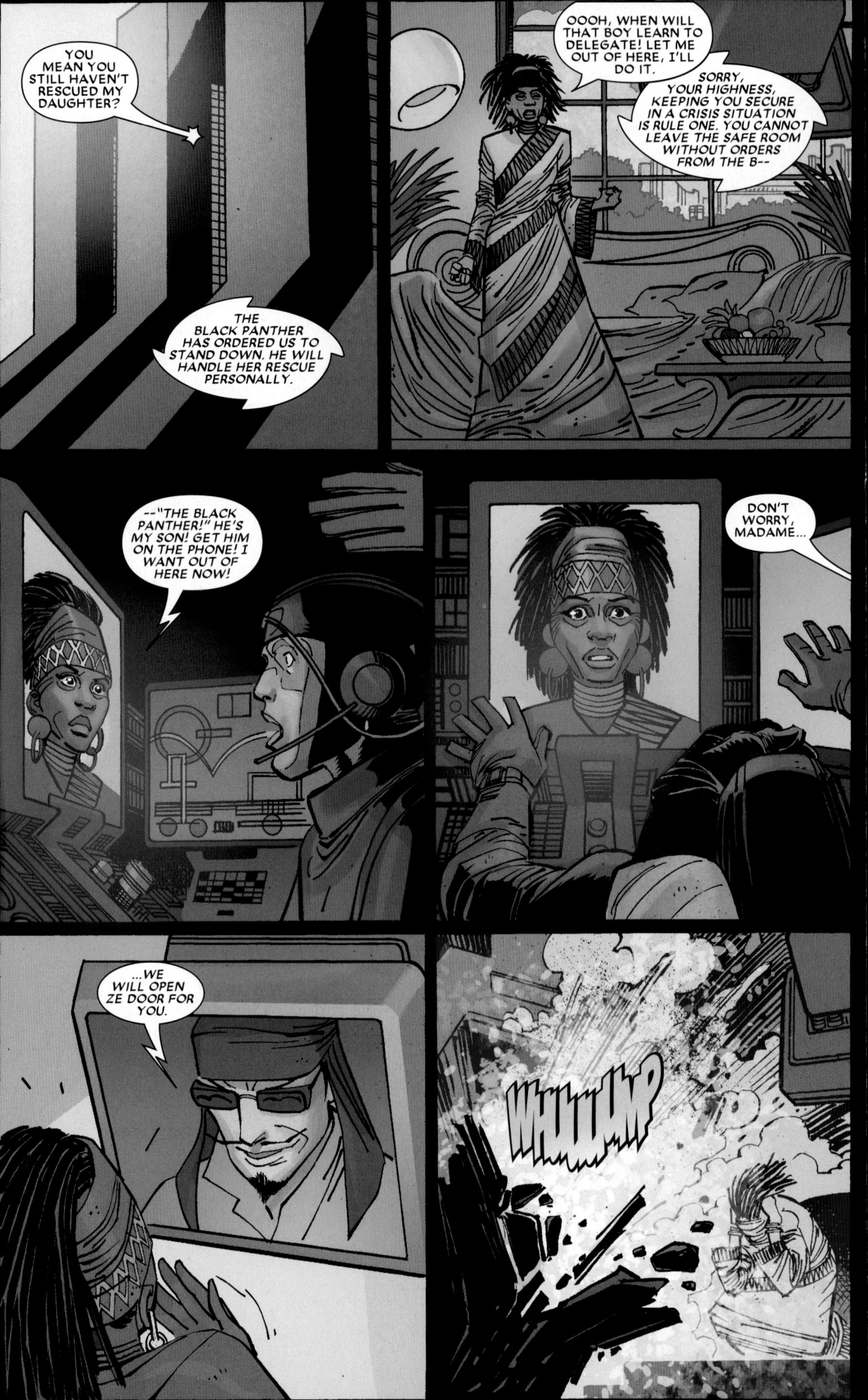
YOU MEAN YOU STILL HAVEN'T RESCUED MY DAUGHTER?
THE BLACK PANTHER HAS ORDERED US TO STAND DOWN. HE WILL HANDLE HER RESCUE PERSONALLY.
OOOH, WHEN WILL THAT BOY LEARN TO DELEGATE! LET ME OUT OF HERE, I'LL DO IT.
SORRY, YOUR HIGHNESS, KEEPING YOU SECURE IN A CRISIS SITUATION IS RULE ONE. YOU CANNOT LEAVE THE SAFE ROOM WITHOUT ORDERS FROM THE B--
--"THE BLACK PANTHER!" HE'S MY SON! GET HIM ON THE PHONE! I WANT OUT OF HERE NOW!
DON'T WORRY, MADAME...
...WE WILL OPEN ZE DOOR FOR YOU.
WHUUMP

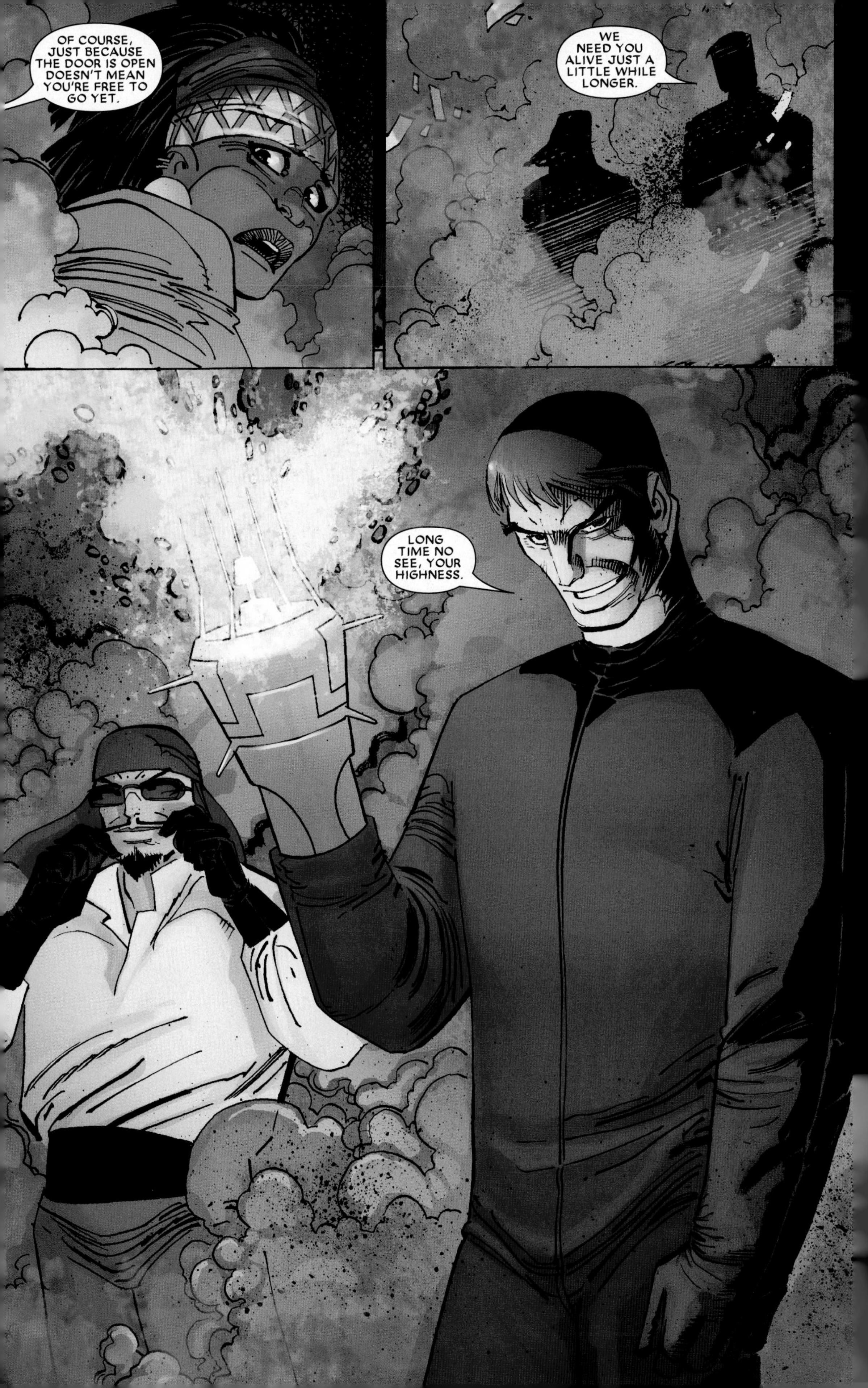
OF COURSE, JUST BECAUSE THE DOOR IS OPEN DOESN'T MEAN YOU'RE FREE TO GO YET.
WE NEED YOU ALIVE JUST A LITTLE WHILE LONGER.
LONG TIME NO SEE, YOUR HIGHNESS.

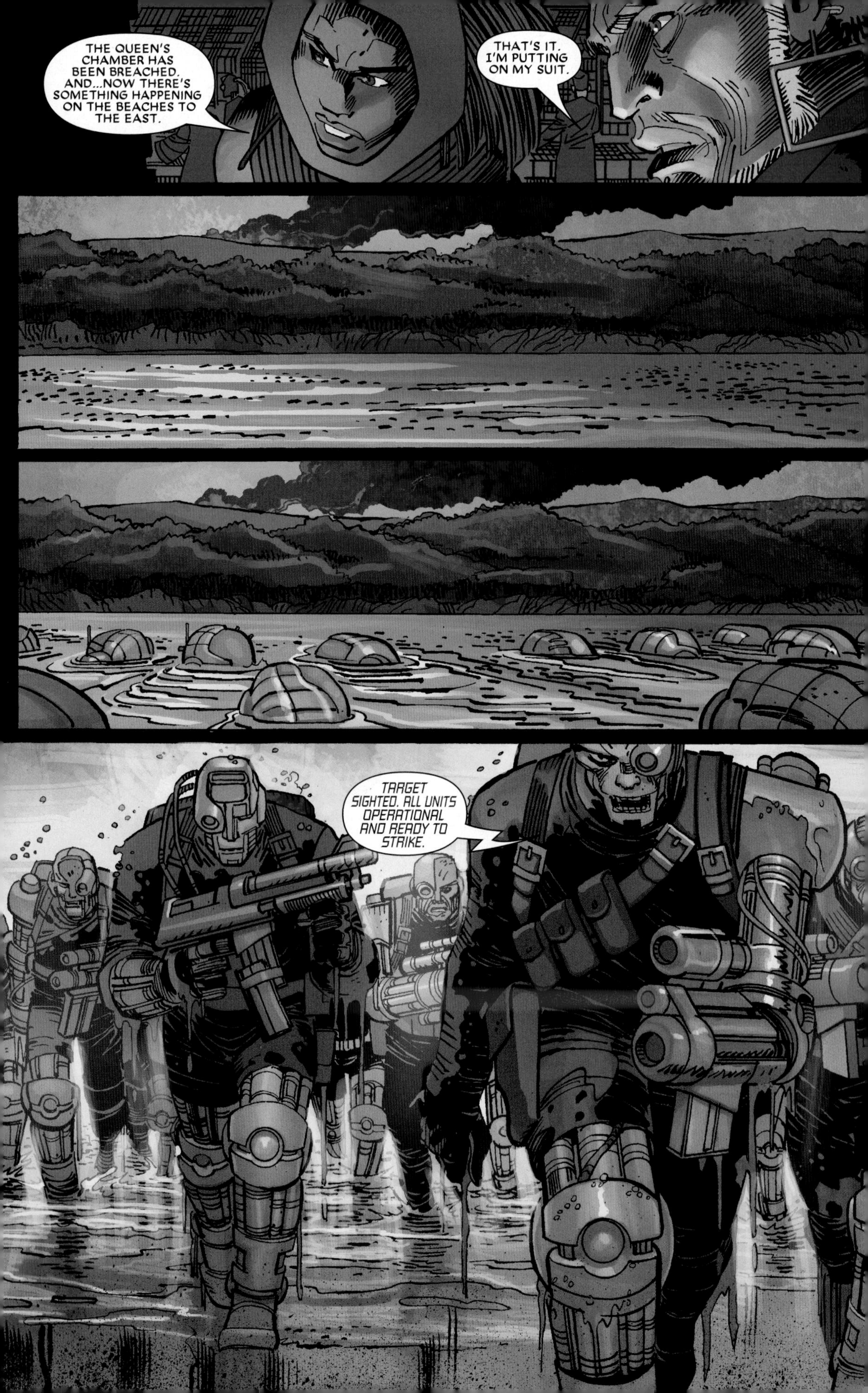
THE QUEEN'S CHAMBER HAS BEEN BREACHED. AND...NOW THERE'S SOMETHING HAPPENING ON THE BEACHES TO THE EAST.
THAT'S IT. I'M PUTTING ON MY SUIT.
TARGET SIGHTED. ALL UNITS OPERATIONAL AND READY TO STRIKE.

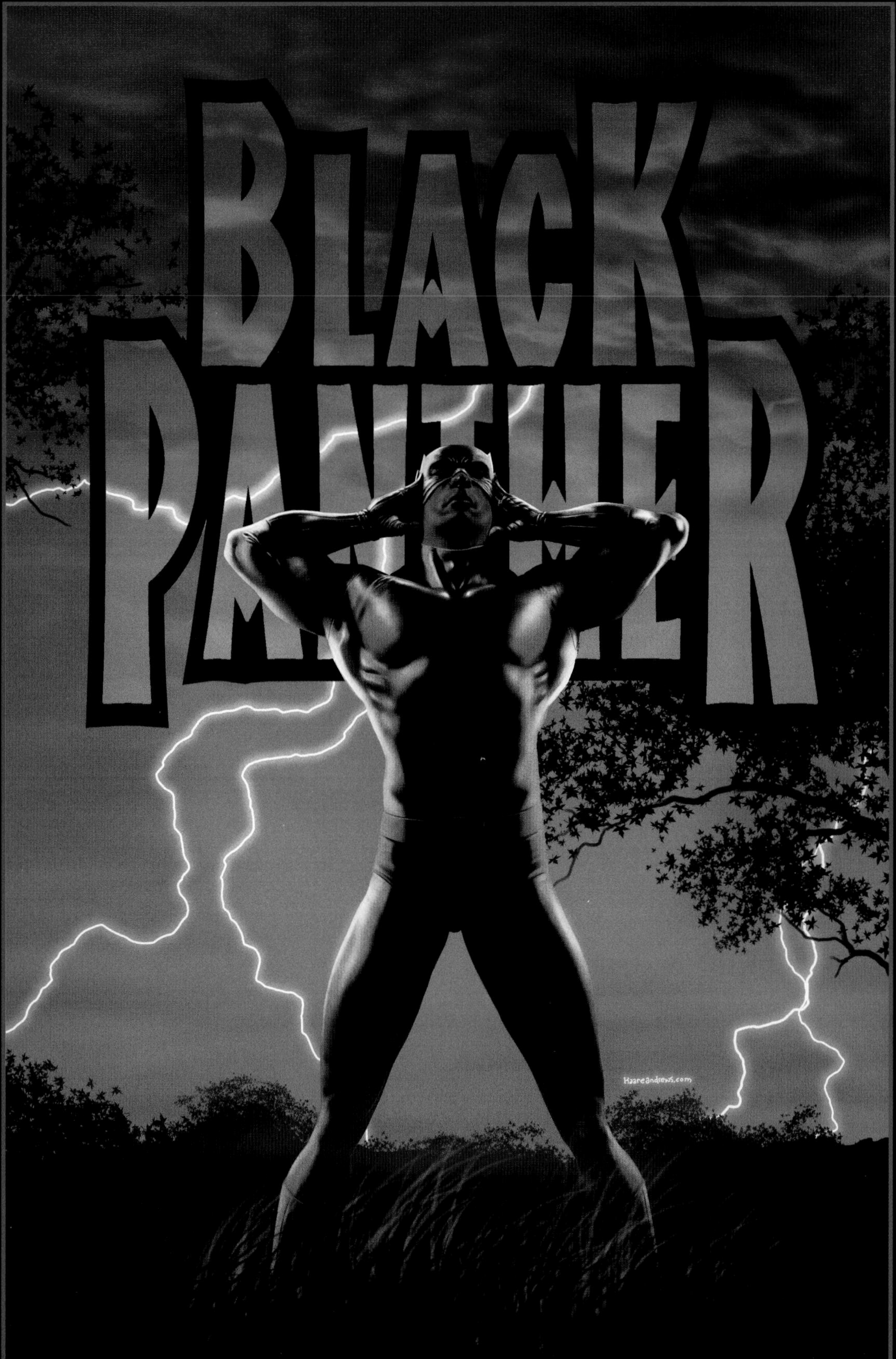
BLACK PANTHER
hiaareandrews.com

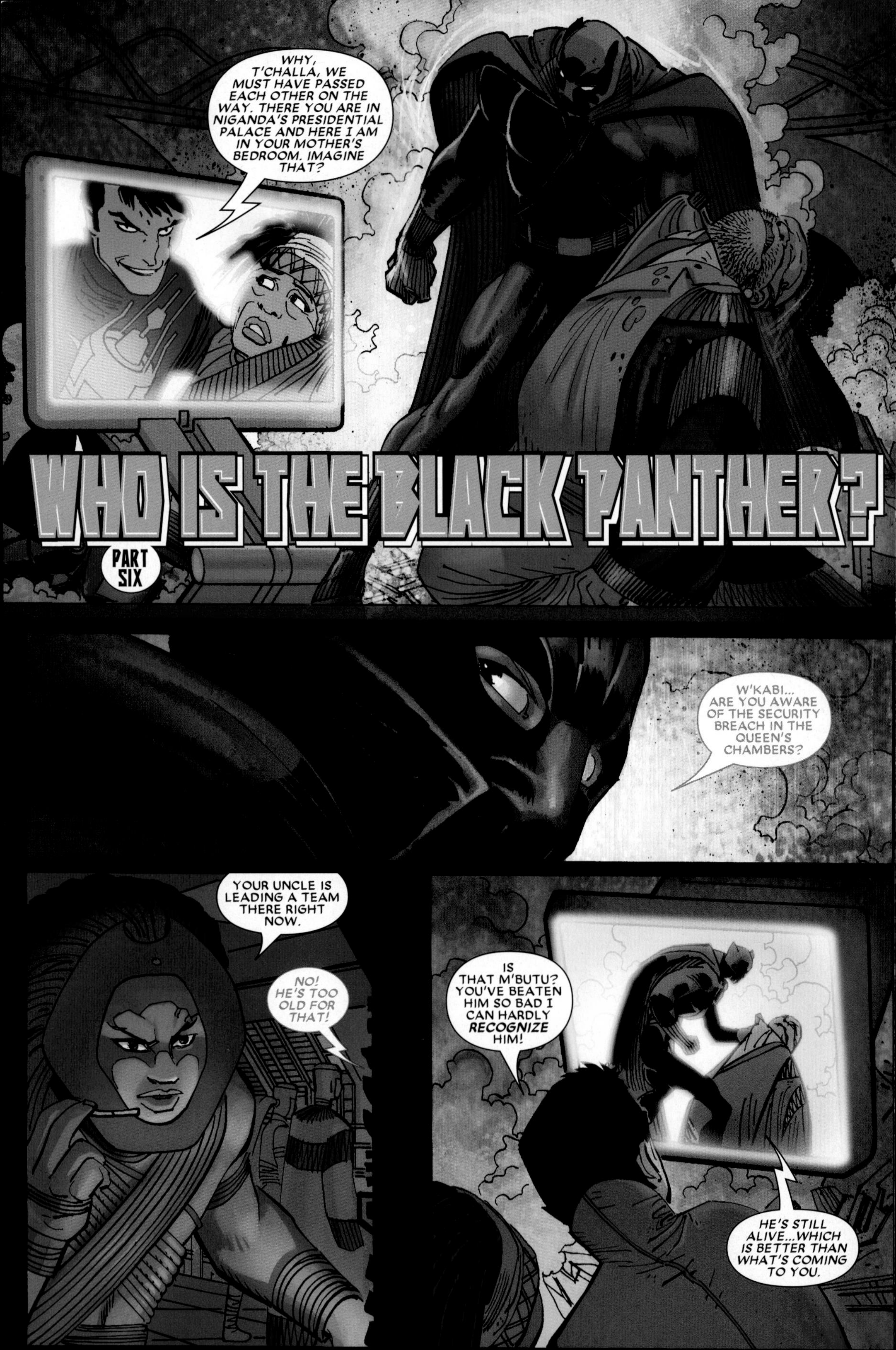
WHY, T'CHALLA, WE MUST HAVE PASSED EACH OTHER ON THE WAY. THERE YOU ARE IN NIGANDA'S PRESIDENTIAL PALACE AND HERE I AM IN YOUR MOTHER'S BEDROOM. IMAGINE THAT?
WHO IS THE BLACK PANTHER?
PART SIX
W'KABI... ARE YOU AWARE OF THE SECURITY BREACH IN THE QUEEN'S CHAMBERS?
YOUR UNCLE IS LEADING A TEAM THERE RIGHT NOW.
NO! HE'S TOO OLD FOR THAT!
IS THAT M'BUTU? YOU'VE BEATEN HIM SO BAD I CAN HARDLY RECOGNIZE HIM!
HE'S STILL ALIVE...WHICH IS BETTER THAN WHAT'S COMING TO YOU.

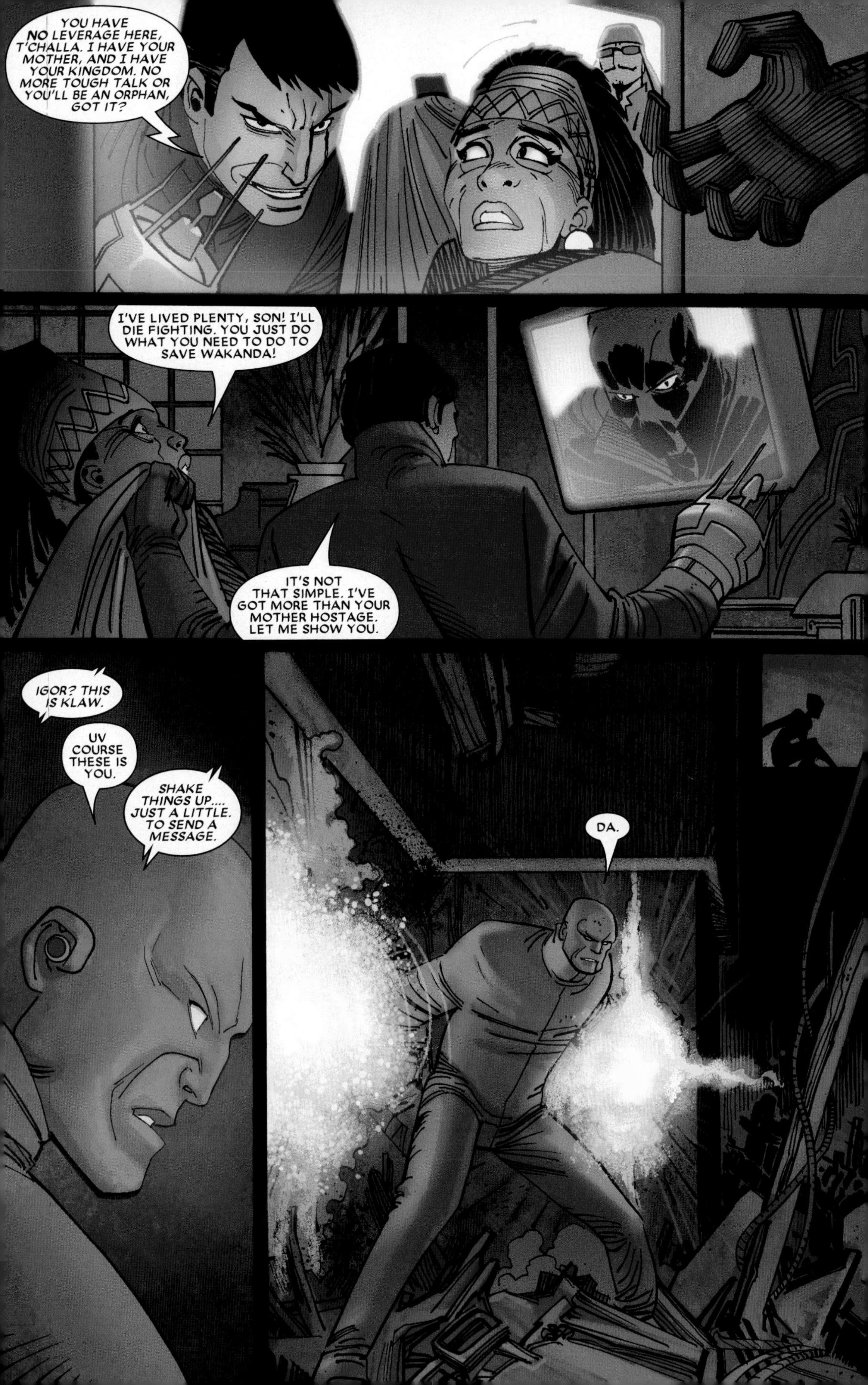
YOU HAVE NO LEVERAGE HERE, T'CHALLA. I HAVE YOUR MOTHER, AND I HAVE YOUR KINGDOM. NO MORE TOUGH TALK OR YOU'LL BE AN ORPHAN, GOT IT?
I'VE LIVED PLENTY, SON! I'LL DIE FIGHTING. YOU JUST DO WHAT YOU NEED TO DO TO SAVE WAKANDA!
IT'S NOT THAT SIMPLE. I'VE GOT MORE THAN YOUR MOTHER HOSTAGE. LET ME SHOW YOU.
IGOR? THIS IS KLAW.
UV COURSE THESE IS YOU.
SHAKE THINGS UP.... JUST A LITTLE. TO SEND A MESSAGE.
DA.

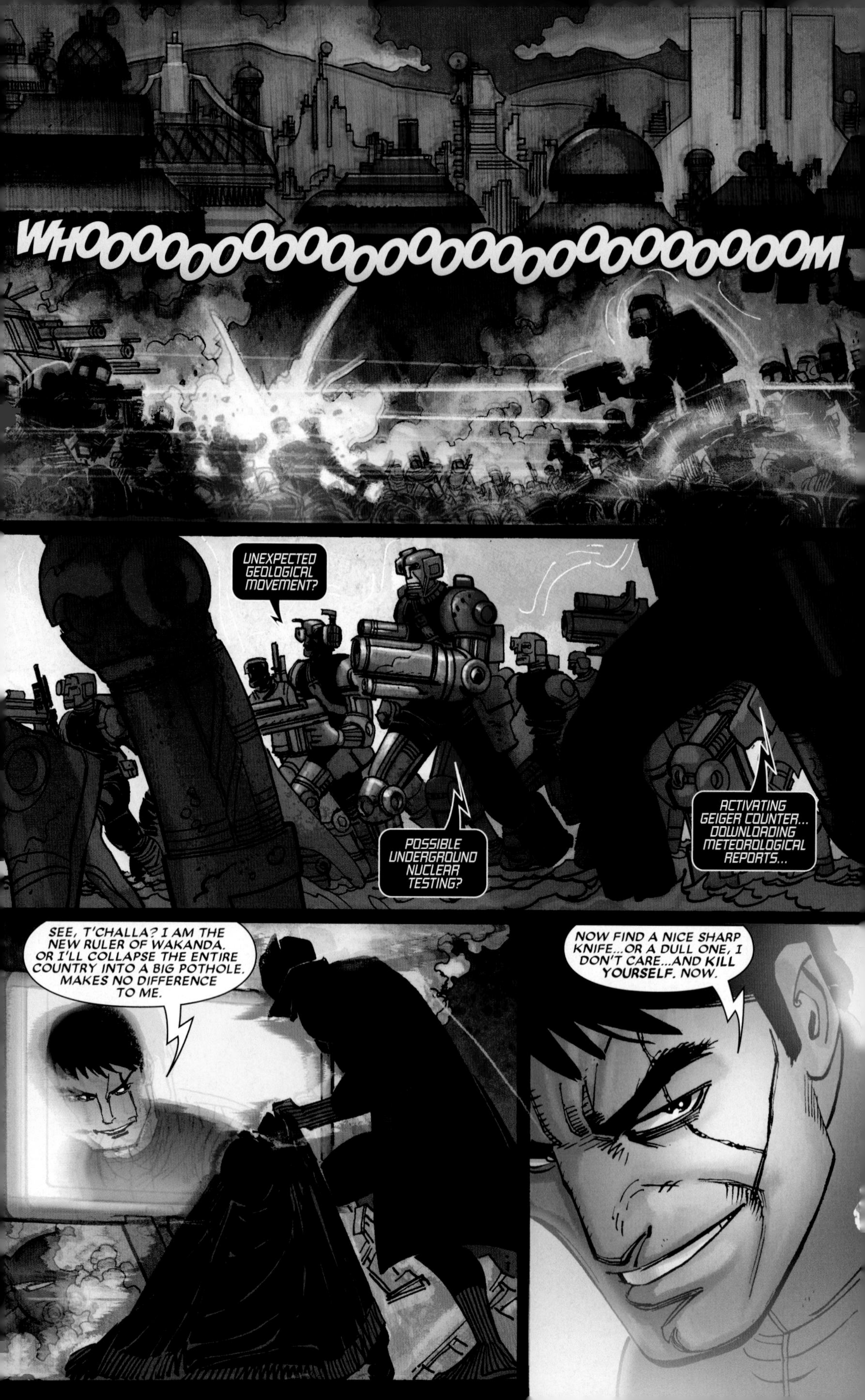

WHOOOOOOOOOOOOOOOOOOOOOOOOOOOM
UNEXPECTED GEOLOGICAL MOVEMENT?
POSSIBLE UNDERGROUND NUCLEAR TESTING?
ACTIVATING GEIGER COUNTER... DOWNLOADING METEOROLOGICAL REPORTS...
SEE, T'CHALLA? I AM THE NEW RULER OF WAKANDA. OR I'LL COLLAPSE THE ENTIRE COUNTRY INTO A BIG POTHOLE. MAKES NO DIFFERENCE TO ME.
NOW FIND A NICE SHARP KNIFE...OR A DULL ONE, I DON'T CARE...AND KILL YOURSELF. NOW.

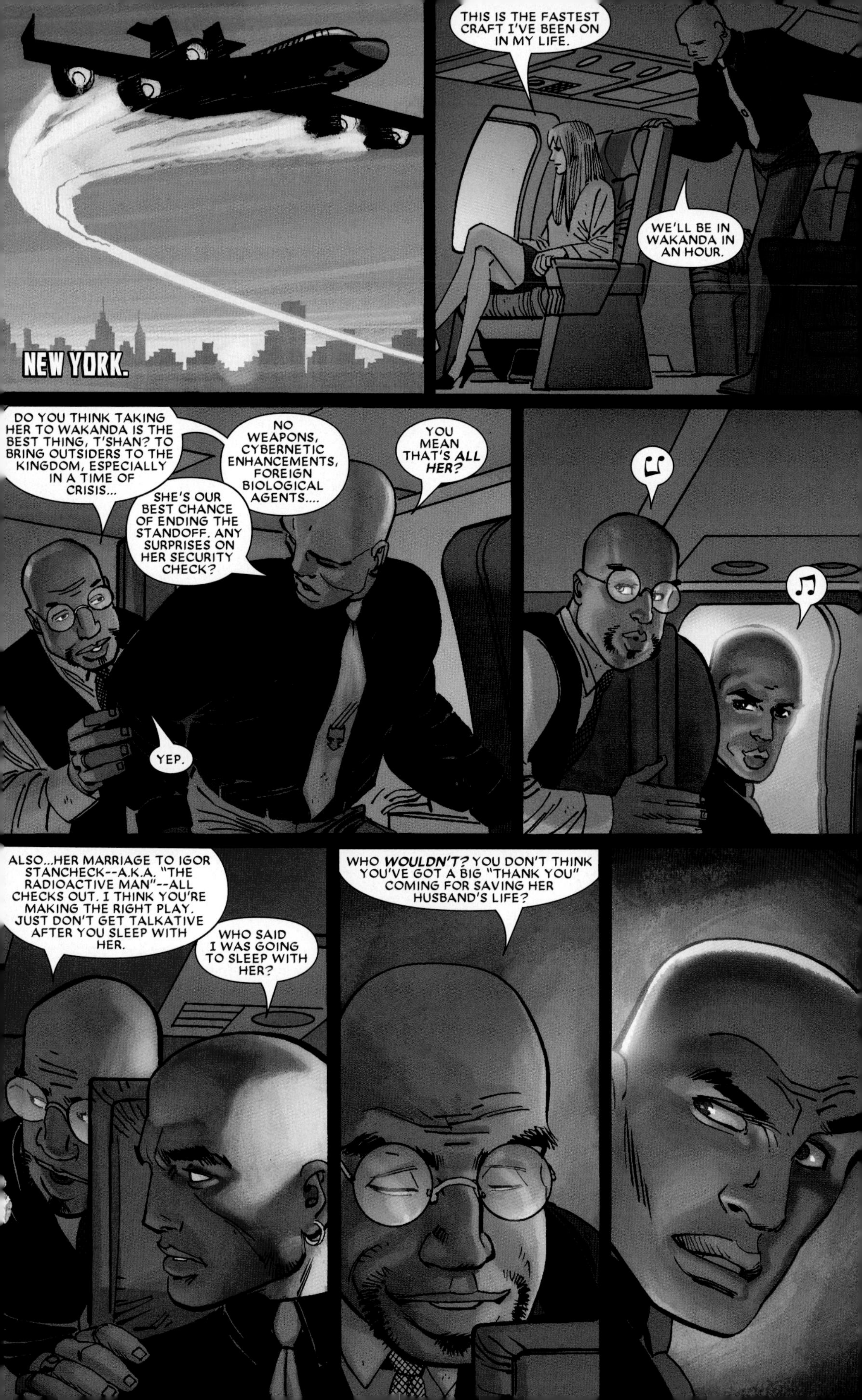
NEW YORK.
THIS IS THE FASTEST CRAFT I'VE BEEN ON IN MY LIFE.
WE'LL BE IN WAKANDA IN AN HOUR.
DO YOU THINK TAKING HER TO WAKANDA IS THE BEST THING, T'SHAN? TO BRING OUTSIDERS TO THE KINGDOM, ESPECIALLY IN A TIME OF CRISIS...
SHE'S OUR BEST CHANCE OF ENDING THE STANDOFF. ANY SURPRISES ON HER SECURITY CHECK?
NO WEAPONS, CYBERNETIC ENHANCEMENTS, FOREIGN BIOLOGICAL AGENTS....
YOU MEAN THAT'S ALL HER?
YEP.
♫
♫
ALSO...HER MARRIAGE TO IGOR STANCHECK--A.K.A. "THE RADIOACTIVE MAN"--ALL CHECKS OUT. I THINK YOU'RE MAKING THE RIGHT PLAY. JUST DON'T GET TALKATIVE AFTER YOU SLEEP WITH HER.
WHO SAID I WAS GOING TO SLEEP WITH HER?
WHO WOULDN'T? YOU DON'T THINK YOU'VE GOT A BIG "THANK YOU" COMING FOR SAVING HER HUSBAND'S LIFE?

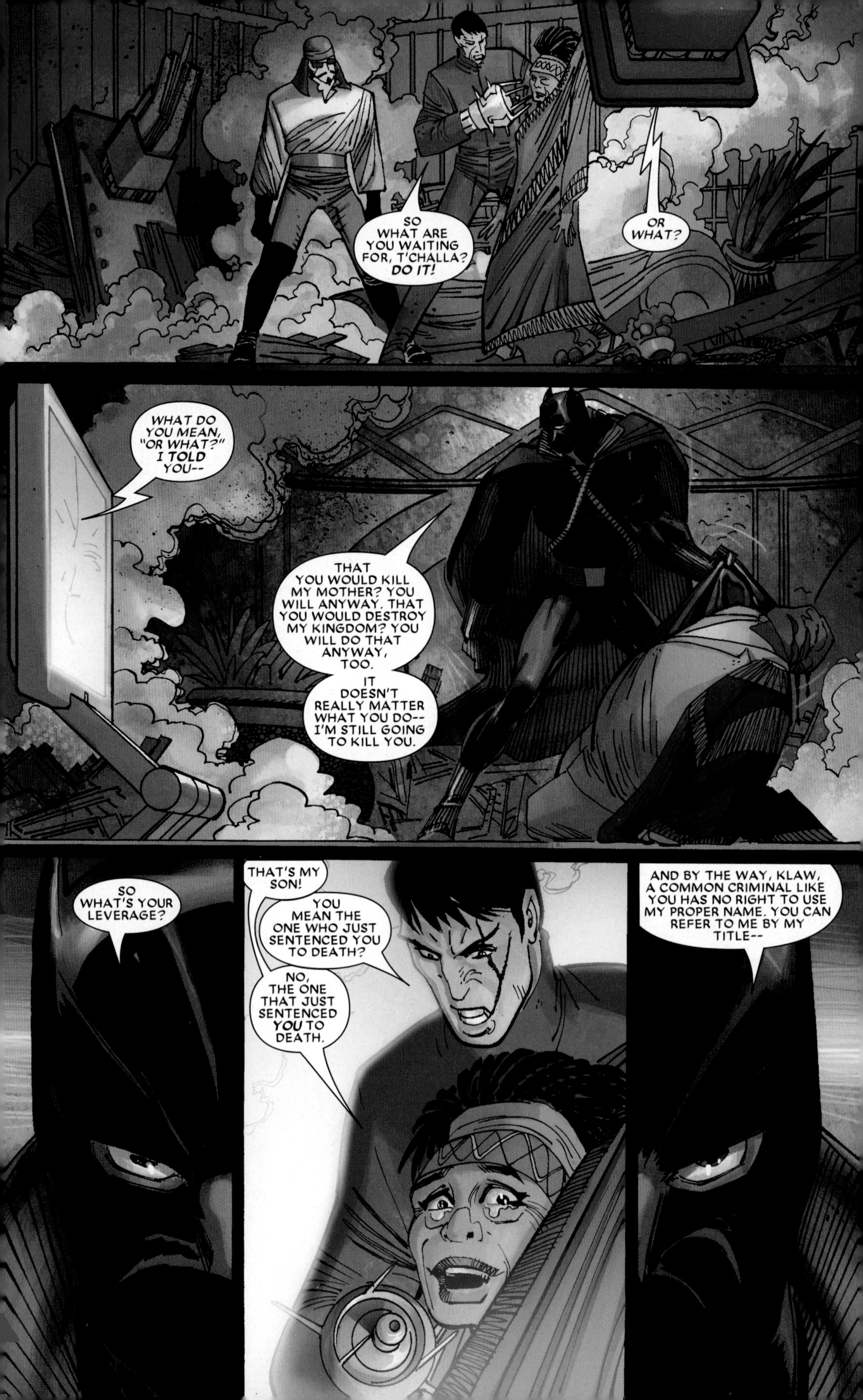
SO WHAT ARE YOU WAITING FOR, T'CHALLA? DO IT!
OR WHAT?
WHAT DO YOU MEAN, "OR WHAT?" I TOLD YOU--
THAT YOU WOULD KILL MY MOTHER? YOU WILL ANYWAY. THAT YOU WOULD DESTROY MY KINGDOM? YOU WILL DO THAT ANYWAY, TOO.
IT DOESN'T REALLY MATTER WHAT YOU DO-- I'M STILL GOING TO KILL YOU.
SO WHAT'S YOUR LEVERAGE?
THAT'S MY SON!
YOU MEAN THE ONE WHO JUST SENTENCED YOU TO DEATH?
NO, THE ONE THAT JUST SENTENCED YOU TO DEATH.
AND BY THE WAY, KLAW, A COMMON CRIMINAL LIKE YOU HAS NO RIGHT TO USE MY PROPER NAME. YOU CAN REFER TO ME BY MY TITLE--

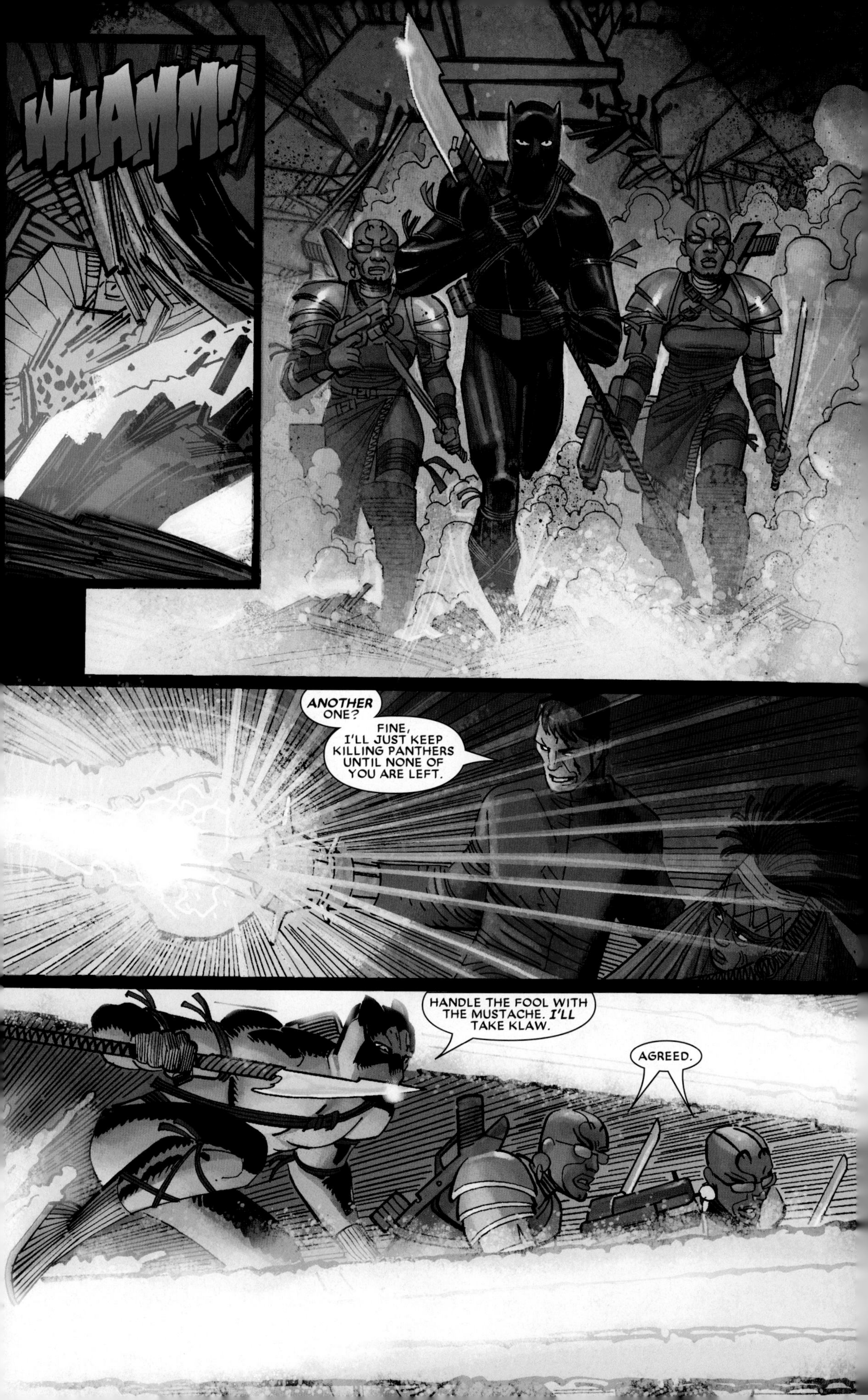
WHAMM!
ANOTHER ONE?
FINE, I'LL JUST KEEP KILLING PANTHERS UNTIL NONE OF YOU ARE LEFT.
HANDLE THE FOOL WITH THE MUSTACHE. I'LL TAKE KLAW.
AGREED.

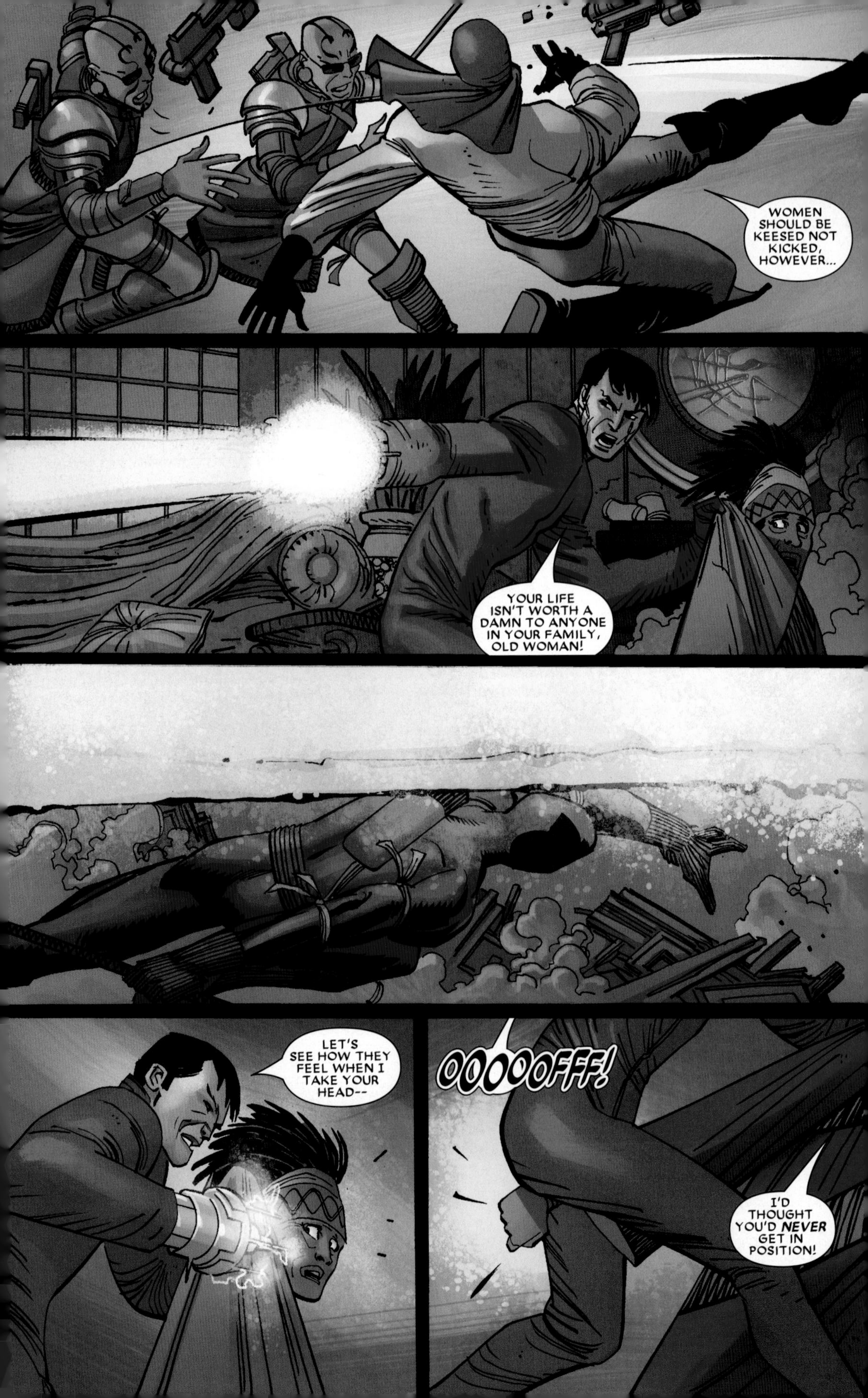
WOMEN SHOULD BE KEESED NOT KICKED, HOWEVER...
YOUR LIFE ISN'T WORTH A DAMN TO ANYONE IN YOUR FAMILY, OLD WOMAN!
LET'S SEE HOW THEY FEEL WHEN I TAKE YOUR HEAD--
OOOOOOFFF!
I'D THOUGHT YOU'D NEVER GET IN POSITION!

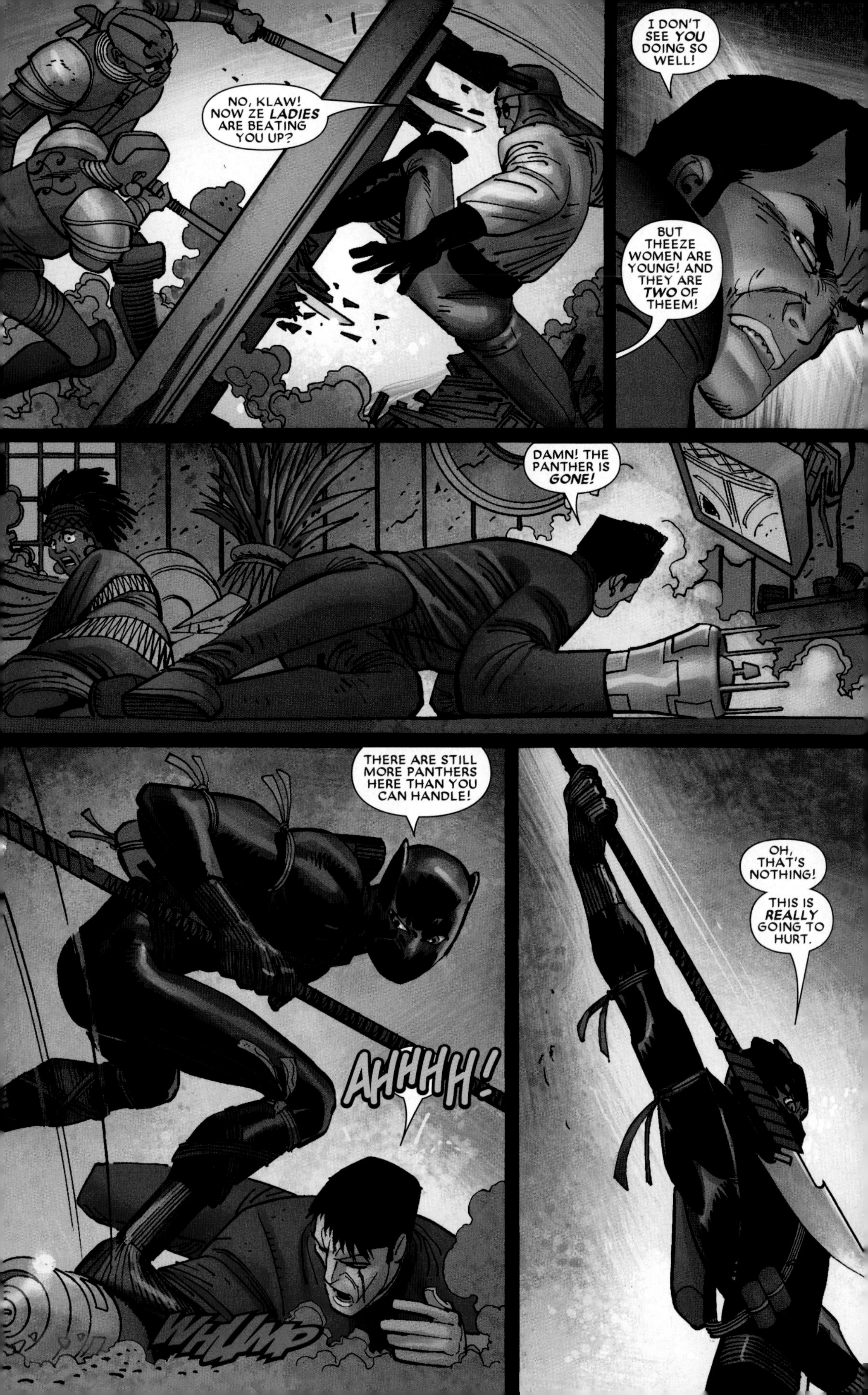
NO, KLAW! NOW ZE LADIES ARE BEATING YOU UP?
I DON'T SEE YOU DOING SO WELL!
BUT THEEZE WOMEN ARE YOUNG! AND THEY ARE TWO OF THEEM!
DAMN! THE PANTHER IS GONE!
THERE ARE STILL MORE PANTHERS HERE THAN YOU CAN HANDLE!
AHHHH!
WHUMP
OH, THAT'S NOTHING!
THIS IS REALLY GOING TO HURT.

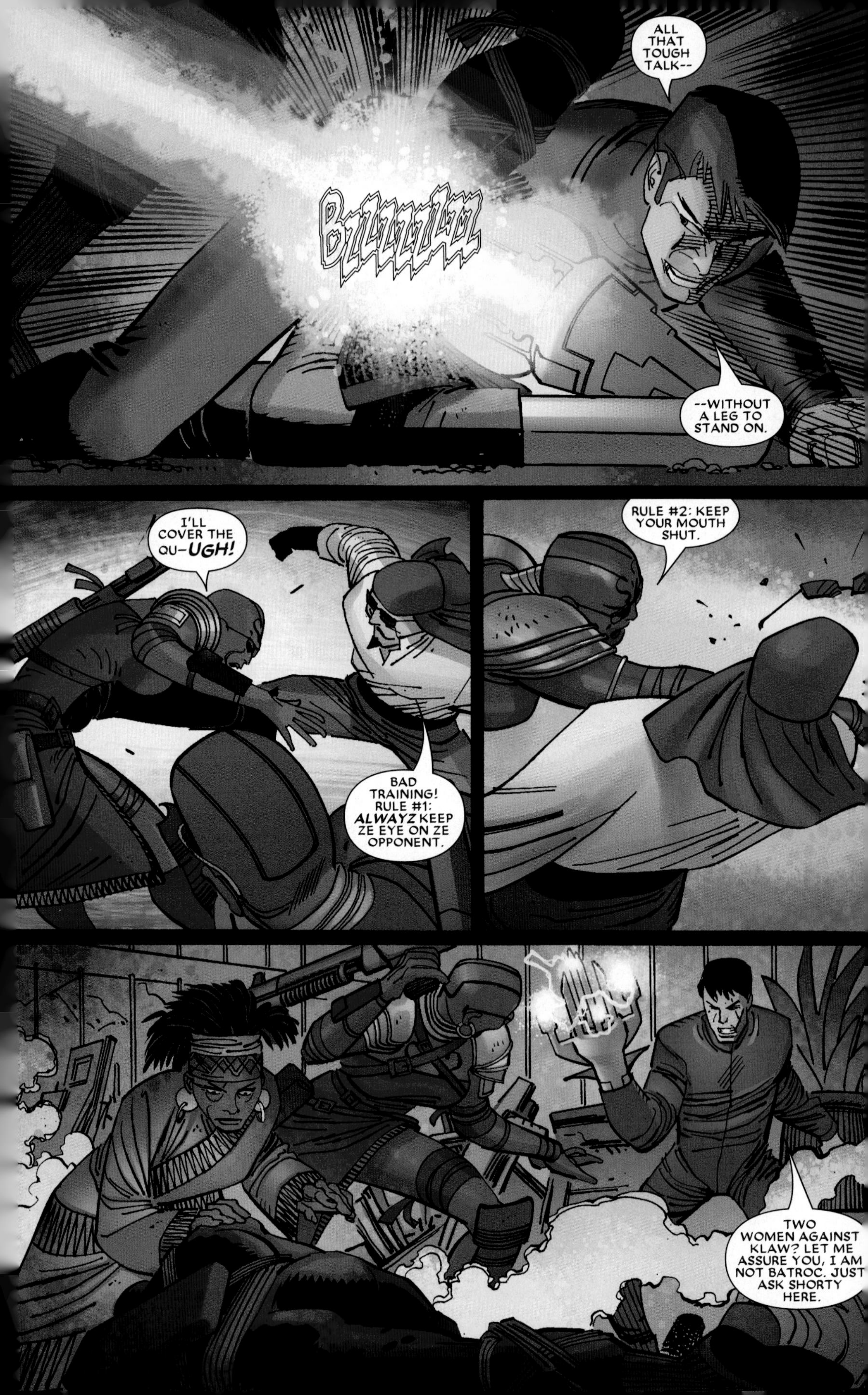
ALL THAT TOUGH TALK--
BZZZZZZZZ
--WITHOUT A LEG TO STAND ON.
I'LL COVER THE QU--UGH!
BAD TRAINING! RULE #1: ALWAYZ KEEP ZE EYE ON ZE OPPONENT.
RULE #2: KEEP YOUR MOUTH SHUT.
TWO WOMEN AGAINST KLAW? LET ME ASSURE YOU, I AM NOT BATROC. JUST ASK SHORTY HERE.

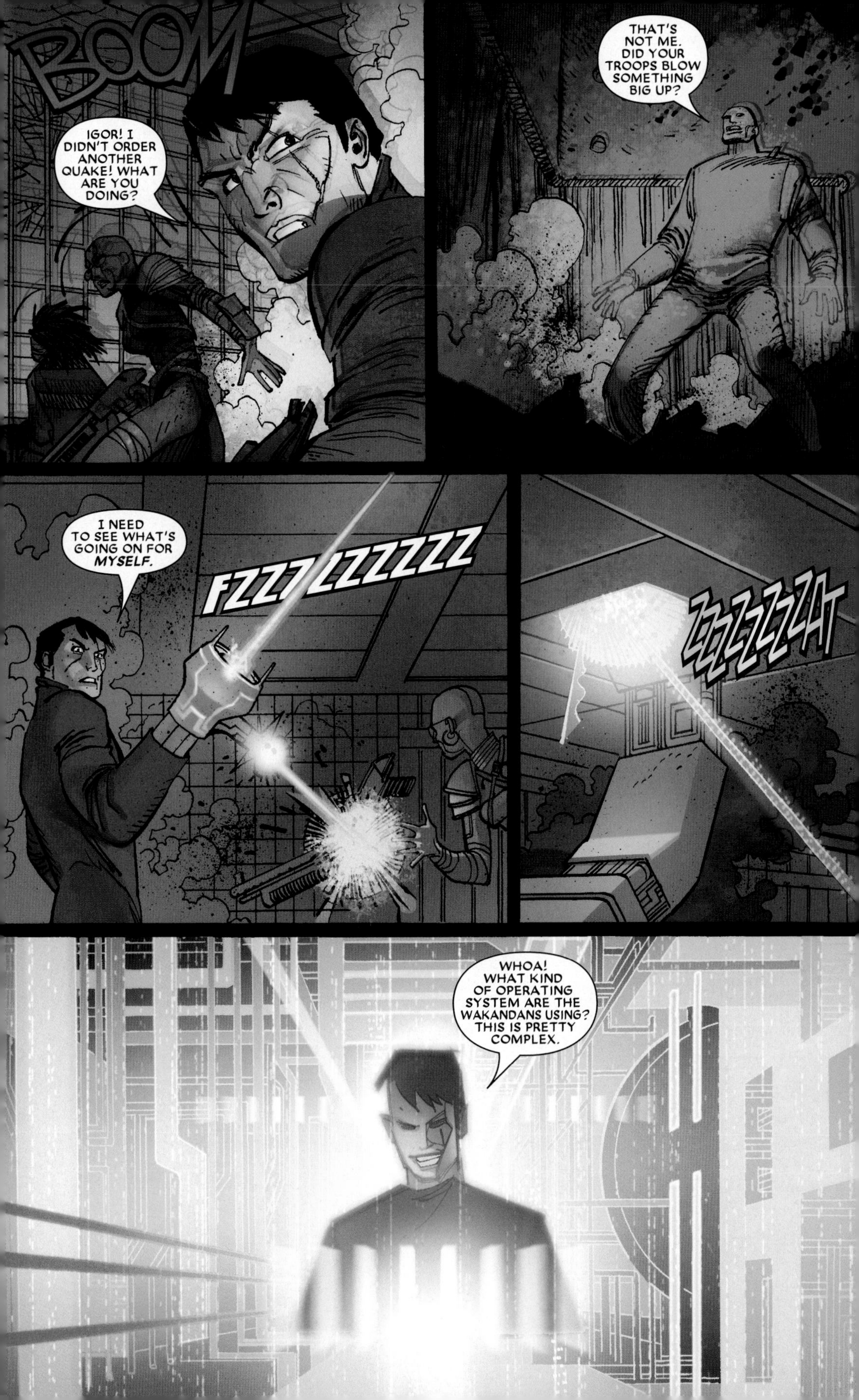
BOOM
IGOR! I DIDN'T ORDER ANOTHER QUAKE! WHAT ARE YOU DOING?
THAT'S NOT ME. DID YOUR TROOPS BLOW SOMETHING BIG UP?
I NEED TO SEE WHAT'S GOING ON FOR *MYSELF*.
FZZZZZZZZZ
ZZZZZZZZAT
WHOA! WHAT KIND OF OPERATING SYSTEM ARE THE WAKANDANS USING? THIS IS PRETTY COMPLEX.

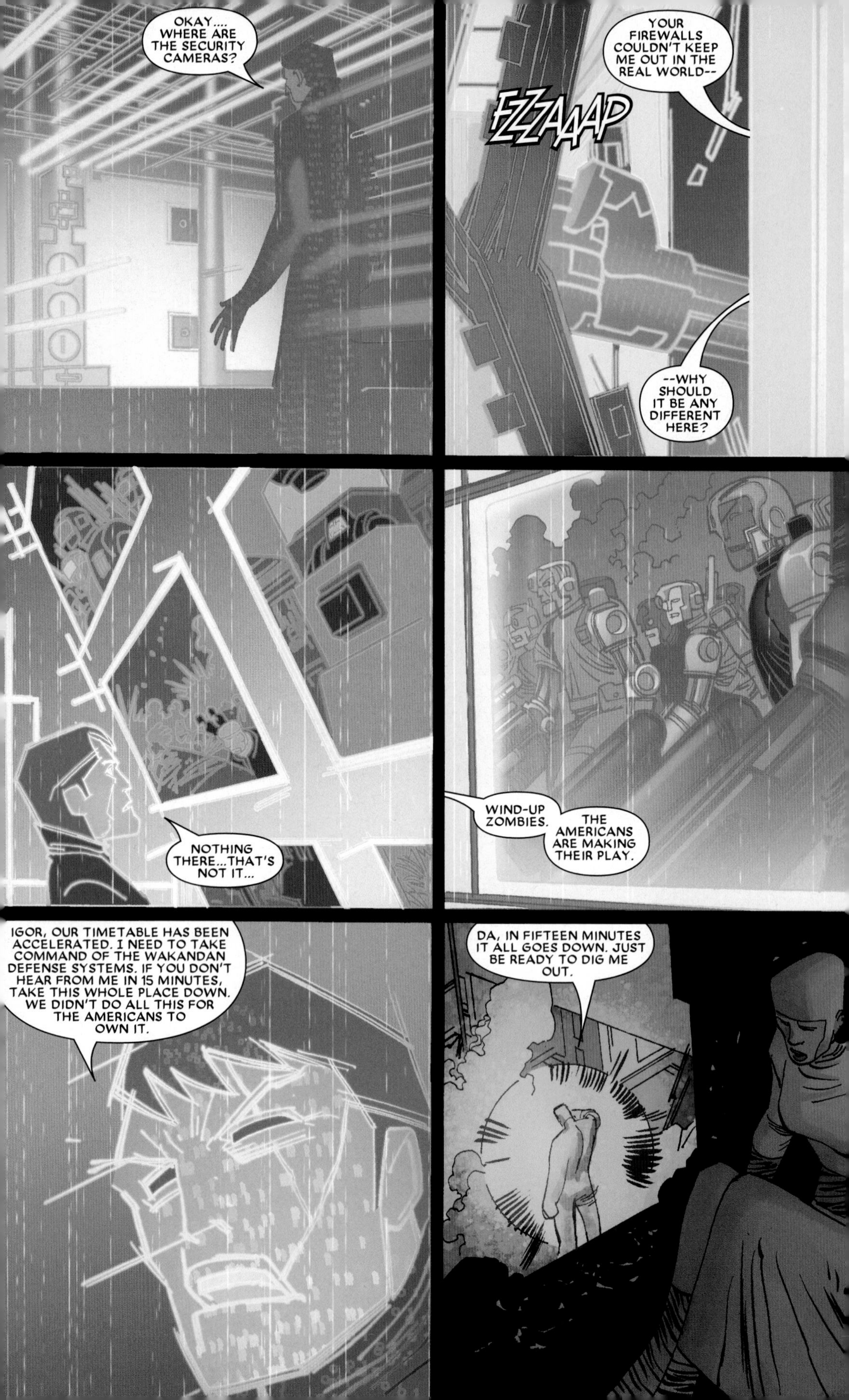
OKAY.... WHERE ARE THE SECURITY CAMERAS?
YOUR FIREWALLS COULDN'T KEEP ME OUT IN THE REAL WORLD--
FZZZAAAP
--WHY SHOULD IT BE ANY DIFFERENT HERE?
NOTHING THERE...THAT'S NOT IT...
WIND-UP ZOMBIES.
THE AMERICANS ARE MAKING THEIR PLAY.
IGOR, OUR TIMETABLE HAS BEEN ACCELERATED. I NEED TO TAKE COMMAND OF THE WAKANDAN DEFENSE SYSTEMS. IF YOU DON'T HEAR FROM ME IN 15 MINUTES, TAKE THIS WHOLE PLACE DOWN. WE DIDN'T DO ALL THIS FOR THE AMERICANS TO OWN IT.
DA, IN FIFTEEN MINUTES IT ALL GOES DOWN. JUST BE READY TO DIG ME OUT.

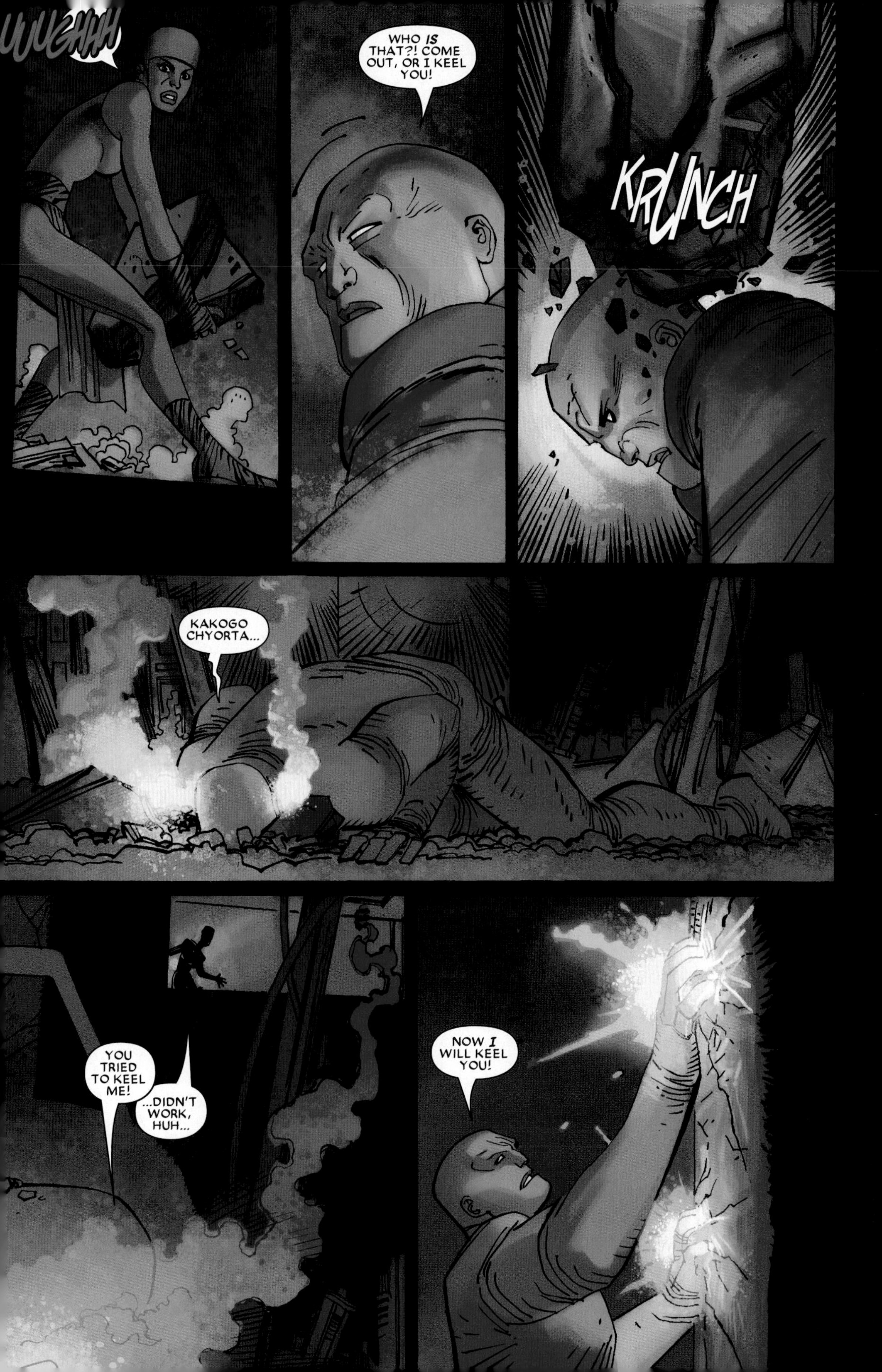
UUUGHHH
WHO IS THAT?! COME OUT, OR I KEEL YOU!
KRUNCH
KAKOGO CHYORTA...
YOU TRIED TO KEEL ME!
...DIDN'T WORK, HUH...
NOW I WILL KEEL YOU!

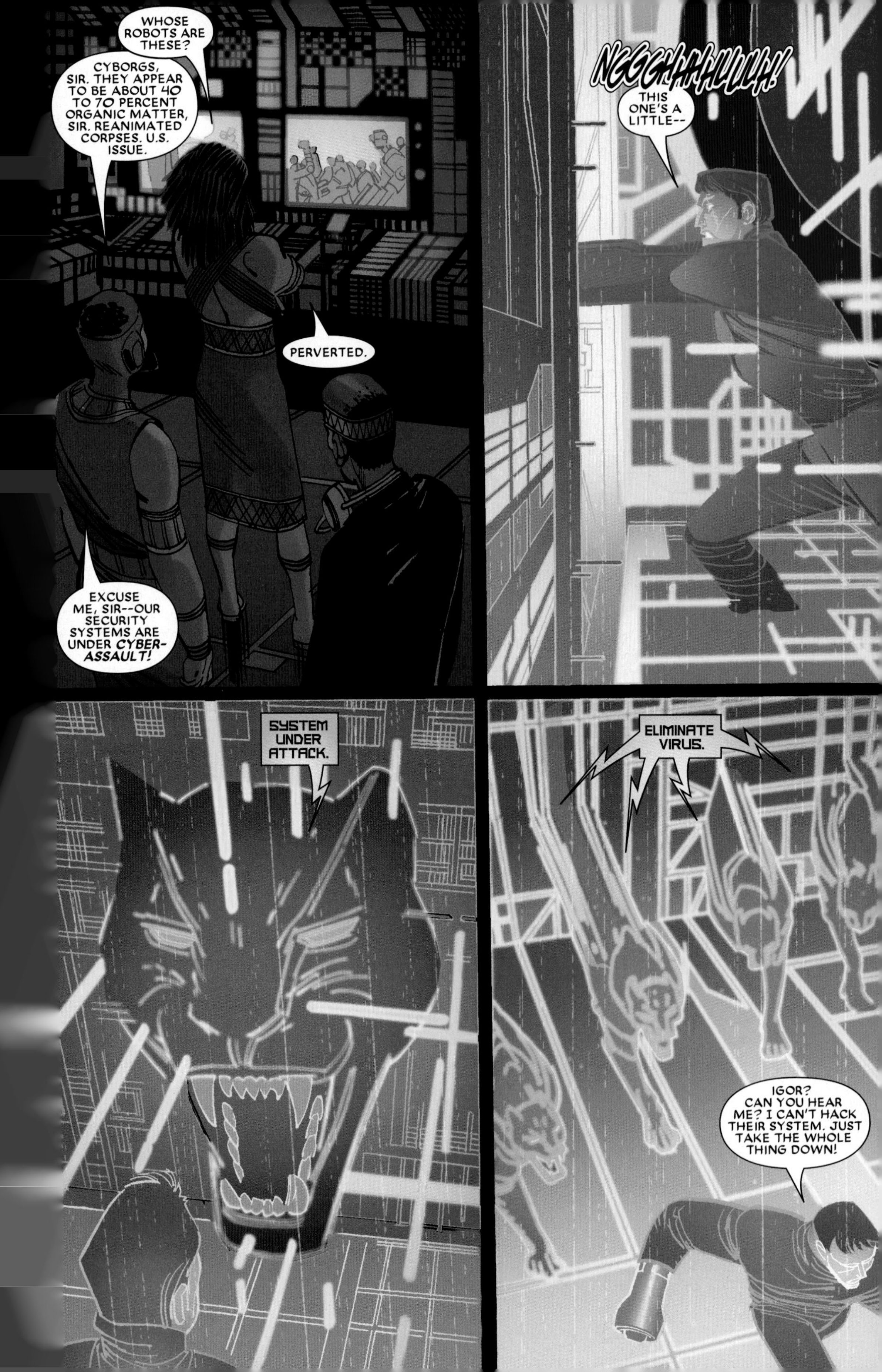
WHOSE ROBOTS ARE THESE?
CYBORGS, SIR. THEY APPEAR TO BE ABOUT 40 TO 70 PERCENT ORGANIC MATTER, SIR. REANIMATED CORPSES. U.S. ISSUE.
PERVERTED.
EXCUSE ME, SIR--OUR SECURITY SYSTEMS ARE UNDER *CYBER-ASSAULT!*
NGGGHHAAHUUUH!
THIS ONE'S A LITTLE--
SYSTEM UNDER ATTACK.
ELIMINATE VIRUS.
IGOR? CAN YOU HEAR ME? I CAN'T HACK THEIR SYSTEM. JUST TAKE THE WHOLE THING DOWN!

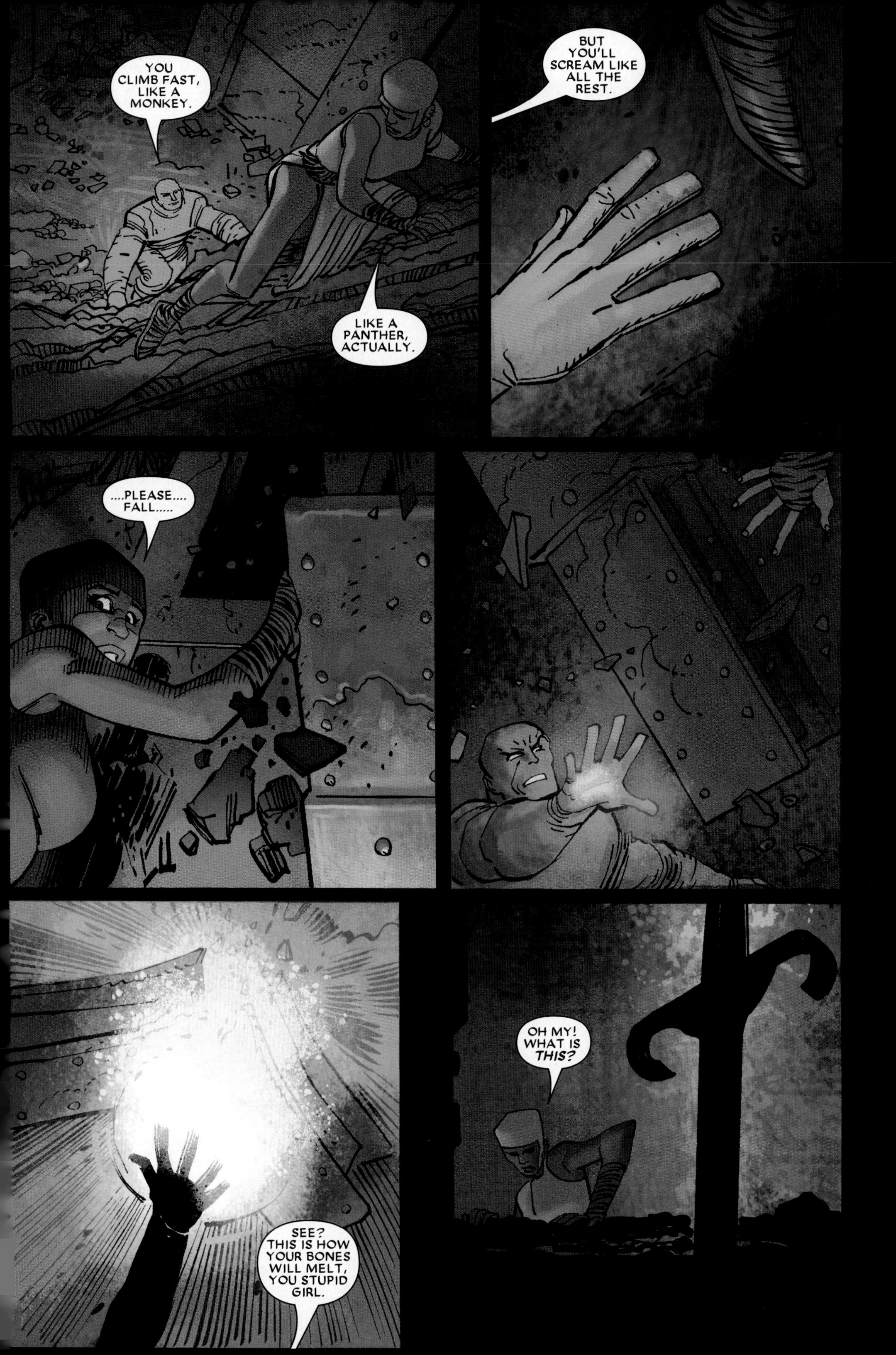
YOU CLIMB FAST, LIKE A MONKEY.
LIKE A PANTHER, ACTUALLY.
BUT YOU'LL SCREAM LIKE ALL THE REST.
....PLEASE.... FALL.....
SEE? THIS IS HOW YOUR BONES WILL MELT, YOU STUPID GIRL.
OH MY! WHAT IS *THIS?*

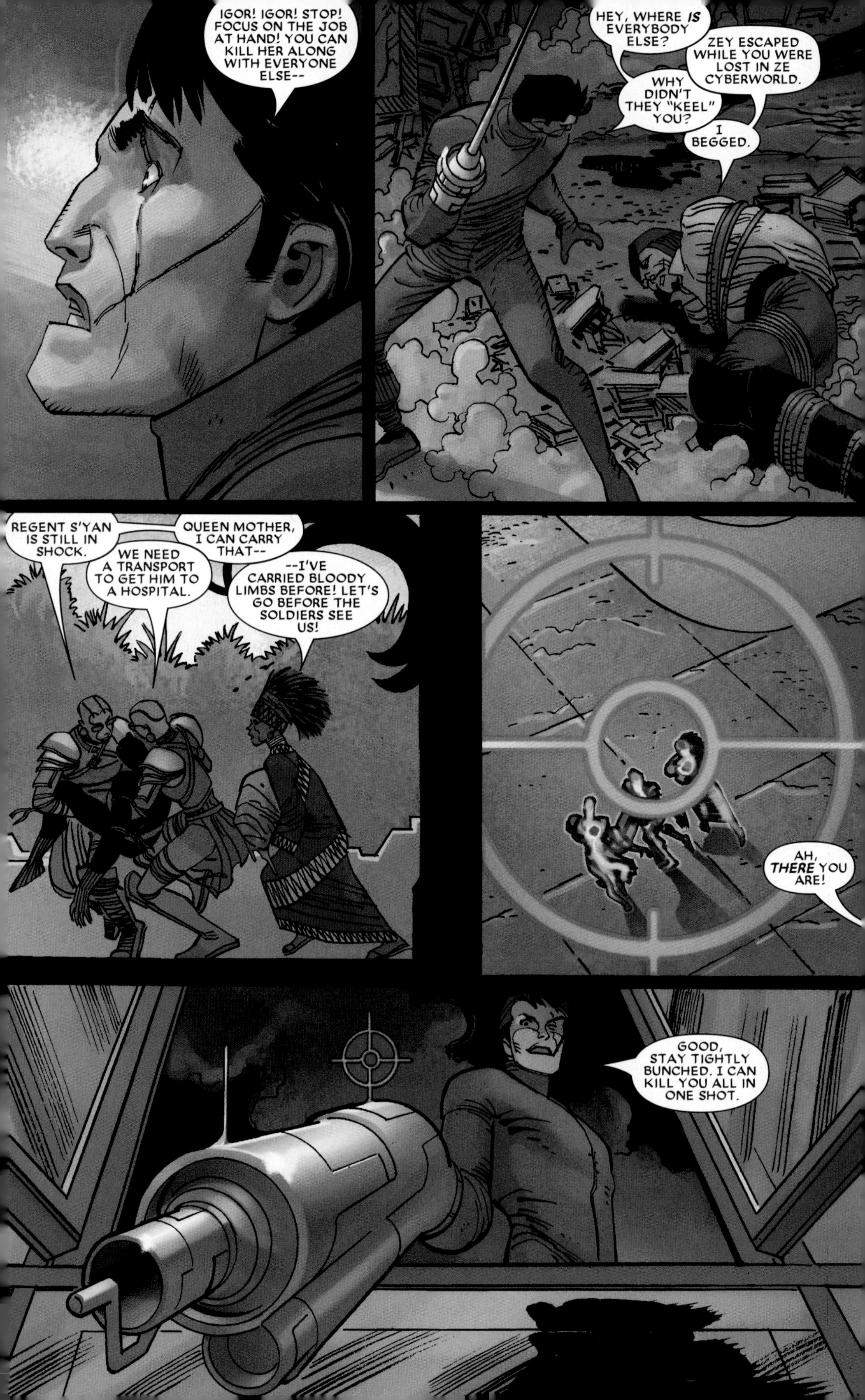
IGOR! IGOR! STOP! FOCUS ON THE JOB AT HAND! YOU CAN KILL HER ALONG WITH EVERYONE ELSE--
HEY, WHERE IS EVERYBODY ELSE?
ZEY ESCAPED WHILE YOU WERE LOST IN ZE CYBERWORLD.
WHY DIDN'T THEY "KEEL" YOU?
I BEGGED.
REGENT S'YAN IS STILL IN SHOCK.
WE NEED A TRANSPORT TO GET HIM TO A HOSPITAL.
QUEEN MOTHER, I CAN CARRY THAT--
--I'VE CARRIED BLOODY LIMBS BEFORE! LET'S GO BEFORE THE SOLDIERS SEE US!
AH, THERE YOU ARE!
GOOD, STAY TIGHTLY BUNCHED. I CAN KILL YOU ALL IN ONE SHOT.

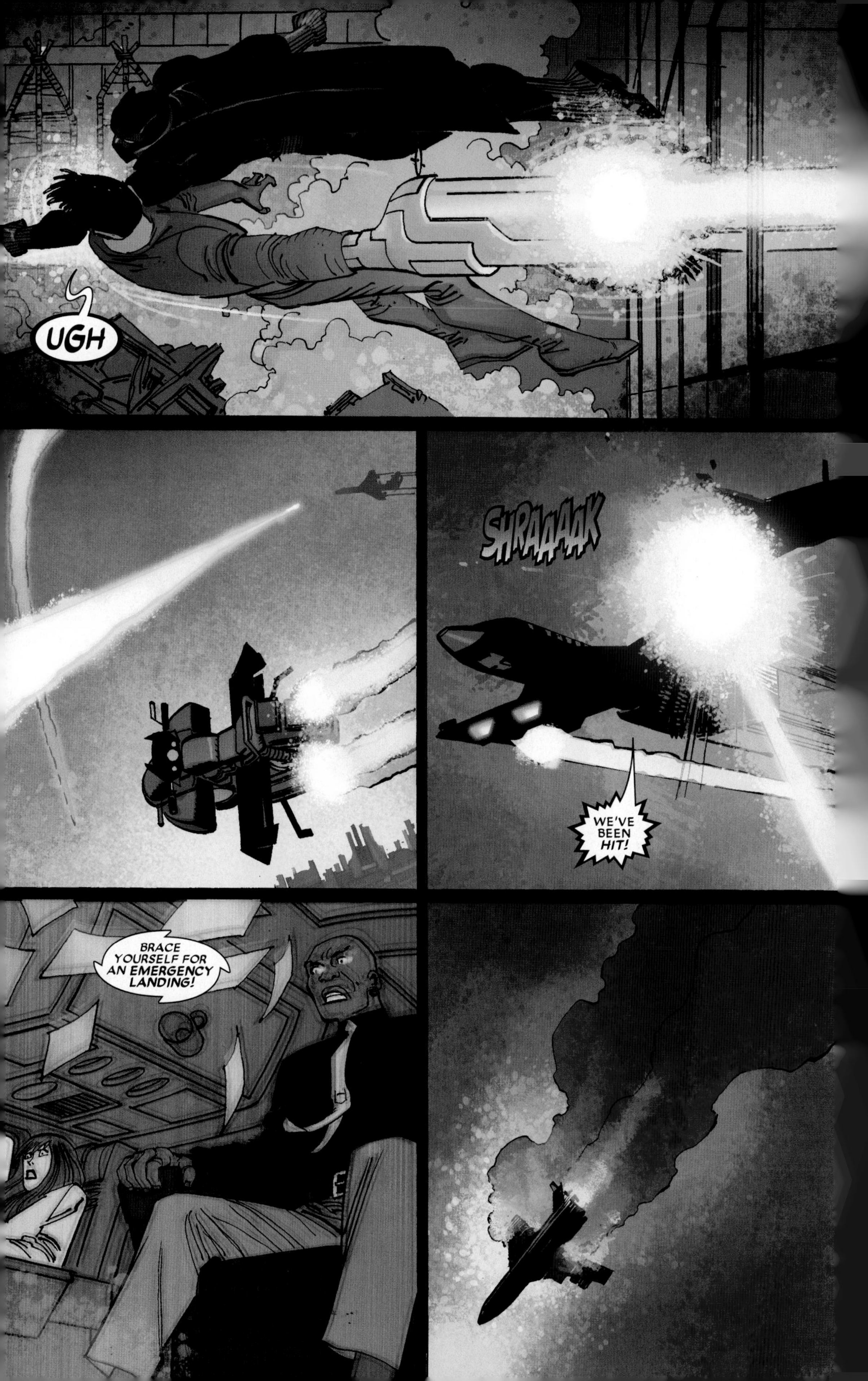
UGH
SHRAAAAK
WE'VE BEEN HIT!
BRACE YOURSELF FOR AN EMERGENCY LANDING!

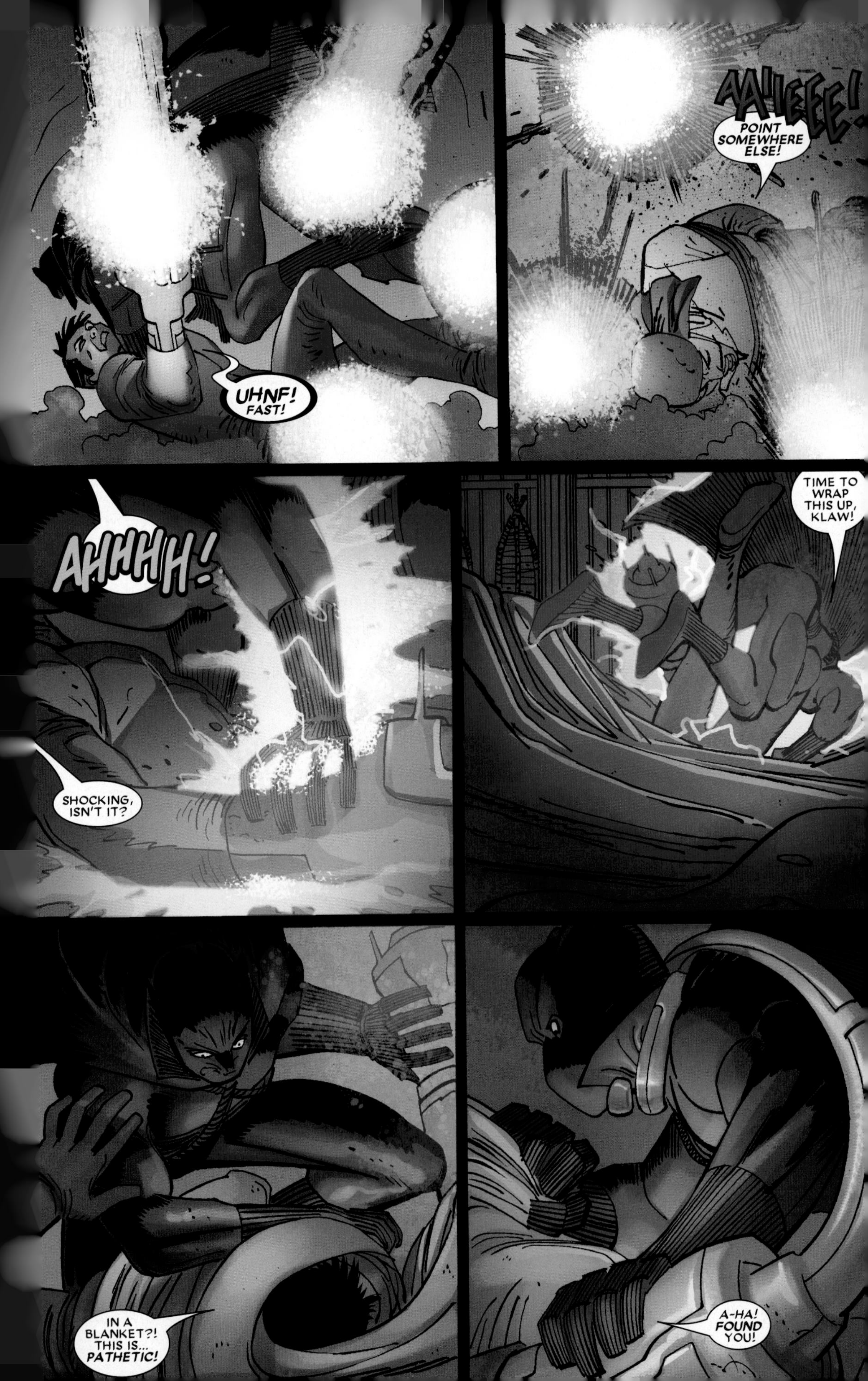
UHNF! FAST!
AA'IEEE!
POINT SOMEWHERE ELSE!
AHHHH!
SHOCKING, ISN'T IT?
TIME TO WRAP THIS UP, KLAW!
IN A BLANKET?! THIS IS... PATHETIC!
A-HA! FOUND YOU!

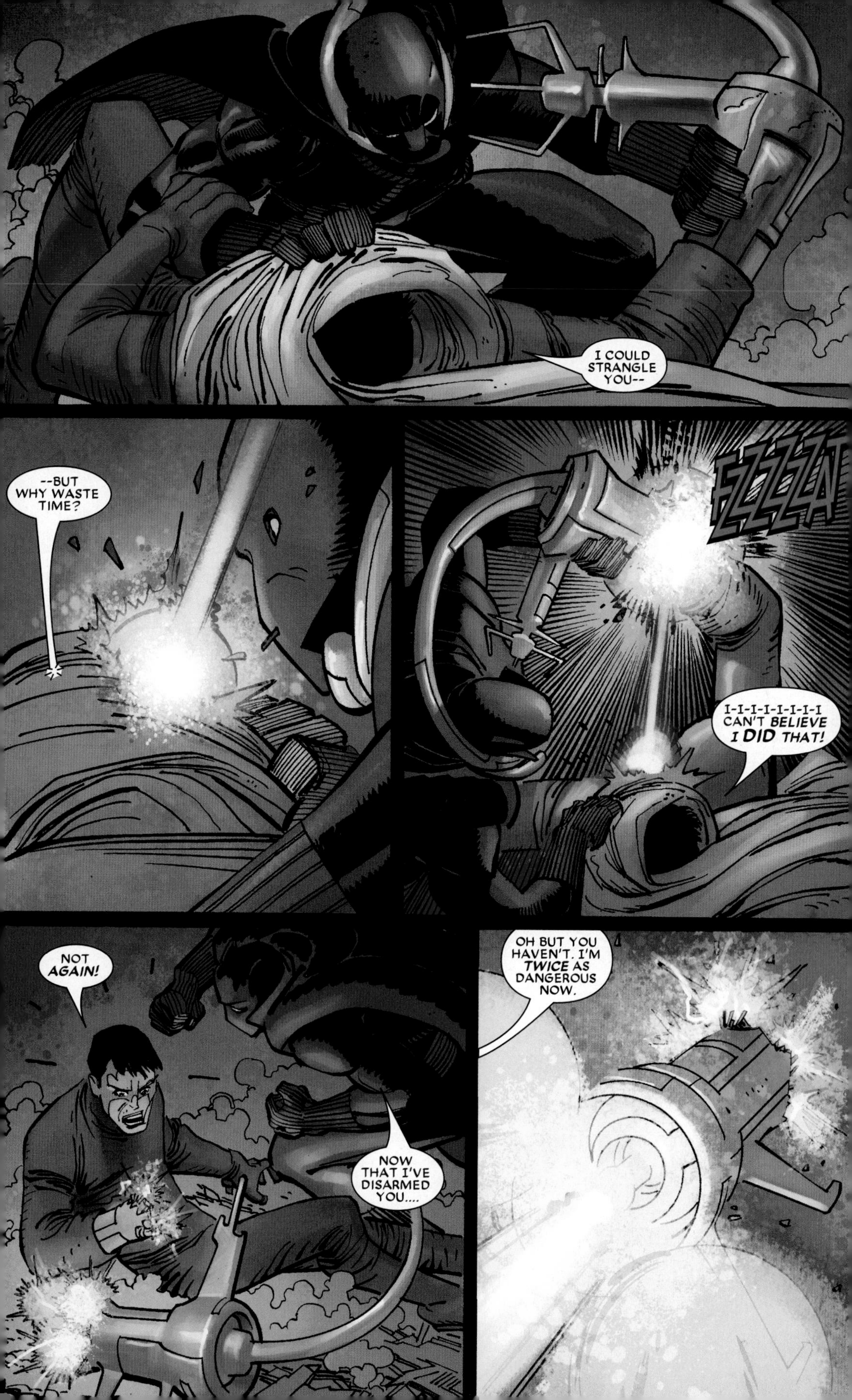
I COULD STRANGLE YOU--
--BUT WHY WASTE TIME?
FZZZZAT
I-I-I-I-I-I-I-I CAN'T *BELIEVE* *I DID* THAT!
NOT *AGAIN!*
NOW THAT I'VE DISARMED YOU....
OH BUT YOU HAVEN'T. I'M *TWICE* AS DANGEROUS NOW.

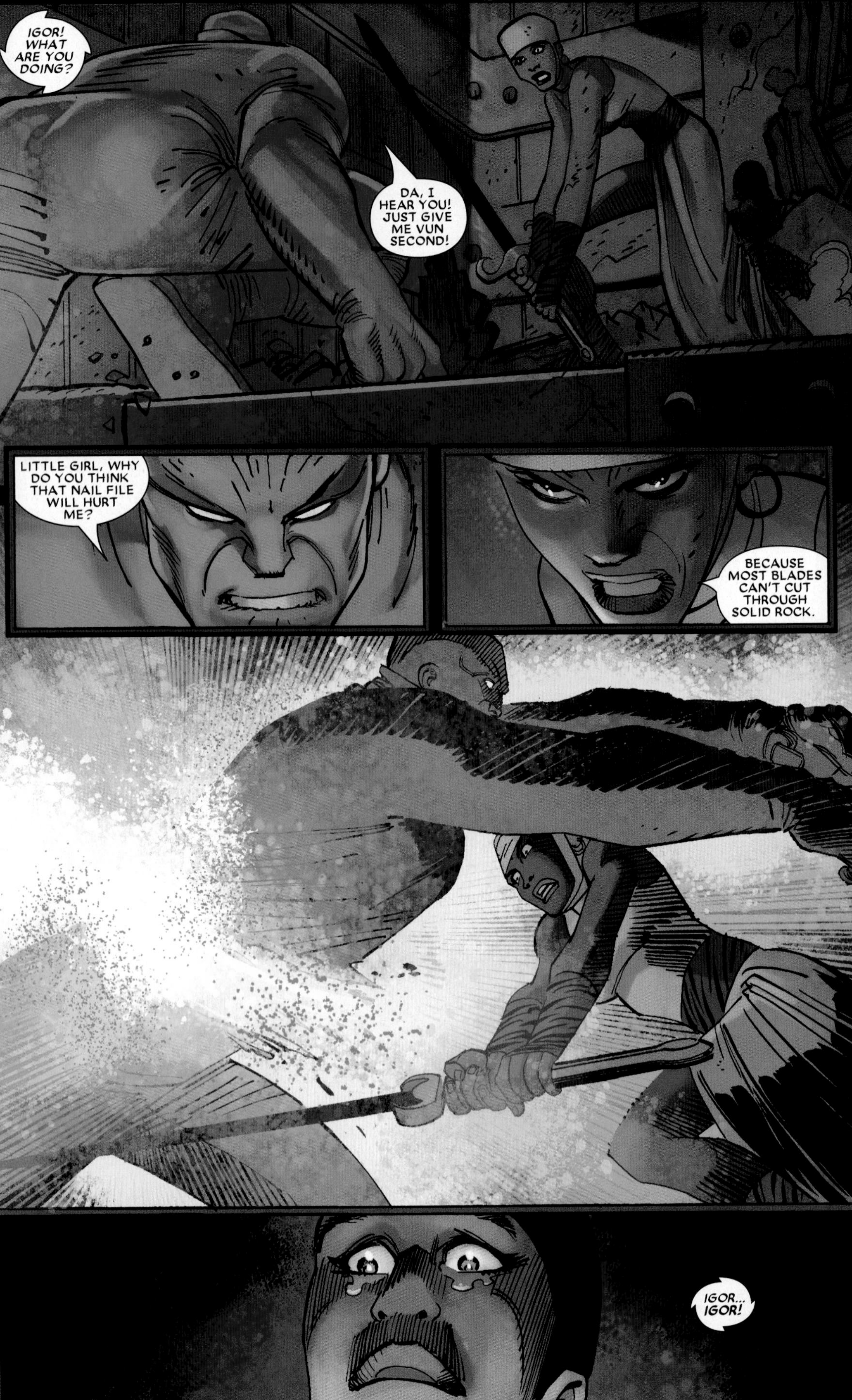
IGOR! WHAT ARE YOU DOING?
DA, I HEAR YOU! JUST GIVE ME VUN SECOND!
LITTLE GIRL, WHY DO YOU THINK THAT NAIL FILE WILL HURT ME?
BECAUSE MOST BLADES CAN'T CUT THROUGH SOLID ROCK.
IGOR... IGOR!

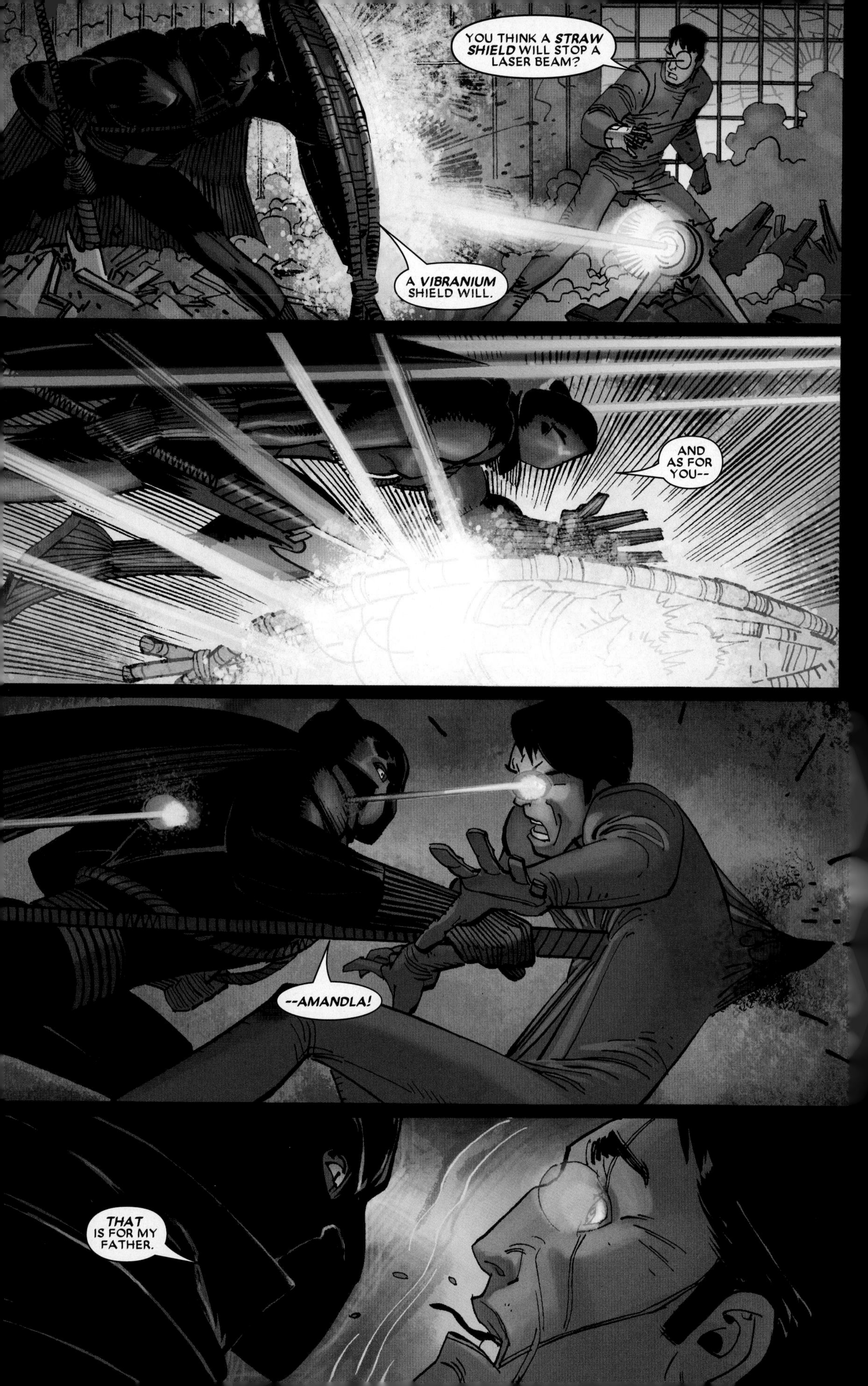
YOU THINK A STRAW SHIELD WILL STOP A LASER BEAM?
A VIBRANIUM SHIELD WILL.
AND AS FOR YOU--
--AMANDLA!
THAT IS FOR MY FATHER.

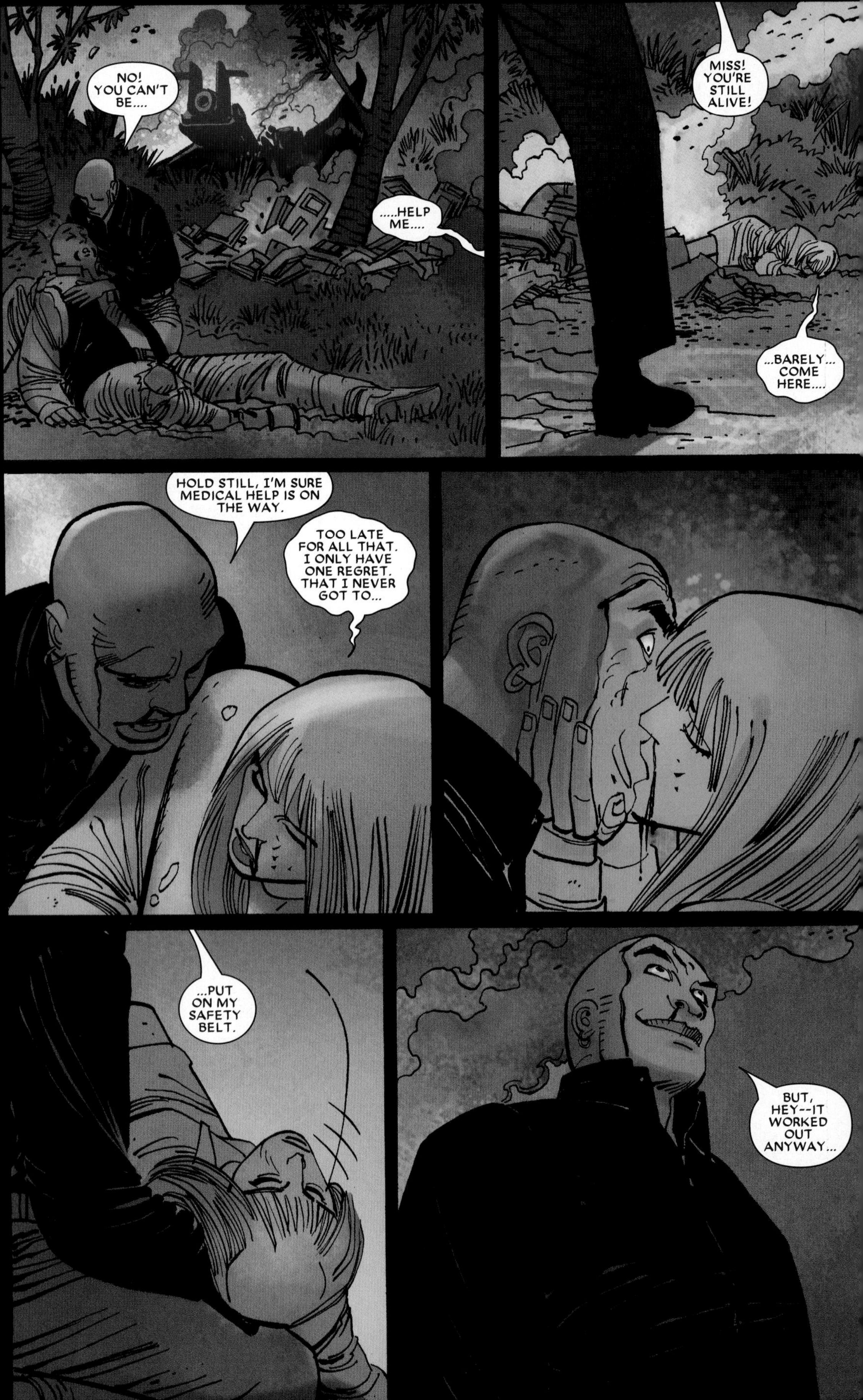
NO! YOU CAN'T BE....
.....HELP ME....
MISS! YOU'RE STILL ALIVE!
...BARELY... COME HERE....
HOLD STILL, I'M SURE MEDICAL HELP IS ON THE WAY.
TOO LATE FOR ALL THAT. I ONLY HAVE ONE REGRET. THAT I NEVER GOT TO...
...PUT ON MY SAFETY BELT.
BUT, HEY--IT WORKED OUT ANYWAY...

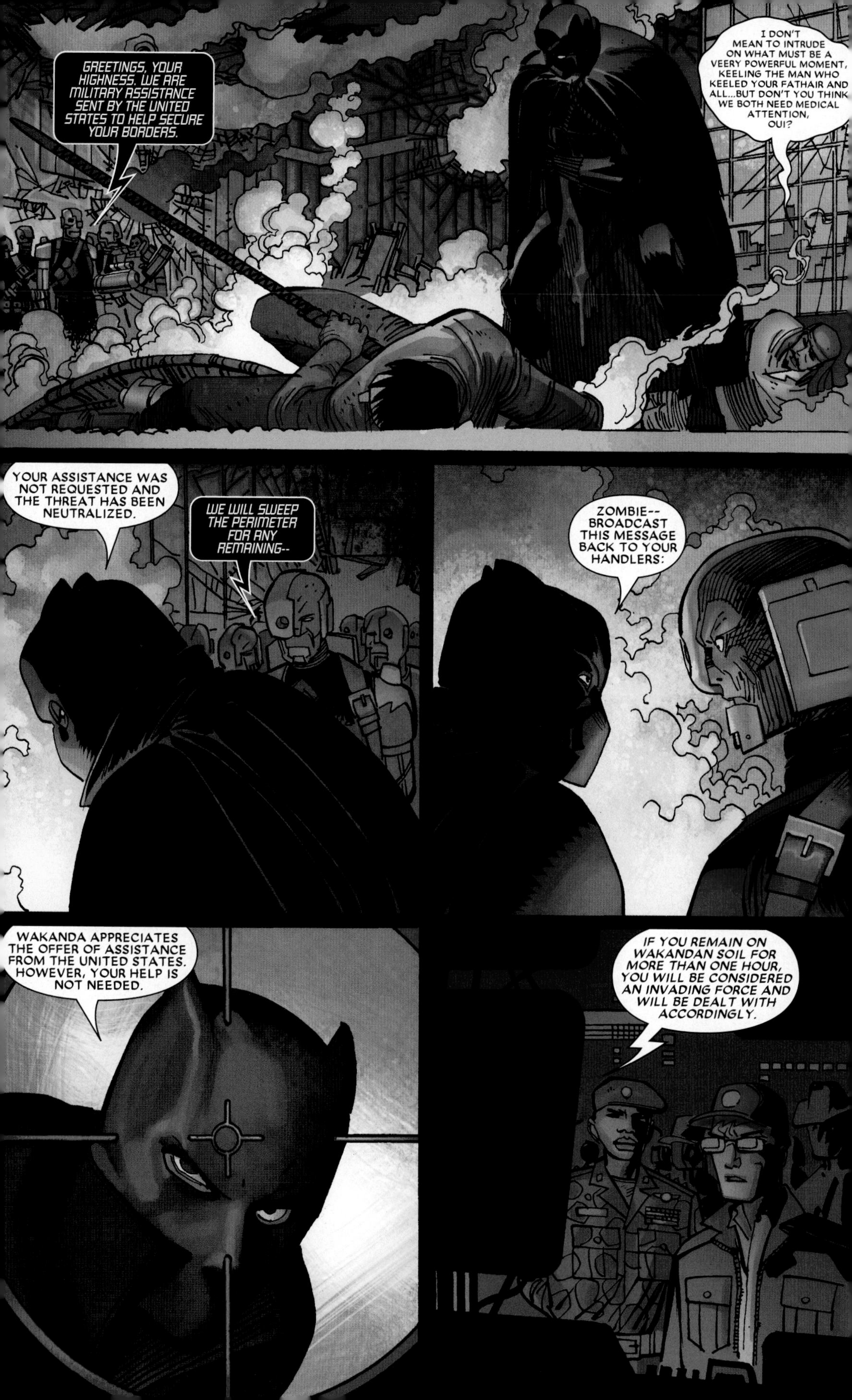
GREETINGS, YOUR HIGHNESS. WE ARE MILITARY ASSISTANCE SENT BY THE UNITED STATES TO HELP SECURE YOUR BORDERS.
I DON'T MEAN TO INTRUDE ON WHAT MUST BE A VEERY POWERFUL MOMENT, KEELING THE MAN WHO KEELED YOUR FATHAIR AND ALL...BUT DON'T YOU THINK WE BOTH NEED MEDICAL ATTENTION, OUI?
YOUR ASSISTANCE WAS NOT REQUESTED AND THE THREAT HAS BEEN NEUTRALIZED.
WE WILL SWEEP THE PERIMETER FOR ANY REMAINING--
ZOMBIE-- BROADCAST THIS MESSAGE BACK TO YOUR HANDLERS:
WAKANDA APPRECIATES THE OFFER OF ASSISTANCE FROM THE UNITED STATES. HOWEVER, YOUR HELP IS NOT NEEDED.
IF YOU REMAIN ON WAKANDAN SOIL FOR MORE THAN ONE HOUR, YOU WILL BE CONSIDERED AN INVADING FORCE AND WILL BE DEALT WITH ACCORDINGLY.

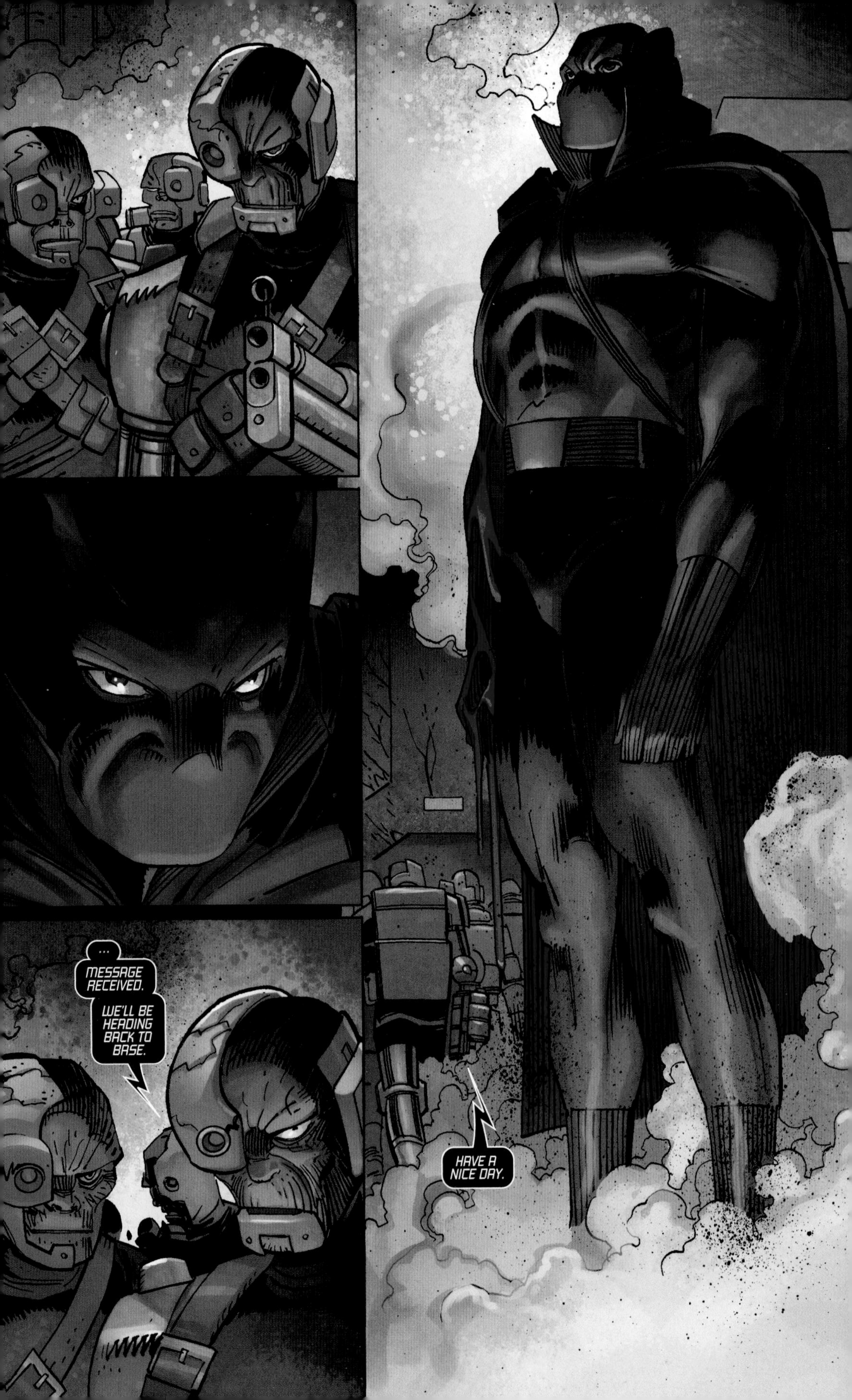
...
MESSAGE RECEIVED.
WE'LL BE HEADING BACK TO BASE.
HAVE A NICE DAY.

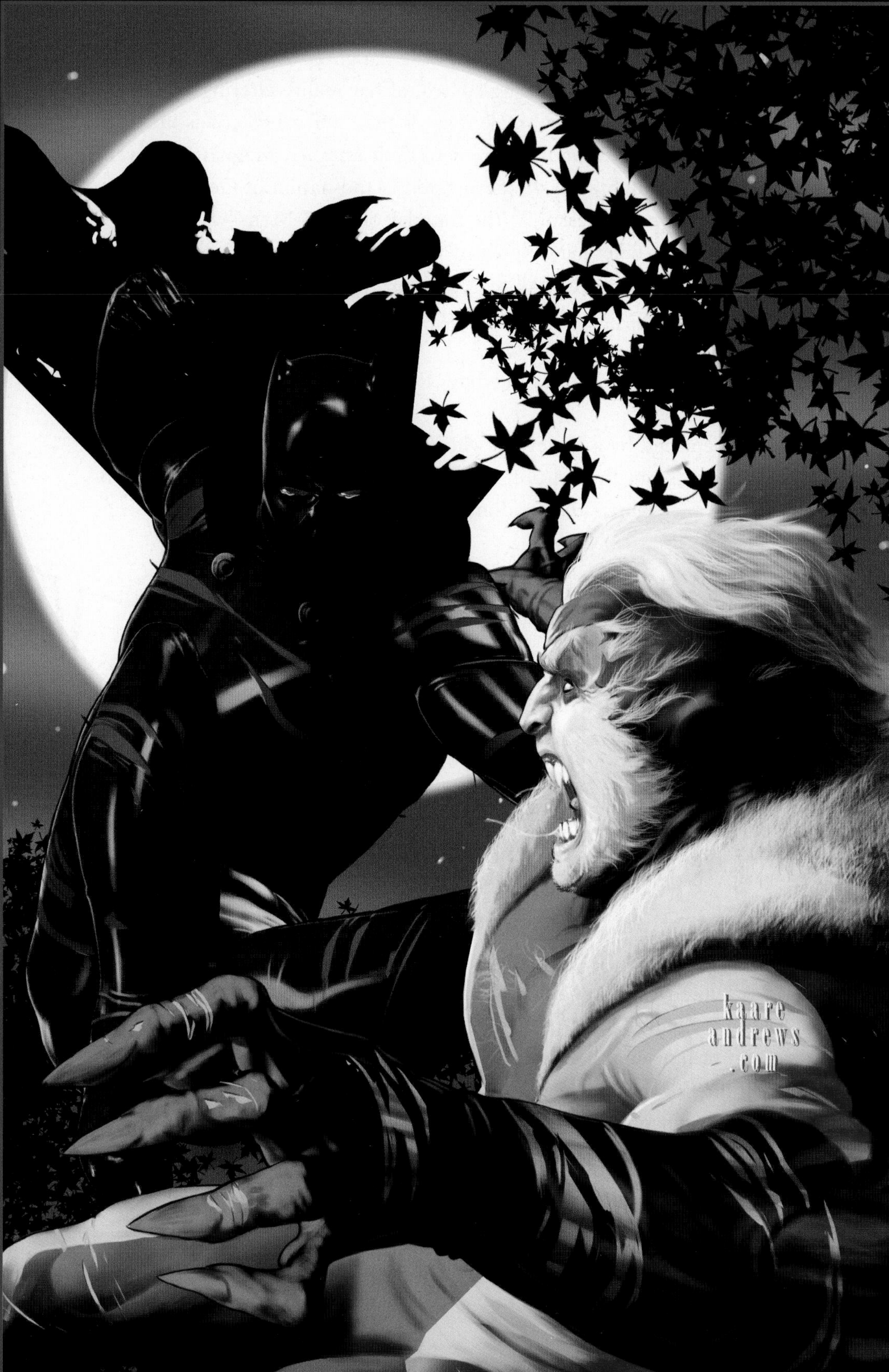
kaare
andrews
.com

The New Avengers and the Astonishing X-Men met to discuss the fate of
Wanda Maximoff, the Scarlet Witch—the daughter of the powerful mutant
terrorist Magneto. After losing control of her reality-altering powers and
suffering a total nervous breakdown, Wanda unleashed chaos upon the
Avengers, killing and injuring many of their number. Magneto intervened
and took his daughter to the devastated island-nation of Genosha, where
Charles Xavier—Professor X, the founder of the X-Men—was to help her
recover. Xavier failed, and now it is up to Wanda's friends and teammates
to decide whether she will live or die. But Magneto, Wanda, and her
brother Pietro disappear...

Then the world burns to white. Reality as we knew it is gone...

...to be replaced by a society in which humans are the oppressed minority
and mutants run the culture, ruling over all existing countries, religions,
and politics. A kingdom united under the House of M.

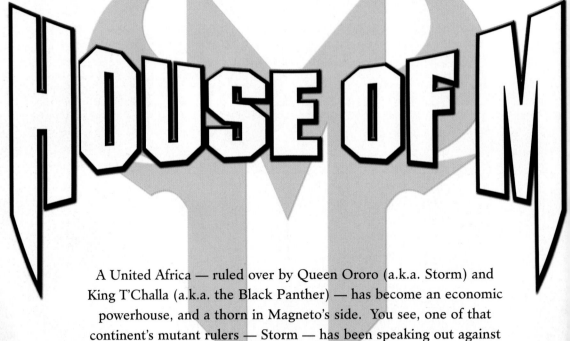

A United Africa — ruled over by Queen Ororo (a.k.a. Storm) and
King T'Challa (a.k.a. the Black Panther) — has become an economic
powerhouse, and a thorn in Magneto's side. You see, one of that
continent's mutant rulers — Storm — has been speaking out against
the persistence of supremacist notions in the mutant-controlled world...
something Magneto simply can't abide.

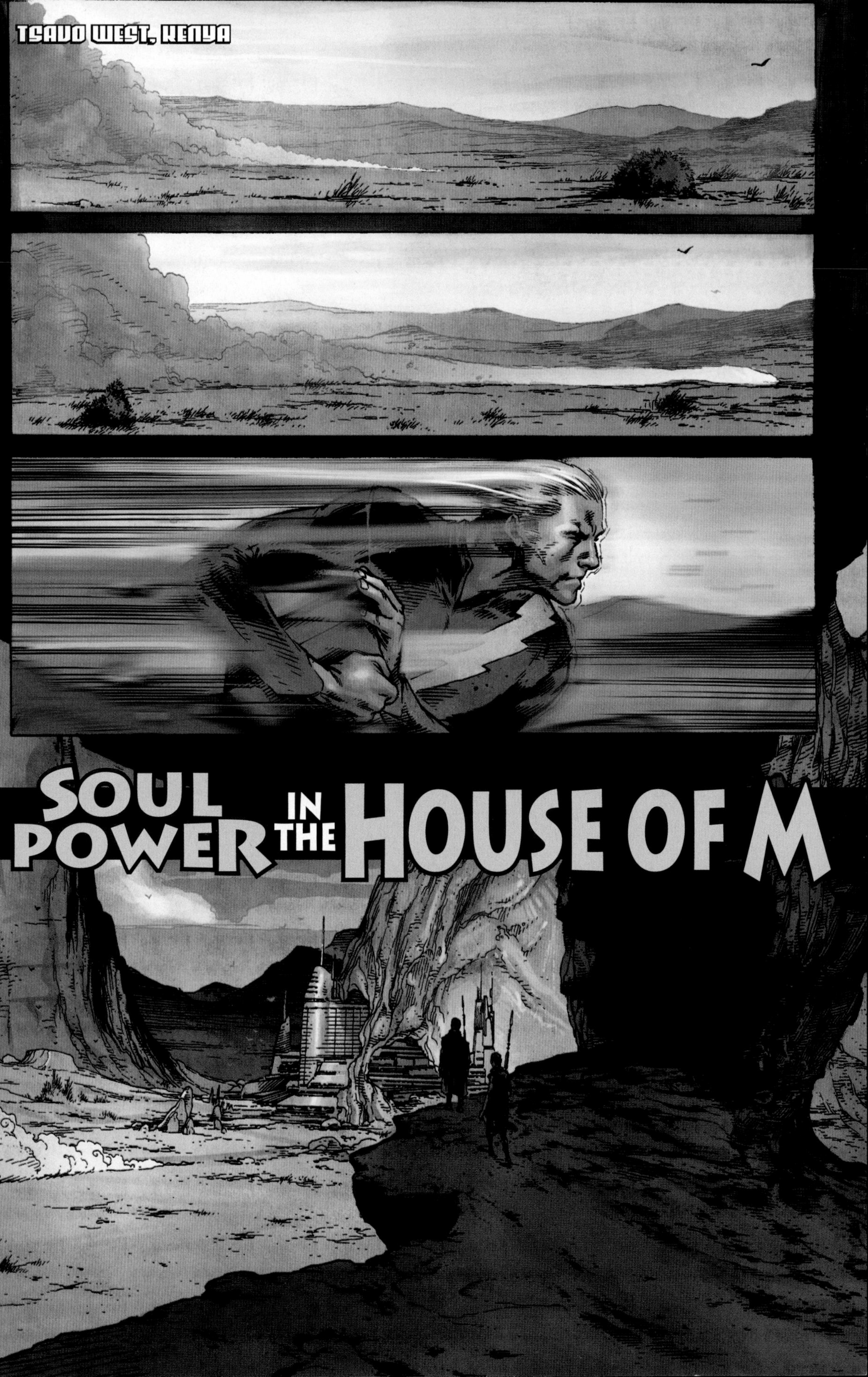
TSAVO WEST, KENYA
SOUL POWER IN THE HOUSE OF M

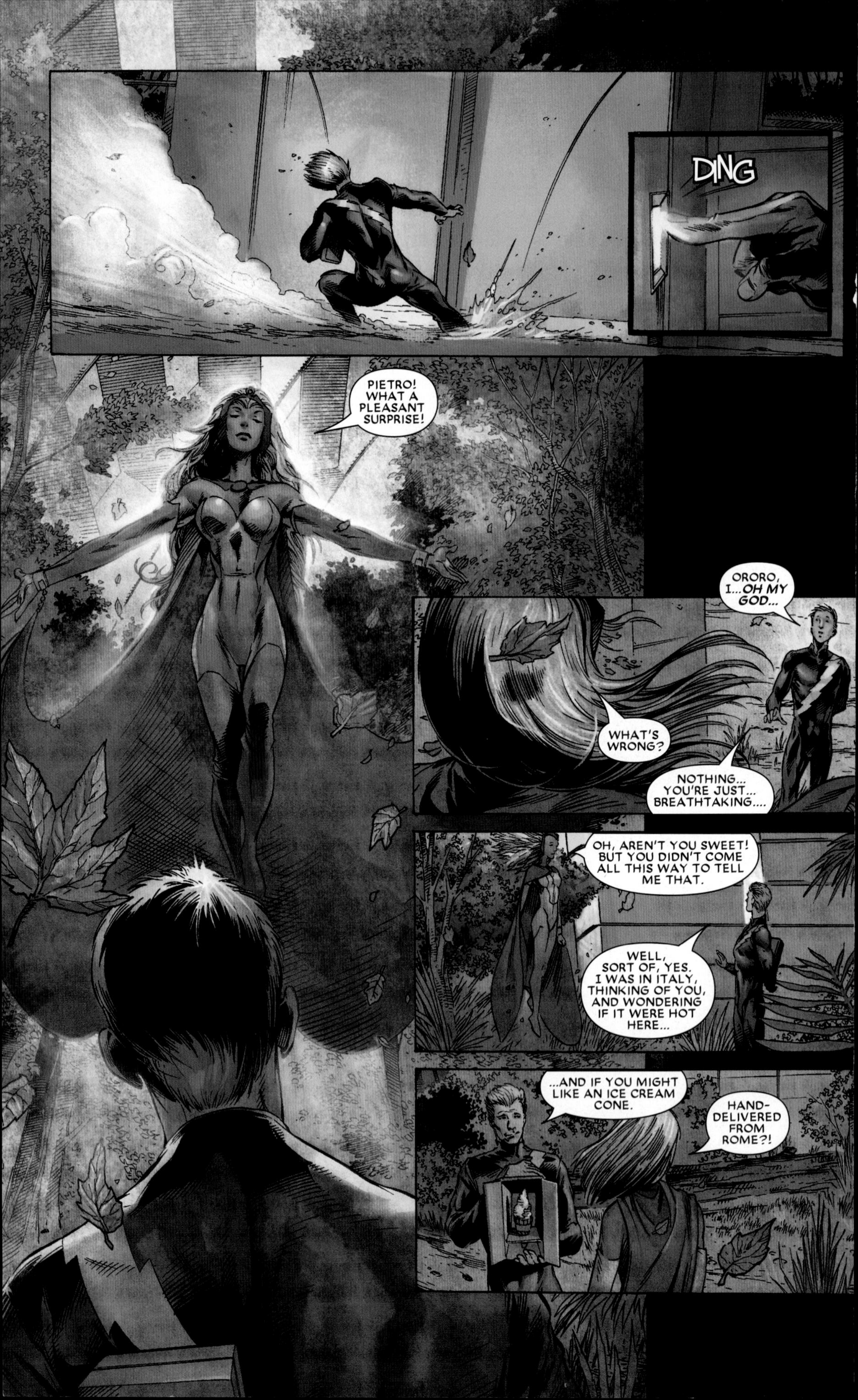
DING
PIETRO! WHAT A PLEASANT SURPRISE!
ORORO, I...OH MY GOD...
WHAT'S WRONG?
NOTHING... YOU'RE JUST... BREATHTAKING....
OH, AREN'T YOU SWEET! BUT YOU DIDN'T COME ALL THIS WAY TO TELL ME THAT.
WELL, SORT OF, YES. I WAS IN ITALY, THINKING OF YOU, AND WONDERING IF IT WERE HOT HERE...
...AND IF YOU MIGHT LIKE AN ICE CREAM CONE.
HAND-DELIVERED FROM ROME?!

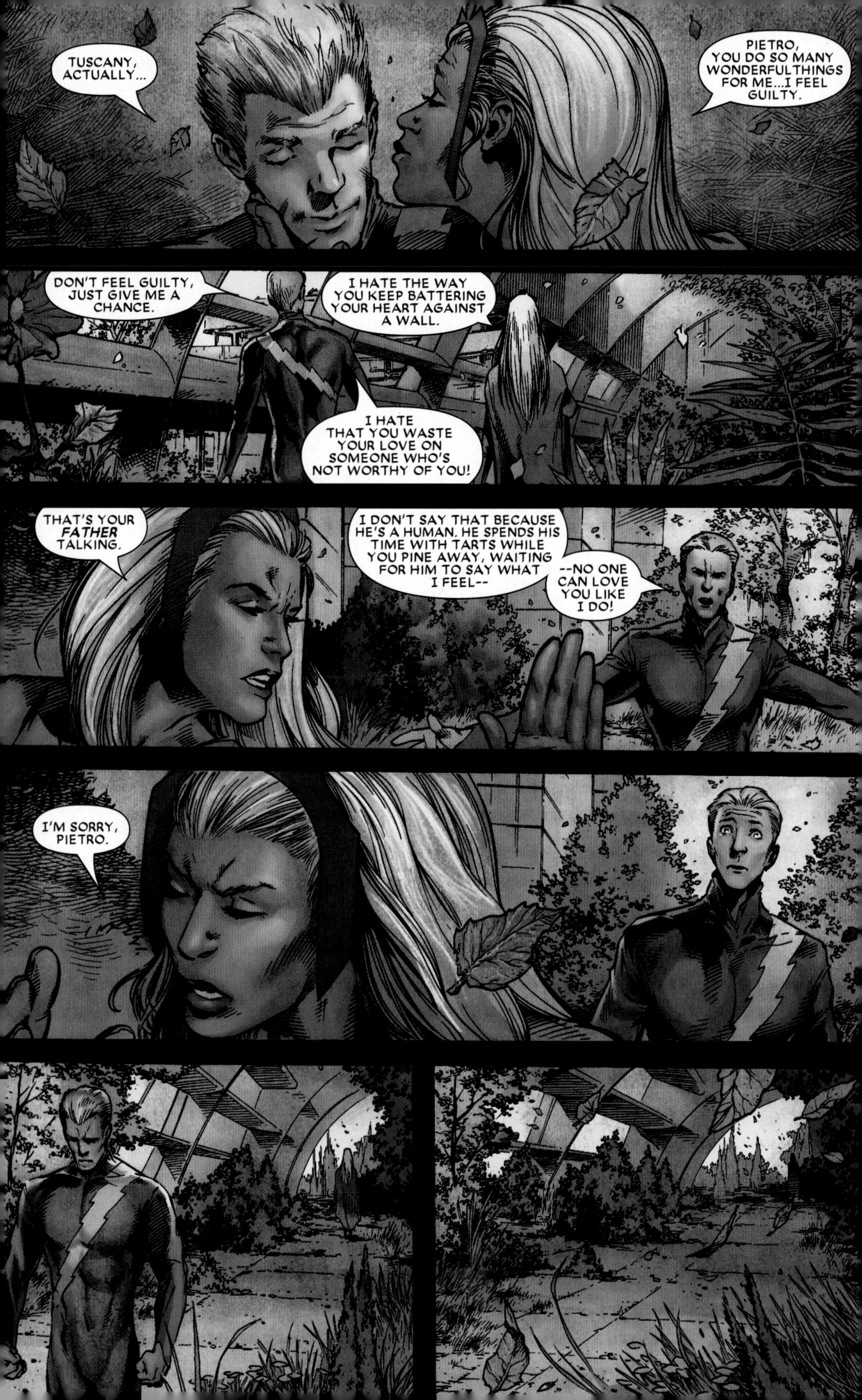
TUSCANY, ACTUALLY...
PIETRO, YOU DO SO MANY WONDERFULTHINGS FOR ME...I FEEL GUILTY.
DON'T FEEL GUILTY, JUST GIVE ME A CHANCE.
I HATE THE WAY YOU KEEP BATTERING YOUR HEART AGAINST A WALL.
I HATE THAT YOU WASTE YOUR LOVE ON SOMEONE WHO'S NOT WORTHY OF YOU!
THAT'S YOUR *FATHER* TALKING.
I DON'T SAY THAT BECAUSE HE'S A HUMAN. HE SPENDS HIS TIME WITH TARTS WHILE YOU PINE AWAY, WAITING FOR HIM TO SAY WHAT I FEEL--
--NO ONE CAN LOVE YOU LIKE I DO!
I'M SORRY, PIETRO.

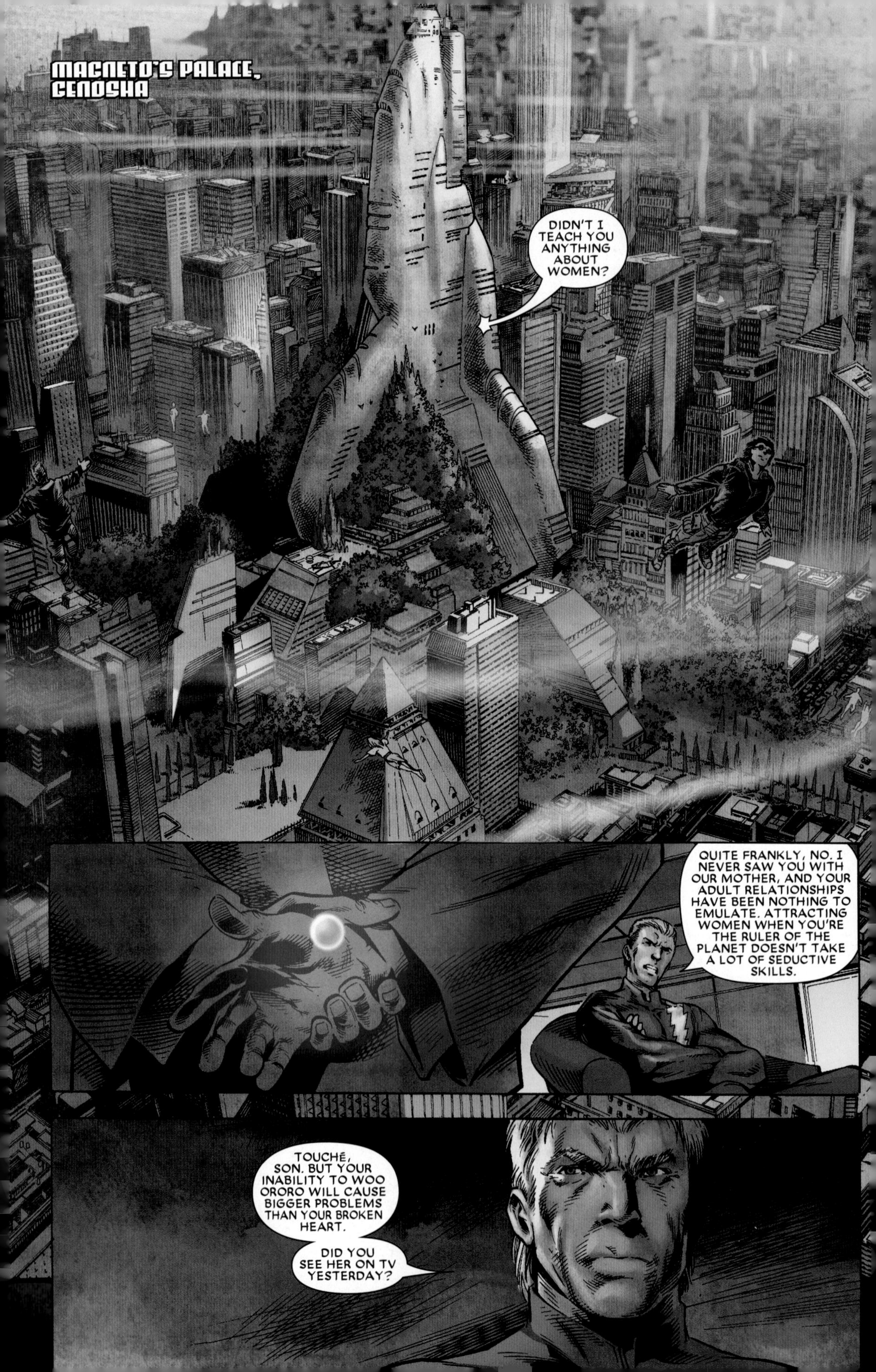
MAGNETO'S PALACE, GENOSHA
DIDN'T I TEACH YOU ANYTHING ABOUT WOMEN?
QUITE FRANKLY, NO. I NEVER SAW YOU WITH OUR MOTHER, AND YOUR ADULT RELATIONSHIPS HAVE BEEN NOTHING TO EMULATE. ATTRACTING WOMEN WHEN YOU'RE THE RULER OF THE PLANET DOESN'T TAKE A LOT OF SEDUCTIVE SKILLS.
TOUCHÉ, SON. BUT YOUR INABILITY TO WOO ORORO WILL CAUSE BIGGER PROBLEMS THAN YOUR BROKEN HEART.
DID YOU SEE HER ON TV YESTERDAY?

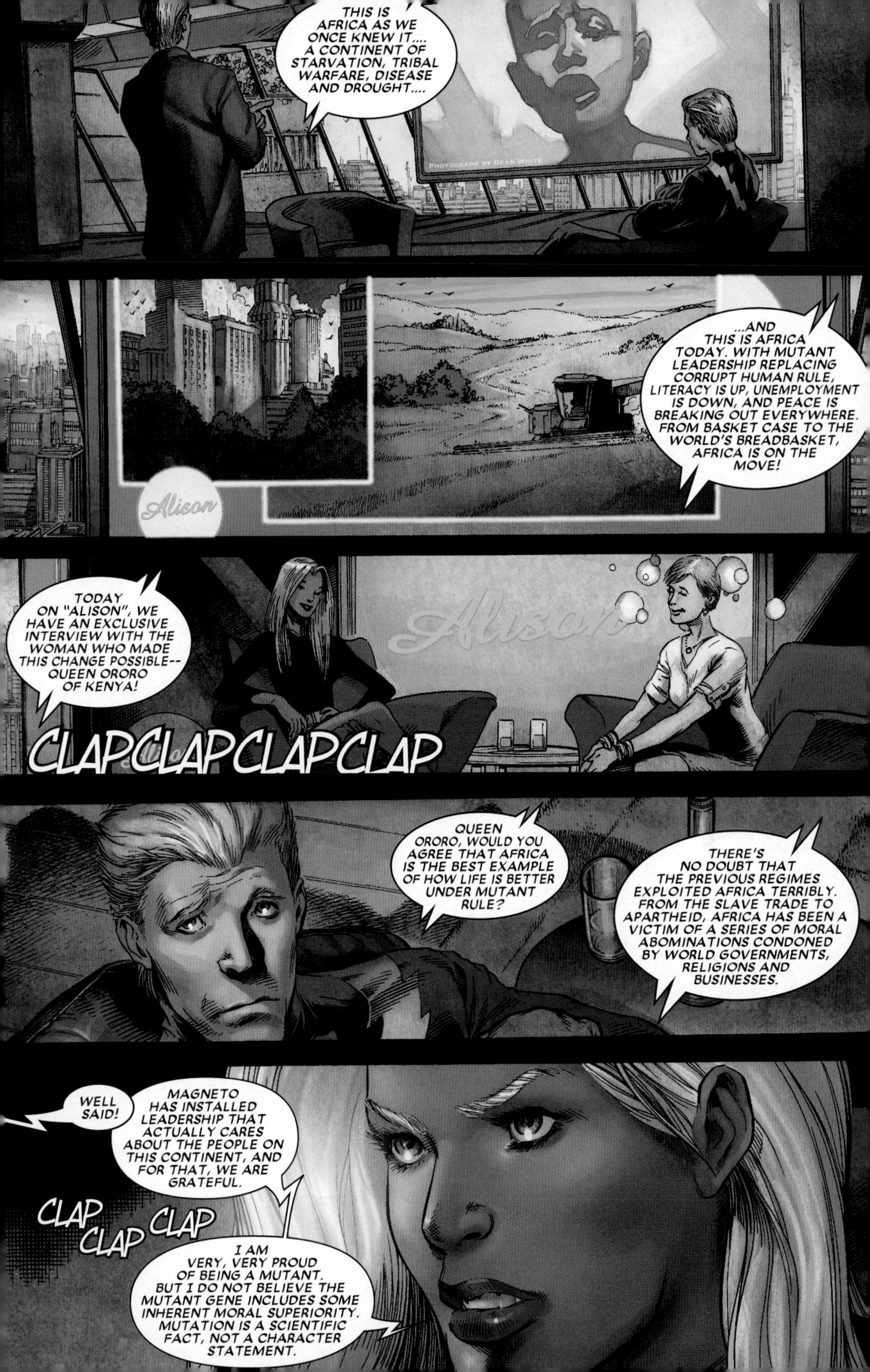
THIS IS AFRICA AS WE ONCE KNEW IT.... A CONTINENT OF STARVATION, TRIBAL WARFARE, DISEASE AND DROUGHT....
PHOTOGRAPH BY DEAN WHITE
...AND THIS IS AFRICA TODAY. WITH MUTANT LEADERSHIP REPLACING CORRUPT HUMAN RULE, LITERACY IS UP, UNEMPLOYMENT IS DOWN, AND PEACE IS BREAKING OUT EVERYWHERE. FROM BASKET CASE TO THE WORLD'S BREADBASKET, AFRICA IS ON THE MOVE!
Alison
TODAY ON "ALISON", WE HAVE AN EXCLUSIVE INTERVIEW WITH THE WOMAN WHO MADE THIS CHANGE POSSIBLE-- QUEEN ORORO OF KENYA!
Alison
CLAPCLAPCLAPCLAP
QUEEN ORORO, WOULD YOU AGREE THAT AFRICA IS THE BEST EXAMPLE OF HOW LIFE IS BETTER UNDER MUTANT RULE?
THERE'S NO DOUBT THAT THE PREVIOUS REGIMES EXPLOITED AFRICA TERRIBLY. FROM THE SLAVE TRADE TO APARTHEID, AFRICA HAS BEEN A VICTIM OF A SERIES OF MORAL ABOMINATIONS CONDONED BY WORLD GOVERNMENTS, RELIGIONS AND BUSINESSES.
WELL SAID!
MAGNETO HAS INSTALLED LEADERSHIP THAT ACTUALLY CARES ABOUT THE PEOPLE ON THIS CONTINENT, AND FOR THAT, WE ARE GRATEFUL.
CLAP CLAP CLAP
I AM VERY, VERY PROUD OF BEING A MUTANT. BUT I DO NOT BELIEVE THE MUTANT GENE INCLUDES SOME INHERENT MORAL SUPERIORITY. MUTATION IS A SCIENTIFIC FACT, NOT A CHARACTER STATEMENT.

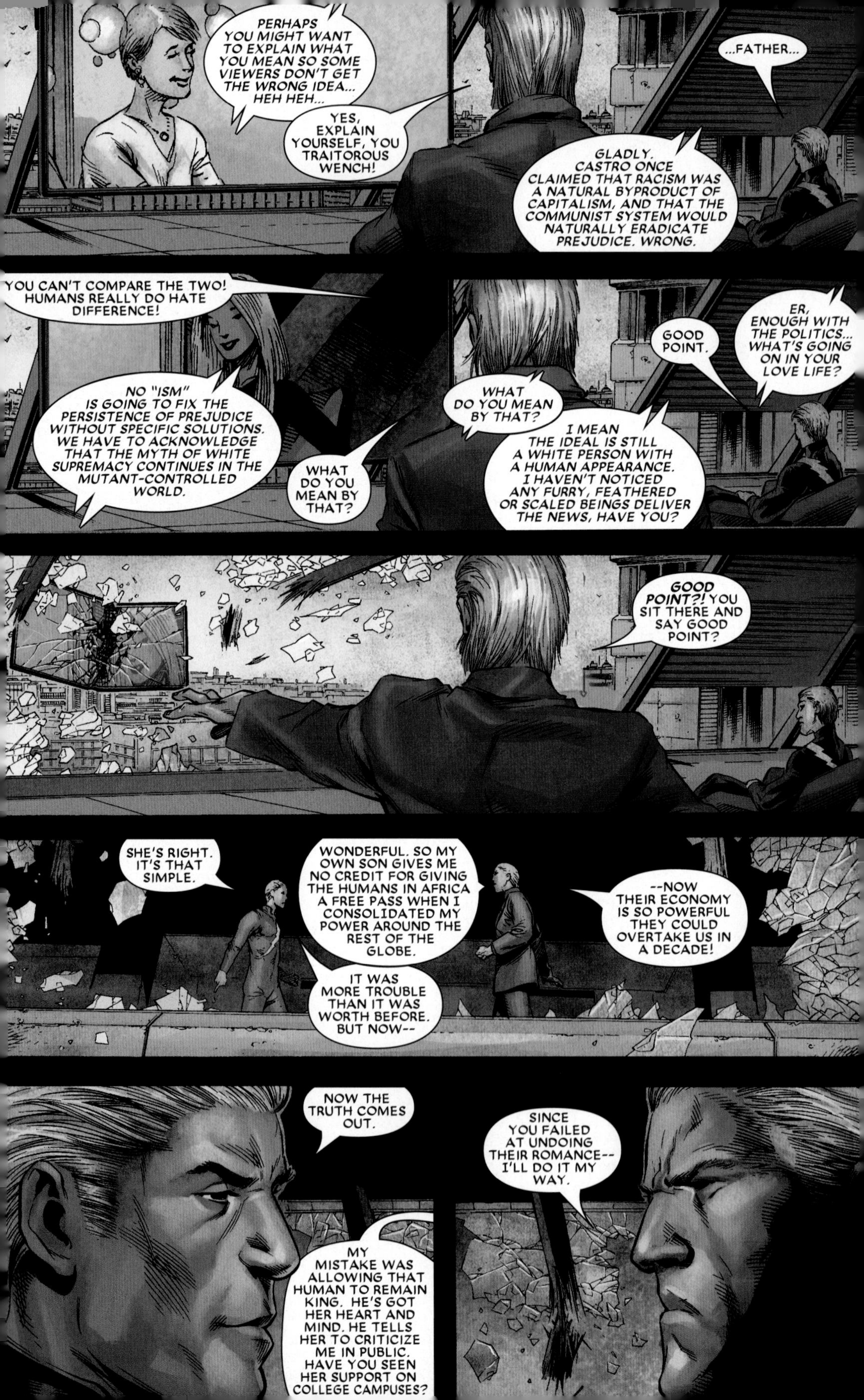

PERHAPS YOU MIGHT WANT TO EXPLAIN WHAT YOU MEAN SO SOME VIEWERS DON'T GET THE WRONG IDEA... HEH HEH...
YES, EXPLAIN YOURSELF, YOU TRAITOROUS WENCH!
...FATHER...
GLADLY. CASTRO ONCE CLAIMED THAT RACISM WAS A NATURAL BYPRODUCT OF CAPITALISM, AND THAT THE COMMUNIST SYSTEM WOULD NATURALLY ERADICATE PREJUDICE. WRONG.
YOU CAN'T COMPARE THE TWO! HUMANS REALLY DO HATE DIFFERENCE!
GOOD POINT.
ER, ENOUGH WITH THE POLITICS... WHAT'S GOING ON IN YOUR LOVE LIFE?
NO "ISM" IS GOING TO FIX THE PERSISTENCE OF PREJUDICE WITHOUT SPECIFIC SOLUTIONS. WE HAVE TO ACKNOWLEDGE THAT THE MYTH OF WHITE SUPREMACY CONTINUES IN THE MUTANT-CONTROLLED WORLD.
WHAT DO YOU MEAN BY THAT?
WHAT DO YOU MEAN BY THAT?
I MEAN THE IDEAL IS STILL A WHITE PERSON WITH A HUMAN APPEARANCE. I HAVEN'T NOTICED ANY FURRY, FEATHERED OR SCALED BEINGS DELIVER THE NEWS, HAVE YOU?
GOOD POINT?! YOU SIT THERE AND SAY GOOD POINT?
SHE'S RIGHT. IT'S THAT SIMPLE.
WONDERFUL. SO MY OWN SON GIVES ME NO CREDIT FOR GIVING THE HUMANS IN AFRICA A FREE PASS WHEN I CONSOLIDATED MY POWER AROUND THE REST OF THE GLOBE.
IT WAS MORE TROUBLE THAN IT WAS WORTH BEFORE. BUT NOW--
--NOW THEIR ECONOMY IS SO POWERFUL THEY COULD OVERTAKE US IN A DECADE!
NOW THE TRUTH COMES OUT.
MY MISTAKE WAS ALLOWING THAT HUMAN TO REMAIN KING. HE'S GOT HER HEART AND MIND. HE TELLS HER TO CRITICIZE ME IN PUBLIC. HAVE YOU SEEN HER SUPPORT ON COLLEGE CAMPUSES?
SINCE YOU FAILED AT UNDOING THEIR ROMANCE--I'LL DO IT MY WAY.

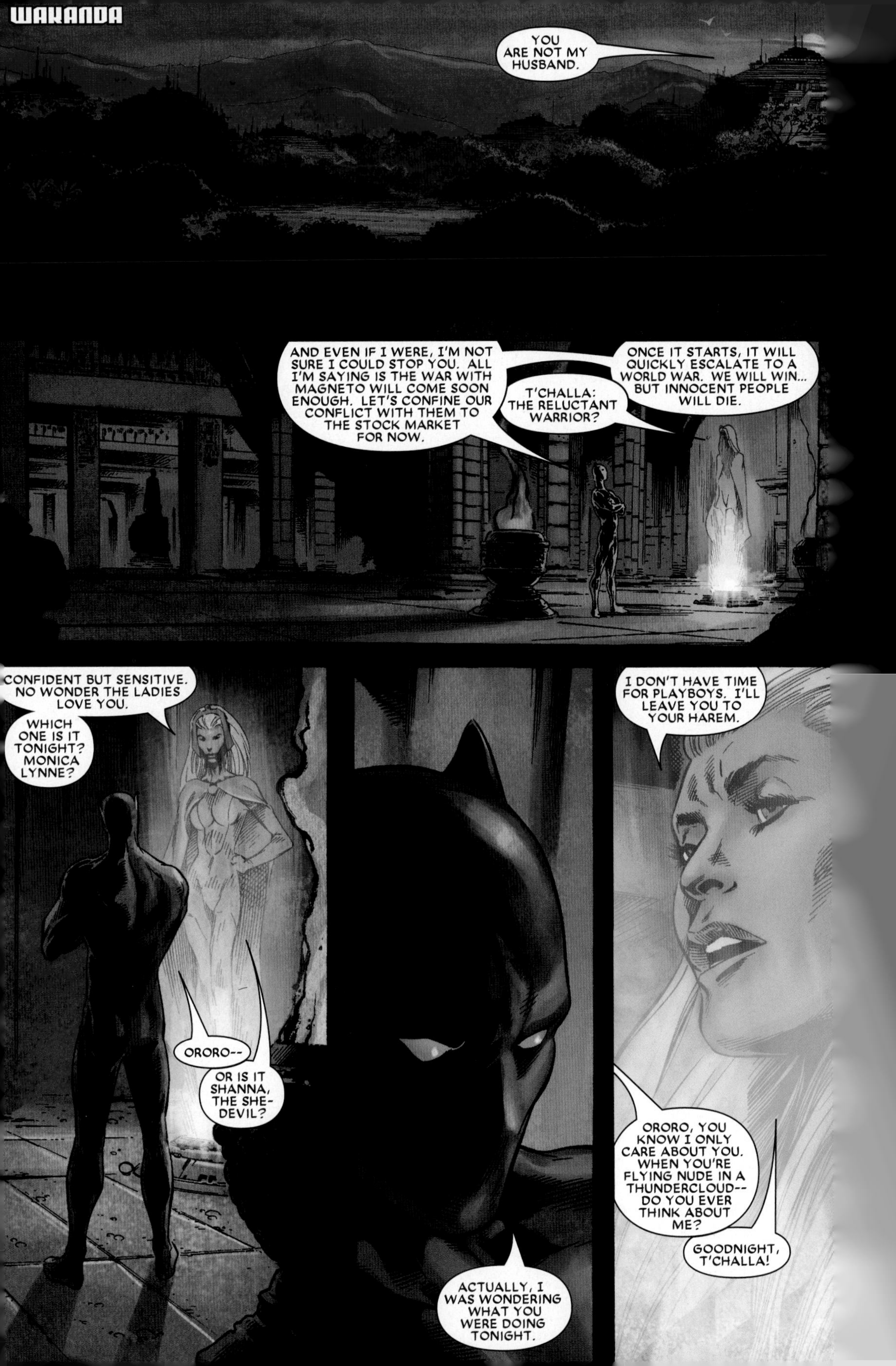
WAKANDA
YOU ARE NOT MY HUSBAND.
AND EVEN IF I WERE, I'M NOT SURE I COULD STOP YOU. ALL I'M SAYING IS THE WAR WITH MAGNETO WILL COME SOON ENOUGH. LET'S CONFINE OUR CONFLICT WITH THEM TO THE STOCK MARKET FOR NOW.
T'CHALLA: THE RELUCTANT WARRIOR?
ONCE IT STARTS, IT WILL QUICKLY ESCALATE TO A WORLD WAR. WE WILL WIN... BUT INNOCENT PEOPLE WILL DIE.
CONFIDENT BUT SENSITIVE. NO WONDER THE LADIES LOVE YOU.
WHICH ONE IS IT TONIGHT? MONICA LYNNE?
ORORO--
OR IS IT SHANNA, THE SHE-DEVIL?
ACTUALLY, I WAS WONDERING WHAT YOU WERE DOING TONIGHT.
I DON'T HAVE TIME FOR PLAYBOYS. I'LL LEAVE YOU TO YOUR HAREM.
ORORO, YOU KNOW I ONLY CARE ABOUT YOU. WHEN YOU'RE FLYING NUDE IN A THUNDERCLOUD-- DO YOU EVER THINK ABOUT ME?
GOODNIGHT, T'CHALLA!

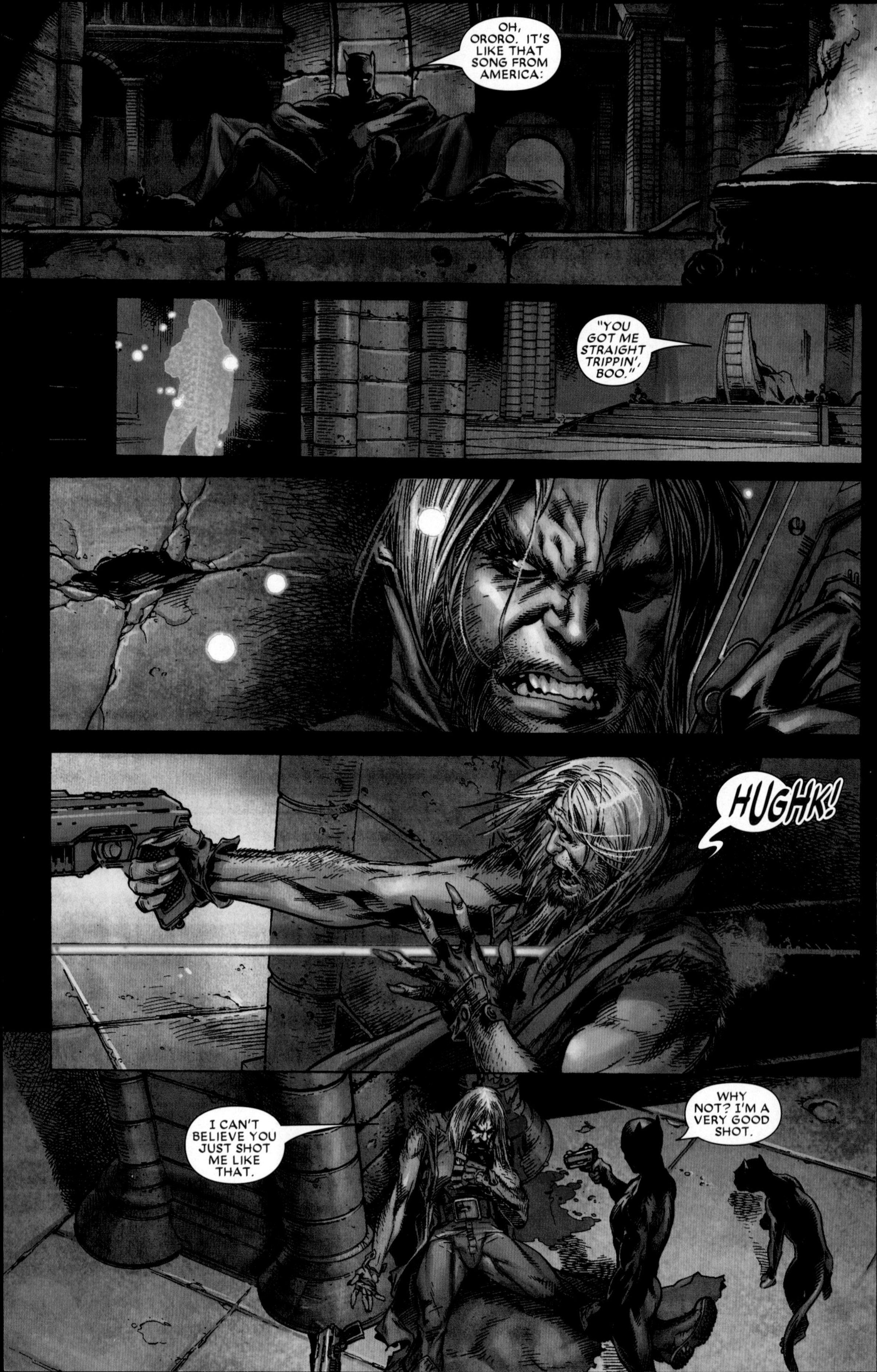
OH, ORORO. IT'S LIKE THAT SONG FROM AMERICA:
"YOU GOT ME STRAIGHT TRIPPIN', BOO."
HUGHK!
I CAN'T BELIEVE YOU JUST SHOT ME LIKE THAT.
WHY NOT? I'M A VERY GOOD SHOT.

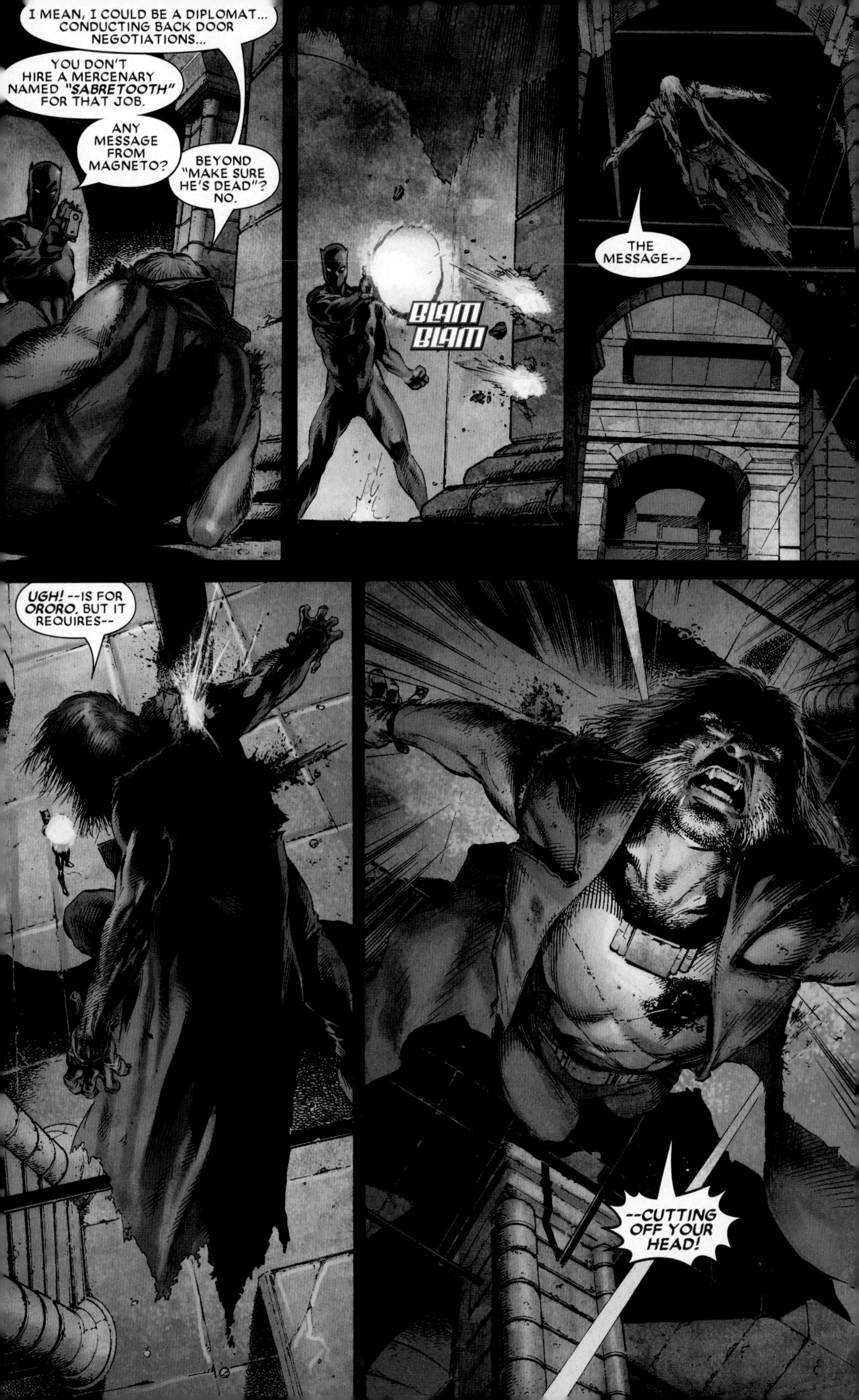
I MEAN, I COULD BE A DIPLOMAT... CONDUCTING BACK DOOR NEGOTIATIONS...
YOU DON'T HIRE A MERCENARY NAMED "SABRETOOTH" FOR THAT JOB.
ANY MESSAGE FROM MAGNETO?
BEYOND "MAKE SURE HE'S DEAD"? NO.
BLAM BLAM
THE MESSAGE--
UGH! --IS FOR ORORO, BUT IT REQUIRES--
--CUTTING OFF YOUR HEAD!

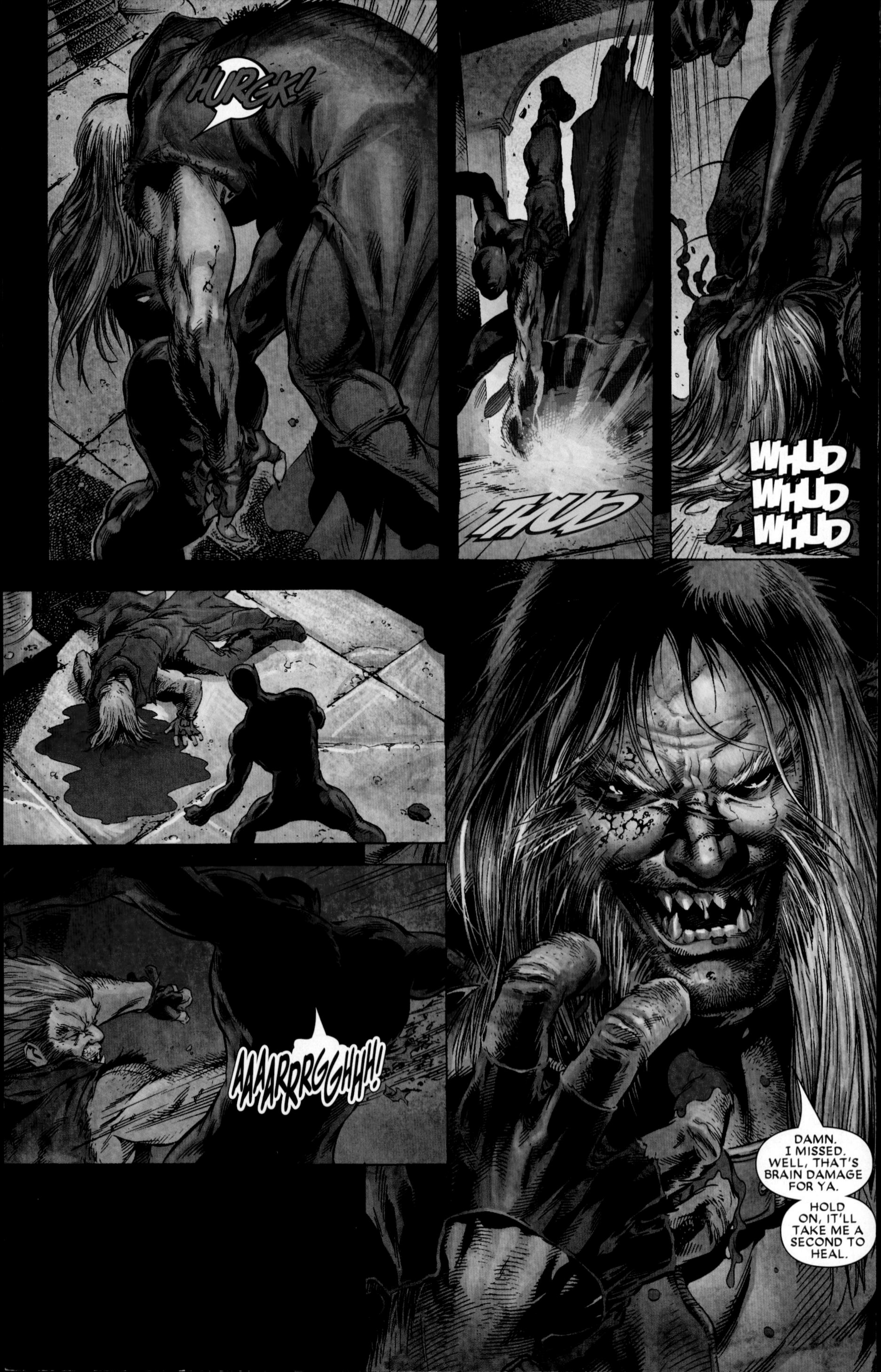
HURGK!
THUD
WHUD
WHUD
WHUD
AAAARRRGHHH!
DAMN. I MISSED. WELL, THAT'S BRAIN DAMAGE FOR YA.
HOLD ON, IT'LL TAKE ME A SECOND TO HEAL.

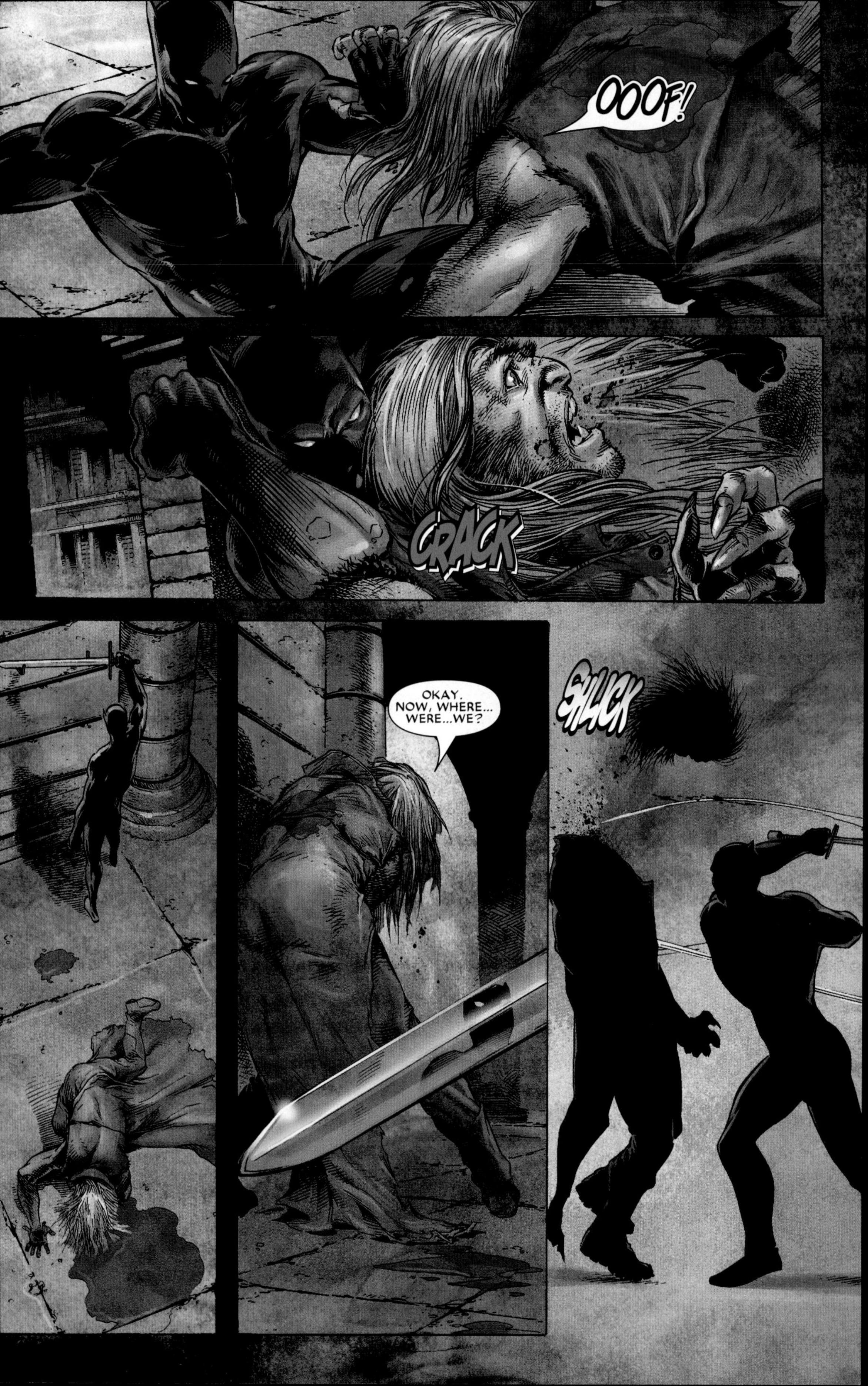
OOOF!
CRACK
OKAY. NOW, WHERE... WERE...WE?
SHLICK

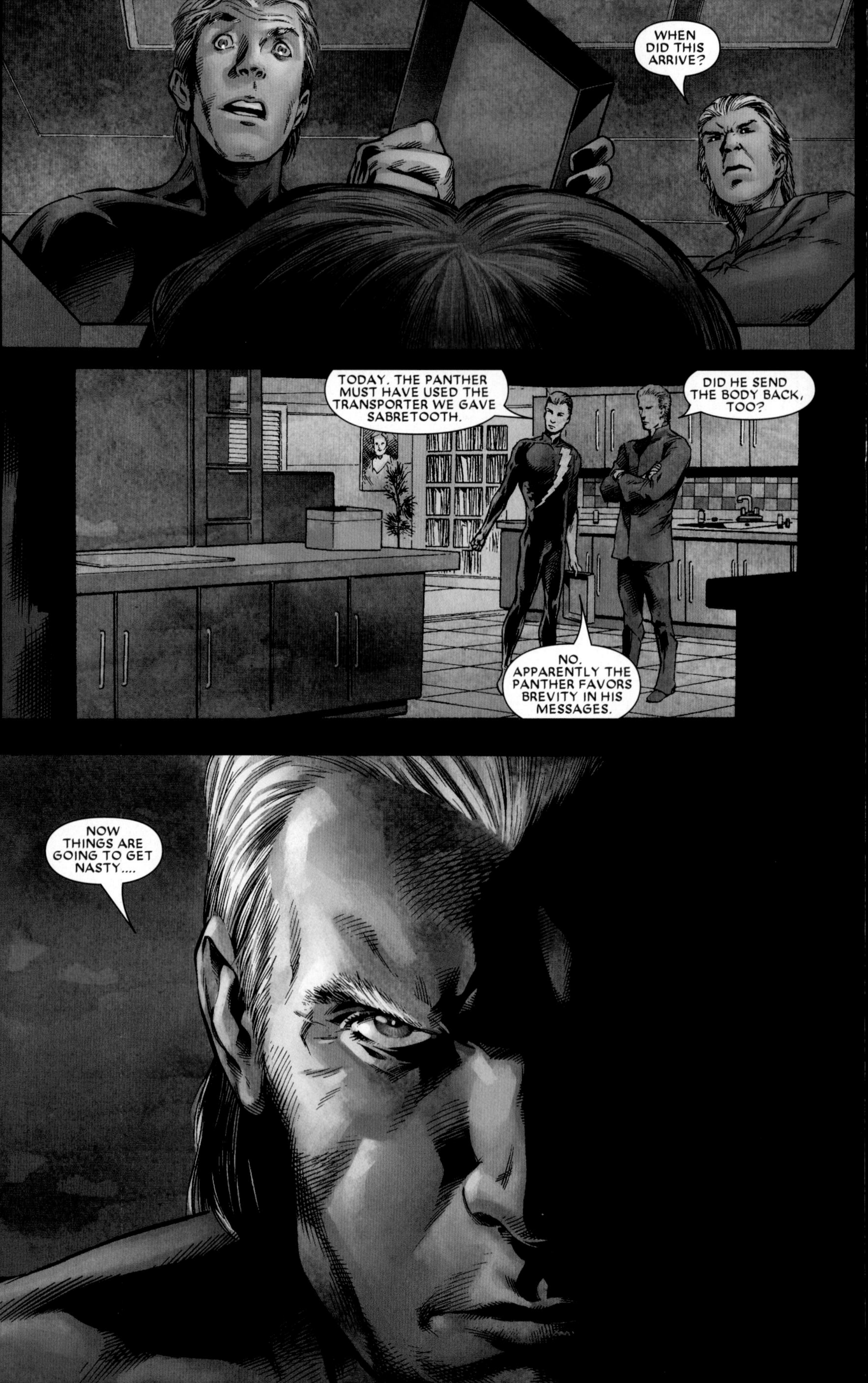
WHEN DID THIS ARRIVE?
TODAY. THE PANTHER MUST HAVE USED THE TRANSPORTER WE GAVE SABRETOOTH.
DID HE SEND THE BODY BACK, TOO?
NO. APPARENTLY THE PANTHER FAVORS BREVITY IN HIS MESSAGES.
NOW THINGS ARE GOING TO GET NASTY....

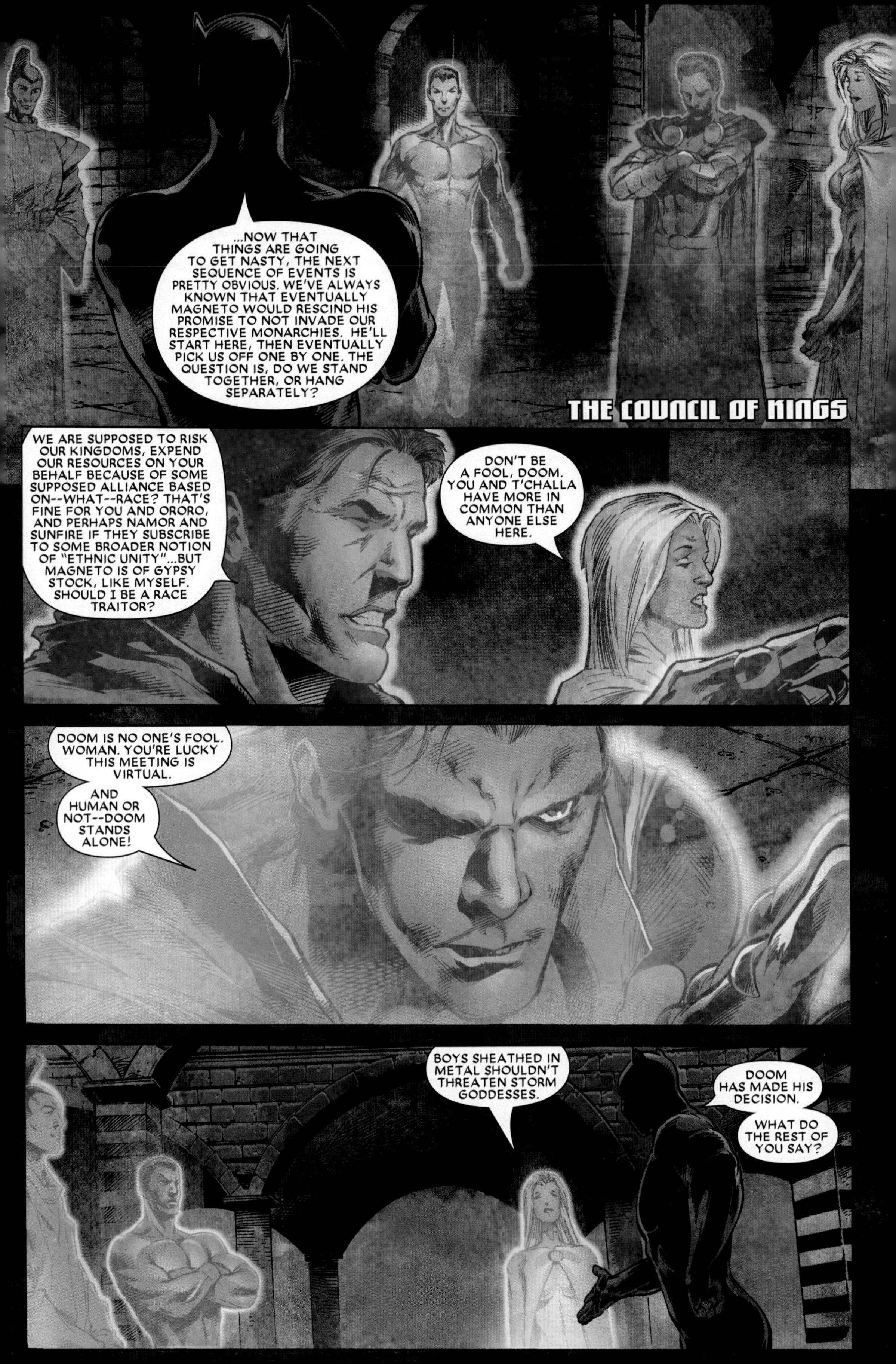
...NOW THAT THINGS ARE GOING TO GET NASTY, THE NEXT SEQUENCE OF EVENTS IS PRETTY OBVIOUS. WE'VE ALWAYS KNOWN THAT EVENTUALLY MAGNETO WOULD RESCIND HIS PROMISE TO NOT INVADE OUR RESPECTIVE MONARCHIES. HE'LL START HERE, THEN EVENTUALLY PICK US OFF ONE BY ONE. THE QUESTION IS, DO WE STAND TOGETHER, OR HANG SEPARATELY?
THE COUNCIL OF KINGS
WE ARE SUPPOSED TO RISK OUR KINGDOMS, EXPEND OUR RESOURCES ON YOUR BEHALF BECAUSE OF SOME SUPPOSED ALLIANCE BASED ON--WHAT--RACE? THAT'S FINE FOR YOU AND ORORO, AND PERHAPS NAMOR AND SUNFIRE IF THEY SUBSCRIBE TO SOME BROADER NOTION OF "ETHNIC UNITY"...BUT MAGNETO IS OF GYPSY STOCK, LIKE MYSELF. SHOULD I BE A RACE TRAITOR?
DON'T BE A FOOL, DOOM. YOU AND T'CHALLA HAVE MORE IN COMMON THAN ANYONE ELSE HERE.
DOOM IS NO ONE'S FOOL. WOMAN. YOU'RE LUCKY THIS MEETING IS VIRTUAL.
AND HUMAN OR NOT--DOOM STANDS ALONE!
BOYS SHEATHED IN METAL SHOULDN'T THREATEN STORM GODDESSES.
DOOM HAS MADE HIS DECISION.
WHAT DO THE REST OF YOU SAY?

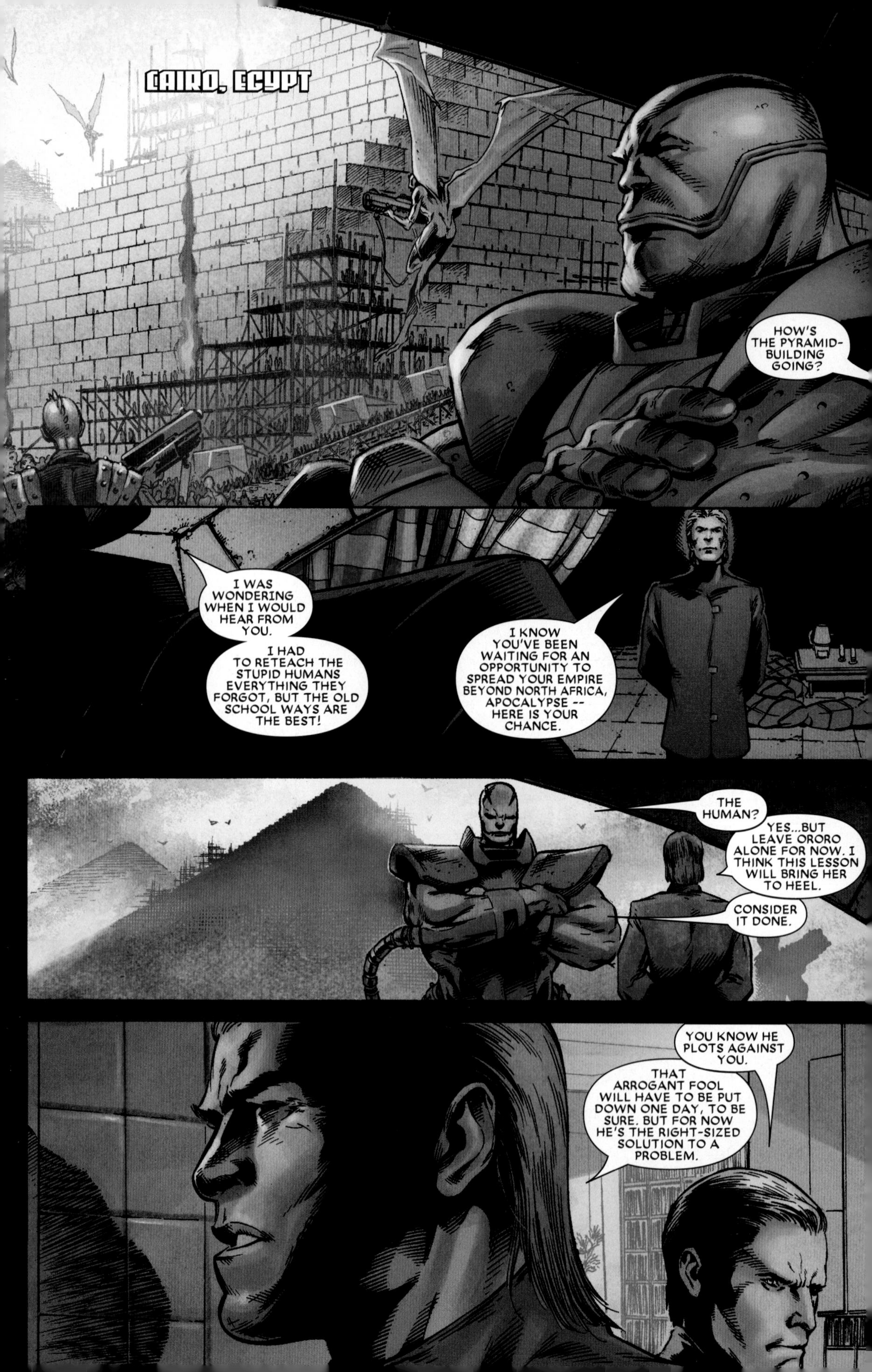
CAIRO, EGYPT
HOW'S THE PYRAMID-BUILDING GOING?
I WAS WONDERING WHEN I WOULD HEAR FROM YOU.
I HAD TO RETEACH THE STUPID HUMANS EVERYTHING THEY FORGOT, BUT THE OLD SCHOOL WAYS ARE THE BEST!
I KNOW YOU'VE BEEN WAITING FOR AN OPPORTUNITY TO SPREAD YOUR EMPIRE BEYOND NORTH AFRICA, APOCALYPSE -- HERE IS YOUR CHANCE.
THE HUMAN?
YES...BUT LEAVE ORORO ALONE FOR NOW. I THINK THIS LESSON WILL BRING HER TO HEEL.
CONSIDER IT DONE.
YOU KNOW HE PLOTS AGAINST YOU.
THAT ARROGANT FOOL WILL HAVE TO BE PUT DOWN ONE DAY, TO BE SURE. BUT FOR NOW HE'S THE RIGHT-SIZED SOLUTION TO A PROBLEM.

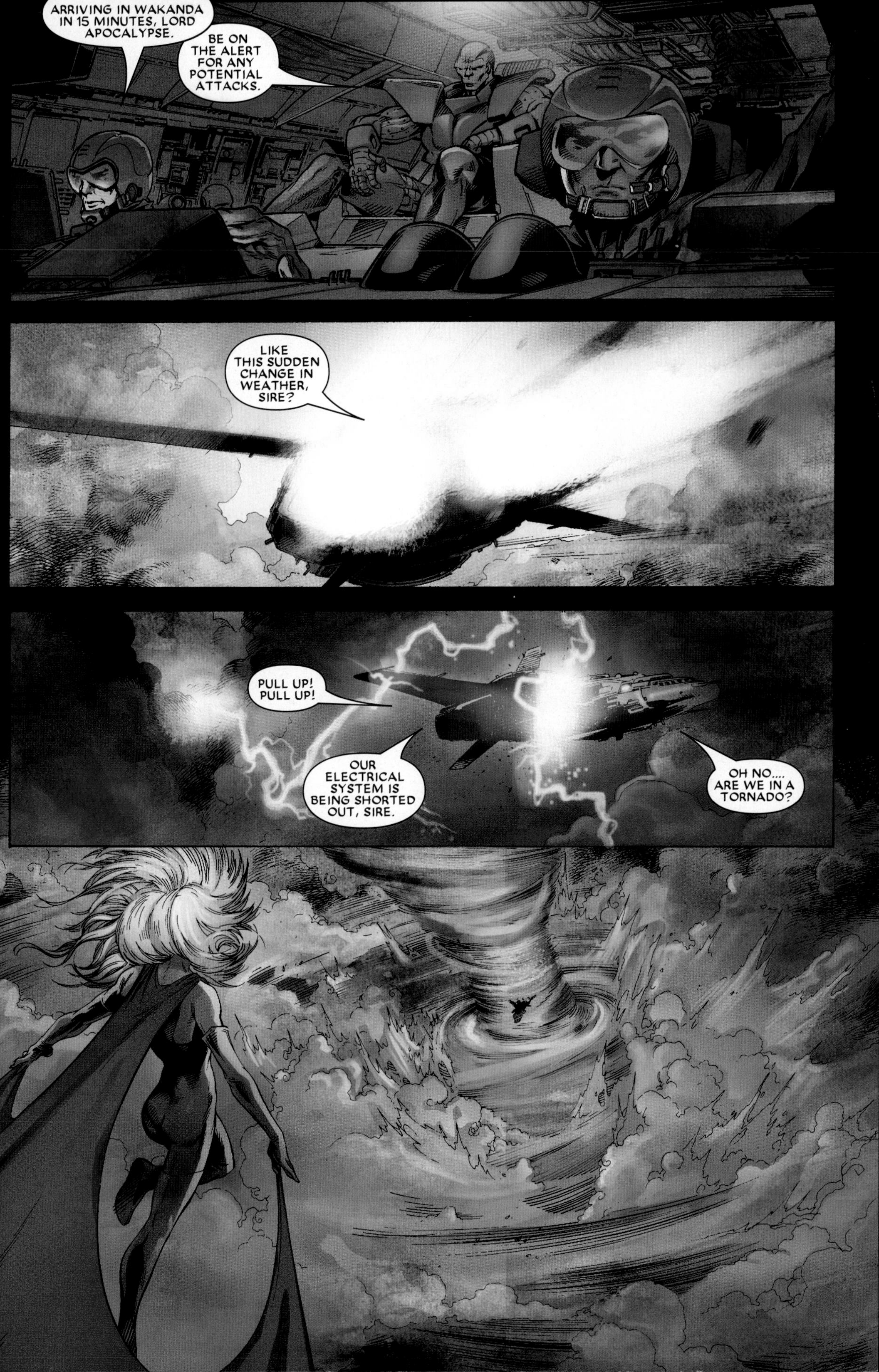
ARRIVING IN WAKANDA IN 15 MINUTES, LORD APOCALYPSE.
BE ON THE ALERT FOR ANY POTENTIAL ATTACKS.
LIKE THIS SUDDEN CHANGE IN WEATHER, SIRE?
PULL UP! PULL UP!
OUR ELECTRICAL SYSTEM IS BEING SHORTED OUT, SIRE.
OH NO.... ARE WE IN A TORNADO?

THE BACKUP TEAM IS ON ITS WAY, SIRE-- *GLGLPPP!*

YOU ARE THE LAPDOG OF MEN WITHOUT HONOR. *IMPERIUS REX!*

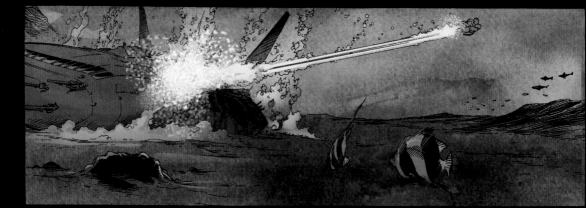

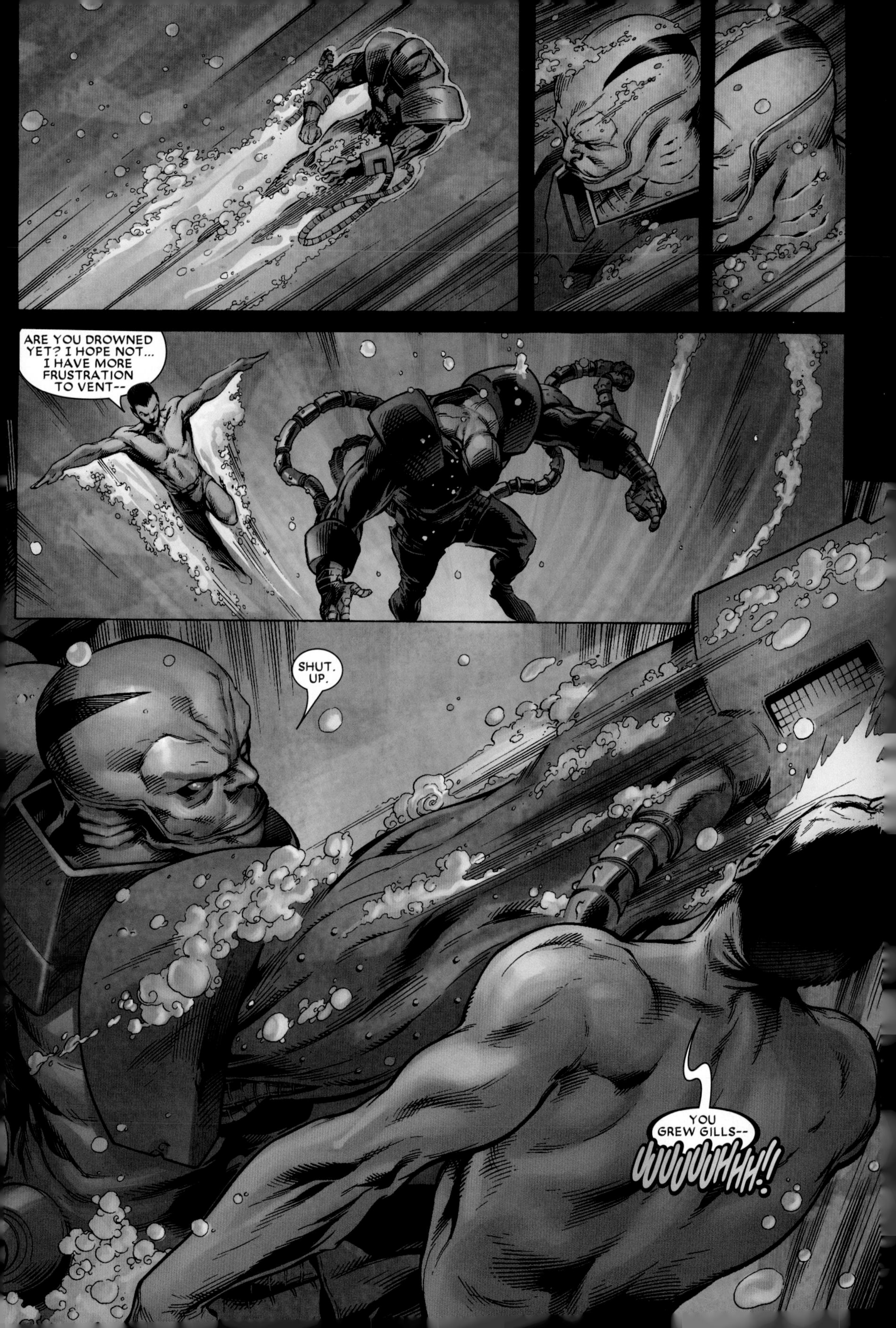
ARE YOU DROWNED YET? I HOPE NOT... I HAVE MORE FRUSTRATION TO VENT--
SHUT. UP.
YOU GREW GILLS--
UUUUUUUHHH!!

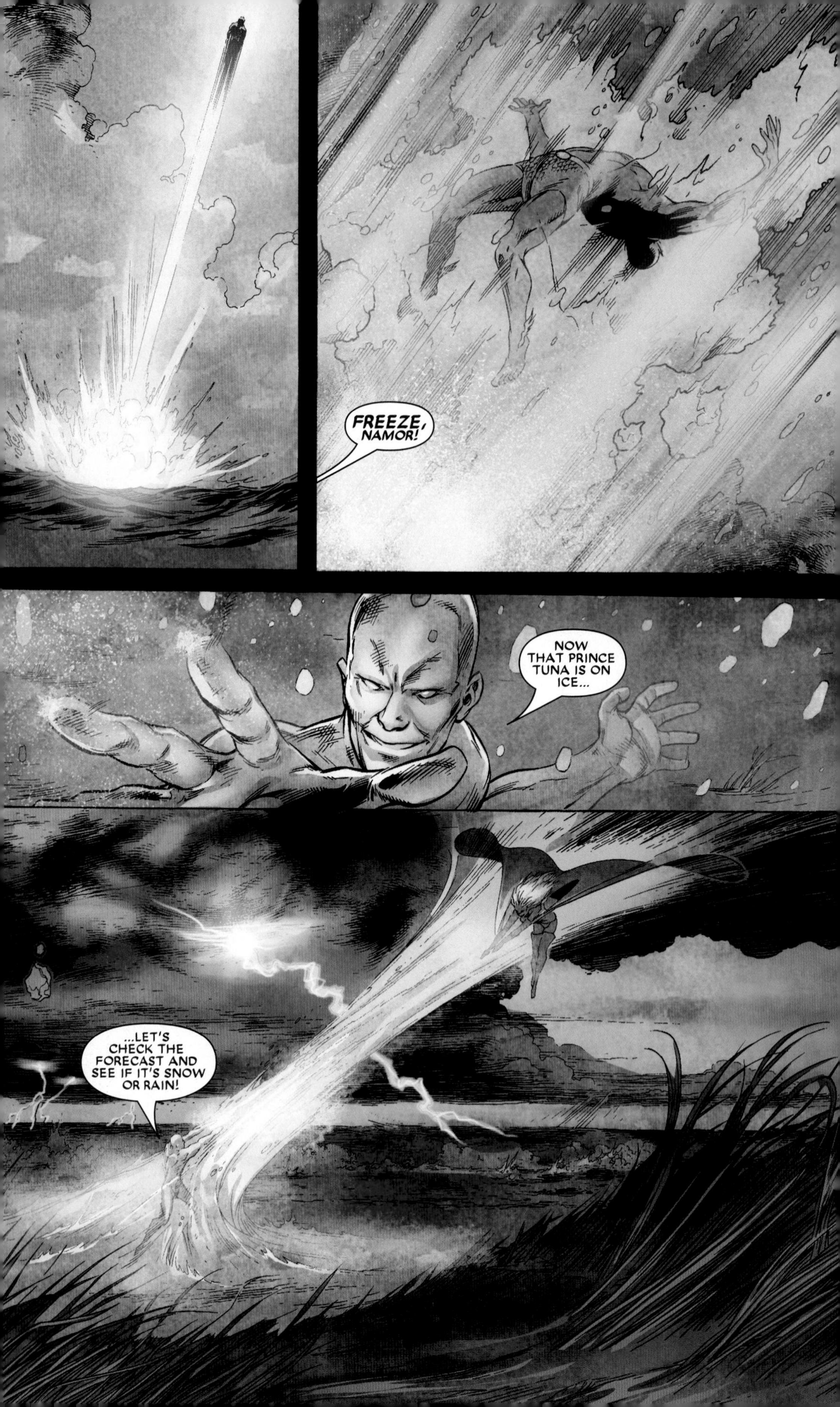
FREEZE, NAMOR!
NOW THAT PRINCE TUNA IS ON ICE...
...LET'S CHECK THE FORECAST AND SEE IF IT'S SNOW OR RAIN!

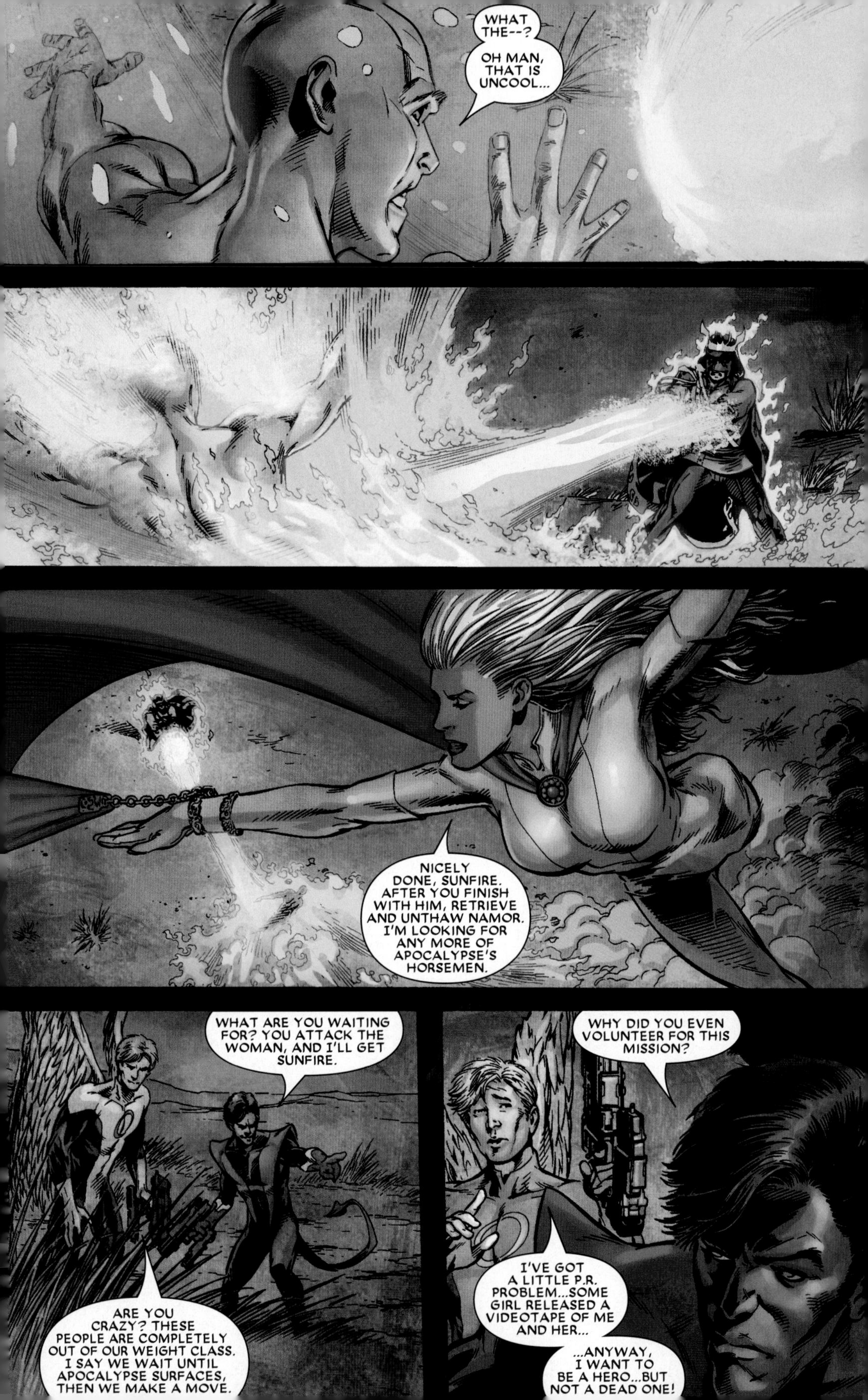
WHAT THE--?
OH MAN, THAT IS UNCOOL...
NICELY DONE, SUNFIRE. AFTER YOU FINISH WITH HIM, RETRIEVE AND UNTHAW NAMOR. I'M LOOKING FOR ANY MORE OF APOCALYPSE'S HORSEMEN.
WHAT ARE YOU WAITING FOR? YOU ATTACK THE WOMAN, AND I'LL GET SUNFIRE.
ARE YOU CRAZY? THESE PEOPLE ARE COMPLETELY OUT OF OUR WEIGHT CLASS. I SAY WE WAIT UNTIL APOCALYPSE SURFACES, THEN WE MAKE A MOVE.
WHY DID YOU EVEN VOLUNTEER FOR THIS MISSION?
I'VE GOT A LITTLE P.R. PROBLEM...SOME GIRL RELEASED A VIDEOTAPE OF ME AND HER...
...ANYWAY, I WANT TO BE A HERO...BUT NOT A DEAD ONE!

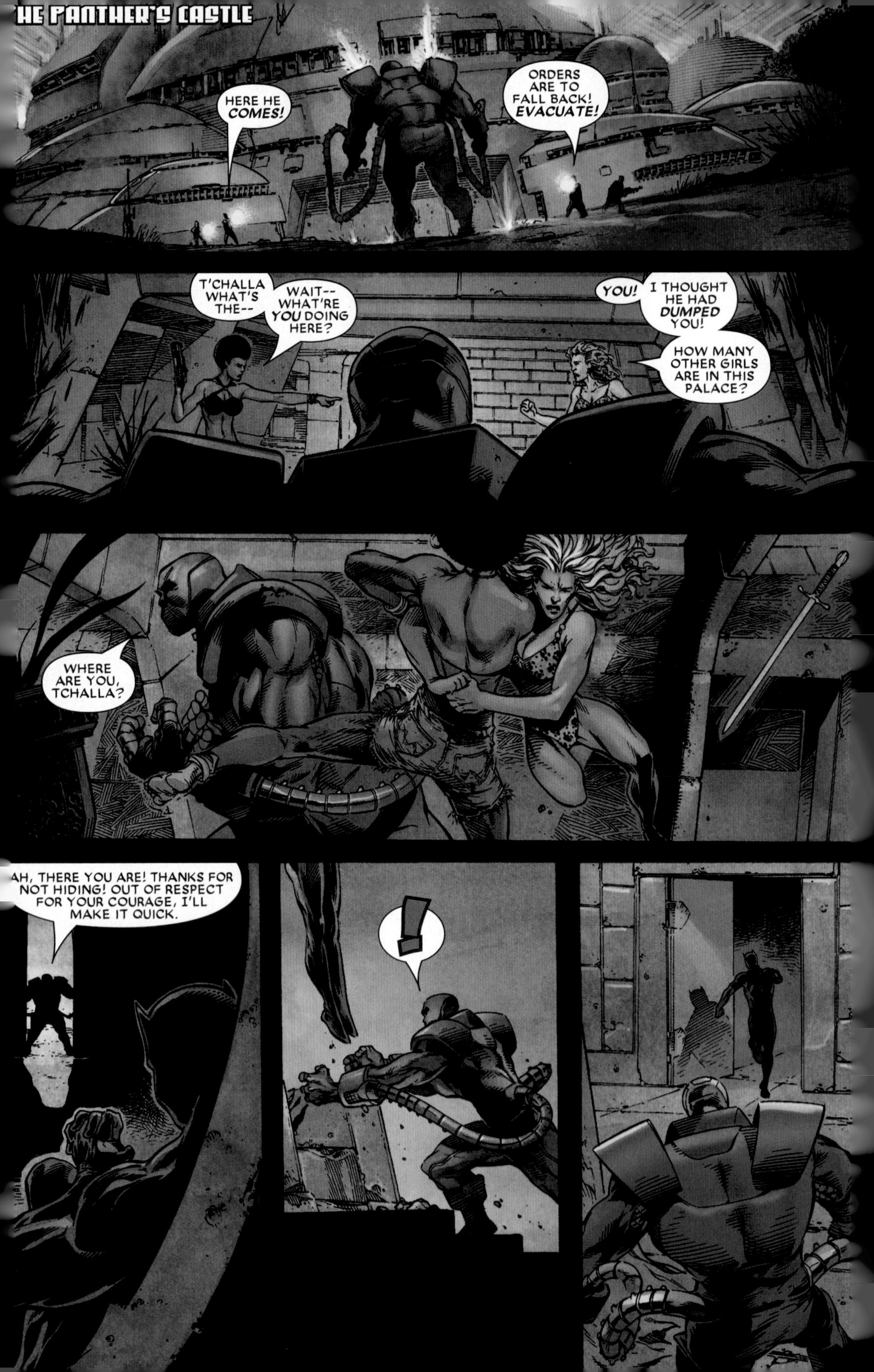

HE PANTHER'S CASTLE
HERE HE COMES!
ORDERS ARE TO FALL BACK! EVACUATE!
T'CHALLA WHAT'S THE--
WAIT-- WHAT'RE YOU DOING HERE?
YOU!
I THOUGHT HE HAD DUMPED YOU!
HOW MANY OTHER GIRLS ARE IN THIS PALACE?
WHERE ARE YOU, TCHALLA?
AH, THERE YOU ARE! THANKS FOR NOT HIDING! OUT OF RESPECT FOR YOUR COURAGE, I'LL MAKE IT QUICK.
!

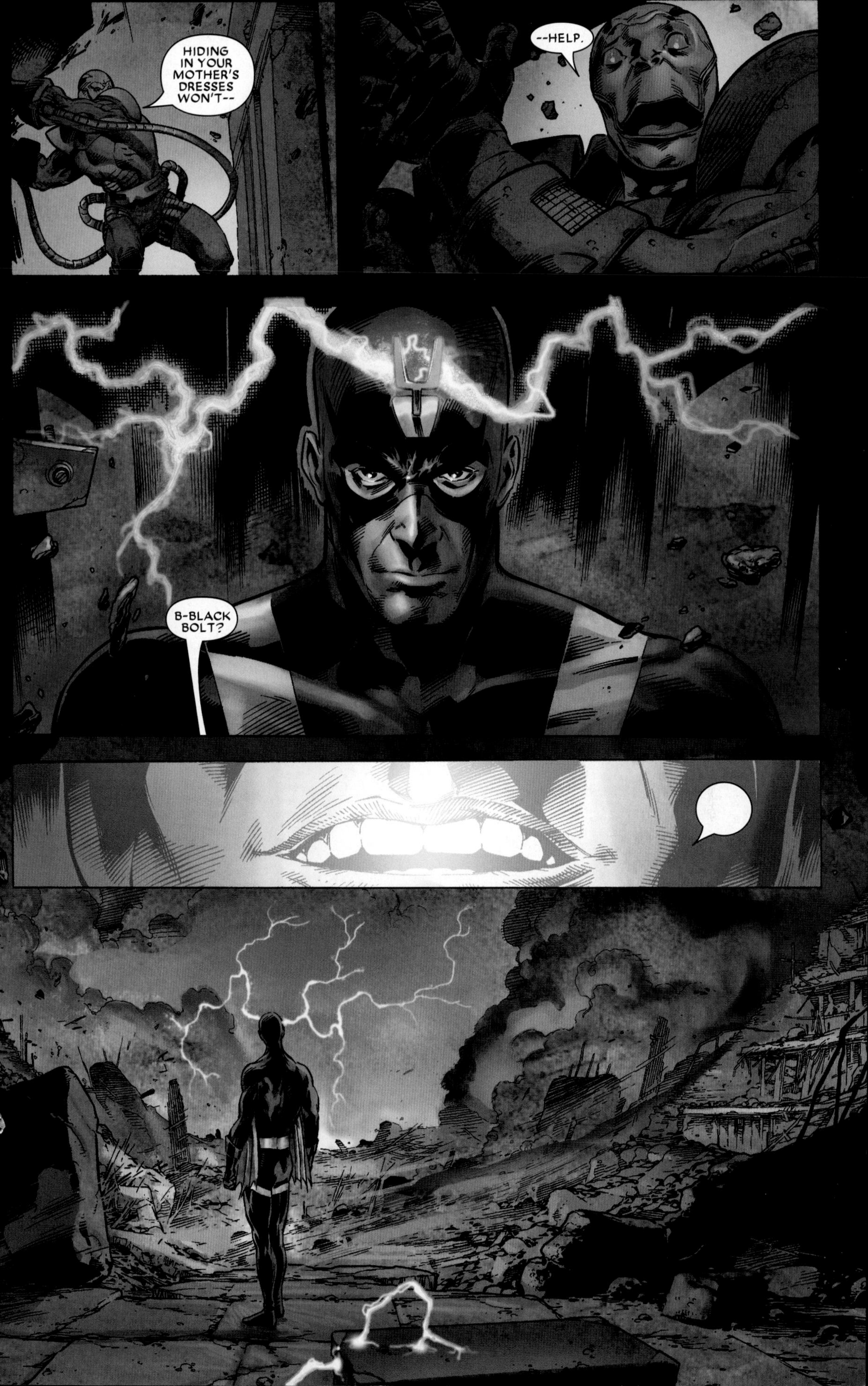
HIDING IN YOUR MOTHER'S DRESSES WON'T--
--HELP.
B-BLACK BOLT?

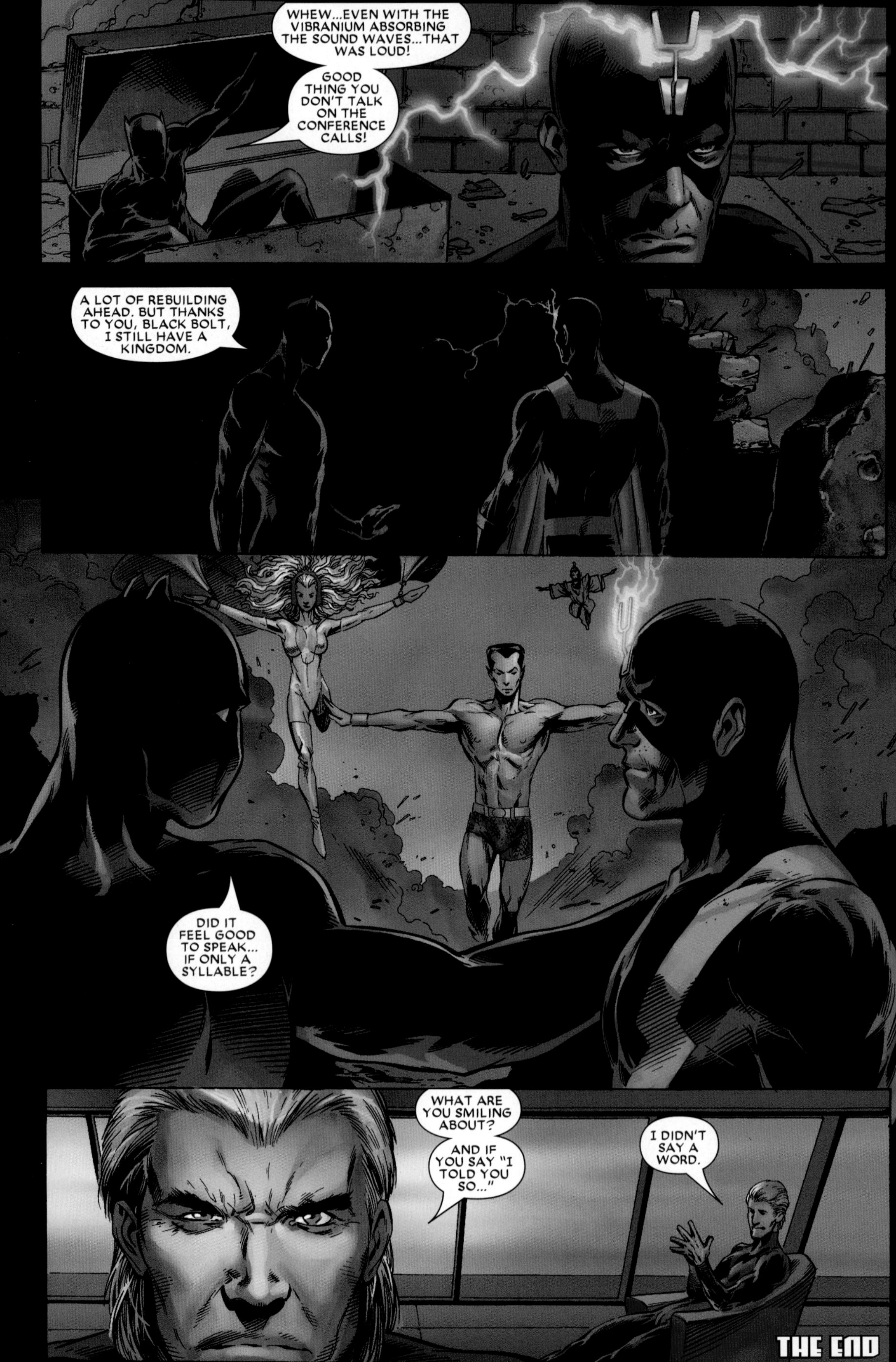
WHEW...EVEN WITH THE VIBRANIUM ABSORBING THE SOUND WAVES...THAT WAS LOUD!
GOOD THING YOU DON'T TALK ON THE CONFERENCE CALLS!
A LOT OF REBUILDING AHEAD. BUT THANKS TO YOU, BLACK BOLT, I STILL HAVE A KINGDOM.
DID IT FEEL GOOD TO SPEAK... IF ONLY A SYLLABLE?
WHAT ARE YOU SMILING ABOUT?
AND IF YOU SAY "I TOLD YOU SO..."
I DIDN'T SAY A WORD.
THE END

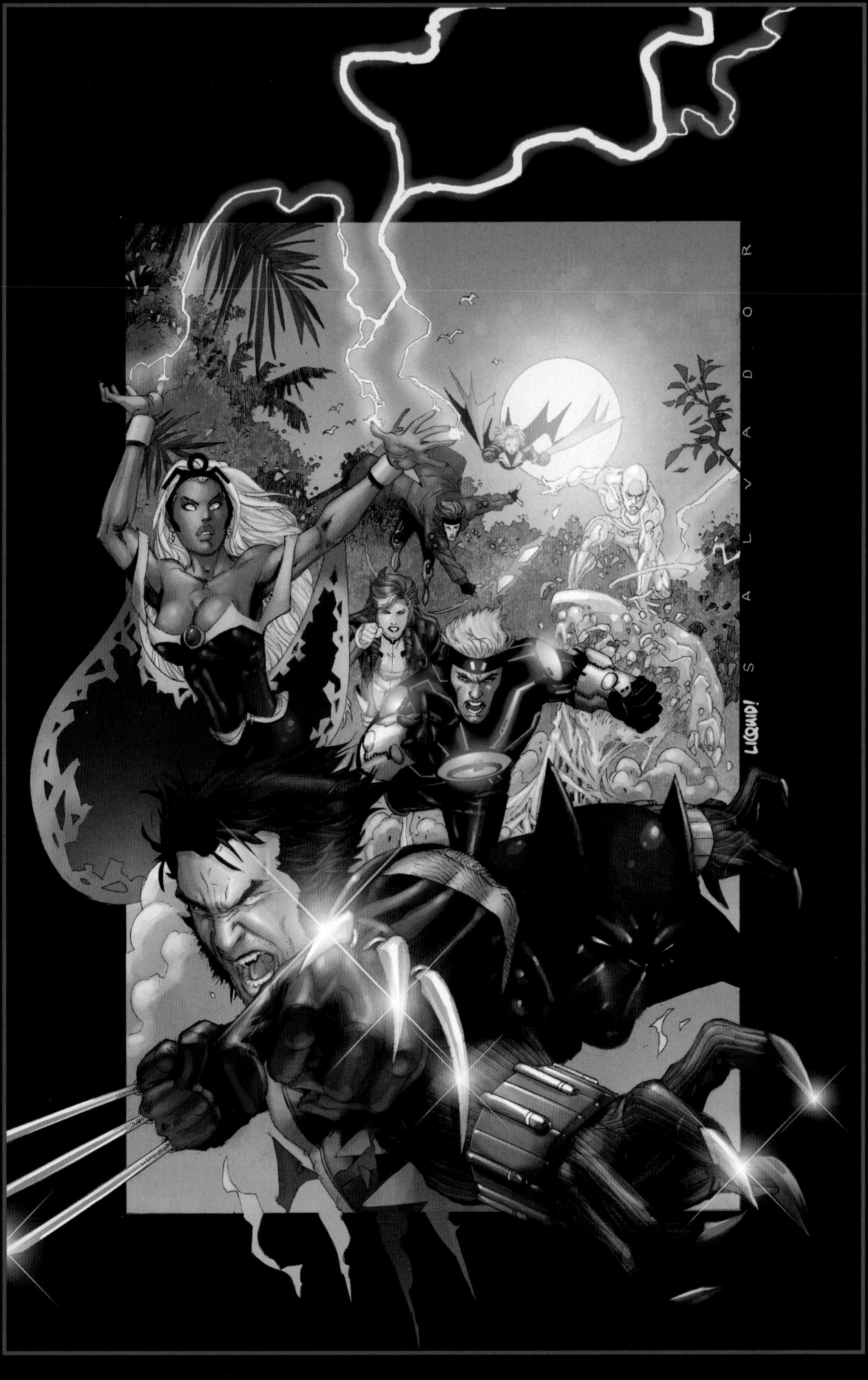
SALVADOR
LIQUID!

X-MEN **175**

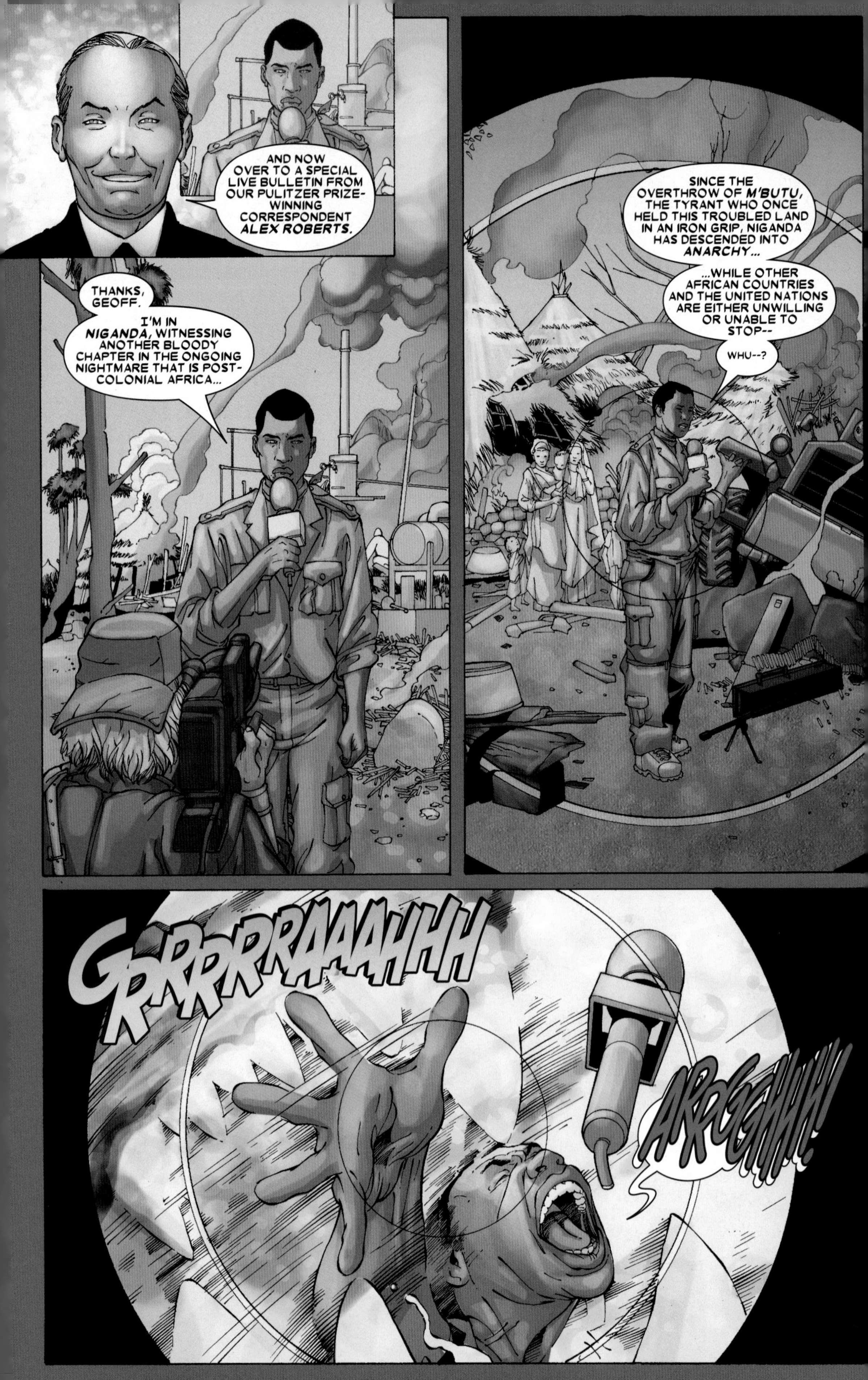
AND NOW OVER TO A SPECIAL LIVE BULLETIN FROM OUR PULITZER PRIZE-WINNING CORRESPONDENT ALEX ROBERTS.
THANKS, GEOFF.
I'M IN NIGANDA, WITNESSING ANOTHER BLOODY CHAPTER IN THE ONGOING NIGHTMARE THAT IS POST-COLONIAL AFRICA...
SINCE THE OVERTHROW OF M'BUTU, THE TYRANT WHO ONCE HELD THIS TROUBLED LAND IN AN IRON GRIP, NIGANDA HAS DESCENDED INTO ANARCHY...
...WHILE OTHER AFRICAN COUNTRIES AND THE UNITED NATIONS ARE EITHER UNWILLING OR UNABLE TO STOP--
WHU--?
GRRRRRAAAAHHH
ARRGGHHH!

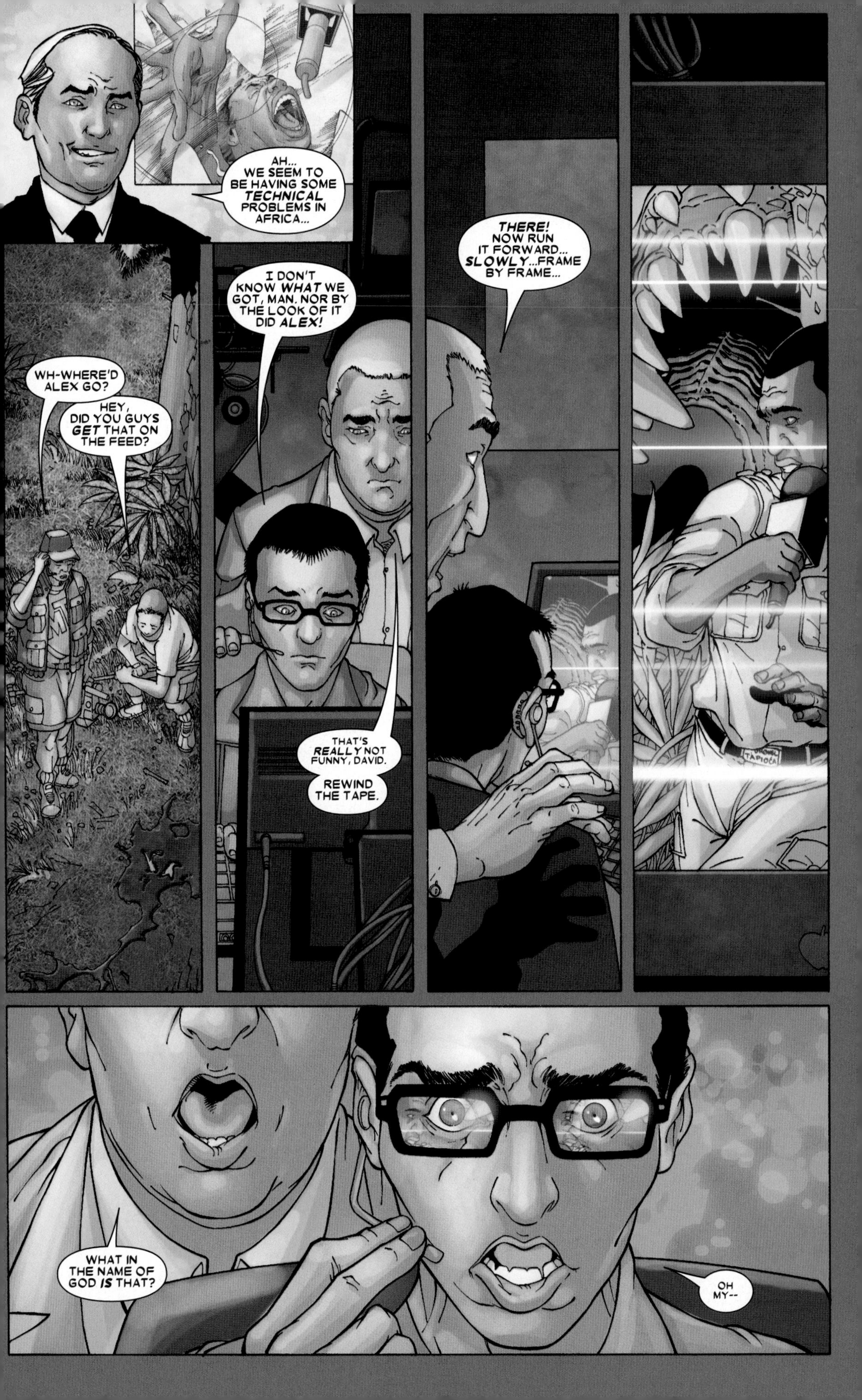
AH...
WE SEEM TO BE HAVING SOME TECHNICAL PROBLEMS IN AFRICA...
WH-WHERE'D ALEX GO?
HEY, DID YOU GUYS GET THAT ON THE FEED?
I DON'T KNOW WHAT WE GOT, MAN. NOR BY THE LOOK OF IT DID ALEX!
THAT'S REALLY NOT FUNNY, DAVID.
REWIND THE TAPE.
THERE! NOW RUN IT FORWARD... SLOWLY...FRAME BY FRAME...
WHAT IN THE NAME OF GOD IS THAT?
OH MY--

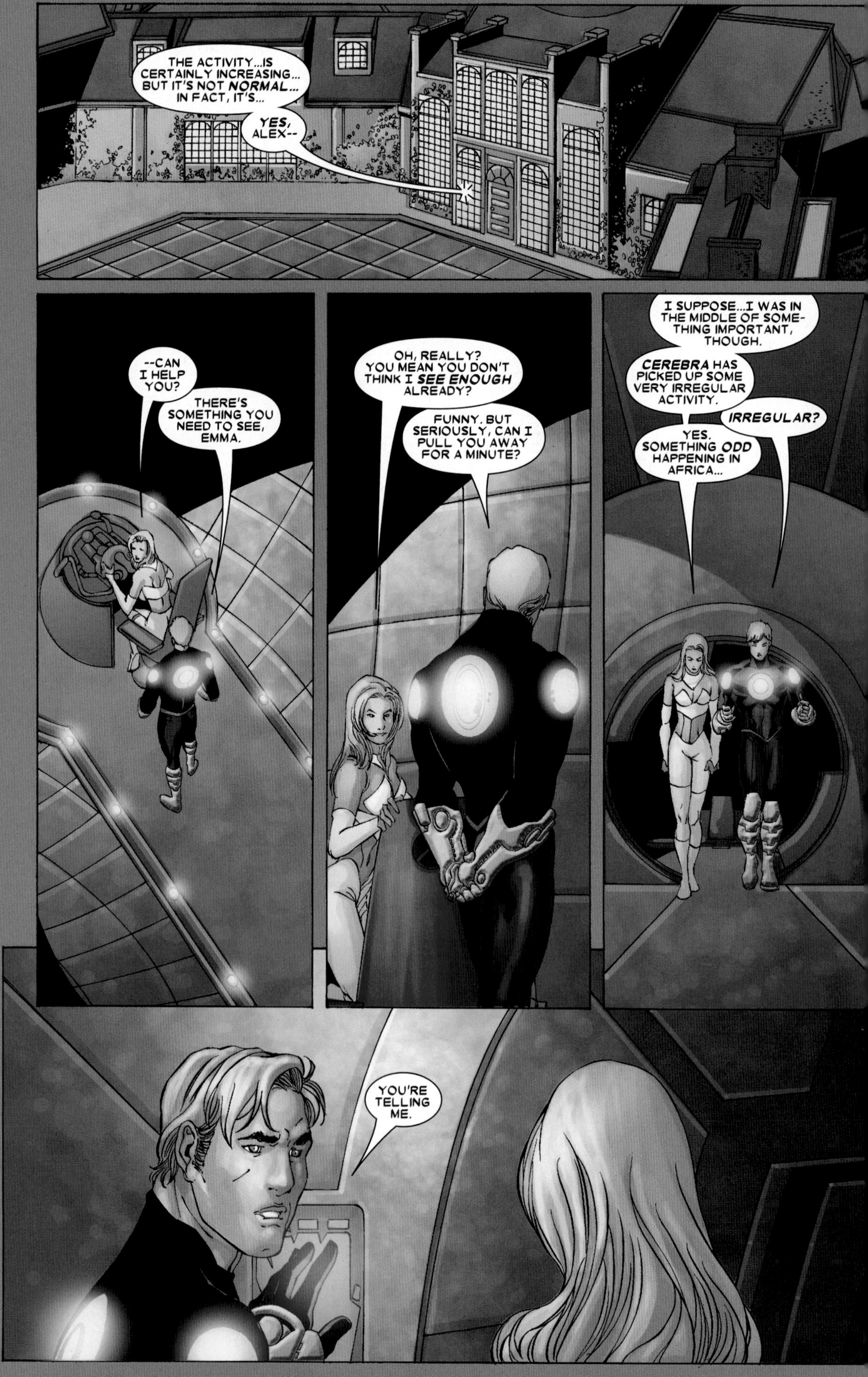
THE ACTIVITY...IS CERTAINLY INCREASING... BUT IT'S NOT NORMAL... IN FACT, IT'S...
YES, ALEX--
--CAN I HELP YOU?
THERE'S SOMETHING YOU NEED TO SEE, EMMA.
OH, REALLY? YOU MEAN YOU DON'T THINK I SEE ENOUGH ALREADY?
FUNNY. BUT SERIOUSLY, CAN I PULL YOU AWAY FOR A MINUTE?
I SUPPOSE...I WAS IN THE MIDDLE OF SOMETHING IMPORTANT, THOUGH.
CEREBRA HAS PICKED UP SOME VERY IRREGULAR ACTIVITY.
IRREGULAR?
YES. SOMETHING ODD HAPPENING IN AFRICA...
YOU'RE TELLING ME.

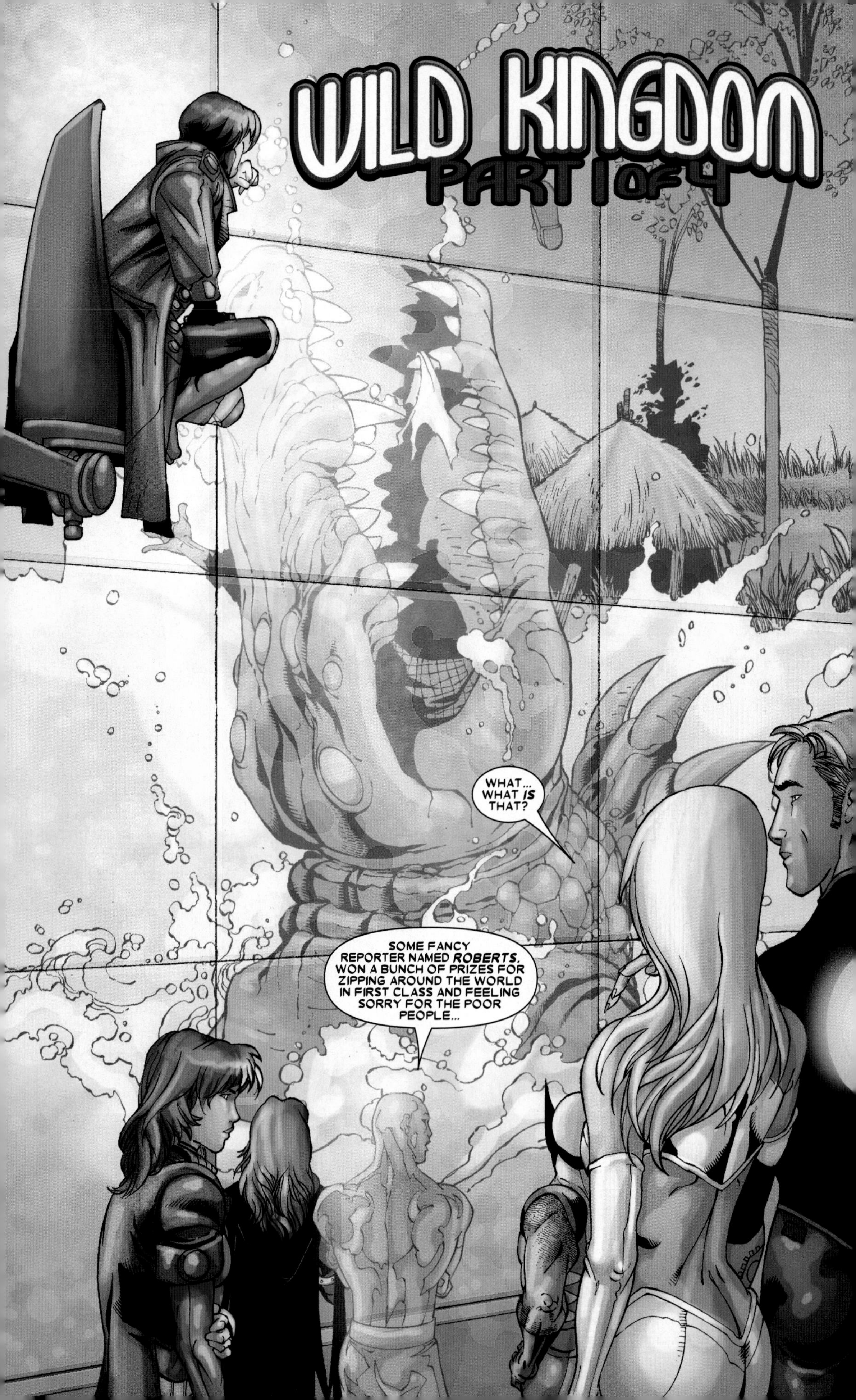
WILD KINGDOM
PART 1 OF 4
WHAT... WHAT IS THAT?
SOME FANCY REPORTER NAMED ROBERTS. WON A BUNCH OF PRIZES FOR ZIPPING AROUND THE WORLD IN FIRST CLASS AND FEELING SORRY FOR THE POOR PEOPLE...

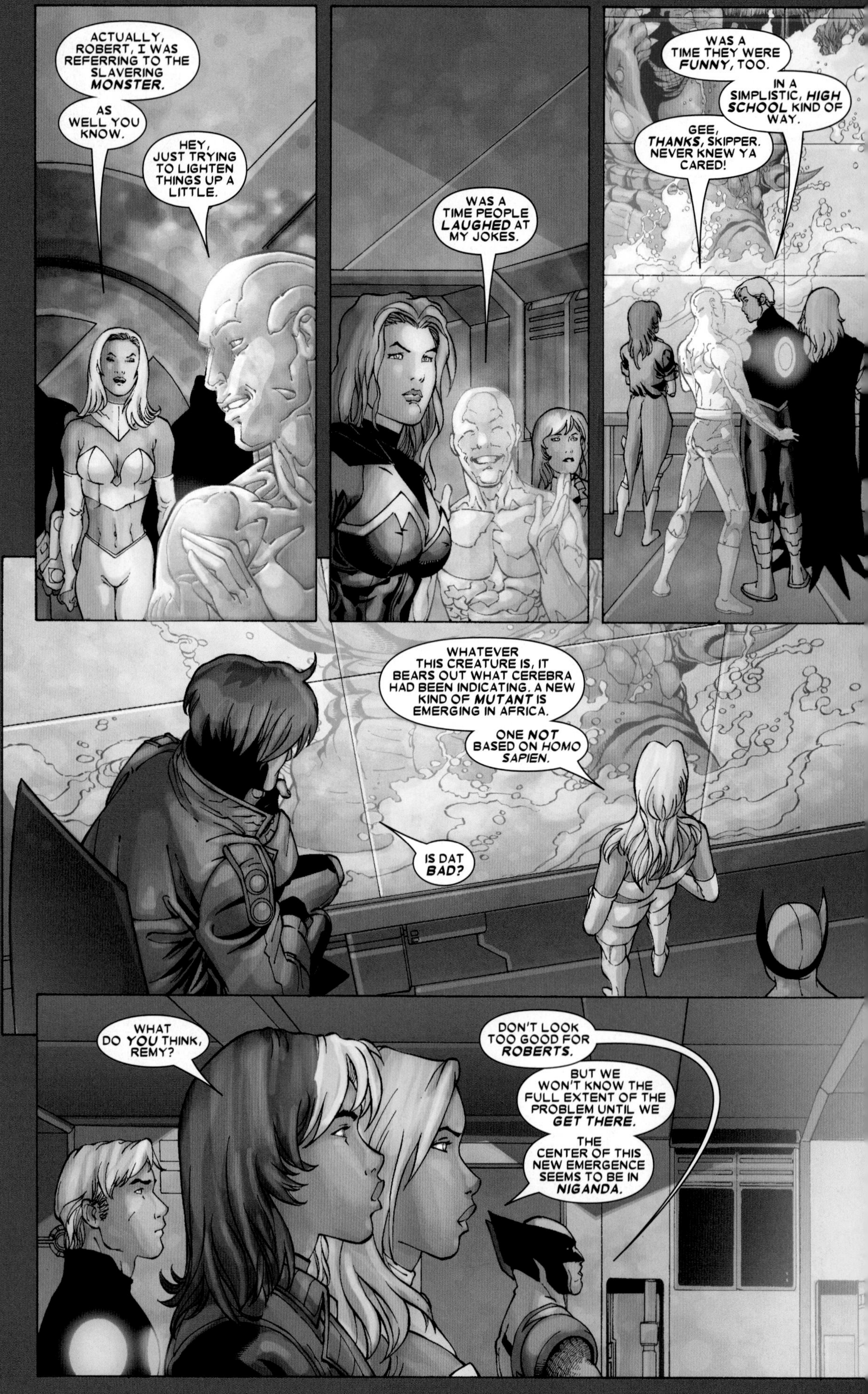
ACTUALLY, ROBERT, I WAS REFERRING TO THE SLAVERING MONSTER.
AS WELL YOU KNOW.
HEY, JUST TRYING TO LIGHTEN THINGS UP A LITTLE.
WAS A TIME PEOPLE LAUGHED AT MY JOKES.
WAS A TIME THEY WERE FUNNY, TOO.
IN A SIMPLISTIC, HIGH SCHOOL KIND OF WAY.
GEE, THANKS, SKIPPER. NEVER KNEW YA CARED!
WHATEVER THIS CREATURE IS, IT BEARS OUT WHAT CEREBRA HAD BEEN INDICATING. A NEW KIND OF MUTANT IS EMERGING IN AFRICA.
ONE NOT BASED ON HOMO SAPIEN.
IS DAT BAD?
WHAT DO YOU THINK, REMY?
DON'T LOOK TOO GOOD FOR ROBERTS.
BUT WE WON'T KNOW THE FULL EXTENT OF THE PROBLEM UNTIL WE GET THERE.
THE CENTER OF THIS NEW EMERGENCE SEEMS TO BE IN NIGANDA.

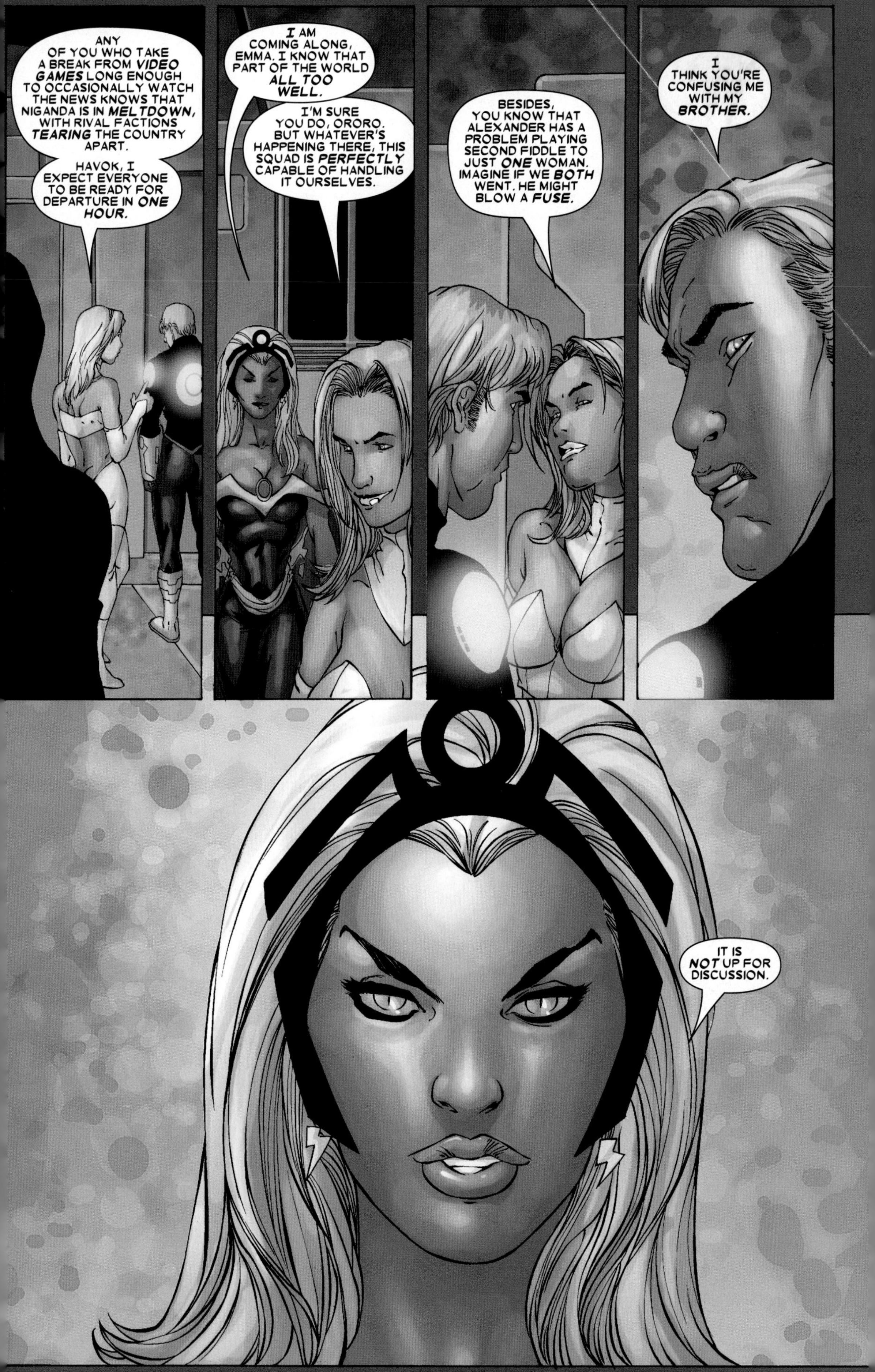
ANY OF YOU WHO TAKE A BREAK FROM VIDEO GAMES LONG ENOUGH TO OCCASIONALLY WATCH THE NEWS KNOWS THAT NIGANDA IS IN MELTDOWN, WITH RIVAL FACTIONS TEARING THE COUNTRY APART.
HAVOK, I EXPECT EVERYONE TO BE READY FOR DEPARTURE IN ONE HOUR.
I AM COMING ALONG, EMMA. I KNOW THAT PART OF THE WORLD ALL TOO WELL.
I'M SURE YOU DO, ORORO. BUT WHATEVER'S HAPPENING THERE, THIS SQUAD IS PERFECTLY CAPABLE OF HANDLING IT OURSELVES.
BESIDES, YOU KNOW THAT ALEXANDER HAS A PROBLEM PLAYING SECOND FIDDLE TO JUST ONE WOMAN. IMAGINE IF WE BOTH WENT. HE MIGHT BLOW A FUSE.
I THINK YOU'RE CONFUSING ME WITH MY BROTHER.
IT IS NOT UP FOR DISCUSSION.

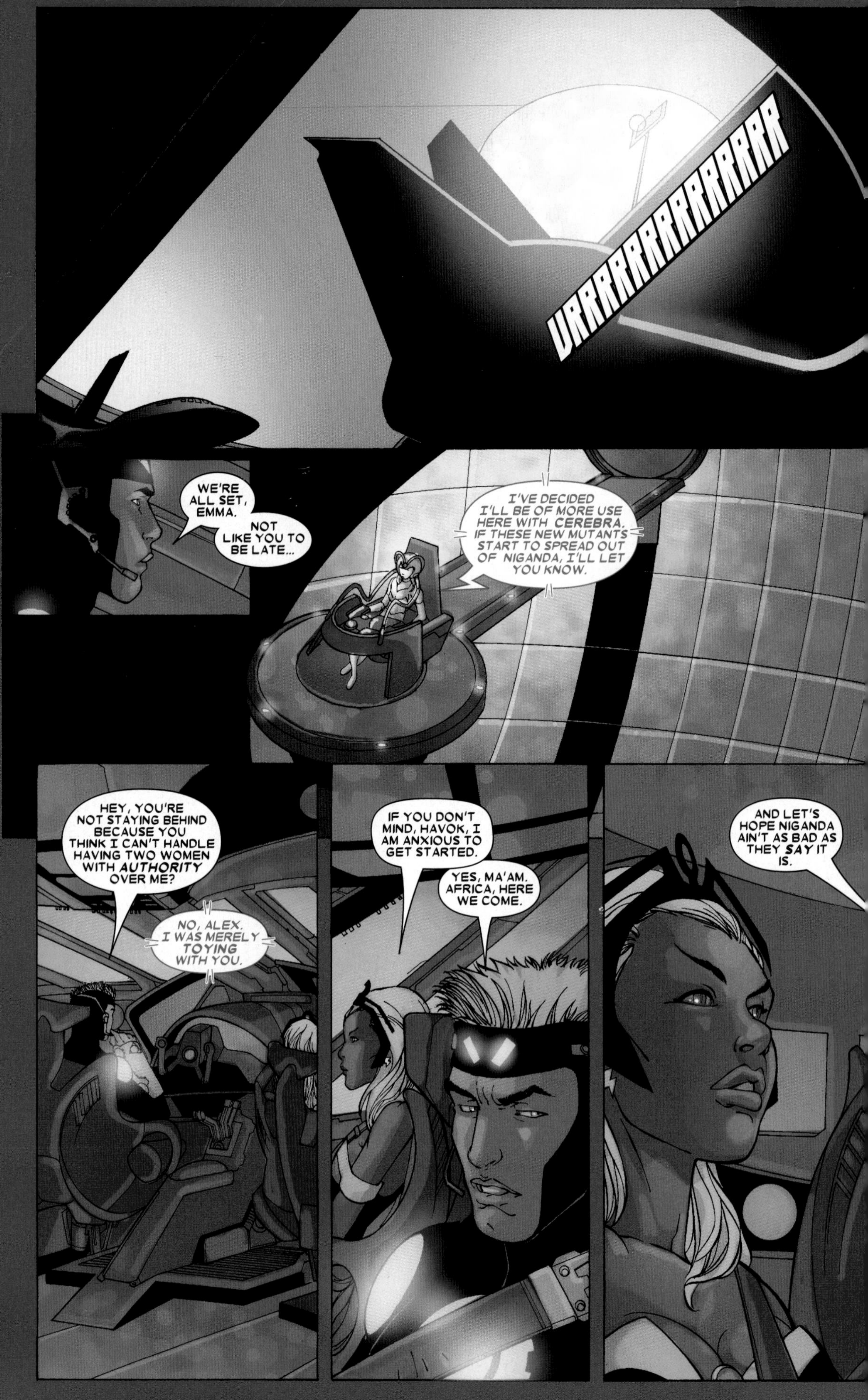
URRRRRRRRRRRRRRRR
WE'RE ALL SET, EMMA.
NOT LIKE YOU TO BE LATE...
I'VE DECIDED I'LL BE OF MORE USE HERE WITH CEREBRA. IF THESE NEW MUTANTS START TO SPREAD OUT OF NIGANDA, I'LL LET YOU KNOW.
HEY, YOU'RE NOT STAYING BEHIND BECAUSE YOU THINK I CAN'T HANDLE HAVING TWO WOMEN WITH *AUTHORITY* OVER ME?
NO, ALEX. I WAS MERELY *TOYING* WITH YOU.
IF YOU DON'T MIND, HAVOK, I AM ANXIOUS TO GET STARTED.
YES, MA'AM. AFRICA, HERE WE COME.
AND LET'S HOPE NIGANDA AIN'T AS BAD AS THEY *SAY* IT IS.

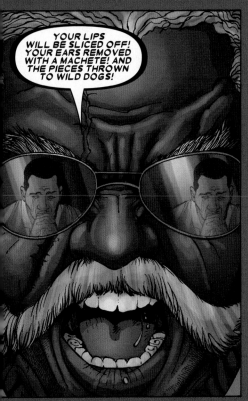

YOUR LIPS WILL BE SLICED OFF! YOUR EARS REMOVED WITH A MACHETE! AND THE PIECES THROWN TO WILD DOGS!

THIS IS THE *USUAL* PUNISHMENT FOR HELPING AN OFFICIAL OF THE NIGANDA PEOPLES' LIBERATION ARMY. BUT I HAVE *OTHER* PLANS...

TH-THAT MAN WAS *DYING!* I WAS SIMPLY DOING MY JOB AS A *PHYSICIAN...* THE HIPPOCRATIC OATH--

WHAPP!

YOU'VE BEEN POLLUTED BY THE *WEST,* PHYSICIAN.

IT'S TIME YOU EMBRACED THE *NEW* AFRICA.

BHAFF

AAHEEE!

OHHH...!

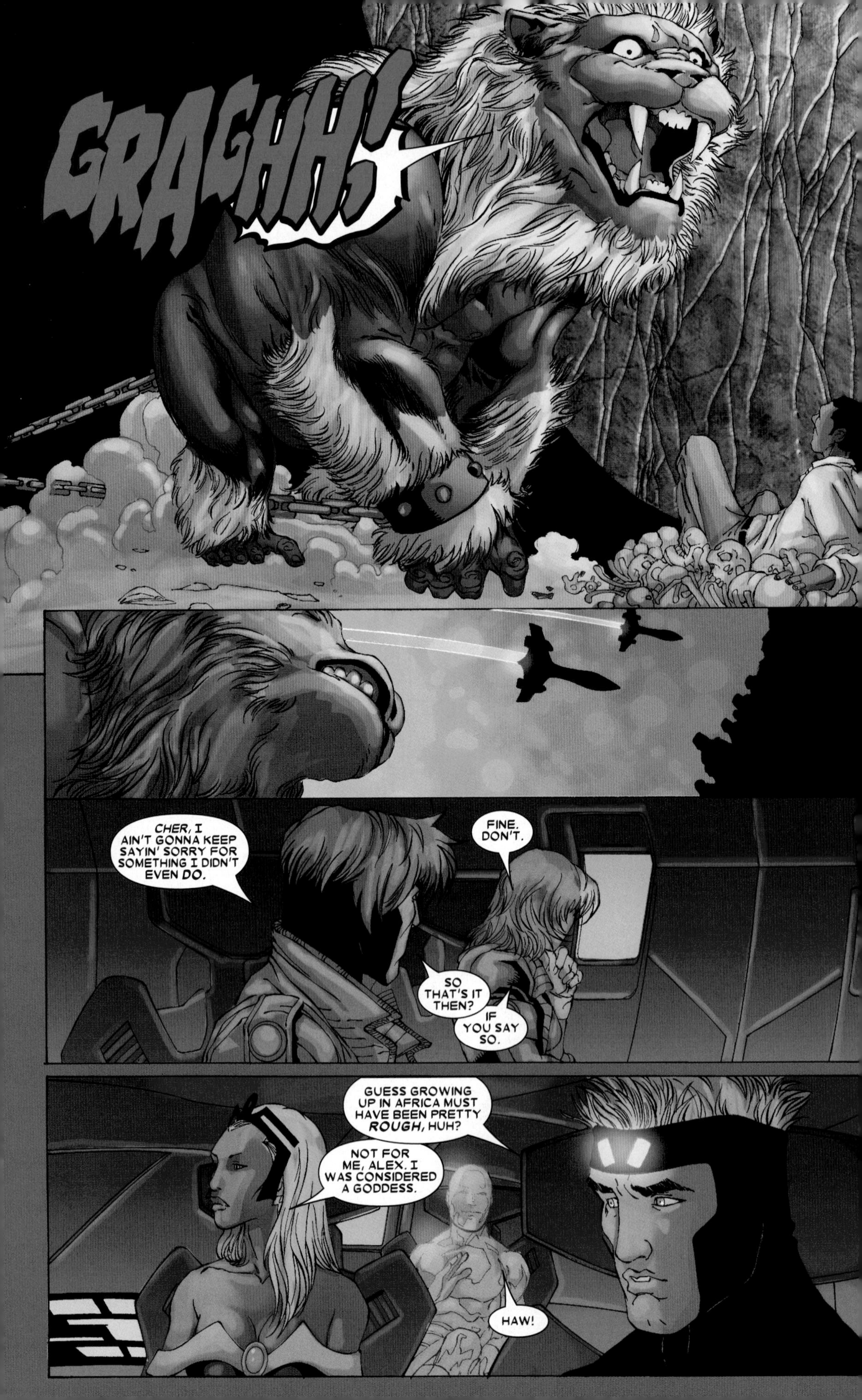
GRAGHH!
CHER, I AIN'T GONNA KEEP SAYIN' SORRY FOR SOMETHING I DIDN'T EVEN DO.
FINE. DON'T.
SO THAT'S IT THEN?
IF YOU SAY SO.
GUESS GROWING UP IN AFRICA MUST HAVE BEEN PRETTY ROUGH, HUH?
NOT FOR ME, ALEX. I WAS CONSIDERED A GODDESS.
HAW!

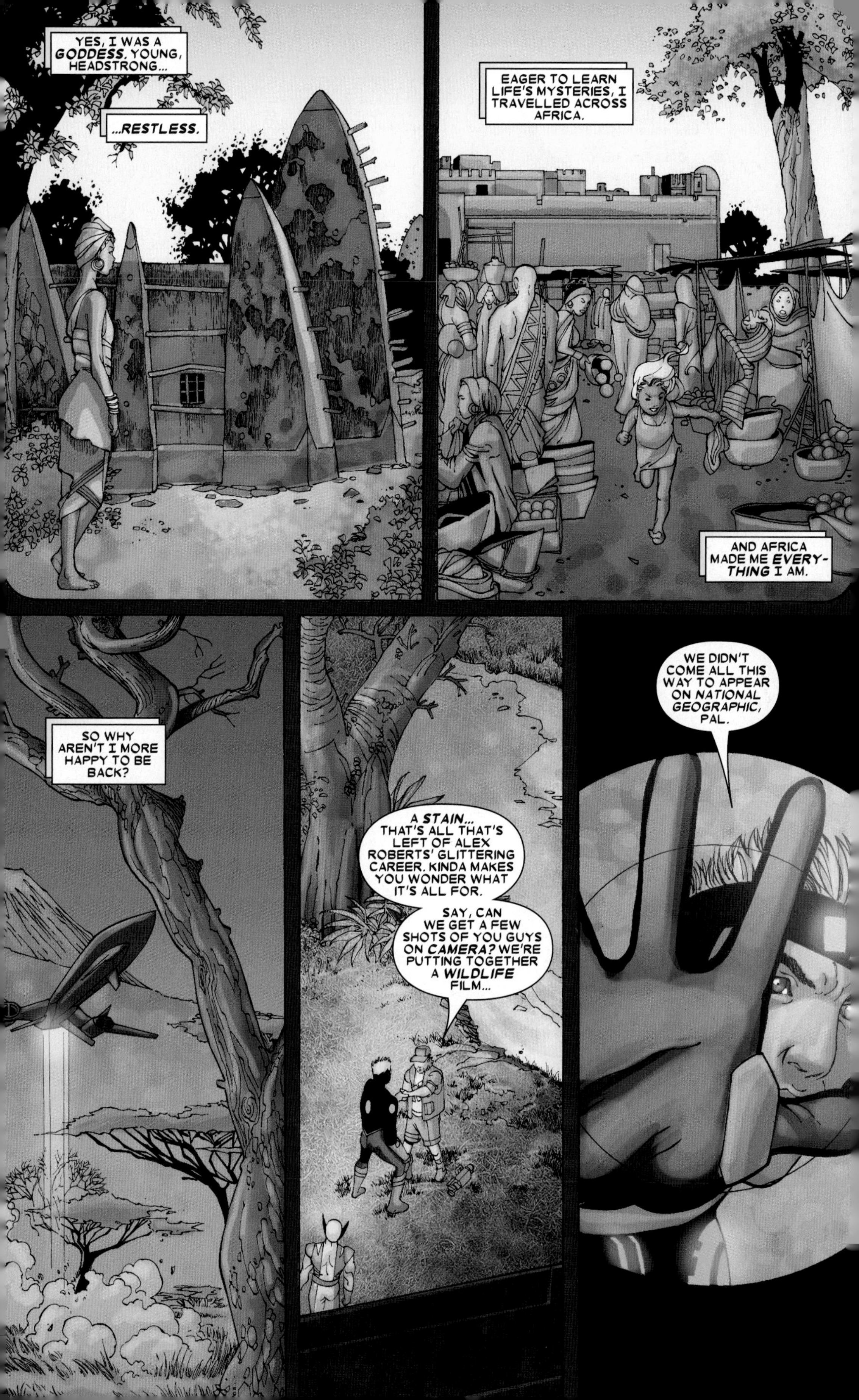
YES, I WAS A GODDESS, YOUNG, HEADSTRONG...
...RESTLESS.
EAGER TO LEARN LIFE'S MYSTERIES, I TRAVELLED ACROSS AFRICA.
AND AFRICA MADE ME EVERY-THING I AM.
SO WHY AREN'T I MORE HAPPY TO BE BACK?
A STAIN... THAT'S ALL THAT'S LEFT OF ALEX ROBERTS' GLITTERING CAREER. KINDA MAKES YOU WONDER WHAT IT'S ALL FOR.
SAY, CAN WE GET A FEW SHOTS OF YOU GUYS ON CAMERA? WE'RE PUTTING TOGETHER A WILDLIFE FILM...
WE DIDN'T COME ALL THIS WAY TO APPEAR ON NATIONAL GEOGRAPHIC, PAL.

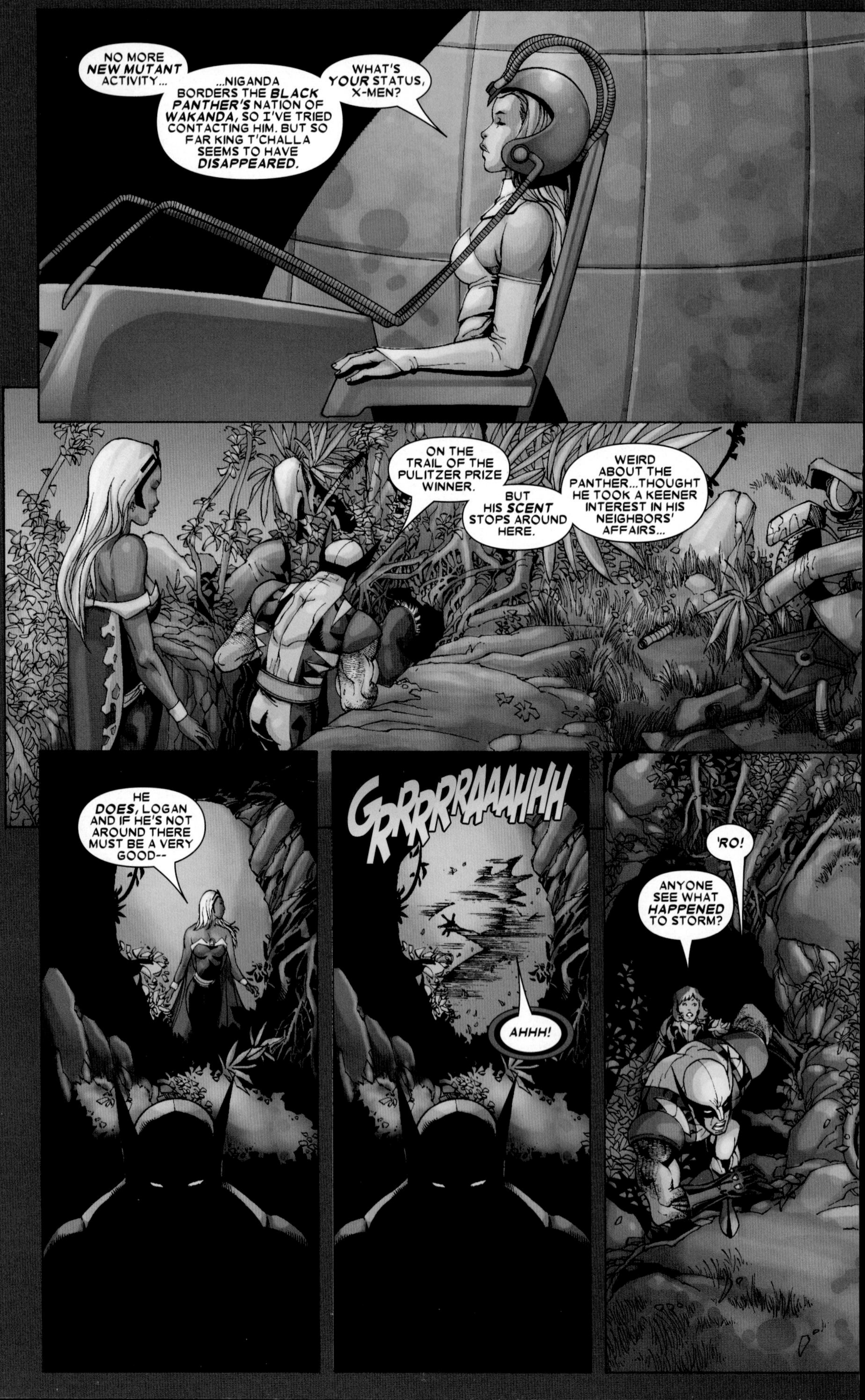
NO MORE NEW MUTANT ACTIVITY...
...NIGANDA BORDERS THE BLACK PANTHER'S NATION OF WAKANDA, SO I'VE TRIED CONTACTING HIM. BUT SO FAR KING T'CHALLA SEEMS TO HAVE DISAPPEARED.
WHAT'S YOUR STATUS, X-MEN?
ON THE TRAIL OF THE PULITZER PRIZE WINNER.
BUT HIS SCENT STOPS AROUND HERE.
WEIRD ABOUT THE PANTHER...THOUGHT HE TOOK A KEENER INTEREST IN HIS NEIGHBORS' AFFAIRS...
HE DOES, LOGAN AND IF HE'S NOT AROUND THERE MUST BE A VERY GOOD--
GRRRRRAAAHHH
AHHH!
'RO!
ANYONE SEE WHAT HAPPENED TO STORM?

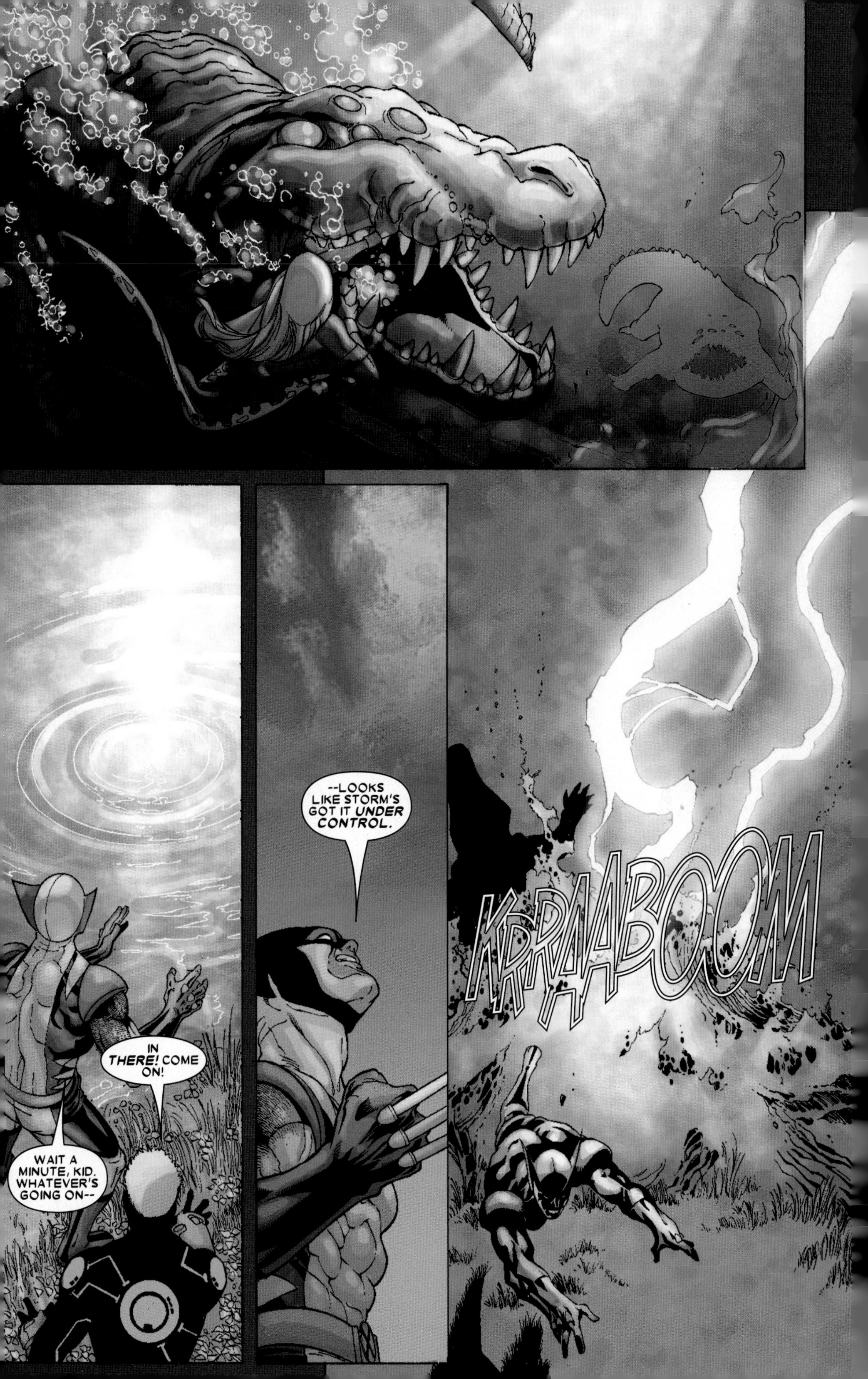
IN THERE! COME ON!
WAIT A MINUTE, KID. WHATEVER'S GOING ON--
--LOOKS LIKE STORM'S GOT IT UNDER CONTROL.
KRRAABOOM

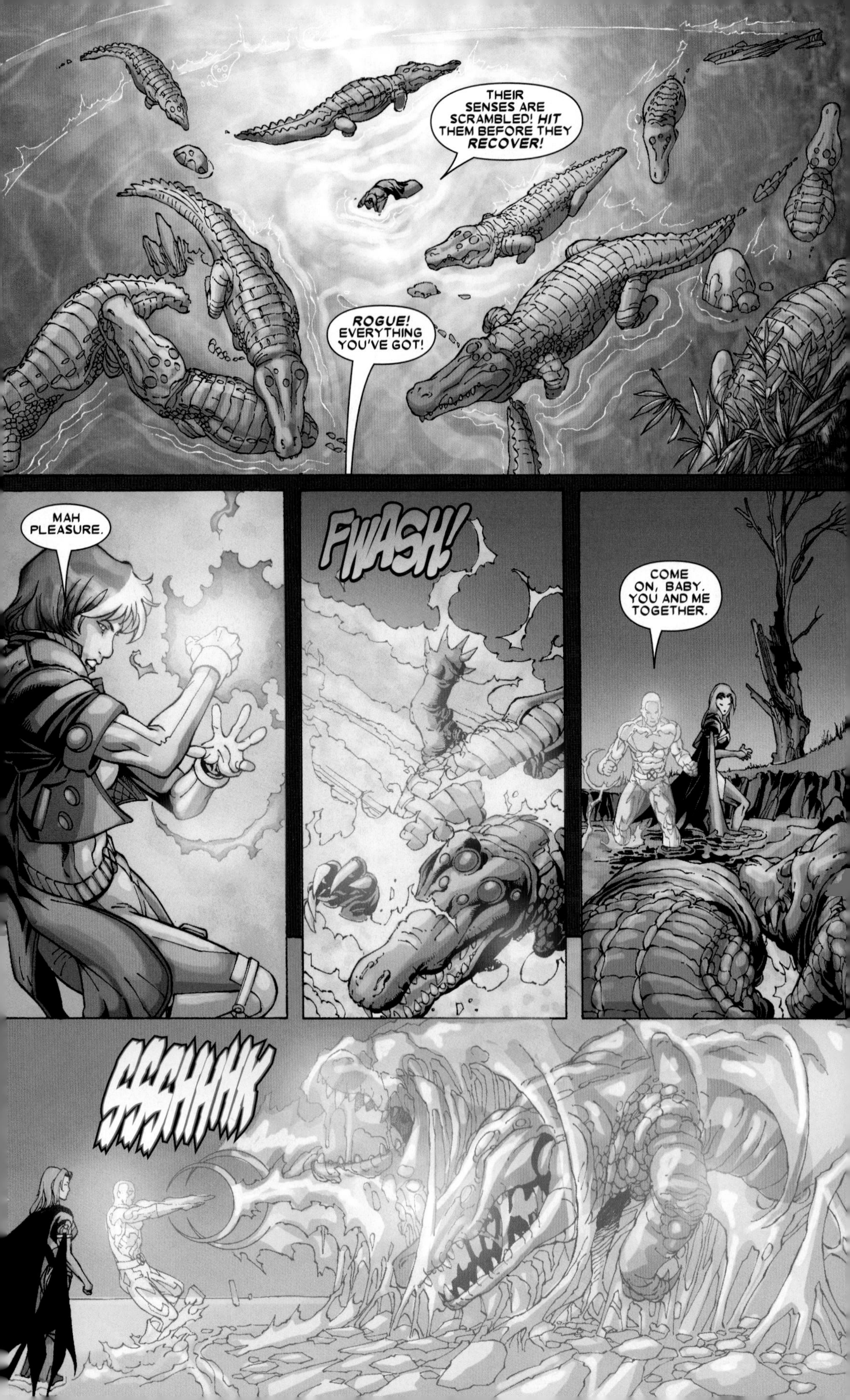
THEIR SENSES ARE SCRAMBLED! HIT THEM BEFORE THEY RECOVER!
ROGUE! EVERYTHING YOU'VE GOT!
MAH PLEASURE.
FWASH!
COME ON, BABY. YOU AND ME TOGETHER.
SSSHHKK

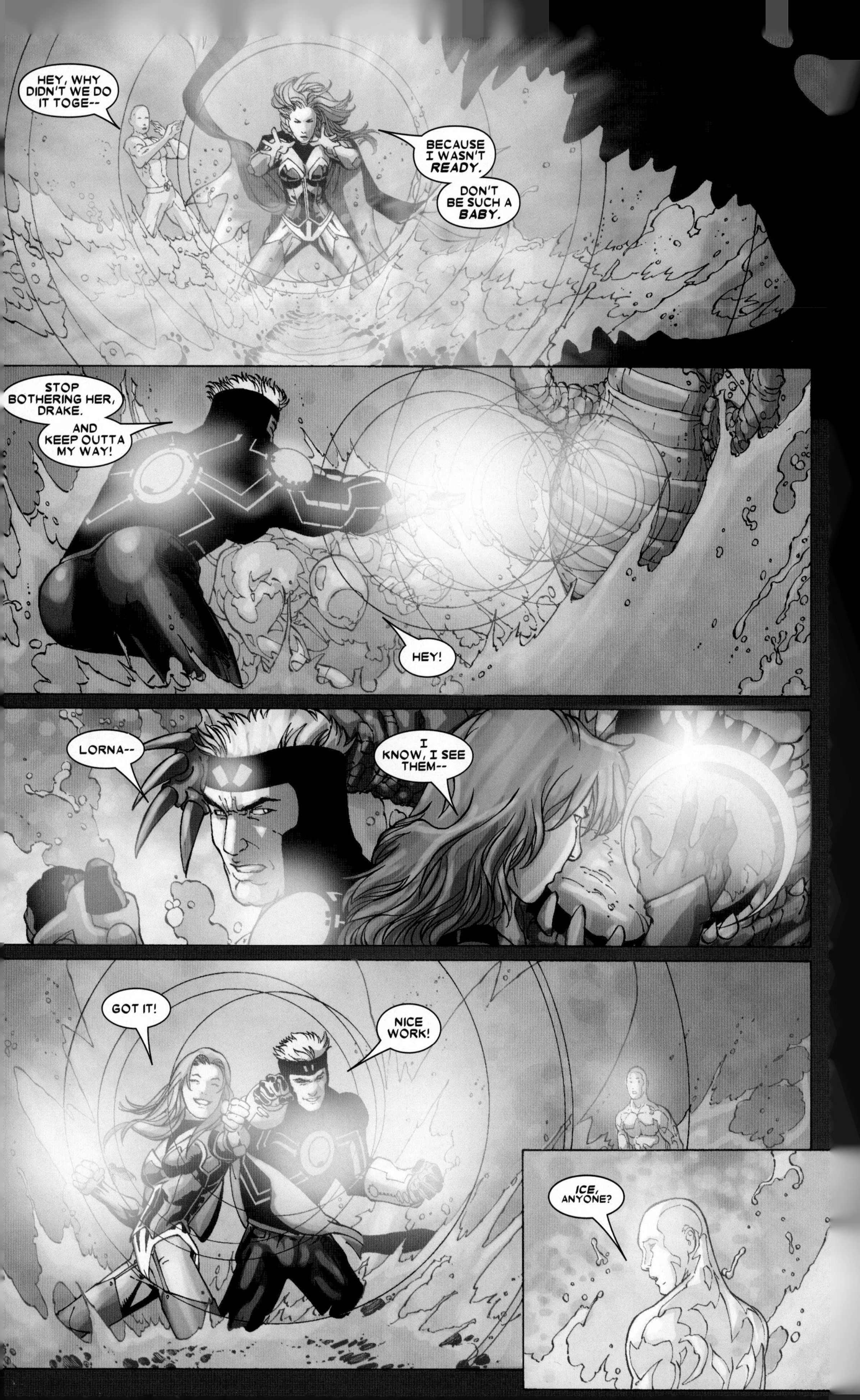
HEY, WHY DIDN'T WE DO IT TOGE--
BECAUSE I WASN'T *READY*.
DON'T BE SUCH A *BABY*.
STOP BOTHERING HER, DRAKE.
AND KEEP OUTTA MY WAY!
HEY!
LORNA--
I KNOW, I SEE THEM--
GOT IT!
NICE WORK!
ICE, ANYONE?

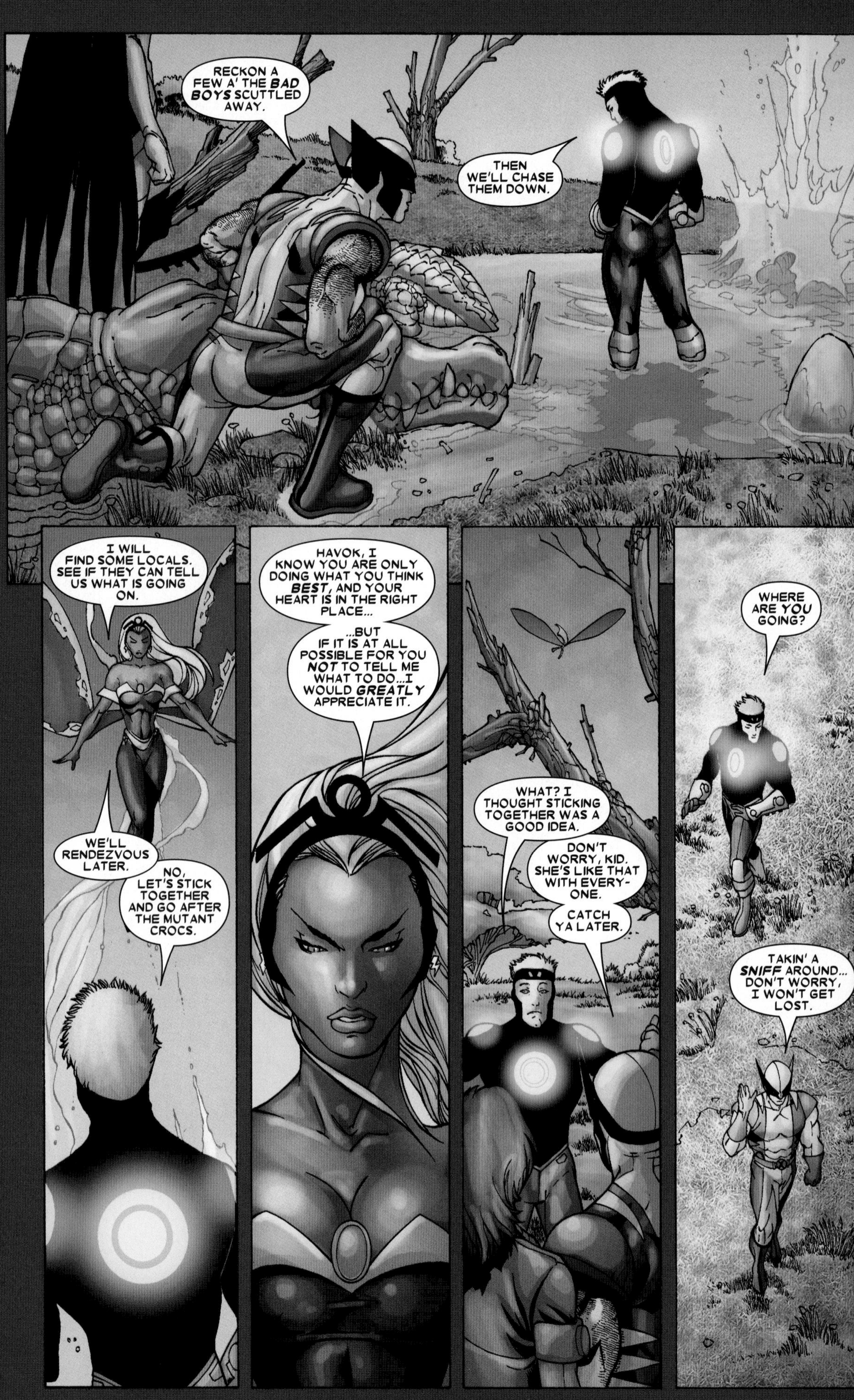
RECKON A FEW A' THE BAD BOYS SCUTTLED AWAY.
THEN WE'LL CHASE THEM DOWN.
I WILL FIND SOME LOCALS. SEE IF THEY CAN TELL US WHAT IS GOING ON.
WE'LL RENDEZVOUS LATER.
NO, LET'S STICK TOGETHER AND GO AFTER THE MUTANT CROCS.
HAVOK, I KNOW YOU ARE ONLY DOING WHAT YOU THINK BEST, AND YOUR HEART IS IN THE RIGHT PLACE...
...BUT IF IT IS AT ALL POSSIBLE FOR YOU NOT TO TELL ME WHAT TO DO...I WOULD GREATLY APPRECIATE IT.
WHAT? I THOUGHT STICKING TOGETHER WAS A GOOD IDEA.
DON'T WORRY, KID. SHE'S LIKE THAT WITH EVERY-ONE.
CATCH YA LATER.
WHERE ARE YOU GOING?
TAKIN' A SNIFF AROUND... DON'T WORRY, I WON'T GET LOST.

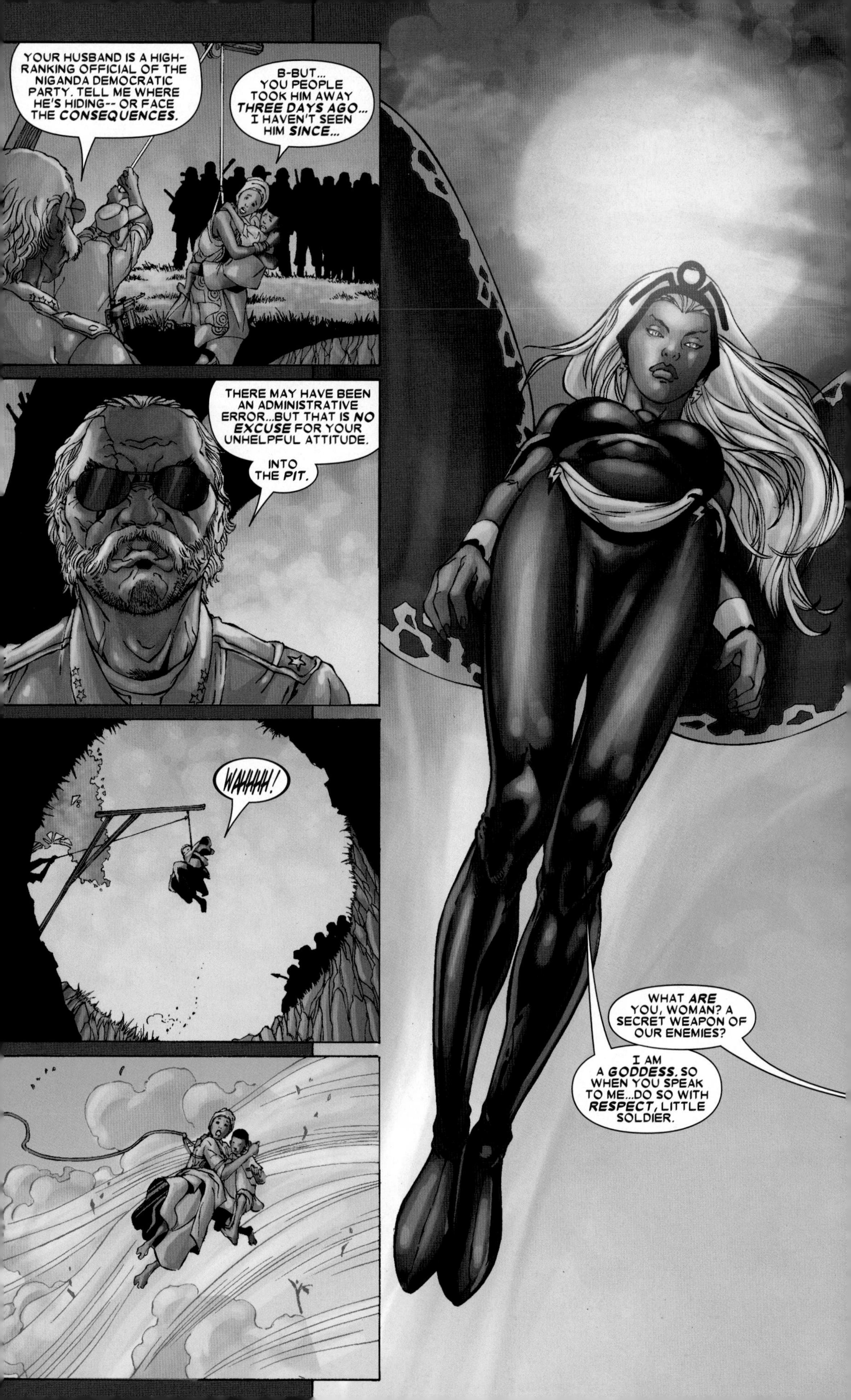
YOUR HUSBAND IS A HIGH-RANKING OFFICIAL OF THE NIGANDA DEMOCRATIC PARTY. TELL ME WHERE HE'S HIDING-- OR FACE THE CONSEQUENCES.
B-BUT... YOU PEOPLE TOOK HIM AWAY THREE DAYS AGO... I HAVEN'T SEEN HIM SINCE...
THERE MAY HAVE BEEN AN ADMINISTRATIVE ERROR...BUT THAT IS NO EXCUSE FOR YOUR UNHELPFUL ATTITUDE.
INTO THE PIT.
WAHHHH!
WHAT ARE YOU, WOMAN? A SECRET WEAPON OF OUR ENEMIES?
I AM A GODDESS. SO WHEN YOU SPEAK TO ME...DO SO WITH RESPECT, LITTLE SOLDIER.

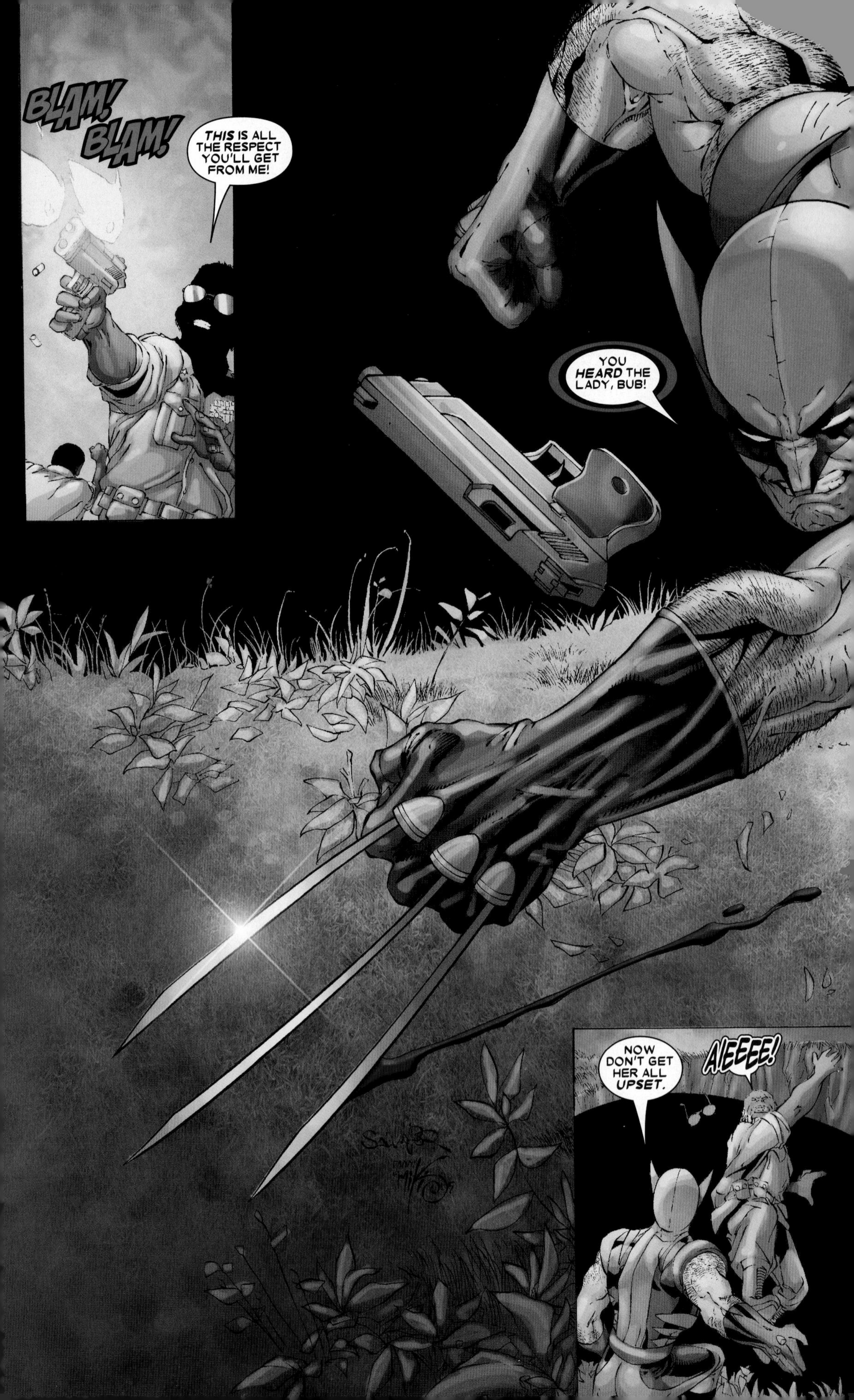
BLAM! BLAM!
THIS IS ALL THE RESPECT YOU'LL GET FROM ME!
YOU HEARD THE LADY, BUB!
NOW DON'T GET HER ALL UPSET.
AIEEEE!

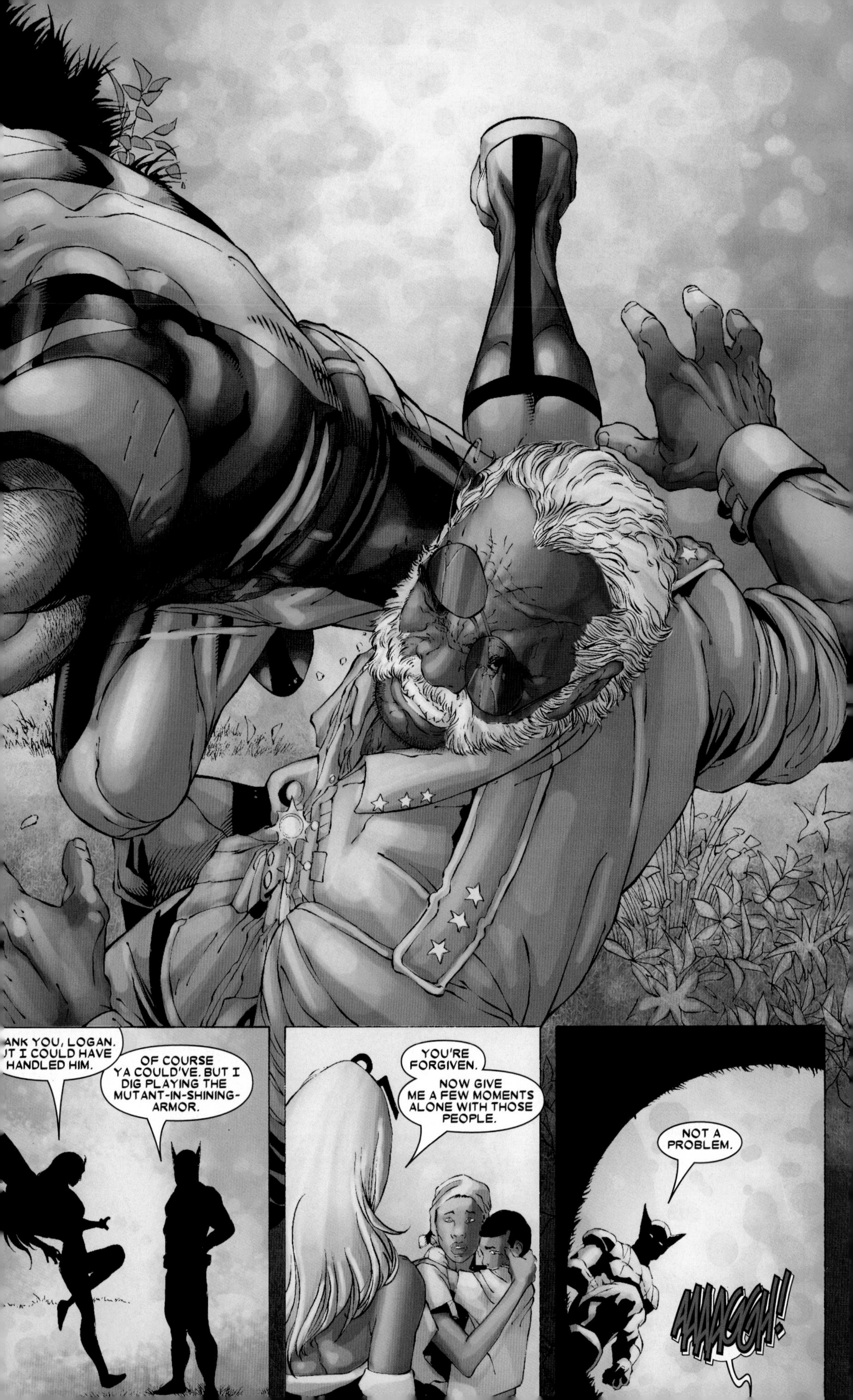
ANK YOU, LOGAN. UT I COULD HAVE HANDLED HIM.
OF COURSE YA COULD'VE. BUT I DIG PLAYING THE MUTANT-IN-SHINING-ARMOR.
YOU'RE FORGIVEN.
NOW GIVE ME A FEW MOMENTS ALONE WITH THOSE PEOPLE.
NOT A PROBLEM.
AAAAGGH!

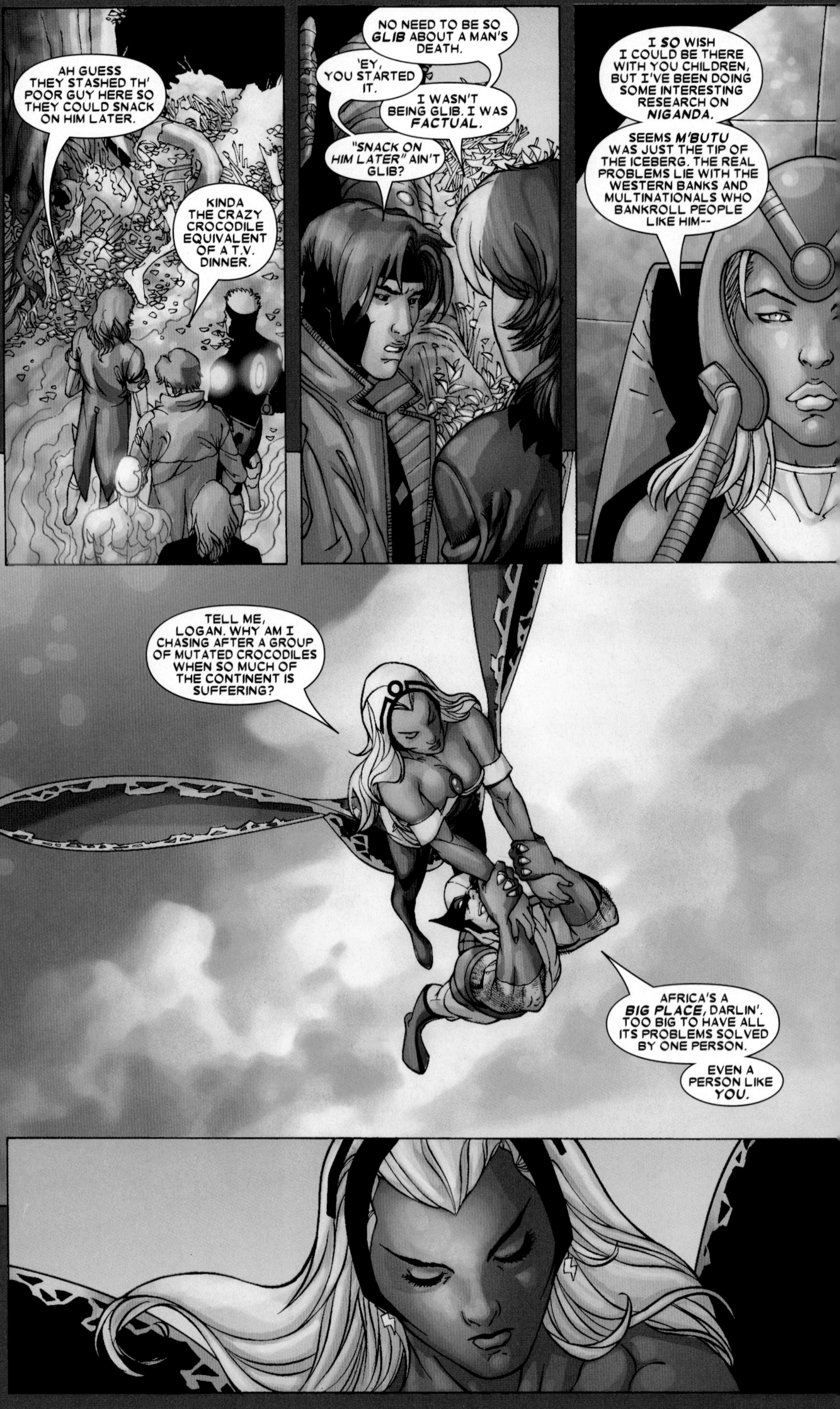
AH GUESS THEY STASHED TH' POOR GUY HERE SO THEY COULD SNACK ON HIM LATER.
KINDA THE CRAZY CROCODILE EQUIVALENT OF A T.V. DINNER.
NO NEED TO BE SO GLIB ABOUT A MAN'S DEATH.
'EY, YOU STARTED IT.
I WASN'T BEING GLIB. I WAS FACTUAL.
"SNACK ON HIM LATER" AIN'T GLIB?
I SO WISH I COULD BE THERE WITH YOU CHILDREN, BUT I'VE BEEN DOING SOME INTERESTING RESEARCH ON NIGANDA.
SEEMS M'BUTU WAS JUST THE TIP OF THE ICEBERG. THE REAL PROBLEMS LIE WITH THE WESTERN BANKS AND MULTINATIONALS WHO BANKROLL PEOPLE LIKE HIM--
TELL ME, LOGAN. WHY AM I CHASING AFTER A GROUP OF MUTATED CROCODILES WHEN SO MUCH OF THE CONTINENT IS SUFFERING?
AFRICA'S A BIG PLACE, DARLIN'. TOO BIG TO HAVE ALL ITS PROBLEMS SOLVED BY ONE PERSON.
EVEN A PERSON LIKE YOU.

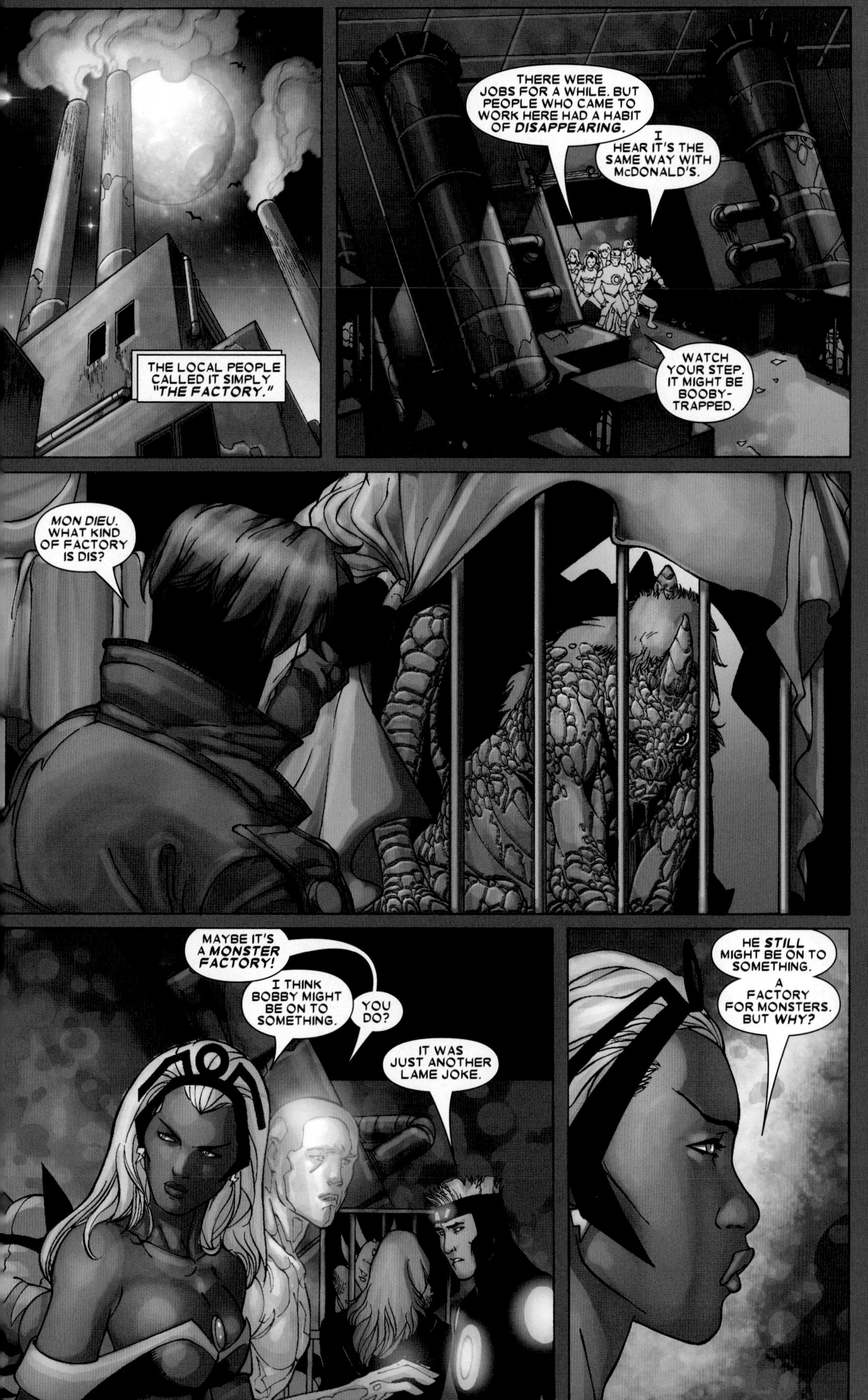
THE LOCAL PEOPLE CALLED IT SIMPLY "THE FACTORY."
THERE WERE JOBS FOR A WHILE. BUT PEOPLE WHO CAME TO WORK HERE HAD A HABIT OF DISAPPEARING.
I HEAR IT'S THE SAME WAY WITH McDONALD'S.
WATCH YOUR STEP. IT MIGHT BE BOOBY-TRAPPED.
MON DIEU. WHAT KIND OF FACTORY IS DIS?
MAYBE IT'S A MONSTER FACTORY!
I THINK BOBBY MIGHT BE ON TO SOMETHING.
YOU DO?
IT WAS JUST ANOTHER LAME JOKE.
HE STILL MIGHT BE ON TO SOMETHING.
A FACTORY FOR MONSTERS. BUT WHY?

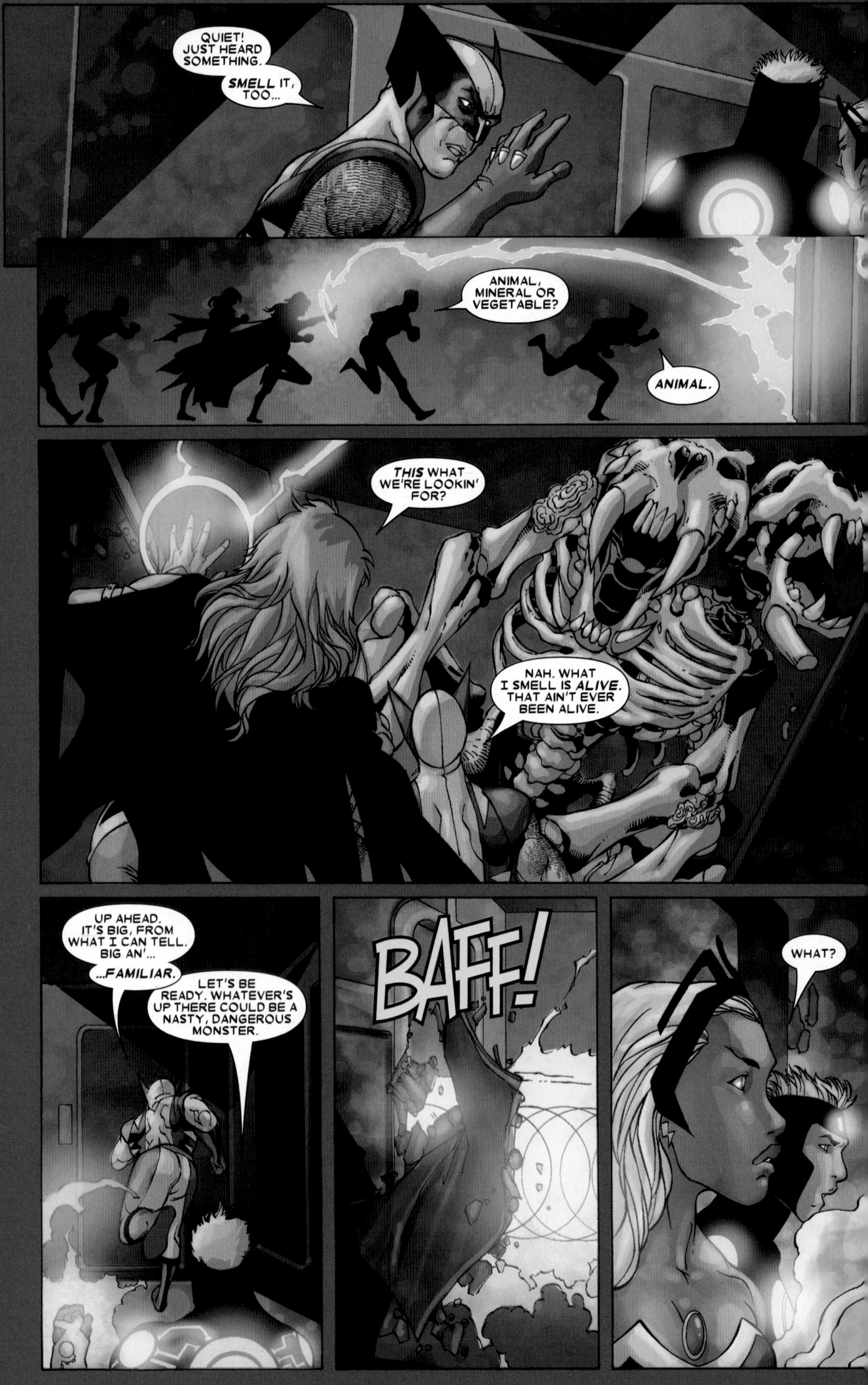
QUIET! JUST HEARD SOMETHING.
SMELL IT, TOO...
ANIMAL, MINERAL OR VEGETABLE?
ANIMAL.
THIS WHAT WE'RE LOOKIN' FOR?
NAH. WHAT I SMELL IS ALIVE. THAT AIN'T EVER BEEN ALIVE.
UP AHEAD. IT'S BIG, FROM WHAT I CAN TELL. BIG AN'...
...FAMILIAR.
LET'S BE READY. WHATEVER'S UP THERE COULD BE A NASTY, DANGEROUS MONSTER.
BAFF!
WHAT?

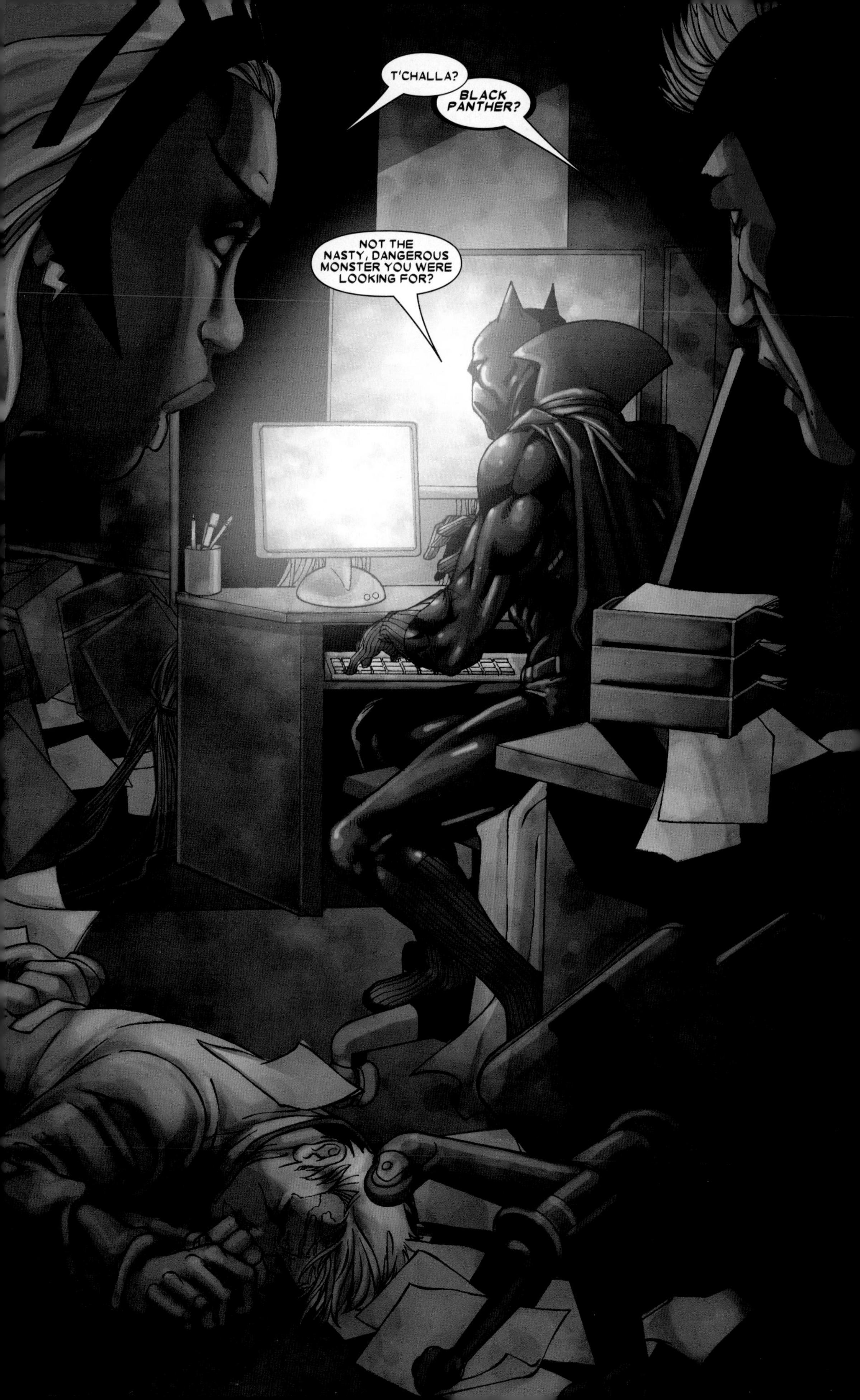
T'CHALLA?
BLACK PANTHER?
NOT THE NASTY, DANGEROUS MONSTER YOU WERE LOOKING FOR?

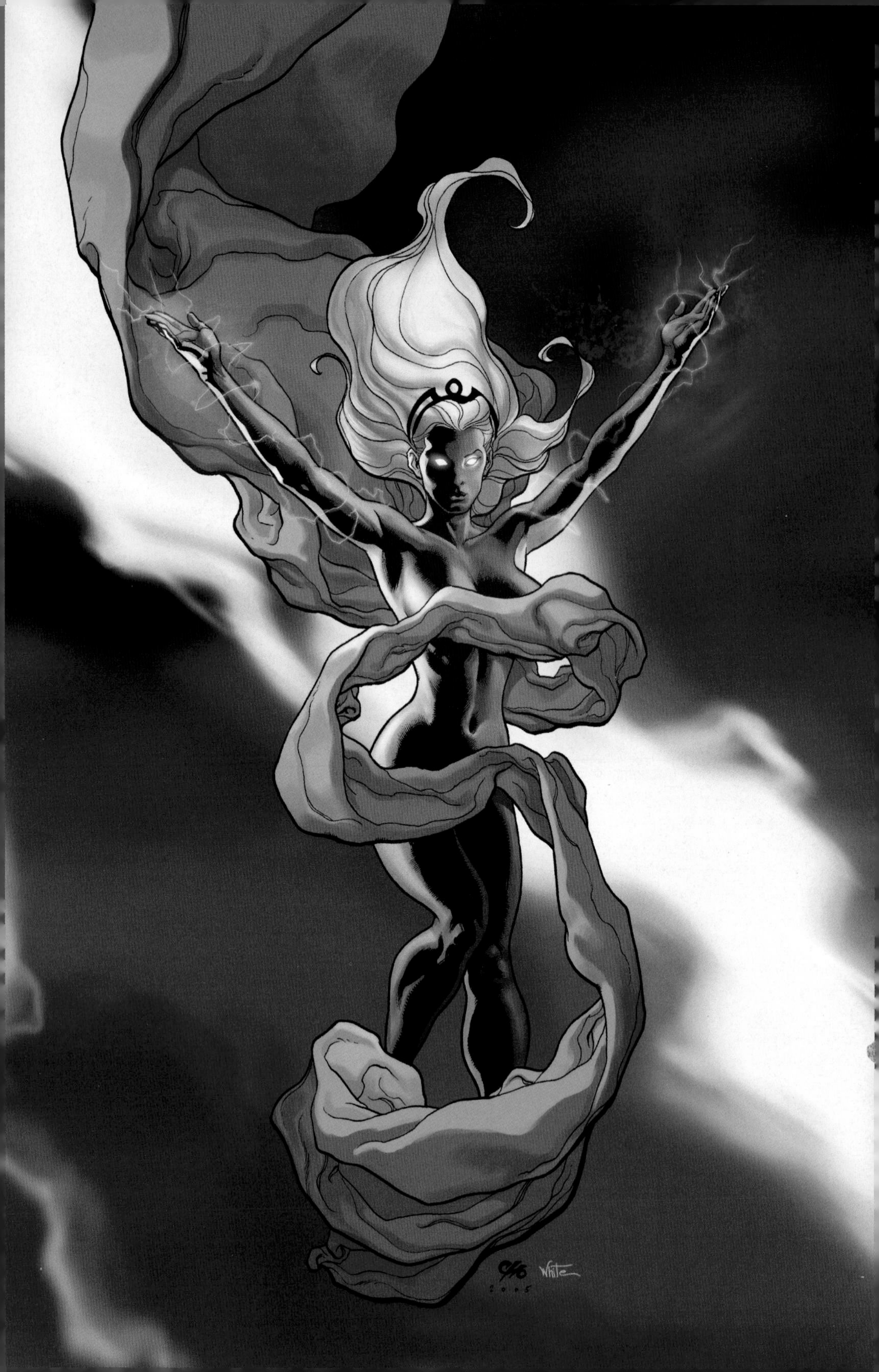
White
2005

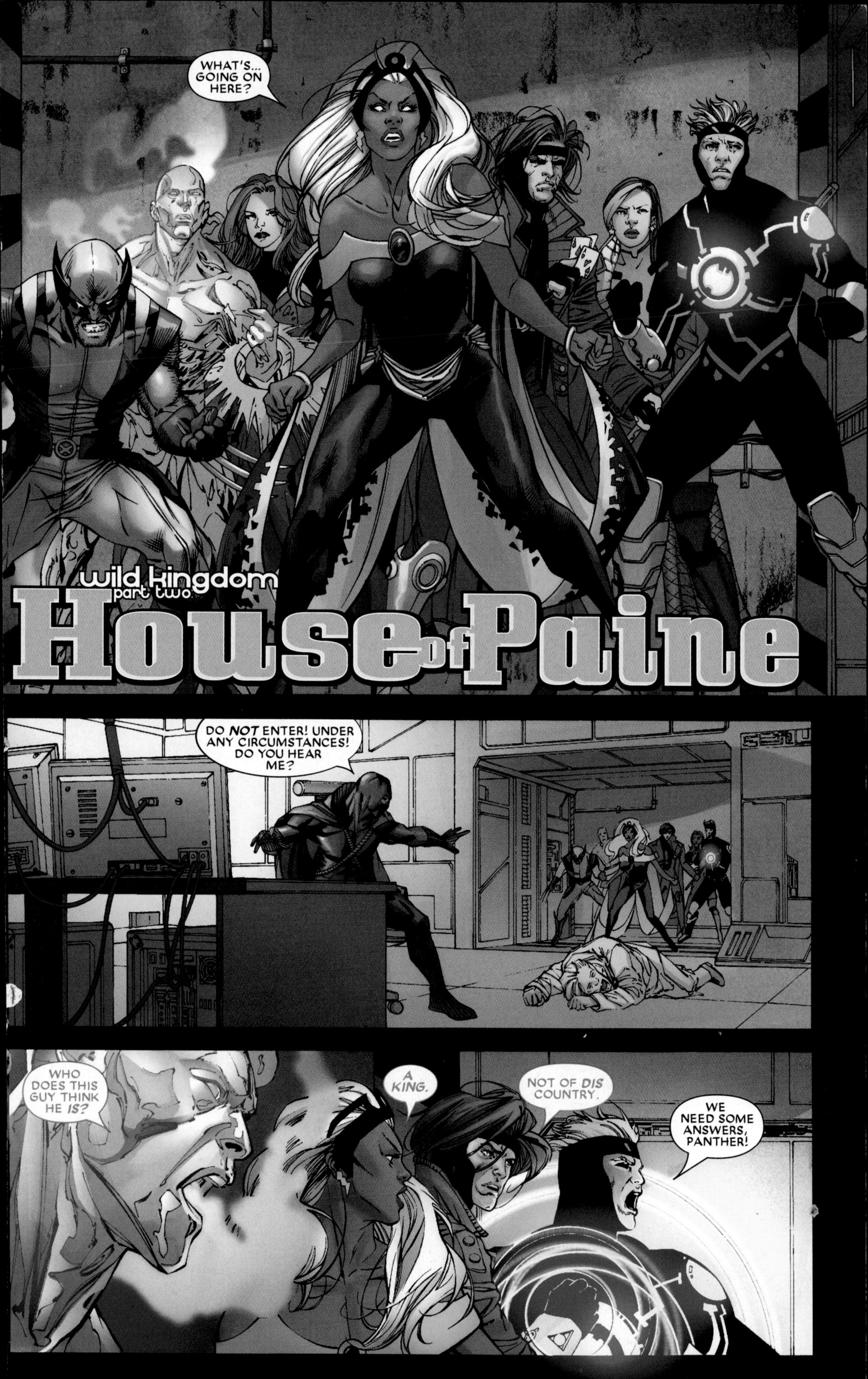
WHAT'S... GOING ON HERE?
wild kingdom
part two:
House of Paine
DO NOT ENTER! UNDER ANY CIRCUMSTANCES! DO YOU HEAR ME?
WHO DOES THIS GUY THINK HE IS?
A KING.
NOT OF DIS COUNTRY.
WE NEED SOME ANSWERS, PANTHER!

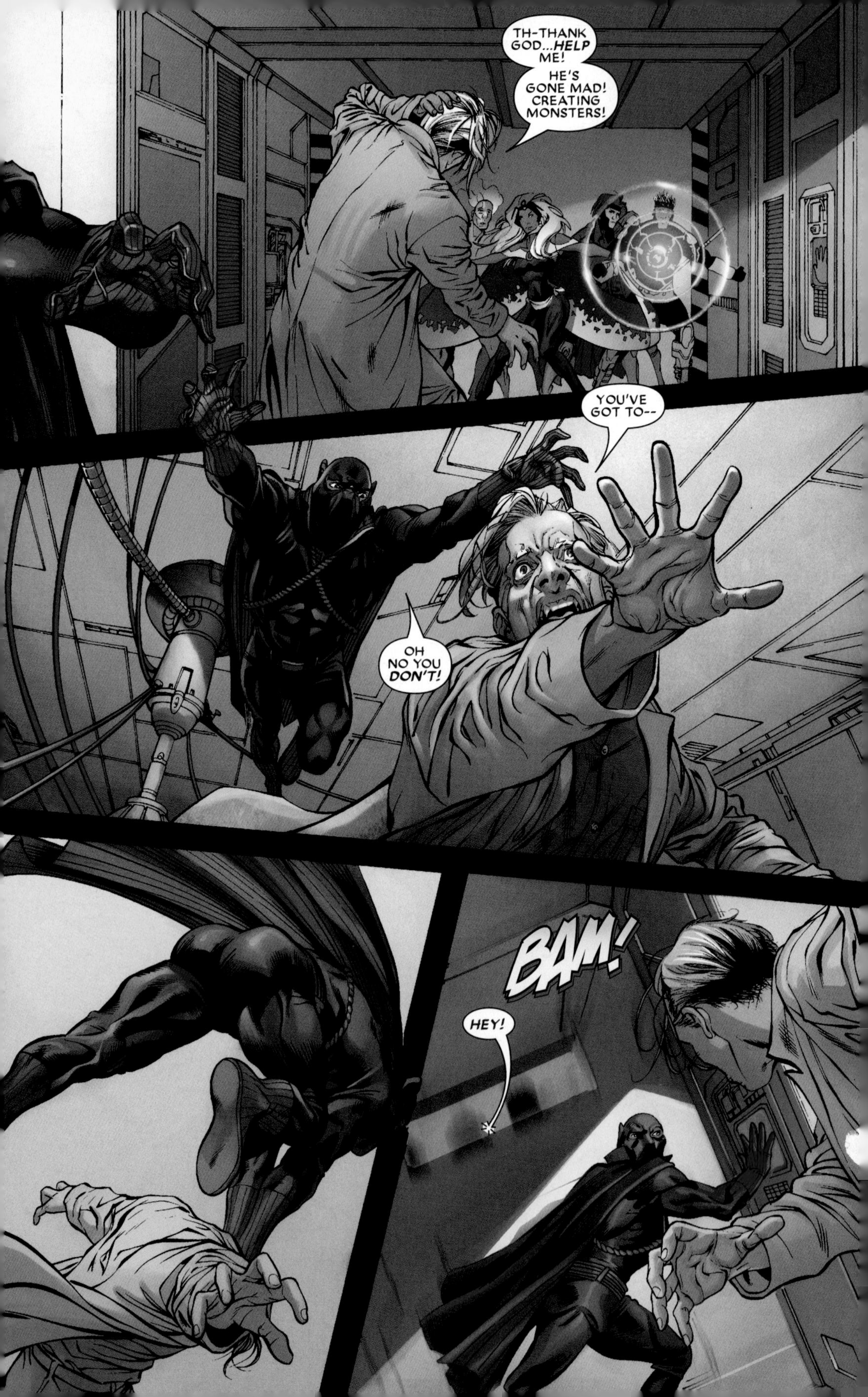

TH-THANK GOD...HELP ME!
HE'S GONE MAD! CREATING MONSTERS!
YOU'VE GOT TO--
OH NO YOU DON'T!
BAM!
HEY!

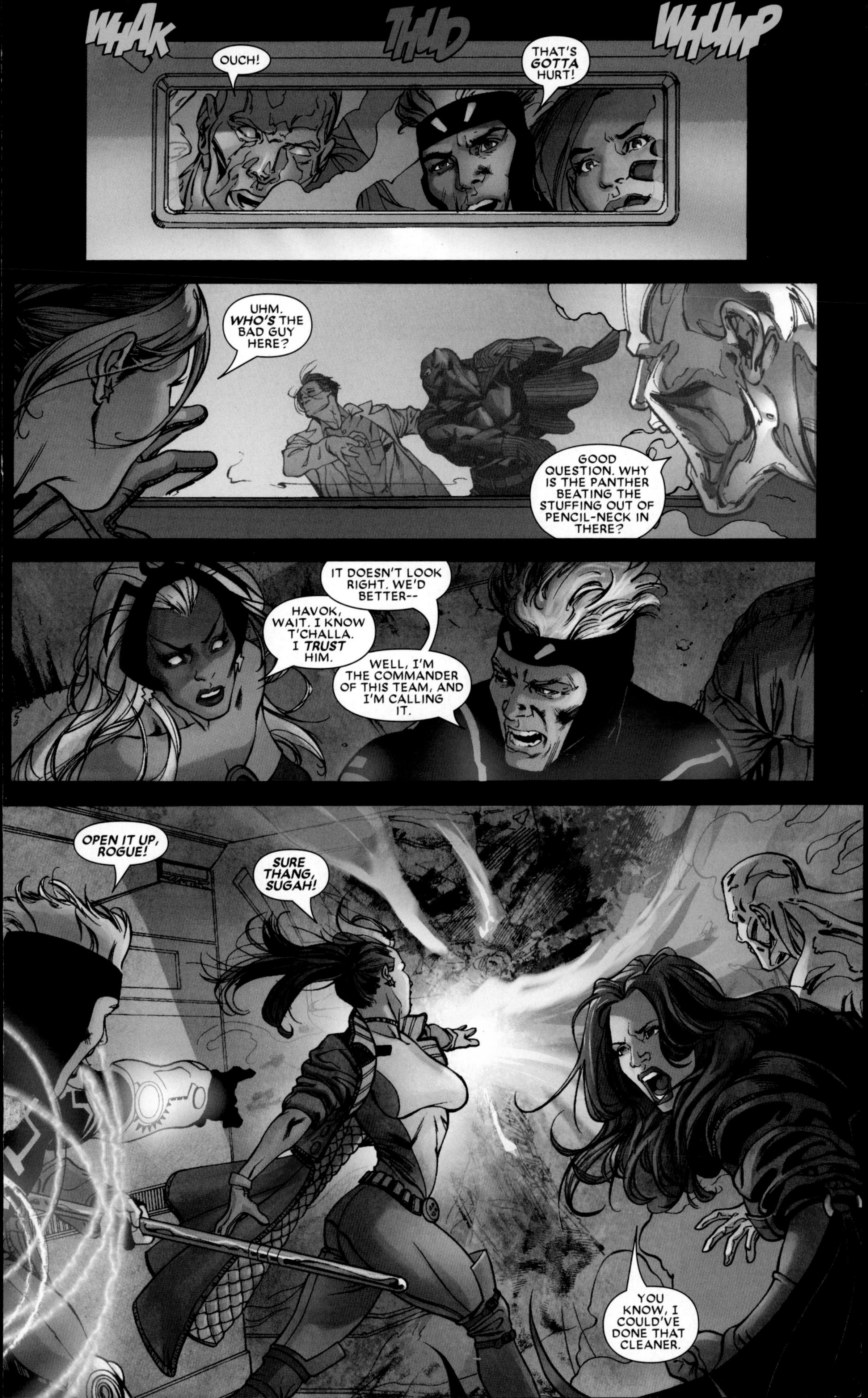
WHAK
THUD
WHUMP
OUCH!
THAT'S GOTTA HURT!
UHM. WHO'S THE BAD GUY HERE?
GOOD QUESTION. WHY IS THE PANTHER BEATING THE STUFFING OUT OF PENCIL-NECK IN THERE?
IT DOESN'T LOOK RIGHT. WE'D BETTER--
HAVOK, WAIT. I KNOW T'CHALLA. I TRUST HIM.
WELL, I'M THE COMMANDER OF THIS TEAM, AND I'M CALLING IT.
OPEN IT UP, ROGUE!
SURE THANG, SUGAH!
YOU KNOW, I COULD'VE DONE THAT CLEANER.

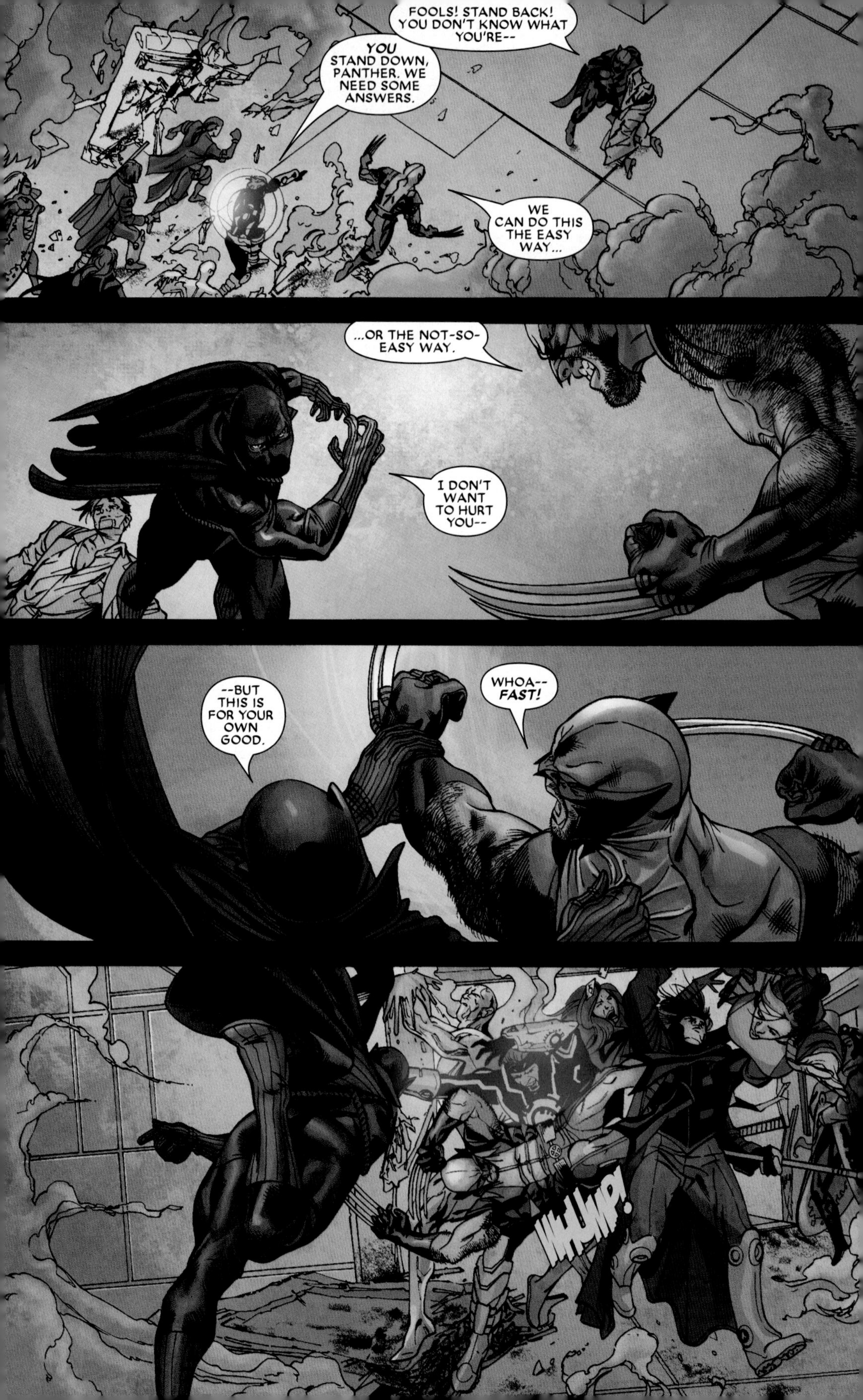
FOOLS! STAND BACK! YOU DON'T KNOW WHAT YOU'RE--
YOU STAND DOWN, PANTHER. WE NEED SOME ANSWERS.
WE CAN DO THIS THE EASY WAY...
...OR THE NOT-SO-EASY WAY.
I DON'T WANT TO HURT YOU--
--BUT THIS IS FOR YOUR OWN GOOD.
WHOA-- FAST!
WHUMP!

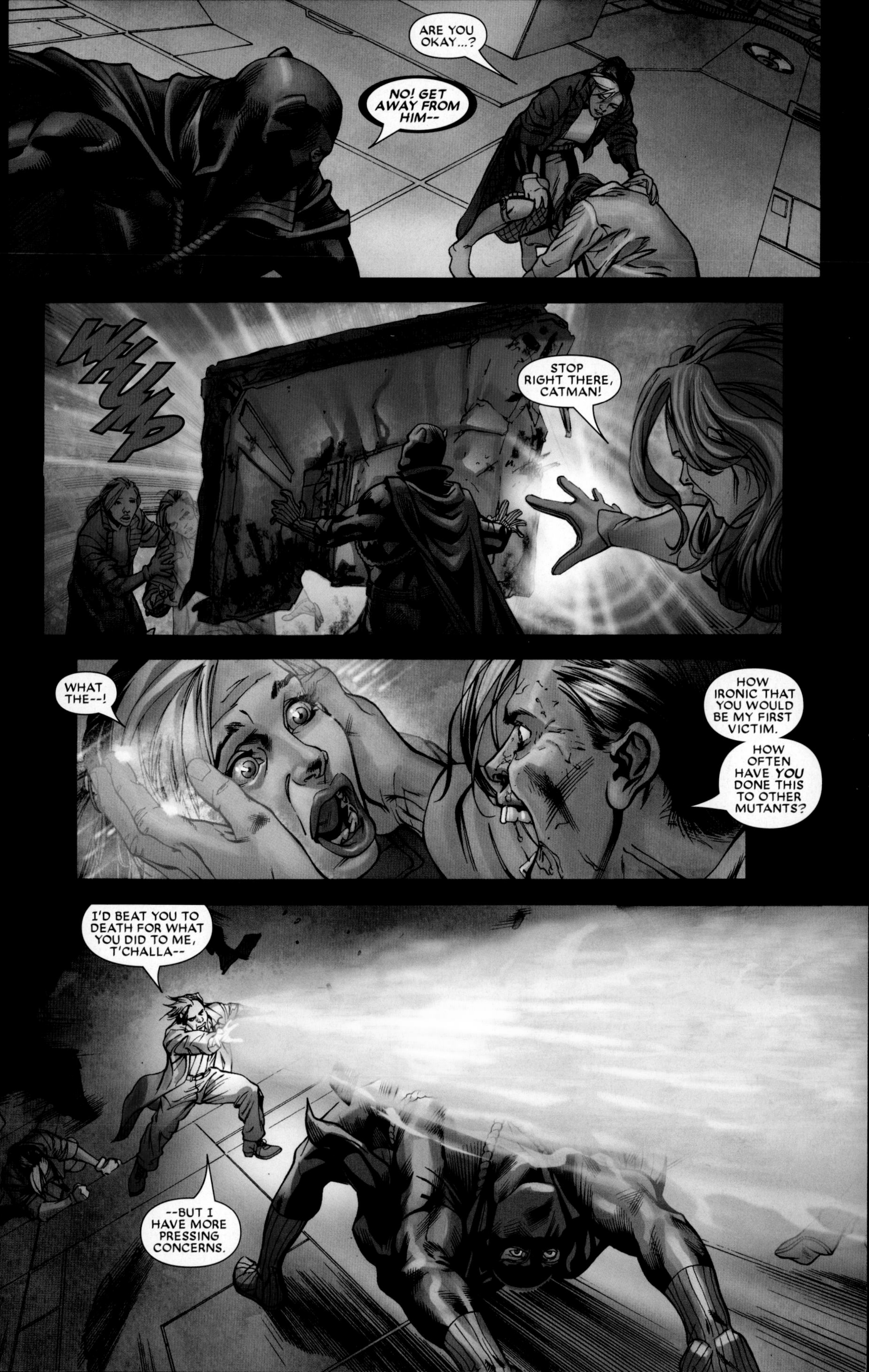
ARE YOU OKAY...?
NO! GET AWAY FROM HIM--
WHUMP
STOP RIGHT THERE, CATMAN!
WHAT THE--!
HOW IRONIC THAT YOU WOULD BE MY FIRST VICTIM.
HOW OFTEN HAVE YOU DONE THIS TO OTHER MUTANTS?
I'D BEAT YOU TO DEATH FOR WHAT YOU DID TO ME, T'CHALLA--
--BUT I HAVE MORE PRESSING CONCERNS.

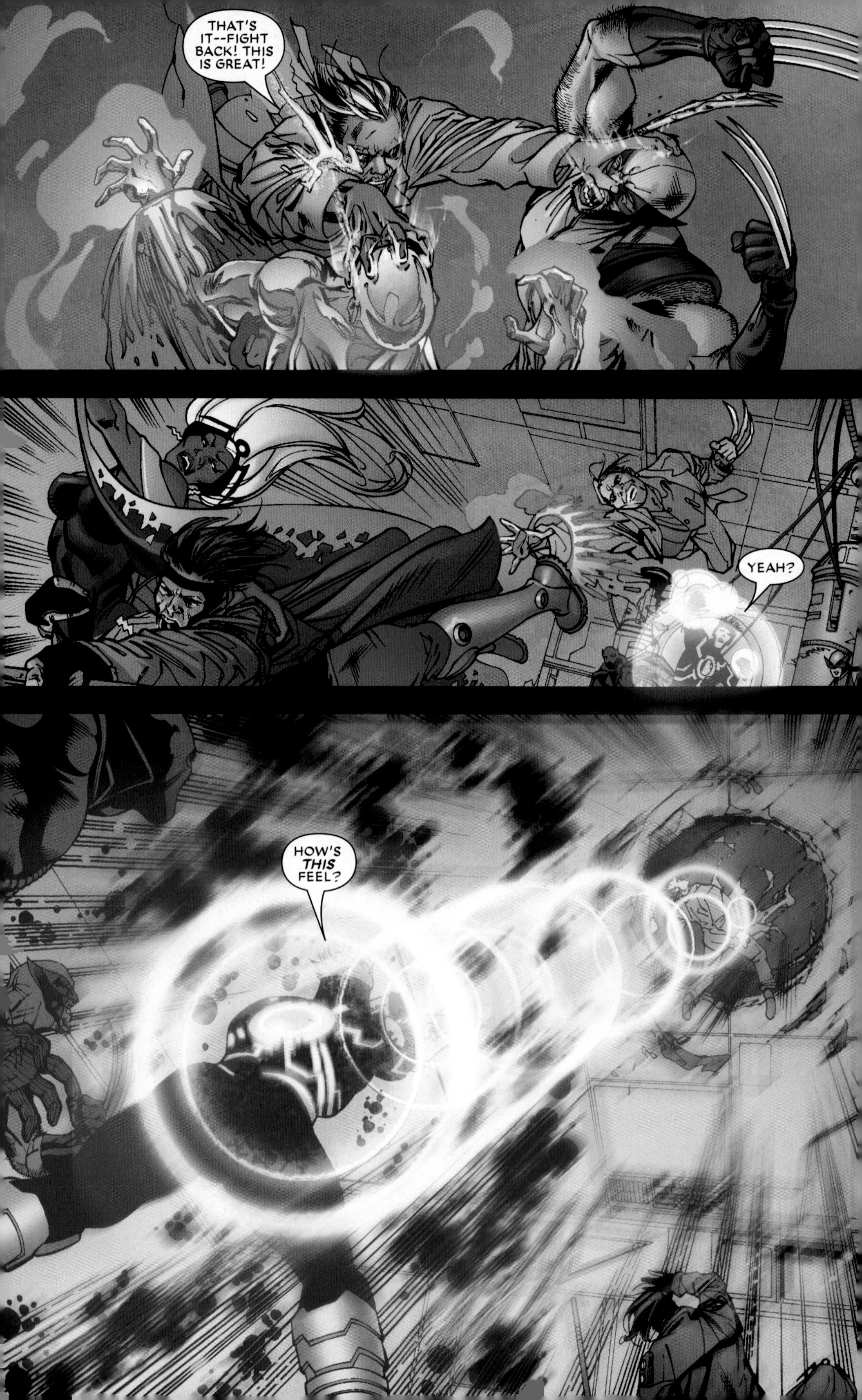
THAT'S IT--FIGHT BACK! THIS IS GREAT!
YEAH?
HOW'S THIS FEEL?

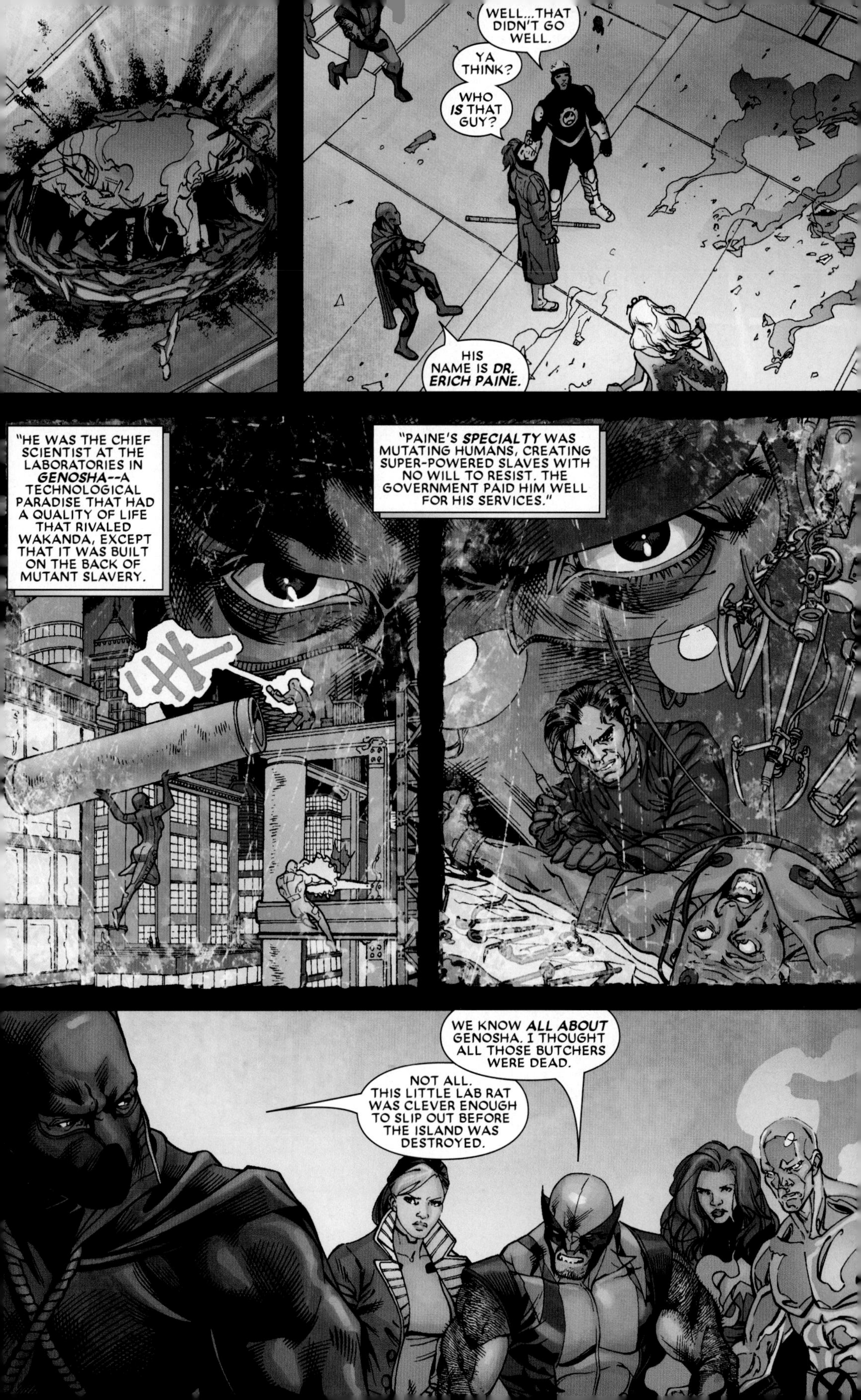
WELL...THAT DIDN'T GO WELL.
YA THINK?
WHO IS THAT GUY?
HIS NAME IS DR. ERICH PAINE.
"HE WAS THE CHIEF SCIENTIST AT THE LABORATORIES IN GENOSHA--A TECHNOLOGICAL PARADISE THAT HAD A QUALITY OF LIFE THAT RIVALED WAKANDA, EXCEPT THAT IT WAS BUILT ON THE BACK OF MUTANT SLAVERY.
"PAINE'S SPECIALTY WAS MUTATING HUMANS, CREATING SUPER-POWERED SLAVES WITH NO WILL TO RESIST. THE GOVERNMENT PAID HIM WELL FOR HIS SERVICES."
WE KNOW ALL ABOUT GENOSHA. I THOUGHT ALL THOSE BUTCHERS WERE DEAD.
NOT ALL. THIS LITTLE LAB RAT WAS CLEVER ENOUGH TO SLIP OUT BEFORE THE ISLAND WAS DESTROYED.

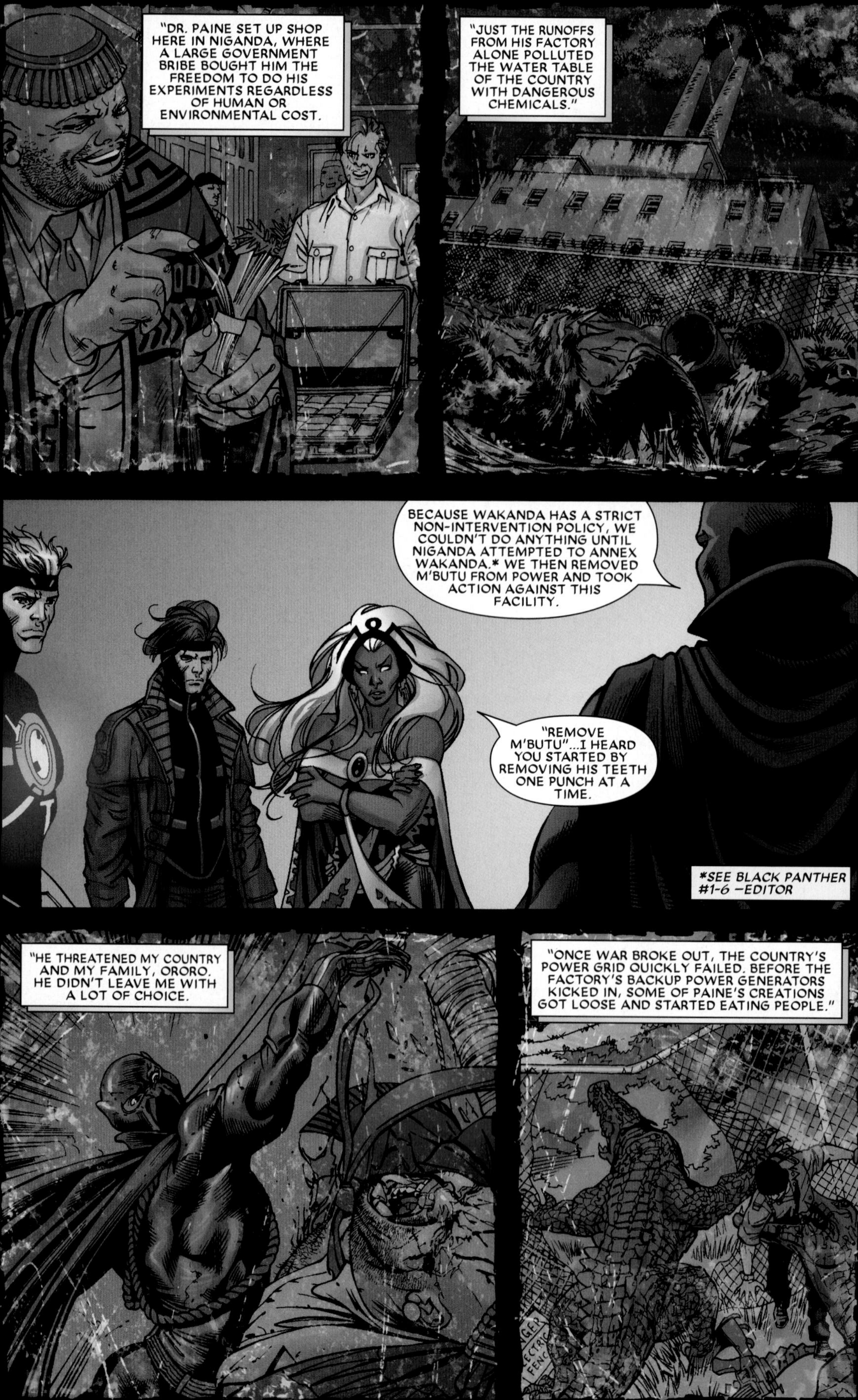
"DR. PAINE SET UP SHOP HERE IN NIGANDA, WHERE A LARGE GOVERNMENT BRIBE BOUGHT HIM THE FREEDOM TO DO HIS EXPERIMENTS REGARDLESS OF HUMAN OR ENVIRONMENTAL COST.
"JUST THE RUNOFFS FROM HIS FACTORY ALONE POLLUTED THE WATER TABLE OF THE COUNTRY WITH DANGEROUS CHEMICALS."
BECAUSE WAKANDA HAS A STRICT NON-INTERVENTION POLICY, WE COULDN'T DO ANYTHING UNTIL NIGANDA ATTEMPTED TO ANNEX WAKANDA.* WE THEN REMOVED M'BUTU FROM POWER AND TOOK ACTION AGAINST THIS FACILITY.
"REMOVE M'BUTU"...I HEARD YOU STARTED BY REMOVING HIS TEETH ONE PUNCH AT A TIME.
*SEE BLACK PANTHER #1-6 —EDITOR
"HE THREATENED MY COUNTRY AND MY FAMILY, ORORO. HE DIDN'T LEAVE ME WITH A LOT OF CHOICE.
"ONCE WAR BROKE OUT, THE COUNTRY'S POWER GRID QUICKLY FAILED. BEFORE THE FACTORY'S BACKUP POWER GENERATORS KICKED IN, SOME OF PAINE'S CREATIONS GOT LOOSE AND STARTED EATING PEOPLE."

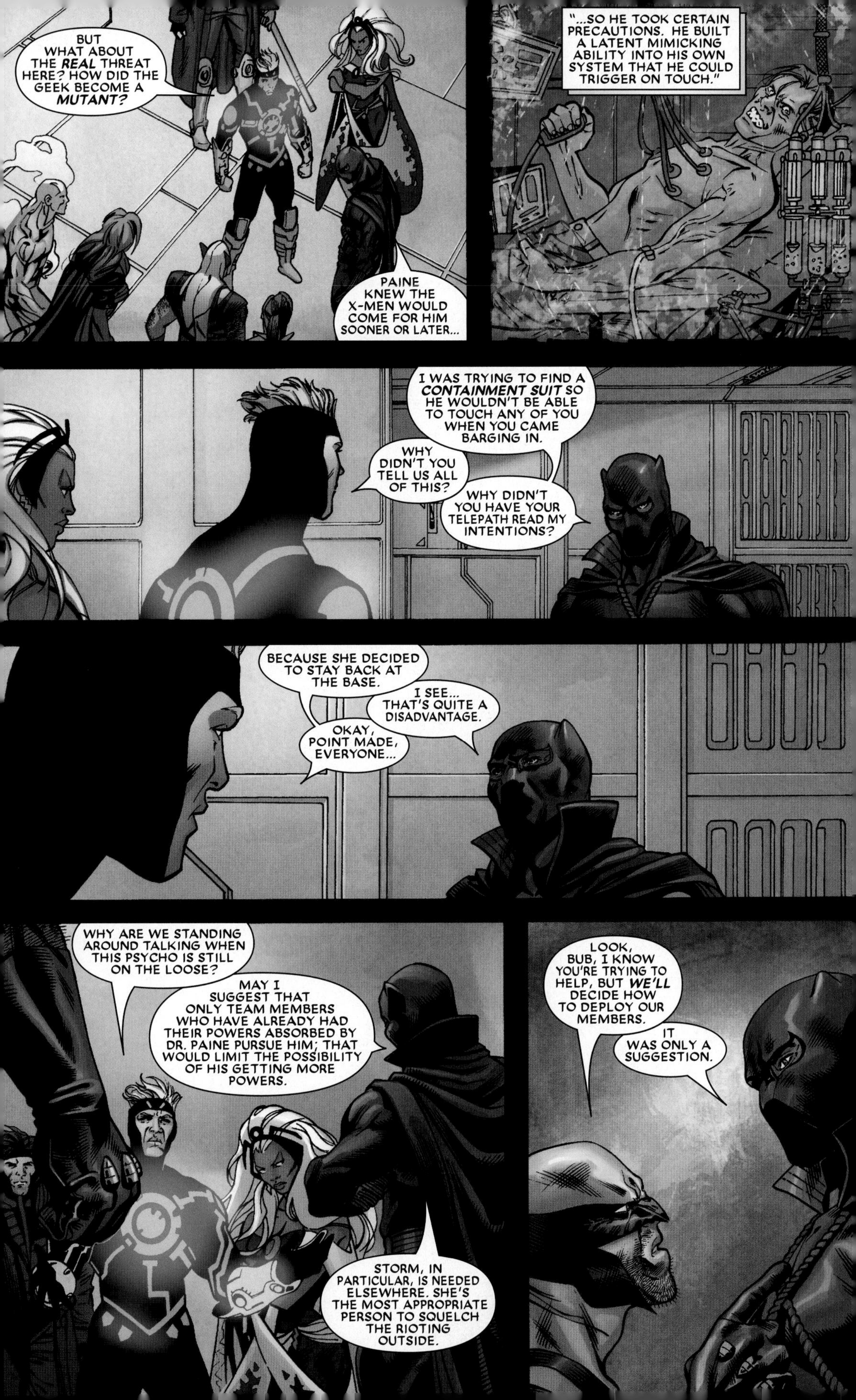
BUT WHAT ABOUT THE REAL THREAT HERE? HOW DID THE GEEK BECOME A MUTANT?
PAINE KNEW THE X-MEN WOULD COME FOR HIM SOONER OR LATER...
"...SO HE TOOK CERTAIN PRECAUTIONS. HE BUILT A LATENT MIMICKING ABILITY INTO HIS OWN SYSTEM THAT HE COULD TRIGGER ON TOUCH."
I WAS TRYING TO FIND A CONTAINMENT SUIT SO HE WOULDN'T BE ABLE TO TOUCH ANY OF YOU WHEN YOU CAME BARGING IN.
WHY DIDN'T YOU TELL US ALL OF THIS?
WHY DIDN'T YOU HAVE YOUR TELEPATH READ MY INTENTIONS?
BECAUSE SHE DECIDED TO STAY BACK AT THE BASE.
I SEE... THAT'S QUITE A DISADVANTAGE.
OKAY, POINT MADE, EVERYONE...
WHY ARE WE STANDING AROUND TALKING WHEN THIS PSYCHO IS STILL ON THE LOOSE?
MAY I SUGGEST THAT ONLY TEAM MEMBERS WHO HAVE ALREADY HAD THEIR POWERS ABSORBED BY DR. PAINE PURSUE HIM; THAT WOULD LIMIT THE POSSIBILITY OF HIS GETTING MORE POWERS.
STORM, IN PARTICULAR, IS NEEDED ELSEWHERE. SHE'S THE MOST APPROPRIATE PERSON TO SQUELCH THE RIOTING OUTSIDE.
LOOK, BUB, I KNOW YOU'RE TRYING TO HELP, BUT WE'LL DECIDE HOW TO DEPLOY OUR MEMBERS.
IT WAS ONLY A SUGGESTION.

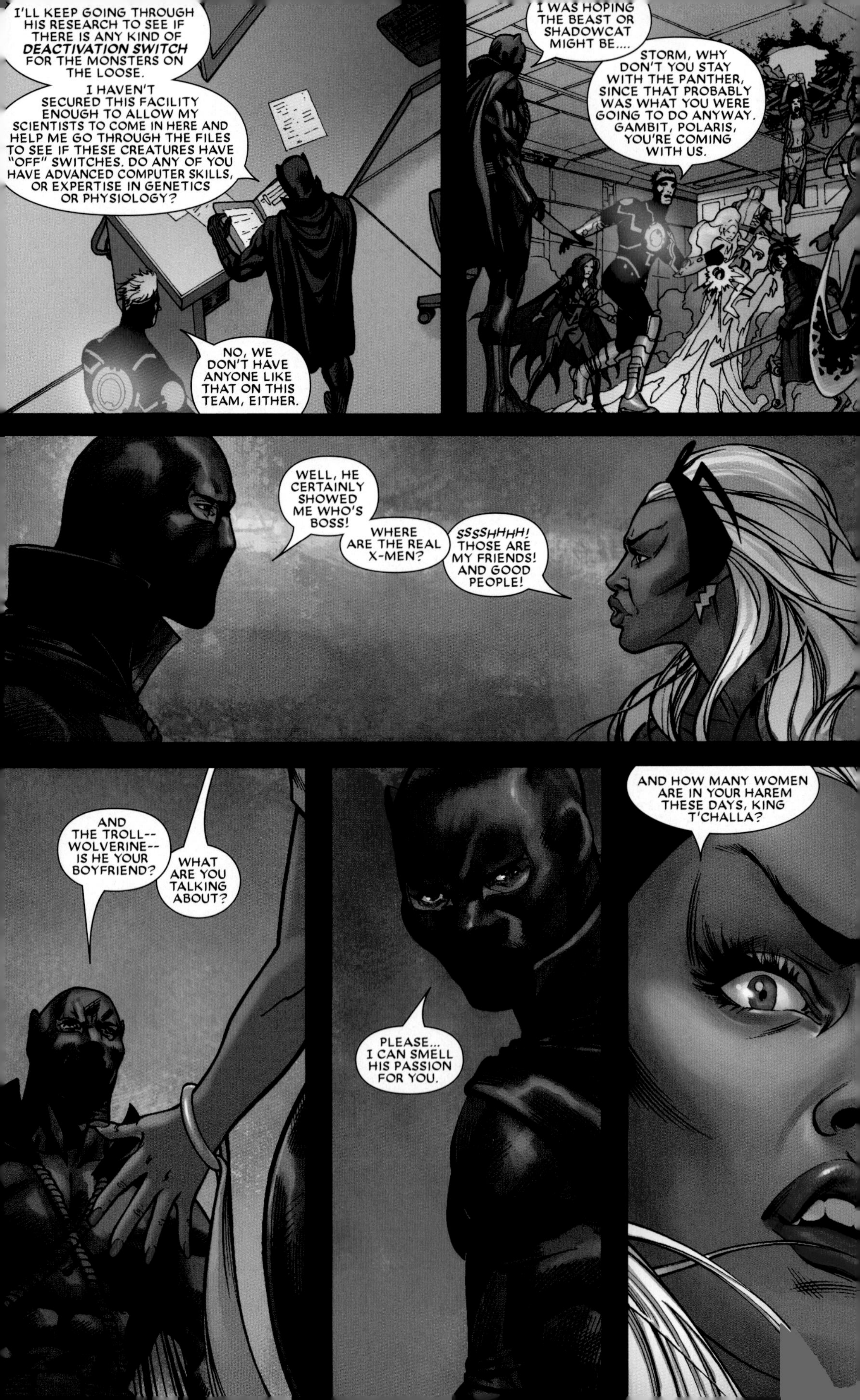

I'LL KEEP GOING THROUGH HIS RESEARCH TO SEE IF THERE IS ANY KIND OF *DEACTIVATION SWITCH* FOR THE MONSTERS ON THE LOOSE.
I HAVEN'T SECURED THIS FACILITY ENOUGH TO ALLOW MY SCIENTISTS TO COME IN HERE AND HELP ME GO THROUGH THE FILES TO SEE IF THESE CREATURES HAVE "OFF" SWITCHES. DO ANY OF YOU HAVE ADVANCED COMPUTER SKILLS, OR EXPERTISE IN GENETICS OR PHYSIOLOGY?
NO, WE DON'T HAVE ANYONE LIKE THAT ON THIS TEAM, EITHER.
I WAS HOPING THE BEAST OR SHADOWCAT MIGHT BE....
STORM, WHY DON'T YOU STAY WITH THE PANTHER, SINCE THAT PROBABLY WAS WHAT YOU WERE GOING TO DO ANYWAY. GAMBIT, POLARIS, YOU'RE COMING WITH US.
WELL, HE CERTAINLY SHOWED ME WHO'S BOSS!
WHERE ARE THE REAL X-MEN?
SSSHHHH! THOSE ARE MY FRIENDS! AND GOOD PEOPLE!
AND THE TROLL-- WOLVERINE-- IS HE YOUR BOYFRIEND?
WHAT ARE YOU TALKING ABOUT?
PLEASE... I CAN SMELL HIS PASSION FOR YOU.
AND HOW MANY WOMEN ARE IN YOUR HAREM THESE DAYS, KING T'CHALLA?

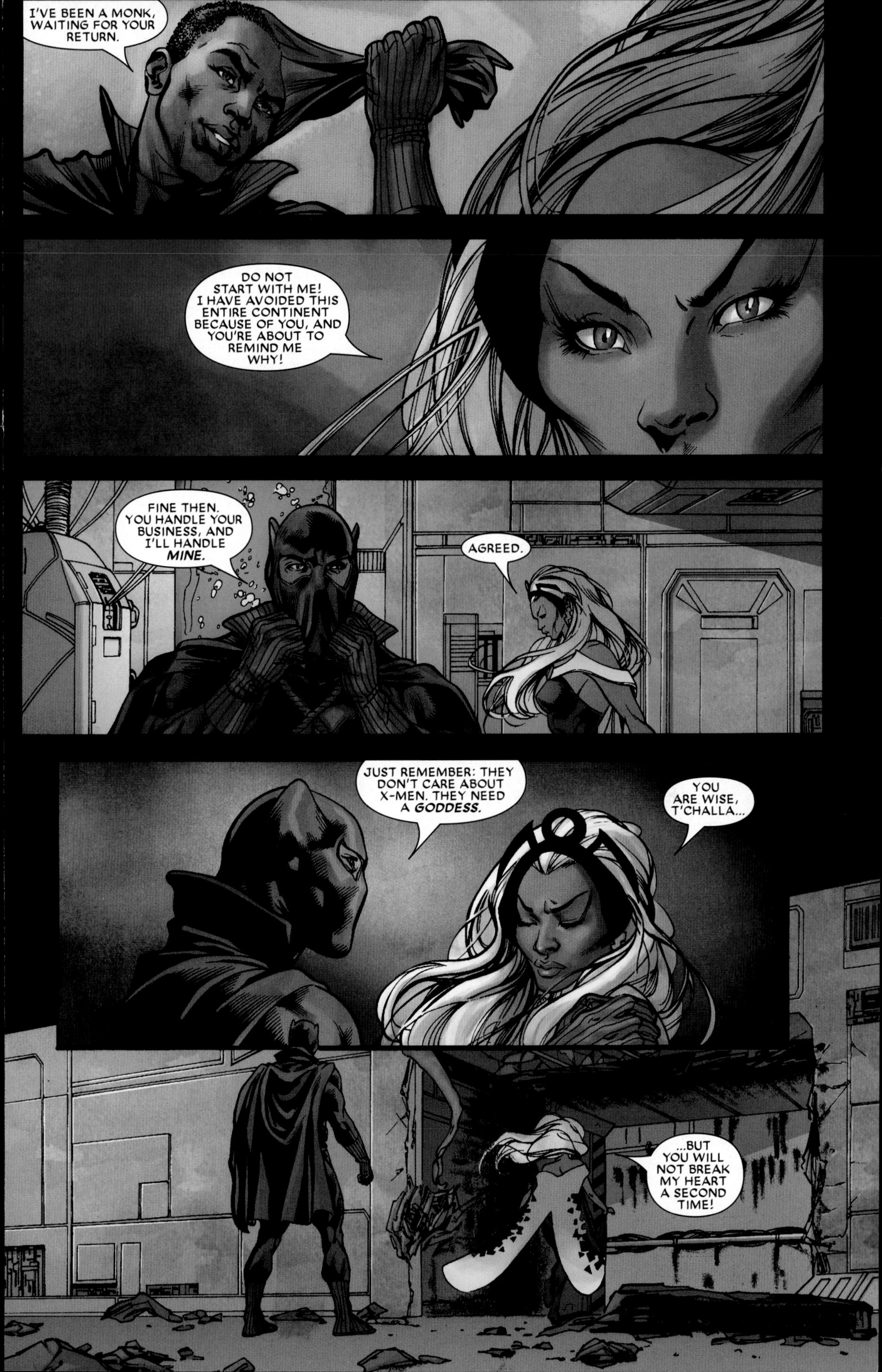
I'VE BEEN A MONK, WAITING FOR YOUR RETURN.
DO NOT START WITH ME! I HAVE AVOIDED THIS ENTIRE CONTINENT BECAUSE OF YOU, AND YOU'RE ABOUT TO REMIND ME WHY!
FINE THEN. YOU HANDLE YOUR BUSINESS, AND I'LL HANDLE *MINE.*
AGREED.
JUST REMEMBER: THEY DON'T CARE ABOUT X-MEN. THEY NEED A *GODDESS.*
YOU ARE WISE, T'CHALLA...
...BUT YOU WILL NOT BREAK MY HEART A SECOND TIME!

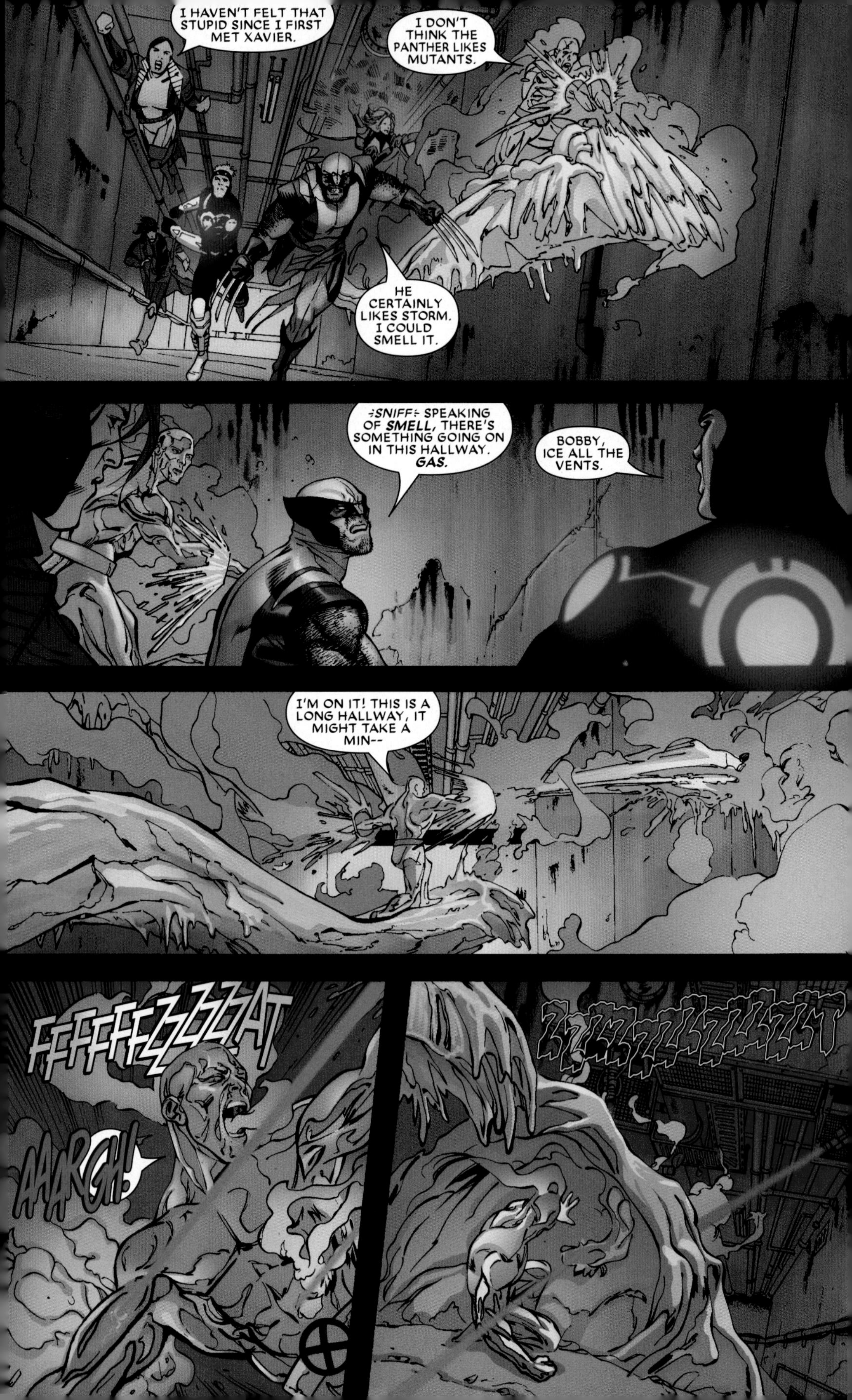
I HAVEN'T FELT THAT STUPID SINCE I FIRST MET XAVIER.
I DON'T THINK THE PANTHER LIKES MUTANTS.
HE CERTAINLY LIKES STORM. I COULD SMELL IT.
÷SNIFF÷ SPEAKING OF SMELL, THERE'S SOMETHING GOING ON IN THIS HALLWAY. GAS.
BOBBY, ICE ALL THE VENTS.
I'M ON IT! THIS IS A LONG HALLWAY, IT MIGHT TAKE A MIN--
FFFFFFZZZZZAT
AAARGH!

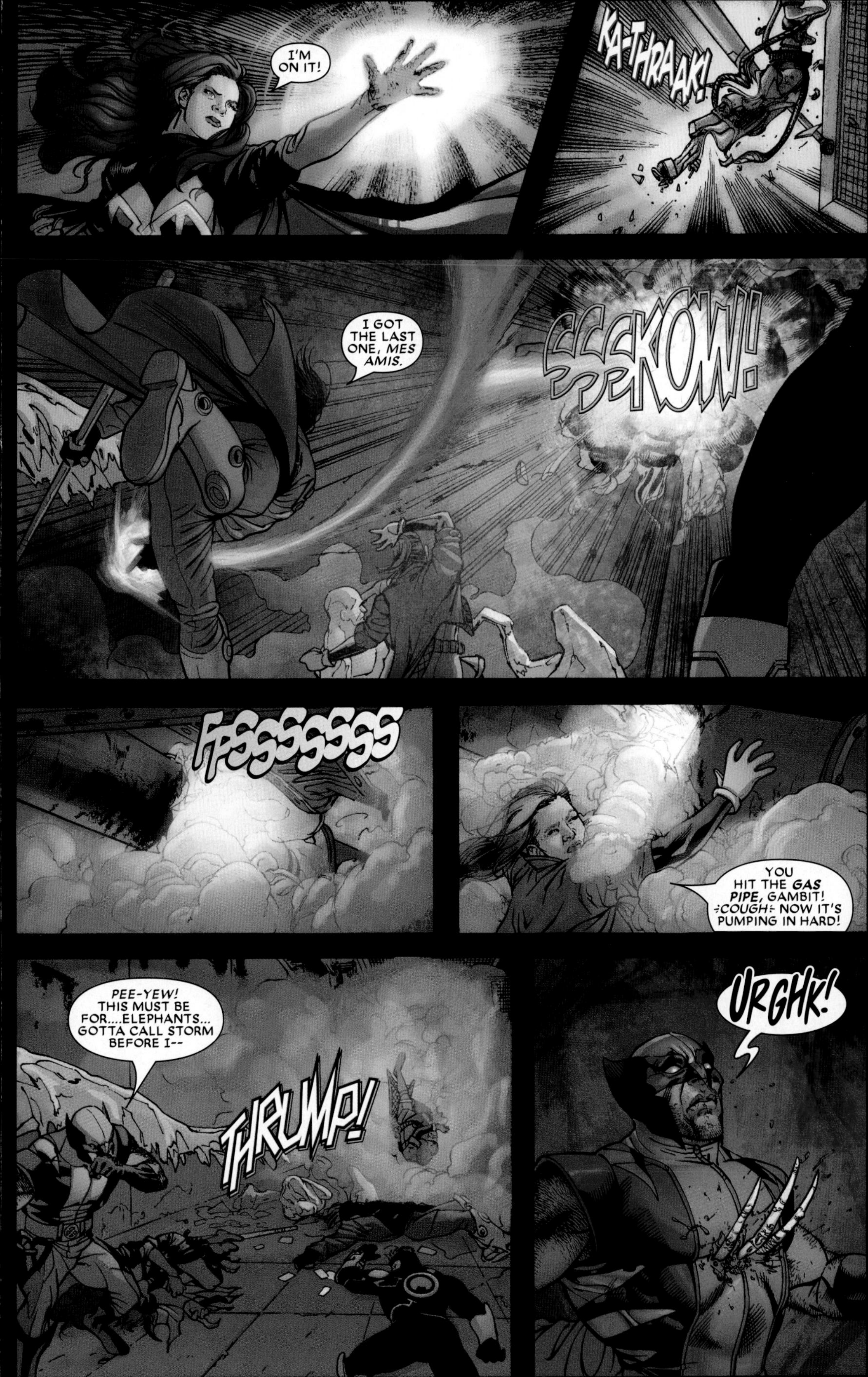
I'M ON IT!
KA-THRAAK!
I GOT THE LAST ONE, MES AMIS.
SSSKOW!
FSSSSSSS
YOU HIT THE GAS PIPE, GAMBIT! =COUGH= NOW IT'S PUMPING IN HARD!
PEE-YEW! THIS MUST BE FOR....ELEPHANTS... GOTTA CALL STORM BEFORE I--
THRUMP!
URGHK!

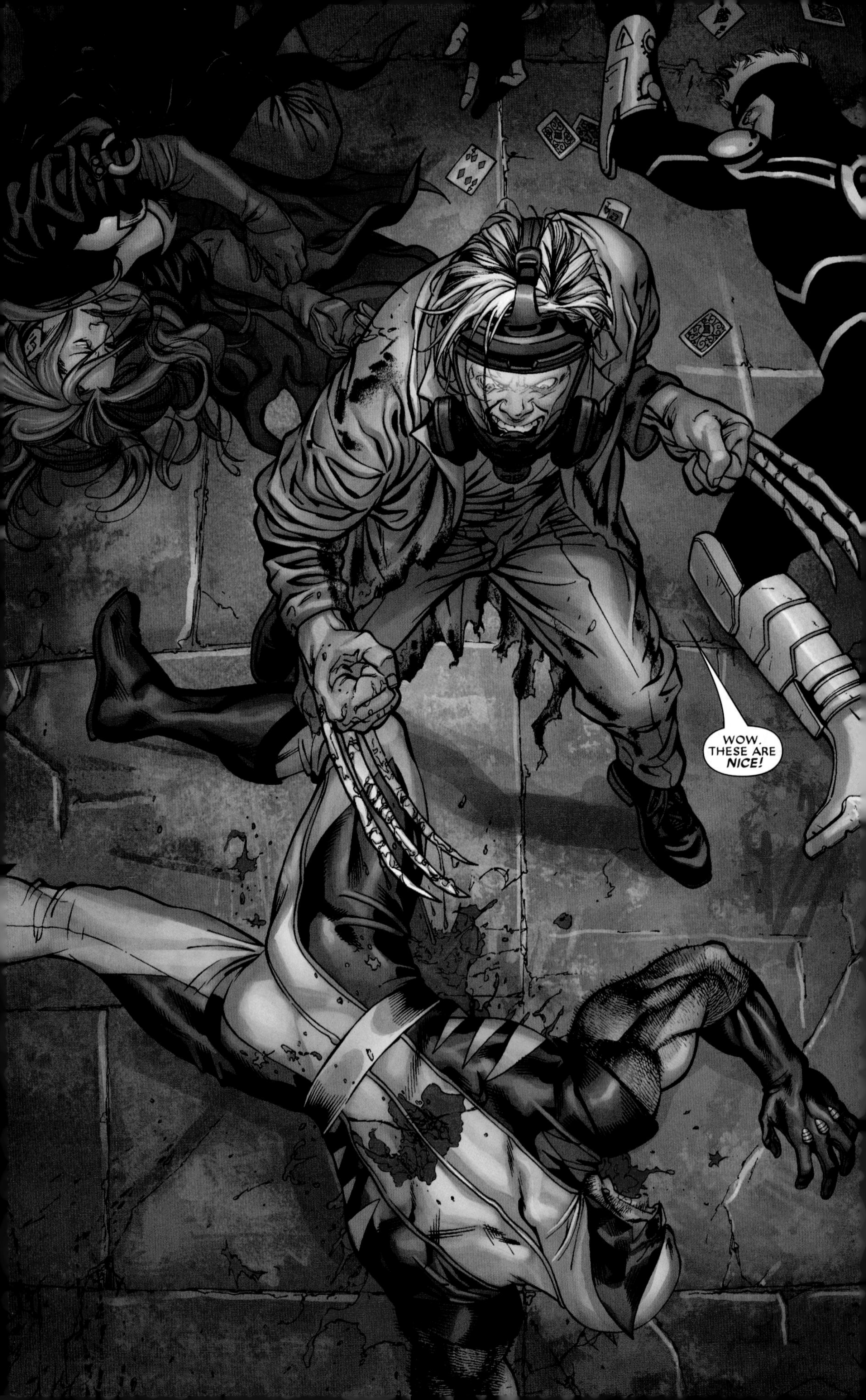
WOW. THESE ARE NICE!

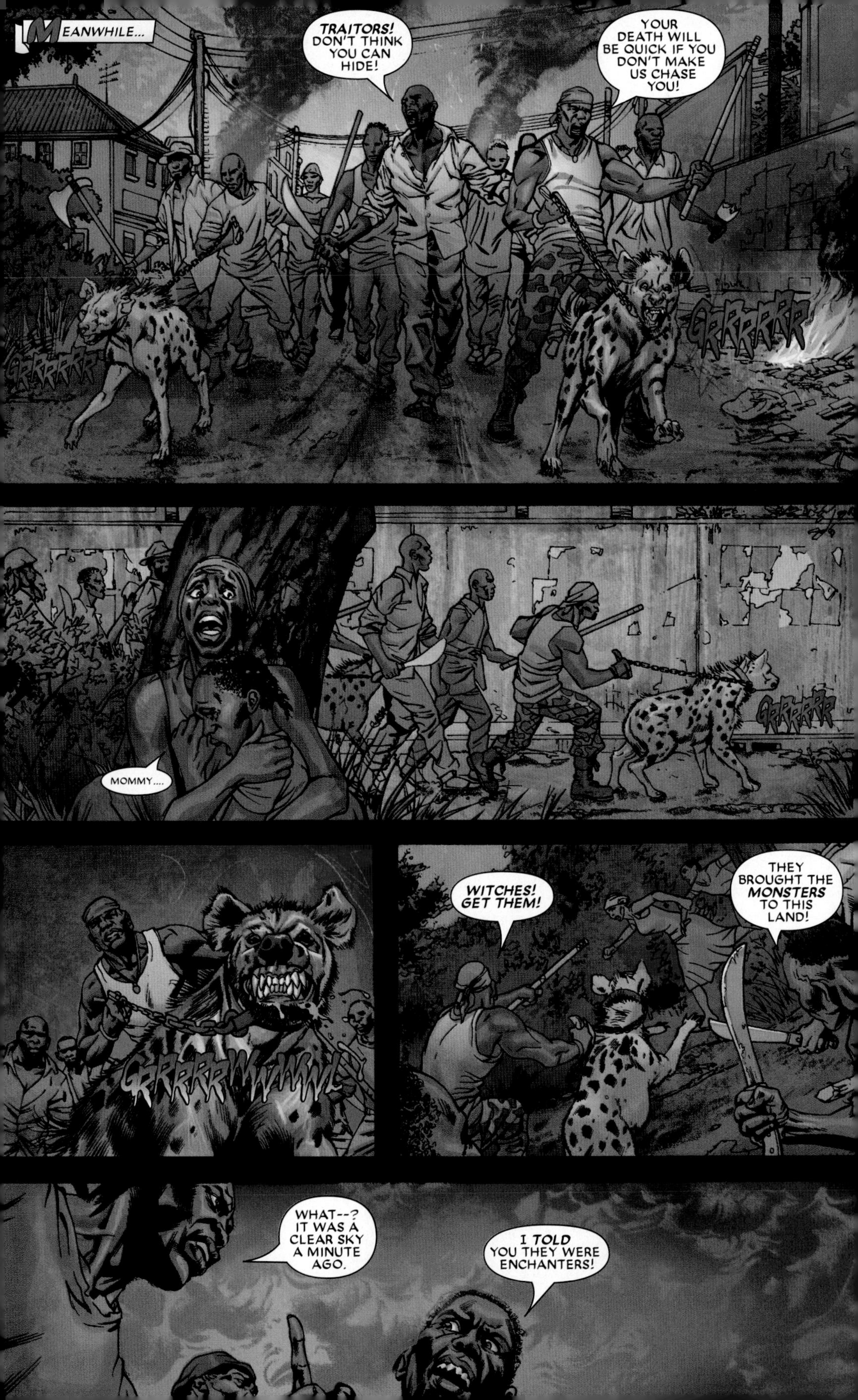
MEANWHILE...
TRAITORS! DON'T THINK YOU CAN HIDE!
YOUR DEATH WILL BE QUICK IF YOU DON'T MAKE US CHASE YOU!
GRRRRRR
GRRRRRRR
MOMMY....
GRRRRRR
GRRRRRWWWWL
WITCHES! GET THEM!
THEY BROUGHT THE MONSTERS TO THIS LAND!
WHAT--? IT WAS A CLEAR SKY A MINUTE AGO.
I TOLD YOU THEY WERE ENCHANTERS!

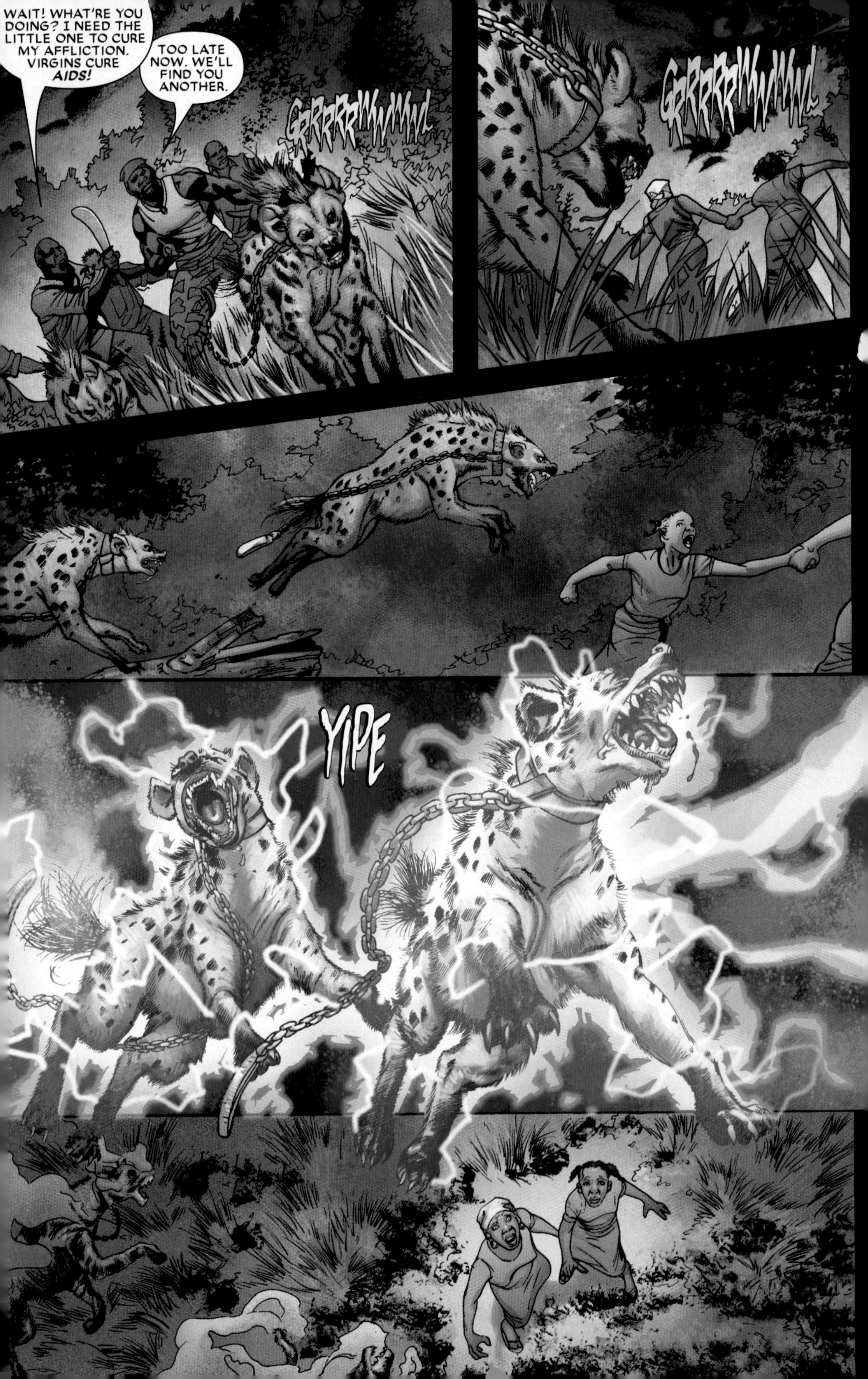
WAIT! WHAT'RE YOU DOING? I NEED THE LITTLE ONE TO CURE MY AFFLICTION. VIRGINS CURE AIDS!
TOO LATE NOW. WE'LL FIND YOU ANOTHER.
GRRRRRWWWWL
GRRRRRWWWWL
YIPE

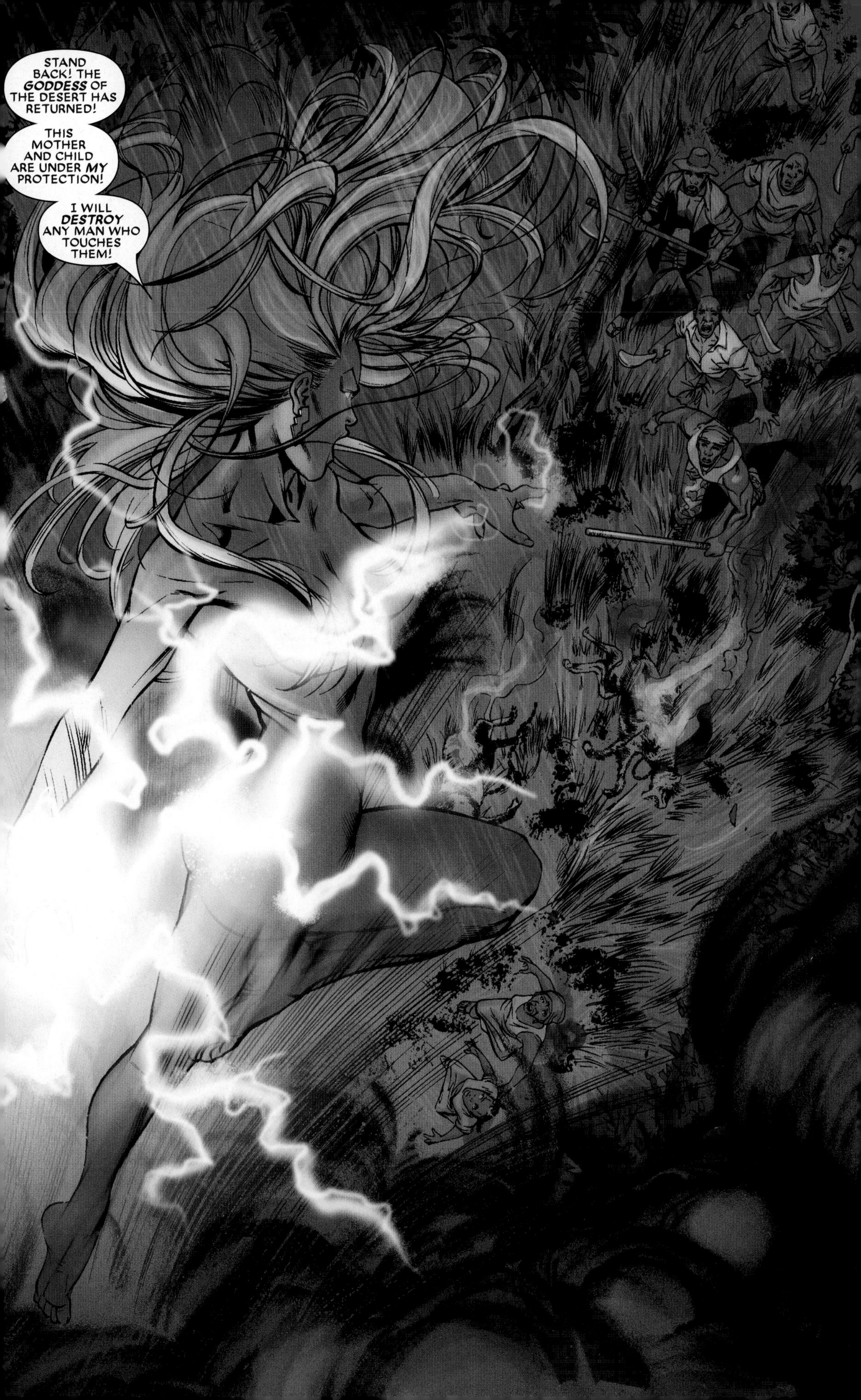
STAND BACK! THE GODDESS OF THE DESERT HAS RETURNED!
THIS MOTHER AND CHILD ARE UNDER MY PROTECTION!
I WILL DESTROY ANY MAN WHO TOUCHES THEM!

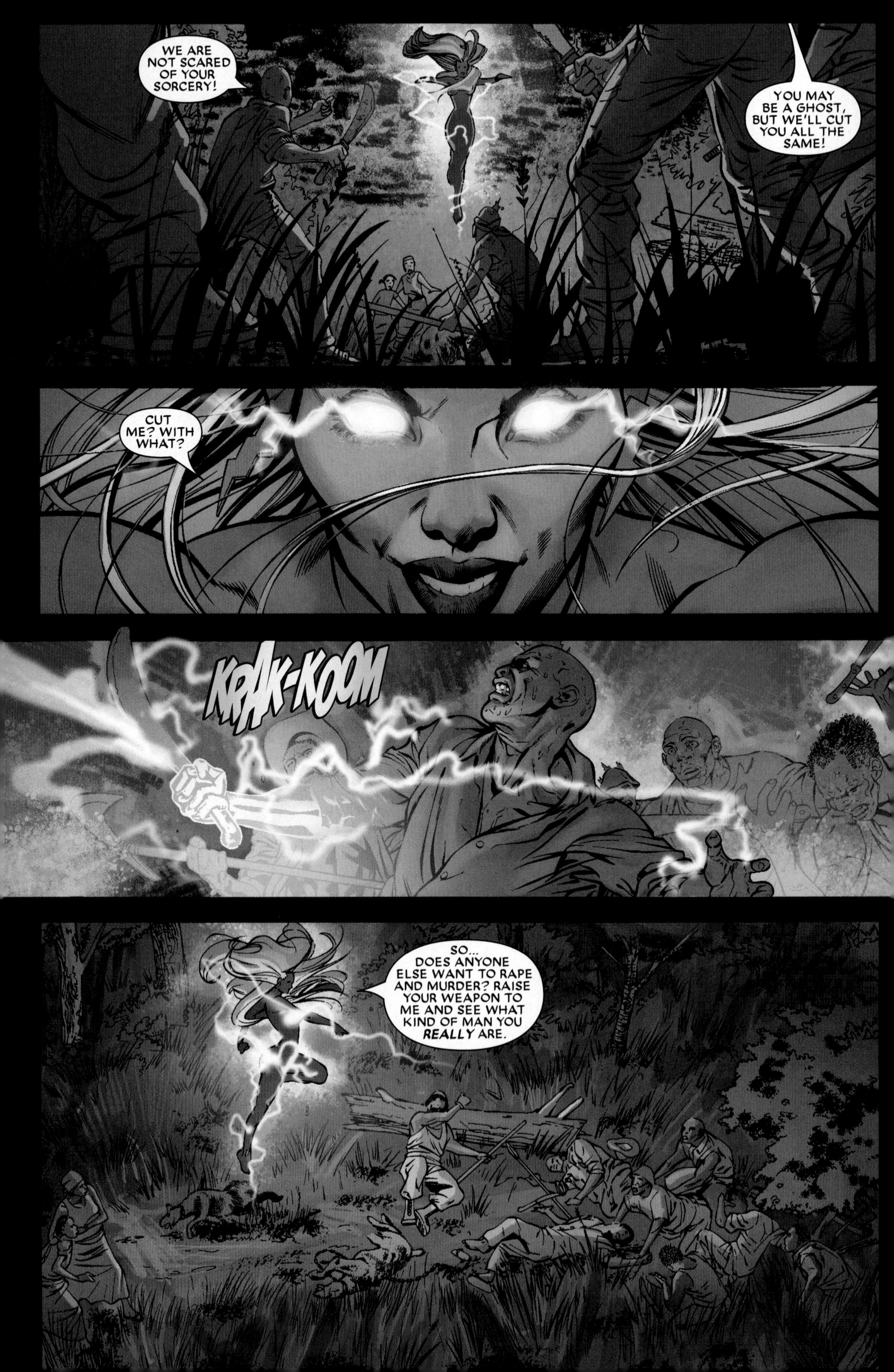
WE ARE NOT SCARED OF YOUR SORCERY!
YOU MAY BE A GHOST, BUT WE'LL CUT YOU ALL THE SAME!
CUT ME? WITH WHAT?
KRAK-KOOM
SO... DOES ANYONE ELSE WANT TO RAPE AND MURDER? RAISE YOUR WEAPON TO ME AND SEE WHAT KIND OF MAN YOU *REALLY* ARE.

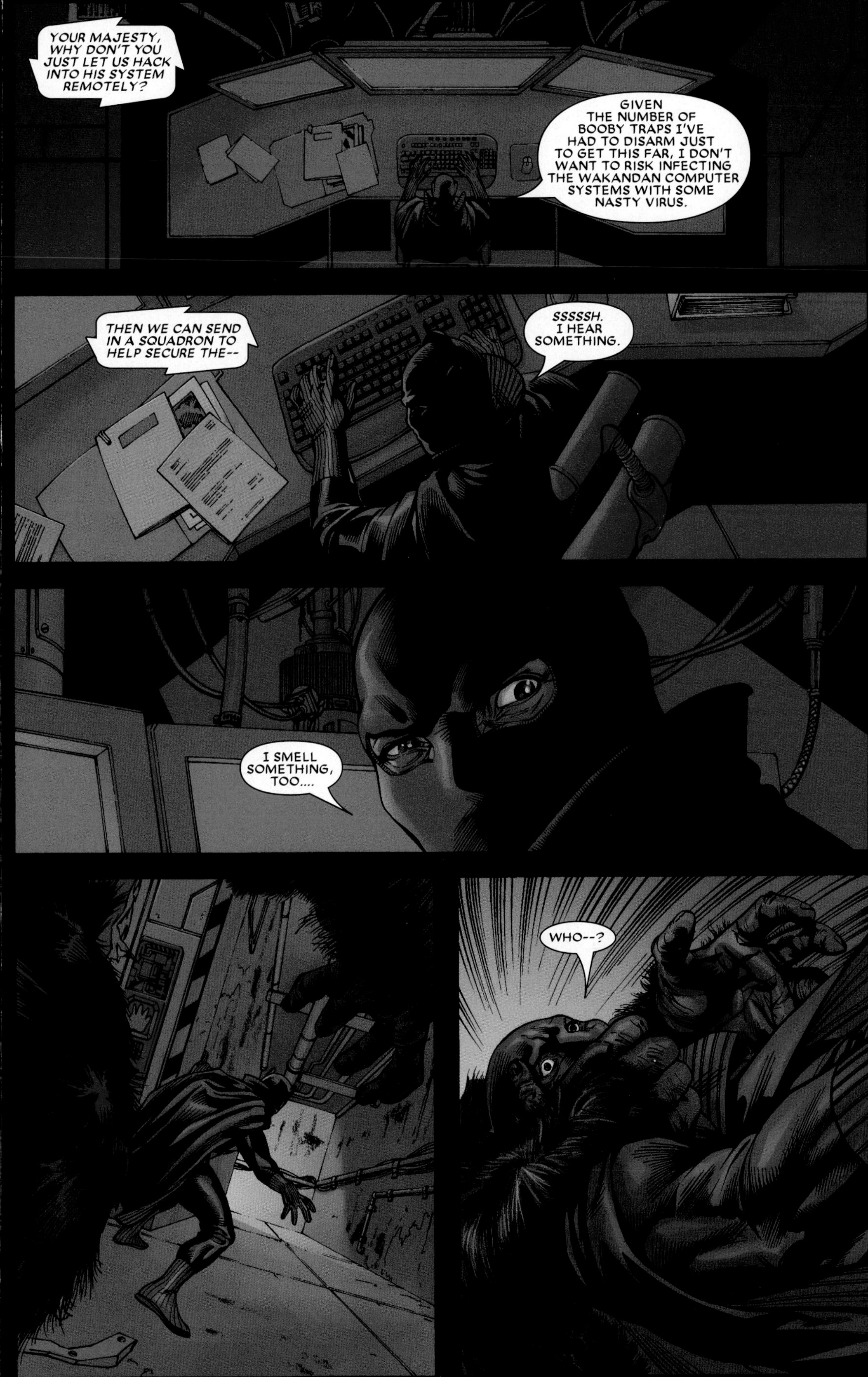
YOUR MAJESTY, WHY DON'T YOU JUST LET US HACK INTO HIS SYSTEM REMOTELY?
GIVEN THE NUMBER OF BOOBY TRAPS I'VE HAD TO DISARM JUST TO GET THIS FAR, I DON'T WANT TO RISK INFECTING THE WAKANDAN COMPUTER SYSTEMS WITH SOME NASTY VIRUS.
THEN WE CAN SEND IN A SQUADRON TO HELP SECURE THE--
SSSSSH. I HEAR SOMETHING.
I SMELL SOMETHING, TOO....
WHO--?

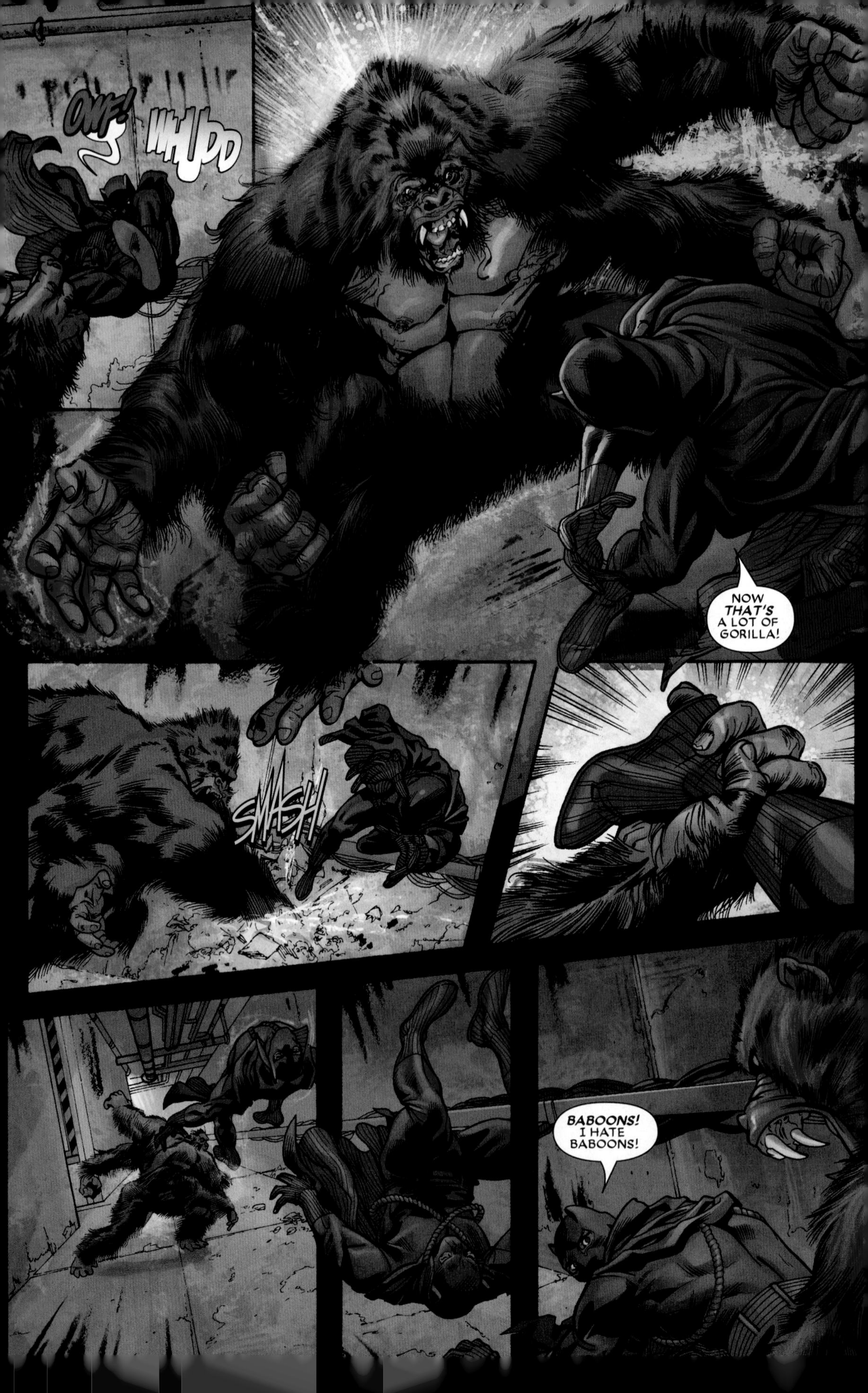
OWF!
WHUDD
NOW THAT'S A LOT OF GORILLA!
SMASH
BABOONS! I HATE BABOONS!

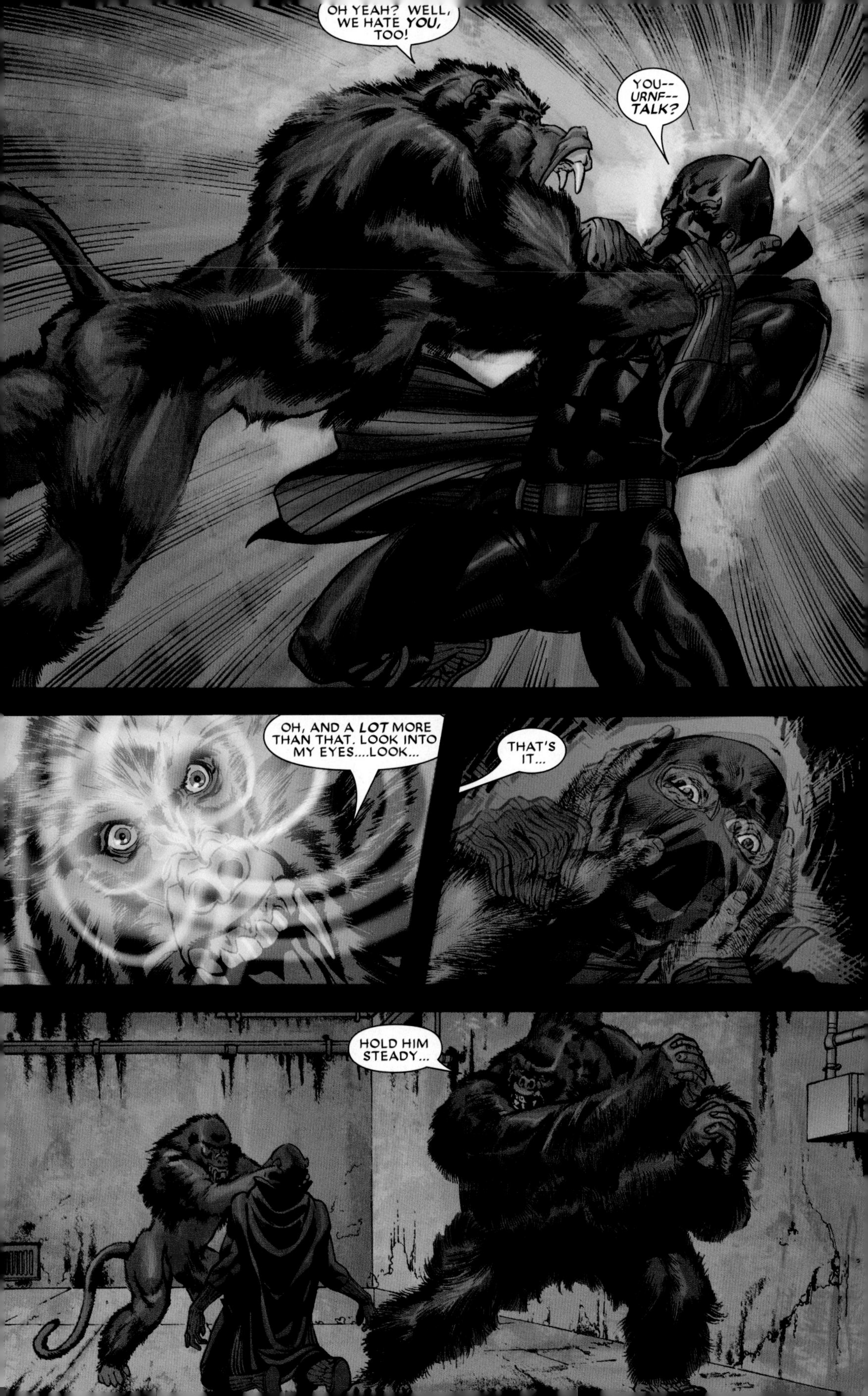
OH YEAH? WELL, WE HATE YOU, TOO!
YOU-- URNF-- TALK?
OH, AND A LOT MORE THAN THAT. LOOK INTO MY EYES....LOOK...
THAT'S IT...
HOLD HIM STEADY...

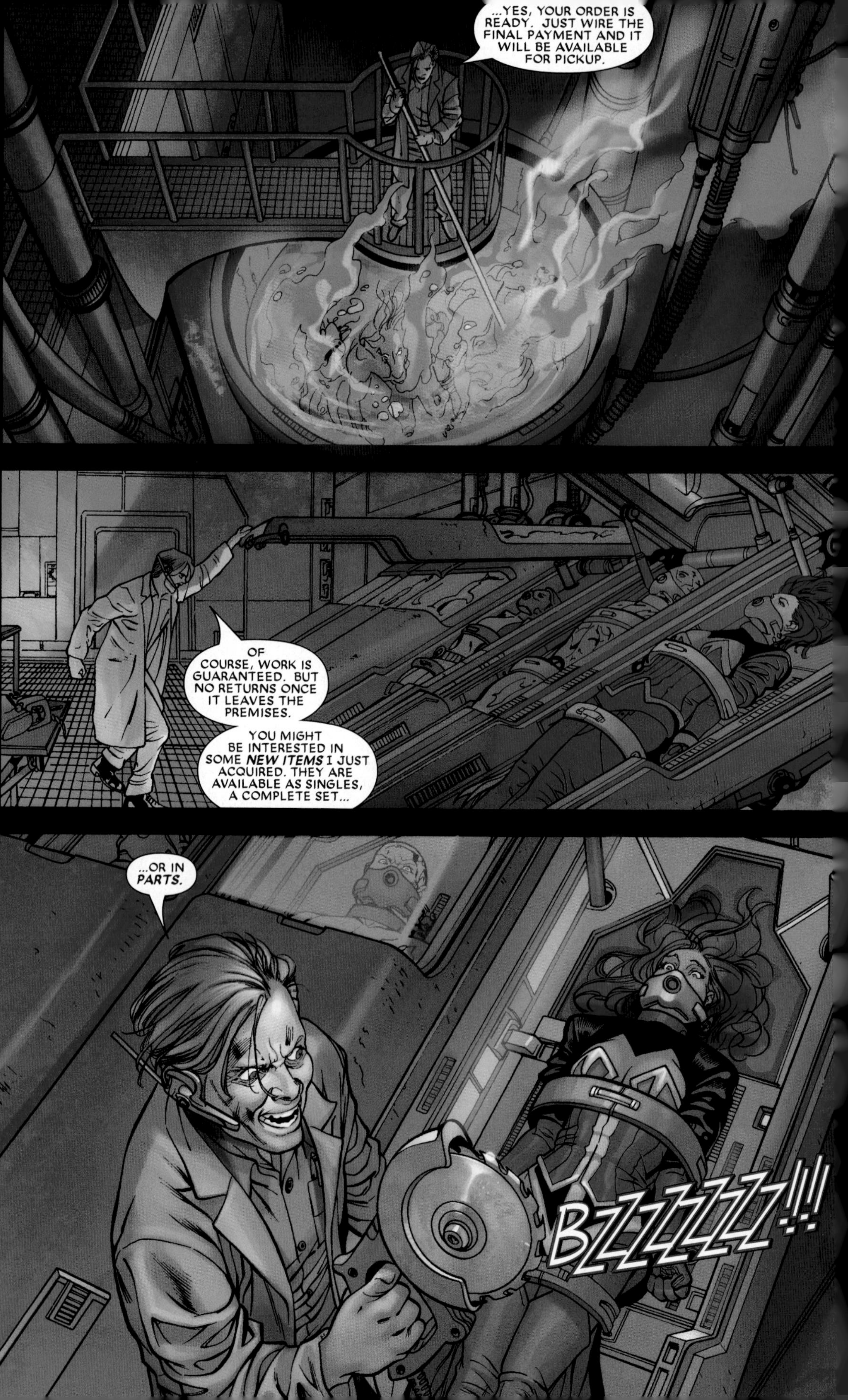
...YES, YOUR ORDER IS READY. JUST WIRE THE FINAL PAYMENT AND IT WILL BE AVAILABLE FOR PICKUP.
OF COURSE, WORK IS GUARANTEED. BUT NO RETURNS ONCE IT LEAVES THE PREMISES.
YOU MIGHT BE INTERESTED IN SOME NEW ITEMS I JUST ACQUIRED. THEY ARE AVAILABLE AS SINGLES, A COMPLETE SET...
...OR IN PARTS.
BZZZZZZZ!!!

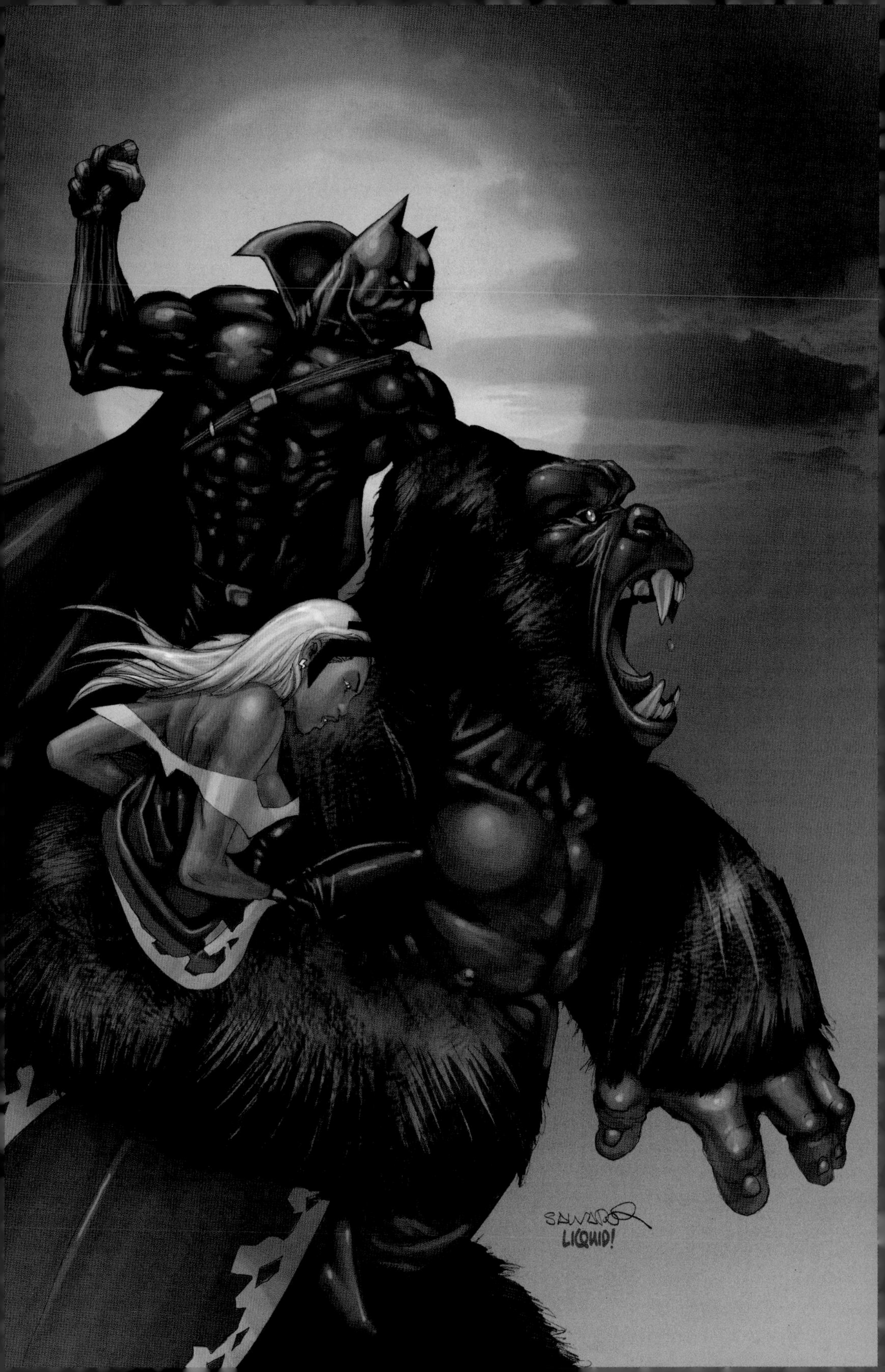
SALVADOR
LICQUID!

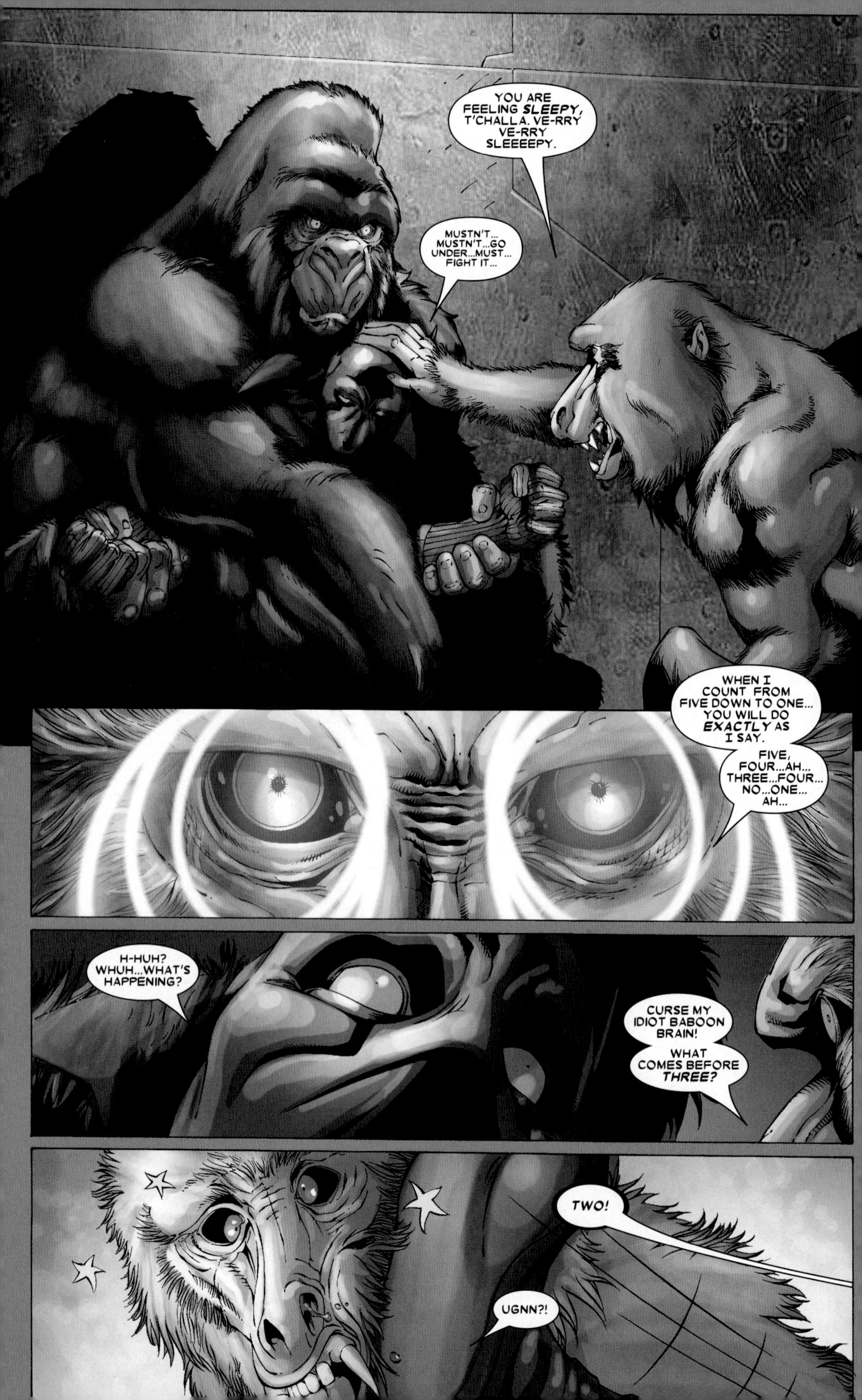
YOU ARE FEELING SLEEPY, T'CHALLA. VE-RRY VE-RRY SLEEEEEPY.
MUSTN'T... MUSTN'T...GO UNDER...MUST... FIGHT IT...
WHEN I COUNT FROM FIVE DOWN TO ONE... YOU WILL DO EXACTLY AS I SAY.
FIVE, FOUR...AH... THREE...FOUR... NO...ONE... AH...
H-HUH? WHUH...WHAT'S HAPPENING?
CURSE MY IDIOT BABOON BRAIN!
WHAT COMES BEFORE THREE?
TWO!
UGNN?!

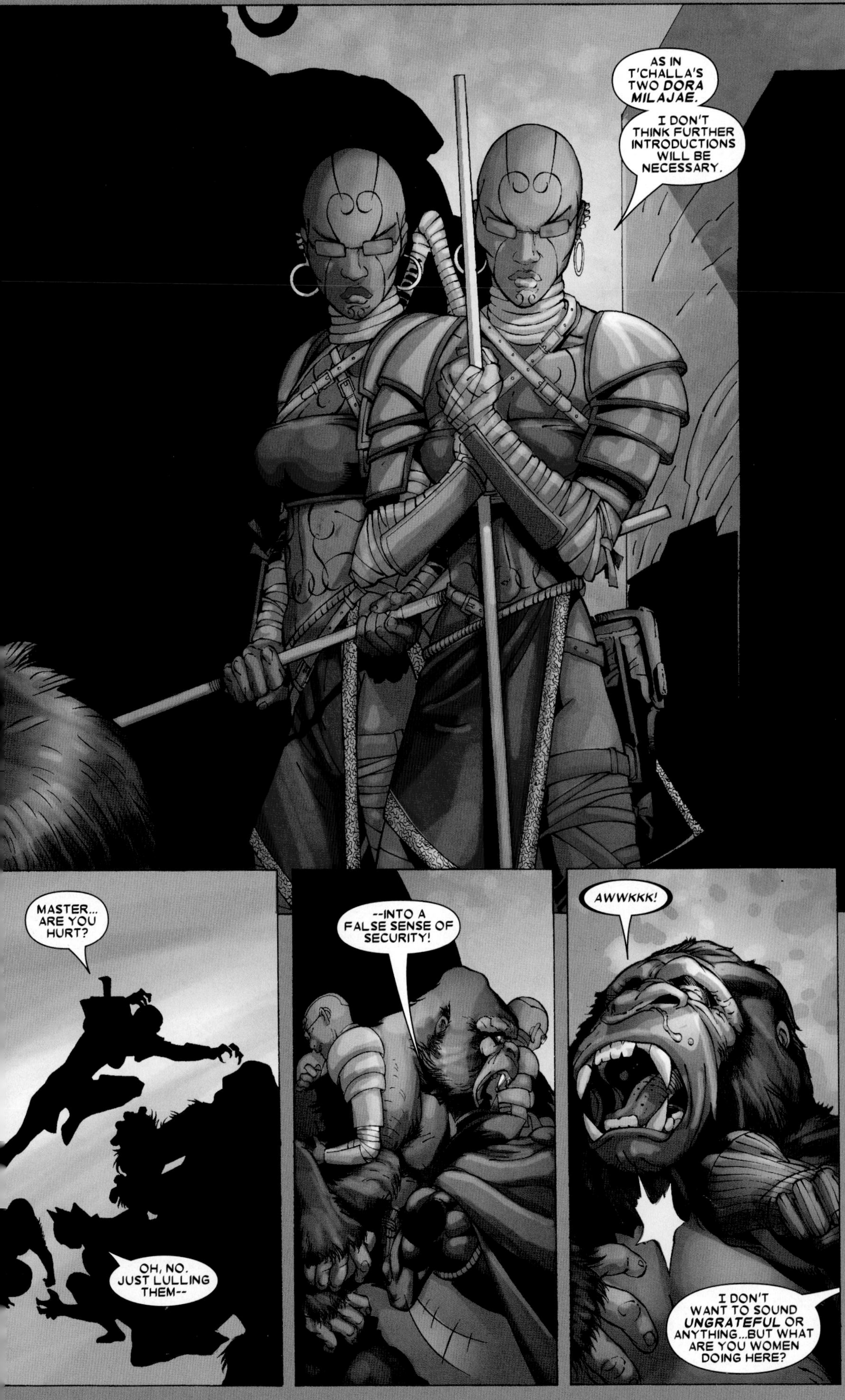
AS IN T'CHALLA'S TWO DORA MILAJAE.
I DON'T THINK FURTHER INTRODUCTIONS WILL BE NECESSARY.
MASTER... ARE YOU HURT?
OH, NO. JUST LULLING THEM--
--INTO A FALSE SENSE OF SECURITY!
AWWKKK!
I DON'T WANT TO SOUND UNGRATEFUL OR ANYTHING...BUT WHAT ARE YOU WOMEN DOING HERE?

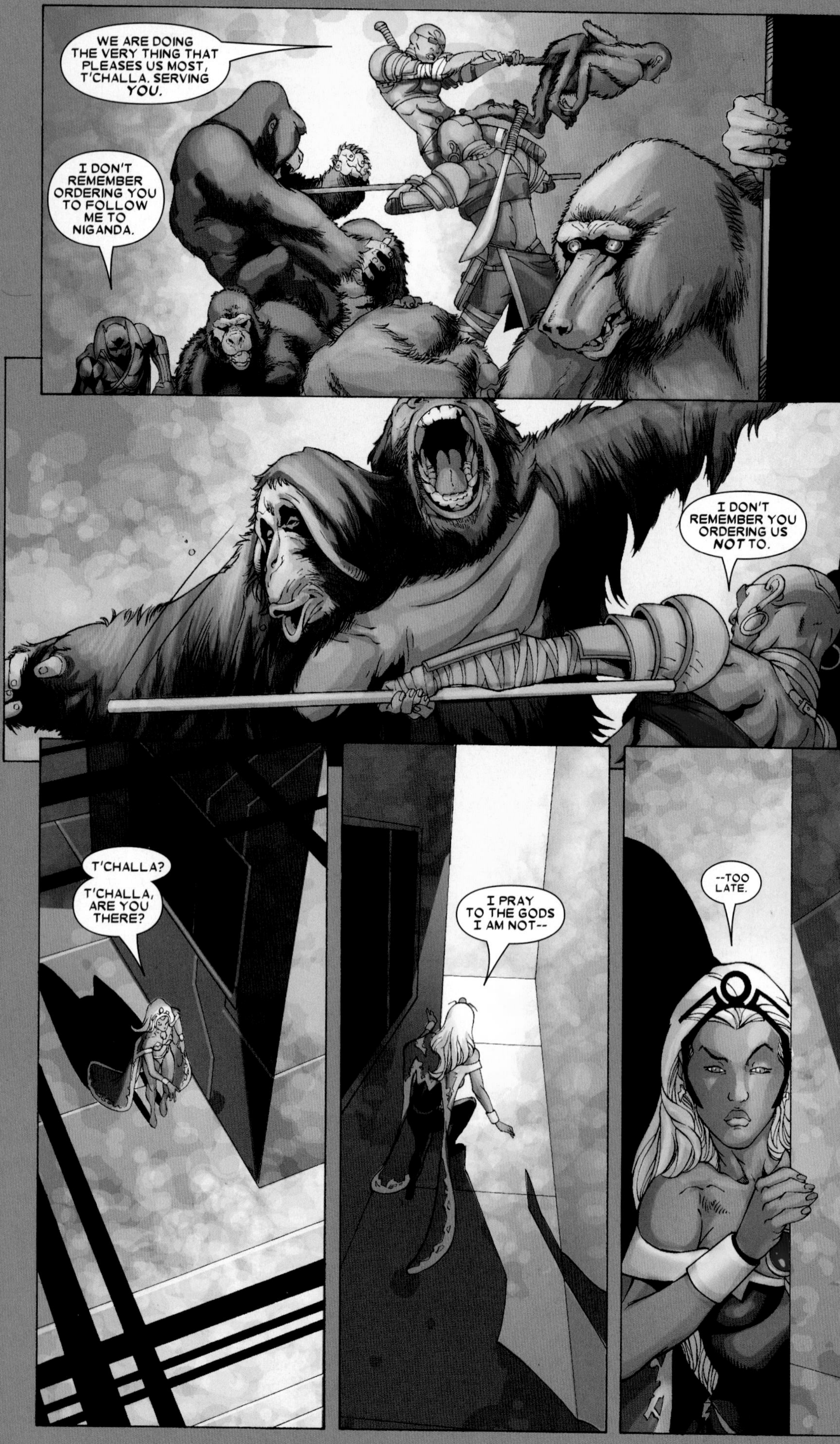
WE ARE DOING THE VERY THING THAT PLEASES US MOST, T'CHALLA. SERVING *YOU*.
I DON'T REMEMBER ORDERING YOU TO FOLLOW ME TO NIGANDA.
I DON'T REMEMBER YOU ORDERING US *NOT* TO.
T'CHALLA?
T'CHALLA, ARE YOU THERE?
I PRAY TO THE GODS I AM NOT--
--TOO LATE.

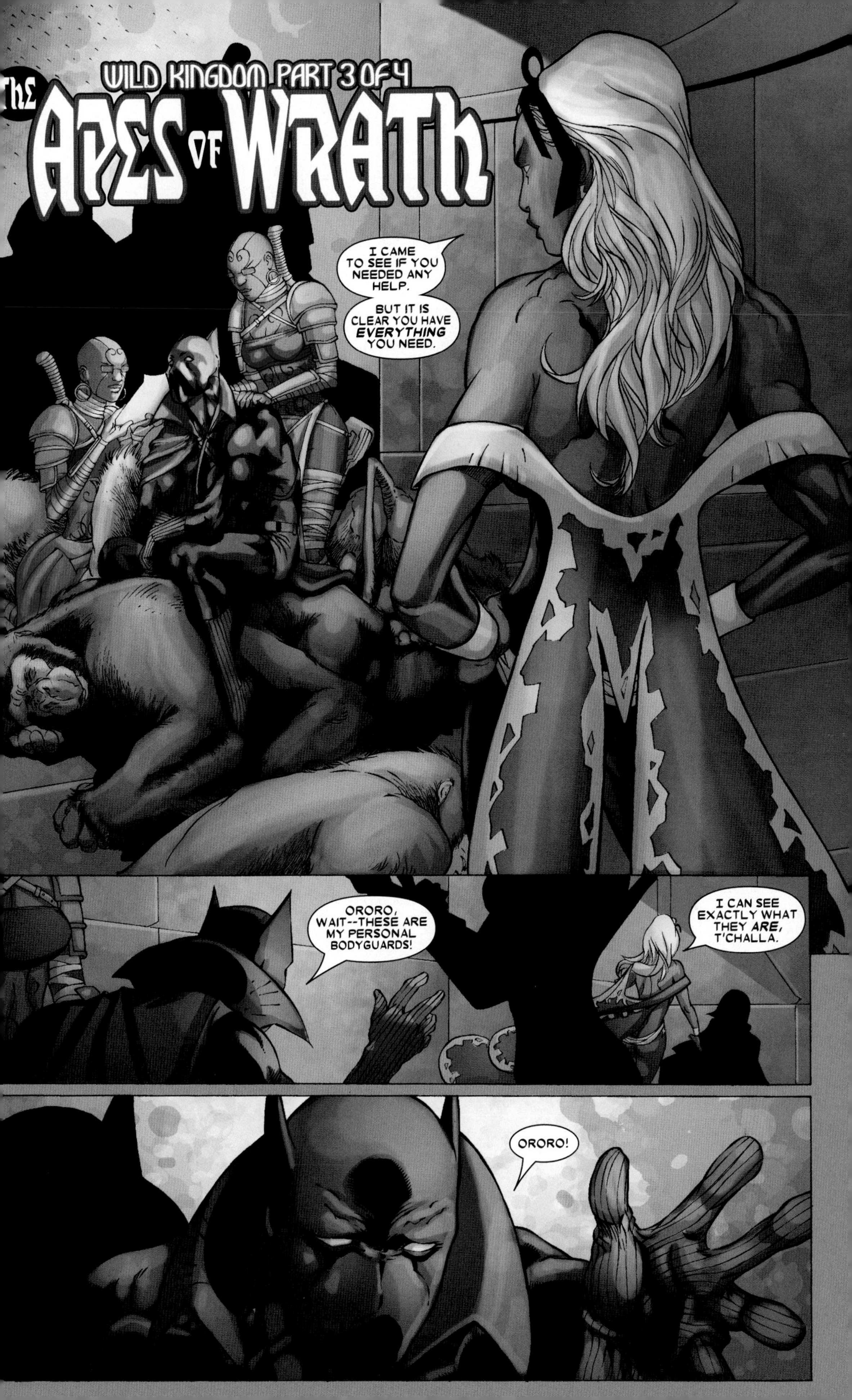

WILD KINGDOM PART 3 OF 4
THE APES OF WRATH
I CAME TO SEE IF YOU NEEDED ANY HELP.
BUT IT IS CLEAR YOU HAVE EVERYTHING YOU NEED.
ORORO, WAIT--THESE ARE MY PERSONAL BODYGUARDS!
I CAN SEE EXACTLY WHAT THEY ARE, T'CHALLA.
ORORO!

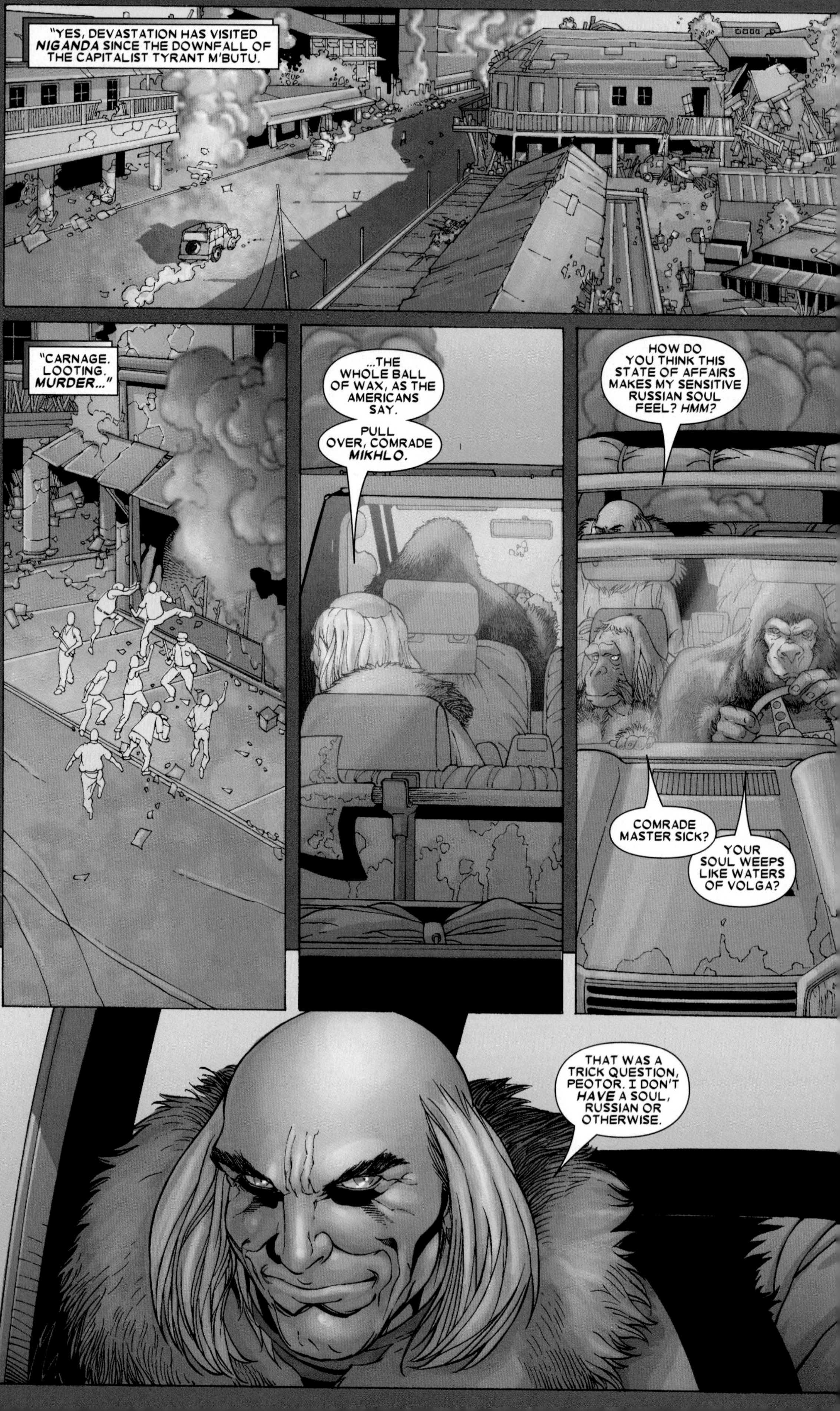
"YES, DEVASTATION HAS VISITED NIGANDA SINCE THE DOWNFALL OF THE CAPITALIST TYRANT M'BUTU.
"CARNAGE. LOOTING. MURDER..."
...THE WHOLE BALL OF WAX, AS THE AMERICANS SAY.
PULL OVER, COMRADE MIKHLO.
HOW DO YOU THINK THIS STATE OF AFFAIRS MAKES MY SENSITIVE RUSSIAN SOUL FEEL? HMM?
COMRADE MASTER SICK?
YOUR SOUL WEEPS LIKE WATERS OF VOLGA?
THAT WAS A TRICK QUESTION, PEOTOR. I DON'T HAVE A SOUL, RUSSIAN OR OTHERWISE.

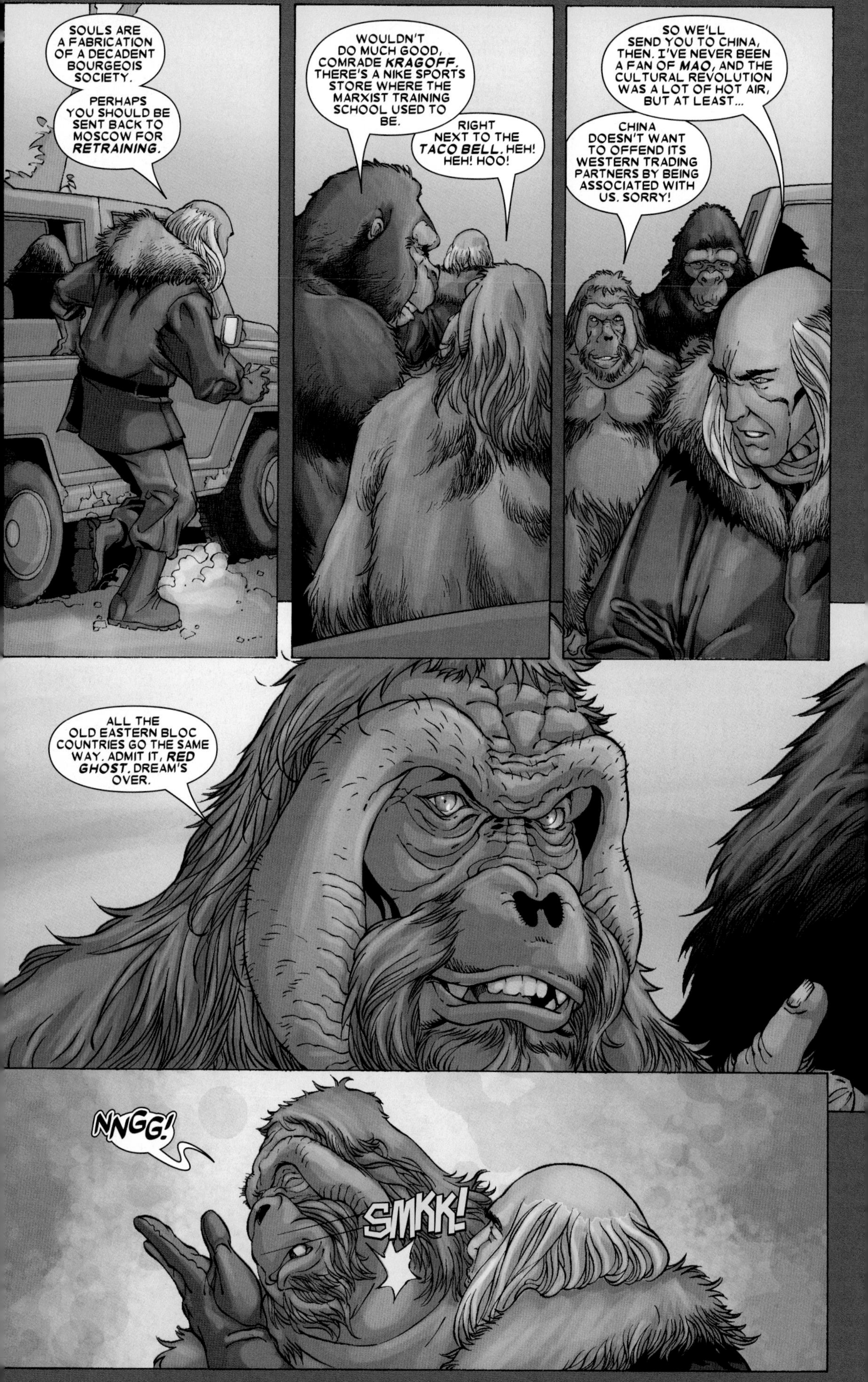
SOULS ARE A FABRICATION OF A DECADENT BOURGEOIS SOCIETY.
PERHAPS YOU SHOULD BE SENT BACK TO MOSCOW FOR RETRAINING.
WOULDN'T DO MUCH GOOD, COMRADE KRAGOFF. THERE'S A NIKE SPORTS STORE WHERE THE MARXIST TRAINING SCHOOL USED TO BE.
RIGHT NEXT TO THE TACO BELL. HEH! HEH! HOO!
SO WE'LL SEND YOU TO CHINA, THEN. I'VE NEVER BEEN A FAN OF MAO, AND THE CULTURAL REVOLUTION WAS A LOT OF HOT AIR, BUT AT LEAST...
CHINA DOESN'T WANT TO OFFEND ITS WESTERN TRADING PARTNERS BY BEING ASSOCIATED WITH US. SORRY!
ALL THE OLD EASTERN BLOC COUNTRIES GO THE SAME WAY. ADMIT IT, RED GHOST. DREAM'S OVER.
NNGG!
SMKK!

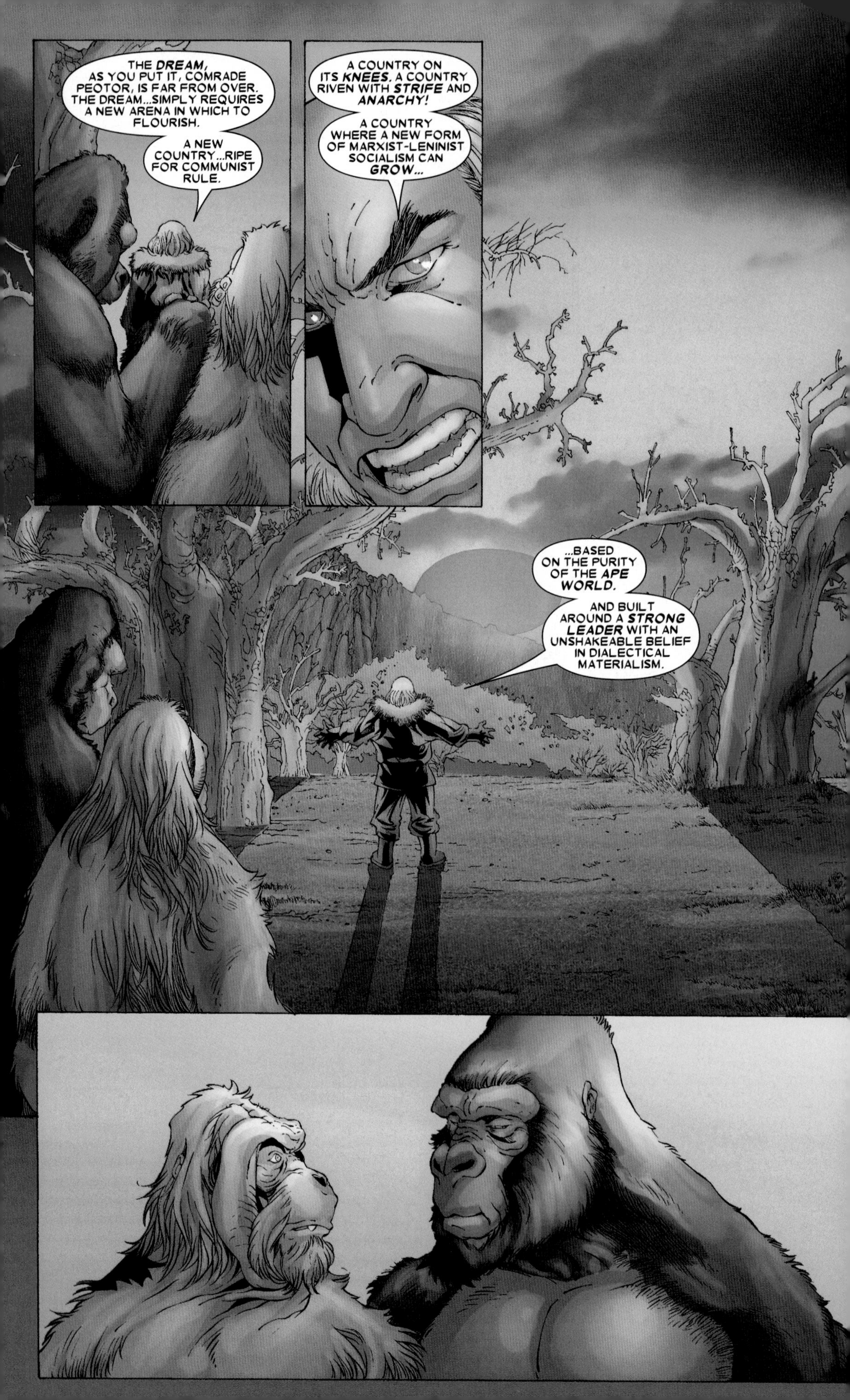
THE DREAM, AS YOU PUT IT, COMRADE PEOTOR, IS FAR FROM OVER. THE DREAM...SIMPLY REQUIRES A NEW ARENA IN WHICH TO FLOURISH.
A NEW COUNTRY...RIPE FOR COMMUNIST RULE.
A COUNTRY ON ITS KNEES, A COUNTRY RIVEN WITH STRIFE AND ANARCHY!
A COUNTRY WHERE A NEW FORM OF MARXIST-LENINIST SOCIALISM CAN GROW...
...BASED ON THE PURITY OF THE APE WORLD.
AND BUILT AROUND A STRONG LEADER WITH AN UNSHAKEABLE BELIEF IN DIALECTICAL MATERIALISM.

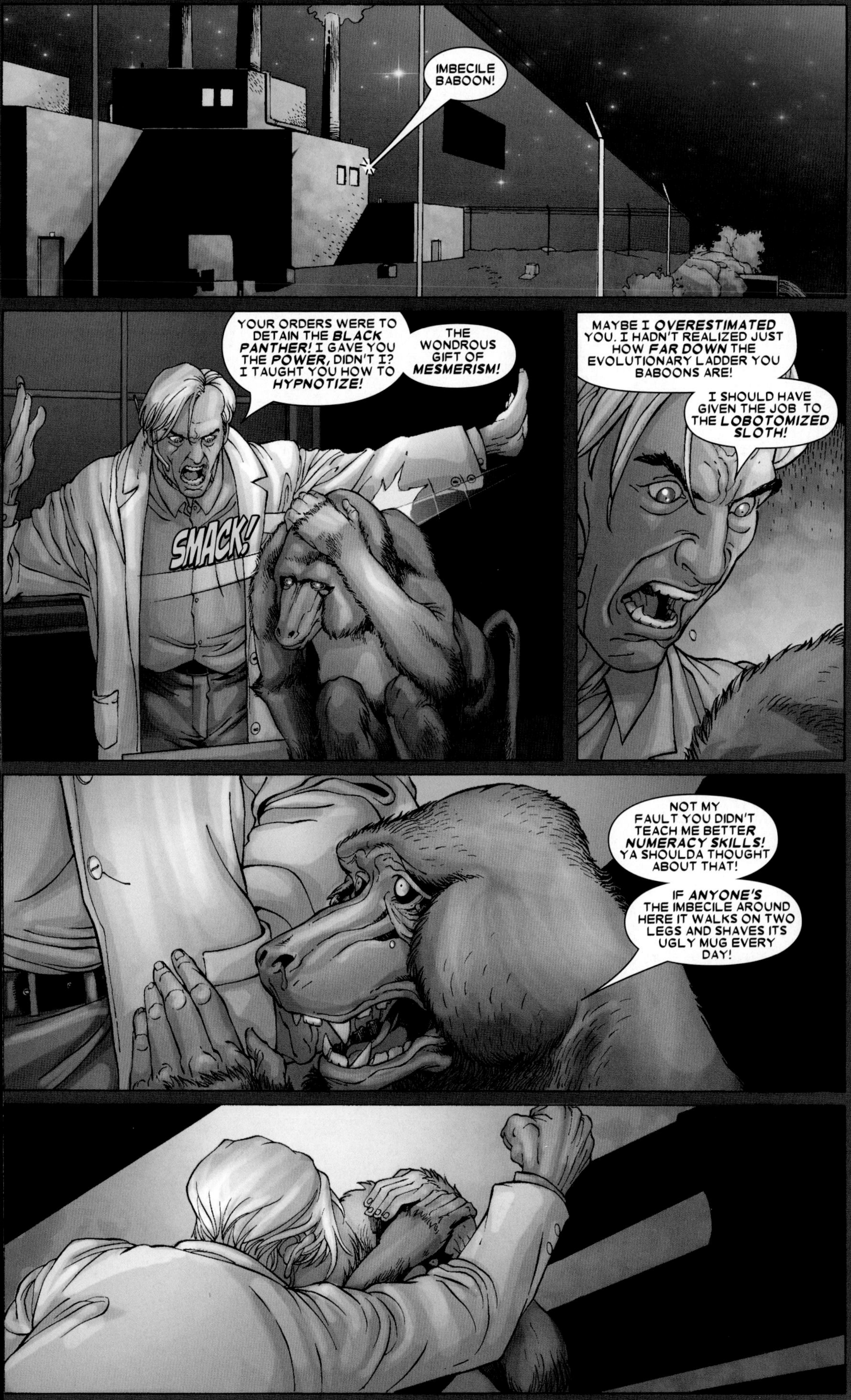
IMBECILE BABOON!
YOUR ORDERS WERE TO DETAIN THE BLACK PANTHER! I GAVE YOU THE POWER, DIDN'T I? I TAUGHT YOU HOW TO HYPNOTIZE!
THE WONDROUS GIFT OF MESMERISM!
SMACK!
MAYBE I OVERESTIMATED YOU. I HADN'T REALIZED JUST HOW FAR DOWN THE EVOLUTIONARY LADDER YOU BABOONS ARE!
I SHOULD HAVE GIVEN THE JOB TO THE LOBOTOMIZED SLOTH!
NOT MY FAULT YOU DIDN'T TEACH ME BETTER NUMERACY SKILLS! YA SHOULDA THOUGHT ABOUT THAT!
IF ANYONE'S THE IMBECILE AROUND HERE IT WALKS ON TWO LEGS AND SHAVES ITS UGLY MUG EVERY DAY!

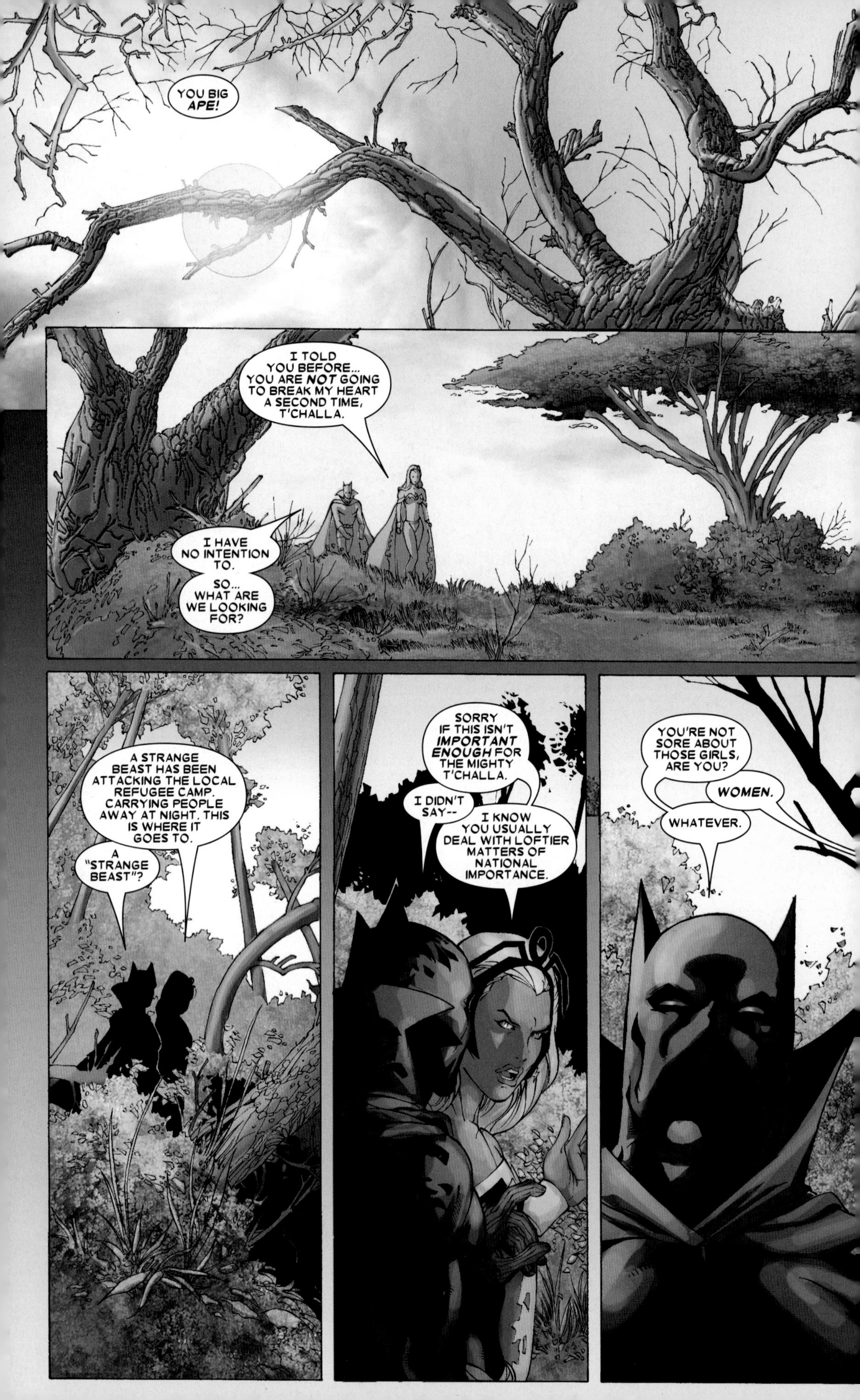

YOU BIG APE!
I TOLD YOU BEFORE... YOU ARE NOT GOING TO BREAK MY HEART A SECOND TIME, T'CHALLA.
I HAVE NO INTENTION TO.
SO... WHAT ARE WE LOOKING FOR?
A STRANGE BEAST HAS BEEN ATTACKING THE LOCAL REFUGEE CAMP. CARRYING PEOPLE AWAY AT NIGHT. THIS IS WHERE IT GOES TO.
A "STRANGE BEAST"?
SORRY IF THIS ISN'T IMPORTANT ENOUGH FOR THE MIGHTY T'CHALLA.
I DIDN'T SAY--
I KNOW YOU USUALLY DEAL WITH LOFTIER MATTERS OF NATIONAL IMPORTANCE.
YOU'RE NOT SORE ABOUT THOSE GIRLS, ARE YOU?
WOMEN.
WHATEVER.

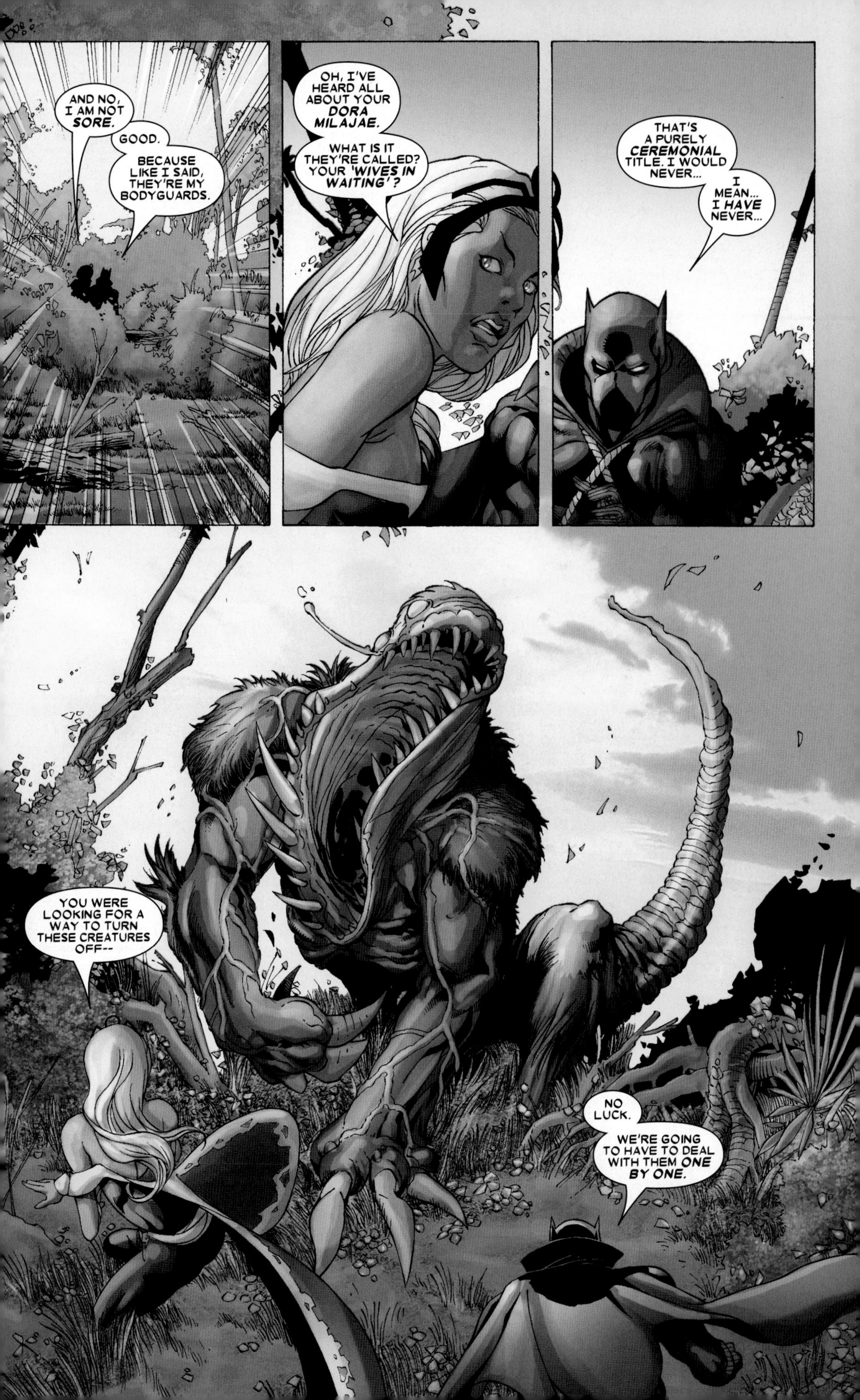
AND NO, I AM NOT SORE.
GOOD.
BECAUSE LIKE I SAID, THEY'RE MY BODYGUARDS.
OH, I'VE HEARD ALL ABOUT YOUR DORA MILAJAE.
WHAT IS IT THEY'RE CALLED? YOUR 'WIVES IN WAITING'?
THAT'S A PURELY CEREMONIAL TITLE. I WOULD NEVER...
I MEAN... I HAVE NEVER...
YOU WERE LOOKING FOR A WAY TO TURN THESE CREATURES OFF--
NO LUCK.
WE'RE GOING TO HAVE TO DEAL WITH THEM ONE BY ONE.

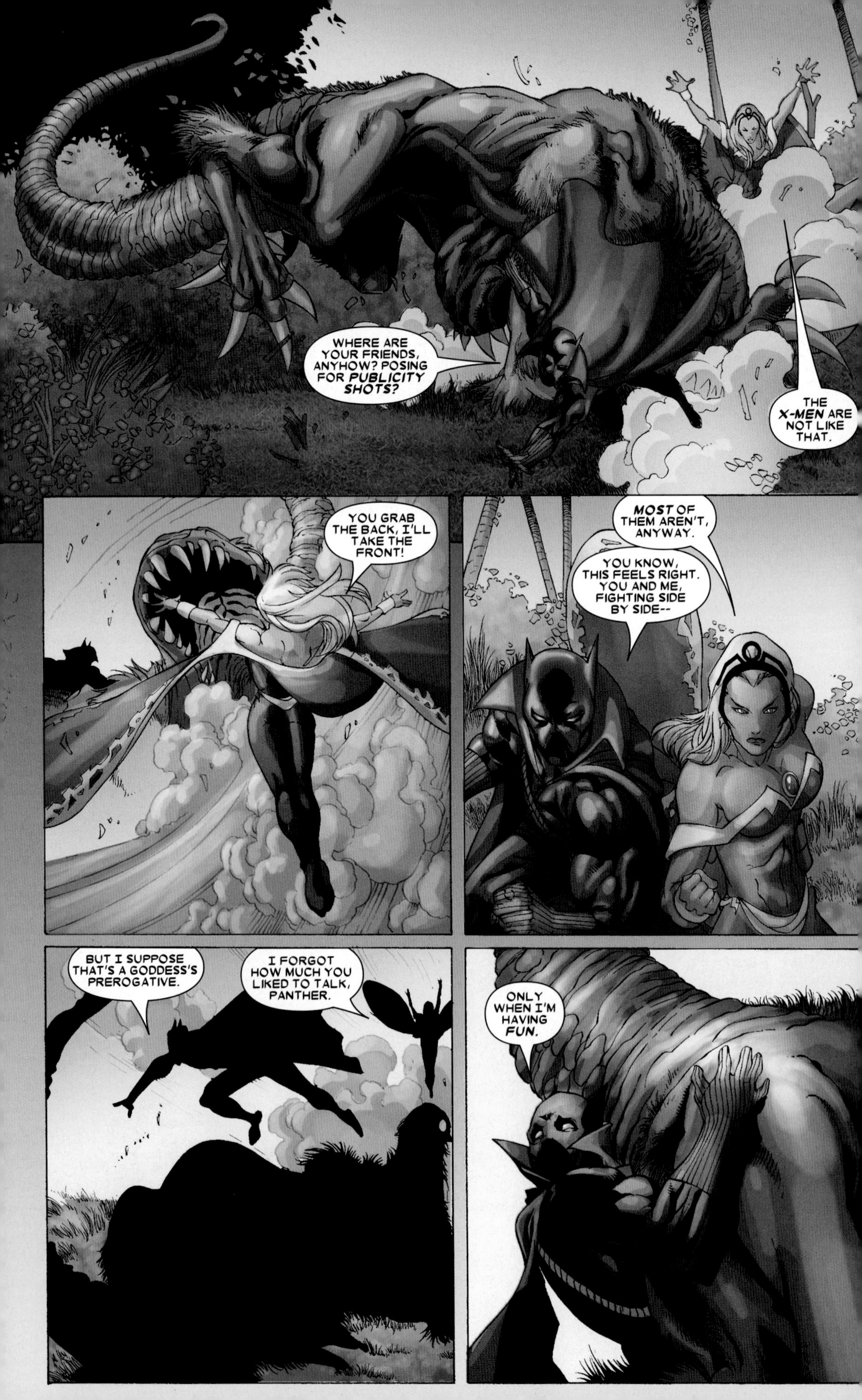
WHERE ARE YOUR FRIENDS, ANYHOW? POSING FOR PUBLICITY SHOTS?
THE X-MEN ARE NOT LIKE THAT.
YOU GRAB THE BACK, I'LL TAKE THE FRONT!
MOST OF THEM AREN'T, ANYWAY.
YOU KNOW, THIS FEELS RIGHT. YOU AND ME, FIGHTING SIDE BY SIDE--
BUT I SUPPOSE THAT'S A GODDESS'S PREROGATIVE.
I FORGOT HOW MUCH YOU LIKED TO TALK, PANTHER.
ONLY WHEN I'M HAVING FUN.

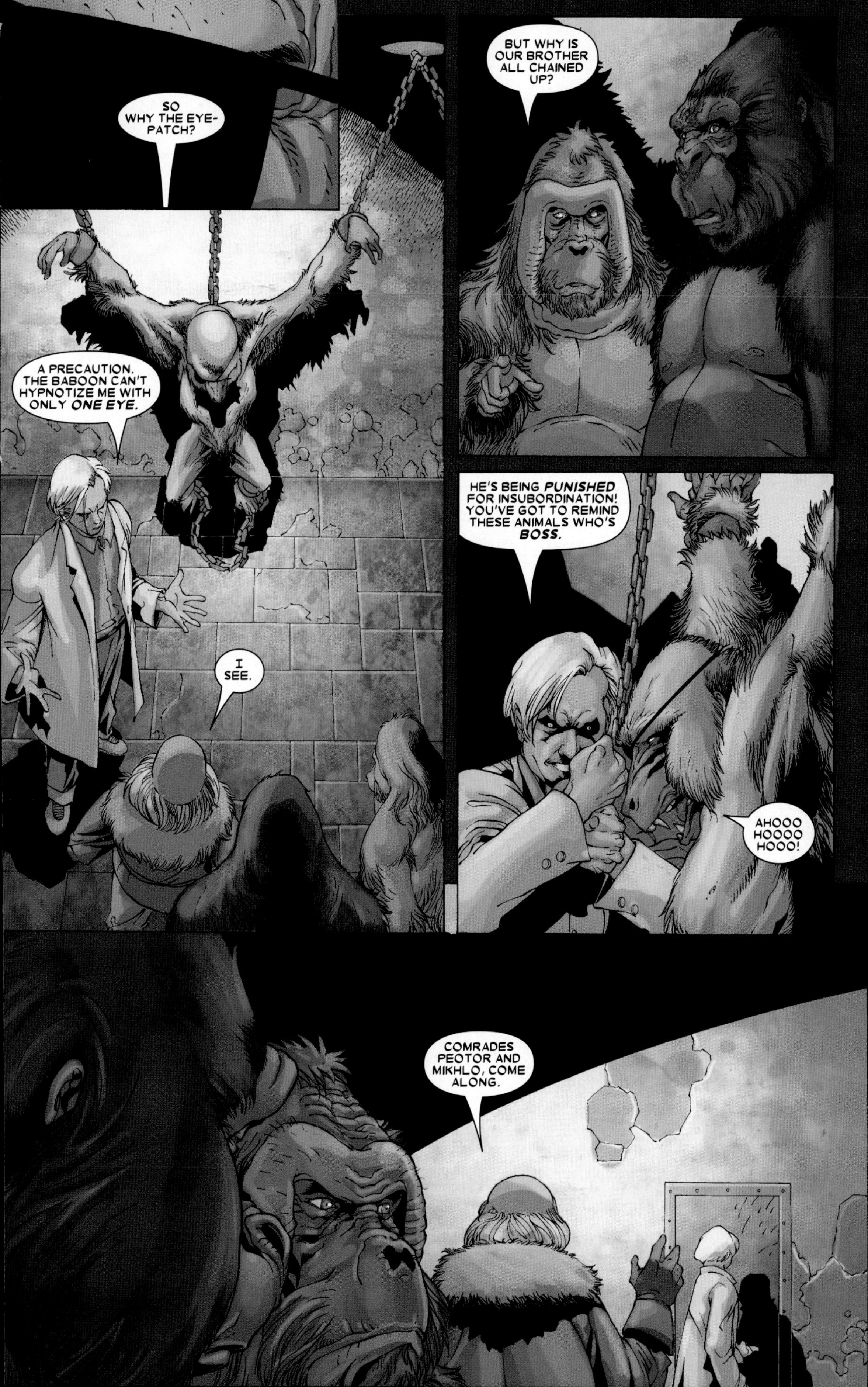
SO WHY THE EYE-PATCH?
A PRECAUTION. THE BABOON CAN'T HYPNOTIZE ME WITH ONLY *ONE EYE.*
I SEE.
BUT WHY IS OUR BROTHER ALL CHAINED UP?
HE'S BEING *PUNISHED* FOR INSUBORDINATION! YOU'VE GOT TO REMIND THESE ANIMALS WHO'S *BOSS.*
AHOOO HOOOO HOOO!
COMRADES PEOTOR AND MIKHLO, COME ALONG.

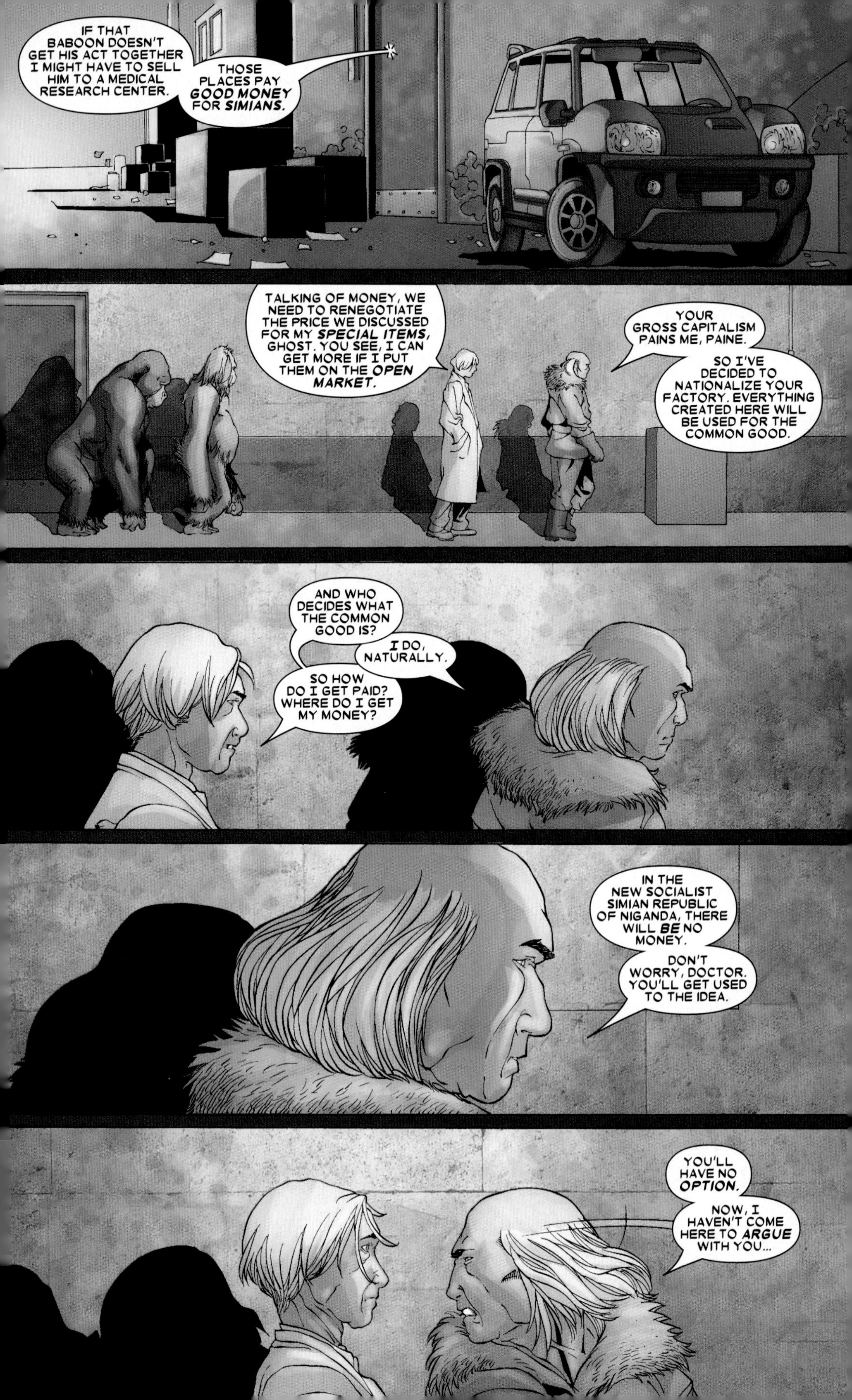
IF THAT BABOON DOESN'T GET HIS ACT TOGETHER I MIGHT HAVE TO SELL HIM TO A MEDICAL RESEARCH CENTER.
THOSE PLACES PAY GOOD MONEY FOR SIMIANS.
TALKING OF MONEY, WE NEED TO RENEGOTIATE THE PRICE WE DISCUSSED FOR MY SPECIAL ITEMS, GHOST. YOU SEE, I CAN GET MORE IF I PUT THEM ON THE OPEN MARKET.
YOUR GROSS CAPITALISM PAINS ME, PAINE.
SO I'VE DECIDED TO NATIONALIZE YOUR FACTORY. EVERYTHING CREATED HERE WILL BE USED FOR THE COMMON GOOD.
AND WHO DECIDES WHAT THE COMMON GOOD IS?
I DO, NATURALLY.
SO HOW DO I GET PAID? WHERE DO I GET MY MONEY?
IN THE NEW SOCIALIST SIMIAN REPUBLIC OF NIGANDA, THERE WILL BE NO MONEY.
DON'T WORRY, DOCTOR. YOU'LL GET USED TO THE IDEA.
YOU'LL HAVE NO OPTION.
NOW, I HAVEN'T COME HERE TO ARGUE WITH YOU...

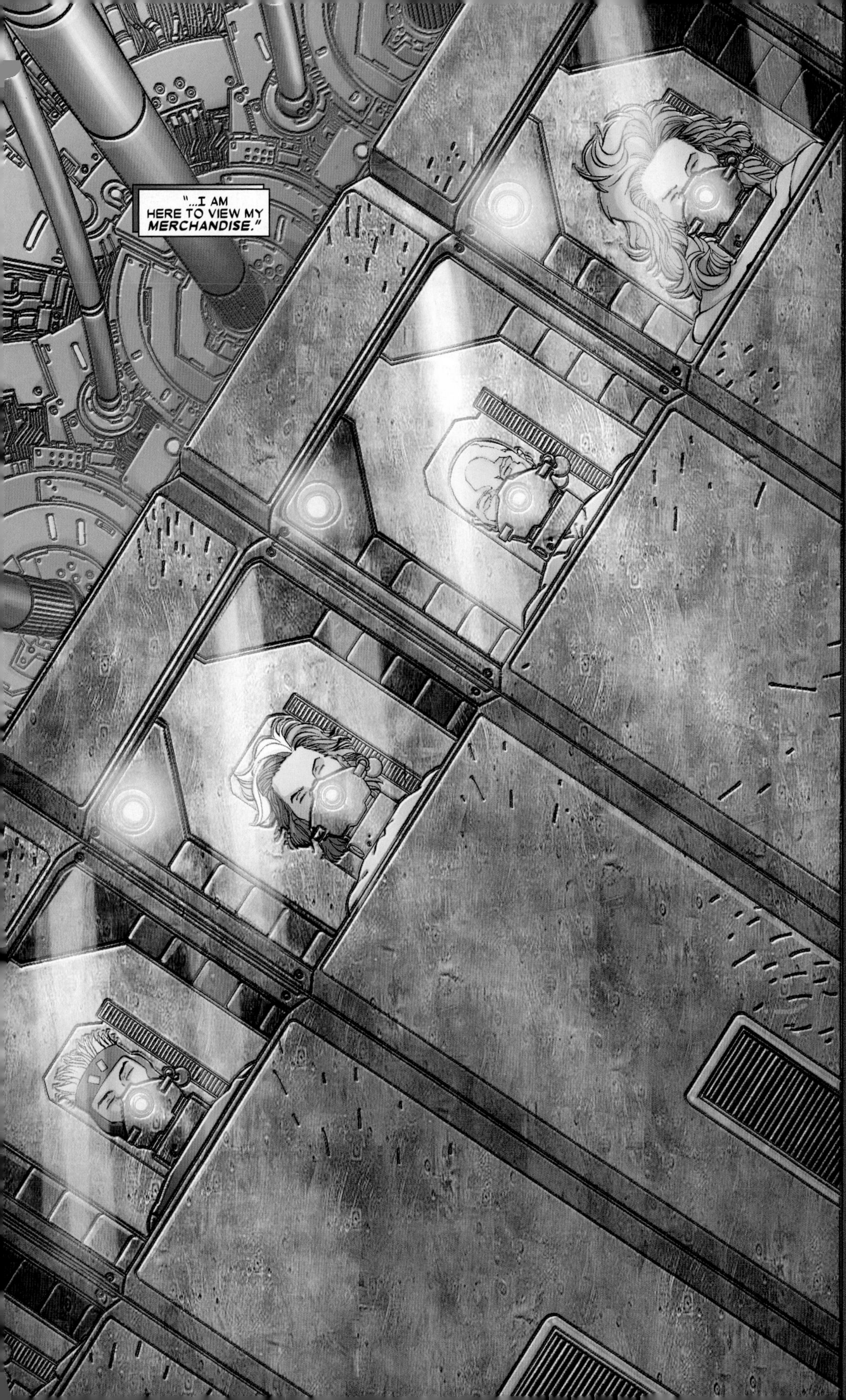
"...I AM HERE TO VIEW MY MERCHANDISE."

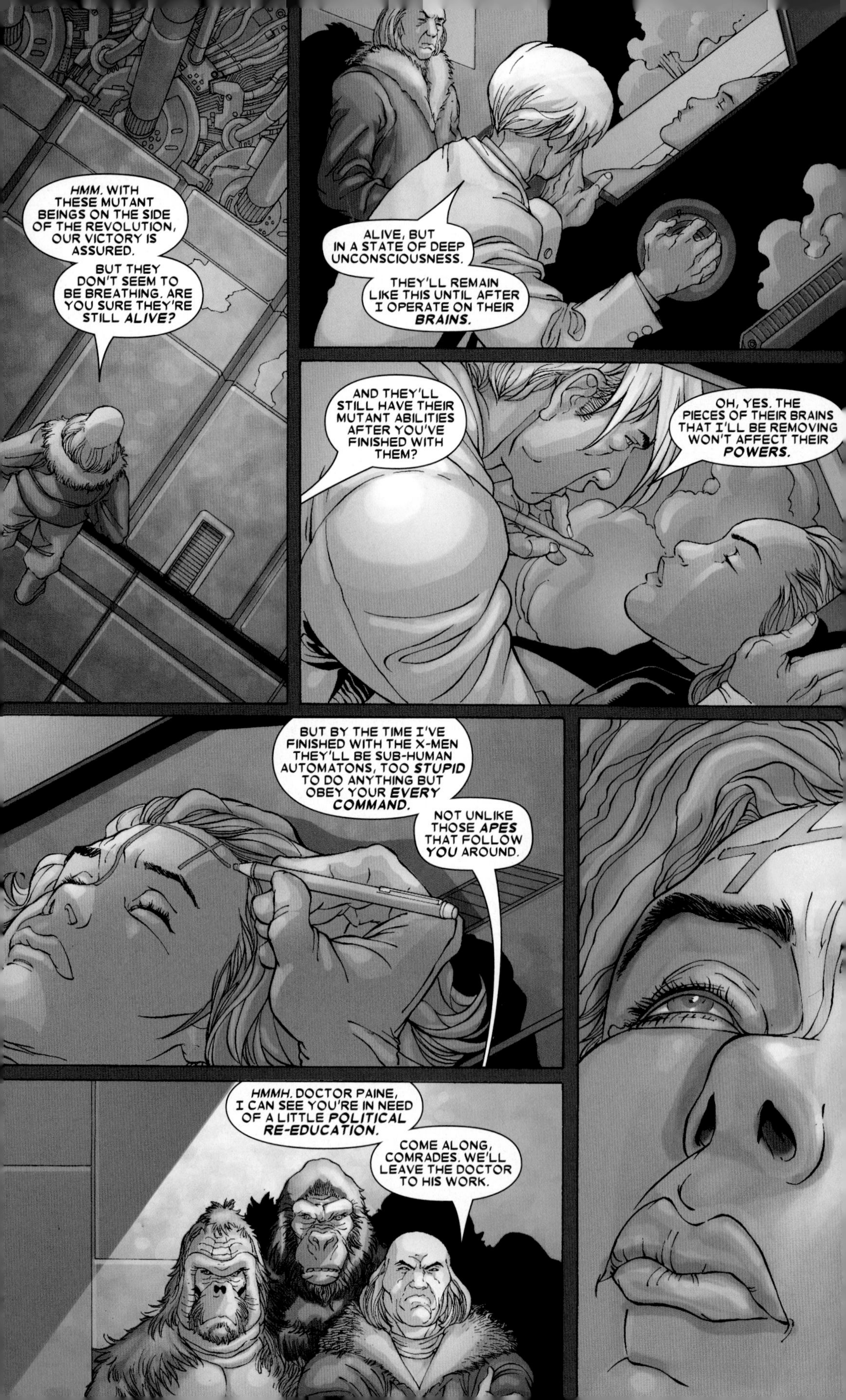
HMM. WITH THESE MUTANT BEINGS ON THE SIDE OF THE REVOLUTION, OUR VICTORY IS ASSURED.
BUT THEY DON'T SEEM TO BE BREATHING. ARE YOU SURE THEY'RE STILL ALIVE?
ALIVE, BUT IN A STATE OF DEEP UNCONSCIOUSNESS.
THEY'LL REMAIN LIKE THIS UNTIL AFTER I OPERATE ON THEIR BRAINS.
AND THEY'LL STILL HAVE THEIR MUTANT ABILITIES AFTER YOU'VE FINISHED WITH THEM?
OH, YES. THE PIECES OF THEIR BRAINS THAT I'LL BE REMOVING WON'T AFFECT THEIR POWERS.
BUT BY THE TIME I'VE FINISHED WITH THE X-MEN THEY'LL BE SUB-HUMAN AUTOMATONS, TOO STUPID TO DO ANYTHING BUT OBEY YOUR EVERY COMMAND.
NOT UNLIKE THOSE APES THAT FOLLOW YOU AROUND.
HMMH. DOCTOR PAINE, I CAN SEE YOU'RE IN NEED OF A LITTLE POLITICAL RE-EDUCATION.
COME ALONG, COMRADES. WE'LL LEAVE THE DOCTOR TO HIS WORK.

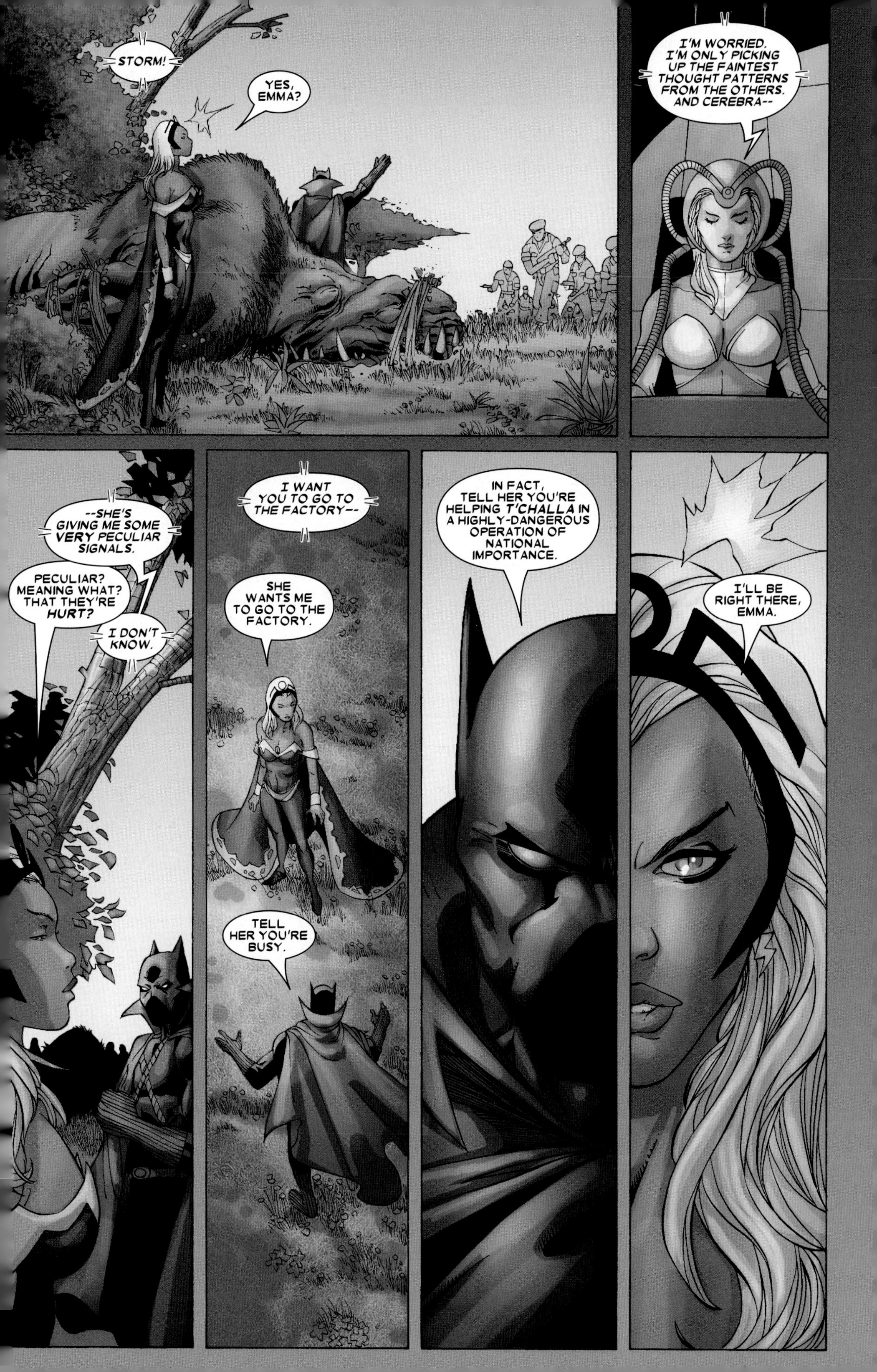
STORM!
YES, EMMA?
I'M WORRIED. I'M ONLY PICKING UP THE FAINTEST THOUGHT PATTERNS FROM THE OTHERS. AND CEREBRA--
--SHE'S GIVING ME SOME VERY PECULIAR SIGNALS.
PECULIAR? MEANING WHAT? THAT THEY'RE HURT?
I DON'T KNOW.
I WANT YOU TO GO TO THE FACTORY--
SHE WANTS ME TO GO TO THE FACTORY.
TELL HER YOU'RE BUSY.
IN FACT, TELL HER YOU'RE HELPING T'CHALLA IN A HIGHLY-DANGEROUS OPERATION OF NATIONAL IMPORTANCE.
I'LL BE RIGHT THERE, EMMA.

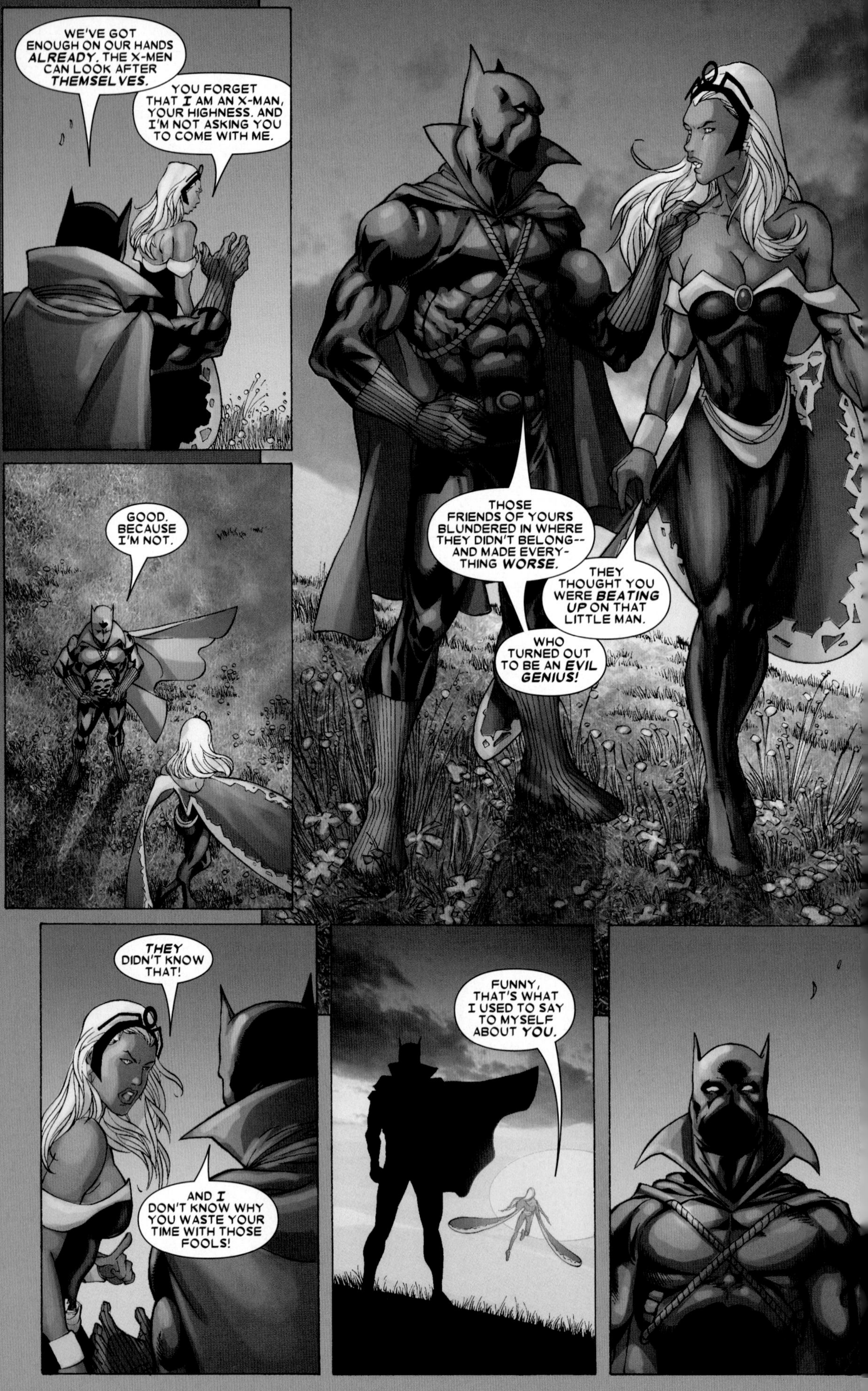

WE'VE GOT ENOUGH ON OUR HANDS ALREADY. THE X-MEN CAN LOOK AFTER THEMSELVES.
YOU FORGET THAT I AM AN X-MAN, YOUR HIGHNESS. AND I'M NOT ASKING YOU TO COME WITH ME.
GOOD. BECAUSE I'M NOT.
THOSE FRIENDS OF YOURS BLUNDERED IN WHERE THEY DIDN'T BELONG--AND MADE EVERY-THING WORSE.
THEY THOUGHT YOU WERE BEATING UP ON THAT LITTLE MAN.
WHO TURNED OUT TO BE AN EVIL GENIUS!
THEY DIDN'T KNOW THAT!
AND I DON'T KNOW WHY YOU WASTE YOUR TIME WITH THOSE FOOLS!
FUNNY, THAT'S WHAT I USED TO SAY TO MYSELF ABOUT YOU.

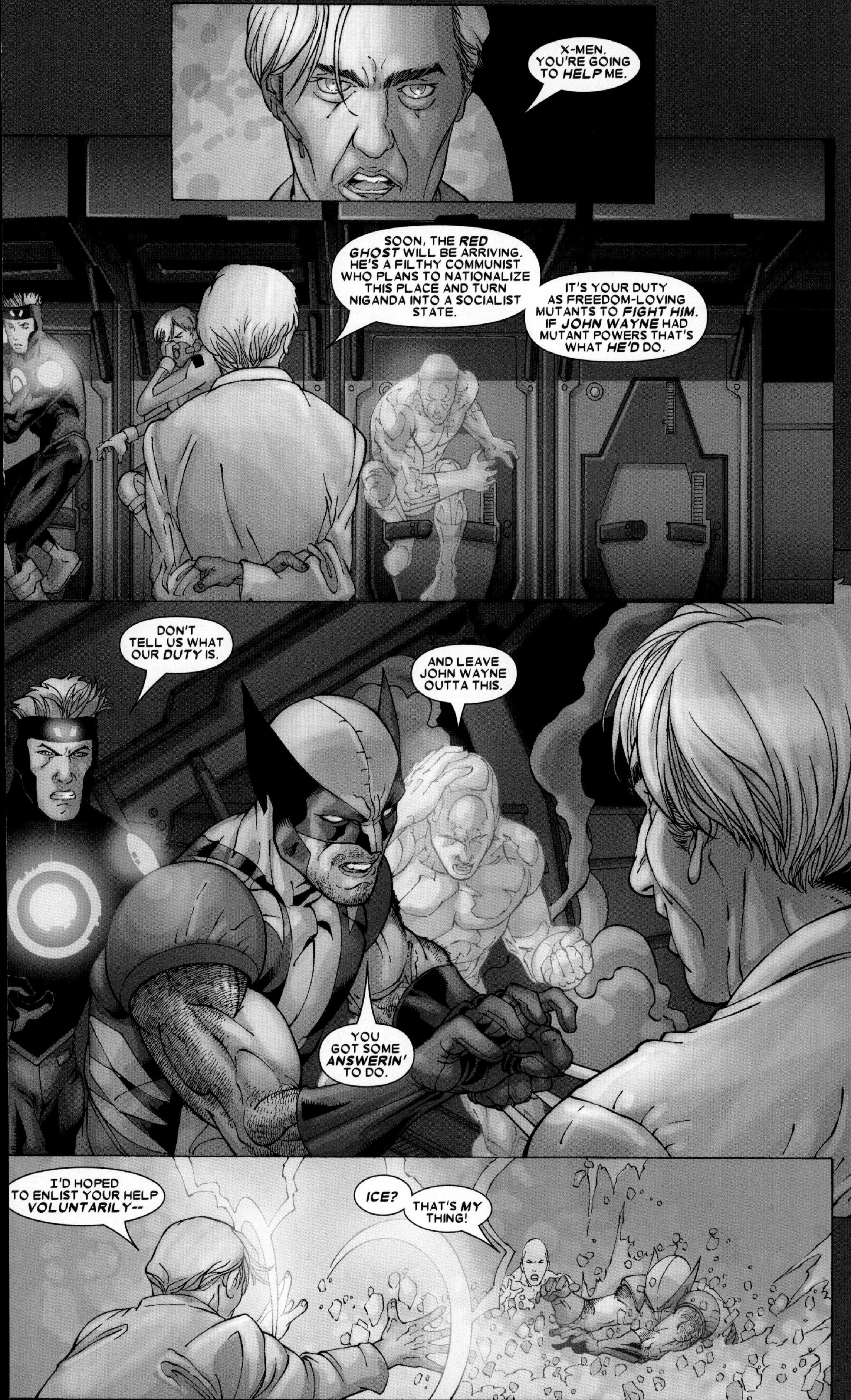
X-MEN. YOU'RE GOING TO *HELP* ME.
SOON, THE *RED GHOST* WILL BE ARRIVING. HE'S A FILTHY COMMUNIST WHO PLANS TO NATIONALIZE THIS PLACE AND TURN NIGANDA INTO A SOCIALIST STATE.
IT'S YOUR DUTY AS FREEDOM-LOVING MUTANTS TO *FIGHT HIM.* IF *JOHN WAYNE* HAD MUTANT POWERS THAT'S WHAT *HE'D* DO.
DON'T TELL US WHAT OUR *DUTY* IS.
AND LEAVE JOHN WAYNE OUTTA THIS.
YOU GOT SOME *ANSWERIN'* TO DO.
I'D HOPED TO ENLIST YOUR HELP *VOLUNTARILY*--
ICE?
THAT'S *MY* THING!

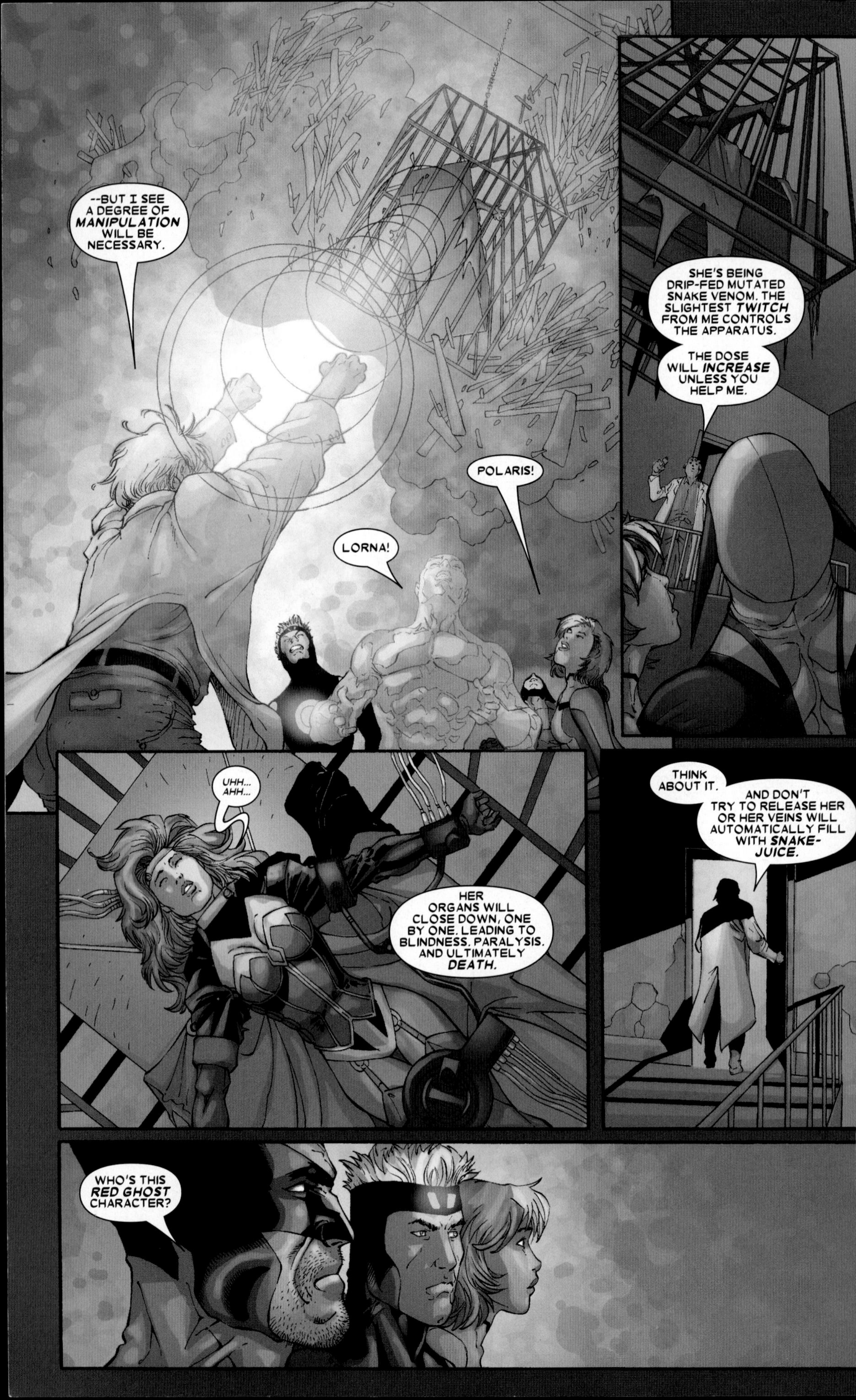
--BUT I SEE A DEGREE OF MANIPULATION WILL BE NECESSARY.
POLARIS!
LORNA!
SHE'S BEING DRIP-FED MUTATED SNAKE VENOM. THE SLIGHTEST TWITCH FROM ME CONTROLS THE APPARATUS.
THE DOSE WILL INCREASE UNLESS YOU HELP ME.
UHH... AHH...
HER ORGANS WILL CLOSE DOWN, ONE BY ONE. LEADING TO BLINDNESS, PARALYSIS, AND ULTIMATELY DEATH.
THINK ABOUT IT.
AND DON'T TRY TO RELEASE HER OR HER VEINS WILL AUTOMATICALLY FILL WITH SNAKE-JUICE.
WHO'S THIS RED GHOST CHARACTER?

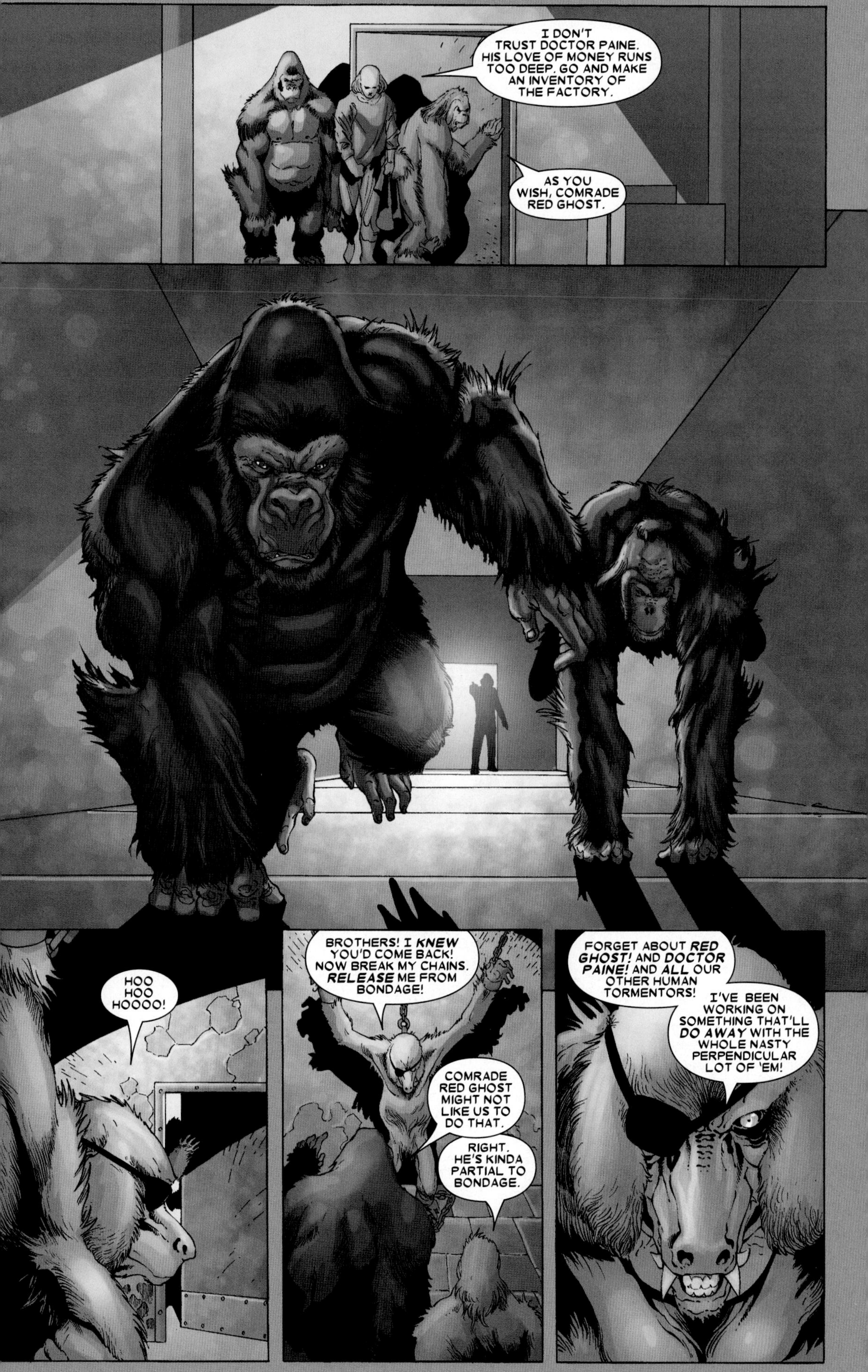
I DON'T TRUST DOCTOR PAINE. HIS LOVE OF MONEY RUNS TOO DEEP. GO AND MAKE AN INVENTORY OF THE FACTORY.
AS YOU WISH, COMRADE RED GHOST.
HOO HOO HOOOO!
BROTHERS! I KNEW YOU'D COME BACK! NOW BREAK MY CHAINS. RELEASE ME FROM BONDAGE!
COMRADE RED GHOST MIGHT NOT LIKE US TO DO THAT.
RIGHT. HE'S KINDA PARTIAL TO BONDAGE.
FORGET ABOUT RED GHOST! AND DOCTOR PAINE! AND ALL OUR OTHER HUMAN TORMENTORS!
I'VE BEEN WORKING ON SOMETHING THAT'LL DO AWAY WITH THE WHOLE NASTY PERPENDICULAR LOT OF 'EM!

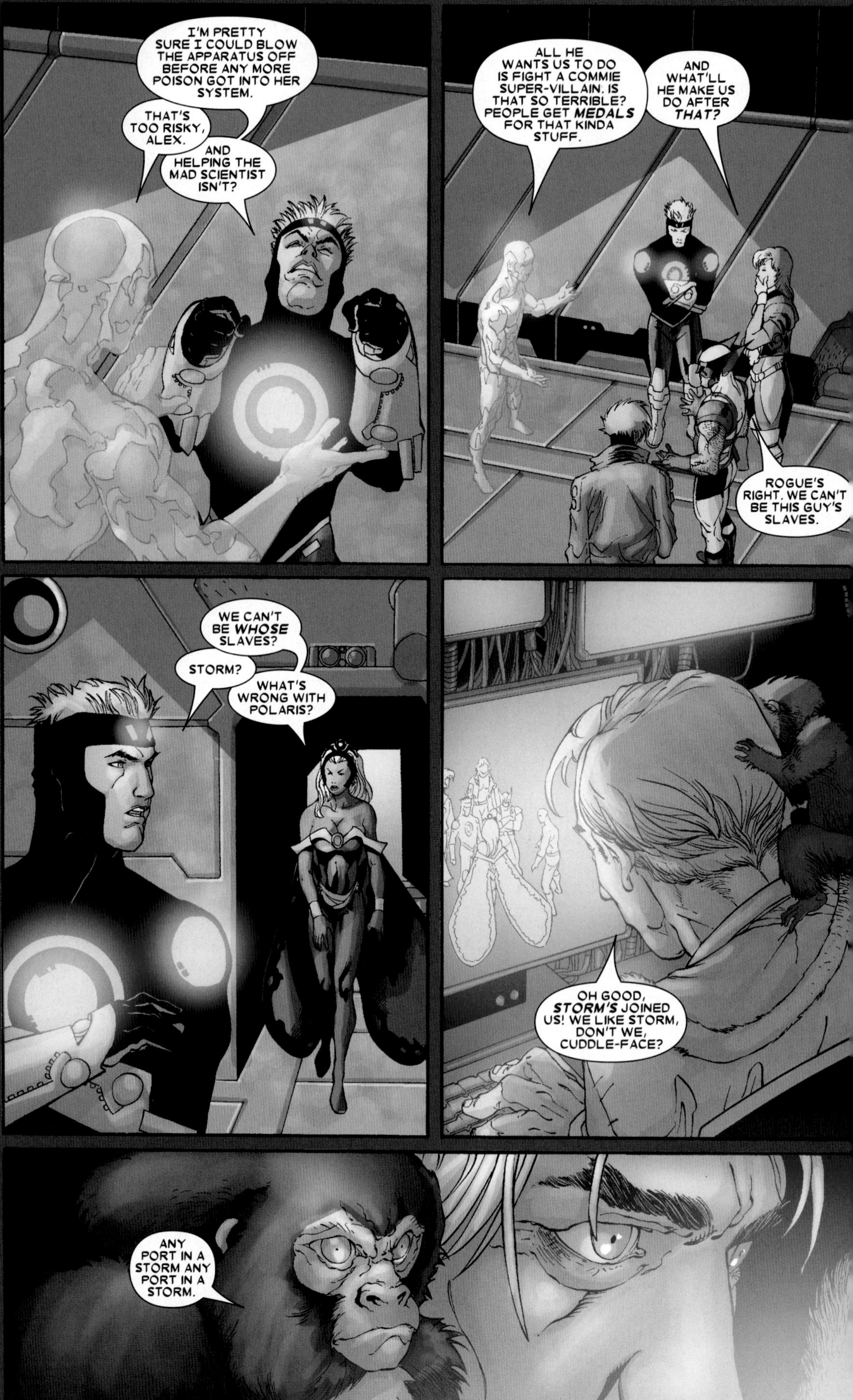
I'M PRETTY SURE I COULD BLOW THE APPARATUS OFF BEFORE ANY MORE POISON GOT INTO HER SYSTEM.
THAT'S TOO RISKY, ALEX.
AND HELPING THE MAD SCIENTIST ISN'T?
ALL HE WANTS US TO DO IS FIGHT A COMMIE SUPER-VILLAIN. IS THAT SO TERRIBLE? PEOPLE GET *MEDALS* FOR THAT KINDA STUFF.
AND WHAT'LL HE MAKE US DO AFTER *THAT?*
ROGUE'S RIGHT. WE CAN'T BE THIS GUY'S SLAVES.
WE CAN'T BE *WHOSE* SLAVES?
STORM?
WHAT'S WRONG WITH POLARIS?
OH GOOD, *STORM'S* JOINED US! WE LIKE STORM, DON'T WE, CUDDLE-FACE?
ANY PORT IN A STORM ANY PORT IN A STORM.

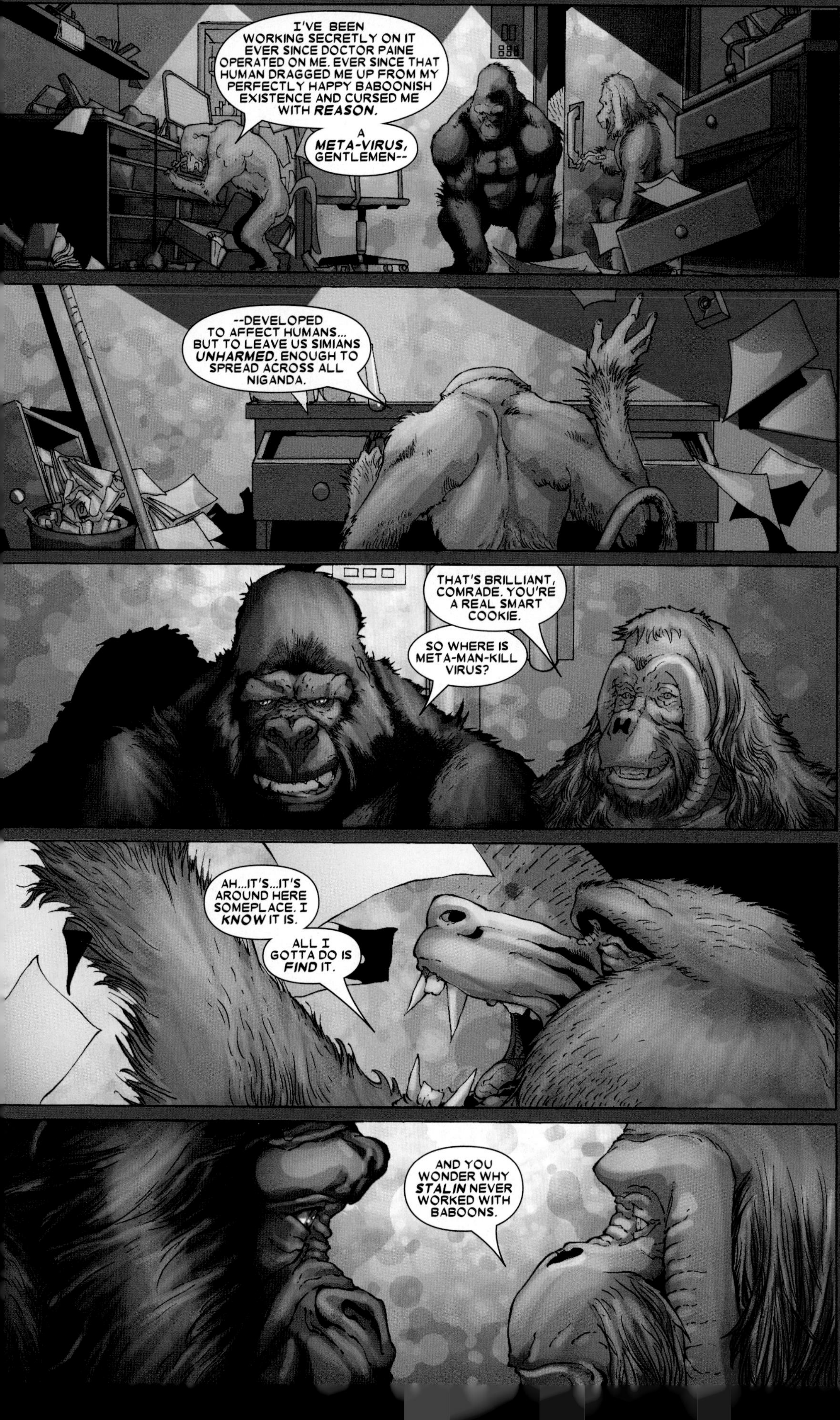
I'VE BEEN WORKING SECRETLY ON IT EVER SINCE DOCTOR PAINE OPERATED ON ME. EVER SINCE THAT HUMAN DRAGGED ME UP FROM MY PERFECTLY HAPPY BABOONISH EXISTENCE AND CURSED ME WITH REASON.
A META-VIRUS, GENTLEMEN--
--DEVELOPED TO AFFECT HUMANS... BUT TO LEAVE US SIMIANS UNHARMED. ENOUGH TO SPREAD ACROSS ALL NIGANDA.
THAT'S BRILLIANT, COMRADE. YOU'RE A REAL SMART COOKIE.
SO WHERE IS META-MAN-KILL VIRUS?
AH...IT'S...IT'S AROUND HERE SOMEPLACE. I KNOW IT IS.
ALL I GOTTA DO IS FIND IT.
AND YOU WONDER WHY STALIN NEVER WORKED WITH BABOONS.

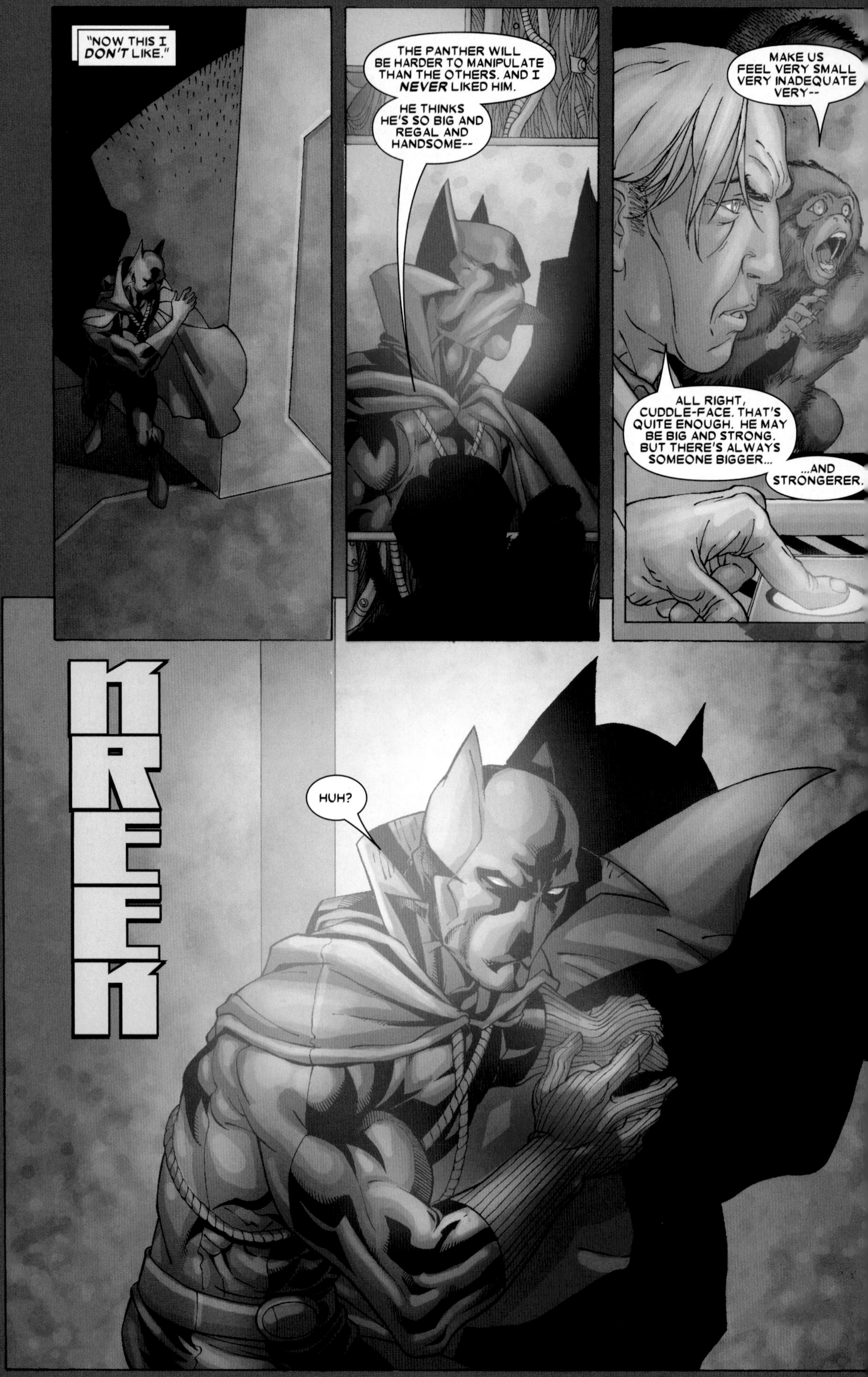
"NOW THIS I DON'T LIKE."
THE PANTHER WILL BE HARDER TO MANIPULATE THAN THE OTHERS. AND I NEVER LIKED HIM.
HE THINKS HE'S SO BIG AND REGAL AND HANDSOME--
MAKE US FEEL VERY SMALL VERY INADEQUATE VERY--
ALL RIGHT, CUDDLE-FACE. THAT'S QUITE ENOUGH. HE MAY BE BIG AND STRONG. BUT THERE'S ALWAYS SOMEONE BIGGER...
...AND STRONGERER.
KREEK
HUH?

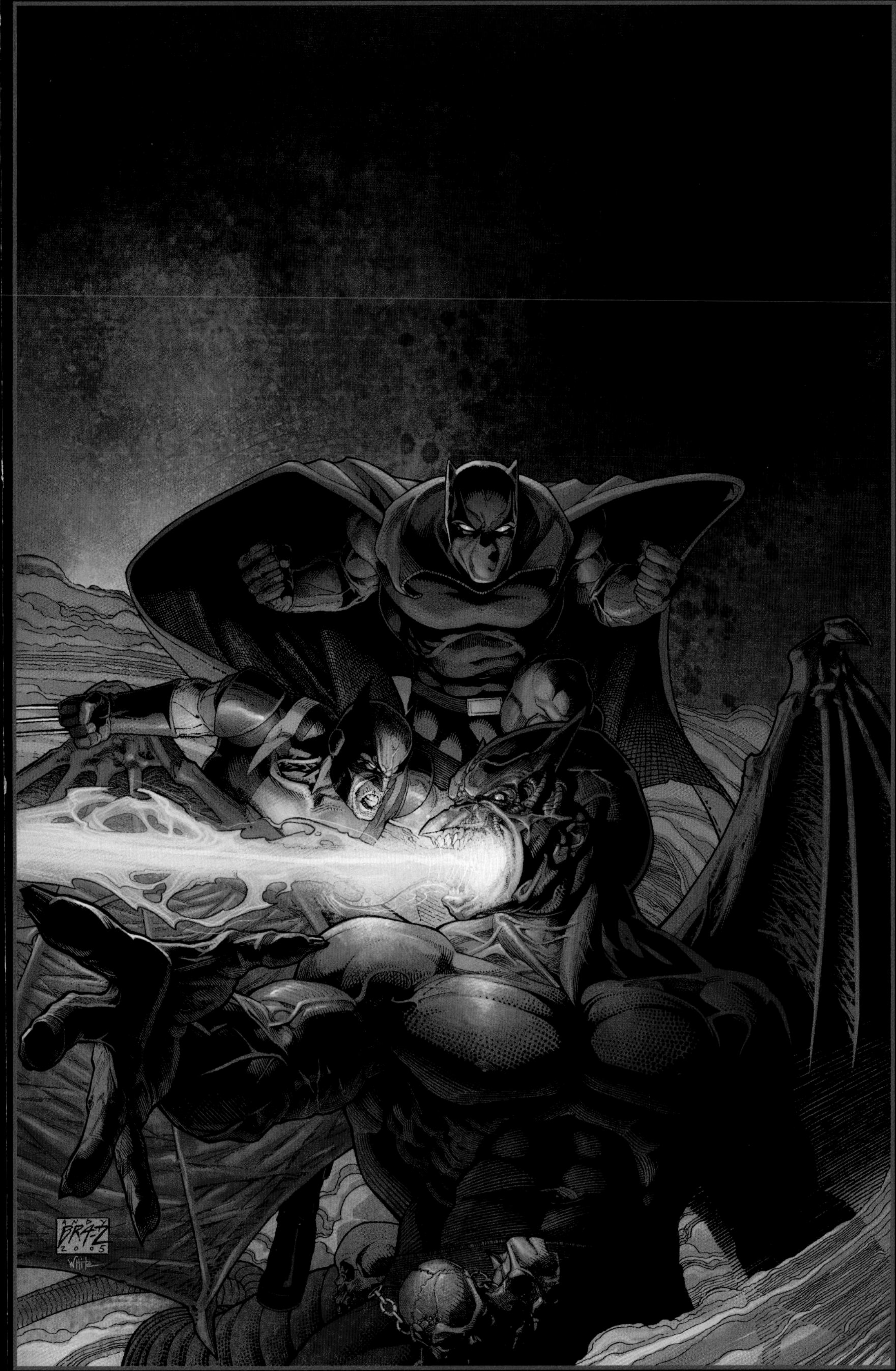

N'IGANDA, AFRICA.

WHAT'S GOING ON? ANOTHER HUNT FOR TRAITORS?

NO...A *MIRACLE* HAS HAPPENED.

THE *GODDESS* HAS RETURNED. SHE BLESSED THAT GIRL IN THE FRONT OF THE LINE!

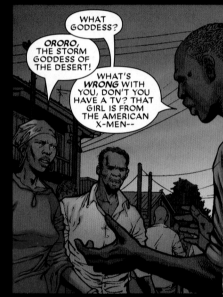

WHAT GODDESS?

ORORO, THE STORM GODDESS OF THE DESERT!

WHAT'S *WRONG* WITH YOU, DON'T YOU HAVE A TV? THAT GIRL IS FROM THE AMERICAN X-MEN--

BLASPHEMER!!!

NO! NO!

MIEEE!

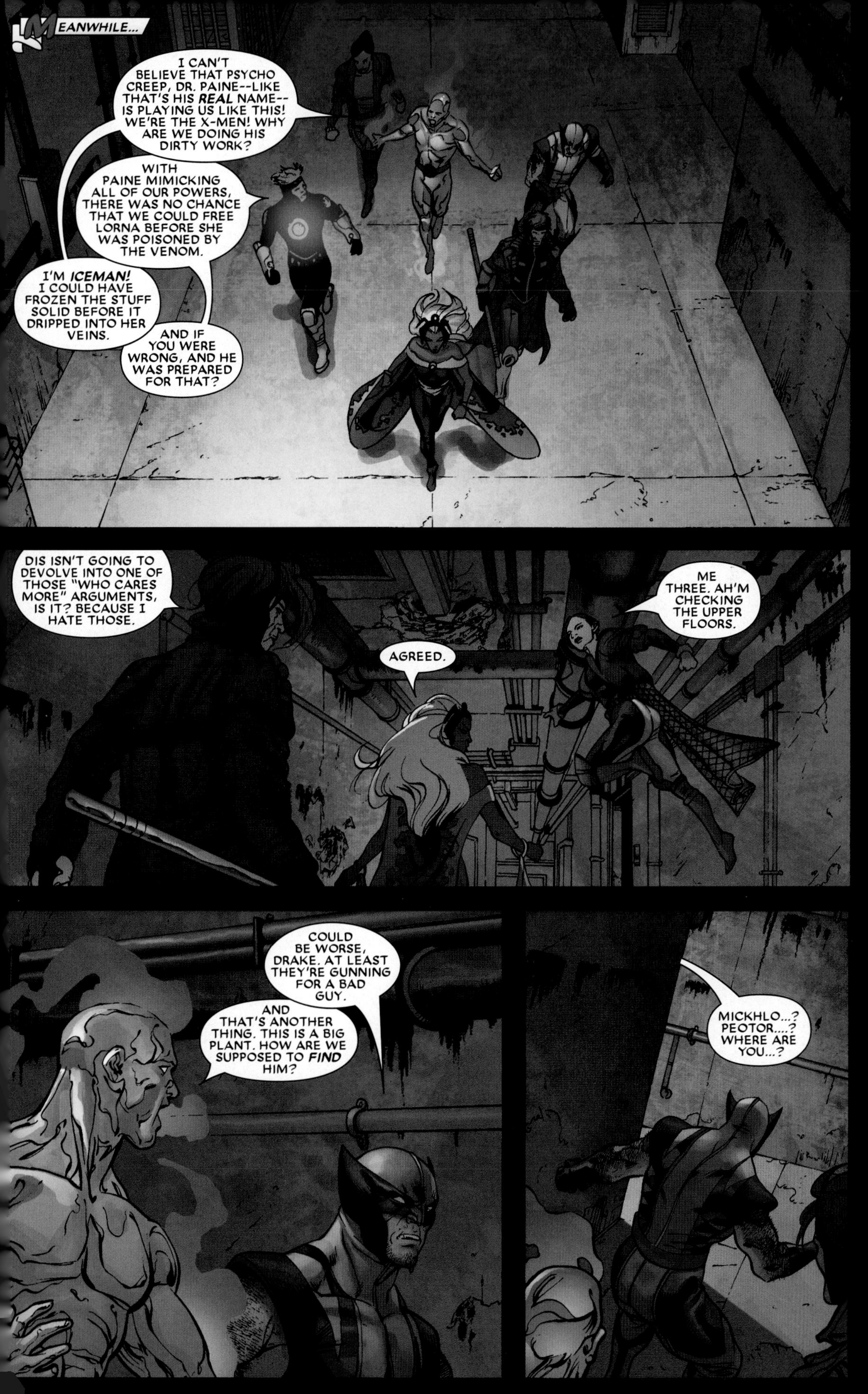
MEANWHILE...
I CAN'T BELIEVE THAT PSYCHO CREEP, DR. PAINE--LIKE THAT'S HIS *REAL* NAME--IS PLAYING US LIKE THIS! WE'RE THE X-MEN! WHY ARE WE DOING HIS DIRTY WORK?
WITH PAINE MIMICKING ALL OF OUR POWERS, THERE WAS NO CHANCE THAT WE COULD FREE LORNA BEFORE SHE WAS POISONED BY THE VENOM.
I'M *ICEMAN!* I COULD HAVE FROZEN THE STUFF SOLID BEFORE IT DRIPPED INTO HER VEINS.
AND IF YOU WERE WRONG, AND HE WAS PREPARED FOR THAT?
DIS ISN'T GOING TO DEVOLVE INTO ONE OF THOSE "WHO CARES MORE" ARGUMENTS, IS IT? BECAUSE I HATE THOSE.
AGREED.
ME THREE. AH'M CHECKING THE UPPER FLOORS.
COULD BE WORSE, DRAKE. AT LEAST THEY'RE GUNNING FOR A BAD GUY.
AND THAT'S ANOTHER THING. THIS IS A BIG PLANT. HOW ARE WE SUPPOSED TO *FIND* HIM?
MICKHLO...? PEOTOR....? WHERE ARE YOU...?

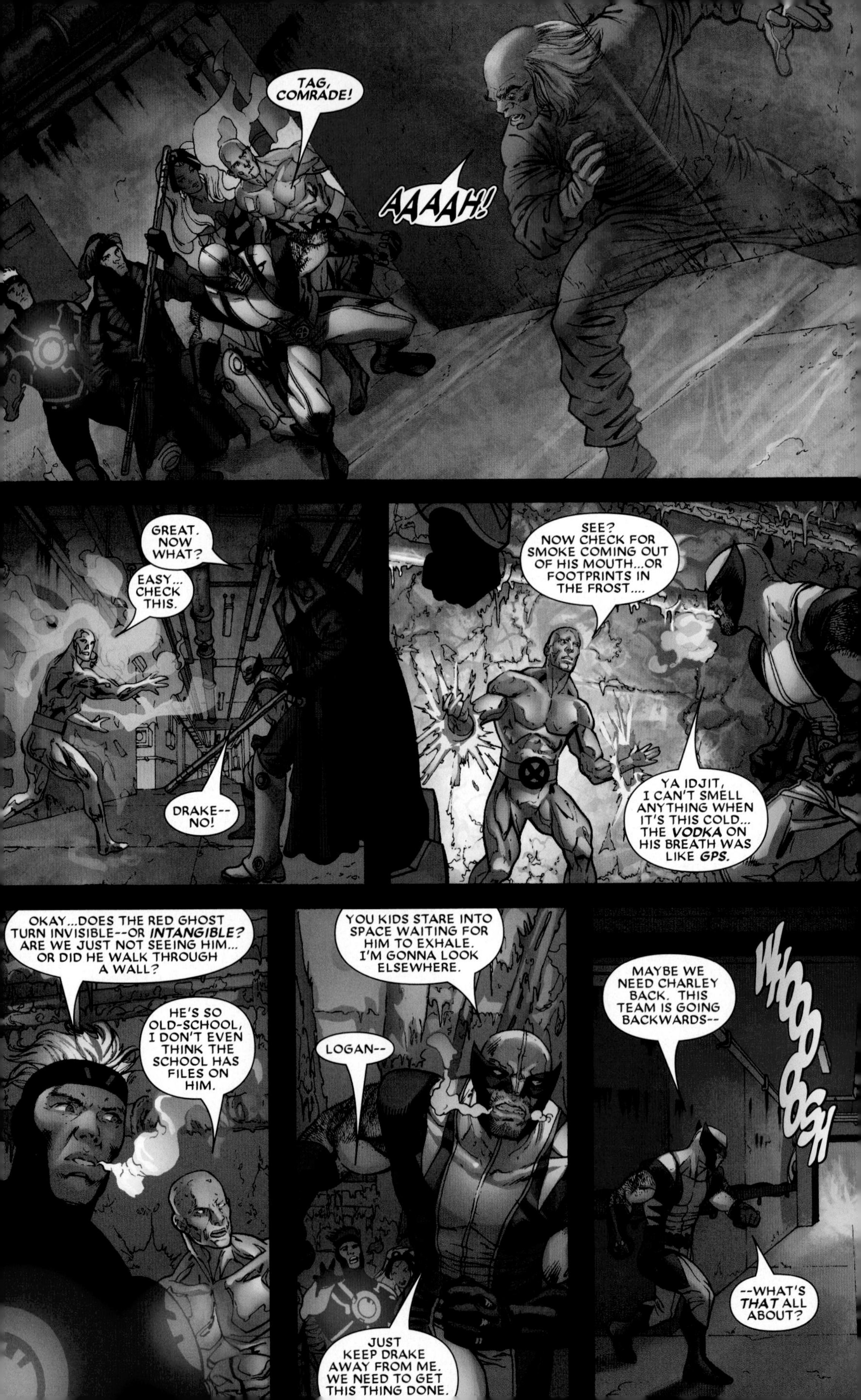
TAG, COMRADE!
AAAAH!
GREAT. NOW WHAT?
EASY... CHECK THIS.
DRAKE-- NO!
SEE? NOW CHECK FOR SMOKE COMING OUT OF HIS MOUTH...OR FOOTPRINTS IN THE FROST....
YA IDJIT, I CAN'T SMELL ANYTHING WHEN IT'S THIS COLD... THE VODKA ON HIS BREATH WAS LIKE GPS.
OKAY...DOES THE RED GHOST TURN INVISIBLE--OR INTANGIBLE? ARE WE JUST NOT SEEING HIM... OR DID HE WALK THROUGH A WALL?
HE'S SO OLD-SCHOOL, I DON'T EVEN THINK THE SCHOOL HAS FILES ON HIM.
YOU KIDS STARE INTO SPACE WAITING FOR HIM TO EXHALE. I'M GONNA LOOK ELSEWHERE.
LOGAN--
JUST KEEP DRAKE AWAY FROM ME. WE NEED TO GET THIS THING DONE.
MAYBE WE NEED CHARLEY BACK. THIS TEAM IS GOING BACKWARDS--
WHOOOOOSH
--WHAT'S THAT ALL ABOUT?

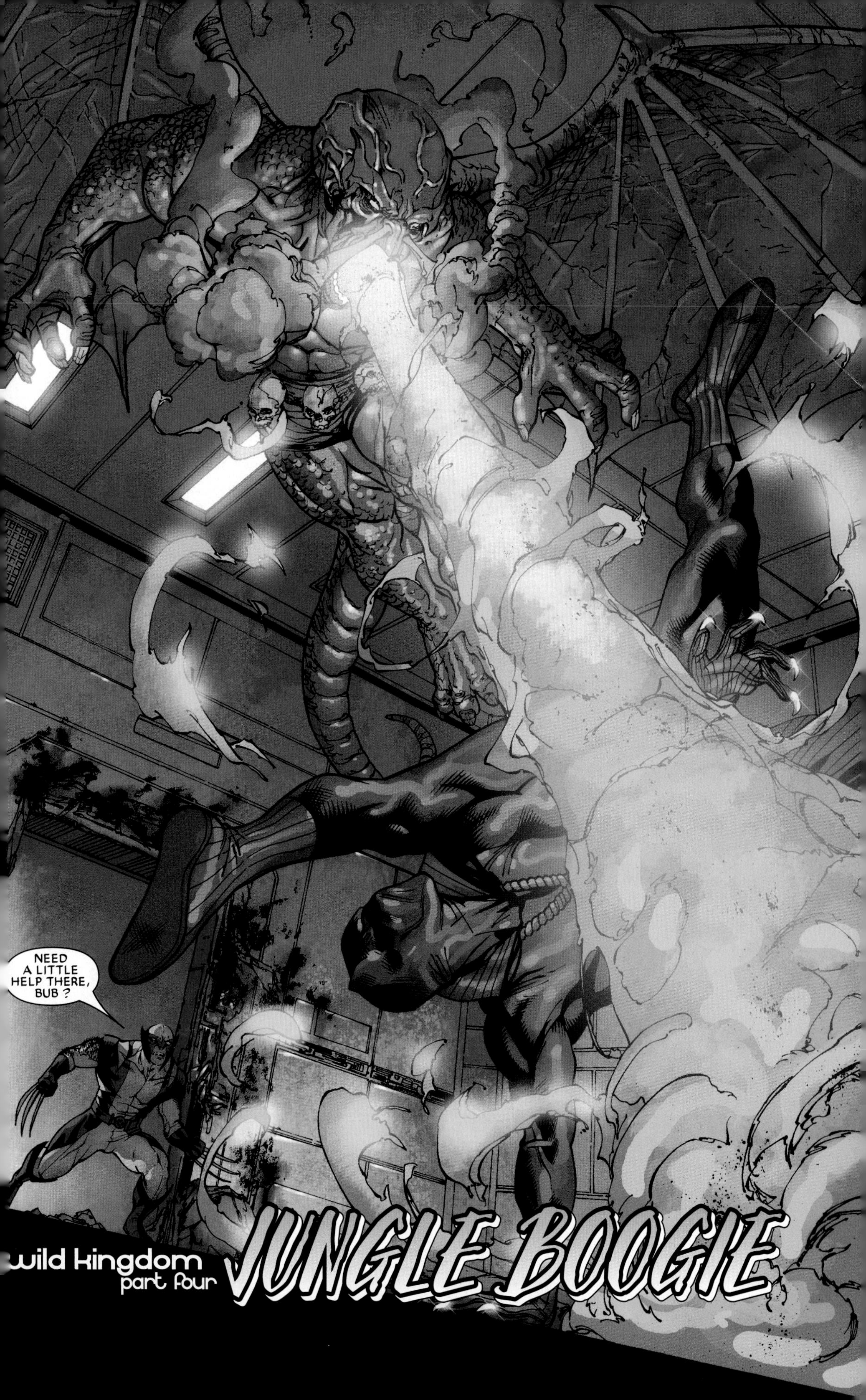
NEED A LITTLE HELP THERE, BUB ?
wild kingdom part four
JUNGLE BOOGIE

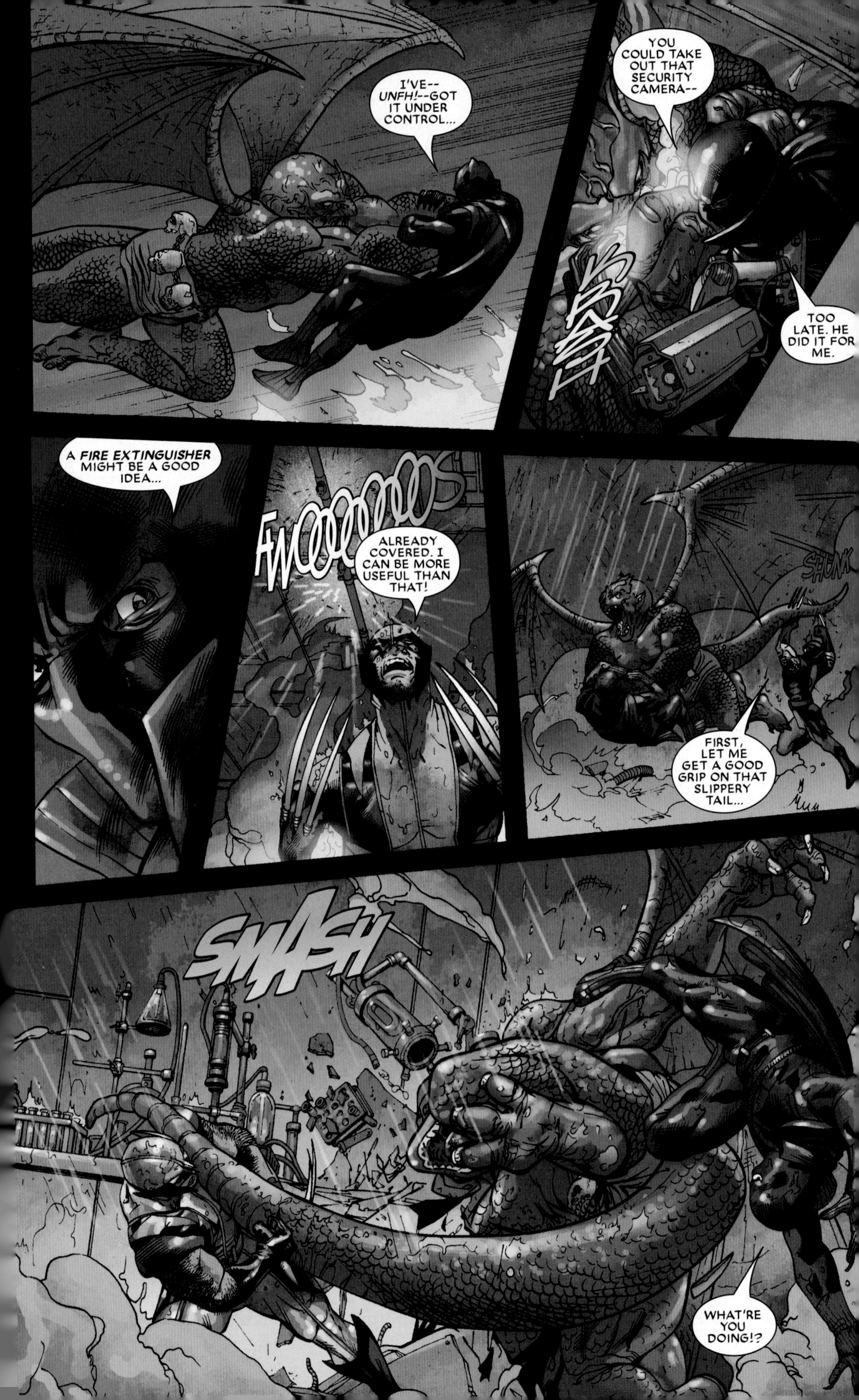
I'VE-- UNFH!--GOT IT UNDER CONTROL...
YOU COULD TAKE OUT THAT SECURITY CAMERA--
TOO LATE. HE DID IT FOR ME.
A FIRE EXTINGUISHER MIGHT BE A GOOD IDEA...
FWOOOOOOOS
ALREADY COVERED. I CAN BE MORE USEFUL THAN THAT!
SHUNK
FIRST, LET ME GET A GOOD GRIP ON THAT SLIPPERY TAIL...
SMASH
WHAT'RE YOU DOING!?

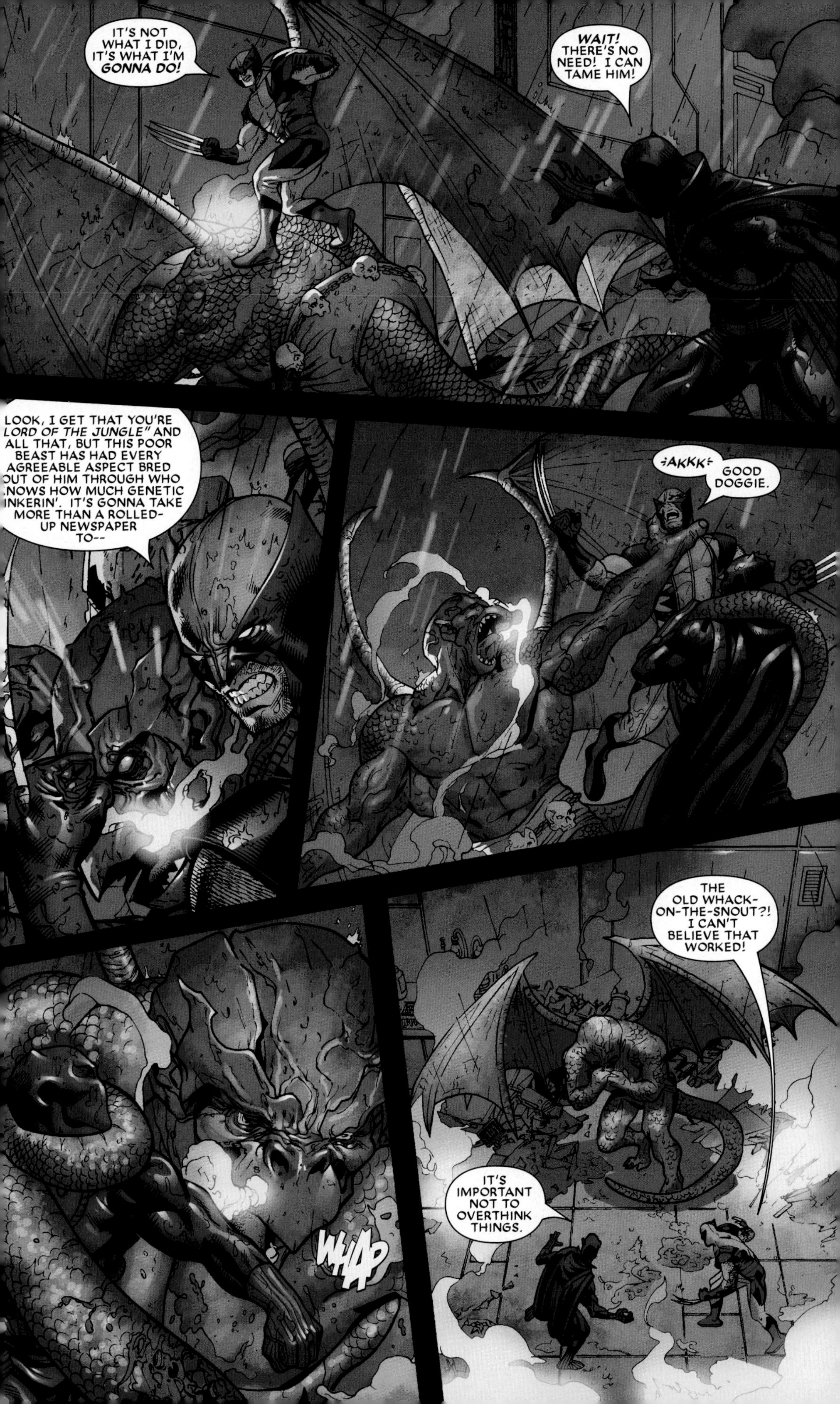

IT'S NOT WHAT I DID, IT'S WHAT I'M GONNA DO!
WAIT! THERE'S NO NEED! I CAN TAME HIM!
LOOK, I GET THAT YOU'RE "LORD OF THE JUNGLE" AND ALL THAT, BUT THIS POOR BEAST HAS HAD EVERY AGREEABLE ASPECT BRED OUT OF HIM THROUGH WHO KNOWS HOW MUCH GENETIC TINKERIN'. IT'S GONNA TAKE MORE THAN A ROLLED-UP NEWSPAPER TO--
AKKK
GOOD DOGGIE.
WHAP
THE OLD WHACK-ON-THE-SNOUT?! I CAN'T BELIEVE THAT WORKED!
IT'S IMPORTANT NOT TO OVERTHINK THINGS.

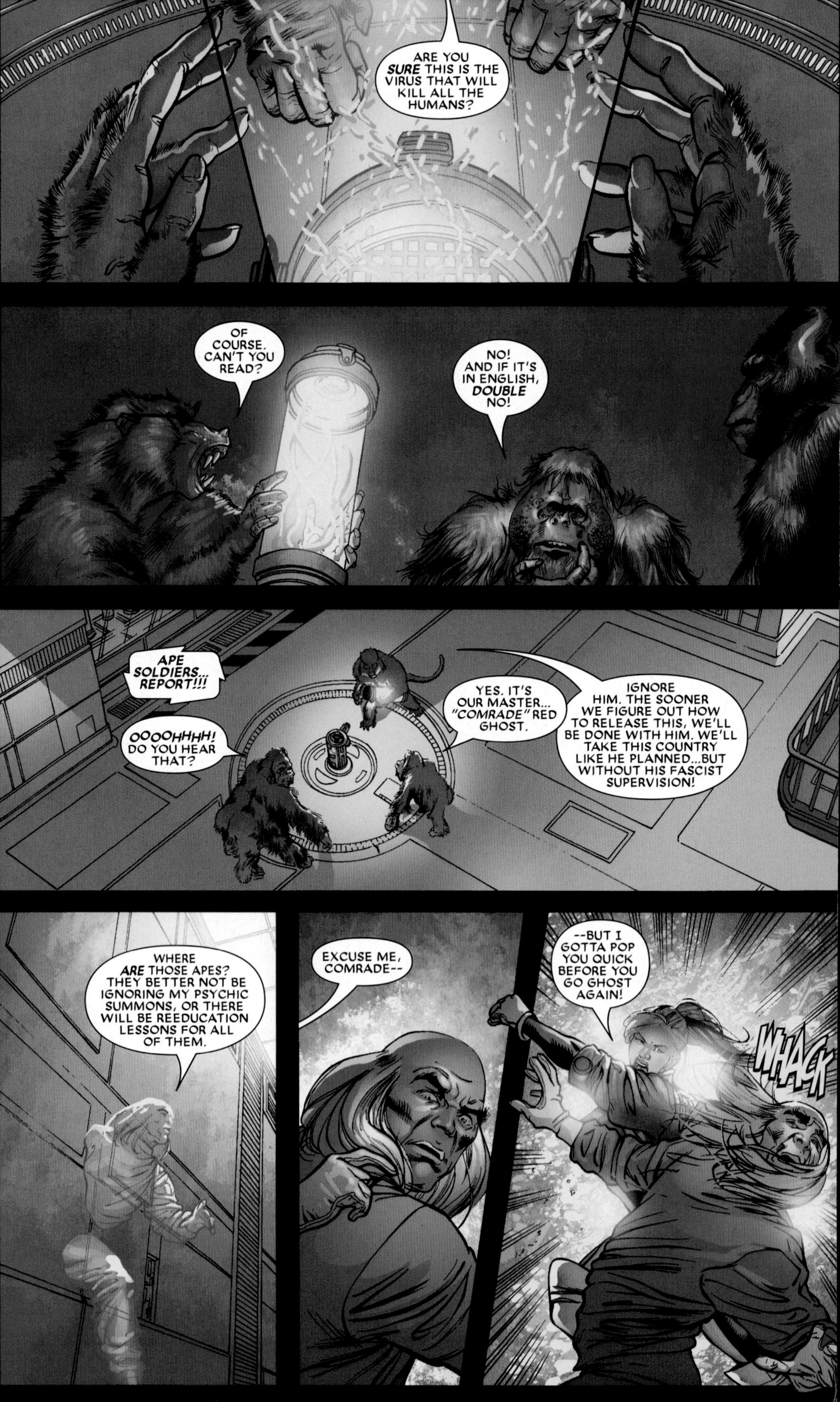

ARE YOU SURE THIS IS THE VIRUS THAT WILL KILL ALL THE HUMANS?
OF COURSE. CAN'T YOU READ?
NO! AND IF IT'S IN ENGLISH, DOUBLE NO!
APE SOLDIERS... REPORT!!!
OOOOHHHH! DO YOU HEAR THAT?
YES. IT'S OUR MASTER... "COMRADE" RED GHOST.
IGNORE HIM. THE SOONER WE FIGURE OUT HOW TO RELEASE THIS, WE'LL BE DONE WITH HIM. WE'LL TAKE THIS COUNTRY LIKE HE PLANNED...BUT WITHOUT HIS FASCIST SUPERVISION!
WHERE ARE THOSE APES? THEY BETTER NOT BE IGNORING MY PSYCHIC SUMMONS, OR THERE WILL BE REEDUCATION LESSONS FOR ALL OF THEM.
EXCUSE ME, COMRADE--
--BUT I GOTTA POP YOU QUICK BEFORE YOU GO GHOST AGAIN!
WHACK

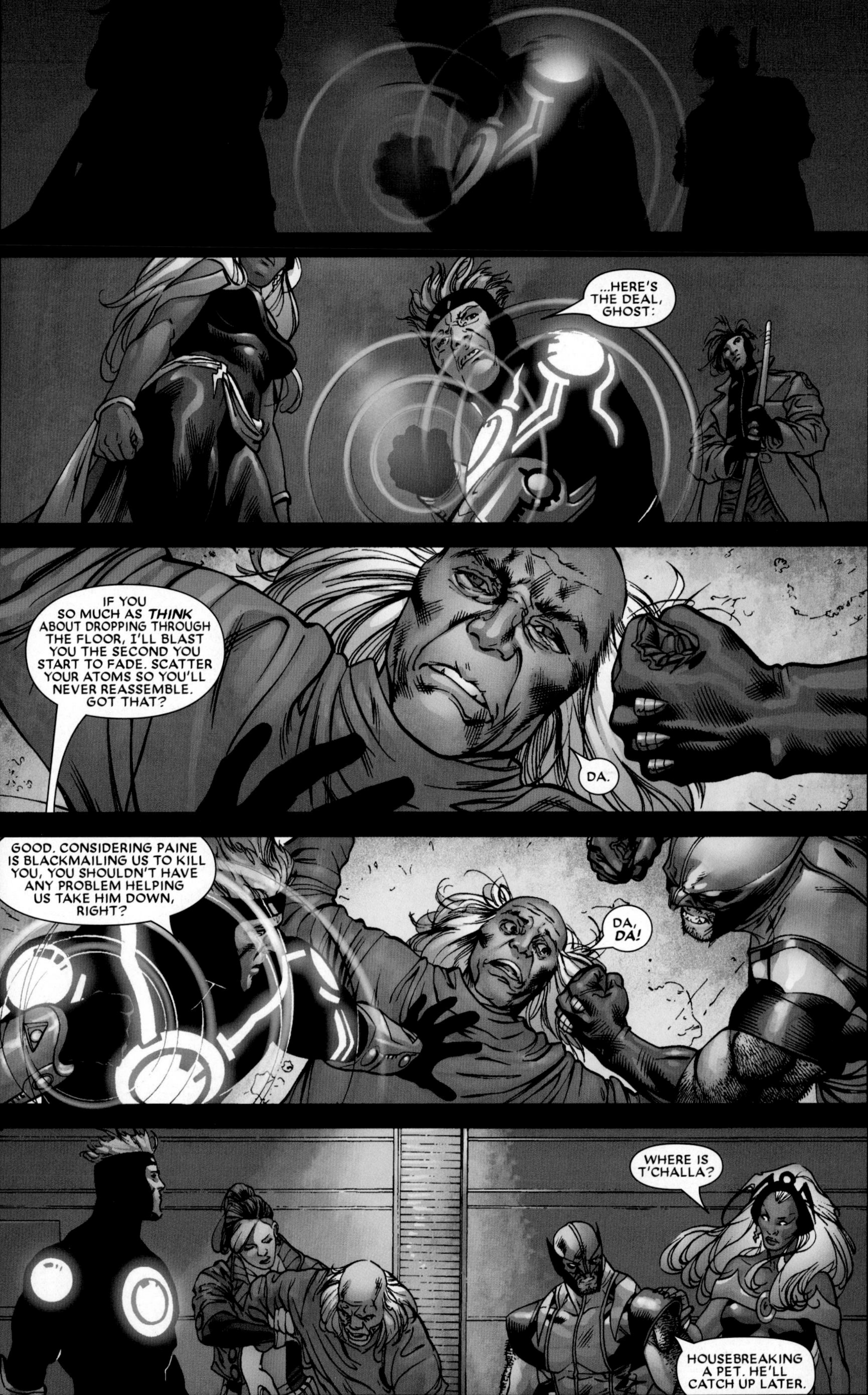
...HERE'S THE DEAL, GHOST:
IF YOU SO MUCH AS *THINK* ABOUT DROPPING THROUGH THE FLOOR, I'LL BLAST YOU THE SECOND YOU START TO FADE. SCATTER YOUR ATOMS SO YOU'LL NEVER REASSEMBLE. GOT THAT?
DA.
GOOD. CONSIDERING PAINE IS BLACKMAILING US TO KILL YOU, YOU SHOULDN'T HAVE ANY PROBLEM HELPING US TAKE HIM DOWN, RIGHT?
DA, *DA!*
WHERE IS T'CHALLA?
HOUSEBREAKING A PET. HE'LL CATCH UP LATER.

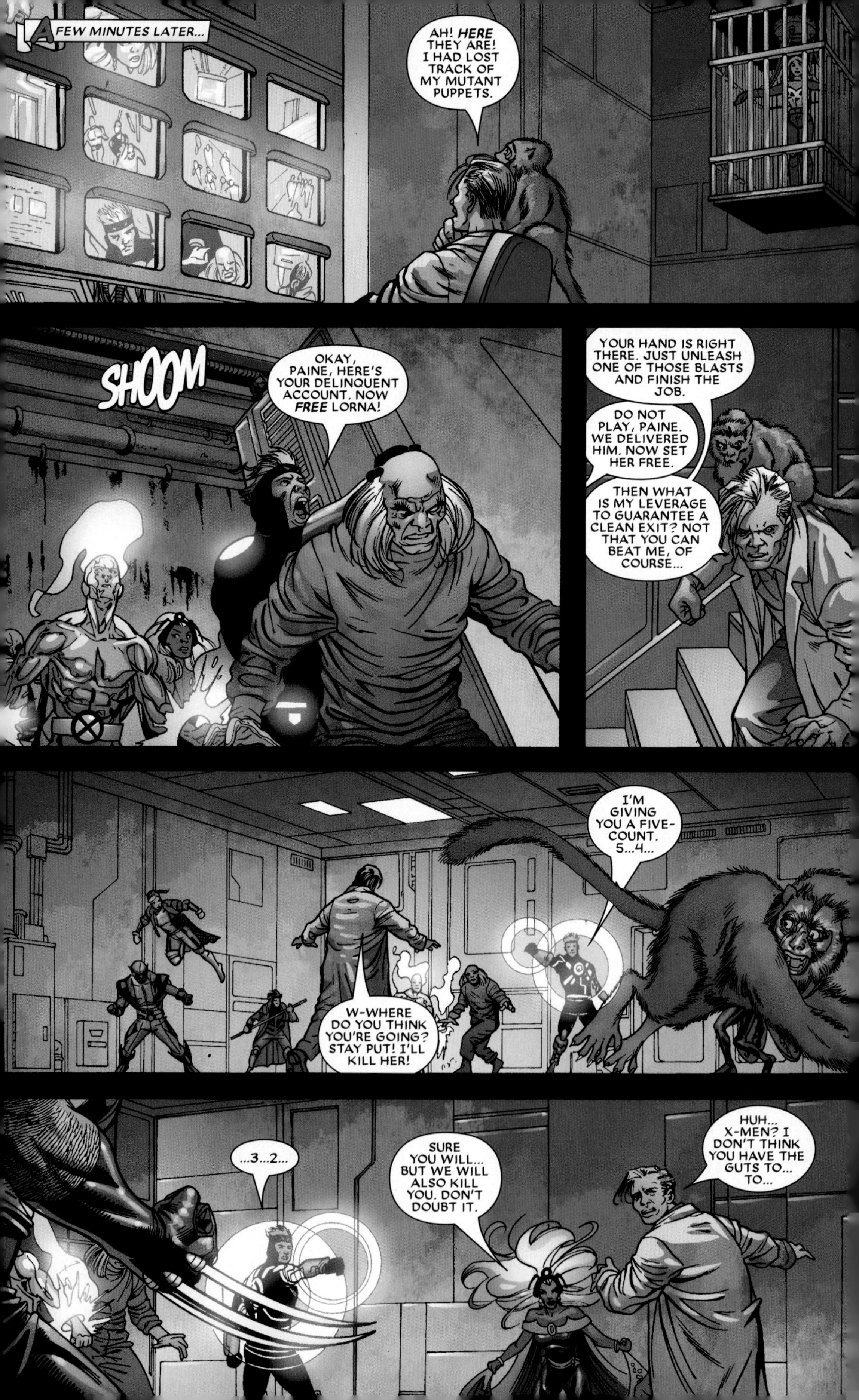
A FEW MINUTES LATER...
AH! HERE THEY ARE! I HAD LOST TRACK OF MY MUTANT PUPPETS.
SHOOM
OKAY, PAINE, HERE'S YOUR DELINQUENT ACCOUNT. NOW FREE LORNA!
YOUR HAND IS RIGHT THERE. JUST UNLEASH ONE OF THOSE BLASTS AND FINISH THE JOB.
DO NOT PLAY, PAINE. WE DELIVERED HIM. NOW SET HER FREE.
THEN WHAT IS MY LEVERAGE TO GUARANTEE A CLEAN EXIT? NOT THAT YOU CAN BEAT ME, OF COURSE...
I'M GIVING YOU A FIVE-COUNT. 5...4...
W-WHERE DO YOU THINK YOU'RE GOING? STAY PUT! I'LL KILL HER!
...3...2...
SURE YOU WILL... BUT WE WILL ALSO KILL YOU. DON'T DOUBT IT.
HUH... X-MEN? I DON'T THINK YOU HAVE THE GUTS TO... TO...

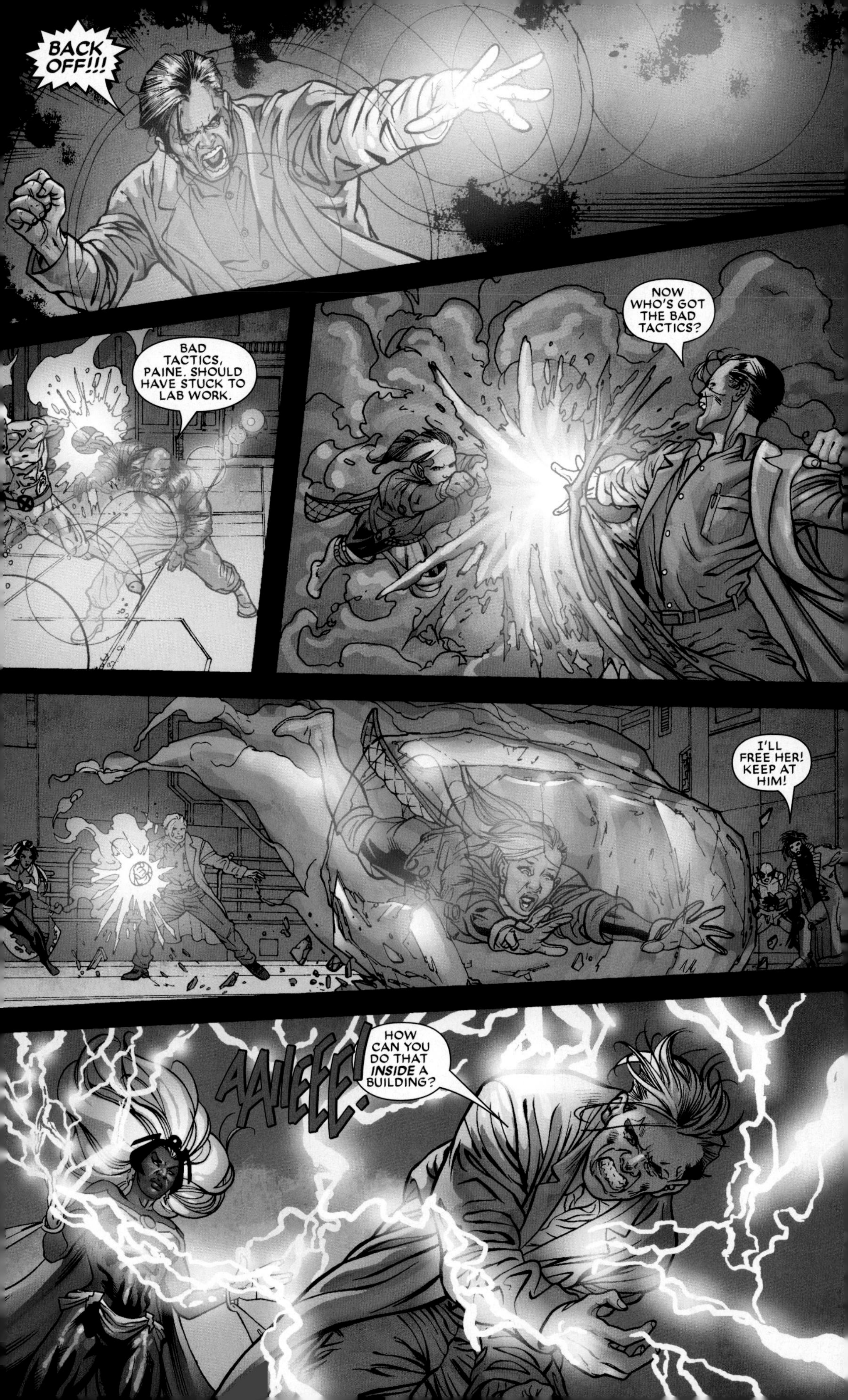
BACK OFF!!!
BAD TACTICS, PAINE. SHOULD HAVE STUCK TO LAB WORK.
NOW WHO'S GOT THE BAD TACTICS?
I'LL FREE HER! KEEP AT HIM!
AAIEEE!
HOW CAN YOU DO THAT INSIDE A BUILDING?

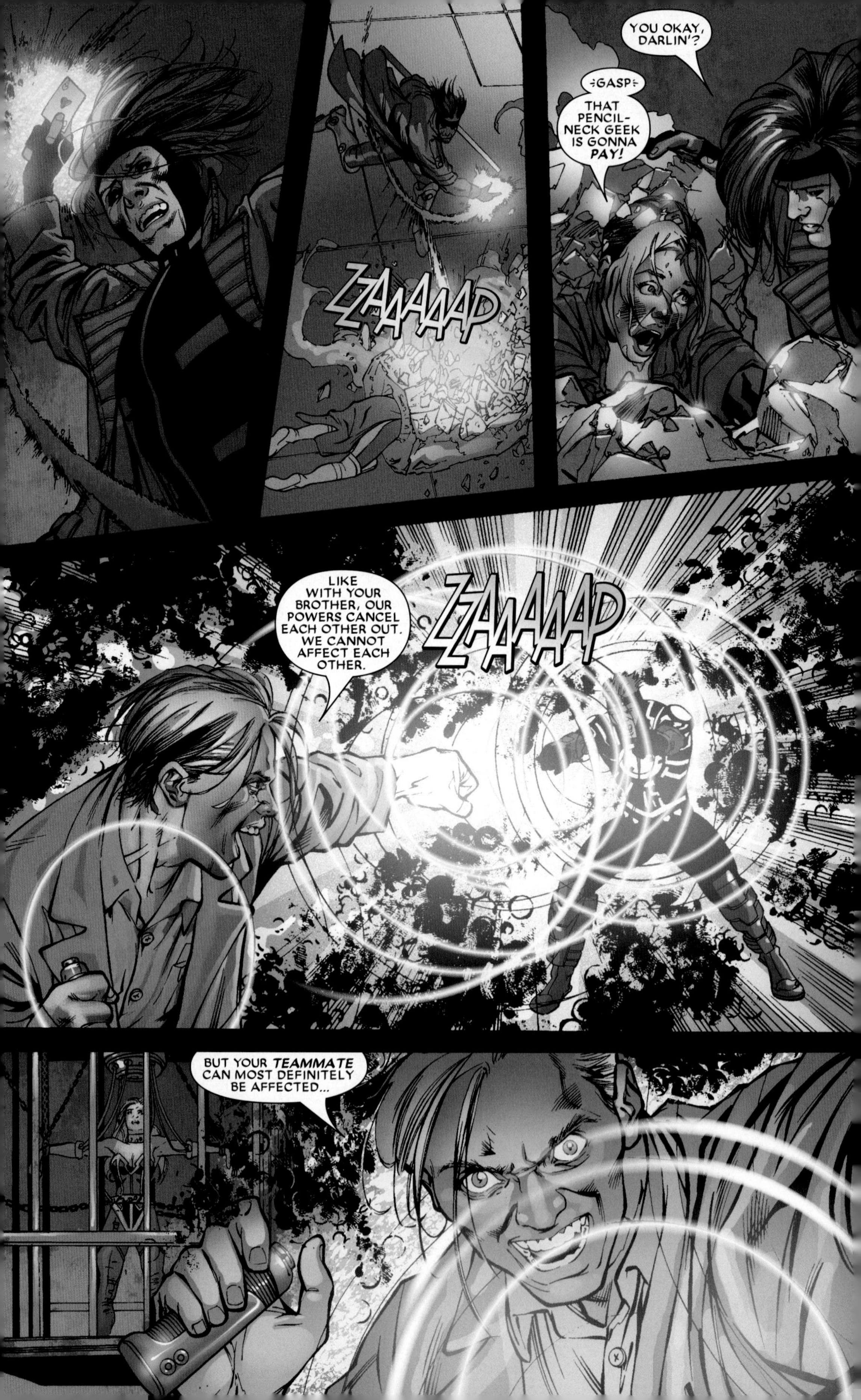
ZZAAAAAP
YOU OKAY, DARLIN'?
GASP
THAT PENCIL-NECK GEEK IS GONNA PAY!
LIKE WITH YOUR BROTHER, OUR POWERS CANCEL EACH OTHER OUT. WE CANNOT AFFECT EACH OTHER.
ZZAAAAAP
BUT YOUR TEAMMATE CAN MOST DEFINITELY BE AFFECTED...

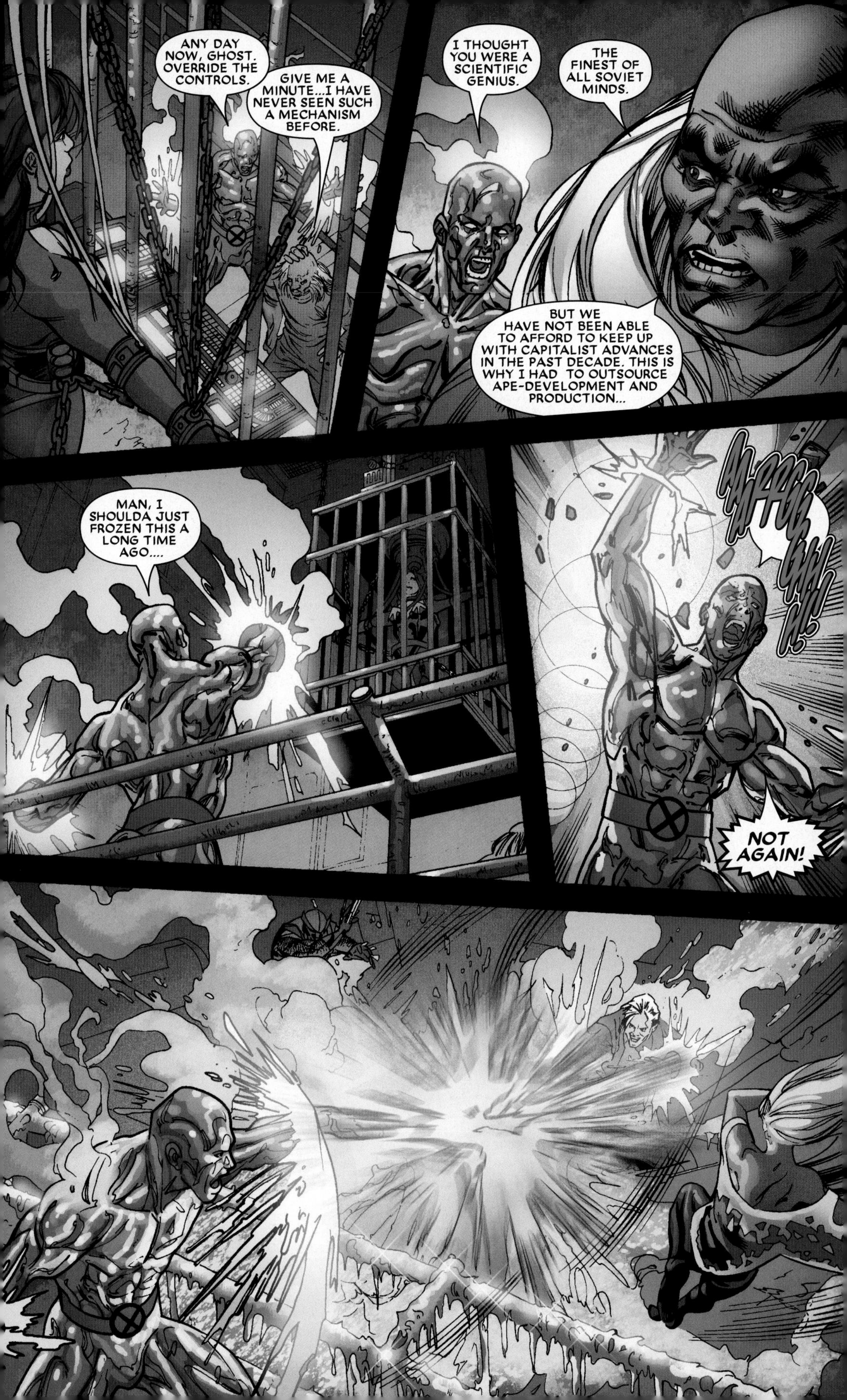

ANY DAY NOW, GHOST. OVERRIDE THE CONTROLS.
GIVE ME A MINUTE...I HAVE NEVER SEEN SUCH A MECHANISM BEFORE.
I THOUGHT YOU WERE A SCIENTIFIC GENIUS.
THE FINEST OF ALL SOVIET MINDS.
BUT WE HAVE NOT BEEN ABLE TO AFFORD TO KEEP UP WITH CAPITALIST ADVANCES IN THE PAST DECADE. THIS IS WHY I HAD TO OUTSOURCE APE-DEVELOPMENT AND PRODUCTION...
MAN, I SHOULDA JUST FROZEN THIS A LONG TIME AGO....
NOT AGAIN!

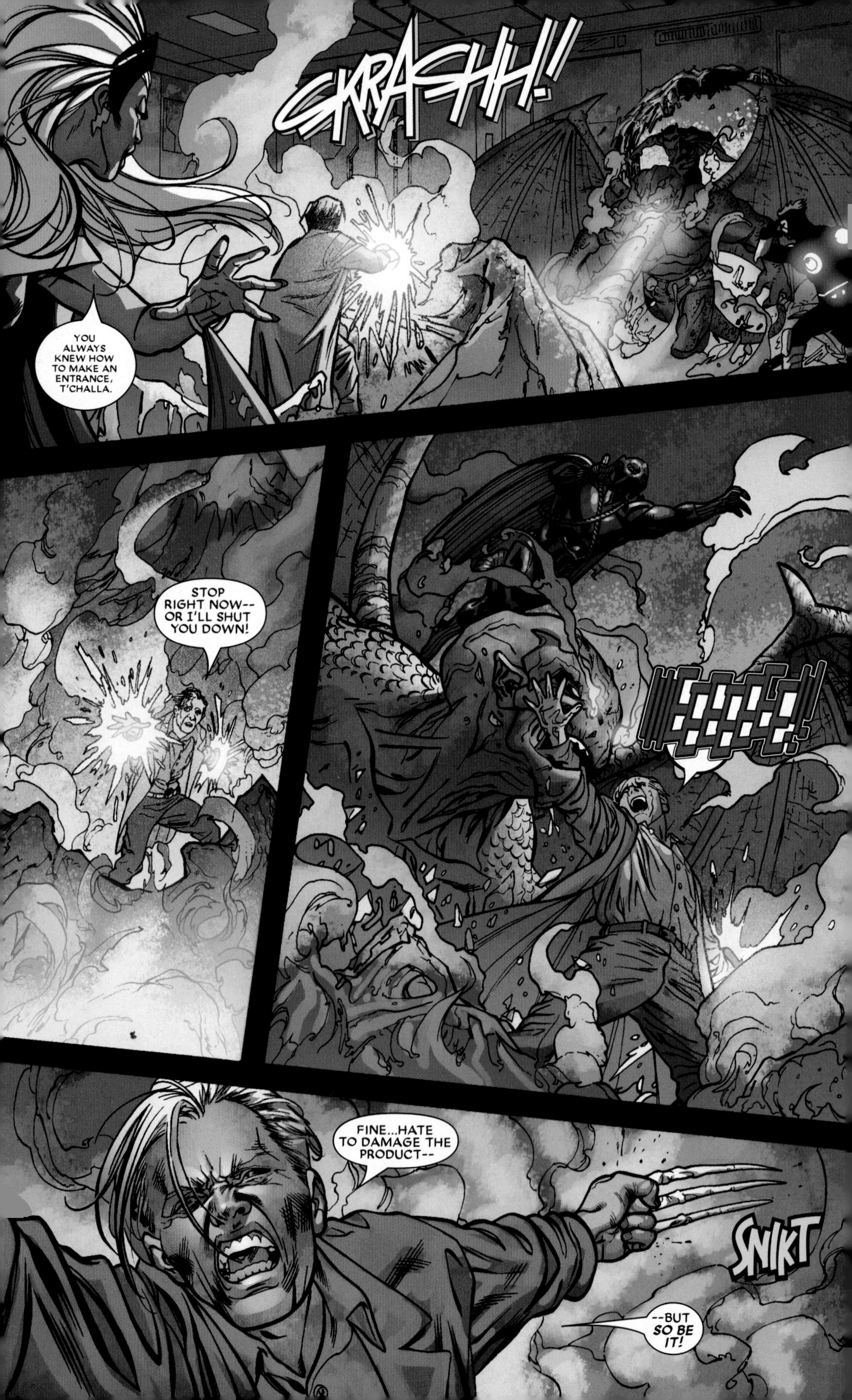
CKRASHH!
YOU ALWAYS KNEW HOW TO MAKE AN ENTRANCE, T'CHALLA.
STOP RIGHT NOW-- OR I'LL SHUT YOU DOWN!
EEEEEE!
FINE...HATE TO DAMAGE THE PRODUCT--
SNIKT
--BUT SO BE IT!

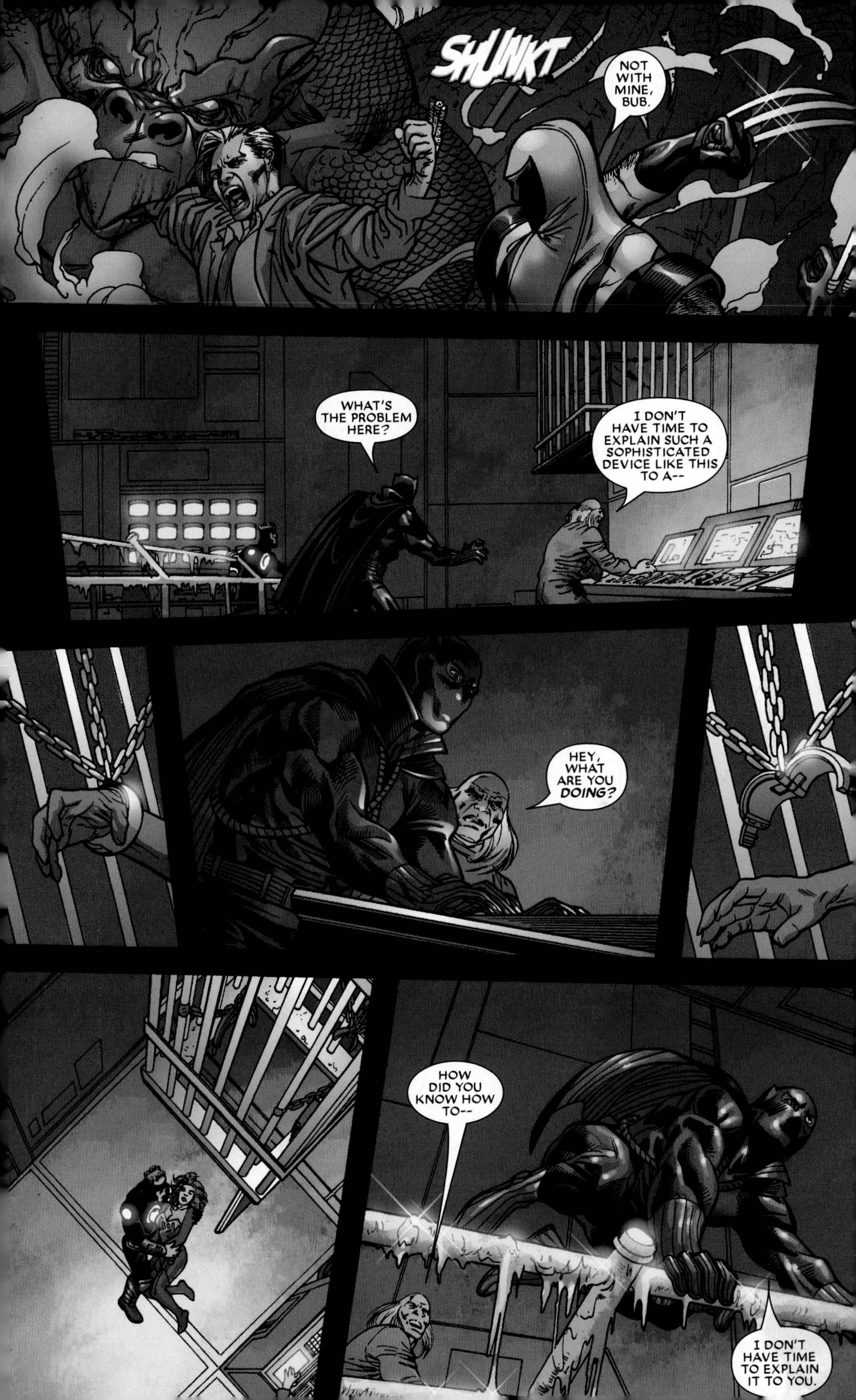
SHUNKT
NOT WITH MINE, BUB.
WHAT'S THE PROBLEM HERE?
I DON'T HAVE TIME TO EXPLAIN SUCH A SOPHISTICATED DEVICE LIKE THIS TO A--
HEY, WHAT ARE YOU *DOING?*
HOW DID YOU KNOW HOW TO--
I DON'T HAVE TIME TO EXPLAIN IT TO YOU.

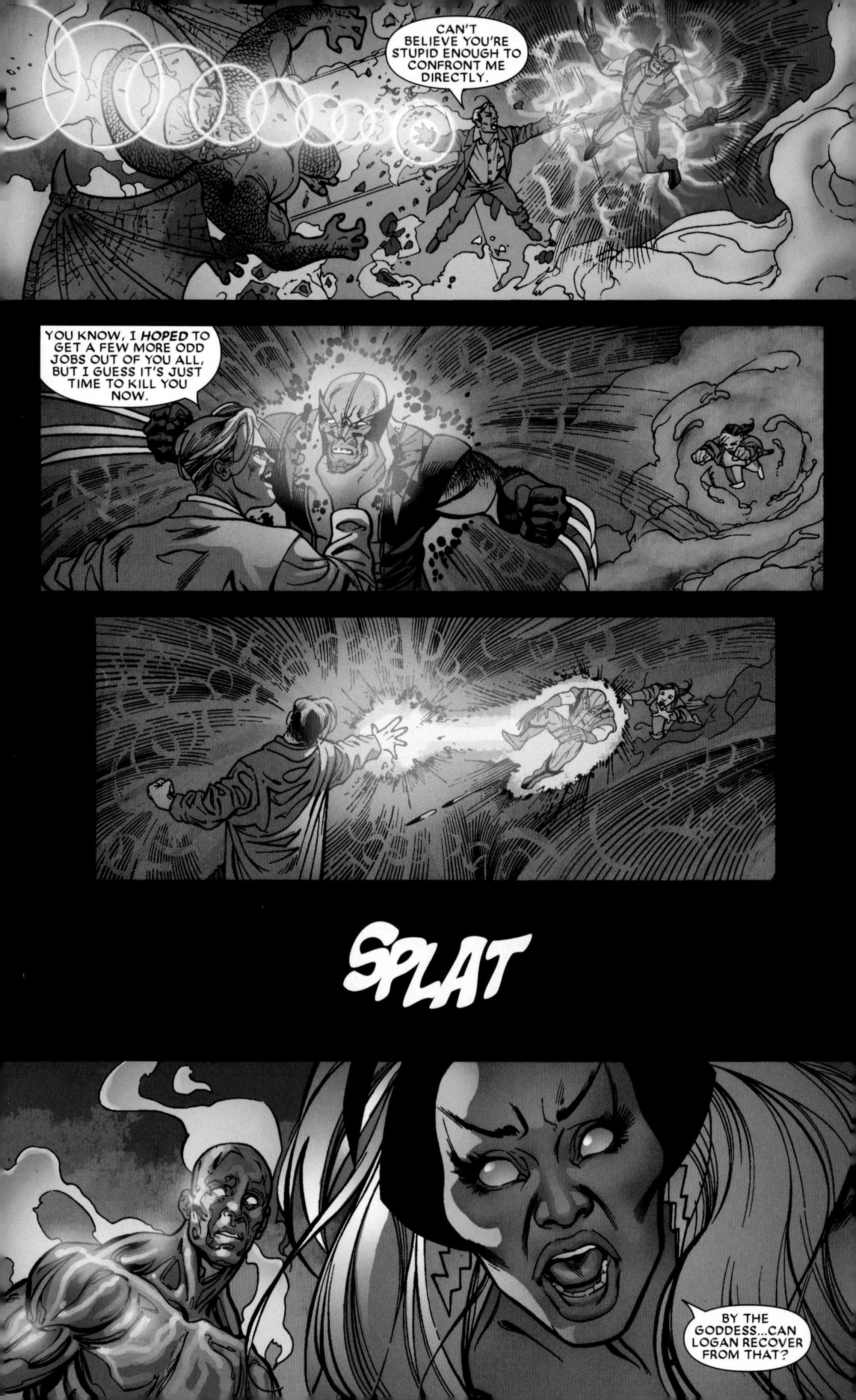
CAN'T BELIEVE YOU'RE STUPID ENOUGH TO CONFRONT ME DIRECTLY.
YOU KNOW, I *HOPED* TO GET A FEW MORE ODD JOBS OUT OF YOU ALL, BUT I GUESS IT'S JUST TIME TO KILL YOU NOW.
SPLAT
BY THE GODDESS...CAN LOGAN RECOVER FROM THAT?

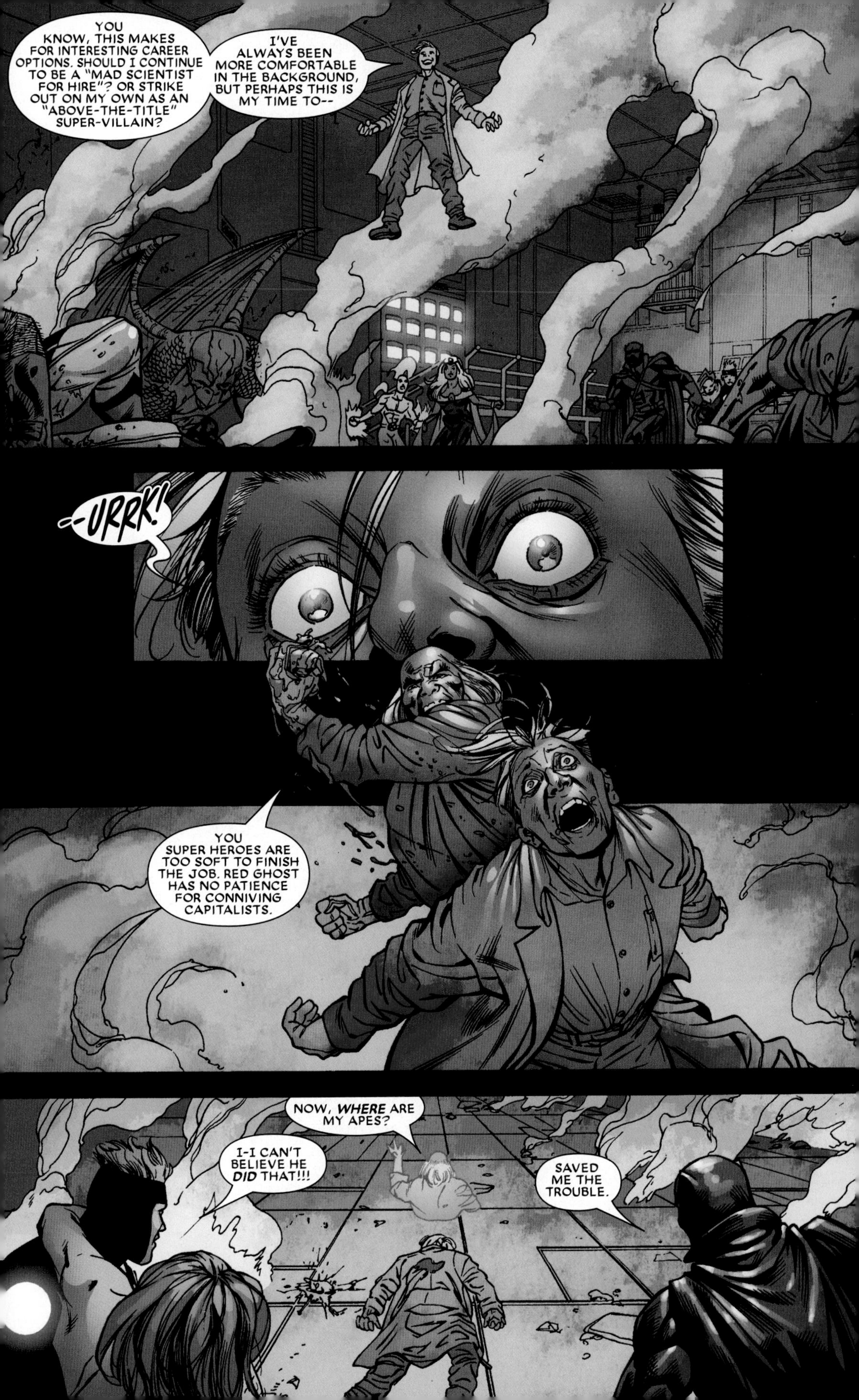
YOU KNOW, THIS MAKES FOR INTERESTING CAREER OPTIONS. SHOULD I CONTINUE TO BE A "MAD SCIENTIST FOR HIRE"? OR STRIKE OUT ON MY OWN AS AN "ABOVE-THE-TITLE" SUPER-VILLAIN?
I'VE ALWAYS BEEN MORE COMFORTABLE IN THE BACKGROUND, BUT PERHAPS THIS IS MY TIME TO--
--URRK!
YOU SUPER HEROES ARE TOO SOFT TO FINISH THE JOB. RED GHOST HAS NO PATIENCE FOR CONNIVING CAPITALISTS.
NOW, WHERE ARE MY APES?
I-I CAN'T BELIEVE HE DID THAT!!!
SAVED ME THE TROUBLE.

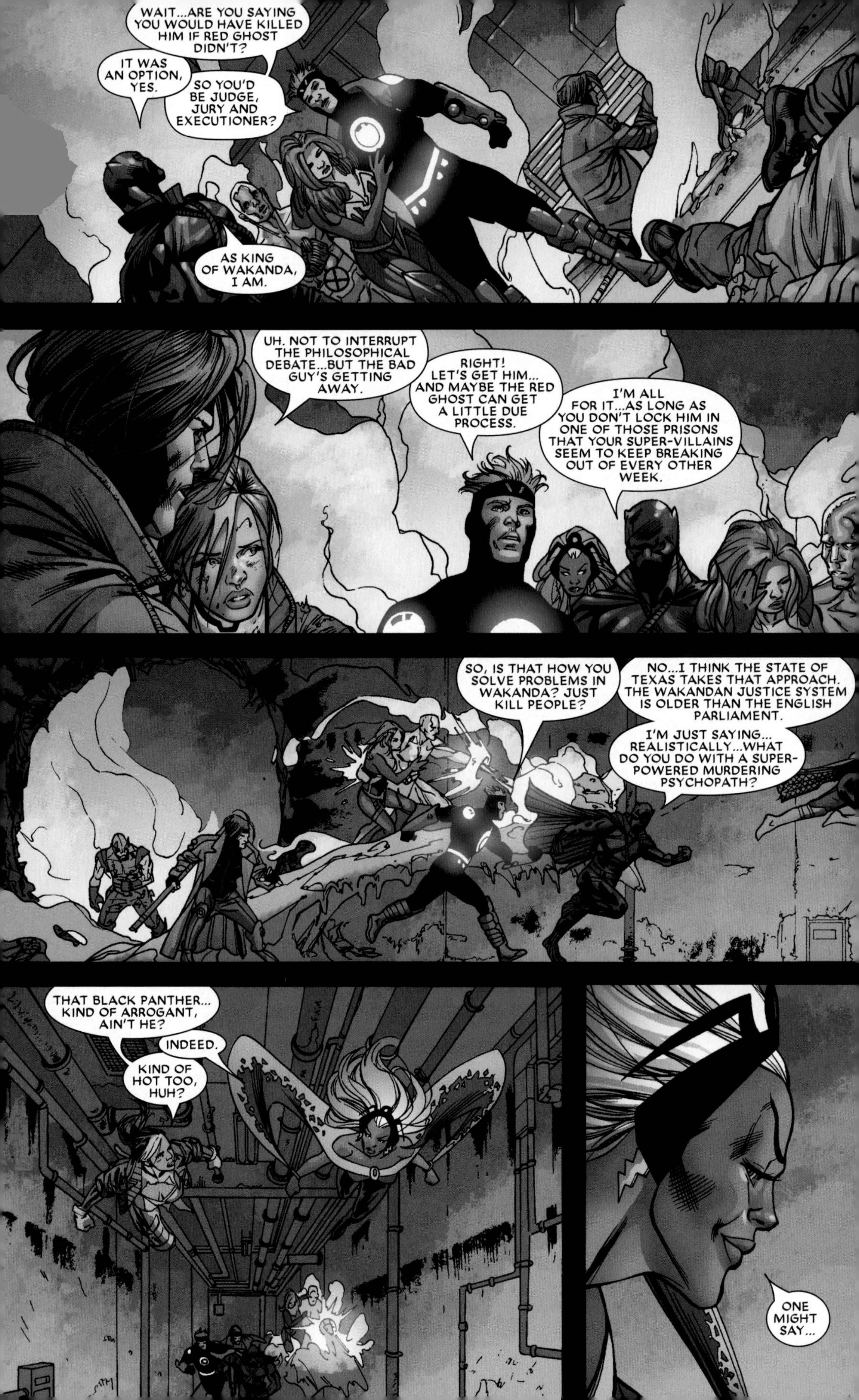
WAIT...ARE YOU SAYING YOU WOULD HAVE KILLED HIM IF RED GHOST DIDN'T?
IT WAS AN OPTION, YES.
SO YOU'D BE JUDGE, JURY AND EXECUTIONER?
AS KING OF WAKANDA, I AM.
UH. NOT TO INTERRUPT THE PHILOSOPHICAL DEBATE...BUT THE BAD GUY'S GETTING AWAY.
RIGHT! LET'S GET HIM... AND MAYBE THE RED GHOST CAN GET A LITTLE DUE PROCESS.
I'M ALL FOR IT...AS LONG AS YOU DON'T LOCK HIM IN ONE OF THOSE PRISONS THAT YOUR SUPER-VILLAINS SEEM TO KEEP BREAKING OUT OF EVERY OTHER WEEK.
SO, IS THAT HOW YOU SOLVE PROBLEMS IN WAKANDA? JUST KILL PEOPLE?
NO...I THINK THE STATE OF TEXAS TAKES THAT APPROACH. THE WAKANDAN JUSTICE SYSTEM IS OLDER THAN THE ENGLISH PARLIAMENT.
I'M JUST SAYING... REALISTICALLY...WHAT DO YOU DO WITH A SUPER-POWERED MURDERING PSYCHOPATH?
THAT BLACK PANTHER... KIND OF ARROGANT, AIN'T HE?
INDEED.
KIND OF HOT TOO, HUH?
ONE MIGHT SAY...

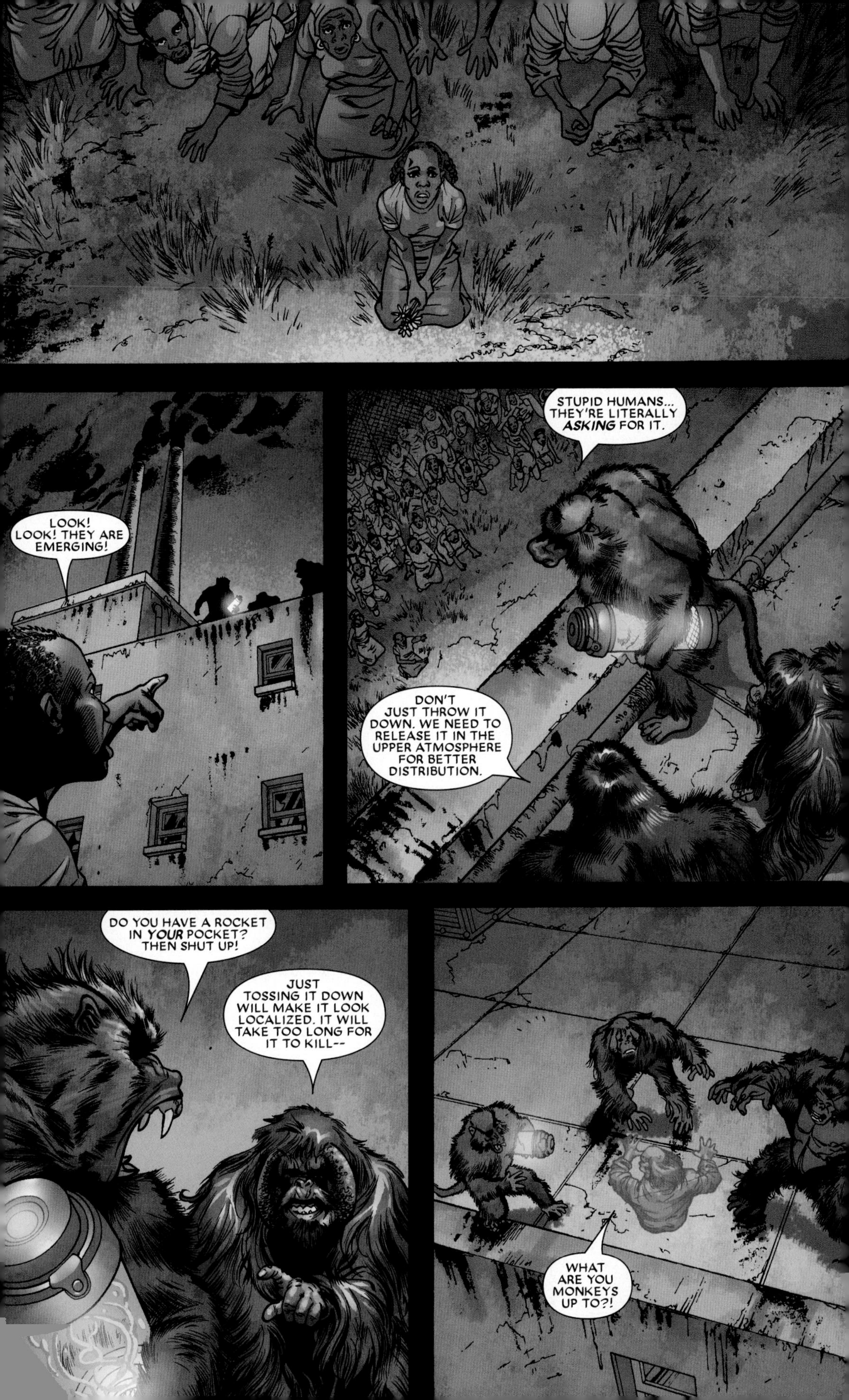
LOOK! LOOK! THEY ARE EMERGING!
STUPID HUMANS... THEY'RE LITERALLY *ASKING* FOR IT.
DON'T JUST THROW IT DOWN. WE NEED TO RELEASE IT IN THE UPPER ATMOSPHERE FOR BETTER DISTRIBUTION.
DO YOU HAVE A ROCKET IN *YOUR* POCKET? THEN SHUT UP!
JUST TOSSING IT DOWN WILL MAKE IT LOOK LOCALIZED. IT WILL TAKE TOO LONG FOR IT TO KILL--
WHAT ARE YOU MONKEYS UP TO?!

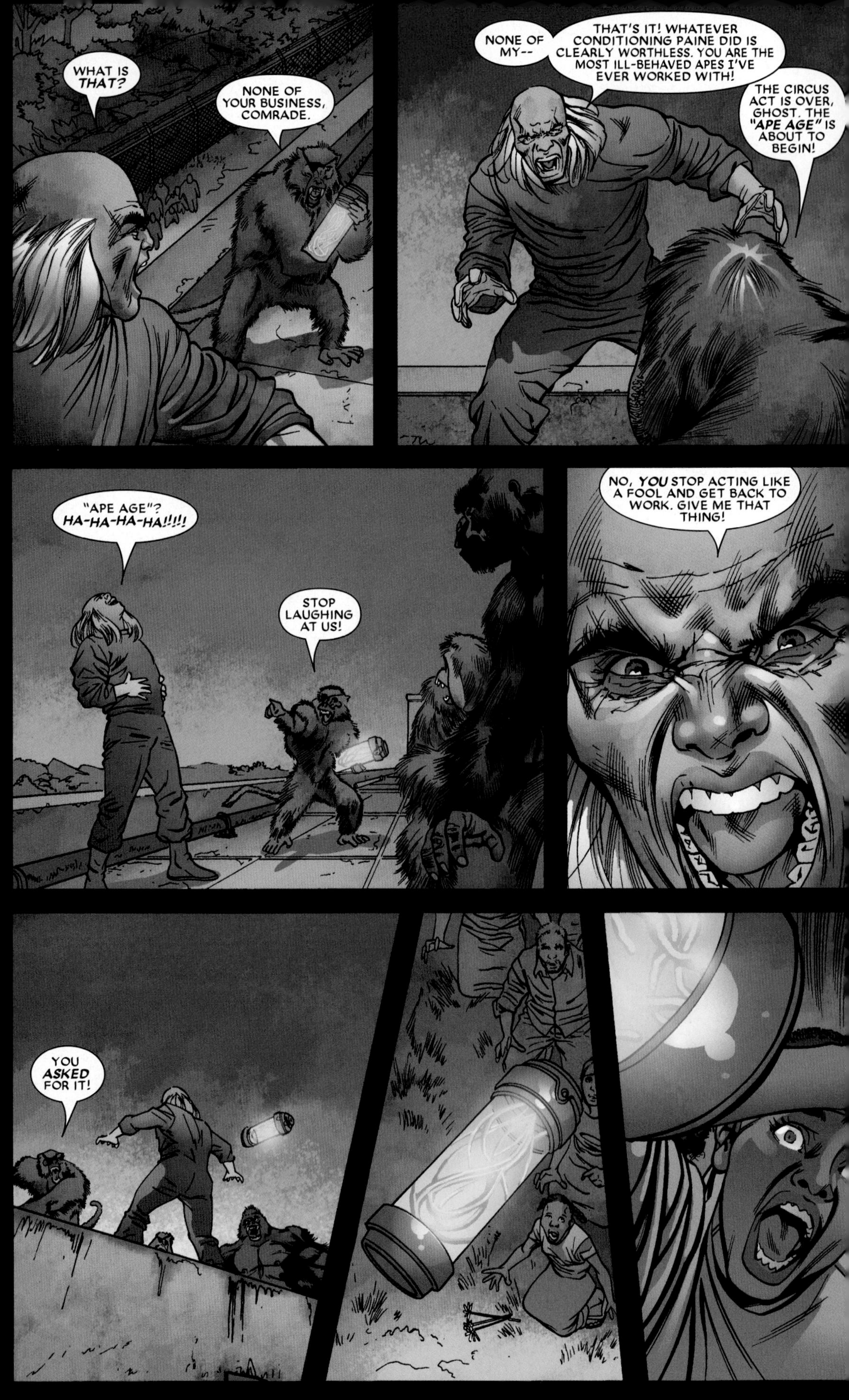
WHAT IS *THAT?*
NONE OF YOUR BUSINESS, COMRADE.
NONE OF MY--
THAT'S IT! WHATEVER CONDITIONING PAINE DID IS CLEARLY WORTHLESS. YOU ARE THE MOST ILL-BEHAVED APES I'VE EVER WORKED WITH!
THE CIRCUS ACT IS OVER, GHOST. THE *"APE AGE"* IS ABOUT TO BEGIN!
"APE AGE"? *HA-HA-HA-HA!!!!!*
STOP LAUGHING AT US!
NO, *YOU* STOP ACTING LIKE A FOOL AND GET BACK TO WORK. GIVE ME THAT THING!
YOU *ASKED* FOR IT!

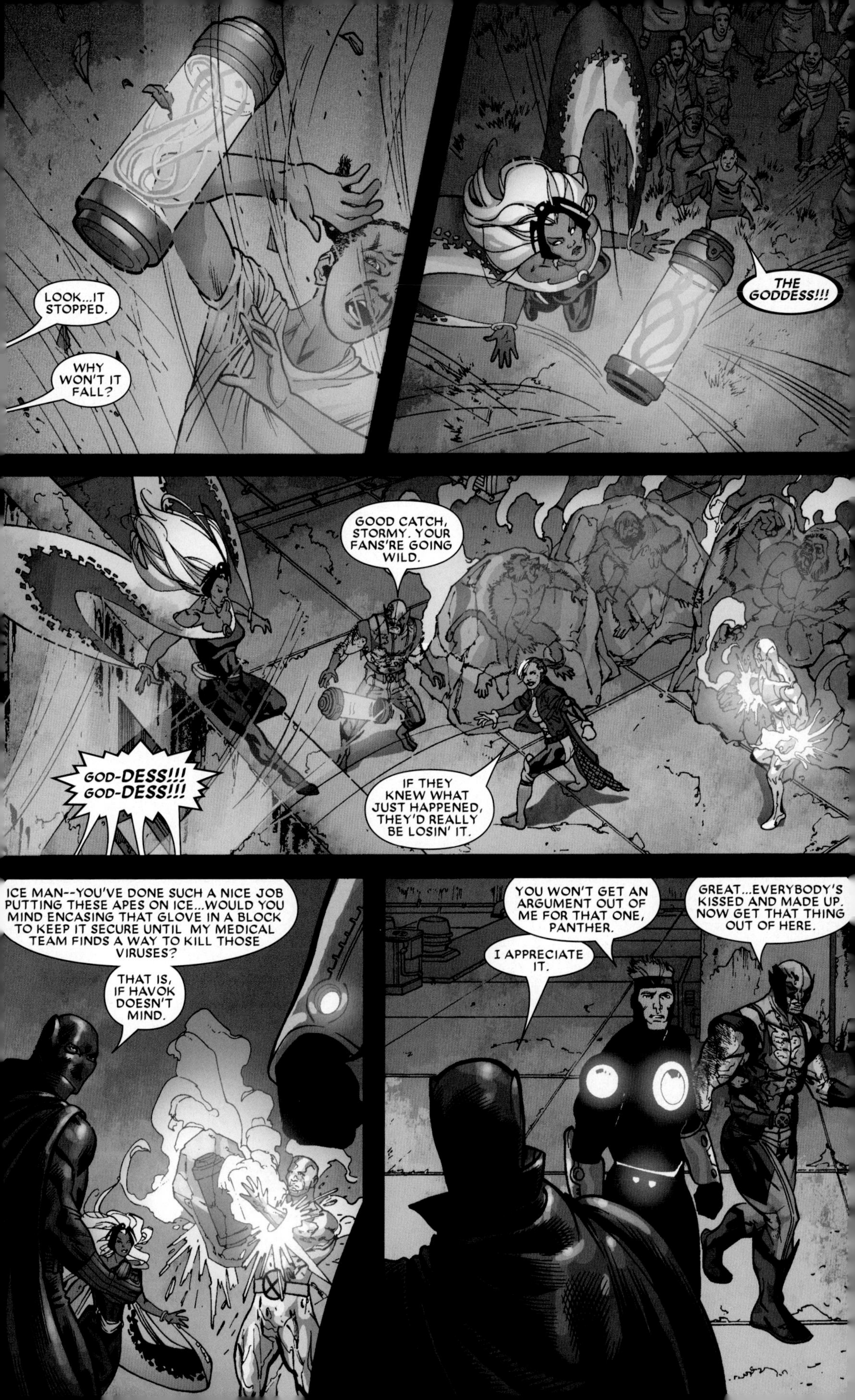
LOOK...IT STOPPED.
WHY WON'T IT FALL?
THE GODDESS!!!
GOOD CATCH, STORMY. YOUR FANS'RE GOING WILD.
GOD-DESS!!! GOD-DESS!!!
IF THEY KNEW WHAT JUST HAPPENED, THEY'D REALLY BE LOSIN' IT.
ICE MAN--YOU'VE DONE SUCH A NICE JOB PUTTING THESE APES ON ICE...WOULD YOU MIND ENCASING THAT GLOVE IN A BLOCK TO KEEP IT SECURE UNTIL MY MEDICAL TEAM FINDS A WAY TO KILL THOSE VIRUSES?
THAT IS, IF HAVOK DOESN'T MIND.
YOU WON'T GET AN ARGUMENT OUT OF ME FOR THAT ONE, PANTHER.
I APPRECIATE IT.
GREAT...EVERYBODY'S KISSED AND MADE UP. NOW GET THAT THING OUT OF HERE.

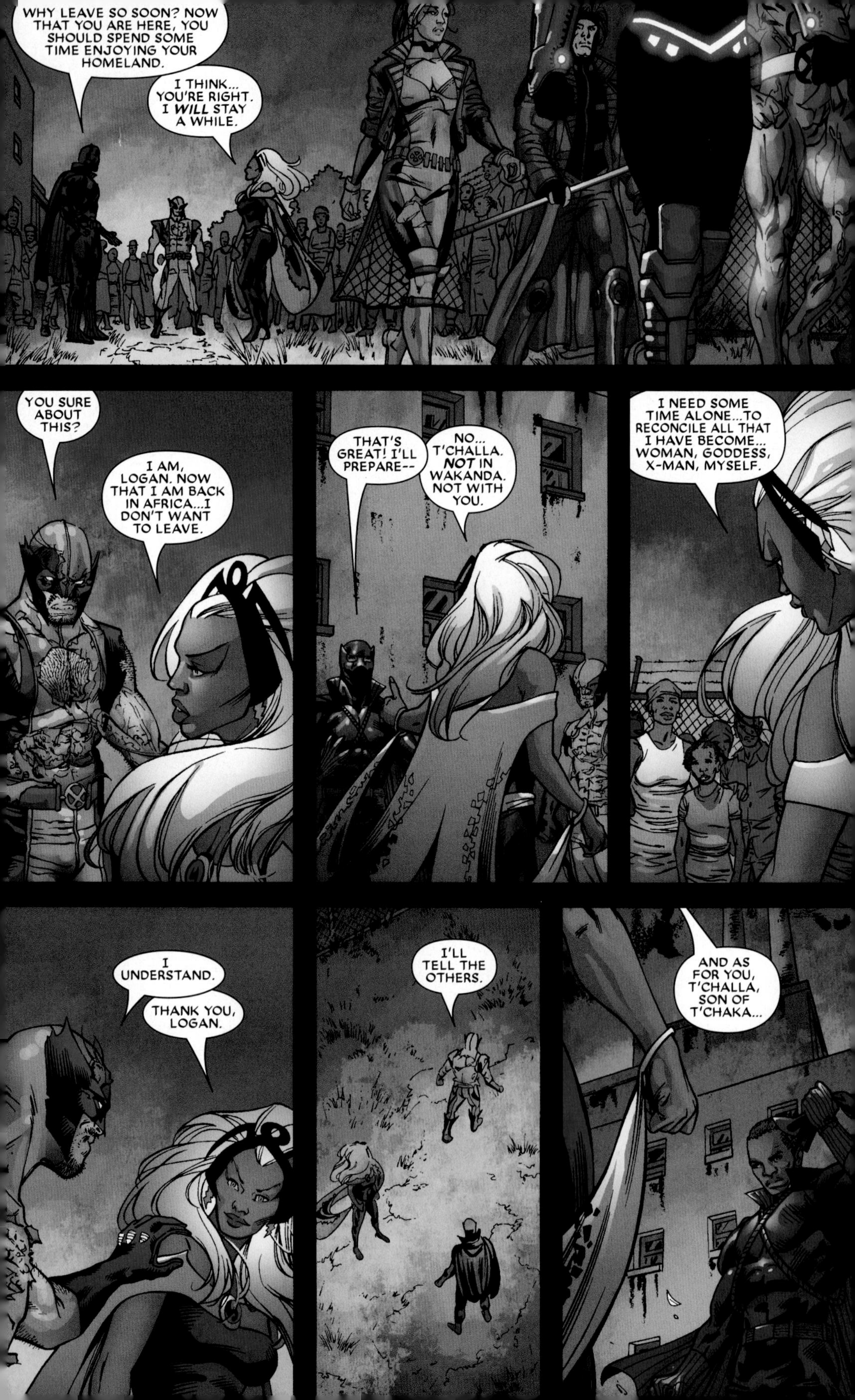
WHY LEAVE SO SOON? NOW THAT YOU ARE HERE, YOU SHOULD SPEND SOME TIME ENJOYING YOUR HOMELAND.
I THINK... YOU'RE RIGHT. I WILL STAY A WHILE.
YOU SURE ABOUT THIS?
I AM, LOGAN. NOW THAT I AM BACK IN AFRICA...I DON'T WANT TO LEAVE.
THAT'S GREAT! I'LL PREPARE--
NO... T'CHALLA. NOT IN WAKANDA. NOT WITH YOU.
I NEED SOME TIME ALONE...TO RECONCILE ALL THAT I HAVE BECOME... WOMAN, GODDESS, X-MAN, MYSELF.
I UNDERSTAND.
THANK YOU, LOGAN.
I'LL TELL THE OTHERS.
AND AS FOR YOU, T'CHALLA, SON OF T'CHAKA...

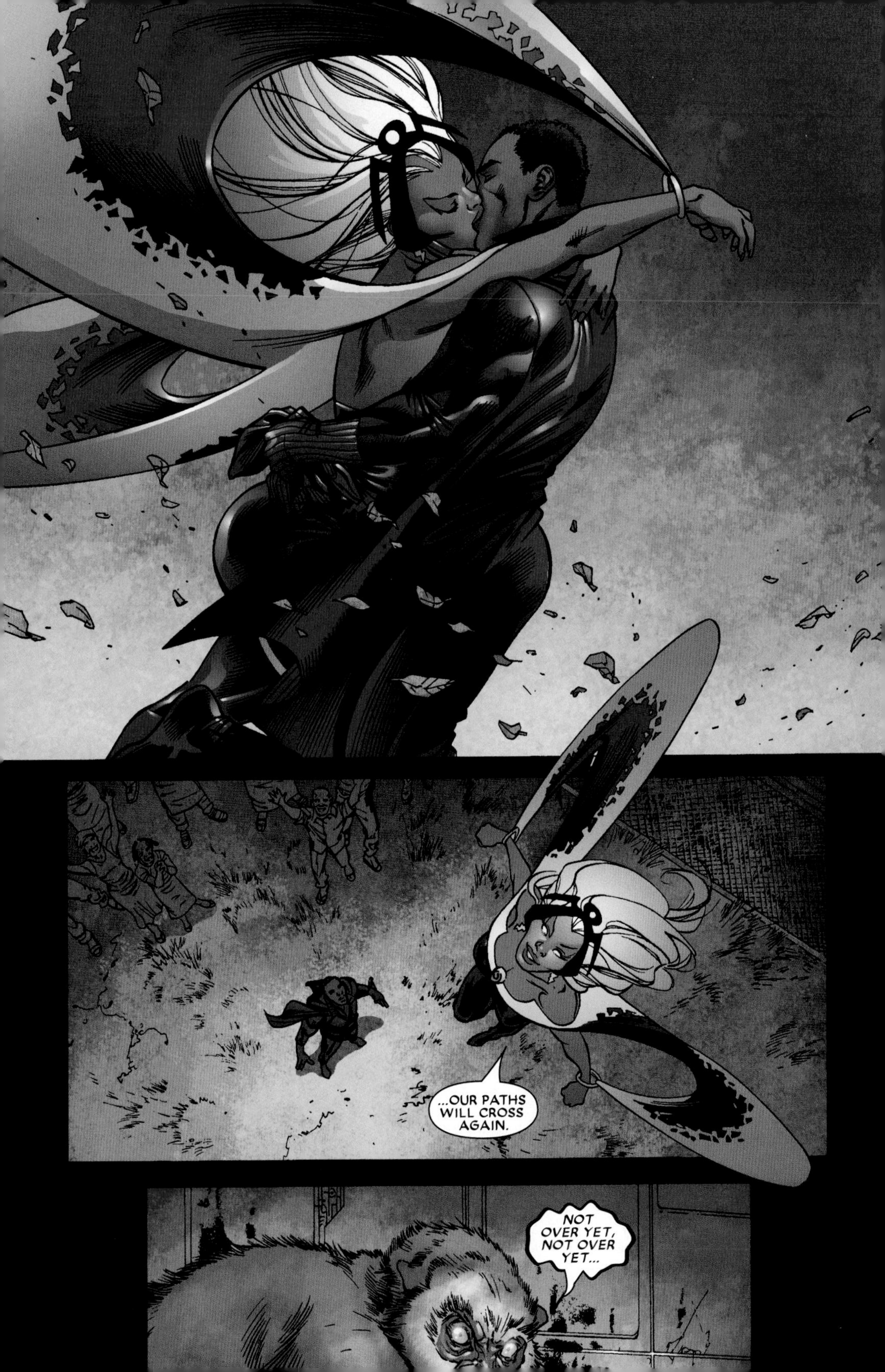
...OUR PATHS WILL CROSS AGAIN.
NOT OVER YET, NOT OVER YET...

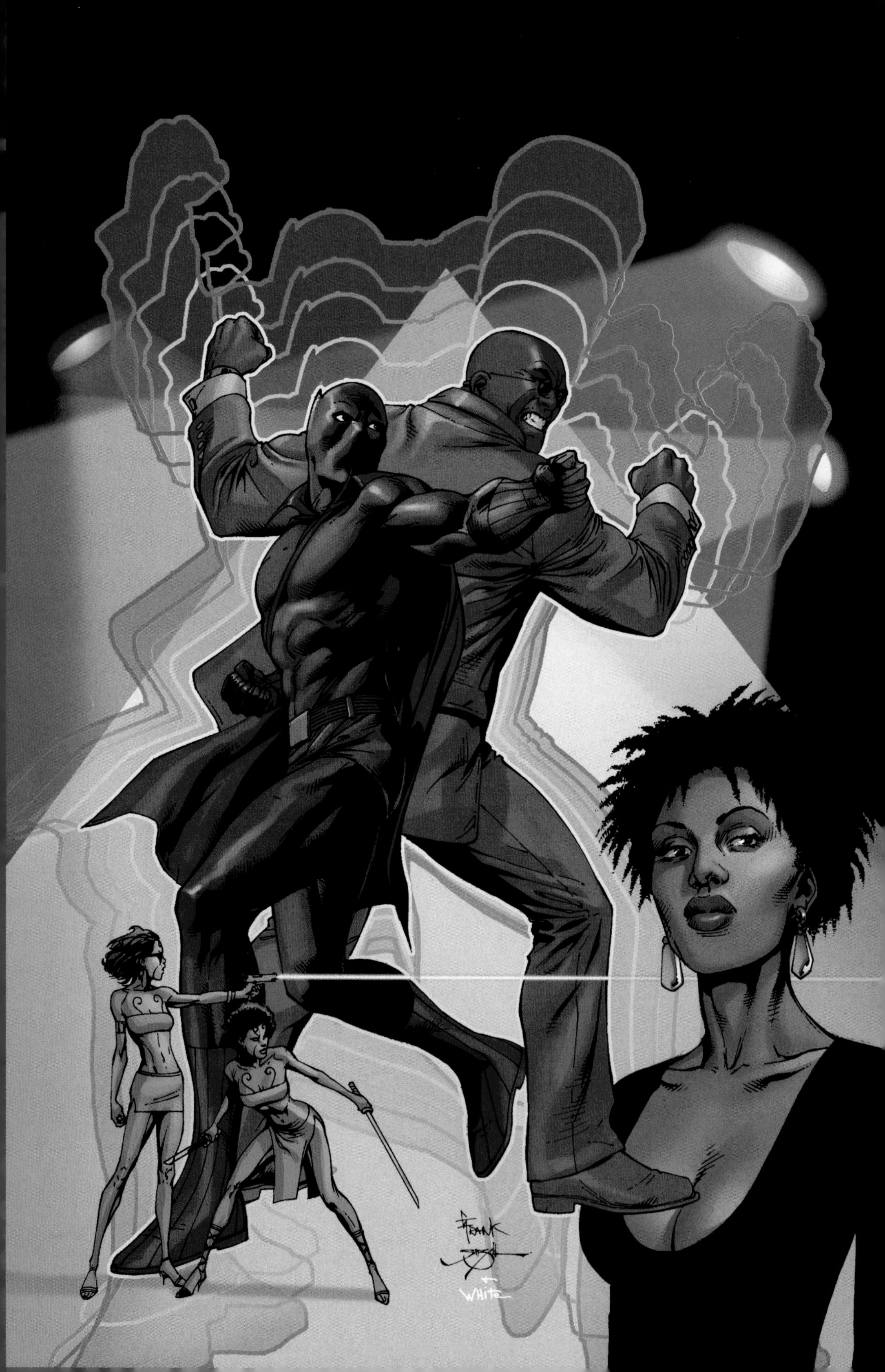
FRANK
+
WHITE

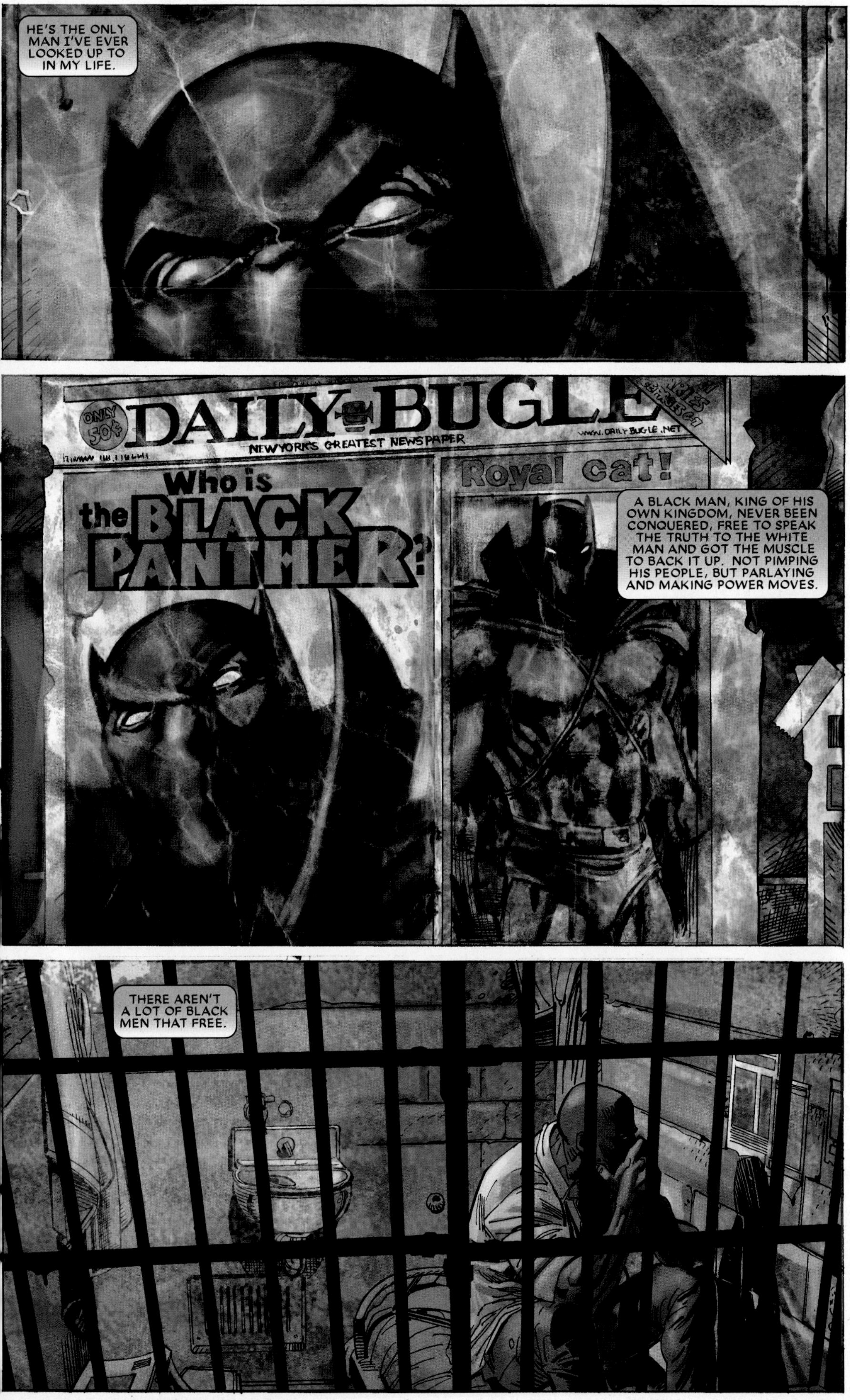
HE'S THE ONLY MAN I'VE EVER LOOKED UP TO IN MY LIFE.
ONLY 50¢
DAILY BUGLE
NEW YORK'S GREATEST NEWSPAPER
WWW.DAILYBUGLE.NET
Who is the BLACK PANTHER?
Royal cat!
A BLACK MAN, KING OF HIS OWN KINGDOM, NEVER BEEN CONQUERED, FREE TO SPEAK THE TRUTH TO THE WHITE MAN AND GOT THE MUSCLE TO BACK IT UP. NOT PIMPING HIS PEOPLE, BUT PARLAYING AND MAKING POWER MOVES.
THERE AREN'T A LOT OF BLACK MEN THAT FREE.

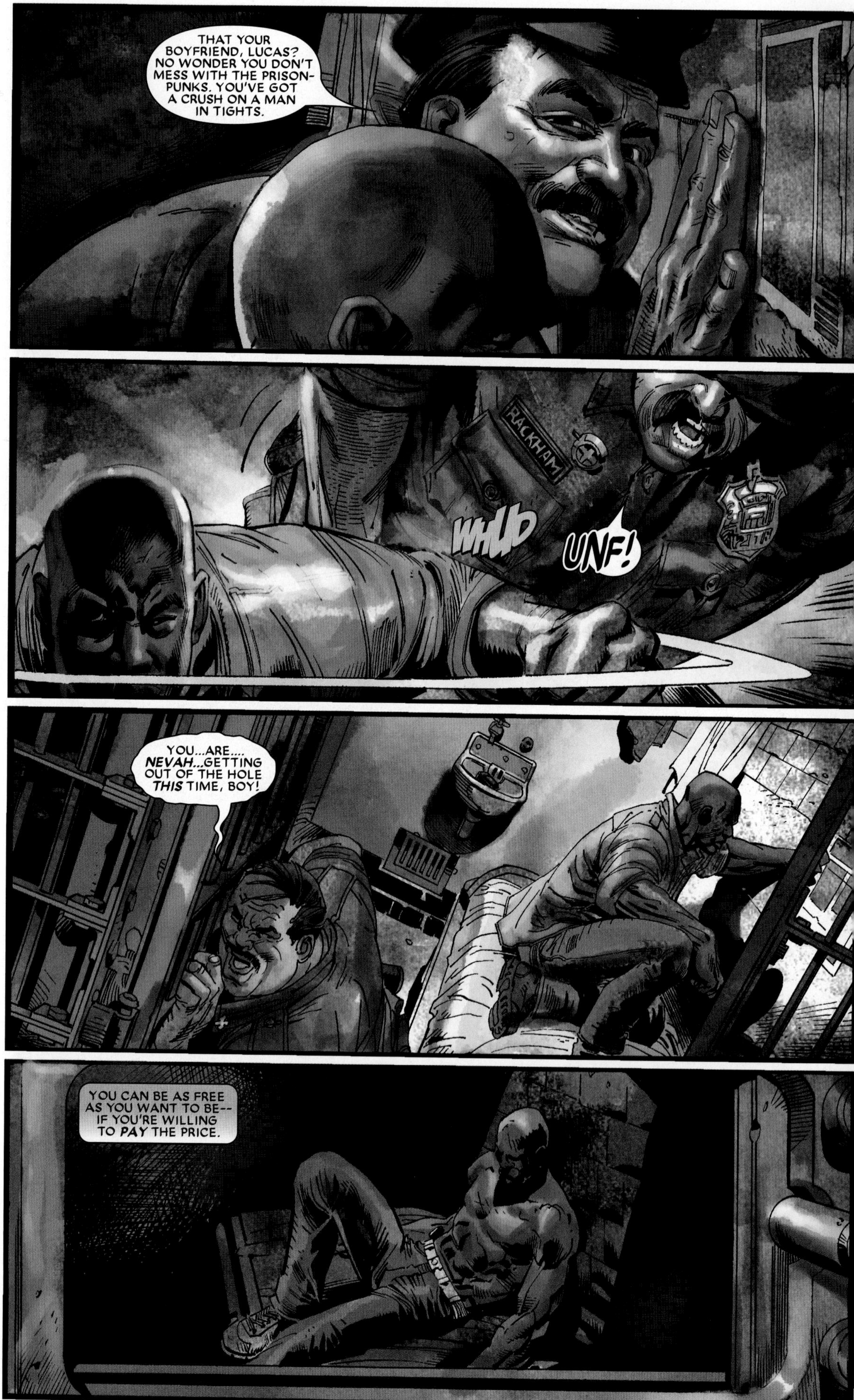
THAT YOUR BOYFRIEND, LUCAS? NO WONDER YOU DON'T MESS WITH THE PRISON-PUNKS. YOU'VE GOT A CRUSH ON A MAN IN TIGHTS.
RACKHAM
WHUD
UNF!
YOU...ARE.... NEVAH...GETTING OUT OF THE HOLE THIS TIME, BOY!
YOU CAN BE AS FREE AS YOU WANT TO BE-- IF YOU'RE WILLING TO PAY THE PRICE.

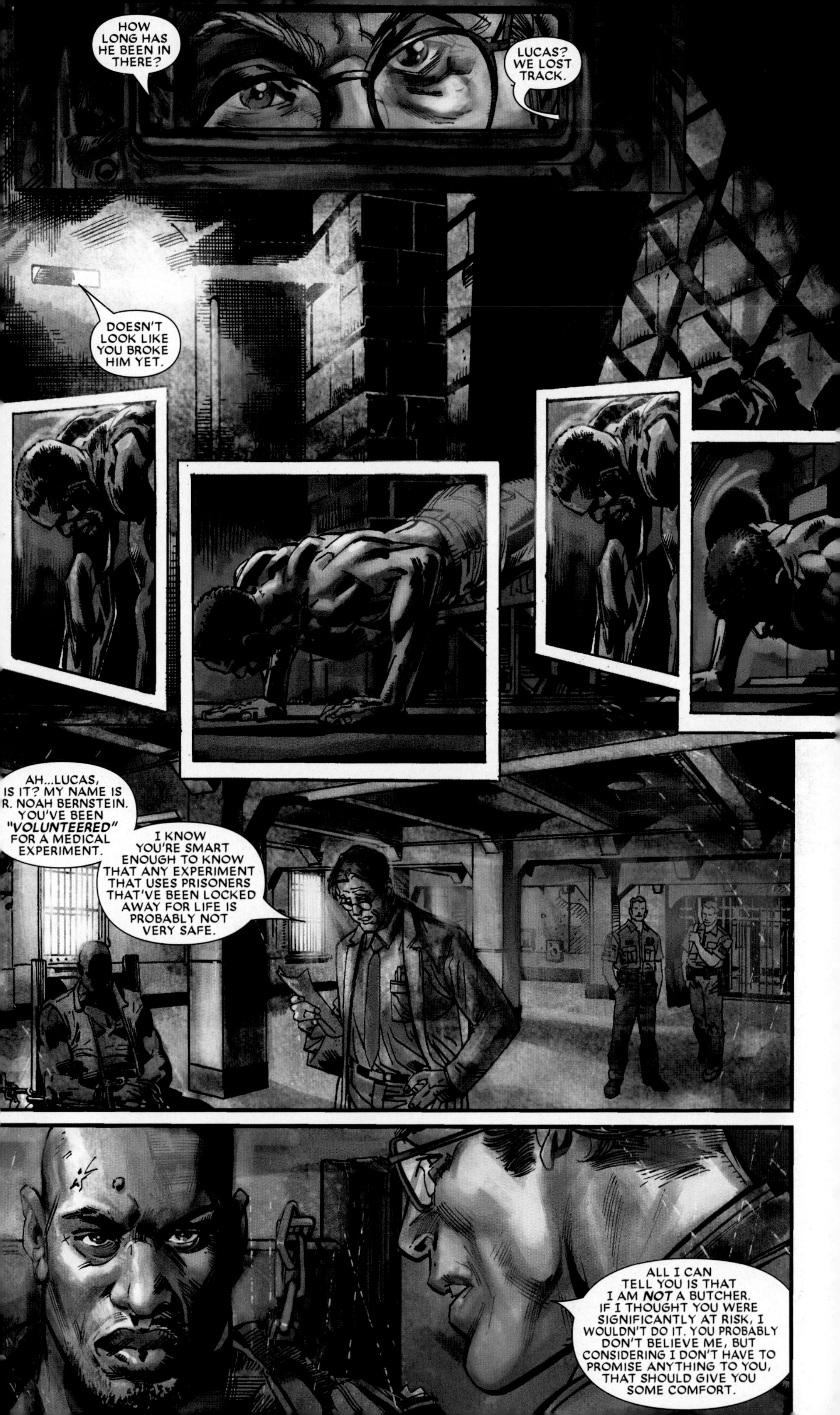
HOW LONG HAS HE BEEN IN THERE?
LUCAS? WE LOST TRACK.
DOESN'T LOOK LIKE YOU BROKE HIM YET.
AH...LUCAS, IS IT? MY NAME IS R. NOAH BERNSTEIN. YOU'VE BEEN "VOLUNTEERED" FOR A MEDICAL EXPERIMENT.
I KNOW YOU'RE SMART ENOUGH TO KNOW THAT ANY EXPERIMENT THAT USES PRISONERS THAT'VE BEEN LOCKED AWAY FOR LIFE IS PROBABLY NOT VERY SAFE.
ALL I CAN TELL YOU IS THAT I AM NOT A BUTCHER. IF I THOUGHT YOU WERE SIGNIFICANTLY AT RISK, I WOULDN'T DO IT. YOU PROBABLY DON'T BELIEVE ME, BUT CONSIDERING I DON'T HAVE TO PROMISE ANYTHING TO YOU, THAT SHOULD GIVE YOU SOME COMFORT.

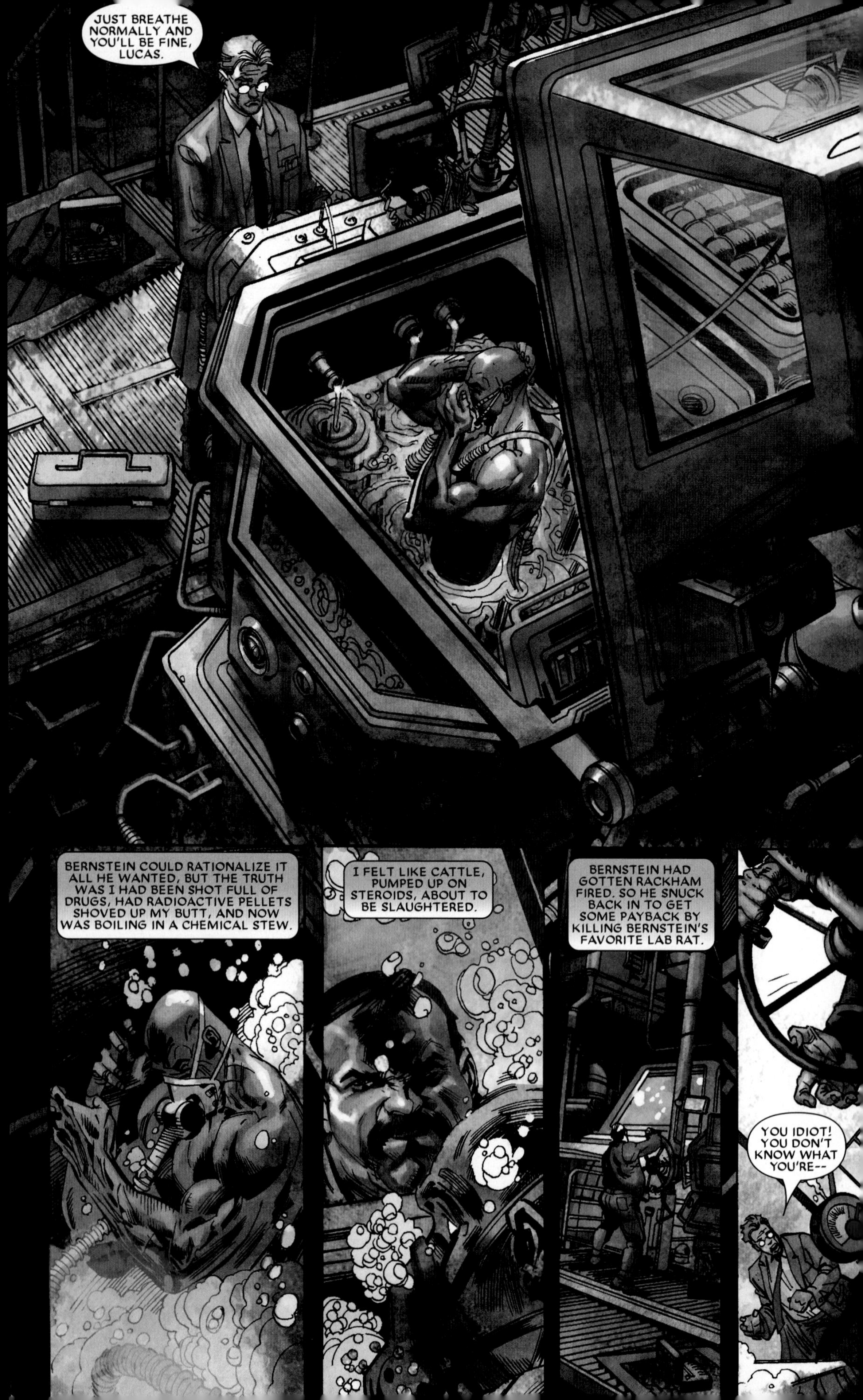
JUST BREATHE NORMALLY AND YOU'LL BE FINE, LUCAS.
BERNSTEIN COULD RATIONALIZE IT ALL HE WANTED, BUT THE TRUTH WAS I HAD BEEN SHOT FULL OF DRUGS, HAD RADIOACTIVE PELLETS SHOVED UP MY BUTT, AND NOW WAS BOILING IN A CHEMICAL STEW.
I FELT LIKE CATTLE, PUMPED UP ON STEROIDS, ABOUT TO BE SLAUGHTERED.
BERNSTEIN HAD GOTTEN RACKHAM FIRED. SO HE SNUCK BACK IN TO GET SOME PAYBACK BY KILLING BERNSTEIN'S FAVORITE LAB RAT.
YOU IDIOT! YOU DON'T KNOW WHAT YOU'RE--

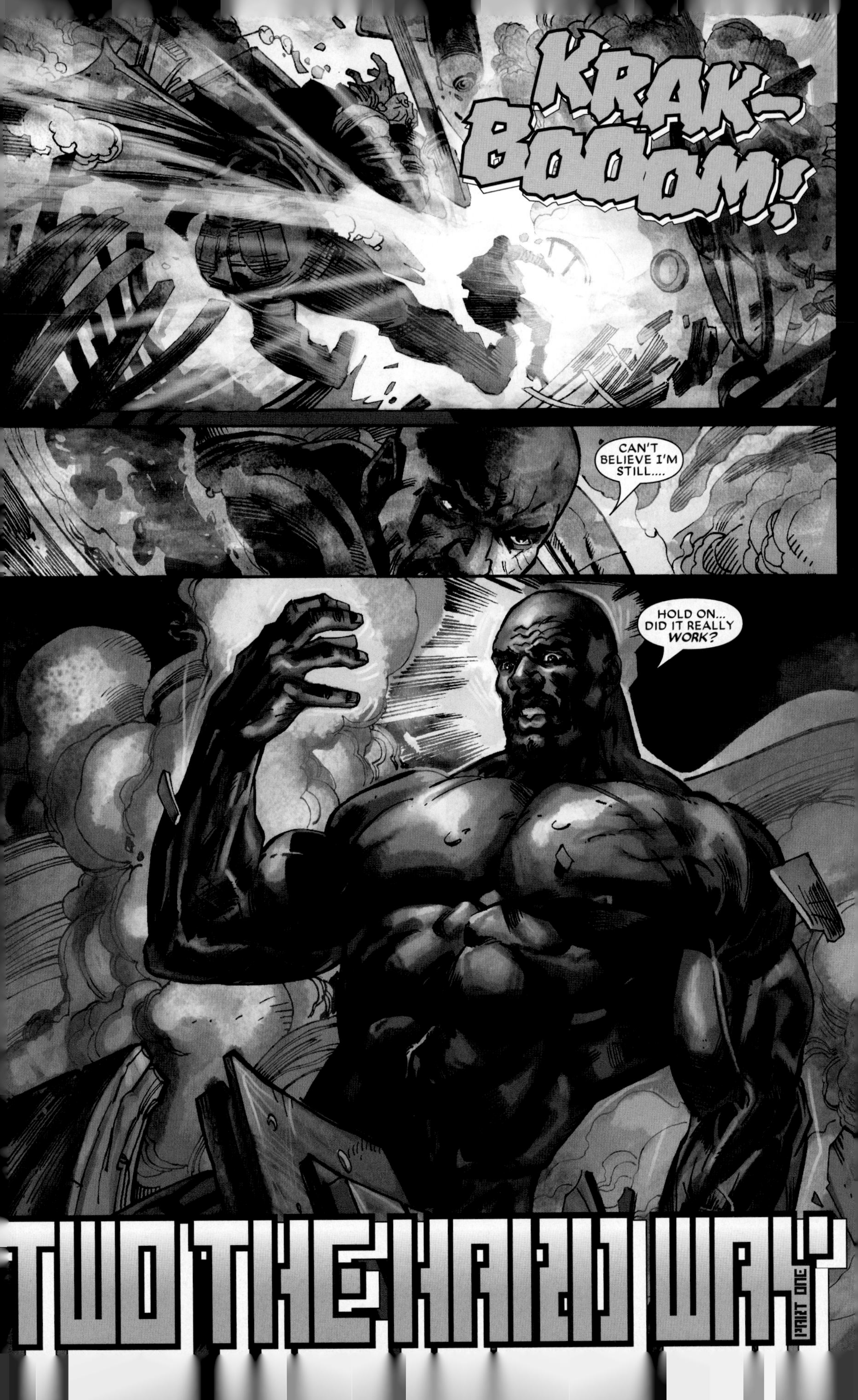
KRAK-BOOOM!
CAN'T BELIEVE I'M STILL....
HOLD ON... DID IT REALLY *WORK?*
TWO THE HARD WAY
PART ONE

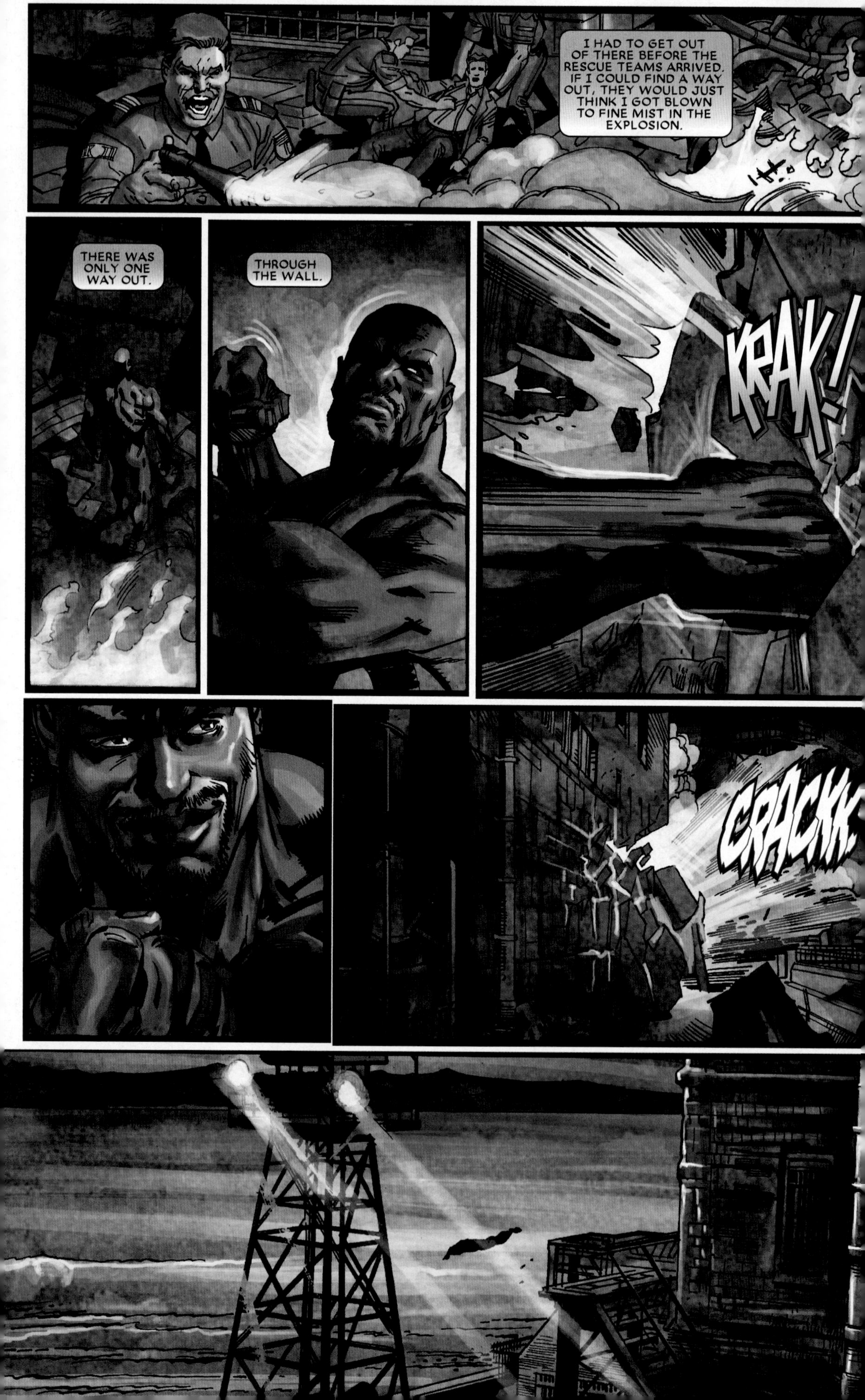
I HAD TO GET OUT OF THERE BEFORE THE RESCUE TEAMS ARRIVED. IF I COULD FIND A WAY OUT, THEY WOULD JUST THINK I GOT BLOWN TO FINE MIST IN THE EXPLOSION.
THERE WAS ONLY ONE WAY OUT.
THROUGH THE WALL.
KRAK!
CRACKK

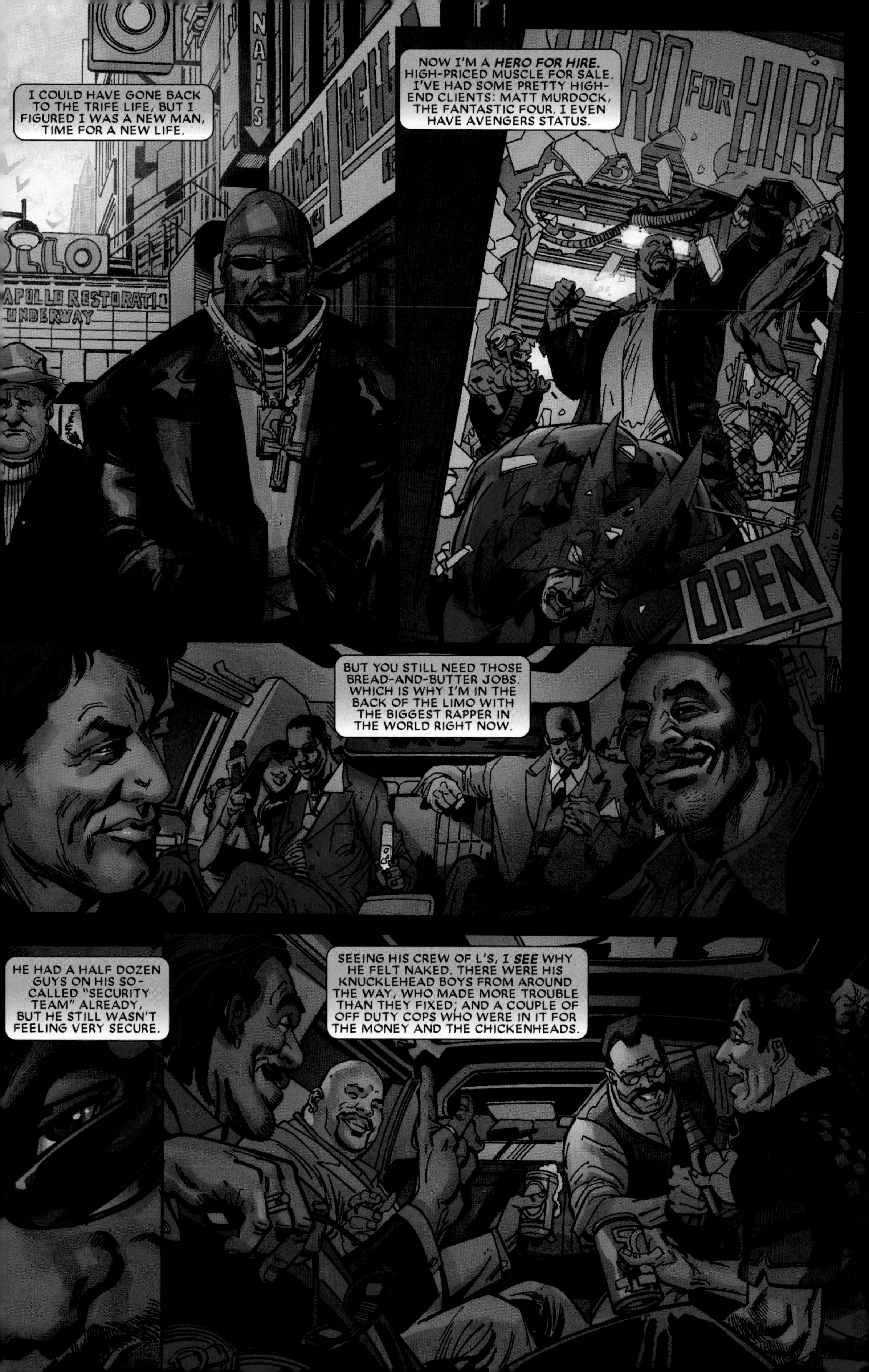
I COULD HAVE GONE BACK TO THE TRIFE LIFE, BUT I FIGURED I WAS A NEW MAN, TIME FOR A NEW LIFE.
NAILS
APOLLO RESTORATI
UNDERWAY
NOW I'M A *HERO FOR HIRE*. HIGH-PRICED MUSCLE FOR SALE. I'VE HAD SOME PRETTY HIGH-END CLIENTS: MATT MURDOCK, THE FANTASTIC FOUR. I EVEN HAVE AVENGERS STATUS.
HERO FOR HIRE
OPEN
BUT YOU STILL NEED THOSE BREAD-AND-BUTTER JOBS. WHICH IS WHY I'M IN THE BACK OF THE LIMO WITH THE BIGGEST RAPPER IN THE WORLD RIGHT NOW.
HE HAD A HALF DOZEN GUYS ON HIS SO-CALLED "SECURITY TEAM" ALREADY, BUT HE STILL WASN'T FEELING VERY SECURE.
SEEING HIS CREW OF L'S, I *SEE* WHY HE FELT NAKED. THERE WERE HIS KNUCKLEHEAD BOYS FROM AROUND THE WAY, WHO MADE MORE TROUBLE THAN THEY FIXED; AND A COUPLE OF OFF DUTY COPS WHO WERE IN IT FOR THE MONEY AND THE CHICKENHEADS.

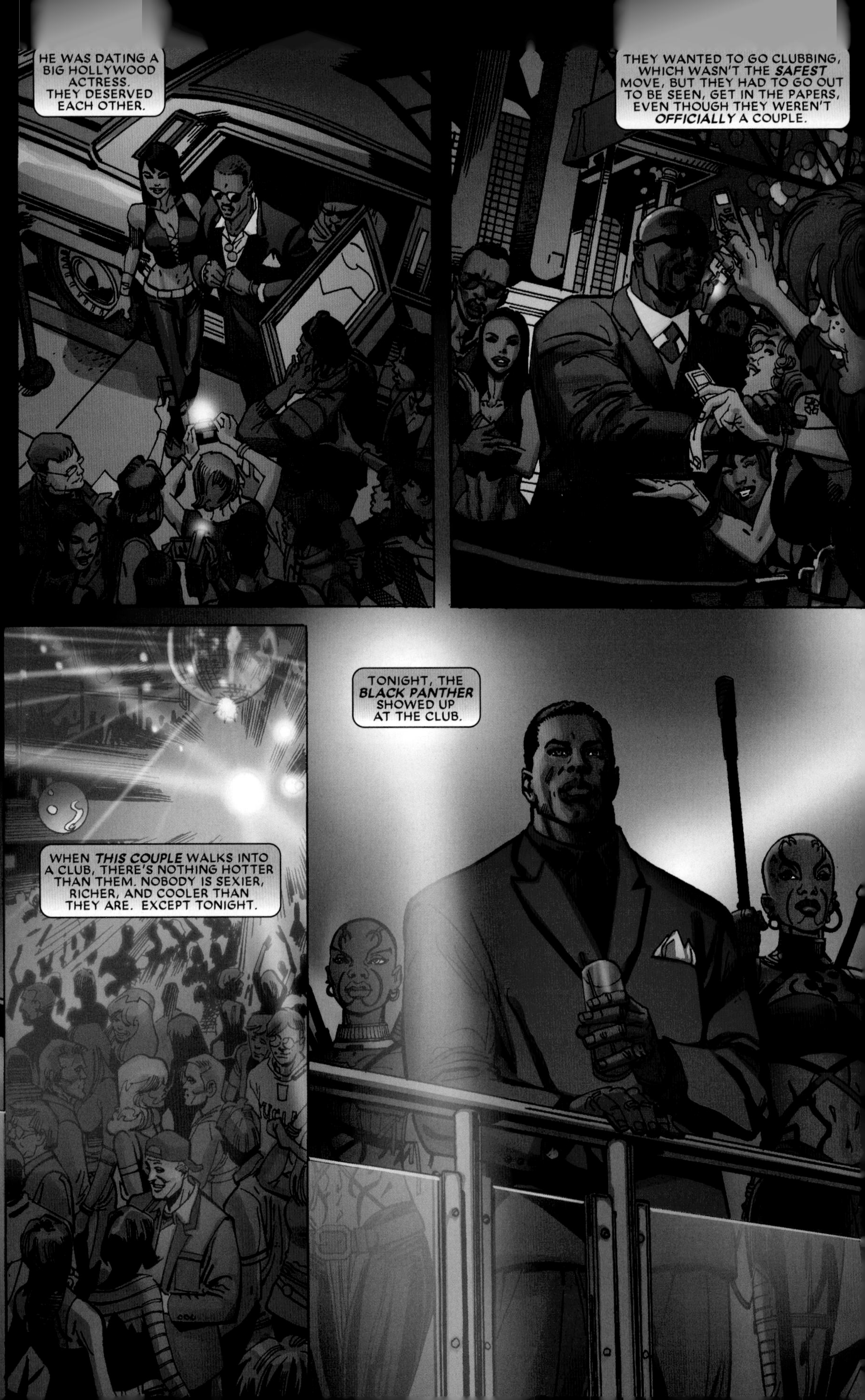
HE WAS DATING A BIG HOLLYWOOD ACTRESS. THEY DESERVED EACH OTHER.
THEY WANTED TO GO CLUBBING, WHICH WASN'T THE *SAFEST* MOVE, BUT THEY HAD TO GO OUT TO BE SEEN, GET IN THE PAPERS, EVEN THOUGH THEY WEREN'T *OFFICIALLY* A COUPLE.
WHEN *THIS COUPLE* WALKS INTO A CLUB, THERE'S NOTHING HOTTER THAN THEM. NOBODY IS SEXIER, RICHER, AND COOLER THAN THEY ARE. EXCEPT TONIGHT.
TONIGHT, THE *BLACK PANTHER* SHOWED UP AT THE CLUB.

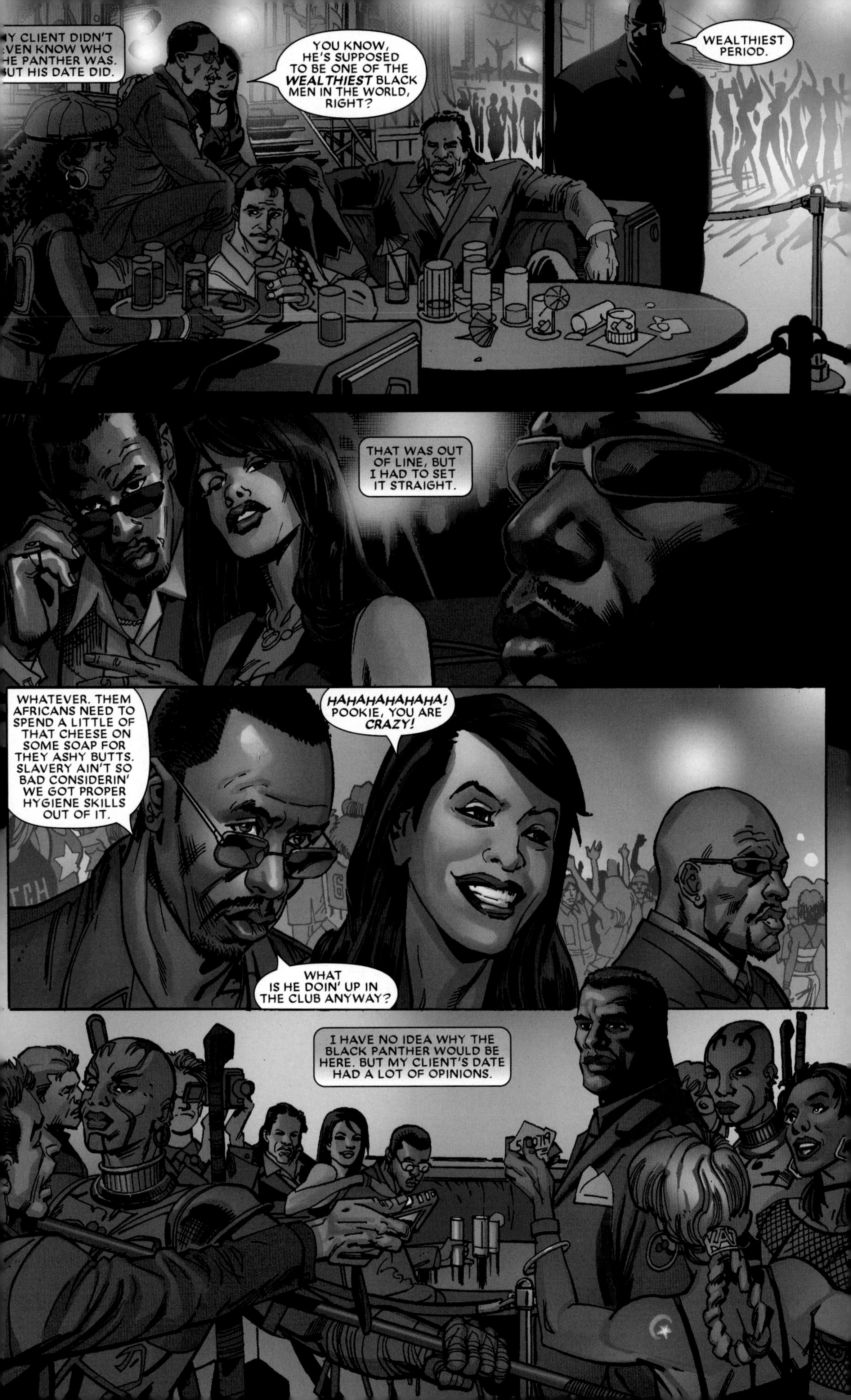
Y CLIENT DIDN'T
VEN KNOW WHO
HE PANTHER WAS.
UT HIS DATE DID.
YOU KNOW, HE'S SUPPOSED TO BE ONE OF THE WEALTHIEST BLACK MEN IN THE WORLD, RIGHT?
WEALTHIEST PERIOD.
THAT WAS OUT OF LINE, BUT I HAD TO SET IT STRAIGHT.
WHATEVER. THEM AFRICANS NEED TO SPEND A LITTLE OF THAT CHEESE ON SOME SOAP FOR THEY ASHY BUTTS. SLAVERY AIN'T SO BAD CONSIDERIN' WE GOT PROPER HYGIENE SKILLS OUT OF IT.
HAHAHAHAHAHA! POOKIE, YOU ARE CRAZY!
WHAT IS HE DOIN' UP IN THE CLUB ANYWAY?
I HAVE NO IDEA WHY THE BLACK PANTHER WOULD BE HERE. BUT MY CLIENT'S DATE HAD A LOT OF OPINIONS.

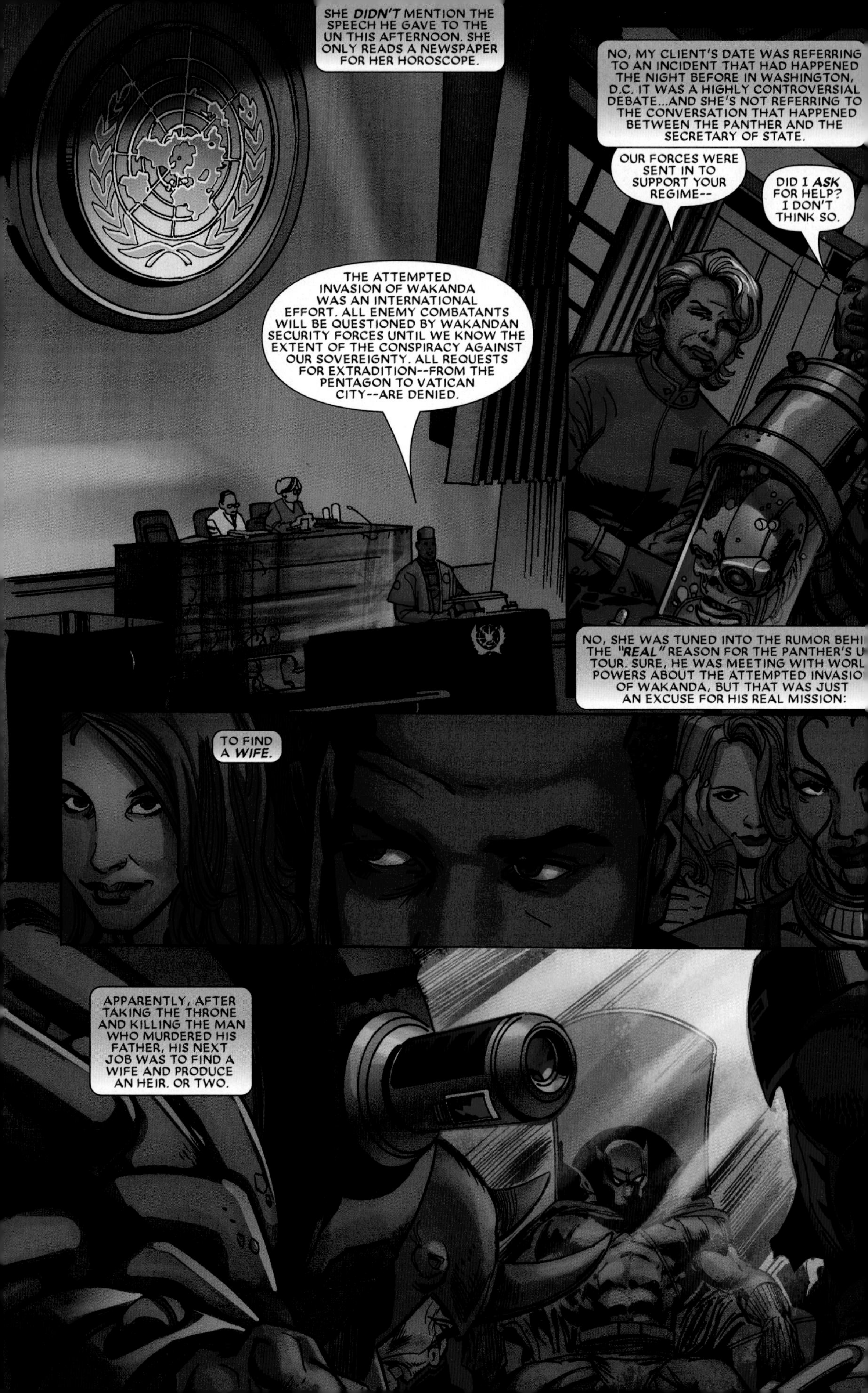

SHE *DIDN'T* MENTION THE SPEECH HE GAVE TO THE UN THIS AFTERNOON. SHE ONLY READS A NEWSPAPER FOR HER HOROSCOPE.
THE ATTEMPTED INVASION OF WAKANDA WAS AN INTERNATIONAL EFFORT. ALL ENEMY COMBATANTS WILL BE QUESTIONED BY WAKANDAN SECURITY FORCES UNTIL WE KNOW THE EXTENT OF THE CONSPIRACY AGAINST OUR SOVEREIGNTY. ALL REQUESTS FOR EXTRADITION--FROM THE PENTAGON TO VATICAN CITY--ARE DENIED.
NO, MY CLIENT'S DATE WAS REFERRING TO AN INCIDENT THAT HAD HAPPENED THE NIGHT BEFORE IN WASHINGTON, D.C. IT WAS A HIGHLY CONTROVERSIAL DEBATE...AND SHE'S NOT REFERRING TO THE CONVERSATION THAT HAPPENED BETWEEN THE PANTHER AND THE SECRETARY OF STATE.
OUR FORCES WERE SENT IN TO SUPPORT YOUR REGIME--
DID I *ASK* FOR HELP? I DON'T THINK SO.
NO, SHE WAS TUNED INTO THE RUMOR BEHI THE *"REAL"* REASON FOR THE PANTHER'S U TOUR. SURE, HE WAS MEETING WITH WORL POWERS ABOUT THE ATTEMPTED INVASIO OF WAKANDA, BUT THAT WAS JUST AN EXCUSE FOR HIS REAL MISSION:
TO FIND A *WIFE.*
APPARENTLY, AFTER TAKING THE THRONE AND KILLING THE MAN WHO MURDERED HIS FATHER, HIS NEXT JOB WAS TO FIND A WIFE AND PRODUCE AN HEIR. OR TWO.

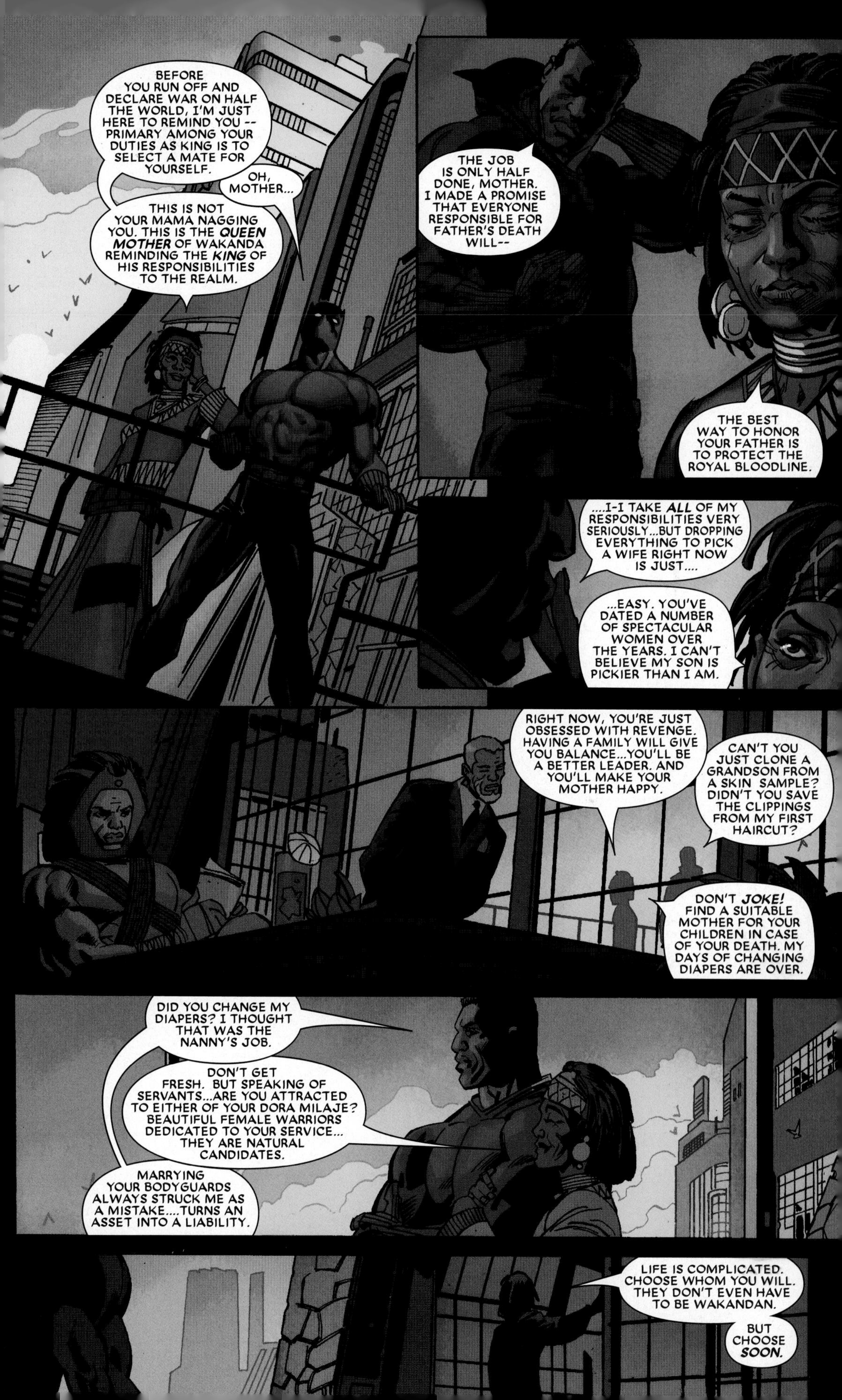
BEFORE YOU RUN OFF AND DECLARE WAR ON HALF THE WORLD, I'M JUST HERE TO REMIND YOU -- PRIMARY AMONG YOUR DUTIES AS KING IS TO SELECT A MATE FOR YOURSELF.
OH, MOTHER...
THIS IS NOT YOUR MAMA NAGGING YOU. THIS IS THE *QUEEN MOTHER* OF WAKANDA REMINDING THE *KING* OF HIS RESPONSIBILITIES TO THE REALM.
THE JOB IS ONLY HALF DONE, MOTHER. I MADE A PROMISE THAT EVERYONE RESPONSIBLE FOR FATHER'S DEATH WILL--
THE BEST WAY TO HONOR YOUR FATHER IS TO PROTECT THE ROYAL BLOODLINE.
....I-I TAKE *ALL* OF MY RESPONSIBILITIES VERY SERIOUSLY...BUT DROPPING EVERYTHING TO PICK A WIFE RIGHT NOW IS JUST....
...EASY. YOU'VE DATED A NUMBER OF SPECTACULAR WOMEN OVER THE YEARS. I CAN'T BELIEVE MY SON IS PICKIER THAN I AM.
RIGHT NOW, YOU'RE JUST OBSESSED WITH REVENGE. HAVING A FAMILY WILL GIVE YOU BALANCE...YOU'LL BE A BETTER LEADER. AND YOU'LL MAKE YOUR MOTHER HAPPY.
CAN'T YOU JUST CLONE A GRANDSON FROM A SKIN SAMPLE? DIDN'T YOU SAVE THE CLIPPINGS FROM MY FIRST HAIRCUT?
DON'T *JOKE!* FIND A SUITABLE MOTHER FOR YOUR CHILDREN IN CASE OF YOUR DEATH. MY DAYS OF CHANGING DIAPERS ARE OVER.
DID YOU CHANGE MY DIAPERS? I THOUGHT THAT WAS THE NANNY'S JOB.
DON'T GET FRESH. BUT SPEAKING OF SERVANTS...ARE YOU ATTRACTED TO EITHER OF YOUR DORA MILAJE? BEAUTIFUL FEMALE WARRIORS DEDICATED TO YOUR SERVICE... THEY ARE NATURAL CANDIDATES.
MARRYING YOUR BODYGUARDS ALWAYS STRUCK ME AS A MISTAKE....TURNS AN ASSET INTO A LIABILITY.
LIFE IS COMPLICATED. CHOOSE WHOM YOU WILL. THEY DON'T EVEN HAVE TO BE WAKANDAN.
BUT CHOOSE *SOON.*

MO' WOMEN, MO' PROBLEMS. THESE YOUNG BOYS WILL LEARN THAT EVENTUALLY. PLUS, IF YOU WANT TO BE REAL GANGSTER ABOUT IT, A FAMILY GETS YOUR MIND RIGHT. LIKE MICHAEL CORLEONE IN "THE GODFATHER." FIRST THING HE DID WHEN HE GOT MADE CAPO WAS TO FIND KAY AND CONVINCE HER TO COME BACK TO HIM.

WHAT'S HE DOING IN *AMERICA* LOOKING FOR A WIFE? HE NEEDS TO FIND A HALF DOZEN MFOOFOO'S OUT IN THE BUSH SOMEWHERE AND ROTATE 'EM IN A HAREM.

YOU MEAN LIKE HOW *YOU* DO IT, BIG DADDY?

THAT'S WHY THE PANTHER WAS IN D.C. TO FIND HIS KAY.

MONICA LYNNE, A NEO-SOUL SINGER OUT OF PHILLY. THEY DATED WHILE HE WAS LEARNING THE DIPLOMATIC GAME IN WASHINGTON. HE WAS OUT OF COLLEGE AND SHE ALREADY HAD A FOLLOWING.

NOW HE'S A KING AND SHE'S A STAR. I GIVE HER CREDIT--SHE MAKES REAL GROWN FOLKS MUSIC. I APPRECIATE HER STUFF AND IT GIVES THE KIDS SOMETHING DECENT TO LISTEN TO.

OH MY GOD, MY HAIRDRESSER'S BOYFRIEND WAS THERE AND *HEARD* THE WHOLE THING.

SO THE PANTHER MEETS HER BACKSTAGE AFTER TH[E] SHOW. YOU'D *THINK* THA[T] AN AFRICAN KING THAT YOU[...] DATING BACK IN THE DAY [...] WHEN YOU DIDN'T EVEN KN[OW] WAS A KING COMES TO AS[K] TO GET MARRIED, YOU'D J[...] FOR JOY, RIGHT? I MEA[N] THAT'S WHAT HAPPENE[D] "COMING TO AMERICA[,]" RIGHT?

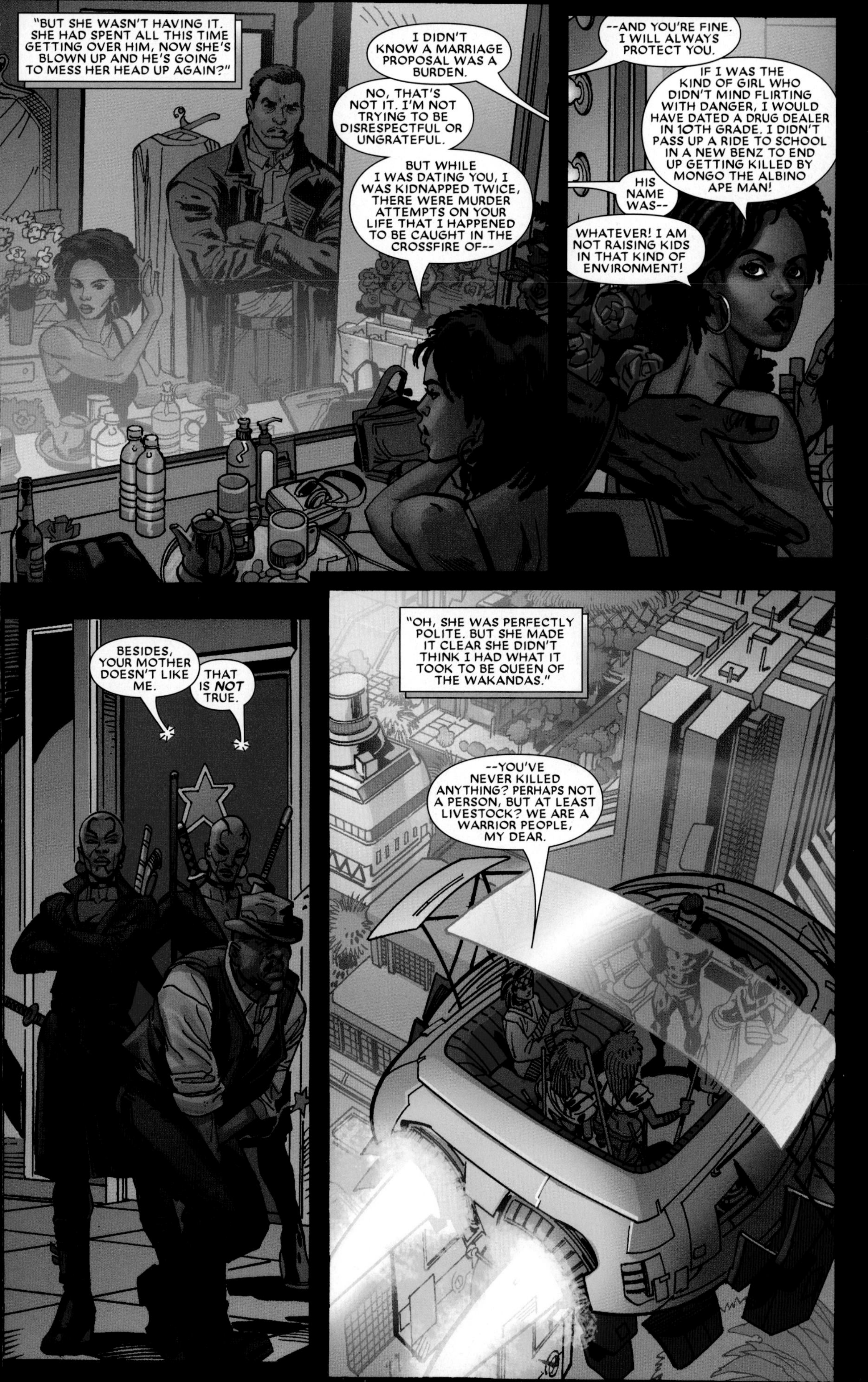
"BUT SHE WASN'T HAVING IT. SHE HAD SPENT ALL THIS TIME GETTING OVER HIM, NOW SHE'S BLOWN UP AND HE'S GOING TO MESS HER HEAD UP AGAIN?"
I DIDN'T KNOW A MARRIAGE PROPOSAL WAS A BURDEN.
NO, THAT'S NOT IT. I'M NOT TRYING TO BE DISRESPECTFUL OR UNGRATEFUL.
BUT WHILE I WAS DATING YOU, I WAS KIDNAPPED TWICE, THERE WERE MURDER ATTEMPTS ON YOUR LIFE THAT I HAPPENED TO BE CAUGHT IN THE CROSSFIRE OF--
--AND YOU'RE FINE. I WILL ALWAYS PROTECT YOU.
IF I WAS THE KIND OF GIRL WHO DIDN'T MIND FLIRTING WITH DANGER, I WOULD HAVE DATED A DRUG DEALER IN 10TH GRADE. I DIDN'T PASS UP A RIDE TO SCHOOL IN A NEW BENZ TO END UP GETTING KILLED BY MONGO THE ALBINO APE MAN!
HIS NAME WAS--
WHATEVER! I AM NOT RAISING KIDS IN THAT KIND OF ENVIRONMENT!
BESIDES, YOUR MOTHER DOESN'T LIKE ME.
THAT IS ***NOT*** TRUE.
"OH, SHE WAS PERFECTLY POLITE. BUT SHE MADE IT CLEAR SHE DIDN'T THINK I HAD WHAT IT TOOK TO BE QUEEN OF THE WAKANDAS."
--YOU'VE NEVER KILLED ANYTHING? PERHAPS NOT A PERSON, BUT AT LEAST LIVESTOCK? WE ARE A WARRIOR PEOPLE, MY DEAR.

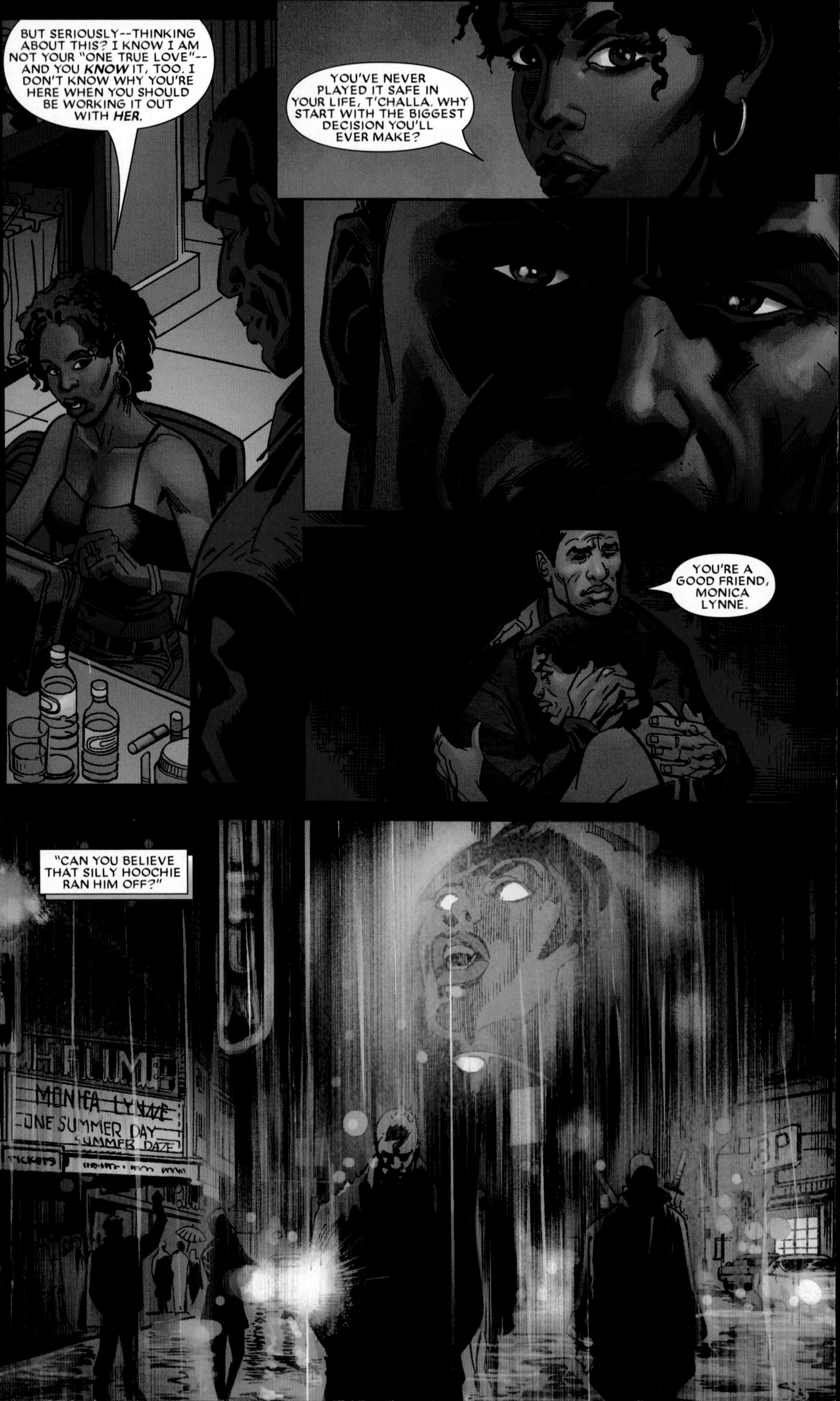
BUT SERIOUSLY--THINKING ABOUT THIS? I KNOW I AM NOT YOUR "ONE TRUE LOVE"--AND YOU *KNOW* IT, TOO. I DON'T KNOW WHY YOU'RE HERE WHEN YOU SHOULD BE WORKING IT OUT WITH *HER.*
YOU'VE NEVER PLAYED IT SAFE IN YOUR LIFE, T'CHALLA. WHY START WITH THE BIGGEST DECISION YOU'LL EVER MAKE?
YOU'RE A GOOD FRIEND, MONICA LYNNE.
"CAN YOU BELIEVE THAT SILLY HOOCHIE RAN HIM OFF?"
MONICA LYNNE
ONE SUMMER DAY
SUMMER DAZE
TICKETS

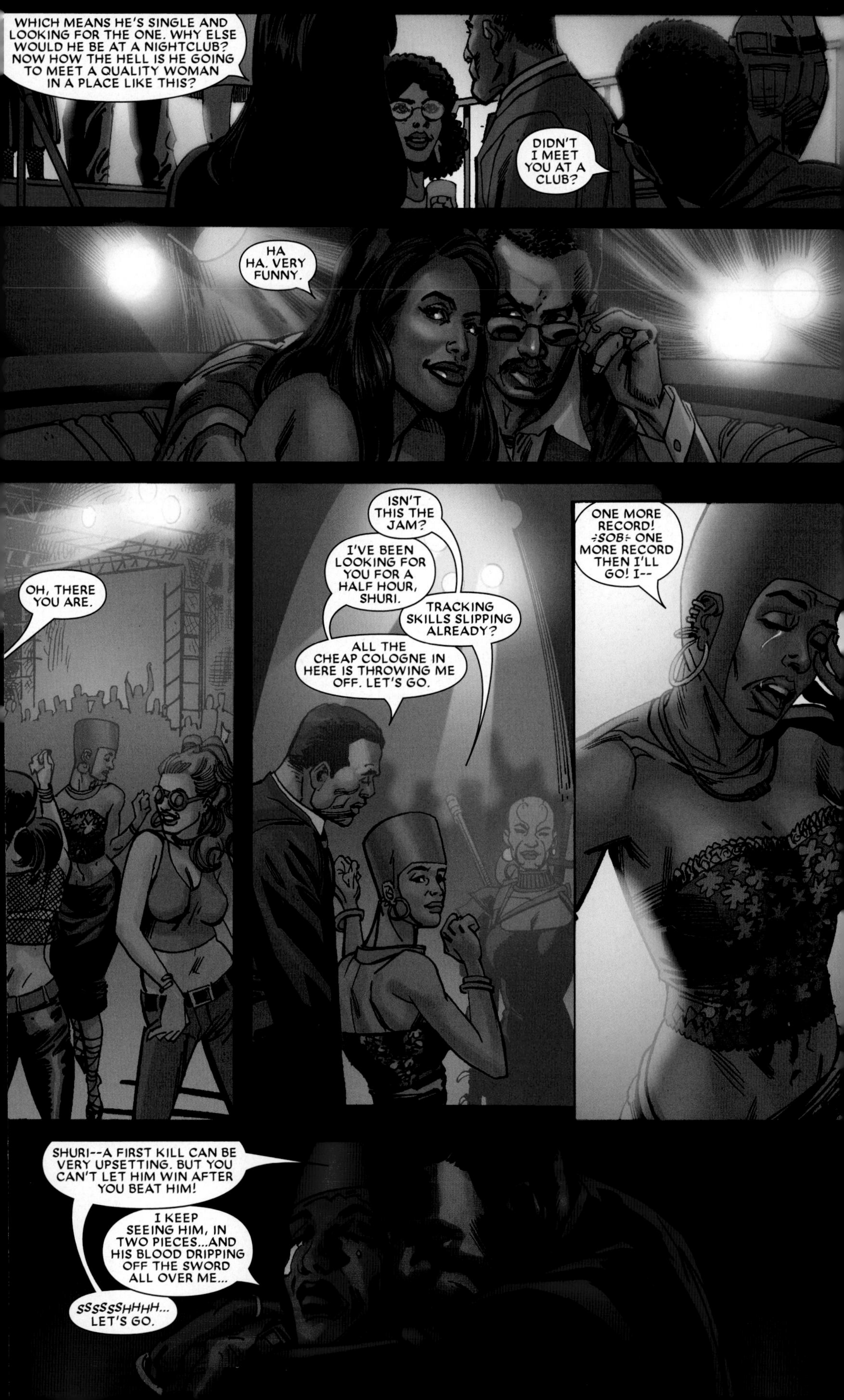
WHICH MEANS HE'S SINGLE AND LOOKING FOR THE ONE. WHY ELSE WOULD HE BE AT A NIGHTCLUB? NOW HOW THE HELL IS HE GOING TO MEET A QUALITY WOMAN IN A PLACE LIKE THIS?
DIDN'T I MEET YOU AT A CLUB?
HA HA. VERY FUNNY.
OH, THERE YOU ARE.
ISN'T THIS THE JAM?
I'VE BEEN LOOKING FOR YOU FOR A HALF HOUR, SHURI.
TRACKING SKILLS SLIPPING ALREADY?
ALL THE CHEAP COLOGNE IN HERE IS THROWING ME OFF. LET'S GO.
ONE MORE RECORD! ÷SOB÷ ONE MORE RECORD THEN I'LL GO! I--
SHURI--A FIRST KILL CAN BE VERY UPSETTING. BUT YOU CAN'T LET HIM WIN AFTER YOU BEAT HIM!
I KEEP SEEING HIM, IN TWO PIECES...AND HIS BLOOD DRIPPING OFF THE SWORD ALL OVER ME...
SSSSSSHHHH... LET'S GO.

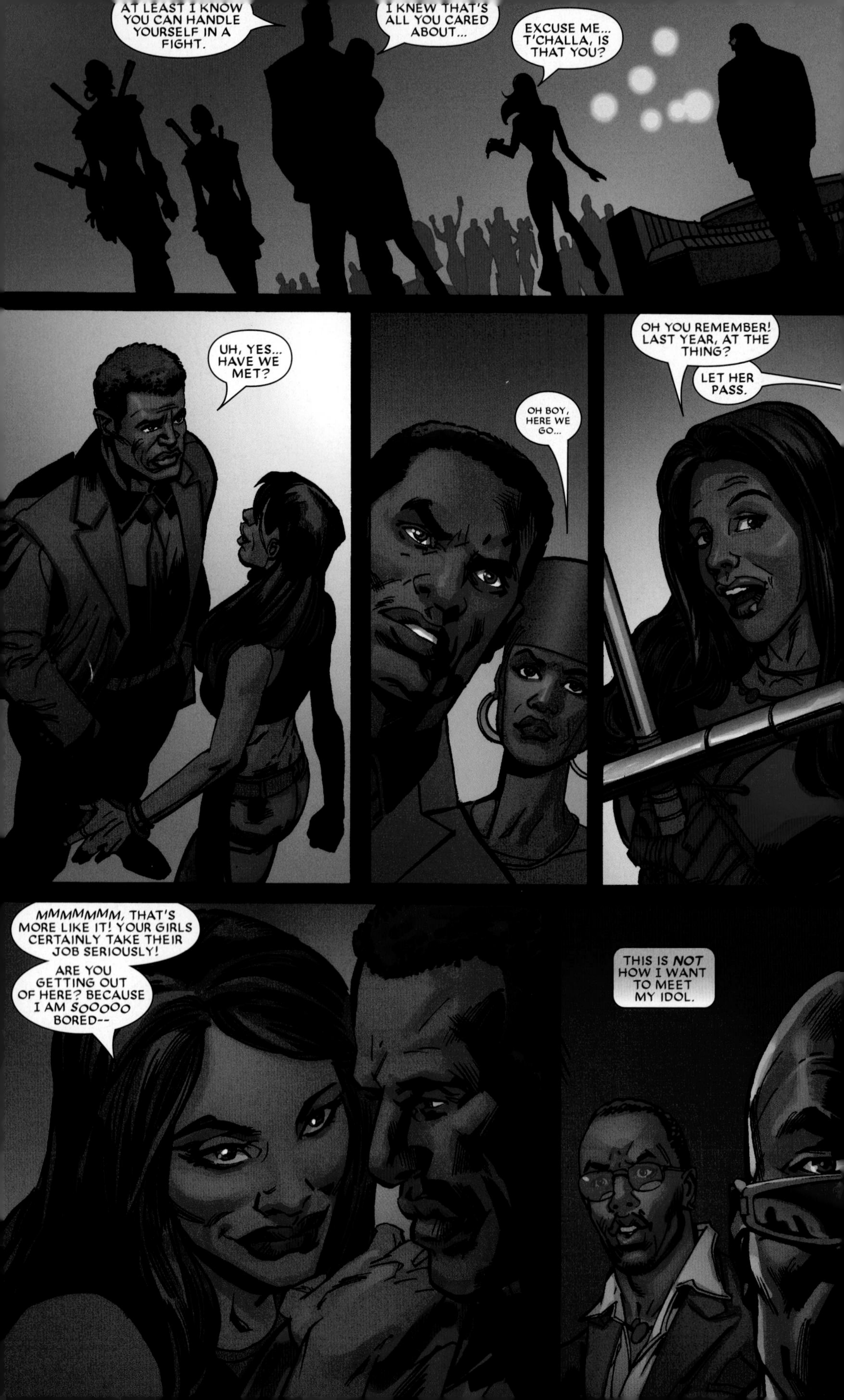
AT LEAST I KNOW YOU CAN HANDLE YOURSELF IN A FIGHT.
I KNEW THAT'S ALL YOU CARED ABOUT...
EXCUSE ME... T'CHALLA, IS THAT YOU?
UH, YES... HAVE WE MET?
OH BOY, HERE WE GO...
OH YOU REMEMBER! LAST YEAR, AT THE THING?
LET HER PASS.
MMMMMMM, THAT'S MORE LIKE IT! YOUR GIRLS CERTAINLY TAKE THEIR JOB SERIOUSLY!
ARE YOU GETTING OUT OF HERE? BECAUSE I AM SOOOOO BORED--
THIS IS NOT HOW I WANT TO MEET MY IDOL.

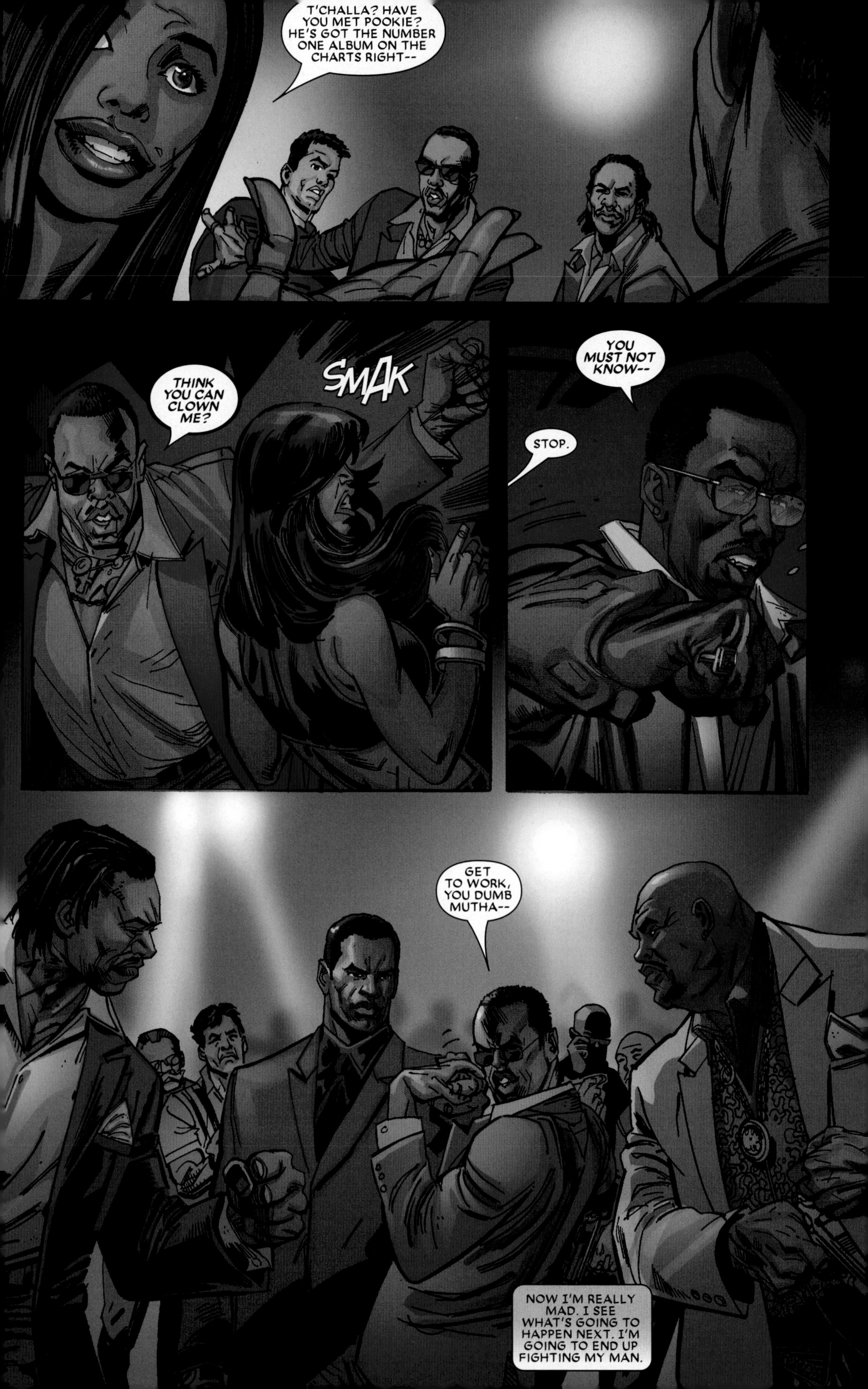
T'CHALLA? HAVE YOU MET POOKIE? HE'S GOT THE NUMBER ONE ALBUM ON THE CHARTS RIGHT--
THINK YOU CAN CLOWN ME?
SMAK
YOU MUST NOT KNOW--
STOP.
GET TO WORK, YOU DUMB MUTHA--
NOW I'M REALLY MAD. I SEE WHAT'S GOING TO HAPPEN NEXT. I'M GOING TO END UP FIGHTING MY MAN.

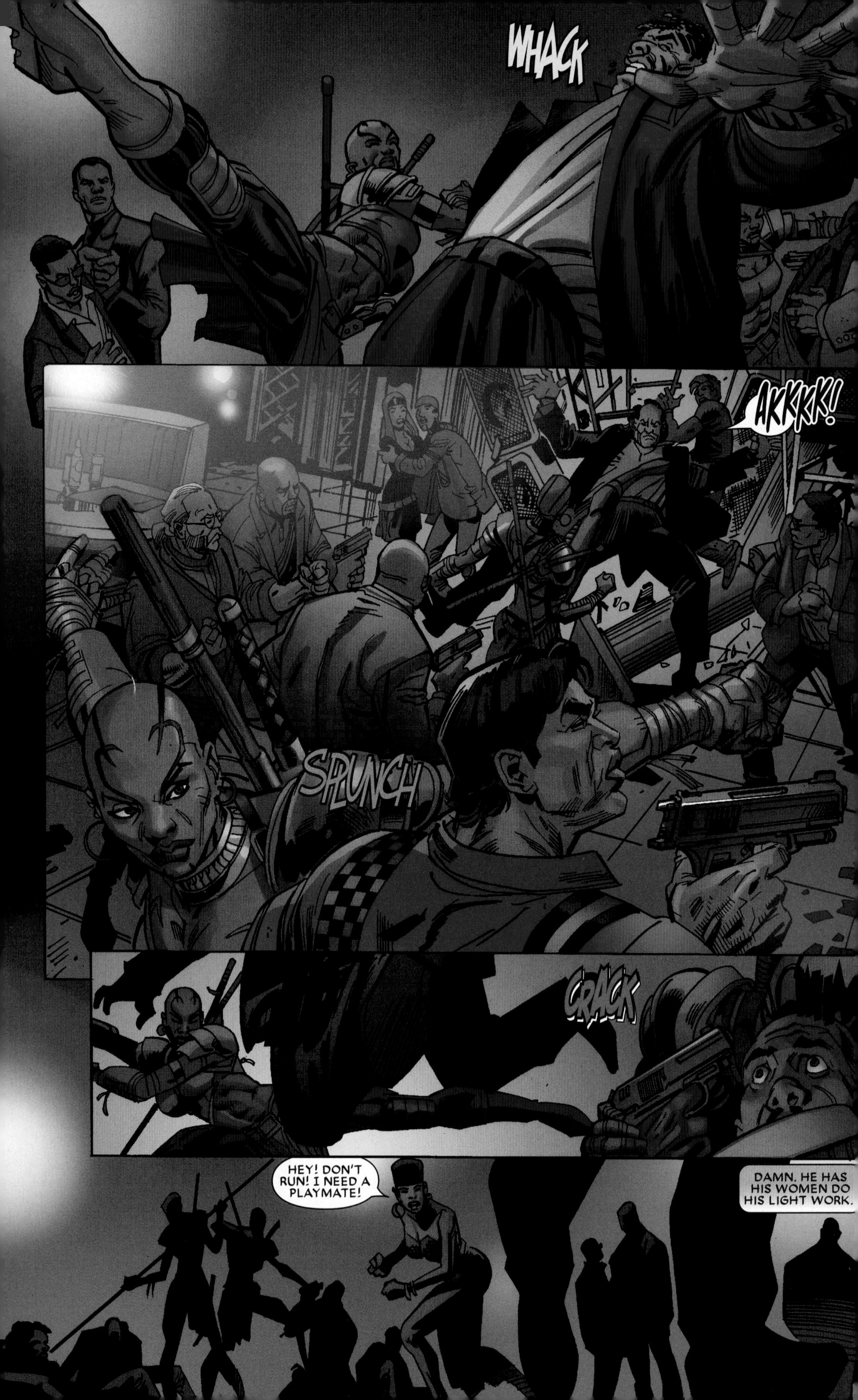
WHACK
AKKKK!
SPLUNCH
CRACK
HEY! DON'T RUN! I NEED A PLAYMATE!
DAMN. HE HAS HIS WOMEN DO HIS LIGHT WORK.

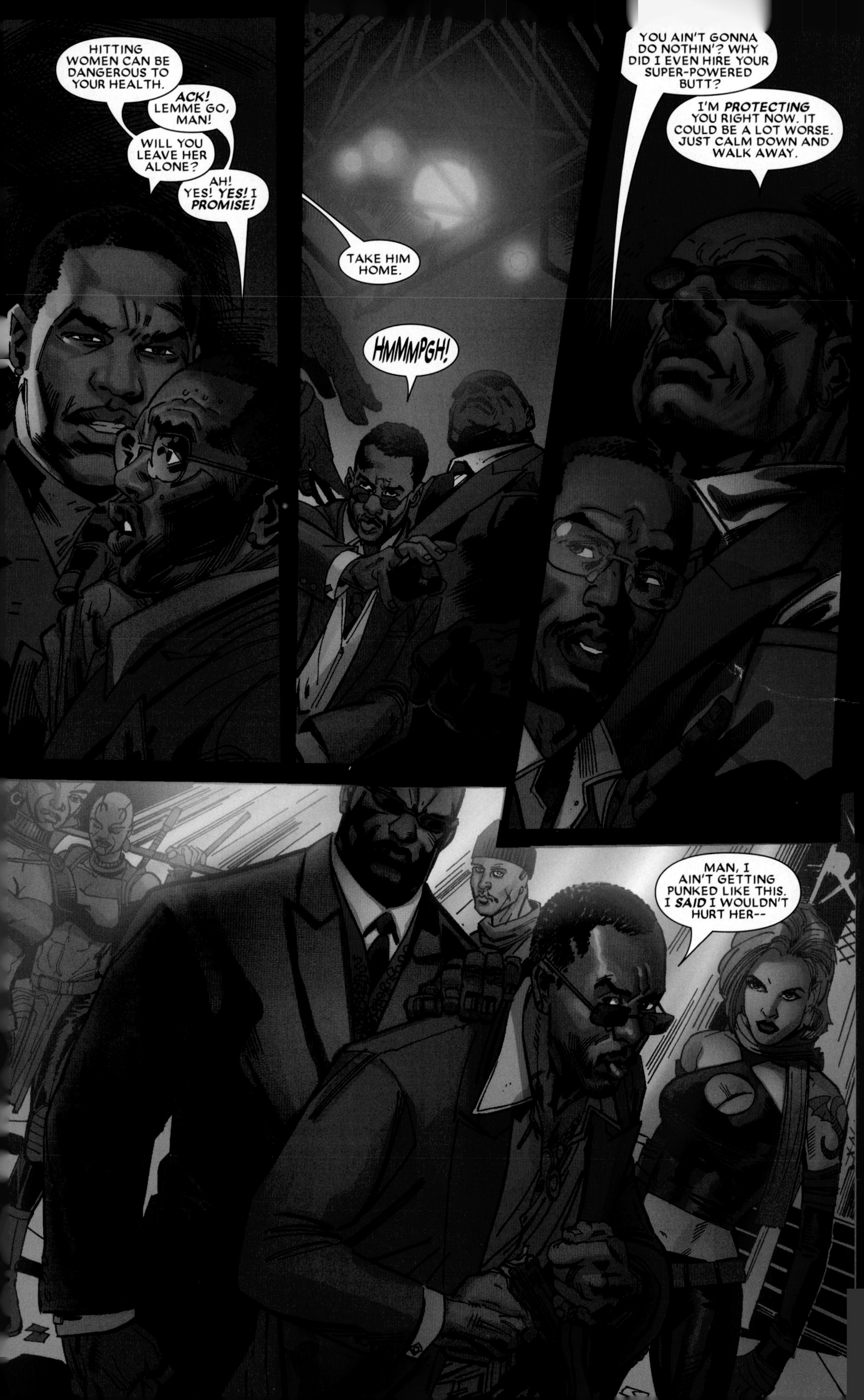
HITTING WOMEN CAN BE DANGEROUS TO YOUR HEALTH.
ACK! LEMME GO, MAN!
WILL YOU LEAVE HER ALONE?
AH! YES! YES! I PROMISE!
TAKE HIM HOME.
HMMMPGH!
YOU AIN'T GONNA DO NOTHIN'? WHY DID I EVEN HIRE YOUR SUPER-POWERED BUTT?
I'M PROTECTING YOU RIGHT NOW. IT COULD BE A LOT WORSE. JUST CALM DOWN AND WALK AWAY.
MAN, I AIN'T GETTING PUNKED LIKE THIS. I SAID I WOULDN'T HURT HER--

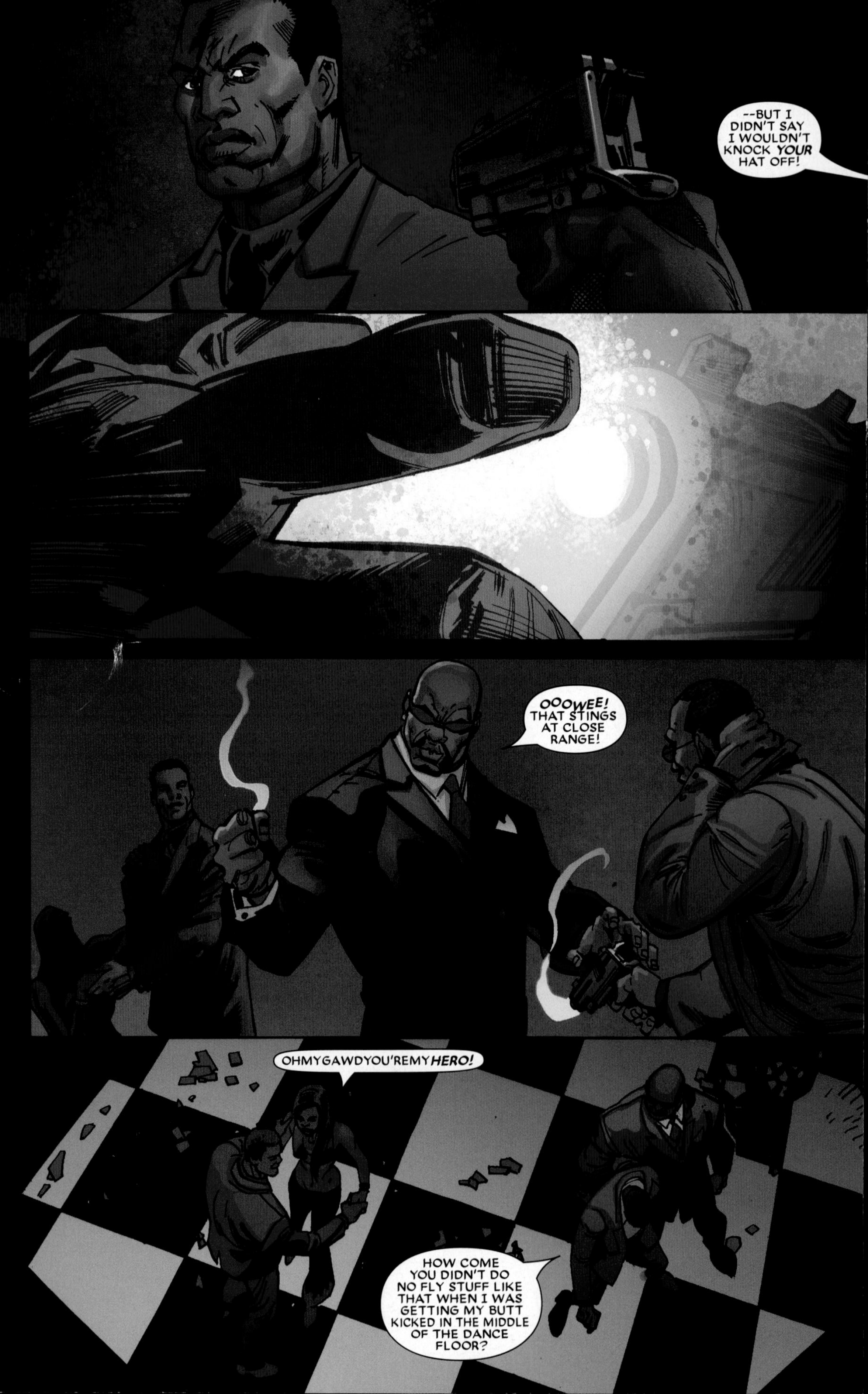
--BUT I DIDN'T SAY I WOULDN'T KNOCK YOUR HAT OFF!
OOOWEE! THAT STINGS AT CLOSE RANGE!
OHMYGAWDYOU'REMYHERO!
HOW COME YOU DIDN'T DO NO FLY STUFF LIKE THAT WHEN I WAS GETTING MY BUTT KICKED IN THE MIDDLE OF THE DANCE FLOOR?

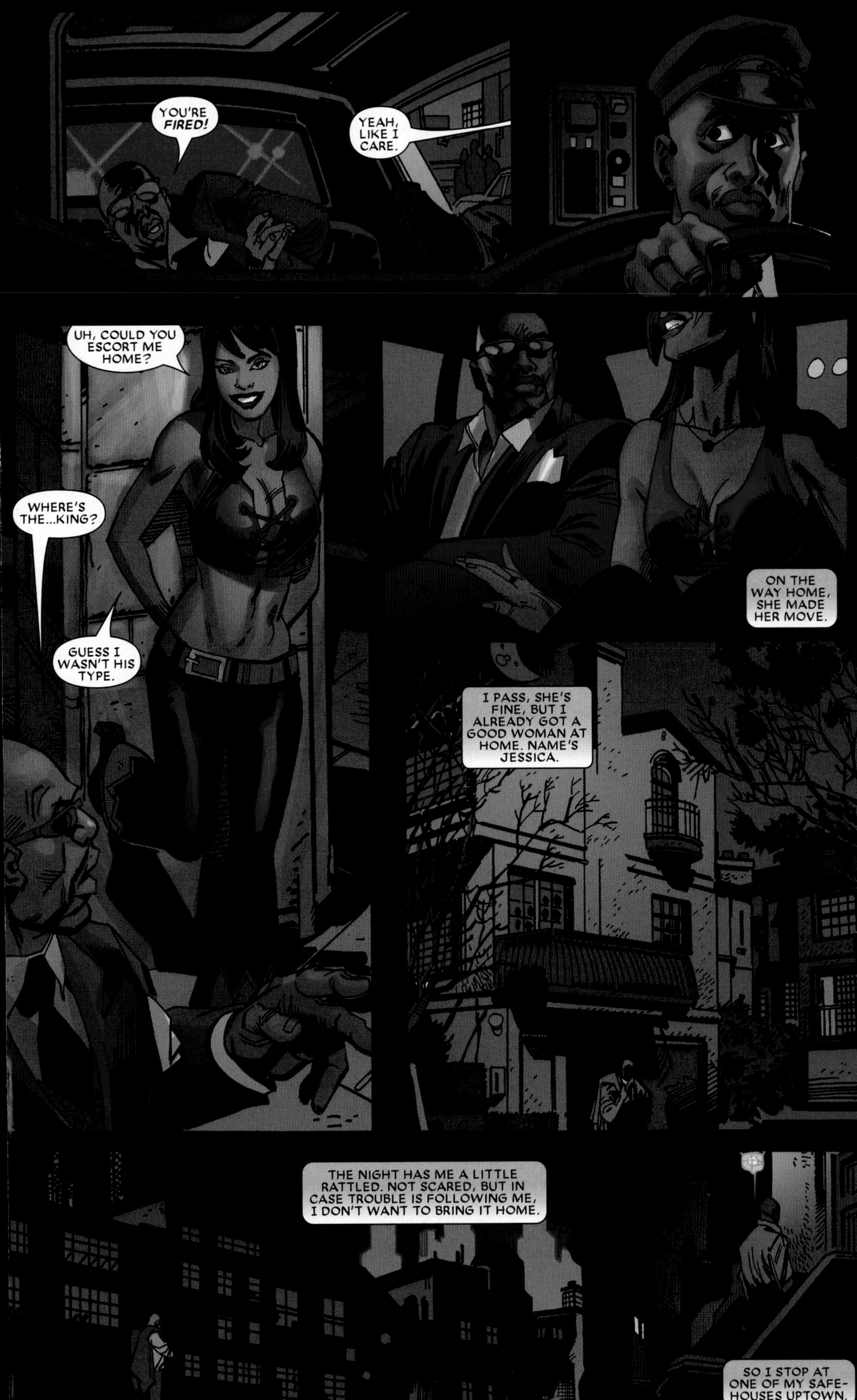
YOU'RE *FIRED!*
YEAH, LIKE I CARE.
UH, COULD YOU ESCORT ME HOME?
WHERE'S THE...KING?
GUESS I WASN'T HIS TYPE.
ON THE WAY HOME, SHE MADE HER MOVE.
I PASS, SHE'S FINE, BUT I ALREADY GOT A GOOD WOMAN AT HOME. NAME'S JESSICA.
THE NIGHT HAS ME A LITTLE RATTLED. NOT SCARED, BUT IN CASE TROUBLE IS FOLLOWING ME, I DON'T WANT TO BRING IT HOME.
SO I STOP AT ONE OF MY SAFE-HOUSES UPTOWN.

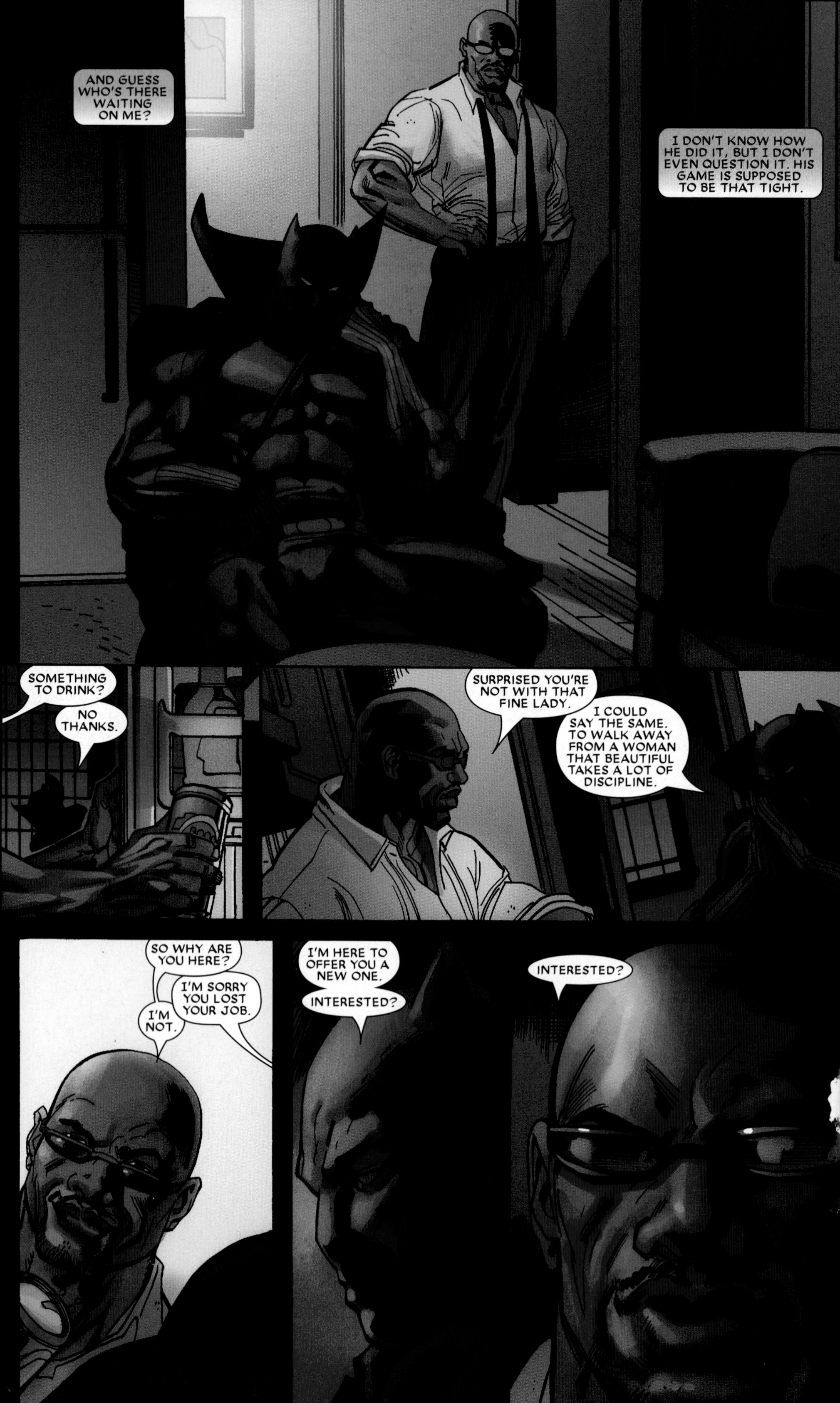
AND GUESS WHO'S THERE WAITING ON ME?
I DON'T KNOW HOW HE DID IT, BUT I DON'T EVEN QUESTION IT. HIS GAME IS SUPPOSED TO BE THAT TIGHT.
SOMETHING TO DRINK?
NO THANKS.
SURPRISED YOU'RE NOT WITH THAT FINE LADY.
I COULD SAY THE SAME. TO WALK AWAY FROM A WOMAN THAT BEAUTIFUL TAKES A LOT OF DISCIPLINE.
SO WHY ARE YOU HERE?
I'M SORRY YOU LOST YOUR JOB.
I'M NOT.
I'M HERE TO OFFER YOU A NEW ONE.
INTERESTED?
INTERESTED?

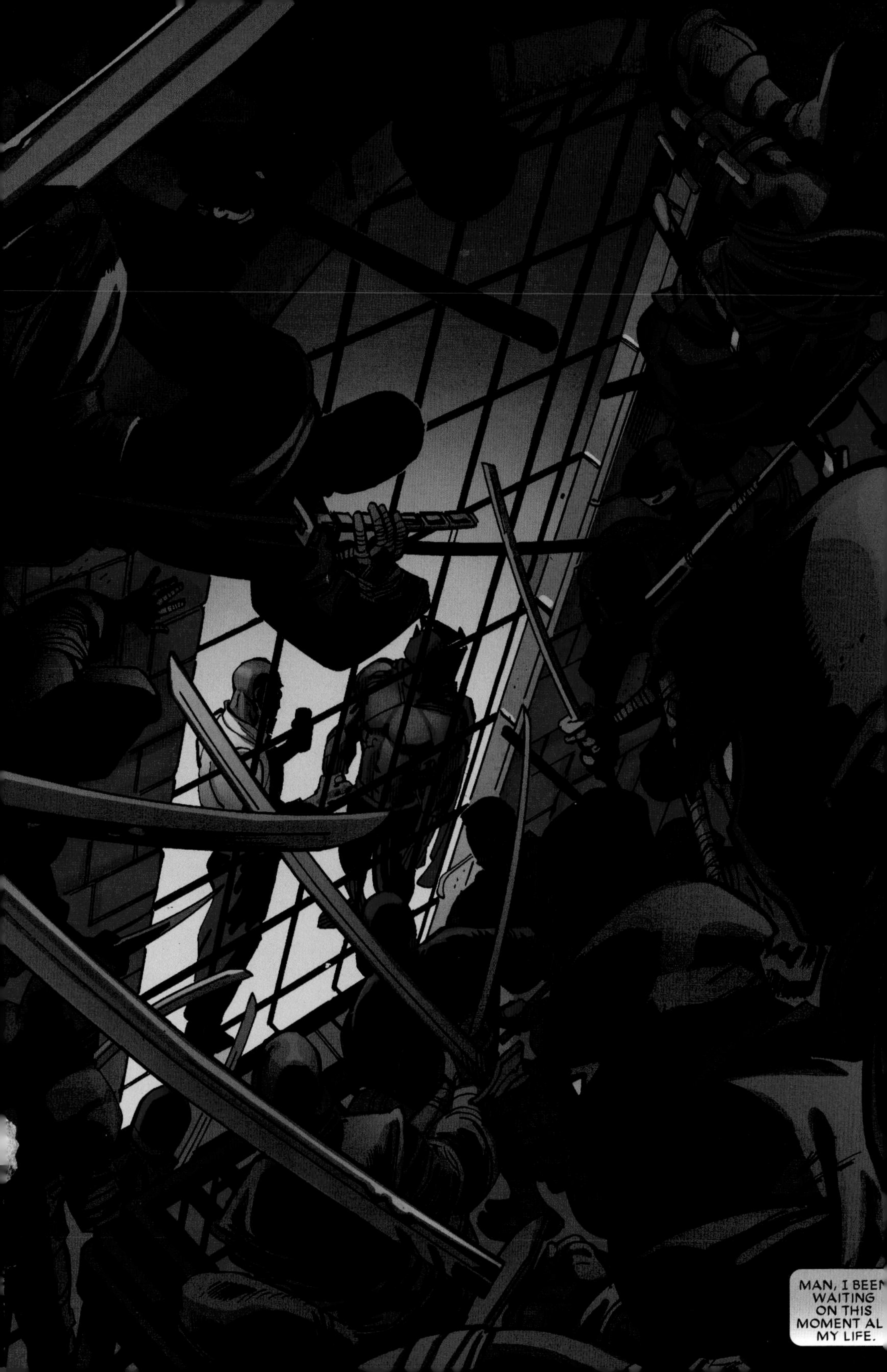
MAN, I BEEN WAITING ON THIS MOMENT AL MY LIFE.

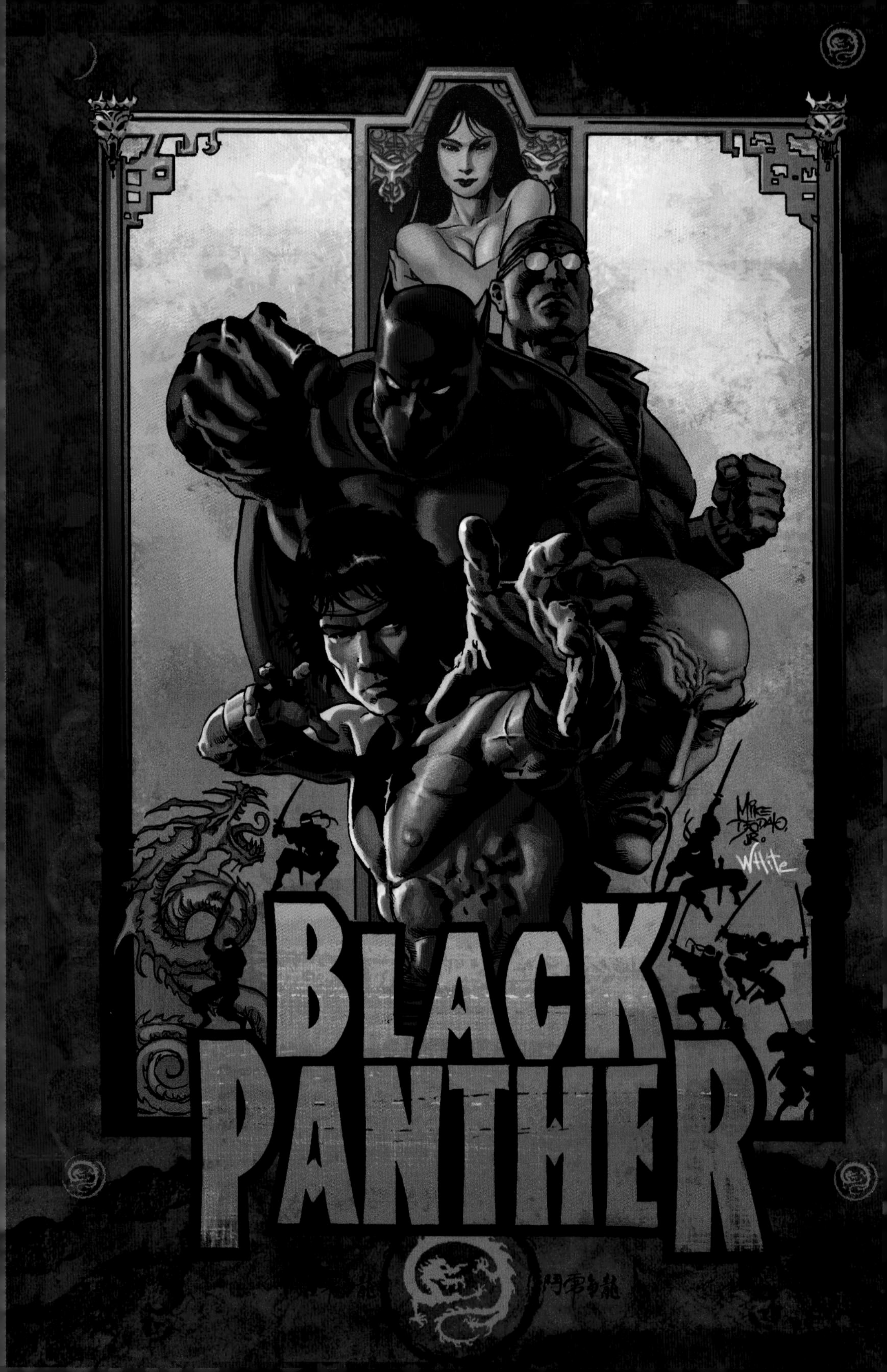
BLACK PANTHER
MIKE DEODATO, JR.
White

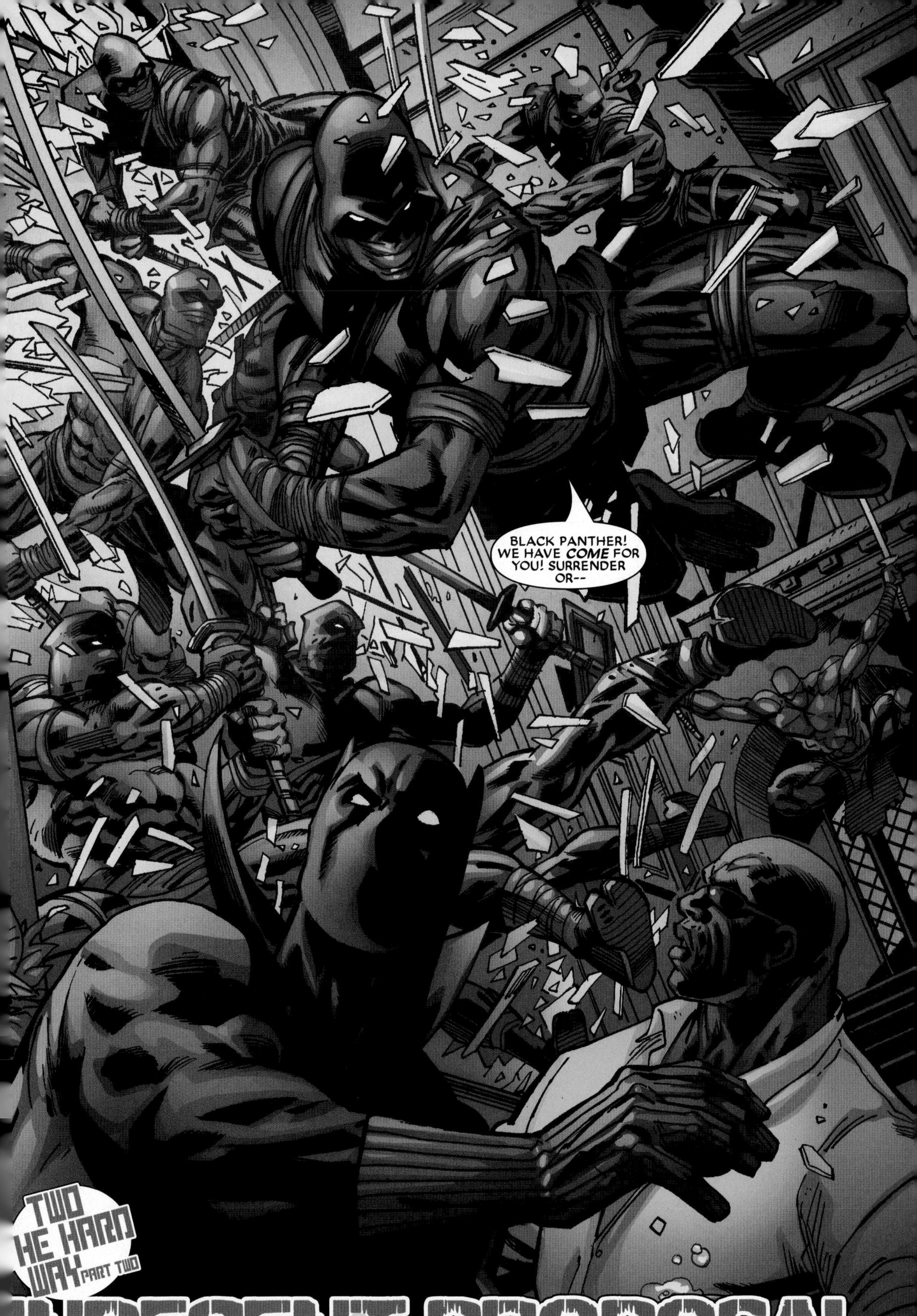
BLACK PANTHER! WE HAVE *COME* FOR YOU! SURRENDER OR--
TWO
HE HARD
WAY PART TWO
INDECENT PROPOSAL

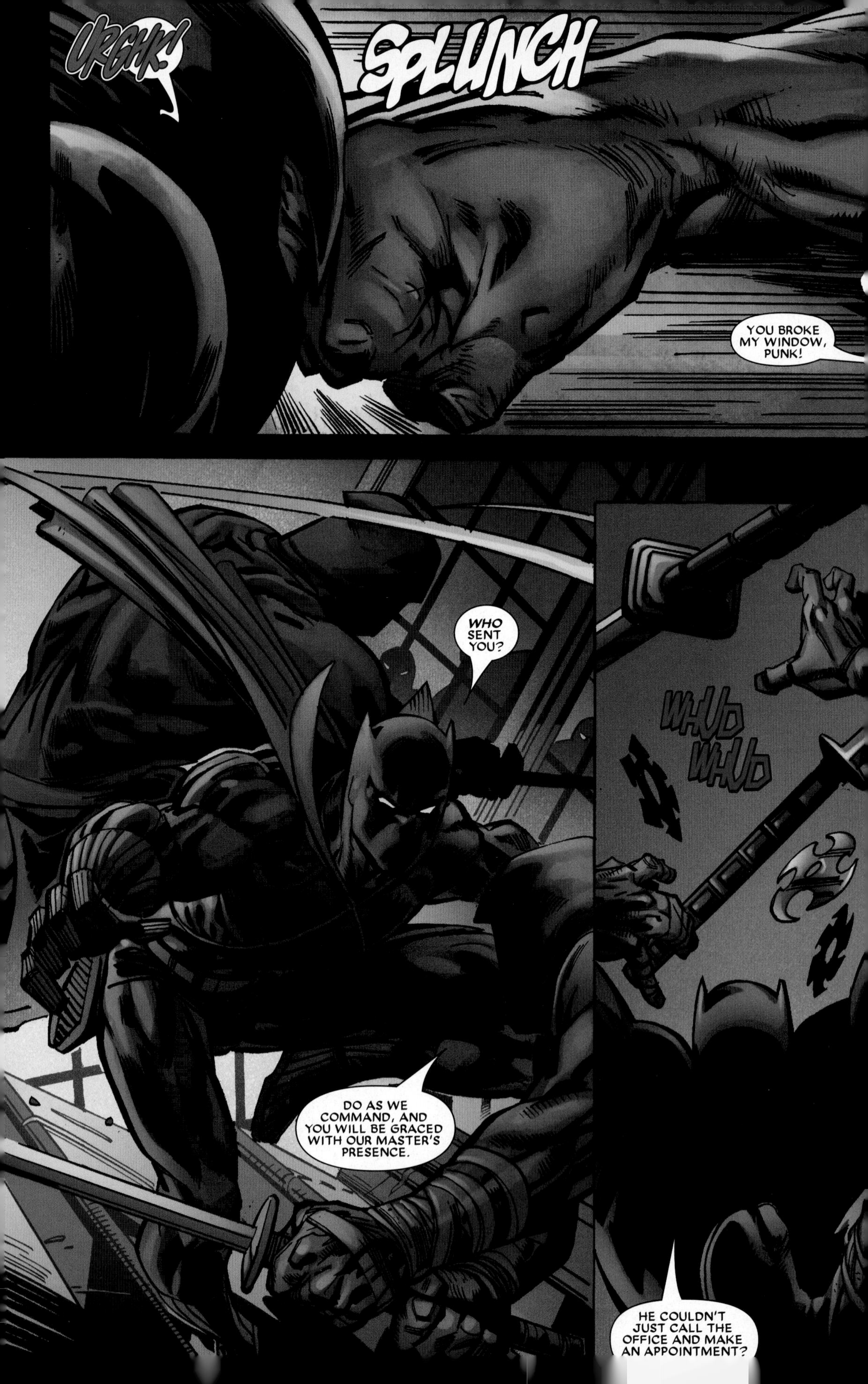
URGHK!
SPLUNCH
YOU BROKE MY WINDOW, PUNK!
WHO SENT YOU?
DO AS WE COMMAND, AND YOU WILL BE GRACED WITH OUR MASTER'S PRESENCE.
WHUD
WHUD
HE COULDN'T JUST CALL THE OFFICE AND MAKE AN APPOINTMENT?

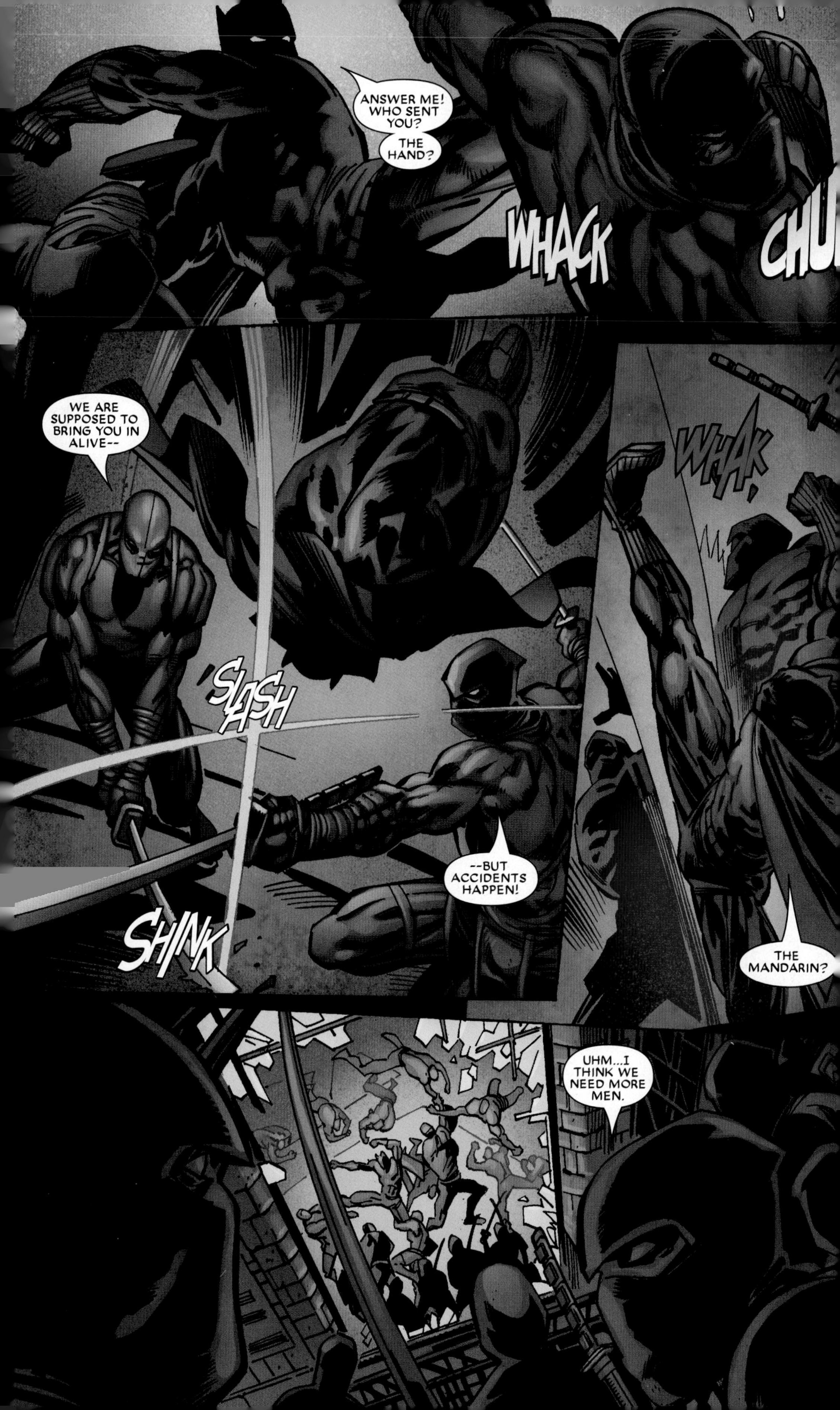
ANSWER ME! WHO SENT YOU?
THE HAND?
WHACK
CHU
WE ARE SUPPOSED TO BRING YOU IN ALIVE--
SLASH
--BUT ACCIDENTS HAPPEN!
SHINK
WHAK
THE MANDARIN?
UHM...I THINK WE NEED MORE MEN.

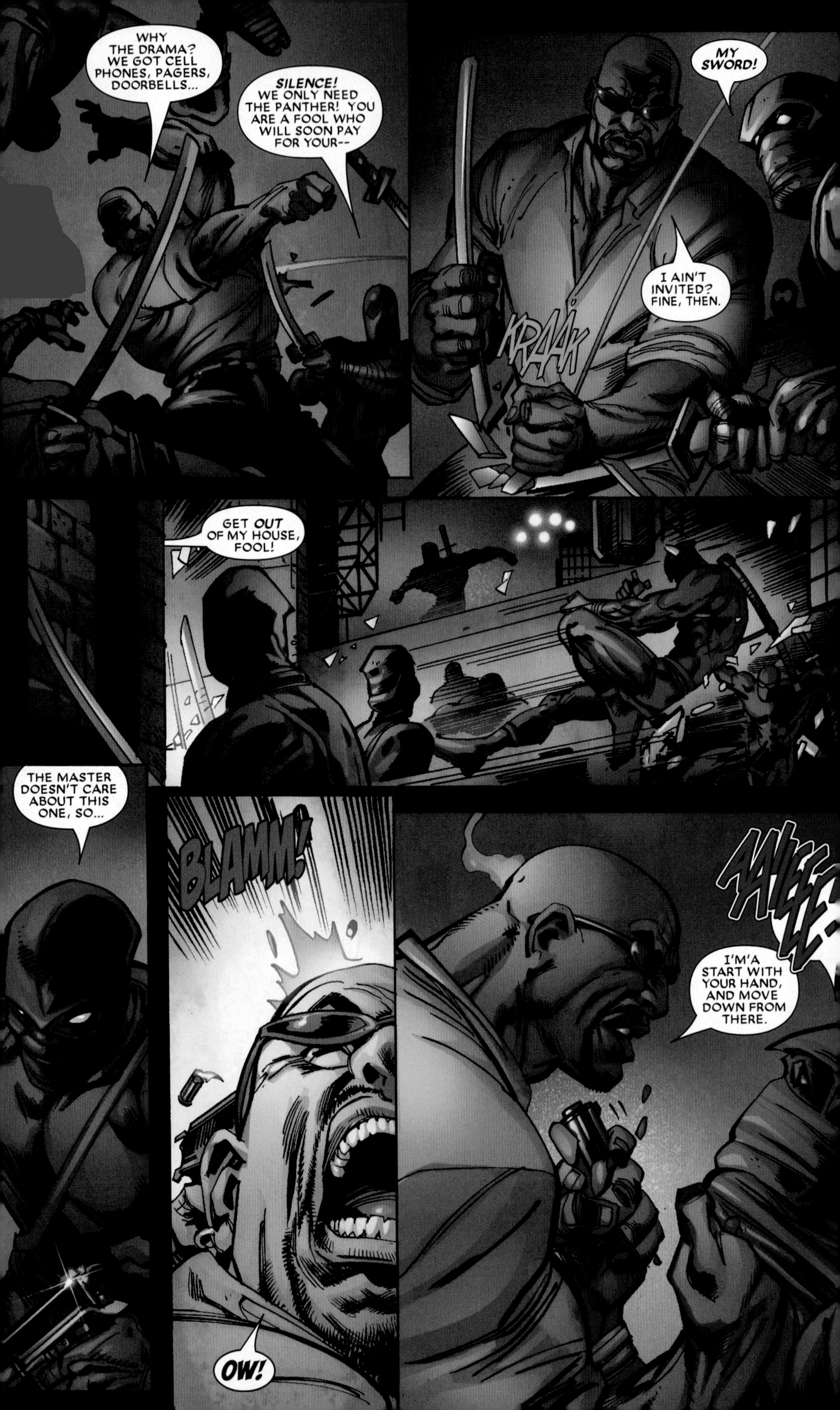
WHY THE DRAMA? WE GOT CELL PHONES, PAGERS, DOORBELLS...
SILENCE! WE ONLY NEED THE PANTHER! YOU ARE A FOOL WHO WILL SOON PAY FOR YOUR--
MY SWORD!
I AIN'T INVITED? FINE, THEN.
KRAAK
GET OUT OF MY HOUSE, FOOL!
THE MASTER DOESN'T CARE ABOUT THIS ONE, SO...
BLAMM!
OW!
I'M'A START WITH YOUR HAND, AND MOVE DOWN FROM THERE.

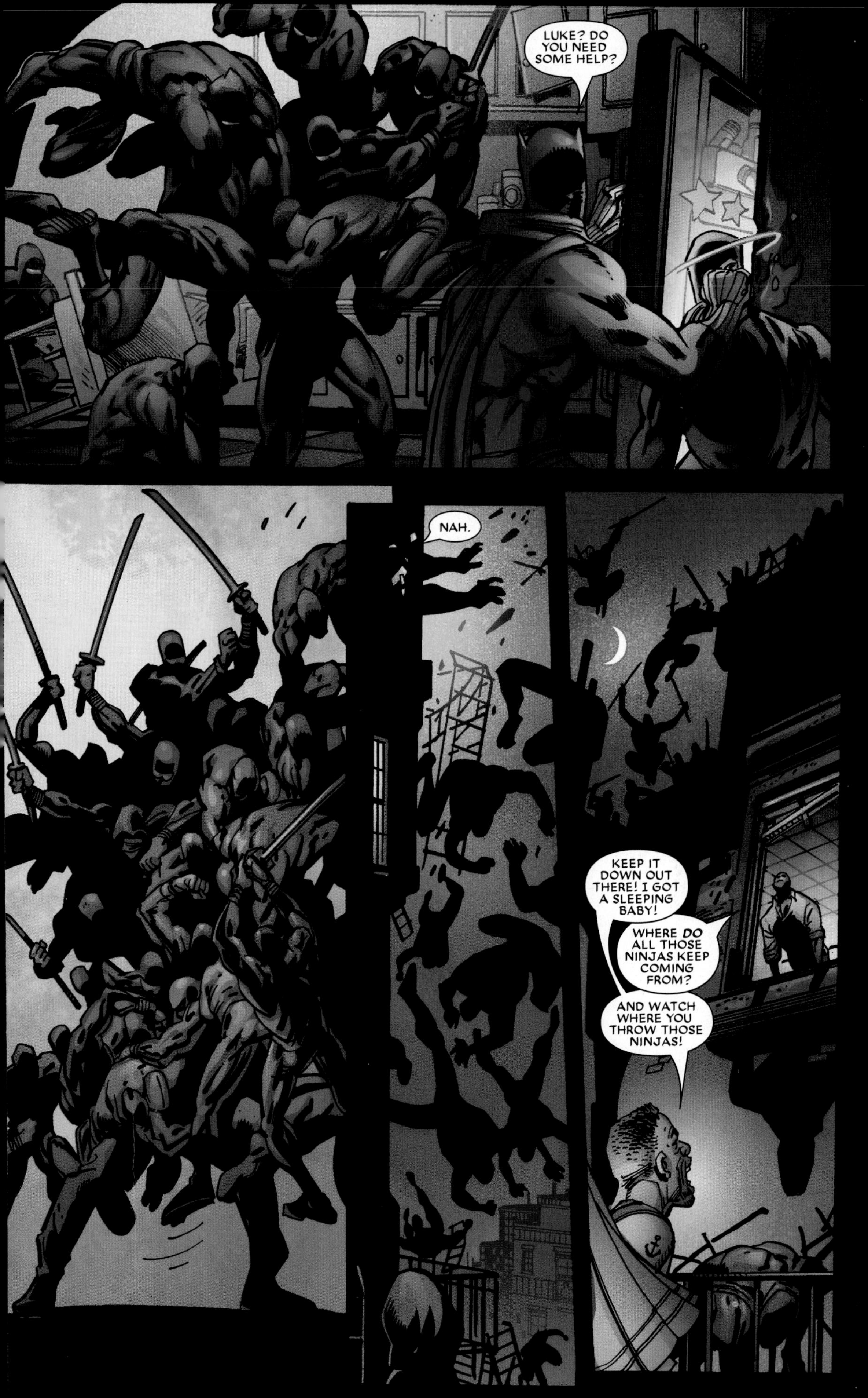
LUKE? DO YOU NEED SOME HELP?
NAH.
KEEP IT DOWN OUT THERE! I GOT A SLEEPING BABY!
WHERE **DO** ALL THOSE NINJAS KEEP COMING FROM?
AND WATCH WHERE YOU THROW THOSE NINJAS!

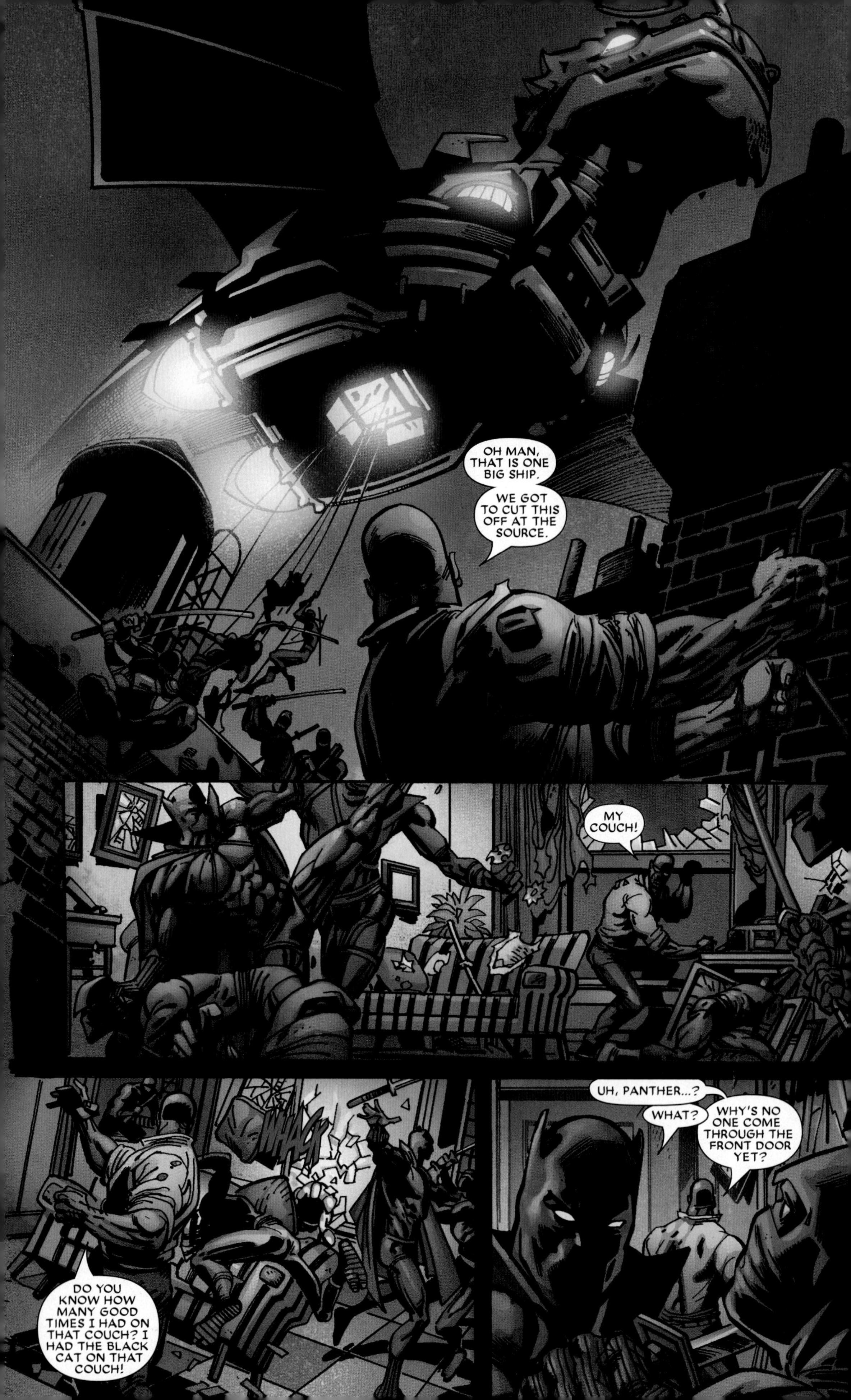
OH MAN, THAT IS ONE BIG SHIP.
WE GOT TO CUT THIS OFF AT THE SOURCE.
MY COUCH!
WHACK
DO YOU KNOW HOW MANY GOOD TIMES I HAD ON THAT COUCH? I HAD THE BLACK CAT ON THAT COUCH!
UH, PANTHER...?
WHAT?
WHY'S NO ONE COME THROUGH THE FRONT DOOR YET?

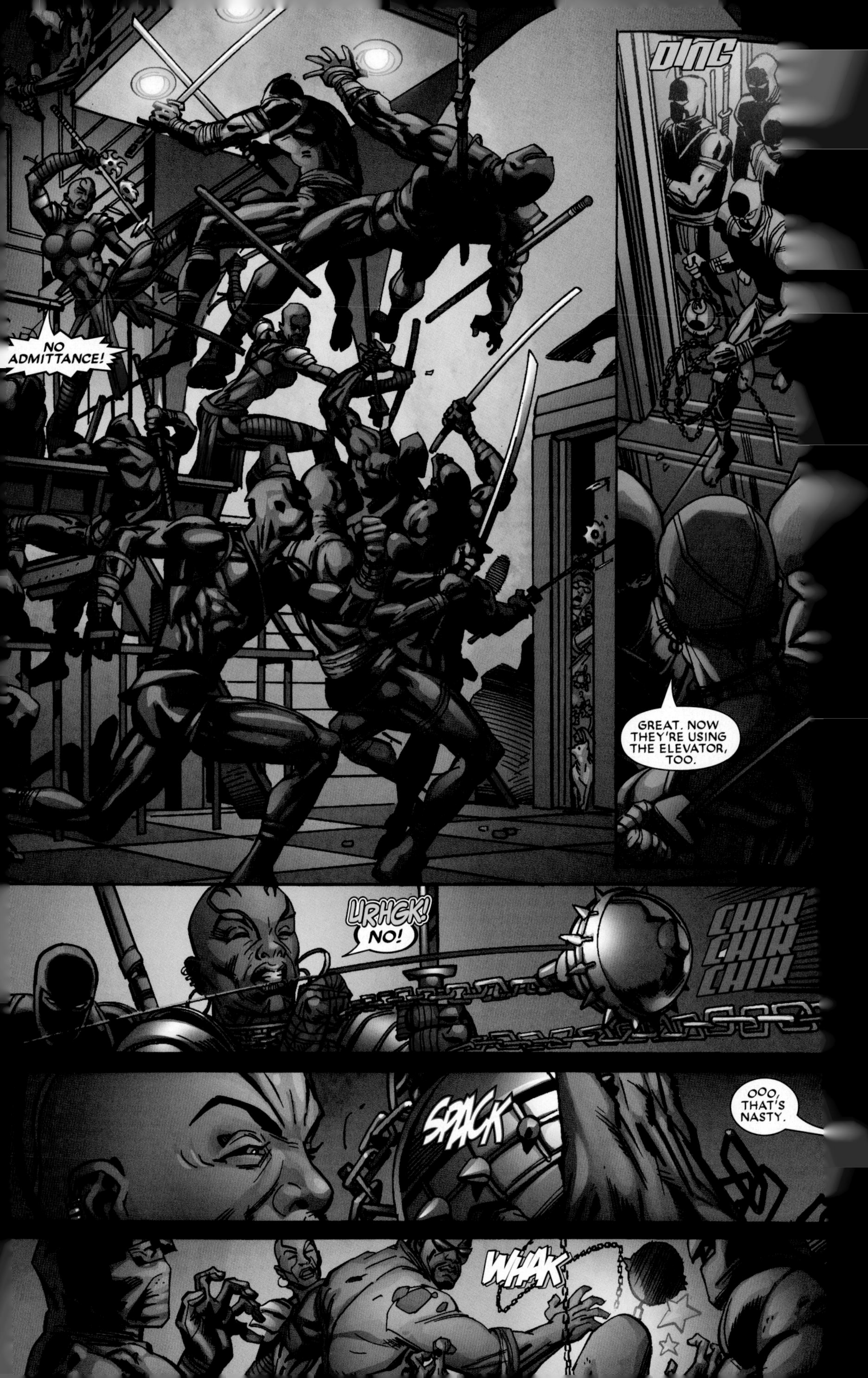
NO ADMITTANCE!
DING
GREAT. NOW THEY'RE USING THE ELEVATOR, TOO.
URHGK! NO!
CHIK CHIK CHIK
SPACK
OOO, THAT'S NASTY.
WHAK

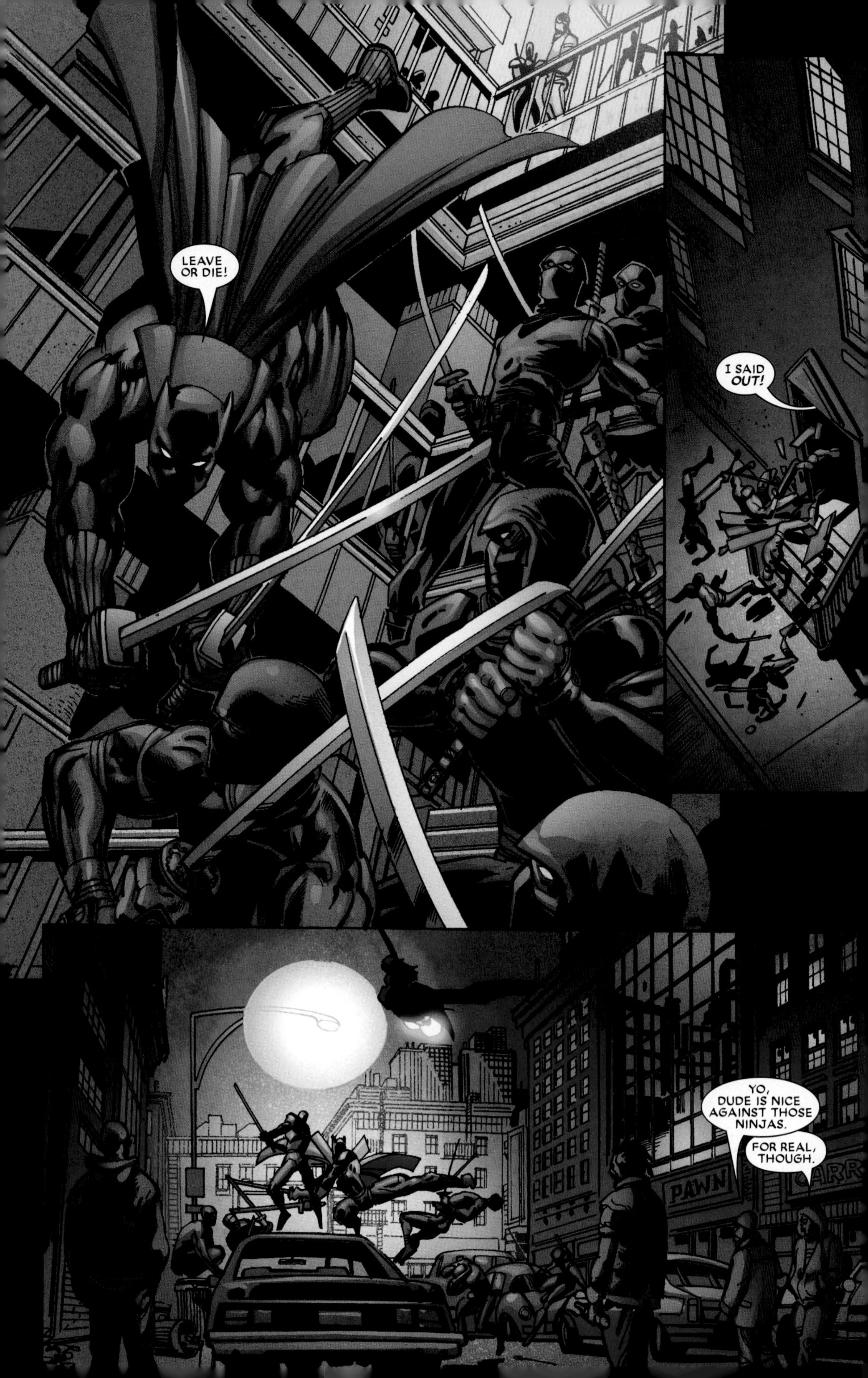
LEAVE OR DIE!
I SAID OUT!
YO, DUDE IS NICE AGAINST THOSE NINJAS.
FOR REAL, THOUGH.
PAWN

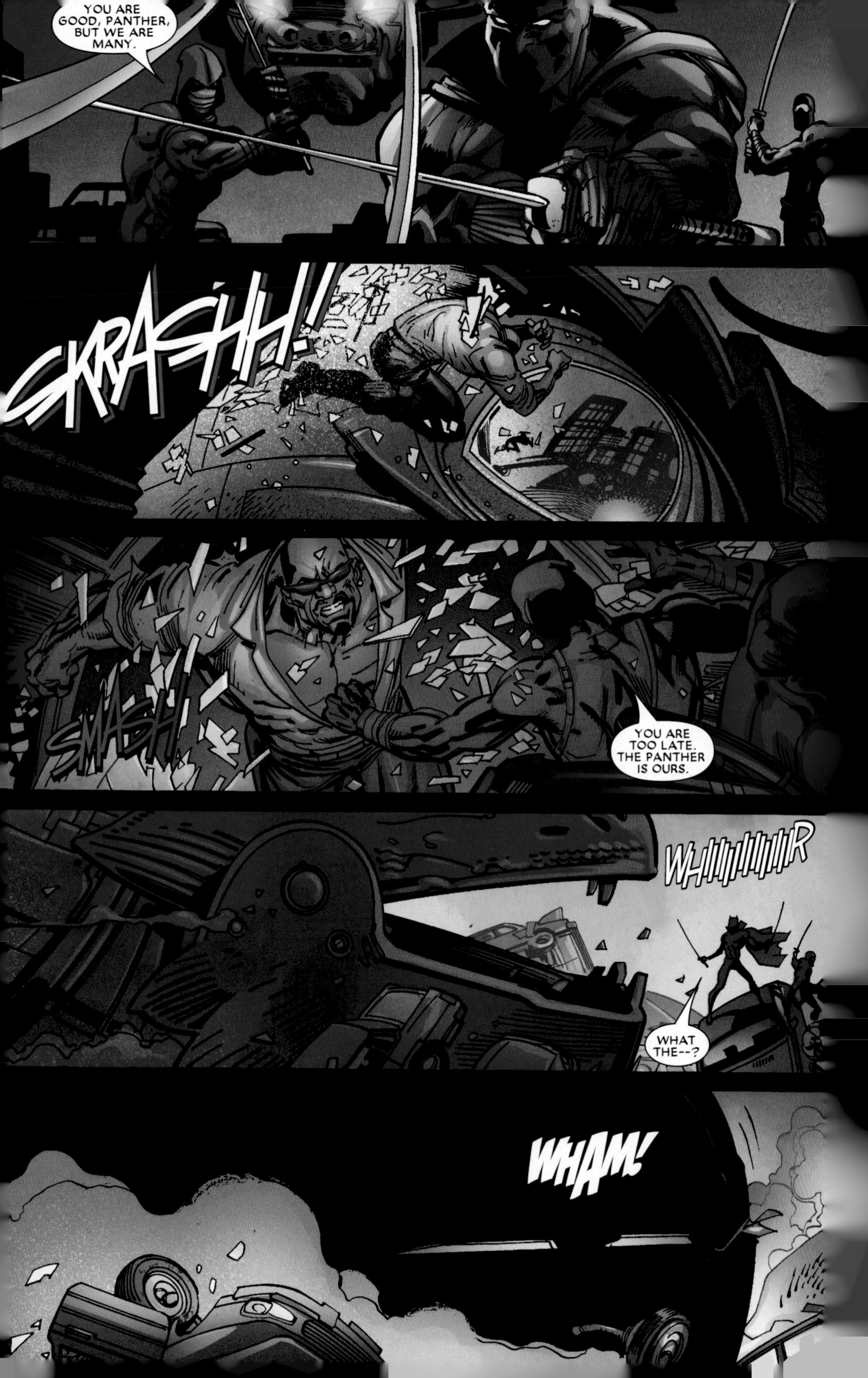
YOU ARE GOOD, PANTHER, BUT WE ARE MANY.
SKRASHH!
SMASH!
YOU ARE TOO LATE. THE PANTHER IS OURS.
WHIIIIIIIIIR
WHAT THE--?
WHAM!

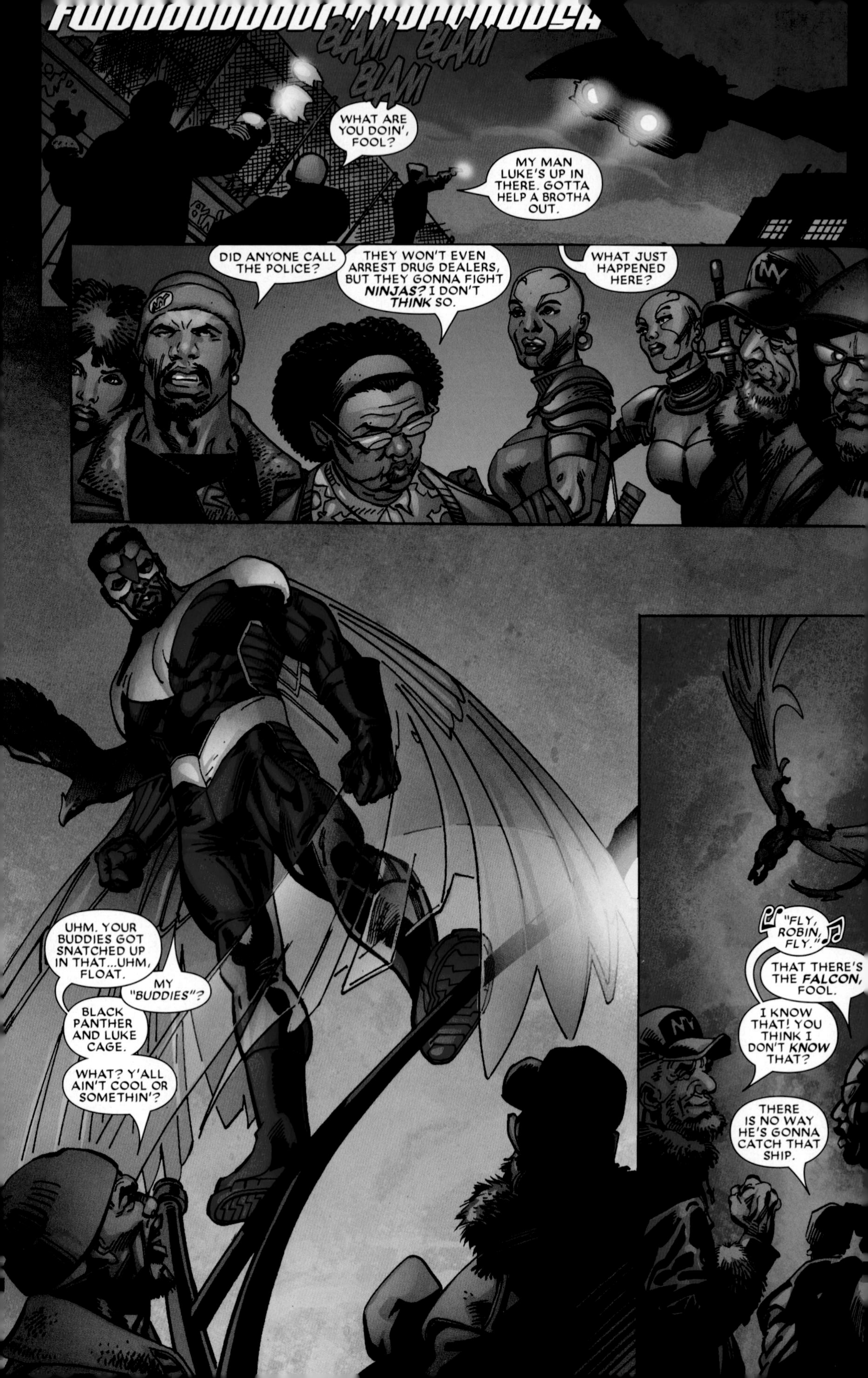
FWDDDDDDDDDOOOOOOOOSH
BLAM BLAM
BLAM
WHAT ARE YOU DOIN', FOOL?
MY MAN LUKE'S UP IN THERE. GOTTA HELP A BROTHA OUT.
DID ANYONE CALL THE POLICE?
THEY WON'T EVEN ARREST DRUG DEALERS, BUT THEY GONNA FIGHT NINJAS? I DON'T THINK SO.
WHAT JUST HAPPENED HERE?
UHM. YOUR BUDDIES GOT SNATCHED UP IN THAT...UHM, FLOAT.
MY "BUDDIES"?
BLACK PANTHER AND LUKE CAGE.
WHAT? Y'ALL AIN'T COOL OR SOMETHIN'?
"FLY, ROBIN, FLY."
THAT THERE'S THE FALCON, FOOL.
I KNOW THAT! YOU THINK I DON'T KNOW THAT?
THERE IS NO WAY HE'S GONNA CATCH THAT SHIP.

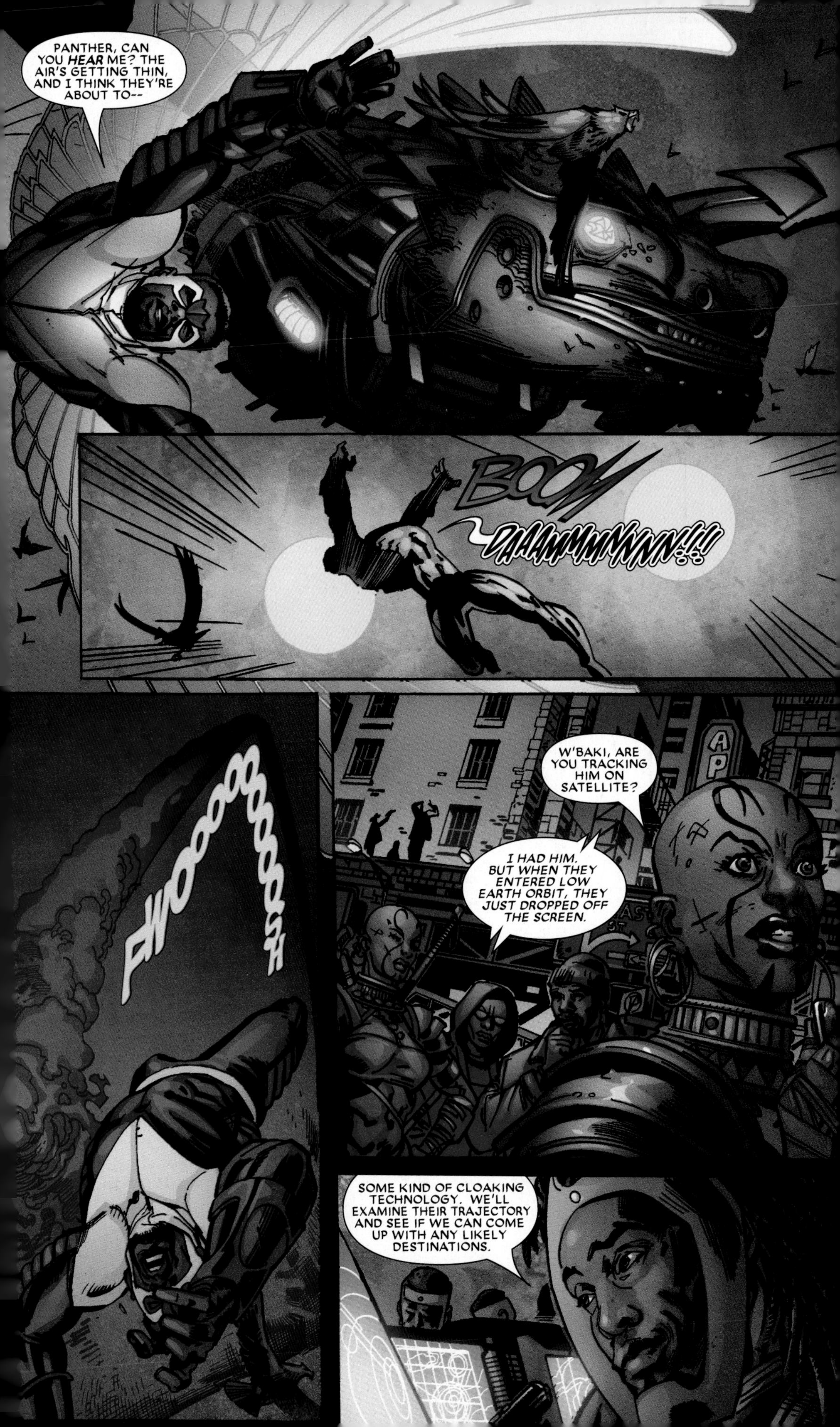
PANTHER, CAN YOU HEAR ME? THE AIR'S GETTING THIN, AND I THINK THEY'RE ABOUT TO--
BOOM
DAAAMMMNNNN!!!
FWOOOOOOOOOSH
W'BAKI, ARE YOU TRACKING HIM ON SATELLITE?
I HAD HIM. BUT WHEN THEY ENTERED LOW EARTH ORBIT, THEY JUST DROPPED OFF THE SCREEN.
SOME KIND OF CLOAKING TECHNOLOGY. WE'LL EXAMINE THEIR TRAJECTORY AND SEE IF WE CAN COME UP WITH ANY LIKELY DESTINATIONS.

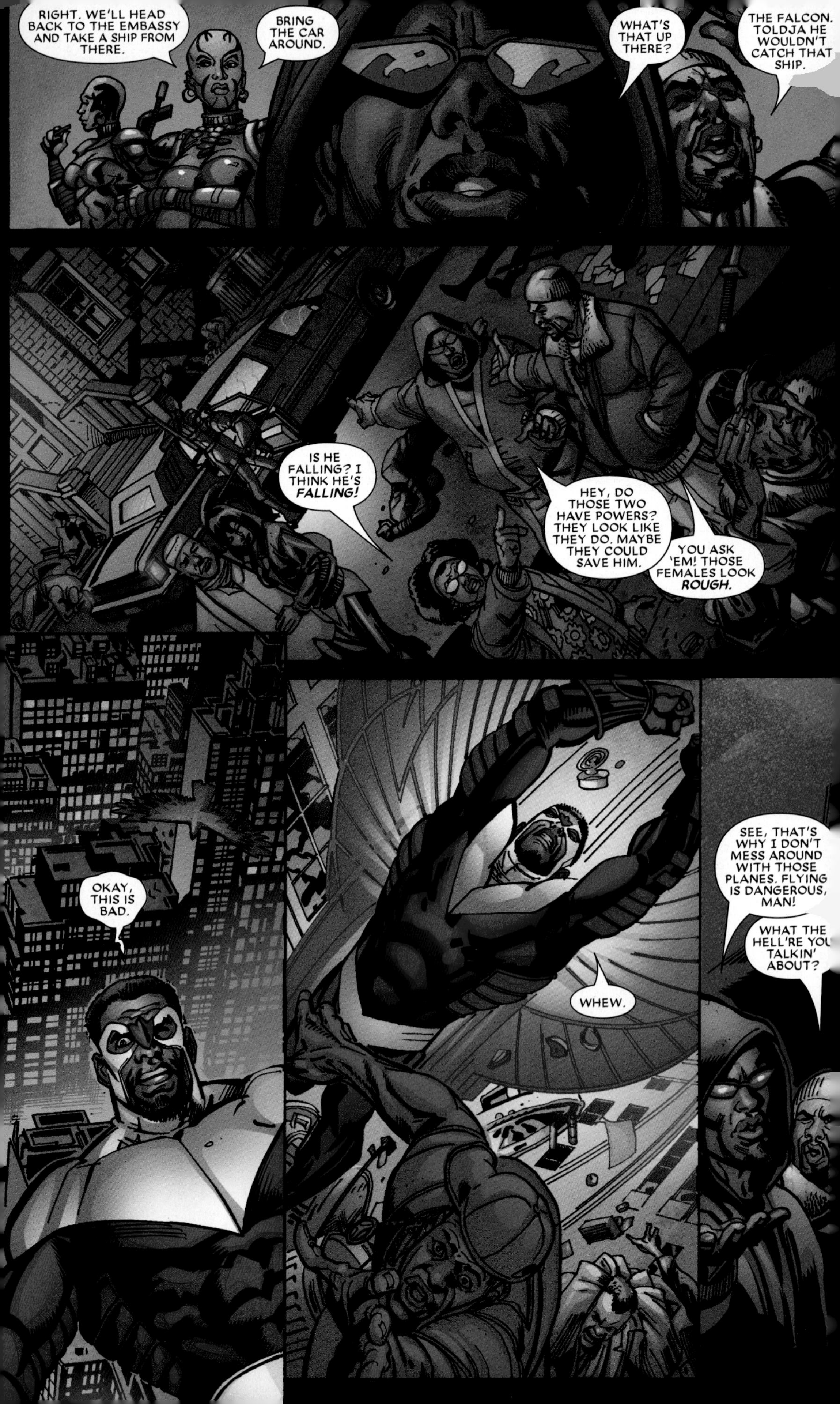

RIGHT. WE'LL HEAD BACK TO THE EMBASSY AND TAKE A SHIP FROM THERE.
BRING THE CAR AROUND.
WHAT'S THAT UP THERE?
THE FALCON. TOLDJA HE WOULDN'T CATCH THAT SHIP.
IS HE FALLING? I THINK HE'S *FALLING!*
HEY, DO THOSE TWO HAVE POWERS? THEY LOOK LIKE THEY DO. MAYBE THEY COULD SAVE HIM.
YOU ASK 'EM! THOSE FEMALES LOOK *ROUGH.*
OKAY, THIS IS BAD.
WHEW.
SEE, THAT'S WHY I DON'T MESS AROUND WITH THOSE PLANES. FLYING IS DANGEROUS, MAN!
WHAT THE HELL'RE YOU TALKIN' ABOUT?

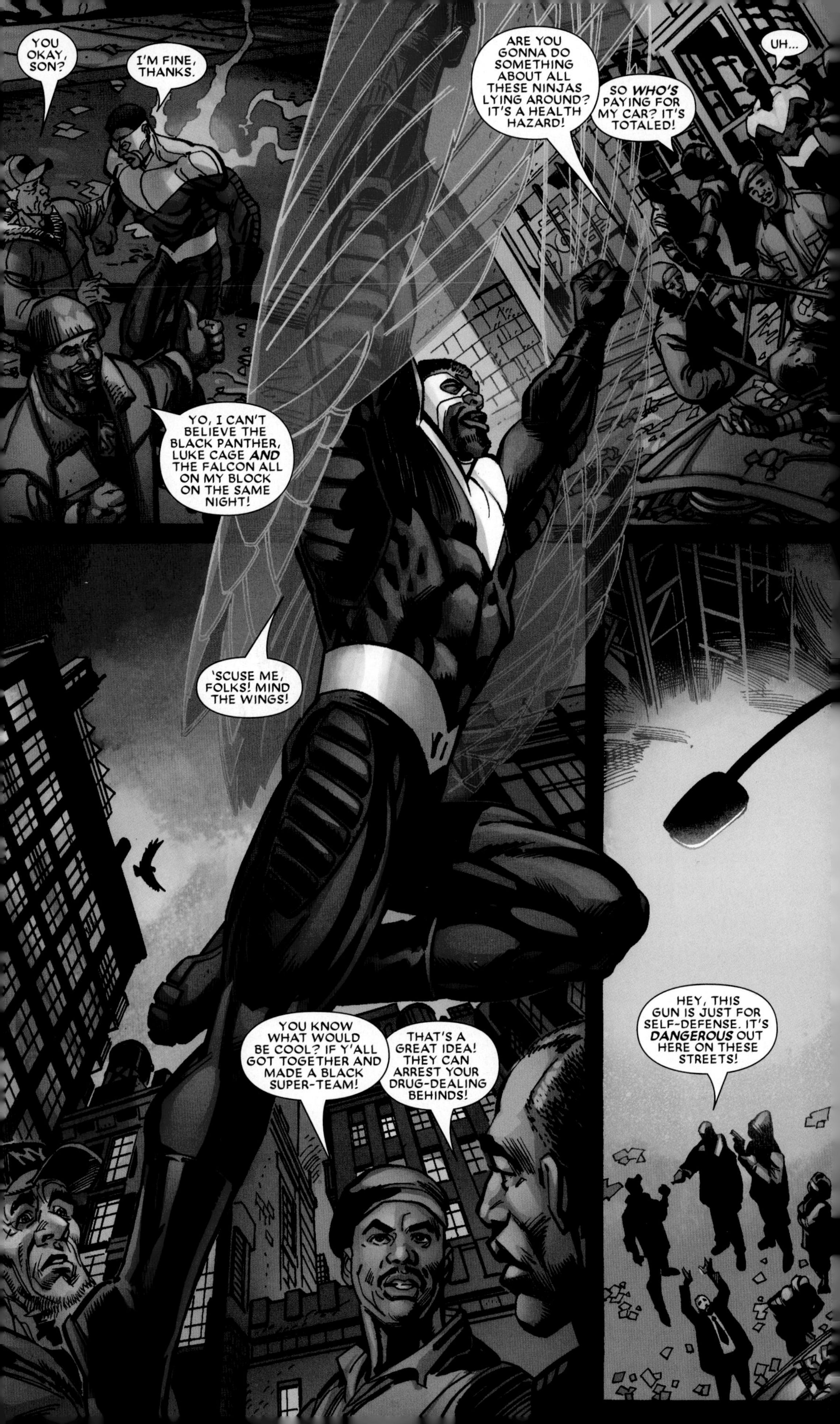
YOU OKAY, SON?
I'M FINE, THANKS.
ARE YOU GONNA DO SOMETHING ABOUT ALL THESE NINJAS LYING AROUND? IT'S A HEALTH HAZARD!
SO WHO'S PAYING FOR MY CAR? IT'S TOTALED!
UH...
YO, I CAN'T BELIEVE THE BLACK PANTHER, LUKE CAGE AND THE FALCON ALL ON MY BLOCK ON THE SAME NIGHT!
'SCUSE ME, FOLKS! MIND THE WINGS!
YOU KNOW WHAT WOULD BE COOL? IF Y'ALL GOT TOGETHER AND MADE A BLACK SUPER-TEAM!
THAT'S A GREAT IDEA! THEY CAN ARREST YOUR DRUG-DEALING BEHINDS!
HEY, THIS GUN IS JUST FOR SELF-DEFENSE. IT'S DANGEROUS OUT HERE ON THESE STREETS!

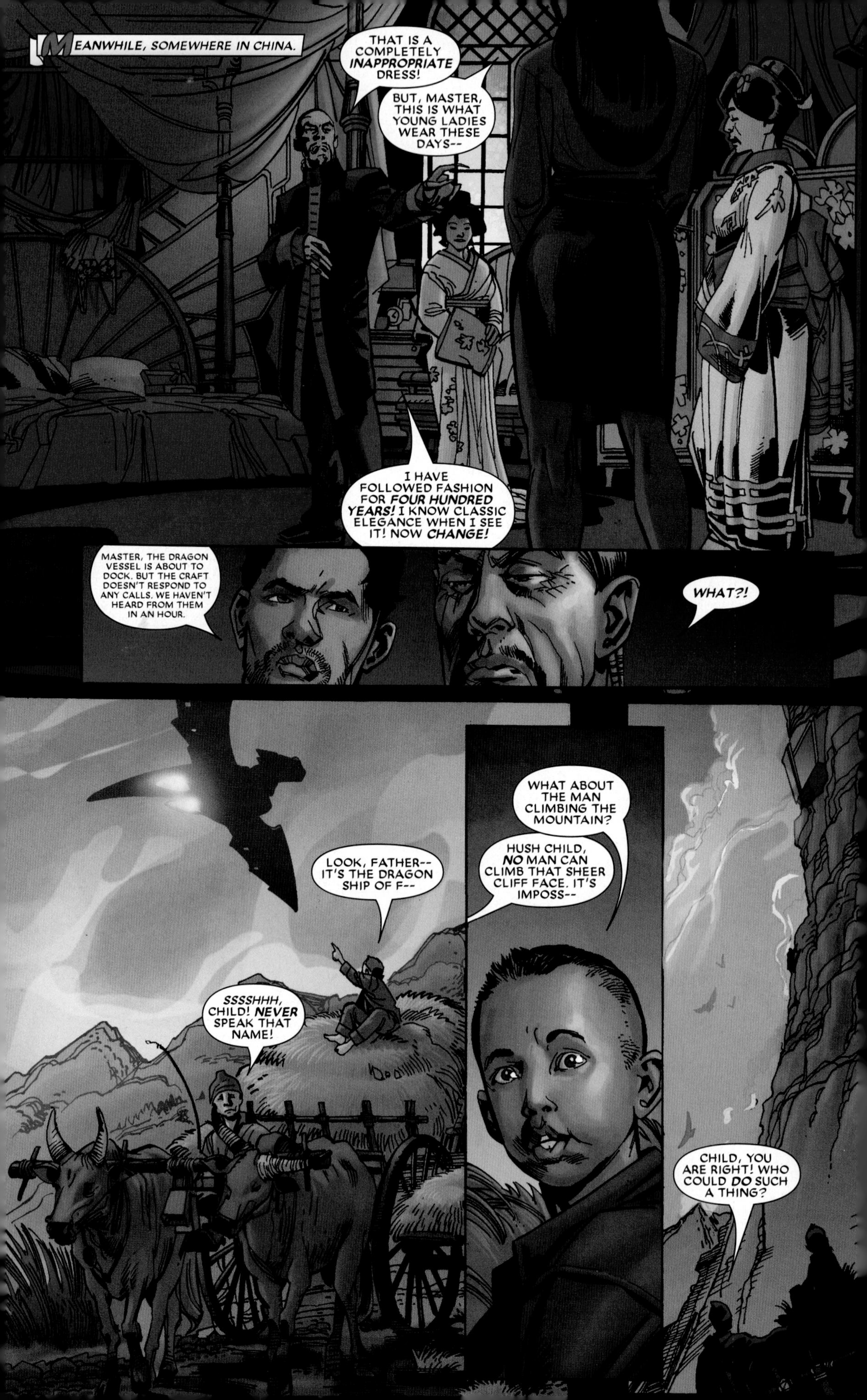
MEANWHILE, SOMEWHERE IN CHINA.
THAT IS A COMPLETELY INAPPROPRIATE DRESS!
BUT, MASTER, THIS IS WHAT YOUNG LADIES WEAR THESE DAYS--
I HAVE FOLLOWED FASHION FOR FOUR HUNDRED YEARS! I KNOW CLASSIC ELEGANCE WHEN I SEE IT! NOW CHANGE!
MASTER, THE DRAGON VESSEL IS ABOUT TO DOCK. BUT THE CRAFT DOESN'T RESPOND TO ANY CALLS. WE HAVEN'T HEARD FROM THEM IN AN HOUR.
WHAT?!
LOOK, FATHER-- IT'S THE DRAGON SHIP OF F--
SSSSHHH, CHILD! NEVER SPEAK THAT NAME!
WHAT ABOUT THE MAN CLIMBING THE MOUNTAIN?
HUSH CHILD, NO MAN CAN CLIMB THAT SHEER CLIFF FACE. IT'S IMPOSS--
CHILD, YOU ARE RIGHT! WHO COULD DO SUCH A THING?

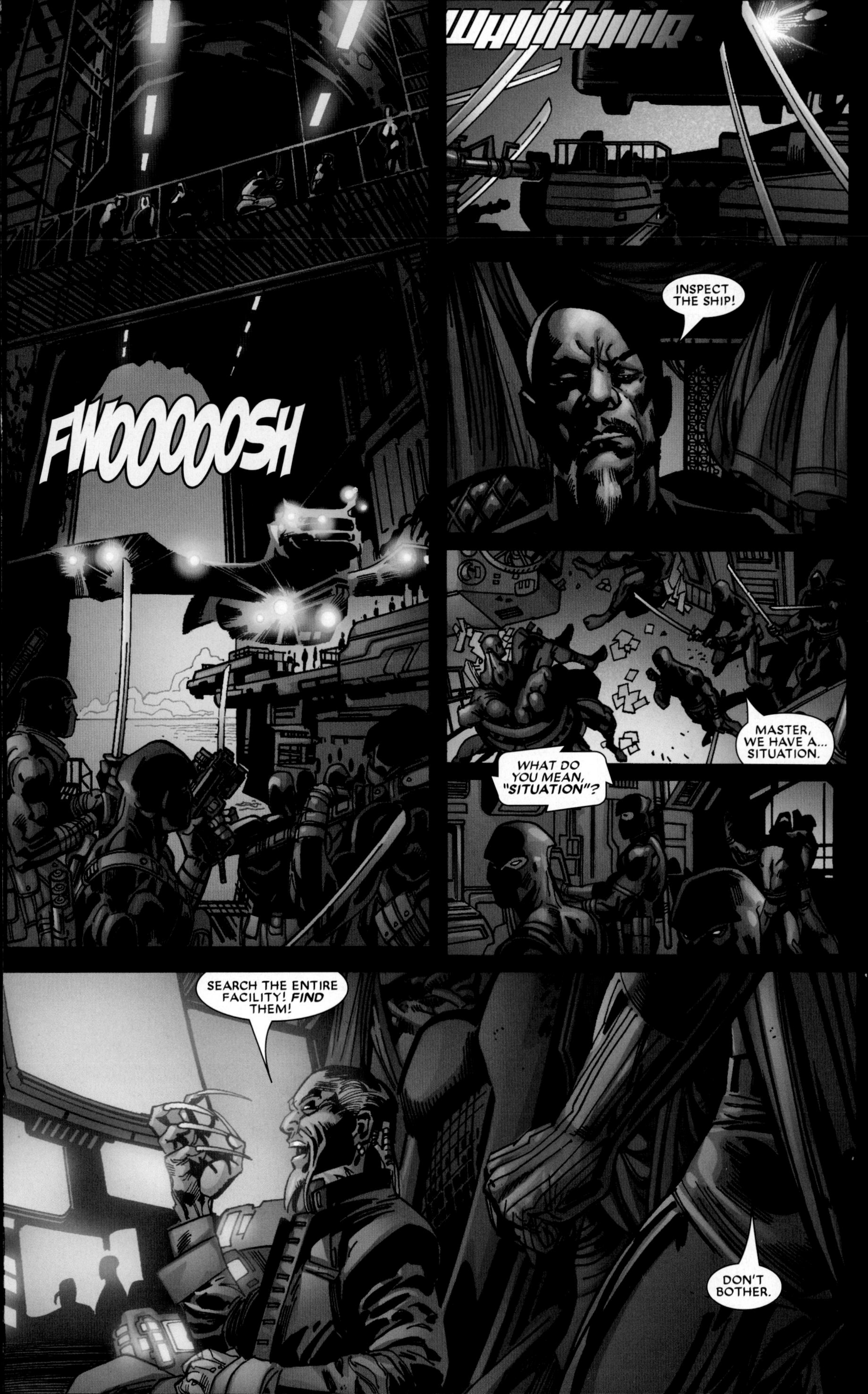
WHIIIIIIIR
FWOOOOOSH
INSPECT THE SHIP!
MASTER, WE HAVE A... SITUATION.
WHAT DO YOU MEAN, "SITUATION"?
SEARCH THE ENTIRE FACILITY! FIND THEM!
DON'T BOTHER.

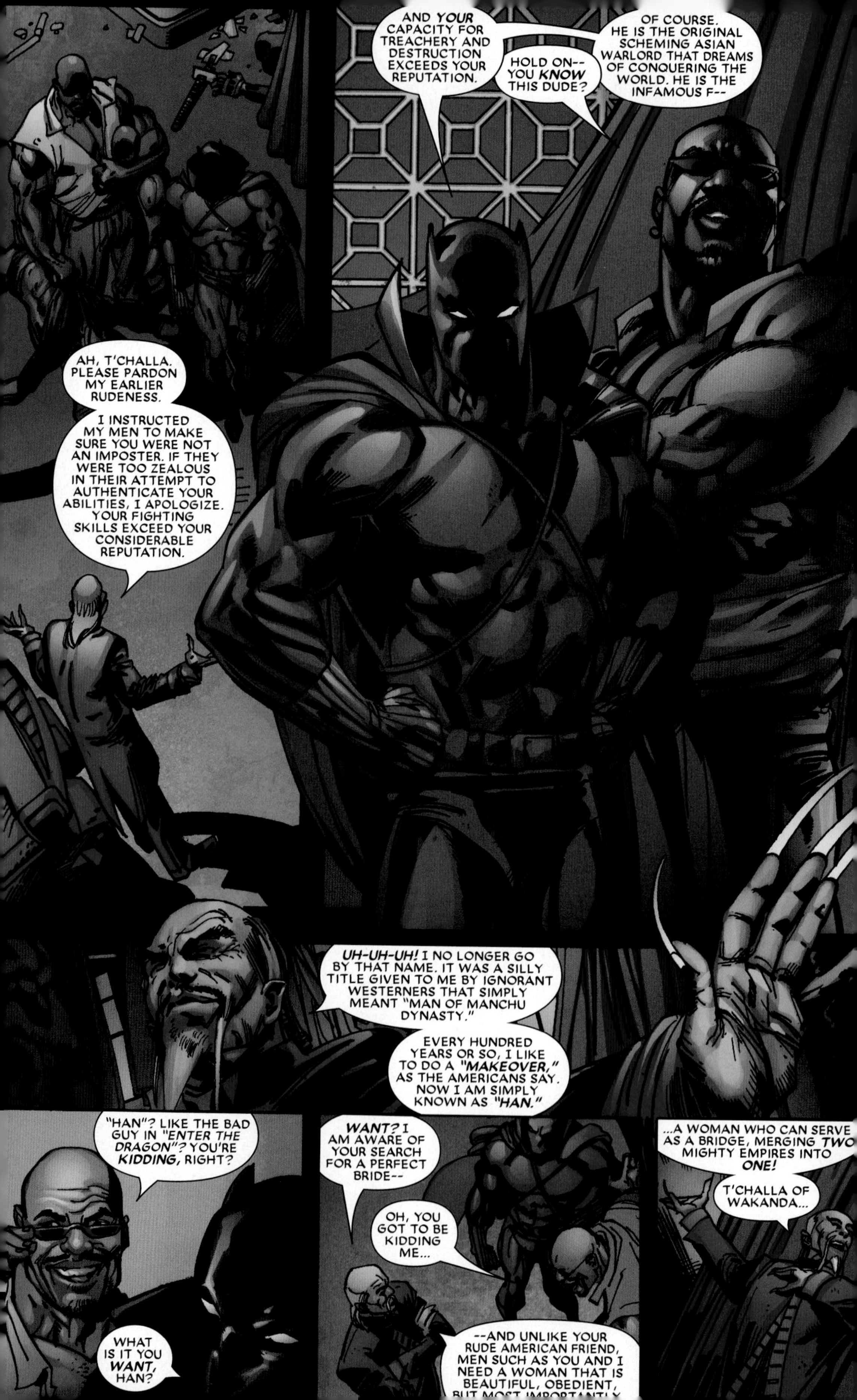
AH, T'CHALLA. PLEASE PARDON MY EARLIER RUDENESS.
I INSTRUCTED MY MEN TO MAKE SURE YOU WERE NOT AN IMPOSTER. IF THEY WERE TOO ZEALOUS IN THEIR ATTEMPT TO AUTHENTICATE YOUR ABILITIES, I APOLOGIZE. YOUR FIGHTING SKILLS EXCEED YOUR CONSIDERABLE REPUTATION.
AND *YOUR* CAPACITY FOR TREACHERY AND DESTRUCTION EXCEEDS YOUR REPUTATION.
HOLD ON-- YOU *KNOW* THIS DUDE?
OF COURSE. HE IS THE ORIGINAL SCHEMING ASIAN WARLORD THAT DREAMS OF CONQUERING THE WORLD. HE IS THE INFAMOUS F--
UH-UH-UH! I NO LONGER GO BY THAT NAME. IT WAS A SILLY TITLE GIVEN TO ME BY IGNORANT WESTERNERS THAT SIMPLY MEANT "MAN OF MANCHU DYNASTY."
EVERY HUNDRED YEARS OR SO, I LIKE TO DO A *"MAKEOVER,"* AS THE AMERICANS SAY. NOW I AM SIMPLY KNOWN AS *"HAN."*
"HAN"? LIKE THE BAD GUY IN *"ENTER THE DRAGON"*? YOU'RE *KIDDING,* RIGHT?
WHAT IS IT YOU *WANT,* HAN?
WANT? I AM AWARE OF YOUR SEARCH FOR A PERFECT BRIDE--
OH, YOU GOT TO BE KIDDING ME...
--AND UNLIKE YOUR RUDE AMERICAN FRIEND, MEN SUCH AS YOU AND I NEED A WOMAN THAT IS BEAUTIFUL, OBEDIENT,
...A WOMAN WHO CAN SERVE AS A BRIDGE, MERGING *TWO* MIGHTY EMPIRES INTO *ONE!*
T'CHALLA OF WAKANDA...

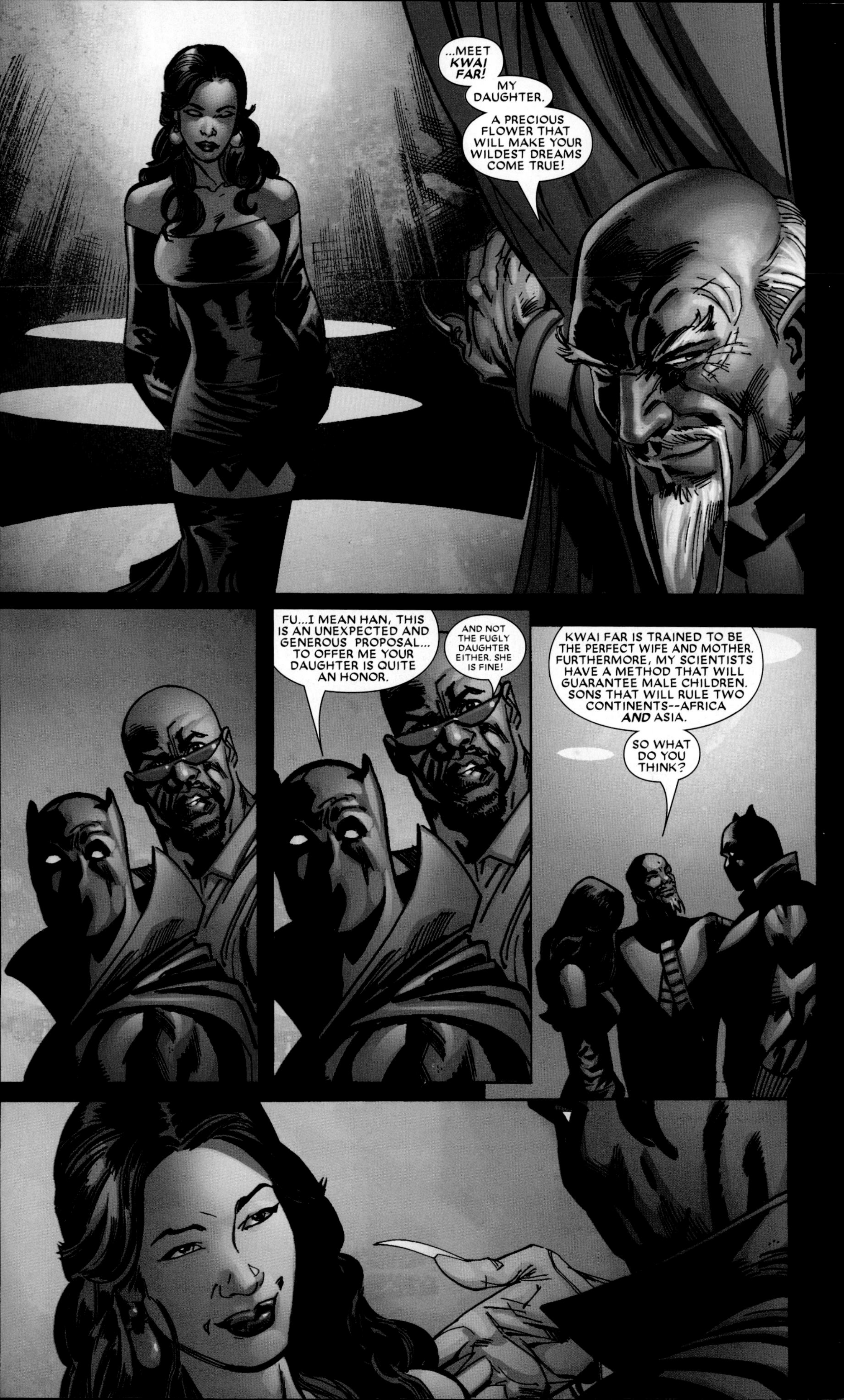
...MEET *KWAI FAR!*
MY DAUGHTER.
A PRECIOUS FLOWER THAT WILL MAKE YOUR WILDEST DREAMS COME TRUE!
FU...I MEAN HAN, THIS IS AN UNEXPECTED AND GENEROUS PROPOSAL... TO OFFER ME YOUR DAUGHTER IS QUITE AN HONOR.
AND NOT THE FUGLY DAUGHTER EITHER. SHE IS FINE!
KWAI FAR IS TRAINED TO BE THE PERFECT WIFE AND MOTHER. FURTHERMORE, MY SCIENTISTS HAVE A METHOD THAT WILL GUARANTEE MALE CHILDREN. SONS THAT WILL RULE TWO CONTINENTS--AFRICA *AND* ASIA.
SO WHAT DO YOU THINK?

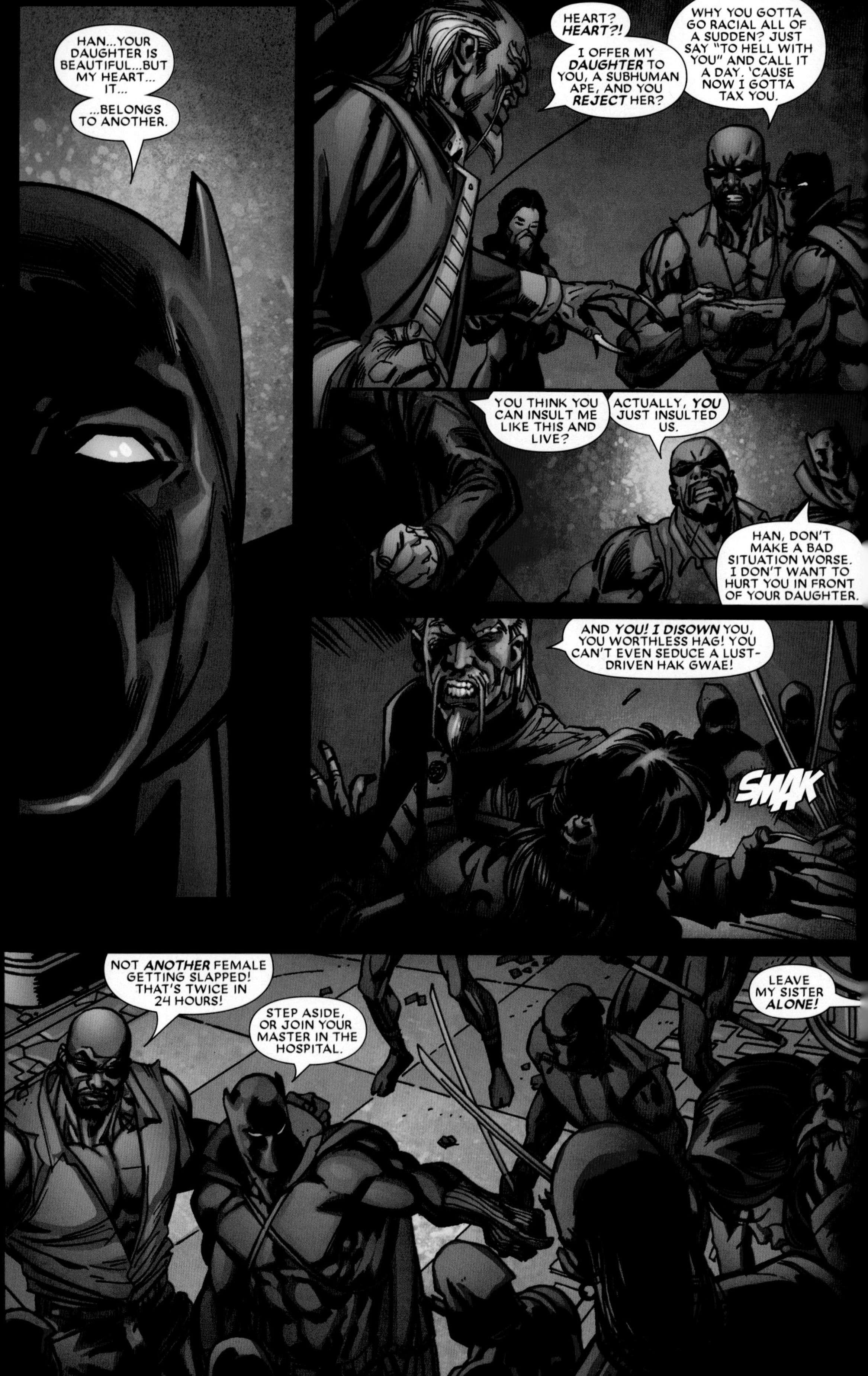

HAN...YOUR DAUGHTER IS BEAUTIFUL...BUT MY HEART... IT...
...BELONGS TO ANOTHER.
HEART? HEART?!
I OFFER MY DAUGHTER TO YOU, A SUBHUMAN APE, AND YOU REJECT HER?
WHY YOU GOTTA GO RACIAL ALL OF A SUDDEN? JUST SAY "TO HELL WITH YOU" AND CALL IT A DAY. 'CAUSE NOW I GOTTA TAX YOU.
YOU THINK YOU CAN INSULT ME LIKE THIS AND LIVE?
ACTUALLY, YOU JUST INSULTED US.
HAN, DON'T MAKE A BAD SITUATION WORSE. I DON'T WANT TO HURT YOU IN FRONT OF YOUR DAUGHTER.
AND YOU! I DISOWN YOU, YOU WORTHLESS HAG! YOU CAN'T EVEN SEDUCE A LUST-DRIVEN HAK GWAE!
SMAK
NOT ANOTHER FEMALE GETTING SLAPPED! THAT'S TWICE IN 24 HOURS!
STEP ASIDE, OR JOIN YOUR MASTER IN THE HOSPITAL.
LEAVE MY SISTER ALONE!

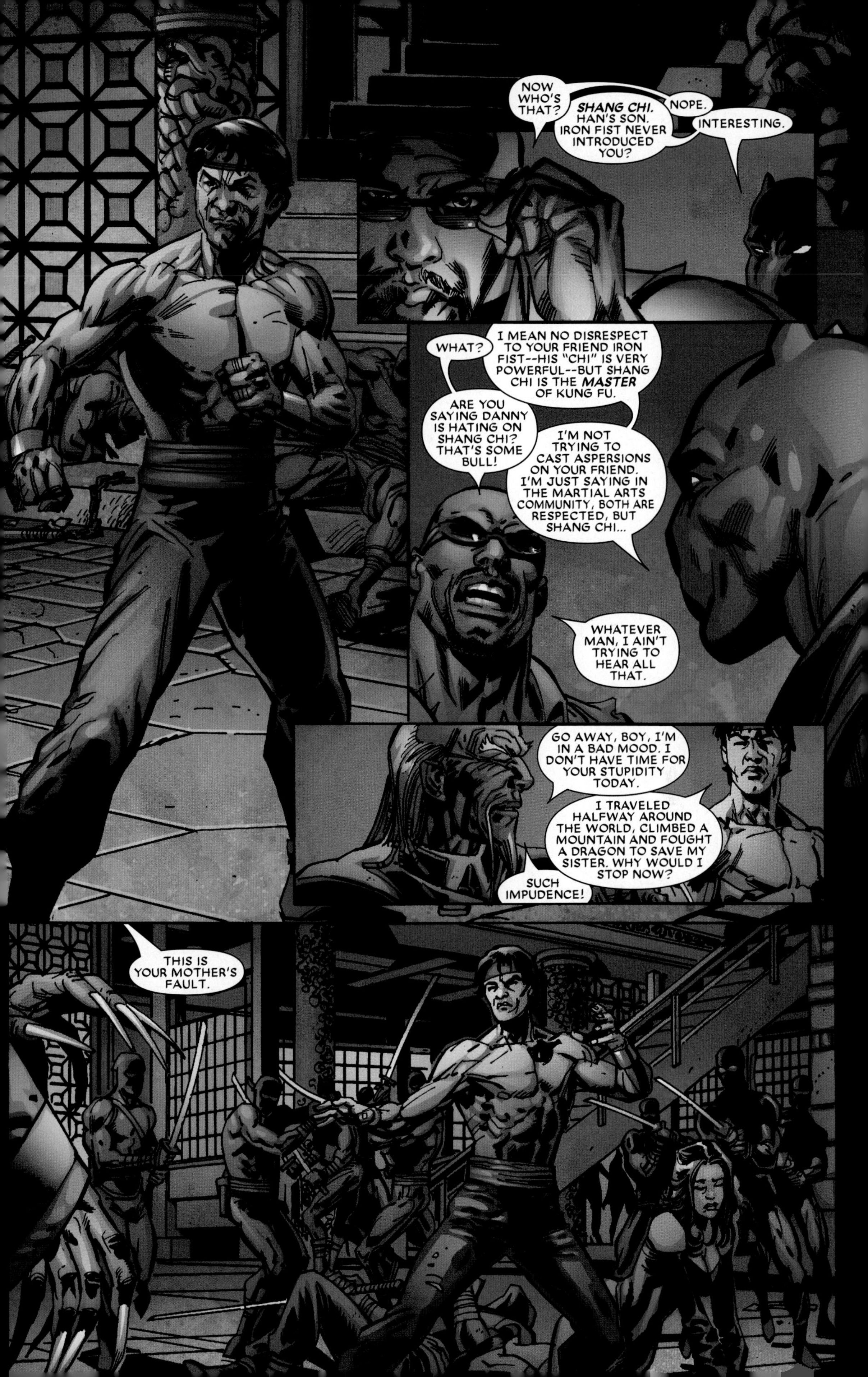
NOW WHO'S THAT?
SHANG CHI. HAN'S SON. IRON FIST NEVER INTRODUCED YOU?
NOPE.
INTERESTING.
WHAT?
I MEAN NO DISRESPECT TO YOUR FRIEND IRON FIST--HIS "CHI" IS VERY POWERFUL--BUT SHANG CHI IS THE MASTER OF KUNG FU.
ARE YOU SAYING DANNY IS HATING ON SHANG CHI? THAT'S SOME BULL!
I'M NOT TRYING TO CAST ASPERSIONS ON YOUR FRIEND. I'M JUST SAYING IN THE MARTIAL ARTS COMMUNITY, BOTH ARE RESPECTED, BUT SHANG CHI...
WHATEVER MAN, I AIN'T TRYING TO HEAR ALL THAT.
GO AWAY, BOY, I'M IN A BAD MOOD. I DON'T HAVE TIME FOR YOUR STUPIDITY TODAY.
I TRAVELED HALFWAY AROUND THE WORLD, CLIMBED A MOUNTAIN AND FOUGHT A DRAGON TO SAVE MY SISTER. WHY WOULD I STOP NOW?
SUCH IMPUDENCE!
THIS IS YOUR MOTHER'S FAULT.

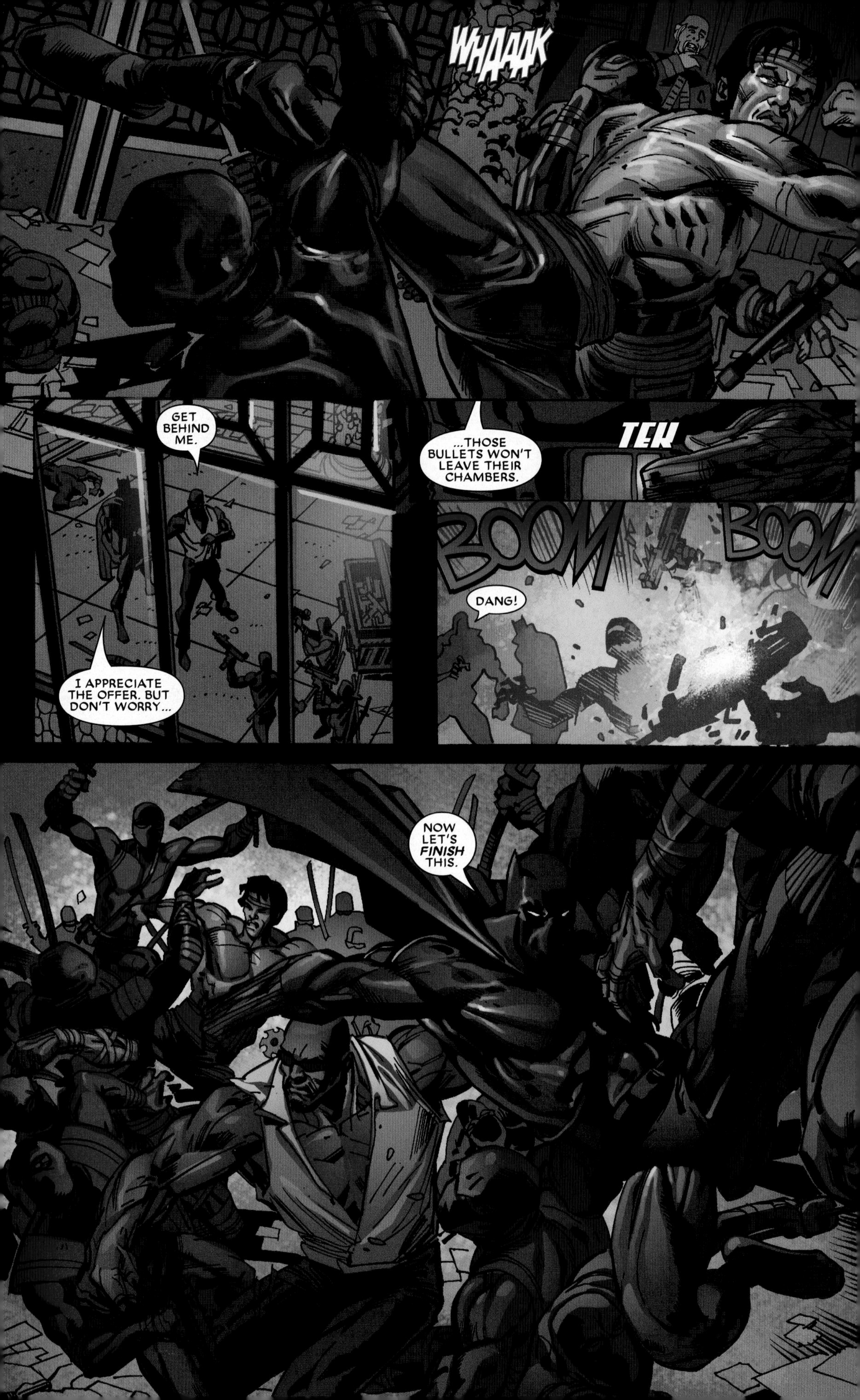
WHAAAK
GET BEHIND ME.
I APPRECIATE THE OFFER. BUT DON'T WORRY...
...THOSE BULLETS WON'T LEAVE THEIR CHAMBERS.
TEK
BOOM
BOOM
DANG!
NOW LET'S FINISH THIS.

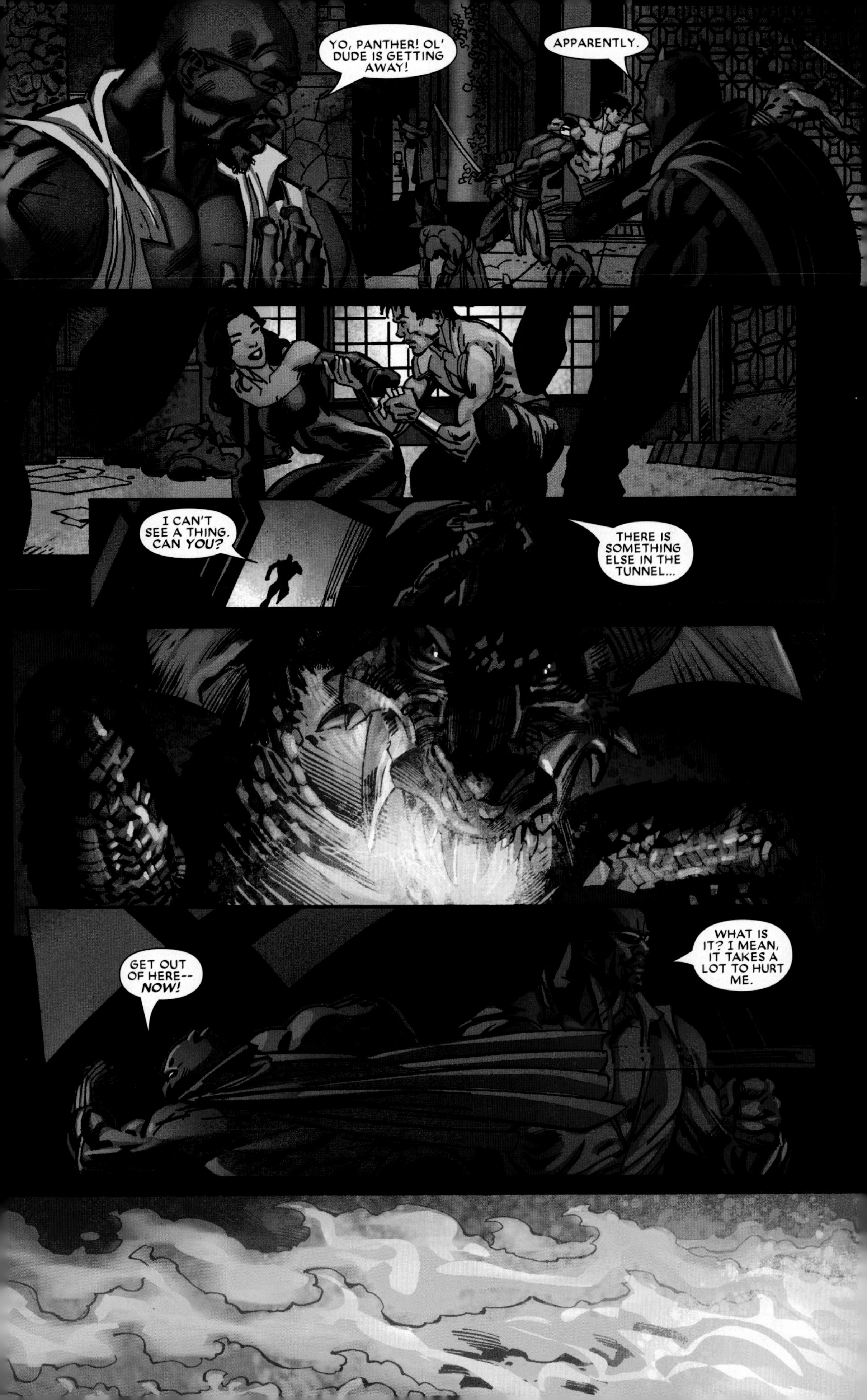
YO, PANTHER! OL' DUDE IS GETTING AWAY!
APPARENTLY.
I CAN'T SEE A THING. CAN YOU?
THERE IS SOMETHING ELSE IN THE TUNNEL...
GET OUT OF HERE-- NOW!
WHAT IS IT? I MEAN, IT TAKES A LOT TO HURT ME.

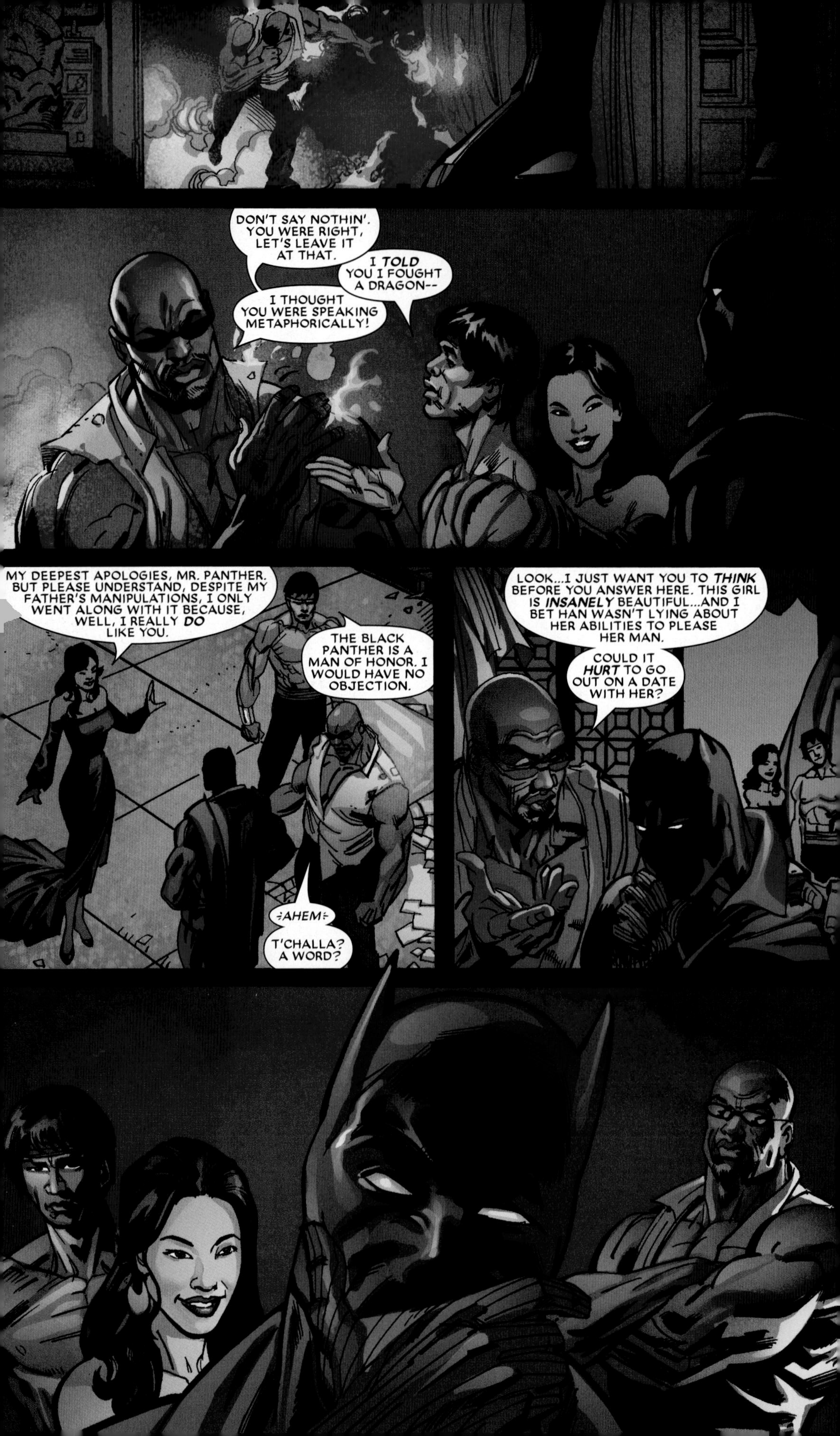
DON'T SAY NOTHIN'. YOU WERE RIGHT, LET'S LEAVE IT AT THAT.
I THOUGHT YOU WERE SPEAKING METAPHORICALLY!
I TOLD YOU I FOUGHT A DRAGON--
MY DEEPEST APOLOGIES, MR. PANTHER. BUT PLEASE UNDERSTAND, DESPITE MY FATHER'S MANIPULATIONS, I ONLY WENT ALONG WITH IT BECAUSE, WELL, I REALLY DO LIKE YOU.
THE BLACK PANTHER IS A MAN OF HONOR. I WOULD HAVE NO OBJECTION.
AHEM
T'CHALLA? A WORD?
LOOK...I JUST WANT YOU TO THINK BEFORE YOU ANSWER HERE. THIS GIRL IS INSANELY BEAUTIFUL...AND I BET HAN WASN'T LYING ABOUT HER ABILITIES TO PLEASE HER MAN.
COULD IT HURT TO GO OUT ON A DATE WITH HER?

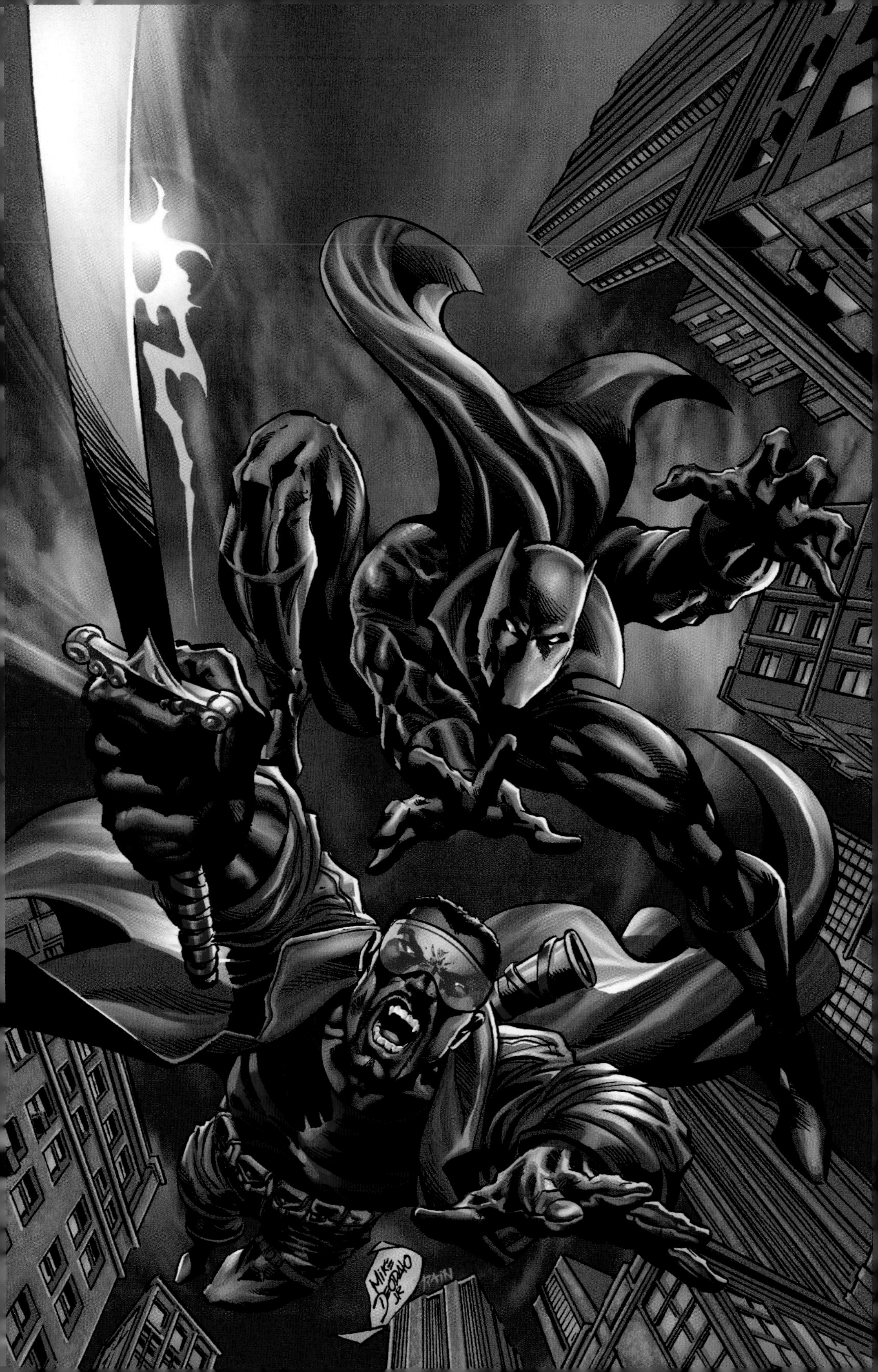

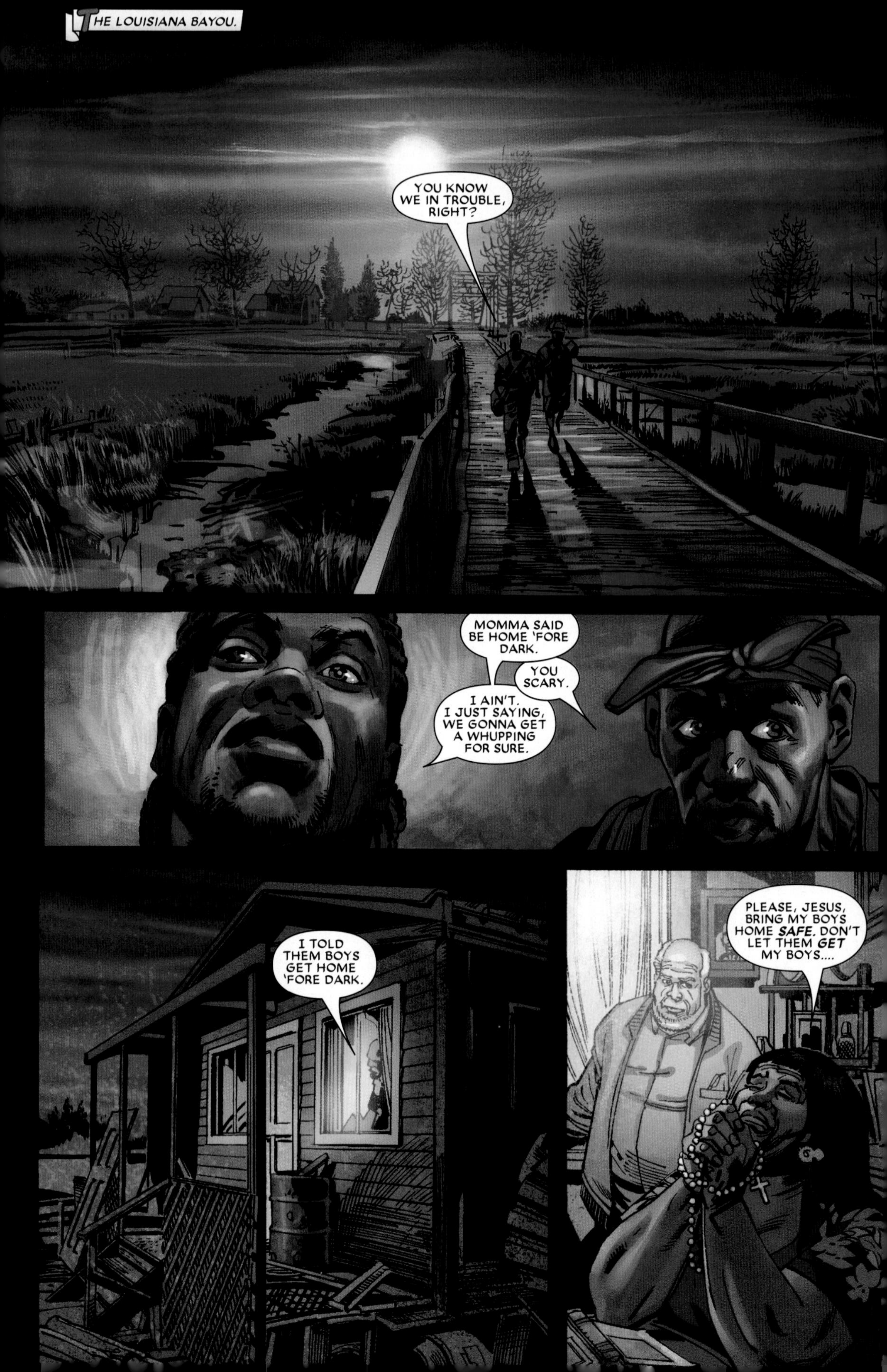
THE LOUISIANA BAYOU.
YOU KNOW WE IN TROUBLE, RIGHT?
MOMMA SAID BE HOME 'FORE DARK.
YOU SCARY.
I AIN'T. I JUST SAYING, WE GONNA GET A WHUPPING FOR SURE.
I TOLD THEM BOYS GET HOME 'FORE DARK.
PLEASE, JESUS, BRING MY BOYS HOME SAFE. DON'T LET THEM GET MY BOYS....

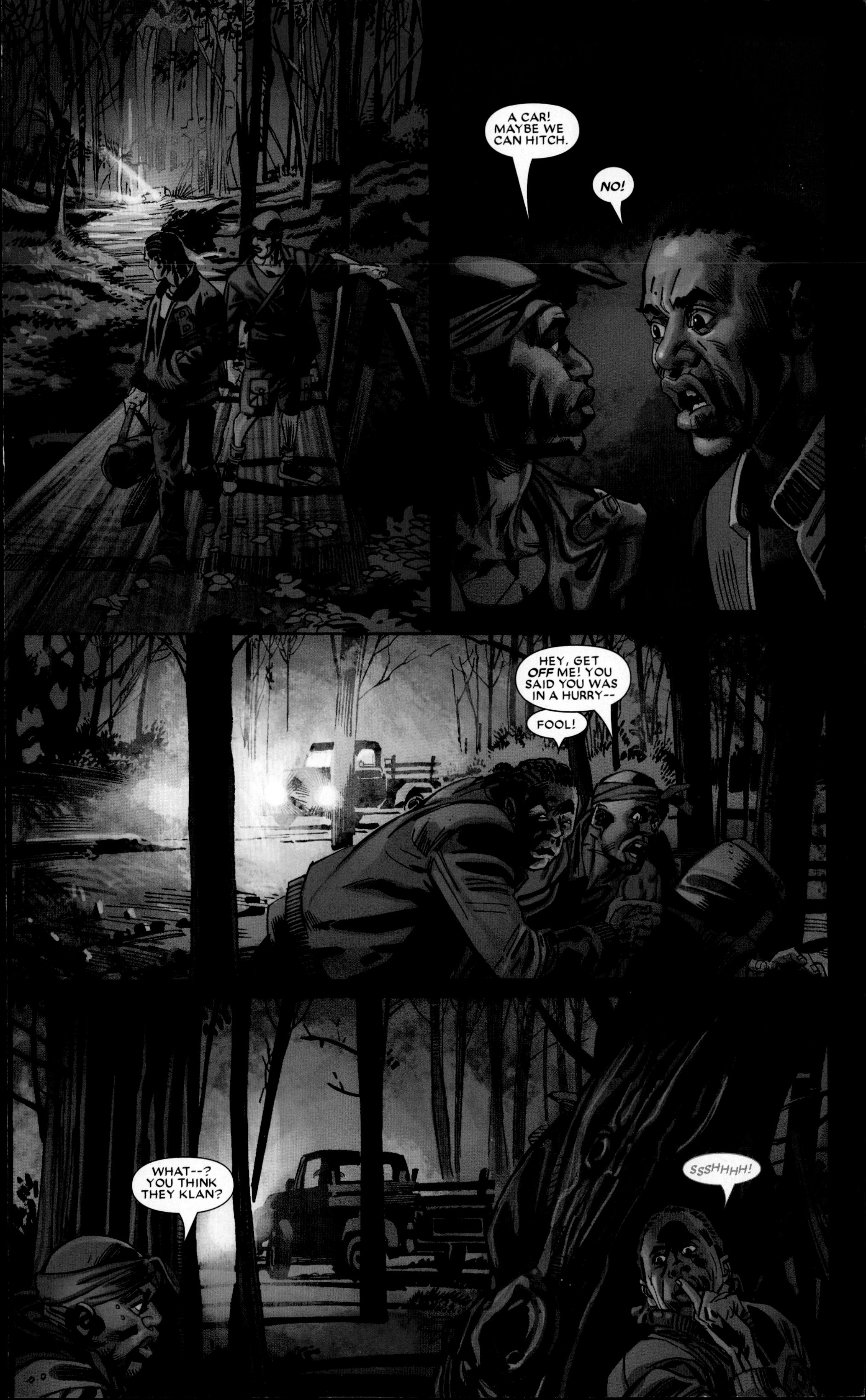
A CAR! MAYBE WE CAN HITCH.
NO!
HEY, GET OFF ME! YOU SAID YOU WAS IN A HURRY--
FOOL!
WHAT--? YOU THINK THEY KLAN?
SSSHHHH!

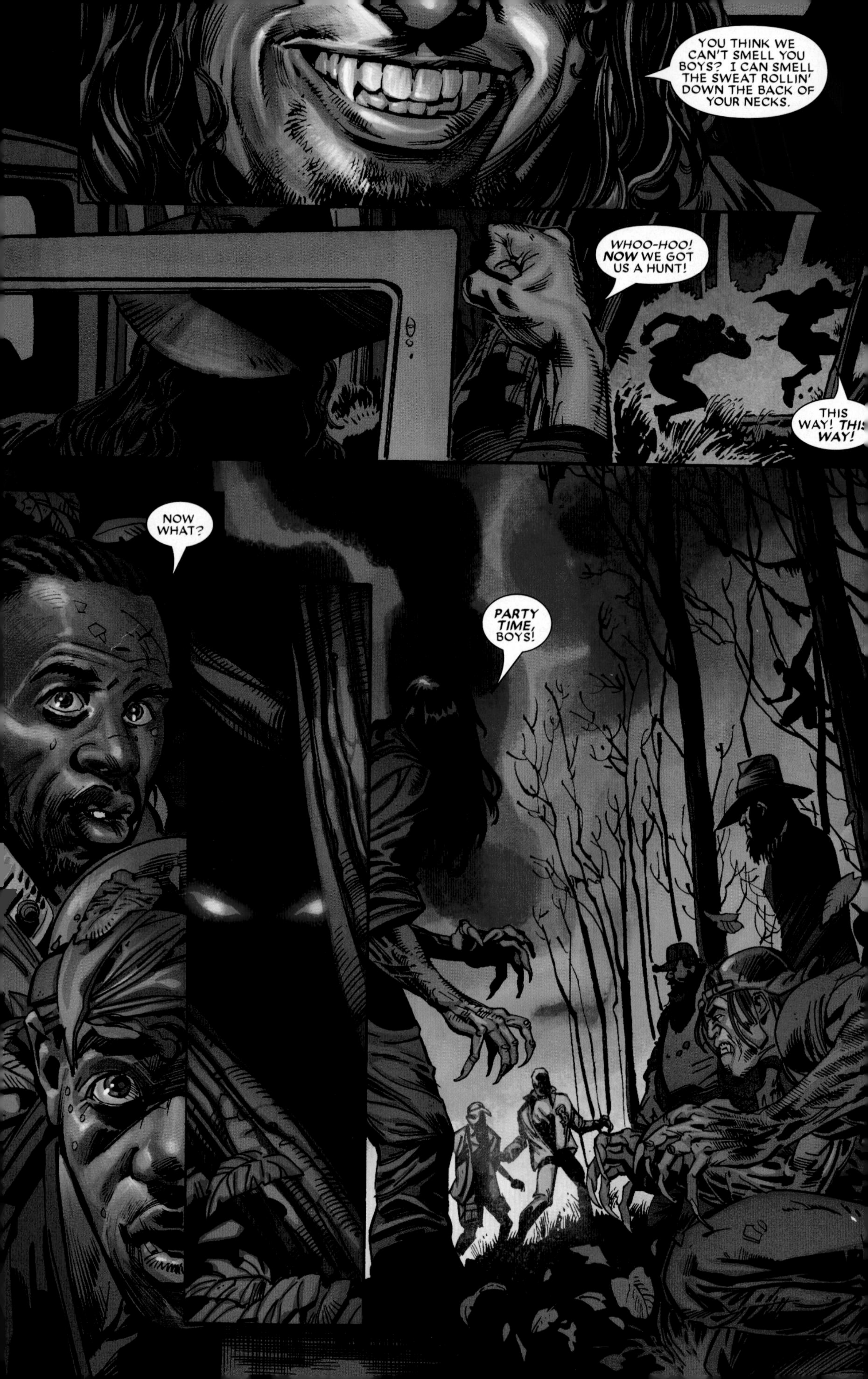

YOU THINK WE CAN'T SMELL YOU BOYS? I CAN SMELL THE SWEAT ROLLIN' DOWN THE BACK OF YOUR NECKS.
WHOO-HOO! NOW WE GOT US A HUNT!
THIS WAY! THIS WAY!
NOW WHAT?
PARTY TIME, BOYS!

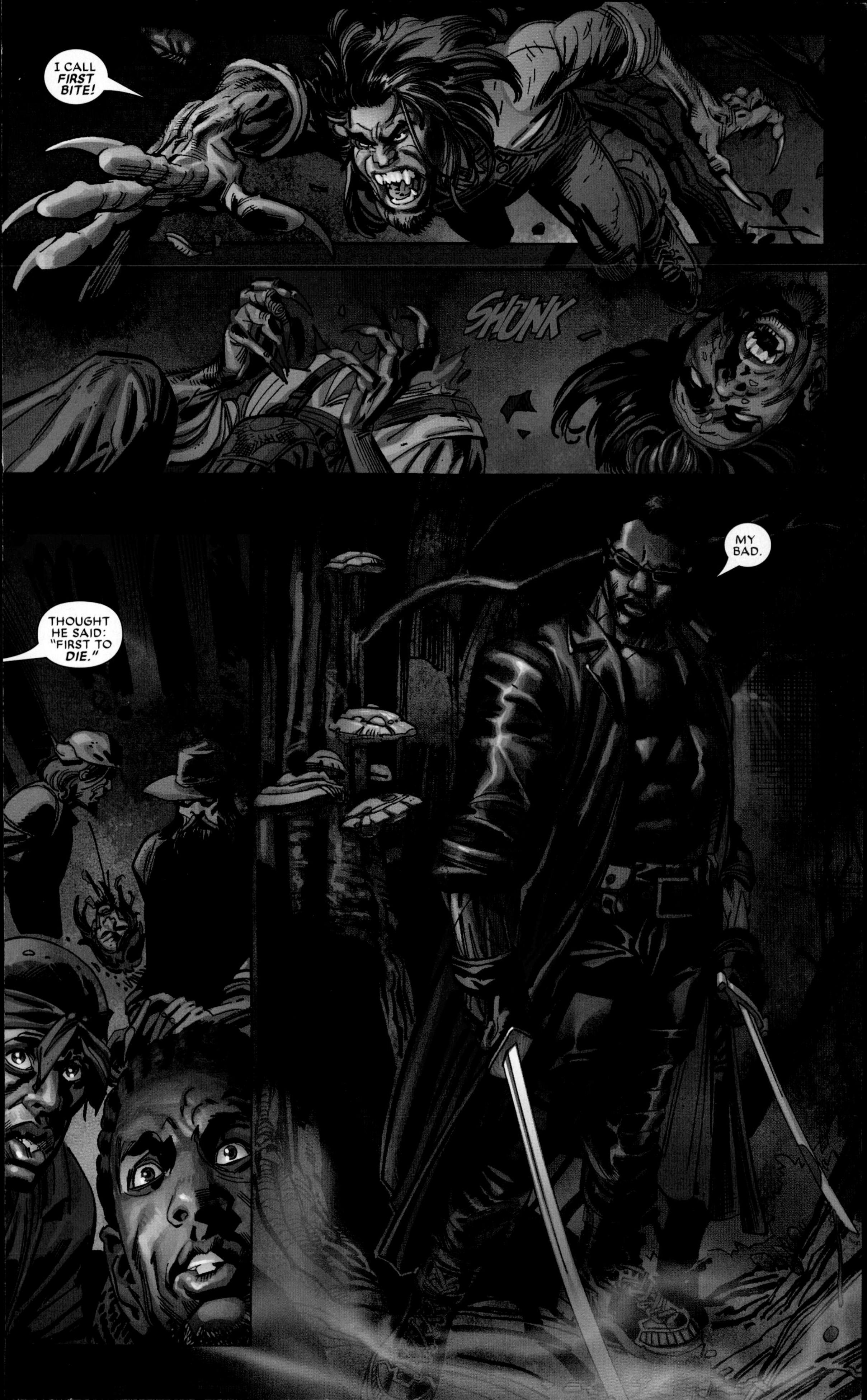
I CALL FIRST BITE!
SHUNK
MY BAD.
THOUGHT HE SAID: "FIRST TO DIE."

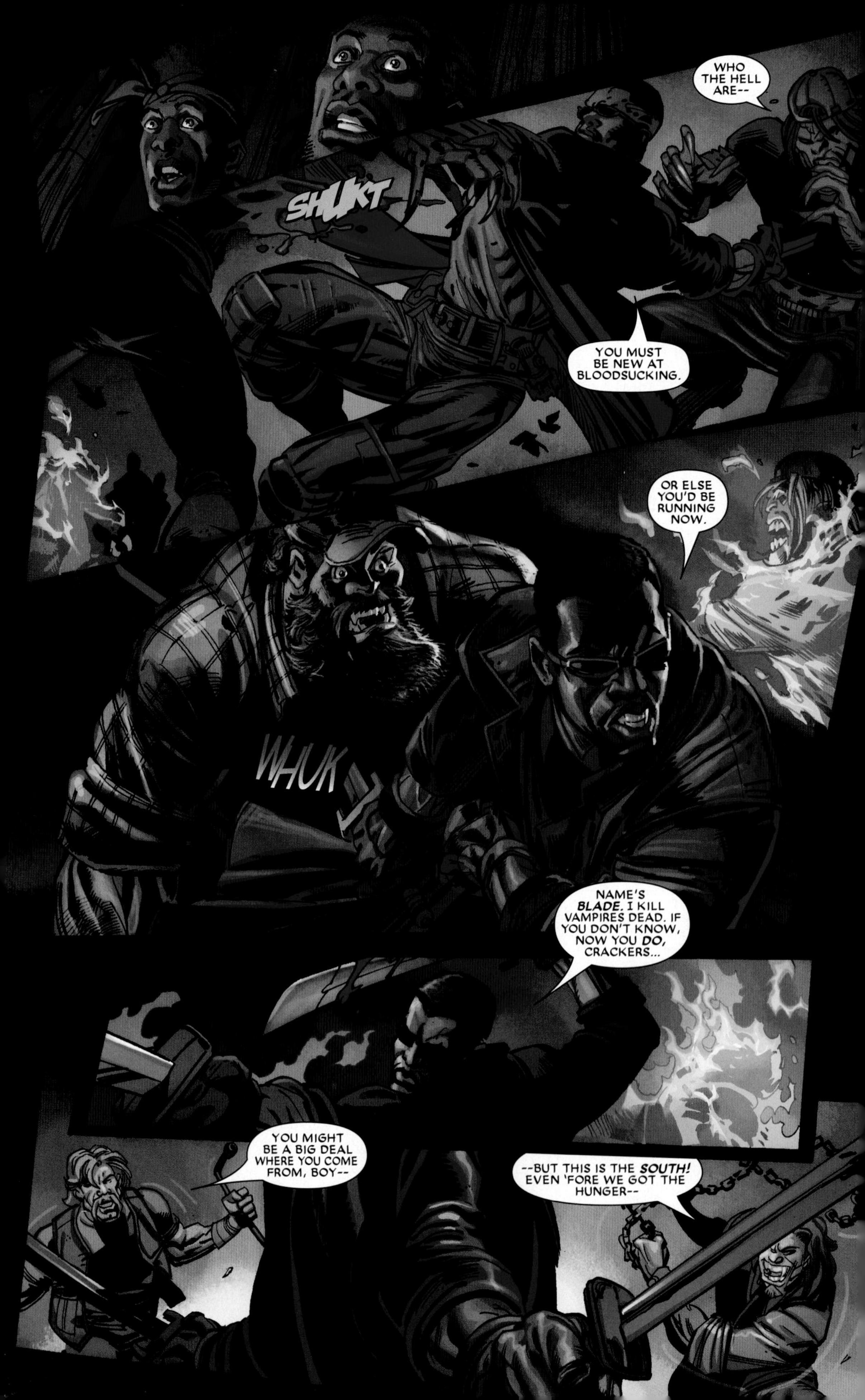
WHO THE HELL ARE--
SHUKT
YOU MUST BE NEW AT BLOODSUCKING.
OR ELSE YOU'D BE RUNNING NOW.
WHUK
NAME'S BLADE. I KILL VAMPIRES DEAD. IF YOU DON'T KNOW, NOW YOU DO, CRACKERS...
YOU MIGHT BE A BIG DEAL WHERE YOU COME FROM, BOY--
--BUT THIS IS THE SOUTH! EVEN 'FORE WE GOT THE HUNGER--

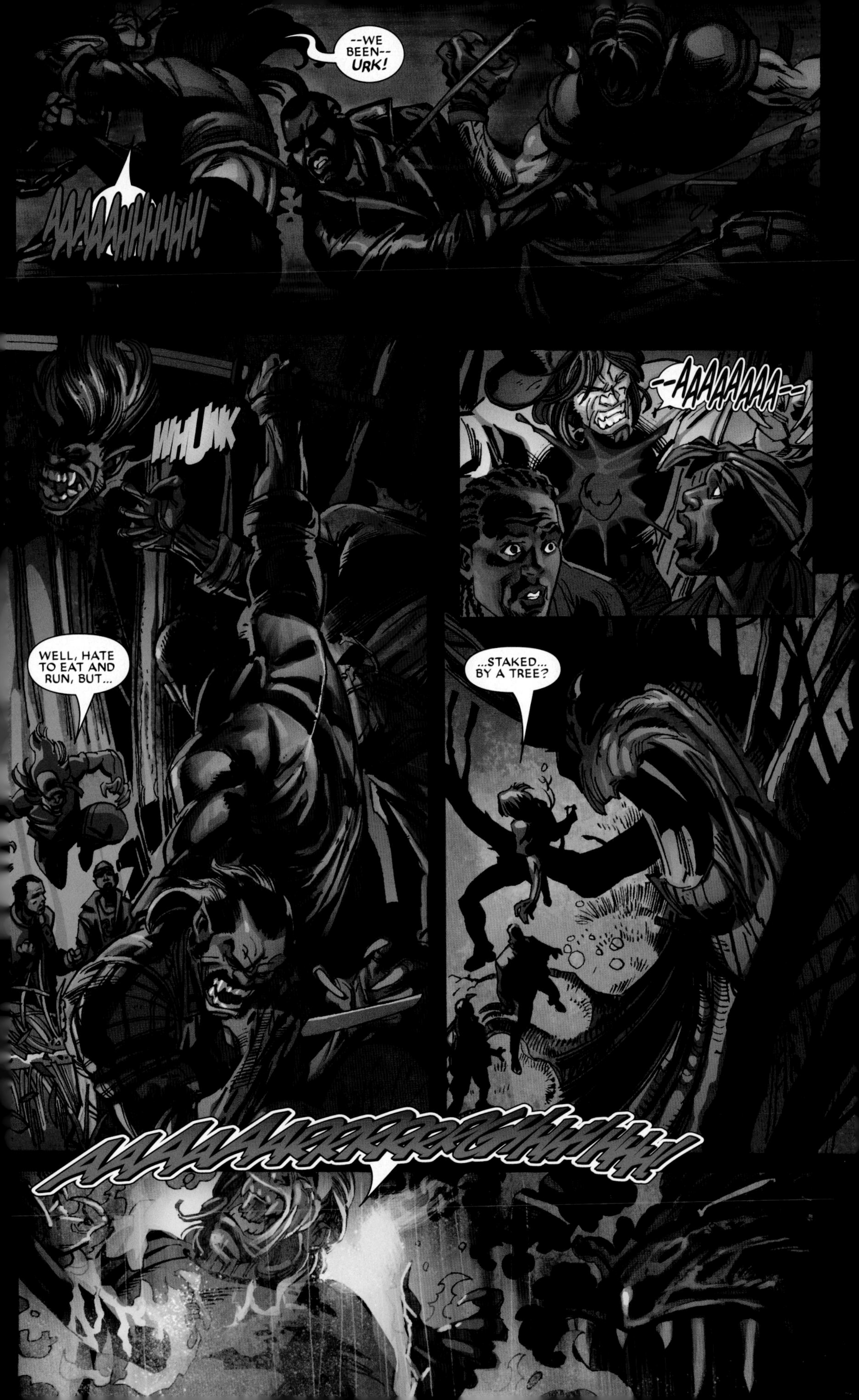
--WE BEEN-- URK!
AAAAAHHHHHH!
WHUNK
--AAAAAAA--
WELL, HATE TO EAT AND RUN, BUT...
...STAKED... BY A TREE?
AAAAAARRRRRGHHHHH!

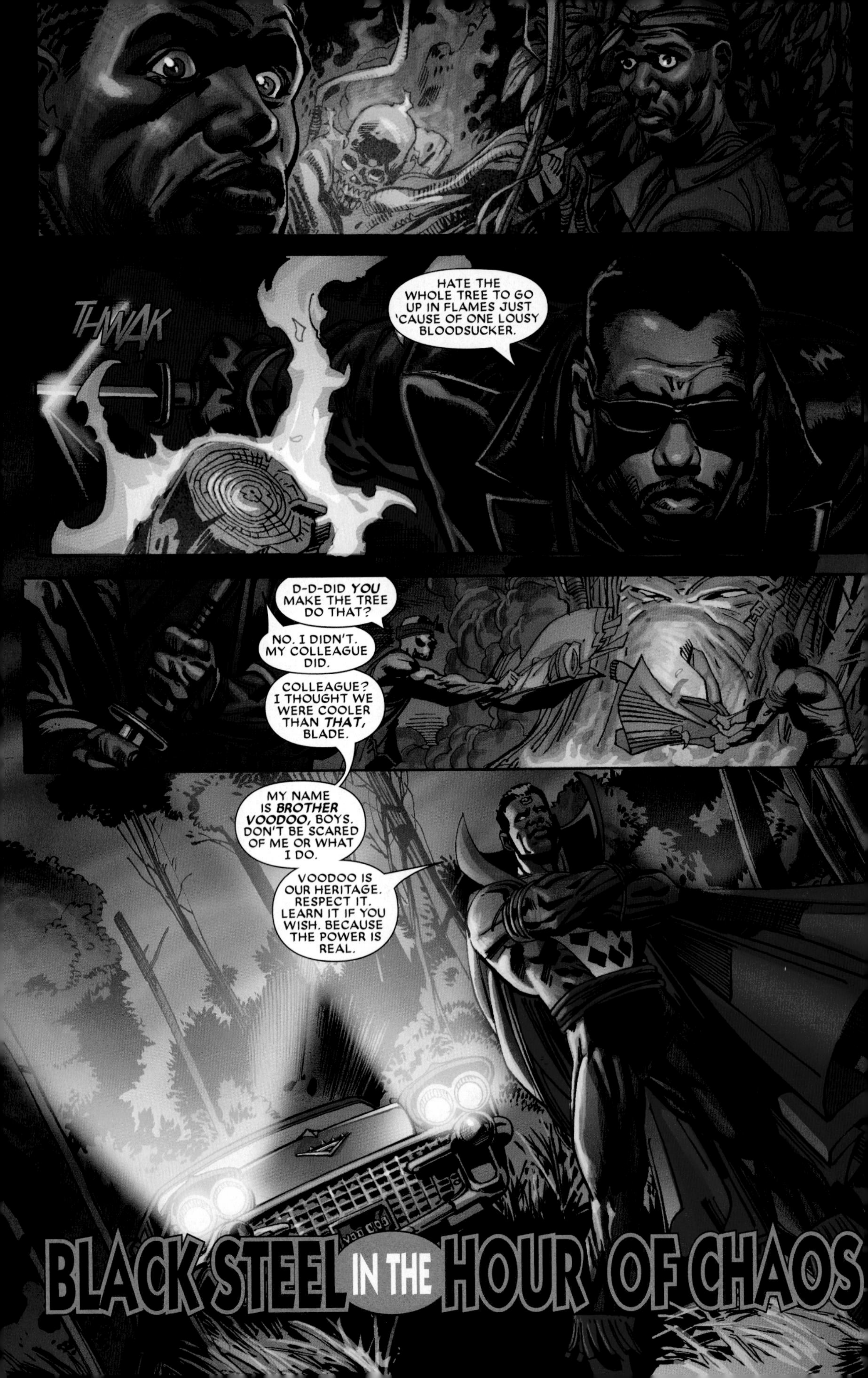
THWAK
HATE THE WHOLE TREE TO GO UP IN FLAMES JUST 'CAUSE OF ONE LOUSY BLOODSUCKER.
D-D-DID *YOU* MAKE THE TREE DO THAT?
NO. I DIDN'T. MY COLLEAGUE DID.
COLLEAGUE? I THOUGHT WE WERE COOLER THAN *THAT,* BLADE.
MY NAME IS ***BROTHER VOODOO,*** BOYS. DON'T BE SCARED OF ME OR WHAT I DO.
VOODOO IS OUR HERITAGE. RESPECT IT. LEARN IT IF YOU WISH. BECAUSE THE POWER IS REAL.
BLACK STEEL IN THE HOUR OF CHAOS

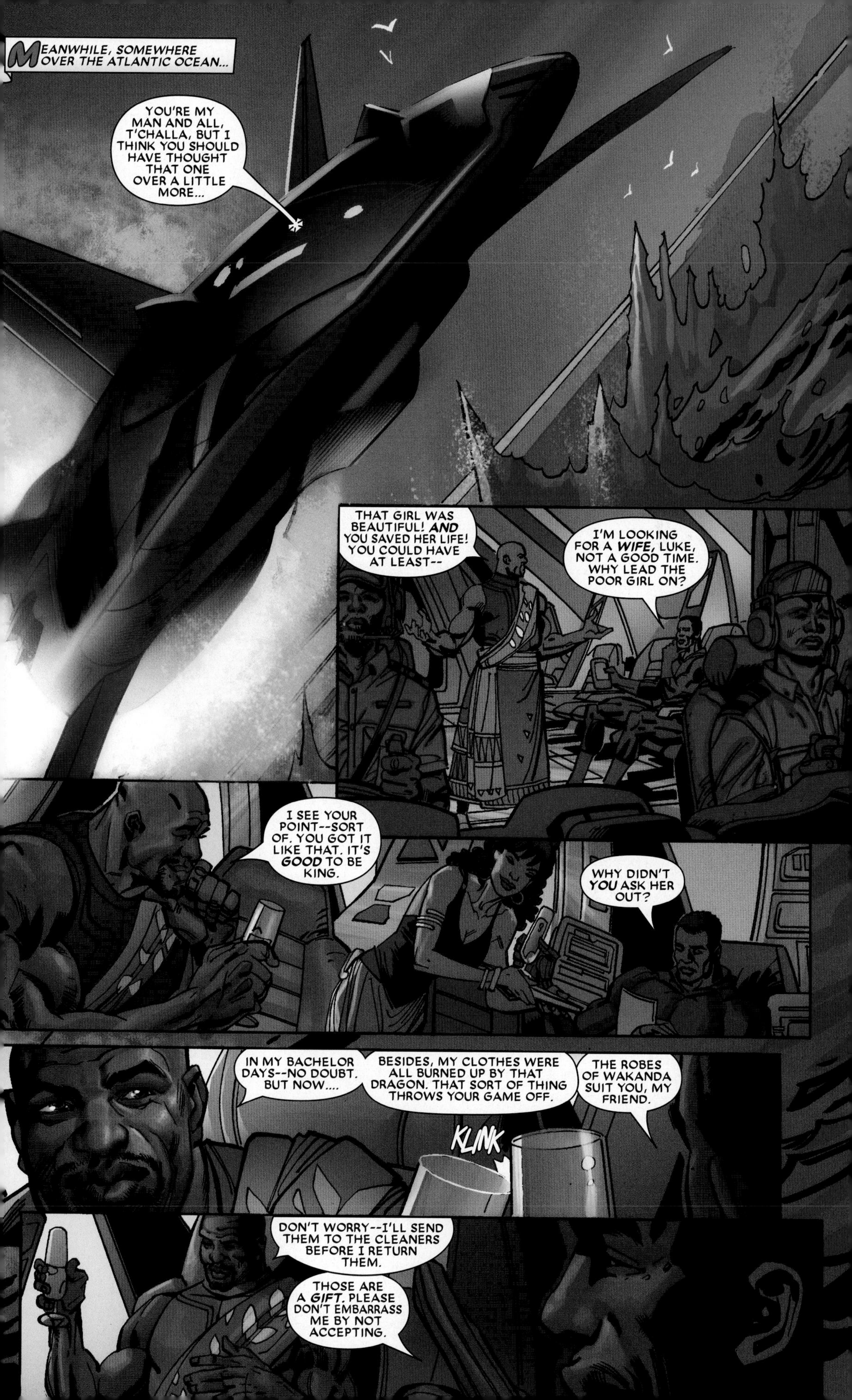
MEANWHILE, SOMEWHERE OVER THE ATLANTIC OCEAN...
YOU'RE MY MAN AND ALL, T'CHALLA, BUT I THINK YOU SHOULD HAVE THOUGHT THAT ONE OVER A LITTLE MORE...
THAT GIRL WAS BEAUTIFUL! AND YOU SAVED HER LIFE! YOU COULD HAVE AT LEAST--
I'M LOOKING FOR A WIFE, LUKE, NOT A GOOD TIME. WHY LEAD THE POOR GIRL ON?
I SEE YOUR POINT--SORT OF. YOU GOT IT LIKE THAT. IT'S GOOD TO BE KING.
WHY DIDN'T YOU ASK HER OUT?
IN MY BACHELOR DAYS--NO DOUBT. BUT NOW....
BESIDES, MY CLOTHES WERE ALL BURNED UP BY THAT DRAGON. THAT SORT OF THING THROWS YOUR GAME OFF.
THE ROBES OF WAKANDA SUIT YOU, MY FRIEND.
KLINK
DON'T WORRY--I'LL SEND THEM TO THE CLEANERS BEFORE I RETURN THEM.
THOSE ARE A GIFT. PLEASE DON'T EMBARRASS ME BY NOT ACCEPTING.

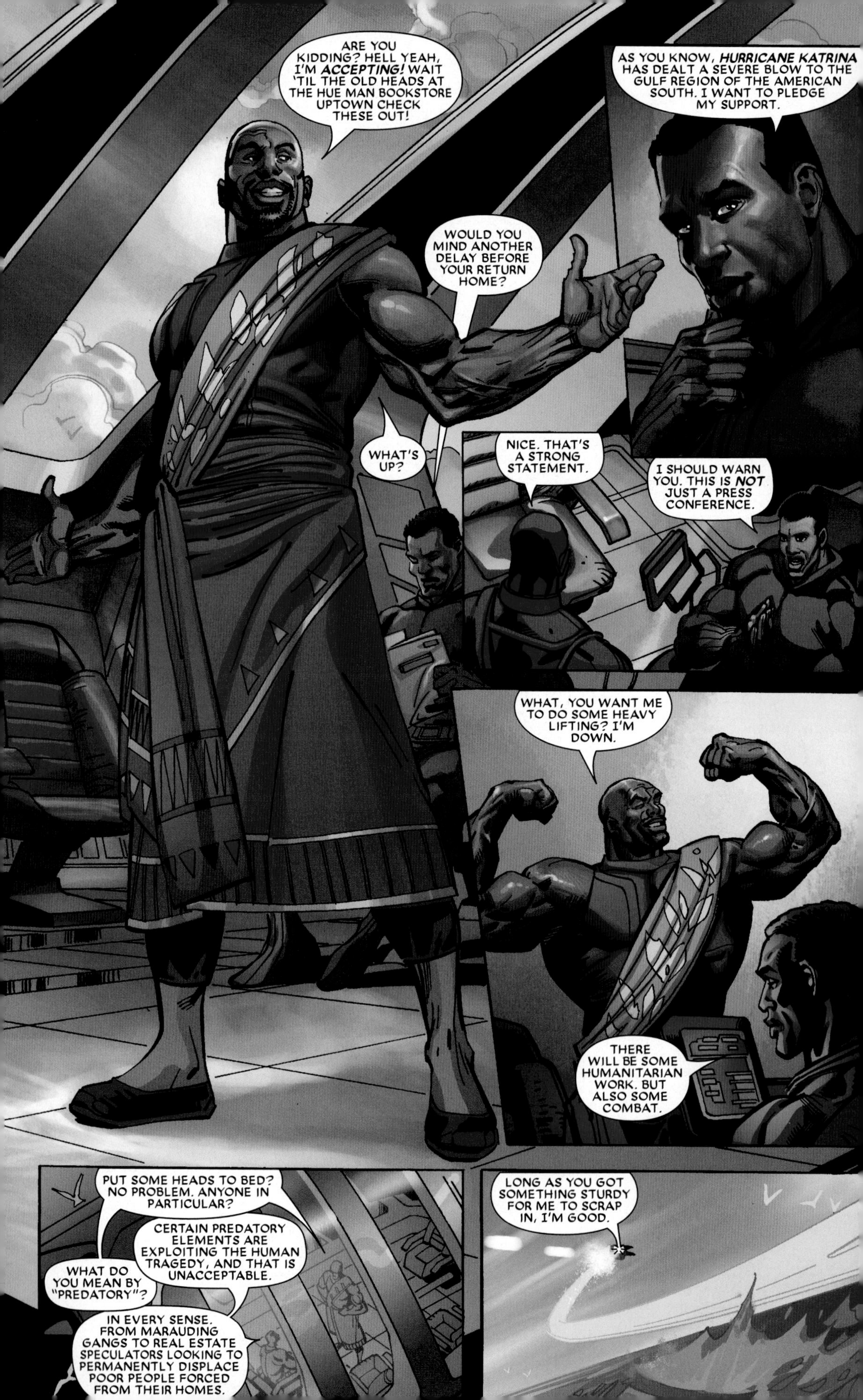
AS YOU KNOW, HURRICANE KATRINA HAS DEALT A SEVERE BLOW TO THE GULF REGION OF THE AMERICAN SOUTH. I WANT TO PLEDGE MY SUPPORT.
ARE YOU KIDDING? HELL YEAH, I'M ACCEPTING! WAIT 'TIL THE OLD HEADS AT THE HUE MAN BOOKSTORE UPTOWN CHECK THESE OUT!
WOULD YOU MIND ANOTHER DELAY BEFORE YOUR RETURN HOME?
WHAT'S UP?
NICE. THAT'S A STRONG STATEMENT.
I SHOULD WARN YOU. THIS IS NOT JUST A PRESS CONFERENCE.
WHAT, YOU WANT ME TO DO SOME HEAVY LIFTING? I'M DOWN.
THERE WILL BE SOME HUMANITARIAN WORK. BUT ALSO SOME COMBAT.
PUT SOME HEADS TO BED? NO PROBLEM. ANYONE IN PARTICULAR?
CERTAIN PREDATORY ELEMENTS ARE EXPLOITING THE HUMAN TRAGEDY, AND THAT IS UNACCEPTABLE.
WHAT DO YOU MEAN BY "PREDATORY"?
IN EVERY SENSE. FROM MARAUDING GANGS TO REAL ESTATE SPECULATORS LOOKING TO PERMANENTLY DISPLACE POOR PEOPLE FORCED FROM THEIR HOMES.
LONG AS YOU GOT SOMETHING STURDY FOR ME TO SCRAP IN, I'M GOOD.

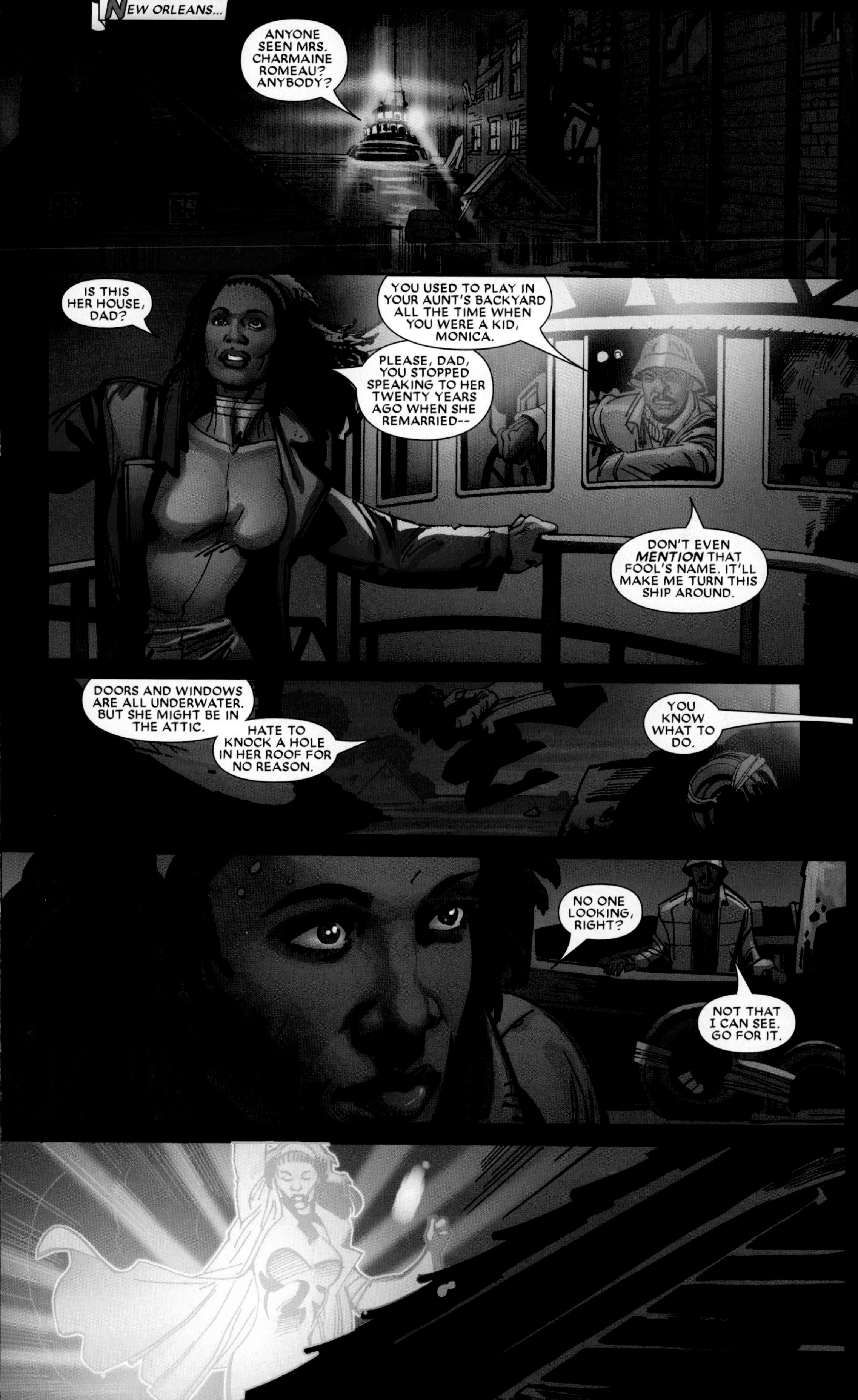
NEW ORLEANS...
ANYONE SEEN MRS. CHARMAINE ROMEAU? ANYBODY?
IS THIS HER HOUSE, DAD?
YOU USED TO PLAY IN YOUR AUNT'S BACKYARD ALL THE TIME WHEN YOU WERE A KID, MONICA.
PLEASE, DAD, YOU STOPPED SPEAKING TO HER TWENTY YEARS AGO WHEN SHE REMARRIED--
DON'T EVEN MENTION THAT FOOL'S NAME. IT'LL MAKE ME TURN THIS SHIP AROUND.
DOORS AND WINDOWS ARE ALL UNDERWATER. BUT SHE MIGHT BE IN THE ATTIC.
HATE TO KNOCK A HOLE IN HER ROOF FOR NO REASON.
YOU KNOW WHAT TO DO.
NO ONE LOOKING, RIGHT?
NOT THAT I CAN SEE. GO FOR IT.

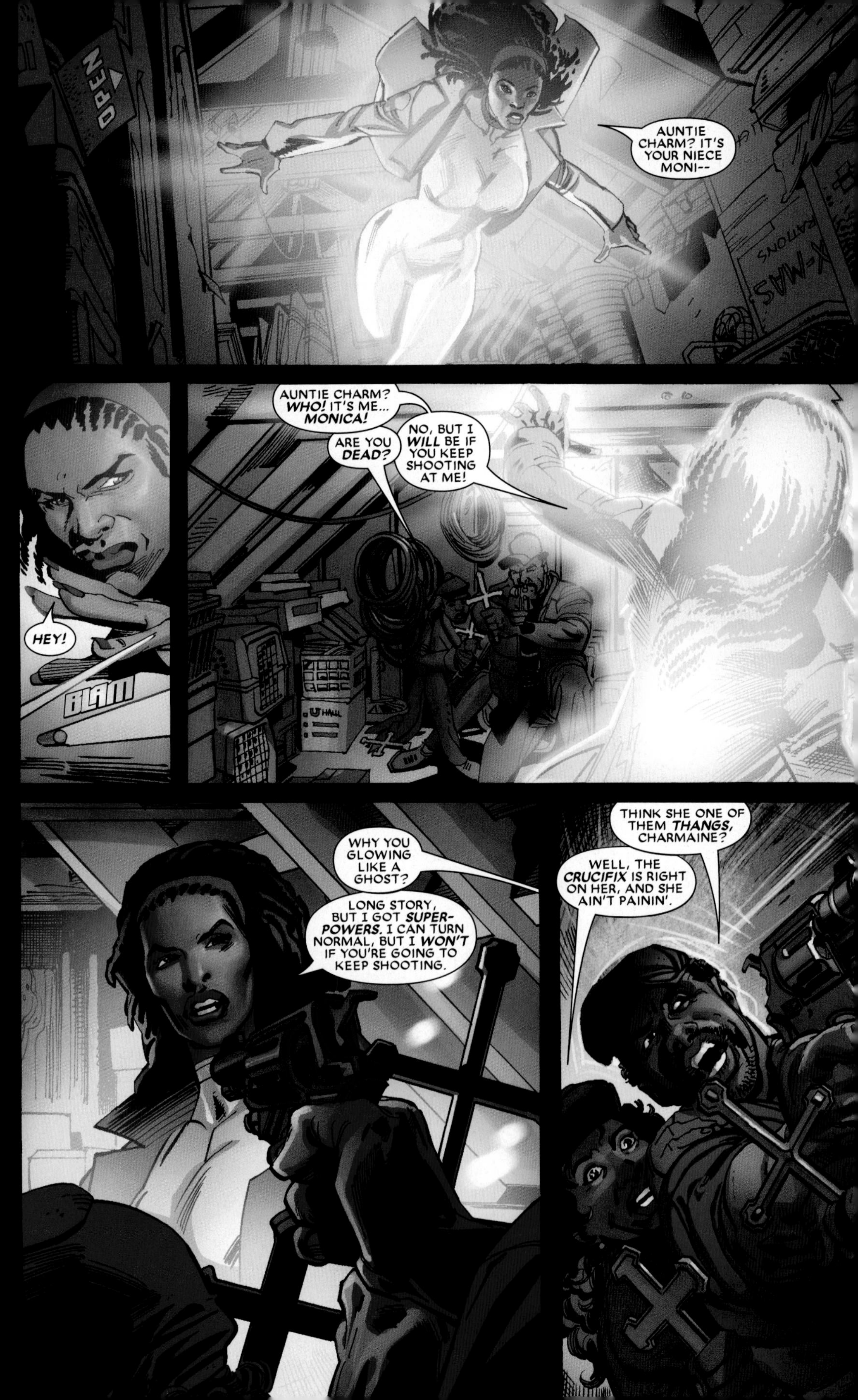
OPEN
AUNTIE CHARM? IT'S YOUR NIECE MONI--
X-MAS DECORATIONS
HEY!
BLAM
AUNTIE CHARM? WHO! IT'S ME... MONICA!
ARE YOU DEAD?
NO, BUT I WILL BE IF YOU KEEP SHOOTING AT ME!
U-HAUL
WHY YOU GLOWING LIKE A GHOST?
LONG STORY, BUT I GOT SUPER-POWERS. I CAN TURN NORMAL, BUT I WON'T IF YOU'RE GOING TO KEEP SHOOTING.
THINK SHE ONE OF THEM THANGS, CHARMAINE?
WELL, THE CRUCIFIX IS RIGHT ON HER, AND SHE AIN'T PAININ'.

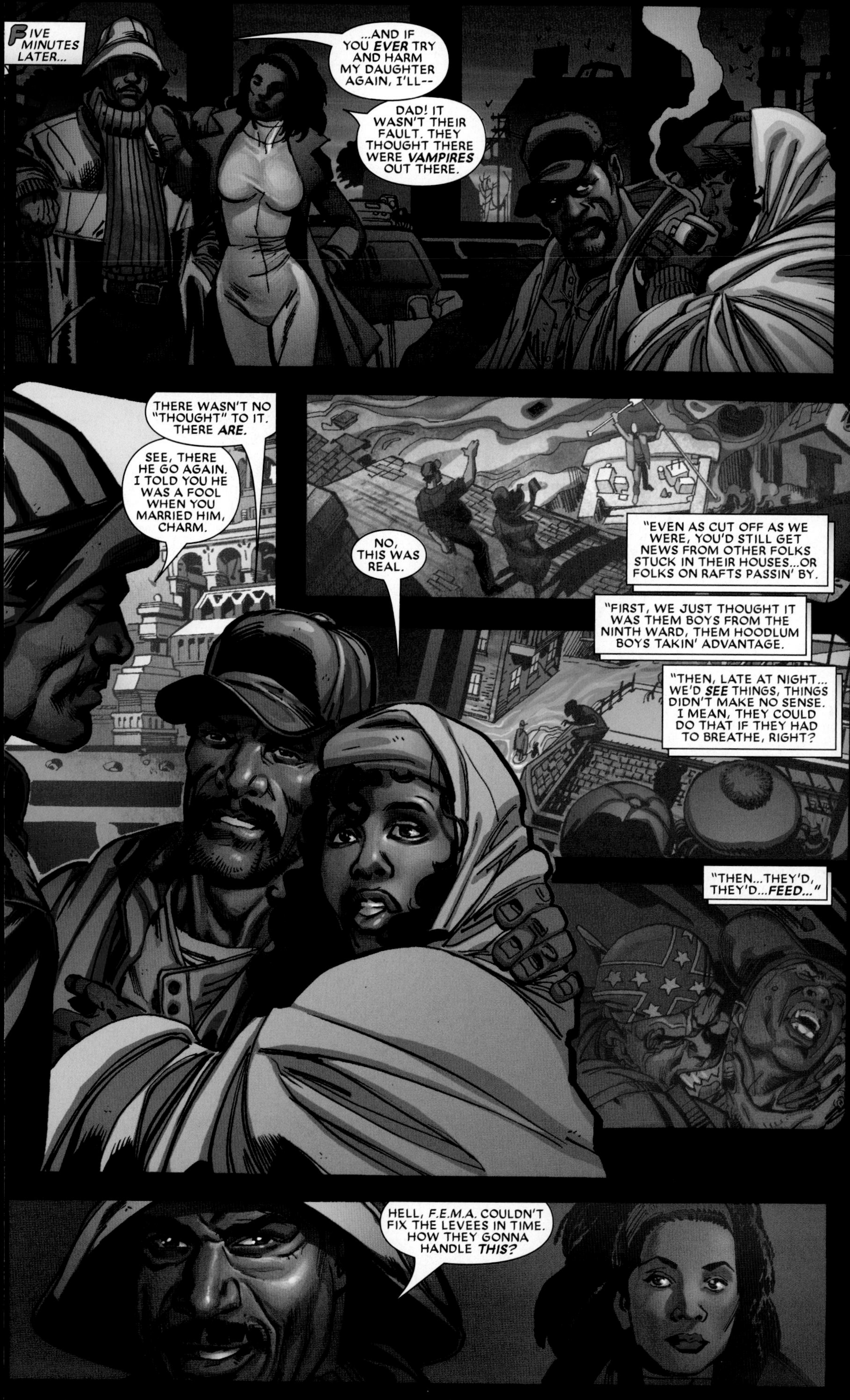
FIVE MINUTES LATER...
...AND IF YOU EVER TRY AND HARM MY DAUGHTER AGAIN, I'LL--
DAD! IT WASN'T THEIR FAULT. THEY THOUGHT THERE WERE VAMPIRES OUT THERE.
THERE WASN'T NO "THOUGHT" TO IT. THERE ARE.
SEE, THERE HE GO AGAIN. I TOLD YOU HE WAS A FOOL WHEN YOU MARRIED HIM, CHARM.
NO, THIS WAS REAL.
"EVEN AS CUT OFF AS WE WERE, YOU'D STILL GET NEWS FROM OTHER FOLKS STUCK IN THEIR HOUSES...OR FOLKS ON RAFTS PASSIN' BY.
"FIRST, WE JUST THOUGHT IT WAS THEM BOYS FROM THE NINTH WARD, THEM HOODLUM BOYS TAKIN' ADVANTAGE.
"THEN, LATE AT NIGHT... WE'D SEE THINGS, THINGS DIDN'T MAKE NO SENSE. I MEAN, THEY COULD DO THAT IF THEY HAD TO BREATHE, RIGHT?
"THEN...THEY'D, THEY'D...FEED..."
HELL, F.E.M.A. COULDN'T FIX THE LEVEES IN TIME. HOW THEY GONNA HANDLE THIS?

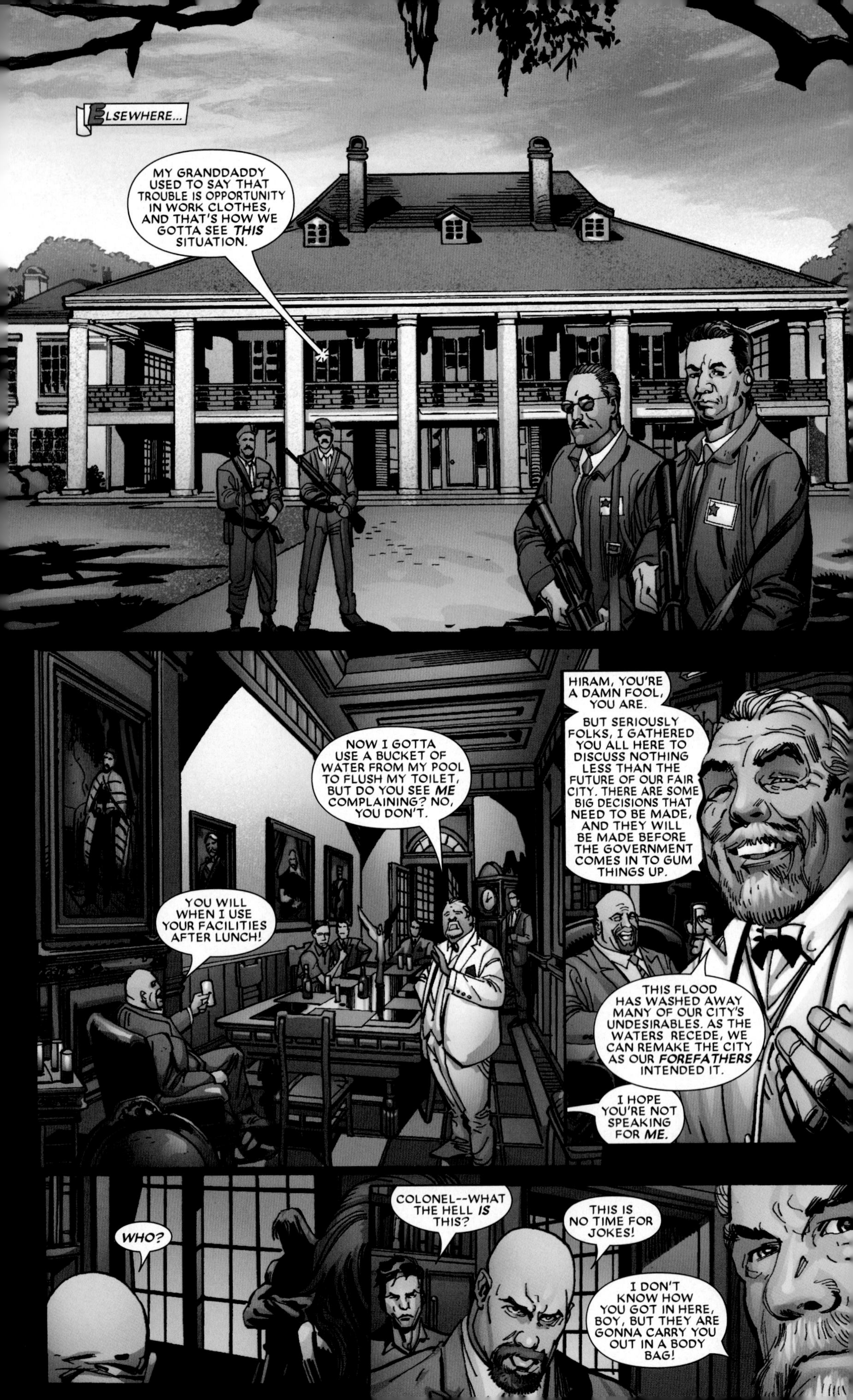
ELSEWHERE...
MY GRANDDADDY USED TO SAY THAT TROUBLE IS OPPORTUNITY IN WORK CLOTHES, AND THAT'S HOW WE GOTTA SEE THIS SITUATION.
NOW I GOTTA USE A BUCKET OF WATER FROM MY POOL TO FLUSH MY TOILET, BUT DO YOU SEE ME COMPLAINING? NO, YOU DON'T.
YOU WILL WHEN I USE YOUR FACILITIES AFTER LUNCH!
HIRAM, YOU'RE A DAMN FOOL, YOU ARE.
BUT SERIOUSLY FOLKS, I GATHERED YOU ALL HERE TO DISCUSS NOTHING LESS THAN THE FUTURE OF OUR FAIR CITY. THERE ARE SOME BIG DECISIONS THAT NEED TO BE MADE, AND THEY WILL BE MADE BEFORE THE GOVERNMENT COMES IN TO GUM THINGS UP.
THIS FLOOD HAS WASHED AWAY MANY OF OUR CITY'S UNDESIRABLES. AS THE WATERS RECEDE, WE CAN REMAKE THE CITY AS OUR FOREFATHERS INTENDED IT.
I HOPE YOU'RE NOT SPEAKING FOR ME.
WHO?
COLONEL--WHAT THE HELL IS THIS?
THIS IS NO TIME FOR JOKES!
I DON'T KNOW HOW YOU GOT IN HERE, BOY, BUT THEY ARE GONNA CARRY YOU OUT IN A BODY BAG!

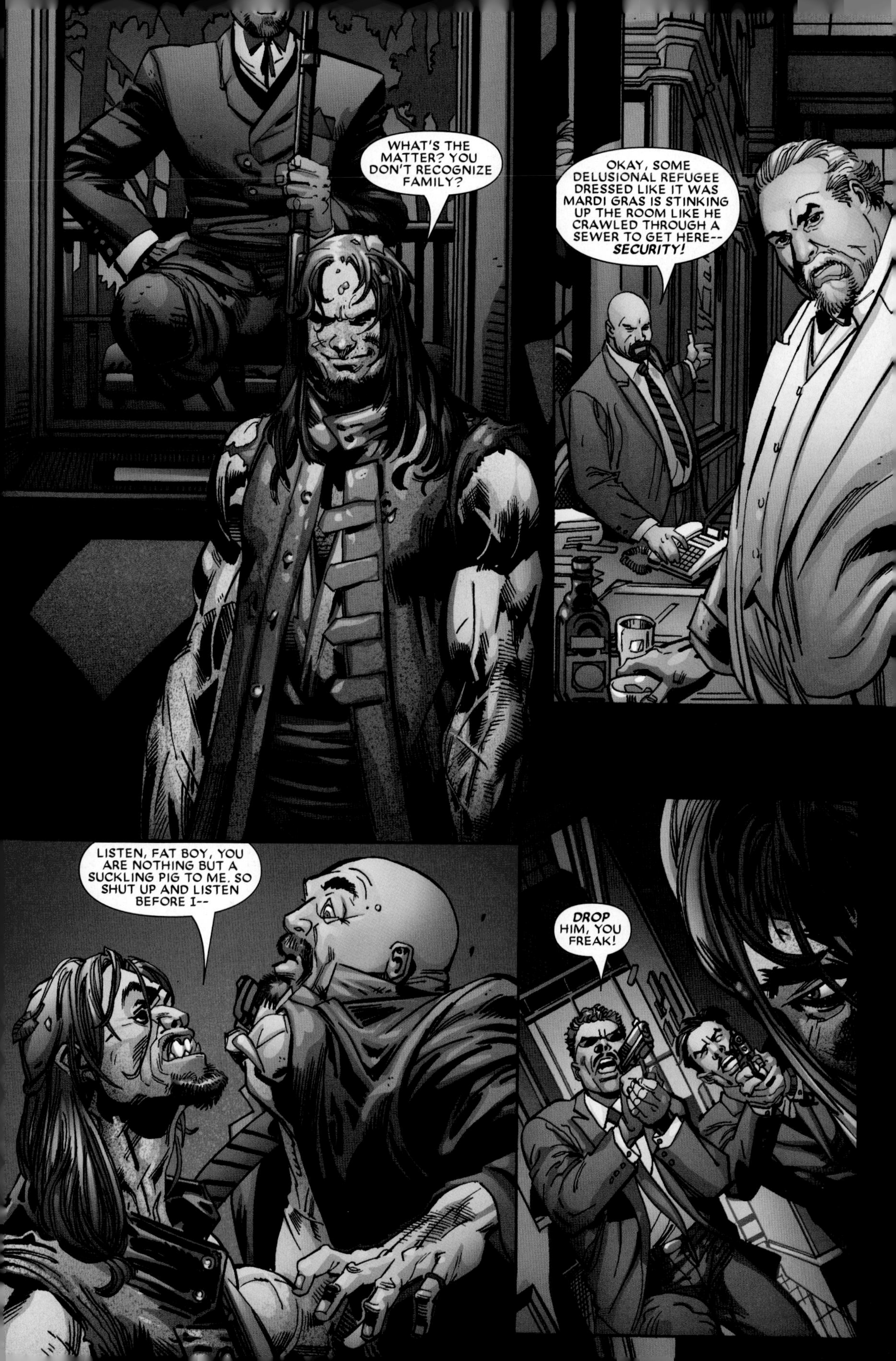
WHAT'S THE MATTER? YOU DON'T RECOGNIZE FAMILY?
OKAY, SOME DELUSIONAL REFUGEE DRESSED LIKE IT WAS MARDI GRAS IS STINKING UP THE ROOM LIKE HE CRAWLED THROUGH A SEWER TO GET HERE-- SECURITY!
LISTEN, FAT BOY, YOU ARE NOTHING BUT A SUCKLING PIG TO ME. SO SHUT UP AND LISTEN BEFORE I--
DROP HIM, YOU FREAK!

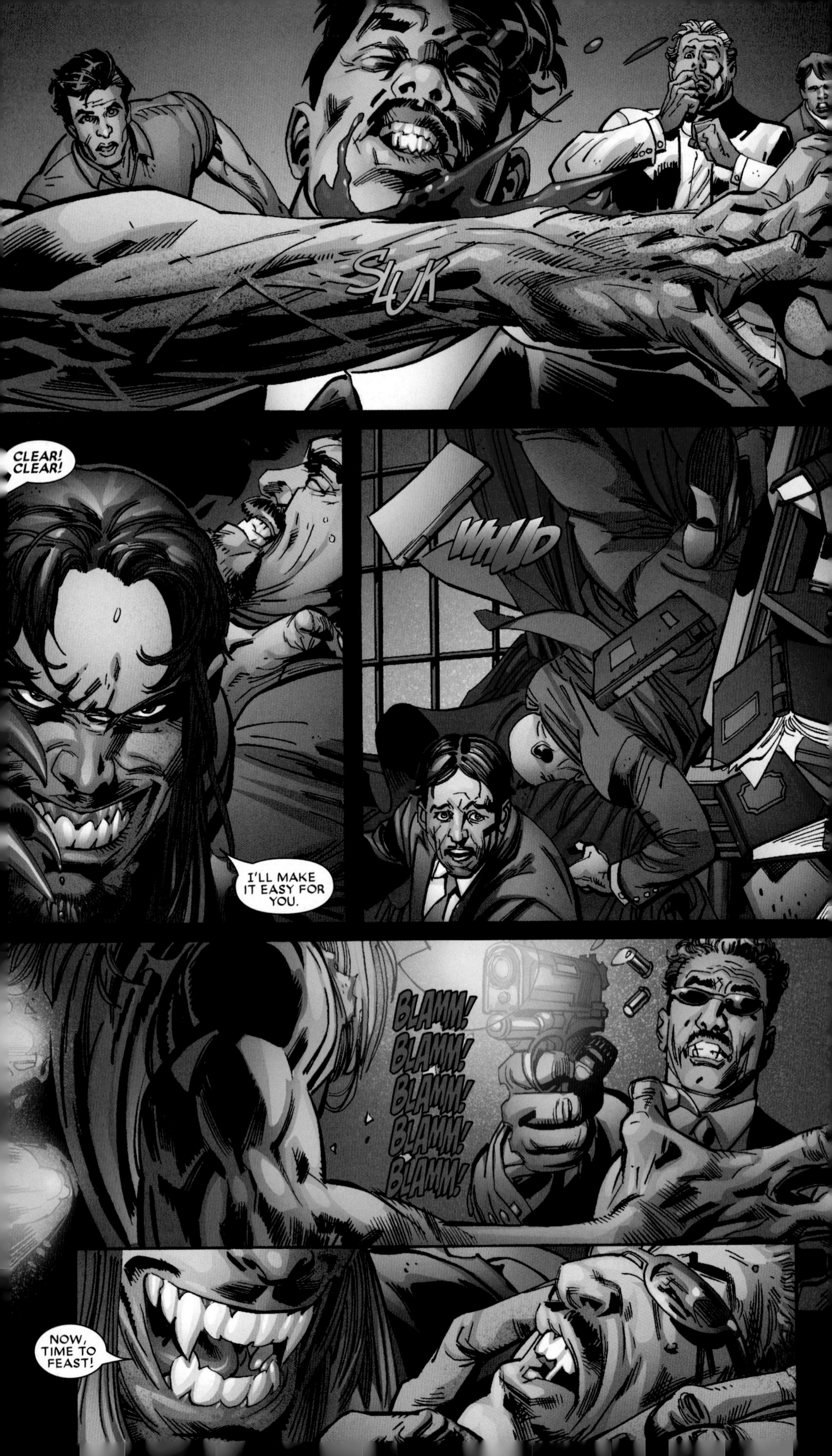
SLUK
CLEAR! CLEAR!
I'LL MAKE IT EASY FOR YOU.
WHUD
BLAMM! BLAMM! BLAMM! BLAMM! BLAMM!
NOW, TIME TO FEAST!

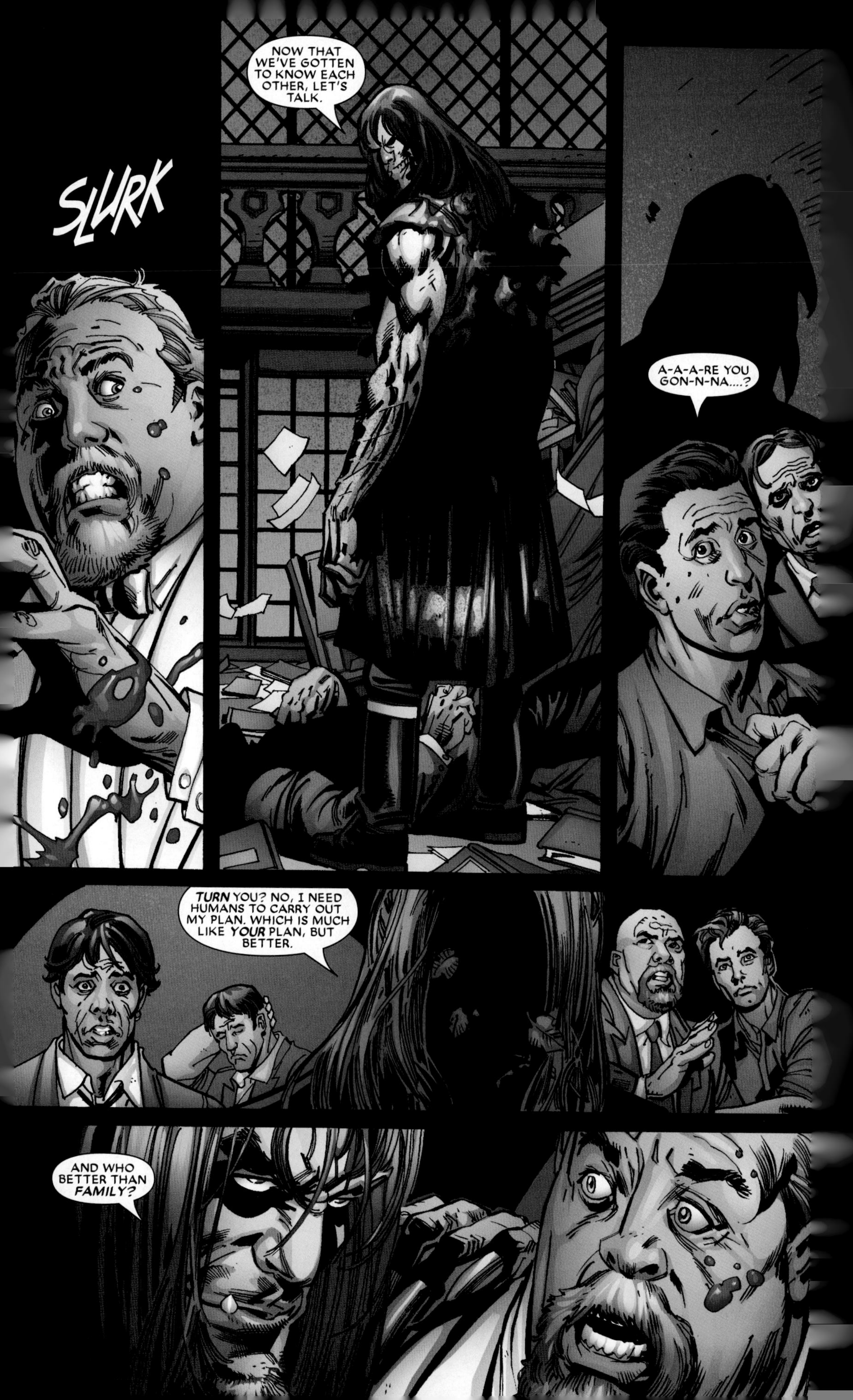
SLURK
NOW THAT WE'VE GOTTEN TO KNOW EACH OTHER, LET'S TALK.
A-A-A-RE YOU GON-N-NA....?
TURN YOU? NO, I NEED HUMANS TO CARRY OUT MY PLAN. WHICH IS MUCH LIKE *YOUR* PLAN, BUT BETTER.
AND WHO BETTER THAN *FAMILY*?

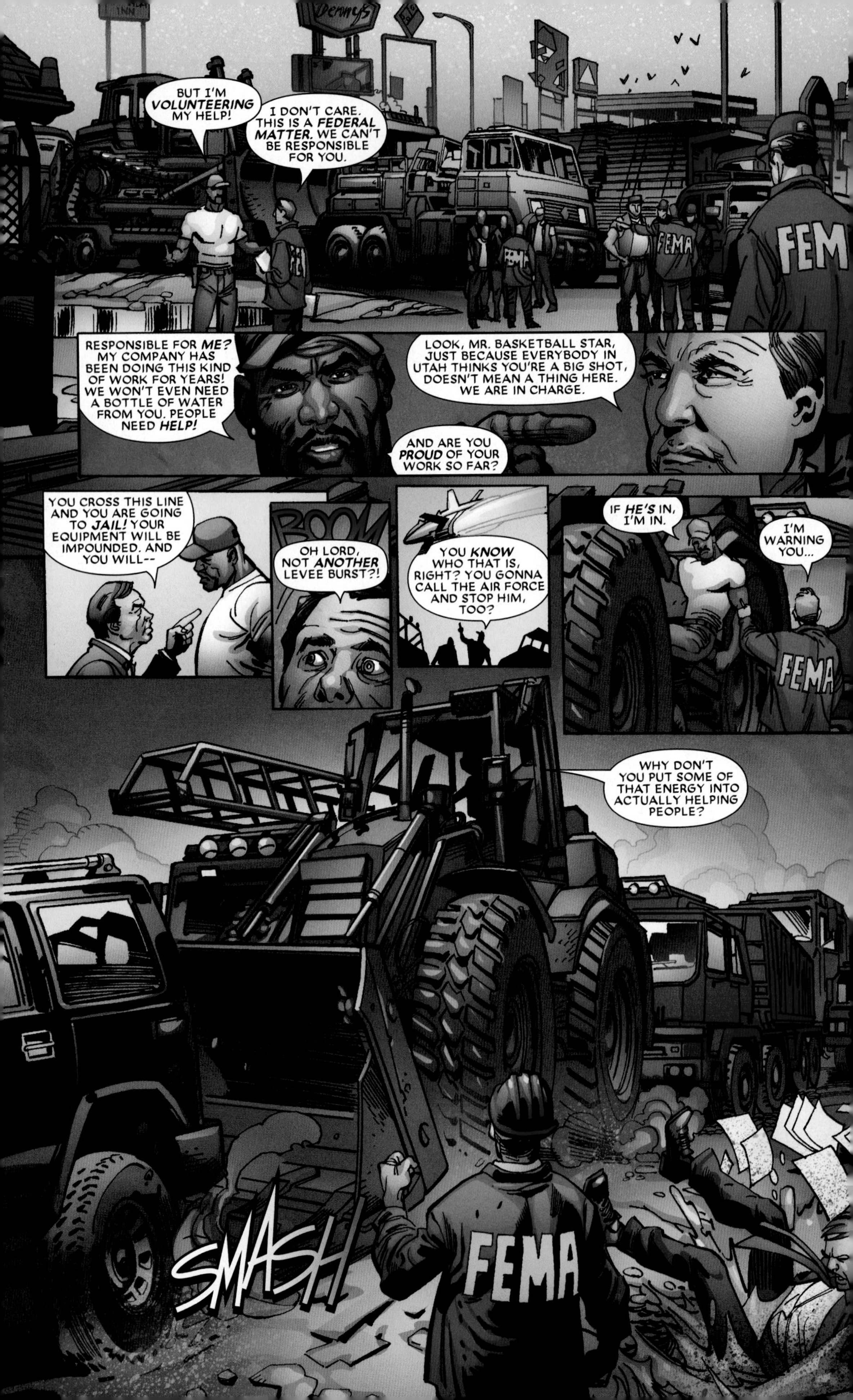
BUT I'M VOLUNTEERING MY HELP!
I DON'T CARE. THIS IS A FEDERAL MATTER. WE CAN'T BE RESPONSIBLE FOR YOU.
FEMA
RESPONSIBLE FOR ME? MY COMPANY HAS BEEN DOING THIS KIND OF WORK FOR YEARS! WE WON'T EVEN NEED A BOTTLE OF WATER FROM YOU. PEOPLE NEED HELP!
LOOK, MR. BASKETBALL STAR, JUST BECAUSE EVERYBODY IN UTAH THINKS YOU'RE A BIG SHOT, DOESN'T MEAN A THING HERE. WE ARE IN CHARGE.
AND ARE YOU PROUD OF YOUR WORK SO FAR?
YOU CROSS THIS LINE AND YOU ARE GOING TO JAIL! YOUR EQUIPMENT WILL BE IMPOUNDED. AND YOU WILL--
BOOM
OH LORD, NOT ANOTHER LEVEE BURST?!
YOU KNOW WHO THAT IS, RIGHT? YOU GONNA CALL THE AIR FORCE AND STOP HIM, TOO?
IF HE'S IN, I'M IN.
I'M WARNING YOU...
FEMA
WHY DON'T YOU PUT SOME OF THAT ENERGY INTO ACTUALLY HELPING PEOPLE?
SMASH
FEMA

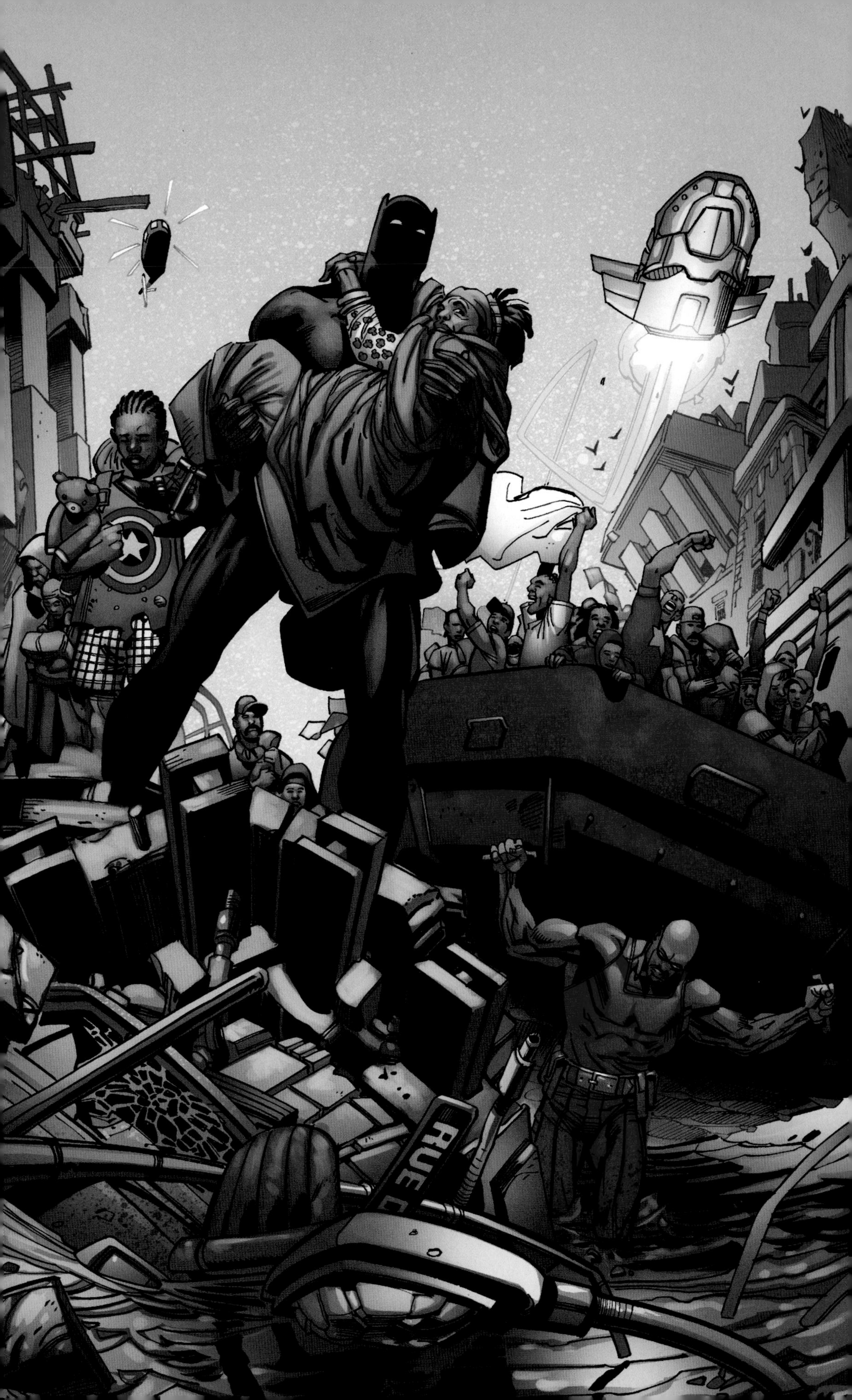
RUE

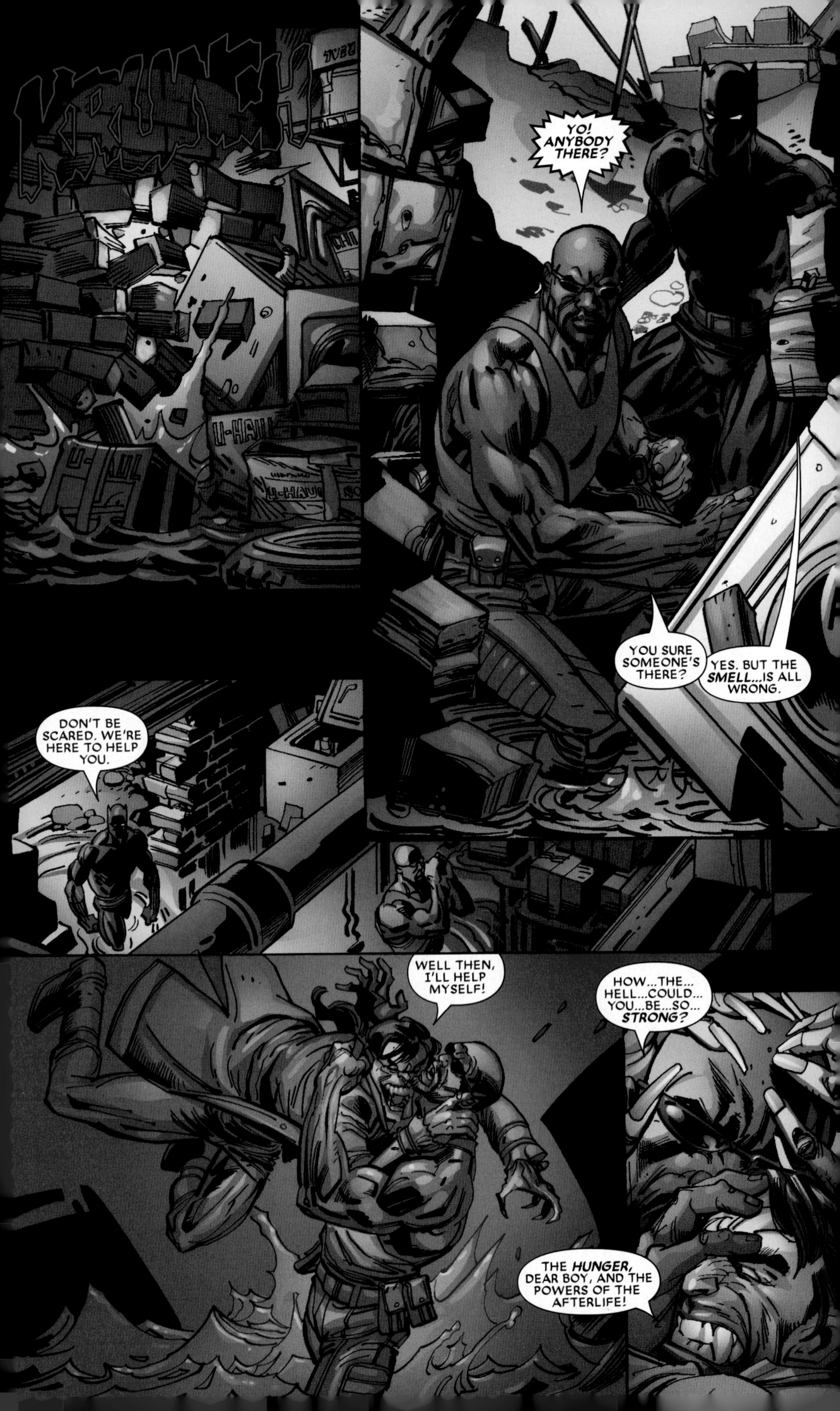
U-HAUL
U-HAUL
U-HAUL
YO! ANYBODY THERE?
YOU SURE SOMEONE'S THERE?
YES. BUT THE SMELL...IS ALL WRONG.
DON'T BE SCARED. WE'RE HERE TO HELP YOU.
WELL THEN, I'LL HELP MYSELF!
HOW...THE... HELL...COULD... YOU...BE...SO... STRONG?
THE HUNGER, DEAR BOY, AND THE POWERS OF THE AFTERLIFE!

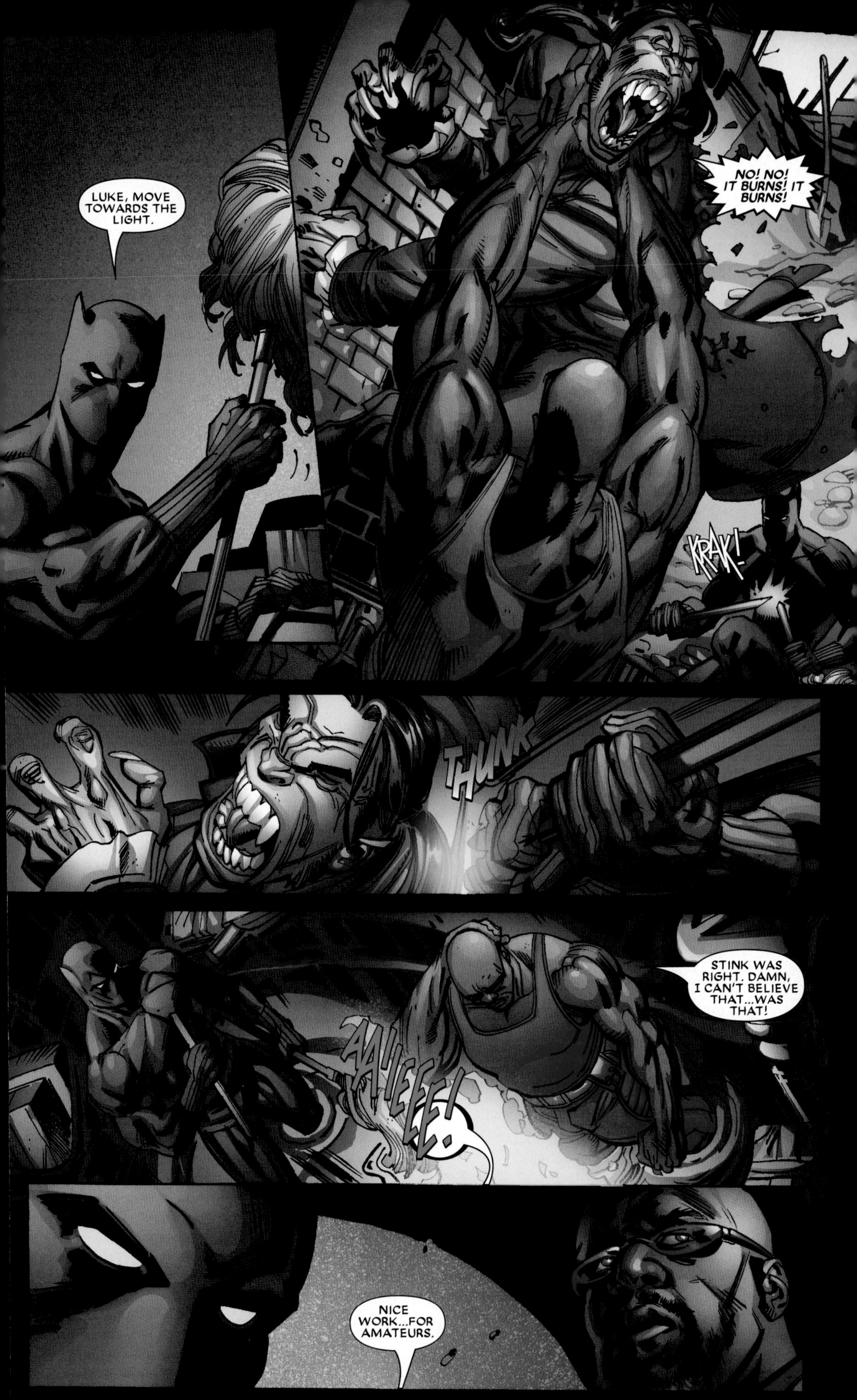
LUKE, MOVE TOWARDS THE LIGHT.
NO! NO! IT BURNS! IT BURNS!
KRAK!
THUNK
STINK WAS RIGHT. DAMN, I CAN'T BELIEVE THAT...WAS THAT!
AAHEEEE!
NICE WORK...FOR AMATEURS.

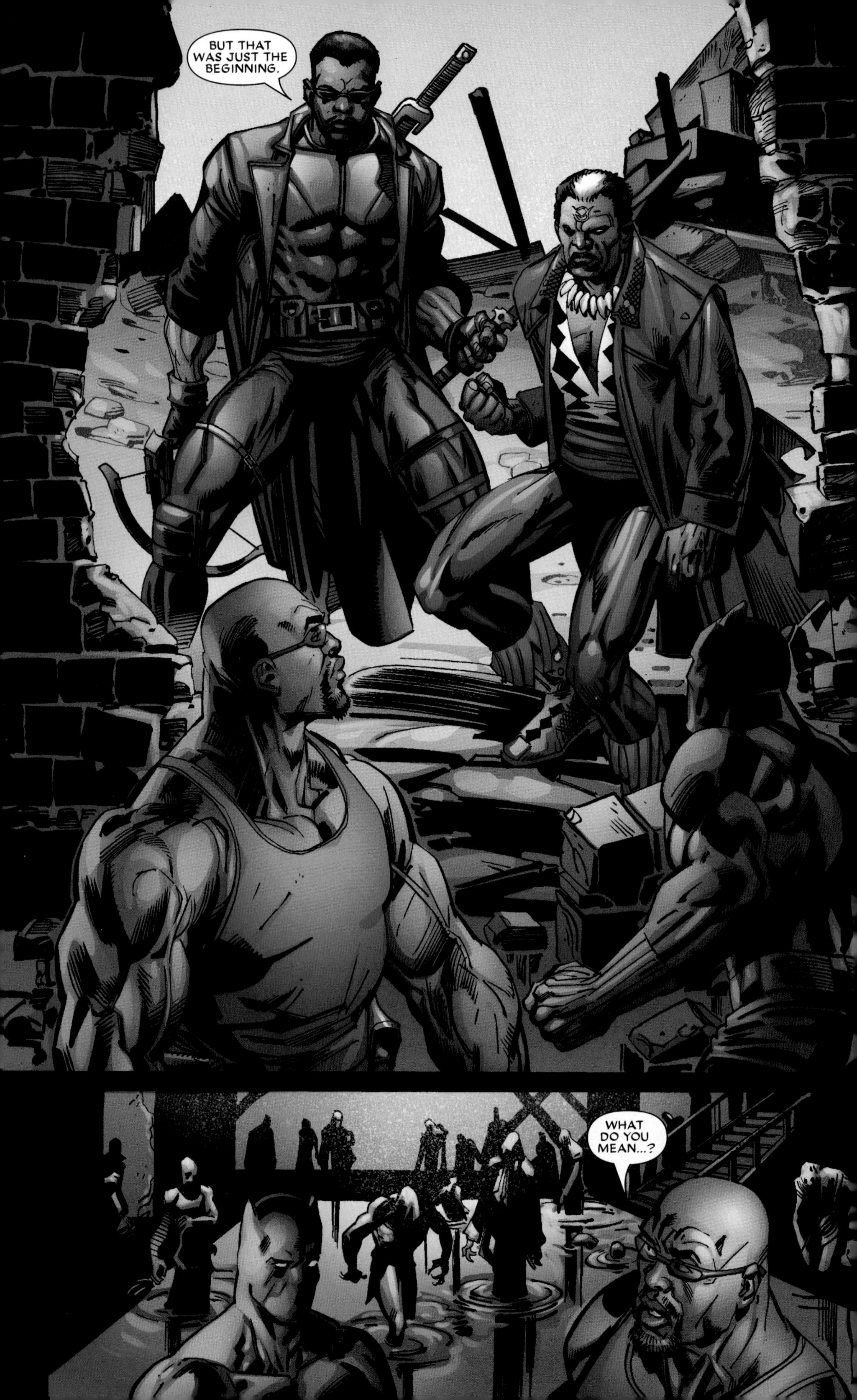
BUT THAT WAS JUST THE BEGINNING.
WHAT DO YOU MEAN...?

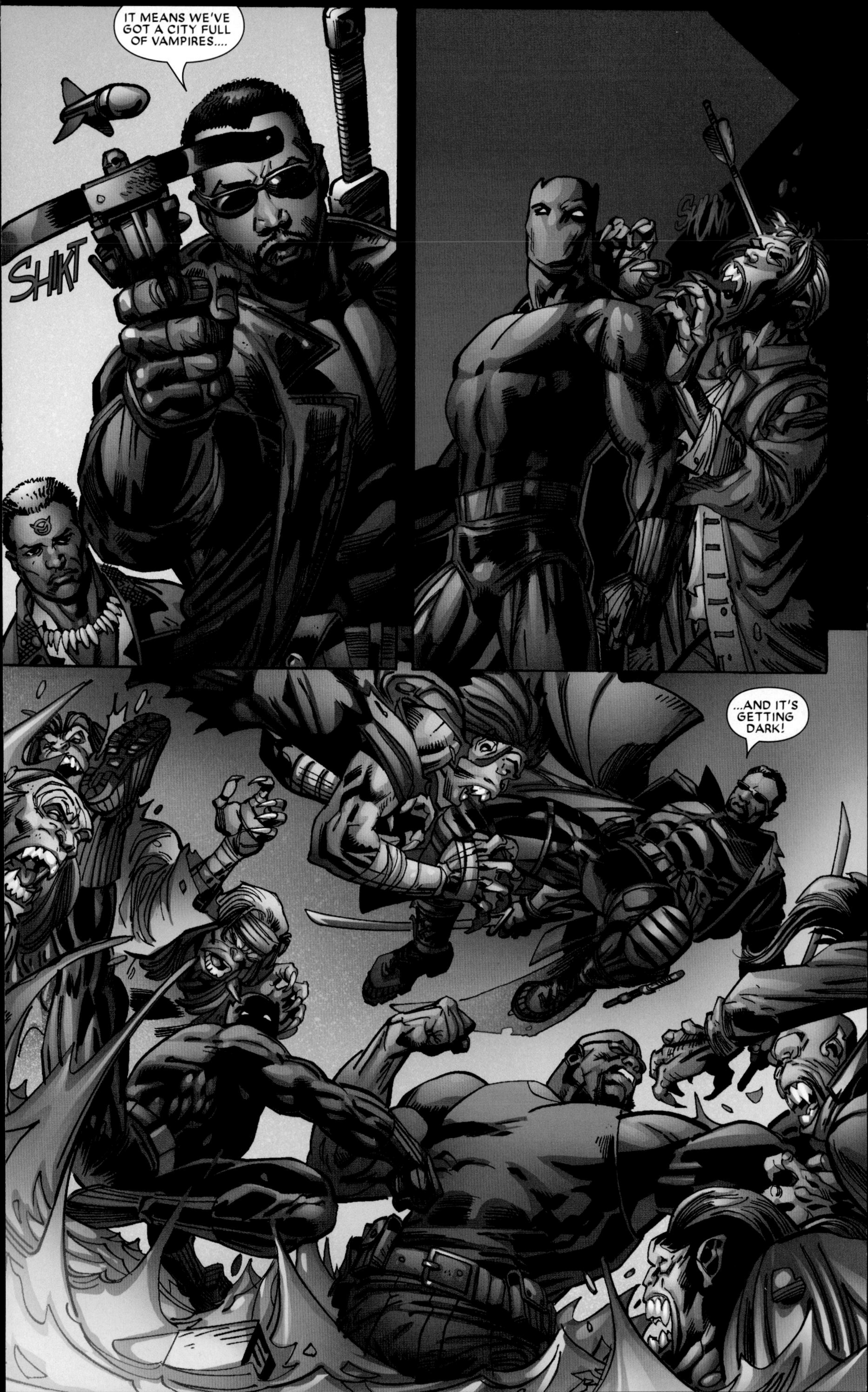
IT MEANS WE'VE GOT A CITY FULL OF VAMPIRES....
SHIKT
SHUNK
...AND IT'S GETTING DARK!

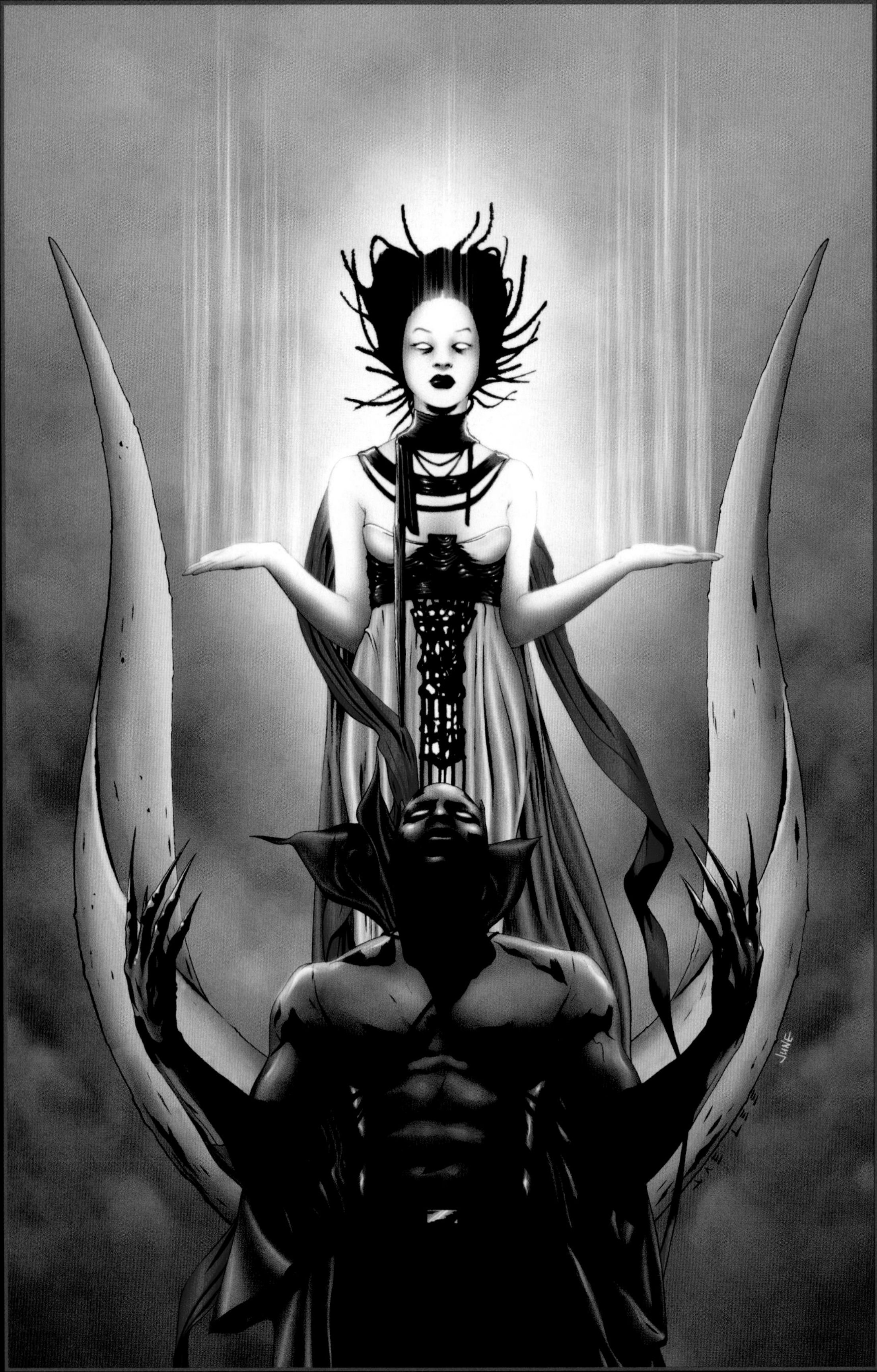
JUNE

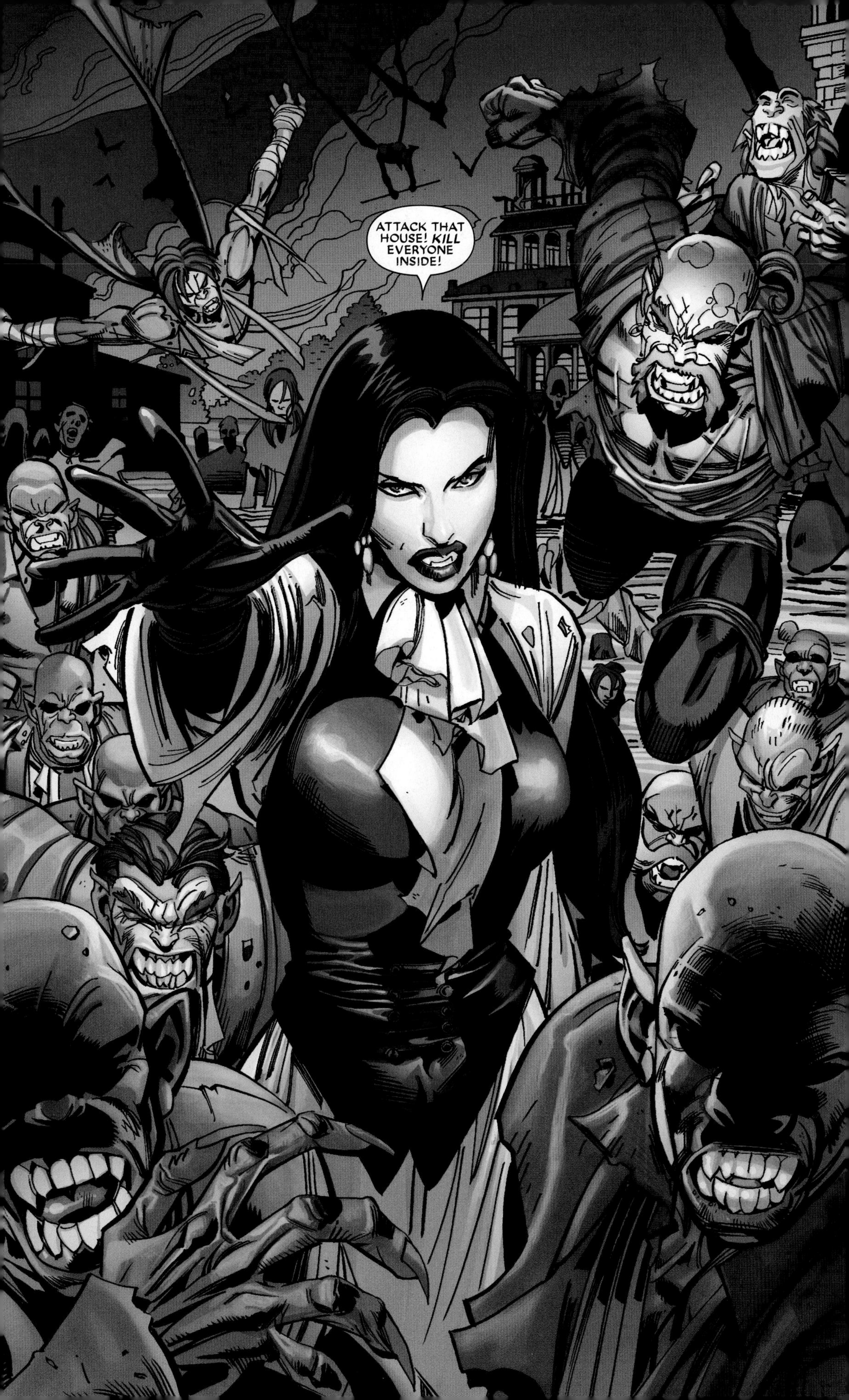
ATTACK THAT HOUSE! *KILL* EVERYONE INSIDE!

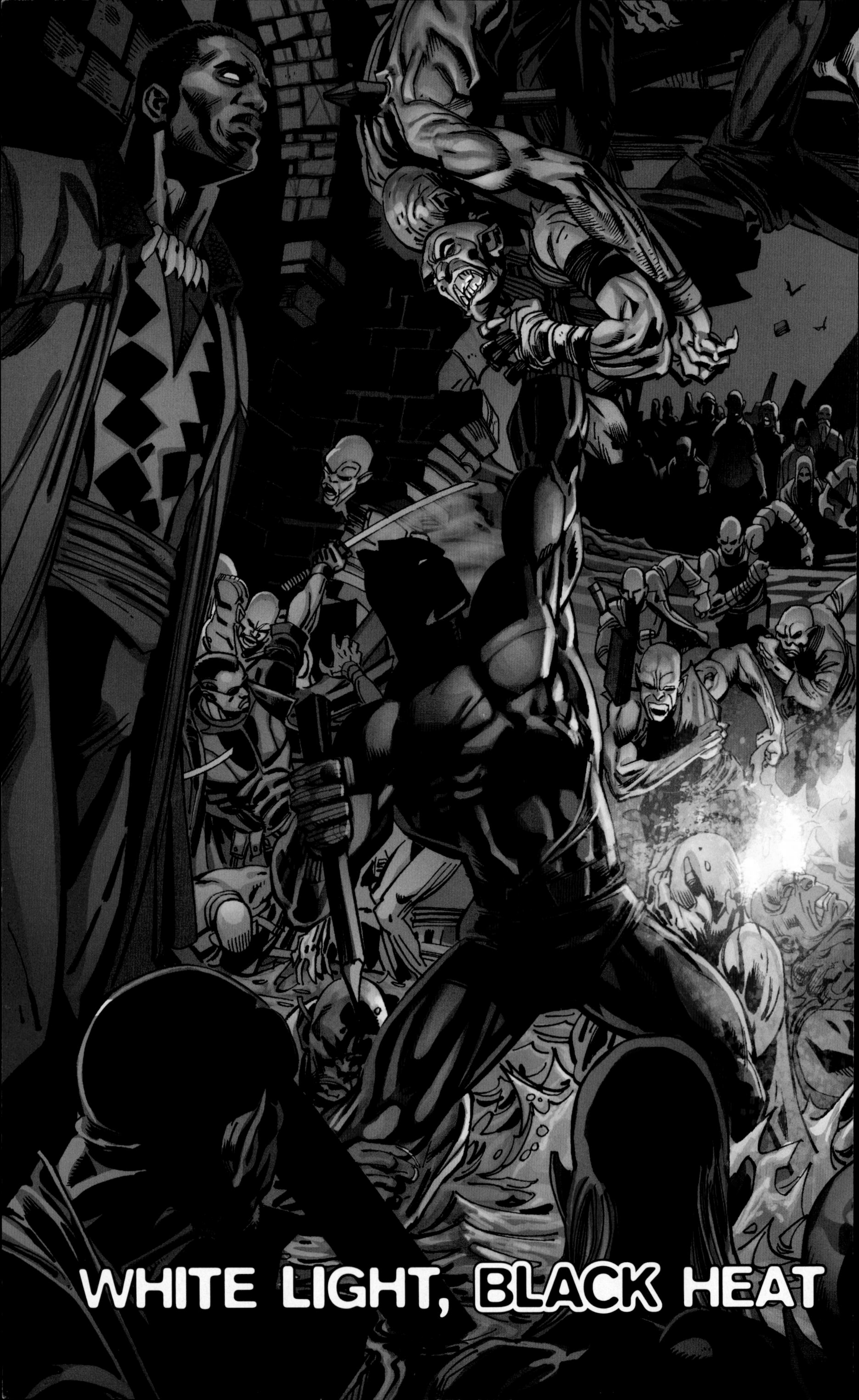
WHITE LIGHT, BLACK HEAT

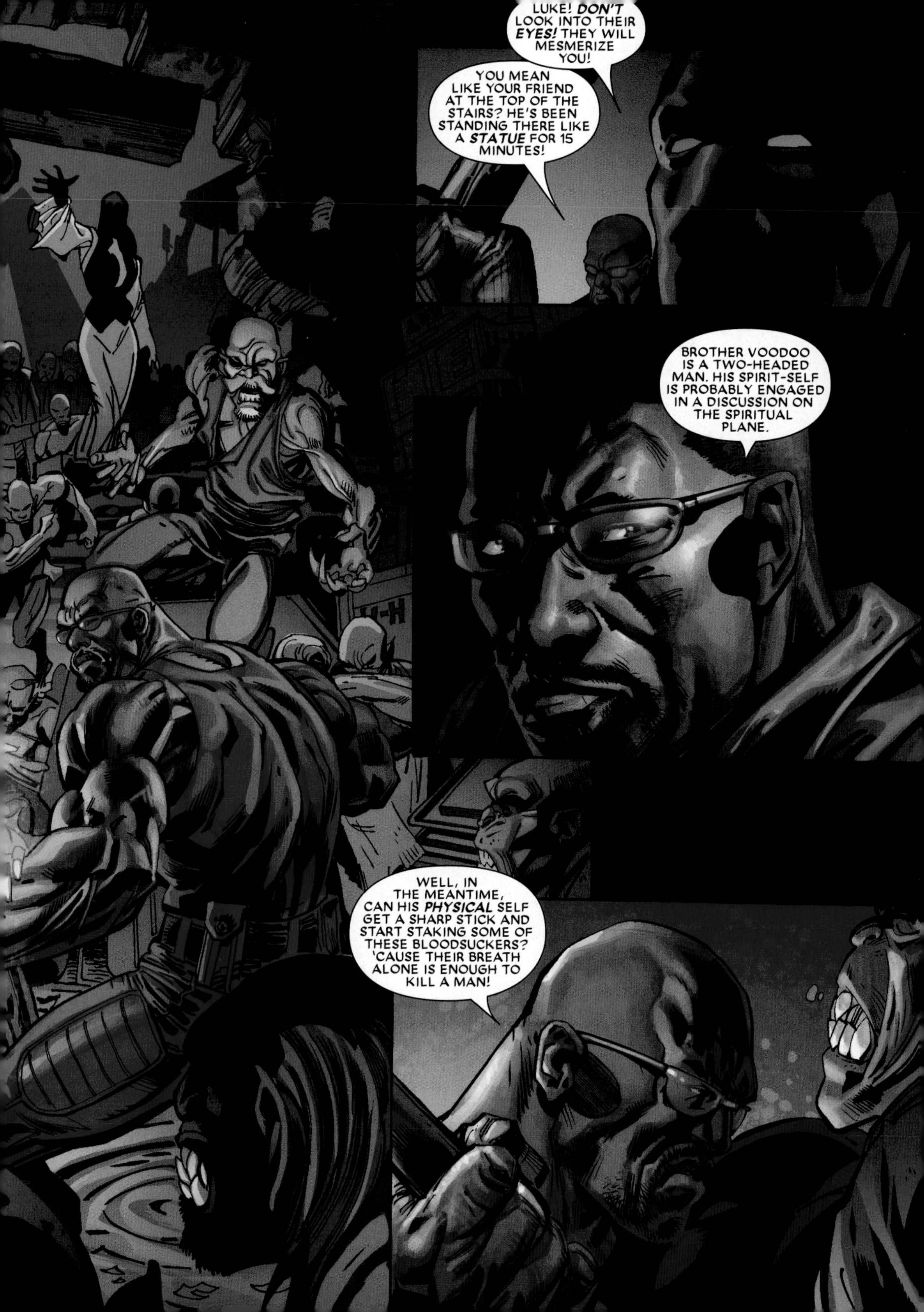
LUKE! DON'T LOOK INTO THEIR EYES! THEY WILL MESMERIZE YOU!
YOU MEAN LIKE YOUR FRIEND AT THE TOP OF THE STAIRS? HE'S BEEN STANDING THERE LIKE A STATUE FOR 15 MINUTES!
BROTHER VOODOO IS A TWO-HEADED MAN. HIS SPIRIT-SELF IS PROBABLY ENGAGED IN A DISCUSSION ON THE SPIRITUAL PLANE.
WELL, IN THE MEANTIME, CAN HIS PHYSICAL SELF GET A SHARP STICK AND START STAKING SOME OF THESE BLOODSUCKERS? 'CAUSE THEIR BREATH ALONE IS ENOUGH TO KILL A MAN!

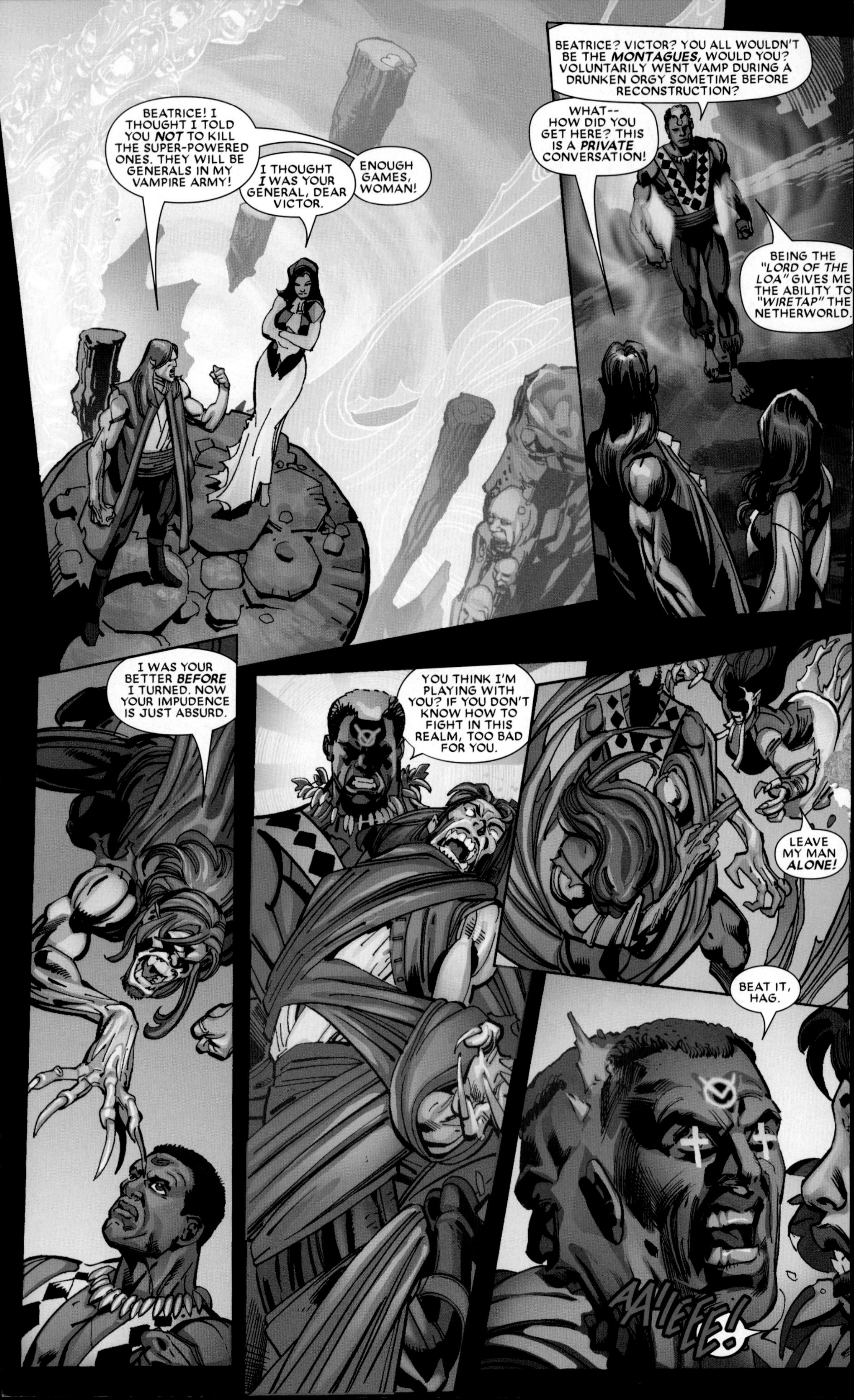
BEATRICE! I THOUGHT I TOLD YOU NOT TO KILL THE SUPER-POWERED ONES. THEY WILL BE GENERALS IN MY VAMPIRE ARMY!
I THOUGHT I WAS YOUR GENERAL, DEAR VICTOR.
ENOUGH GAMES, WOMAN!
BEATRICE? VICTOR? YOU ALL WOULDN'T BE THE MONTAGUES, WOULD YOU? VOLUNTARILY WENT VAMP DURING A DRUNKEN ORGY SOMETIME BEFORE RECONSTRUCTION?
WHAT-- HOW DID YOU GET HERE? THIS IS A PRIVATE CONVERSATION!
BEING THE "LORD OF THE LOA" GIVES ME THE ABILITY TO "WIRETAP" THE NETHERWORLD.
I WAS YOUR BETTER BEFORE I TURNED. NOW YOUR IMPUDENCE IS JUST ABSURD.
YOU THINK I'M PLAYING WITH YOU? IF YOU DON'T KNOW HOW TO FIGHT IN THIS REALM, TOO BAD FOR YOU.
LEAVE MY MAN ALONE!
BEAT IT, HAG.
AAIEEEE!

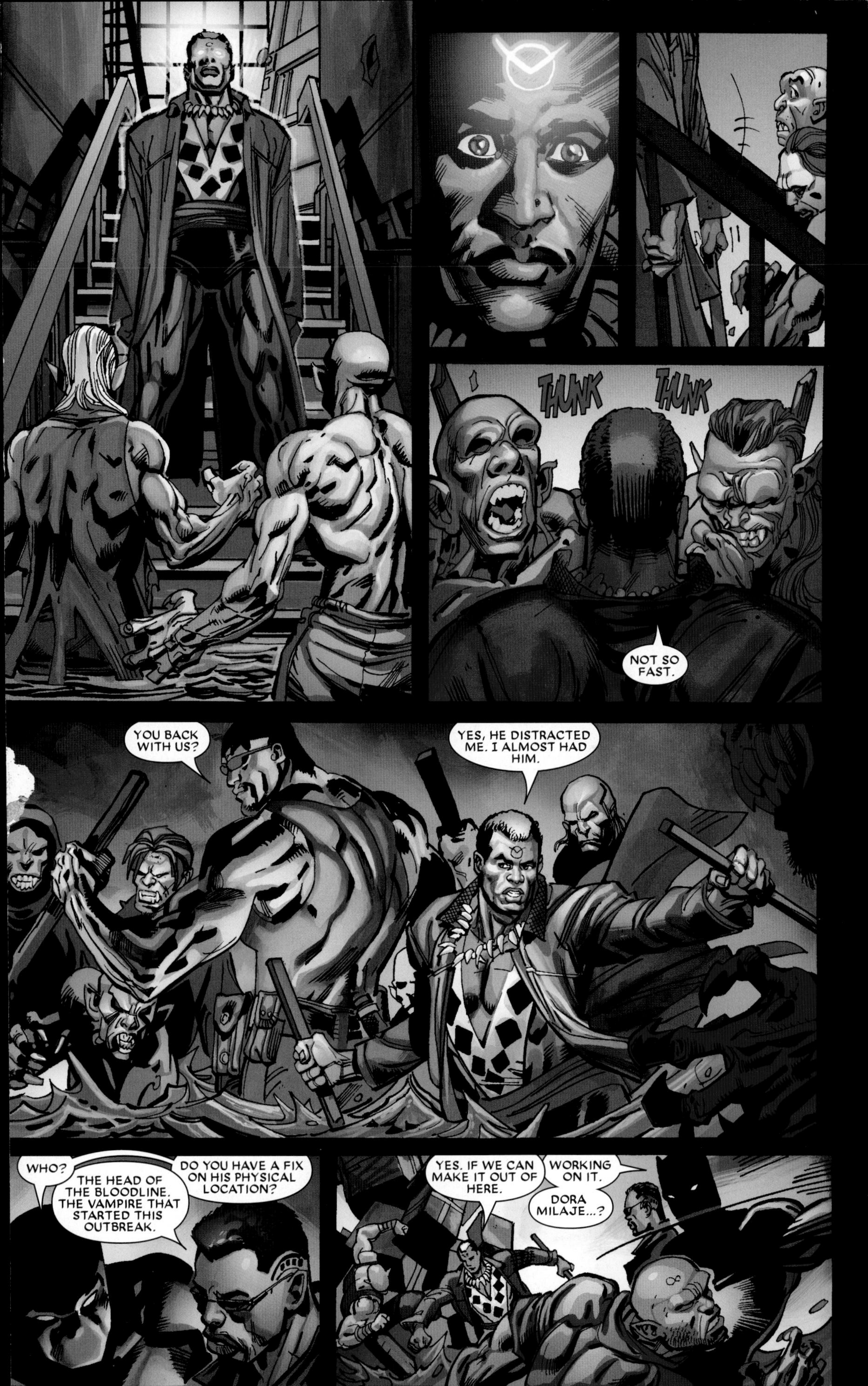
THUNK
THUNK
NOT SO FAST.
YOU BACK WITH US?
YES, HE DISTRACTED ME. I ALMOST HAD HIM.
WHO?
THE HEAD OF THE BLOODLINE. THE VAMPIRE THAT STARTED THIS OUTBREAK.
DO YOU HAVE A FIX ON HIS PHYSICAL LOCATION?
YES. IF WE CAN MAKE IT OUT OF HERE.
WORKING ON IT.
DORA MILAJE...?

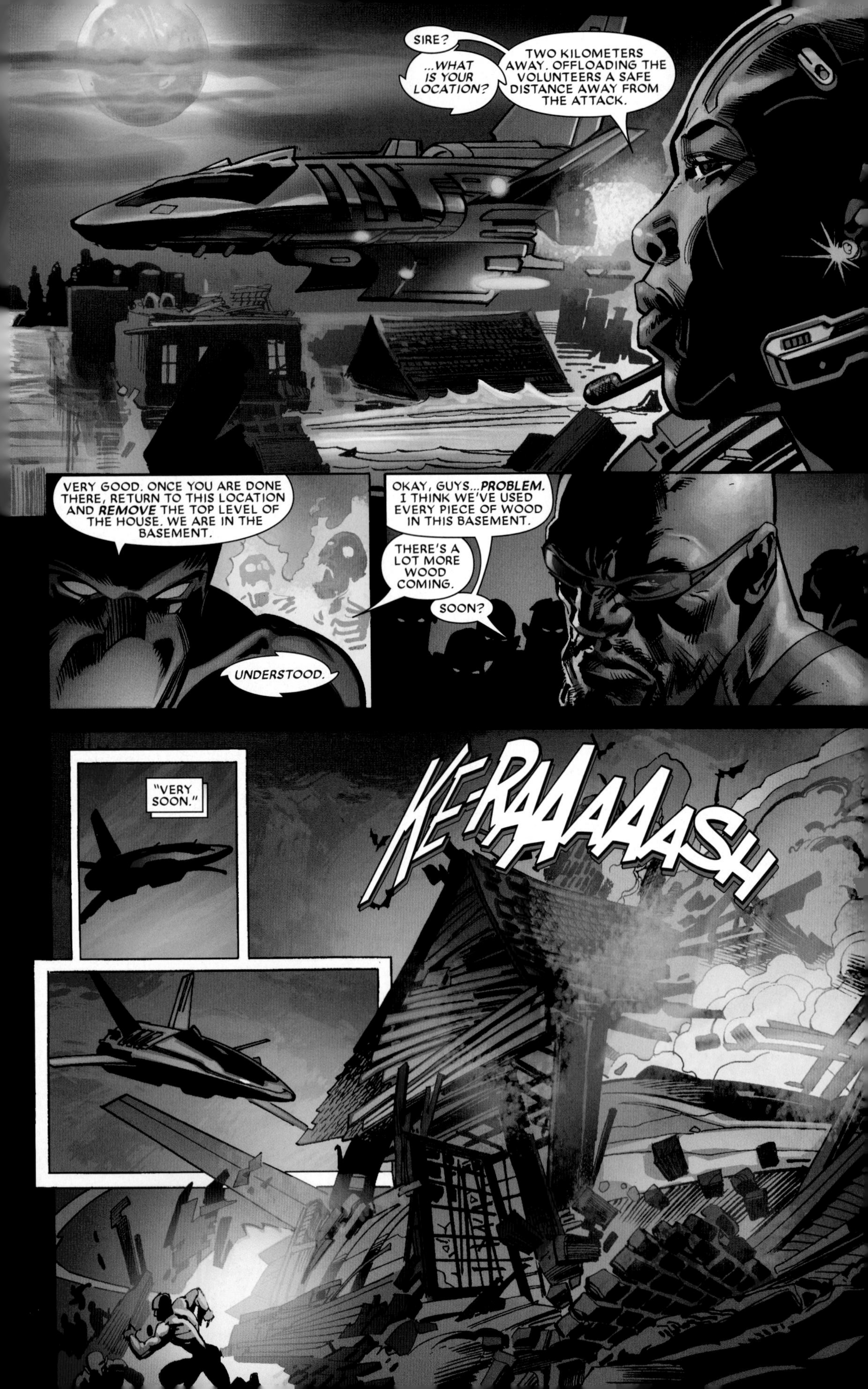
SIRE?
...WHAT IS YOUR LOCATION?
TWO KILOMETERS AWAY. OFFLOADING THE VOLUNTEERS A SAFE DISTANCE AWAY FROM THE ATTACK.
VERY GOOD. ONCE YOU ARE DONE THERE, RETURN TO THIS LOCATION AND REMOVE THE TOP LEVEL OF THE HOUSE. WE ARE IN THE BASEMENT.
UNDERSTOOD.
OKAY, GUYS...PROBLEM. I THINK WE'VE USED EVERY PIECE OF WOOD IN THIS BASEMENT.
THERE'S A LOT MORE WOOD COMING.
SOON?
"VERY SOON."
KE-RAAAAASH

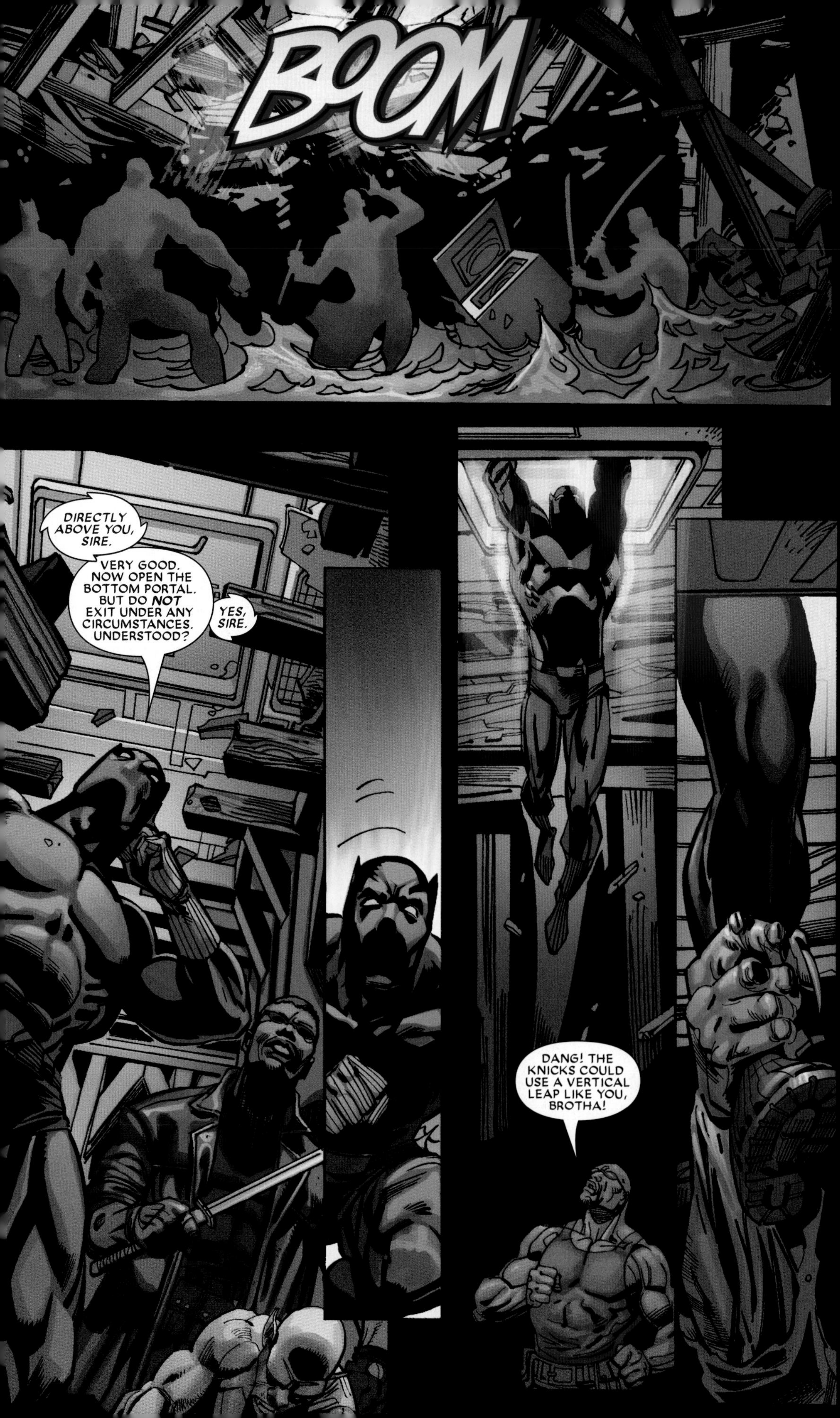
BOOM
DIRECTLY ABOVE YOU, SIRE.
VERY GOOD. NOW OPEN THE BOTTOM PORTAL. BUT DO NOT EXIT UNDER ANY CIRCUMSTANCES. UNDERSTOOD?
YES, SIRE.
DANG! THE KNICKS COULD USE A VERTICAL LEAP LIKE YOU, BROTHA!

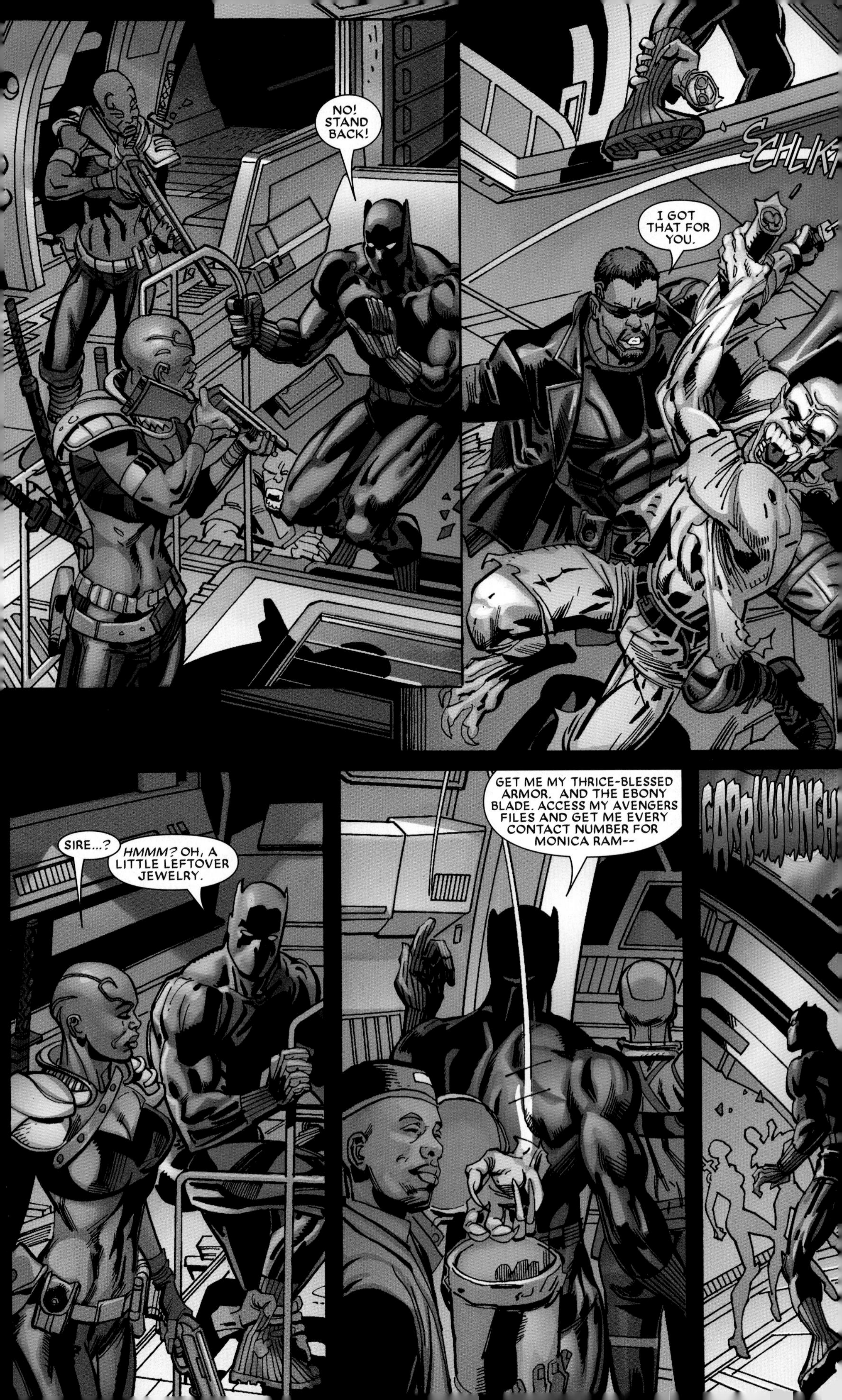
NO! STAND BACK!
SCHLIK!
I GOT THAT FOR YOU.
SIRE...?
HMMM? OH, A LITTLE LEFTOVER JEWELRY.
GET ME MY THRICE-BLESSED ARMOR. AND THE EBONY BLADE. ACCESS MY AVENGERS FILES AND GET ME EVERY CONTACT NUMBER FOR MONICA RAM--
CARRUUUNCH

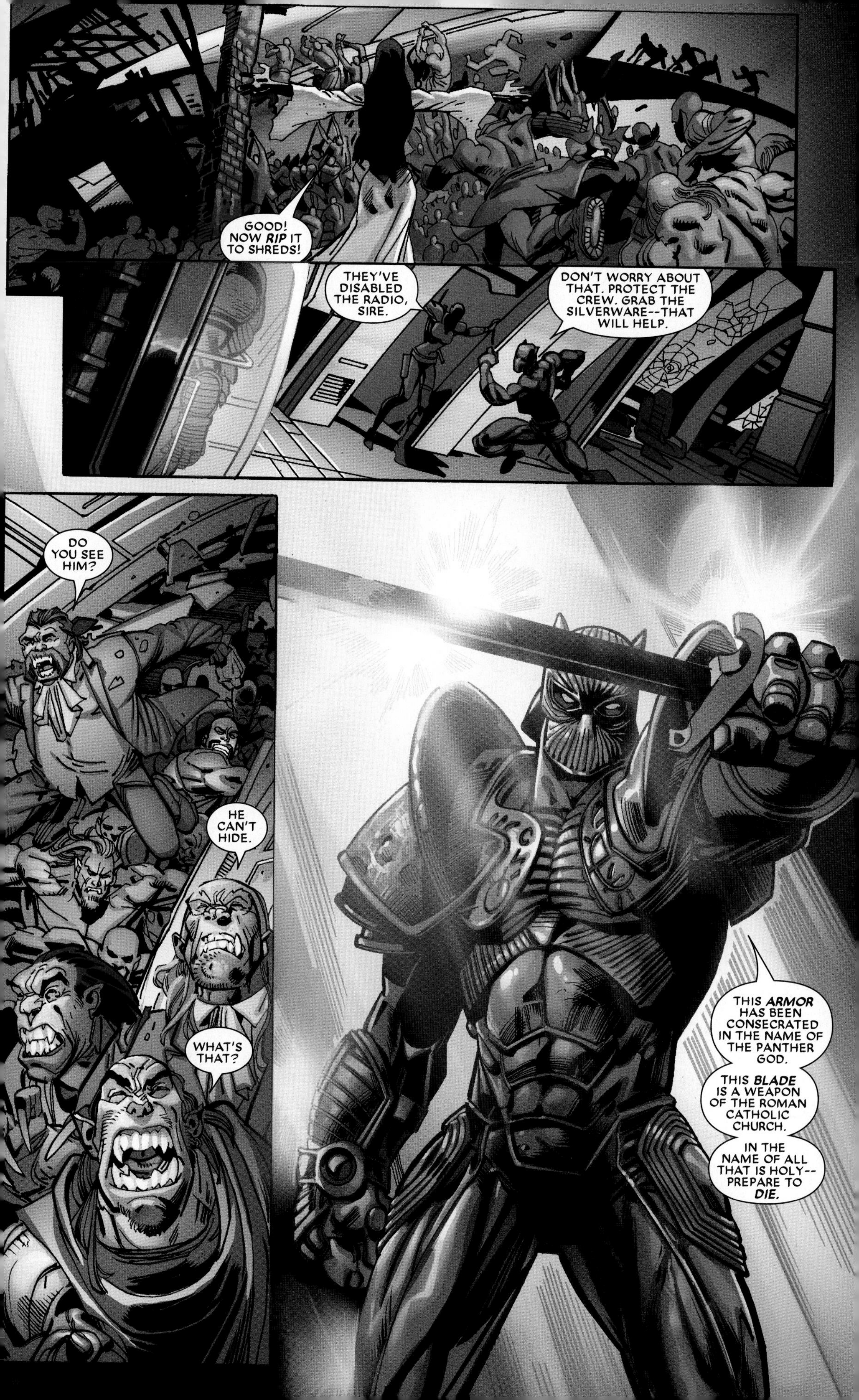
GOOD! NOW RIP IT TO SHREDS!
THEY'VE DISABLED THE RADIO, SIRE.
DON'T WORRY ABOUT THAT. PROTECT THE CREW. GRAB THE SILVERWARE--THAT WILL HELP.
DO YOU SEE HIM?
HE CAN'T HIDE.
WHAT'S THAT?
THIS ARMOR HAS BEEN CONSECRATED IN THE NAME OF THE PANTHER GOD.
THIS BLADE IS A WEAPON OF THE ROMAN CATHOLIC CHURCH.
IN THE NAME OF ALL THAT IS HOLY-- PREPARE TO DIE.

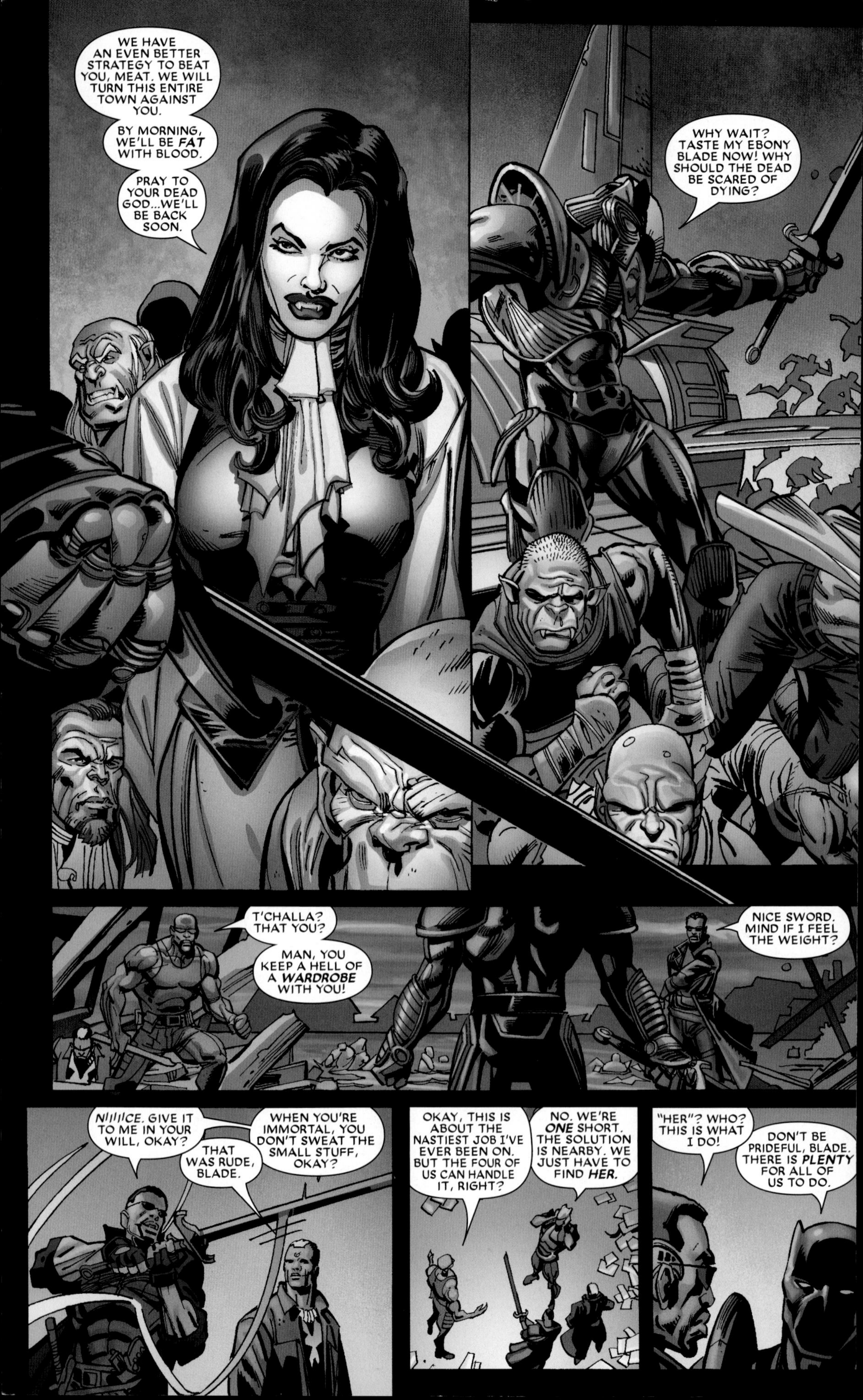
WE HAVE AN EVEN BETTER STRATEGY TO BEAT YOU, MEAT. WE WILL TURN THIS ENTIRE TOWN AGAINST YOU.
BY MORNING, WE'LL BE FAT WITH BLOOD.
PRAY TO YOUR DEAD GOD...WE'LL BE BACK SOON.
WHY WAIT? TASTE MY EBONY BLADE NOW! WHY SHOULD THE DEAD BE SCARED OF DYING?
T'CHALLA? THAT YOU?
MAN, YOU KEEP A HELL OF A WARDROBE WITH YOU!
NICE SWORD. MIND IF I FEEL THE WEIGHT?
NIIIICE. GIVE IT TO ME IN YOUR WILL, OKAY?
WHEN YOU'RE IMMORTAL, YOU DON'T SWEAT THE SMALL STUFF, OKAY?
THAT WAS RUDE, BLADE.
OKAY, THIS IS ABOUT THE NASTIEST JOB I'VE EVER BEEN ON. BUT THE FOUR OF US CAN HANDLE IT, RIGHT?
NO. WE'RE ONE SHORT. THE SOLUTION IS NEARBY. WE JUST HAVE TO FIND HER.
"HER"? WHO? THIS IS WHAT I DO!
DON'T BE PRIDEFUL, BLADE. THERE IS PLENTY FOR ALL OF US TO DO.

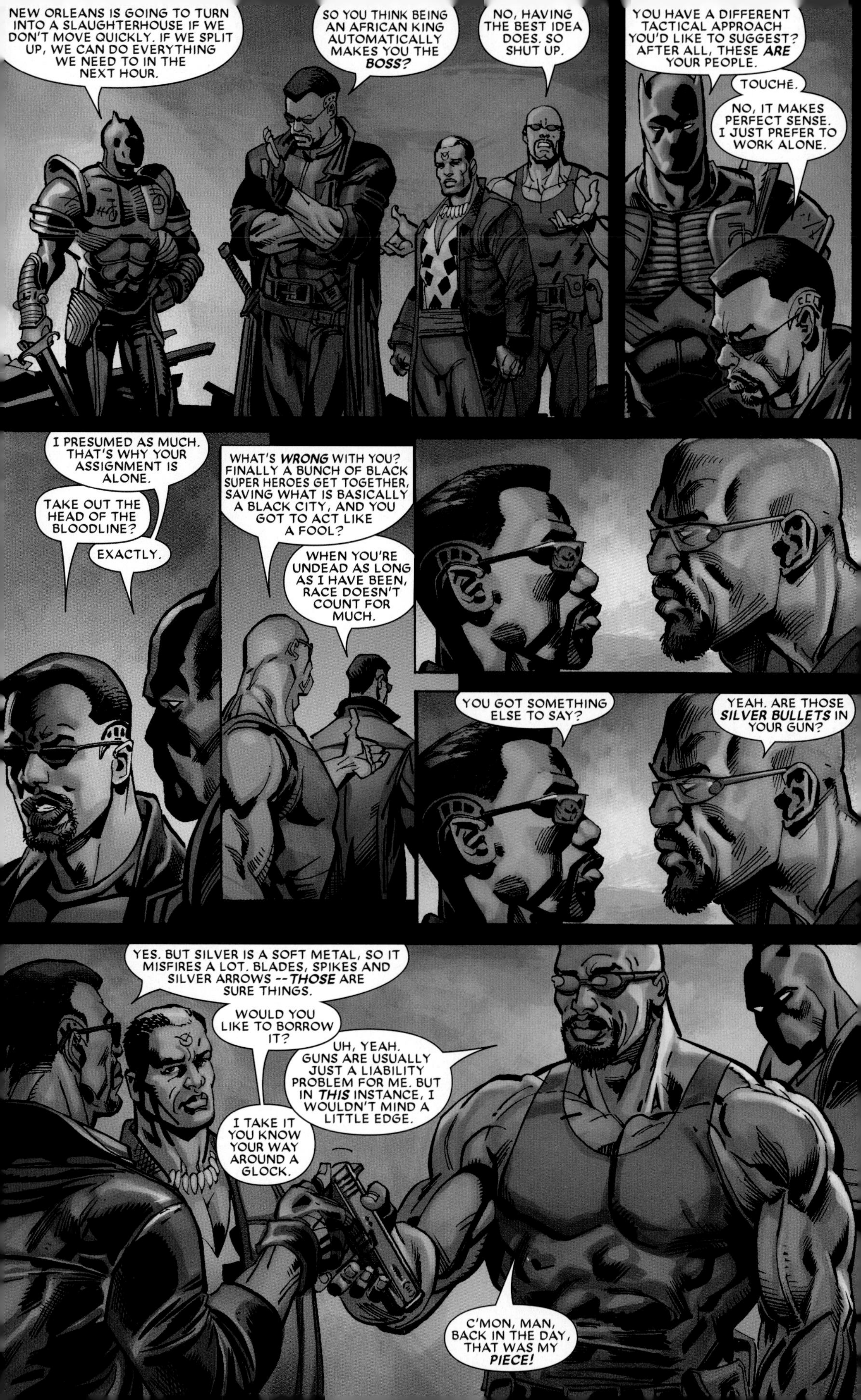
NEW ORLEANS IS GOING TO TURN INTO A SLAUGHTERHOUSE IF WE DON'T MOVE QUICKLY. IF WE SPLIT UP, WE CAN DO EVERYTHING WE NEED TO IN THE NEXT HOUR.
SO YOU THINK BEING AN AFRICAN KING AUTOMATICALLY MAKES YOU THE *BOSS?*
NO, HAVING THE BEST IDEA DOES. SO SHUT UP.
YOU HAVE A DIFFERENT TACTICAL APPROACH YOU'D LIKE TO SUGGEST? AFTER ALL, THESE *ARE* YOUR PEOPLE.
TOUCHÉ.
NO, IT MAKES PERFECT SENSE. I JUST PREFER TO WORK ALONE.
I PRESUMED AS MUCH. THAT'S WHY YOUR ASSIGNMENT IS ALONE.
TAKE OUT THE HEAD OF THE BLOODLINE?
EXACTLY.
WHAT'S *WRONG* WITH YOU? FINALLY A BUNCH OF BLACK SUPER HEROES GET TOGETHER, SAVING WHAT IS BASICALLY A BLACK CITY, AND YOU GOT TO ACT LIKE A FOOL?
WHEN YOU'RE UNDEAD AS LONG AS I HAVE BEEN, RACE DOESN'T COUNT FOR MUCH.
YOU GOT SOMETHING ELSE TO SAY?
YEAH. ARE THOSE *SILVER BULLETS* IN YOUR GUN?
YES. BUT SILVER IS A SOFT METAL, SO IT MISFIRES A LOT. BLADES, SPIKES AND SILVER ARROWS -- *THOSE* ARE SURE THINGS.
WOULD YOU LIKE TO BORROW IT?
UH, YEAH. GUNS ARE USUALLY JUST A LIABILITY PROBLEM FOR ME. BUT IN *THIS* INSTANCE, I WOULDN'T MIND A LITTLE EDGE.
I TAKE IT YOU KNOW YOUR WAY AROUND A GLOCK.
C'MON, MAN, BACK IN THE DAY, THAT WAS MY *PIECE!*

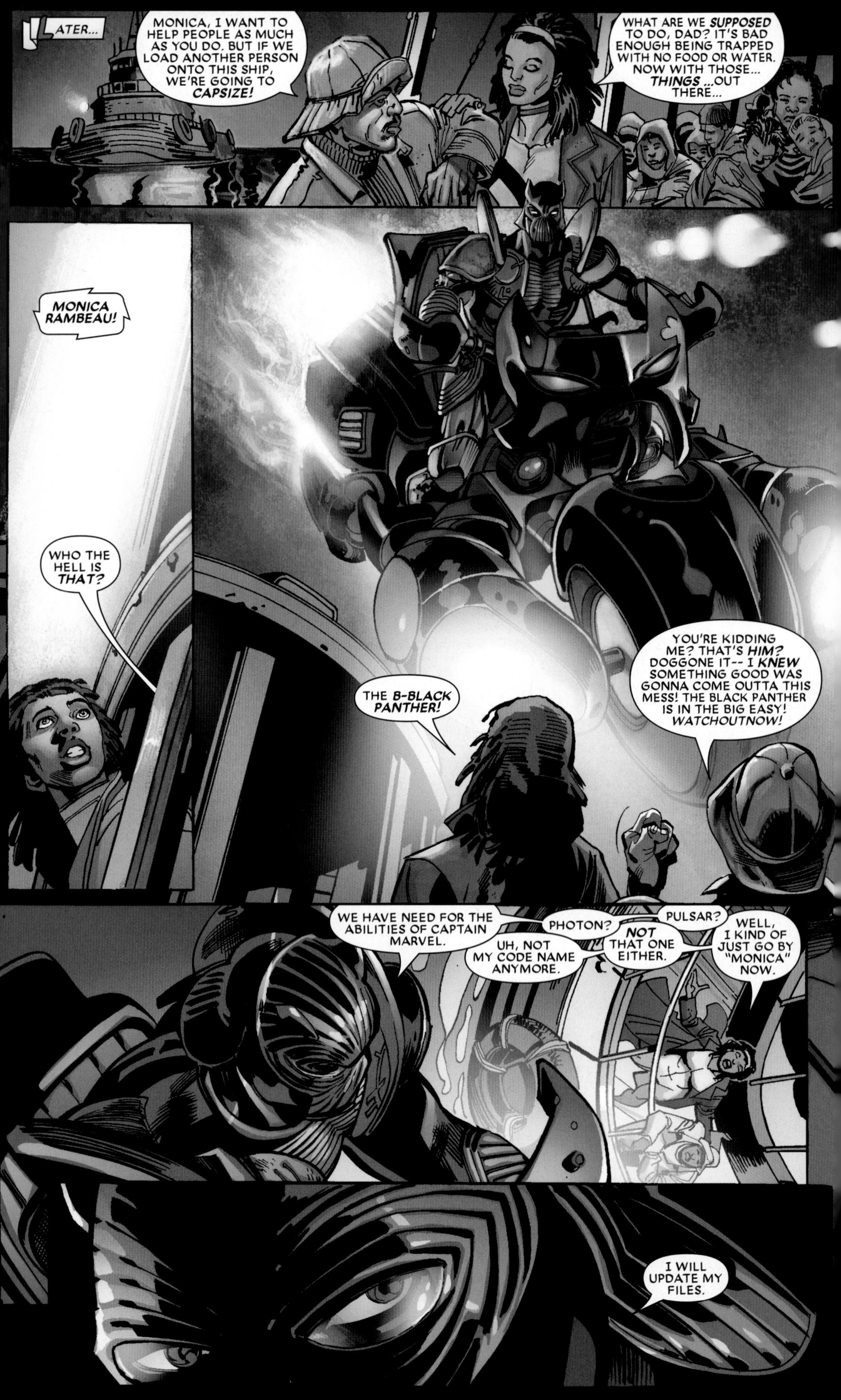
LATER...
MONICA, I WANT TO HELP PEOPLE AS MUCH AS YOU DO. BUT IF WE LOAD ANOTHER PERSON ONTO THIS SHIP, WE'RE GOING TO *CAPSIZE!*
WHAT ARE WE *SUPPOSED* TO DO, DAD? IT'S BAD ENOUGH BEING TRAPPED WITH NO FOOD OR WATER. NOW WITH THOSE... *THINGS*...OUT THERE...
MONICA RAMBEAU!
WHO THE HELL IS *THAT?*
THE *B-BLACK PANTHER!*
YOU'RE KIDDING ME? THAT'S *HIM?* DOGGONE IT-- I *KNEW* SOMETHING GOOD WAS GONNA COME OUTTA THIS MESS! THE BLACK PANTHER IS IN THE BIG EASY! *WATCHOUTNOW!*
WE HAVE NEED FOR THE ABILITIES OF CAPTAIN MARVEL.
UH, NOT MY CODE NAME ANYMORE.
PHOTON?
NOT THAT ONE EITHER.
PULSAR?
WELL, I KIND OF JUST GO BY "MONICA" NOW.
I WILL UPDATE MY FILES.

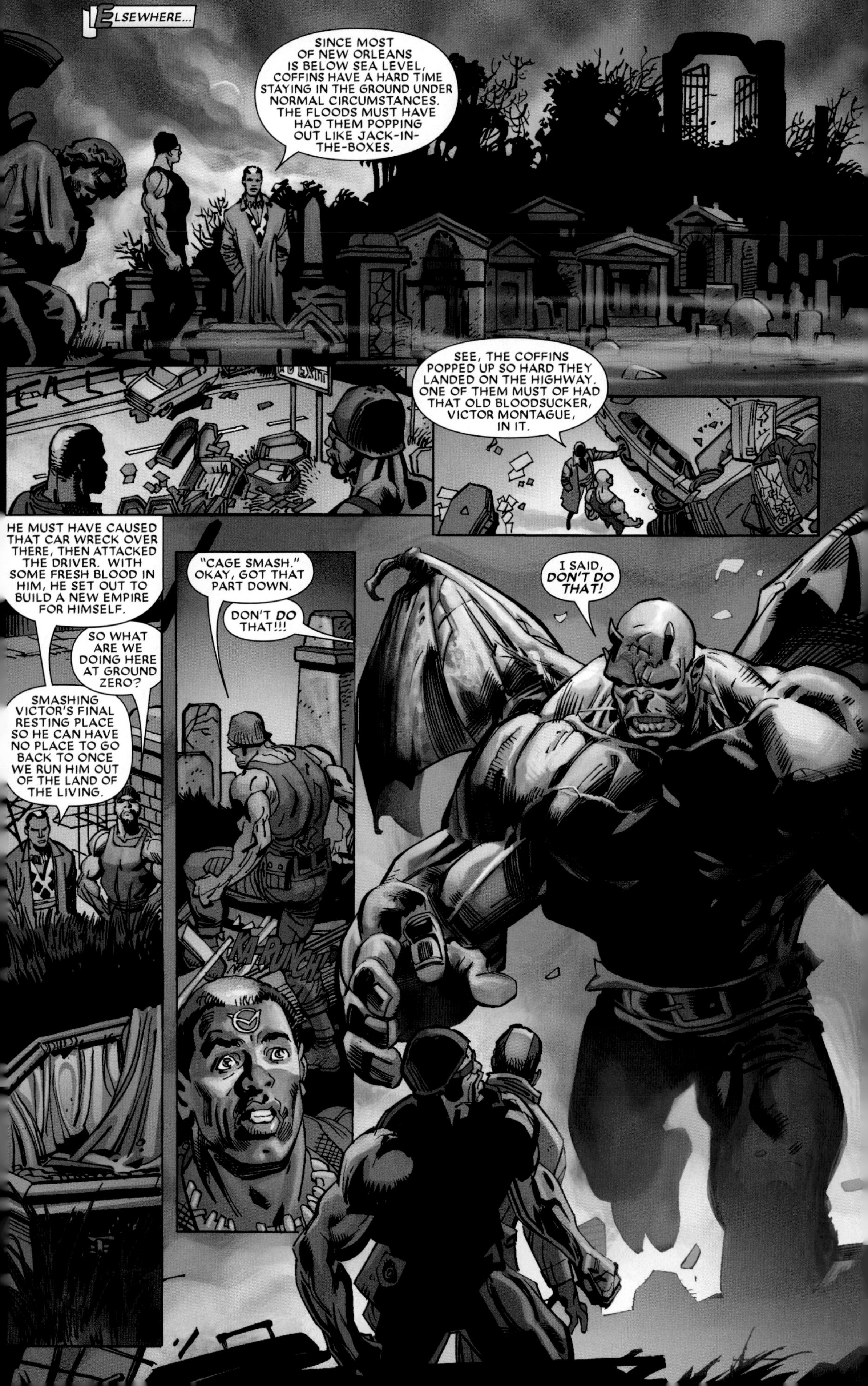
ELSEWHERE...
SINCE MOST OF NEW ORLEANS IS BELOW SEA LEVEL, COFFINS HAVE A HARD TIME STAYING IN THE GROUND UNDER NORMAL CIRCUMSTANCES. THE FLOODS MUST HAVE HAD THEM POPPING OUT LIKE JACK-IN-THE-BOXES.
SEE, THE COFFINS POPPED UP SO HARD THEY LANDED ON THE HIGHWAY. ONE OF THEM MUST OF HAD THAT OLD BLOODSUCKER, VICTOR MONTAGUE, IN IT.
HE MUST HAVE CAUSED THAT CAR WRECK OVER THERE, THEN ATTACKED THE DRIVER. WITH SOME FRESH BLOOD IN HIM, HE SET OUT TO BUILD A NEW EMPIRE FOR HIMSELF.
SO WHAT ARE WE DOING HERE AT GROUND ZERO?
SMASHING VICTOR'S FINAL RESTING PLACE SO HE CAN HAVE NO PLACE TO GO BACK TO ONCE WE RUN HIM OUT OF THE LAND OF THE LIVING.
"CAGE SMASH." OKAY, GOT THAT PART DOWN.
DON'T DO THAT!!!
KA-RUNCH!
I SAID, DON'T DO THAT!

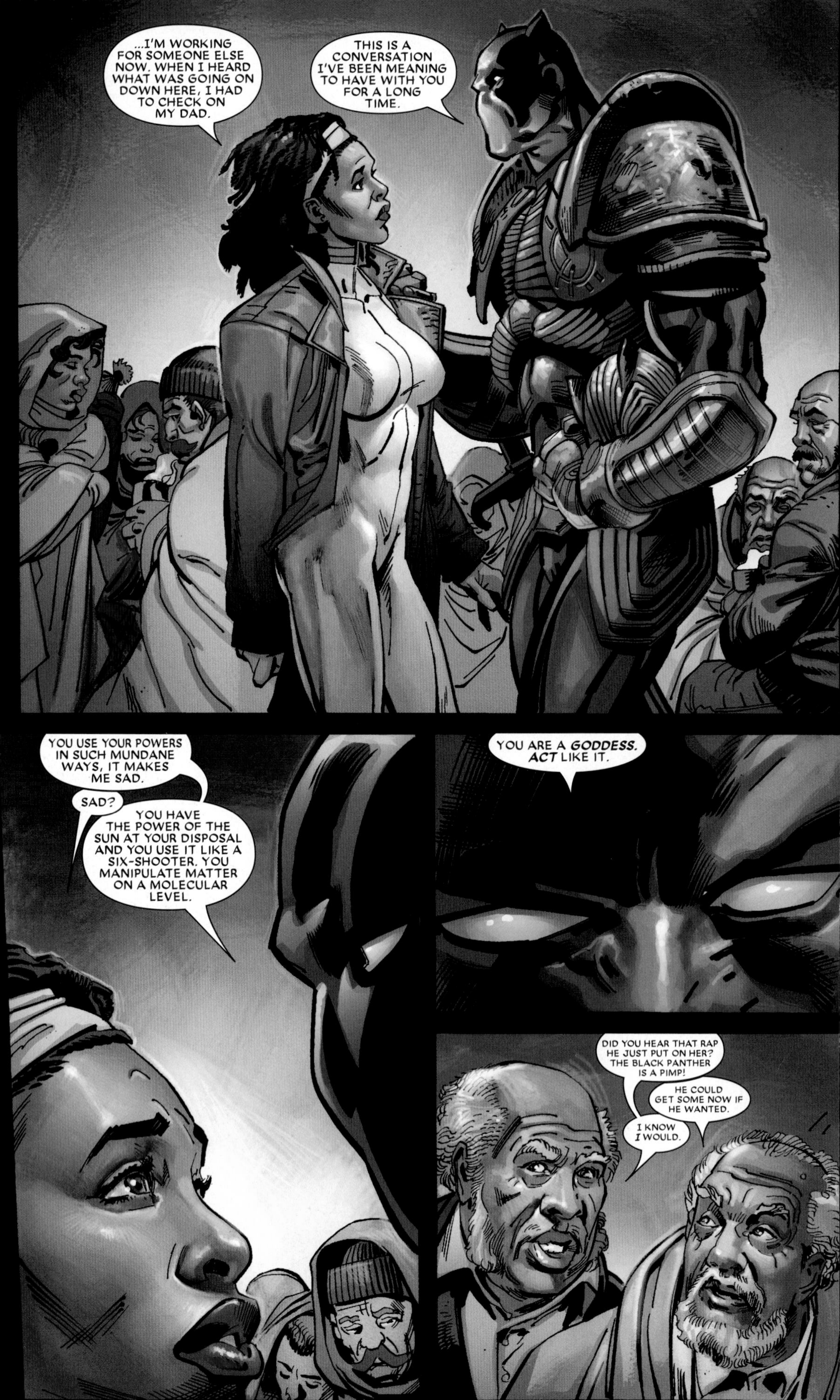
...I'M WORKING FOR SOMEONE ELSE NOW. WHEN I HEARD WHAT WAS GOING ON DOWN HERE, I HAD TO CHECK ON MY DAD.
THIS IS A CONVERSATION I'VE BEEN MEANING TO HAVE WITH YOU FOR A LONG TIME.
YOU USE YOUR POWERS IN SUCH MUNDANE WAYS, IT MAKES ME SAD.
SAD?
YOU HAVE THE POWER OF THE SUN AT YOUR DISPOSAL AND YOU USE IT LIKE A SIX-SHOOTER. YOU MANIPULATE MATTER ON A MOLECULAR LEVEL.
YOU ARE A *GODDESS.* *ACT* LIKE IT.
DID YOU HEAR THAT RAP HE JUST PUT ON HER? THE BLACK PANTHER IS A PIMP!
HE COULD GET SOME NOW IF HE WANTED.
I KNOW *I* WOULD.

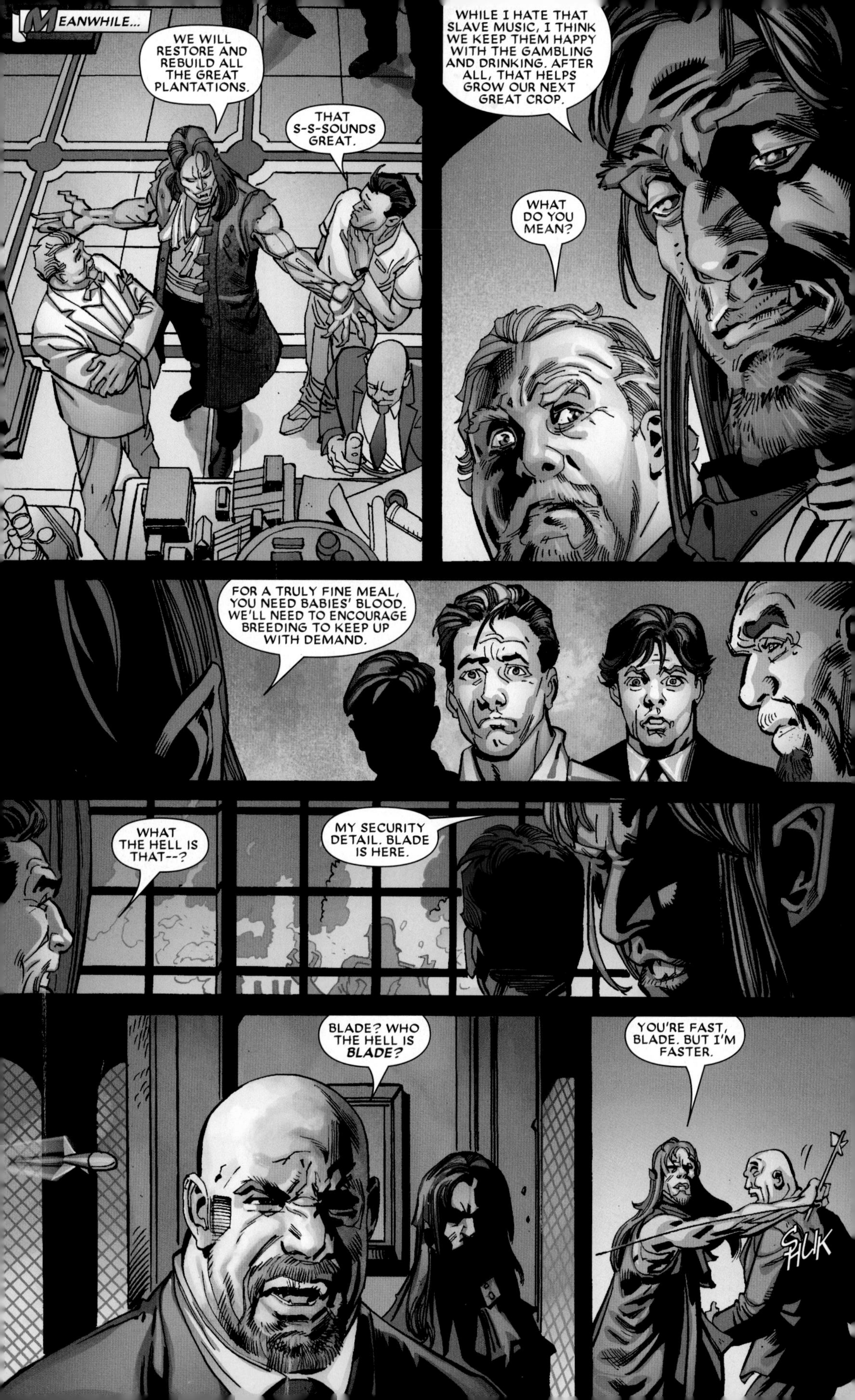
MEANWHILE...
WE WILL RESTORE AND REBUILD ALL THE GREAT PLANTATIONS.
THAT S-S-SOUNDS GREAT.
WHILE I HATE THAT SLAVE MUSIC, I THINK WE KEEP THEM HAPPY WITH THE GAMBLING AND DRINKING. AFTER ALL, THAT HELPS GROW OUR NEXT GREAT CROP.
WHAT DO YOU MEAN?
FOR A TRULY FINE MEAL, YOU NEED BABIES' BLOOD. WE'LL NEED TO ENCOURAGE BREEDING TO KEEP UP WITH DEMAND.
WHAT THE HELL IS THAT--?
MY SECURITY DETAIL. BLADE IS HERE.
BLADE? WHO THE HELL IS *BLADE?*
YOU'RE FAST, BLADE. BUT I'M FASTER.
SHUK

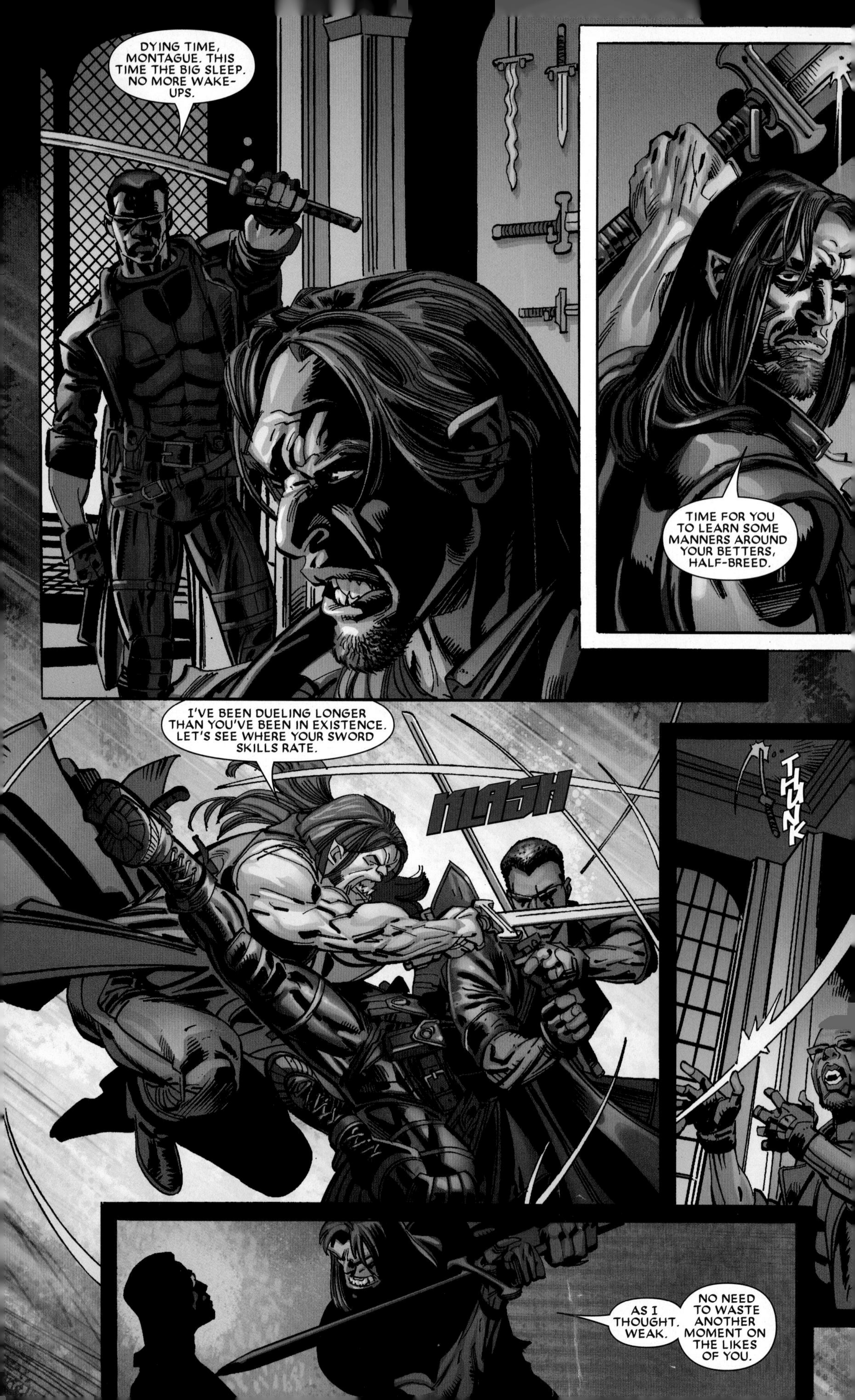
DYING TIME, MONTAGUE. THIS TIME THE BIG SLEEP. NO MORE WAKE-UPS.
TIME FOR YOU TO LEARN SOME MANNERS AROUND YOUR BETTERS, HALF-BREED.
I'VE BEEN DUELING LONGER THAN YOU'VE BEEN IN EXISTENCE. LET'S SEE WHERE YOUR SWORD SKILLS RATE.
KLASH
THUNK
AS I THOUGHT. WEAK.
NO NEED TO WASTE ANOTHER MOMENT ON THE LIKES OF YOU.

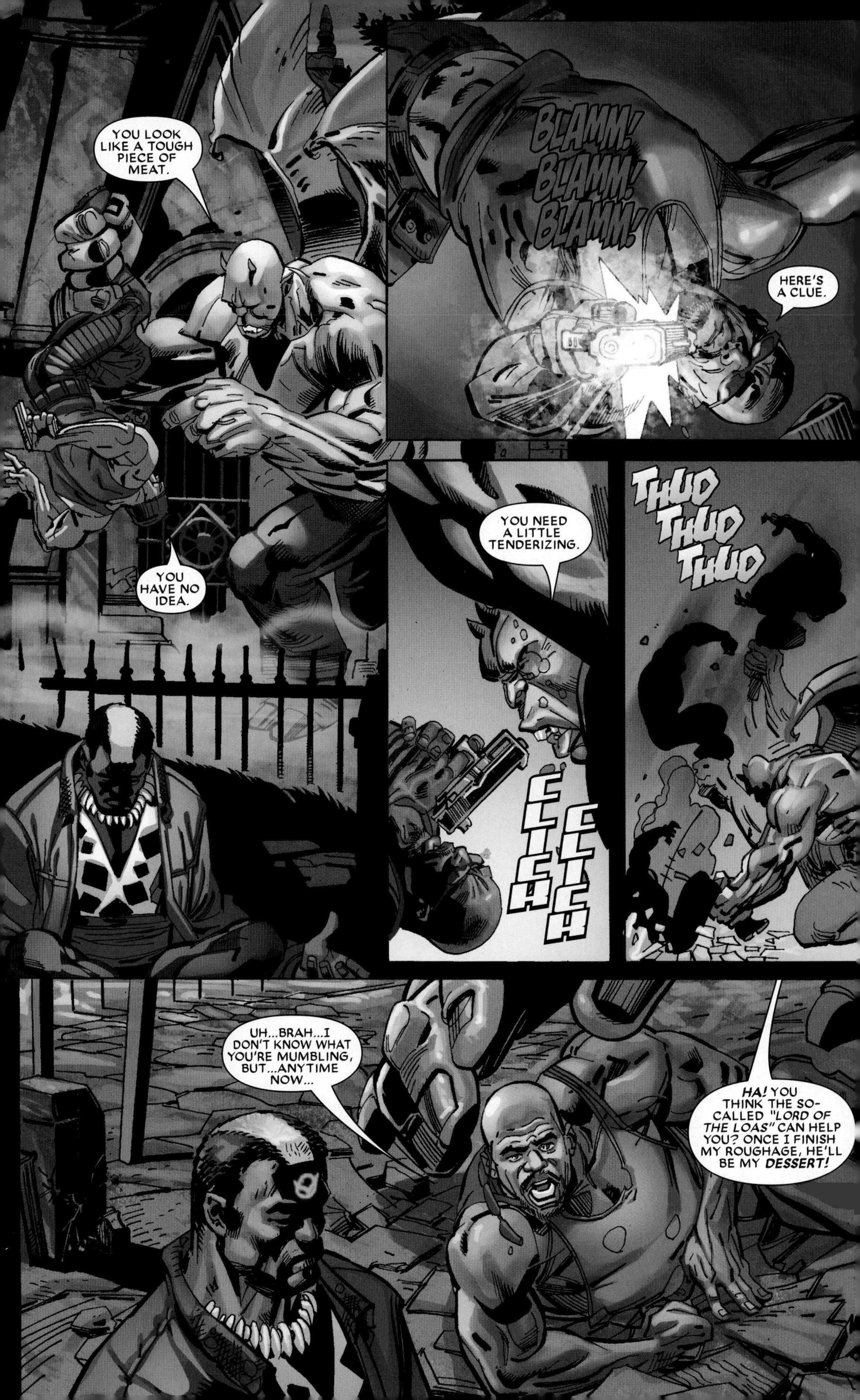
YOU LOOK LIKE A TOUGH PIECE OF MEAT.
BLAMM! BLAMM! BLAMM!
HERE'S A CLUE.
YOU HAVE NO IDEA.
YOU NEED A LITTLE TENDERIZING.
CLICH CLICH
THUD THUD THUD
UH...BRAH...I DON'T KNOW WHAT YOU'RE MUMBLING, BUT...ANYTIME NOW...
HA! YOU THINK THE SO-CALLED "LORD OF THE LOAS" CAN HELP YOU? ONCE I FINISH MY ROUGHAGE, HE'LL BE MY DESSERT!

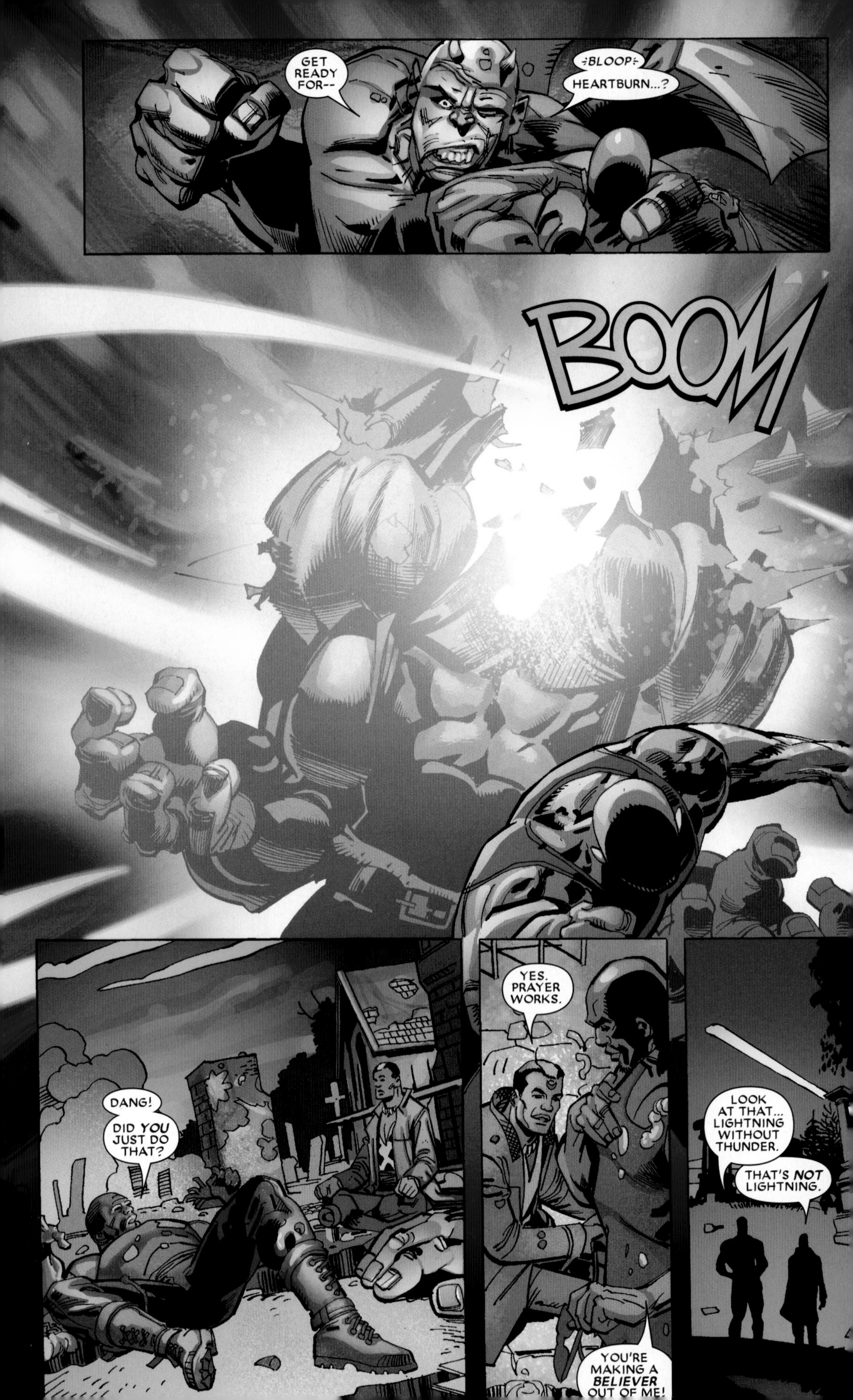
GET READY FOR--
÷BLOOP÷
HEARTBURN...?
BOOM
DANG!
DID YOU JUST DO THAT?
YES. PRAYER WORKS.
YOU'RE MAKING A BELIEVER OUT OF ME!
LOOK AT THAT... LIGHTNING WITHOUT THUNDER.
THAT'S NOT LIGHTNING.

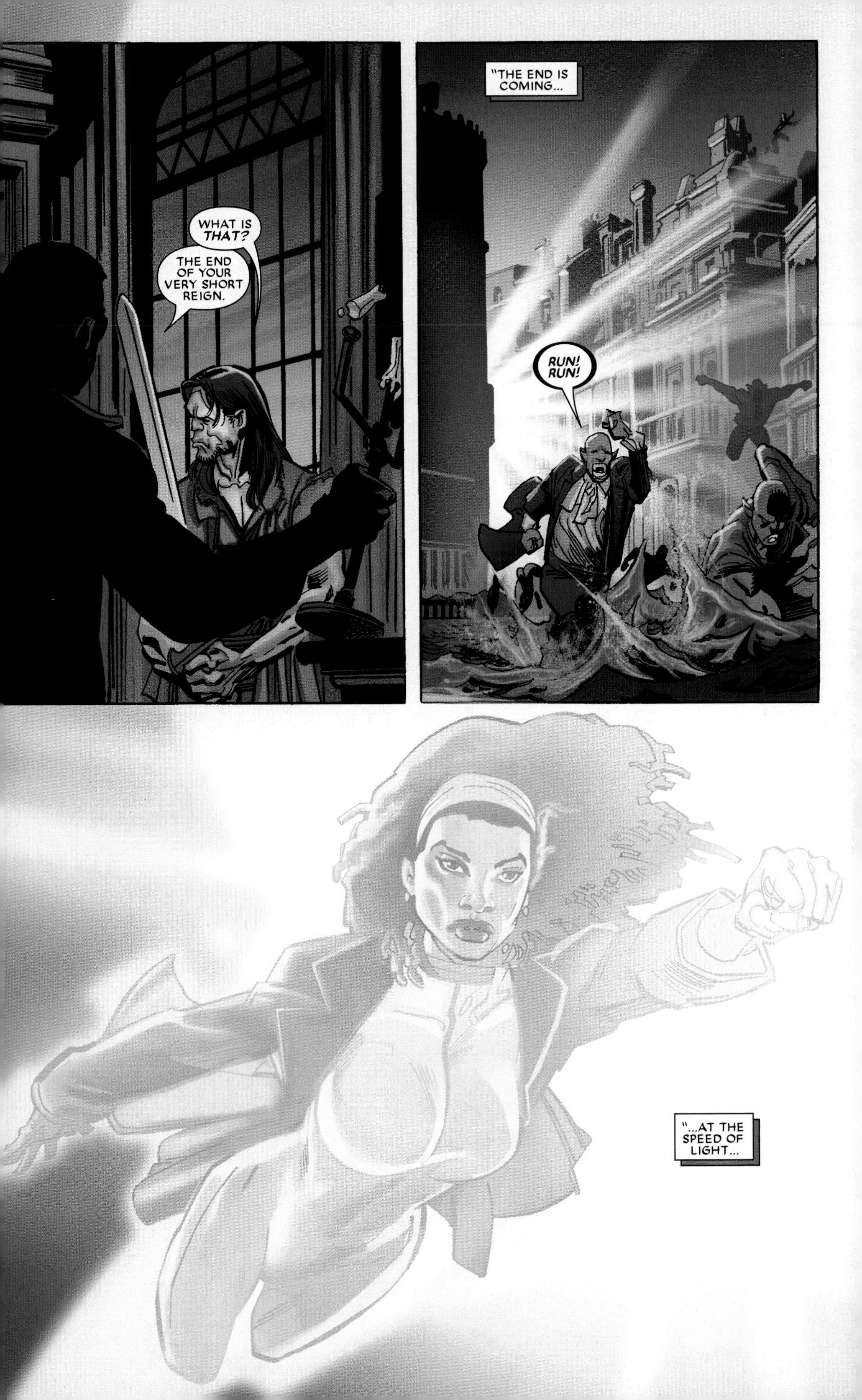
WHAT IS THAT?
THE END OF YOUR VERY SHORT REIGN.
"THE END IS COMING...
RUN! RUN!
"...AT THE SPEED OF LIGHT...

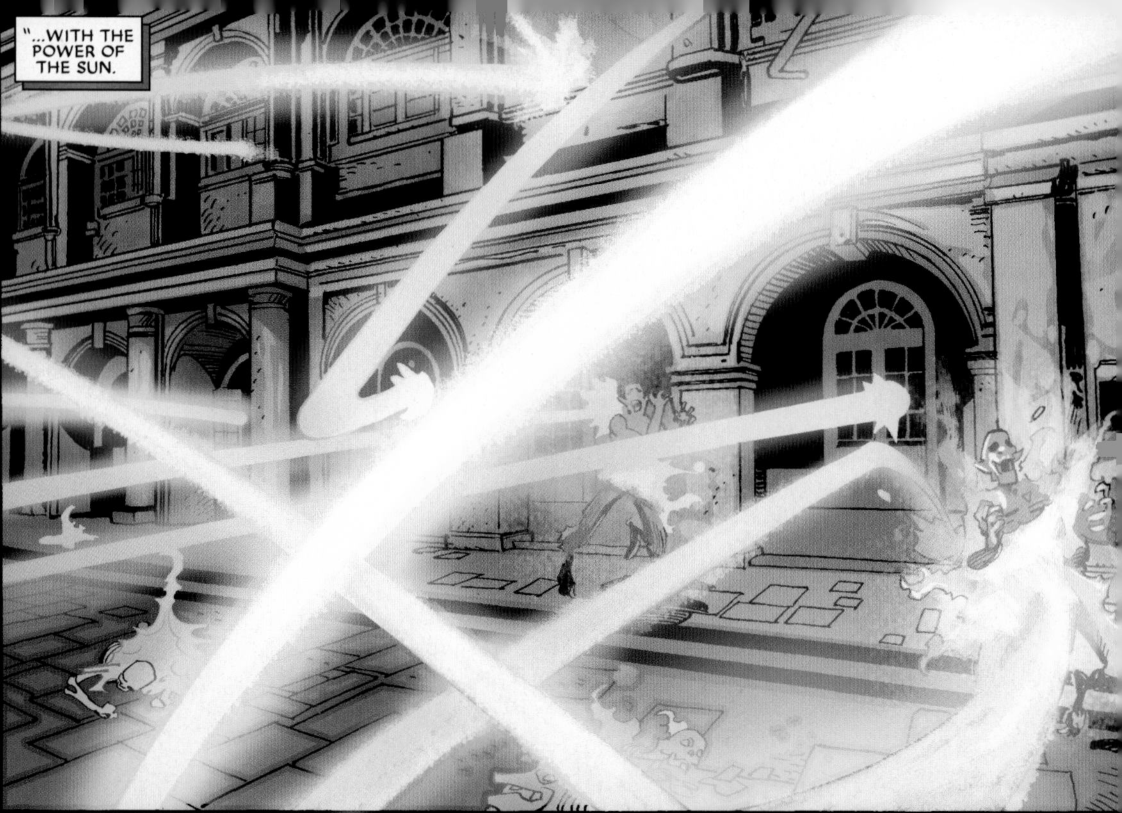
"...WITH THE POWER OF THE SUN.

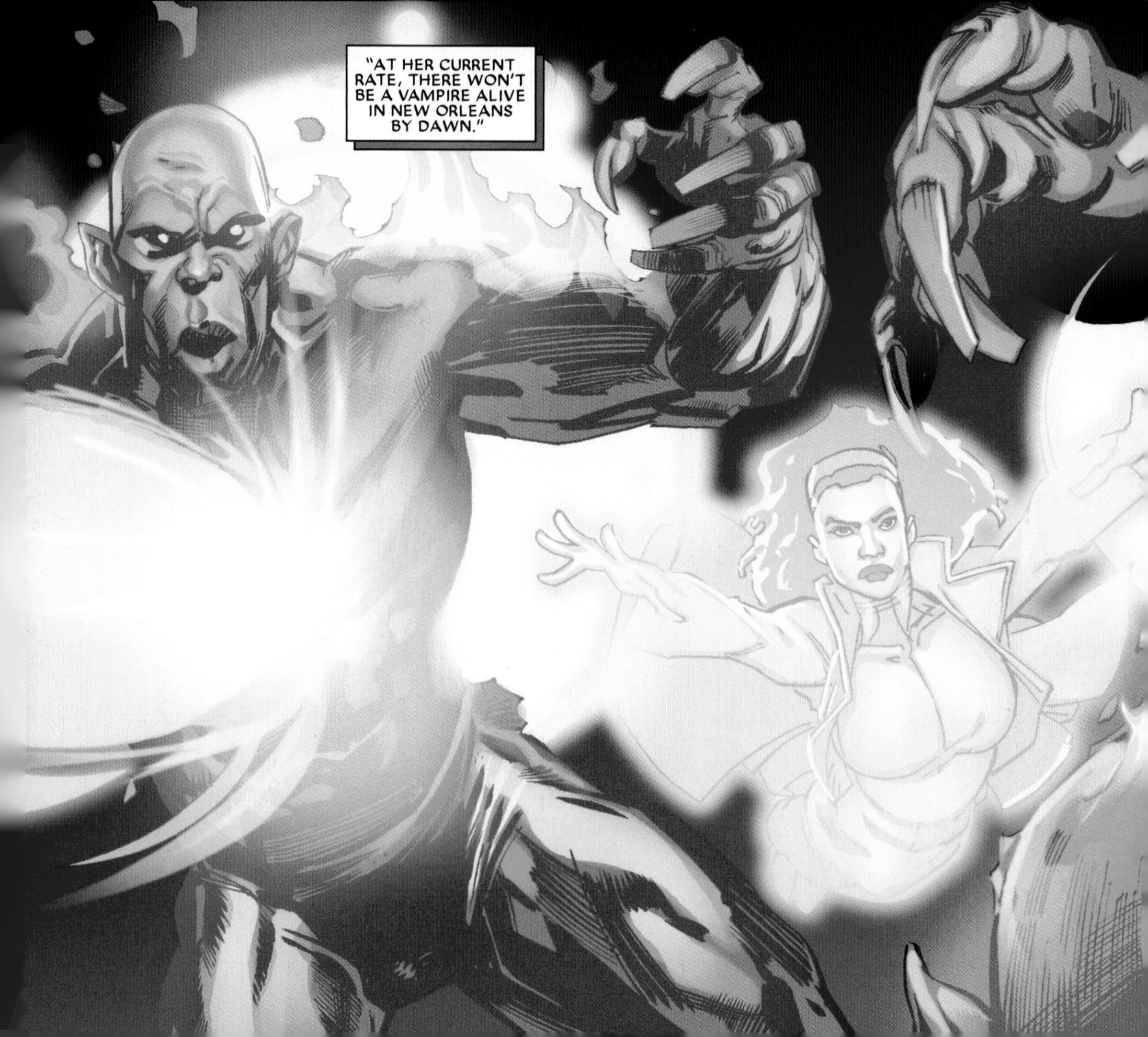
"AT HER CURRENT RATE, THERE WON'T BE A VAMPIRE ALIVE IN NEW ORLEANS BY DAWN."

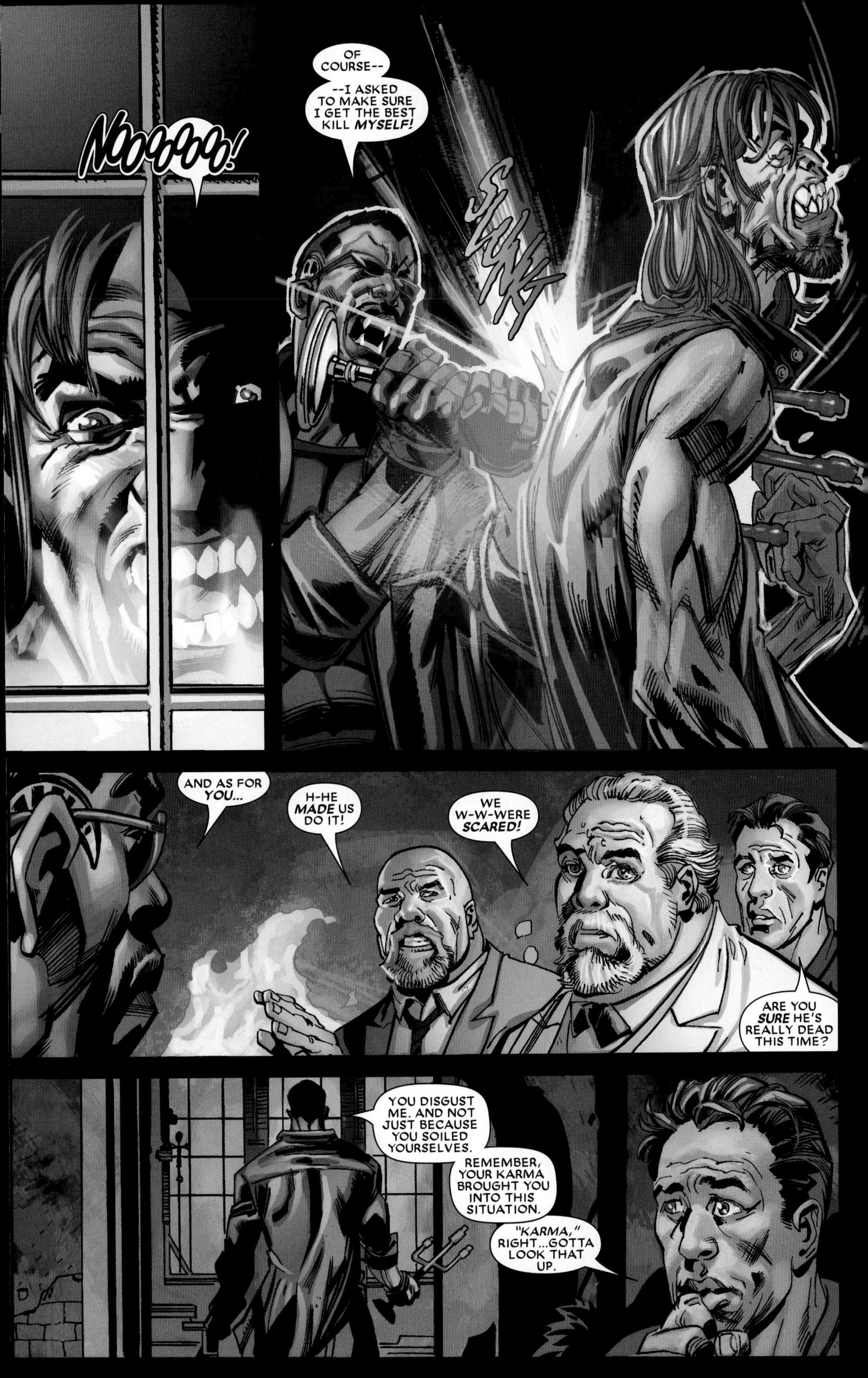

NOOOOOOO!
OF COURSE--
--I ASKED TO MAKE SURE I GET THE BEST KILL *MYSELF!*
SLUNK
AND AS FOR *YOU*...
H-HE *MADE* US DO IT!
WE W-W-WERE *SCARED!*
ARE YOU *SURE* HE'S REALLY DEAD THIS TIME?
YOU DISGUST ME. AND NOT JUST BECAUSE YOU SOILED YOURSELVES.
REMEMBER, YOUR KARMA BROUGHT YOU INTO THIS SITUATION.
"KARMA," RIGHT...GOTTA LOOK THAT UP.

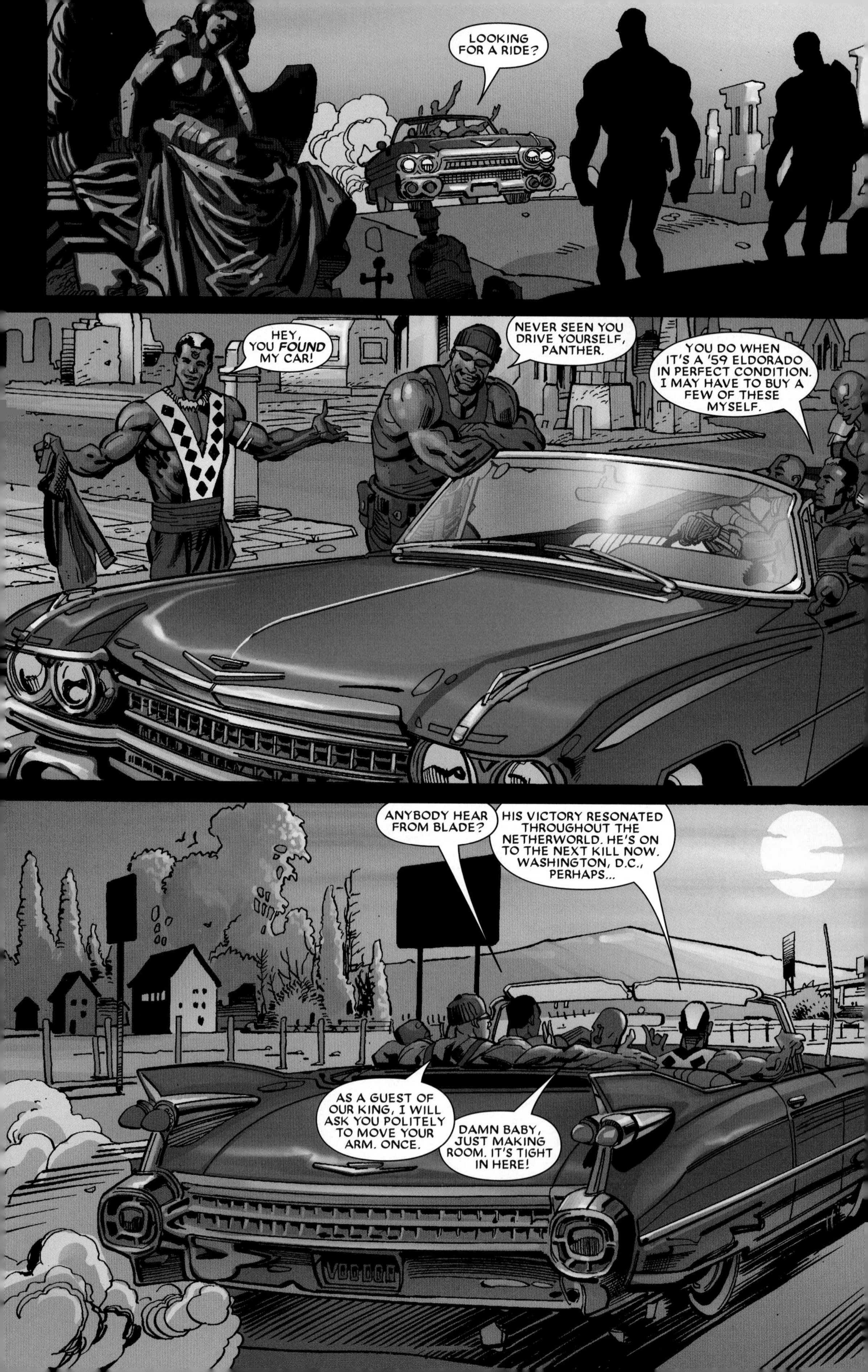

LOOKING FOR A RIDE?
HEY, YOU *FOUND* MY CAR!
NEVER SEEN YOU DRIVE YOURSELF, PANTHER.
YOU DO WHEN IT'S A '59 ELDORADO IN PERFECT CONDITION. I MAY HAVE TO BUY A FEW OF THESE MYSELF.
ANYBODY HEAR FROM BLADE?
HIS VICTORY RESONATED THROUGHOUT THE NETHERWORLD. HE'S ON TO THE NEXT KILL NOW. WASHINGTON, D.C., PERHAPS...
AS A GUEST OF OUR KING, I WILL ASK YOU POLITELY TO MOVE YOUR ARM. ONCE.
DAMN BABY, JUST MAKING ROOM. IT'S TIGHT IN HERE!

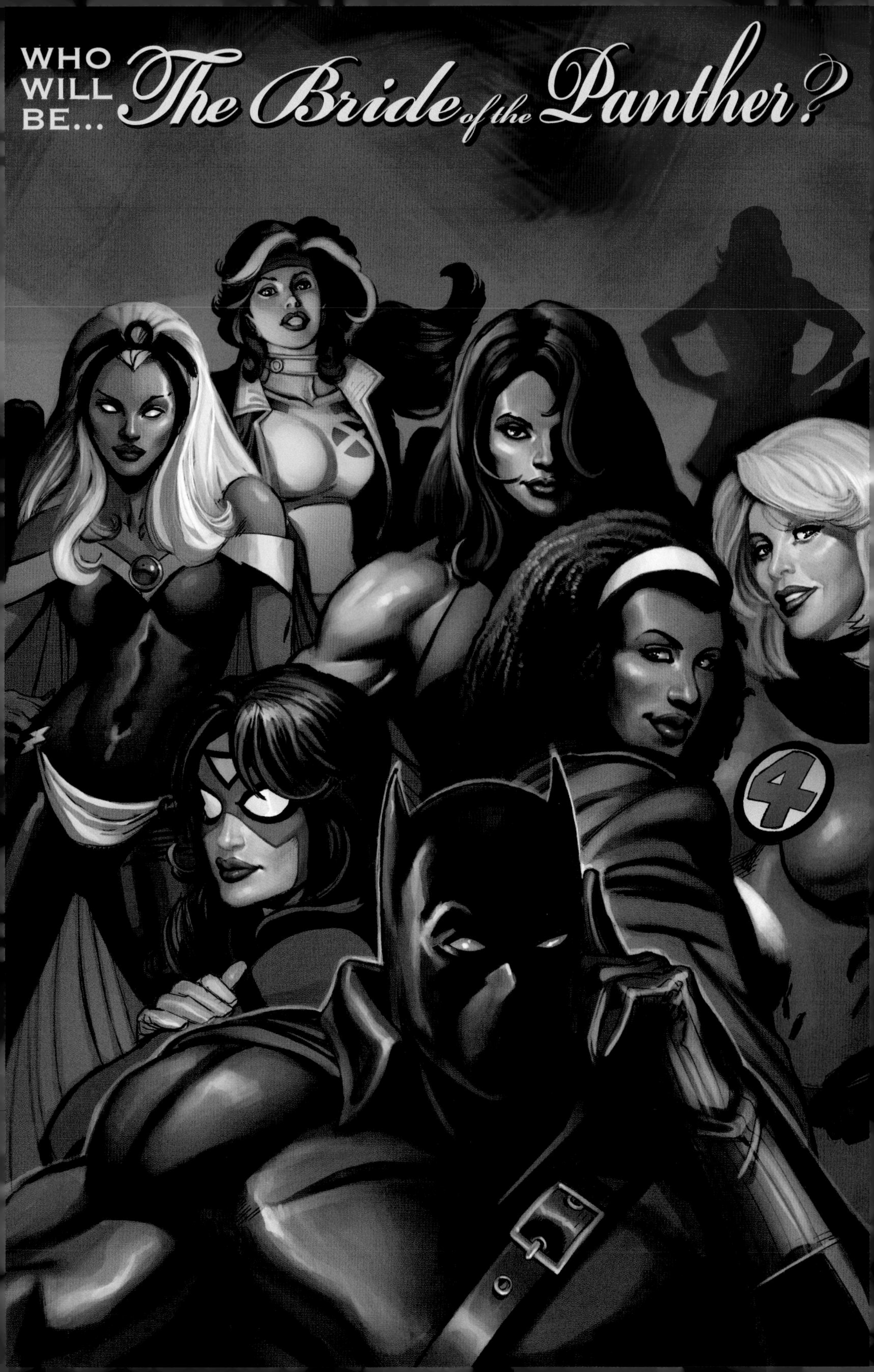
WHO WILL BE... The Bride of the Panther?
4

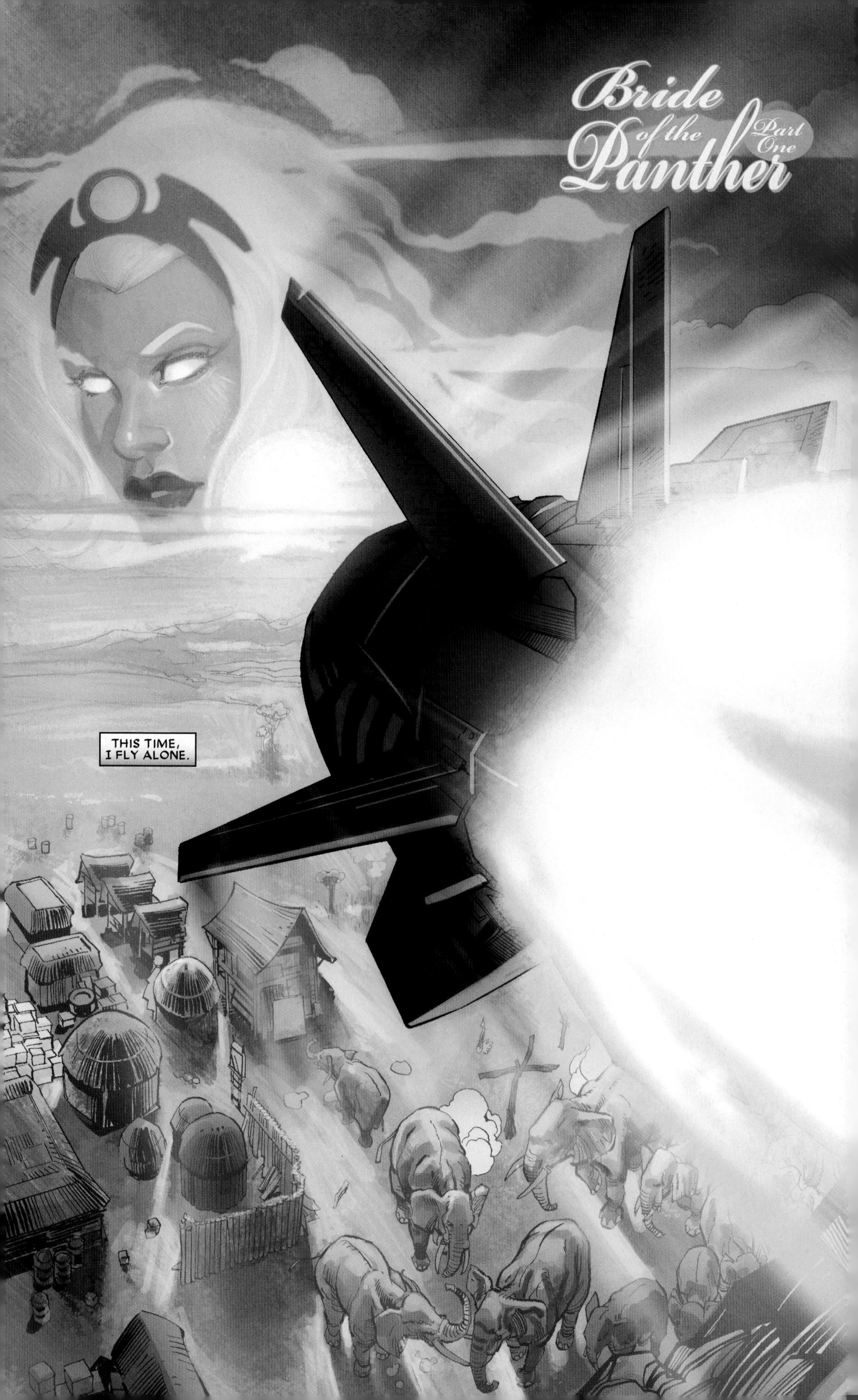
Bride of the Panther
Part One
THIS TIME, I FLY ALONE.

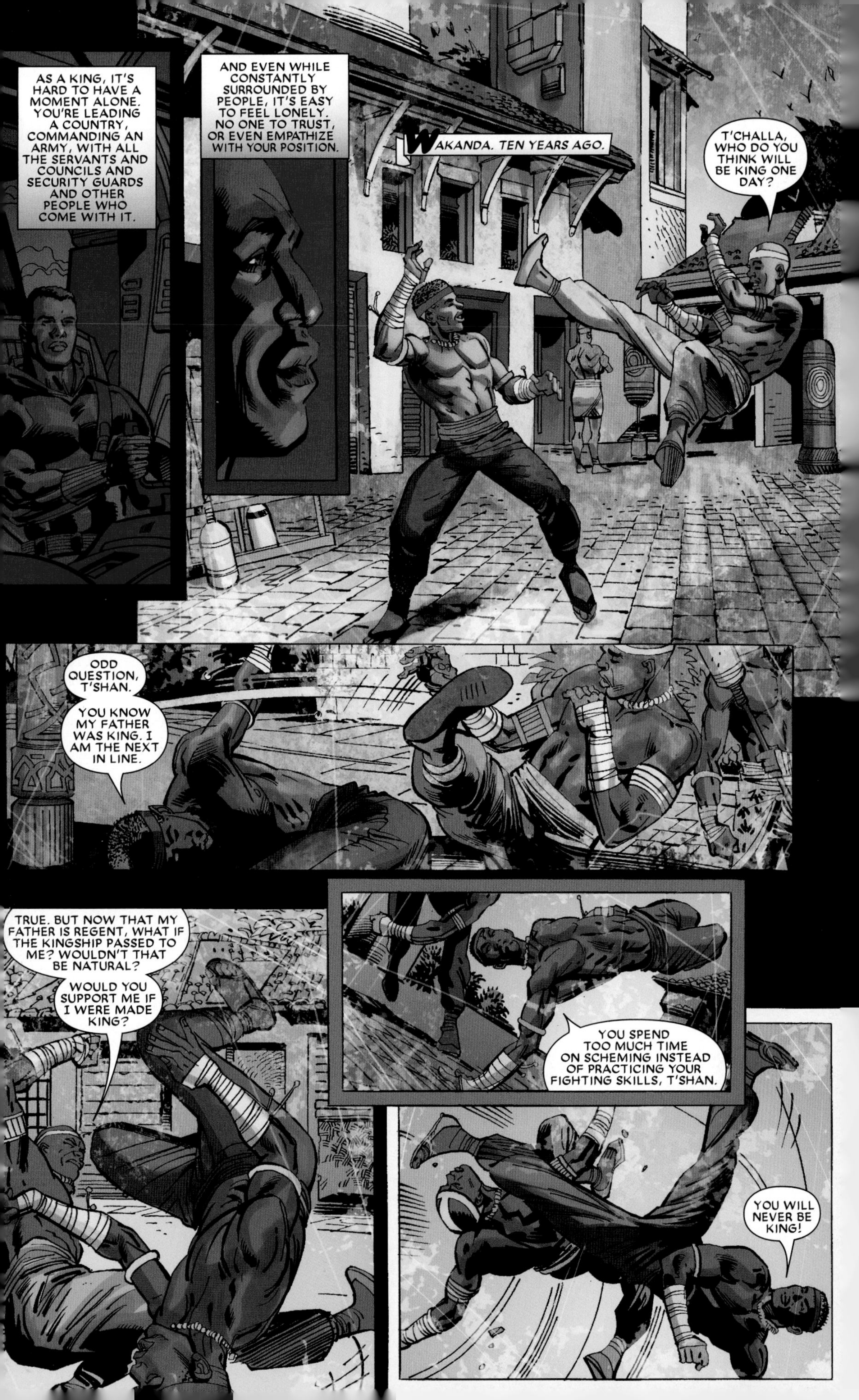
AS A KING, IT'S HARD TO HAVE A MOMENT ALONE. YOU'RE LEADING A COUNTRY, COMMANDING AN ARMY, WITH ALL THE SERVANTS AND COUNCILS AND SECURITY GUARDS AND OTHER PEOPLE WHO COME WITH IT.
AND EVEN WHILE CONSTANTLY SURROUNDED BY PEOPLE, IT'S EASY TO FEEL LONELY. NO ONE TO TRUST, OR EVEN EMPATHIZE WITH YOUR POSITION.
WAKANDA. TEN YEARS AGO.
T'CHALLA, WHO DO YOU THINK WILL BE KING ONE DAY?
ODD QUESTION, T'SHAN.
YOU KNOW MY FATHER WAS KING. I AM THE NEXT IN LINE.
TRUE. BUT NOW THAT MY FATHER IS REGENT, WHAT IF THE KINGSHIP PASSED TO ME? WOULDN'T THAT BE NATURAL?
WOULD YOU SUPPORT ME IF I WERE MADE KING?
YOU SPEND TOO MUCH TIME ON SCHEMING INSTEAD OF PRACTICING YOUR FIGHTING SKILLS, T'SHAN.
YOU WILL NEVER BE KING!

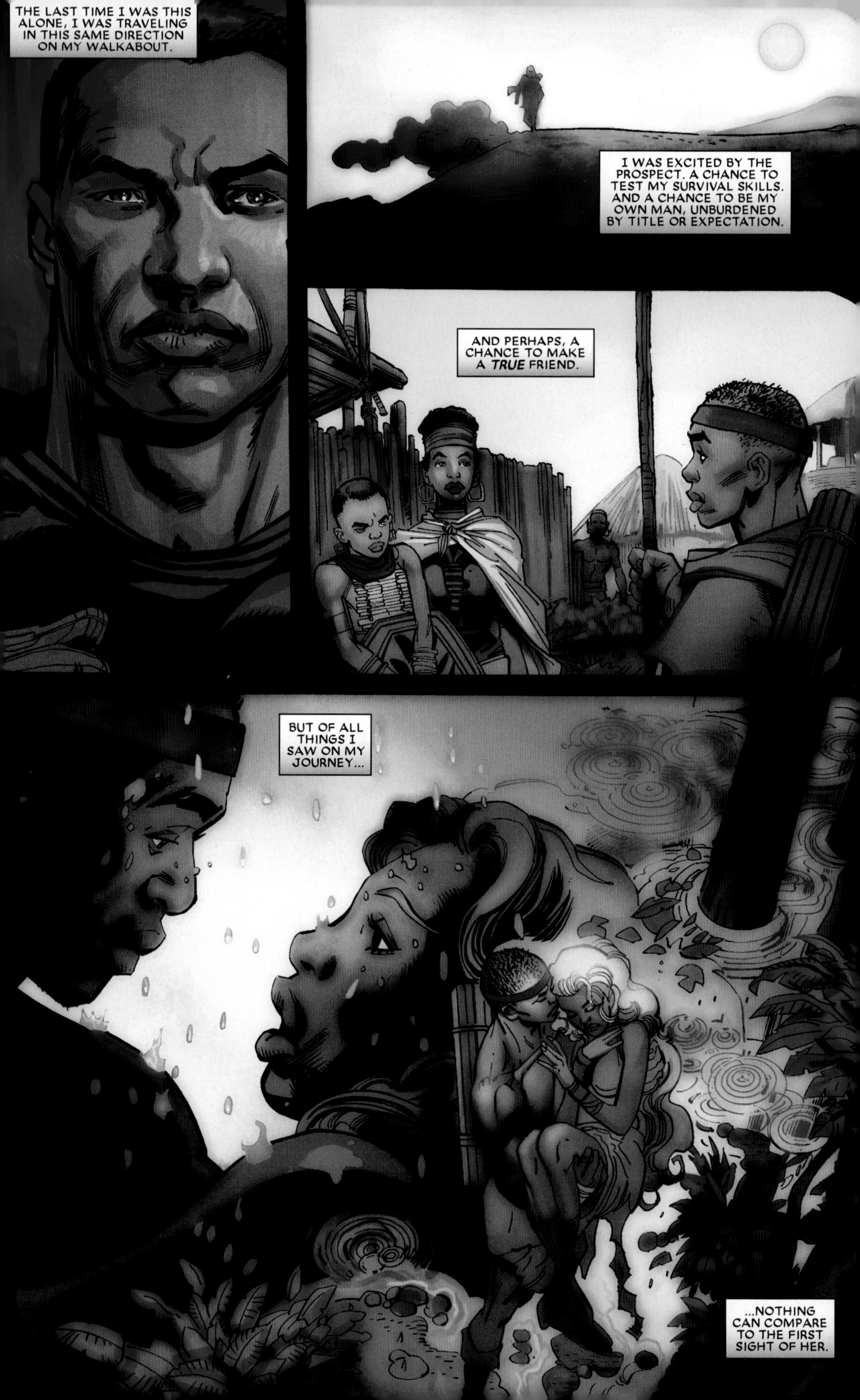
THE LAST TIME I WAS THIS ALONE, I WAS TRAVELING IN THIS SAME DIRECTION ON MY WALKABOUT.
I WAS EXCITED BY THE PROSPECT. A CHANCE TO TEST MY SURVIVAL SKILLS. AND A CHANCE TO BE MY OWN MAN, UNBURDENED BY TITLE OR EXPECTATION.
AND PERHAPS, A CHANCE TO MAKE A TRUE FRIEND.
BUT OF ALL THINGS I SAW ON MY JOURNEY...
...NOTHING CAN COMPARE TO THE FIRST SIGHT OF HER.

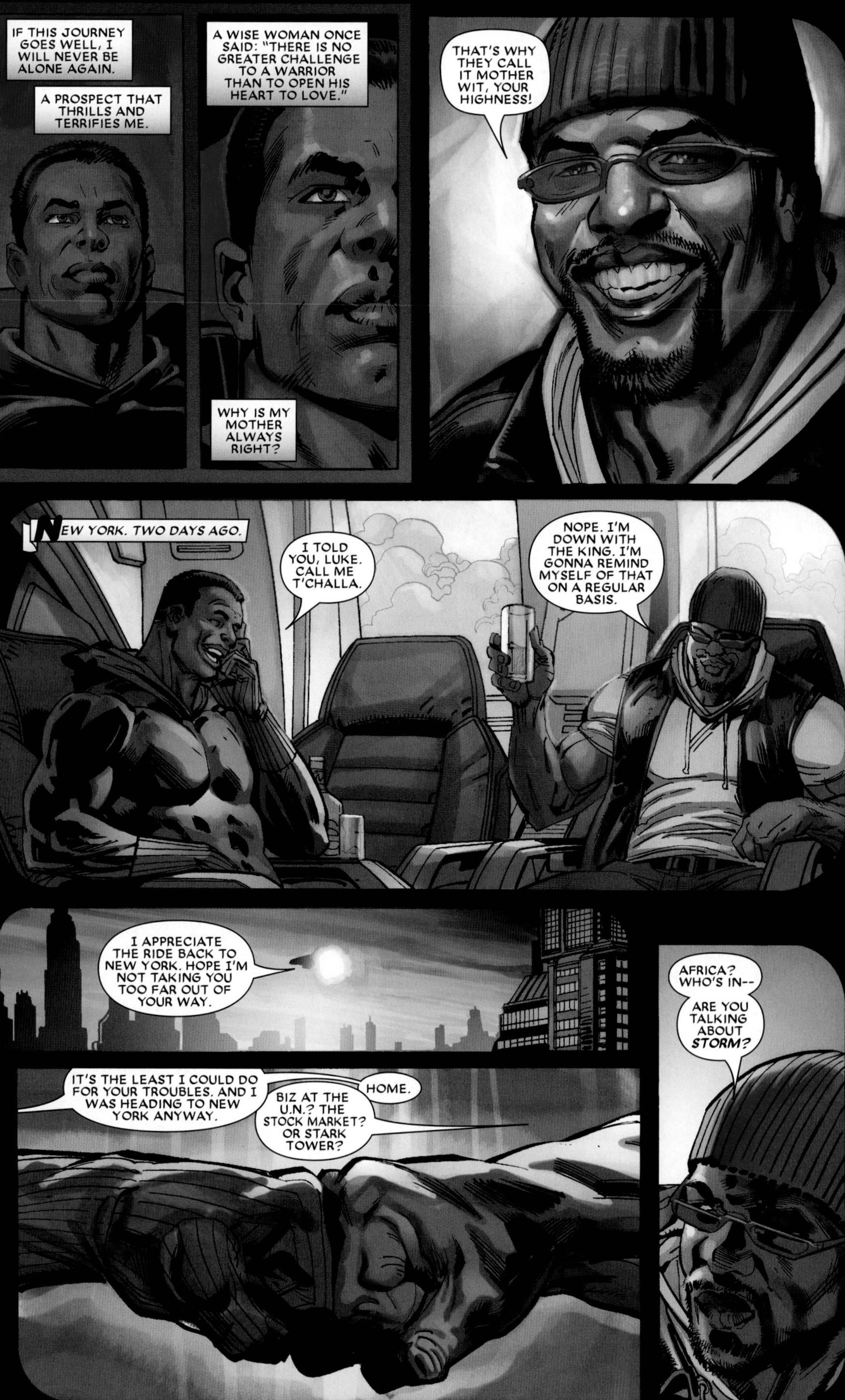
IF THIS JOURNEY GOES WELL, I WILL NEVER BE ALONE AGAIN.
A PROSPECT THAT THRILLS AND TERRIFIES ME.
A WISE WOMAN ONCE SAID: "THERE IS NO GREATER CHALLENGE TO A WARRIOR THAN TO OPEN HIS HEART TO LOVE."
WHY IS MY MOTHER ALWAYS RIGHT?
THAT'S WHY THEY CALL IT MOTHER WIT, YOUR HIGHNESS!
NEW YORK. TWO DAYS AGO.
I TOLD YOU, LUKE. CALL ME T'CHALLA.
NOPE. I'M DOWN WITH THE KING. I'M GONNA REMIND MYSELF OF THAT ON A REGULAR BASIS.
I APPRECIATE THE RIDE BACK TO NEW YORK. HOPE I'M NOT TAKING YOU TOO FAR OUT OF YOUR WAY.
IT'S THE LEAST I COULD DO FOR YOUR TROUBLES. AND I WAS HEADING TO NEW YORK ANYWAY.
BIZ AT THE U.N.? THE STOCK MARKET? OR STARK TOWER?
HOME.
AFRICA? WHO'S IN--
ARE YOU TALKING ABOUT STORM?

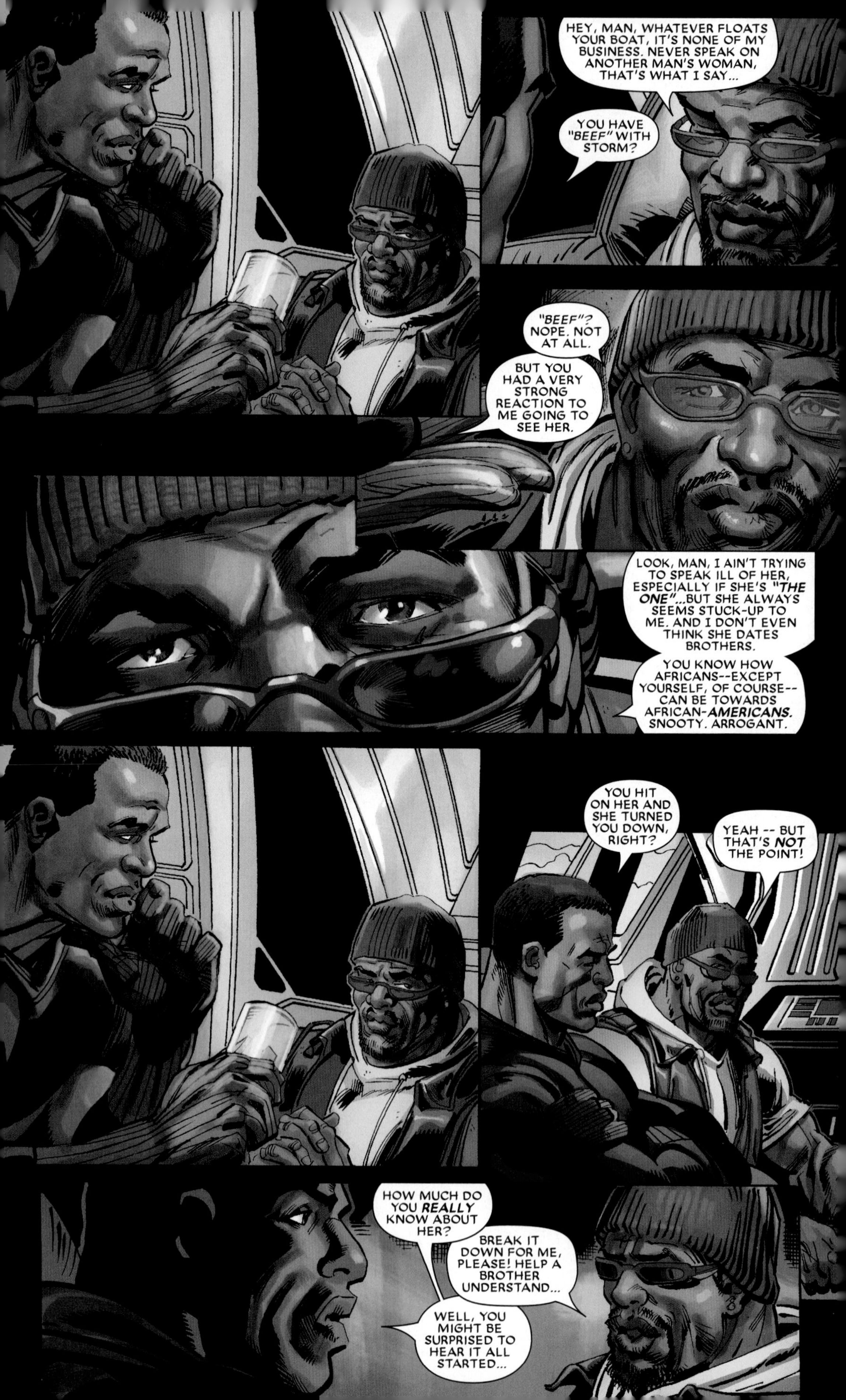
HEY, MAN, WHATEVER FLOATS YOUR BOAT, IT'S NONE OF MY BUSINESS. NEVER SPEAK ON ANOTHER MAN'S WOMAN, THAT'S WHAT I SAY...
YOU HAVE "BEEF" WITH STORM?
"BEEF"? NOPE. NOT AT ALL.
BUT YOU HAD A VERY STRONG REACTION TO ME GOING TO SEE HER.
LOOK, MAN, I AIN'T TRYING TO SPEAK ILL OF HER, ESPECIALLY IF SHE'S "THE ONE"...BUT SHE ALWAYS SEEMS STUCK-UP TO ME. AND I DON'T EVEN THINK SHE DATES BROTHERS.
YOU KNOW HOW AFRICANS--EXCEPT YOURSELF, OF COURSE--CAN BE TOWARDS AFRICAN-AMERICANS. SNOOTY. ARROGANT.
YOU HIT ON HER AND SHE TURNED YOU DOWN, RIGHT?
YEAH -- BUT THAT'S NOT THE POINT!
HOW MUCH DO YOU REALLY KNOW ABOUT HER?
BREAK IT DOWN FOR ME, PLEASE! HELP A BROTHER UNDERSTAND...
WELL, YOU MIGHT BE SURPRISED TO HEAR IT ALL STARTED...

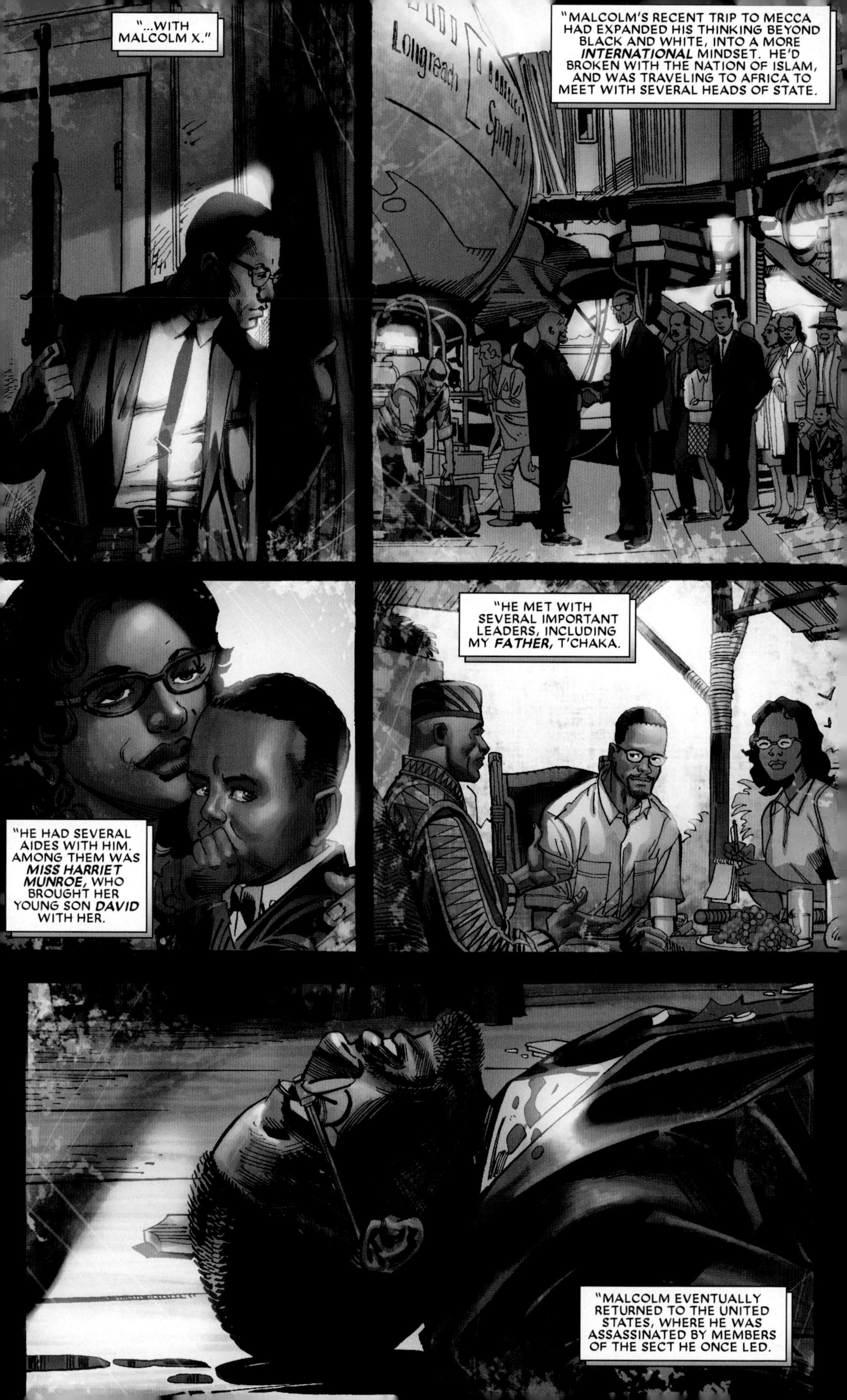
"...WITH MALCOLM X."
"MALCOLM'S RECENT TRIP TO MECCA HAD EXPANDED HIS THINKING BEYOND BLACK AND WHITE, INTO A MORE INTERNATIONAL MINDSET. HE'D BROKEN WITH THE NATION OF ISLAM, AND WAS TRAVELING TO AFRICA TO MEET WITH SEVERAL HEADS OF STATE.
Longreach
"HE HAD SEVERAL AIDES WITH HIM. AMONG THEM WAS MISS HARRIET MUNROE, WHO BROUGHT HER YOUNG SON DAVID WITH HER.
"HE MET WITH SEVERAL IMPORTANT LEADERS, INCLUDING MY FATHER, T'CHAKA.
"MALCOLM EVENTUALLY RETURNED TO THE UNITED STATES, WHERE HE WAS ASSASSINATED BY MEMBERS OF THE SECT HE ONCE LED.

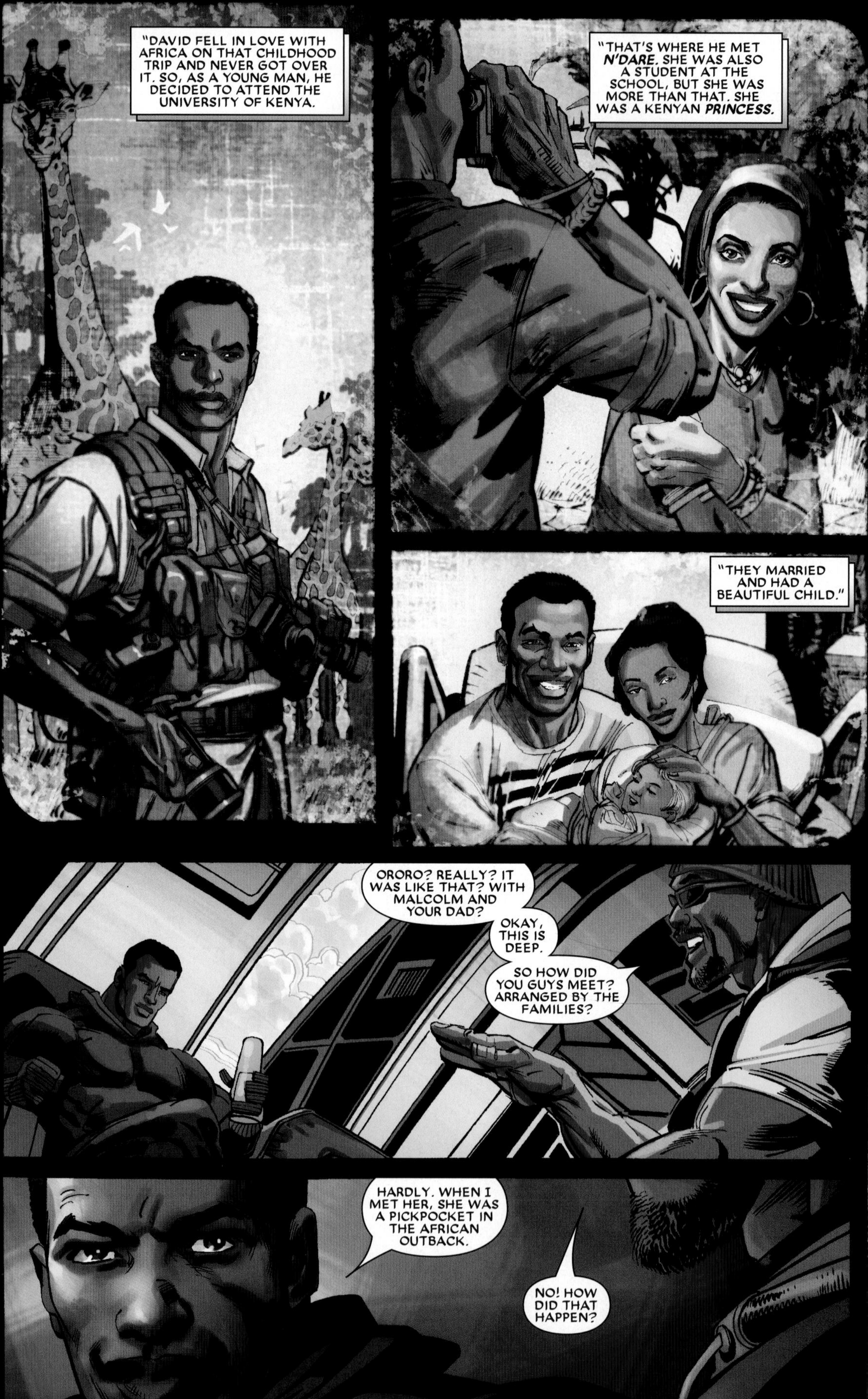
"DAVID FELL IN LOVE WITH AFRICA ON THAT CHILDHOOD TRIP AND NEVER GOT OVER IT. SO, AS A YOUNG MAN, HE DECIDED TO ATTEND THE UNIVERSITY OF KENYA.
"THAT'S WHERE HE MET N'DARE. SHE WAS ALSO A STUDENT AT THE SCHOOL, BUT SHE WAS MORE THAN THAT. SHE WAS A KENYAN PRINCESS.
"THEY MARRIED AND HAD A BEAUTIFUL CHILD."
ORORO? REALLY? IT WAS LIKE THAT? WITH MALCOLM AND YOUR DAD?
OKAY, THIS IS DEEP.
SO HOW DID YOU GUYS MEET? ARRANGED BY THE FAMILIES?
HARDLY. WHEN I MET HER, SHE WAS A PICKPOCKET IN THE AFRICAN OUTBACK.
NO! HOW DID THAT HAPPEN?

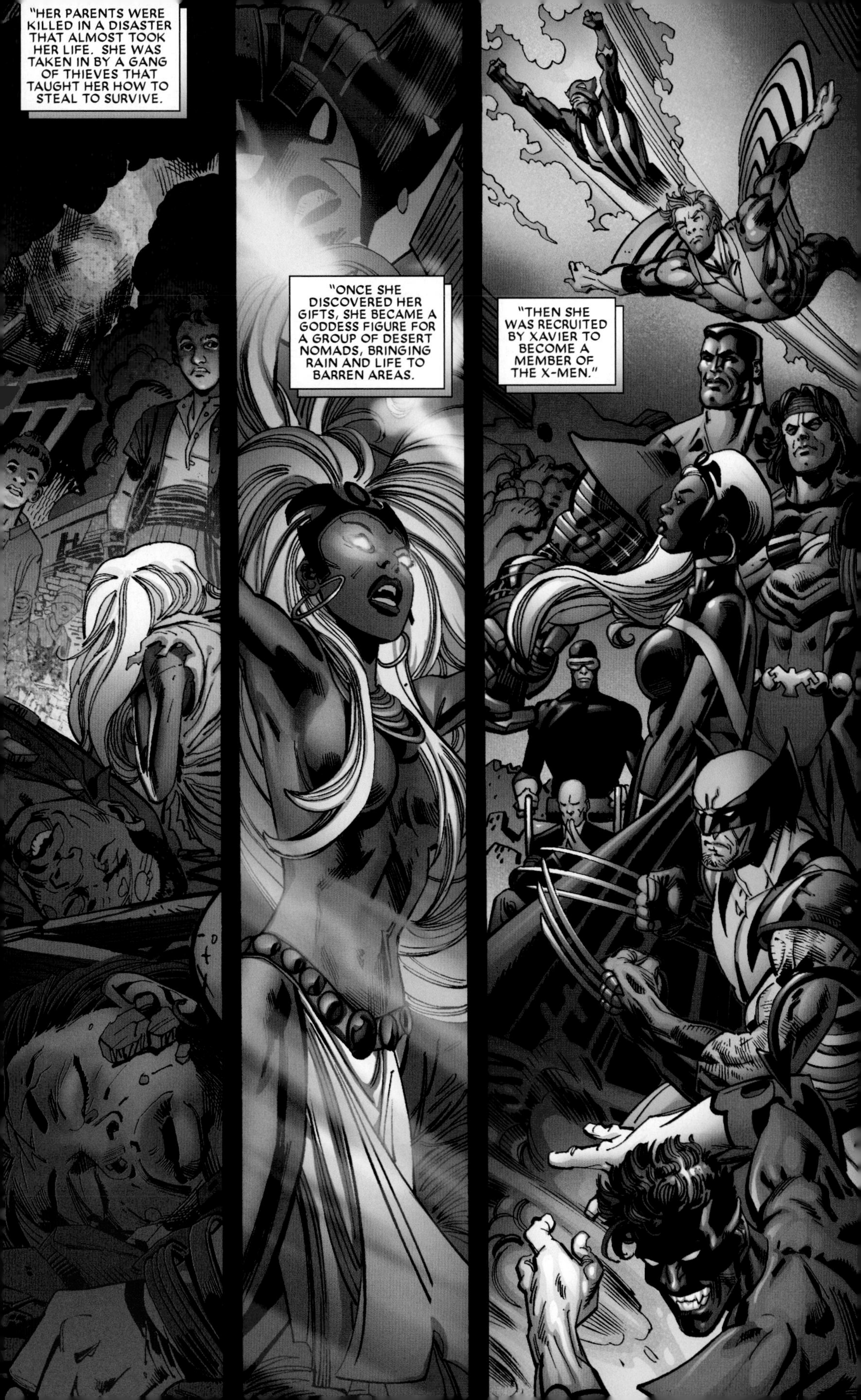
"HER PARENTS WERE KILLED IN A DISASTER THAT ALMOST TOOK HER LIFE. SHE WAS TAKEN IN BY A GANG OF THIEVES THAT TAUGHT HER HOW TO STEAL TO SURVIVE.
"ONCE SHE DISCOVERED HER GIFTS, SHE BECAME A GODDESS FIGURE FOR A GROUP OF DESERT NOMADS, BRINGING RAIN AND LIFE TO BARREN AREAS.
"THEN SHE WAS RECRUITED BY XAVIER TO BECOME A MEMBER OF THE X-MEN."

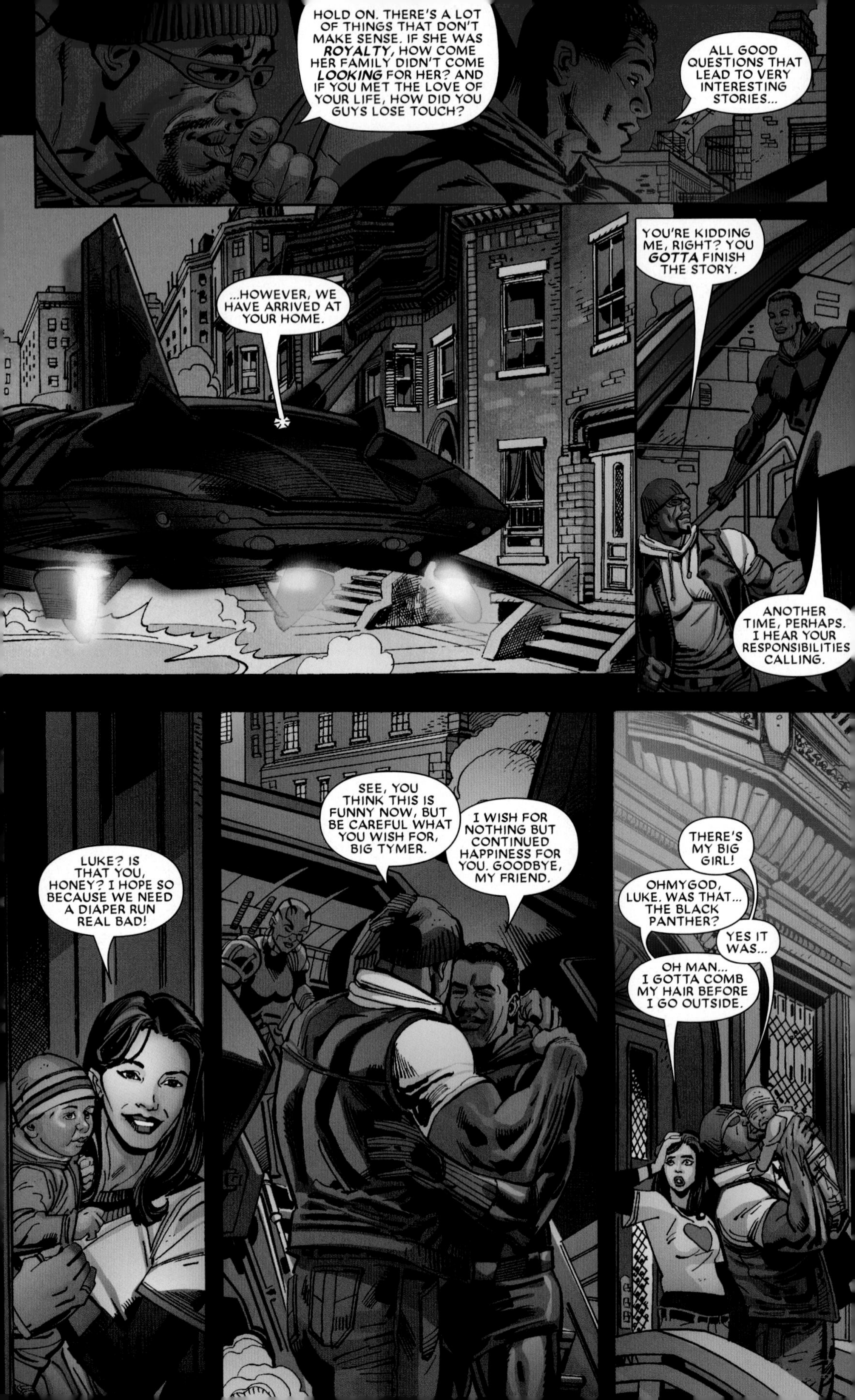
HOLD ON. THERE'S A LOT OF THINGS THAT DON'T MAKE SENSE. IF SHE WAS ROYALTY, HOW COME HER FAMILY DIDN'T COME LOOKING FOR HER? AND IF YOU MET THE LOVE OF YOUR LIFE, HOW DID YOU GUYS LOSE TOUCH?
ALL GOOD QUESTIONS THAT LEAD TO VERY INTERESTING STORIES...
...HOWEVER, WE HAVE ARRIVED AT YOUR HOME.
YOU'RE KIDDING ME, RIGHT? YOU GOTTA FINISH THE STORY.
ANOTHER TIME, PERHAPS. I HEAR YOUR RESPONSIBILITIES CALLING.
LUKE? IS THAT YOU, HONEY? I HOPE SO BECAUSE WE NEED A DIAPER RUN REAL BAD!
SEE, YOU THINK THIS IS FUNNY NOW, BUT BE CAREFUL WHAT YOU WISH FOR, BIG TYMER.
I WISH FOR NOTHING BUT CONTINUED HAPPINESS FOR YOU. GOODBYE, MY FRIEND.
THERE'S MY BIG GIRL!
OHMYGOD, LUKE. WAS THAT... THE BLACK PANTHER?
YES IT WAS...
OH MAN... I GOTTA COMB MY HAIR BEFORE I GO OUTSIDE.

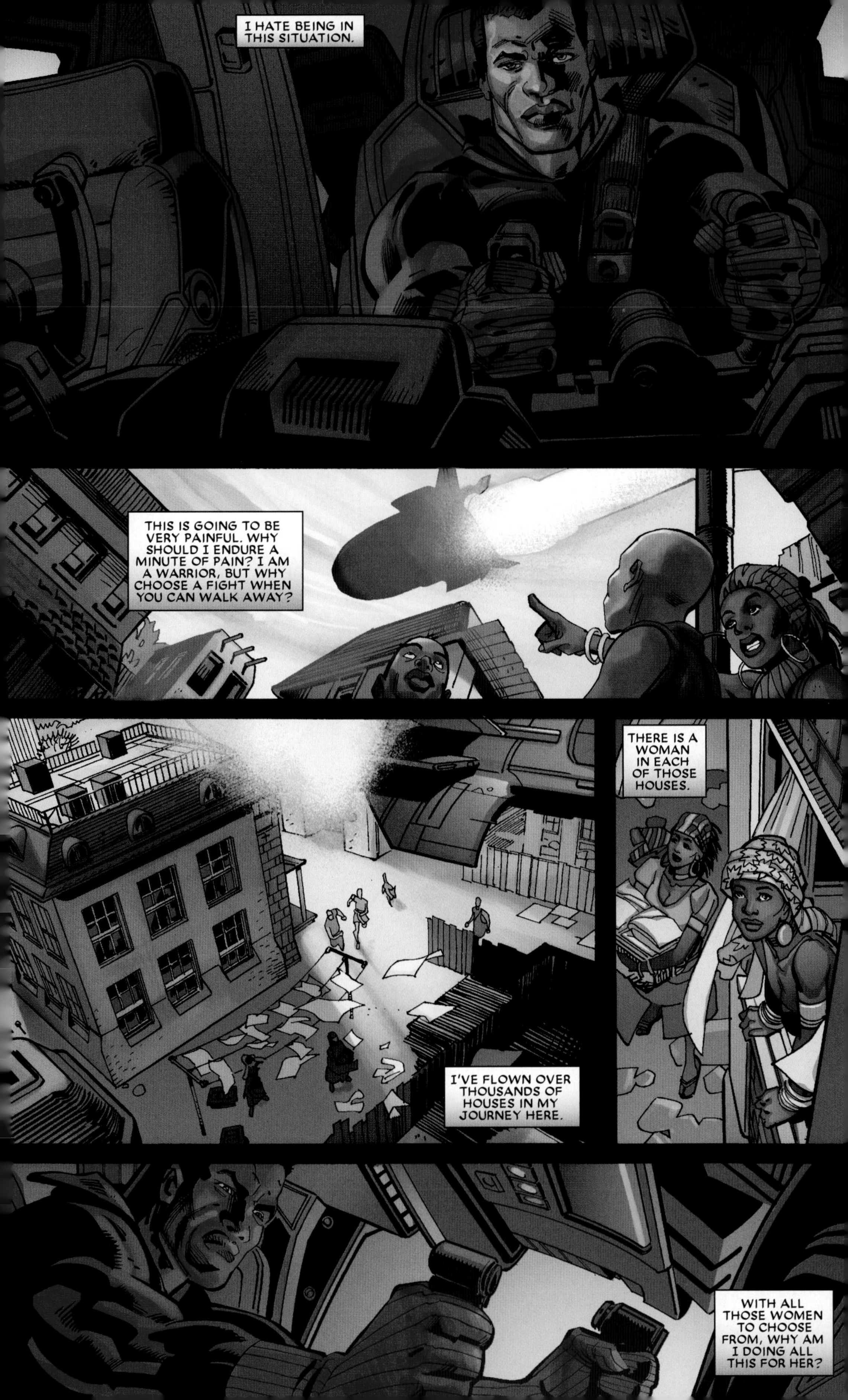
I HATE BEING IN THIS SITUATION.
THIS IS GOING TO BE VERY PAINFUL. WHY SHOULD I ENDURE A MINUTE OF PAIN? I AM A WARRIOR, BUT WHY CHOOSE A FIGHT WHEN YOU CAN WALK AWAY?
I'VE FLOWN OVER THOUSANDS OF HOUSES IN MY JOURNEY HERE.
THERE IS A WOMAN IN EACH OF THOSE HOUSES.
WITH ALL THOSE WOMEN TO CHOOSE FROM, WHY AM I DOING ALL THIS FOR HER?

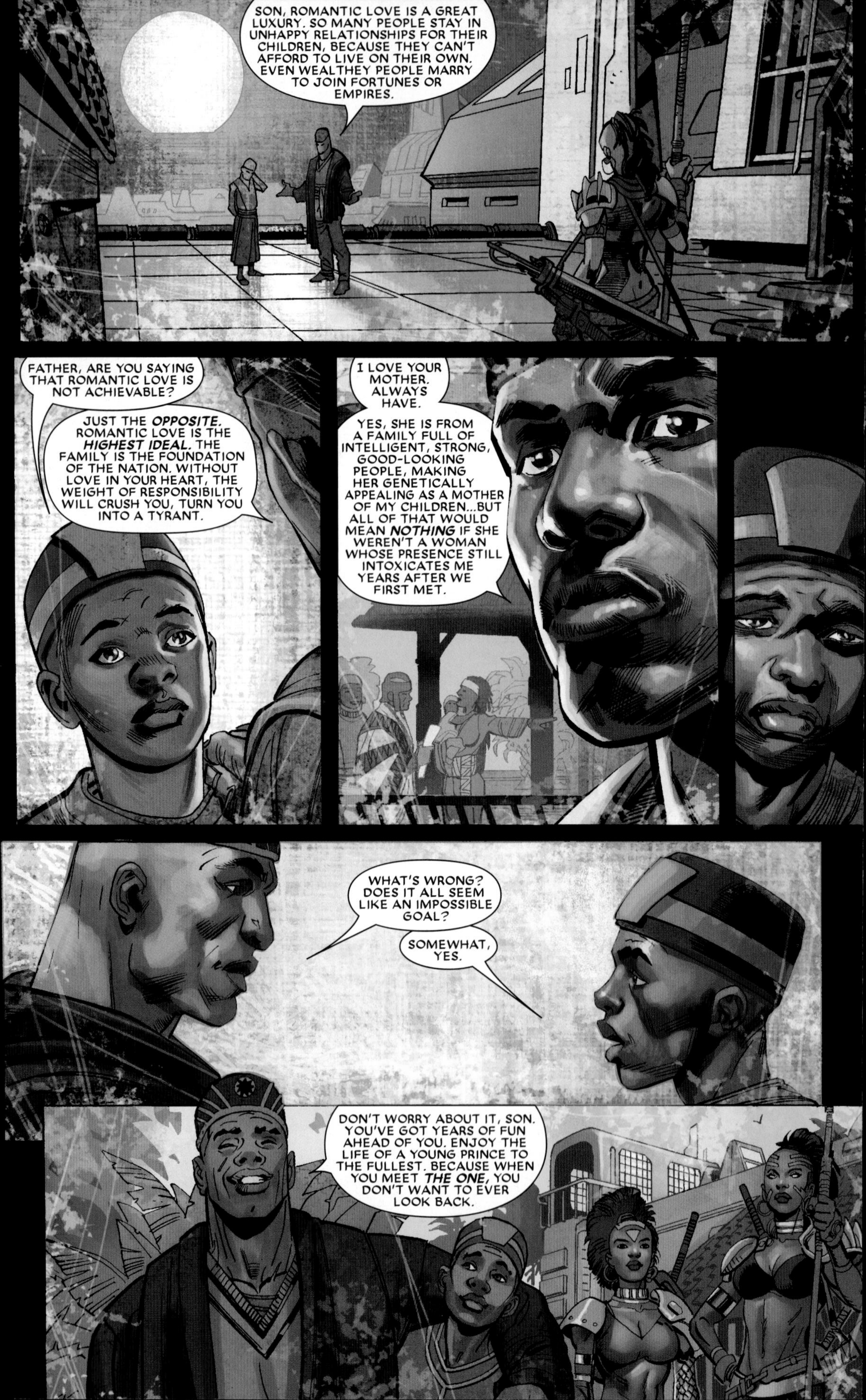
SON, ROMANTIC LOVE IS A GREAT LUXURY. SO MANY PEOPLE STAY IN UNHAPPY RELATIONSHIPS FOR THEIR CHILDREN, BECAUSE THEY CAN'T AFFORD TO LIVE ON THEIR OWN. EVEN WEALTHEY PEOPLE MARRY TO JOIN FORTUNES OR EMPIRES.
FATHER, ARE YOU SAYING THAT ROMANTIC LOVE IS NOT ACHIEVABLE?
JUST THE *OPPOSITE.* ROMANTIC LOVE IS THE ***HIGHEST IDEAL.*** THE FAMILY IS THE FOUNDATION OF THE NATION. WITHOUT LOVE IN YOUR HEART, THE WEIGHT OF RESPONSIBILITY WILL CRUSH YOU, TURN YOU INTO A TYRANT.
I LOVE YOUR MOTHER. ALWAYS HAVE.
YES, SHE IS FROM A FAMILY FULL OF INTELLIGENT, STRONG, GOOD-LOOKING PEOPLE, MAKING HER GENETICALLY APPEALING AS A MOTHER OF MY CHILDREN...BUT ALL OF THAT WOULD MEAN ***NOTHING*** IF SHE WEREN'T A WOMAN WHOSE PRESENCE STILL INTOXICATES ME YEARS AFTER WE FIRST MET.
WHAT'S WRONG? DOES IT ALL SEEM LIKE AN IMPOSSIBLE GOAL?
SOMEWHAT, YES.
DON'T WORRY ABOUT IT, SON. YOU'VE GOT YEARS OF FUN AHEAD OF YOU. ENJOY THE LIFE OF A YOUNG PRINCE TO THE FULLEST. BECAUSE WHEN YOU MEET ***THE ONE,*** YOU DON'T WANT TO EVER LOOK BACK.

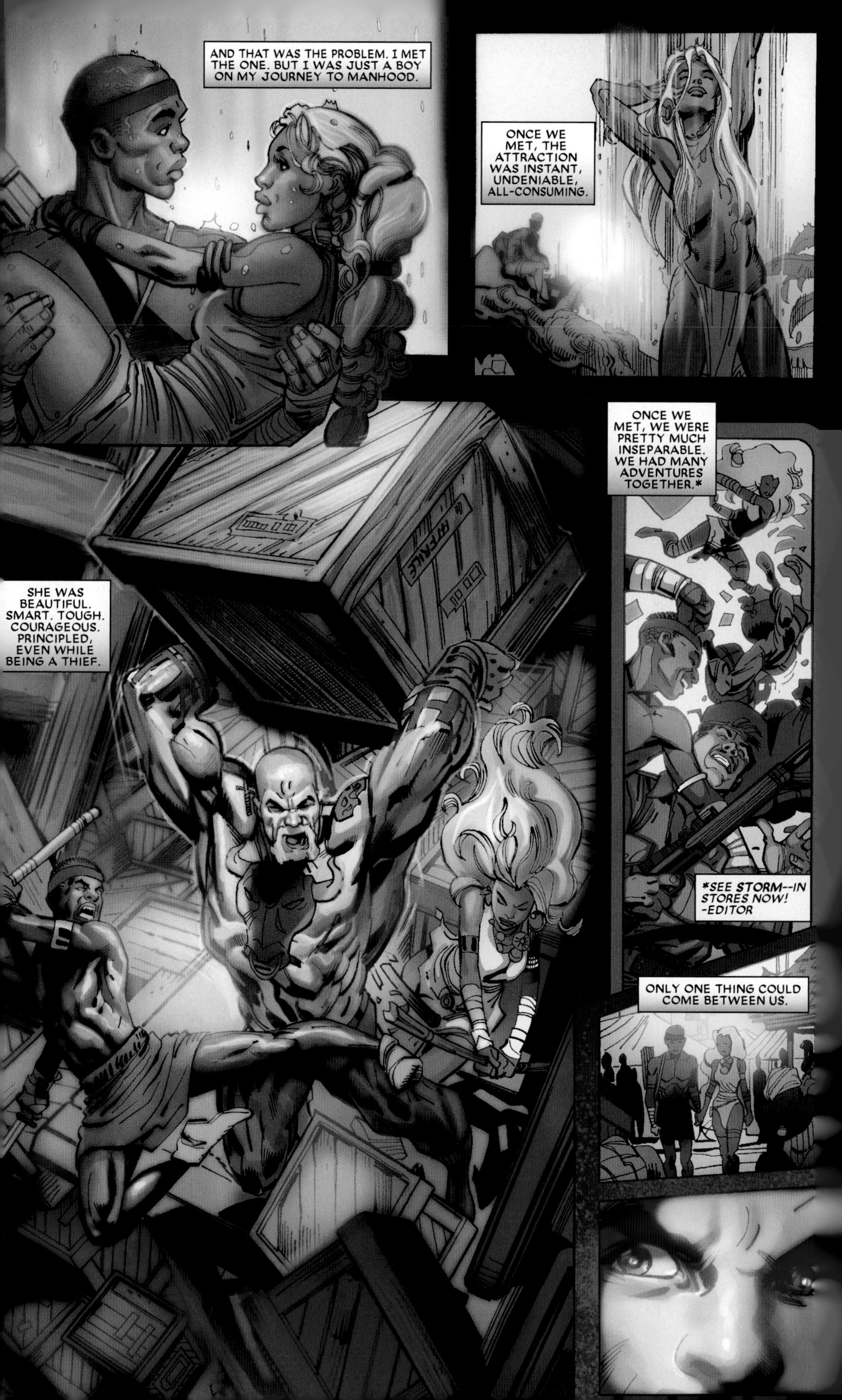

AND THAT WAS THE PROBLEM. I MET THE ONE. BUT I WAS JUST A BOY ON MY JOURNEY TO MANHOOD.
ONCE WE MET, THE ATTRACTION WAS INSTANT, UNDENIABLE, ALL-CONSUMING.
SHE WAS BEAUTIFUL. SMART. TOUGH. COURAGEOUS. PRINCIPLED, EVEN WHILE BEING A THIEF.
ONCE WE MET, WE WERE PRETTY MUCH INSEPARABLE. WE HAD MANY ADVENTURES TOGETHER.*
*SEE STORM--IN STORES NOW! -EDITOR
ONLY ONE THING COULD COME BETWEEN US.

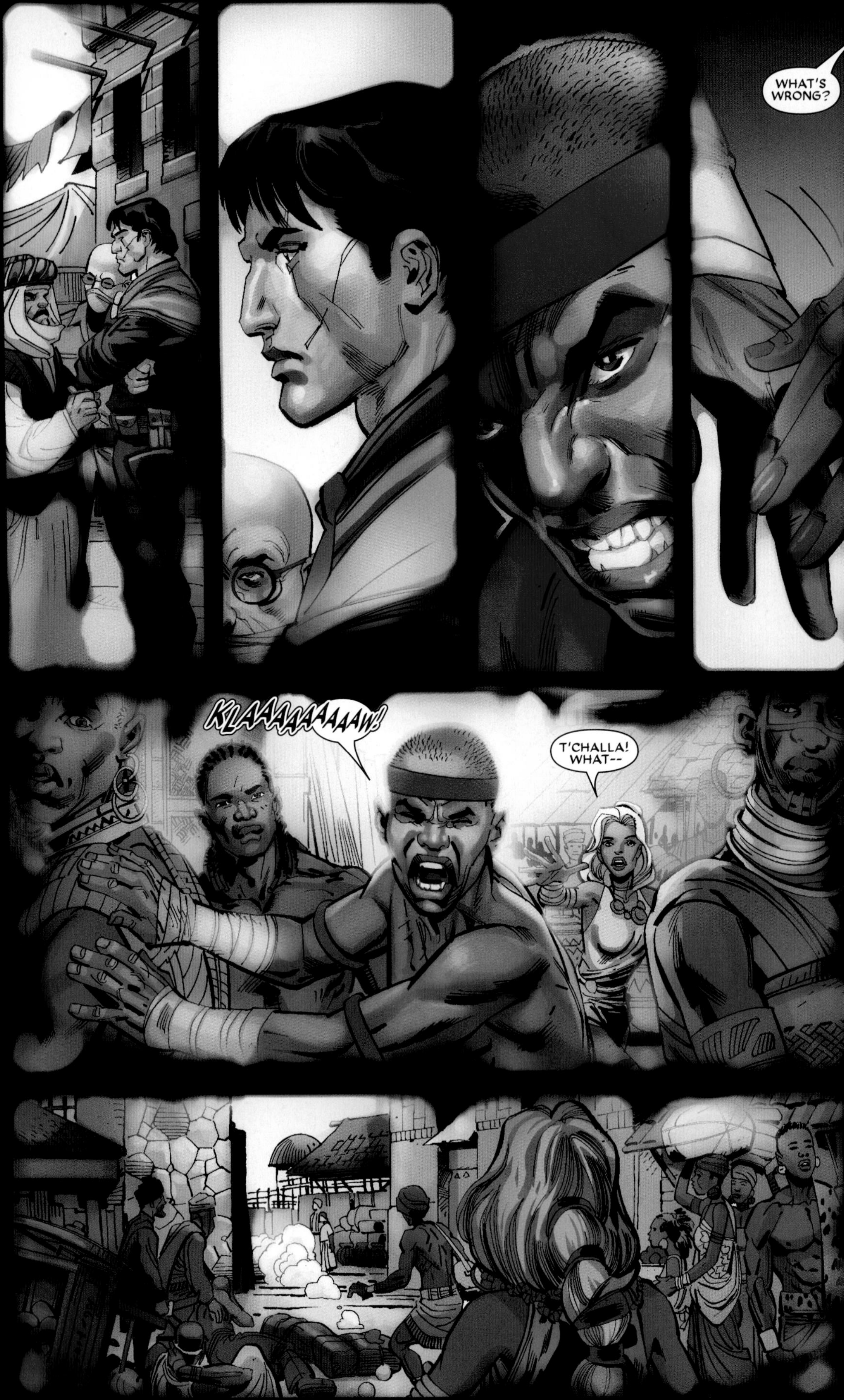
WHAT'S WRONG?
KLAAAAAAAAAW!
T'CHALLA! WHAT--

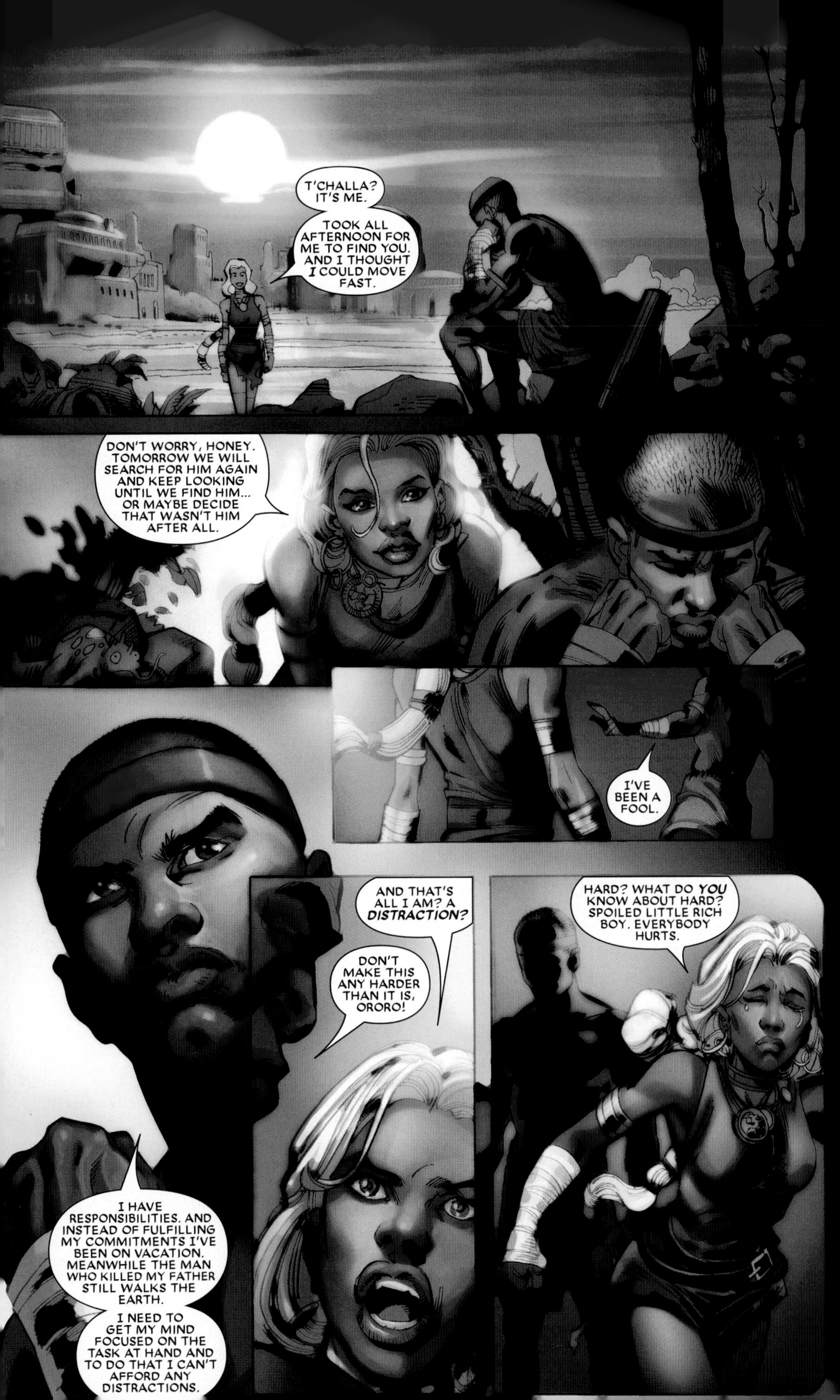
T'CHALLA? IT'S ME.
TOOK ALL AFTERNOON FOR ME TO FIND YOU. AND I THOUGHT *I* COULD MOVE FAST.
DON'T WORRY, HONEY. TOMORROW WE WILL SEARCH FOR HIM AGAIN AND KEEP LOOKING UNTIL WE FIND HIM... OR MAYBE DECIDE THAT WASN'T HIM AFTER ALL.
I'VE BEEN A FOOL.
I HAVE RESPONSIBILITIES. AND INSTEAD OF FULFILLING MY COMMITMENTS I'VE BEEN ON VACATION. MEANWHILE THE MAN WHO KILLED MY FATHER STILL WALKS THE EARTH.
I NEED TO GET MY MIND FOCUSED ON THE TASK AT HAND AND TO DO THAT I CAN'T AFFORD ANY DISTRACTIONS.
AND THAT'S ALL I AM? A *DISTRACTION?*
DON'T MAKE THIS ANY HARDER THAN IT IS, ORORO!
HARD? WHAT DO *YOU* KNOW ABOUT HARD? SPOILED LITTLE RICH BOY. EVERYBODY HURTS.

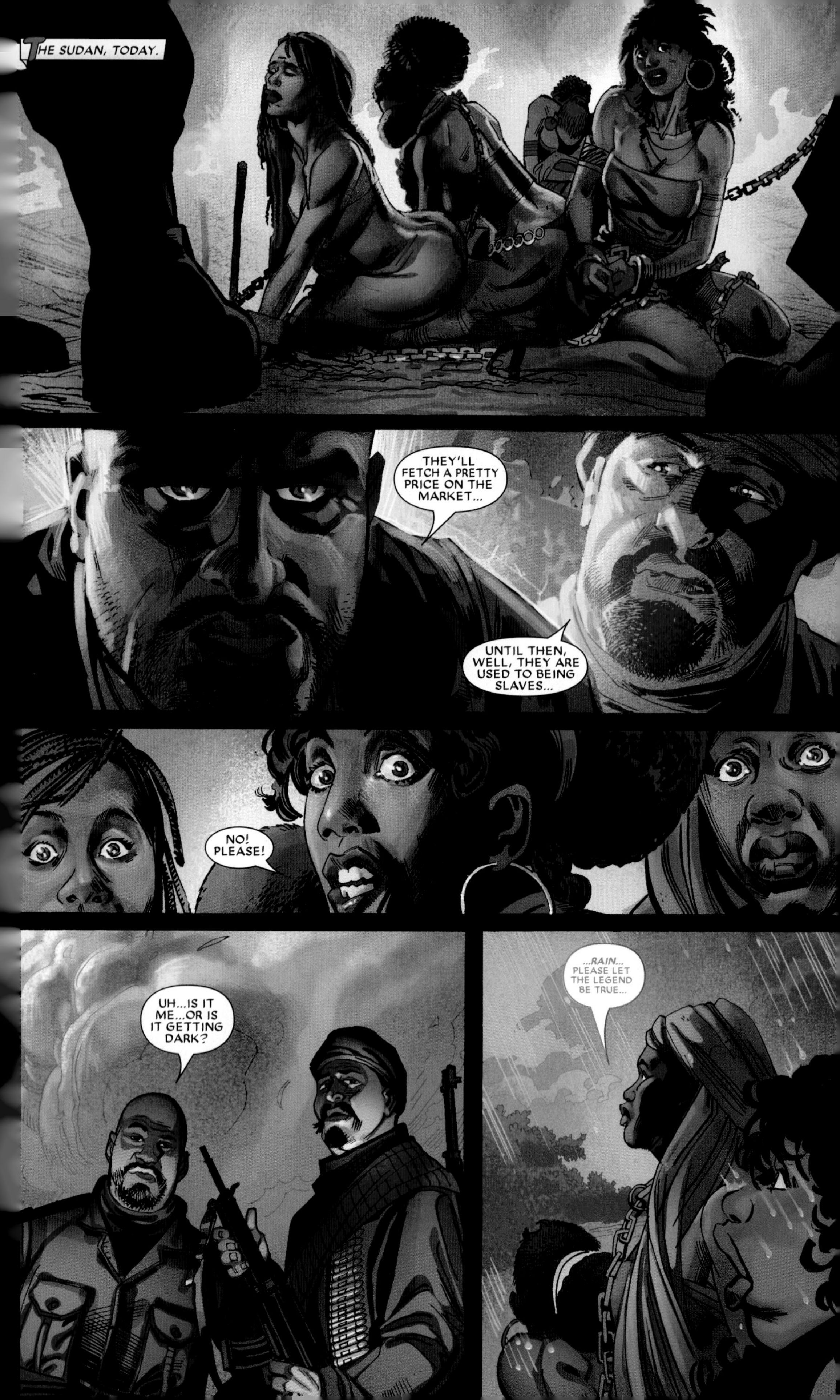
THE SUDAN, TODAY.
THEY'LL FETCH A PRETTY PRICE ON THE MARKET...
UNTIL THEN, WELL, THEY ARE USED TO BEING SLAVES...
NO! PLEASE!
UH...IS IT ME...OR IS IT GETTING DARK?
...RAIN... PLEASE LET THE LEGEND BE TRUE...

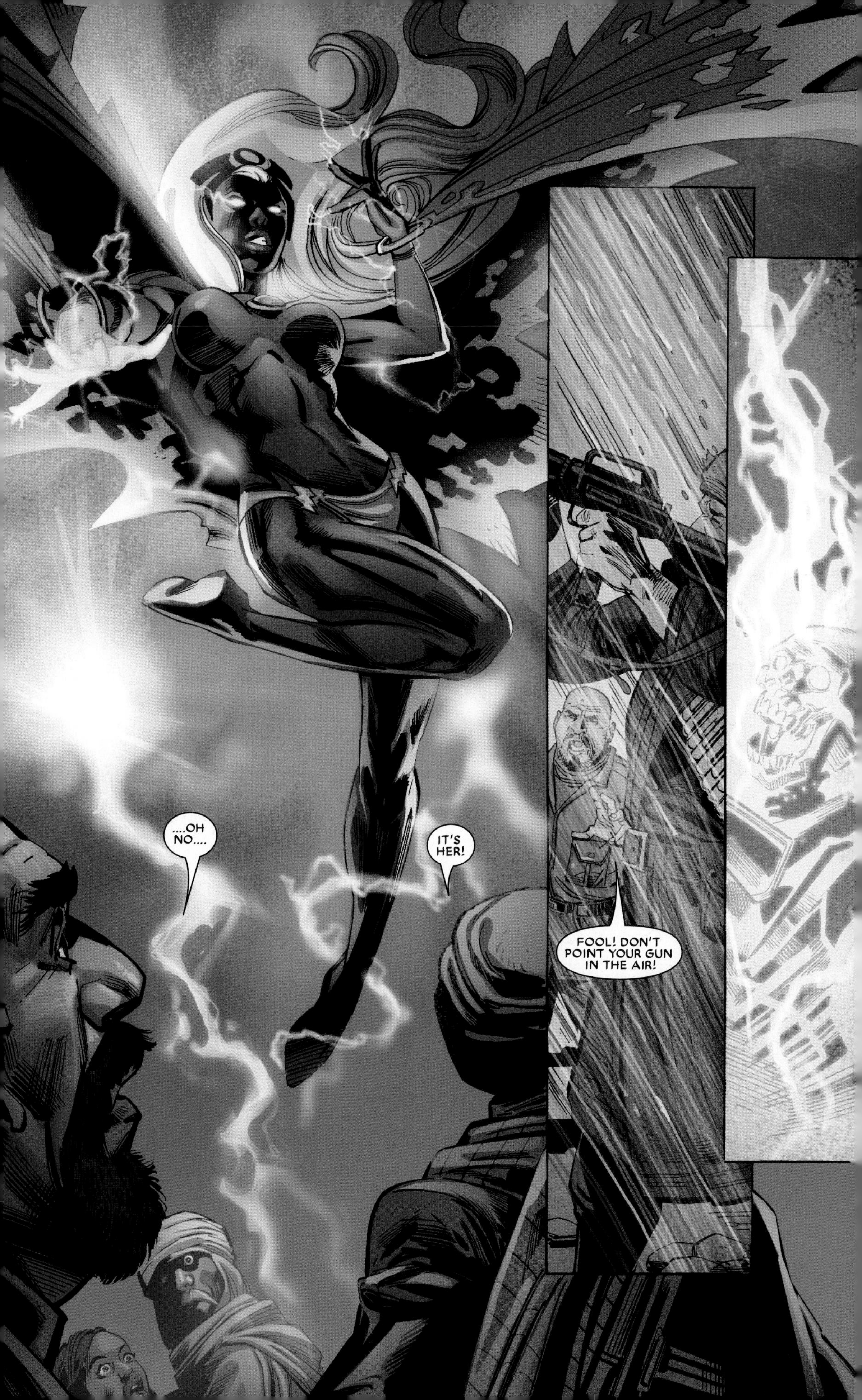

....OH NO....
IT'S HER!
FOOL! DON'T POINT YOUR GUN IN THE AIR!

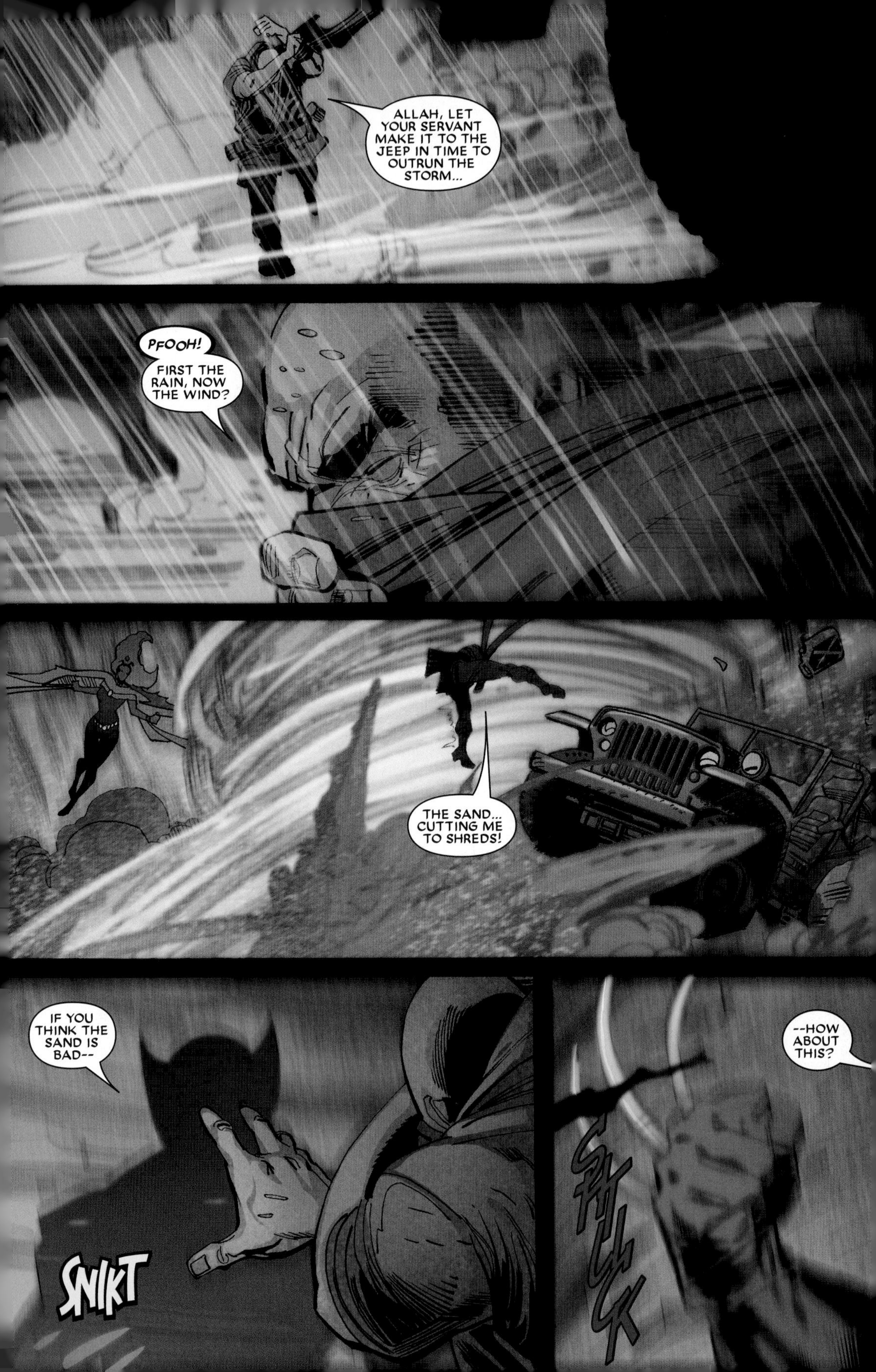
ALLAH, LET YOUR SERVANT MAKE IT TO THE JEEP IN TIME TO OUTRUN THE STORM...
PFOOH!
FIRST THE RAIN, NOW THE WIND?
THE SAND... CUTTING ME TO SHREDS!
IF YOU THINK THE SAND IS BAD--
SNIKT
--HOW ABOUT THIS?
SHUCK

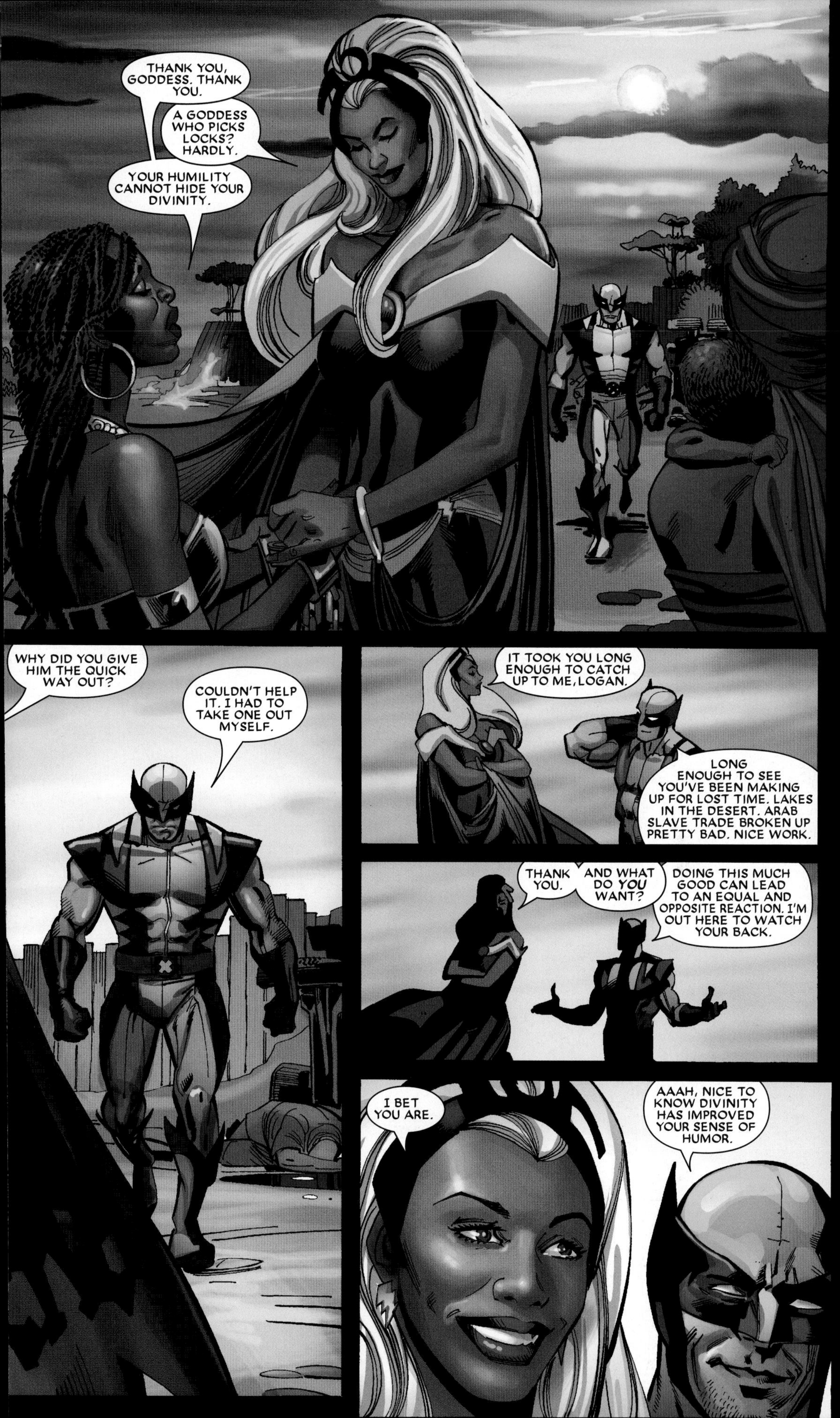
THANK YOU, GODDESS. THANK YOU.
A GODDESS WHO PICKS LOCKS? HARDLY.
YOUR HUMILITY CANNOT HIDE YOUR DIVINITY.
WHY DID YOU GIVE HIM THE QUICK WAY OUT?
COULDN'T HELP IT. I HAD TO TAKE ONE OUT MYSELF.
IT TOOK YOU LONG ENOUGH TO CATCH UP TO ME, LOGAN.
LONG ENOUGH TO SEE YOU'VE BEEN MAKING UP FOR LOST TIME. LAKES IN THE DESERT. ARAB SLAVE TRADE BROKEN UP PRETTY BAD. NICE WORK.
THANK YOU.
AND WHAT DO YOU WANT?
DOING THIS MUCH GOOD CAN LEAD TO AN EQUAL AND OPPOSITE REACTION. I'M OUT HERE TO WATCH YOUR BACK.
I BET YOU ARE.
AAAH, NICE TO KNOW DIVINITY HAS IMPROVED YOUR SENSE OF HUMOR.

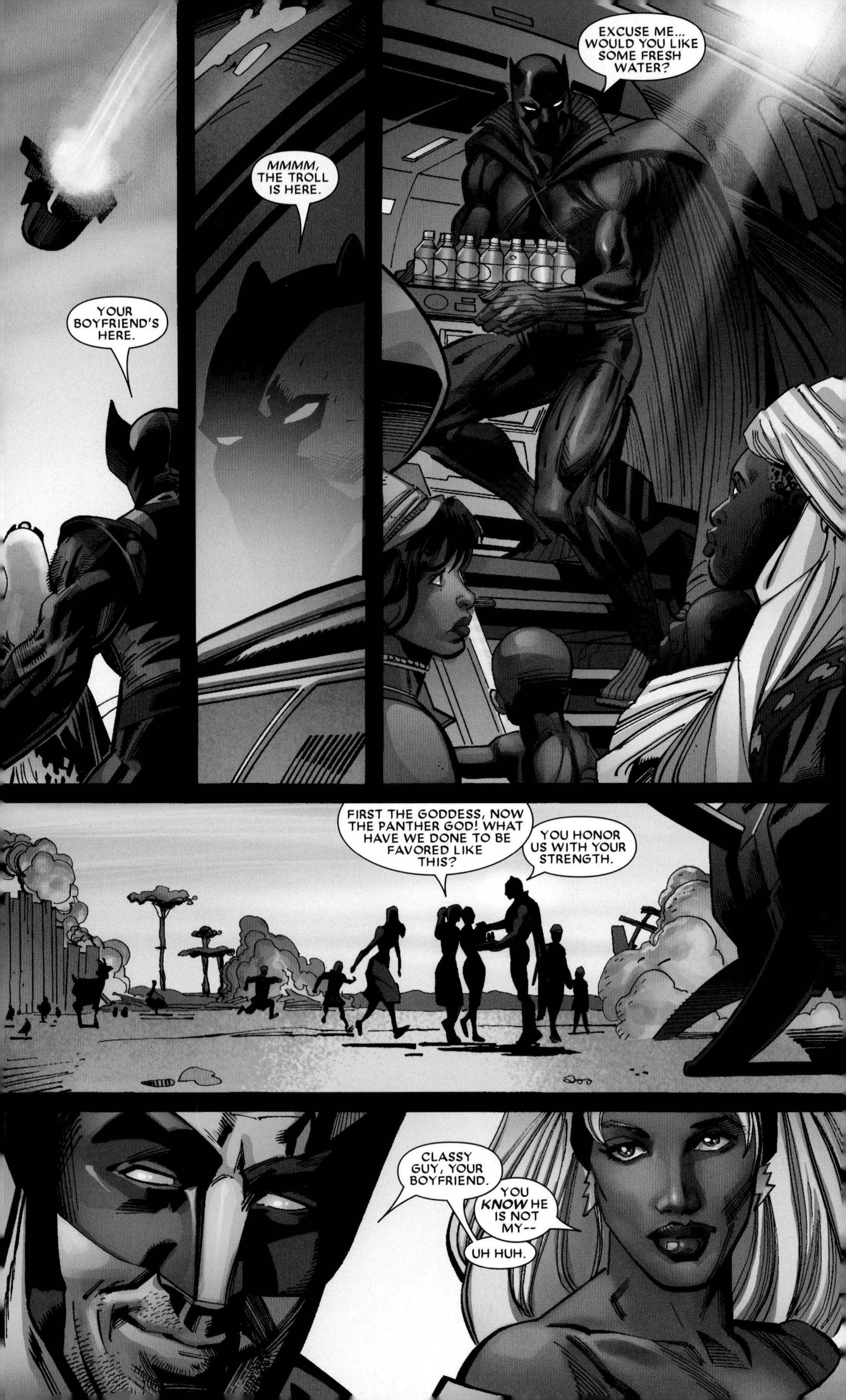
YOUR BOYFRIEND'S HERE.
MMMM, THE TROLL IS HERE.
EXCUSE ME... WOULD YOU LIKE SOME FRESH WATER?
FIRST THE GODDESS, NOW THE PANTHER GOD! WHAT HAVE WE DONE TO BE FAVORED LIKE THIS?
YOU HONOR US WITH YOUR STRENGTH.
CLASSY GUY, YOUR BOYFRIEND.
YOU KNOW HE IS NOT MY--
UH HUH.

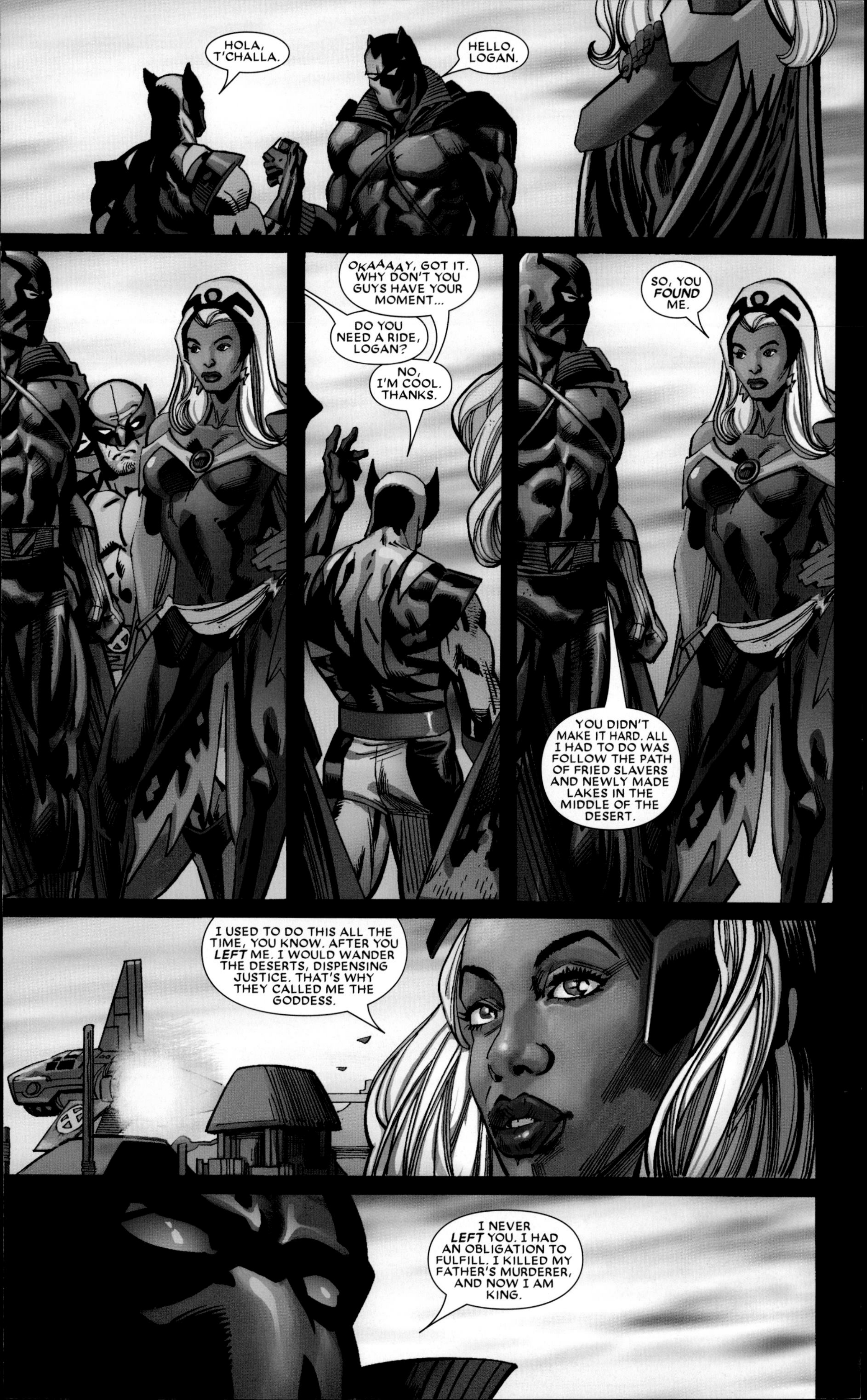
HOLA, T'CHALLA.
HELLO, LOGAN.
OKAAAAY, GOT IT. WHY DON'T YOU GUYS HAVE YOUR MOMENT...
DO YOU NEED A RIDE, LOGAN?
NO, I'M COOL. THANKS.
SO, YOU FOUND ME.
YOU DIDN'T MAKE IT HARD. ALL I HAD TO DO WAS FOLLOW THE PATH OF FRIED SLAVERS AND NEWLY MADE LAKES IN THE MIDDLE OF THE DESERT.
I USED TO DO THIS ALL THE TIME, YOU KNOW. AFTER YOU LEFT ME. I WOULD WANDER THE DESERTS, DISPENSING JUSTICE. THAT'S WHY THEY CALLED ME THE GODDESS.
I NEVER LEFT YOU. I HAD AN OBLIGATION TO FULFILL. I KILLED MY FATHER'S MURDERER, AND NOW I AM KING.

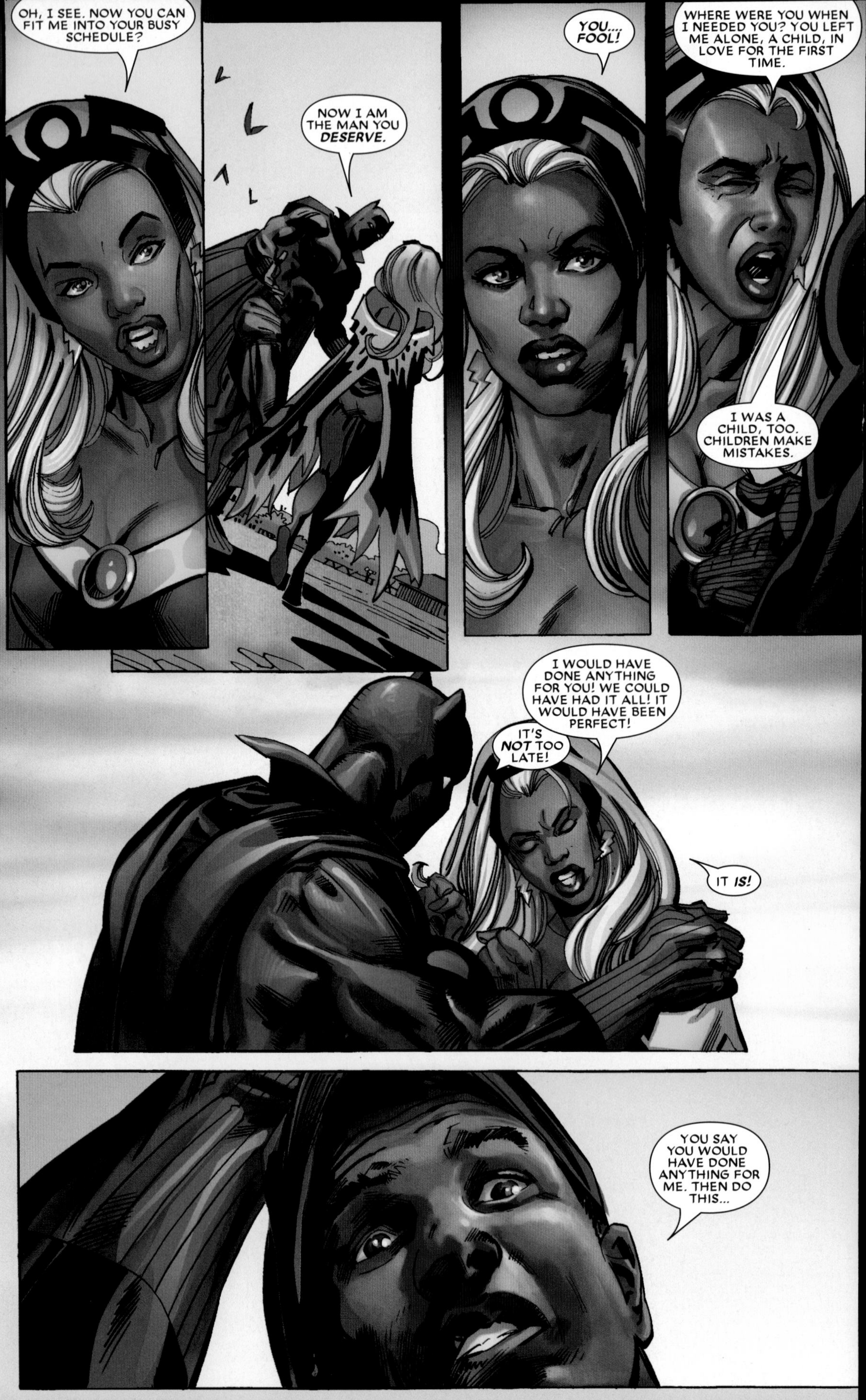

OH, I SEE. NOW YOU CAN FIT ME INTO YOUR BUSY SCHEDULE?
NOW I AM THE MAN YOU DESERVE.
YOU... FOOL!
WHERE WERE YOU WHEN I NEEDED YOU? YOU LEFT ME ALONE, A CHILD, IN LOVE FOR THE FIRST TIME.
I WAS A CHILD, TOO. CHILDREN MAKE MISTAKES.
I WOULD HAVE DONE ANYTHING FOR YOU! WE COULD HAVE HAD IT ALL! IT WOULD HAVE BEEN PERFECT!
IT'S NOT TOO LATE!
IT IS!
YOU SAY YOU WOULD HAVE DONE ANYTHING FOR ME. THEN DO THIS...

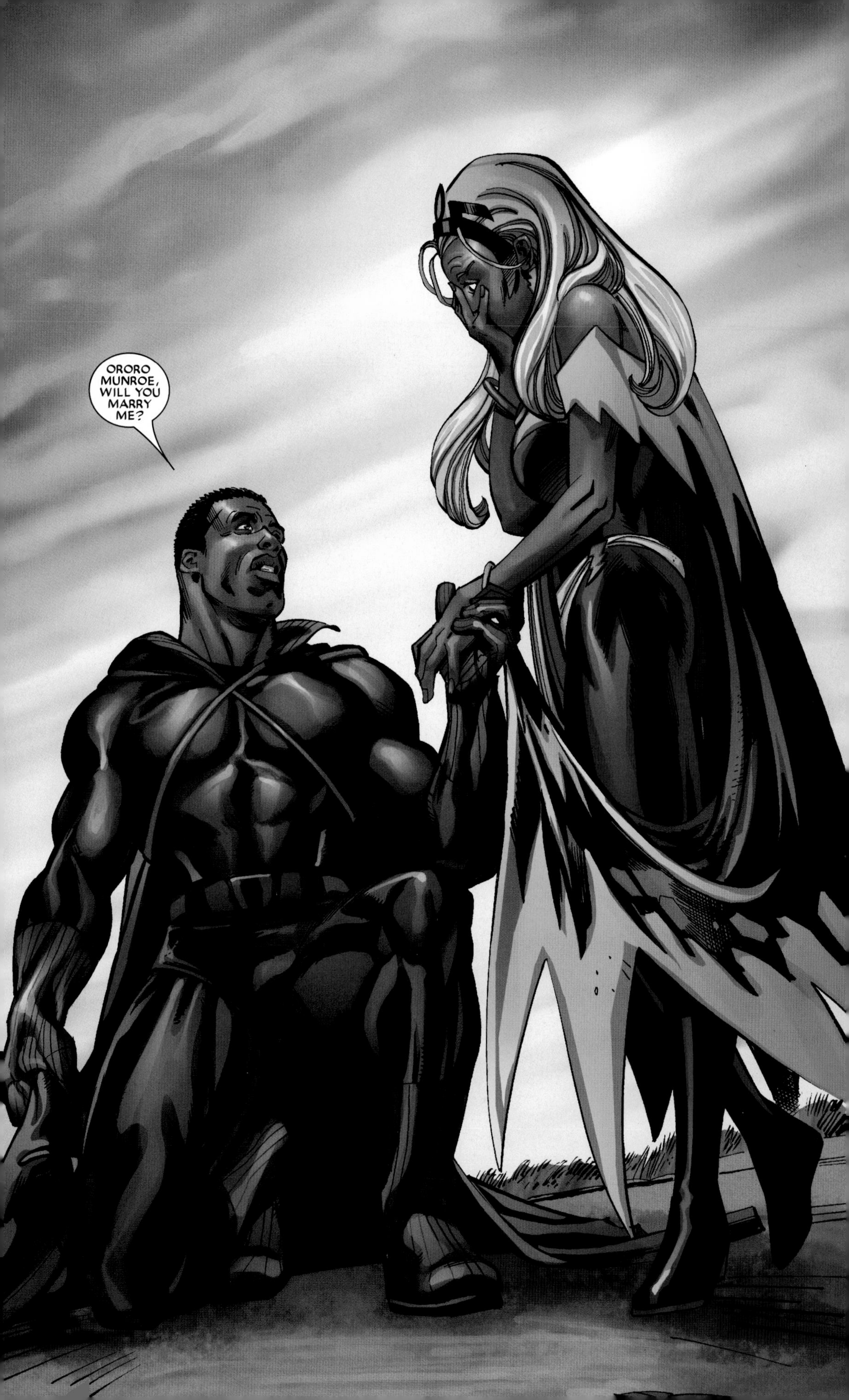
ORORO MUNROE, WILL YOU MARRY ME?

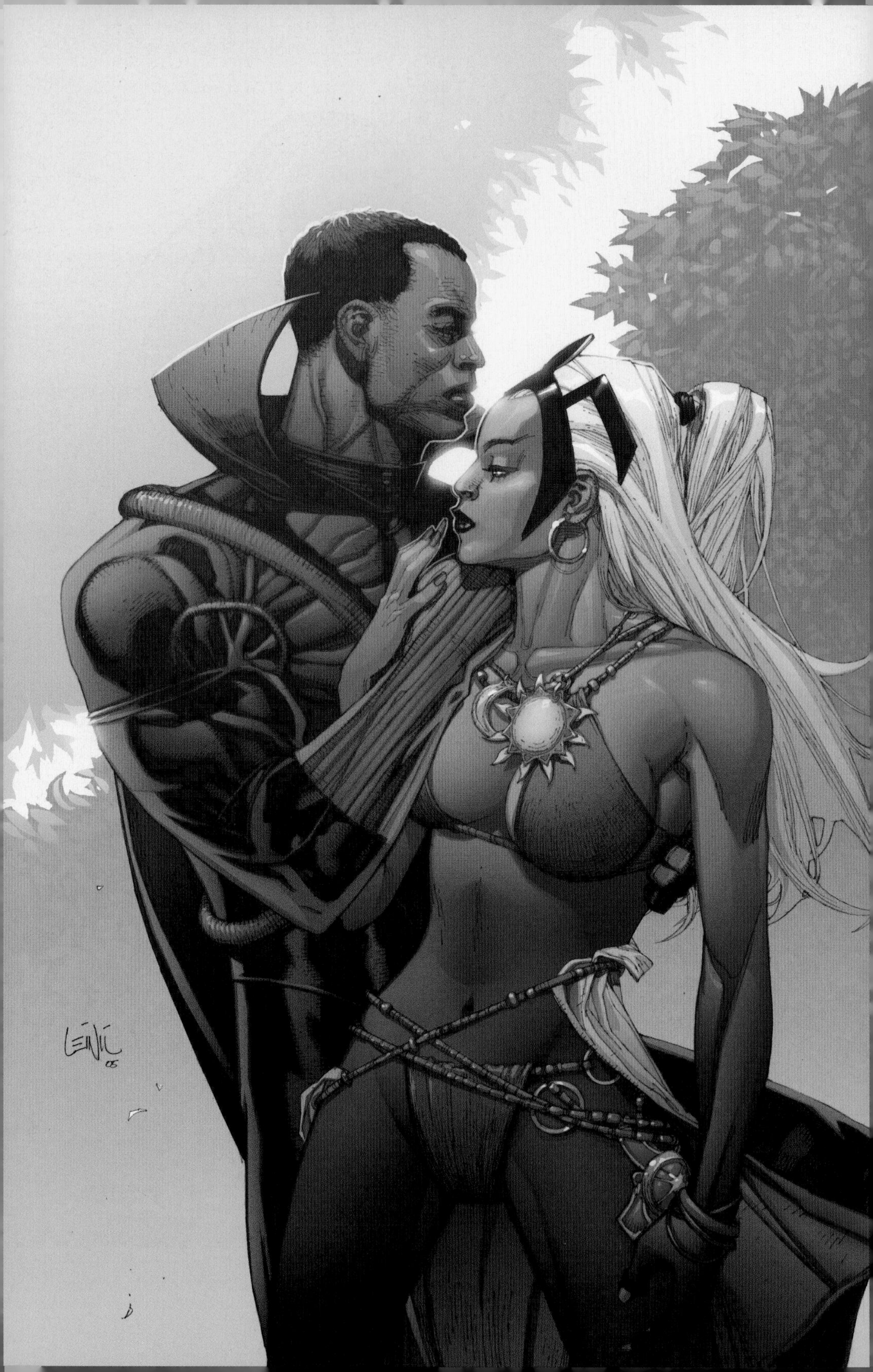

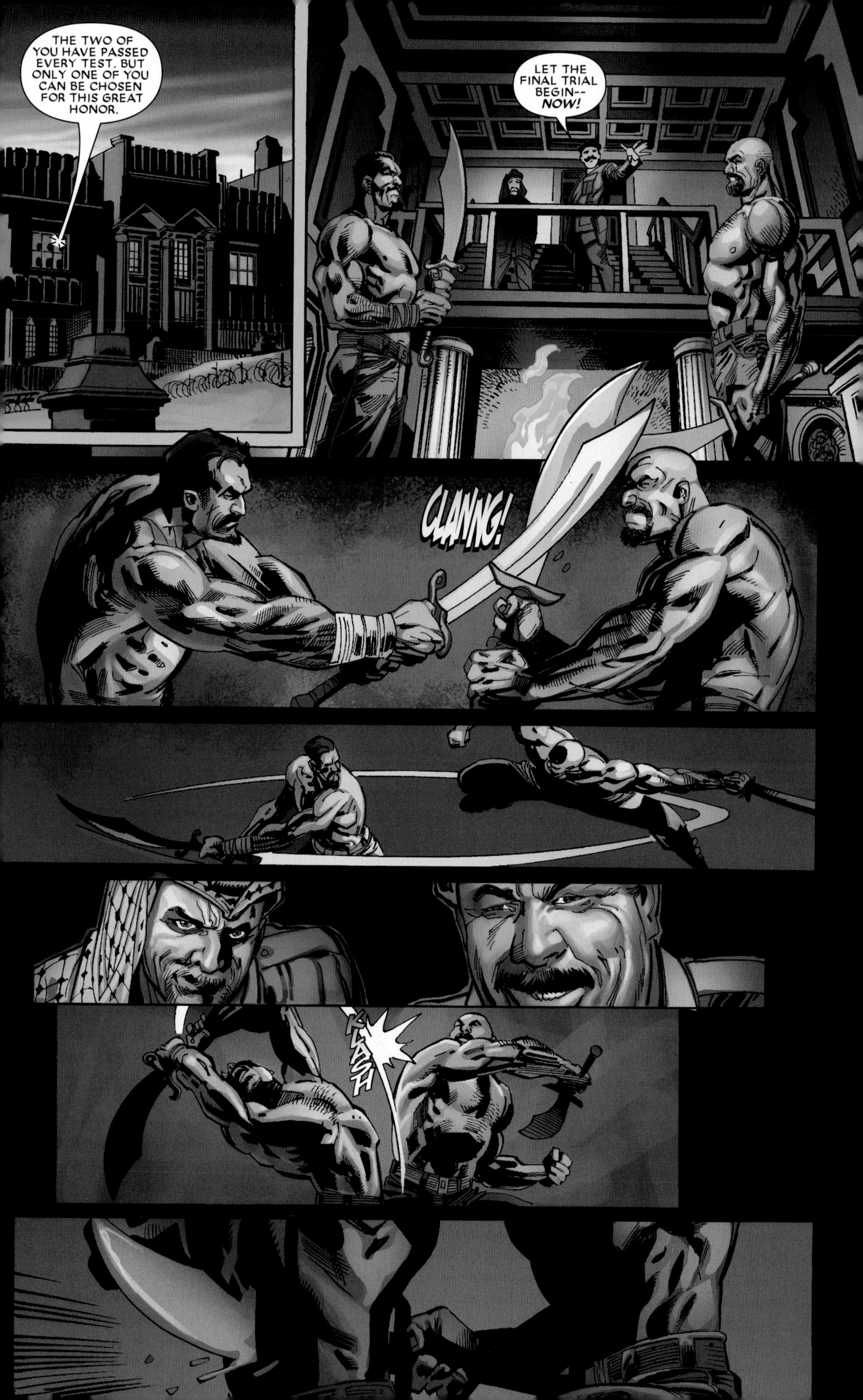
THE TWO OF YOU HAVE PASSED EVERY TEST. BUT ONLY ONE OF YOU CAN BE CHOSEN FOR THIS GREAT HONOR.
LET THE FINAL TRIAL BEGIN-- NOW!
CLANNG!
KLASH

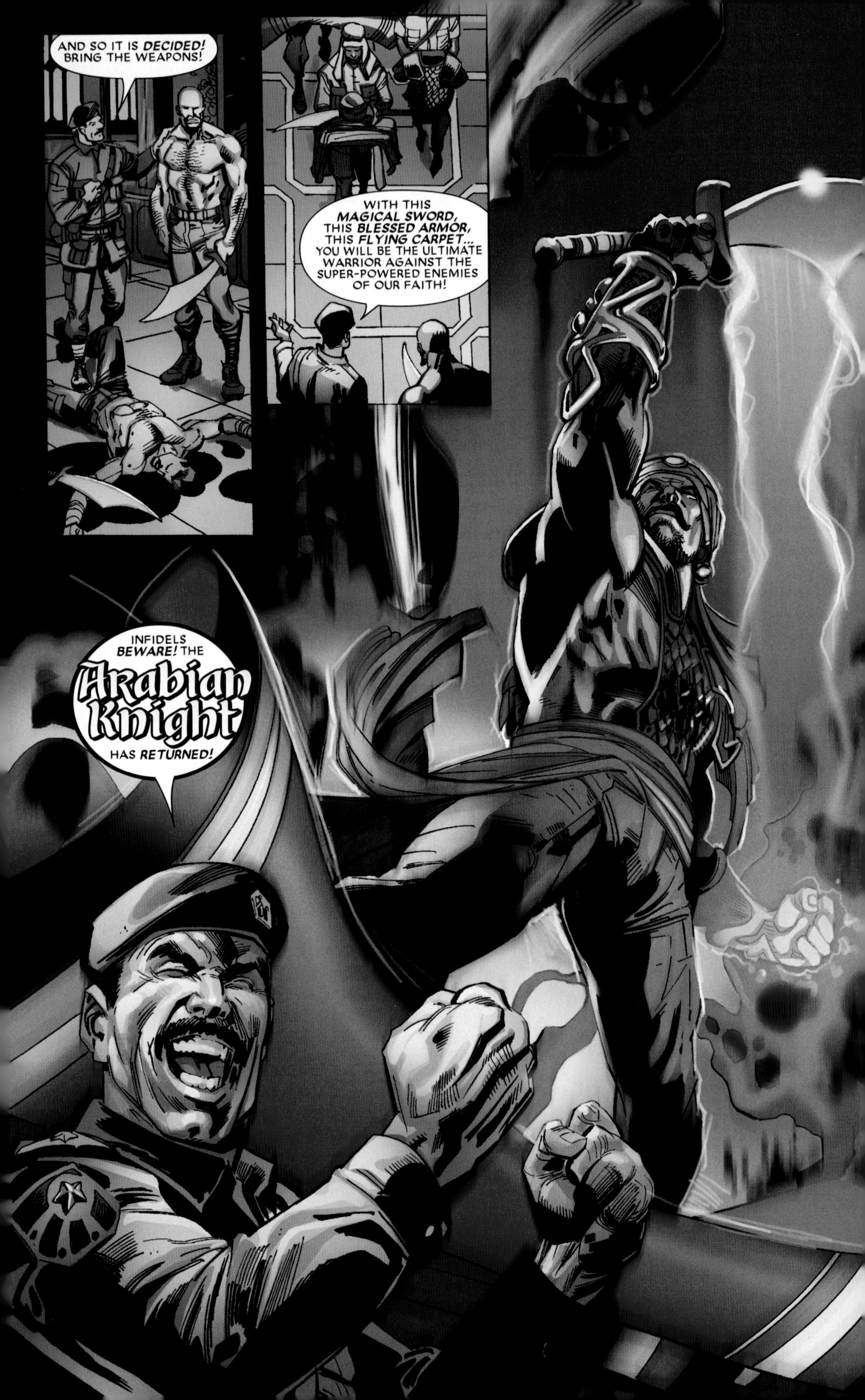
AND SO IT IS DECIDED! BRING THE WEAPONS!
WITH THIS MAGICAL SWORD, THIS BLESSED ARMOR, THIS FLYING CARPET... YOU WILL BE THE ULTIMATE WARRIOR AGAINST THE SUPER-POWERED ENEMIES OF OUR FAITH!
INFIDELS BEWARE! THE Arabian Knight HAS RETURNED!

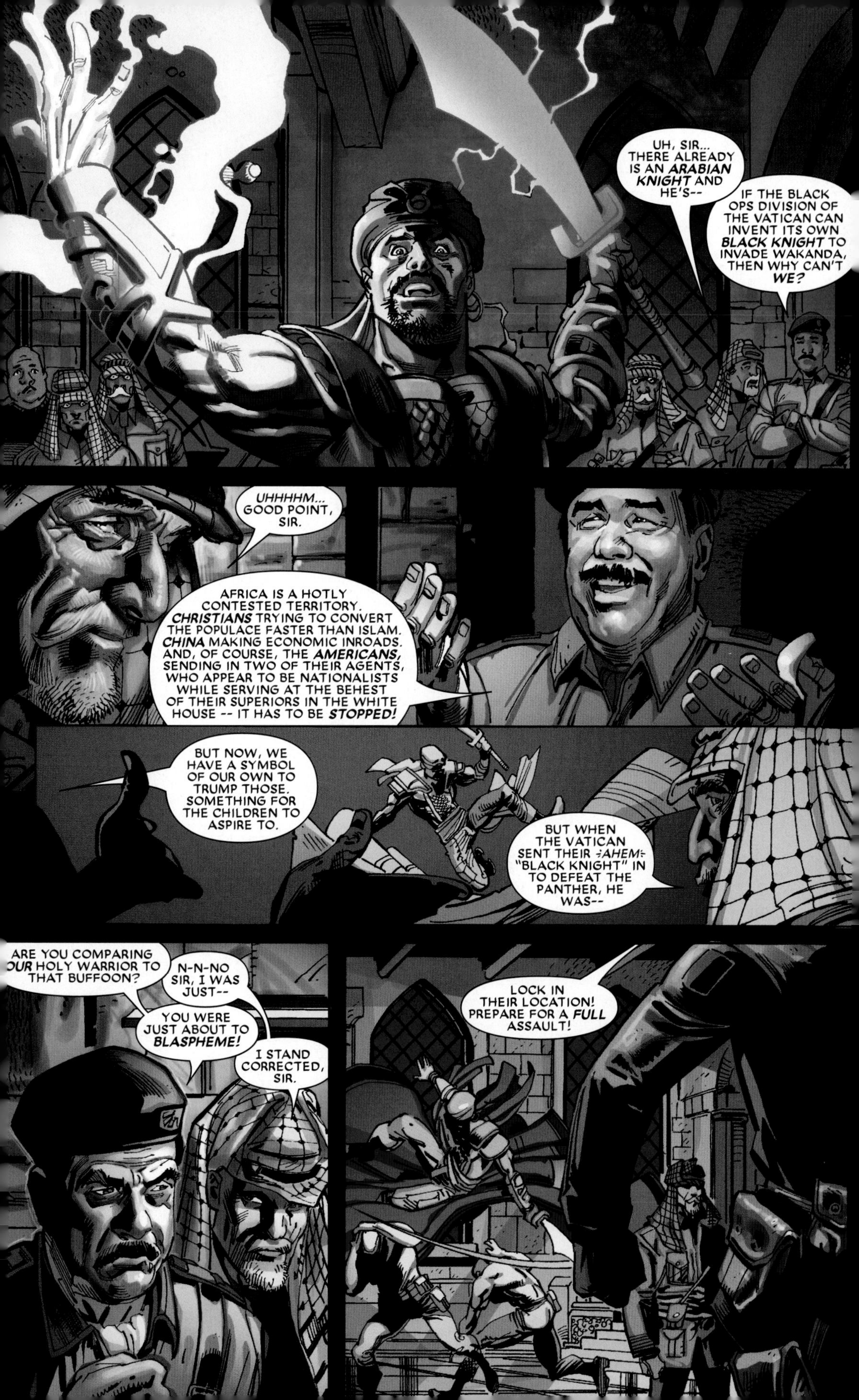

UH, SIR... THERE ALREADY IS AN ARABIAN KNIGHT AND HE'S--
IF THE BLACK OPS DIVISION OF THE VATICAN CAN INVENT ITS OWN BLACK KNIGHT TO INVADE WAKANDA, THEN WHY CAN'T WE?
UHHHHM... GOOD POINT, SIR.
AFRICA IS A HOTLY CONTESTED TERRITORY. CHRISTIANS TRYING TO CONVERT THE POPULACE FASTER THAN ISLAM. CHINA MAKING ECONOMIC INROADS. AND, OF COURSE, THE AMERICANS, SENDING IN TWO OF THEIR AGENTS, WHO APPEAR TO BE NATIONALISTS WHILE SERVING AT THE BEHEST OF THEIR SUPERIORS IN THE WHITE HOUSE -- IT HAS TO BE STOPPED!
BUT NOW, WE HAVE A SYMBOL OF OUR OWN TO TRUMP THOSE. SOMETHING FOR THE CHILDREN TO ASPIRE TO.
BUT WHEN THE VATICAN SENT THEIR -AHEM- "BLACK KNIGHT" IN TO DEFEAT THE PANTHER, HE WAS--
ARE YOU COMPARING OUR HOLY WARRIOR TO THAT BUFFOON?
N-N-NO SIR, I WAS JUST--
YOU WERE JUST ABOUT TO BLASPHEME!
I STAND CORRECTED, SIR.
LOCK IN THEIR LOCATION! PREPARE FOR A FULL ASSAULT!

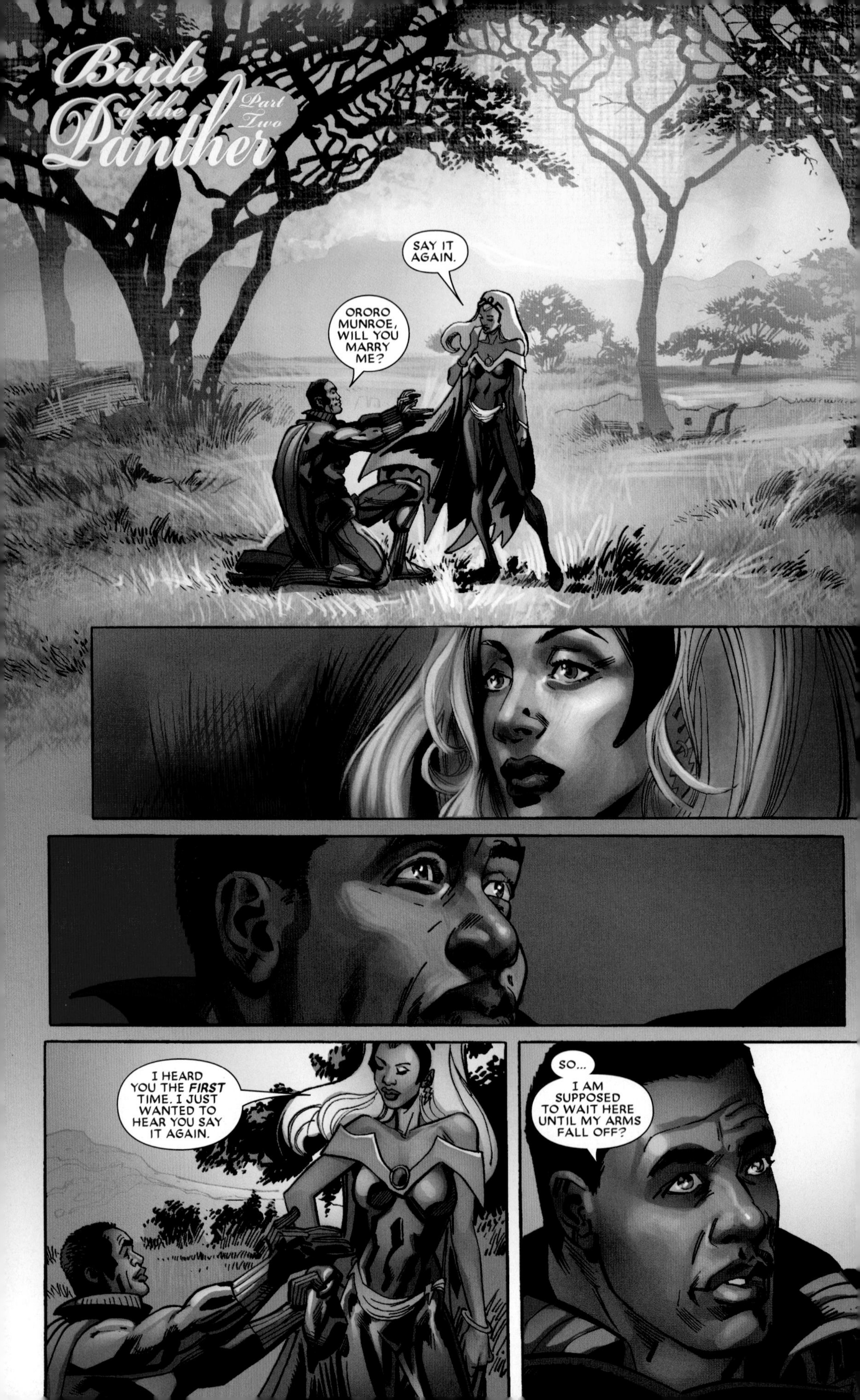
Bride of the Panther
Part Two
SAY IT AGAIN.
ORORO MUNROE, WILL YOU MARRY ME?
I HEARD YOU THE FIRST TIME. I JUST WANTED TO HEAR YOU SAY IT AGAIN.
SO...
I AM SUPPOSED TO WAIT HERE UNTIL MY ARMS FALL OFF?

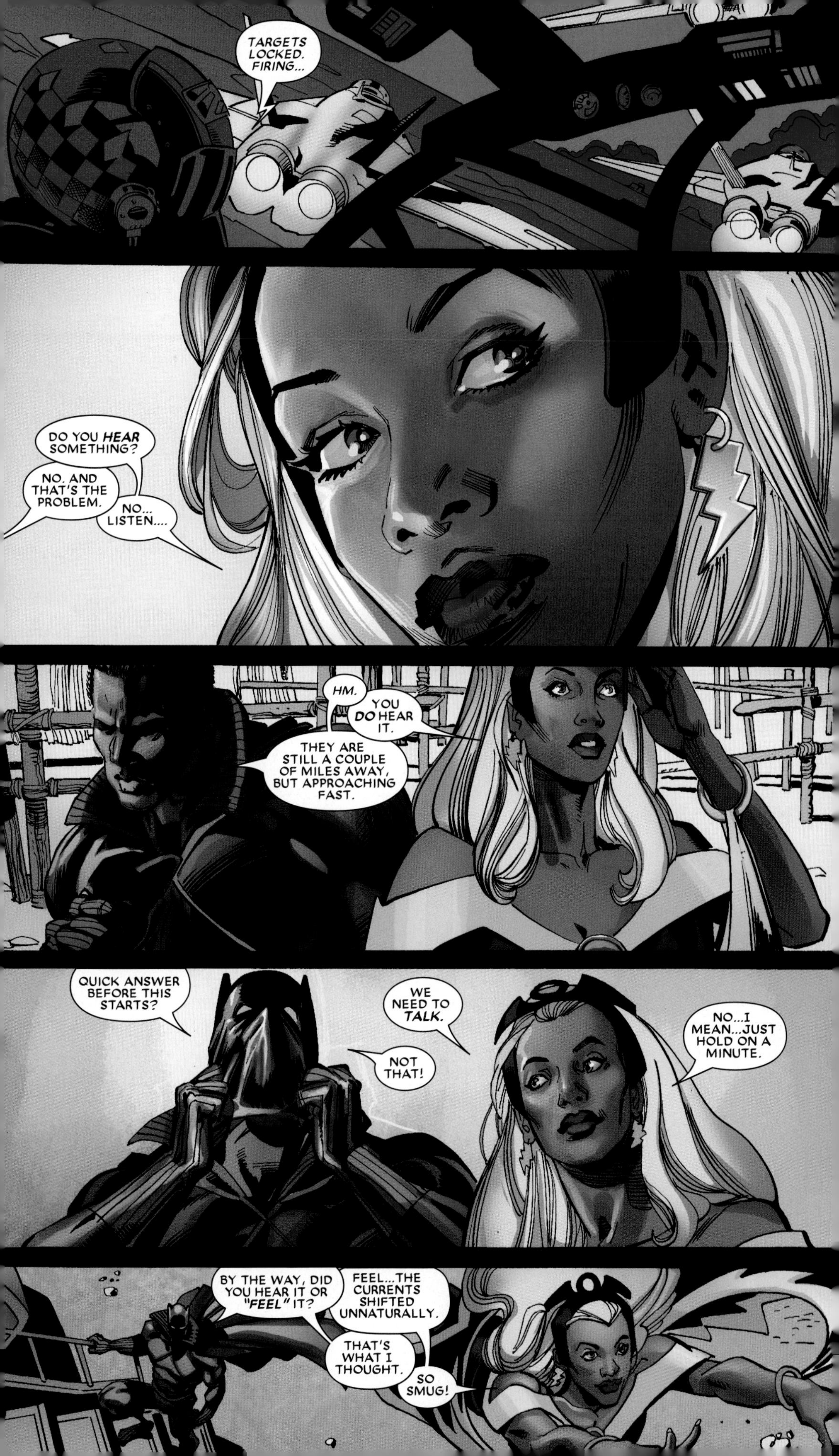
TARGETS LOCKED. FIRING...
DO YOU HEAR SOMETHING?
NO. AND THAT'S THE PROBLEM.
NO... LISTEN....
HM.
YOU DO HEAR IT.
THEY ARE STILL A COUPLE OF MILES AWAY, BUT APPROACHING FAST.
QUICK ANSWER BEFORE THIS STARTS?
WE NEED TO TALK.
NOT THAT!
NO...I MEAN...JUST HOLD ON A MINUTE.
BY THE WAY, DID YOU HEAR IT OR "FEEL" IT?
FEEL...THE CURRENTS SHIFTED UNNATURALLY.
THAT'S WHAT I THOUGHT.
SO SMUG!

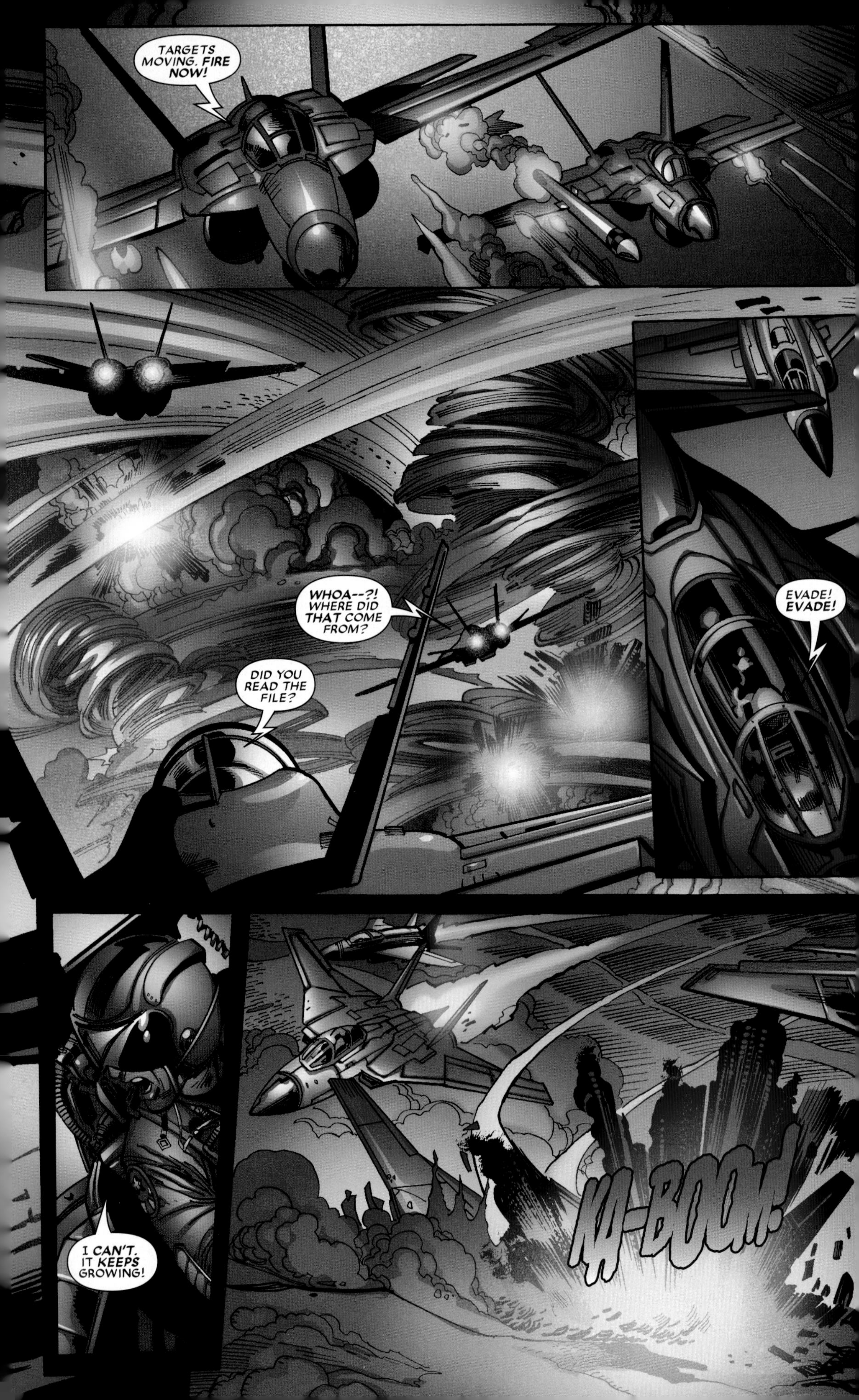
TARGETS MOVING. FIRE NOW!
WHOA--?! WHERE DID THAT COME FROM?
DID YOU READ THE FILE?
EVADE! EVADE!
I CAN'T. IT KEEPS GROWING!
KA-BOOM!

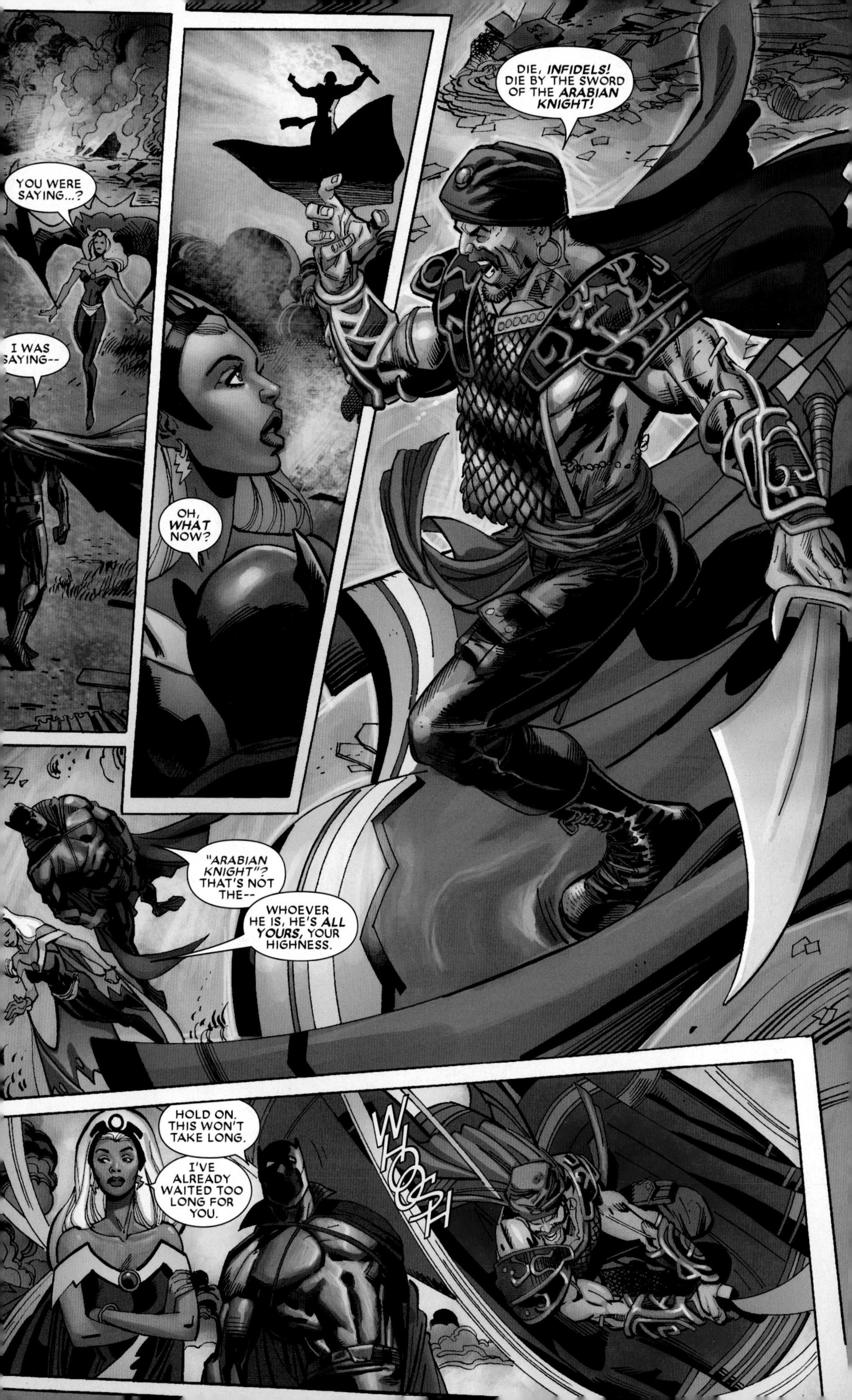
YOU WERE SAYING...?
I WAS SAYING--
OH, WHAT NOW?
DIE, INFIDELS! DIE BY THE SWORD OF THE ARABIAN KNIGHT!
"ARABIAN KNIGHT"? THAT'S NOT THE--
WHOEVER HE IS, HE'S ALL YOURS, YOUR HIGHNESS.
HOLD ON. THIS WON'T TAKE LONG.
I'VE ALREADY WAITED TOO LONG FOR YOU.
WHOOSH

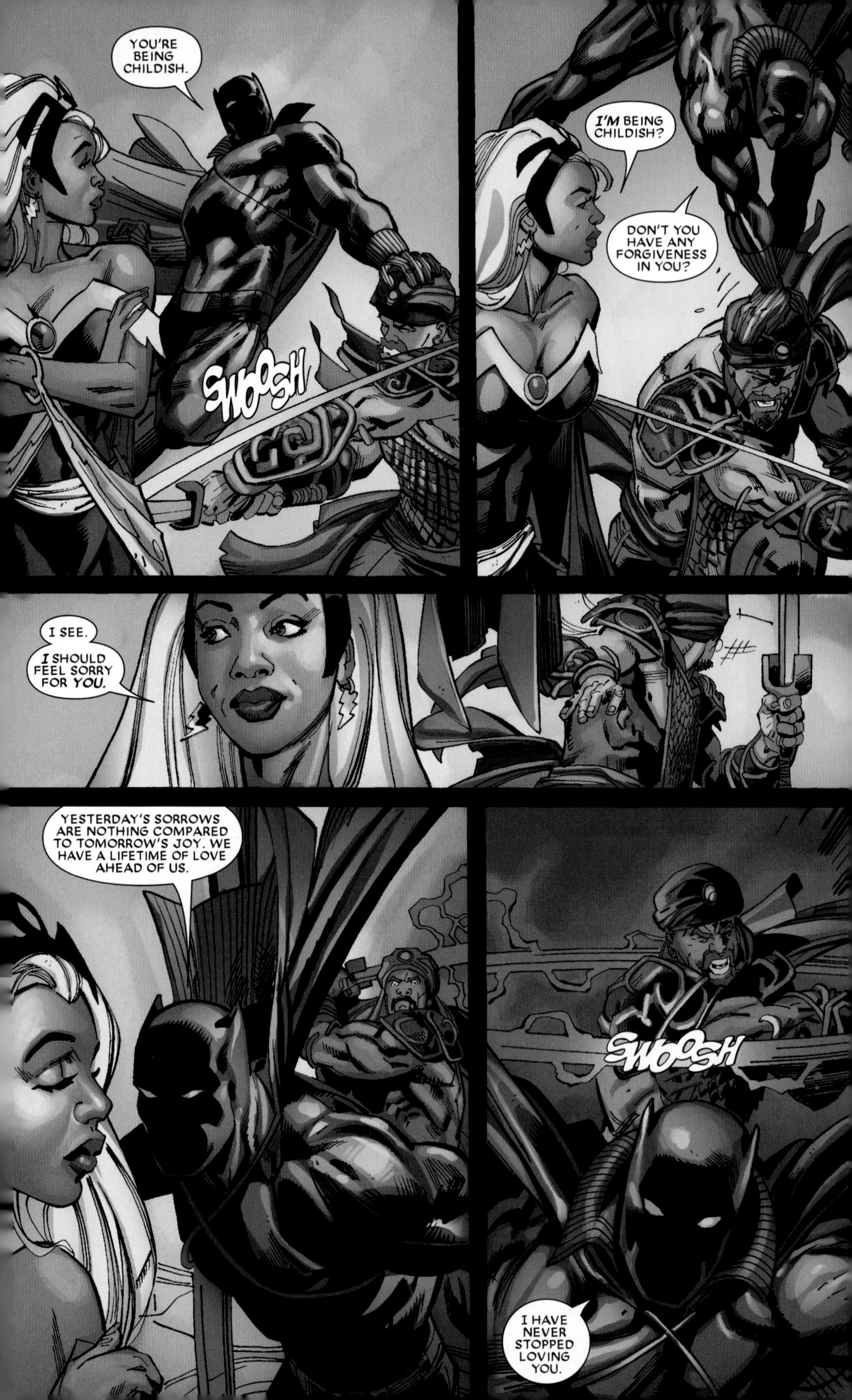

YOU'RE BEING CHILDISH.
SWOOSH
I'M BEING CHILDISH?
DON'T YOU HAVE ANY FORGIVENESS IN YOU?
I SEE.
I SHOULD FEEL SORRY FOR YOU.
YESTERDAY'S SORROWS ARE NOTHING COMPARED TO TOMORROW'S JOY. WE HAVE A LIFETIME OF LOVE AHEAD OF US.
SWOOSH
I HAVE NEVER STOPPED LOVING YOU.

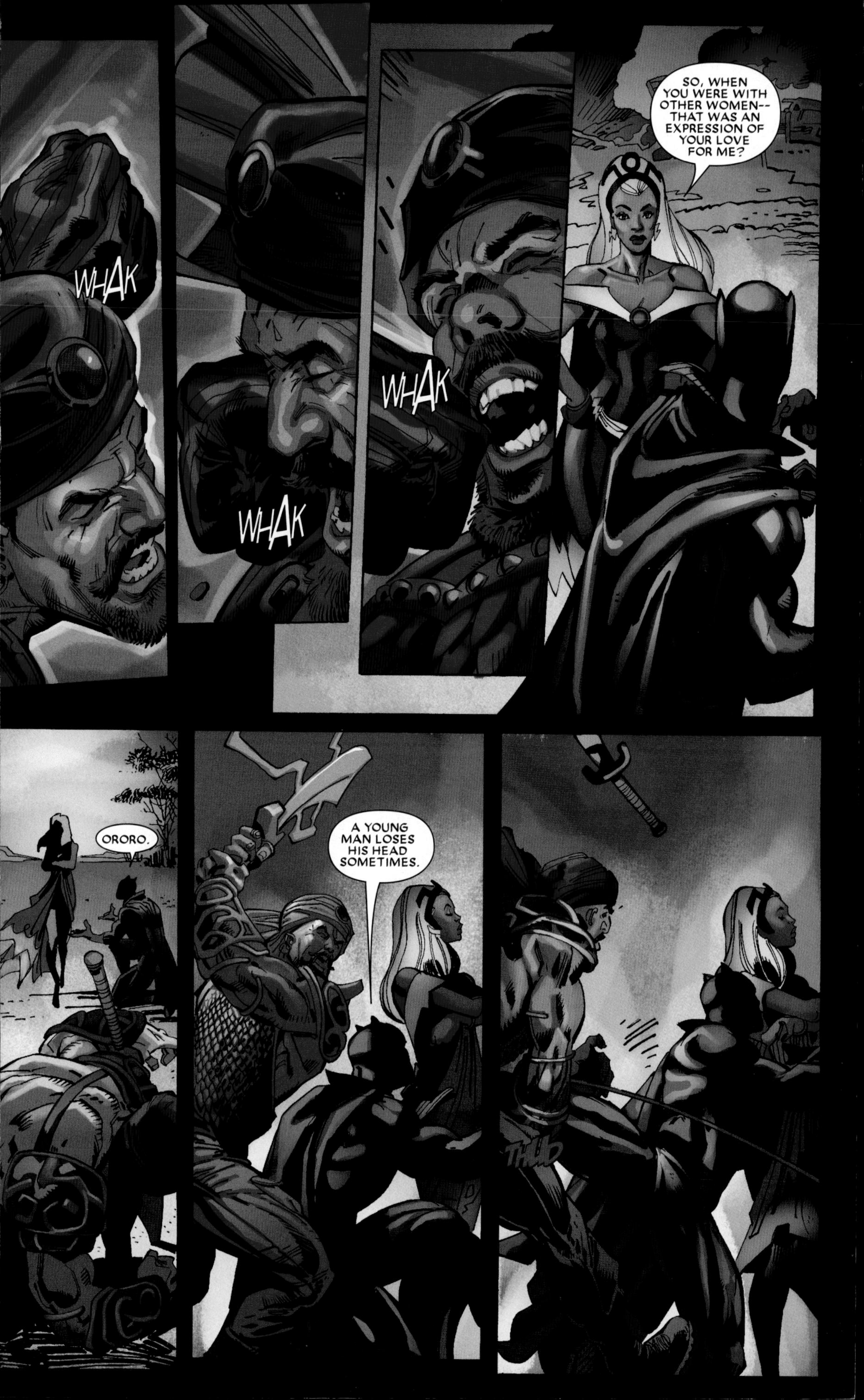

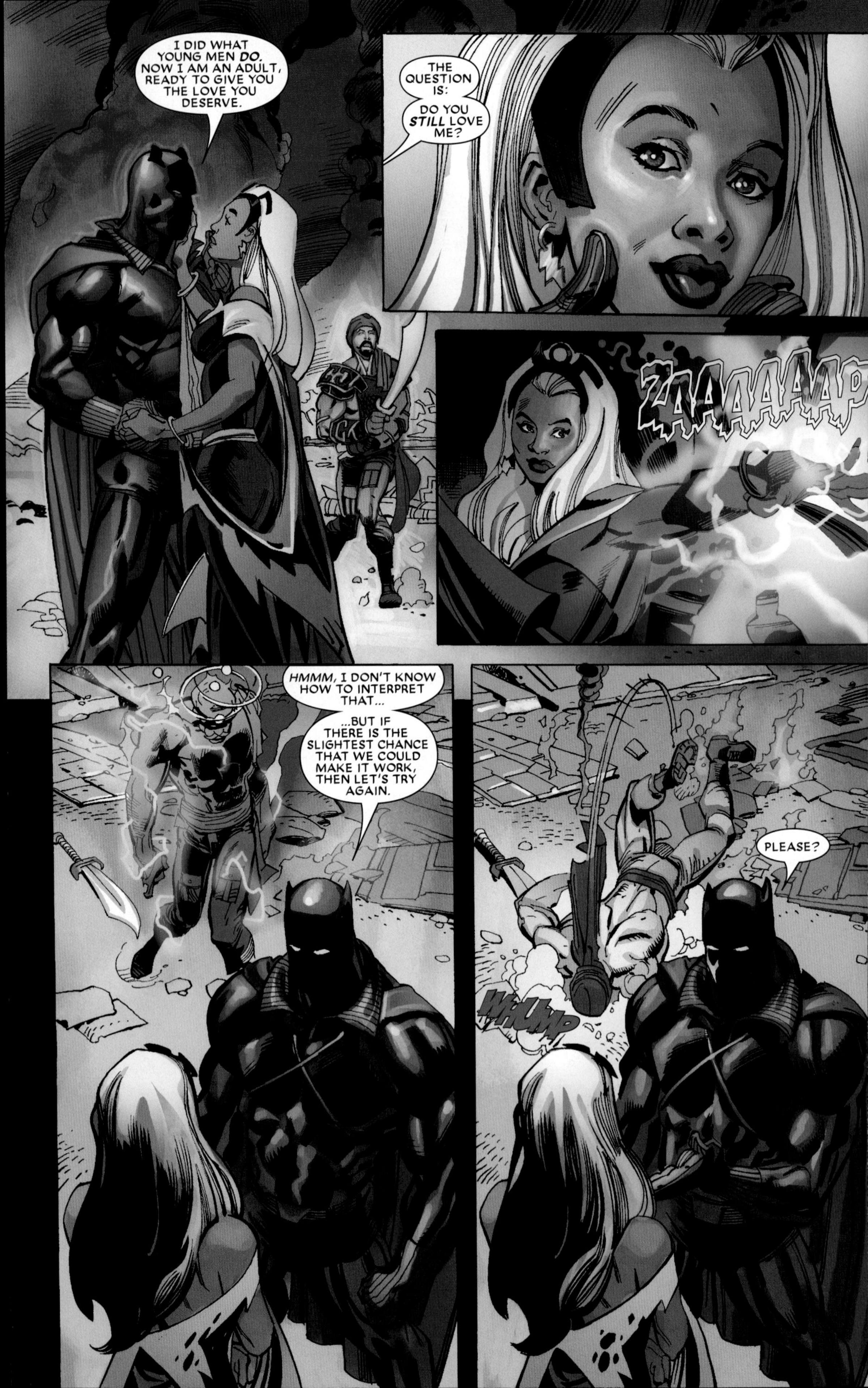

I DID WHAT YOUNG MEN *DO.* NOW I AM AN ADULT, READY TO GIVE YOU THE LOVE YOU DESERVE.
THE QUESTION IS:
DO YOU *STILL* LOVE ME?
ZAAAAAAP
HMMM, I DON'T KNOW HOW TO INTERPRET THAT...
...BUT IF THERE IS THE SLIGHTEST CHANCE THAT WE COULD MAKE IT WORK, THEN LET'S TRY AGAIN.
WHUMP
PLEASE?

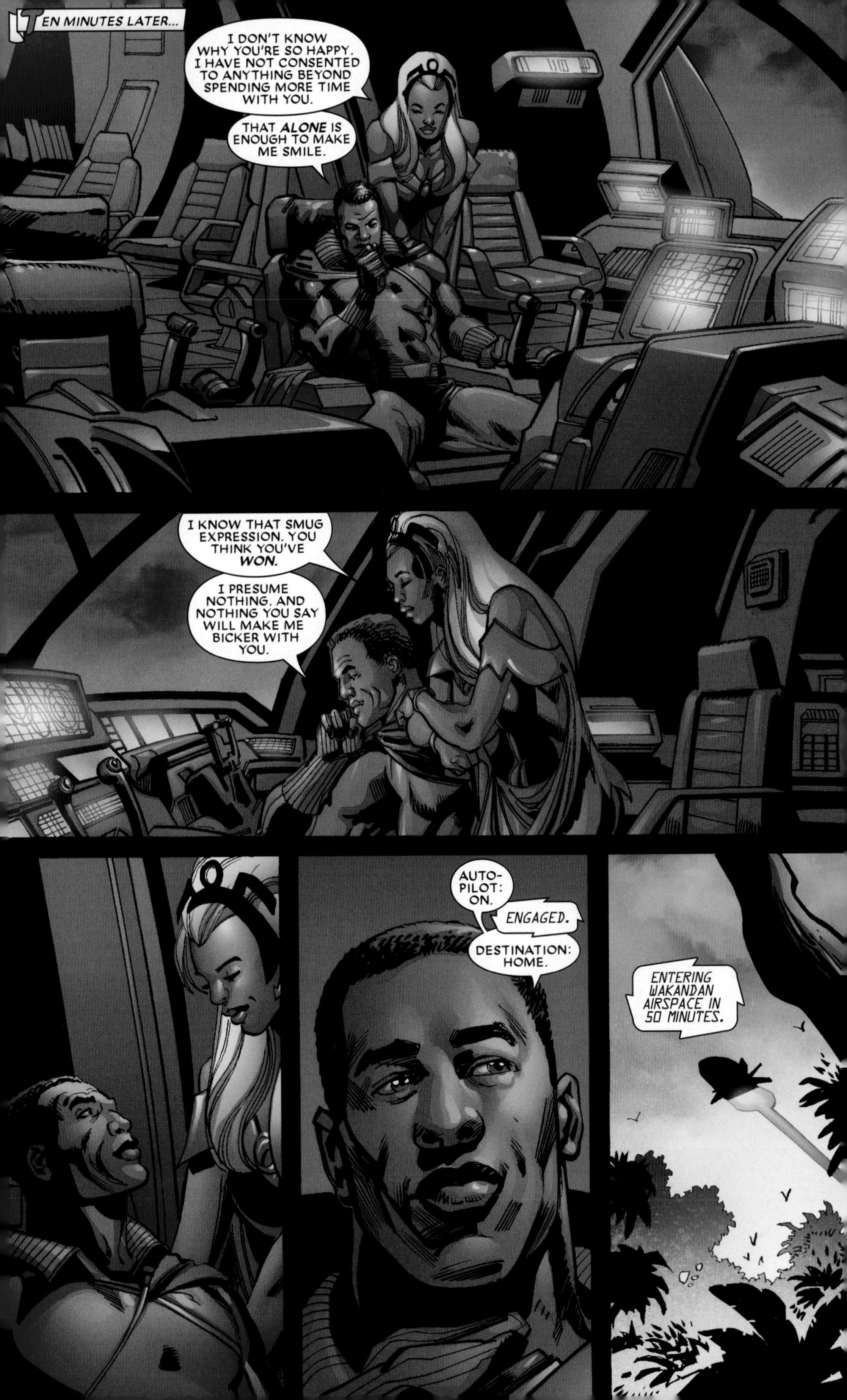
TEN MINUTES LATER...
I DON'T KNOW WHY YOU'RE SO HAPPY. I HAVE NOT CONSENTED TO ANYTHING BEYOND SPENDING MORE TIME WITH YOU.
THAT ALONE IS ENOUGH TO MAKE ME SMILE.
I KNOW THAT SMUG EXPRESSION. YOU THINK YOU'VE WON.
I PRESUME NOTHING. AND NOTHING YOU SAY WILL MAKE ME BICKER WITH YOU.
AUTO-PILOT: ON.
ENGAGED.
DESTINATION: HOME.
ENTERING WAKANDAN AIRSPACE IN 50 MINUTES.

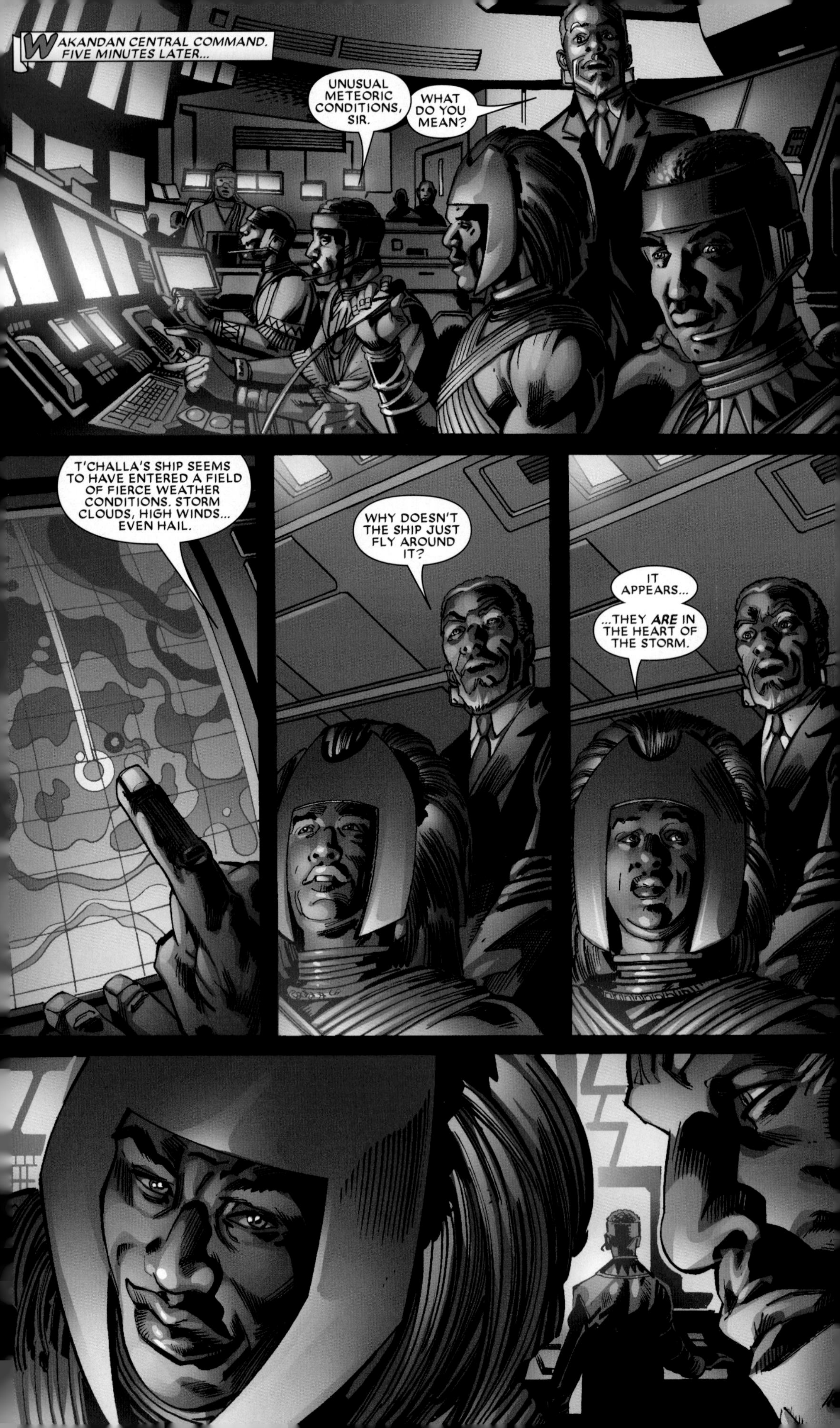
WAKANDAN CENTRAL COMMAND. FIVE MINUTES LATER...
UNUSUAL METEORIC CONDITIONS, SIR.
WHAT DO YOU MEAN?
T'CHALLA'S SHIP SEEMS TO HAVE ENTERED A FIELD OF FIERCE WEATHER CONDITIONS. STORM CLOUDS, HIGH WINDS... EVEN HAIL.
WHY DOESN'T THE SHIP JUST FLY AROUND IT?
IT APPEARS...
...THEY ARE IN THE HEART OF THE STORM.

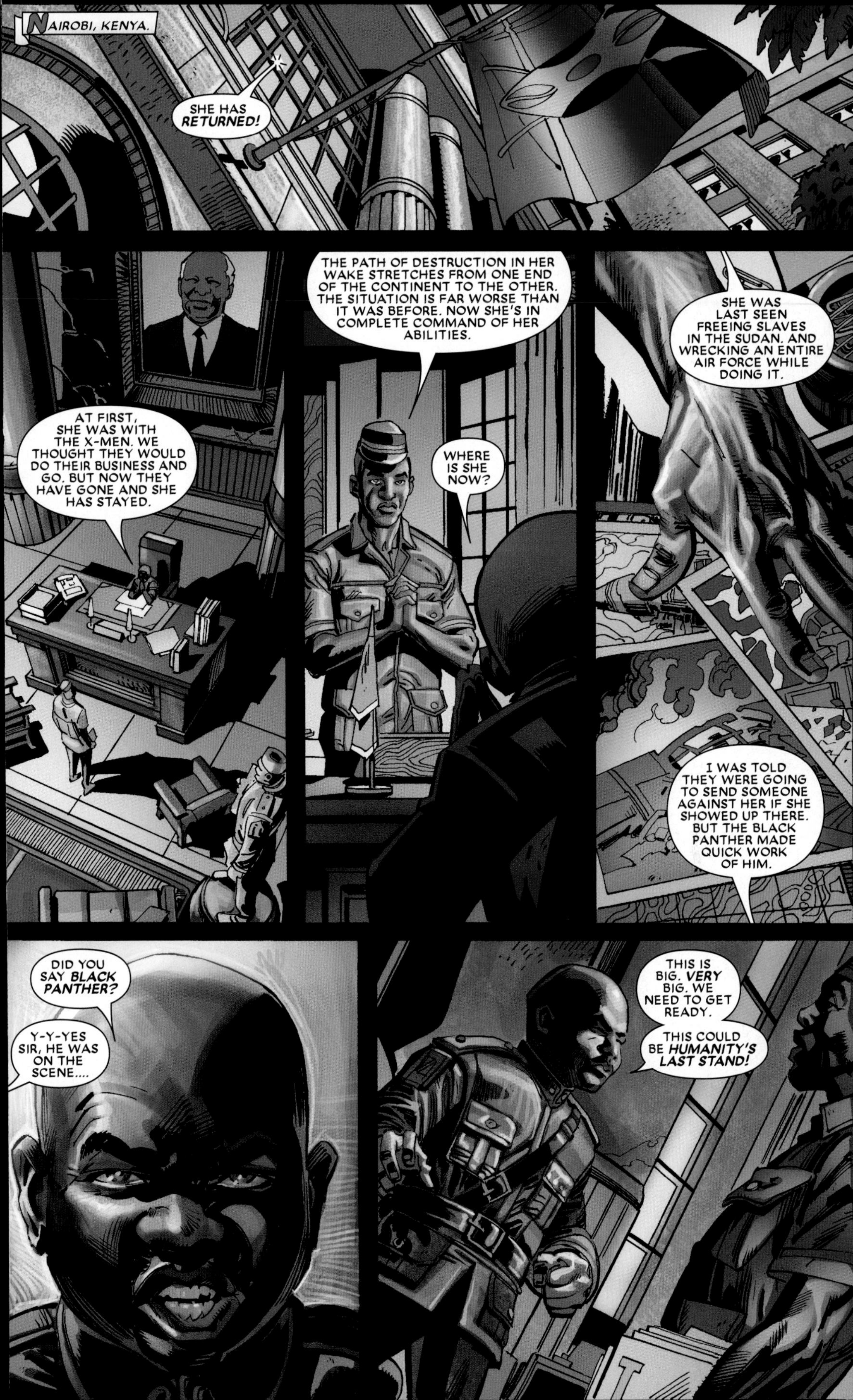
NAIROBI, KENYA.
SHE HAS RETURNED!
AT FIRST, SHE WAS WITH THE X-MEN. WE THOUGHT THEY WOULD DO THEIR BUSINESS AND GO. BUT NOW THEY HAVE GONE AND SHE HAS STAYED.
THE PATH OF DESTRUCTION IN HER WAKE STRETCHES FROM ONE END OF THE CONTINENT TO THE OTHER. THE SITUATION IS FAR WORSE THAN IT WAS BEFORE. NOW SHE'S IN COMPLETE COMMAND OF HER ABILITIES.
WHERE IS SHE NOW?
SHE WAS LAST SEEN FREEING SLAVES IN THE SUDAN. AND WRECKING AN ENTIRE AIR FORCE WHILE DOING IT.
I WAS TOLD THEY WERE GOING TO SEND SOMEONE AGAINST HER IF SHE SHOWED UP THERE. BUT THE BLACK PANTHER MADE QUICK WORK OF HIM.
DID YOU SAY BLACK PANTHER?
Y-Y-YES SIR, HE WAS ON THE SCENE....
THIS IS BIG. VERY BIG. WE NEED TO GET READY.
THIS COULD BE HUMANITY'S LAST STAND!

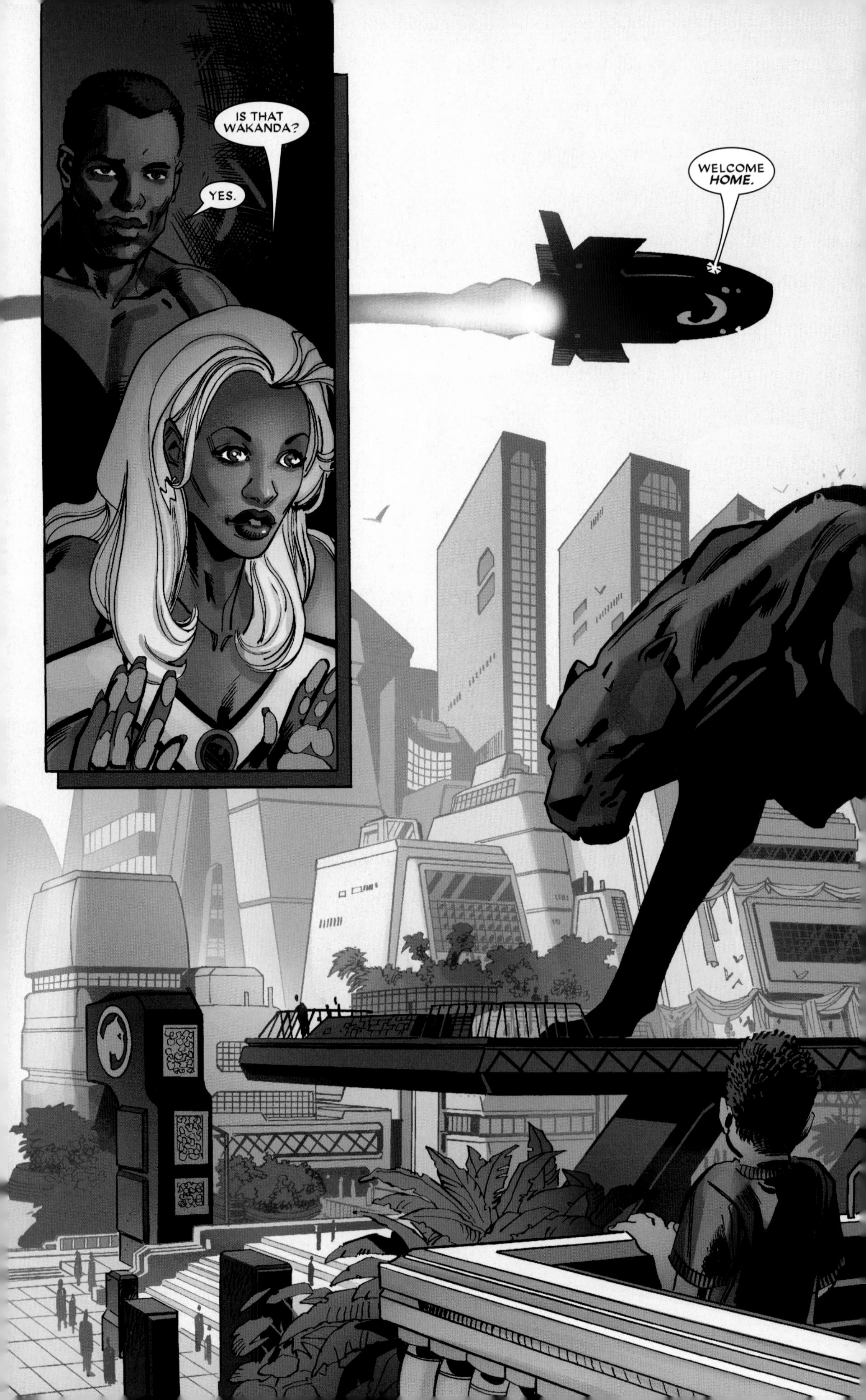
IS THAT WAKANDA?
YES.
WELCOME HOME.

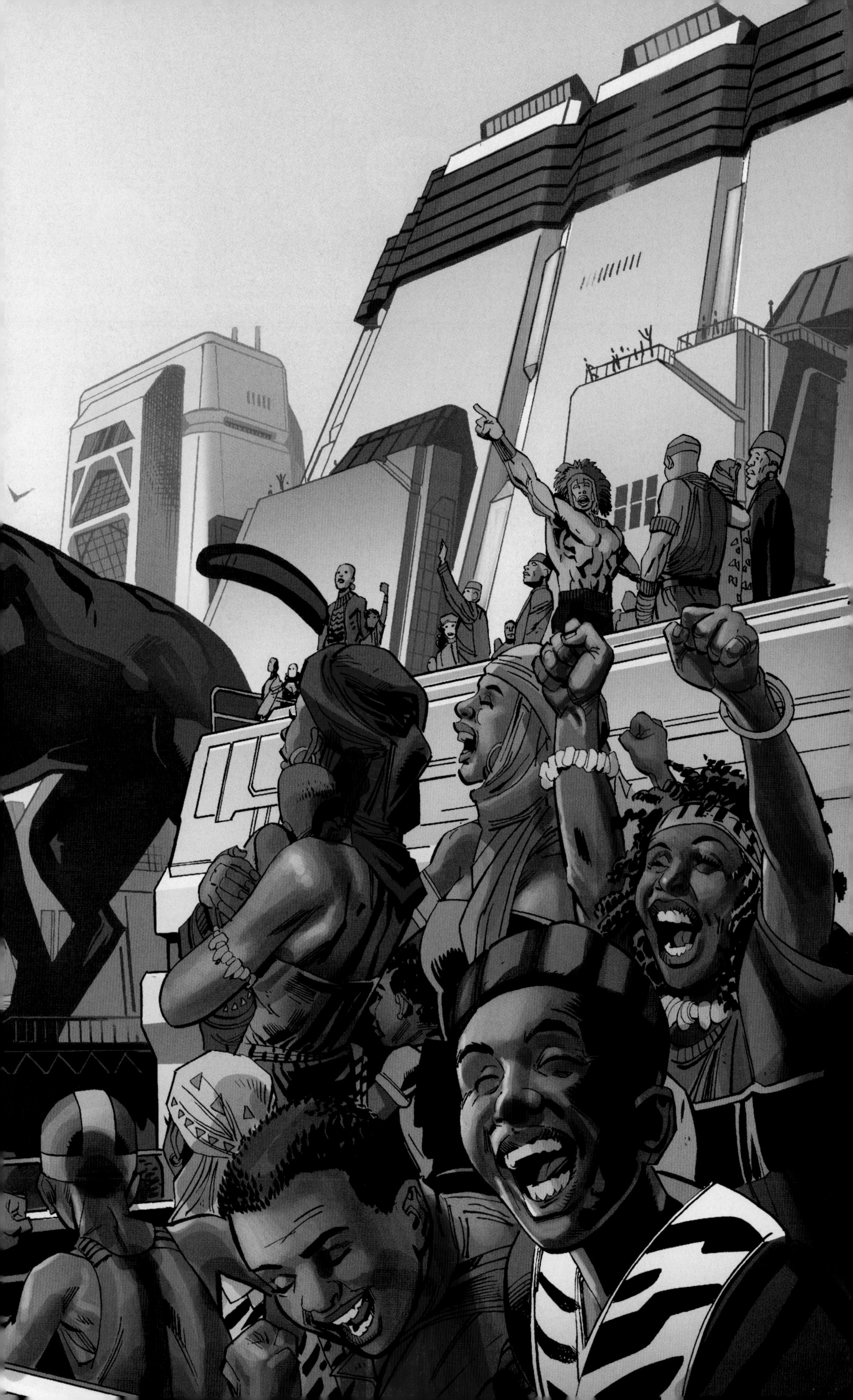

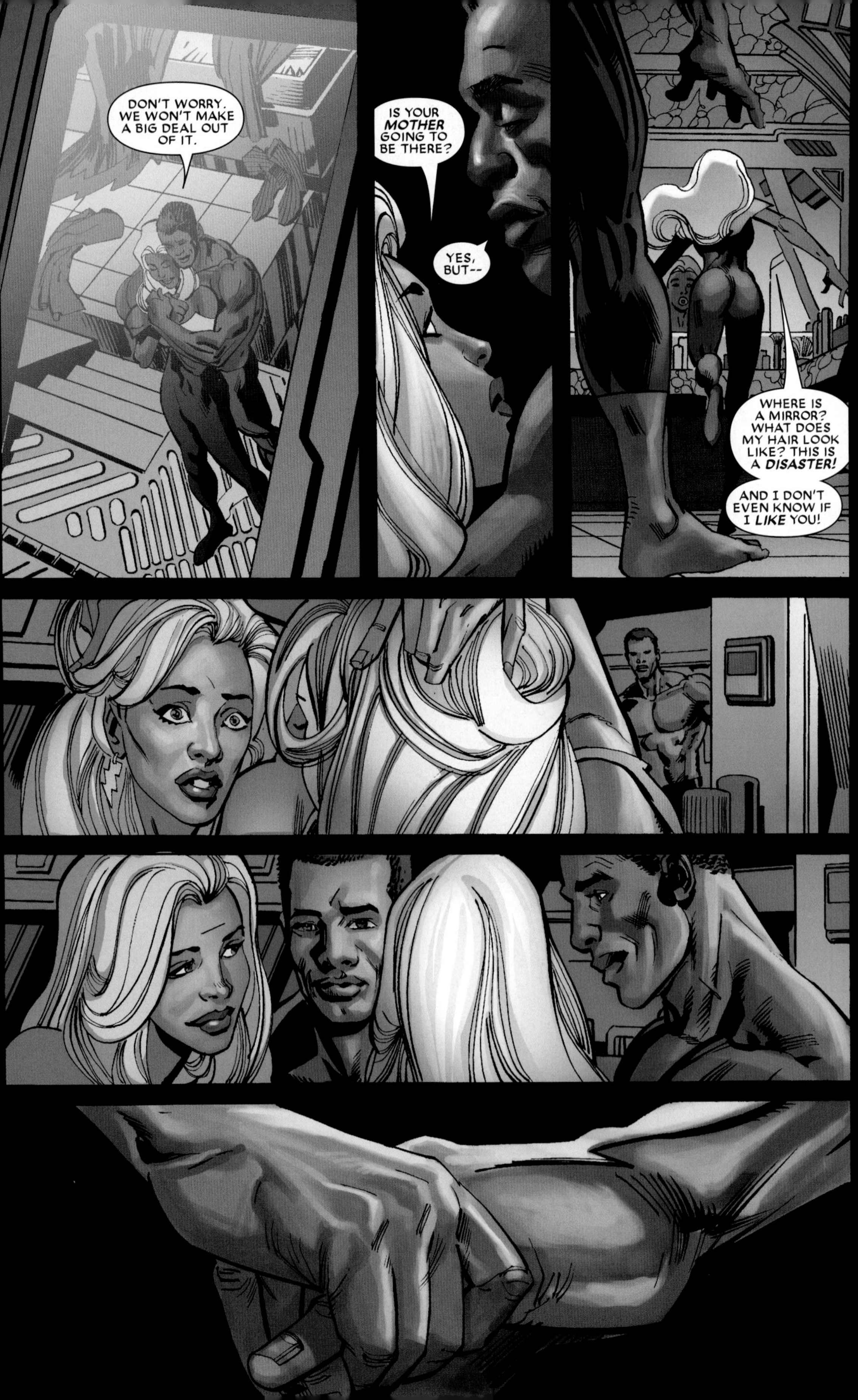

DON'T WORRY. WE WON'T MAKE A BIG DEAL OUT OF IT.
IS YOUR **MOTHER** GOING TO BE THERE?
YES, BUT--
WHERE IS A MIRROR? WHAT DOES MY HAIR LOOK LIKE? THIS IS A ***DISASTER!***
AND I DON'T EVEN KNOW IF I ***LIKE*** YOU!

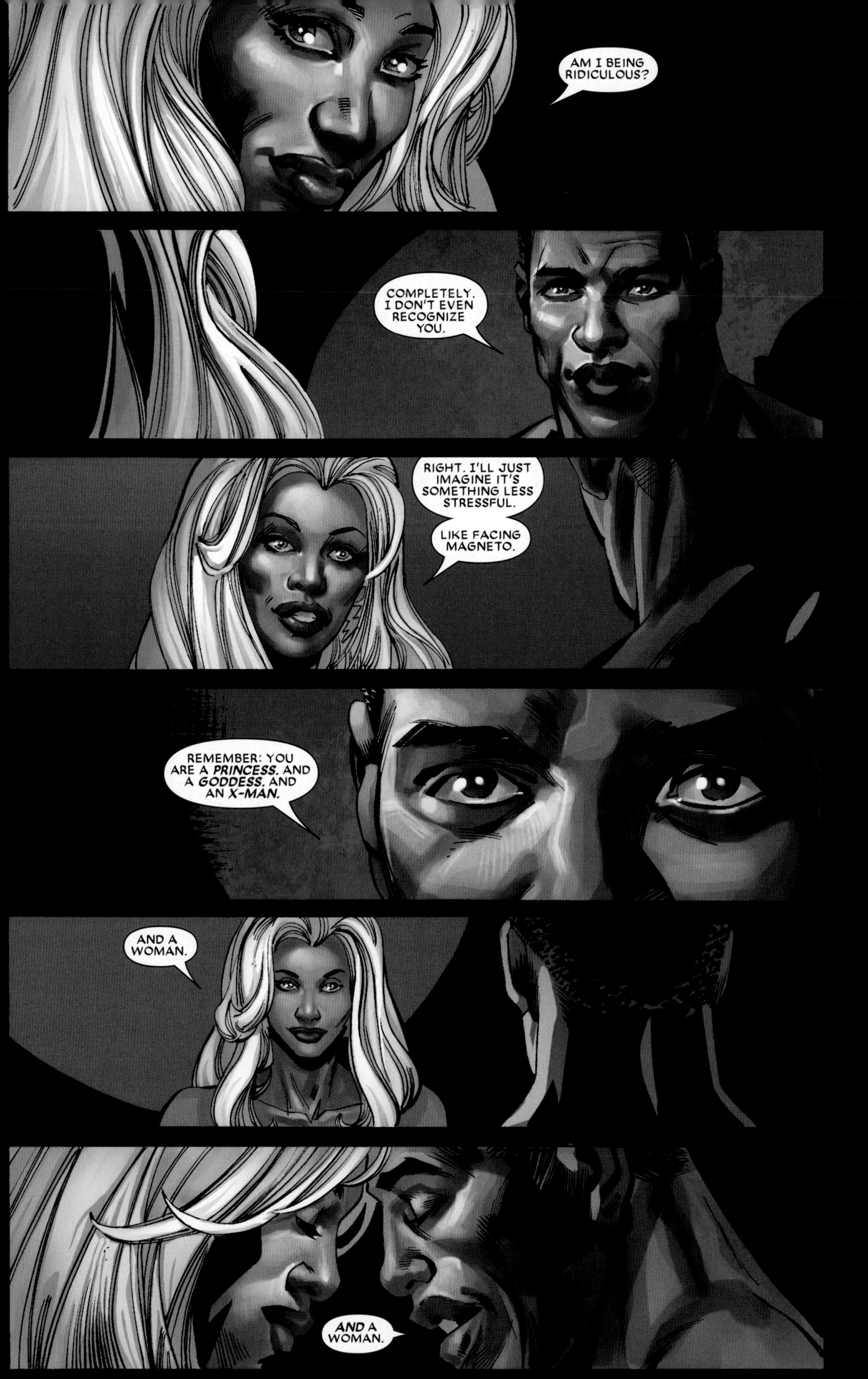
AM I BEING RIDICULOUS?
COMPLETELY. I DON'T EVEN RECOGNIZE YOU.
RIGHT. I'LL JUST IMAGINE IT'S SOMETHING LESS STRESSFUL.
LIKE FACING MAGNETO.
REMEMBER: YOU ARE A *PRINCESS.* AND A *GODDESS.* AND AN *X-MAN.*
AND A WOMAN.
AND A WOMAN.

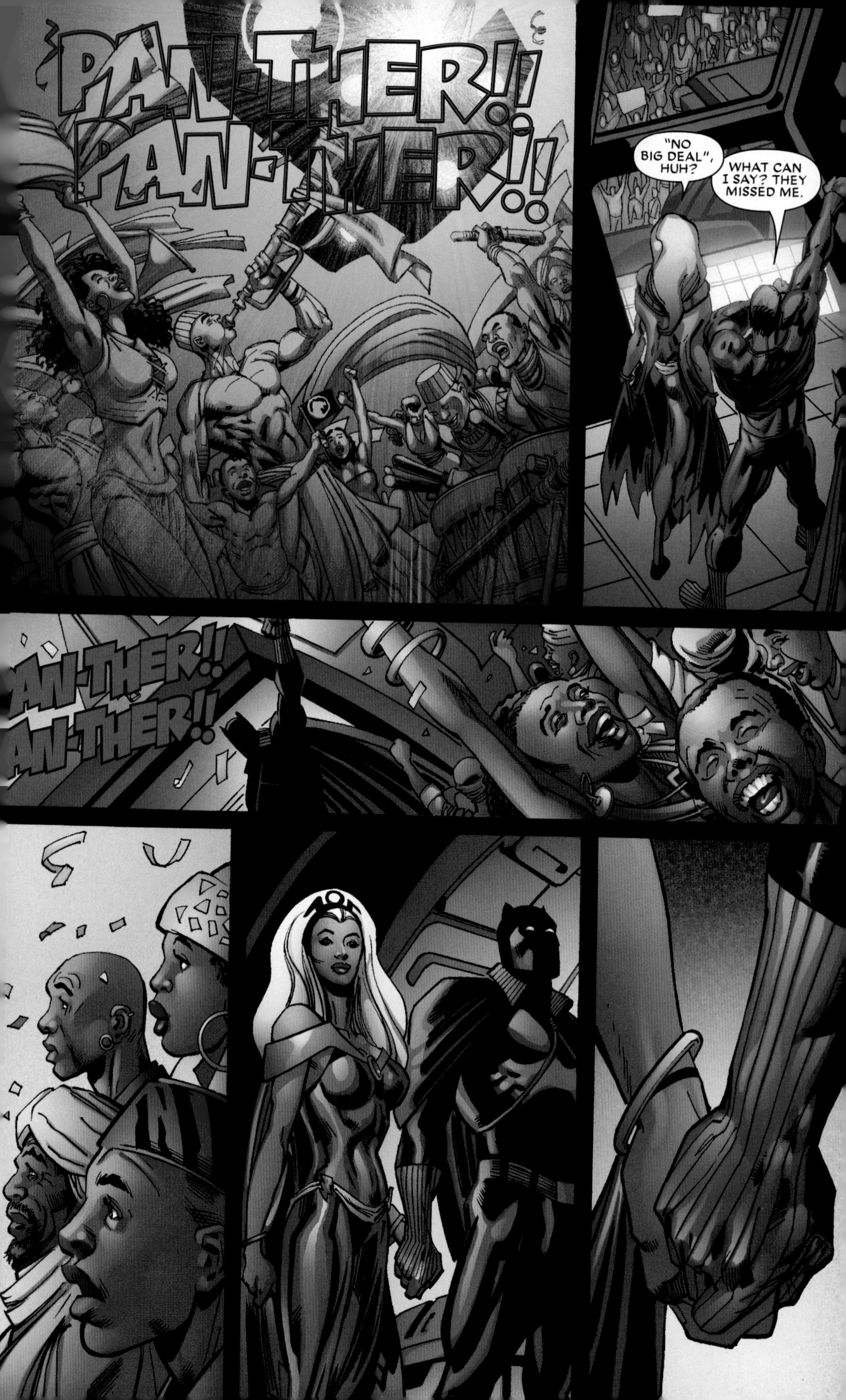
PAN-THER!!
PAN-THER!!
"NO BIG DEAL", HUH?
WHAT CAN I SAY? THEY MISSED ME.
AN-THER!!
AN-THER!!

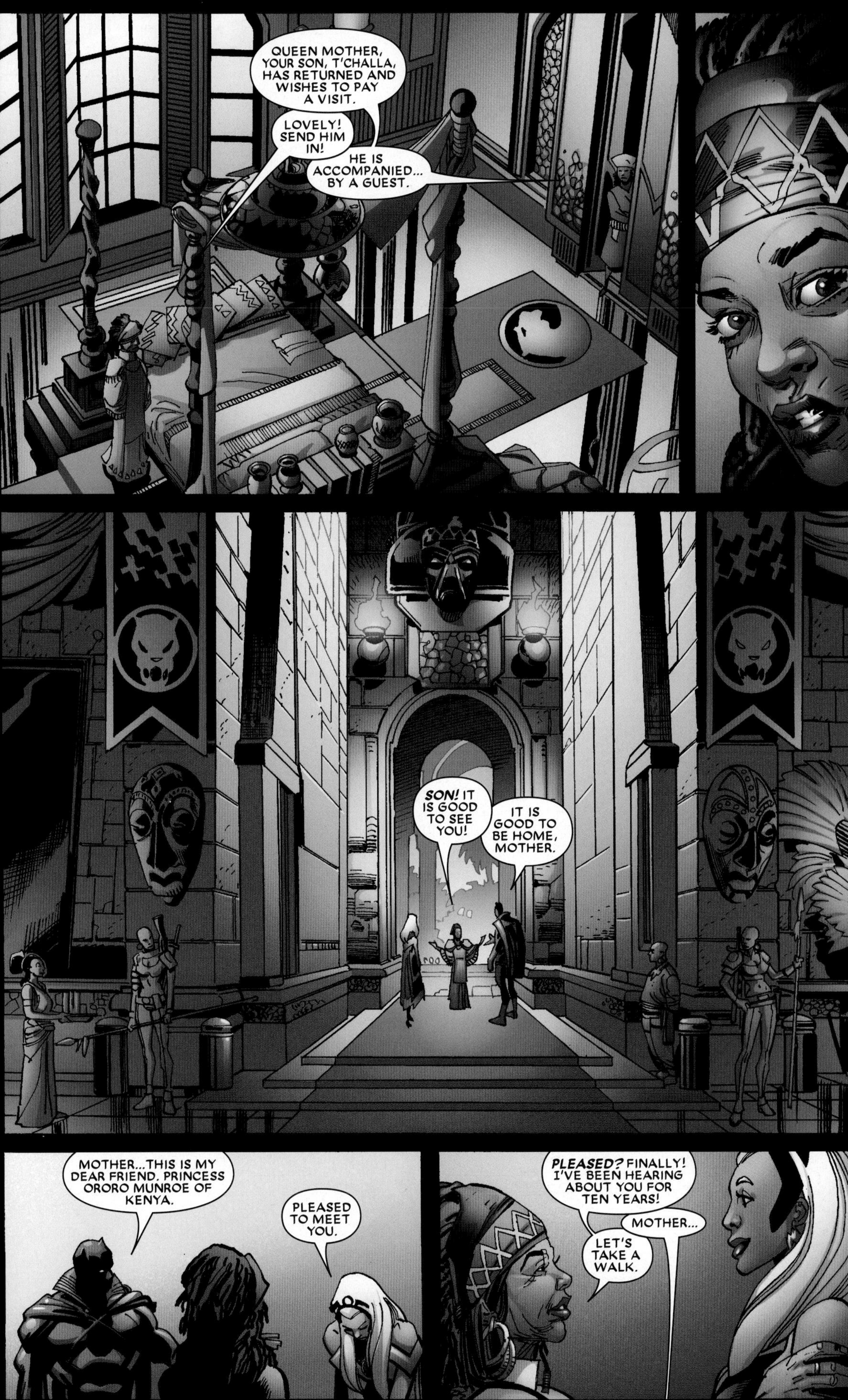
QUEEN MOTHER, YOUR SON, T'CHALLA, HAS RETURNED AND WISHES TO PAY A VISIT.
LOVELY! SEND HIM IN!
HE IS ACCOMPANIED... BY A GUEST.
SON! IT IS GOOD TO SEE YOU!
IT IS GOOD TO BE HOME, MOTHER.
MOTHER...THIS IS MY DEAR FRIEND. PRINCESS ORORO MUNROE OF KENYA.
PLEASED TO MEET YOU.
PLEASED? FINALLY! I'VE BEEN HEARING ABOUT YOU FOR TEN YEARS!
MOTHER...
LET'S TAKE A WALK.

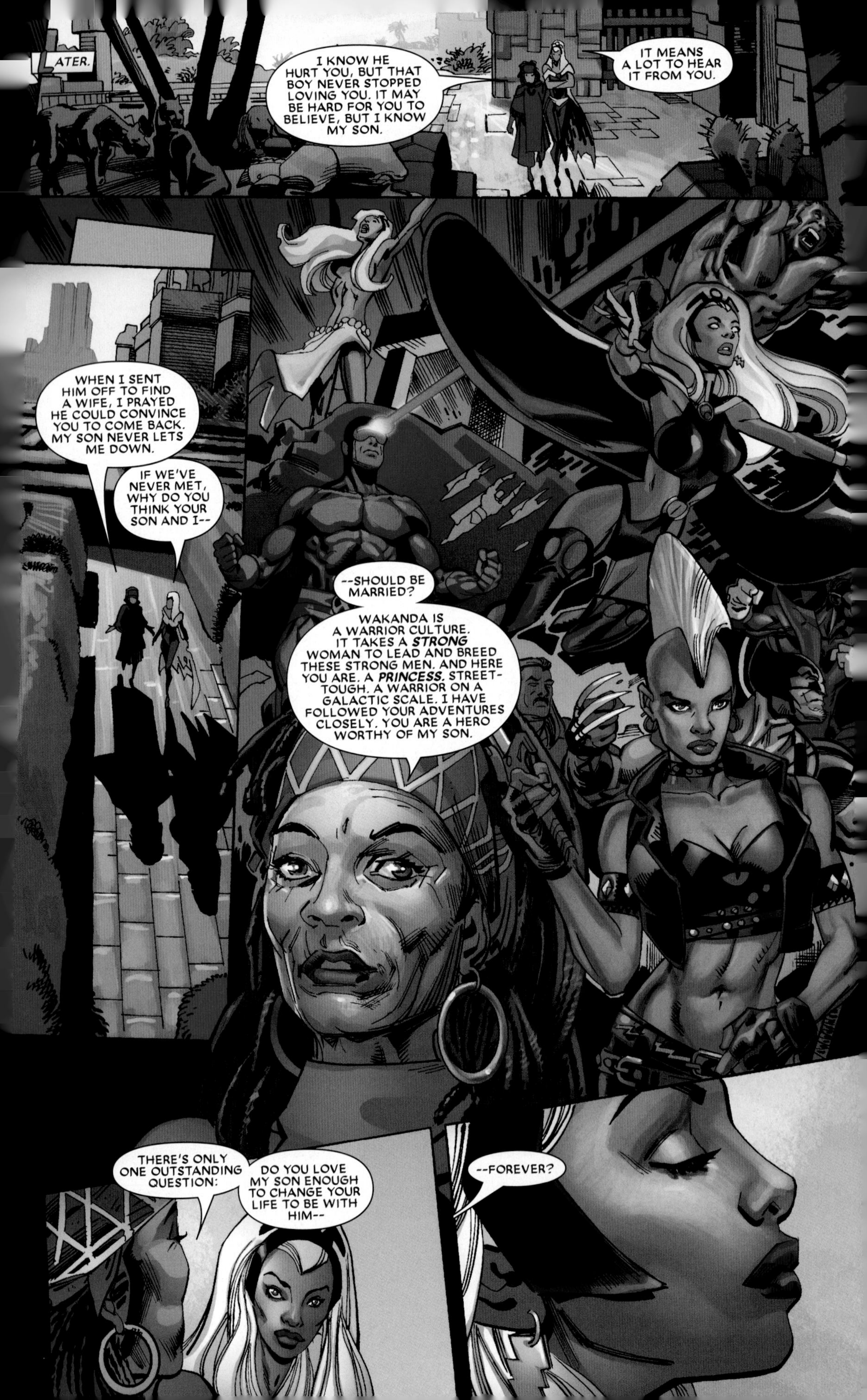
LATER.
I KNOW HE HURT YOU, BUT THAT BOY NEVER STOPPED LOVING YOU. IT MAY BE HARD FOR YOU TO BELIEVE, BUT I KNOW MY SON.
IT MEANS A LOT TO HEAR IT FROM YOU.
WHEN I SENT HIM OFF TO FIND A WIFE, I PRAYED HE COULD CONVINCE YOU TO COME BACK. MY SON NEVER LETS ME DOWN.
IF WE'VE NEVER MET, WHY DO YOU THINK YOUR SON AND I--
--SHOULD BE MARRIED?
WAKANDA IS A WARRIOR CULTURE. IT TAKES A **STRONG** WOMAN TO LEAD AND BREED THESE STRONG MEN. AND HERE YOU ARE. A **PRINCESS.** STREET-TOUGH. A WARRIOR ON A GALACTIC SCALE. I HAVE FOLLOWED YOUR ADVENTURES CLOSELY. YOU ARE A HERO WORTHY OF MY SON.
THERE'S ONLY ONE OUTSTANDING QUESTION:
DO YOU LOVE MY SON ENOUGH TO CHANGE YOUR LIFE TO BE WITH HIM--
--FOREVER?

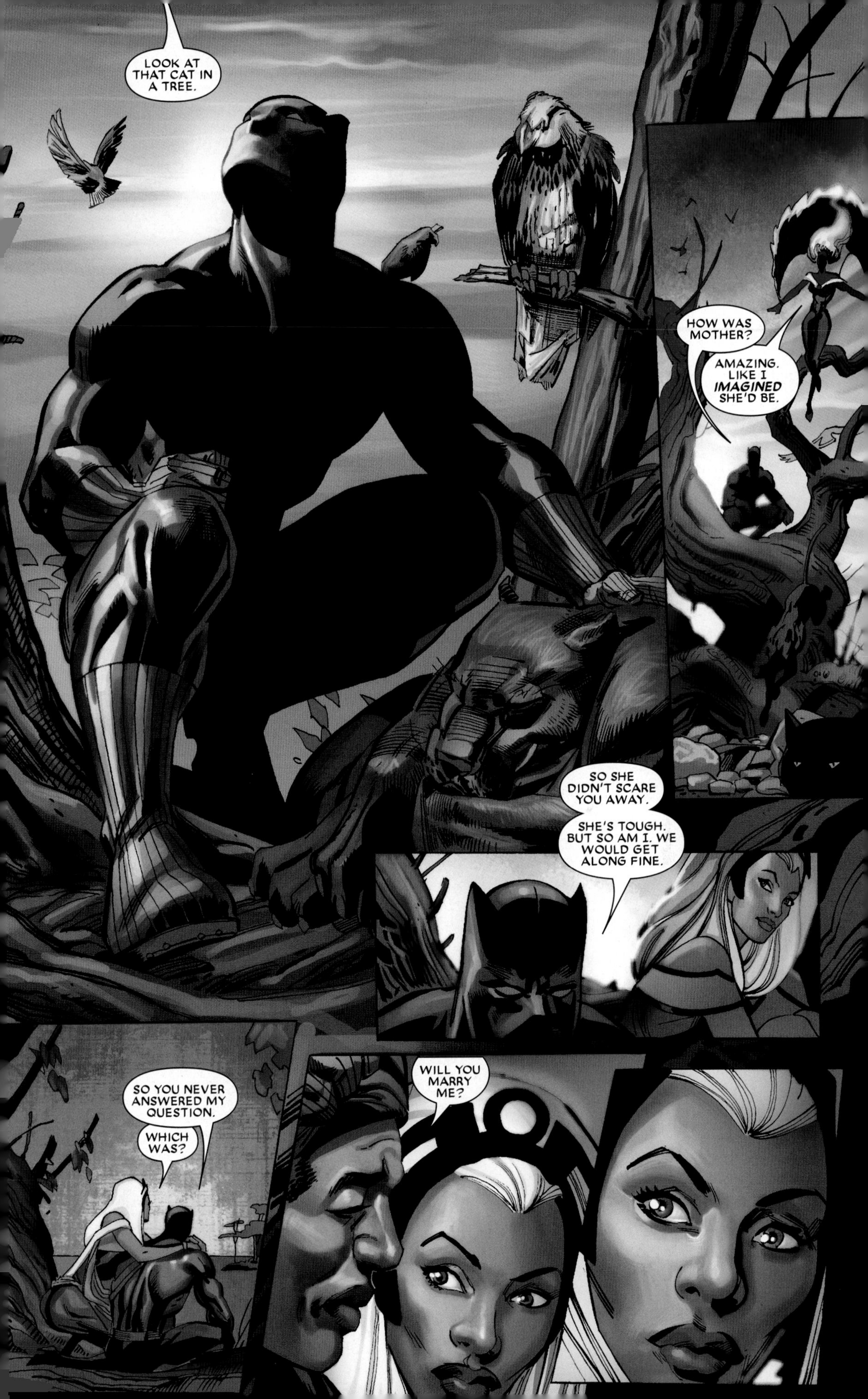

LOOK AT THAT CAT IN A TREE.
HOW WAS MOTHER?
AMAZING. LIKE I *IMAGINED* SHE'D BE.
SO SHE DIDN'T SCARE YOU AWAY.
SHE'S TOUGH. BUT SO AM I. WE WOULD GET ALONG FINE.
SO YOU NEVER ANSWERED MY QUESTION.
WHICH WAS?
WILL YOU MARRY ME?

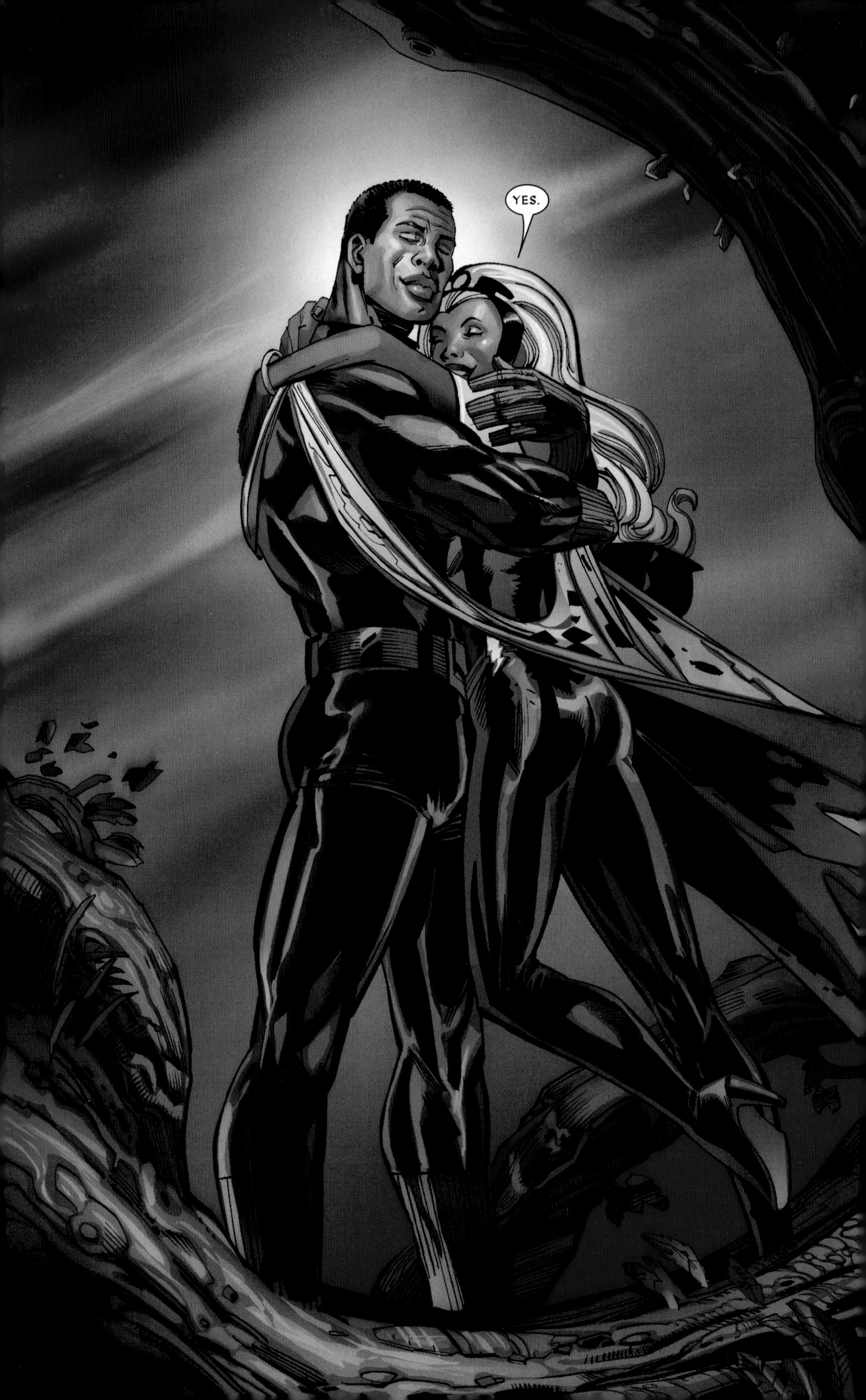
YES.

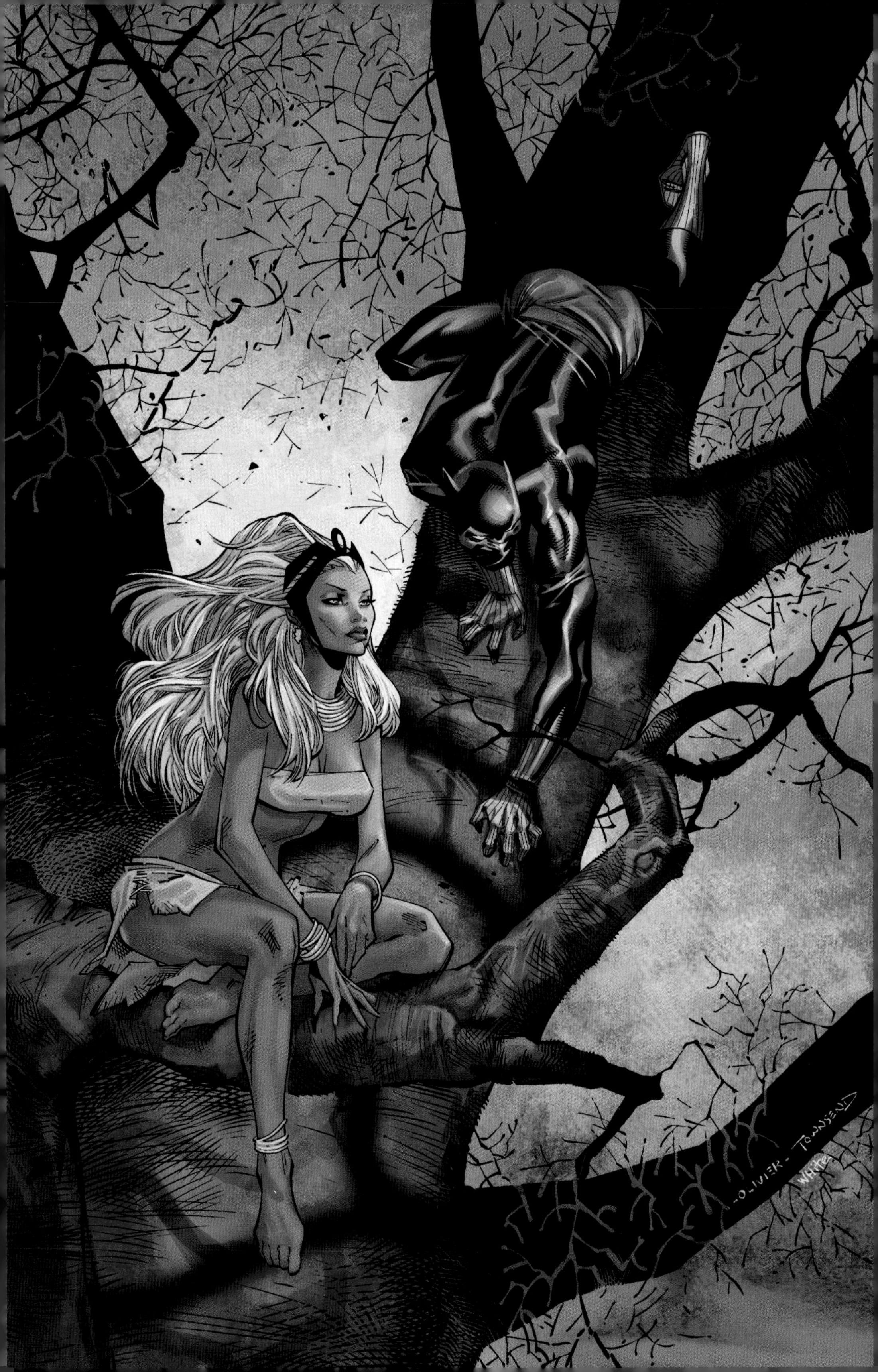
-OLIVIER- TOWNSEND
WHITE

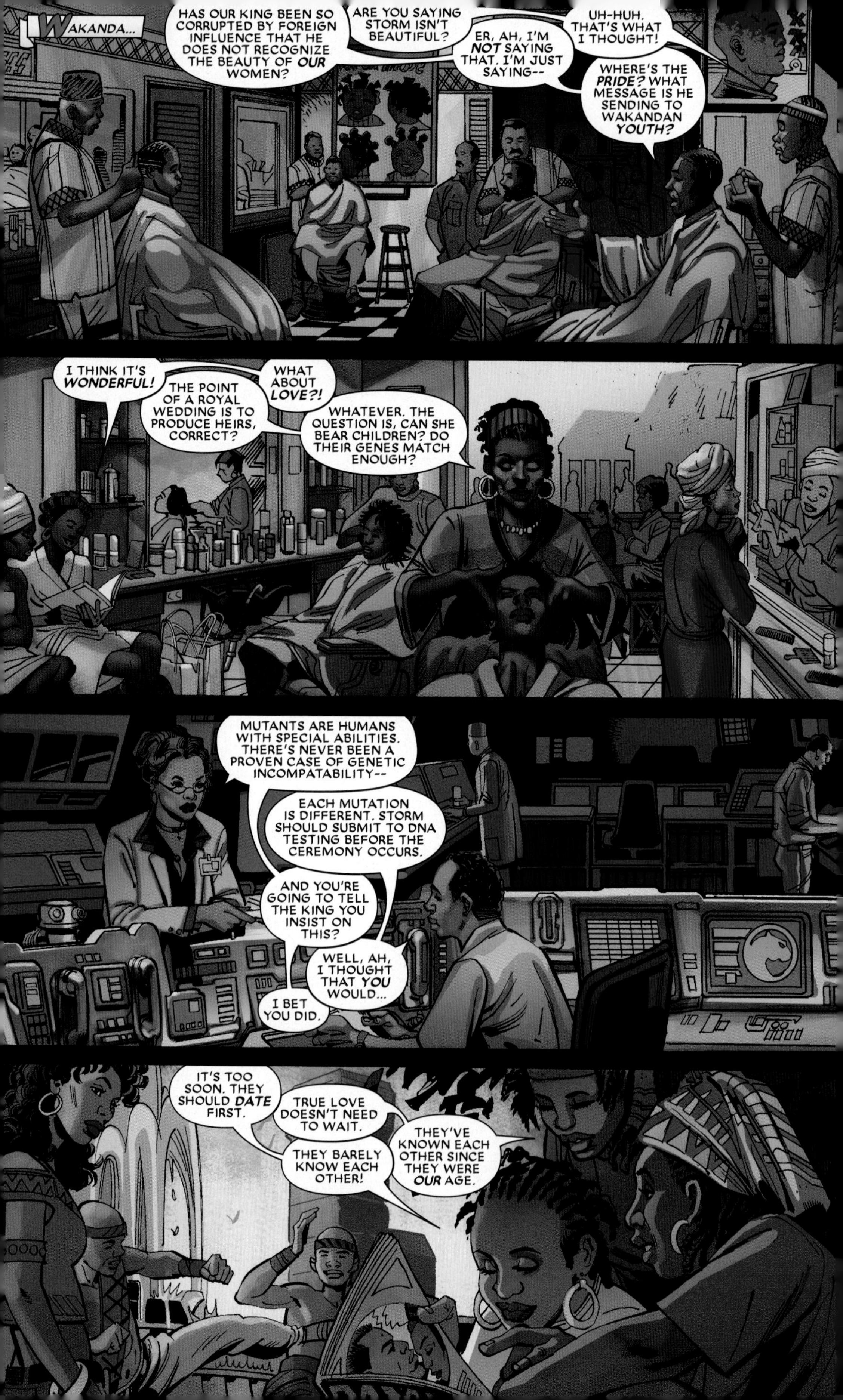
WAKANDA...
HAS OUR KING BEEN SO CORRUPTED BY FOREIGN INFLUENCE THAT HE DOES NOT RECOGNIZE THE BEAUTY OF *OUR* WOMEN?
ARE YOU SAYING STORM ISN'T BEAUTIFUL?
ER, AH, I'M *NOT* SAYING THAT. I'M JUST SAYING--
UH-HUH. THAT'S WHAT I THOUGHT!
WHERE'S THE *PRIDE?* WHAT MESSAGE IS HE SENDING TO WAKANDAN *YOUTH?*
I THINK IT'S *WONDERFUL!*
THE POINT OF A ROYAL WEDDING IS TO PRODUCE HEIRS, CORRECT?
WHAT ABOUT *LOVE?!*
WHATEVER. THE QUESTION IS, CAN SHE BEAR CHILDREN? DO THEIR GENES MATCH ENOUGH?
MUTANTS ARE HUMANS WITH SPECIAL ABILITIES. THERE'S NEVER BEEN A PROVEN CASE OF GENETIC INCOMPATABILITY--
EACH MUTATION IS DIFFERENT. STORM SHOULD SUBMIT TO DNA TESTING BEFORE THE CEREMONY OCCURS.
AND YOU'RE GOING TO TELL THE KING YOU INSIST ON THIS?
WELL, AH, I THOUGHT THAT *YOU* WOULD...
I BET YOU DID.
IT'S TOO SOON. THEY SHOULD *DATE* FIRST.
TRUE LOVE DOESN'T NEED TO WAIT.
THEY BARELY KNOW EACH OTHER!
THEY'VE KNOWN EACH OTHER SINCE THEY WERE *OUR* AGE.

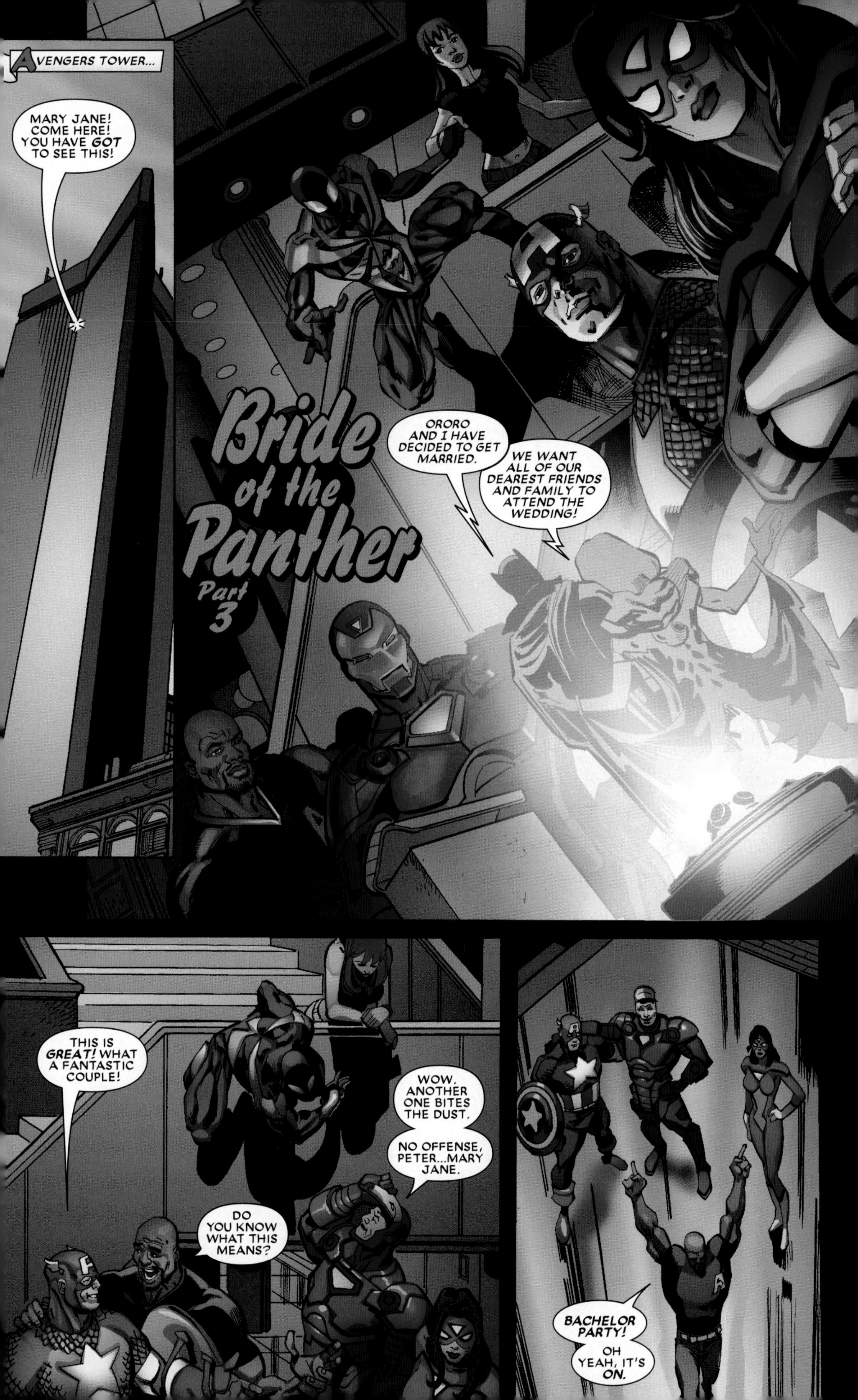
AVENGERS TOWER...
MARY JANE! COME HERE! YOU HAVE GOT TO SEE THIS!
Bride of the Panther
Part 3
ORORO AND I HAVE DECIDED TO GET MARRIED.
WE WANT ALL OF OUR DEAREST FRIENDS AND FAMILY TO ATTEND THE WEDDING!
THIS IS GREAT! WHAT A FANTASTIC COUPLE!
WOW. ANOTHER ONE BITES THE DUST.
NO OFFENSE, PETER...MARY JANE.
DO YOU KNOW WHAT THIS MEANS?
BACHELOR PARTY!
OH YEAH, IT'S ON.

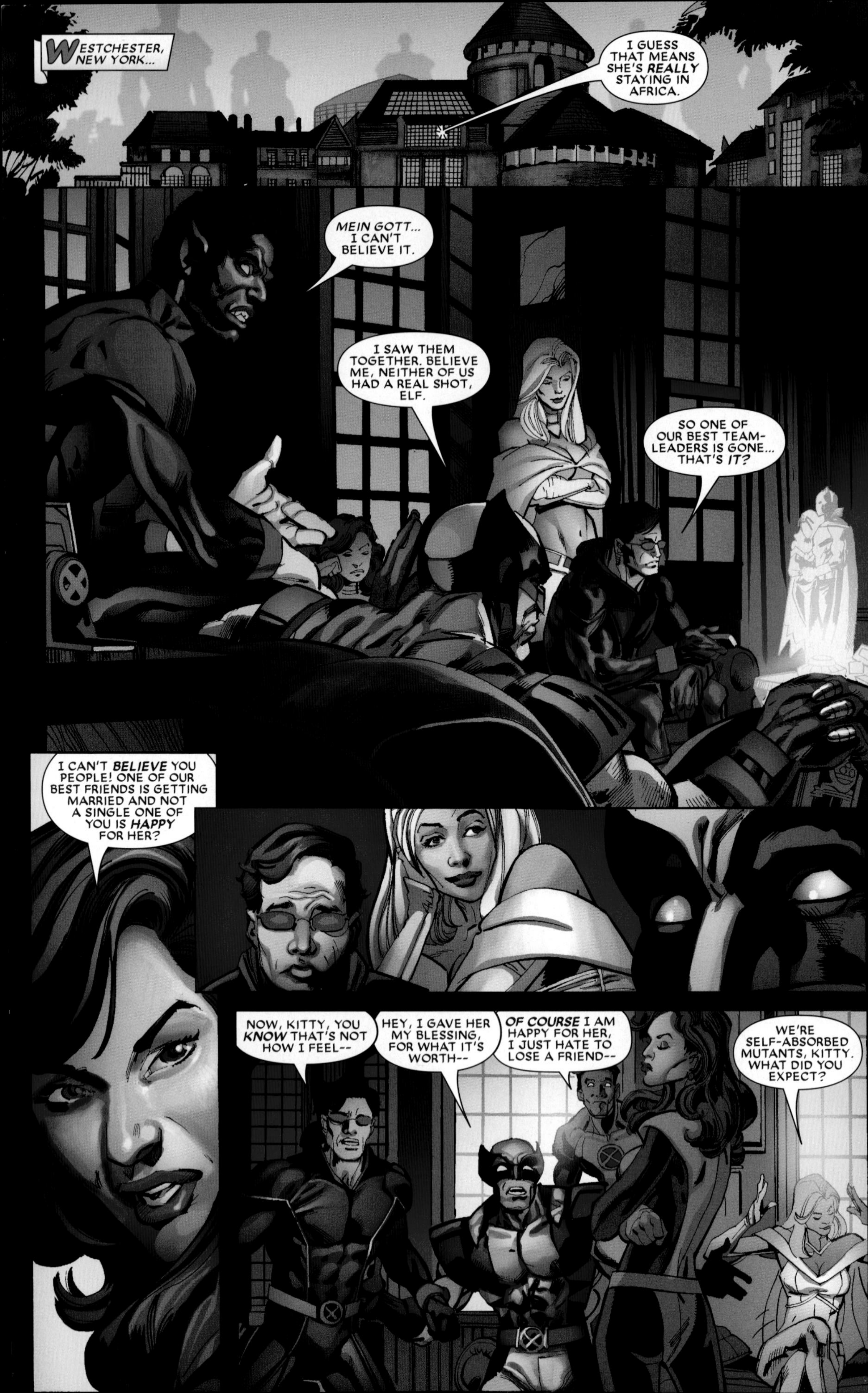
WESTCHESTER, NEW YORK...
I GUESS THAT MEANS SHE'S REALLY STAYING IN AFRICA.
MEIN GOTT... I CAN'T BELIEVE IT.
I SAW THEM TOGETHER. BELIEVE ME, NEITHER OF US HAD A REAL SHOT, ELF.
SO ONE OF OUR BEST TEAM-LEADERS IS GONE... THAT'S IT?
I CAN'T BELIEVE YOU PEOPLE! ONE OF OUR BEST FRIENDS IS GETTING MARRIED AND NOT A SINGLE ONE OF YOU IS HAPPY FOR HER?
NOW, KITTY, YOU KNOW THAT'S NOT HOW I FEEL--
HEY, I GAVE HER MY BLESSING, FOR WHAT IT'S WORTH--
OF COURSE I AM HAPPY FOR HER, I JUST HATE TO LOSE A FRIEND--
WE'RE SELF-ABSORBED MUTANTS, KITTY. WHAT DID YOU EXPECT?

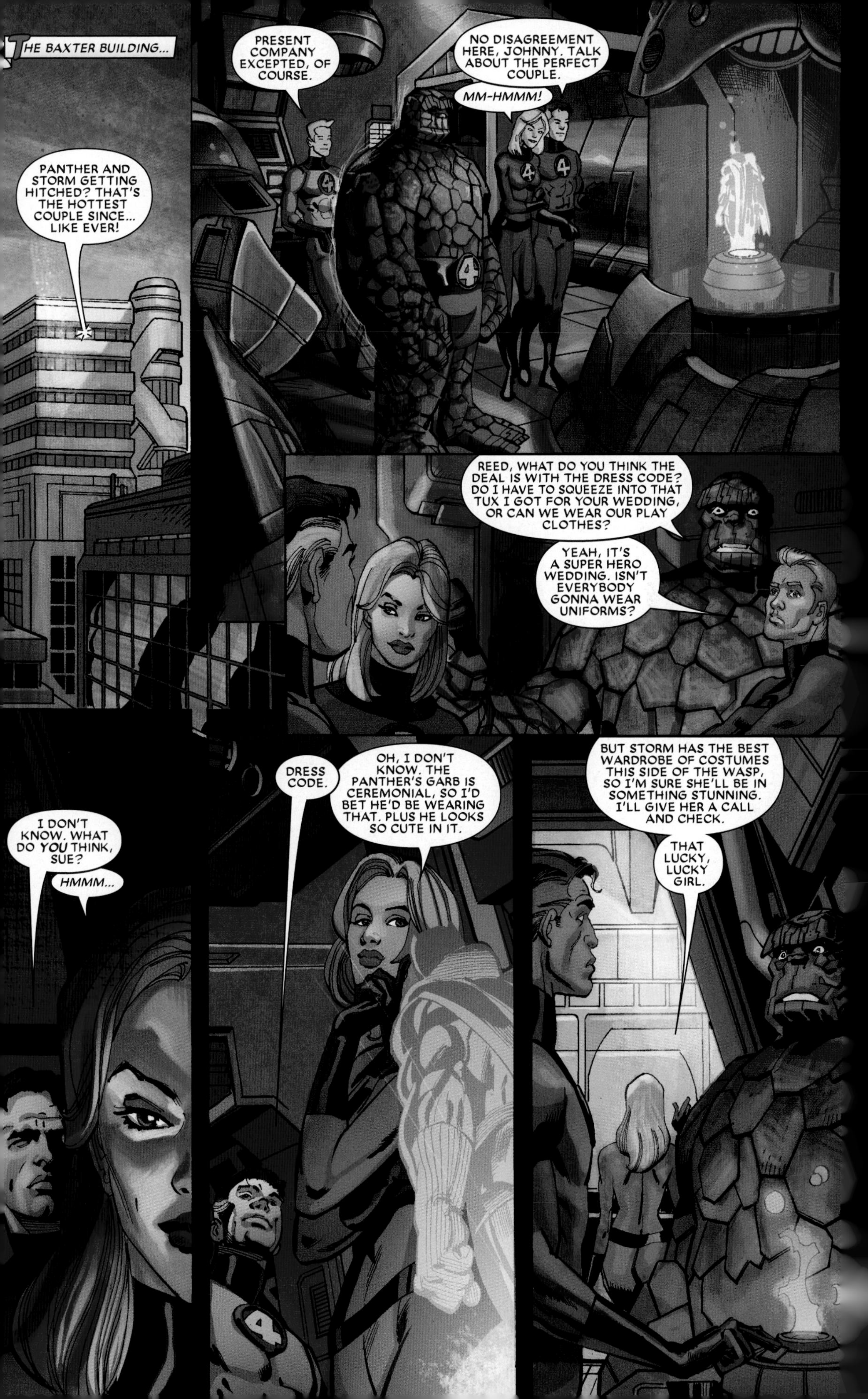
THE BAXTER BUILDING...
PANTHER AND STORM GETTING HITCHED? THAT'S THE HOTTEST COUPLE SINCE... LIKE EVER!
PRESENT COMPANY EXCEPTED, OF COURSE.
NO DISAGREEMENT HERE, JOHNNY. TALK ABOUT THE PERFECT COUPLE.
MM-HMMM!
REED, WHAT DO YOU THINK THE DEAL IS WITH THE DRESS CODE? DO I HAVE TO SQUEEZE INTO THAT TUX I GOT FOR YOUR WEDDING, OR CAN WE WEAR OUR PLAY CLOTHES?
YEAH, IT'S A SUPER HERO WEDDING. ISN'T EVERYBODY GONNA WEAR UNIFORMS?
I DON'T KNOW. WHAT DO YOU THINK, SUE?
HMMM...
DRESS CODE.
OH, I DON'T KNOW. THE PANTHER'S GARB IS CEREMONIAL, SO I'D BET HE'D BE WEARING THAT. PLUS HE LOOKS SO CUTE IN IT.
BUT STORM HAS THE BEST WARDROBE OF COSTUMES THIS SIDE OF THE WASP, SO I'M SURE SHE'LL BE IN SOMETHING STUNNING. I'LL GIVE HER A CALL AND CHECK.
THAT LUCKY, LUCKY GIRL.

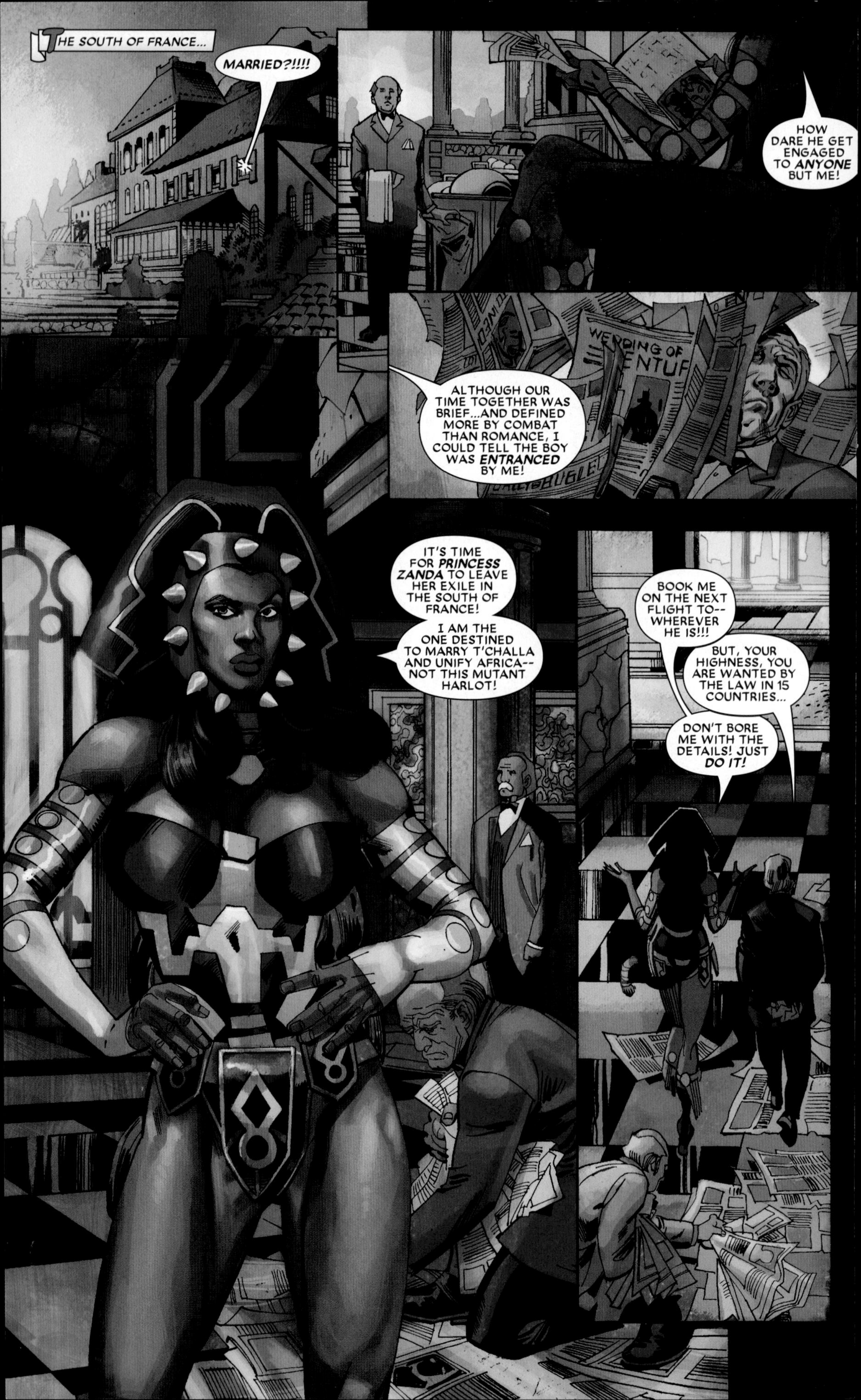
THE SOUTH OF FRANCE...
MARRIED?!!!!
HOW DARE HE GET ENGAGED TO ANYONE BUT ME!
WEDDING OF CENTUR
ALTHOUGH OUR TIME TOGETHER WAS BRIEF...AND DEFINED MORE BY COMBAT THAN ROMANCE, I COULD TELL THE BOY WAS ENTRANCED BY ME!
IT'S TIME FOR PRINCESS ZANDA TO LEAVE HER EXILE IN THE SOUTH OF FRANCE!
I AM THE ONE DESTINED TO MARRY T'CHALLA AND UNIFY AFRICA-- NOT THIS MUTANT HARLOT!
BOOK ME ON THE NEXT FLIGHT TO-- WHEREVER HE IS!!!
BUT, YOUR HIGHNESS, YOU ARE WANTED BY THE LAW IN 15 COUNTRIES...
DON'T BORE ME WITH THE DETAILS! JUST DO IT!

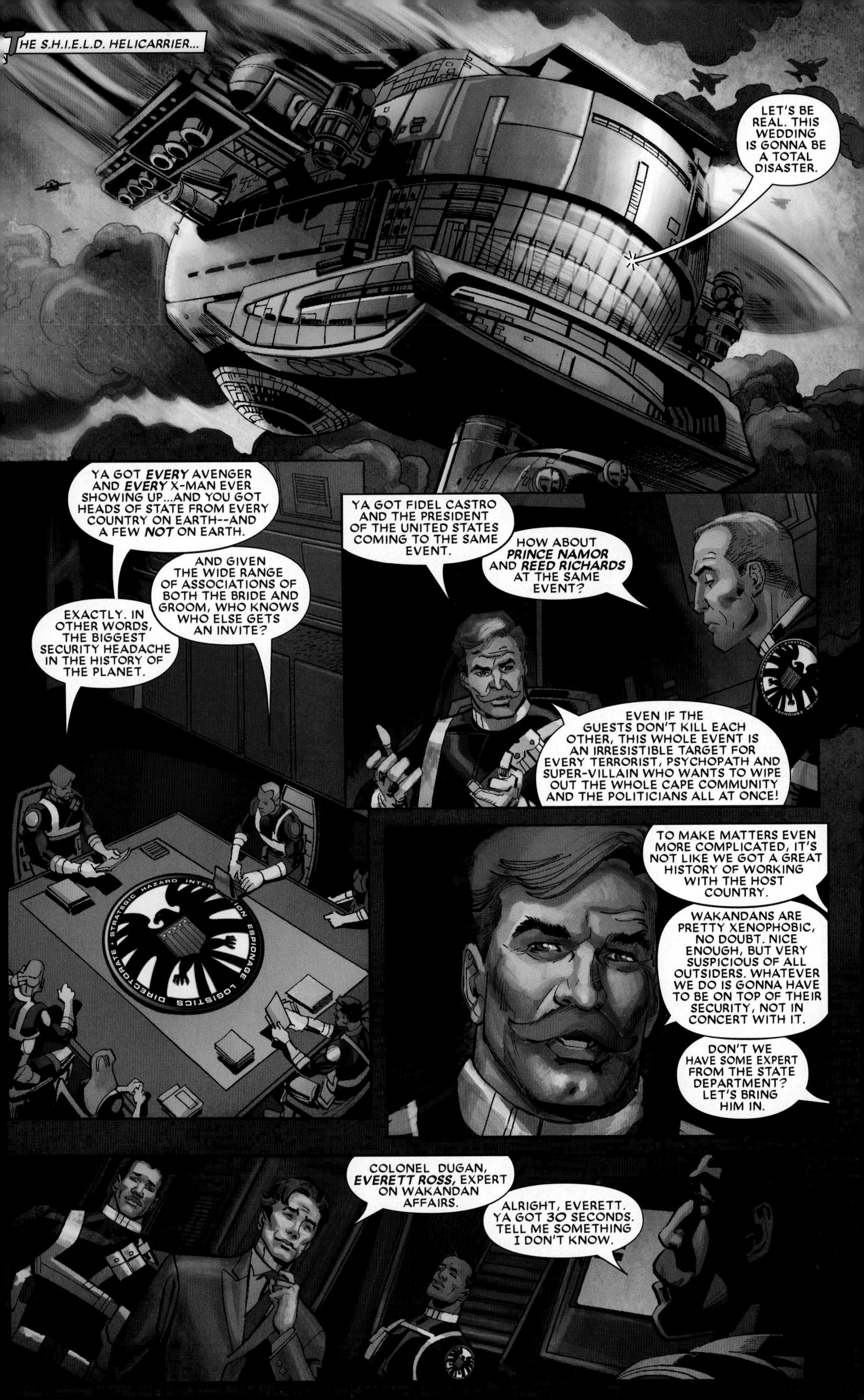
THE S.H.I.E.L.D. HELICARRIER...
LET'S BE REAL. THIS WEDDING IS GONNA BE A TOTAL DISASTER.
YA GOT EVERY AVENGER AND EVERY X-MAN EVER SHOWING UP...AND YOU GOT HEADS OF STATE FROM EVERY COUNTRY ON EARTH--AND A FEW NOT ON EARTH.
AND GIVEN THE WIDE RANGE OF ASSOCIATIONS OF BOTH THE BRIDE AND GROOM, WHO KNOWS WHO ELSE GETS AN INVITE?
EXACTLY. IN OTHER WORDS, THE BIGGEST SECURITY HEADACHE IN THE HISTORY OF THE PLANET.
YA GOT FIDEL CASTRO AND THE PRESIDENT OF THE UNITED STATES COMING TO THE SAME EVENT.
HOW ABOUT PRINCE NAMOR AND REED RICHARDS AT THE SAME EVENT?
EVEN IF THE GUESTS DON'T KILL EACH OTHER, THIS WHOLE EVENT IS AN IRRESISTIBLE TARGET FOR EVERY TERRORIST, PSYCHOPATH AND SUPER-VILLAIN WHO WANTS TO WIPE OUT THE WHOLE CAPE COMMUNITY AND THE POLITICIANS ALL AT ONCE!
STRATEGIC HAZARD INTERVENTION ESPIONAGE LOGISTICS DIRECTORATE
TO MAKE MATTERS EVEN MORE COMPLICATED, IT'S NOT LIKE WE GOT A GREAT HISTORY OF WORKING WITH THE HOST COUNTRY.
WAKANDANS ARE PRETTY XENOPHOBIC, NO DOUBT. NICE ENOUGH, BUT VERY SUSPICIOUS OF ALL OUTSIDERS. WHATEVER WE DO IS GONNA HAVE TO BE ON TOP OF THEIR SECURITY, NOT IN CONCERT WITH IT.
DON'T WE HAVE SOME EXPERT FROM THE STATE DEPARTMENT? LET'S BRING HIM IN.
COLONEL DUGAN, EVERETT ROSS, EXPERT ON WAKANDAN AFFAIRS.
ALRIGHT, EVERETT. YA GOT 30 SECONDS. TELL ME SOMETHING I DON'T KNOW.

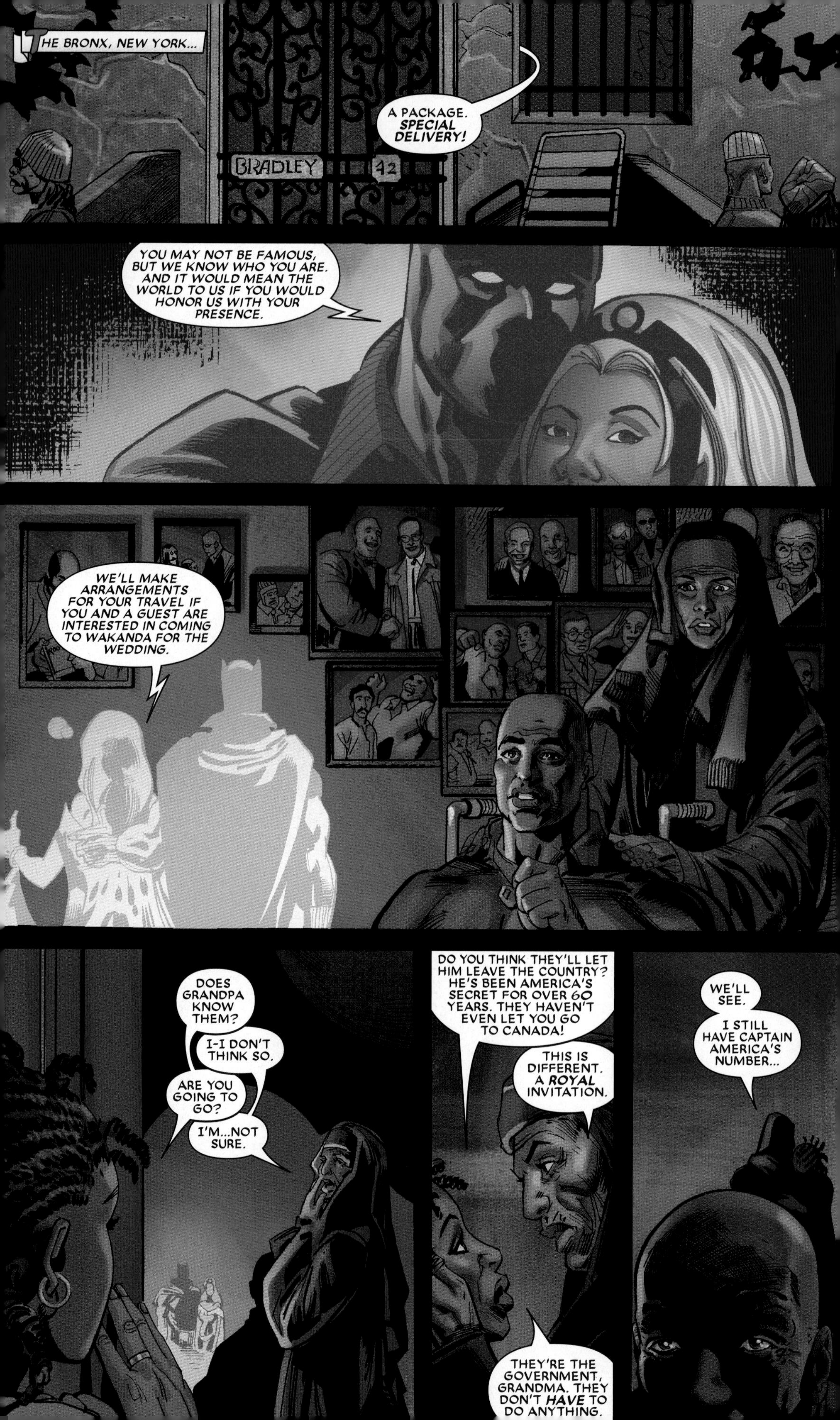
THE BRONX, NEW YORK...
A PACKAGE. SPECIAL DELIVERY!
BRADLEY
42
YOU MAY NOT BE FAMOUS, BUT WE KNOW WHO YOU ARE. AND IT WOULD MEAN THE WORLD TO US IF YOU WOULD HONOR US WITH YOUR PRESENCE.
WE'LL MAKE ARRANGEMENTS FOR YOUR TRAVEL IF YOU AND A GUEST ARE INTERESTED IN COMING TO WAKANDA FOR THE WEDDING.
DOES GRANDPA KNOW THEM?
I-I DON'T THINK SO.
ARE YOU GOING TO GO?
I'M...NOT SURE.
DO YOU THINK THEY'LL LET HIM LEAVE THE COUNTRY? HE'S BEEN AMERICA'S SECRET FOR OVER 60 YEARS. THEY HAVEN'T EVEN LET YOU GO TO CANADA!
THIS IS DIFFERENT. A ROYAL INVITATION.
THEY'RE THE GOVERNMENT, GRANDMA. THEY DON'T HAVE TO DO ANYTHING.
WE'LL SEE.
I STILL HAVE CAPTAIN AMERICA'S NUMBER...

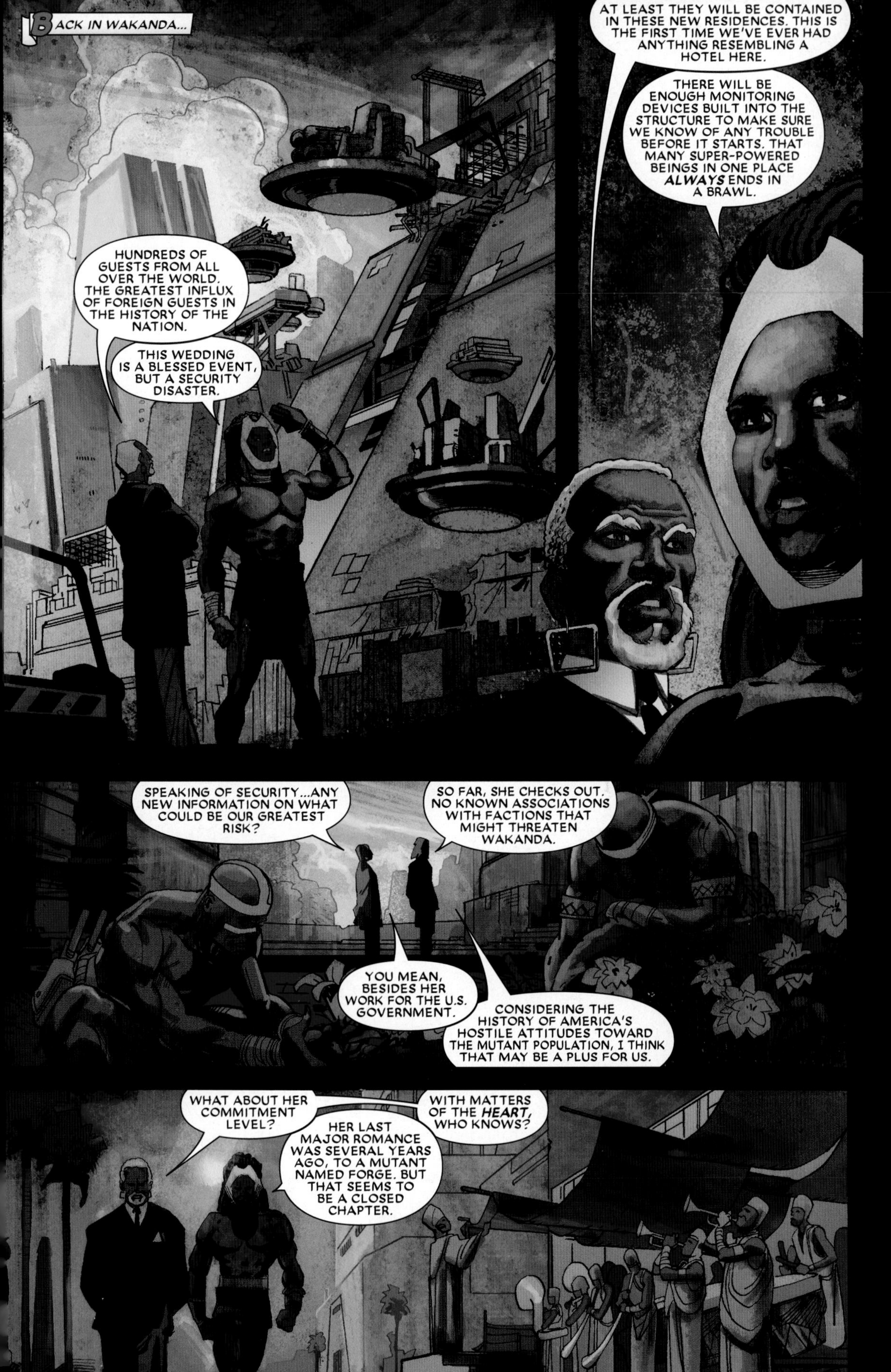
BACK IN WAKANDA...
HUNDREDS OF GUESTS FROM ALL OVER THE WORLD. THE GREATEST INFLUX OF FOREIGN GUESTS IN THE HISTORY OF THE NATION.
THIS WEDDING IS A BLESSED EVENT, BUT A SECURITY DISASTER.
AT LEAST THEY WILL BE CONTAINED IN THESE NEW RESIDENCES. THIS IS THE FIRST TIME WE'VE EVER HAD ANYTHING RESEMBLING A HOTEL HERE.
THERE WILL BE ENOUGH MONITORING DEVICES BUILT INTO THE STRUCTURE TO MAKE SURE WE KNOW OF ANY TROUBLE BEFORE IT STARTS. THAT MANY SUPER-POWERED BEINGS IN ONE PLACE *ALWAYS* ENDS IN A BRAWL.
SPEAKING OF SECURITY...ANY NEW INFORMATION ON WHAT COULD BE OUR GREATEST RISK?
SO FAR, SHE CHECKS OUT. NO KNOWN ASSOCIATIONS WITH FACTIONS THAT MIGHT THREATEN WAKANDA.
YOU MEAN, BESIDES HER WORK FOR THE U.S. GOVERNMENT.
CONSIDERING THE HISTORY OF AMERICA'S HOSTILE ATTITUDES TOWARD THE MUTANT POPULATION, I THINK THAT MAY BE A PLUS FOR US.
WHAT ABOUT HER COMMITMENT LEVEL?
WITH MATTERS OF THE *HEART,* WHO KNOWS?
HER LAST MAJOR ROMANCE WAS SEVERAL YEARS AGO, TO A MUTANT NAMED FORGE. BUT THAT SEEMS TO BE A CLOSED CHAPTER.

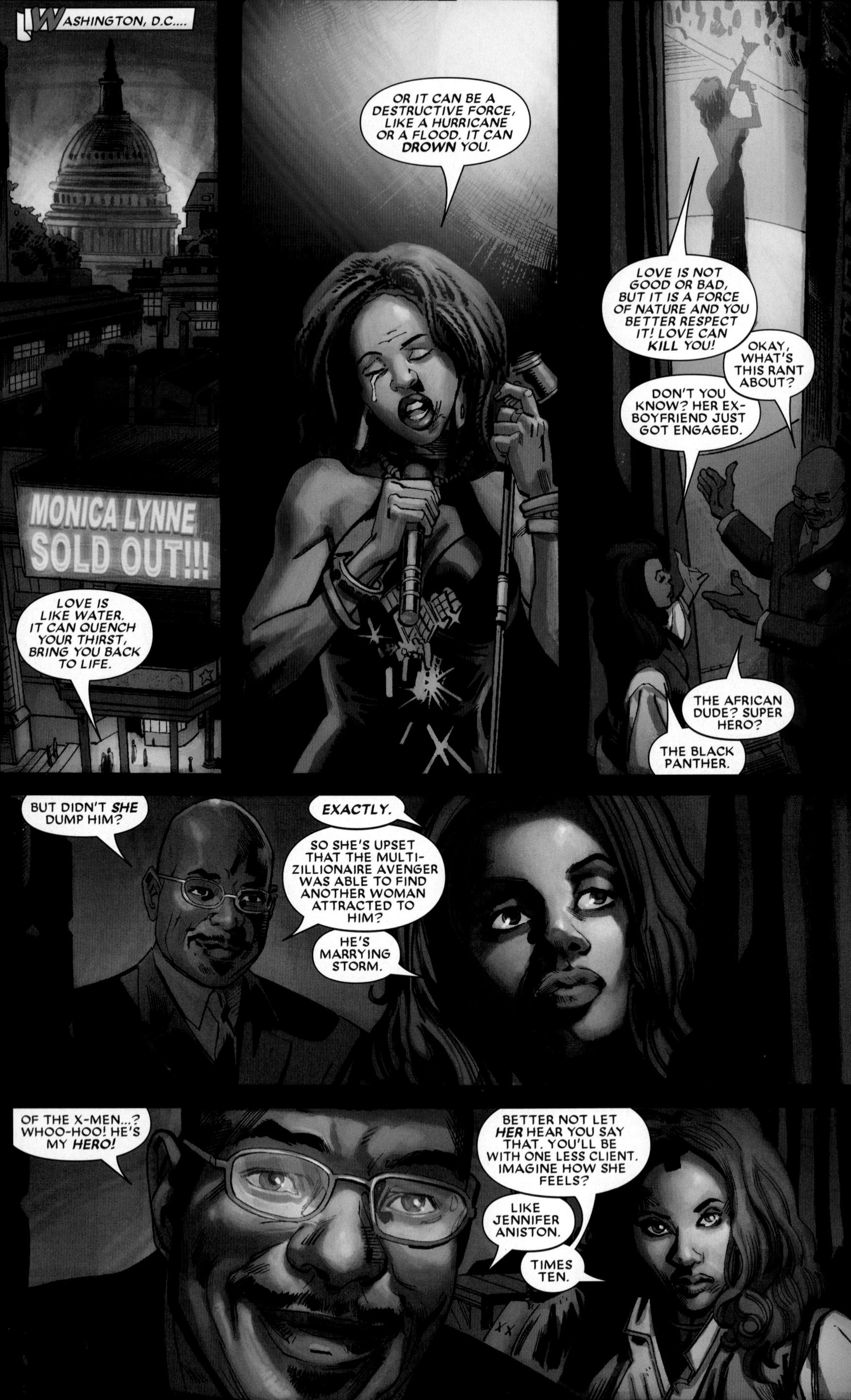
WASHINGTON, D.C....
MONICA LYNNE SOLD OUT!!!
LOVE IS LIKE WATER. IT CAN QUENCH YOUR THIRST, BRING YOU BACK TO LIFE.
OR IT CAN BE A DESTRUCTIVE FORCE, LIKE A HURRICANE OR A FLOOD. IT CAN DROWN YOU.
LOVE IS NOT GOOD OR BAD, BUT IT IS A FORCE OF NATURE AND YOU BETTER RESPECT IT! LOVE CAN KILL YOU!
OKAY, WHAT'S THIS RANT ABOUT?
DON'T YOU KNOW? HER EX-BOYFRIEND JUST GOT ENGAGED.
THE AFRICAN DUDE? SUPER HERO?
THE BLACK PANTHER.
BUT DIDN'T SHE DUMP HIM?
EXACTLY.
SO SHE'S UPSET THAT THE MULTI-ZILLIONAIRE AVENGER WAS ABLE TO FIND ANOTHER WOMAN ATTRACTED TO HIM?
HE'S MARRYING STORM.
OF THE X-MEN...? WHOO-HOO! HE'S MY HERO!
BETTER NOT LET HER HEAR YOU SAY THAT. YOU'LL BE WITH ONE LESS CLIENT. IMAGINE HOW SHE FEELS?
LIKE JENNIFER ANISTON.
TIMES TEN.

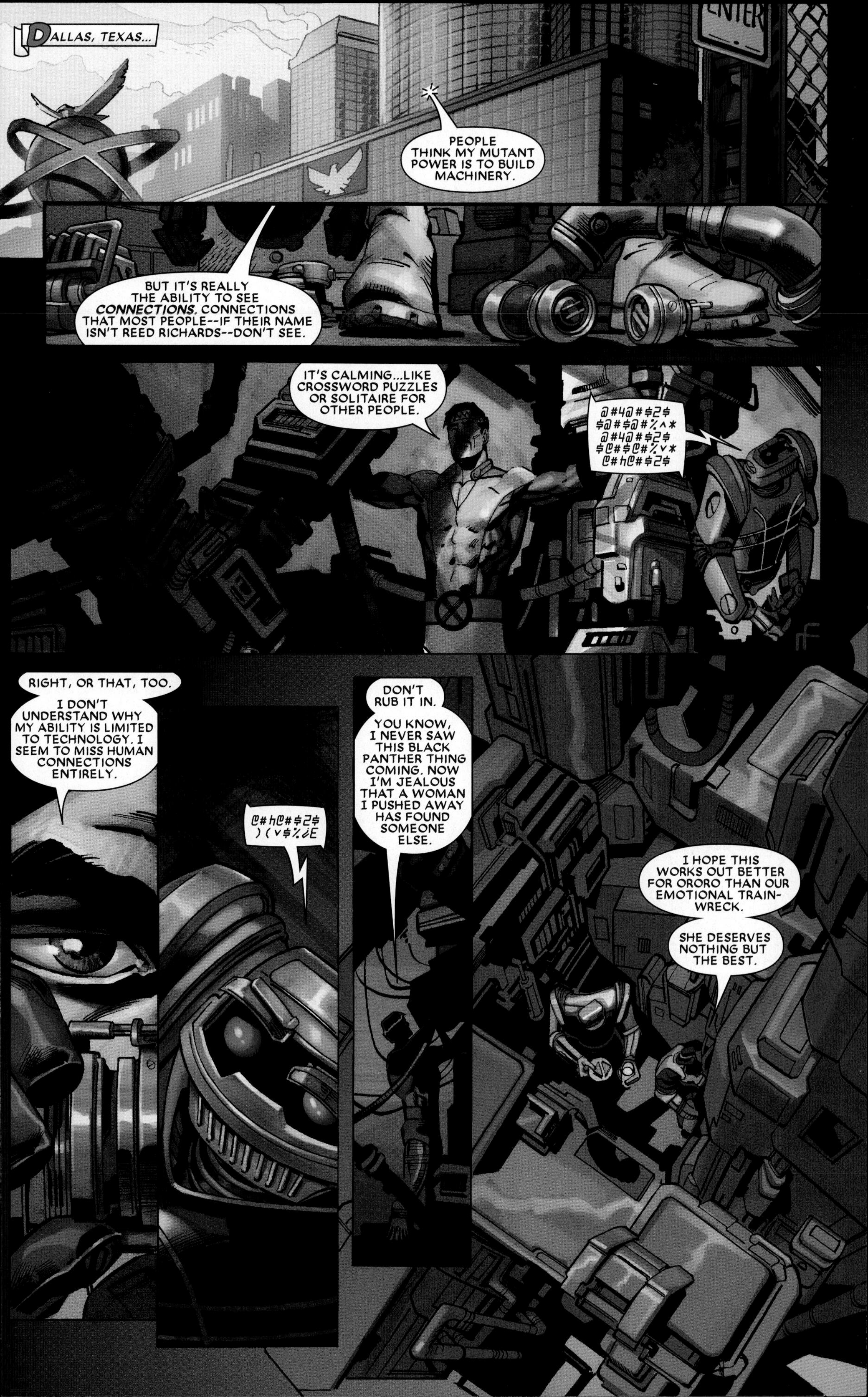
DALLAS, TEXAS...
PEOPLE THINK MY MUTANT POWER IS TO BUILD MACHINERY.
BUT IT'S REALLY THE ABILITY TO SEE CONNECTIONS. CONNECTIONS THAT MOST PEOPLE--IF THEIR NAME ISN'T REED RICHARDS--DON'T SEE.
IT'S CALMING...LIKE CROSSWORD PUZZLES OR SOLITAIRE FOR OTHER PEOPLE.
RIGHT, OR THAT, TOO.
I DON'T UNDERSTAND WHY MY ABILITY IS LIMITED TO TECHNOLOGY. I SEEM TO MISS HUMAN CONNECTIONS ENTIRELY.
DON'T RUB IT IN.
YOU KNOW, I NEVER SAW THIS BLACK PANTHER THING COMING. NOW I'M JEALOUS THAT A WOMAN I PUSHED AWAY HAS FOUND SOMEONE ELSE.
I HOPE THIS WORKS OUT BETTER FOR ORORO THAN OUR EMOTIONAL TRAIN-WRECK.
SHE DESERVES NOTHING BUT THE BEST.

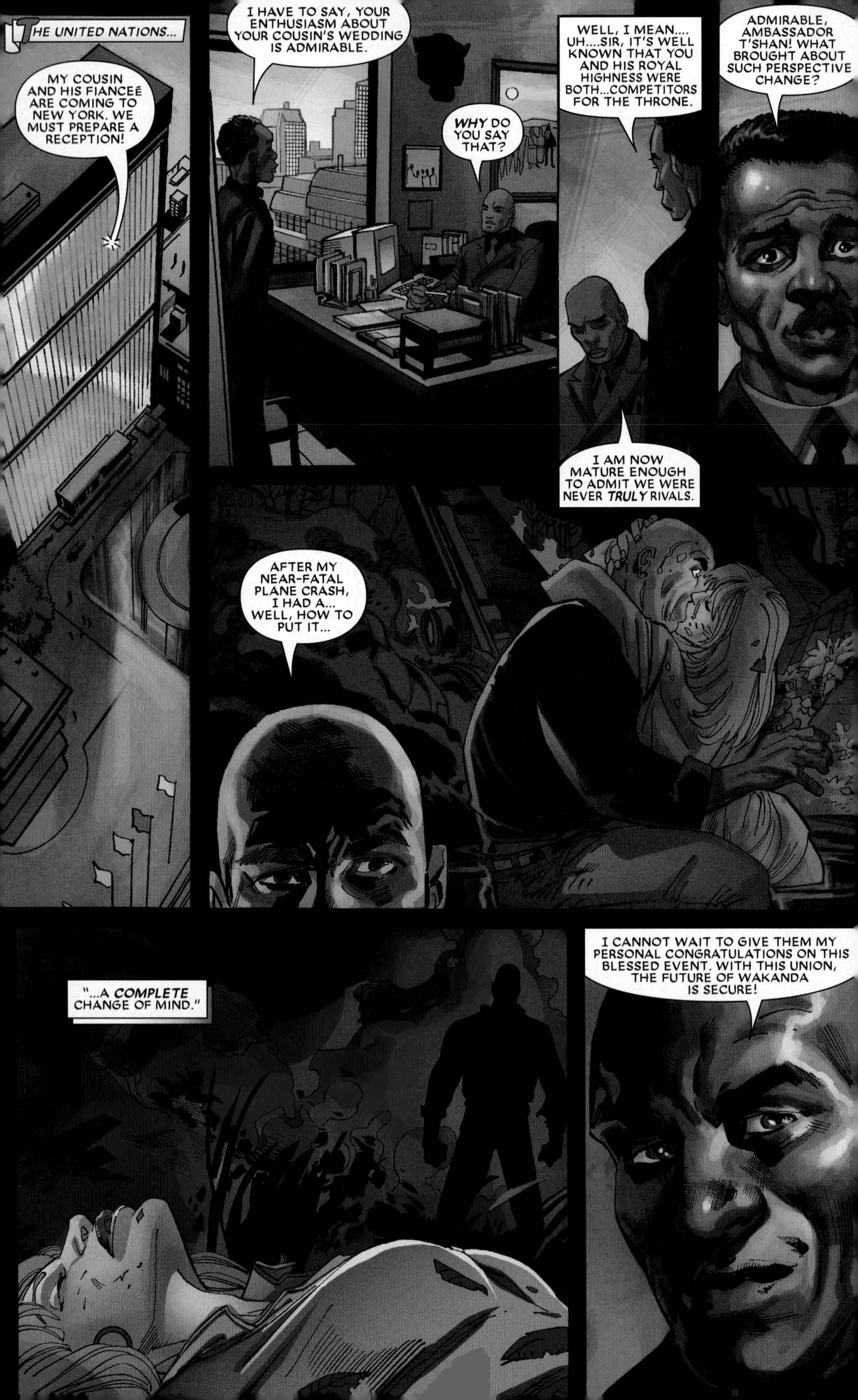
THE UNITED NATIONS...
MY COUSIN AND HIS FIANCÉE ARE COMING TO NEW YORK. WE MUST PREPARE A RECEPTION!
I HAVE TO SAY, YOUR ENTHUSIASM ABOUT YOUR COUSIN'S WEDDING IS ADMIRABLE.
WHY DO YOU SAY THAT?
WELL, I MEAN.... UH....SIR, IT'S WELL KNOWN THAT YOU AND HIS ROYAL HIGHNESS WERE BOTH...COMPETITORS FOR THE THRONE.
I AM NOW MATURE ENOUGH TO ADMIT WE WERE NEVER TRULY RIVALS.
ADMIRABLE, AMBASSADOR T'SHAN! WHAT BROUGHT ABOUT SUCH PERSPECTIVE CHANGE?
AFTER MY NEAR-FATAL PLANE CRASH, I HAD A... WELL, HOW TO PUT IT...
"...A COMPLETE CHANGE OF MIND."
I CANNOT WAIT TO GIVE THEM MY PERSONAL CONGRATULATIONS ON THIS BLESSED EVENT. WITH THIS UNION, THE FUTURE OF WAKANDA IS SECURE!

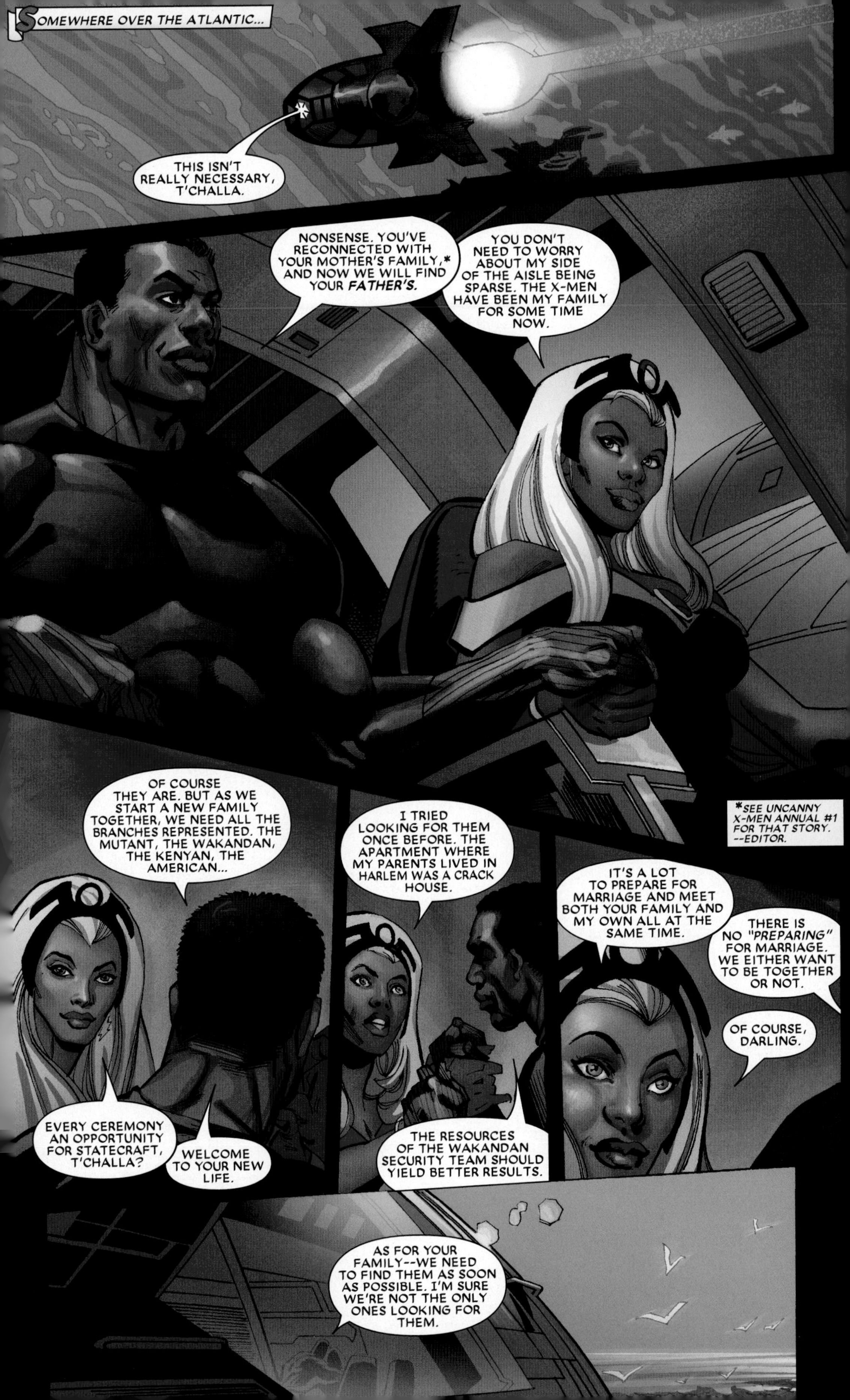
SOMEWHERE OVER THE ATLANTIC...
THIS ISN'T REALLY NECESSARY, T'CHALLA.
NONSENSE. YOU'VE RECONNECTED WITH YOUR MOTHER'S FAMILY,* AND NOW WE WILL FIND YOUR FATHER'S.
YOU DON'T NEED TO WORRY ABOUT MY SIDE OF THE AISLE BEING SPARSE. THE X-MEN HAVE BEEN MY FAMILY FOR SOME TIME NOW.
*SEE UNCANNY X-MEN ANNUAL #1 FOR THAT STORY. --EDITOR.
OF COURSE THEY ARE. BUT AS WE START A NEW FAMILY TOGETHER, WE NEED ALL THE BRANCHES REPRESENTED. THE MUTANT, THE WAKANDAN, THE KENYAN, THE AMERICAN...
EVERY CEREMONY AN OPPORTUNITY FOR STATECRAFT, T'CHALLA?
WELCOME TO YOUR NEW LIFE.
I TRIED LOOKING FOR THEM ONCE BEFORE. THE APARTMENT WHERE MY PARENTS LIVED IN HARLEM WAS A CRACK HOUSE.
THE RESOURCES OF THE WAKANDAN SECURITY TEAM SHOULD YIELD BETTER RESULTS.
IT'S A LOT TO PREPARE FOR MARRIAGE AND MEET BOTH YOUR FAMILY AND MY OWN ALL AT THE SAME TIME.
THERE IS NO "PREPARING" FOR MARRIAGE. WE EITHER WANT TO BE TOGETHER OR NOT.
OF COURSE, DARLING.
AS FOR YOUR FAMILY--WE NEED TO FIND THEM AS SOON AS POSSIBLE. I'M SURE WE'RE NOT THE ONLY ONES LOOKING FOR THEM.

NEW JERSEY...

GRANDDAD, 24'S ABOUT TO START!

I GOT NO TIME FOR THAT NONSENSE, BOY. WHY WOULD I--

DING DONG

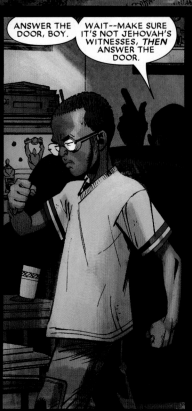

ANSWER THE DOOR, BOY.

WAIT--MAKE SURE IT'S NOT JEHOVAH'S WITNESSES, THEN ANSWER THE DOOR.

WHO IS IT, BOY?

GRANDPA, YOU'RE NOT GONNA BELIEVE THIS...

IT'S HYDRA.

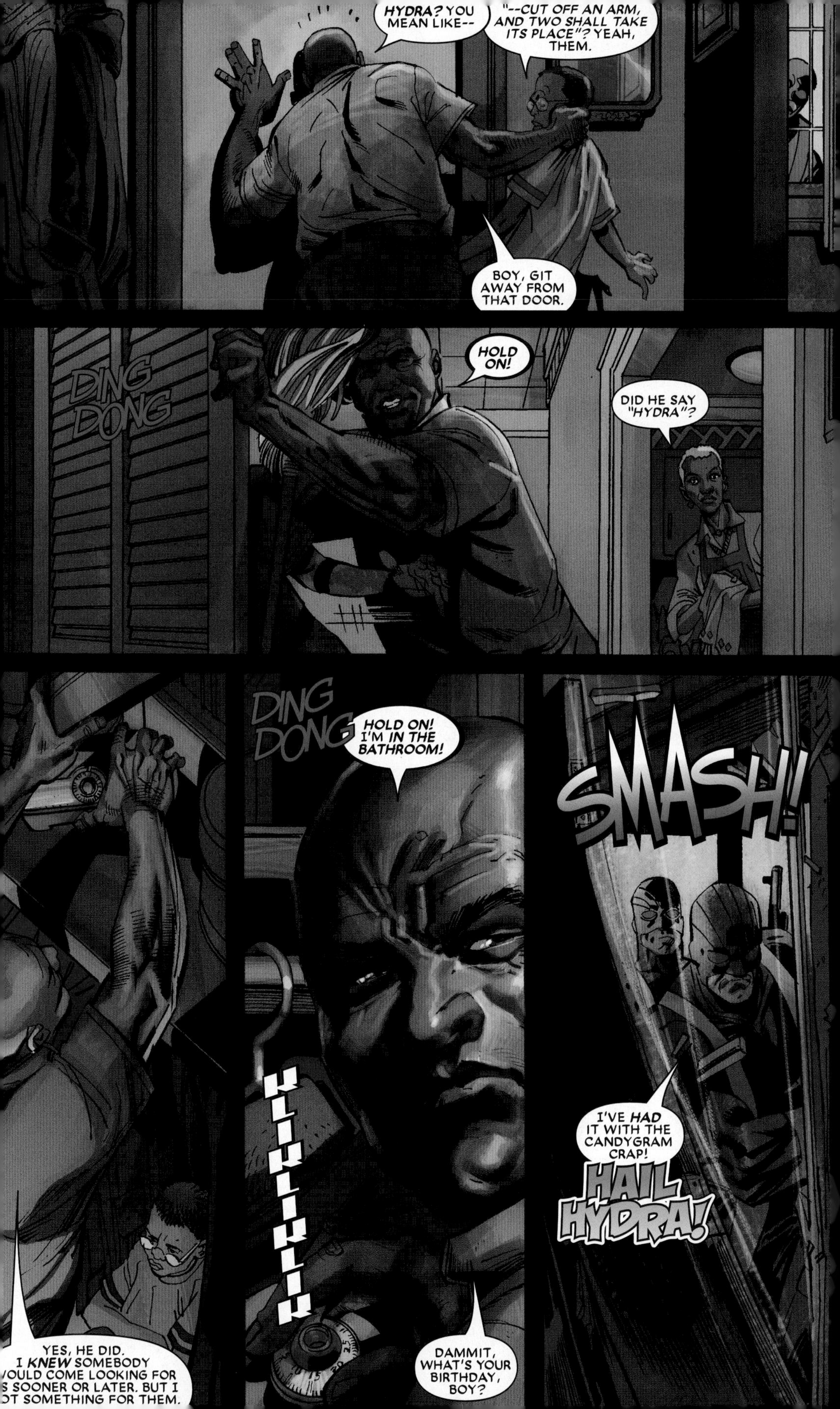

HYDRA? YOU MEAN LIKE--
"--CUT OFF AN ARM, AND TWO SHALL TAKE ITS PLACE"? YEAH, THEM.
BOY, GIT AWAY FROM THAT DOOR.
DING DONG
HOLD ON!
DID HE SAY "HYDRA"?
YES, HE DID. I KNEW SOMEBODY
DING DONG
HOLD ON! I'M IN THE BATHROOM!
KLIKLIKLIK
DAMMIT, WHAT'S YOUR BIRTHDAY, BOY?
SMASH!
I'VE HAD IT WITH THE CANDYGRAM CRAP!
HAIL HYDRA!

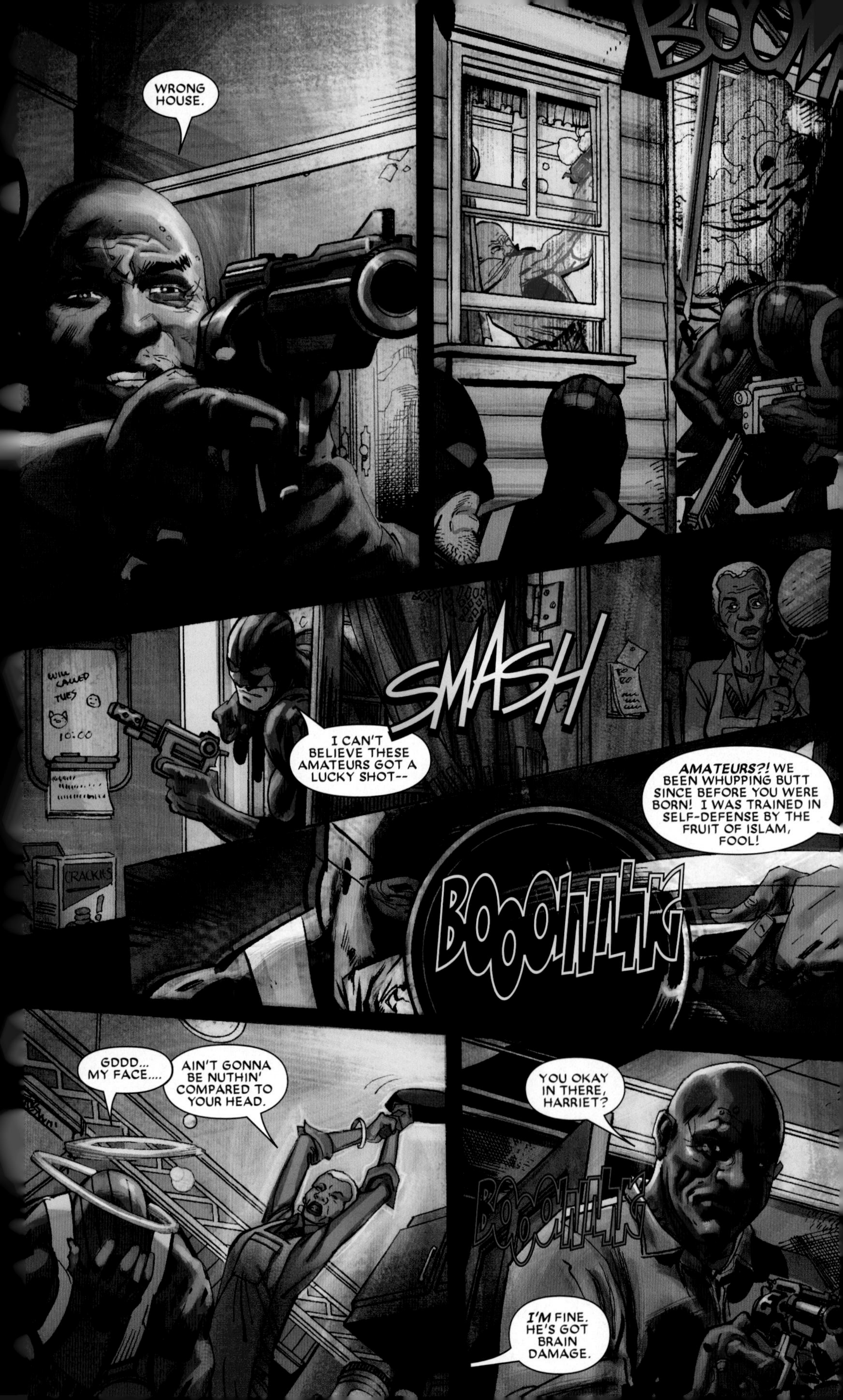
WRONG HOUSE.
BOOOM
WILL CALLED TUES 10:00
CRACKIES
SMASH
I CAN'T BELIEVE THESE AMATEURS GOT A LUCKY SHOT--
AMATEURS?! WE BEEN WHUPPING BUTT SINCE BEFORE YOU WERE BORN! I WAS TRAINED IN SELF-DEFENSE BY THE FRUIT OF ISLAM, FOOL!
BOOOWNNNG
GDDD... MY FACE....
AIN'T GONNA BE NUTHIN' COMPARED TO YOUR HEAD.
YOU OKAY IN THERE, HARRIET?
BOOOWNNNG
I'M FINE. HE'S GOT BRAIN DAMAGE.

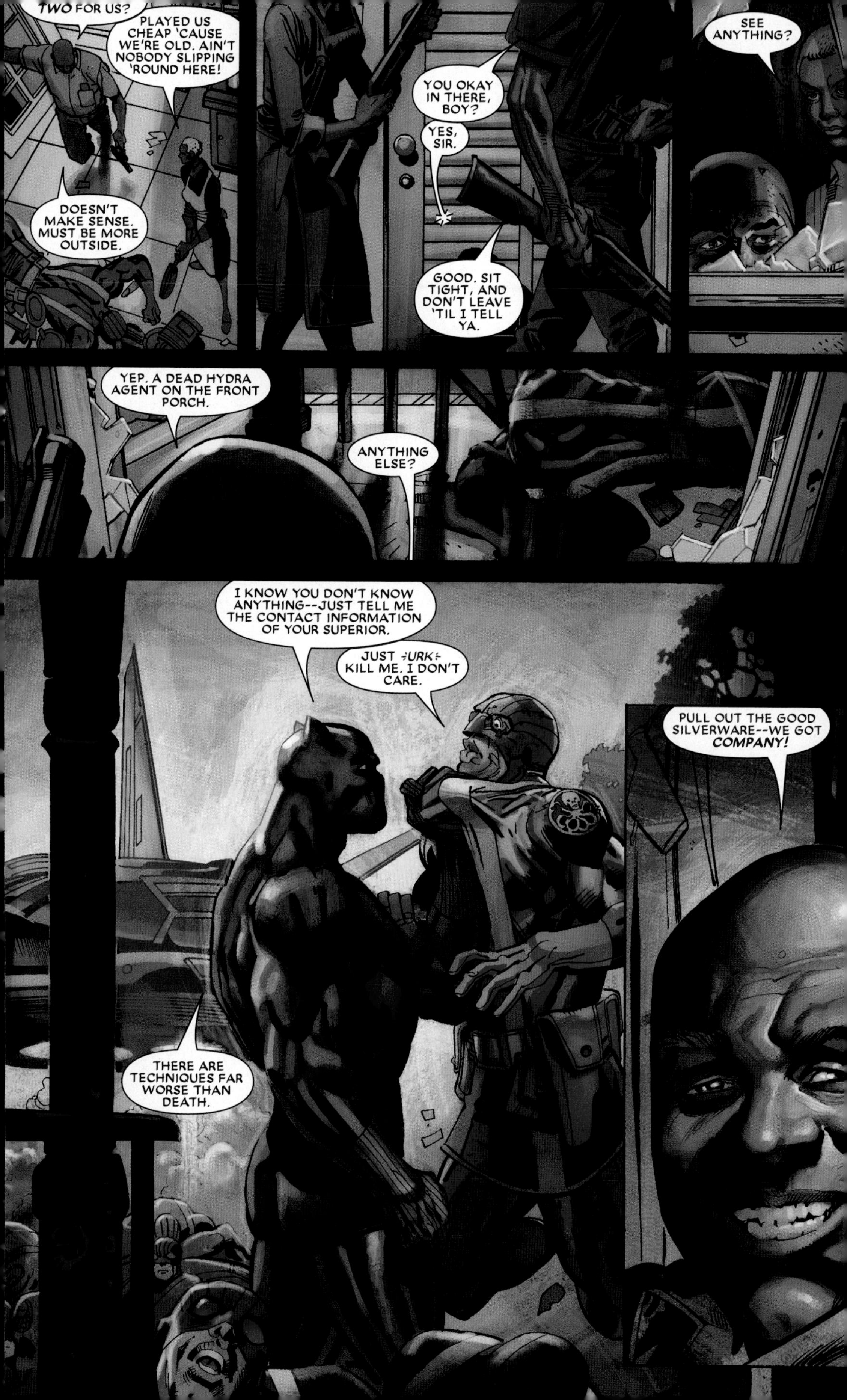
TWO FOR US?
PLAYED US CHEAP 'CAUSE WE'RE OLD. AIN'T NOBODY SLIPPING 'ROUND HERE!
DOESN'T MAKE SENSE. MUST BE MORE OUTSIDE.
YOU OKAY IN THERE, BOY?
YES, SIR.
GOOD. SIT TIGHT, AND DON'T LEAVE 'TIL I TELL YA.
SEE ANYTHING?
YEP. A DEAD HYDRA AGENT ON THE FRONT PORCH.
ANYTHING ELSE?
I KNOW YOU DON'T KNOW ANYTHING--JUST TELL ME THE CONTACT INFORMATION OF YOUR SUPERIOR.
JUST ≑URK≑ KILL ME. I DON'T CARE.
THERE ARE TECHNIQUES FAR WORSE THAN DEATH.
PULL OUT THE GOOD SILVERWARE--WE GOT COMPANY!

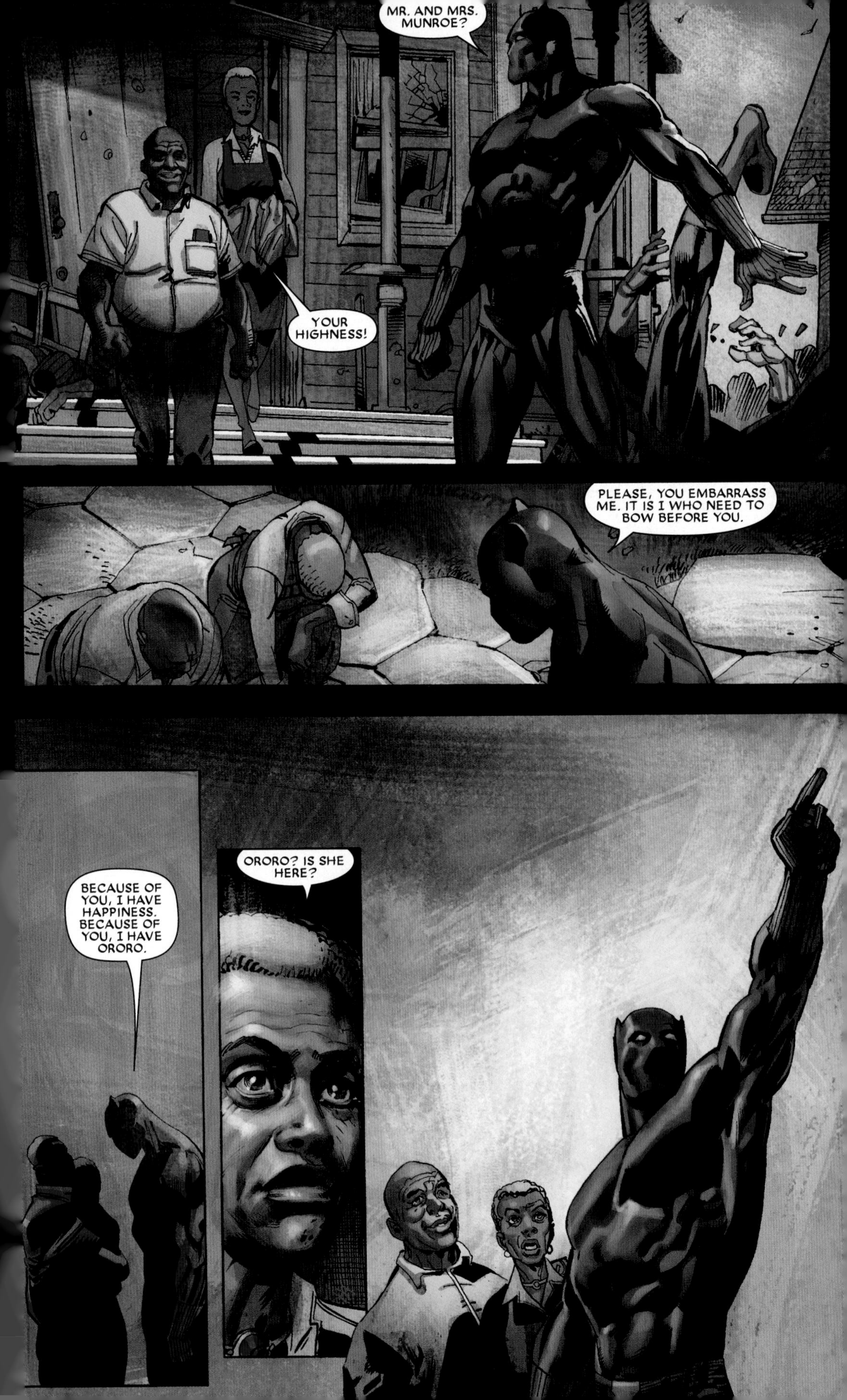
MR. AND MRS. MUNROE?
YOUR HIGHNESS!
PLEASE, YOU EMBARRASS ME. IT IS I WHO NEED TO BOW BEFORE YOU.
BECAUSE OF YOU, I HAVE HAPPINESS. BECAUSE OF YOU, I HAVE ORORO.
ORORO? IS SHE HERE?

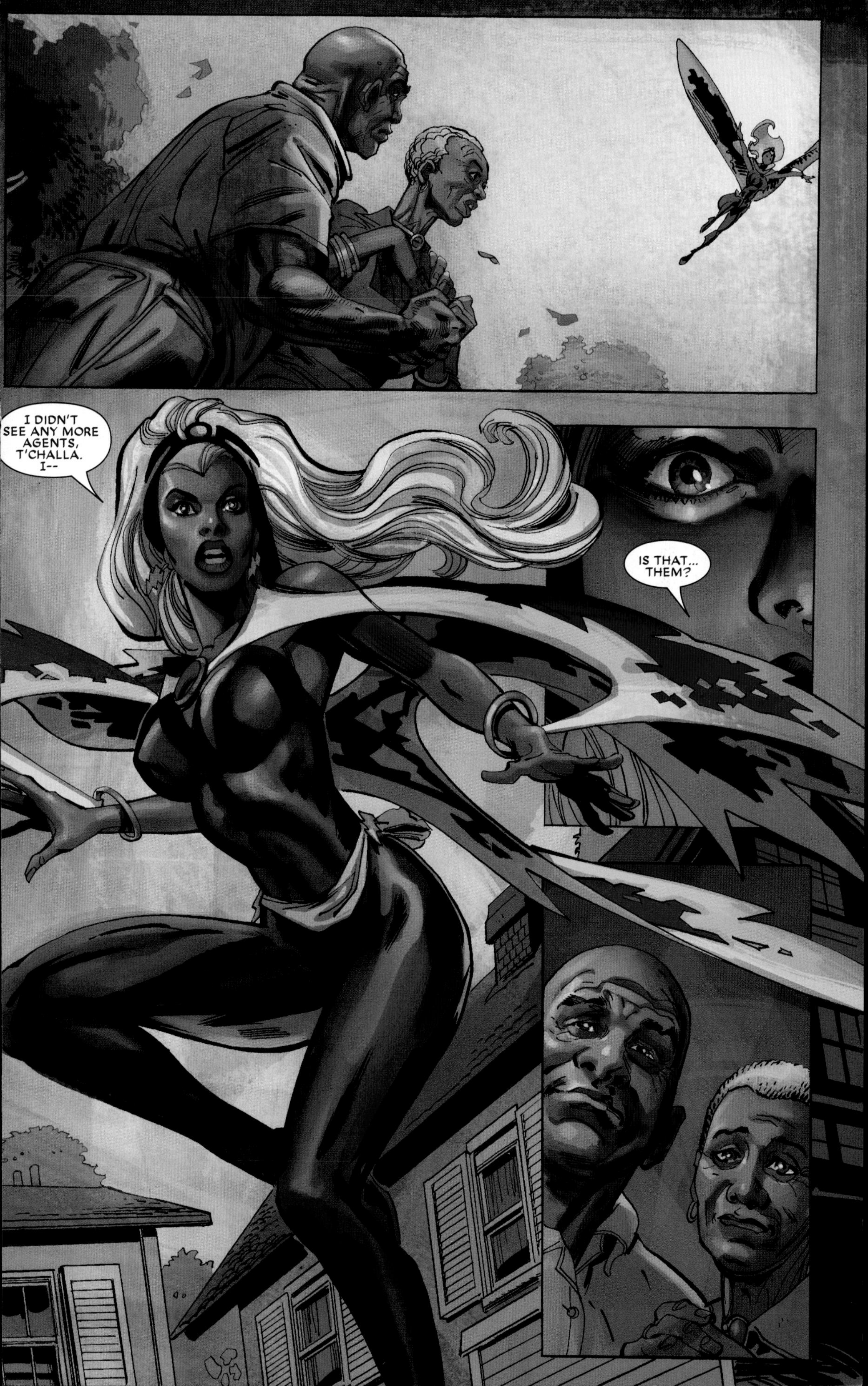
I DIDN'T SEE ANY MORE AGENTS, T'CHALLA. I--
IS THAT... THEM?

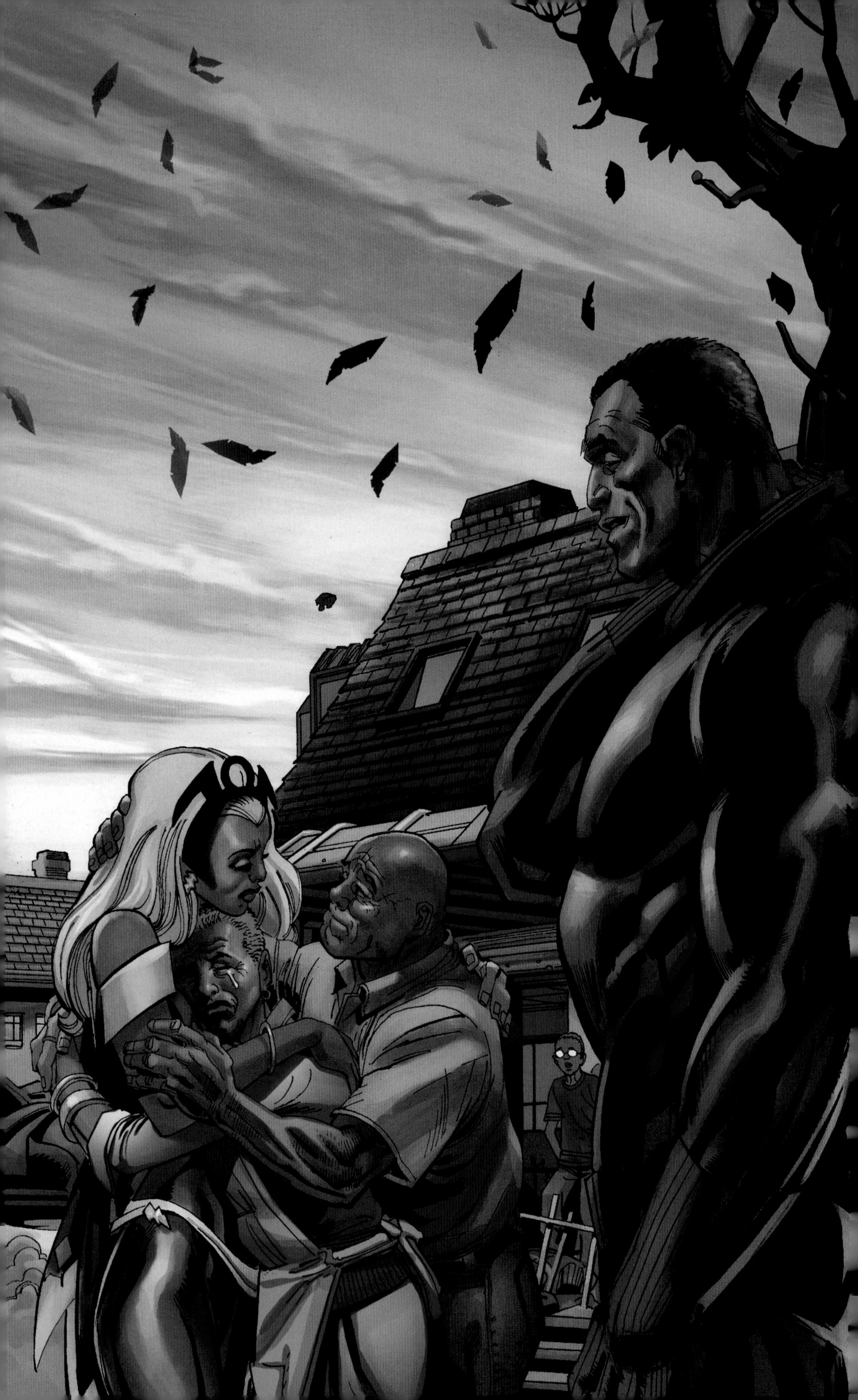

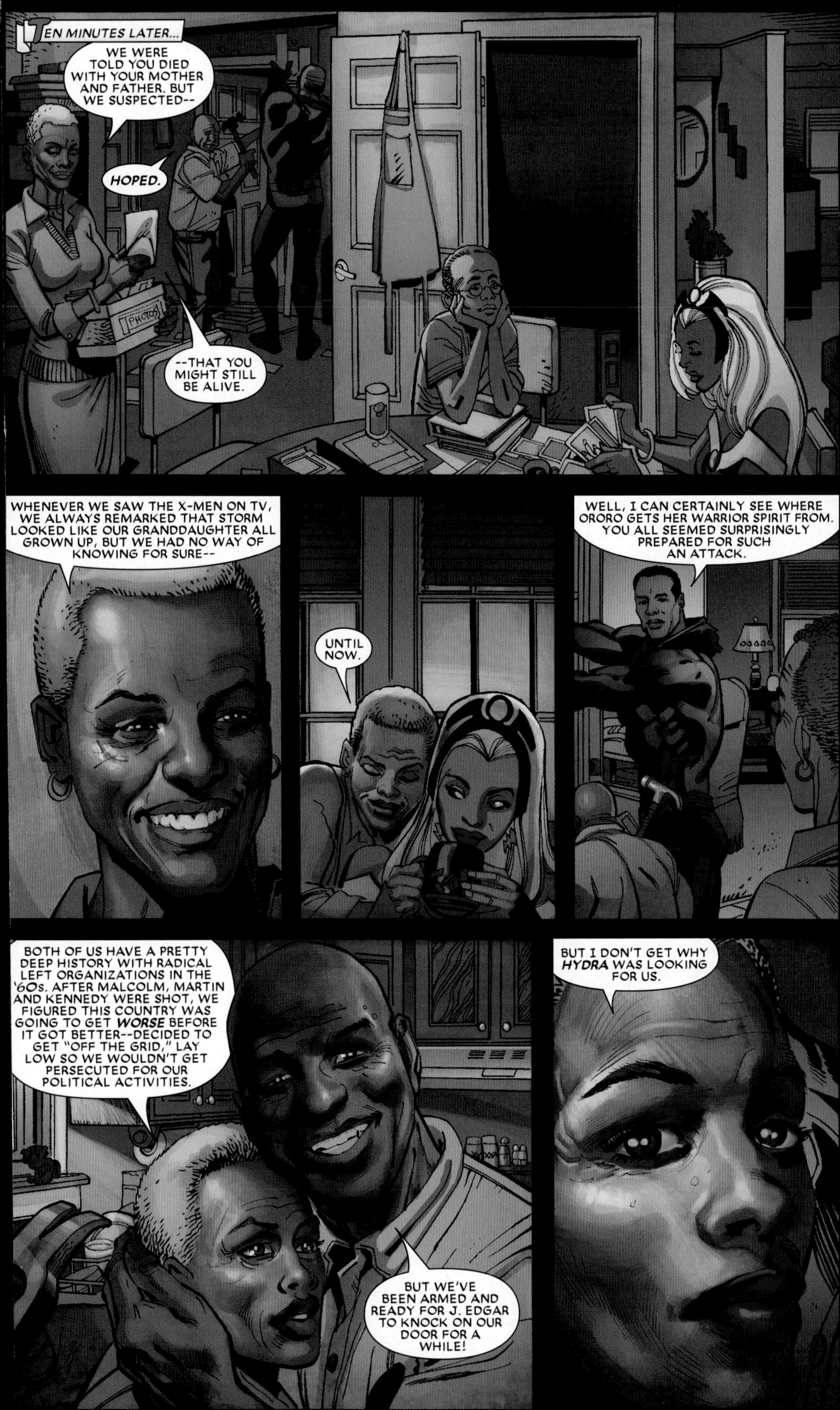
TEN MINUTES LATER...
WE WERE TOLD YOU DIED WITH YOUR MOTHER AND FATHER. BUT WE SUSPECTED--
HOPED.
PHOTOS
--THAT YOU MIGHT STILL BE ALIVE.
WHENEVER WE SAW THE X-MEN ON TV, WE ALWAYS REMARKED THAT STORM LOOKED LIKE OUR GRANDDAUGHTER ALL GROWN UP, BUT WE HAD NO WAY OF KNOWING FOR SURE--
UNTIL NOW.
WELL, I CAN CERTAINLY SEE WHERE ORORO GETS HER WARRIOR SPIRIT FROM. YOU ALL SEEMED SURPRISINGLY PREPARED FOR SUCH AN ATTACK.
BOTH OF US HAVE A PRETTY DEEP HISTORY WITH RADICAL LEFT ORGANIZATIONS IN THE '60s. AFTER MALCOLM, MARTIN AND KENNEDY WERE SHOT, WE FIGURED THIS COUNTRY WAS GOING TO GET WORSE BEFORE IT GOT BETTER--DECIDED TO GET "OFF THE GRID," LAY LOW SO WE WOULDN'T GET PERSECUTED FOR OUR POLITICAL ACTIVITIES.
BUT WE'VE BEEN ARMED AND READY FOR J. EDGAR TO KNOCK ON OUR DOOR FOR A WHILE!
BUT I DON'T GET WHY HYDRA WAS LOOKING FOR US.

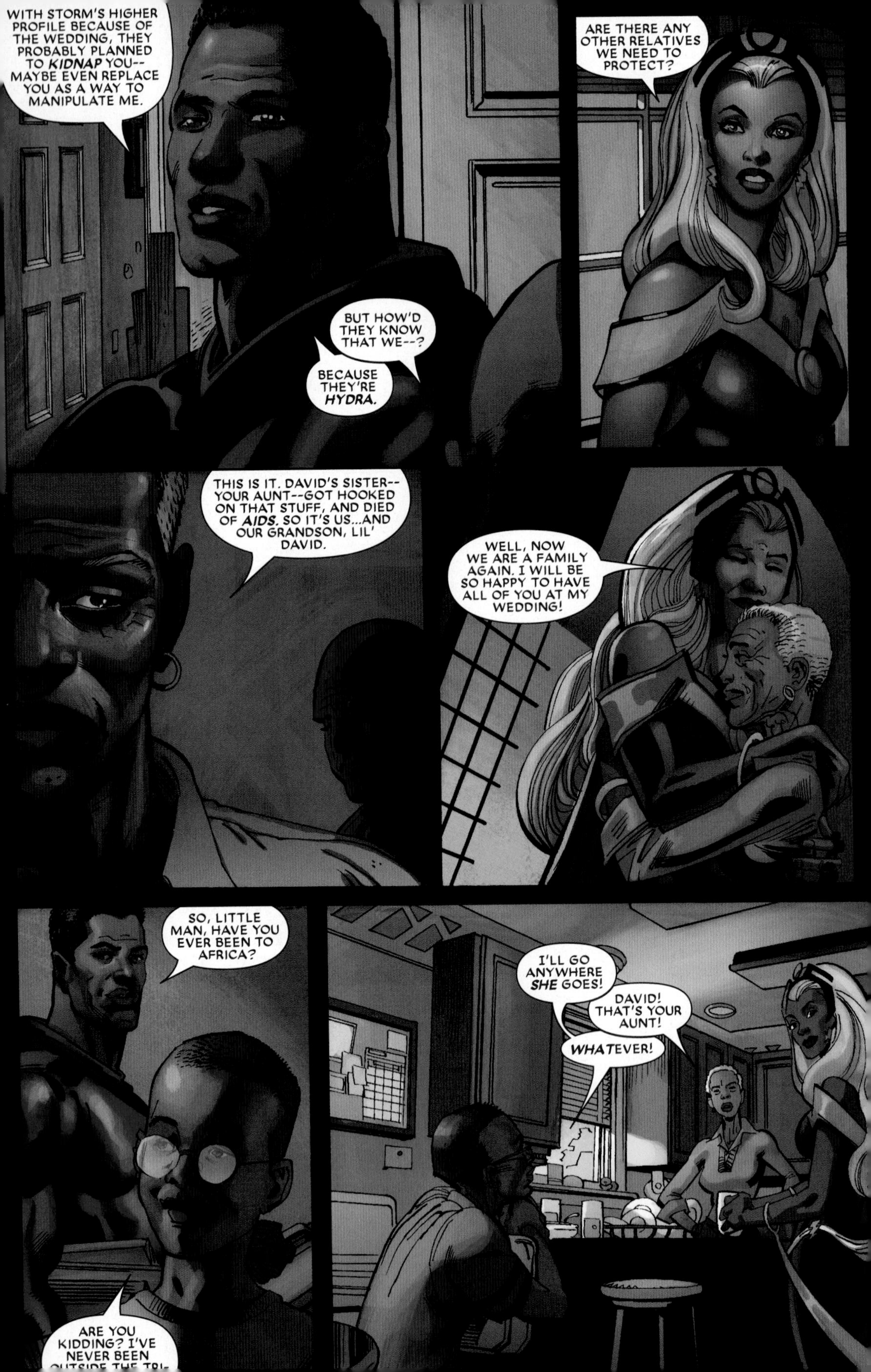
WITH STORM'S HIGHER PROFILE BECAUSE OF THE WEDDING, THEY PROBABLY PLANNED TO KIDNAP YOU-- MAYBE EVEN REPLACE YOU AS A WAY TO MANIPULATE ME.
BUT HOW'D THEY KNOW THAT WE--?
BECAUSE THEY'RE HYDRA.
ARE THERE ANY OTHER RELATIVES WE NEED TO PROTECT?
THIS IS IT. DAVID'S SISTER-- YOUR AUNT--GOT HOOKED ON THAT STUFF, AND DIED OF AIDS. SO IT'S US...AND OUR GRANDSON, LIL' DAVID.
WELL, NOW WE ARE A FAMILY AGAIN. I WILL BE SO HAPPY TO HAVE ALL OF YOU AT MY WEDDING!
SO, LITTLE MAN, HAVE YOU EVER BEEN TO AFRICA?
ARE YOU KIDDING? I'VE NEVER BEEN
I'LL GO ANYWHERE SHE GOES!
DAVID! THAT'S YOUR AUNT!
WHATEVER!

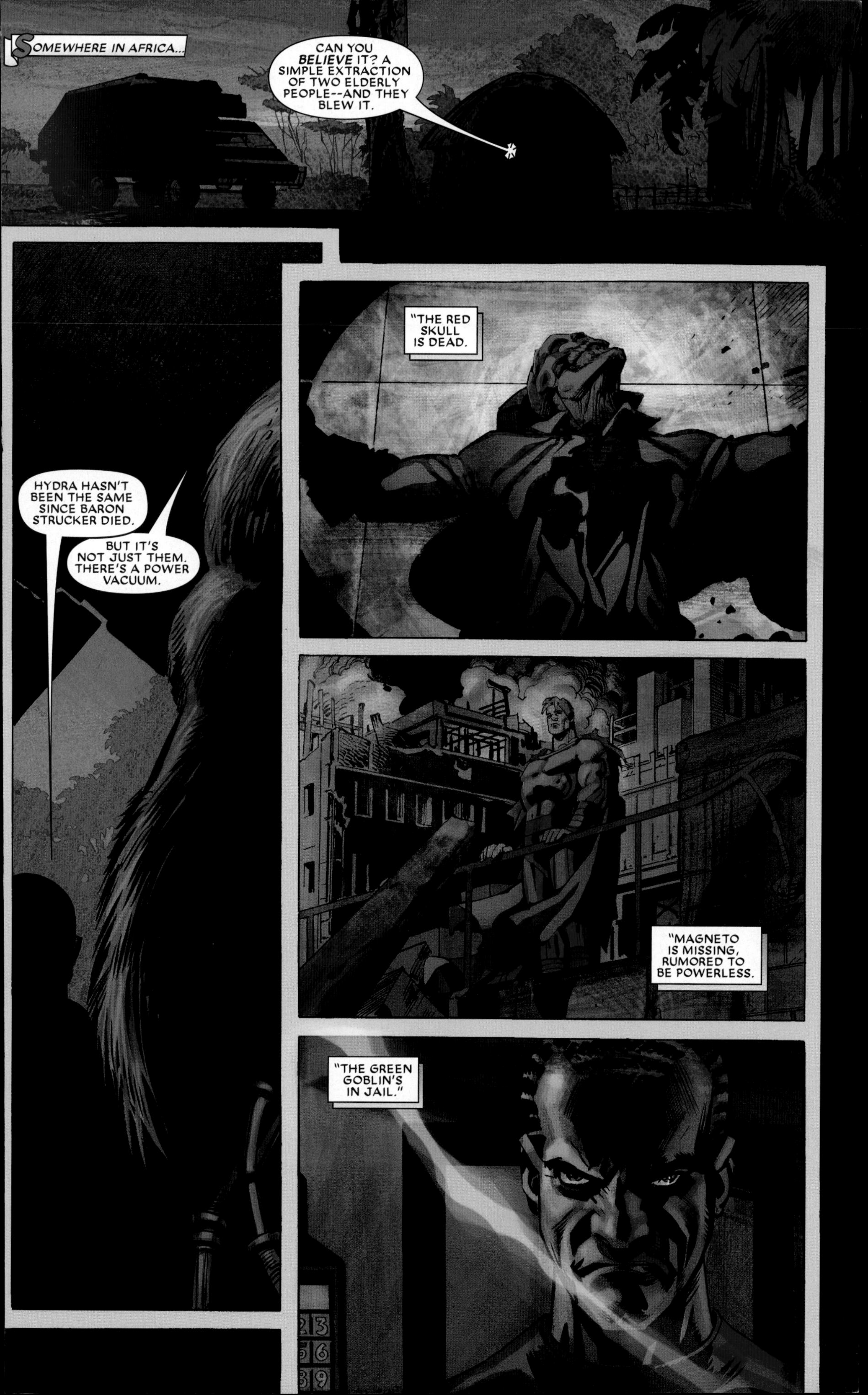
SOMEWHERE IN AFRICA...
CAN YOU BELIEVE IT? A SIMPLE EXTRACTION OF TWO ELDERLY PEOPLE--AND THEY BLEW IT.
"THE RED SKULL IS DEAD.
HYDRA HASN'T BEEN THE SAME SINCE BARON STRUCKER DIED.
BUT IT'S NOT JUST THEM. THERE'S A POWER VACUUM.
"MAGNETO IS MISSING, RUMORED TO BE POWERLESS.
"THE GREEN GOBLIN'S IN JAIL."

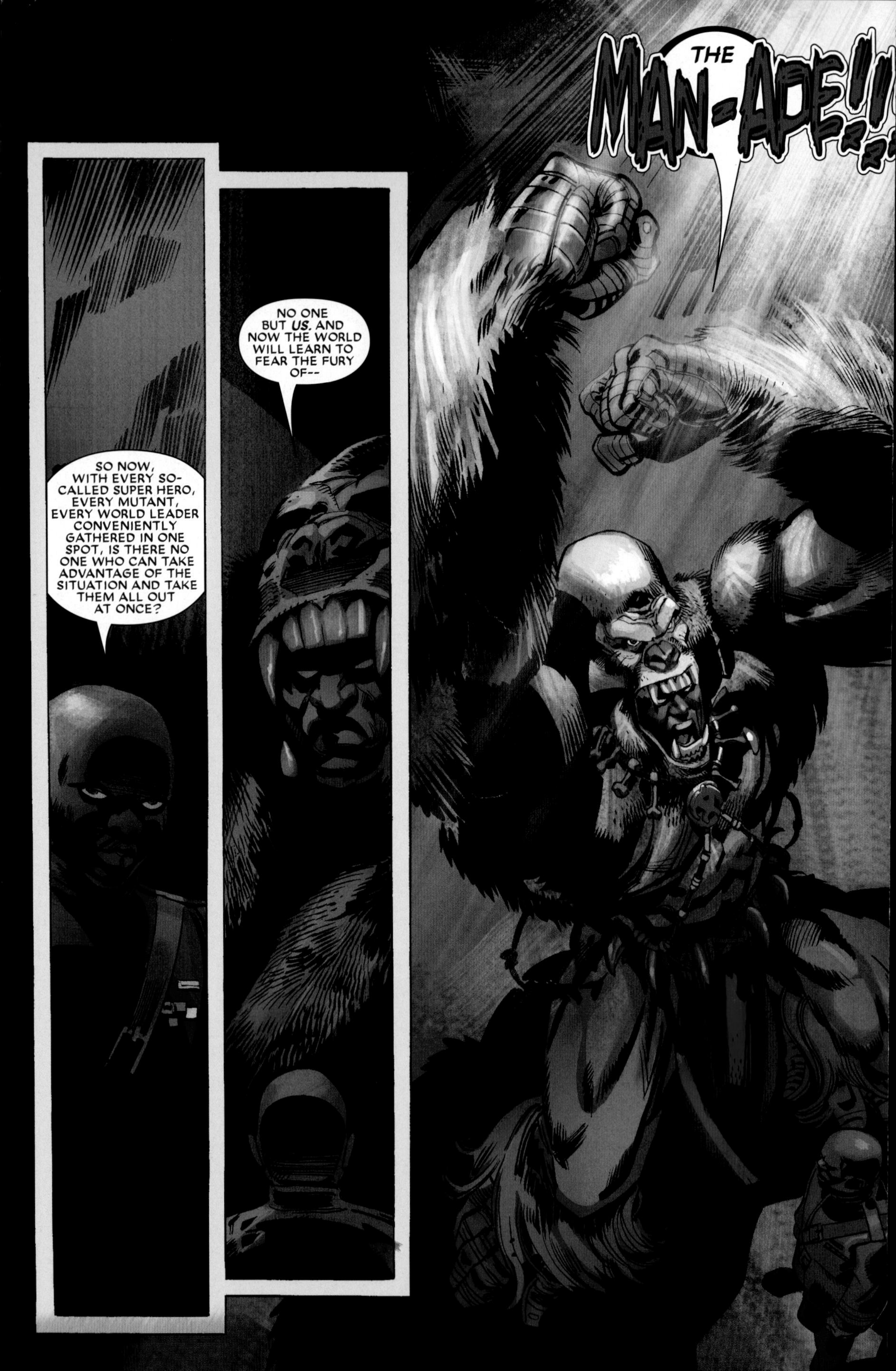
SO NOW, WITH EVERY SO-CALLED SUPER HERO, EVERY MUTANT, EVERY WORLD LEADER CONVENIENTLY GATHERED IN ONE SPOT, IS THERE NO ONE WHO CAN TAKE ADVANTAGE OF THE SITUATION AND TAKE THEM ALL OUT AT ONCE?
NO ONE BUT US. AND NOW THE WORLD WILL LEARN TO FEAR THE FURY OF--
THE MAN-APE!!

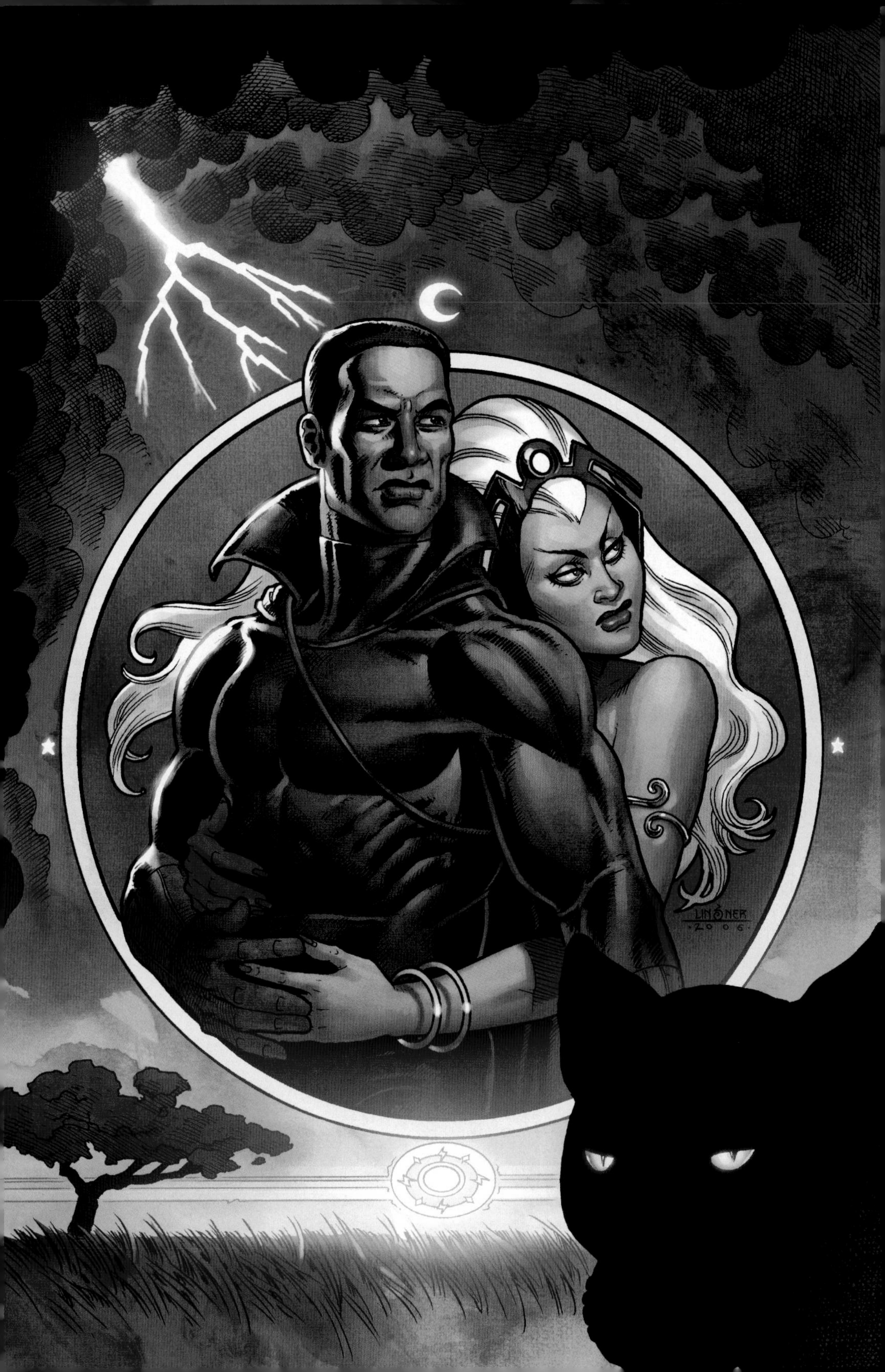
LINSNER
2006

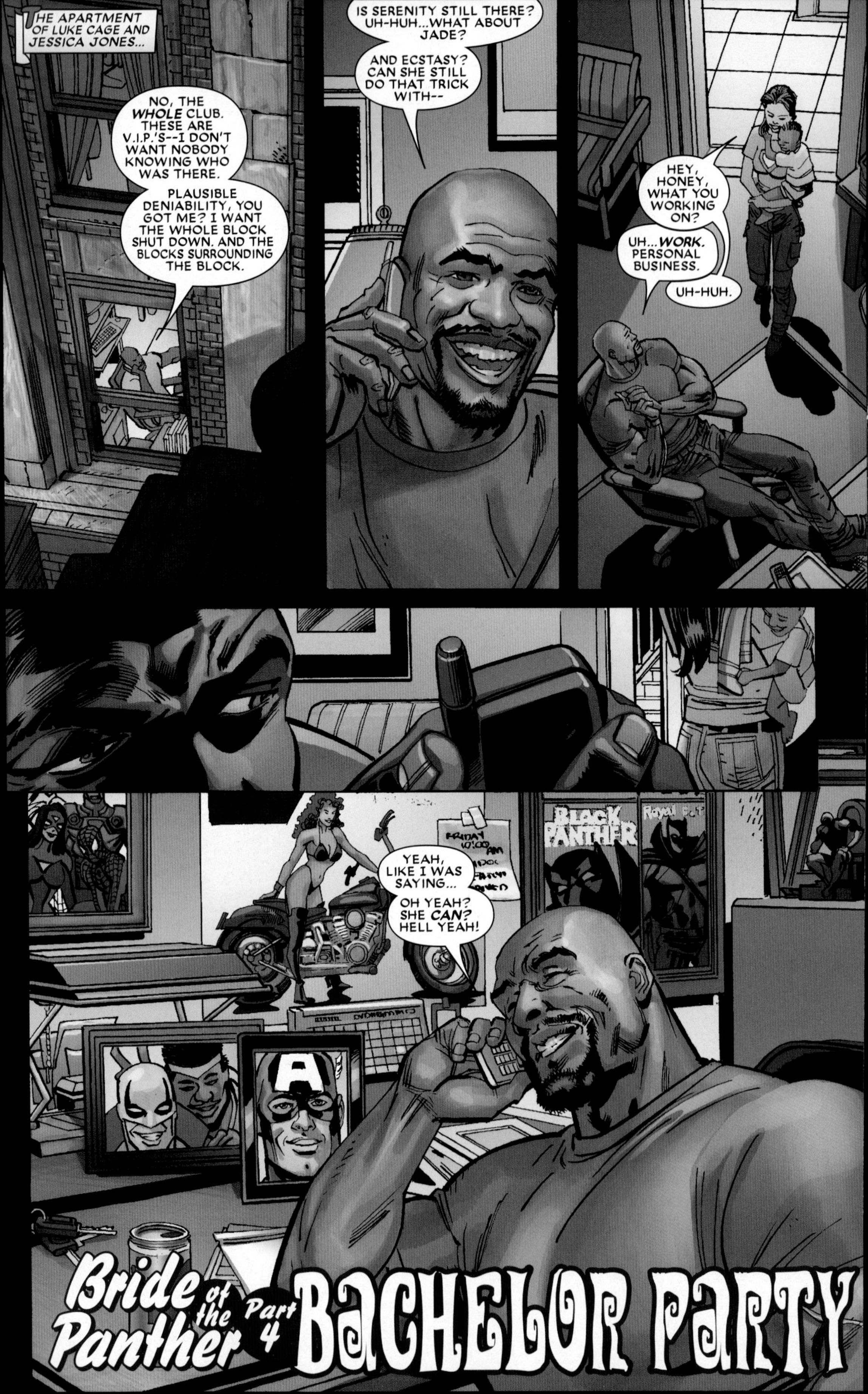
THE APARTMENT OF LUKE CAGE AND JESSICA JONES...
NO, THE WHOLE CLUB. THESE ARE V.I.P.'S--I DON'T WANT NOBODY KNOWING WHO WAS THERE.
PLAUSIBLE DENIABILITY, YOU GOT ME? I WANT THE WHOLE BLOCK SHUT DOWN. AND THE BLOCKS SURROUNDING THE BLOCK.
IS SERENITY STILL THERE? UH-HUH...WHAT ABOUT JADE?
AND ECSTASY? CAN SHE STILL DO THAT TRICK WITH--
HEY, HONEY, WHAT YOU WORKING ON?
UH...WORK. PERSONAL BUSINESS.
UH-HUH.
YEAH, LIKE I WAS SAYING...
OH YEAH? SHE CAN? HELL YEAH!
BLACK PANTHER
Bride of the Panther Part 4
BACHELOR PARTY

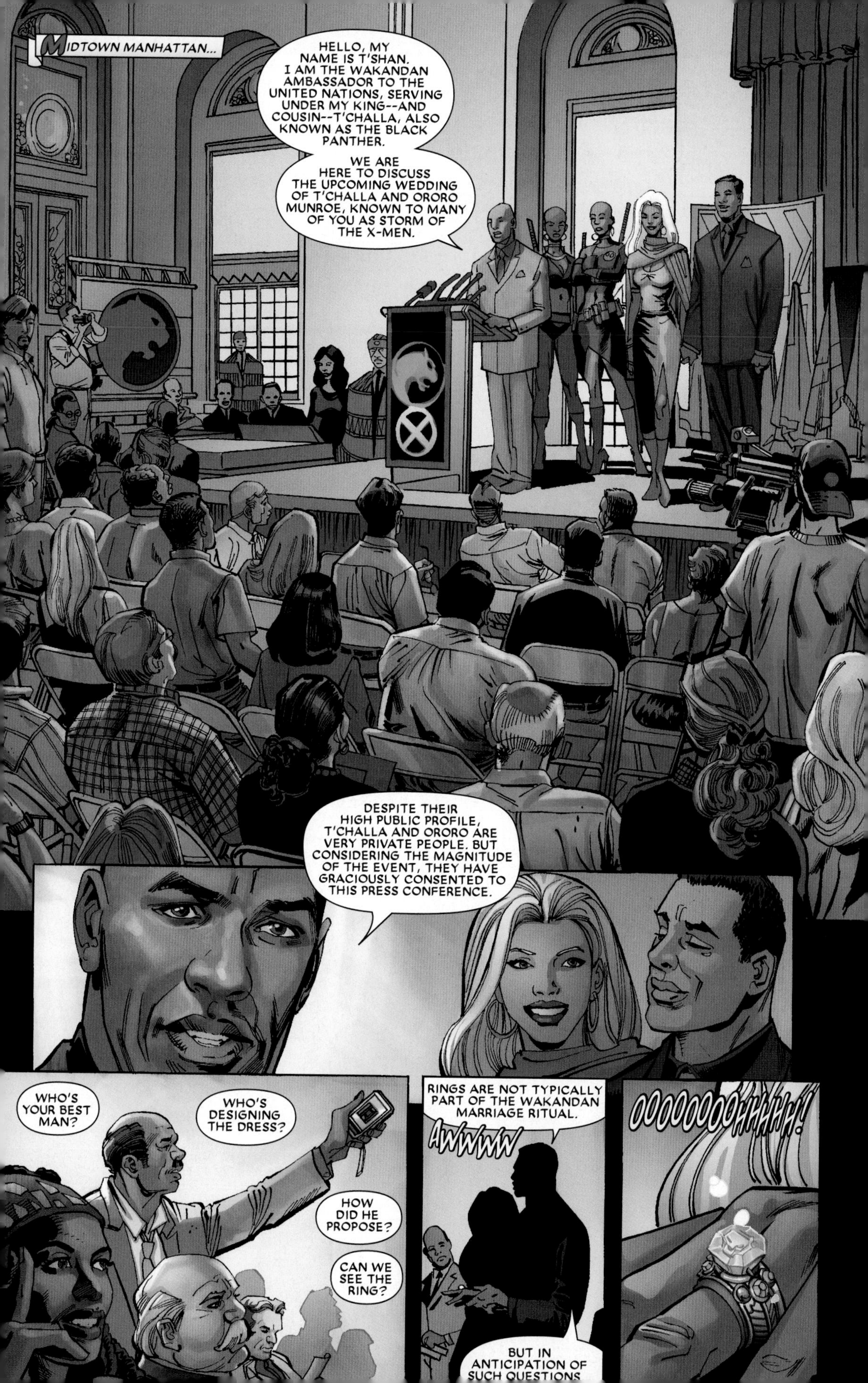
MIDTOWN MANHATTAN...
HELLO, MY NAME IS T'SHAN. I AM THE WAKANDAN AMBASSADOR TO THE UNITED NATIONS, SERVING UNDER MY KING--AND COUSIN--T'CHALLA, ALSO KNOWN AS THE BLACK PANTHER.
WE ARE HERE TO DISCUSS THE UPCOMING WEDDING OF T'CHALLA AND ORORO MUNROE, KNOWN TO MANY OF YOU AS STORM OF THE X-MEN.
DESPITE THEIR HIGH PUBLIC PROFILE, T'CHALLA AND ORORO ARE VERY PRIVATE PEOPLE. BUT CONSIDERING THE MAGNITUDE OF THE EVENT, THEY HAVE GRACIOUSLY CONSENTED TO THIS PRESS CONFERENCE.
WHO'S YOUR BEST MAN?
WHO'S DESIGNING THE DRESS?
HOW DID HE PROPOSE?
CAN WE SEE THE RING?
RINGS ARE NOT TYPICALLY PART OF THE WAKANDAN MARRIAGE RITUAL.
AWWWW
BUT IN ANTICIPATION OF SUCH QUESTIONS
OOOOOOOOHHHHH!

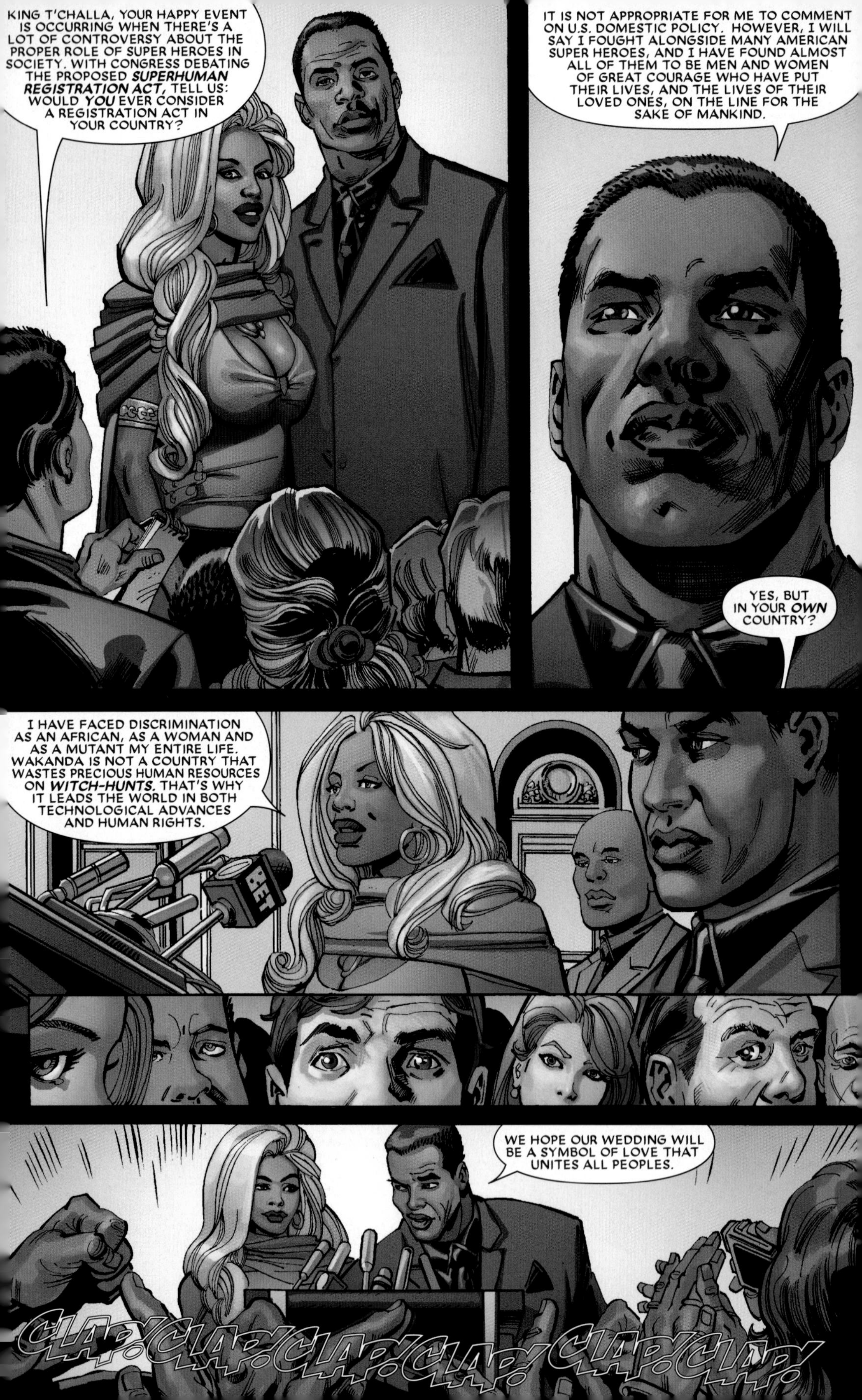
KING T'CHALLA, YOUR HAPPY EVENT IS OCCURRING WHEN THERE'S A LOT OF CONTROVERSY ABOUT THE PROPER ROLE OF SUPER HEROES IN SOCIETY. WITH CONGRESS DEBATING THE PROPOSED *SUPERHUMAN REGISTRATION ACT*, TELL US: WOULD *YOU* EVER CONSIDER A REGISTRATION ACT IN YOUR COUNTRY?
IT IS NOT APPROPRIATE FOR ME TO COMMENT ON U.S. DOMESTIC POLICY. HOWEVER, I WILL SAY I FOUGHT ALONGSIDE MANY AMERICAN SUPER HEROES, AND I HAVE FOUND ALMOST ALL OF THEM TO BE MEN AND WOMEN OF GREAT COURAGE WHO HAVE PUT THEIR LIVES, AND THE LIVES OF THEIR LOVED ONES, ON THE LINE FOR THE SAKE OF MANKIND.
YES, BUT IN YOUR *OWN* COUNTRY?
I HAVE FACED DISCRIMINATION AS AN AFRICAN, AS A WOMAN AND AS A MUTANT MY ENTIRE LIFE. WAKANDA IS NOT A COUNTRY THAT WASTES PRECIOUS HUMAN RESOURCES ON *WITCH-HUNTS.* THAT'S WHY IT LEADS THE WORLD IN BOTH TECHNOLOGICAL ADVANCES AND HUMAN RIGHTS.
BET
WE HOPE OUR WEDDING WILL BE A SYMBOL OF LOVE THAT UNITES ALL PEOPLES.
CLAP! CLAP! CLAP! CLAP! CLAP! CLAP! CLAP!

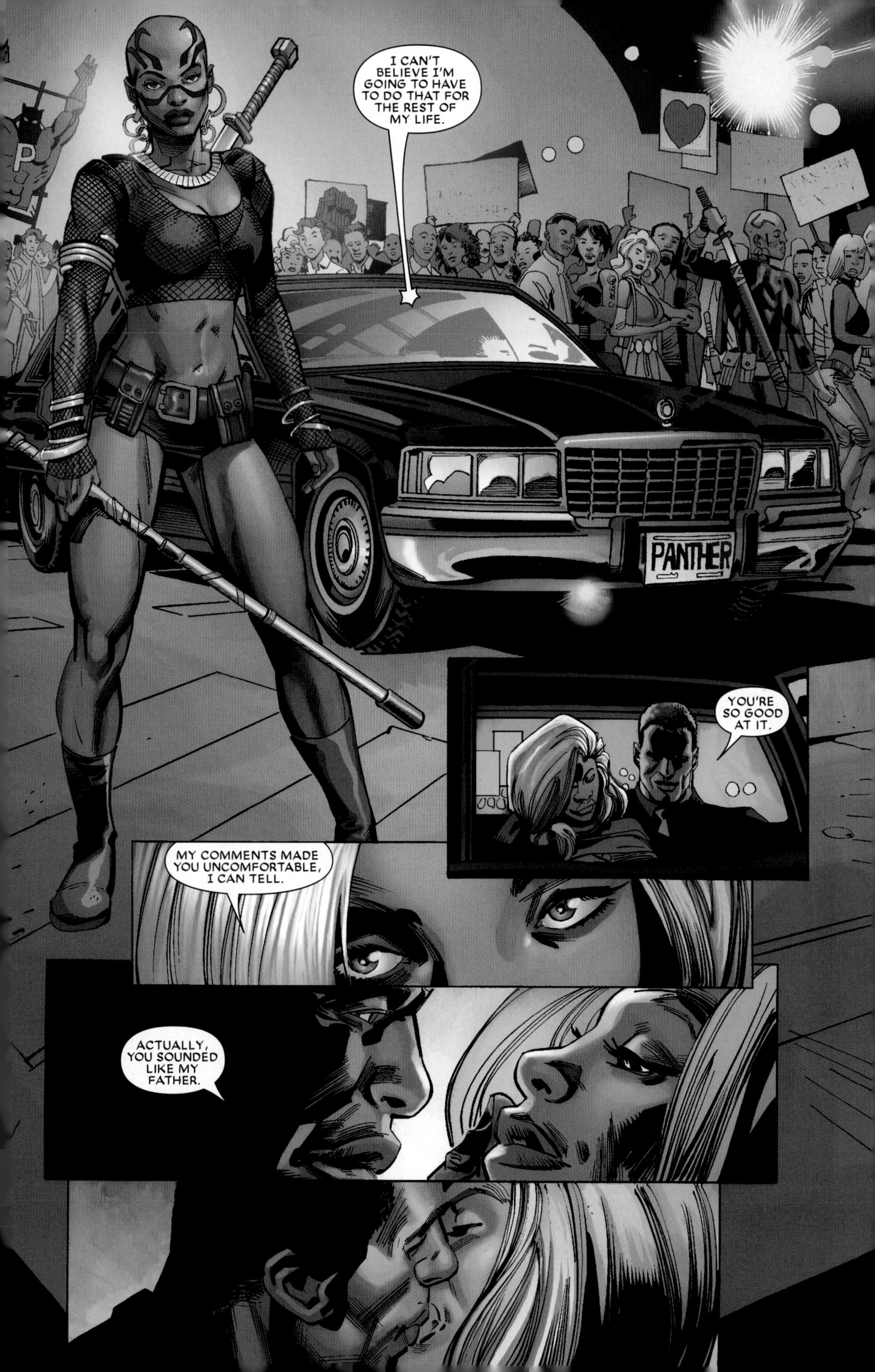
I CAN'T BELIEVE I'M GOING TO HAVE TO DO THAT FOR THE REST OF MY LIFE.
PANTHER
YOU'RE SO GOOD AT IT.
MY COMMENTS MADE YOU UNCOMFORTABLE, I CAN TELL.
ACTUALLY, YOU SOUNDED LIKE MY FATHER.

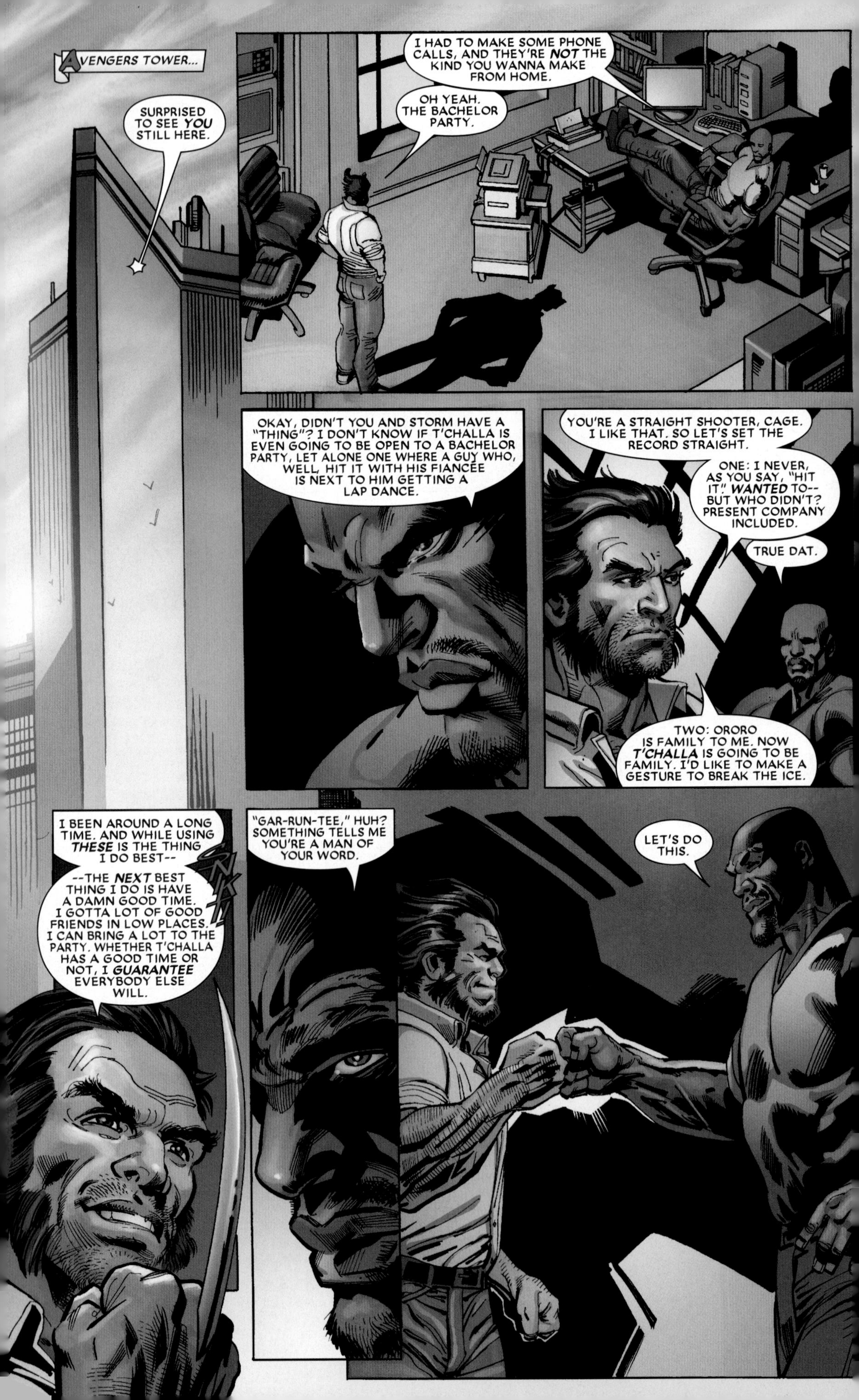
AVENGERS TOWER...
SURPRISED TO SEE YOU STILL HERE.
I HAD TO MAKE SOME PHONE CALLS, AND THEY'RE NOT THE KIND YOU WANNA MAKE FROM HOME.
OH YEAH. THE BACHELOR PARTY.
OKAY, DIDN'T YOU AND STORM HAVE A "THING"? I DON'T KNOW IF T'CHALLA IS EVEN GOING TO BE OPEN TO A BACHELOR PARTY, LET ALONE ONE WHERE A GUY WHO, WELL, HIT IT WITH HIS FIANCÉE IS NEXT TO HIM GETTING A LAP DANCE.
YOU'RE A STRAIGHT SHOOTER, CAGE. I LIKE THAT. SO LET'S SET THE RECORD STRAIGHT.
ONE: I NEVER, AS YOU SAY, "HIT IT." WANTED TO-- BUT WHO DIDN'T? PRESENT COMPANY INCLUDED.
TRUE DAT.
TWO: ORORO IS FAMILY TO ME. NOW T'CHALLA IS GOING TO BE FAMILY. I'D LIKE TO MAKE A GESTURE TO BREAK THE ICE.
I BEEN AROUND A LONG TIME. AND WHILE USING THESE IS THE THING I DO BEST--
SNIKT
--THE NEXT BEST THING I DO IS HAVE A DAMN GOOD TIME. I GOTTA LOT OF GOOD FRIENDS IN LOW PLACES. I CAN BRING A LOT TO THE PARTY. WHETHER T'CHALLA HAS A GOOD TIME OR NOT, I GUARANTEE EVERYBODY ELSE WILL.
"GAR-RUN-TEE," HUH? SOMETHING TELLS ME YOU'RE A MAN OF YOUR WORD.
LET'S DO THIS.

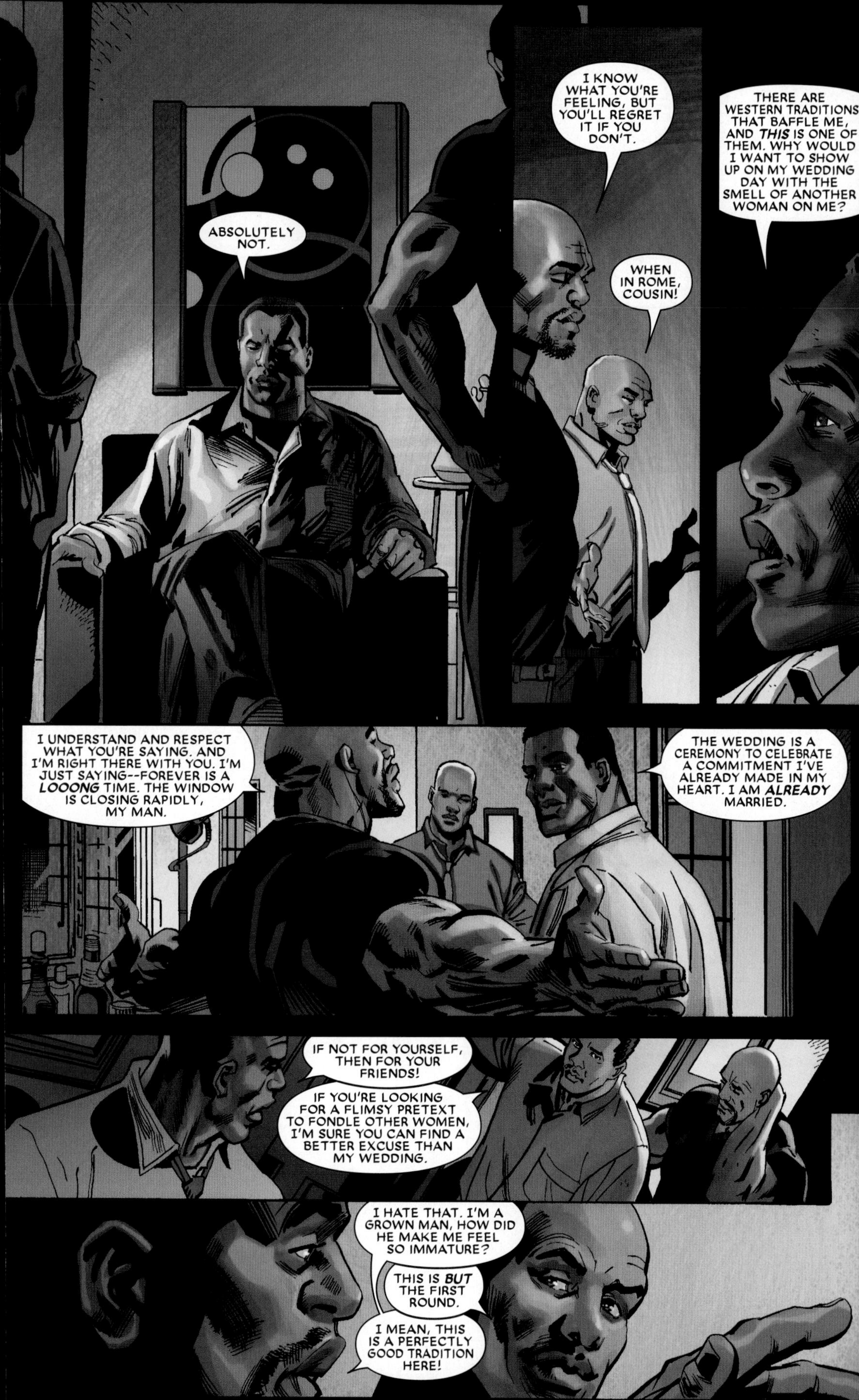
ABSOLUTELY NOT.
I KNOW WHAT YOU'RE FEELING, BUT YOU'LL REGRET IT IF YOU DON'T.
WHEN IN ROME, COUSIN!
THERE ARE WESTERN TRADITIONS THAT BAFFLE ME, AND THIS IS ONE OF THEM. WHY WOULD I WANT TO SHOW UP ON MY WEDDING DAY WITH THE SMELL OF ANOTHER WOMAN ON ME?
I UNDERSTAND AND RESPECT WHAT YOU'RE SAYING. AND I'M RIGHT THERE WITH YOU. I'M JUST SAYING--FOREVER IS A LOOONG TIME. THE WINDOW IS CLOSING RAPIDLY, MY MAN.
THE WEDDING IS A CEREMONY TO CELEBRATE A COMMITMENT I'VE ALREADY MADE IN MY HEART. I AM ALREADY MARRIED.
IF NOT FOR YOURSELF, THEN FOR YOUR FRIENDS!
IF YOU'RE LOOKING FOR A FLIMSY PRETEXT TO FONDLE OTHER WOMEN, I'M SURE YOU CAN FIND A BETTER EXCUSE THAN MY WEDDING.
I HATE THAT. I'M A GROWN MAN, HOW DID HE MAKE ME FEEL SO IMMATURE?
THIS IS BUT THE FIRST ROUND.
I MEAN, THIS IS A PERFECTLY GOOD TRADITION HERE!

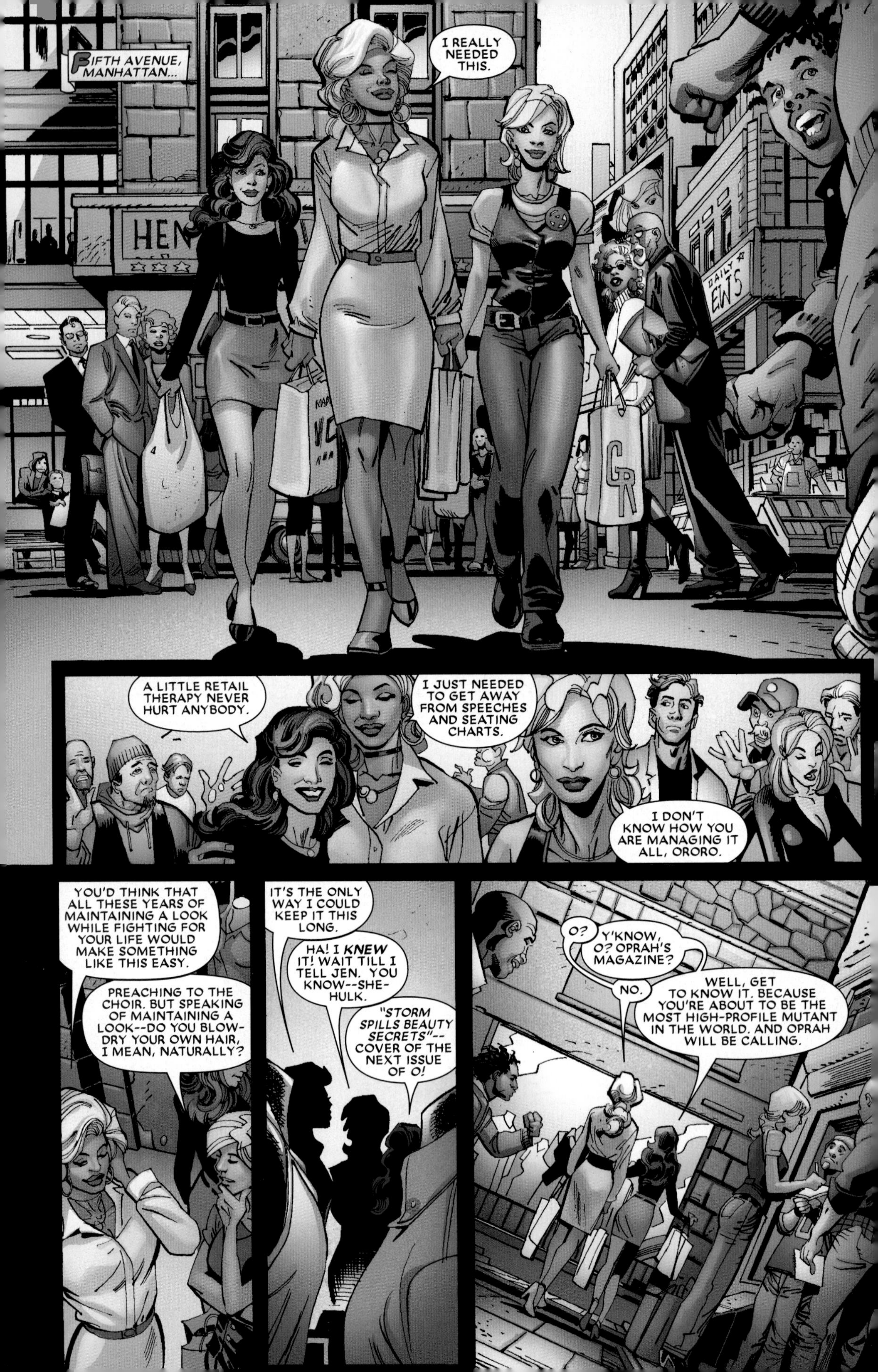
FIFTH AVENUE, MANHATTAN...
I REALLY NEEDED THIS.
HEN
DAILY NEWS
A LITTLE RETAIL THERAPY NEVER HURT ANYBODY.
I JUST NEEDED TO GET AWAY FROM SPEECHES AND SEATING CHARTS.
I DON'T KNOW HOW YOU ARE MANAGING IT ALL, ORORO.
YOU'D THINK THAT ALL THESE YEARS OF MAINTAINING A LOOK WHILE FIGHTING FOR YOUR LIFE WOULD MAKE SOMETHING LIKE THIS EASY.
PREACHING TO THE CHOIR. BUT SPEAKING OF MAINTAINING A LOOK--DO YOU BLOW-DRY YOUR OWN HAIR, I MEAN, NATURALLY?
IT'S THE ONLY WAY I COULD KEEP IT THIS LONG.
HA! I *KNEW* IT! WAIT TILL I TELL JEN. YOU KNOW--SHE-HULK.
"STORM SPILLS BEAUTY SECRETS"--COVER OF THE NEXT ISSUE OF *O!*
O?
Y'KNOW, O? OPRAH'S MAGAZINE?
NO.
WELL, GET TO KNOW IT. BECAUSE YOU'RE ABOUT TO BE THE MOST HIGH-PROFILE MUTANT IN THE WORLD. AND OPRAH WILL BE CALLING.

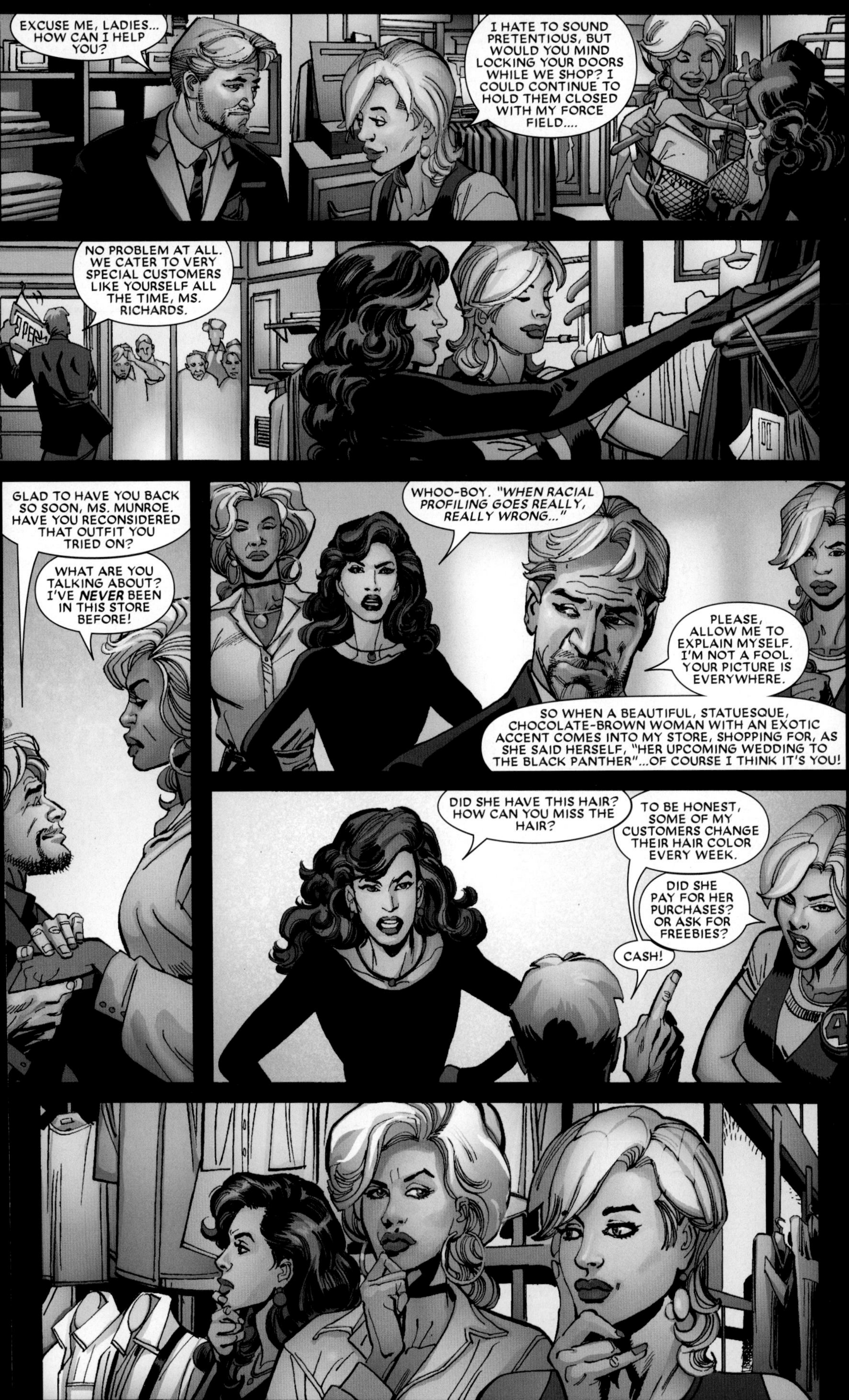
EXCUSE ME, LADIES... HOW CAN I HELP YOU?
I HATE TO SOUND PRETENTIOUS, BUT WOULD YOU MIND LOCKING YOUR DOORS WHILE WE SHOP? I COULD CONTINUE TO HOLD THEM CLOSED WITH MY FORCE FIELD....
NO PROBLEM AT ALL. WE CATER TO VERY SPECIAL CUSTOMERS LIKE YOURSELF ALL THE TIME, MS. RICHARDS.
GLAD TO HAVE YOU BACK SO SOON, MS. MUNROE. HAVE YOU RECONSIDERED THAT OUTFIT YOU TRIED ON?
WHAT ARE YOU TALKING ABOUT? I'VE ***NEVER*** BEEN IN THIS STORE BEFORE!
WHOO-BOY. "*WHEN RACIAL PROFILING GOES REALLY, REALLY WRONG...*"
PLEASE, ALLOW ME TO EXPLAIN MYSELF. I'M NOT A FOOL. YOUR PICTURE IS EVERYWHERE.
SO WHEN A BEAUTIFUL, STATUESQUE, CHOCOLATE-BROWN WOMAN WITH AN EXOTIC ACCENT COMES INTO MY STORE, SHOPPING FOR, AS SHE SAID HERSELF, "HER UPCOMING WEDDING TO THE BLACK PANTHER"...OF COURSE I THINK IT'S YOU!
DID SHE HAVE THIS HAIR? HOW CAN YOU MISS THE HAIR?
TO BE HONEST, SOME OF MY CUSTOMERS CHANGE THEIR HAIR COLOR EVERY WEEK.
DID SHE PAY FOR HER PURCHASES? OR ASK FOR FREEBIES?
CASH!

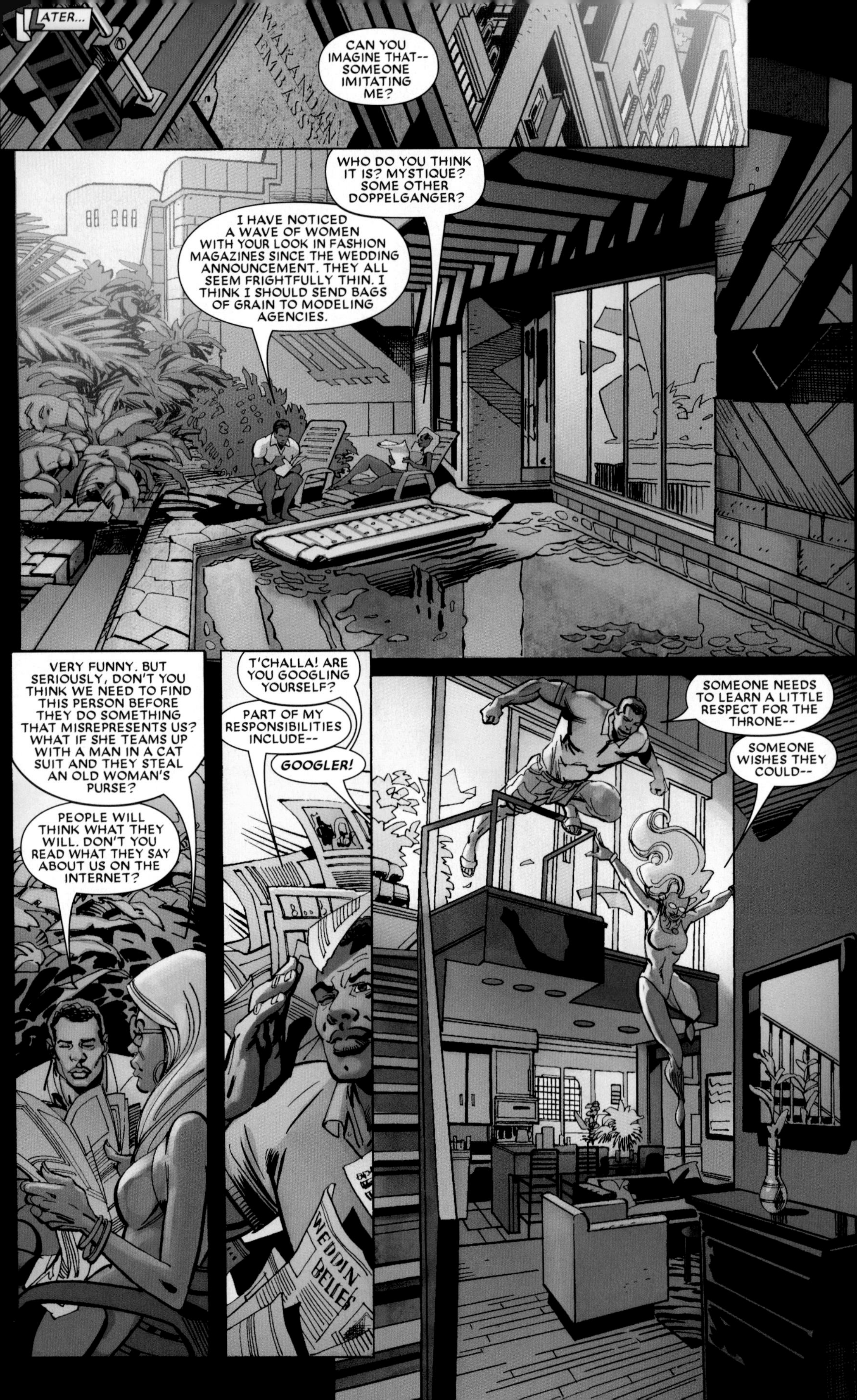
LATER...
CAN YOU IMAGINE THAT-- SOMEONE IMITATING ME?
WHO DO YOU THINK IT IS? MYSTIQUE? SOME OTHER DOPPELGANGER?
I HAVE NOTICED A WAVE OF WOMEN WITH YOUR LOOK IN FASHION MAGAZINES SINCE THE WEDDING ANNOUNCEMENT. THEY ALL SEEM FRIGHTFULLY THIN. I THINK I SHOULD SEND BAGS OF GRAIN TO MODELING AGENCIES.
VERY FUNNY. BUT SERIOUSLY, DON'T YOU THINK WE NEED TO FIND THIS PERSON BEFORE THEY DO SOMETHING THAT MISREPRESENTS US? WHAT IF SHE TEAMS UP WITH A MAN IN A CAT SUIT AND THEY STEAL AN OLD WOMAN'S PURSE?
PEOPLE WILL THINK WHAT THEY WILL. DON'T YOU READ WHAT THEY SAY ABOUT US ON THE INTERNET?
T'CHALLA! ARE YOU GOOGLING YOURSELF?
PART OF MY RESPONSIBILITIES INCLUDE--
GOOGLER!
SOMEONE NEEDS TO LEARN A LITTLE RESPECT FOR THE THRONE--
SOMEONE WISHES THEY COULD--

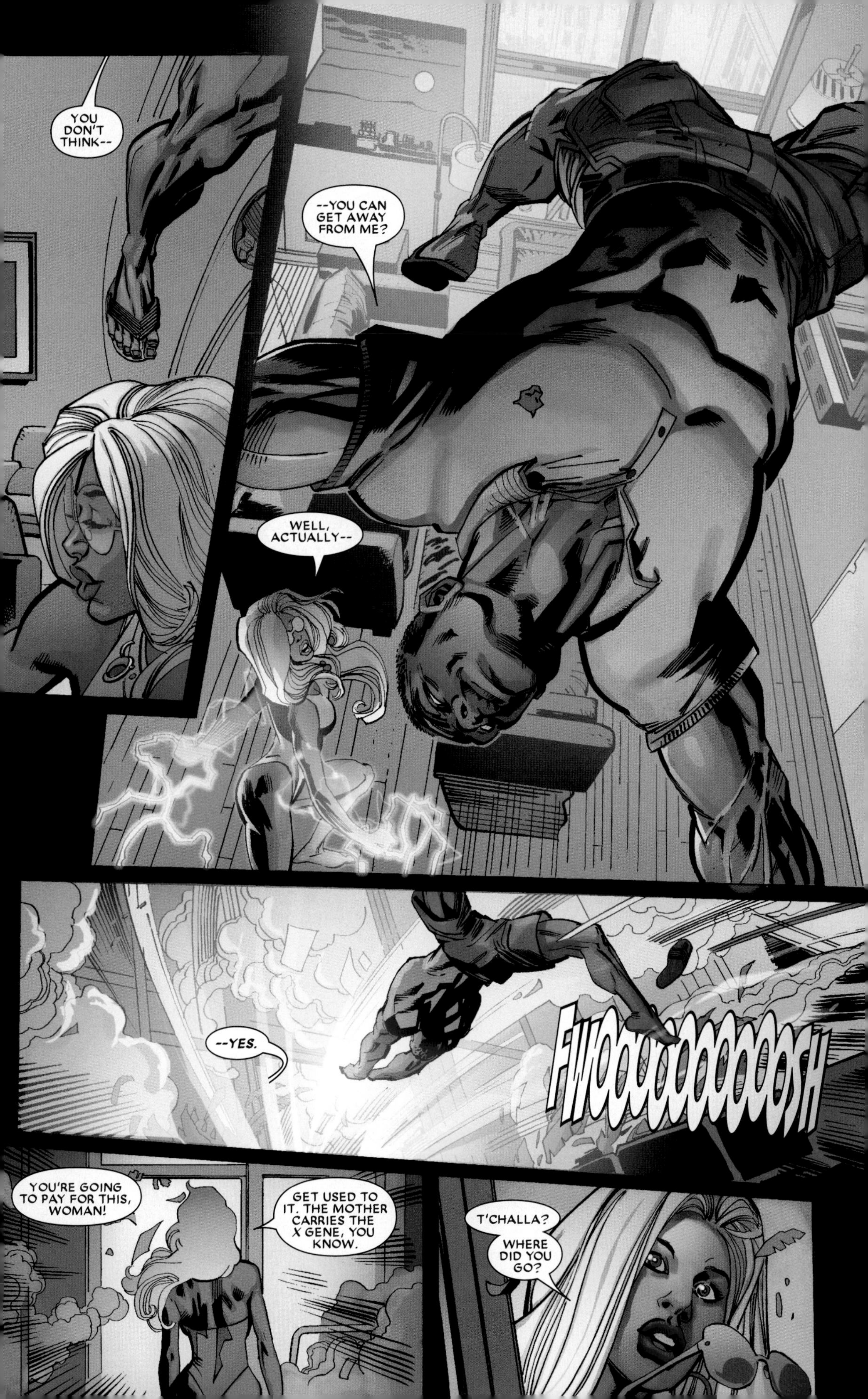
YOU DON'T THINK--
--YOU CAN GET AWAY FROM ME?
WELL, ACTUALLY--
--YES.
FWOOOOOOOOOOSH
YOU'RE GOING TO PAY FOR THIS, WOMAN!
GET USED TO IT. THE MOTHER CARRIES THE X GENE, YOU KNOW.
T'CHALLA?
WHERE DID YOU GO?

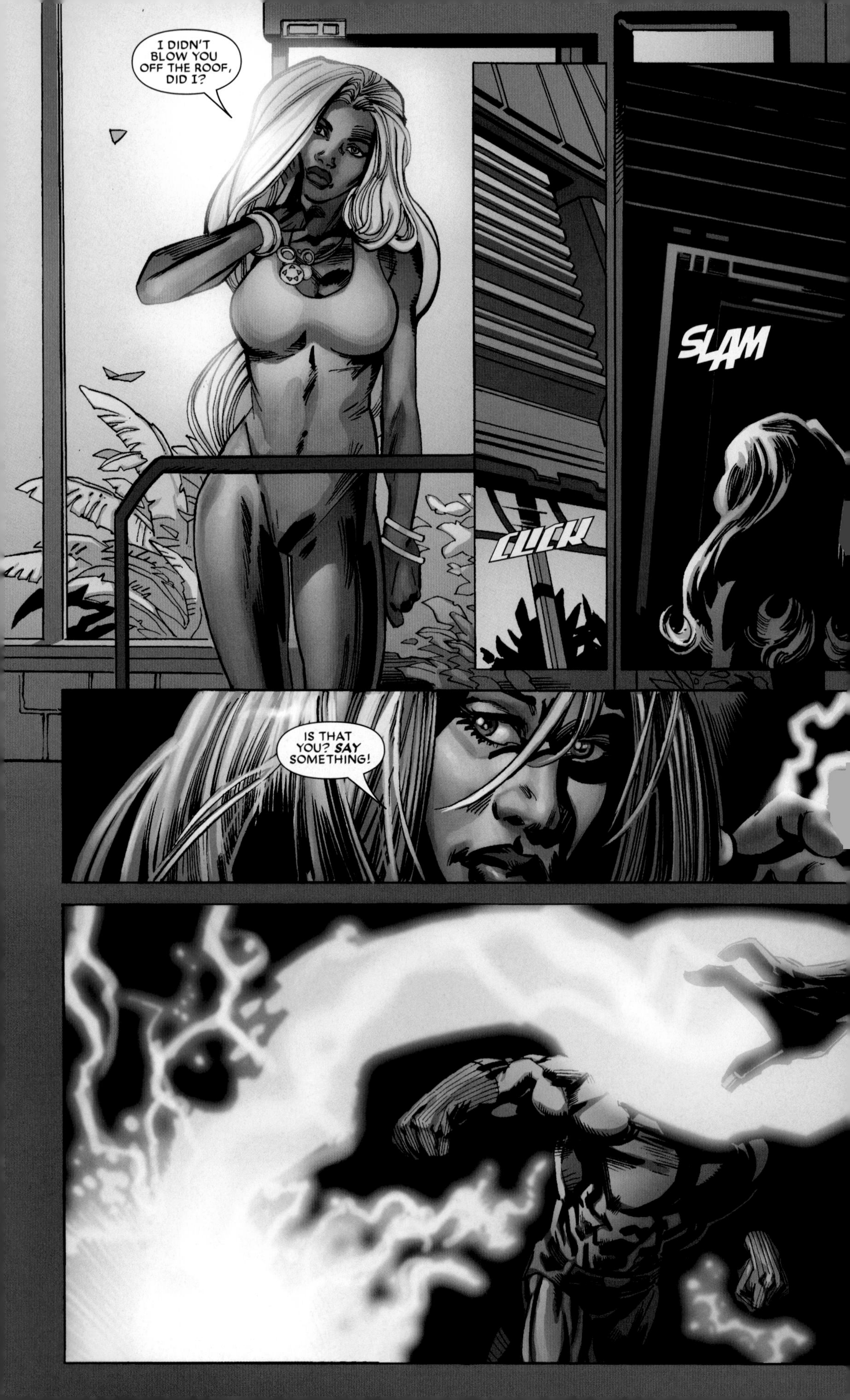
I DIDN'T BLOW YOU OFF THE ROOF, DID I?
CLICK
SLAM
IS THAT YOU? SAY SOMETHING!

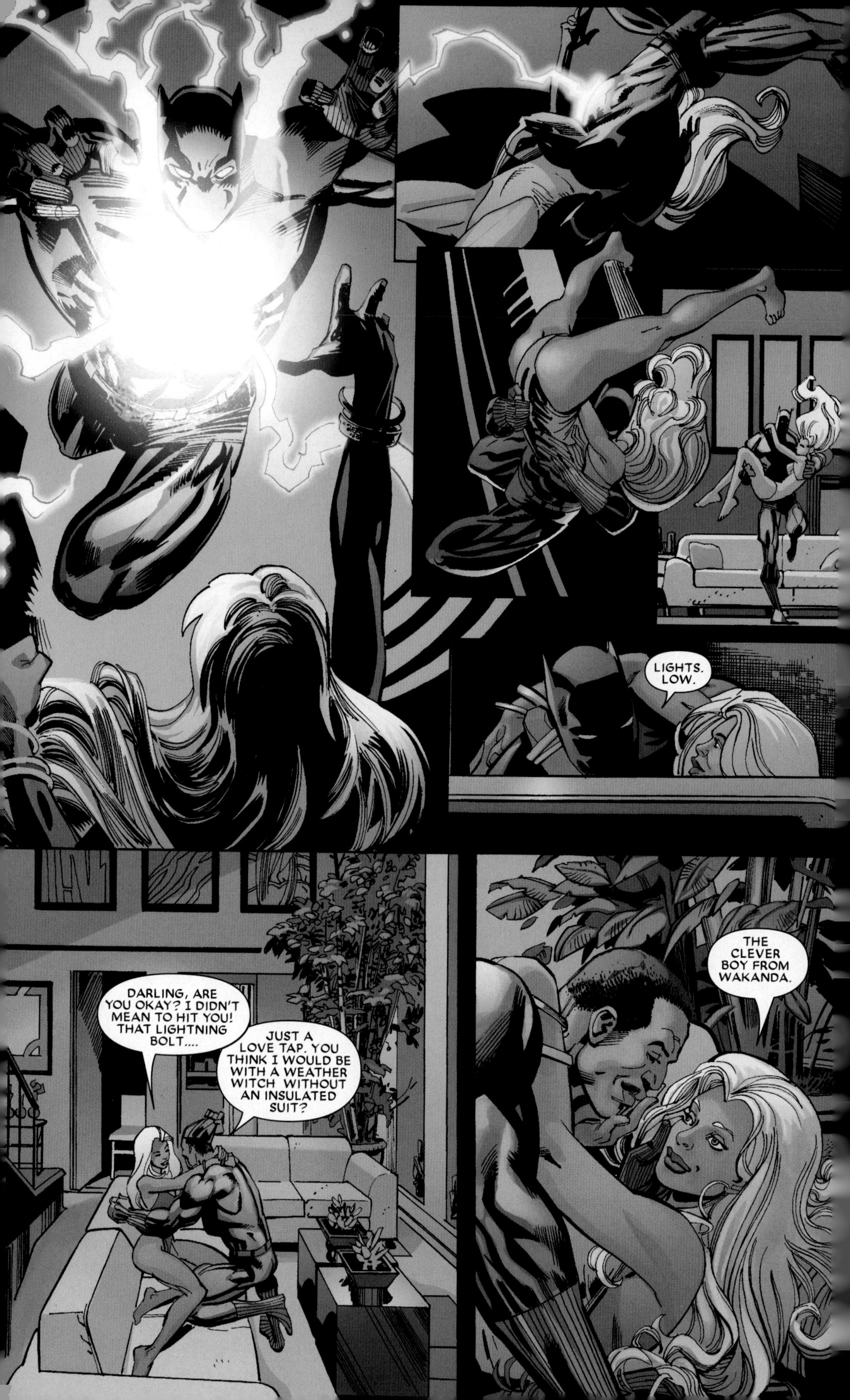
LIGHTS. LOW.
DARLING, ARE YOU OKAY? I DIDN'T MEAN TO HIT YOU! THAT LIGHTNING BOLT....
JUST A LOVE TAP. YOU THINK I WOULD BE WITH A WEATHER WITCH WITHOUT AN INSULATED SUIT?
THE CLEVER BOY FROM WAKANDA.

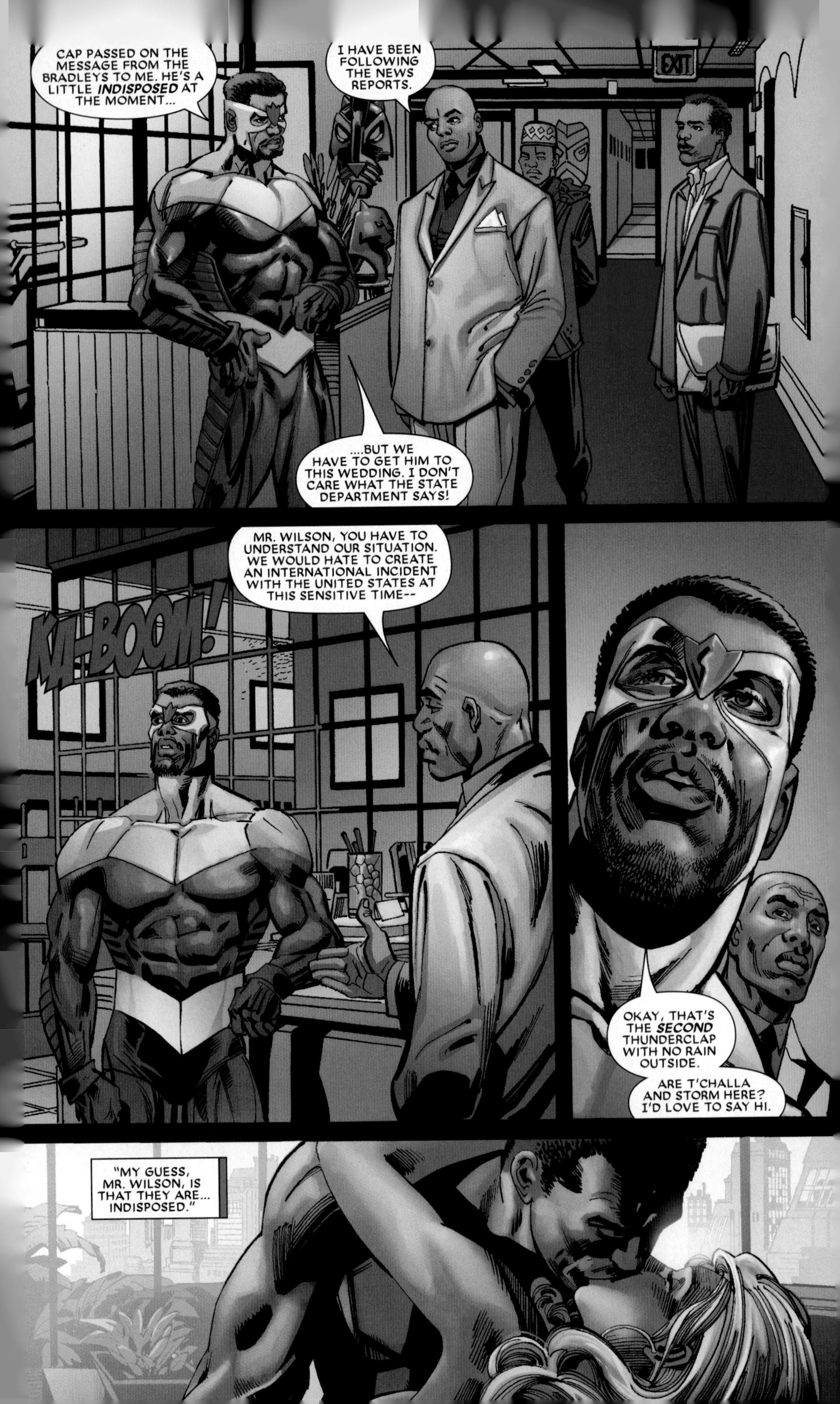
CAP PASSED ON THE MESSAGE FROM THE BRADLEYS TO ME. HE'S A LITTLE *INDISPOSED* AT THE MOMENT...
I HAVE BEEN FOLLOWING THE NEWS REPORTS.
EXIT
...BUT WE HAVE TO GET HIM TO THIS WEDDING. I DON'T CARE WHAT THE STATE DEPARTMENT SAYS!
MR. WILSON, YOU HAVE TO UNDERSTAND OUR SITUATION. WE WOULD HATE TO CREATE AN INTERNATIONAL INCIDENT WITH THE UNITED STATES AT THIS SENSITIVE TIME--
KA-BOOM!
OKAY, THAT'S THE *SECOND* THUNDERCLAP WITH NO RAIN OUTSIDE.
ARE T'CHALLA AND STORM HERE? I'D LOVE TO SAY HI.
"MY GUESS, MR. WILSON, IS THAT THEY ARE... INDISPOSED."

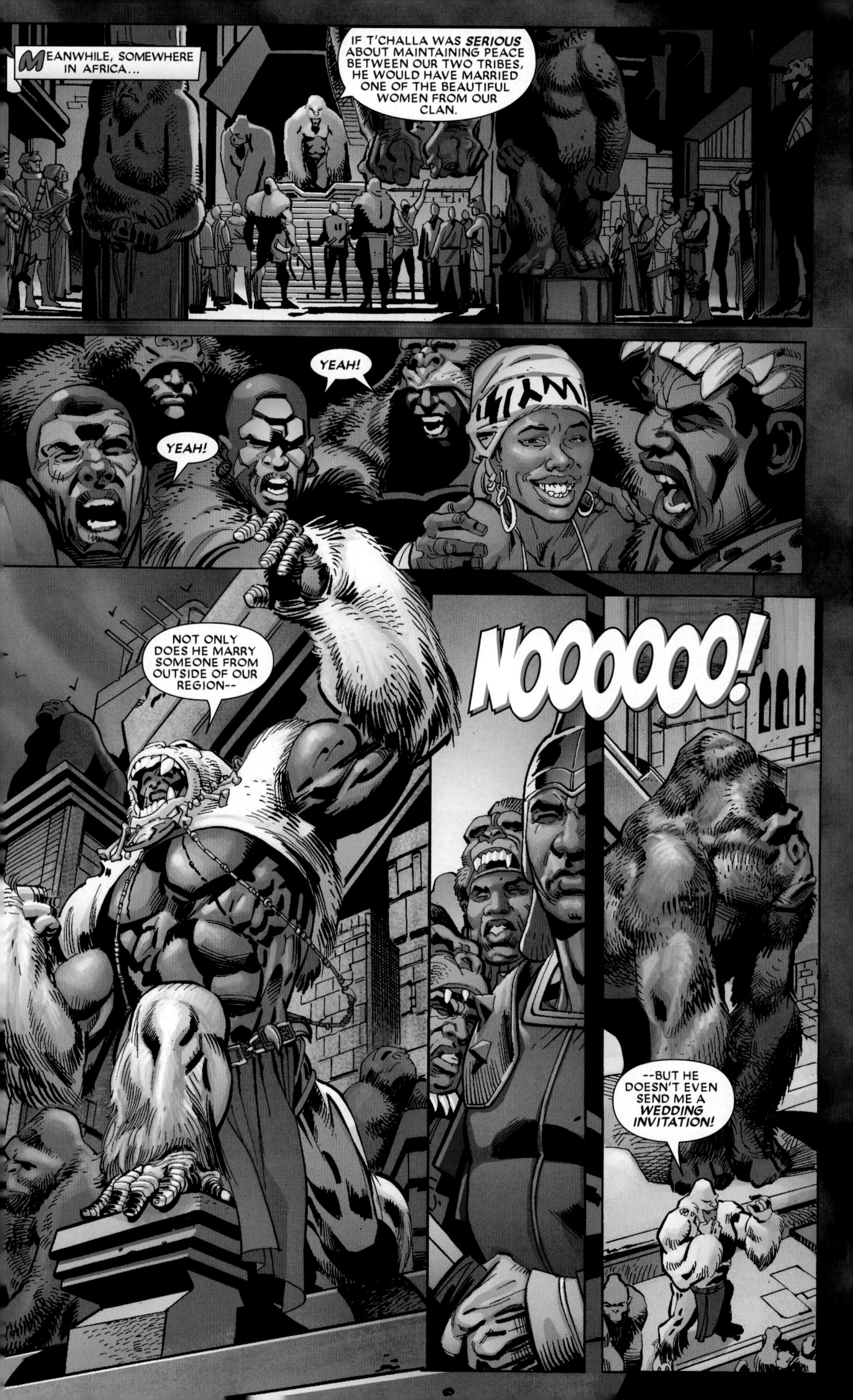
MEANWHILE, SOMEWHERE IN AFRICA...
IF T'CHALLA WAS SERIOUS ABOUT MAINTAINING PEACE BETWEEN OUR TWO TRIBES, HE WOULD HAVE MARRIED ONE OF THE BEAUTIFUL WOMEN FROM OUR CLAN.
YEAH!
YEAH!
NOT ONLY DOES HE MARRY SOMEONE FROM OUTSIDE OF OUR REGION--
NOOOOOO!
--BUT HE DOESN'T EVEN SEND ME A WEDDING INVITATION!

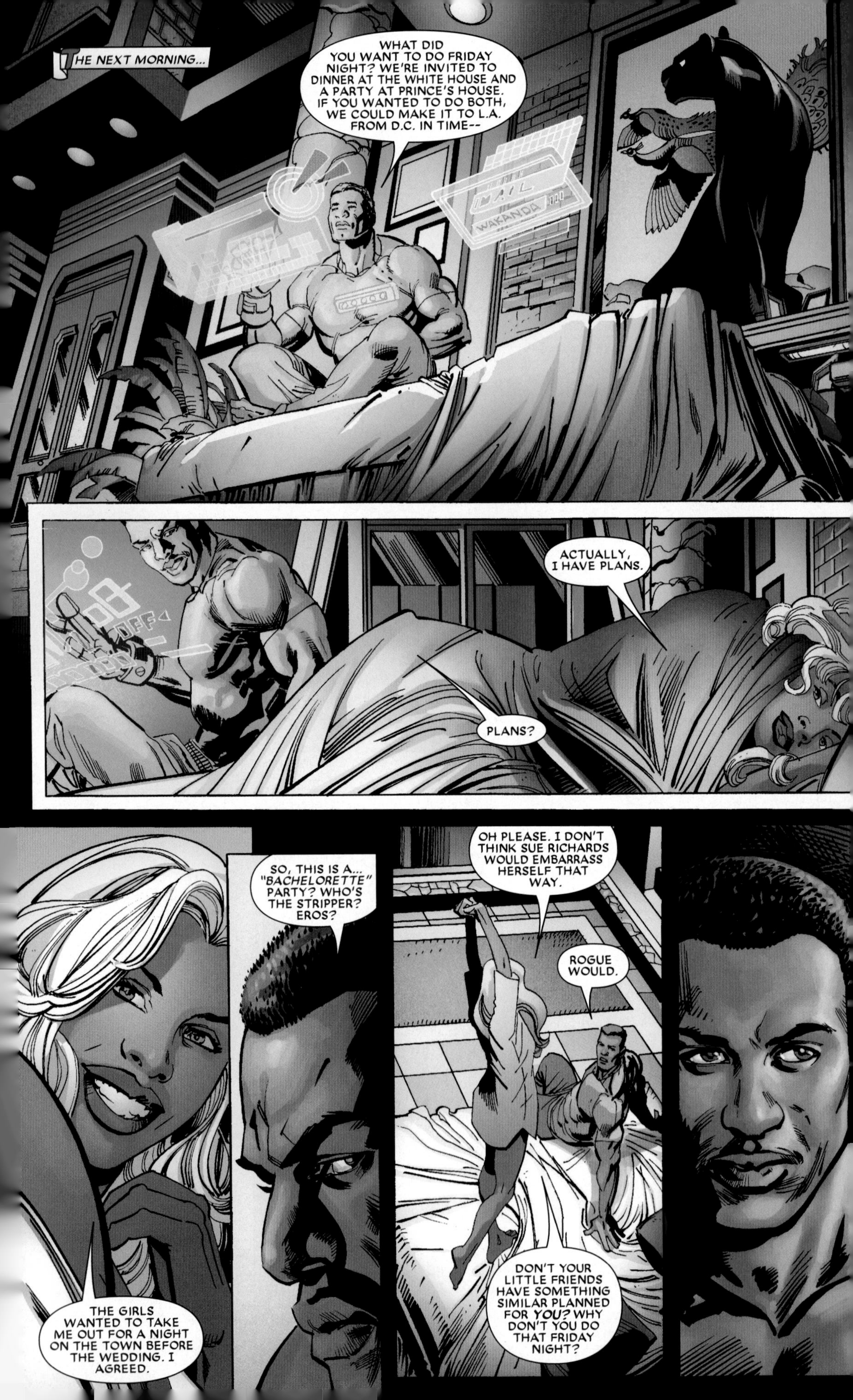
THE NEXT MORNING...
WHAT DID YOU WANT TO DO FRIDAY NIGHT? WE'RE INVITED TO DINNER AT THE WHITE HOUSE AND A PARTY AT PRINCE'S HOUSE. IF YOU WANTED TO DO BOTH, WE COULD MAKE IT TO L.A. FROM D.C. IN TIME--
MAIL
WAKANDA
ACTUALLY, I HAVE PLANS.
PLANS?
THE GIRLS WANTED TO TAKE ME OUT FOR A NIGHT ON THE TOWN BEFORE THE WEDDING. I AGREED.
SO, THIS IS A... "BACHELORETTE" PARTY? WHO'S THE STRIPPER? EROS?
OH PLEASE. I DON'T THINK SUE RICHARDS WOULD EMBARRASS HERSELF THAT WAY.
ROGUE WOULD.
DON'T YOUR LITTLE FRIENDS HAVE SOMETHING SIMILAR PLANNED FOR *YOU?* WHY DON'T YOU DO THAT FRIDAY NIGHT?

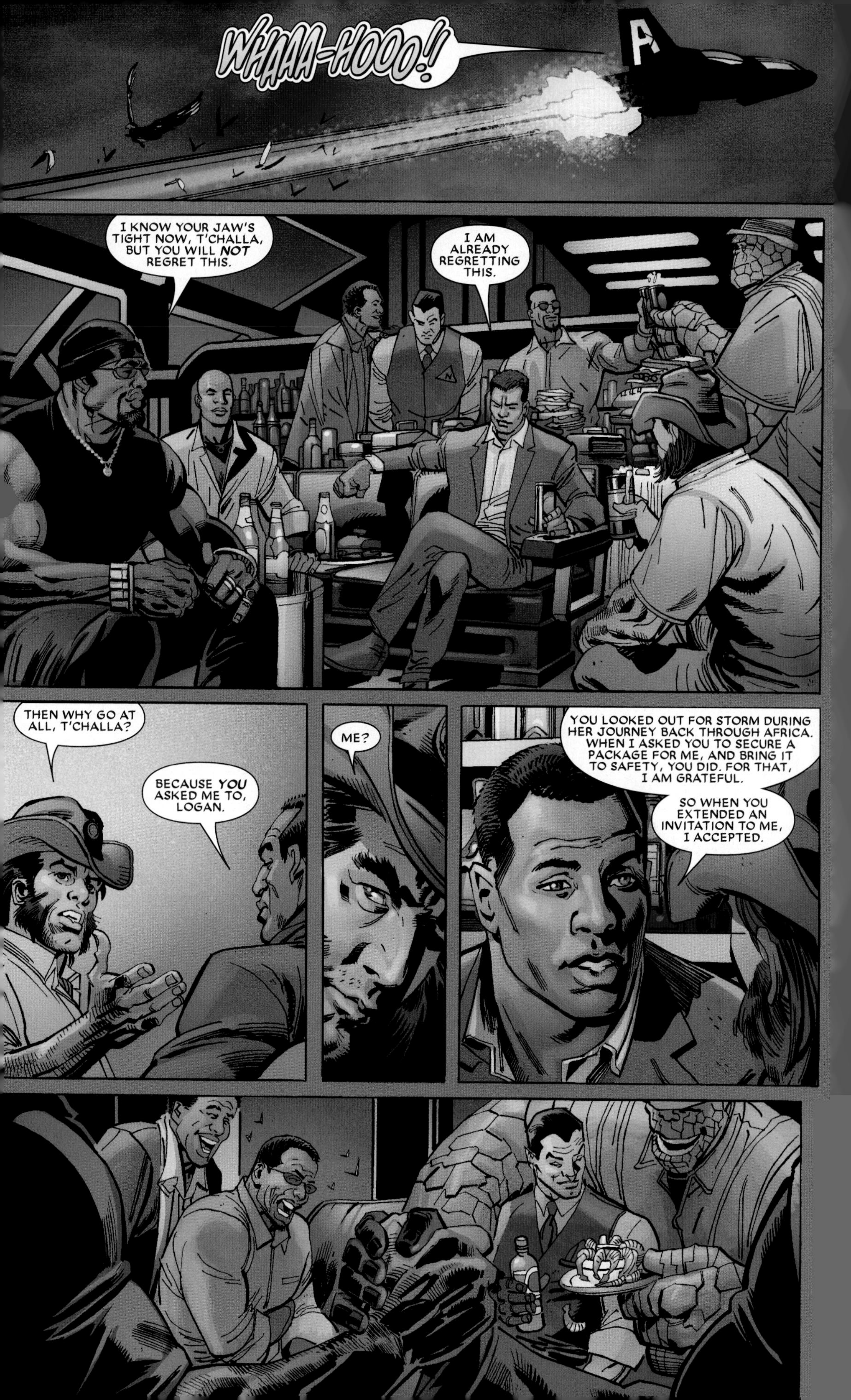
WHAAA-HOOO!!
I KNOW YOUR JAW'S TIGHT NOW, T'CHALLA, BUT YOU WILL **NOT** REGRET THIS.
I AM ALREADY REGRETTING THIS.
THEN WHY GO AT ALL, T'CHALLA?
BECAUSE **YOU** ASKED ME TO, LOGAN.
ME?
YOU LOOKED OUT FOR STORM DURING HER JOURNEY BACK THROUGH AFRICA. WHEN I ASKED YOU TO SECURE A PACKAGE FOR ME, AND BRING IT TO SAFETY, YOU DID. FOR THAT, I AM GRATEFUL.
SO WHEN YOU EXTENDED AN INVITATION TO ME, I ACCEPTED.

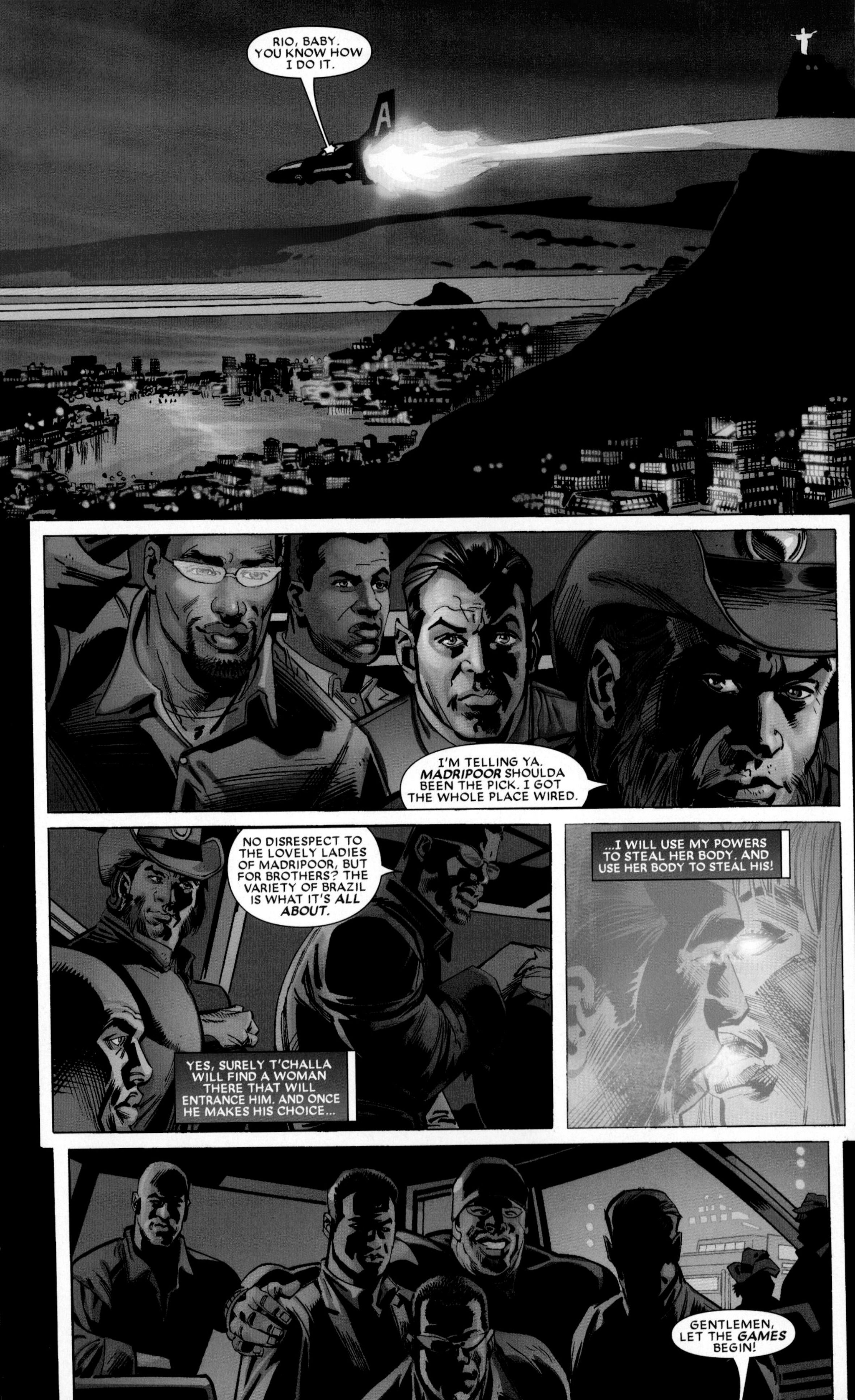
RIO, BABY. YOU KNOW HOW I DO IT.
I'M TELLING YA. MADRIPOOR SHOULDA BEEN THE PICK. I GOT THE WHOLE PLACE WIRED.
NO DISRESPECT TO THE LOVELY LADIES OF MADRIPOOR, BUT FOR BROTHERS? THE VARIETY OF BRAZIL IS WHAT IT'S ALL ABOUT.
YES, SURELY T'CHALLA WILL FIND A WOMAN THERE THAT WILL ENTRANCE HIM. AND ONCE HE MAKES HIS CHOICE...
...I WILL USE MY POWERS TO STEAL HER BODY. AND USE HER BODY TO STEAL HIS!
GENTLEMEN, LET THE GAMES BEGIN!

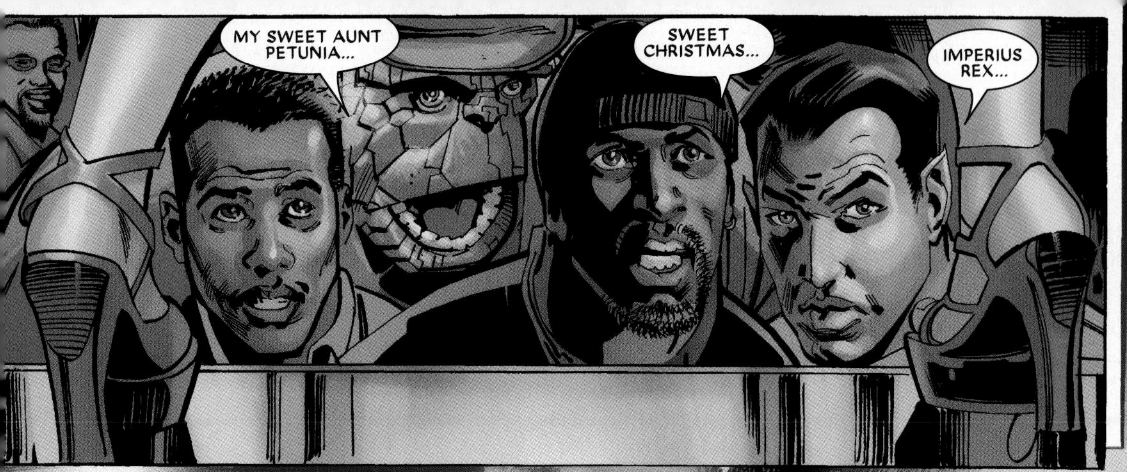
MY SWEET AUNT PETUNIA...
SWEET CHRISTMAS...
IMPERIUS REX...

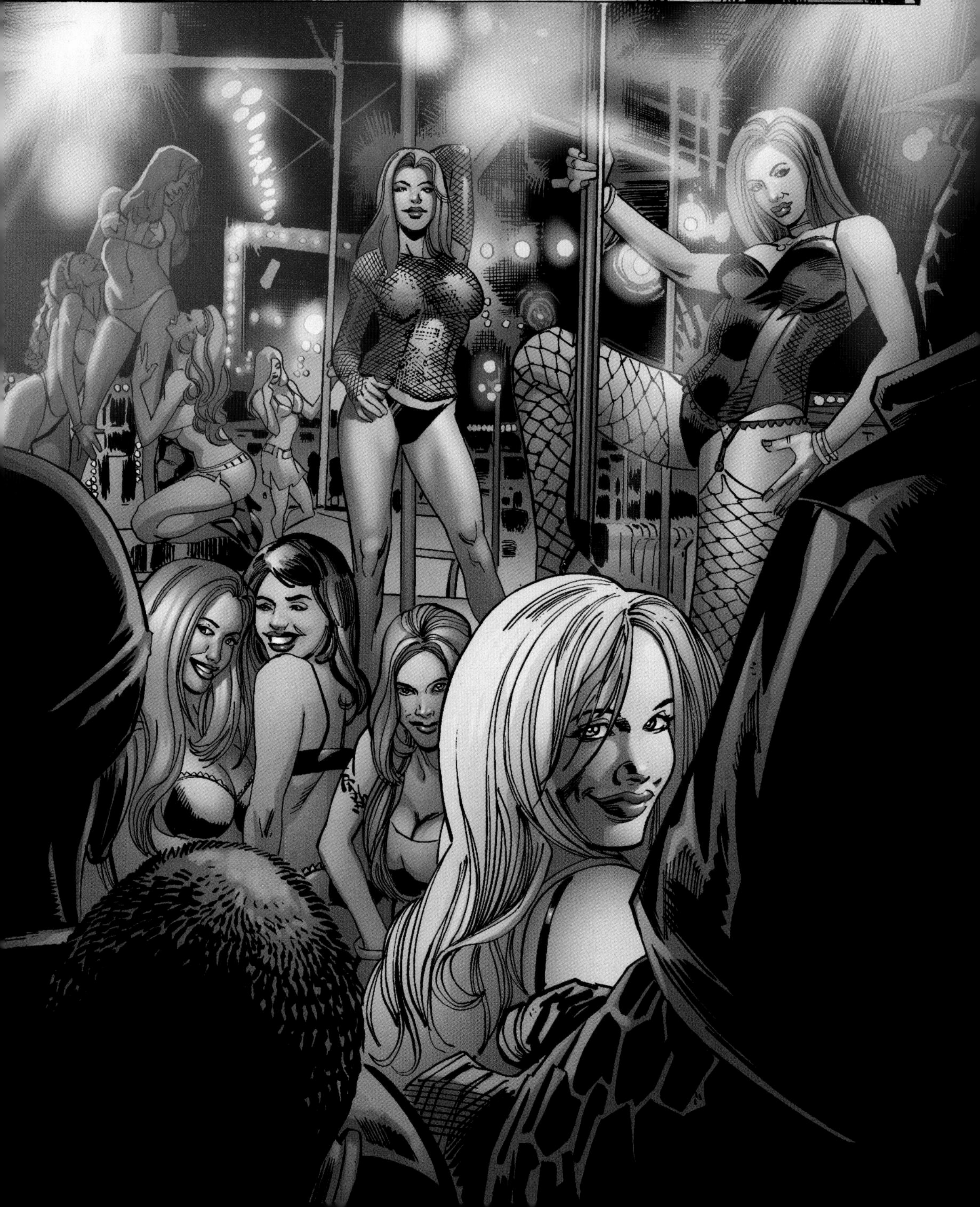

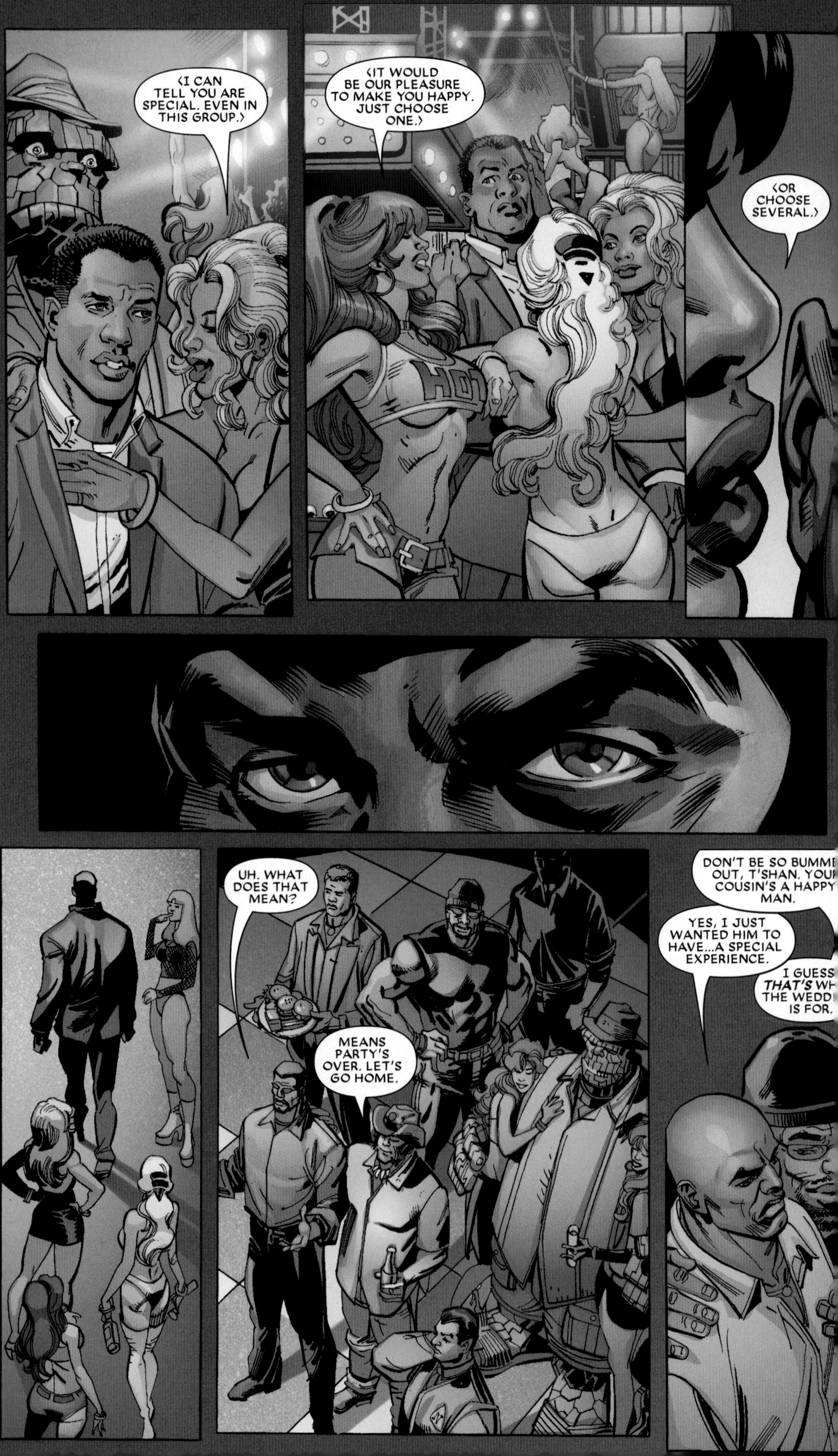
‹I CAN TELL YOU ARE SPECIAL. EVEN IN THIS GROUP.›
‹IT WOULD BE OUR PLEASURE TO MAKE YOU HAPPY. JUST CHOOSE ONE.›
HOT
‹OR CHOOSE SEVERAL.›
UH. WHAT DOES THAT MEAN?
MEANS PARTY'S OVER. LET'S GO HOME.
DON'T BE SO BUMME
OUT, T'SHAN. YOU
COUSIN'S A HAPPY MAN.
YES, I JUST WANTED HIM TO HAVE...A SPECIAL EXPERIENCE.
I GUESS
THAT'S W
THE WEDD
IS FOR.

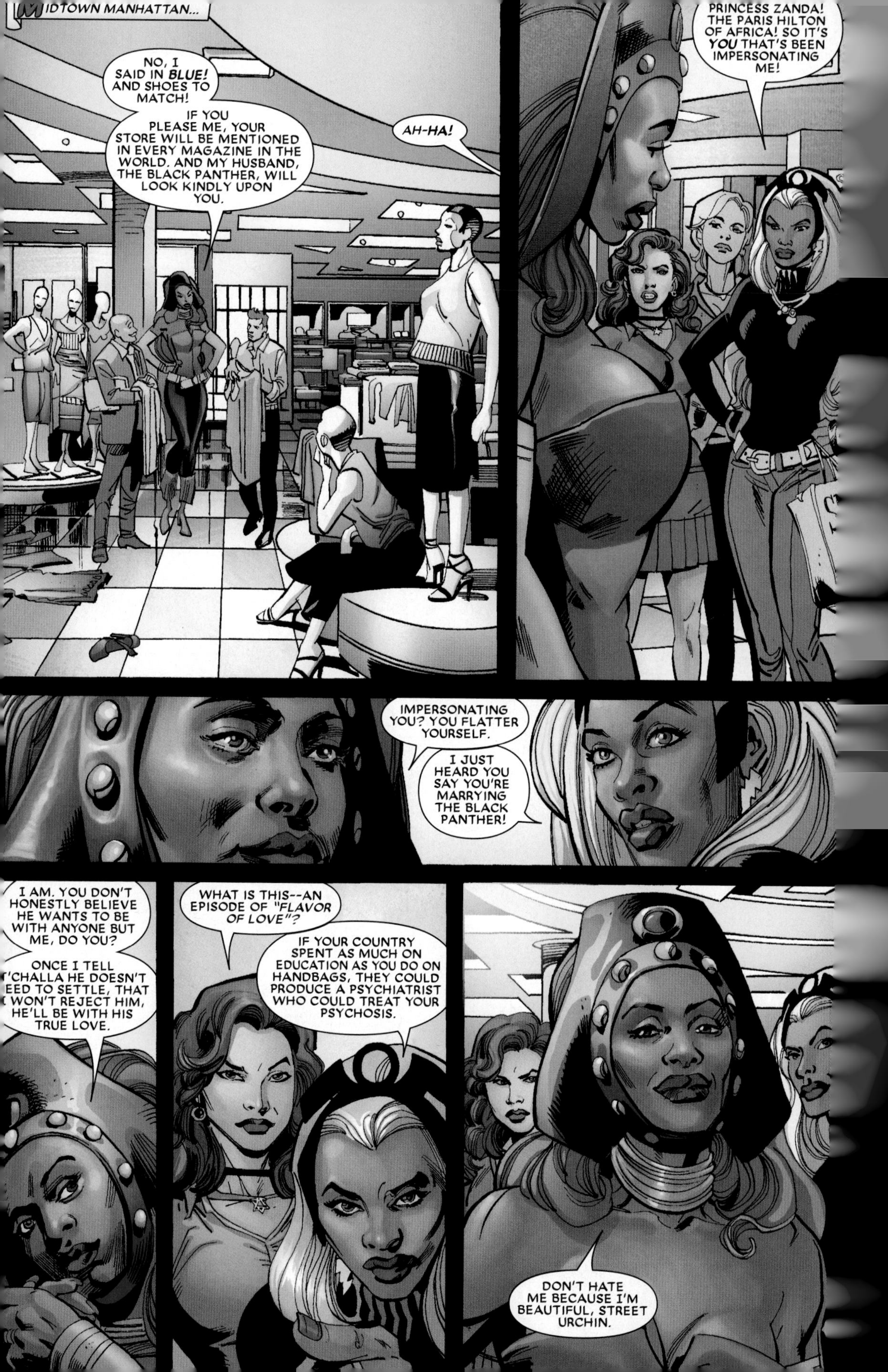
IDTOWN MANHATTAN...
NO, I SAID IN BLUE! AND SHOES TO MATCH!
IF YOU PLEASE ME, YOUR STORE WILL BE MENTIONED IN EVERY MAGAZINE IN THE WORLD. AND MY HUSBAND, THE BLACK PANTHER, WILL LOOK KINDLY UPON YOU.
AH-HA!
PRINCESS ZANDA! THE PARIS HILTON OF AFRICA! SO IT'S YOU THAT'S BEEN IMPERSONATING ME!
IMPERSONATING YOU? YOU FLATTER YOURSELF.
I JUST HEARD YOU SAY YOU'RE MARRYING THE BLACK PANTHER!
I AM. YOU DON'T HONESTLY BELIEVE HE WANTS TO BE WITH ANYONE BUT ME, DO YOU?
ONCE I TELL 'CHALLA HE DOESN'T EED TO SETTLE, THAT WON'T REJECT HIM, HE'LL BE WITH HIS TRUE LOVE.
WHAT IS THIS--AN EPISODE OF "FLAVOR OF LOVE"?
IF YOUR COUNTRY SPENT AS MUCH ON EDUCATION AS YOU DO ON HANDBAGS, THEY COULD PRODUCE A PSYCHIATRIST WHO COULD TREAT YOUR PSYCHOSIS.
DON'T HATE ME BECAUSE I'M BEAUTIFUL, STREET URCHIN.

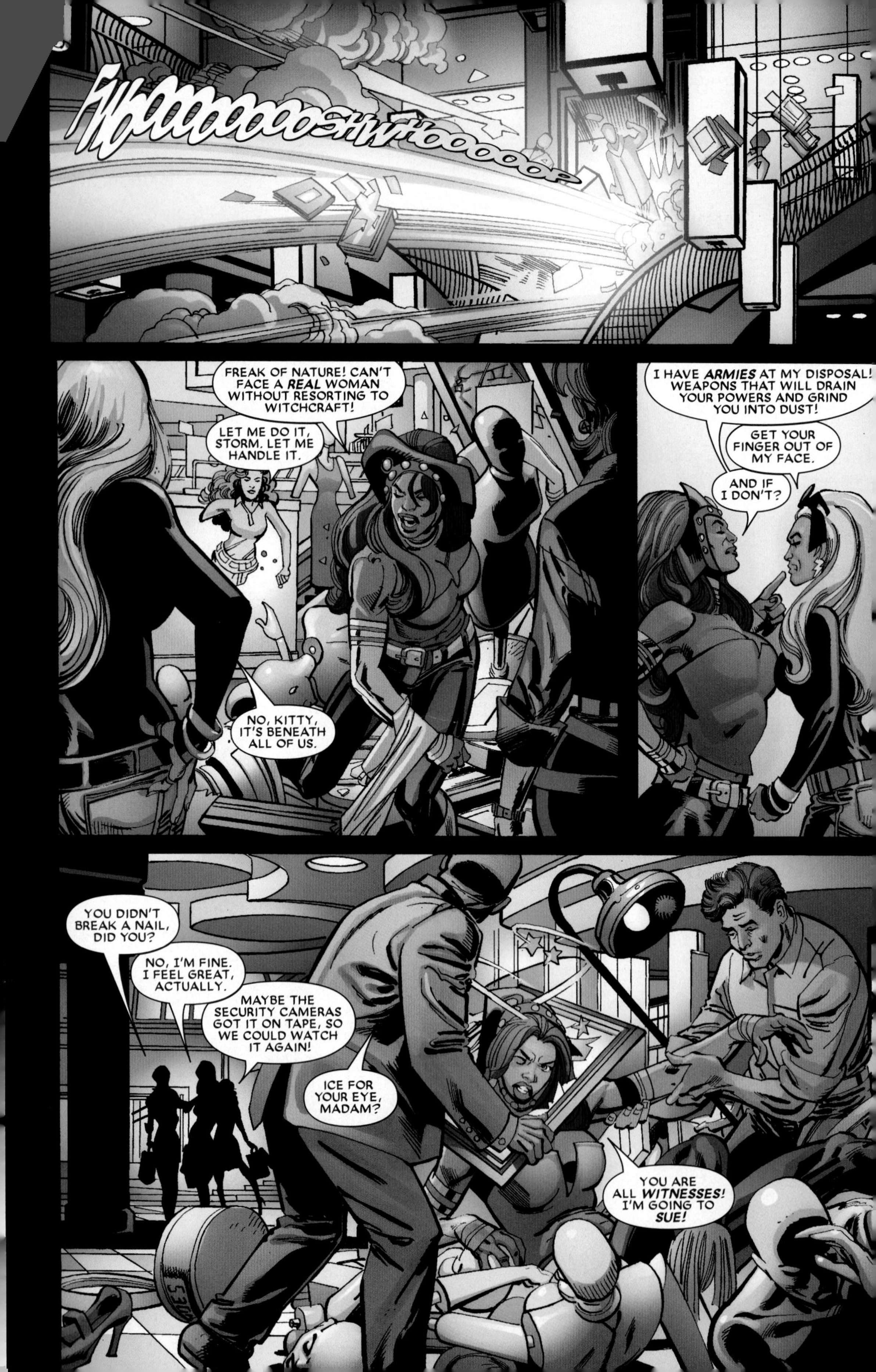

FWOOOOOOOOSHWHOOOOOOP
FREAK OF NATURE! CAN'T FACE A *REAL* WOMAN WITHOUT RESORTING TO WITCHCRAFT!
LET ME DO IT, STORM. LET ME HANDLE IT.
NO, KITTY, IT'S BENEATH ALL OF US.
I HAVE *ARMIES* AT MY DISPOSAL! WEAPONS THAT WILL DRAIN YOUR POWERS AND GRIND YOU INTO DUST!
GET YOUR FINGER OUT OF MY FACE.
AND IF I DON'T?
YOU DIDN'T BREAK A NAIL, DID YOU?
NO, I'M FINE. I FEEL GREAT, ACTUALLY.
MAYBE THE SECURITY CAMERAS GOT IT ON TAPE, SO WE COULD WATCH IT AGAIN!
ICE FOR YOUR EYE, MADAM?
YOU ARE ALL *WITNESSES!* I'M GOING TO *SUE!*

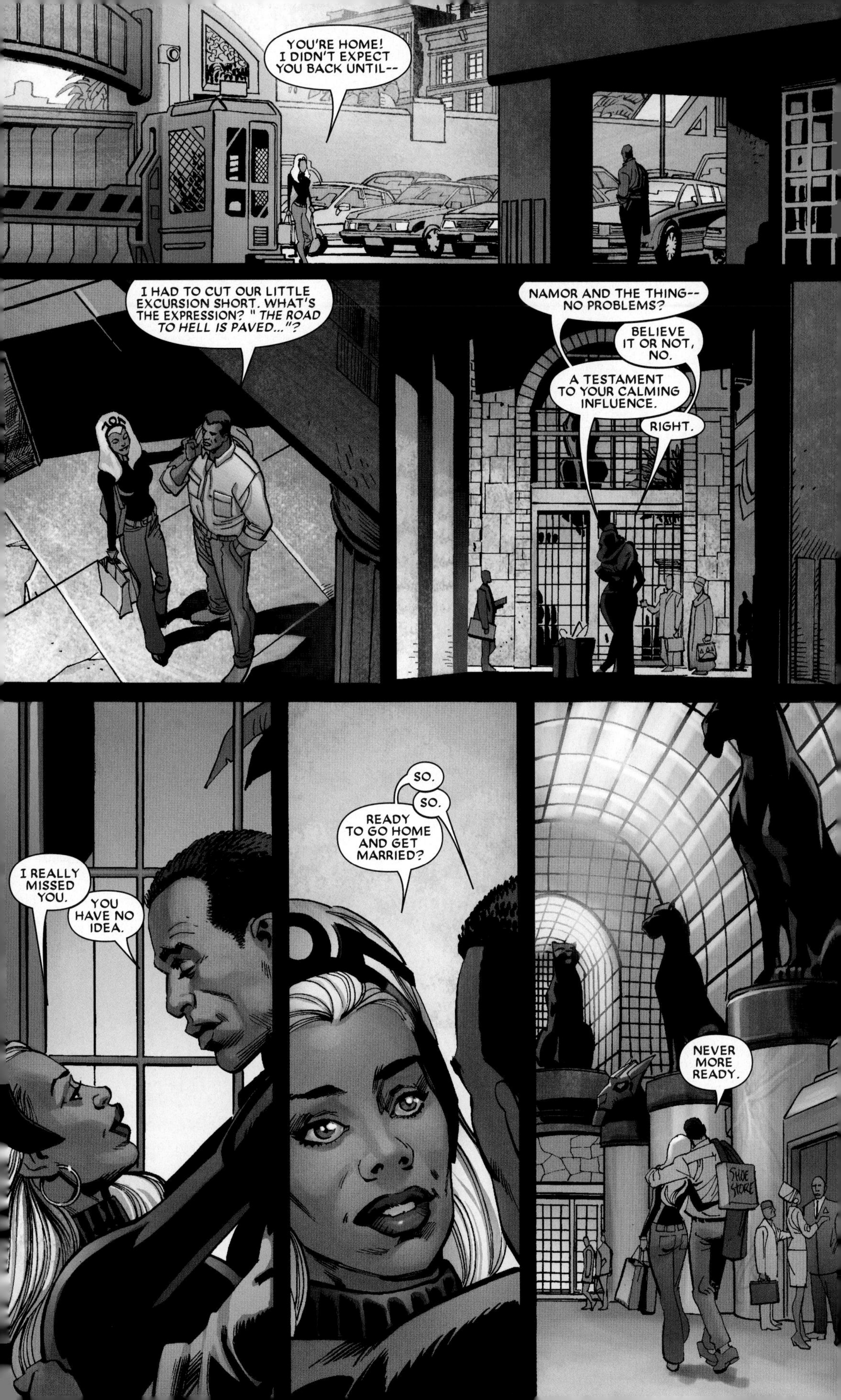

YOU'RE HOME! I DIDN'T EXPECT YOU BACK UNTIL--
I HAD TO CUT OUR LITTLE EXCURSION SHORT. WHAT'S THE EXPRESSION? " THE ROAD TO HELL IS PAVED..."?
NAMOR AND THE THING-- NO PROBLEMS?
BELIEVE IT OR NOT, NO.
A TESTAMENT TO YOUR CALMING INFLUENCE.
RIGHT.
I REALLY MISSED YOU.
YOU HAVE NO IDEA.
SO.
SO.
READY TO GO HOME AND GET MARRIED?
NEVER MORE READY.
SHOE STORE

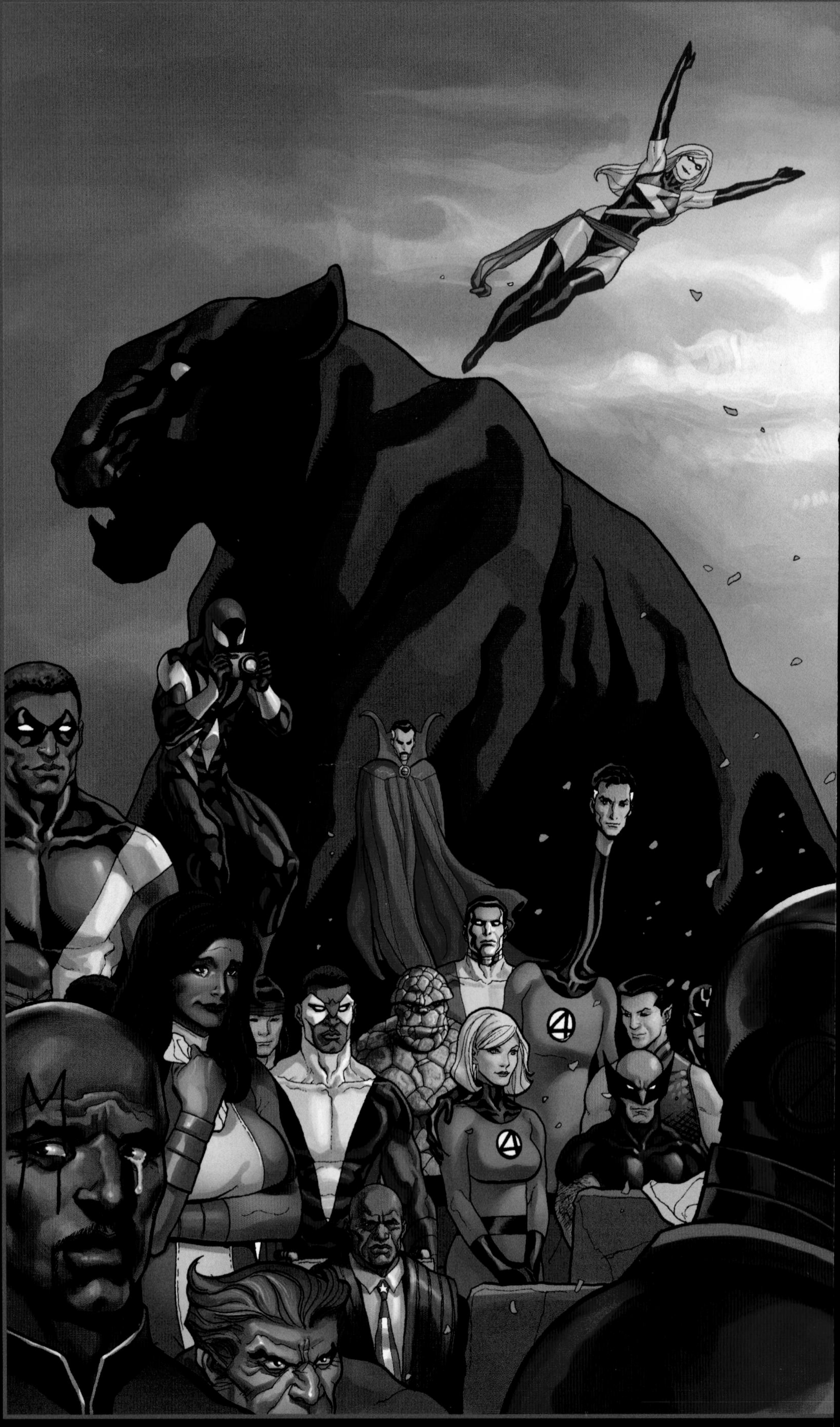

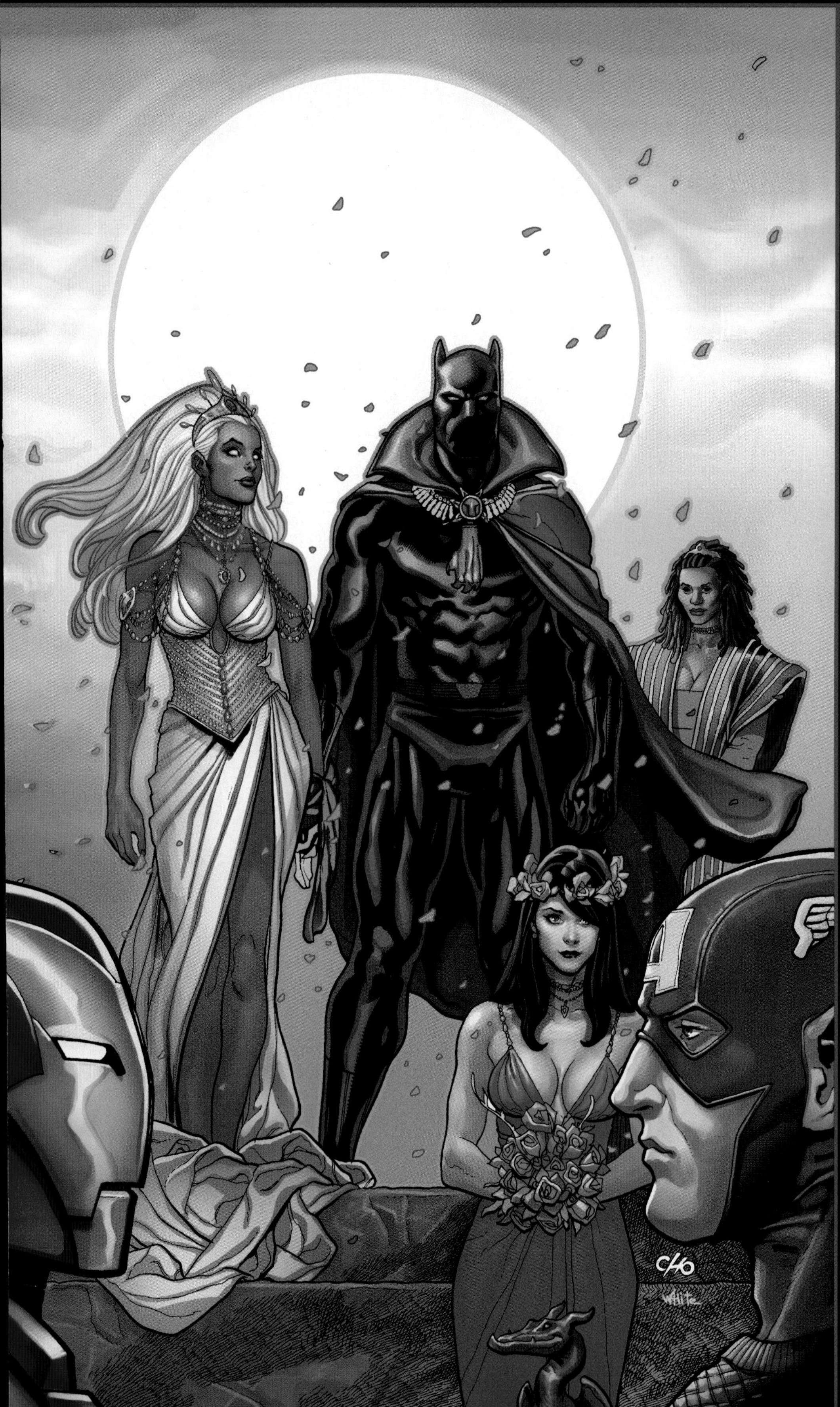
CHO
White

BRIDE OF THE PANTHER, PART 5: **HERE COME A STORM**

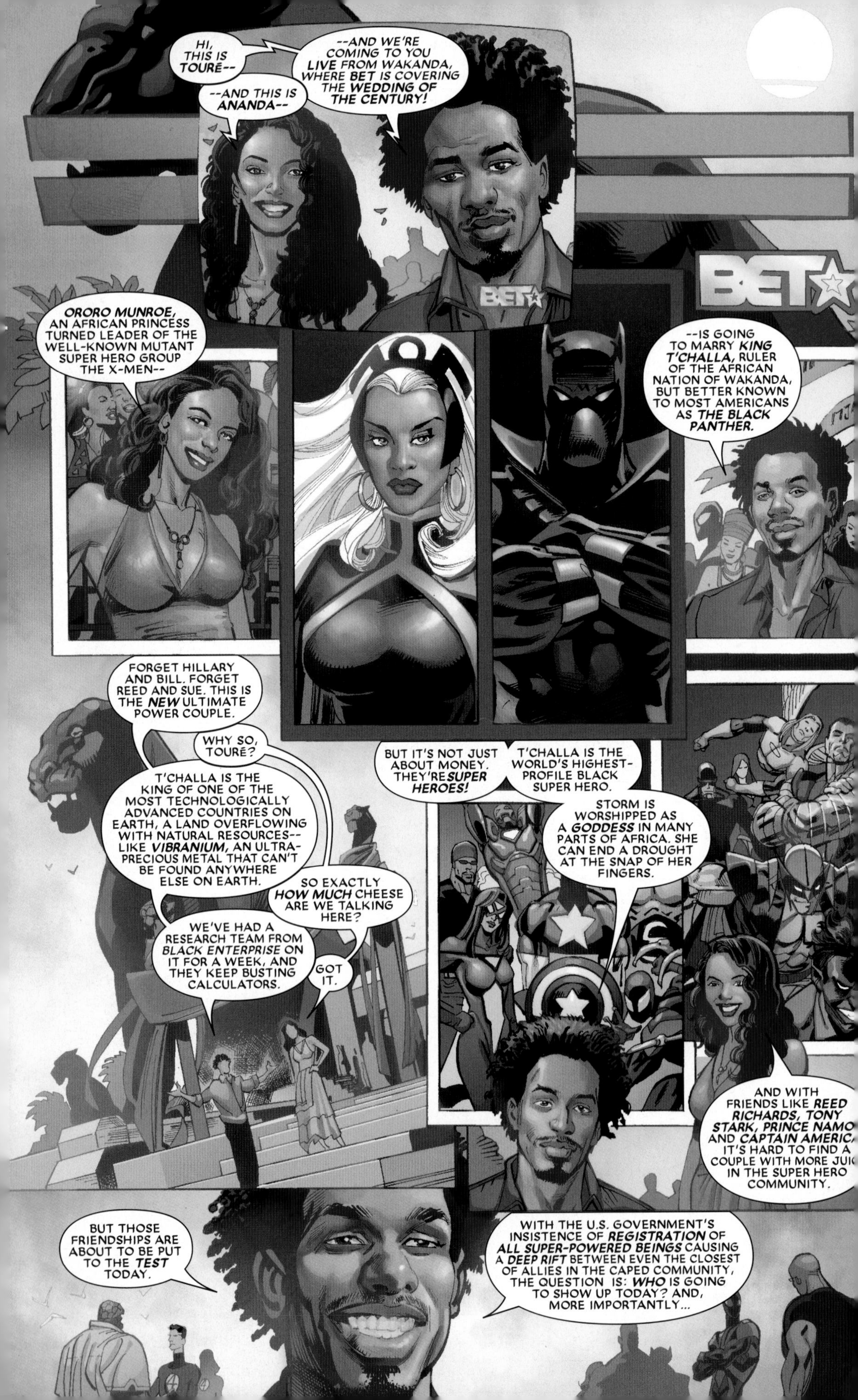
HI, THIS IS TOURÉ--
--AND THIS IS ANANDA--
--AND WE'RE COMING TO YOU LIVE FROM WAKANDA, WHERE BET IS COVERING THE WEDDING OF THE CENTURY!
BET
ORORO MUNROE, AN AFRICAN PRINCESS TURNED LEADER OF THE WELL-KNOWN MUTANT SUPER HERO GROUP THE X-MEN--
--IS GOING TO MARRY KING T'CHALLA, RULER OF THE AFRICAN NATION OF WAKANDA, BUT BETTER KNOWN TO MOST AMERICANS AS THE BLACK PANTHER.
FORGET HILLARY AND BILL. FORGET REED AND SUE. THIS IS THE NEW ULTIMATE POWER COUPLE.
WHY SO, TOURÉ?
T'CHALLA IS THE KING OF ONE OF THE MOST TECHNOLOGICALLY ADVANCED COUNTRIES ON EARTH, A LAND OVERFLOWING WITH NATURAL RESOURCES-- LIKE VIBRANIUM, AN ULTRA-PRECIOUS METAL THAT CAN'T BE FOUND ANYWHERE ELSE ON EARTH.
SO EXACTLY HOW MUCH CHEESE ARE WE TALKING HERE?
WE'VE HAD A RESEARCH TEAM FROM BLACK ENTERPRISE ON IT FOR A WEEK, AND THEY KEEP BUSTING CALCULATORS.
GOT IT.
BUT IT'S NOT JUST ABOUT MONEY. THEY'RE SUPER HEROES!
T'CHALLA IS THE WORLD'S HIGHEST-PROFILE BLACK SUPER HERO.
STORM IS WORSHIPPED AS A GODDESS IN MANY PARTS OF AFRICA. SHE CAN END A DROUGHT AT THE SNAP OF HER FINGERS.
AND WITH FRIENDS LIKE REED RICHARDS, TONY STARK, PRINCE NAMO AND CAPTAIN AMERIC IT'S HARD TO FIND A COUPLE WITH MORE JUI IN THE SUPER HERO COMMUNITY.
BUT THOSE FRIENDSHIPS ARE ABOUT TO BE PUT TO THE TEST TODAY.
WITH THE U.S. GOVERNMENT'S INSISTENCE OF REGISTRATION OF ALL SUPER-POWERED BEINGS CAUSING A DEEP RIFT BETWEEN EVEN THE CLOSEST OF ALLIES IN THE CAPED COMMUNITY, THE QUESTION IS: WHO IS GOING TO SHOW UP TODAY? AND, MORE IMPORTANTLY...

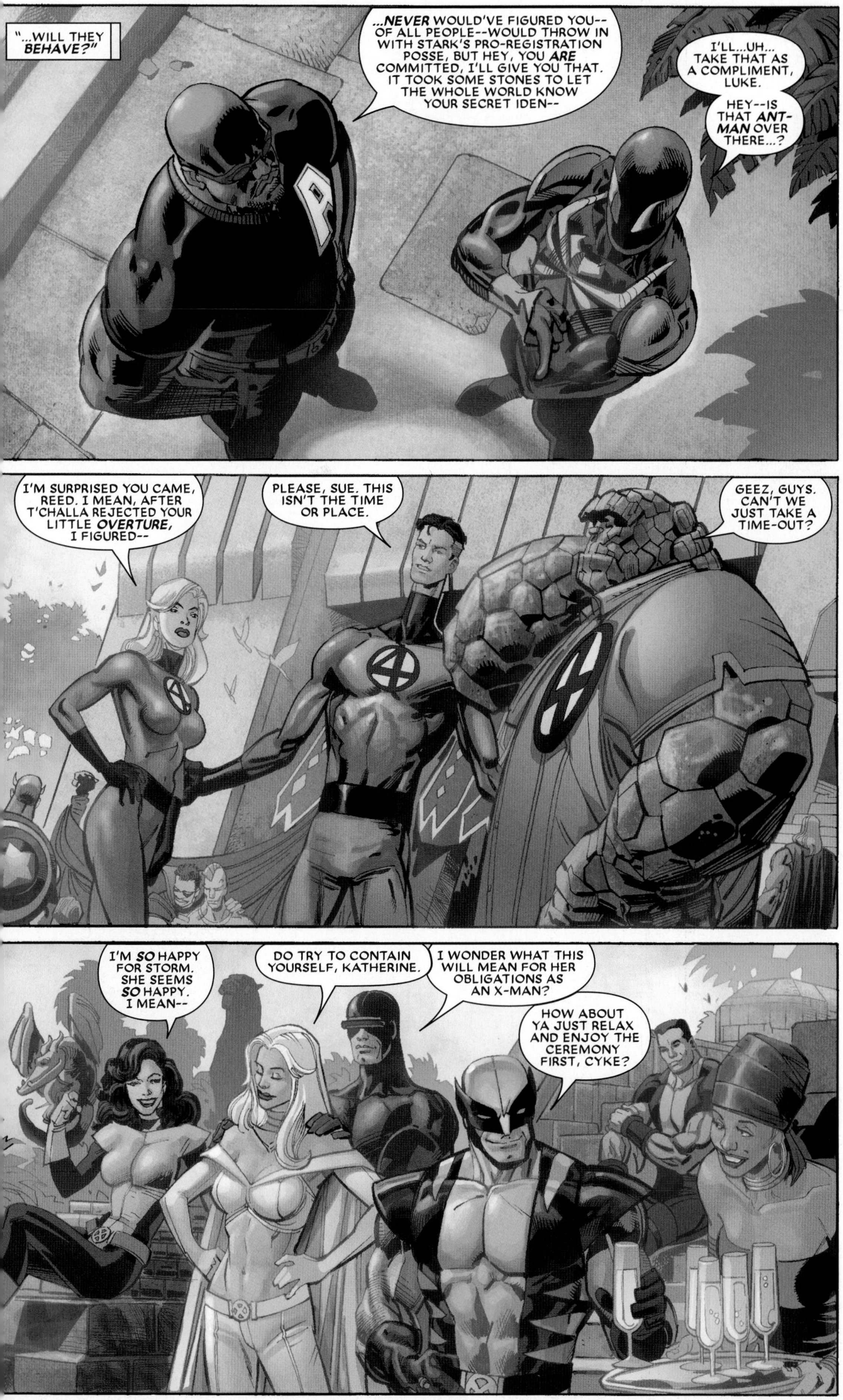
"...WILL THEY *BEHAVE?*"
...NEVER WOULD'VE FIGURED YOU-- OF ALL PEOPLE--WOULD THROW IN WITH STARK'S PRO-REGISTRATION POSSE, BUT HEY, YOU *ARE* COMMITTED, I'LL GIVE YOU THAT. IT TOOK SOME STONES TO LET THE WHOLE WORLD KNOW YOUR SECRET IDEN--
I'LL...UH... TAKE THAT AS A COMPLIMENT, LUKE.
HEY--IS THAT *ANT-MAN* OVER THERE...?
I'M SURPRISED YOU CAME, REED. I MEAN, AFTER T'CHALLA REJECTED YOUR LITTLE *OVERTURE,* I FIGURED--
PLEASE, SUE. THIS ISN'T THE TIME OR PLACE.
GEEZ, GUYS. CAN'T WE JUST TAKE A TIME-OUT?
I'M *SO* HAPPY FOR STORM. SHE SEEMS *SO* HAPPY. I MEAN--
DO TRY TO CONTAIN YOURSELF, KATHERINE.
I WONDER WHAT THIS WILL MEAN FOR HER OBLIGATIONS AS AN X-MAN?
HOW ABOUT YA JUST RELAX AND ENJOY THE CEREMONY FIRST, CYKE?

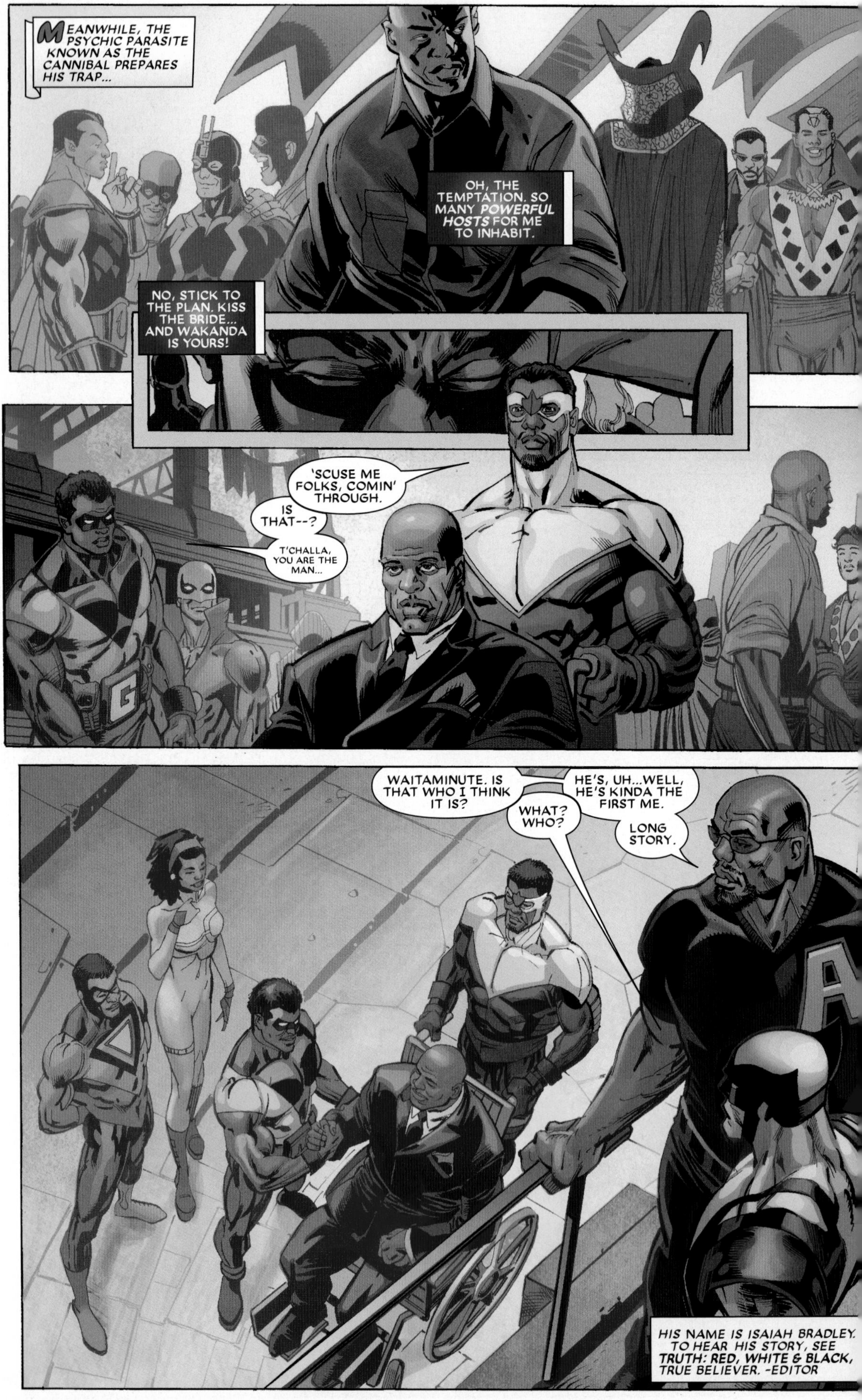
MEANWHILE, THE PSYCHIC PARASITE KNOWN AS THE CANNIBAL PREPARES HIS TRAP...
OH, THE TEMPTATION. SO MANY POWERFUL HOSTS FOR ME TO INHABIT.
NO, STICK TO THE PLAN. KISS THE BRIDE... AND WAKANDA IS YOURS!
'SCUSE ME FOLKS, COMIN' THROUGH.
IS THAT--?
T'CHALLA, YOU ARE THE MAN...
WAITAMINUTE. IS THAT WHO I THINK IT IS?
WHAT? WHO?
HE'S, UH...WELL, HE'S KINDA THE FIRST ME.
LONG STORY.
HIS NAME IS ISAIAH BRADLEY. TO HEAR HIS STORY, SEE TRUTH: RED, WHITE & BLACK, TRUE BELIEVER. -EDITOR

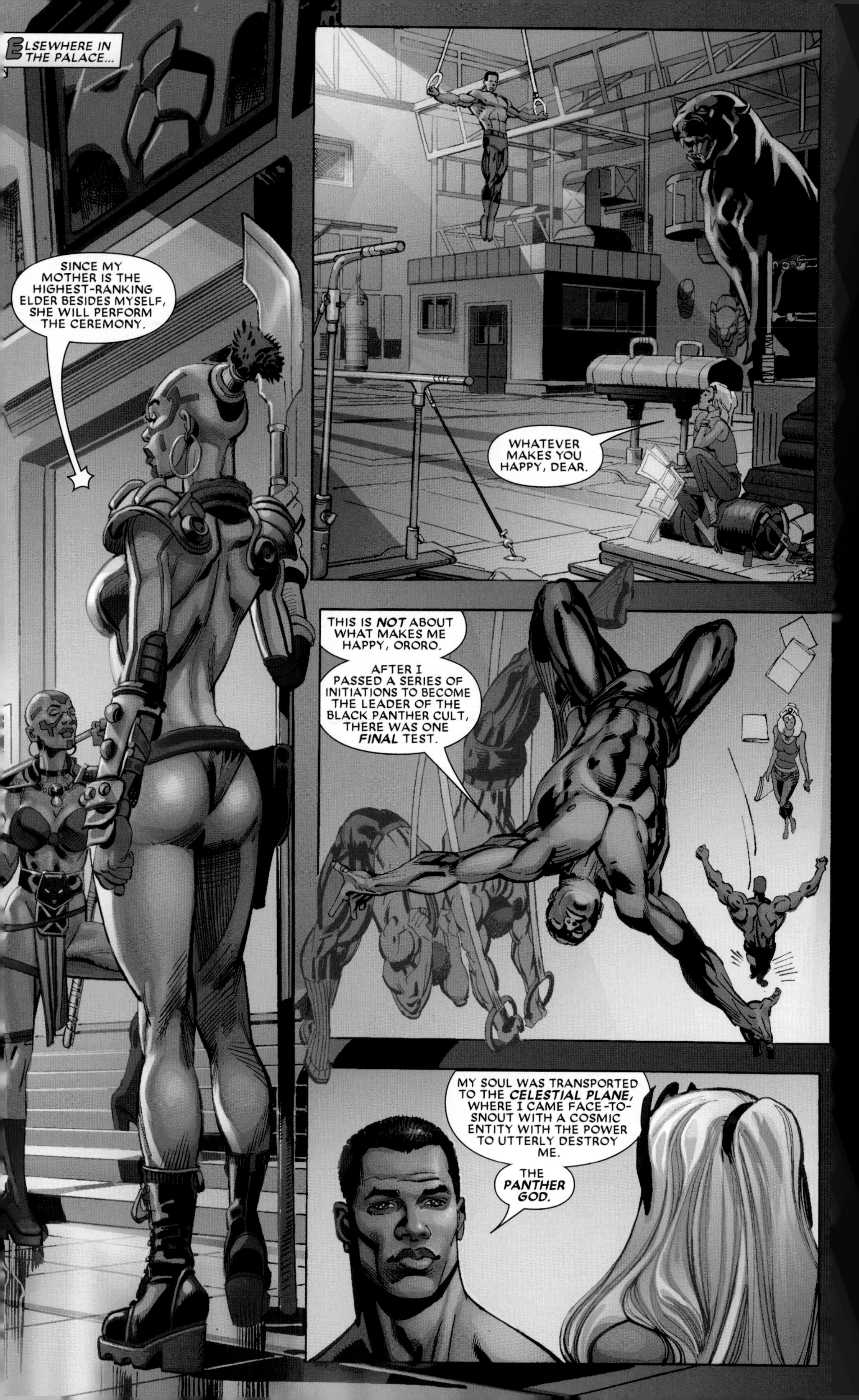
ELSEWHERE IN THE PALACE...
SINCE MY MOTHER IS THE HIGHEST-RANKING ELDER BESIDES MYSELF, SHE WILL PERFORM THE CEREMONY.
WHATEVER MAKES YOU HAPPY, DEAR.
THIS IS **NOT** ABOUT WHAT MAKES ME HAPPY, ORORO.
AFTER I PASSED A SERIES OF INITIATIONS TO BECOME THE LEADER OF THE BLACK PANTHER CULT, THERE WAS ONE **FINAL** TEST.
MY SOUL WAS TRANSPORTED TO THE **CELESTIAL PLANE,** WHERE I CAME FACE-TO-SNOUT WITH A COSMIC ENTITY WITH THE POWER TO UTTERLY DESTROY ME.
THE **PANTHER GOD.**

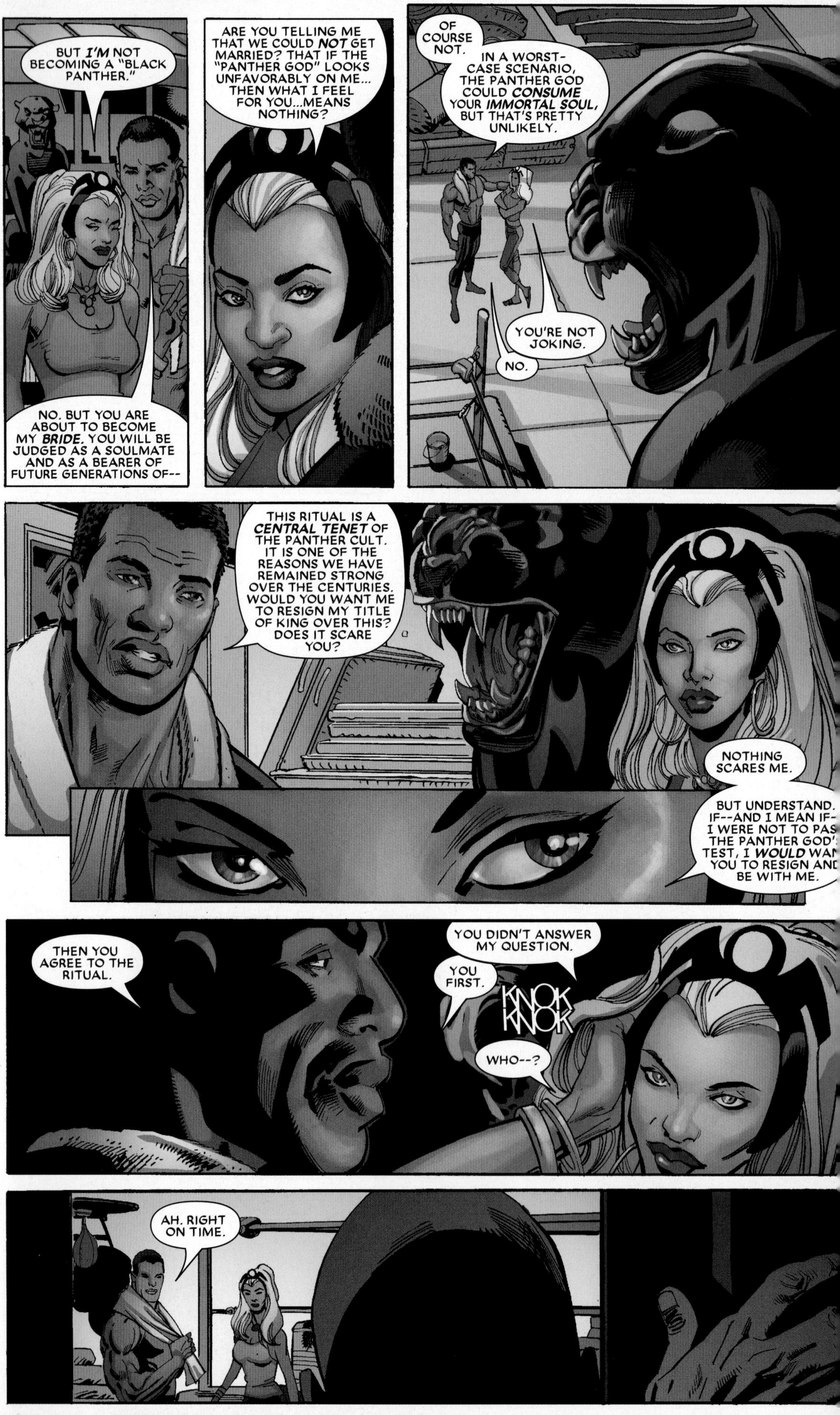
BUT I'M NOT BECOMING A "BLACK PANTHER."
NO. BUT YOU ARE ABOUT TO BECOME MY BRIDE. YOU WILL BE JUDGED AS A SOULMATE AND AS A BEARER OF FUTURE GENERATIONS OF--
ARE YOU TELLING ME THAT WE COULD NOT GET MARRIED? THAT IF THE "PANTHER GOD" LOOKS UNFAVORABLY ON ME... THEN WHAT I FEEL FOR YOU...MEANS NOTHING?
OF COURSE NOT.
IN A WORST-CASE SCENARIO, THE PANTHER GOD COULD CONSUME YOUR IMMORTAL SOUL, BUT THAT'S PRETTY UNLIKELY.
YOU'RE NOT JOKING.
NO.
THIS RITUAL IS A CENTRAL TENET OF THE PANTHER CULT. IT IS ONE OF THE REASONS WE HAVE REMAINED STRONG OVER THE CENTURIES. WOULD YOU WANT ME TO RESIGN MY TITLE OF KING OVER THIS? DOES IT SCARE YOU?
NOTHING SCARES ME.
BUT UNDERSTAND. IF--AND I MEAN IF--I WERE NOT TO PAS THE PANTHER GOD' TEST, I WOULD WAN YOU TO RESIGN AND BE WITH ME.
THEN YOU AGREE TO THE RITUAL.
YOU DIDN'T ANSWER MY QUESTION.
YOU FIRST.
KNOK KNOK
WHO--?
AH. RIGHT ON TIME.

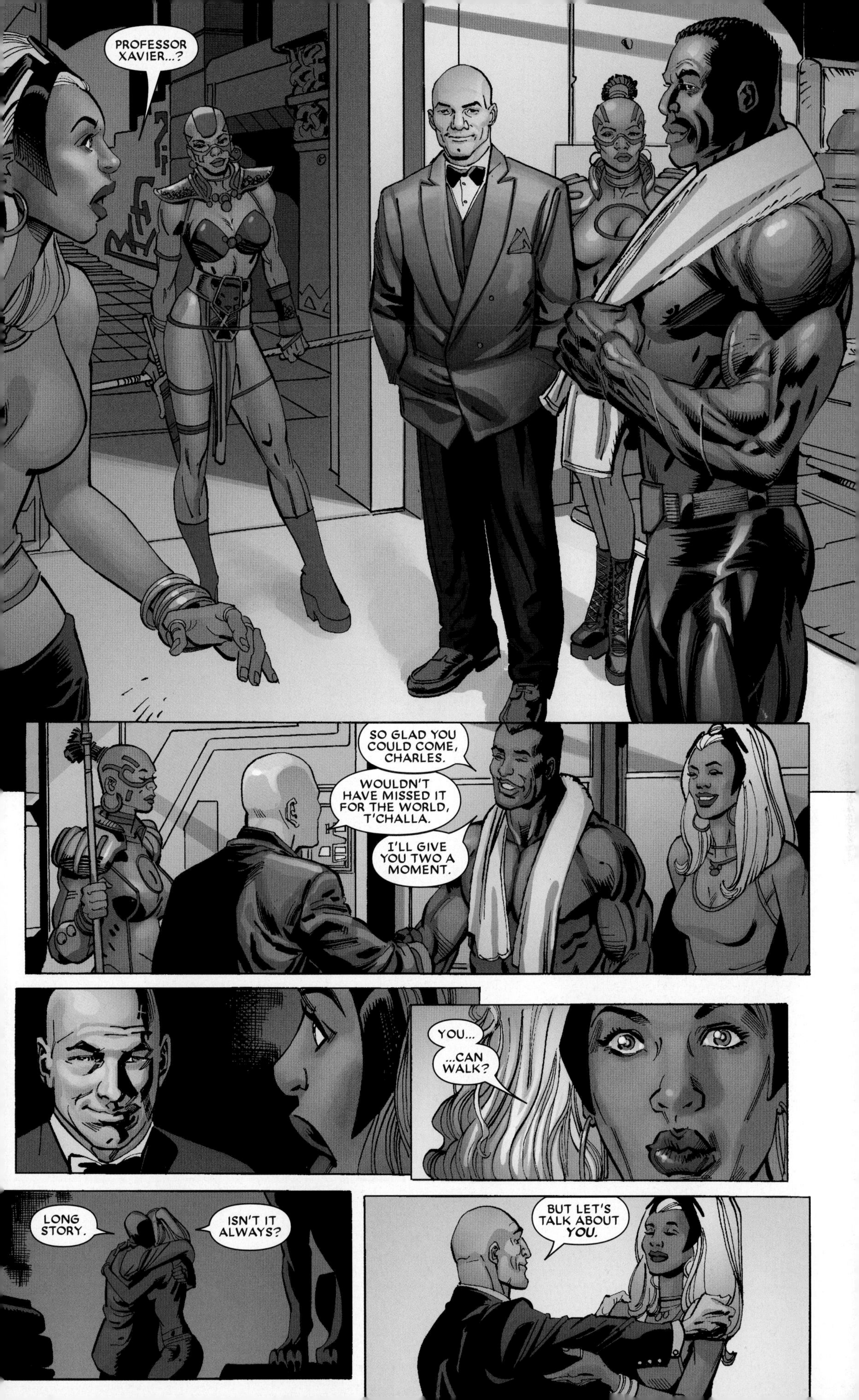

PROFESSOR XAVIER...?
SO GLAD YOU COULD COME, CHARLES.
WOULDN'T HAVE MISSED IT FOR THE WORLD, T'CHALLA.
I'LL GIVE YOU TWO A MOMENT.
YOU...
...CAN WALK?
LONG STORY.
ISN'T IT ALWAYS?
BUT LET'S TALK ABOUT *YOU.*

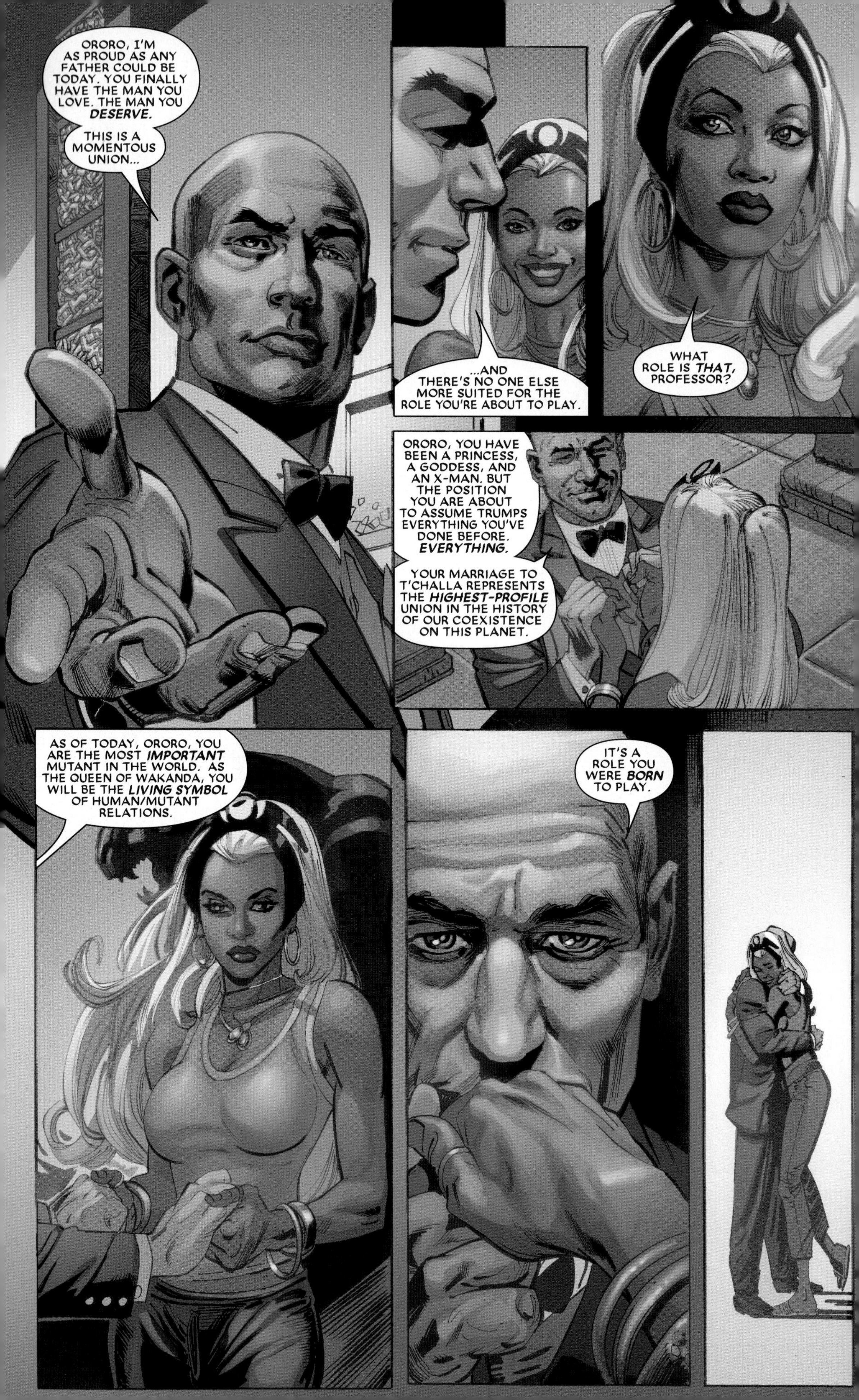

ORORO, I'M AS PROUD AS ANY FATHER COULD BE TODAY. YOU FINALLY HAVE THE MAN YOU LOVE. THE MAN YOU DESERVE.
THIS IS A MOMENTOUS UNION...
...AND THERE'S NO ONE ELSE MORE SUITED FOR THE ROLE YOU'RE ABOUT TO PLAY.
WHAT ROLE IS THAT, PROFESSOR?
ORORO, YOU HAVE BEEN A PRINCESS, A GODDESS, AND AN X-MAN. BUT THE POSITION YOU ARE ABOUT TO ASSUME TRUMPS EVERYTHING YOU'VE DONE BEFORE. EVERYTHING.
YOUR MARRIAGE TO T'CHALLA REPRESENTS THE HIGHEST-PROFILE UNION IN THE HISTORY OF OUR COEXISTENCE ON THIS PLANET.
AS OF TODAY, ORORO, YOU ARE THE MOST IMPORTANT MUTANT IN THE WORLD. AS THE QUEEN OF WAKANDA, YOU WILL BE THE LIVING SYMBOL OF HUMAN/MUTANT RELATIONS.
IT'S A ROLE YOU WERE BORN TO PLAY.

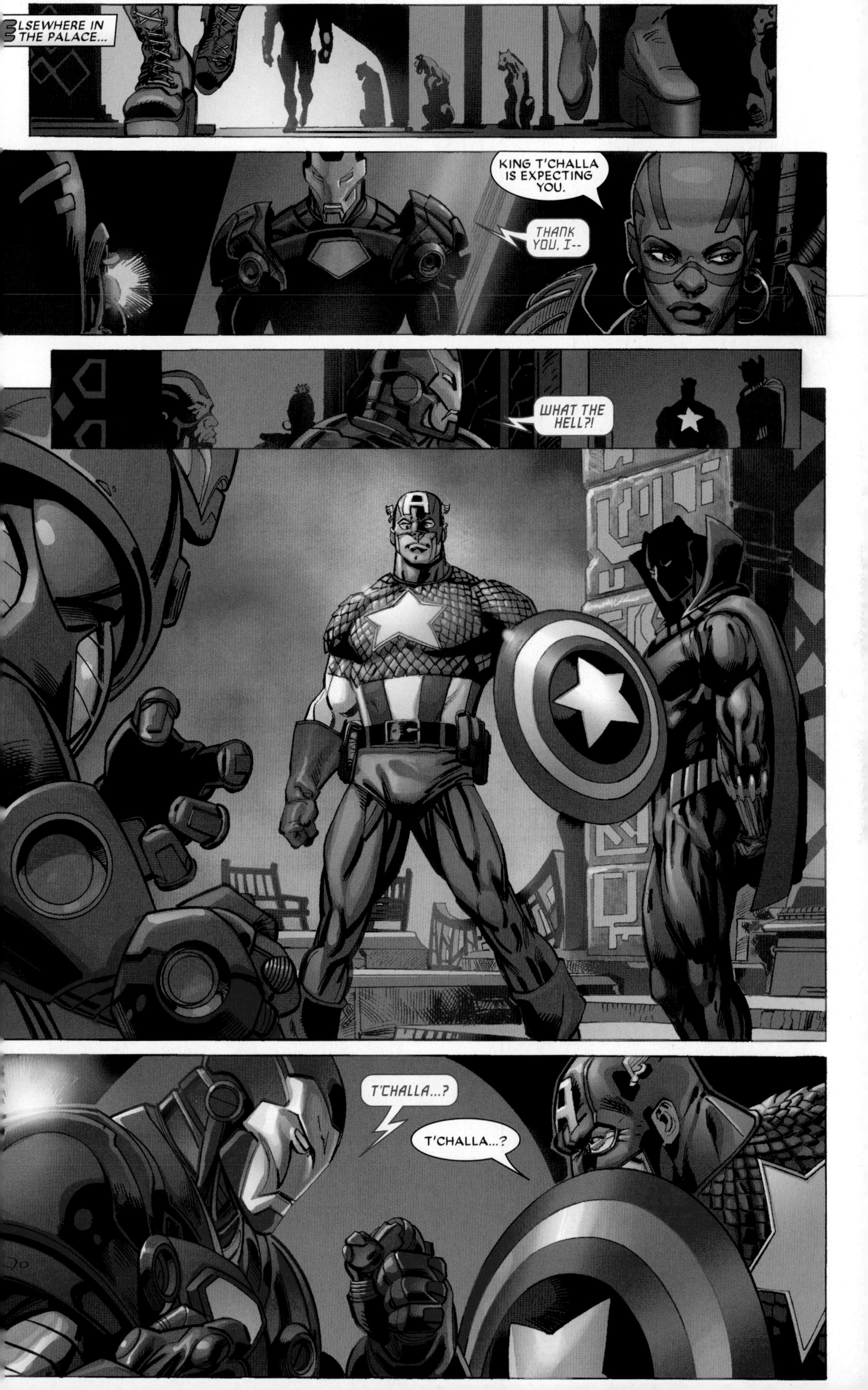
ELSEWHERE IN THE PALACE...
KING T'CHALLA IS EXPECTING YOU.
THANK YOU, I--
WHAT THE HELL?!
T'CHALLA...?
T'CHALLA...?

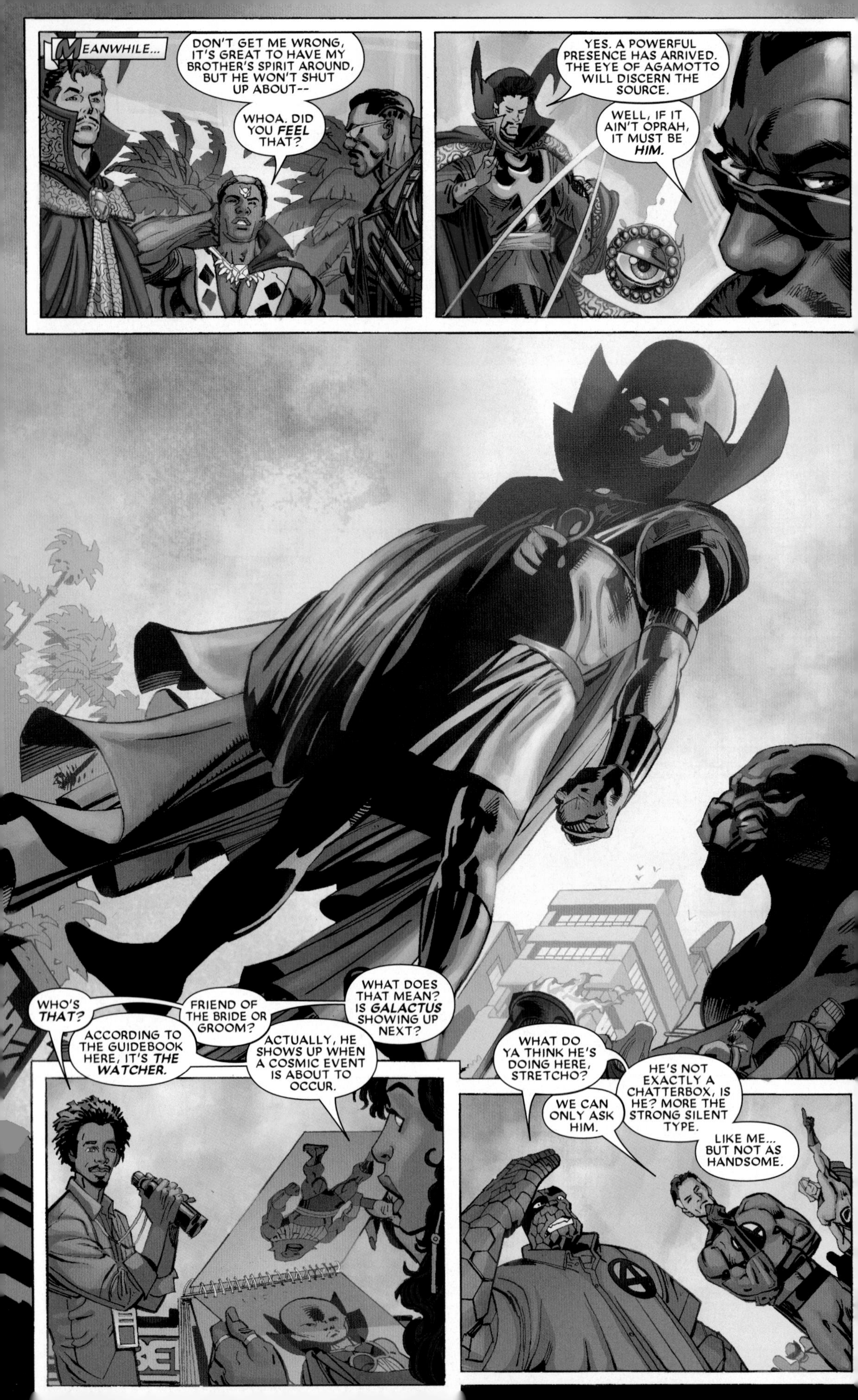
MEANWHILE...
DON'T GET ME WRONG, IT'S GREAT TO HAVE MY BROTHER'S SPIRIT AROUND, BUT HE WON'T SHUT UP ABOUT--
WHOA. DID YOU FEEL THAT?
YES. A POWERFUL PRESENCE HAS ARRIVED. THE EYE OF AGAMOTTO WILL DISCERN THE SOURCE.
WELL, IF IT AIN'T OPRAH, IT MUST BE HIM.
WHO'S THAT?
FRIEND OF THE BRIDE OR GROOM?
WHAT DOES THAT MEAN? IS GALACTUS SHOWING UP NEXT?
ACCORDING TO THE GUIDEBOOK HERE, IT'S THE WATCHER.
ACTUALLY, HE SHOWS UP WHEN A COSMIC EVENT IS ABOUT TO OCCUR.
WHAT DO YA THINK HE'S DOING HERE, STRETCHO?
WE CAN ONLY ASK HIM.
HE'S NOT EXACTLY A CHATTERBOX, IS HE? MORE THE STRONG SILENT TYPE.
LIKE ME... BUT NOT AS HANDSOME.

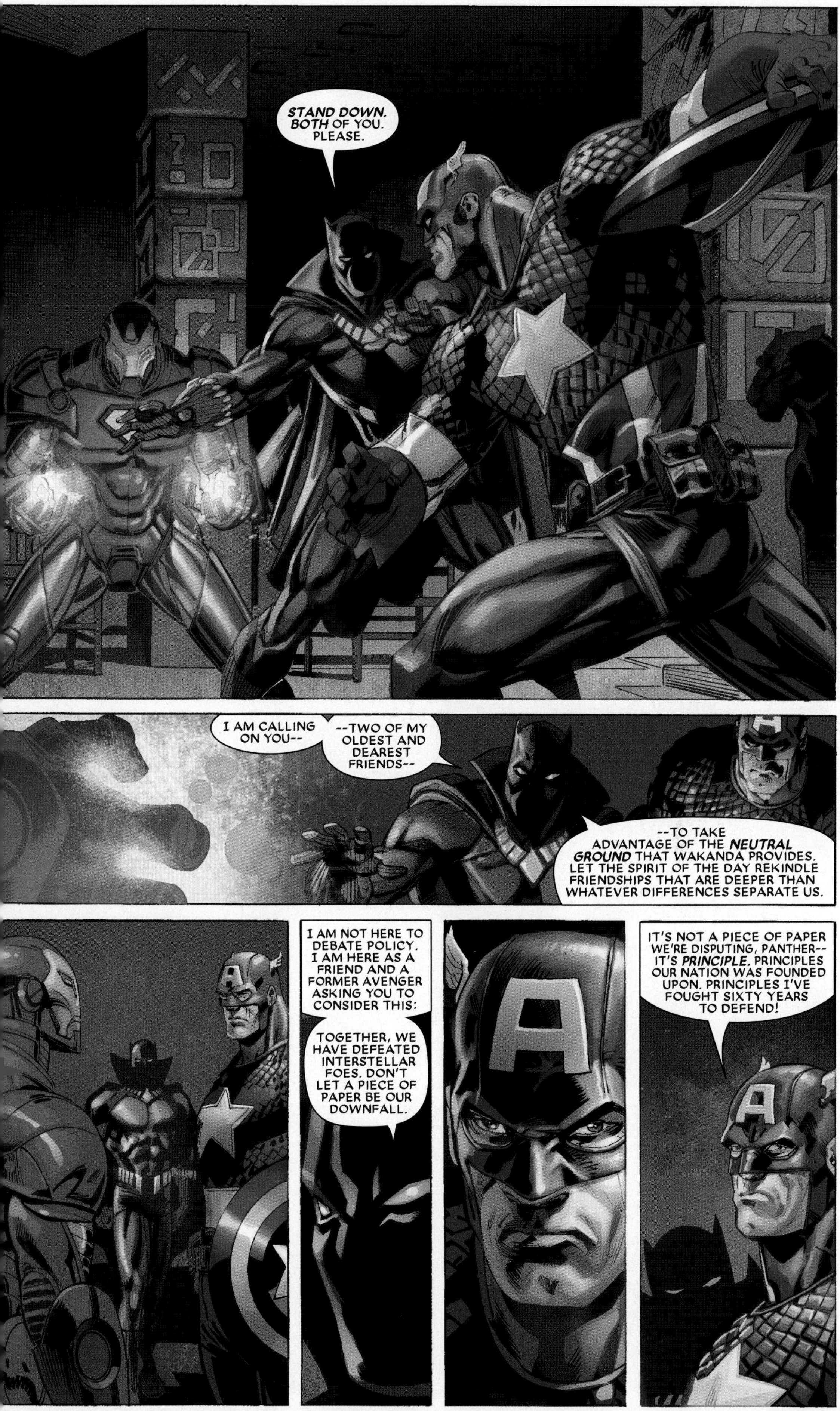
STAND DOWN. BOTH OF YOU. PLEASE.
I AM CALLING ON YOU--
--TWO OF MY OLDEST AND DEAREST FRIENDS--
--TO TAKE ADVANTAGE OF THE NEUTRAL GROUND THAT WAKANDA PROVIDES. LET THE SPIRIT OF THE DAY REKINDLE FRIENDSHIPS THAT ARE DEEPER THAN WHATEVER DIFFERENCES SEPARATE US.
I AM NOT HERE TO DEBATE POLICY. I AM HERE AS A FRIEND AND A FORMER AVENGER ASKING YOU TO CONSIDER THIS:
TOGETHER, WE HAVE DEFEATED INTERSTELLAR FOES. DON'T LET A PIECE OF PAPER BE OUR DOWNFALL.
IT'S NOT A PIECE OF PAPER WE'RE DISPUTING, PANTHER-- IT'S PRINCIPLE. PRINCIPLES OUR NATION WAS FOUNDED UPON. PRINCIPLES I'VE FOUGHT SIXTY YEARS TO DEFEND!

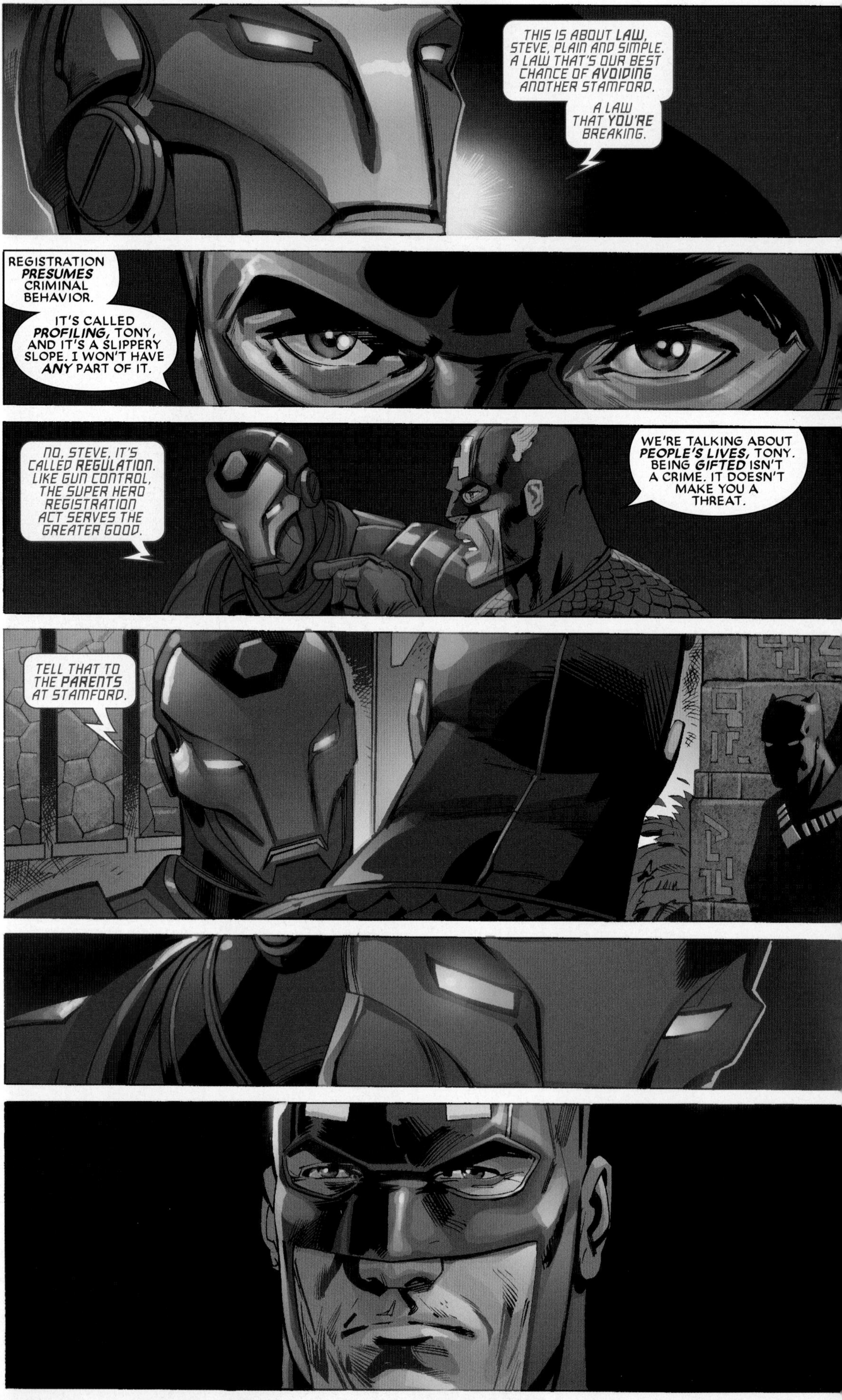

THIS IS ABOUT LAW, STEVE, PLAIN AND SIMPLE. A LAW THAT'S OUR BEST CHANCE OF AVOIDING ANOTHER STAMFORD.
A LAW THAT YOU'RE BREAKING.
REGISTRATION PRESUMES CRIMINAL BEHAVIOR.
IT'S CALLED PROFILING, TONY, AND IT'S A SLIPPERY SLOPE. I WON'T HAVE ANY PART OF IT.
NO, STEVE, IT'S CALLED REGULATION. LIKE GUN CONTROL, THE SUPER HERO REGISTRATION ACT SERVES THE GREATER GOOD.
WE'RE TALKING ABOUT PEOPLE'S LIVES, TONY. BEING GIFTED ISN'T A CRIME. IT DOESN'T MAKE YOU A THREAT.
TELL THAT TO THE PARENTS AT STAMFORD.

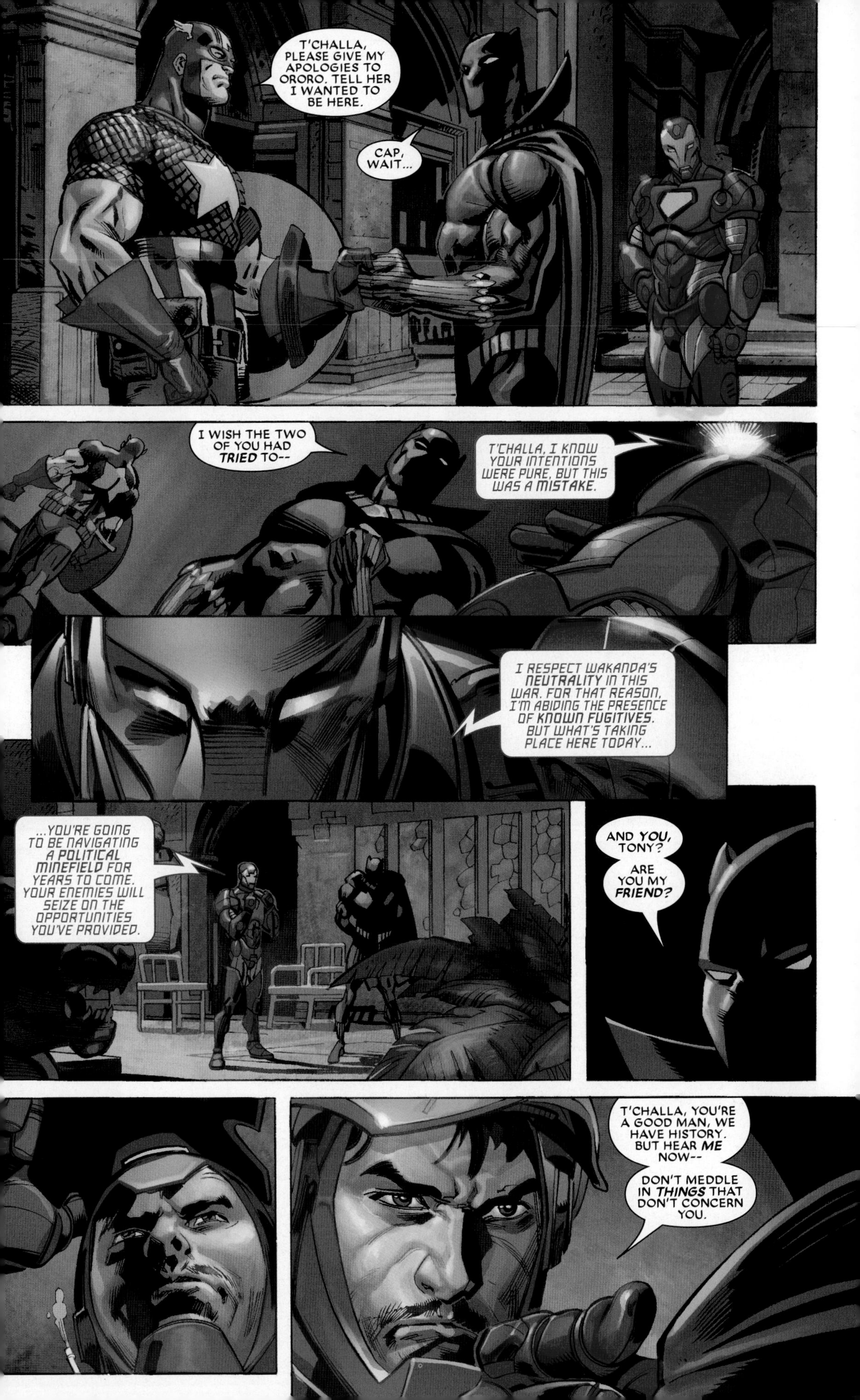

T'CHALLA, PLEASE GIVE MY APOLOGIES TO ORORO. TELL HER I WANTED TO BE HERE.
CAP, WAIT...
I WISH THE TWO OF YOU HAD TRIED TO--
T'CHALLA, I KNOW YOUR INTENTIONS WERE PURE, BUT THIS WAS A MISTAKE.
I RESPECT WAKANDA'S NEUTRALITY IN THIS WAR. FOR THAT REASON, I'M ABIDING THE PRESENCE OF KNOWN FUGITIVES. BUT WHAT'S TAKING PLACE HERE TODAY...
...YOU'RE GOING TO BE NAVIGATING A POLITICAL MINEFIELD FOR YEARS TO COME. YOUR ENEMIES WILL SEIZE ON THE OPPORTUNITIES YOU'VE PROVIDED.
AND YOU, TONY? ARE YOU MY FRIEND?
T'CHALLA, YOU'RE A GOOD MAN, WE HAVE HISTORY. BUT HEAR ME NOW--
DON'T MEDDLE IN THINGS THAT DON'T CONCERN YOU.

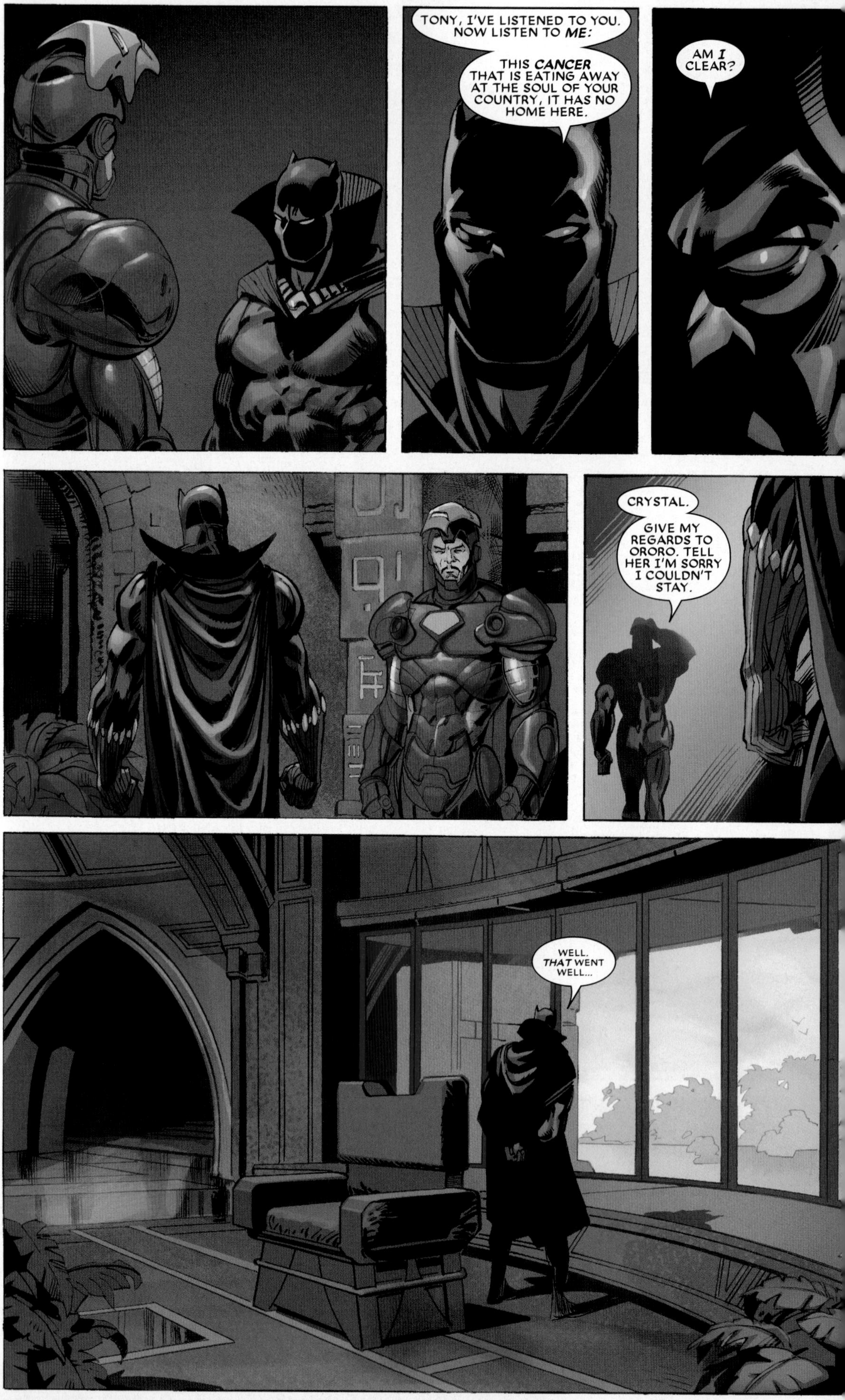
TONY, I'VE LISTENED TO YOU. NOW LISTEN TO *ME:*
THIS *CANCER* THAT IS EATING AWAY AT THE SOUL OF YOUR COUNTRY, IT HAS NO HOME HERE.
AM *I* CLEAR?
CRYSTAL.
GIVE MY REGARDS TO ORORO. TELL HER I'M SORRY I COULDN'T STAY.
WELL. *THAT* WENT WELL...

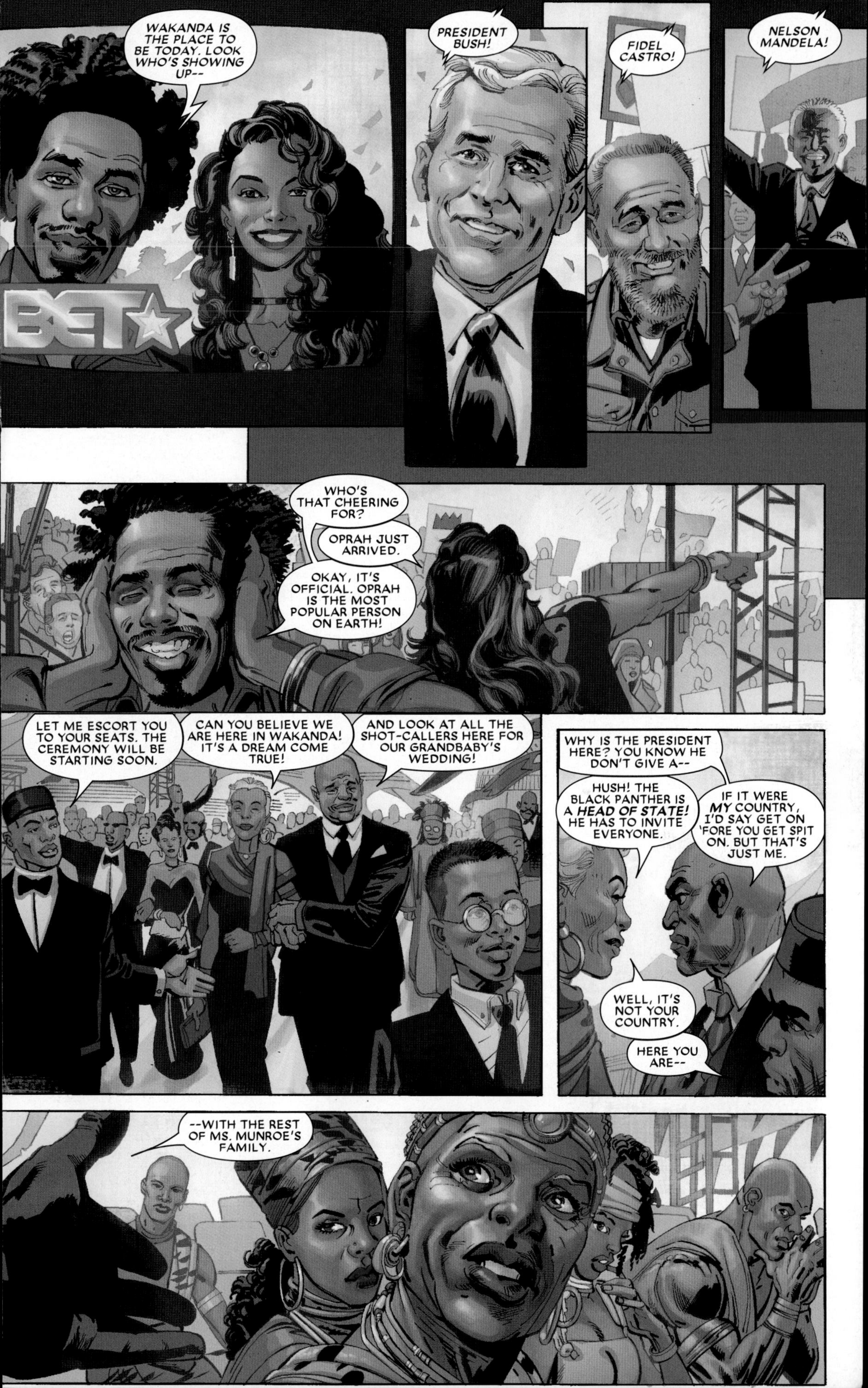
WAKANDA IS THE PLACE TO BE TODAY. LOOK WHO'S SHOWING UP--
BET
PRESIDENT BUSH!
FIDEL CASTRO!
NELSON MANDELA!
WHO'S THAT CHEERING FOR?
OPRAH JUST ARRIVED.
OKAY, IT'S OFFICIAL. OPRAH IS THE MOST POPULAR PERSON ON EARTH!
LET ME ESCORT YOU TO YOUR SEATS. THE CEREMONY WILL BE STARTING SOON.
CAN YOU BELIEVE WE ARE HERE IN WAKANDA! IT'S A DREAM COME TRUE!
AND LOOK AT ALL THE SHOT-CALLERS HERE FOR OUR GRANDBABY'S WEDDING!
WHY IS THE PRESIDENT HERE? YOU KNOW HE DON'T GIVE A--
HUSH! THE BLACK PANTHER IS A HEAD OF STATE! HE HAS TO INVITE EVERYONE.
IF IT WERE MY COUNTRY, I'D SAY GET ON 'FORE YOU GET SPIT ON. BUT THAT'S JUST ME.
WELL, IT'S NOT YOUR COUNTRY.
HERE YOU ARE--
--WITH THE REST OF MS. MUNROE'S FAMILY.

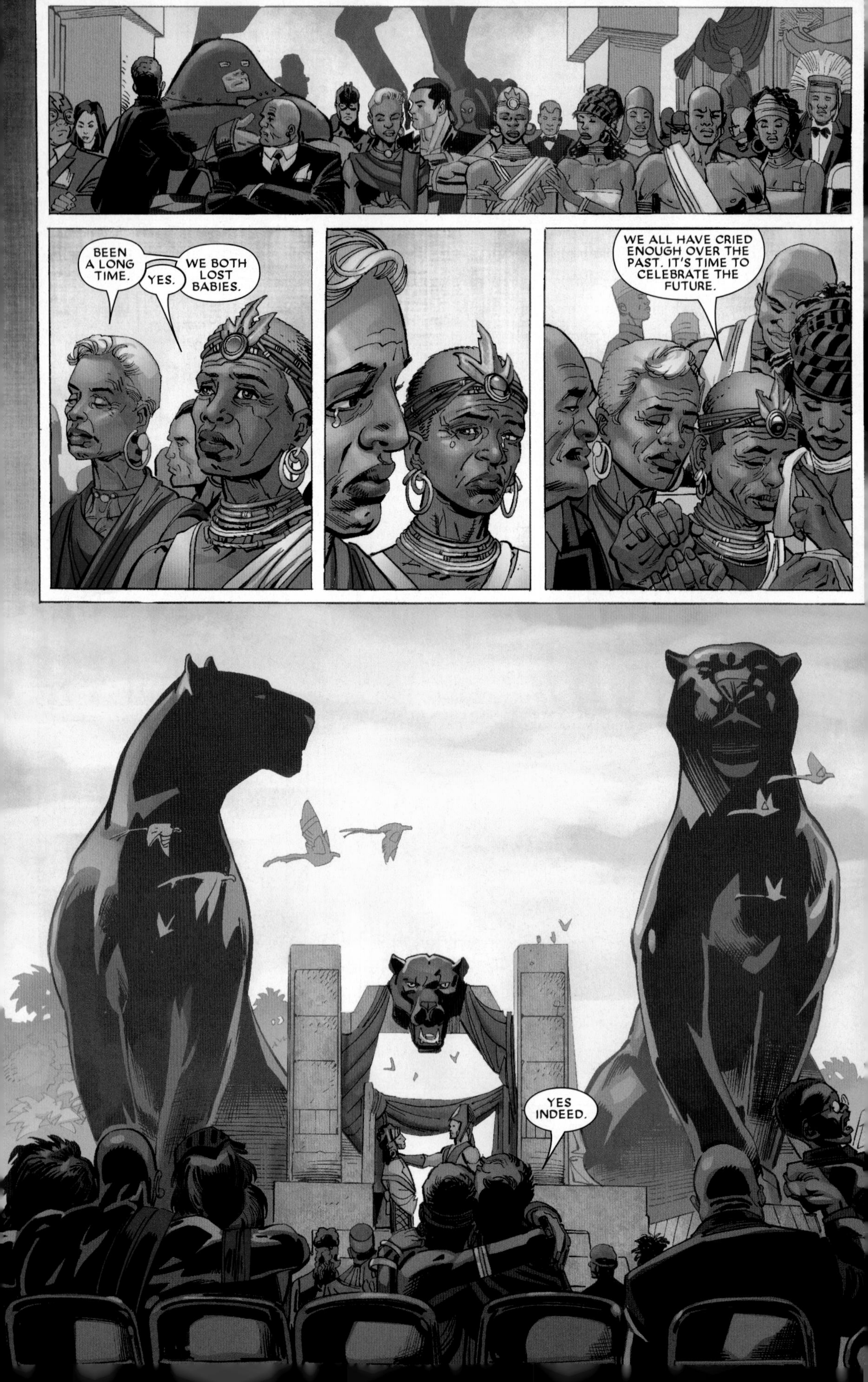
BEEN A LONG TIME.
YES.
WE BOTH LOST BABIES.
WE ALL HAVE CRIED ENOUGH OVER THE PAST. IT'S TIME TO CELEBRATE THE FUTURE.
YES INDEED.

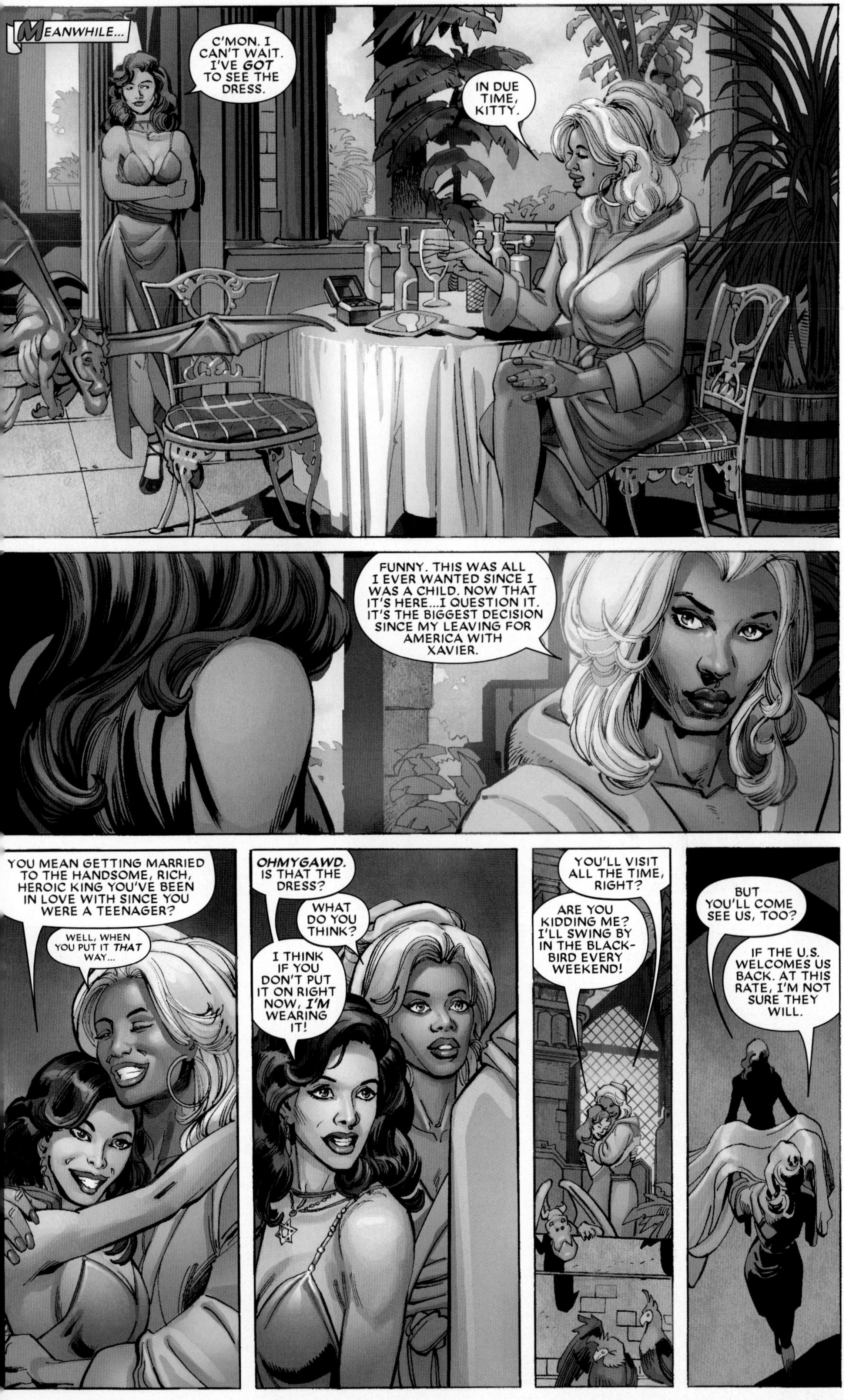
MEANWHILE...
C'MON. I CAN'T WAIT. I'VE GOT TO SEE THE DRESS.
IN DUE TIME, KITTY.
FUNNY. THIS WAS ALL I EVER WANTED SINCE I WAS A CHILD. NOW THAT IT'S HERE...I QUESTION IT. IT'S THE BIGGEST DECISION SINCE MY LEAVING FOR AMERICA WITH XAVIER.
YOU MEAN GETTING MARRIED TO THE HANDSOME, RICH, HEROIC KING YOU'VE BEEN IN LOVE WITH SINCE YOU WERE A TEENAGER?
WELL, WHEN YOU PUT IT THAT WAY...
OHMYGAWD. IS THAT THE DRESS?
WHAT DO YOU THINK?
I THINK IF YOU DON'T PUT IT ON RIGHT NOW, I'M WEARING IT!
YOU'LL VISIT ALL THE TIME, RIGHT?
ARE YOU KIDDING ME? I'LL SWING BY IN THE BLACK-BIRD EVERY WEEKEND!
BUT YOU'LL COME SEE US, TOO?
IF THE U.S. WELCOMES US BACK. AT THIS RATE, I'M NOT SURE THEY WILL.

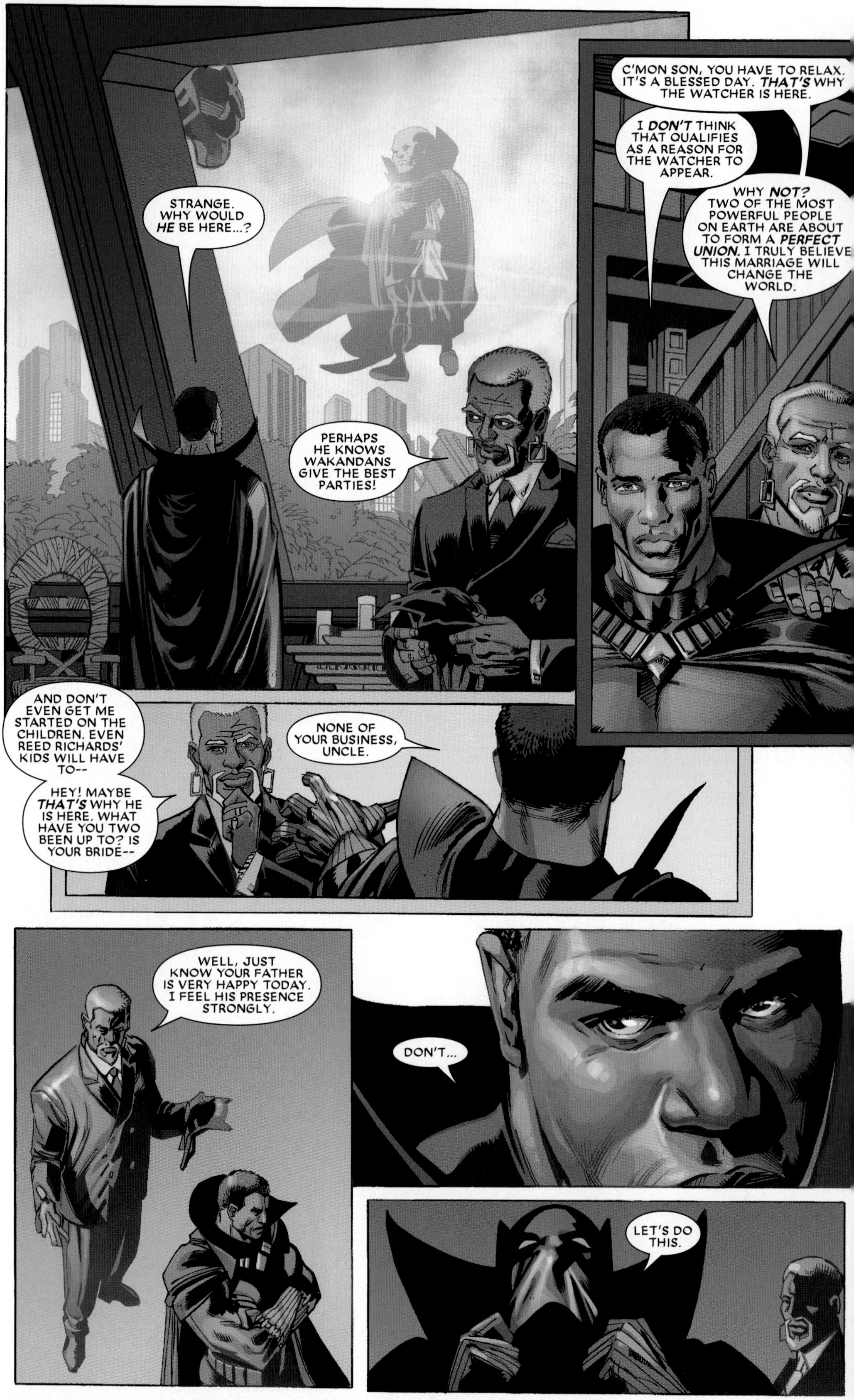
STRANGE. WHY WOULD *HE* BE HERE...?
PERHAPS HE KNOWS WAKANDANS GIVE THE BEST PARTIES!
C'MON SON, YOU HAVE TO RELAX. IT'S A BLESSED DAY. *THAT'S* WHY THE WATCHER IS HERE.
I *DON'T* THINK THAT QUALIFIES AS A REASON FOR THE WATCHER TO APPEAR.
WHY *NOT?* TWO OF THE MOST POWERFUL PEOPLE ON EARTH ARE ABOUT TO FORM A *PERFECT UNION.* I TRULY BELIEVE THIS MARRIAGE WILL CHANGE THE WORLD.
AND DON'T EVEN GET ME STARTED ON THE CHILDREN. EVEN REED RICHARDS' KIDS WILL HAVE TO--
HEY! MAYBE *THAT'S* WHY HE IS HERE. WHAT HAVE YOU TWO BEEN UP TO? IS YOUR BRIDE--
NONE OF YOUR BUSINESS, UNCLE.
WELL, JUST KNOW YOUR FATHER IS VERY HAPPY TODAY. I FEEL HIS PRESENCE STRONGLY.
DON'T...
LET'S DO THIS.

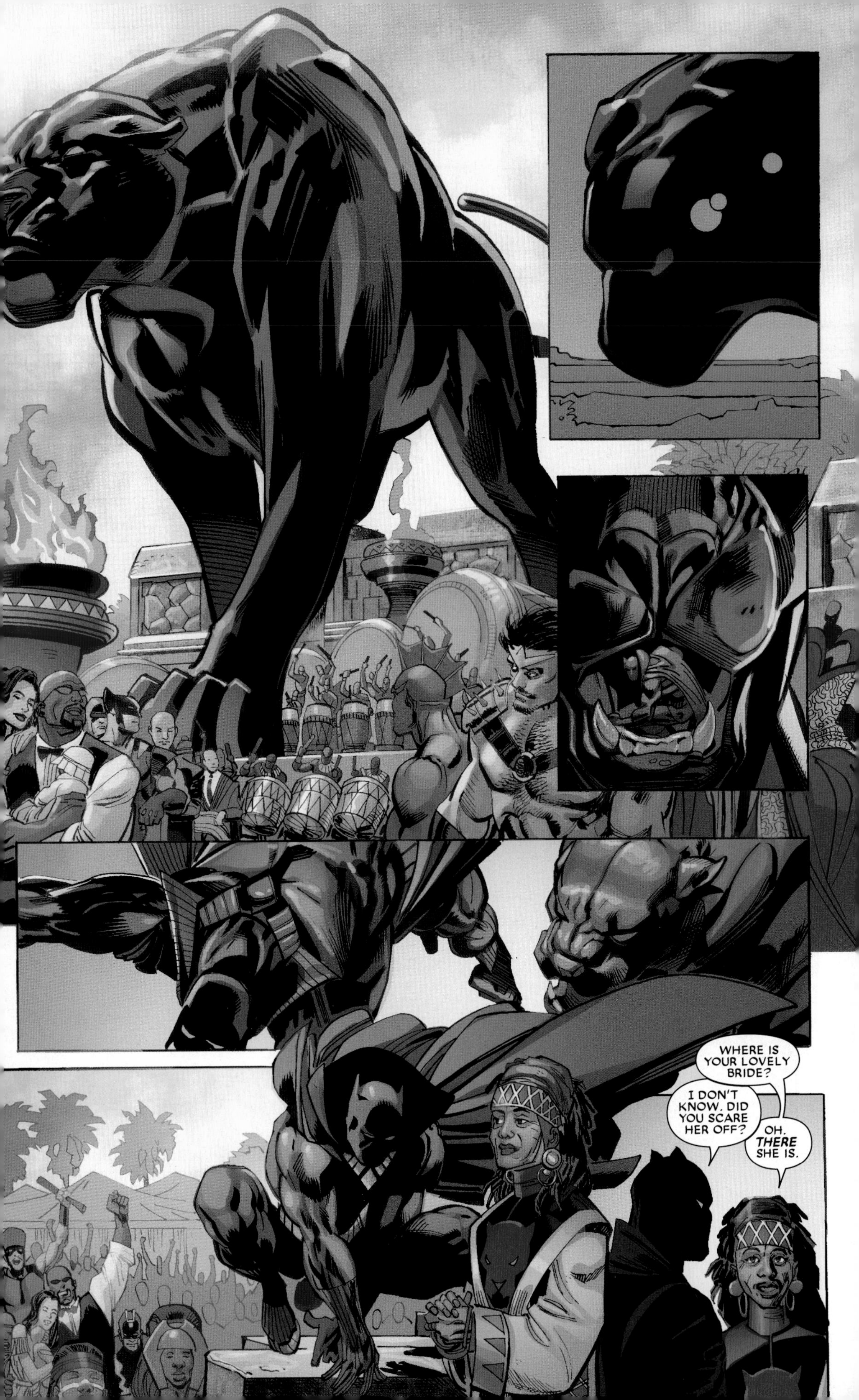
WHERE IS YOUR LOVELY BRIDE?
I DON'T KNOW. DID YOU SCARE HER OFF?
OH. *THERE* SHE IS.

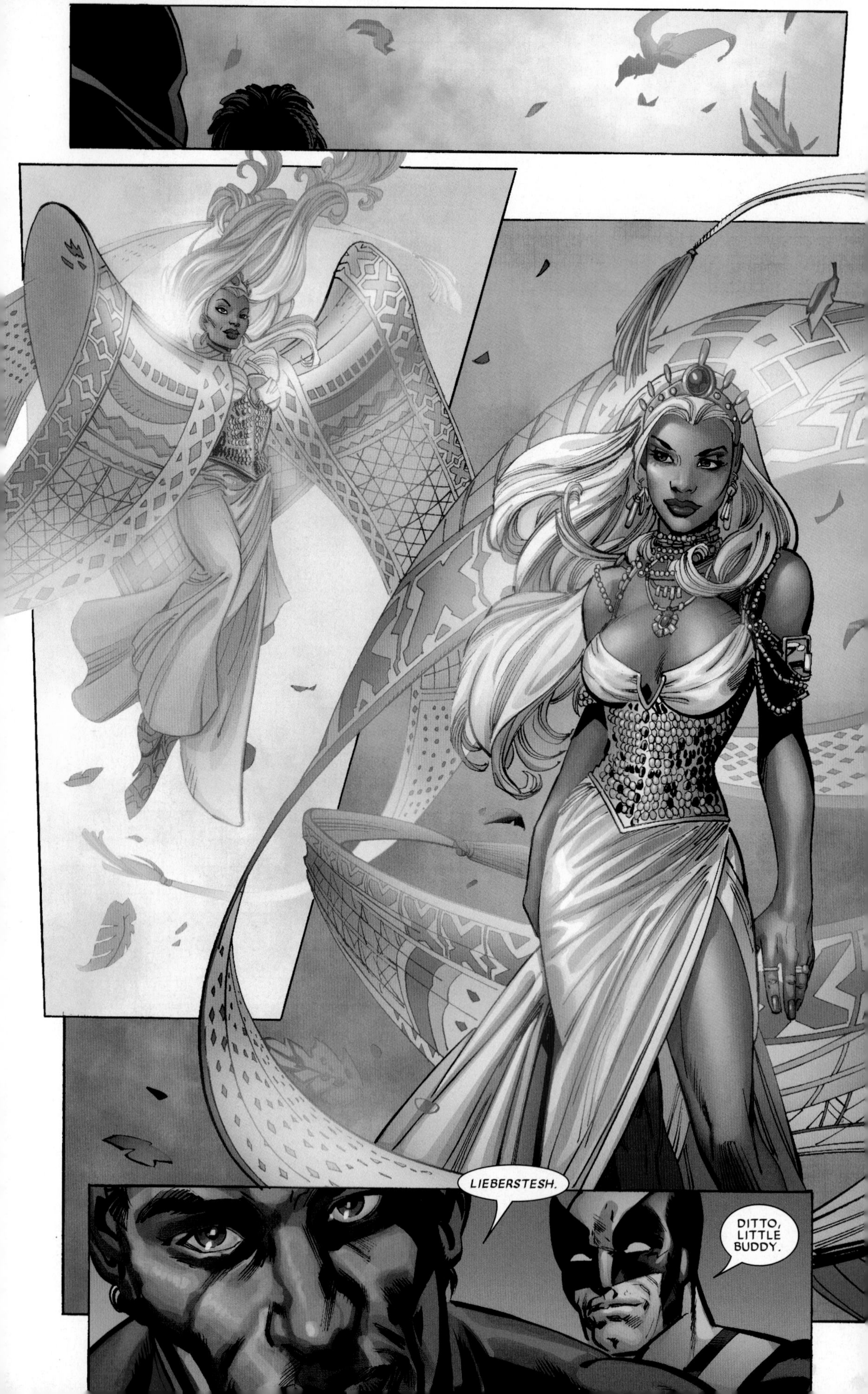
LIEBERSTESH.
DITTO, LITTLE BUDDY.

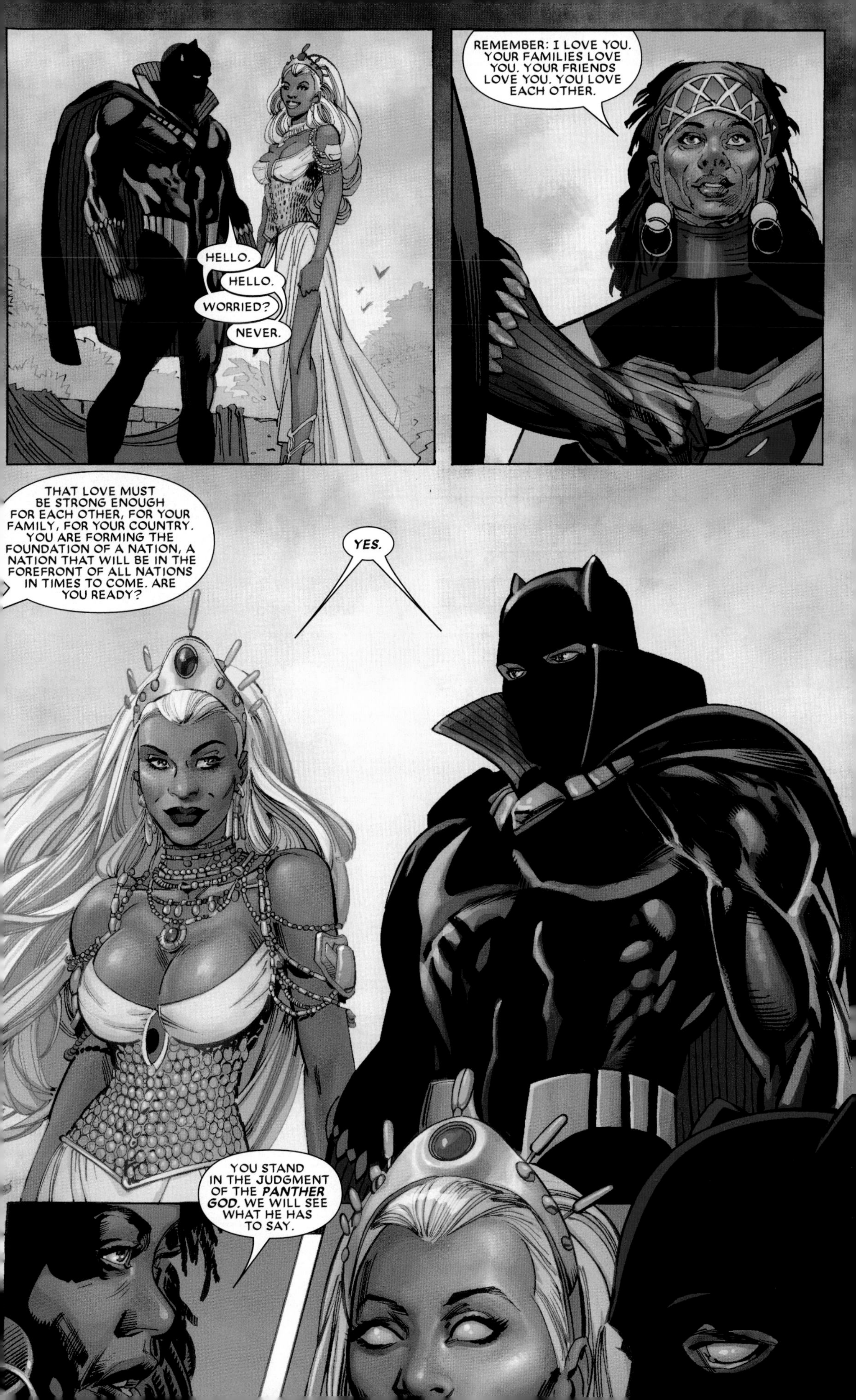
HELLO.
HELLO.
WORRIED?
NEVER.
REMEMBER: I LOVE YOU. YOUR FAMILIES LOVE YOU. YOUR FRIENDS LOVE YOU. YOU LOVE EACH OTHER.
THAT LOVE MUST BE STRONG ENOUGH FOR EACH OTHER, FOR YOUR FAMILY, FOR YOUR COUNTRY. YOU ARE FORMING THE FOUNDATION OF A NATION, A NATION THAT WILL BE IN THE FOREFRONT OF ALL NATIONS IN TIMES TO COME. ARE YOU READY?
YES.
YOU STAND IN THE JUDGMENT OF THE PANTHER GOD. WE WILL SEE WHAT HE HAS TO SAY.

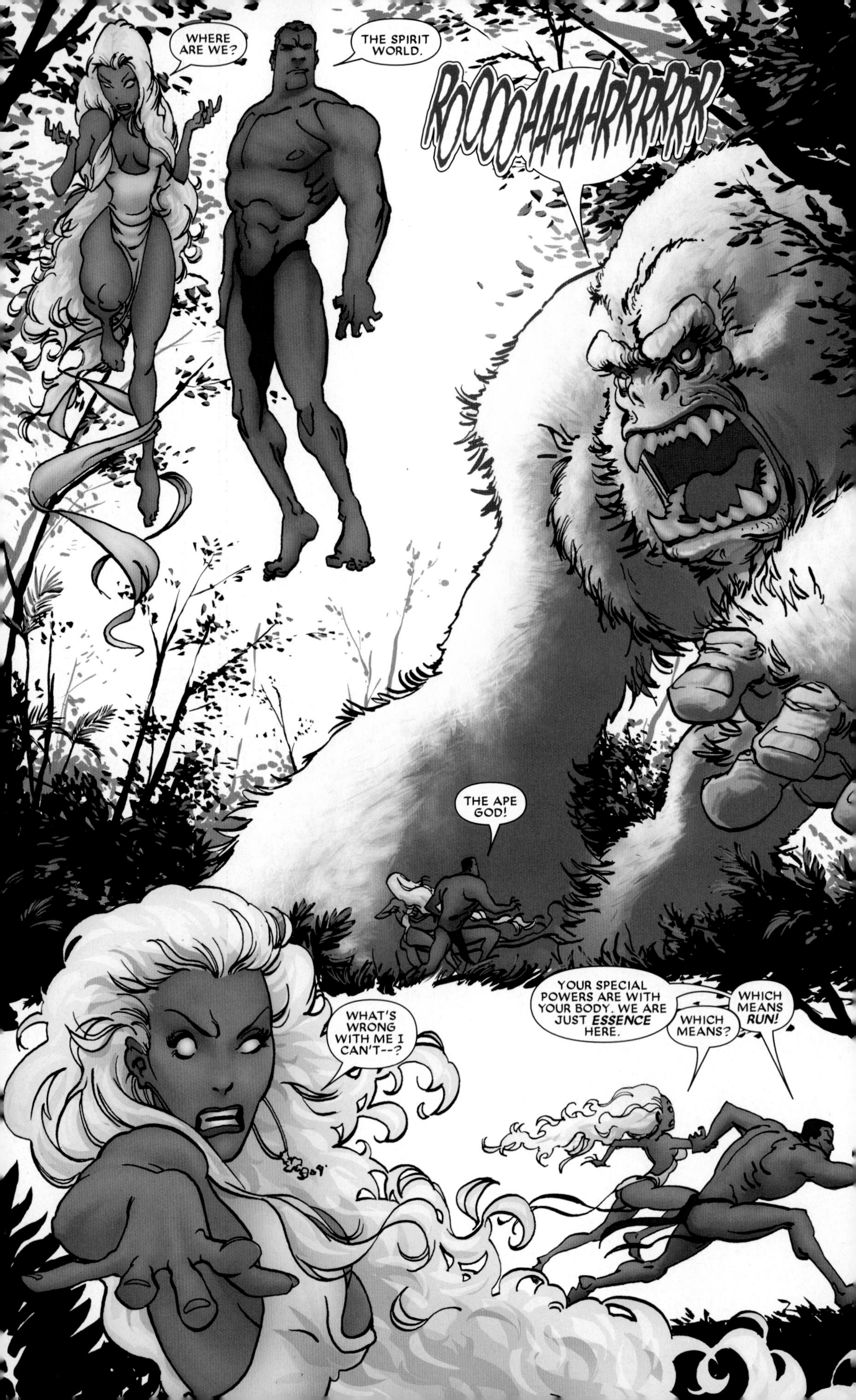
WHERE ARE WE?
THE SPIRIT WORLD.
ROOOOAAAAARRRRRR
THE APE GOD!
WHAT'S WRONG WITH ME I CAN'T--?
YOUR SPECIAL POWERS ARE WITH YOUR BODY. WE ARE JUST ESSENCE HERE.
WHICH MEANS?
WHICH MEANS RUN!

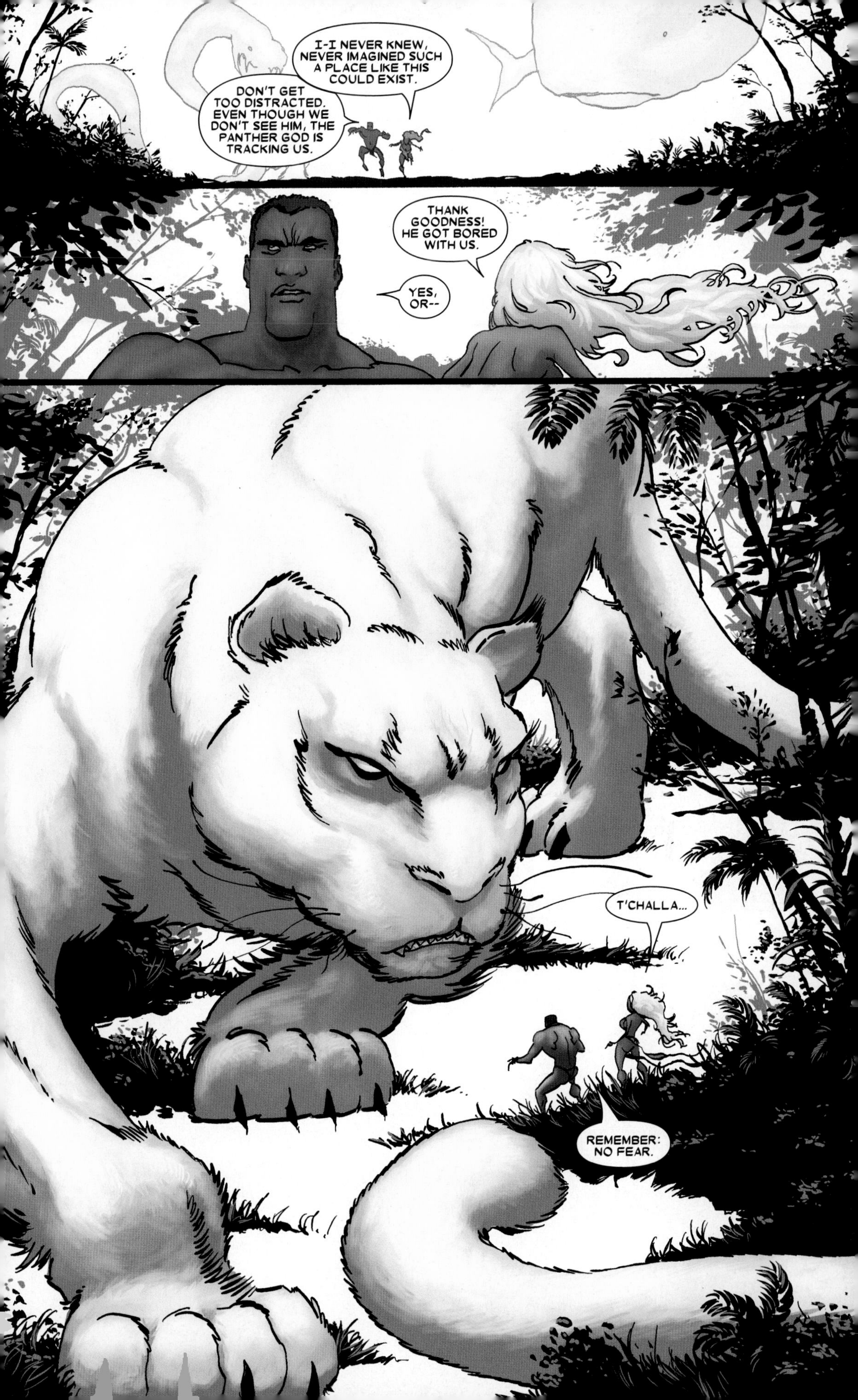
I-I NEVER KNEW, NEVER IMAGINED SUCH A PLACE LIKE THIS COULD EXIST.
DON'T GET TOO DISTRACTED. EVEN THOUGH WE DON'T SEE HIM, THE PANTHER GOD IS TRACKING US.
THANK GOODNESS! HE GOT BORED WITH US.
YES, OR--
T'CHALLA...
REMEMBER: NO FEAR.

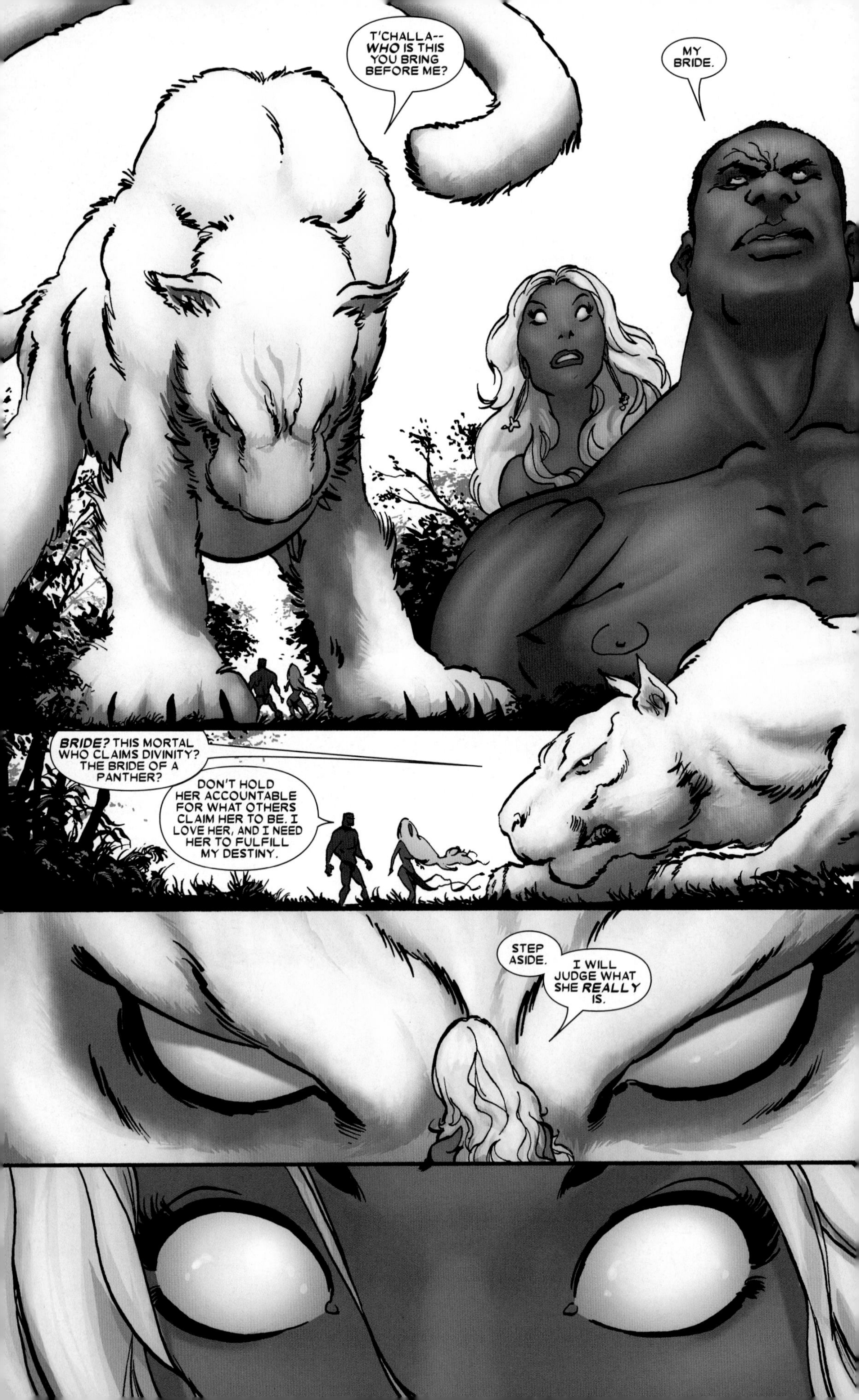
T'CHALLA-- WHO IS THIS YOU BRING BEFORE ME?
MY BRIDE.
BRIDE? THIS MORTAL WHO CLAIMS DIVINITY? THE BRIDE OF A PANTHER?
DON'T HOLD HER ACCOUNTABLE FOR WHAT OTHERS CLAIM HER TO BE. I LOVE HER, AND I NEED HER TO FULFILL MY DESTINY.
STEP ASIDE.
I WILL JUDGE WHAT SHE REALLY IS.

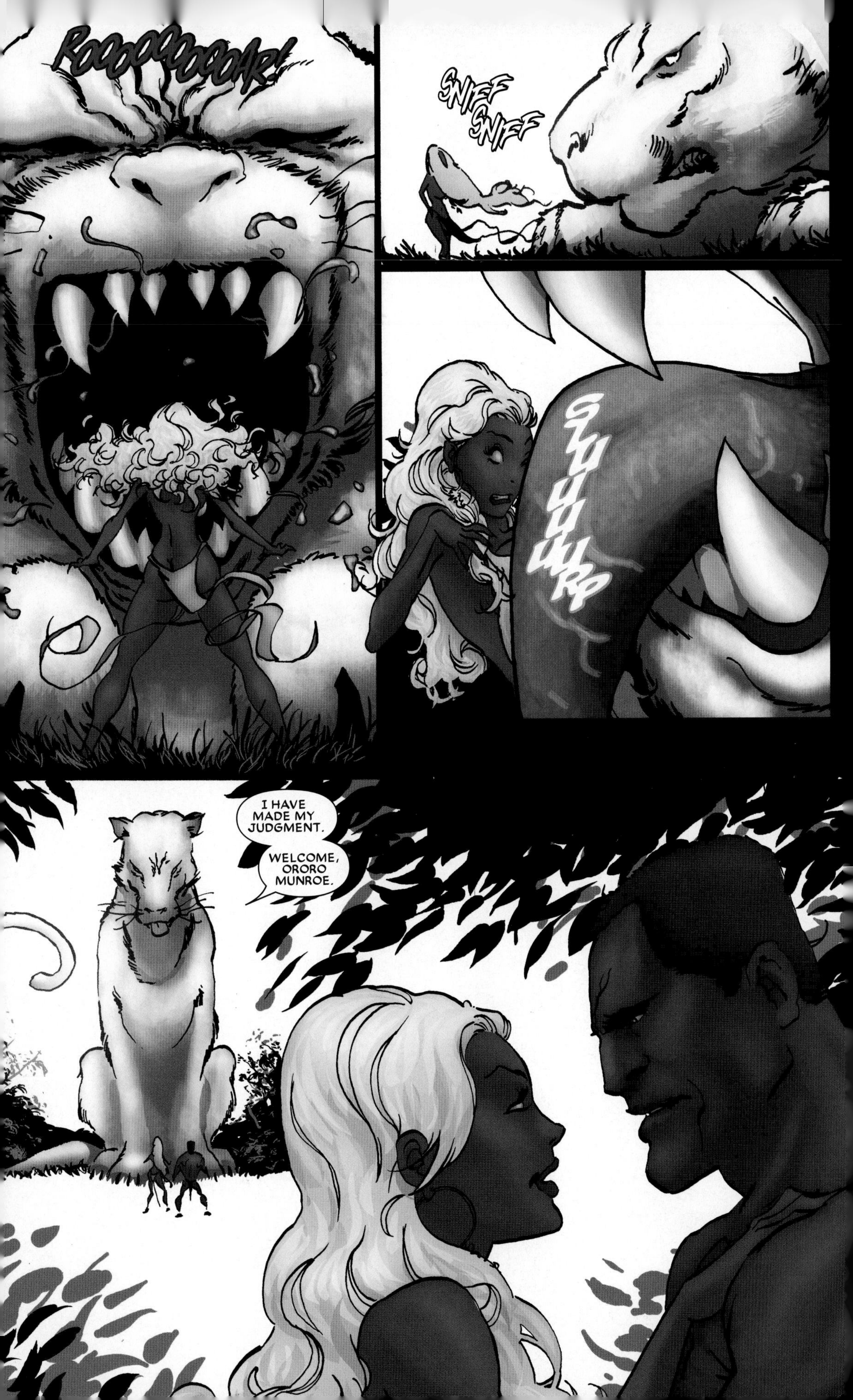
ROOOOOOOOOAR!
SNIFF SNIFF
I HAVE MADE MY JUDGMENT.
WELCOME, ORORO MUNROE.

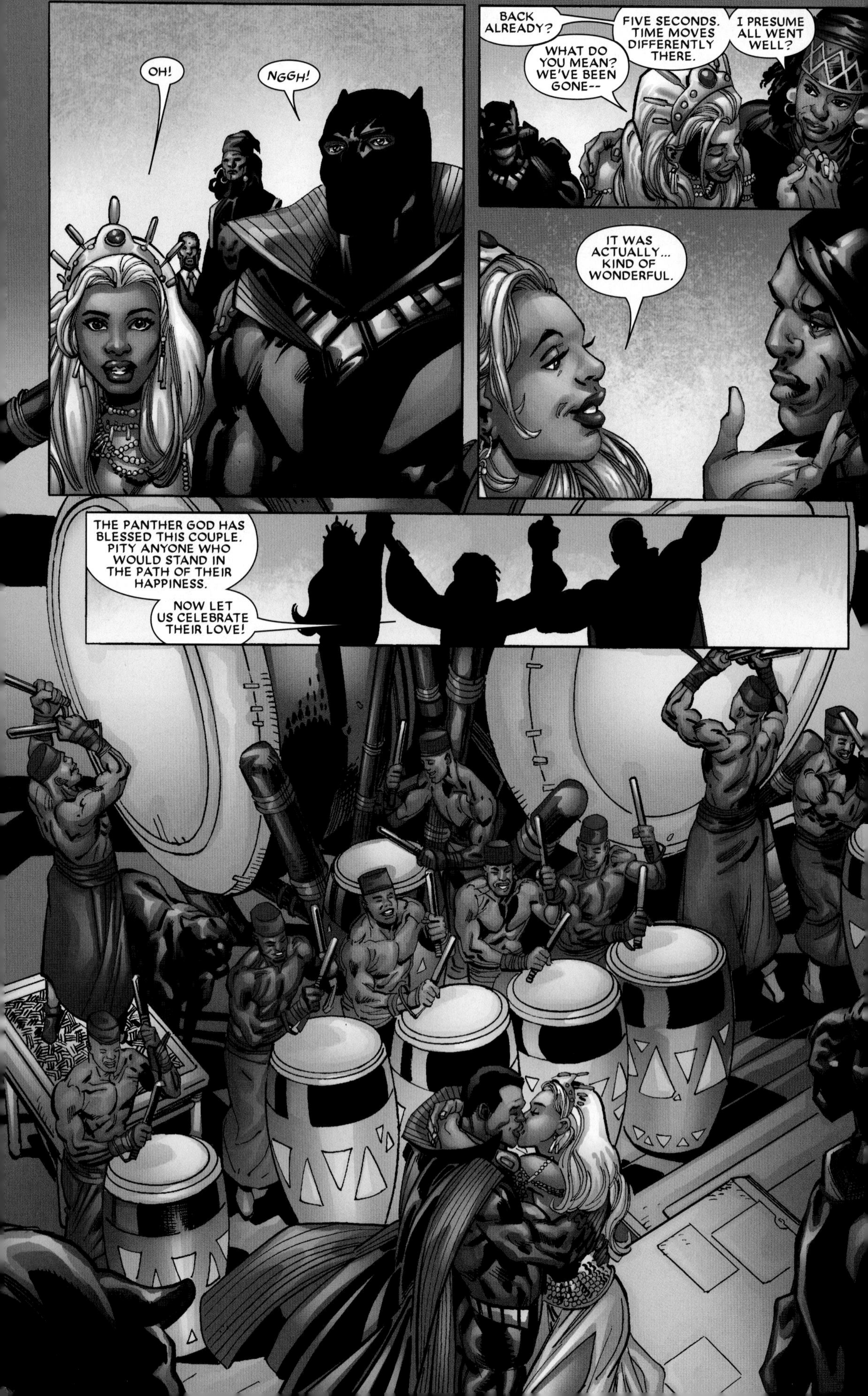
OH!
NGGH!
BACK ALREADY?
WHAT DO YOU MEAN? WE'VE BEEN GONE--
FIVE SECONDS. TIME MOVES DIFFERENTLY THERE.
I PRESUME ALL WENT WELL?
IT WAS ACTUALLY... KIND OF WONDERFUL.
THE PANTHER GOD HAS BLESSED THIS COUPLE. PITY ANYONE WHO WOULD STAND IN THE PATH OF THEIR HAPPINESS.
NOW LET US CELEBRATE THEIR LOVE!

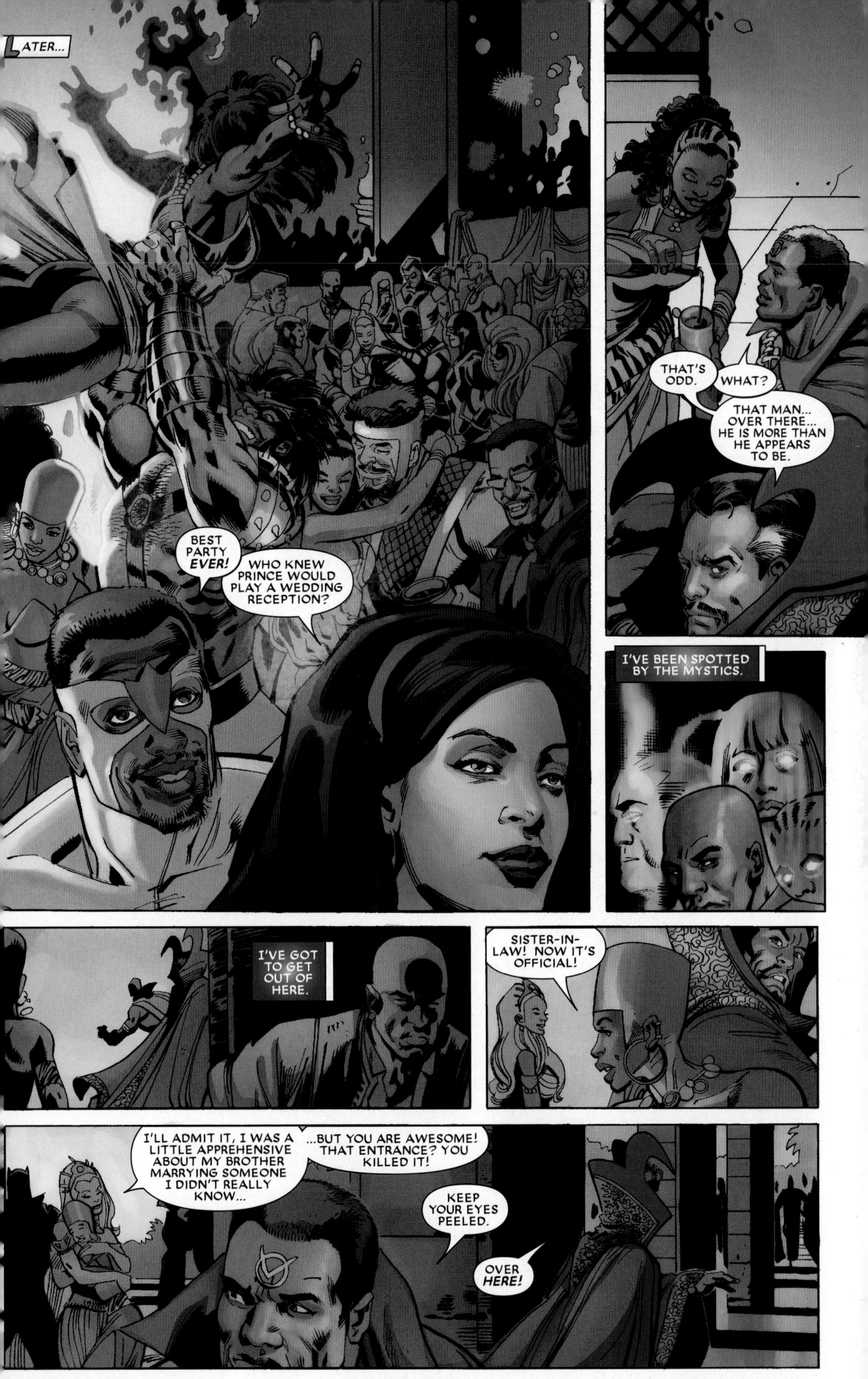
LATER...
BEST PARTY EVER!
WHO KNEW PRINCE WOULD PLAY A WEDDING RECEPTION?
THAT'S ODD.
WHAT?
THAT MAN... OVER THERE... HE IS MORE THAN HE APPEARS TO BE.
I'VE BEEN SPOTTED BY THE MYSTICS.
I'VE GOT TO GET OUT OF HERE.
SISTER-IN-LAW! NOW IT'S OFFICIAL!
I'LL ADMIT IT, I WAS A LITTLE APPREHENSIVE ABOUT MY BROTHER MARRYING SOMEONE I DIDN'T REALLY KNOW...
...BUT YOU ARE AWESOME! THAT ENTRANCE? YOU KILLED IT!
KEEP YOUR EYES PEELED.
OVER HERE!

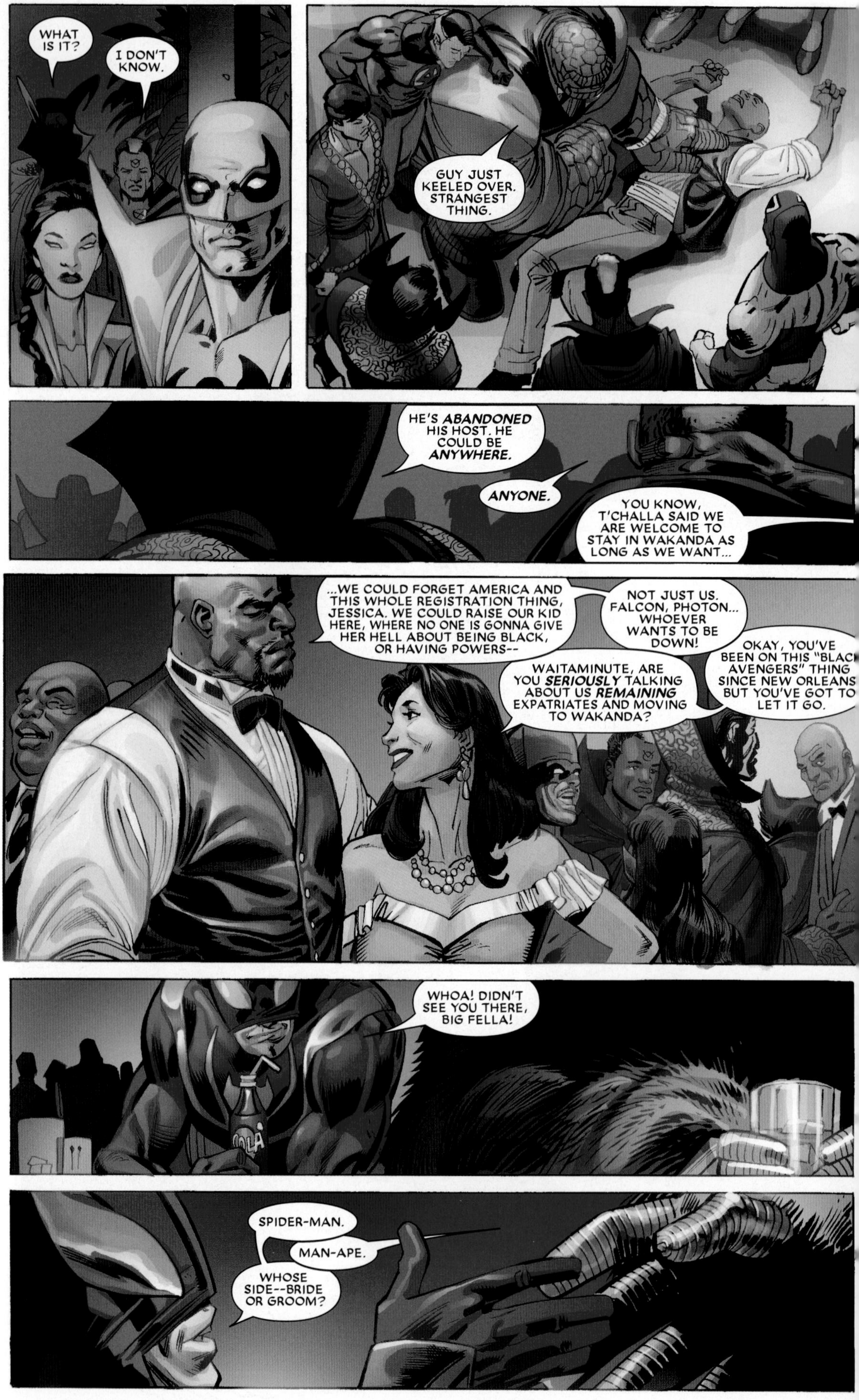
WHAT IS IT?
I DON'T KNOW.
GUY JUST KEELED OVER. STRANGEST THING.
HE'S ABANDONED HIS HOST. HE COULD BE ANYWHERE.
ANYONE.
YOU KNOW, T'CHALLA SAID WE ARE WELCOME TO STAY IN WAKANDA AS LONG AS WE WANT...
...WE COULD FORGET AMERICA AND THIS WHOLE REGISTRATION THING, JESSICA. WE COULD RAISE OUR KID HERE, WHERE NO ONE IS GONNA GIVE HER HELL ABOUT BEING BLACK, OR HAVING POWERS--
NOT JUST US. FALCON, PHOTON... WHOEVER WANTS TO BE DOWN!
WAITAMINUTE, ARE YOU SERIOUSLY TALKING ABOUT US REMAINING EXPATRIATES AND MOVING TO WAKANDA?
OKAY, YOU'VE BEEN ON THIS "BLAC AVENGERS" THING SINCE NEW ORLEANS BUT YOU'VE GOT TO LET IT GO.
WHOA! DIDN'T SEE YOU THERE, BIG FELLA!
SPIDER-MAN.
MAN-APE.
WHOSE SIDE--BRIDE OR GROOM?

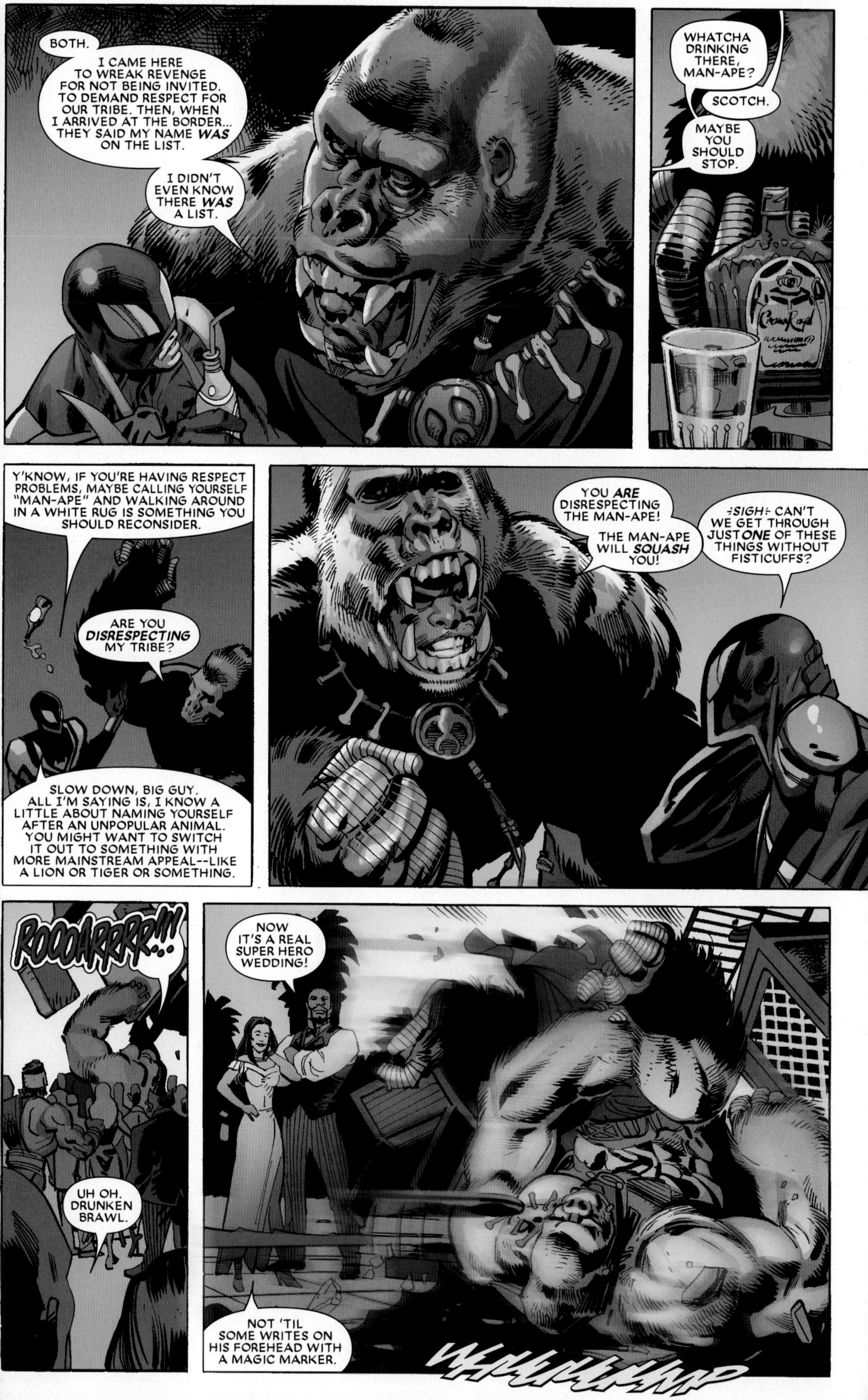
BOTH.
I CAME HERE TO WREAK REVENGE FOR NOT BEING INVITED. TO DEMAND RESPECT FOR OUR TRIBE. THEN, WHEN I ARRIVED AT THE BORDER... THEY SAID MY NAME *WAS* ON THE LIST.
I DIDN'T EVEN KNOW THERE *WAS* A LIST.
WHATCHA DRINKING THERE, MAN-APE?
SCOTCH.
MAYBE YOU SHOULD STOP.
Y'KNOW, IF YOU'RE HAVING RESPECT PROBLEMS, MAYBE CALLING YOURSELF "MAN-APE" AND WALKING AROUND IN A WHITE RUG IS SOMETHING YOU SHOULD RECONSIDER.
ARE YOU *DISRESPECTING* MY TRIBE?
SLOW DOWN, BIG GUY. ALL I'M SAYING IS, I KNOW A LITTLE ABOUT NAMING YOURSELF AFTER AN UNPOPULAR ANIMAL. YOU MIGHT WANT TO SWITCH IT OUT TO SOMETHING WITH MORE MAINSTREAM APPEAL--LIKE A LION OR TIGER OR SOMETHING.
YOU *ARE* DISRESPECTING THE MAN-APE!
THE MAN-APE WILL *SQUASH* YOU!
÷SIGH÷ CAN'T WE GET THROUGH JUST *ONE* OF THESE THINGS WITHOUT FISTICUFFS?
ROOOARRRR!!!
UH OH. DRUNKEN BRAWL.
NOW IT'S A REAL SUPER HERO WEDDING!
NOT 'TIL SOME WRITES ON HIS FOREHEAD WITH A MAGIC MARKER.
WHUMMMP

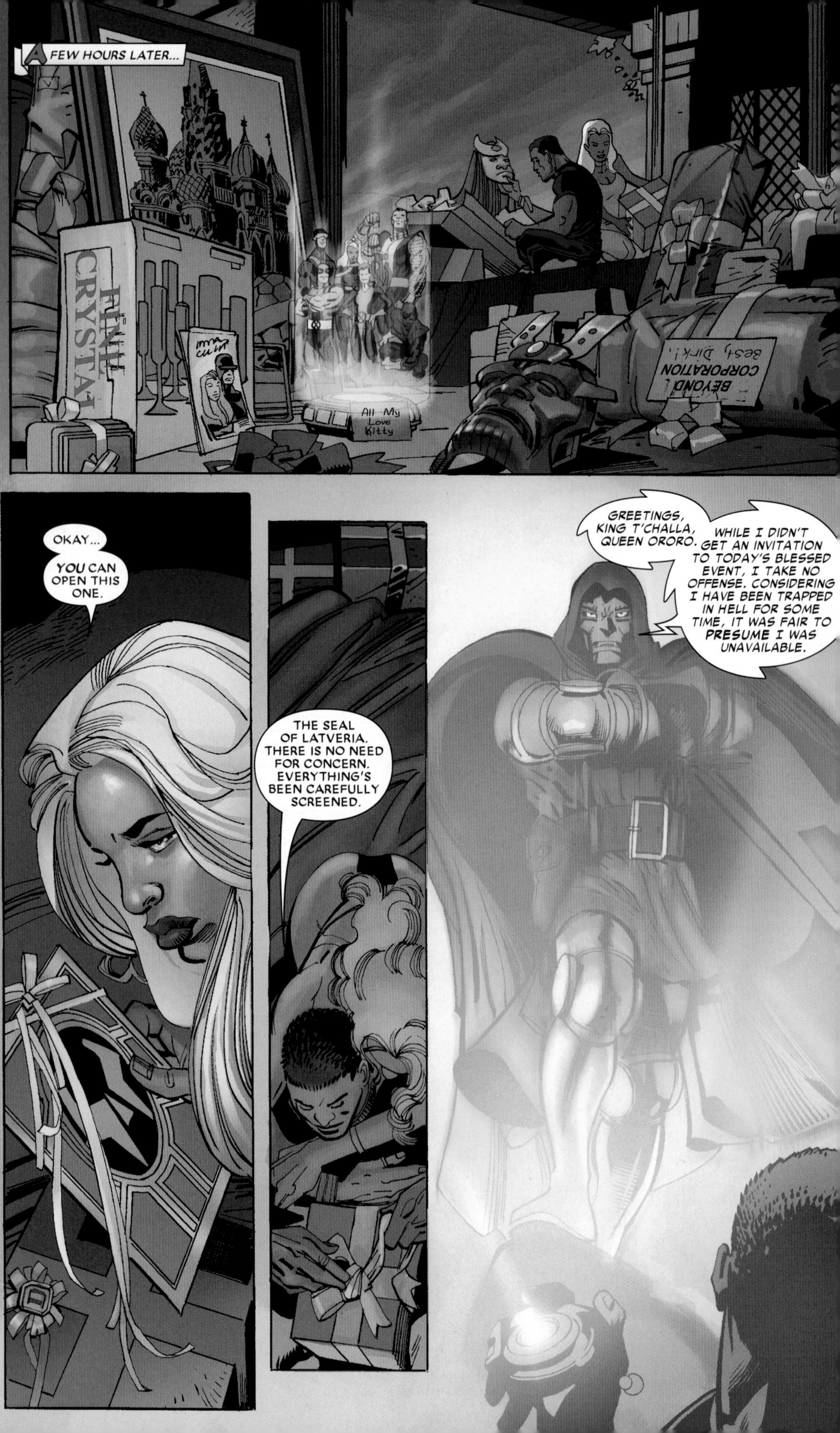
A FEW HOURS LATER...
FINE CRYSTAL
All My Love Kitty
BEYOND CORPORATION
Best, Dirk!
OKAY... YOU CAN OPEN THIS ONE.
THE SEAL OF LATVERIA. THERE IS NO NEED FOR CONCERN. EVERYTHING'S BEEN CAREFULLY SCREENED.
GREETINGS, KING T'CHALLA, QUEEN ORORO.
WHILE I DIDN'T GET AN INVITATION TO TODAY'S BLESSED EVENT, I TAKE NO OFFENSE. CONSIDERING I HAVE BEEN TRAPPED IN HELL FOR SOME TIME, IT WAS FAIR TO PRESUME I WAS UNAVAILABLE.

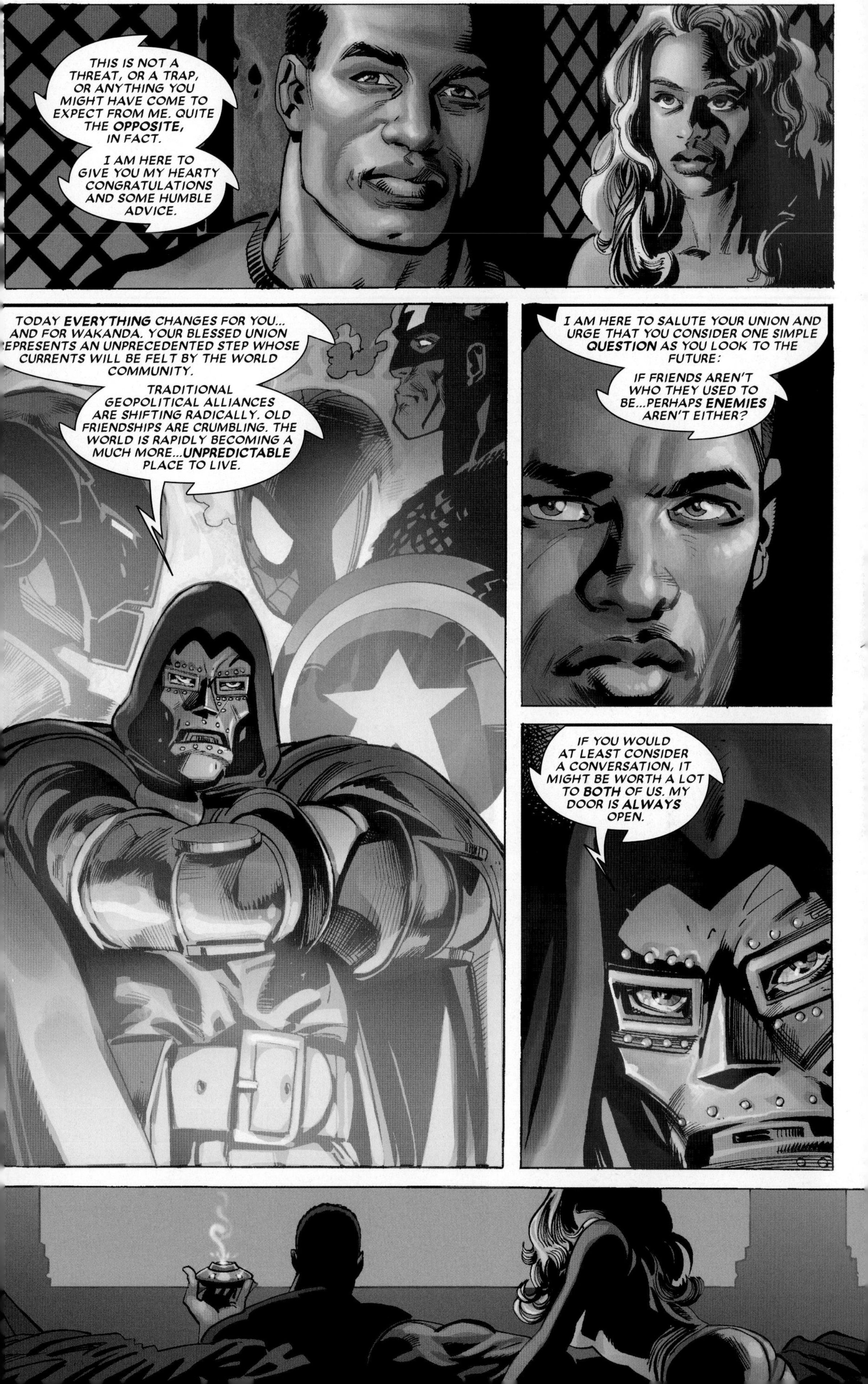
THIS IS NOT A THREAT, OR A TRAP, OR ANYTHING YOU MIGHT HAVE COME TO EXPECT FROM ME. QUITE THE **OPPOSITE,** IN FACT.
I AM HERE TO GIVE YOU MY HEARTY CONGRATULATIONS AND SOME HUMBLE ADVICE.
TODAY **EVERYTHING** CHANGES FOR YOU... AND FOR WAKANDA. YOUR BLESSED UNION REPRESENTS AN UNPRECEDENTED STEP WHOSE CURRENTS WILL BE FELT BY THE WORLD COMMUNITY.
TRADITIONAL GEOPOLITICAL ALLIANCES ARE SHIFTING RADICALLY. OLD FRIENDSHIPS ARE CRUMBLING. THE WORLD IS RAPIDLY BECOMING A MUCH MORE...**UNPREDICTABLE** PLACE TO LIVE.
I AM HERE TO SALUTE YOUR UNION AND URGE THAT YOU CONSIDER ONE SIMPLE **QUESTION** AS YOU LOOK TO THE FUTURE:
IF FRIENDS AREN'T WHO THEY USED TO BE...PERHAPS **ENEMIES** AREN'T EITHER?
IF YOU WOULD AT LEAST CONSIDER A CONVERSATION, IT MIGHT BE WORTH A LOT TO **BOTH** OF US. MY DOOR IS **ALWAYS** OPEN.

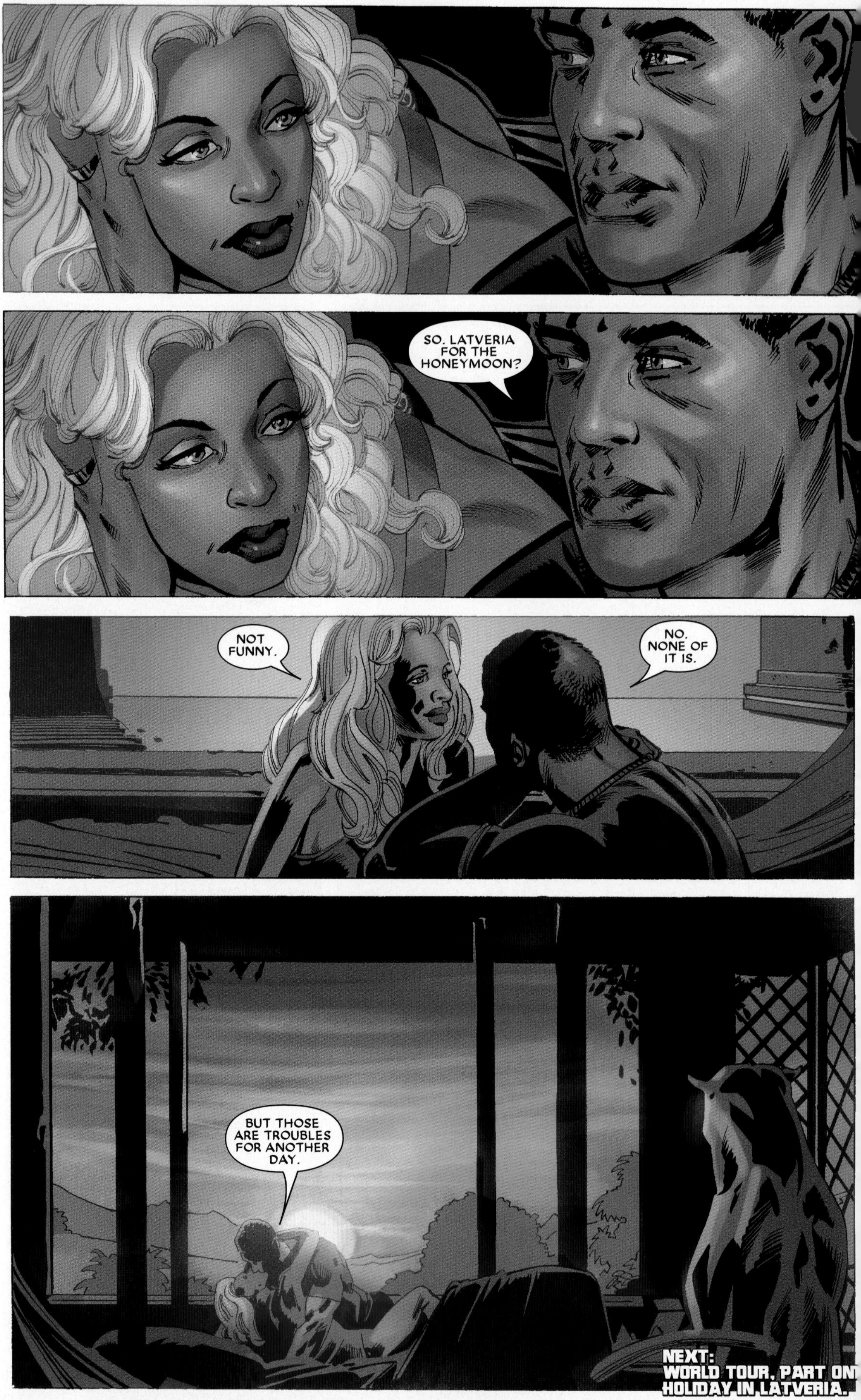
SO. LATVERIA FOR THE HONEYMOON?
NOT FUNNY.
NO. NONE OF IT IS.
BUT THOSE ARE TROUBLES FOR ANOTHER DAY.
NEXT: WORLD TOUR, PART ON HOLIDAY IN LATVERIA.

ARTICLE BY **REGINALD HUDLIN**

THE BLACK PANTHER

A HISTORICAL OVERVIEW AND A LOOK TO THE FUTURE

When the Black Panther debuted in the '60s, he was so cool, so perfect a character in concept and execution it's hard to believe it was done by two white guys. But when the white guys in question were Stan Lee and Jack Kirby, then it makes sense. But to truly appreciate their achievement, it's worth putting it in context: No black super hero before or after the Black Panther is as cool as the Black Panther. Sure, others come close. Luke Cage is as brilliant a Marvel response to blaxploitation as Nick Fury, Agent of S.H.I.E.L.D. was to the James Bond/super spy trend. And the Milestone line of comics was wonderful and smart.

But the Black Panther is STILL The Man.

He's the king of his own country! He's rich! He's tough enough to defeat the Fantastic Four <u>and</u> Captain America! He's suave and sophisticated! He's got cool super-technology! And his name is...THE BLACK PANTHER. Just the name alone was so ahead of its time. (I wonder if the Black Panther Party in Oakland had gotten famous first, would Stan have used the name anyway? Well, he didn't change it, so double-kudos to him!)

The Panther's appearances in the Lee/Kirby issues of the FANTASTIC FOUR and CAPTAIN AMERICA were great, but nothing after that has been able to recapture the original magic. He never made much of an impression on me during any of his AVENGERS stints, and I never liked the McGregor-written series in JUNGLE ACTION. I even preferred the loopy but fun late Kirby series to McGregor's morose characters tha endlessly droned on with overflowing captions with even more yakkety yakking Enough already!

The Priest run on the PANTHER gave a much-needed shot in the arm to the character. His power level was restored to the point that the Panther had contingency plans to take on Galactus Great! And he got two beautiful female bodyguards/concubines who can kick @$$. Great! He kicked it with fellow regents Namor and Doom. Great! He joined the Avengers to spy on them? The best idea yet!

The question is, how do we take the character to the next level?

Let's start by defining who he IS.

The Black Panther is the Black Captain America. He's the embodiment of the ideals of a people. As Americans we feel good when we read Captain America because he reminds us of the potential of how good America can be if, of course, we have the convictions to live by the principles the country was founded on. As a black person, the Black Panther should represent the fulfillment of the potential of the Motherland.

For a long time, the Black American equivalent of that ideal was represented by Sidney Poitier, a man who maintained his dignity even in degrading situations But since the '80s, that ideal has shifted In the post-integration, post-Reagan era the new ideal is Spike Lee or Sean "Puffy" Combs, the artist/businessman hero who profits from his own cultural integrity. In other words, the man who has it all — the money, the politics and the cool and style of black culture.

What those celebrities named, along with Malcolm X, Miles Davis and Muhammad Ali, all have in common, is the knowledge that the act of being a black man in white America is an inherent act of rebellion. They are WILLING to be bad@$$es.

That's what hip hop is all about. Being a bad@$$. Everyone wants to be a bad@$$. That's why white kids have always loved black music — whether it's jazz, rock and roll or hip hop, black music is the music of bad@$$es, and plugging into that culture makes a suburban white kid feel like a bad@$$, too. And for a generation of white kids who have grown up without an "Elvis"— a white interpreter of black culture — their appreciation of edgy street culture is shocking even to me.

I say all this because the harder the Panther is, the more appealing he is to both black AND white audiences.

All we've got to do is let the Panther be who he is set up to be. After all, he's a Wakandan. Wakandans are so bad@$$ THEY'VE NEVER BEEN CONQUERED.

This is important. There are some countries that are like doormats — everybody's kicked their @$$ at one point or another. But there are other peoples in the world — Vietnam comes to mind — that kick the @$$ of everyone who messes with them, superpower or not.

The Wakandans are such people. I figure every 50 years or so, somebody tries to make a move on them, and they have to prove the point to that generation of would-be conquerors:

DON'T EVEN TRY IT!

The independence of the Wakandan people has got to be galling to the rest of the world for a lot of reasons. First of all, the rest of Africa has been carved up like a Christmas turkey. England, Germany, France, Belgium, the United States, the Soviet Union, Islamic and Christian invaders...so many empires have taken large chunks of land and resources for their own. Even after the independence movements of the '60s, any leader that was too competent got killed (like, say, Patrice Lumumba). So the colonial powers still controlled their territories through greedy thugs like Bokassa and Mubutu.

Not only does Wakanda's independence block the total dominance of Africa by colonial powers, its cultural evolution has gone unchecked for centuries. They were ahead of us a thousand years ago. And no one has colonized them, burned their books, erased their language, or broken their spirits.

Unfettered by the yoke of colonization, they have created a hi-tech, ecologically sound paradise that makes the rest of the world seem primitive by comparison. If the right company got their hands on their gadgets, their medicines, their R&D, they would vault themselves a century ahead of their competitors.

But the Wakandans can't be bought out. This isn't a bunch of starving orphans pimped by dictators who'll sell out for a sizable contribution to their Swiss bank account. Wakandans are led by the Black Panthers, a warrior cult that serves as the religious, political and military head of the country. That tower in the center of the country is like a big middle finger to the rest of the world — literally. Their borders are tightly shut and they deal with the world on their own terms... or not at all.

The first scene of the book would be in the 10th century. Start on some neighboring tribe walking across the savannah looking for its next conquest. They roll on Wakanda. But the Wakandans kick their @$$, using man-sized beartraps crossbows and other technology that even Europeans didn't have at the time.

Cut to the turn of the century. The Boers have just finished conquering South Africa and are now moving on Wakanda. They've got rifles, they've got gatling guns. But the Wakandans have a magnetic-based weapon that causes the Boer weapons to backfire, maiming and killing half their troops. The Panthers then move in, leaving one man alive, as they usually do, to spread the word — DON'T EVEN THINK ABOUT IT.

We see Captain America getting his butt whipped by T'Chaka during World War Two. Yeah, they will whip anybody's butt.

Okay, let me stop. I'm starting on scenes and I haven't even given an overview yet.

The first six issues of the book will be a re-telling of the Panther's origin. That hasn't been done during this incarnation of the Panther, and is the best way to set the tone for the book.

It will be a version without the Fantastic Four, much like the Lee/Kirby SILVER SURFER graphic novel from the '70s, which retold his origin without the FF's involvement in the story.

The first six issues will essentially be my version of what the BLACK PANTHER MOVIE should be. But no matter what happens with the movie, or if the movie ever happens, there will be a TPB that people can pick up and see the character done right. No matter how horrible the Joel Schumacher BATMAN movies are, they cannot erase the greatness of THE DARK KNIGHT RETURNS or BATMAN: YEAR ONE. Hopefully, this book will do the same for T'Challa.

I know some people at Marvel feel the Panther's base being in Africa is a problem. It shouldn't be. The Panther should move back and forth between Wakanda and the rest of the world the same way Thor moves between Asgard and Earth. He's an INTERNATIONAL player who's equally at home at the Davos Conference in Switzerland, meeting with Colin Powell in D.C., kicking it in Harlem with Bill Clinton and Al Sharpton, and brokering deals off the coast of Cuba with Fidel Castro and Prince Namor.

A great hero is defined by his villains. The Panther doesn't have his equivalents to Dr. Doom, the Red Skull, or Magneto. Instead he's got a guy wearing a white gorilla fur. I don't even know that loser's name, but he will never be seen inside the pages of the book I write.

Since the first story arc will be his origin, the main villain will be Klaw...but not the Murderous Master of Sound that he was in the 1960s. No way. Our villain is a South African who was named after his ancestor, who was one of the Boers who led the abortive attempt to invade Wakanda a century ago. In an act of revenge for the murder of his great-grandfather, and as part of a conspiracy to overthrow Wakanda, Klaw murdered T'Chaka. As he was about to kill the rest of the royal family, T'Challa, T'Chaka's son, blows Klaw's hand off, LITERALLY disarming him.

Now Klaw is equipped with a cybernetic hand that can turn into any number of murderous devices. He's invading Wakanda again, with a small commando squad of superpowered killers, to kill T'Challa and take over Wakanda.

But he's not the only person with the bright idea to invade Wakanda. Is the Panther ready to wage war at home — on multiple fronts?

And will he be betrayed from within?

Okay, that's not a whole pitch, but it's a start. I won't get into the second story arc with Cage, Shang-Chi, Photon and Storm...but that's gonna be even better.

— REGINALD HUDLIN

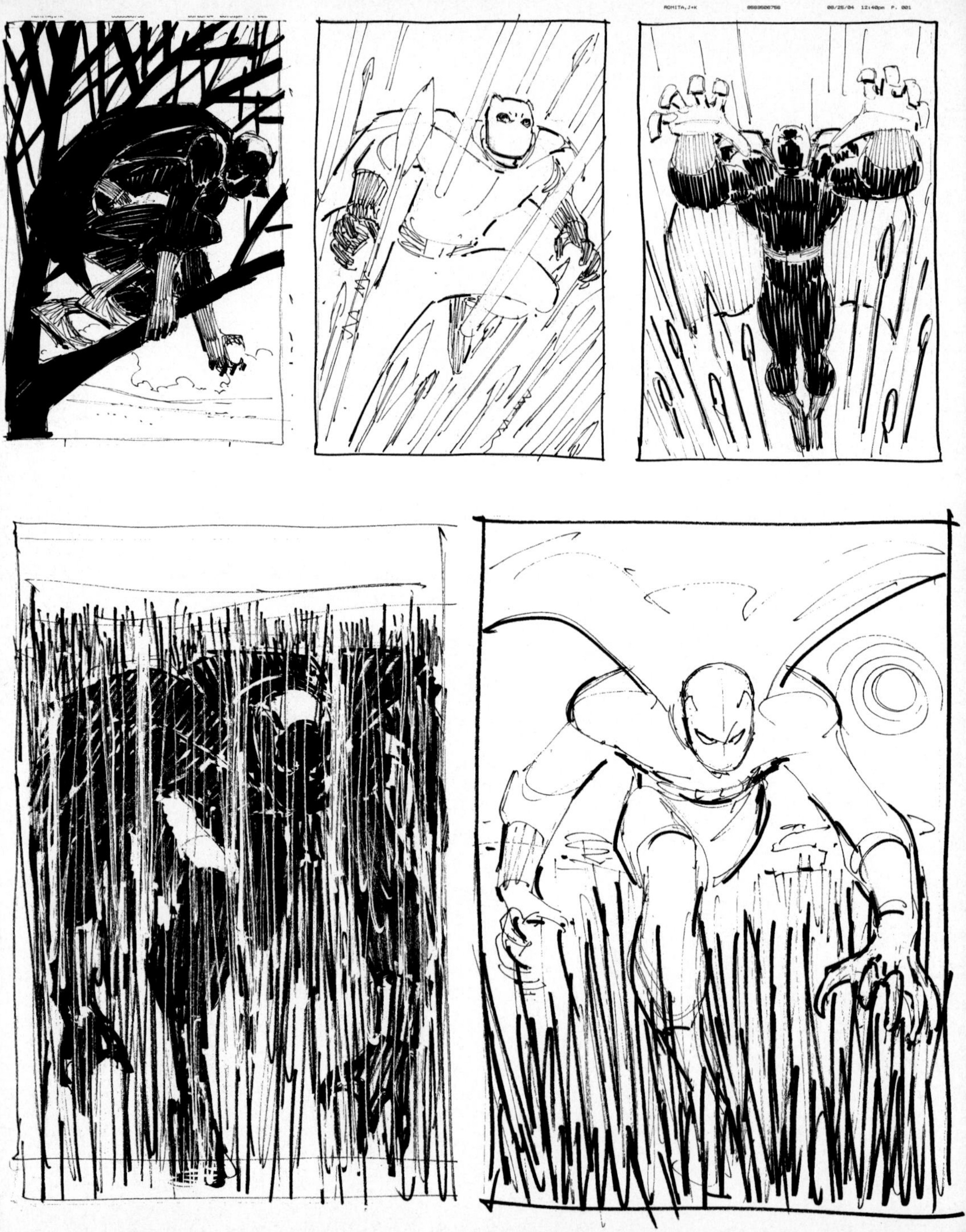
ROMITA,J+K
12:40pm P. 001

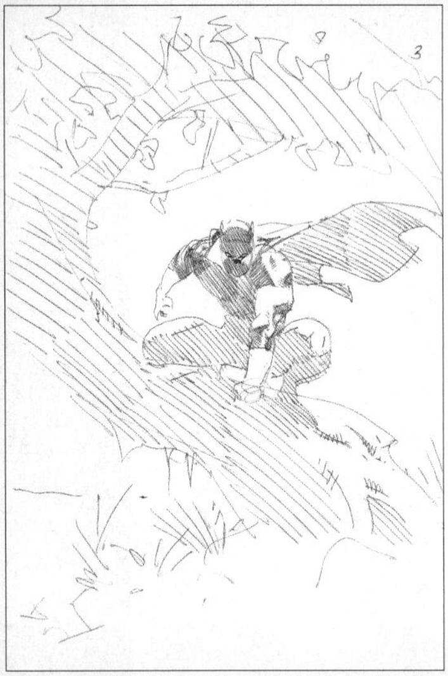
3
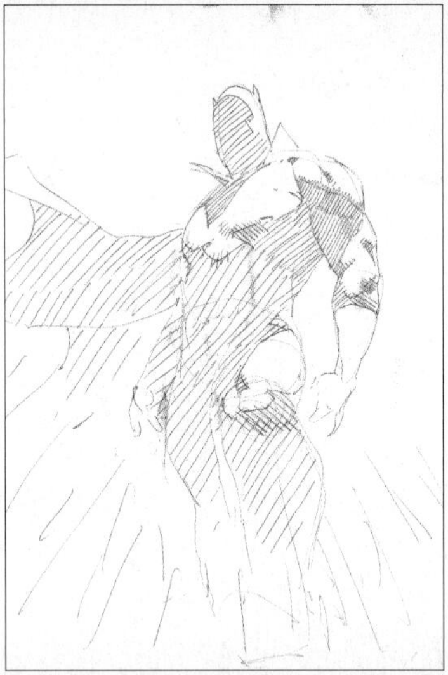
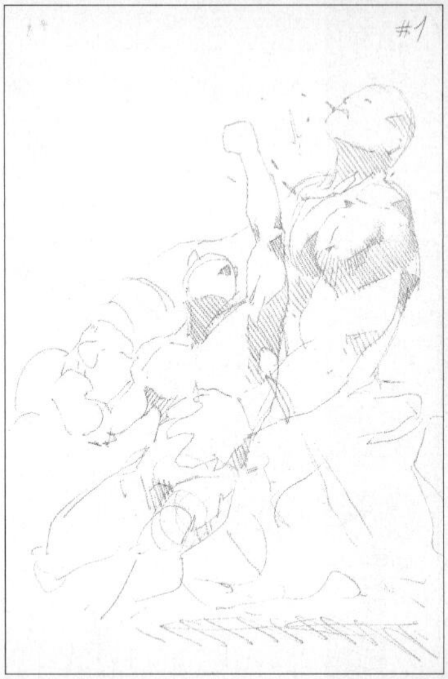
#1

BLACK PANTHER #6 COVER SKETCHES BY **ESAD RIBIĆ**

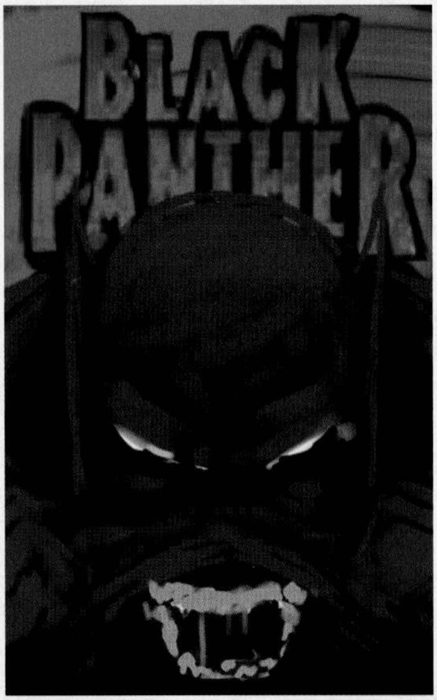
BLACK PANTHER
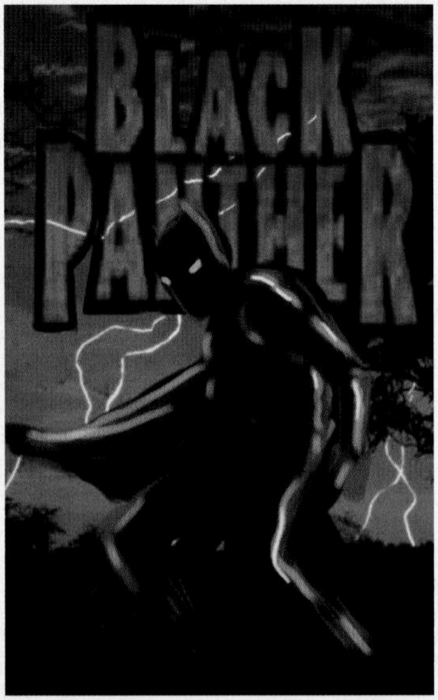
BLACK PANTHER
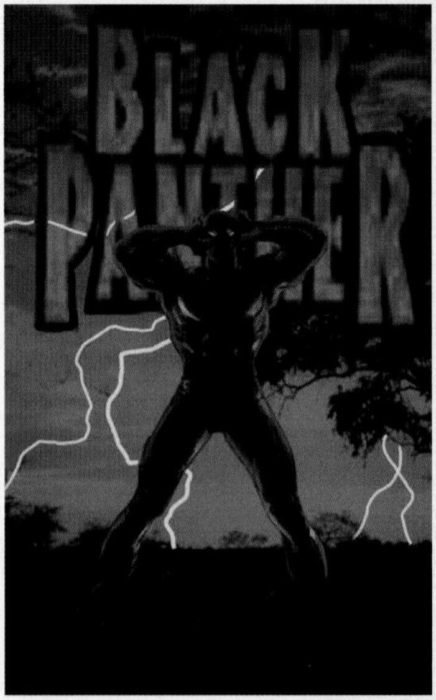
BLACK PANTHER

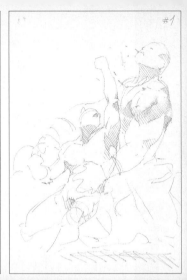

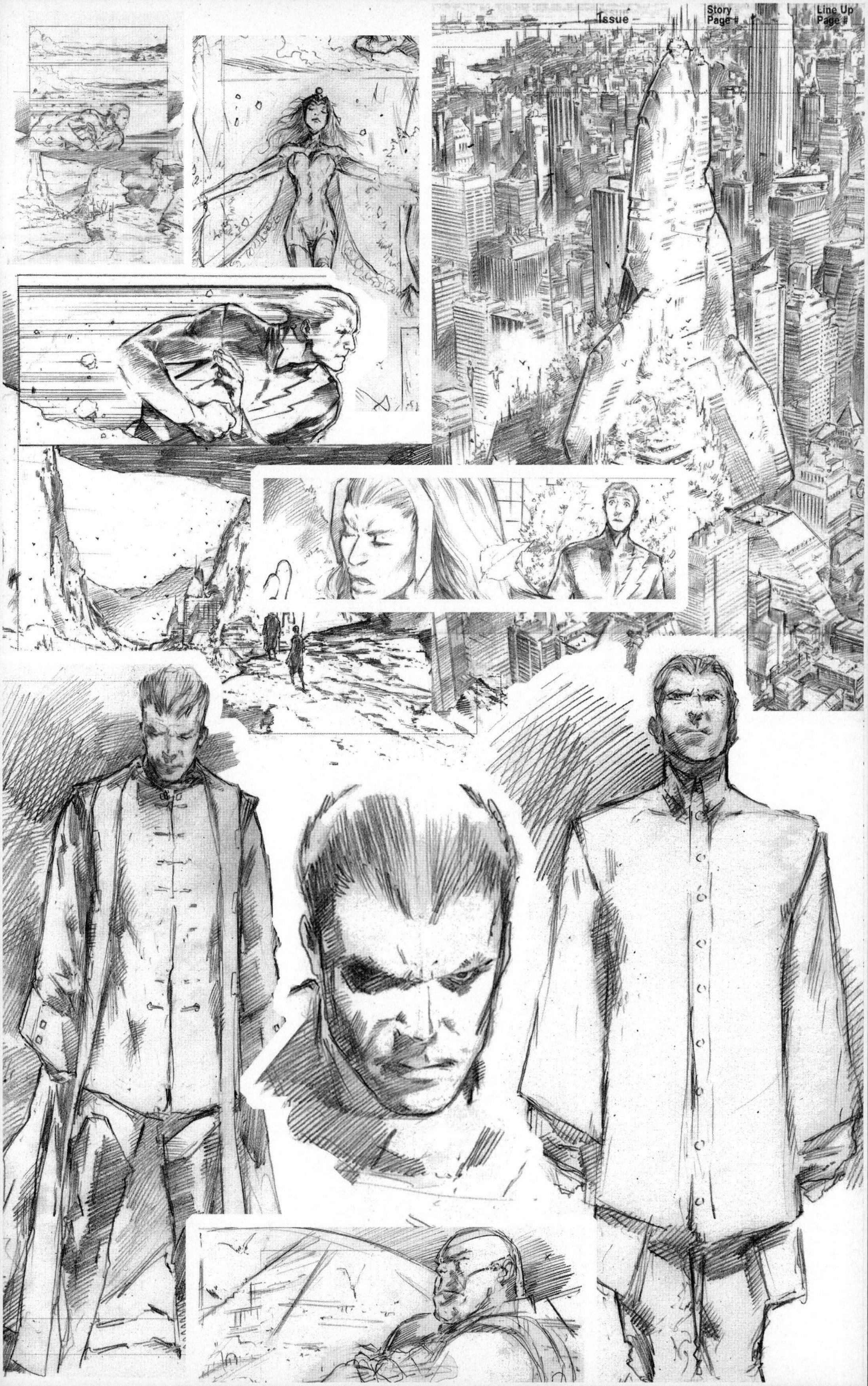
Issue
Story Page #
Line Up Page #

DIVINING THE DESIGN...

by Jim McCann

Many months ago, when we at Marvel knew the Black Panther was going to pop the question, we knew that we had our work cut out for us. I mean, this wasn't just any wedding, this would be a **royal** wedding! The guest list would need to be scrutinized, seating arrangements delicately balanced, and security tightened. After all, we are in the middle of a **Civil War**! However, before any of that could be addressed, we knew we had an even bigger challenge: we had to get a dress!

Who could be worthy of dressing one of our most revered characters? Storm is not only the most recognizable female character, but one of the most stylish and savvy women at Marvel. So, we called up our friends at CBS Daytime and the wonderful Maria Aguero had just the man for the challenge. Shawn Dudley, Costume Designer for *Guiding Light*, has designed dresses for heroes, villains, and divas, so who better to dress a mutant goddess?

So, what exactly goes into designing a dress for the Wedding of the Century? A lot, it seems. A few weeks ago, our pals at Comic Book Resources sat down with Shawn to discuss his process. At that point in time, the dress was designed and Frank Cho worked off that design to draw the cover to *Black Panther* #18. What follows is that interview.

STORM'S GUIDING LIGHT: SHAWN DUDLEY REVEALS

DESIGNER SECRETS

by <u>Arune Singh</u>, *Staff Writer, Comic Book Resources*

It's no secret that the wedding of Storm and the Black Panther is quite unusual for <u>Marvel Comics</u>. Fans have debated the merits of the relationship, with some feeling each character has "better" suitors, but there's no doubt that this union is at the very least something with many storytelling possibilities. The union occurs in July's "Black Panther" #18, but Marvel and TV Guide recently unveiled the wedding dress to be worn by the famous member of the X-Men (and portrayed by Halle Berry in the films), designed by daytime drama Costume Designer Shawn Dudley. Dudley's work on <u>CBS'</u> "Guiding Light" has earned him many accolades, so along with Alyson Hui, his associate designer, he was happy to tackle this iconic comic book character. CBR News recently spoke with Dudley via phone at his New York offices, in between his search for the perfect outfit to compliment the popular Tom Pelphry, who plays Jonathan Randall, on "Guiding Light."

Shawn, thanks for taking the time to talk with us. So how did you get involved with the wedding of Black Panther & Storm?

The initiative started at Marvel, since they wanted to do a promotional with an outside source, to design the basic look for this wedding dress, whether it was from a

top notch wedding designer like Vera Wang or whomever. Marvel eventually narrowed it down to where it was more a costume idea — they didn't want a traditional Western style wedding dress design. They had contacts at ABC and CBS, and asked costume designers to come up with initial design ideas. We seemed to have taken the design concept to where Marvel wanted it and did some in-depth research, came up with the concept, explored the traditions of this kind of wedding and voila, we got the job.

So then what inspired the look of the dress?

We had to do a lot of research because, and I'm a bit embarrassed to say this, I only knew Storm from the big splashy Hollywood movie, so I needed to get in there and find out who Storm was in her comic world. We approached design the same way we approach any design, namely to get inside the character because they have a life, and the dress needs to reflect that. We were not going to design just any dress for Storm: it had to be appropriate for her. We really had to go back and explore the different periods in her story. There's some periods with her hair pulled back, another where she came back from Japan looking very edgy and street. She tends to reflect the journey she's on. Also, this is set as a royal wedding and we wanted the dress to seem appropriately regal. We also went in and did research on different tribal aspects and symbolism, because the writer really wanted to play up the fact that it is going to be set in Africa. Black Panther has his history with Africa and Storm has her history with Africa. We needed

to mix all of that in, along with our additional research. We also turned to various fashion designers from Thierry Mugler, Vivenne Westwood, and vintage Gianni Versace. These were fashion designers who used exaggerated lines and proportions and that unique quality that embodied what we were going for with Storm's dress. We also looked at vintage designs from Erte and the Hollywood costume designer, Adrian. We also designed a beautiful ceremonial cape that she will wear for entrance that hasn't been seen yet. The cape has a gold handpainted and beaded design using African kente cloth and mud cloth design. She makes her grand entrance and the cape is removed to show the wedding gown underneath.

In the press release, you mentioned that the comic book version of the dress differed from your actual design.

[laughs]

Could you explain the differences?

We designed something that was more in keeping with our classic design technique. We paint our renderings in watercolors and it just creates a very different feeling for the dress, as opposed to the artists rendering for the comic book. Our lines are softer, body features aren't quite as exaggerated, and it's just much more in that theatrical style rendering that we're used to. That was the hard part, wrapping our heads around the fact that this wasn't a garment to be produced into a real garment, so it wouldn't be a fully realized project, and we tried to keep in mind how the artists in the comic book world create movement and fabrics. We wanted to make sure that we gave them enough elements to get those looks. We knew she would walk, and possibly fly, and we wanted to make sure those elements were in the costume. We also tried to work in her mother's ruby, and mentioned it to the Marvel guys, but she had lost it somewhere down the road, but they were able to make it so that the ruby comes back to her. When I saw the final version, by Frank Cho, I was a little surprised [laughs] to see it and compare the two. She's much sexier and has a little more bust action going on in the comic book, and I understand it, but I can't go that far with it, because it's not my nature as a designer. It was hard to let our baby go to

someone else, but I'm happy with what he did with it.

So is it safe to assume you were a fan of comics as a kid? You seem to understand the storytelling language.

Oh yeah. I was really more into those weird, kind of scary horror comics from the sixties and seventies. Those were my favorites and I had so many hand-me-downs from my uncle. They creeped me out... but I loved it. I also had some of the classic Disney comics, and kept track of Spider-Man. In New Mexico, where I used to live, the Albuquerque Journal used to run Spider-Man everyday and my grandmother would dutifully cut it out everyday and once a month I'd get a packet of comics she'd cut out for me.

Did you try to work on the film?

No, that's L.A, a whole

different world, but my dream job was *Lord of The Rings*. I almost did go for it. But I found out that they were in production in New Zealand and I would have dropped everything in my life to go work there. I'm one of those

Lord Of The Rings fanatics. I still have my original copies that I first read when I was 13.

Uh oh [laughs]

I even designed those costumes in college, when I studied design.

Did they look like the film's costumes?

They were close. There's an iconic look to many of the characters, so it's hard not to be similar.

Now we know that soap fans and comic fans are equally intense -- and equally vocal. But both mediums, for lack of a better term, are in a certain amount of decline from their glory days. Looking at both industries, how do you think they can increase viewership?

I think they can do it, but there needs to be a real understanding of the contemporary audience. The attention span is much shorter and I think that affects soaps and comics: if you've got a long running storyline, then the audience needs faster resolution and something new all the time. I don't think they're willing to invest that kind of time into the storyline. You see these younger people — I don't want to say kids, but they sort of are — are always looking forward to the next thing, from the iPod to the X-Box, it's the new generation that gets them excited. They get excited about a brand and we have to address that brand issue. I don't know as much about comics as I do about soaps, but we shy away from contemporary storytelling and we seem to sanitize certain

things because we think the audience wants that...but the audience is leaving us. There's so much violence, peer pressure, status objects...all so much more apparent now. I'm generation X and I think there's a bigger generation gap than ever before, which we need to address, since people in their twenties are so much savvier than we expect. We underestimate them.

Well, we don't underestimate you — so will you be doing more comic book work?

If they ask me, I'd love to. It allows me to be creative in ways that I can't be on the show.

DESIGN IN MOTION

Once the dress had been designed and used by Frank Cho, it was time for interior artist Scot Eaton to put that design in motion. I recently sat down with Shawn once more to show him the final result: Storm's "walk" down the aisle. The moment had arrived! So, how did it all come together? Read on, True Believer!

Shawn, once again, thank you for doing this!

Not at all a problem! It's been great!

Ok, so moment of truth. Here it is, Storm in the gown, "in action" as it were. First reaction?

My first reaction was to laugh. But I laughed in a good way mostly because I was sur-

prised to see the transformation and almost final product. I'm amazed to see this design come to life in a way that's very different than what I usually do. I usually see the design through to the end on a live person. I've been able to touch and feel and work with a costume in person. In this form we had to really suspend disbelief and visualize the design on paper and through the beautiful artwork on the page. I think it looks pretty cool.

Now that you've had a chance to see it in four-color, do you think it works the way you envisioned it?

I do think that it mostly works the way I and my assistant, Alyson, envisioned it. We knew that subtle changes would happen as the design was interpreted by each artist. I had to really sit back and force myself to not get involved. And that's really hard for me to do. Its our design, so we're a little possessive. As I look at it though, I'm very pleased with the final product.

Wonderful! I'm glad we did your design justice! You designed the cape for dramatic effect; what do you think about how it was used in the comic?

I think the cape works from what I can tell. My intention for the cape was to be a presentational moment. When Storm first appears at the wedding ceremony, we first see her in this full ceremonial cape befitting the royal aspect of the wedding. She removes it to than reveal her gown and the wedding ceremony begins. But I do love the movement in the cape and the sweep of the panels.

Aside from Storm's dress, what's your favorite costume you've ever designed?

I don't know that I have one favorite costume that I've designed. I learned an interesting lesson back in the day as a theatre design student and that was we should never be fully satisfied with our designs...there's always something more that we could have done or achieved. And when that day comes when we are satisfied with our design, then that's the day it's over. As designers and artists, we should always be learning something new and striving for perfection and looking for that new way to help tell the story.

Great advice! Any final thoughts?

Final thoughts? Yes...I'm just glad to have had the chance to collaborate on a very unique and challenging project. The type of project that really pushes us to think outside the box.

Well, we are thankful for the time and energy! Here's hoping we get to work together again soon!

———————

So, there you have it. From concept to design to wedding day--everything it takes to dress a goddess! As you can tell, it's quite an undertaking! Here's hoping this is the last wedding for a while. Wait, I'm getting a call... What's that? WHO is having a baby? Wow! The fans are going to be shocked! Ok, thanks for the heads up. Hmmm... I wonder if Shawn can design baby clothes...

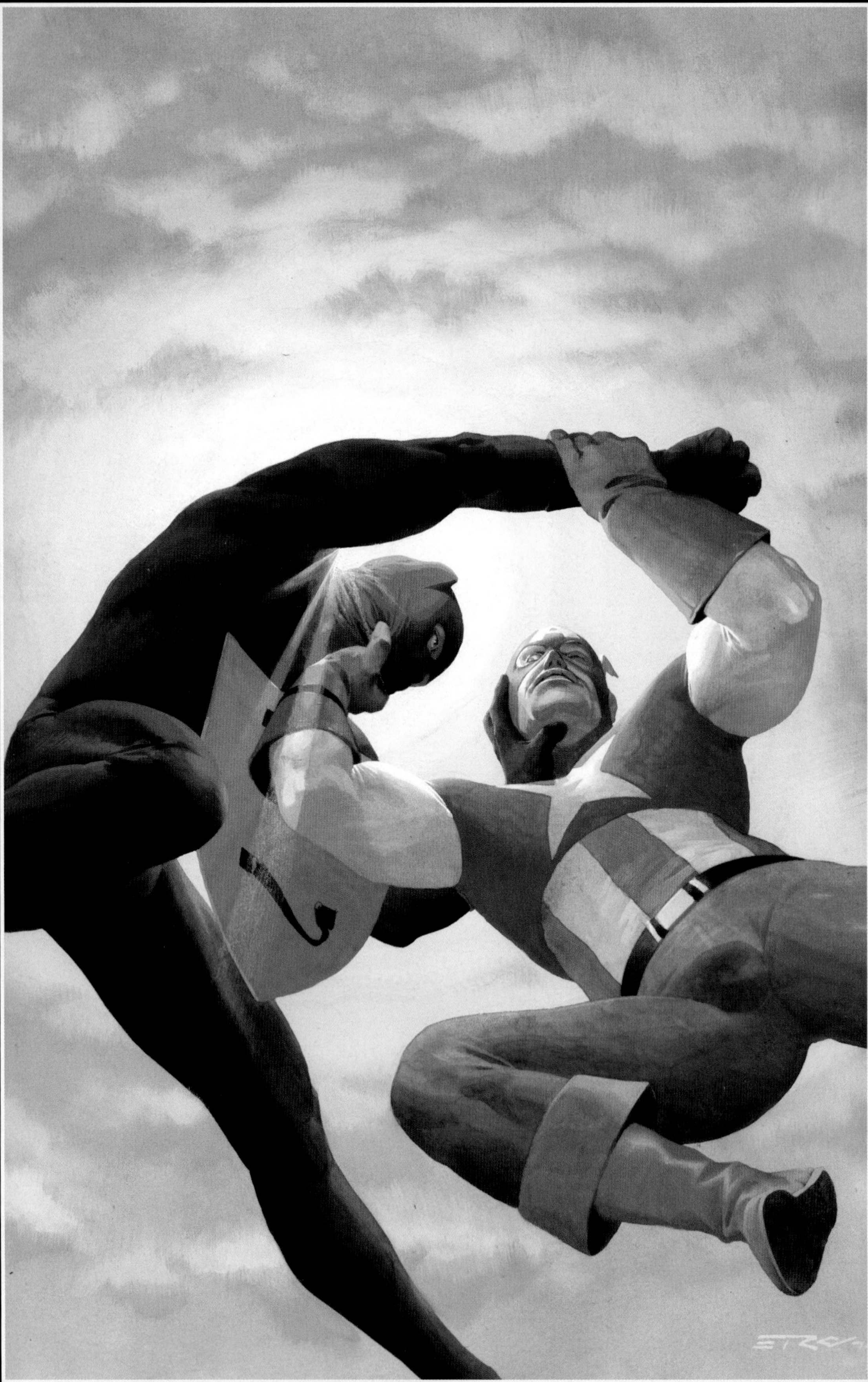

BLACK PANTHER #1 2ND-PRINTING VARIANT BY **ESAD RIBIĆ**

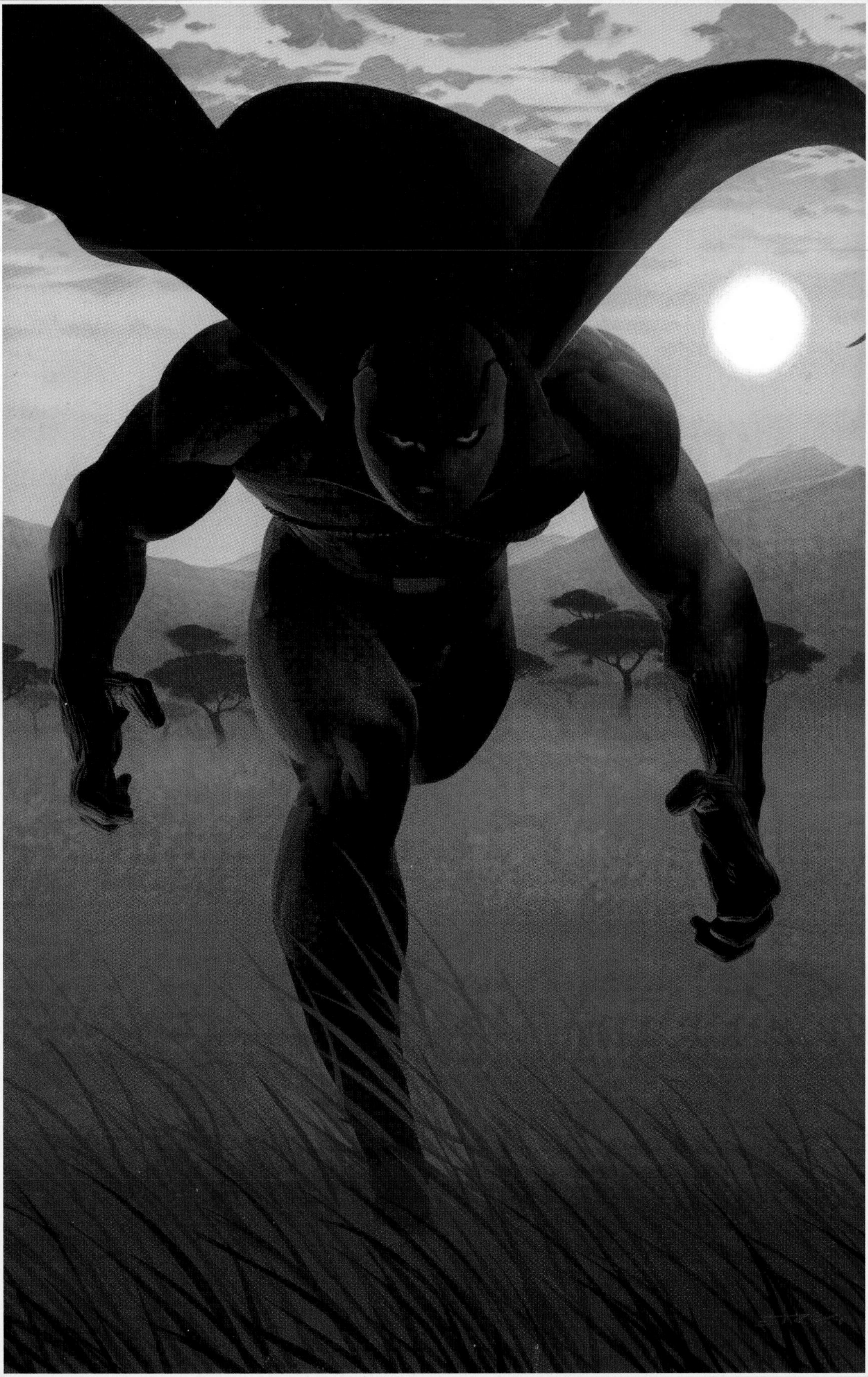

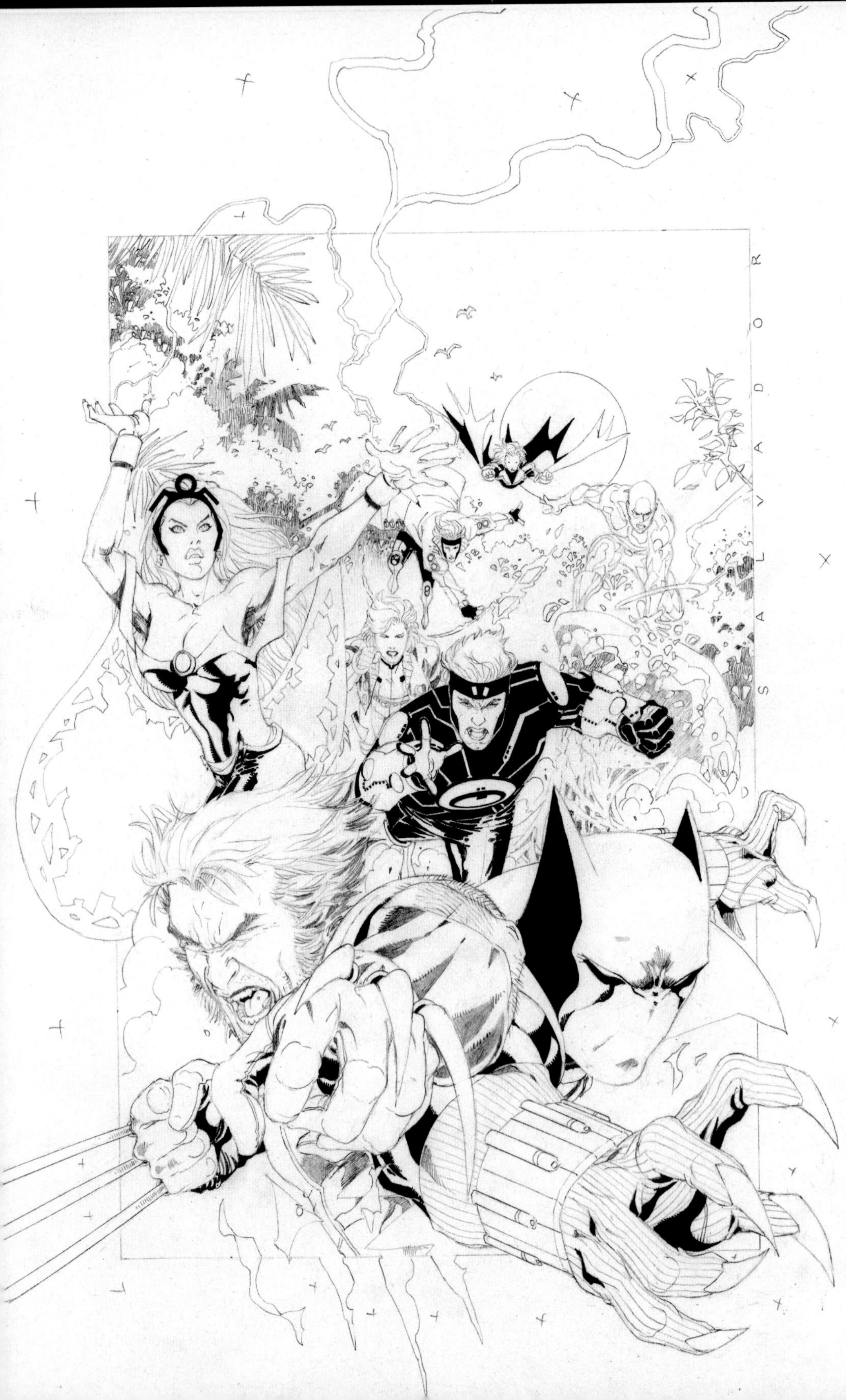
SALVADOR

BLACK PANTHER #8 2ND-PRINTING VARIANT BY **FRANK CHO**

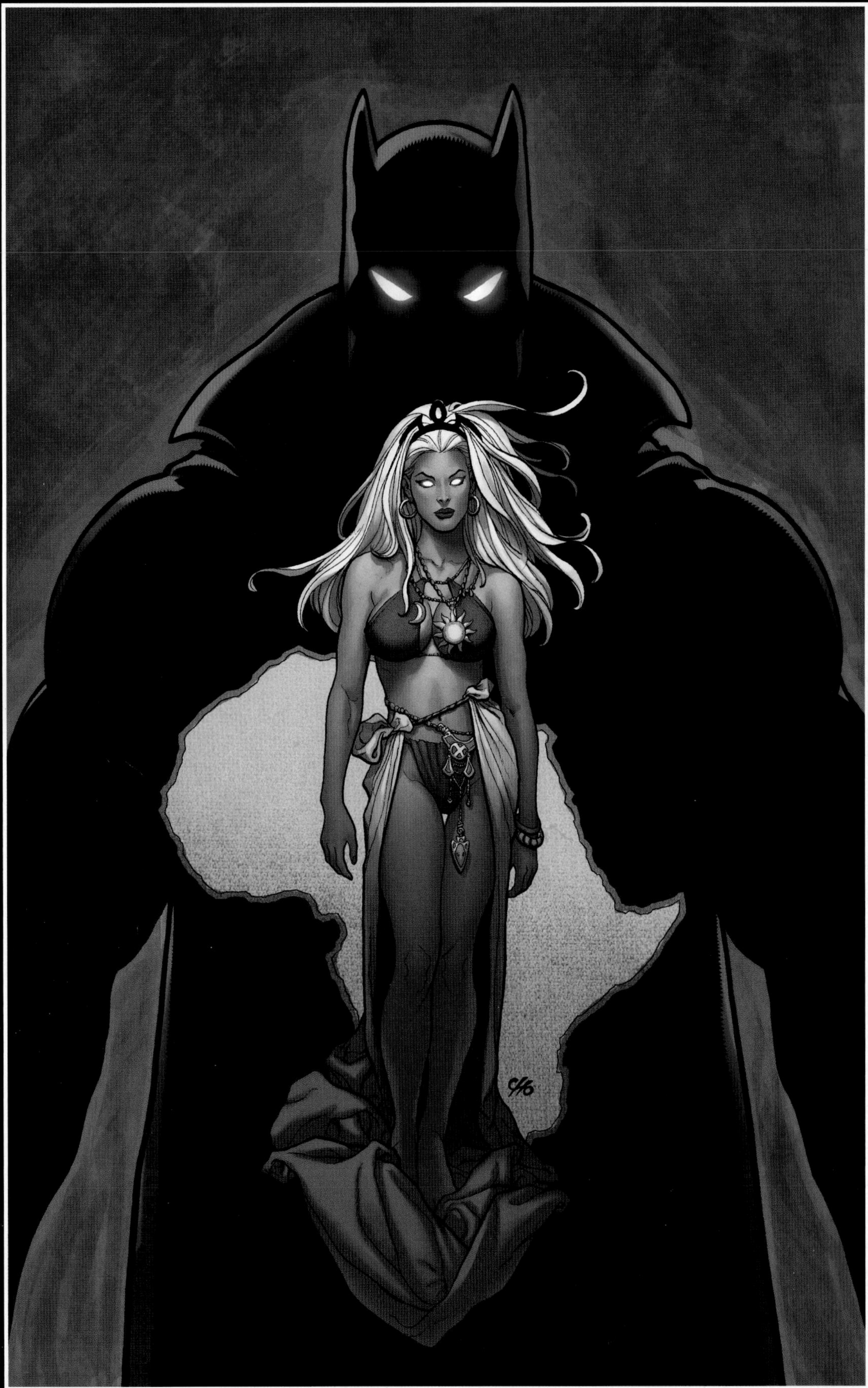

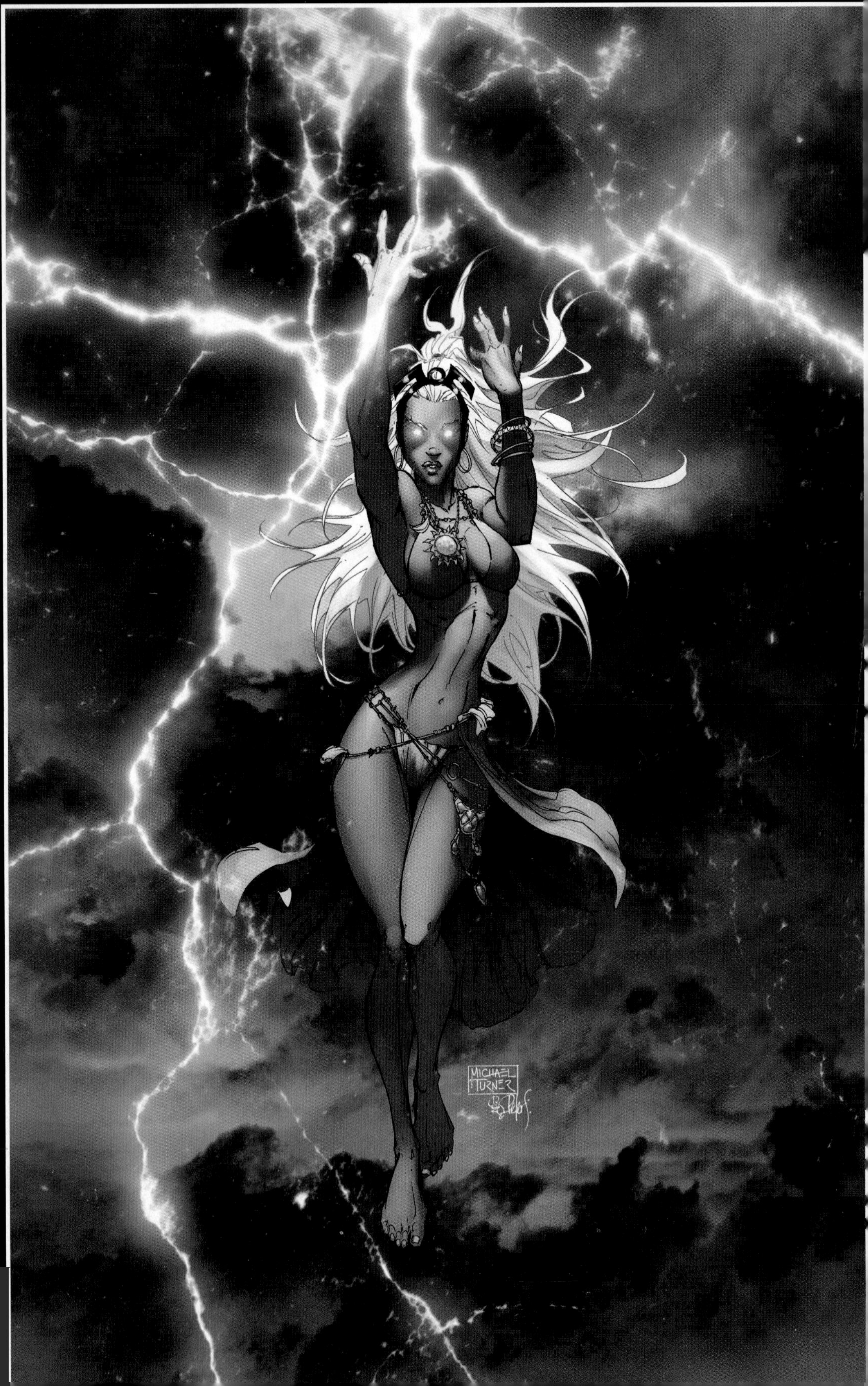
MICHAEL TURNER